Signatures

TEACHER'S EDITION

OUT OF THE BLUE

Senior Authors

Roger C. Farr
Dorothy S. Strickland

Authors

Richard F. Abrahamson
Alma Flor Ada
Barbara Bowen Coulter
Bernice E. Cullinan
Margaret A. Gallego
W. Dorsey Hammond
Nancy Roser
Junko Yokota
Hallie Kay Yopp

Senior Consultant

Asa G. Hilliard III

Consultants

Lee Bennett Hopkins
David A. Monti
Rosalia Salinas

HARCOURT BRACE & COMPANY

Orlando Atlanta Austin Boston San Francisco
Chicago Dallas New York Toronto London

OUT OF THE BLUE

SIGNATURES

Harcourt Brace & Company

Acknowledgments appear in the back of this book.

Printed in the United States of America

ISBN 0-15-310119-9

1 2 3 4 5 6 7 8 9 10 030 00 99 98

Meet Our Authors!

SENIOR AUTHORS

Dr. Roger C. Farr

Chancellors' Professor of Education and Director of the Center for Reading and Language Studies, Indiana University, Bloomington

RESEARCH CONTRIBUTIONS: Assessment, Portfolios, Reading-Writing Strategies, Staff Development

Dr. Dorothy S. Strickland

The State of New Jersey Professor of Reading, Rutgers University

RESEARCH CONTRIBUTIONS: Emergent Literacy, Linguistic and Cultural Diversity, Intervention, Phonics in Literature-based Curriculum, Integrated Language Arts

AUTHORS

Dr. Richard F. Abrahamson

Professor of Literature for Children and Young Adults, University of Houston

RESEARCH CONTRIBUTIONS: Children's Literature, Strategic Reading, Reading Nonfiction

Dr. Alma Flor Ada

Director of Doctoral Studies in the International Multicultural Program, University of San Francisco

RESEARCH CONTRIBUTIONS: Bilingual Education, ESL, Family Involvement

Dr. Barbara Bowen Coulter

Director, Communication Arts, Detroit Public Schools

RESEARCH CONTRIBUTIONS: Multicultural Education, Spelling and Vocabulary, Staff Development

Dr. Bernice E. Cullinan

Professor of Reading, New York University

RESEARCH CONTRIBUTIONS: Children's Literature, Emergent Literacy, Intervention, Integrated Language Arts

Dr. Margaret A. Gallego

Visiting Researcher at Laboratory of Comparative Human Cognition, University of California, San Diego

RESEARCH CONTRIBUTIONS: ESL, Bilingual Education, Second Language Support, Culturally Relevant Curriculum

Dr. W. Dorsey Hammond

Professor of Education, Oakland University of Rochester, Michigan

RESEARCH CONTRIBUTIONS: Reading Comprehension, Reader Response, Staff Development, Critical Thinking, Classroom Management

Dr. Nancy Roser

Professor, Language and Literacy Studies, University of Texas, Austin

RESEARCH CONTRIBUTIONS: Beginning Reading, Book Discussions, Early Childhood, Emergent Literacy, Phonics in Literature-based Curriculum, Reading Comprehension

Dr. Junko Yokota

Associate Professor, Reading/Language Arts Department, National-Louis University, Evanston, Illinois

RESEARCH CONTRIBUTIONS: Multicultural Literature, Children's Literature

Dr. Hallie Kay Yopp

Professor, Department of Elementary Bilingual and Reading Education, California State University, Fullerton

RESEARCH CONTRIBUTIONS: Phonemic Awareness, Early Childhood

CONSULTANTS

Dr. David A. Monti

Professor, Reading and Language Arts Department, Central Connecticut State University, New Britain, Connecticut

RESEARCH CONTRIBUTIONS: During-learning Strategies, Flexible Grouping

Dr. Asa G. Hilliard III

Fuller E. Callaway Professor of Urban Education, Department of Educational Foundations, Georgia State University, Atlanta

RESEARCH CONTRIBUTIONS: Multicultural Education

Dr. Lee Bennett Hopkins

Poet, Author, Anthologist

RESEARCH CONTRIBUTIONS: Poetry, Children's Literature

Dr. Rosalia Salinas

Director of Bilingual Education, San Diego County Office of Education and Director of California Literature Project, Spanish

RESEARCH CONTRIBUTIONS: ESL, Bilingual Education

Dear Educator,

Signatures is a fully integrated reading and language arts program that will leave a lasting mark on your students' literacy—and also on their lives. The program is based on principles of effective reading and language arts instruction that emerge consistently from both research and practical experience:

High-quality trade-book literature should be accessible to *every* child in the classroom. The core of *Signatures* is its collection of high-quality, authentic children's literature, created by award-winning authors and illustrators and selected to represent not only a variety of genres and styles but also the pluralistic nature of our society. Meaningful thematic units encourage students to relate the selections to each other, to readings in other content areas, and to their own life experiences.

Skills and strategies are essential for success in school and in the real world. *Signatures* literature serves as the springboard for instruction in skills and strategies that will help students develop into fluent, lifelong readers and articulate, effective communicators. Cross-curricular content supports comprehensive development of reading, writing, listening, speaking and thinking skills presented in an easy-to-use yet flexible format.

Intervention strategies can help teachers meet the needs of *all* learners. The variety of materials and strategies available in *Signatures* will help teachers customize their teaching practices to meet the needs of all students in the broadest possible range of classroom environments.

Flexible grouping and classroom management are more important than ever in today's classrooms. *Signatures* is designed with abundant teacher-support for meeting the challenges of classroom management in the context of theme-based instruction.

Signatures will help you provide your students with the tools and strategies they need to make their imprint on the world around them.

Sincerely,
The *Signatures* Authors

Contents

TELL A
TRICKY
TALE

Resource Materials

OUT OF THE BLUE

Previewing the Cover

Have children study the cover illustration and describe what they see. Ask volunteers to tell what they know about coyotes or birds like the ones shown in the scene. Then discuss with children what they think the title *Out of the Blue* means. Encourage them to tell how they think the art and the title go together.

Explain that the cover was created by Gerald McDermott, the same artist who painted the pictures for "Coyote," a story in the Student Anthology. You may want to share the following information about the artist.

> **Gerald McDermott chose his shapes and colors carefully. Each shape on the crow's pendant means something. The triangle stands for thunderclouds and the three bars stand for rain. McDermott used bright, rich colors to add more life to the characters. Gerald McDermott is a famous author and illustrator. He received a Caldecott Medal for *Arrow to the Sun*.**

Predicting What's Inside

DISCUSS THE LETTER WITH CHILDREN. Direct children's attention to the letter from the authors at the beginning of the book. Ask them to think about why the authors of their book would write a letter to them. Then read the letter aloud. Ask children to tell you what kinds of surprises they think they will read about.

ACQUAINT CHILDREN WITH THE ORGANIZATION OF THE BOOK. Ask children to preview the Contents on pages 6–11. Read aloud the theme titles with children. Ask them what they think the stories and poems in each theme will be about.

HELP CHILDREN EXAMINE END-OF-BOOK CONTENT. Have children find the Glossary, beginning on page 349 of the Student Anthology. Then ask them how they think this part of the book might help them. Page R190 contains information about introducing children to the Glossary.

Senior Authors
Roger C. Farr
Dorothy S. Strickland

Authors
Richard F. Abrahamson • Alma Flor Ada • Barbara Bowen Coulter
Bernice E. Cullinan • Margaret A. Gallego
W. Dorsey Hammond
Nancy Roser • Junko Yokota • Hallie Kay Yopp

Senior Consultant
Asa G. Hilliard III

Consultants
Lee Bennett Hopkins • Stephen Krashen • David A. Monti • Rosalia Salinas

Harcourt Brace & Company
Orlando Atlanta Austin Boston San Francisco Chicago Dallas New York Toronto London

Acknowledgments appear in the back of this work.

Printed in the United States of America

ISBN 0-15-310106-7

1 2 3 4 5 6 7 8 9 10 048 2000 99 98

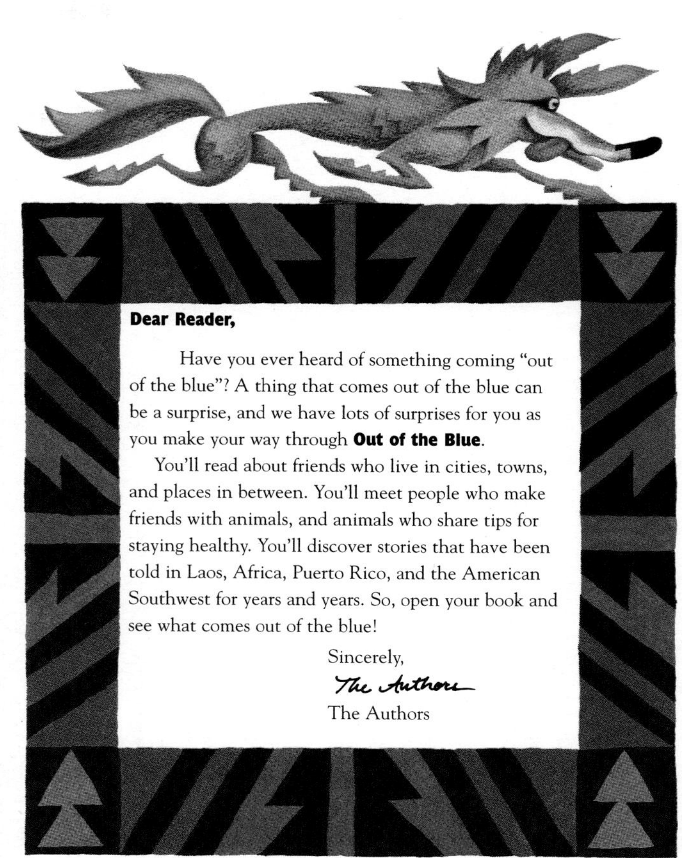

Dear Reader,

Have you ever heard of something coming "out of the blue"? A thing that comes out of the blue can be a surprise, and we have lots of surprises for you as you make your way through **Out of the Blue**.

You'll read about friends who live in cities, towns, and places in between. You'll meet people who make friends with animals, and animals who share tips for staying healthy. You'll discover stories that have been told in Laos, Africa, Puerto Rico, and the American Southwest for years and years. So, open your book and see what comes out of the blue!

Sincerely,

The Authors

The Authors

Celebrate Me!

CONTENTS

CONTENTS

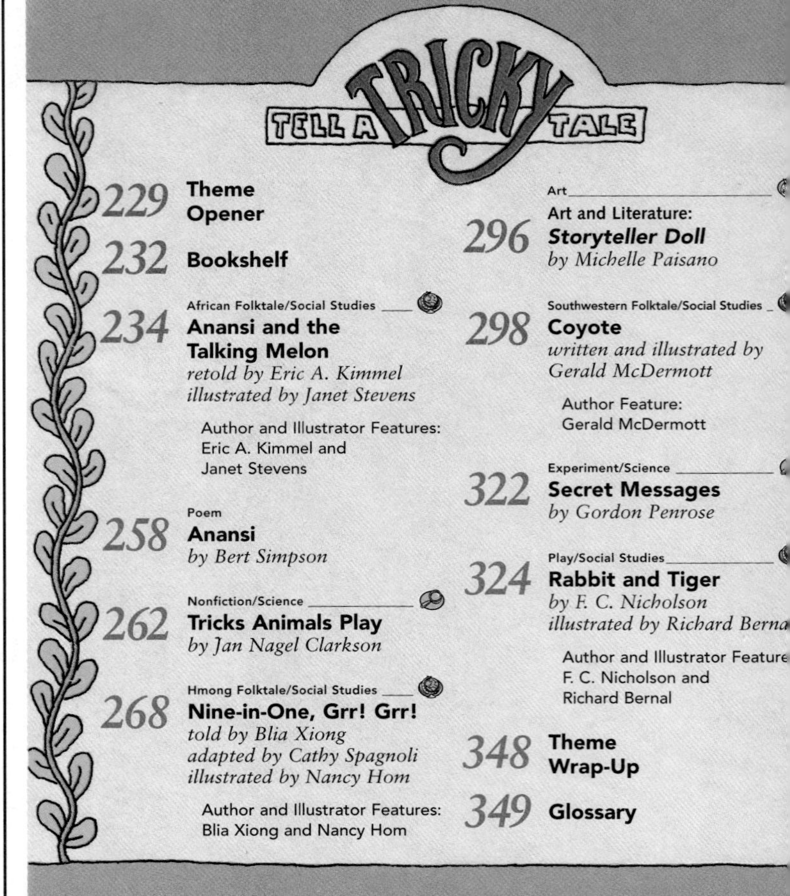

TELL A TRICKY TALE

THEME I

Celebrate Me!

Theme 1

Learning About Oneself

CELEBRATE ME!

Everyone has unique gifts to offer.

In this theme, learning what is special about ourselves and the people we know is cause for celebration.

Theme Overview

Celebrate Me!

Learning About Oneself

As children develop an appreciation of their own abilities and those of other people, they begin to recognize that each person is a one-of-a-kind package of talents. Selections in this theme help children gain respect for the unique qualities that make each of them and every other person extraordinary.

This Is the Way We Go to School

by Edith Baer T21–T68

"One by one or two by two—
Come along, it's fun to do!"

A catchy rhyming text leads readers to think about lifestyles of children who are like them in some ways and different from them in other ways.

This Is the Way We Go to School
A Book About Children Around the World
by EDITH BAER
Illustrated by STEVE BJÖRKMAN

We Have a New Girl in Class by Aliki T46
This poem helps children understand the feelings of a new child at school.

How Do You Feel? by Aliki T47
Pictures and words illustrate a wide variety of emotions that children experience at one time or another.

What's for Lunch? by Samantha Bonar T69–T72
This photo essay prompts readers to consider what children in other countries eat for lunch.

Emily and Alice Again by Joyce Champion T73–T116

"Alice nodded. 'OK, I'll trade!' Alice gave Emily her new sunglasses. Emily gave Alice her only sister."

Emily learns that sunglasses are no substitute for a little sister, and in this humorous story readers are reminded of how much fun a sibling can be.

ART AND LITERATURE: *Ronde des Enfants* by Pablo Picasso T117–T118

The joys of movement and dance are expressed in this painting of children doing a traditional French dance.

Max Found Two Sticks by Brian Pinkney T119–T170

"Tippy-tip . . . tat-tat. He created the rhythm of the light rain falling against the front windows."

This story of a boy who discovers his talent for drumming demonstrates how children can develop their gifts in everyday situations.

Balloon Tom-Tom by Eddie Herschel Oates T171–T174

Readers can follow these step-by-step directions to make their own drums.

Dinosaurs Alive and Well! by Laurie Krasny Brown and Marc Brown T175–T222

"There's a lot you can do to take care of yourself and become the healthiest, happiest person you can be!"

This amusing guide to good health gives children advice for taking care of their bodies and coping with their feelings.

Flexible Grouping

THIS IS THE WAY WE GO TO SCHOOL T21–T68

	BELOW-LEVEL READERS	ABOVE-LEVEL READERS	ESL	BILINGUAL
1 READING AND RESPONDING Build Background and Concepts Vocabulary Strategies Strategic Reading Response Corner	**BEFORE** reading the selection, use the Previewing the Literature page of the *Intervention Strategies Manual* (p. 2). **TEACHER-LED GROUP** **AFTER** reading the selection, children can make and preview their Take-Home/Keep-at-Home Book *New School, New Friends.* **TEACHER-LED GROUP**	**AFTER** reading the selection, have children choose and complete a Response Corner activity. **COOPERATIVE GROUPS** **AFTER** reading the selection and the poems, have children read a book by Aliki Brandenberg. **COOPERATIVE GROUPS**	**AFTER** reading the selection, do a "picture walk" through the Instant Reader *Rabbit and Turtle Go to School* so that children may read it independently. **TEACHER-LED GROUP** **WHILE** reading the selection, children can listen to *Literature Cassette 1* as they follow along. **PAIRS**	**BEFORE** reading the anthology selection, choose the translation in the appropriate *Anthology Translation Booklet* and have children take it home to share. **INDEPENDENT** **INSTEAD OF** Strategic Reading, share with Spanish-speaking children *Hermanas* in CIELO ABIERTO. Share with Chinese-speaking children *All in a Day* from the *Multi-Language Library.* **TEACHER-LED GROUP**
2 INTEGRATING LANGUAGE ARTS Idea Bank Writer's Workshop Grammar Spelling Vocabulary Workshop	**WHILE** doing the Writer's Workshop, help children use the *Language Handbook* (p. 10) as a model of sentences about pictures. **TEACHER-LED GROUP** **DURING** the Spelling lesson, refer to *Integrated Spelling* Teacher's Edition Lesson 1 for additional support lessons. **TEACHER-LED GROUP**	**AFTER** the Idea Bank activities, have children complete the *Writer's Magazine* (pp. 2–5). **INDEPENDENT** **AFTER** the Writer's Workshop, have children complete the Writing Self-Assessment Checklist and add their sentences to their portfolios. **INDEPENDENT**	**BEFORE** the Writer's Workshop, use the Responding to the Literature page of the *Sheltered English/ESL Manual* (p. 5). **TEACHER-LED GROUP**	**DURING** the Writer's Workshop, use CIELO ABIERTO *Teacher's Handbook* page 71 to have children write a description. **TEACHER-LED GROUP** **INSTEAD OF** completing the Grammar lesson, refer to page 11 in *Hermanas Teacher's Guide.* **TEACHER-LED GROUP**
3 LEARNING THROUGH THE LITERATURE Direct Skills Instruction Integrated Curriculum Reading Trade Books Theme Project	**WHILE** children review the Phonics and Decoding lesson, use the *Intervention Strategies Manual.* (pp. 6–7) **INDEPENDENT** **WHILE** others work in centers, children can choose and complete a Curriculum Card activity. **COOPERATIVE GROUPS**	**WHILE** others work on Practice Activities, have children select and read a Trade Book that reflects sequence. (p.T63) **INDEPENDENT**	**DURING** the Comprehension Strategy lesson, review time-order words by cutting out individual frames of cartoon strips from newspapers for children to arrange in time order. (p.T63) **TEACHER-LED GROUP** **WHILE** others work in groups, work with children to make and read the Take-Home/Keep-at-Home Book *New School, New Friends.* **TEACHER-LED GROUP**	**WHILE** others work in groups, have children complete the ongoing cross-curricular project. See page 2 in *Hermanas Teacher's Guide.* **COOPERATIVE GROUPS**

EMILY AND ALICE AGAIN T73–T116

	BELOW-LEVEL READERS	ABOVE-LEVEL READERS	ESL	BILINGUAL
1 READING AND RESPONDING Build Background and Concepts Vocabulary Strategies Strategic Reading Response Corner	**WHILE** reading the selection, use the Guided Reading page of the *Intervention Strategies Manual* (p. 9). **TEACHER-LED GROUP** **AFTER** reading the selection, have children read an *Instant Reader* with a partner. **PAIRS**	**WHILE** children read the selection in small groups, have them use Reader Response Card 3 (Plot). **COOPERATIVE GROUPS** **AFTER** children read the selection, have them select a faraway island they would like to visit, use reference books to do research, and report to classmates. (p. T86) **INDEPENDENT**	**BEFORE** reading the selection, complete the reproducible page of the *Sheltered English/ESL Manual* (p. 7). **TEACHER-LED GROUP** **AFTER** reading the selection, have children read an *Instant Reader* with a more fluent partner. **PAIRS**	**AFTER** reading the anthology selection, choose the translation in the appropriate *Anthology Translation Booklet* and have children take it home to share. **INDEPENDENT** **INSTEAD OF** Strategic Reading, share with Spanish-speaking children poetry from *Dulce es la sal* in CIELO ABIERTO. Share *The Mouse Bride* from the *Multi-Language Library* with Hmong-speaking children. **TEACHER-LED GROUP**
2 INTEGRATING LANGUAGE ARTS Idea Bank Writer's Workshop Grammar Spelling Vocabulary Workshop	**AFTER** the Grammar lesson, have children read Phonics Practice Reader 1. **INDEPENDENT** **WHILE** doing the Writer's Workshop, children may use the *Language Handbook* (pp. 6–7) to model a personal story. **INDEPENDENT**	**WHILE** others work in groups, have children choose and complete an Idea Bank activity. **COOPERATIVE GROUPS** **AFTER** completing Idea Bank activities, children can complete the *Writer's Magazine* (pp. 6–9). **INDEPENDENT**	**BEFORE** the Writer's Workshop, use the Responding to the Literature page of the *Sheltered English/ESL Manual* (p. 9). **TEACHER-LED GROUP** **DURING** the Spelling lesson, use *Integrated Spelling* Teacher's Edition Lesson 2. **TEACHER-LED GROUP**	**DURING** the Writer's Workshop, use the writing activity in the Activities for Responding to the Poem in *Dulce es la sal Teacher's Guide*. **TEACHER-LED GROUP** **INSTEAD OF** using the Vocabulary Workshop activities, use one of the Activities for Responding to the Poem in *Dulce es la sal Teacher's Guide*. **TEACHER-LED GROUP**
3 LEARNING THROUGH THE LITERATURE Direct Skills Instruction Integrated Curriculum Reading Trade Books Theme Project	**WHILE** children review the Phonics and Decoding lesson, use the phonics pages in the *Intervention Strategies Manual.* (pp. 12–13) **TEACHER-LED GROUP** **WHILE** others work in groups, children can make and read the Take-Home/Keep-at-Home Book *The Case of the Missing Lunch.* **PAIRS**	**AFTER** the Phonics and Decoding lesson, have children complete the *Phonics Activity Book* (pp. 4-5). **INDEPENDENT**	**WHILE** others work in centers, children can read *What Do You Like?* an *ESL/Title I Library* book. **PAIRS**	**WHILE** others are sharing trade books, have children choose a book from the *Multi-Language Library* to take home and share with family members. **INDEPENDENT**

Flexible Grouping

MAX FOUND TWO STICKS T119–T170

	BELOW-LEVEL READERS	ABOVE-LEVEL READERS	ESL	BILINGUAL
1 READING AND RESPONDING Build Background and Concepts Vocabulary Strategies Strategic Reading Response Corner	**WHILE** reading the selection, use the Guided Reading page of the *Intervention Strategies Manual* (p.15). **TEACHER-LED GROUP** **WHILE** reading the selection, partners can take turns being Max using two pencils and can answer the questions on Reader Response Card 5 (Free Response). **TEACHER-LED GROUP**	**AFTER** reading the selection, children can write an alternative story ending in their personal journals. **INDEPENDENT** **WHILE** you work with others, children can complete a Response Corner Activity. **COOPERATIVE GROUPS**	**AFTER** reading the selection, do a "picture walk" through an *Instant Reader* so that children may read it independently. **TEACHER-LED GROUP**	**AFTER** reading the anthology selection, choose the translation in the appropriate *Anthology Translation Booklet* and have children take it home to share. **INDEPENDENT** **INSTEAD OF** Strategic Reading, share with Spanish-speaking children works from *En un lugar muy lejano . . .* in CIELO ABIERTO. **TEACHER-LED GROUP**
2 INTEGRATING LANGUAGE ARTS Idea Bank Writer's Workshop Grammar Spelling Vocabulary Workshop	**WHILE** others work on Idea Bank activities, pull out a needs-based group for review of short vowel /a/. **TEACHER-LED GROUP** **AFTER** the Idea Bank activities, children can make and read storybooks using sentence strips (p. R54) from the story. **INDEPENDENT**	**WHILE** doing the Writer's Workshop, children may use the *Language Handbook* (pp. 8–9) to model a story. **INDEPENDENT** **AFTER** the Writer's Workshop, children can enter their stories using *The Amazing Writing Machine.* **PAIRS**	**WHILE** others work on Idea Bank activities, children can complete an activity from Intervention Strategies. (pp.T152–T153) **COOPERATIVE GROUPS** **DURING** the Spelling lesson, refer to *Integrated Spelling* Teacher's Edition Lesson 3 for additional support lessons. **TEACHER-LED GROUP**	**DURING** the Writer's Workshop, use the Personal Writing Profile on page 16 of *En un lugar muy lejano . . . Teacher's Guide.* **COOPERATIVE GROUPS**
3 LEARNING THROUGH THE LITERATURE Direct Skills Instruction Integrated Curriculum Reading Trade Books Theme Project	**AFTER** the Phonics and Decoding lesson, guide children in completing *Practice Book* page 30. **TEACHER-LED GROUP** **AFTER** the Study Skills lesson, children can use the art in *KID PIX* when creating their pennants in the Three Cheers for Tests! activity. **COOPERATIVE GROUPS**	**WHILE** others work in groups, have children complete the Theme Project. (p.T170) **COOPERATIVE GROUPS**	**AFTER** the Phonics and Decoding lesson, children can complete the *Phonics Activity Book* (p. 7). **TEACHER-LED GROUP** **WHILE** others read Trade Books, read *Who Is Tapping at My Window?* from the *ESL/Title I Library.* **INDEPENDENT**	**WHILE** others are working in groups, have children choose a book from the *Multi-Language Library* to take home and share with family members. **INDEPENDENT**

DINOSAURS ALIVE AND WELL! T175–T222

	BELOW-LEVEL READERS	ABOVE-LEVEL READERS	ESL	BILINGUAL
1 READING AND RESPONDING Build Background and Concepts Vocabulary Strategies Strategic Reading Response Corner	**BEFORE** reading the selection, do a "picture walk" through the selection. **TEACHER-LED GROUP** **AFTER** reading the selection, guide partners in rereading it, using Reader Response Card 6 (Written Conversation). **PAIRS**	**WHILE** others complete the strategic reading, have children choose and complete an Idea Bank activity. **COOPERATIVE GROUPS**	**BEFORE** reading the selection, use the Introducing the Literature pages of the *Sheltered English/ESL Manual* (pp. 14-16). **TEACHER-LED GROUP** **AFTER** reading the selection, have children complete the reproducible page of the *Sheltered English/ESL Manual* (p. 15). **INDEPENDENT**	**AFTER** reading the anthology selection, choose the translation in the appropriate *Anthology Translation Booklet* and have children take it home to share. **INDEPENDENT** **INSTEAD OF** Strategic Reading, share with Spanish-speaking children a play from *Escenas y alegrías* in CIELO ABIERTO. **TEACHER-LED GROUP**
2 INTEGRATING LANGUAGE ARTS Idea Bank Writer's Workshop Grammar Spelling Vocabulary Workshop	**WHILE** other children complete Idea Bank activities, help children complete the *Writer's Magazine* (pp. 12–15). **TEACHER-LED GROUP** **WHILE** others work on Spelling, pull out a needs-based group for *Integrated Spelling* Teacher's Edition Lesson 4. **TEACHER-LED GROUP**	**AFTER** the Writer's Workshop, children can enter their how-to sentences using *The Amazing Writing Machine.* **COOPERATIVE GROUPS** **WHILE** you work with others on the Phonics and Decoding lesson, children can use maps to look for and list place names that begin with *wr, kn,* and *gn.* (p.T215) **COOPERATIVE GROUPS**	**DURING** the Vocabulary Workshop, ask children to share antonym pairs in their first languages, and then tell them the English equivalents. (p.T213) **TEACHER-LED GROUP**	**INSTEAD OF** the Idea Bank activities, use one of the Responding to the Script activities in *Escenas y alegrías Teacher's Guide.* **TEACHER-LED GROUP**
3 LEARNING THROUGH THE LITERATURE Direct Skills Instruction Integrated Curriculum Reading Trade Books Theme Project	**WHILE** reviewing the Phonics lesson, use the *Intervention Strategies Manual* (pp. 24-25). **TEACHER-LED GROUP** **AFTER** reading a Trade Book, such as *Max* or *Tacky the Penguin,* have children write their reactions in their personal journals. **INDEPENDENT**	**WHILE** others work on the Phonics and Decoding lesson, children can complete the *Phonics Activity Book* (p.10). **INDEPENDENT**	**AFTER** the Phonics and Decoding lesson, pull out a needs-based group for review of consonant digraphs. **TEACHER-LED GROUP**	**WHILE** others are sharing trade books, have children choose a book from the *Multi-Language Library* to take home to share with family members. **INDEPENDENT**

Ongoing Assessment Strategies

PORTFOLIOS

WHAT IS A PORTFOLIO?

A portfolio is an ongoing collection of a child's reading and writing. It can be an easily accessible folder, box, space on a shelf, or computer disk in which student writing is collected. Begun early in the school year, it is a continually growing collection of both work in progress and finished work. A working portfolio provides assessment, instruction, and development opportunities.

A child benefits from a portfolio because it

- encourages reflection about reading and writing development.
- serves as a springboard to more reading and writing.
- aids in the development of self-assessment strategies.

A teacher benefits from a portfolio because it

- reflects a child's literacy development.
- provides a forum for discussion of a child's reading and writing interests and attitudes.
- supplies continuous informal assessment opportunities and provides opportunities to adjust instruction in order to meet goals.

A wide range of reading and writing activities can be included in the portfolios, such as reading and writing logs; lists of stories read or stories to read; pictures; prewriting ideas; rough and final drafts of free and assigned writing; journals meant to be read by others; and portfolio conference notes.

See the Organizing My Portfolio Checklist on page T234 and the SIGNATURES *Portfolio Assessment Teacher's Guide.*

ASSESSMENT TOOLBOX

Views on assessment (the process of gathering information) and evaluation (the process of judging that information) have evolved in recent years to support a more holistic approach to literacy development. We now recognize that no single tool or strategy is sufficient for viewing all aspects of a child's literacy development.

In addition to formal tools such as the SIGNATURES *Skills Assessment, Holistic Reading Assessment,* and *Integrated Performance Assessment,* you might use one or more of the following strategies to integrate instruction and assessment:

- Observation Checklists or Kid Watching to guide observations of literacy behaviors and development
- Portfolios, or similar ongoing collections of a child's work
- Student Self-Assessment Checklists to gain insight into a child's perception of his or her strengths and weaknesses and to help children begin to take responsibility for their own learning
- Miscue Analysis, or Running Records, to assess an individual's decoding and meaning construction strategies
- Attitudes and Interests Inventories for planning learning activities
- Individual Reading Inventories for assessing the way a child decodes and constructs meaning
- Anecdotal Records to track children's progress and behaviors as they interact with other students, materials, and/or curriculum
- Retellings, oral or written, to gain knowledge about how a child constructs meaning

End-of-Theme Formal Assessment Tools

SKILLS ASSESSMENT

Multiple-choice diagnostic tests that measure mastery of the following skills:

- Reading: vocabulary, *r*-controlled vowel (/är/*ar*), and sequence
- Language: word order, sentences, naming part of sentence, joining naming parts, telling part of sentence, and joining telling parts

HOLISTIC READING ASSESSMENT

Reading passages with multiple-choice and open-ended questions to assess children's application of literal, inferential, and critical thinking in a global and holistic manner

INTEGRATED PERFORMANCE ASSESSMENT

Performance tasks to gain a comprehensive view of a child's reading and writing progress. Children read and respond to "On a Hot, Hot Day" by Nicki Weiss. Children demonstrate expressive writing in story form. One or both sections may be used.

Celebrate Me!

as anyone ever told you that you're special? Well, you are! aybe you are a good friend. Maybe you know how to make ople laugh. There could be something else that you do ell. Everyone is special in some way. And that's what makes e interesting!

13

THEME 1

Celebrate Me!

DISCUSSING THE THEME

Invite children to read about the theme on page 13. Encourage volunteers to tell how they are special. Then draw attention to the sentences *Everyone is special in some way. And that's what makes life interesting!* Discuss what the sentences mean. Ask children for examples of ways that being different from one another helps to make life interesting.

Previewing the Theme Literature

Read the table of contents on pages 14–15 with children. If they are familiar with any of the selections, poets, authors, or illustrators, ask them to share what they know.

Brainstorm with children ways that people are special. As the discussion unfolds, help children see that all of us are unique in some way. Make a group list of the different ways people are special. Display the list, and invite children to add to it as they read the selections in the theme.

Ask children to recall stories they have read in which the characters learned something about themselves or showed that they are special in some way. Volunteers can describe the characters for classmates.

CELEBRATE ME!

Bookshelf

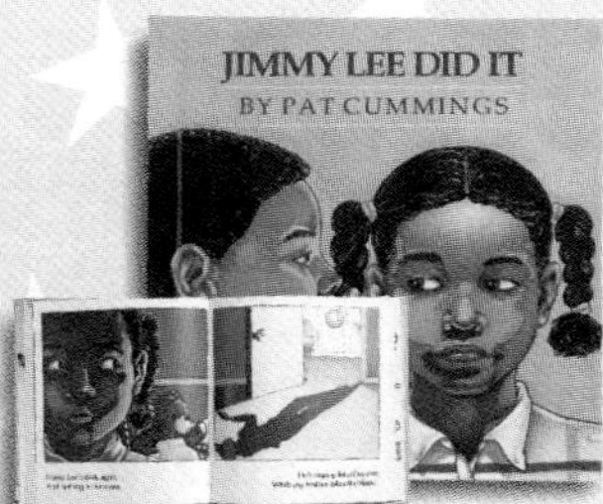

Jimmy Lee Did It
written and illustrated
by Pat Cummings

When things go wrong, Artie blames someone called Jimmy Lee. Artie's sister Angel tries to catch Jimmy Lee in the act. Can she do it?

Signatures Library
Award-Winning Author

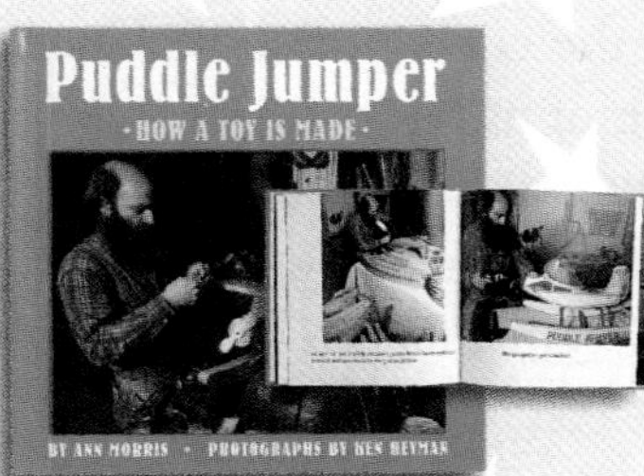

Puddle Jumper: How a Toy Is Made
by Ann Morris

Sarah helps her dad make a puddle jumper. What is it? How is it made? You'll soon find out!

Signatures Library
Award-Winning Author

Emily and Alice
by Joyce Champion

Emily and Alice learn that it isn't always easy to be best friends.

Award-Winning Illustrator

Edward the Emu
by Sheena Knowles

Edward the emu visits other animals in the zoo to see what they are like.

Lionel at Large
by Stephen Krensky

Every day is different for Lionel, and he makes the best of it.

Award-Winning Author

16 17

The Signatures Library

***Jimmy Lee Did It,* written and illustrated by Pat Cummings, tells about a boy who tells his sister that the messes all over their house are the work of someone called Jimmy Lee.**

***Puddle Jumper: How a Toy Is Made* by Ann Morris is a photo essay about Sarah and her father, a toymaker. Sarah watches and helps her dad as he designs, plans, and builds his newest wooden toy, called a Puddle Jumper.**

Strategies for reading *Jimmy Lee Did It* appear with the "Emily and Alice Again" lesson on page T114. Strategies for *Puddle Jumper: How a Toy Is Made* appear with the "Max Found Two Sticks" lesson on page T168.

Comprehensive lesson plans are available on T226–T233.

Related Reading

These trade books offer children further opportunities to work with the Celebrate Me! theme.

ESL/Title I Library

These easy-to-read library books connect to the theme Celebrate Me!: *What Do You Like?* by Michael Grejniec; *Who Is Tapping At My Window?* by A. G. Deming.

THEME PROJECT OVERVIEW

A Book About Me

THEME OVERVIEW

The selections in this theme emphasize the concept that whether our experiences are similar or different, each of us has qualities that make us unique and special. This project will help children recognize ways in which they are uniquely themselves. Each lesson in the theme is followed by a Project Checkpoint that will help children complete the project.

PROJECT PLANNER

QUESTION: What makes me so special? (Investigation)

STAGES		GOALS
	PROJECT LAUNCH (p.T19) 1-2 days	**Examine the idea that children are all different.** • Form groups based on interests, and note differences within the group. • Draw personal webs to use as book covers.
	CHECKPOINT 1 (p.T68) 3-4 days	**Explore children's school experiences.** • Draw pictures or maps showing how they go to school. • Create a list of rules for traveling safely to school.
	CHECKPOINT 2 (p.T116) 2-3 days	**Examine the uniqueness of each one's family.** • Make a class list of titles that show family relationship. • Draw and write about time spent with families.
	CHECKPOINT 3 (p.T170) 2-4 days	**Think about their futures.** • Discuss how Max discovered his rhythm and what he can do to use his talent as he grows up. • Examine own interests and how to use them in a career. • Write steps they can take to reach their goals.
	CHECKPOINT 4 (p.T222) 3-4 days	**Measure themselves, record measurements, and then assemble their books.** • Work with partners to measure height, hand span, and foot length. Make fingerprint records. • Collect book pages, add a title, and assemble books.
	PROJECT PRESENTATIONS (p.T224) 3-4 days	**Share the books.** • Read other children's books and share three new things they learned about each child. • Display books in school or a library for a week. Invite family members and friends to the opening of the display.

STUDENTS ACQUIRING ENGLISH

Encourage children to express their ideas in English and in their primary languages.

MULTIPLE INTELLIGENCES

Encourage children with strong **visual/spatial** skills to experiment with designs and share design ideas.

INQUIRY PROJECT IDEAS

Some children may wish to explore other means of self-examination. They may share ideas after

- reading a book about a child their age.
- exploring the origins of their first or last names.

PROJECT LAUNCH

LAUNCH OPTIONS

HOW YOU'VE CHANGED! **(WHOLE GROUP)** **Ask children to bring in pictures of themselves from their younger years and write their names on the back of each print. Arrange the photos along the chalk ledge. Have groups of children take turns looking at the pictures and trying to match photos to classmates.**	**Look Back on Learning** **(SMALL GROUP)** **Have children think of something they have learned recently. Ask a child to share one thing he or she has learned, such as riding a bike, playing an instrument, reading, or making a snack. Starting with a child sitting next to the first one, children take turns sharing something they have learned.**

WHOLE-GROUP DISCUSSION

Ask children if it is easy or hard to remember things that happened a while ago. Prompt discussion with such questions as *Did someone take your picture the first time you rode a bike? What do people in your family do to remember family events?*

FORM PROJECT GROUPS

Have children form groups based on interests, such as keeping pets, outdoor games, school subjects, or favorite foods. Tell groups to talk about their interests and to notice ways that individuals within the group differ from each other, even though they share an interest.

Tell children to write about themselves in the shape of a wheel. To do this, children should

- **write their names in the middle of a sheet of paper, and draw wheel spokes outward from their names.**
- **On each spoke, they write something about themselves, what they like, or their interests.**

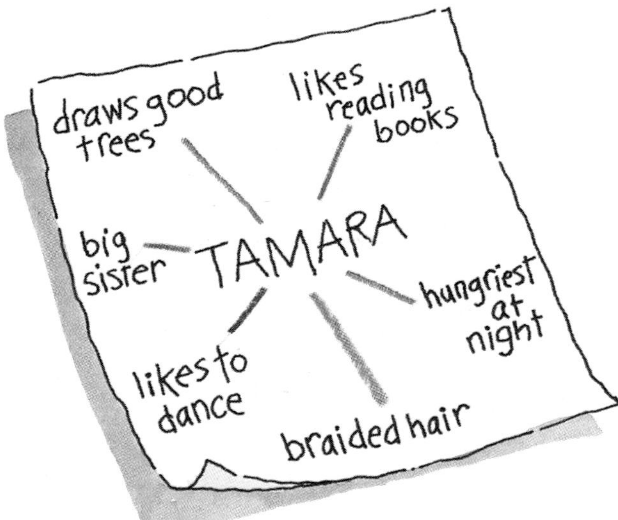

Project Card 1 can be found as a copying master on page R25.

THEME PROJECT LAUNCH 1

Celebrate Me!

A Book About Me

SOMETHING TO THINK ABOUT

1. Think of what you like . . .
   to make   to eat   to look at
2. Talk with a group that likes one of the same things you do. Find out how all the group members are different.
3. Write your name. Draw a wheel around it and write down all the things you like.

riding my bike / dogs / peanut butter / Benjy / reading / waking up early / cartoons

Project Card 1

DID YOU KNOW?

- **Fingerprints aren't our only unique physical identifiers. Other one-of-a-kind indicators are the shape of our kneecaps and the shape of our ears.**
- **In ancient times, wealthy people had statues made of themselves so others would always remember them.**

PROJECT MANAGEMENT

ADDITIONAL RESOURCES

BOOKS

***Just Me* by Marie Hall Ets. Puffin, 1978.**

***I'm Terrific* by Marjorie Weinman Sharmat. Holiday, 1977.**

***Honey, I Love: And Other Love Poems* by Eloise Greenfield. HarperCollins, 1978.**

TECHNOLOGY

FORMAL ASSESSMENT

Prompts for self- and peer assessment and a rubric for teacher assessment are provided on page T225.

Planning a Literacy Event

Grand Opening Begin planning the Grand Opening of a display of children's books as a culminating activity at the completion of the theme. This will give children a chance to share their published work with a wider audience.

- Set a date for the Grand Opening.
- Ask a local library or the school if your class can exhibit their books for one week, starting with the opening day.
- If possible, arrange to have refreshments for the event.
- Children can write invitations to the opening to family and friends.
- Appoint a food committee whose job it will be to decide on refreshments and assign tasks for their preparation.

Enlisting Parents as Partners

Reading: The Key to Success During conferences, parents may ask for ideas to get their children reading. Offer these suggestions:

- ☑ Encourage your child to read, whether it's a street sign or a list of ice cream flavors.
- ☑ Be sure to praise your young reader's efforts.
- ☑ Let your child see you reading and enjoying what you read.
- ☑ Read to your child. Talk about what you read.

TECHNOLOGY

The *At Home in Our Schools* videocassette contains numerous ideas for family involvement projects.

Surfing the Internet? See Issues and Ideas School↔Home Idea Bank on the Harcourt Brace Home Page: http://www.hbschool.com

The *Family Involvement Newsletter* for this theme contains further suggestions on this topic and other topics of interest to parents.

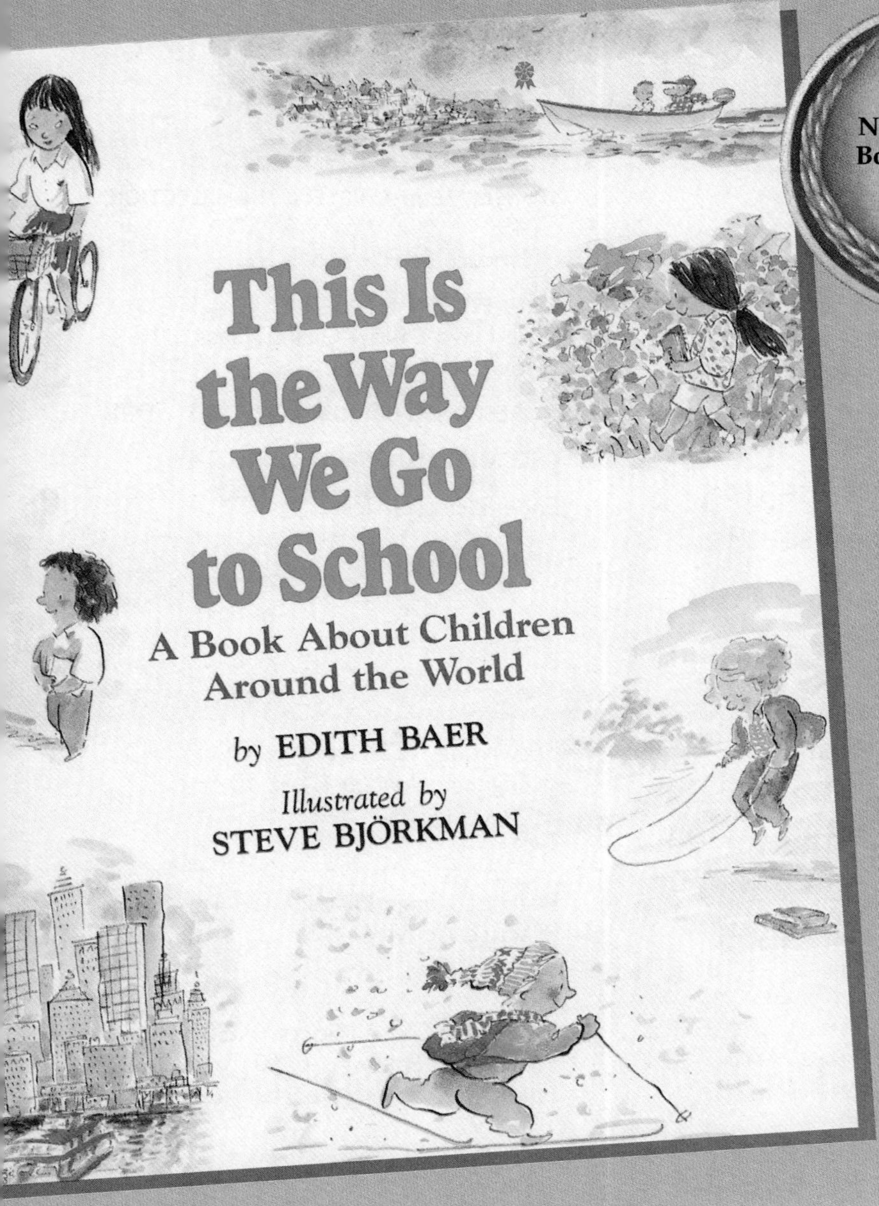

This Is the Way We Go to School
A Book About Children Around the World
by EDITH BAER
Illustrated by STEVE BJÖRKMAN

Notable Trade Book in Social Studies

THEME: LEARNING ABOUT ONESELF

Celebrate Me!

In "This Is the Way We Go to School," children begin to think about the rest of the world. As they read about how children in other places travel to school, they see that every place is different and that people can do things differently—an important part of understanding and celebrating their world and themselves!

Linking Poetry to Nonfiction

Children experience poems about being a new student and about all kinds of feelings.

SELECTION SUMMARY

Genre: Rhyming Nonfiction

This rhyming story takes children on a journey around the globe to see the many ways people travel in different places. First, they meet children who are getting to school by jogging and by riding a bus. As the adventure unfolds, they also learn how children in faraway places and other climates travel to and from school.

Edith Baer

ABOUT THE AUTHOR AND THE ILLUSTRATOR

EDITH BAER has been an author and teacher for years. Her books are enjoyed all over the world. This story is a Notable Trade Book in Social Studies.

STEVE BJÖRKMAN drew pictures for greeting cards before he illustrated children's books. The experience helped him as he developed and created the award-winning illustrations for *This Is the Way We Go to School.*

For more information about the author and the illustrator, see page T45.

Steve Björkman

SUGGESTED LESSON PLANNER

▶ ***This Is the Way We Go to School***

	DAY 1	DAY 2
PART 1 Reading Listening Speaking Viewing **Key Words** mountain against sometimes shoes air start	**BUILD BACKGROUND** T24 **VOCABULARY STRATEGIES** T24–T25 *Chart/Transparency 1* *Practice Book* pp. 3–4 **READING THE SELECTION** T26–T45 Options for Reading T26–T27 *Response Card 5* *Literature Cassette 1* **REVIEW PREDICTIONS/PURPOSE** T44 **APPRECIATING THE LITERATURE** T44 NOTE: Children may read the selection on Day 2.	**SUMMARIZE AND RETELL THE SELECTION** T45 *Practice Book* p. 5 **READ POETRY** T46–T47 "We Have a New Girl in Class," "How Do You Feel?" ◆ **RESPONSE CORNER ACTIVITIES** T48 **CHECKING COMPREHENSION** T49 *End-of-Selection Test*
PART 2 Writer's Workshop	**SENTENCES ABOUT A PICTURE** Thinking as Writers T54 *Chart/Transparency 2*	Prewriting T54 *Language Handbook* p. 10 *Kid Pix*
Grammar	✓ **SENTENCES** Teach the Concept T56 Daily Language Practice (1–2) R18	Daily Language Practice (3–4) R18 Practice Activity T57
Spelling	**WORDS WITH SHORT *o*** *top lot mom pond box* *hop fox hot doll jog* Pretest/Self-Check T58 *Integrated Spelling Teacher's Edition* pp. T21, T268	Open and Closed Sorts T58 *Integrated Spelling* p. 10 *Integrated Spelling Teacher's Edition* p. T22
PART 3 Phonics	✓ ***R*-CONTROLLED VOWEL: /är/*ar*** Phonics-Vocabulary Connection T25	✓ ***R*-CONTROLLED VOWEL: /är/*ar*** (Introduce) T60 *Big Book of Rhymes* p. 4 *Phonics Practice Book* pp. 133–134
Skills and Strategies	◆ **INTEGRATED CURRICULUM** *The World Around Me* **Art** T64 **Social Studies** T64 **Math** T65 **Science** T65  *Thinkin' Things Collection 1: Flying Shapes; Thinkin' Things Collection 2: 2–3 D Blox; Imagination Express, Destination: Ocean*	**COMPREHENSION SKILL** T62–T63 ✓ Sequence (Introduce) *Practice Book* p. 10
	Use the Intervention Strategies note on page T39 to help **below-level readers**.	Use the Challenge note on page T63 for **above-level readers**.

NOTE: An alternative lesson plan for **below-level readers** appears on *Intervention Strategies Manual* pp. 2–7. A lesson for **students acquiring English** appears on *Sheltered English/ESL Manual* pp. 2–5.

DAY 3	DAY 4	DAY 5
◆ **IDEA BANK ACTIVITIES** Listening and Speaking T52 Real-Life Reading: Reading Transportation Signs T52 Oral Language T53 Kinesthetic T53 *Writer's Magazine* pp. 2–5 School–Home Connection 1 R48  	**VOCABULARY WORKSHOP** T59 Reviewing Key Words Story Strips R52 Rhyming Words *Practice Book* p. 8 *Take-Home/Keep-at-Home Book: New School, New Friends* **READING TRADE BOOKS** T66–T67  Take-Home Book	**READING TRADE BOOKS** T61, T63, T65, T66–T67  Instant Reader™ Instant Reader™
Drafting T54 *Language Handbook* pp. 10–11 *The Amazing Writing Machine*	Responding and Revising T55	Proofreading and Publishing T55
Daily Language Practice (5–6) R18 Practice Activity T57 *Language Handbook* pp. 36–37	Daily Language Practice (7–8) R18 Practice Activity T57 *Grammar Practice Book* pp. 13–14	Daily Language Practice (9–12) R18 *Practice Book* p. 6
Discuss the Generalization T58 *Integrated Spelling* p. 11 *Integrated Spelling Teacher's Edition* p. T23	Apply to Writing T58 *Integrated Spelling* pp. 12–13 *Integrated Spelling Teacher's Edition* pp. T24–T25	Posttest T58 *Practice Book* p. 7 *Integrated Spelling Teacher's Edition* p. T26
✓ ***R*-CONTROLLED VOWEL: /är/*ar*** T60 *Phonics Practice Reader 11: Smart Riddles*	✓ ***R*-CONTROLLED VOWEL: /är/*ar*** T61 *Practice Book* p. 9 *Bailey's Book House* (Read-A-Rhyme)	✓ ***R*-CONTROLLED VOWEL: /är/*ar*** T61 *Phonics Activity Book* p. 1
PHONICS AND DECODING MINILESSON T29 Short Vowel: /o/*o* *(Maintain)* *Phonics Activity Book* p. 2 *Phonics Game Board Pattern Book* p. 2 *Phonics Practice Reader 1: How Odd* *Phonics Practice Book* pp. 28–32 *Practice Book* p. 11	**PHONICS AND DECODING MINILESSON** T35 Initial Clusters with s (Maintain) *Phonics Activity Book* p. 3 *Phonics Game Board Pattern Book* p. 29 *Phonics Practice Book* pp. 187–188 *Practice Book* p. 12	**GRAMMAR MINILESSON** T39 ✓ Capitalizing Names (Review) *Language Handbook* pp. 58–59 Theme Project Checkpoint 1 T68
Use the Students Acquiring English note on page T67 for **ESL readers**.	Have children read "What's for Lunch?," pages 42–43, to connect nonfiction about food with the selection they just read.	To help children build fluency, use the *Instant Readers™ Rabbit and Turtle Go to School* and *A World of Fun* on pages T50–T51.

✓ = Tested Skill
◆ = Optional activities that may be used to adjust pacing throughout the lesson
Titles in *italics* are optional materials.

Reading and Responding

BUILDING BACKGROUND AND CONCEPTS

PRIOR KNOWLEDGE

Discuss ways to travel. Tape up a large sheet of paper. Write the following title at the top of the chart: *Ways We Travel*. For starters, have children tell how they travel to school. Then ask them to think of other ways people travel. Encourage them to list ways people travel in the community. Add the suggestions to the chart. Display a globe, and explain to children that they will be reading about how children who live in the United States and in other parts of the world travel to school.

Ways We Travel	
school bus	bike
car	walk

VOCABULARY STRATEGIES

KEY WORDS DEFINED

mountain high hill
sometimes not always
air what we breathe
against in preparation for; to be safe from
shoes coverings for the feet
start to begin

SUPPORT WORDS

Display the words *aboard, ashore, cable cars, ferry, radio, through*, and *trolley*. Discuss their meanings and have them used in sentences.

INTEGRATED SPELLING

SPELLING PRETEST: page T58
SPELLING GENERALIZATION: Words with short *o*

Intervention Strategies

For children who may have difficulty reading "This Is the Way We Go to School," support is available in *Intervention Strategies Manual*, pages 2–7, and on page T39 and T50–T51 in this lesson.

STUDENTS ACQUIRING ENGLISH

See *Sheltered English/ESL Manual*, pages 2–5.

"I like to present this story as a kind of guessing game. After children read each group of pages, I have them use the pictures and words, especially the proper nouns, to guess the city, state, or country where each child lives. Most of the pictures contain clues, and sometimes, the words provided give a place away. Occasionally, clues are absent or subtle. A guessing game is fun, and it encourages children to look closely at the story."

CUEING SYSTEMS

Have children read new vocabulary. Display Chart/Transparency 1, or write the words and sentences on the board. Have children read words they might know.

Ask a volunteer to read the first sentence aloud. When the child comes to the word *mountain*, ask children to suggest a word that would make sense in the sentence. As suggestions are made, ask:

> **Does the word make sense in the sentence?**
> **What parts of the word help you figure it out?**

Have children read the rest of the story, using clues within the words as well as other words in a sentence to help them figure out unknown words.

CHART/TRANSPARENCY 1

mountain	sometimes	air
against	shoes	start

I live on a mountain. I like to walk to school. Sometimes the air is cold. On a windy day, I like to be bundled up against the wind. On warm days, I take off my shoes and socks and go walking. On other days, it will start to rain. Then I run to school!

HANDS-ON ACTIVITY

Make word cards. Distribute six index cards to each child. Write the Key Words on the board. Then have children follow these directions:

- Write the word that rhymes with *chart. (start)*
- Write the word that begins like *short. (shoes)*
- Write the word that means "a high hill." *(mountain)*
- Write the word that rhymes with *chair* and *bear. (air)*
- Write the word that is made from two smaller words. *(sometimes)*
- Write the word that ends like *past* and *best. (against)*

Invite children to draw a picture and write a sentence for each word. Have children add the words to individual Word Files. These can be recipe boxes that have alphabet divider cards inside.

This Is the Way We Go to School

Name ______________________

Cut out the words. Then read each sentence. Use one word to complete each sentence. Glue the word in the right place. Then read the story to a friend.

1. My family sometimes goes hiking.
2. We start early in the morning.
3. It's important to wear strong shoes.

against / air / mountain / shoes / sometimes / start

PRACTICE BOOK, pages 3–4

PHONICS-VOCABULARY CONNECTION

WORD PLAY

Write the Key Word *start* on the board and read the word with children. Then show them how to replace the *st* with a *c* to make *cart*. Again, read the new word with children.

Write these letters on the board: *d, p, ch, sm*. Have children use consonant substitution to make four more words to add to the list. Then, read the words aloud as a group. Talk about how the letter *a* sounds in all of the words. Explain that when *a* is followed by *r*, the *ar* sounds like the vowel sound in *star*.

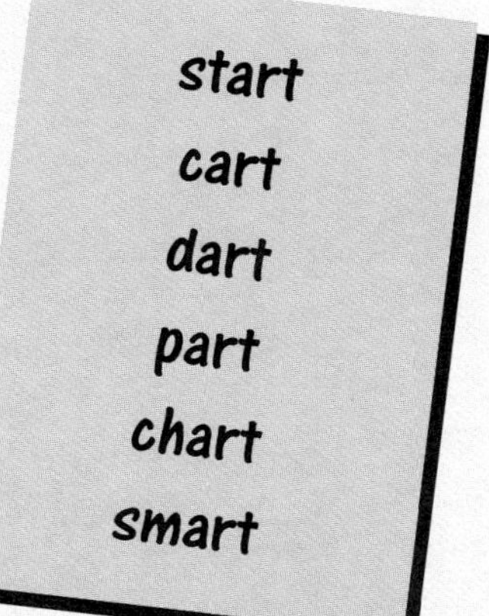

The concept of the *r*-controlled vowel /är/*ar* is further developed on pages T60-T61.

Strategic Reading

STRATEGY FOCUS: SEQUENCING

Display a sheet of chart paper, and write this heading at the top: *What Good Readers Do.* Talk about things good readers do to help themselves understand what they are reading. Then introduce the strategy for this lesson, sequencing. As children begin to read new selections, have them suggest strategies that good readers use. Post the list, and encourage children to refer to it during their reading.

What Good Readers Do
Think about what happens first, next, and last in a story

MODEL **Writers write stories in an order that makes sense. Things happen first, next, and last. When I think about the order of the things that happen, it helps me understand and remember the story.**

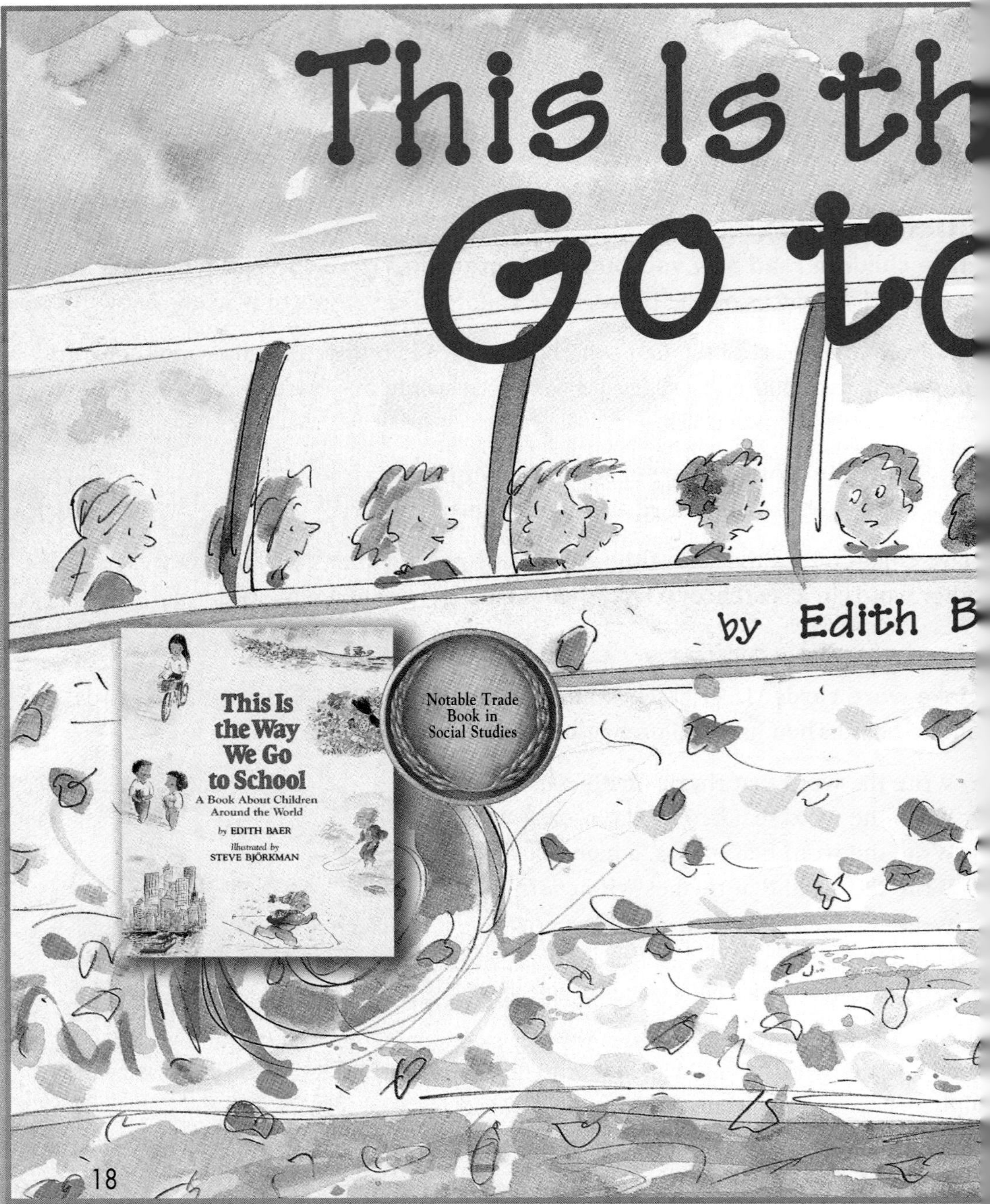

This Is th
Go t
by Edith B

This Is the Way We Go to School
A Book About Children Around the World
by EDITH BAER
Illustrated by STEVE BJÖRKMAN

Notable Trade Book in Social Studies

18

TIPS FOR CLASSROOM MANAGEMENT

SMALL GROUP

INDEPENDENT READING

Have children read "This Is the Way We Go to School" silently. Encourage them to take time to examine the pictures as they read the text. As children finish, have them write in their personal journal which way to travel was their favorite and why.

COOPERATIVE READING

PARTNER READING Make Reader Response Card 5 (Free Response), page R22, available for pairs to use as they read. Partners might choose to take turns reading every other page or read in unison.

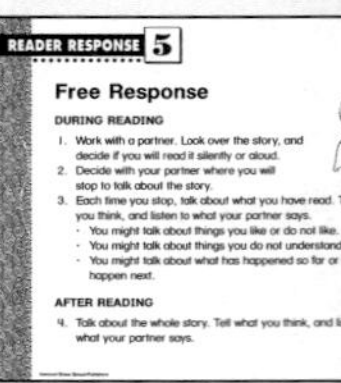

Response Card

Way We School

strated by Steve Björkman

19

PREVIEWING/ SETTING PURPOSES

Have children read the story title on pages 18 and 19. Suggest that children flip through the first few pages to preview the story. Ask them to predict what the story might be about and what they might learn about traveling. Have children write their predictions in their journals. Then help children set their purposes for reading.

How to Make a Journal

Have children begin their personal journals. They can use any kind of notebook they like. Tell them that they will be using these journals to record their predictions about the stories they'll be reading and confirm their predictions after reading.

WHOLE CLASS

STRATEGIC READING

Choose some or all of the suggestions and questions under Strategic Reading, pages T26–T44, to guide a discussion and model the STRATEGY FOCUS of Sequencing.

SHARED READING

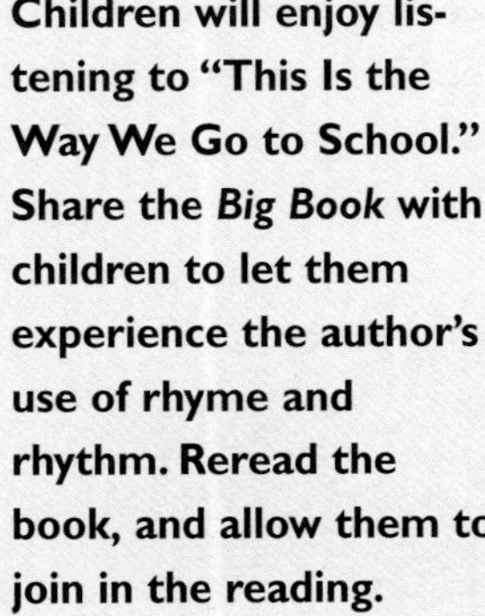

Children will enjoy listening to "This Is the Way We Go to School." Share the *Big Book* with children to let them experience the author's use of rhyme and rhythm. Reread the book, and allow them to join in the reading.

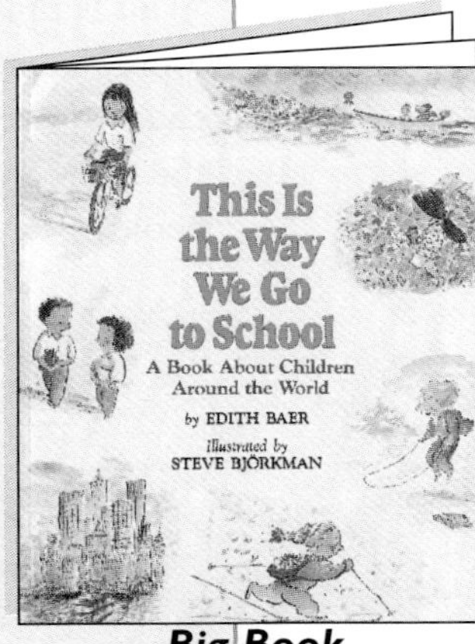

Big Book

Strategic Reading

MODELING A STRATEGY

PAGES 20–21 Before children read, have them look carefully at the pictures and talk about what they think the pages will be about. Then, after children have read, have them look again at the picture on page 21. Model how the picture illustrates what they are reading about in the story. **Think aloud:** *In the picture, I see two children on foot and one on roller skates. The story says "Liz and Larry . . . wear their jogging shoes to school." I can guess that the two children on foot are Liz and Larry. From the words, I can guess that they're jogging to school.*

RELATING PICTURES TO TEXT

One by one or two by two—
Come along, it's fun to do!

Ellen takes it nice and slow,
time to watch the flowers grow.

20

LISTENING CENTER

"This Is the Way We Go to School" is available on *Literature Cassette 1*. Some children may benefit from listening to the story and following along in their books.

PHONICS IN ACTION

Have children find the words *come* and *nice* on page 20. Ask children what is different about the sound that the letter *c* stands for in *nice* and *come*. Point out that the letter *c* can stand for two sounds—the /k/ sound as in *come* or the /s/ sound as in *nice*.

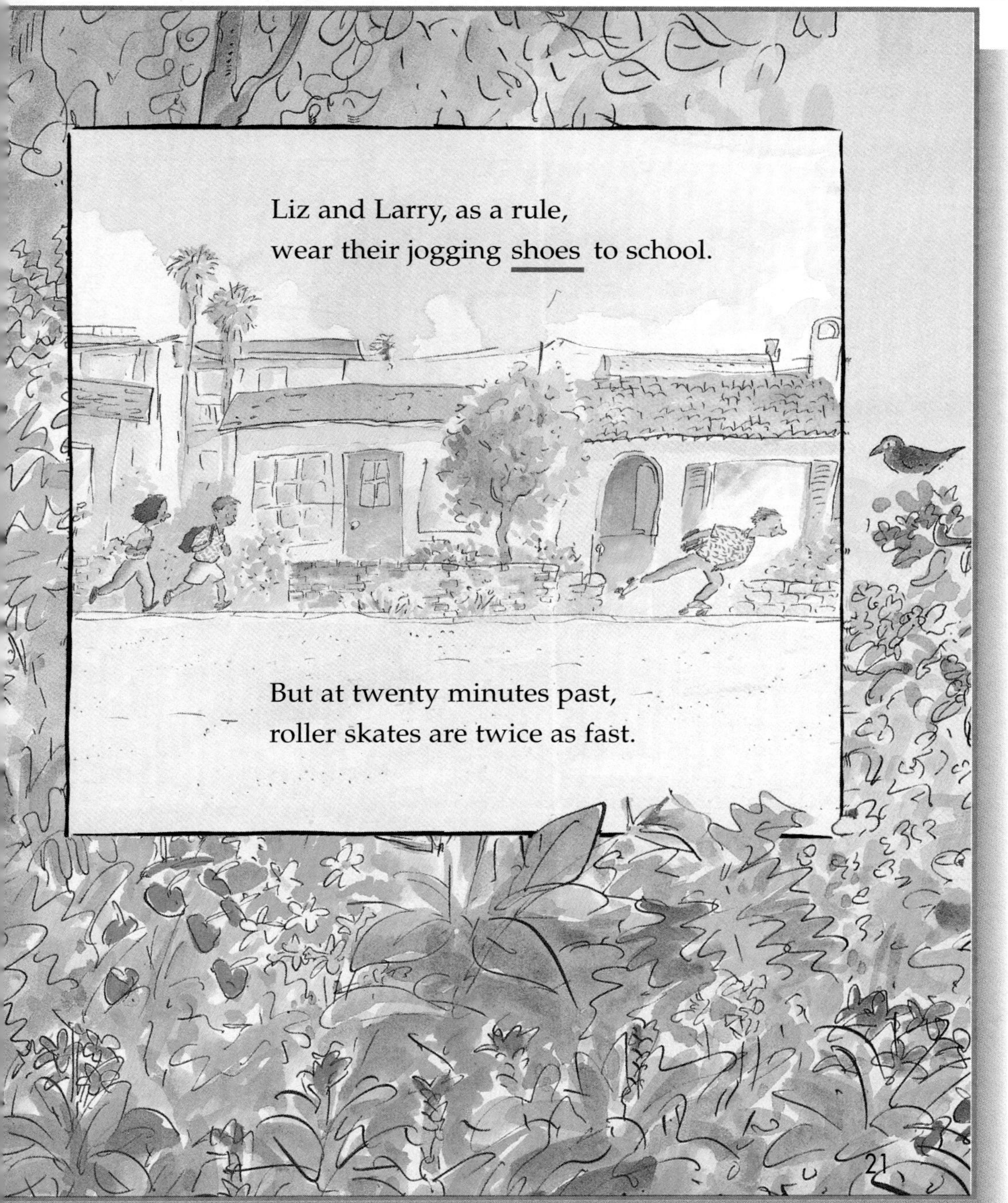

Liz and Larry, as a rule,
wear their jogging shoes to school.

But at twenty minutes past,
roller skates are twice as fast.

21

MINILESSON

MAINTAIN: PHONICS AND DECODING

Short Vowel: /o/*o*

INFORMAL ASSESSMENT

As children read, notice whether they can decode words with the short *o* sound.

TEACH/MODEL

Ask a volunteer to read aloud the sentence about Liz and Larry on page 21:

Liz and Larry, as a rule,
wear their jogging shoes to school.

Write the word *jog* on the board; then write the words *mop, hot, spot,* and *Molly.* Read each word aloud, encouraging children to read along with you. Ask what all the words have in common. Point out that all the words have the same vowel sound, the short *o.*

PRACTICE/APPLY

Distribute these letter cards to pairs of children: *o, p, c, h, m, t.* Have them form the word *hop.* Invite partners to use the cards to form other words. Have pairs keep lists of the words that they form and then share their lists.

PHONICS ACTIVITY BOOK, page 2

For further reinforcement, you may want to use Sounds Like Fox, *Phonics Game Board Pattern Book,* page 2.

PHONICS PRACTICE READER 1

PHONICS PRACTICE BOOK, pages 28–32

MULTI-AGE CLASSROOMS

Have children work in groups to list all the kinds of flowers they can name. Bring the groups together, and compile a list. Younger children can draw pictures to go with the flower names they know, while older children can research the flowers.

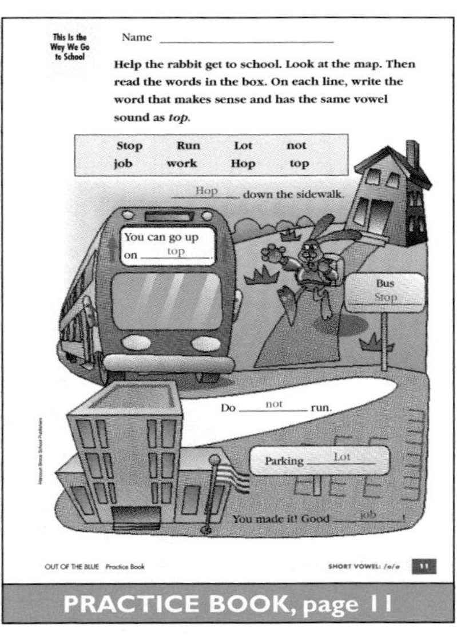

This Is the Way We Go to School

Name ______________

Help the rabbit get to school. Look at the map. Then read the words in the box. On each line, write the word that makes sense and has the same vowel sound as *top*.

Stop	Run	Lot	not
job	work	Hop	top

OUT OF THE BLUE Practice Book — SHORT VOWEL: /o/o — 11

PRACTICE BOOK, page 11

Strategic Reading

MODELING A STRATEGY

PAGES 22–23 Ask children to look at the pictures and predict what the pages will be about. Model your thinking: *I see a car, a school bus, and a boat. I think these pages will tell about traveling to school by car, bus, and boat.*

After reading these pages, children will probably be familiar with the pattern and rhythm of the selection. Review with them the names and the methods of transportation mentioned so far. Ask them to think about the pattern of the story and predict what the next two pages will be about. **SEQUENCING**

And the fastest way by far
is by school bus or by car!

22

MATH CONNECTION

SHAPES **Work with children to generate a list of words that name simple shapes, such as *circle, square, rectangle,* and *triangle*. Then, display a photograph or drawing of a school bus. Work as a group to identify these shapes on a school bus.**

Jenny, Jerry, Pete, and Perry ride the Staten Island Ferry.

23

Student Self-Assessment 

USING READING STRATEGIES

When children are reading in small groups, provide a time for them to talk about the good reading strategies they use and the strategies they observe their classmates using. Encourage children to talk among themselves about which reading strategies have helped them.

SOCIAL STUDIES

STATEN ISLAND FERRY

The Staten Island Ferry operates between Staten Island and Manhattan. It is a main way to travel between the two islands. In addition to having the ferry, Staten Island is connected to other parts of New York and New Jersey by four bridges.

EXPANDING VOCABULARY

Have children find the word *Island* on page 23. Ask children to tell what they already know about islands. If necessary, explain that an island is a piece of land completely surrounded by water. If there are any islands in your area, name them for children. If you have a map or globe in the classroom, point out some of the major islands.

Strategic Reading

MODELING A STRATEGY

PAGES 24–26 After children read the pages, model how to use context clues to figure out what the El is. **Think aloud:** *I know from the story that Michael and Miguel can "see the rooftops." The El must be transportation that is above the ground. From the seats and windows shown in the pictures, I think it's a bus or train.* USING CONTEXT CLUES

Cable cars take Jack and Jill
up the hill—

and down the hill.

24

AUTHOR'S CRAFT

Have children suggest reasons why Edith Baer may have chosen Jack and Jill as the names for the two children on page 24. You may want to recite the rhyme "Jack and Jill" with children. Then ask children to speculate about why the author may have wanted them to think of another rhyme while reading this rhyming story.

A CLOSER LOOK

Notice that Björkman often includes real buildings and landmarks in his well-researched illustrations. For example, the pyramid-shaped building on page 24 is an actual office building called the Transamerica Pyramid, located in San Francisco, California.

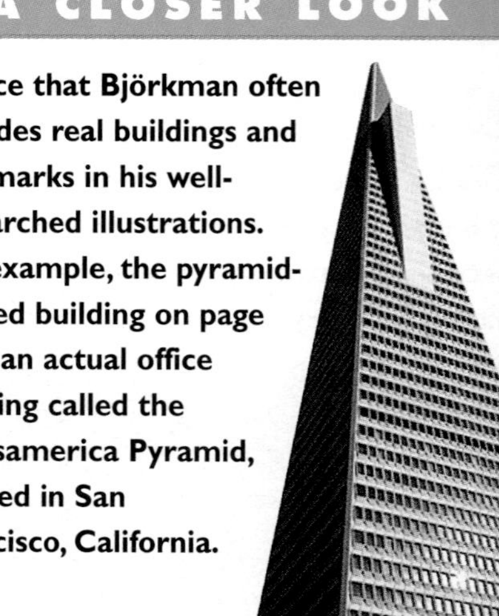

Michael and his friend Miguel see the rooftops from the El.

25

Student Self-Assessment

FIX-UP STRATEGY: USING PICTURE CLUES

If children did not understand what a cable car is, ask them what they could have done to figure out the meaning. Tell children that, as they read, they should look carefully at the pictures for clues to help them better understand unfamiliar words and the plot of the story.

SOCIAL STUDIES

CABLE CARS The cable cars of San Francisco have been in operation since the mid-1870s. Because the city is built on more than forty steep hills, it is difficult for buses to climb them. Instead, the cable cars, which have no power of their own, run on rails and are pulled by a moving cable under the street.

MEETING INDIVIDUAL NEEDS

STUDENTS ACQUIRING ENGLISH Have children find the word *El* on page 25. Children who speak Spanish might be confused because the word *el* means *he* in Spanish and is also sometimes used as an article meaning *the*. Explain that *El* is actually a shortened form of the words *Elevated Railroad*, and that the railroads run on tracks above the ground.

Strategic Reading

APPLYING A STRATEGY

PAGES 27–29 Have children look at the illustrations. Point out that Bianca, Beppo, and Benedetto live in Venice, Italy, while Niels and Solveig live in Norway. Now children can begin to see something about the sequence of the story. Have children read to find out how these children travel to school. Help children name some places already mentioned. Point out that all these places are in the United States. Invite children to notice that the story has now moved to cities and countries around the world. Point out that knowing this pattern can help them understand the story better.
SEQUENCING

PHONICS IN ACTION

Have children find these words on page 26: *plain, day, Jane*. Write the words on the board, and have the words read aloud. Ask how the words are alike. Point out that even though all three words have the long *a* sound, the vowel sound in each word is spelled with different letters.

MULTICULTURAL CONNECTION

The Amish live simple lives in farm communities without the use of electricity. Although the Amish use horses to till their fields and pull their buggies, they use refrigerated trucks to take their produce and cheeses to farmers' markets in large cities.

Bianca, Beppo, Benedetto
ride aboard the *vaporetto.*

Bundled up
against the breeze,
Niels and Solveig
go on skis.

27

MINILESSON

MAINTAIN: PHONICS AND DECODING

Initial Clusters with *s*

INFORMAL ASSESSMENT

When children read, notice whether they can decode words that begin with an *s* cluster.

TEACH/MODEL

Write the following words from pages 26 and 27 on the board: *start, skis.* Ask how the two words are alike. Remind children that when a consonant is blended with the letter *s* at the beginning of a word, both consonant sounds are heard.

PRACTICE/APPLY

Organize children into six groups and assign one of these consonant clusters to each group: *sk, sl, sm, sn, st, sw.* Have children work to list as many words as they can that begin with their cluster. Bring groups together to share their words. Record the words on a chart and encourage children to add words that they find in their reading.

sk	sl	sm	sn	st	sw
skates	slow	smoke	snow	start	swing
sky	sled	smell	snail	stop	sweep
skirt	sleep	small	sniff	story	swan
skip		smart		stand	sweet
skin				star	
				stick	
				stone	

PHONICS ACTIVITY BOOK, page 3

For further reinforcement, you may want to use I Spy. . . , *Phonics Game Board Pattern Book,* page 29.

PHONICS PRACTICE BOOK, pages 187–188

EXPANDING VOCABULARY

Explain that *vaporetto* is an Italian word meaning "steamboat." As children look at the illustration on page 27, they will probably note that there are actually two types of water transportation illustrated. Explain that the boat from which the girl is waving is the vaporetto — the other is called a gondola.

Name ______________

This Is the Way We Go to School

Write a word from the box to complete the poem. Be sure your word makes sense.

snow speak spun skunk ski
scarf stop skin sneak

A skunk in a scarf
Went out to ski.
He spun all around
And then said, "Dear me!
This snow was fun
Up at the top,
But now I don't
Know how to stop!"

12 INITIAL CLUSTERS WITH *s* OUT OF THE BLUE Practice Book

PRACTICE BOOK, page 12

Cooperative Reading

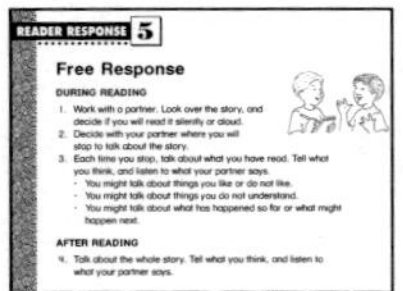
Response Card 5

As children use **Reader Response Card 5** (Free Response) during reading, you may wish to ask a question or two like the following to encourage discussion and assess the group's progress.

1. **What is your favorite way to travel to school so far? Why do you like it?**
2. **Describe how the illustrations help you to understand the places described in the story.**

PHONICS IN ACTION

Write these words from pages 28–29 on the board, and ask a volunteer to read them aloud: *peak, leaves, trees, keep.* Ask how the words are alike. Remind children that the letters *ea* and *ee* can both stand for the long e sound.

SOCIAL STUDIES

SWISS CABLE CARS Sepp and Heidi travel by a special kind of cable railway called a funicular, which is used on mountain peaks. The cars hang above the ground from cables that are strung between towers.

MUSIC CONNECTION

WILLIAM TELL The Swiss have many tales that they enjoy sharing—one is the famous legend of William Tell, who is remembered as one of the bravest fighters for Switzerland's freedom. As they work, children may enjoy listening to the *William Tell* overture, written by Gioacchino Rossini in 1829.

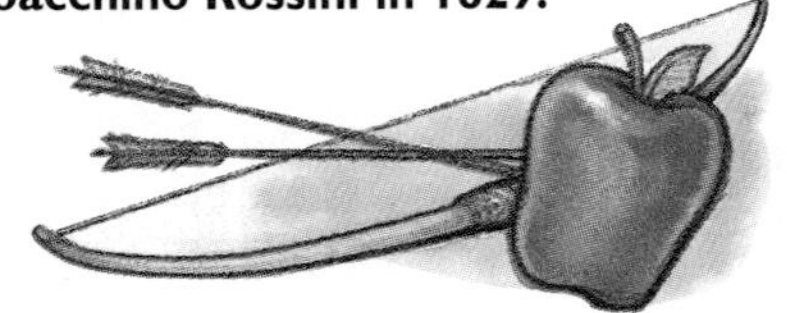

Strategic Reading

APPLYING A STRATEGY

PAGES 30–33 Have children look at the pages and talk about where they think the children live and how the children travel to school. Then, have children read the pages to confirm their ideas.
DRAWING CONCLUSIONS

Kay and Fay and Flo and Joe go to school by radio.

Bicycles bring
Mei and Ling
through the traffic
of Nanjing.

30

SOCIAL STUDIES

CHINA Nanjing is a large city in China. Bicycles are a major form of transportation in China, and both adults and children ride them regularly.
It's not easy to buy bicycles in China, though, because they are very expensive and there is often a waiting period.

CROSS-CULTURAL VIEWPOINT

Mei and Ling are common given names for girls in Chinese culture. The name *Mei* means "beautiful" or "charming." The name *Ling* refers to a musical instrument, a very small bell, and to the delicate sound this bell makes when rung. Have children find out why they were given their names and whether their names have a special meaning.

And beneath the dripping sky,
Ram is riding high and dry.

William comes
ashore by boat,
counting sea gulls
while afloat.

31

Tested Skill

MINILESSON

REVIEW: GRAMMAR

Capitalizing Names

INFORMAL ASSESSMENT

When children write their names during the school day, notice whether they consistently capitalize the first letter.

TEACH/MODEL

Reread pages 30 and 31 of the story with children. Ask volunteers to tell the names they see on these pages. As children say the names, write them on the board. Ask what is special about writing people's names. (Names begin with capital letters.) Remind children that each part of a person's name—first, middle, and last—begins with a capital letter.

PRACTICE/APPLY

Play a name game with children. Ask each child to write his or her name on a slip of paper. Then children fold the slips of paper and place them into a bag or other container. One at a time, children pick a name and read it to classmates. The child who chooses the name tells the capital letter that each part of the name begins with. The child whose name was on the paper takes the next turn.

LANGUAGE HANDBOOK
Special Names and Titles of People, pages 58–59

Intervention Strategies

USING CUEING SYSTEMS **Have children repeat this sentence:** ***When I read and I get stuck on a word, it helps me sometimes to look at the first letter of the word and the picture on the page.*** **Have children share any words they might have had trouble with and how they figured out the word.**

Critical Thinking Questions

1. **Why do you think some of the children walk to school and others ride in vehicles?** (Possible responses: Some children walk because their school is close to their homes and because the weather is nice; some children ride because the school is far away.) CRITICAL: UNDERSTANDING CHARACTERS' ACTIONS

2. **What is another way children could travel to school? Why would they travel in that way?** (Responses will vary, but children should support their answers.) CRITICAL: SPECULATING

Carlos takes the town in stride.

32

Luz prefers the countryside.

EXPANDING VOCABULARY

Read the sentence *Carlos takes the town in stride* and explain that a stride is a kind of step. Explain further that the expression *to take in stride* has its roots in this meaning: "to accept willingly and even gladly." Invite volunteers to walk in a way that shows they're "taking life in stride."

And the famous Metro line
suits Igor and Ilyana fine.

Go by Copter?
By Skidoo?
Somewhere, sometimes,
some kids do!
You come, too!
We'll look for you.

33

Informal Assessment

RELATING TO PERSONAL EXPERIENCES

Good readers make links between literature and their own lives. After children read about all the different kinds of travel in the story, encourage them to tell which kinds of transportation they've used to get to places that are nearby, such as school, and to places that are farther away.

SOCIAL STUDIES

FACT FINDER

Moscow is Russia's transportation center. The people of Moscow are very proud of their elegant—and famous—subway system called the Metro. Over 7 million people ride the Metro every day. Many of its 140 stations are decorated with chandeliers, paintings, statues, stained glass, and marble panels.

A CLOSER LOOK

Have children look at page 33 and use the illustrations to figure out that *copter* is a shortened version of the word *helicopter* and that a Skidoo is a snowmobile used to travel over snow and ice.

Strategic Reading

APPLYING A STRATEGY

PAGES 34–36 Have children look at the map on pages 34–35 and the list on page 36. Discuss how the numbers on the map correspond to the list. Help children locate on the map where they live, and ask them to share their observations about where the children live. Then have children choose two kinds of transportation or two places discussed in the story and tell how they are alike and different. **COMPARING AND CONTRASTING**

1. Ellen
2. Liz and Larry and the skater
3. The bus and car riders
4. Jenny, Jerry, Pete, and Perry
5. Jack and Jill
6. Michael and Miguel
7. Jake and Jane
8. Mitch and Molly
9. Bianca, Beppo, and Benedett
10. Niels and Solveig
11. Ahmed
12. Mira

34

REAL-LIFE CONNECTION

Many children may have seen other states, countries, and cultures only in book and magazine pictures, on television, or in movies. Invite children who have visited or lived in other states and countries to share their experiences. Invite them to bring photographs and objects to show to classmates.

SOCIAL STUDIES CONNECTION

MAPS AND GLOBES Show children how the information on a flat map translates to a globe. Display a globe and help children locate the continents and oceans that are shown on the map on pages 34 and 35. Be sure to emphasize that a globe is another way to show the same information that is on the map.

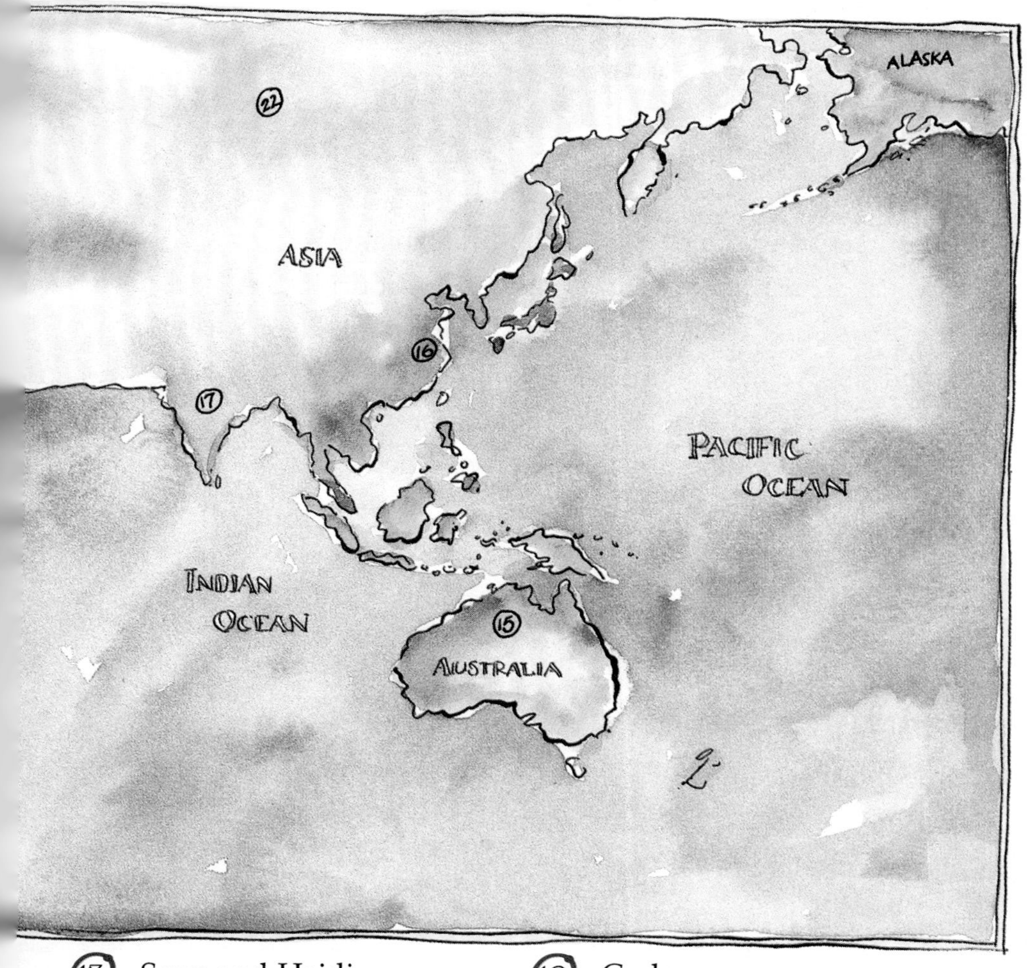

13 Sepp and Heidi
14 Akinyi
15 Kay, Fay, Flo, and Joe
16 Mei and Ling
17 Ram
18 William
19 Carlos
20 Luz
21 Igor and Ilyana
22 The Copter passengers
23 The Skidoo passengers

35

NOTES

Here's a place to list ideas or activities that you would like to use the next time you teach this lesson.

IDEA BANK

LOOKING AT MAPS **Geography comes to life in *The Golden Atlas for Children* by Neil Morris (Western, 1994). This is a rich resource of 21 maps along with interesting details and insights about the world's continents and countries. Use this book or let children look at other maps and share what they learn.**

Returning to the Predictions/Purpose

Earlier in the lesson, children began their personal journals and wrote about what they thought they would learn about traveling. Invite children to share their work and talk about what they did learn about traveling.

Appreciating the Literature

With the whole class or a small group, have an open discussion about the story.

- **What do you think the author wanted you to learn from reading this story?**
- **What did the story make you think about?**

This Is Where We Live

Ellen lives in Hawaii, U.S.A.
Liz and Larry and the skater live in California, U.S.A.
The bus and car riders live in Raytown, Missouri, U.S.A.
Jenny, Jerry, Pete, and Perry live in Staten Island, New York, U.S.A.
Jack and Jill live in San Francisco, California, U.S.A.
Michael and Miguel live in Chicago, Illinois, U.S.A.
Jake and Jane live in Lancaster, Pennsylvania, U.S.A.
Mitch and Molly live in Philadelphia, Pennsylvania, U.S.A.
Bianca, Beppo, and Benedetto live in Venice, Italy.
Niels and Solveig live in Norway.
Ahmed lives in Egypt.
Mira lives in Israel.
Sepp and Heidi live in Switzerland.
Akinyi lives in Kenya.
Kay, Fay, Flo, and Joe live in Australia.
Mei and Ling live in China.
Ram lives in India.
William lives in Maine, U.S.A.
Carlos and Luz live in Mexico.
Igor and Ilyana live in Moscow, Russia.
The Copter passengers live in Siberia, Russia.
The Skidoo passengers live in Canada.

36

SCHOOL↔HOME CONNECTION

Have children ask their families about people they know in other places and about the city or country from which their parents or other family members originally came. Encourage children to find the places on a map or globe and point them out to classmates.

Edith Baer Passport

Name: Edith Baer

Place of Birth: Germany

Childhood: Edith came to the United States alone when she was only a teenager. She left Germany during World War II.

School: She worked hard all day and went to school at night.

Family: Married. She has two children and two grandchildren.

Job: Edith Baer is an author and a college writing teacher. She writes books, magazine stories, and poems. People all over the world read her work.

Steve Björkman Passport

Name: Steve Björkman

Address: California

Family: Married. He has three children.

Job: He used to draw pictures for ads and greeting cards. Now he draws pictures for children's books. *This Is the Way We Go to School* is one of the first books that he has done.

Other: Steve liked drawing pictures for cards. It gave him practice drawing lots of people, animals, and places. This helped him when he started to draw pictures for children's books.

37

About the Author and Illustrator

PAGE 37 Have children read page 37. Talk with them about how authors and illustrators use their personal experiences to create stories and art.

Edith Baer's books are enjoyed by children all over the world. She has written fiction, nonfiction, and poetry. She has also worked as a college teacher to help people learn how to write. Baer and Björkman have collaborated again to create *This Is the Way We Eat Our Lunch: A Book About Children Around the World* (Scholastic, 1995).

Steve Björkman created art for ads and greeting cards before trying children's book illustration. Learning to draw all kinds of people and all kinds of things helped him to illustrate children's books.

SUMMARIZE AND RETELL

Story Travelogue

Display the following chart on the board or use the Chart on page R198 as a transparency. Help children sum up what they've learned about places and travel by completing the chart. Then have children use the chart to retell "This Is the Way We Go to School." See *Practice Book* page 5.

Who?	Where?	How?

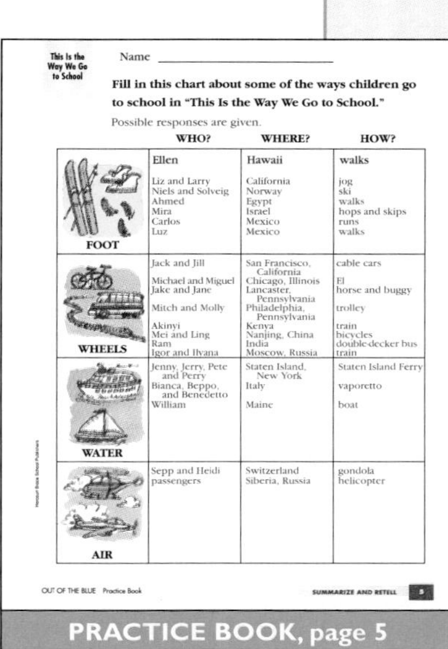

This Is the Way We Go to School

Name ____________________

Fill in this chart about some of the ways children go to school in "This Is the Way We Go to School."

Possible responses are given.

	WHO?	WHERE?	HOW?
FOOT	Ellen Liz and Larry Niels and Solveig Ahmed Mira Carlos Luz	Hawaii California Norway Egypt Israel Mexico Mexico	walks jog ski walks hops and skips runs walks
WHEELS	Jack and Jill Michael and Miguel Jake and Jane Mitch and Molly Akinyi Mei and Ling Ram Igor and Ilyana	San Francisco, California Chicago, Illinois Lancaster, Pennsylvania Philadelphia, Pennsylvania Kenya Nanjing, China India Moscow, Russia	cable cars El horse and buggy trolley train bicycles double-decker bus train
WATER	Jenny, Jerry, Pete and Perry Bianca, Beppo, and Benedetto William	Staten Island, New York Italy Maine	Staten Island Ferry vaporetto boat
AIR	Sepp and Heidi passengers	Switzerland Siberia, Russia	gondola helicopter

OUT OF THE BLUE Practice Book — SUMMARIZE AND RETELL 5

PRACTICE BOOK, page 5

POEMS

We Have a New Girl in Class

How Do You Feel?

by Aliki

INTRODUCING THE POEMS Have children look at the poems on pages 38 and 39. Ask a volunteer to read aloud the poems' titles. Discuss children's ideas about what the poems might be about.

SHARING THE POEMS Have children read the poems to themselves. Then read the poems to children. Talk about the words in the poems that describe feelings. List the words on the board.

Invite children to talk about other words that describe feelings, and add them to the list. Discuss the feelings expressed in both poems. Encourage children to share their opinions of both poems and any experiences they may have brought to mind.

ABOUT THE POEMS

Discuss with children the difference between what the new girl is thinking and what her classmates are saying in the first poem. Encourage children to talk about how the girl must feel.

Ask children to take turns acting out one of the feelings in the second poem. Classmates can try to guess which feeling each child chose.

POET'S CRAFT

Tell children that Aliki illustrates her writing, so the words and pictures work together to show others her ideas. Ask children why they think the new girl's words are stacked up over her head. Talk about how the pictures add to "How Do You Feel?"

About the Poet

Aliki Brandenberg writes children's books because she loves writing and drawing. She started to draw during her preschool years.

The beginning of Aliki's *How a Book Is Made* reflects her feelings about books. The first page shows a cat turning the pages of a book and saying, "I like books. I like the way a book feels. I like the way a book smells. I like to turn each page, read each word, look at the pictures."

The two poems in this lesson come from Aliki's book *Feelings*. In addition to this book, Aliki has written more than forty children's books, many of them award-winning, including *We Are Best Friends, Dinosaur Bones, My Visit to the Aquarium, Communication, Mummies Made in Egypt*, and *Corn Is Maize: The Gift of the Indians*.

EXTRA SUPPORT **Some children may be confused by what is happening in "We Have a New Girl in Class." Explain that the new girl isn't speaking aloud to the other children; the poem is her thoughts as she looks at the children.**

RESPONSE CORNER ACTIVITIES

CREATE A SONG

OFF WE GO!

PAGE 40 As children work on their songs, help them think of other possible tunes they might use, such as "Row, Row, Row Your Boat" or "Twinkle, Twinkle Little Star." Encourage children to use a variety of words from the chart in their song verses. Then invite each group to sing its song and teach it to classmates. MUSIC

MAKE A CLASS BOOK

HOW WOULD YOU GO?

PAGE 41 Suggest children look back at the story to refresh their memories of the different children and choose one child they would like to travel with. Encourage partners to share their finished sentences and pictures.

Assemble children's drawings and writing into a loose-leaf binder, or have volunteers make and decorate a book cover and write a title, such as "On the Go." READING/WRITING

Response Corner

CREATE A SONG

Off We Go!

Make up a song about going to school.

1. Work as a whole group. Make a chart to show how the children in the story travel to school. Add your ideas to the chart.

Land	Sea	Air
walk	ferry	ski lift
jog	vaporetto	helicopter
roller skates		

2. Work with a small group. Make up a song about how you go to school. You can use a tune you know, like "London Bridge." Use the chart for ideas.

We can ride on roller skates, roller skates, roller skates. We can ride on roller skates, all the way to school.

40

VARYING THE ACTIVITY

In the **Off We Go!** activity, children can use instruments to play a tune or to create a rhythm to accompany their song.

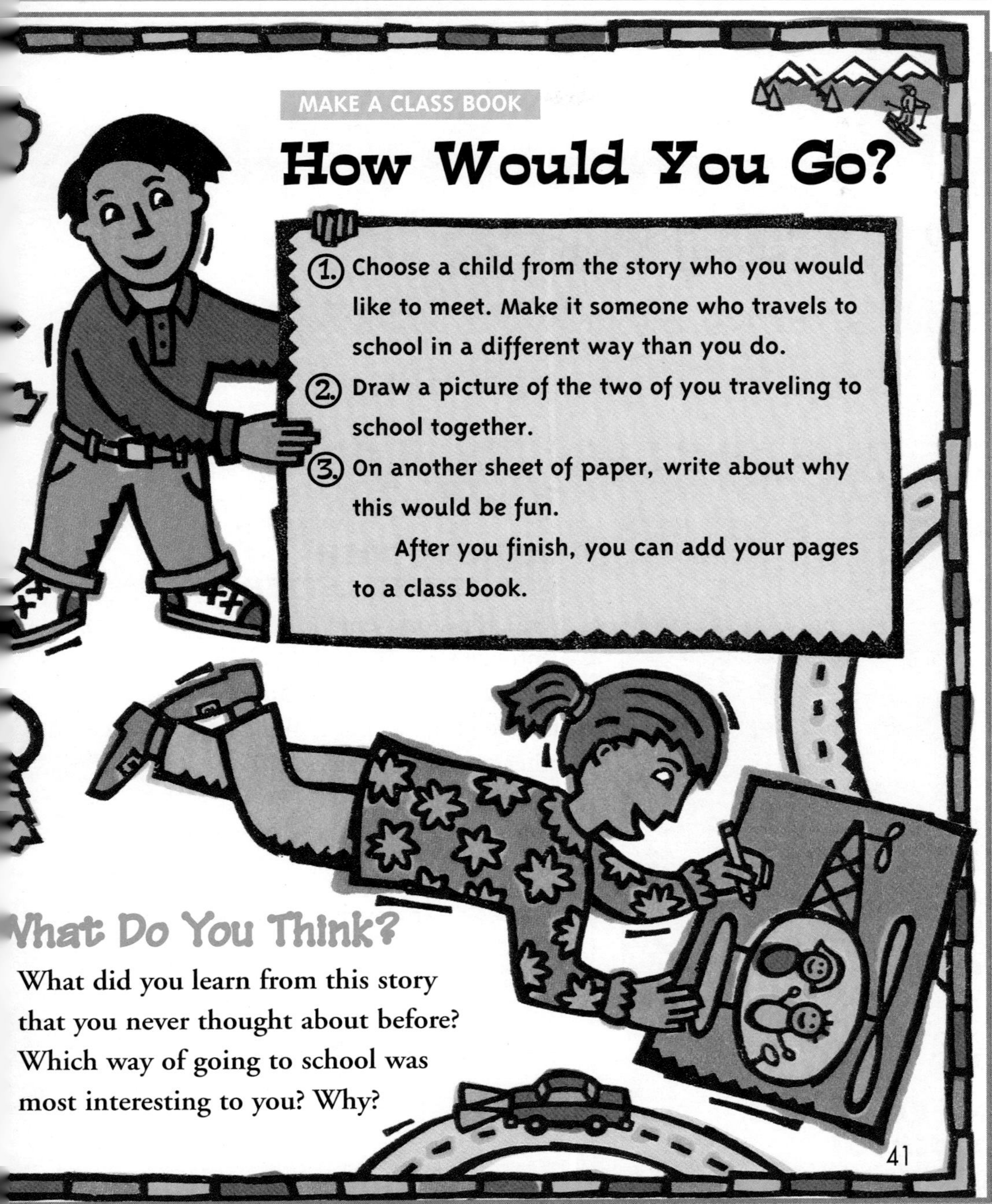

MAKE A CLASS BOOK

How Would You Go?

1. Choose a child from the story who you would like to meet. Make it someone who travels to school in a different way than you do.
2. Draw a picture of the two of you traveling to school together.
3. On another sheet of paper, write about why this would be fun.

After you finish, you can add your pages to a class book.

What Do You Think?

What did you learn from this story that you never thought about before? Which way of going to school was most interesting to you? Why?

41

CHECKING COMPREHENSION

What Do You Think?

1. **What did you learn from this story that you never thought about before?** (Possible responses: I learned that some kids ski to school, and that sounds like fun; some kids listen to school over the radio.) **DESCRIPTIVE RESPONSE**
2. **Which way of going to school was most interesting to you? Why?** (Responses will vary. Children should support their answers.) **PERSONAL RESPONSE**

An additional question for extending reading.

3. **What is your favorite way to travel? Make up a rhyme to tell about it.** (Rhymes will vary, but should be about a favorite way to travel.) **CRITICAL/CREATIVE ANALYSIS**

STUDENTS ACQUIRING ENGLISH

Encourage children acquiring English to share words that describe ways to travel to school in their first language and include them, along with a translation, on the chart. Then encourage groups to include the non-English, as well as the English, words in their songs.

Informal Assessment

Observe groups of children as they make up songs.

- ☑ Do children offer suggestions and ideas for their song?
- ☑ Do children use a variety of words from the chart?
- ☑ Do children work together to share their song with classmates?

Intervention Strategies

Instant Readers™

Predictable and Patterned Little Books That Build Fluency

*** BOOK LEVEL: 9–10**

VOCABULARY:
mountain, start

PHONIC ELEMENTS:
R*-controlled vowel: /är/*ar*; Short vowel: /o/*o*; Initial clusters with *s

PHONOGRAM:
-ark

SUMMARY:
In this version of Aesop's fable, Rabbit and Turtle race to school.

Informal Assessment ✓

Are children able to

- ☑ appropriately add words to a sentence?
- ☑ use initial consonant clusters to form new words?

Reading a New Book

INTRODUCING *RABBIT AND TURTLE GO TO SCHOOL*

To familiarize children with the fable "The Tortoise and the Hare," you may wish to read a version of the story or tell it to children. As you share the cover and title of *Rabbit and Turtle Go to School*, explain that this is another version of the story. As you share the pictures, discuss the race and how the two animals get to school.

READING THE STORY

Have children read the story with a partner to find out how and why Turtle wins the race.

WORKING WITH WORDS AND LETTERS

Write the story sentence *Rabbit ran fast* on a sentence strip. Have children cut apart the sentence and reassemble it. Add the word *very,* and ask the group to put it in the correct place. Add other words or phrases to the sentence.

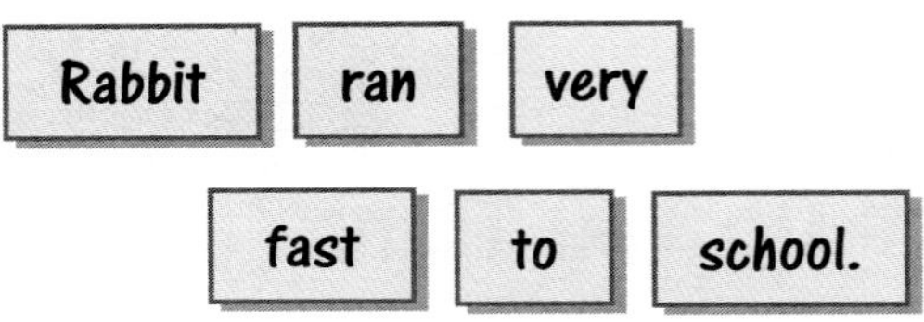

WRITING SENTENCES

Have each child write a sentence about how he or she gets to school.

Additional activities are provided on pages 4–5 of the *Intervention Strategies Manual*.

* **BOOK LEVEL: 13–14**

VOCABULARY:
shoes, sometimes

PHONIC ELEMENTS:
R-controlled vowel: /är/*ar*; Short vowel: /o/*o*; Initial clusters with *s*

SUMMARY:
All around the world, children love to play—often with the same kinds of materials.

Reading a New Book

INTRODUCING *A WORLD OF FUN*

Ask children what kinds of games they like to play with friends. List the games on chart paper, pointing out any similarities (which ones use a ball, a bat, and so on). Explain that children all over the world love to play. Share the illustrations with children, and ask them how the games look like the ones they enjoy.

READING THE STORY

Have children read the story with a partner to find out about games all over the world. Suggest that they talk about the pictures to help them read the text.

WORKING WITH WORDS AND LETTERS

Write the words *step*, *stones*, and *stick* on a write-on, wipe-off board. Ask children how the words are alike, and have a volunteer erase all the letters except the *st* at the beginning of each word. With children brainstorm other words that have the same beginning sounds (such as *star, stir,* and *stomach*). Work together to write the words, using decoding strategies.

WRITING INSTRUCTIONS

Have children write the directions for a favorite game. Use numbers 1–4 to help children focus on the sequence of the game.

1. First,
2. Next,
3. Then,
4. Last,

ESL/Title I Reading

But Not Like Mine by Margery Facklam

Working with "This Is the Way We Go to School"

SYNTACTIC CUES Assist children with the rhyme and rhythm of the story by reading aloud two or three pages with a small group of children. As you read, point to the words, and tap your hand on a desktop. Have children join in, clapping to the rhythm. Repeat this several times until children feel confident in their ability to hear the rhythm of the language.

TECHNOLOGY

INSTANT READERS™

ELECTRONIC EDITION

***Rabbit and Turtle Go to School* and *A World of Fun* are available on CD-ROM. Pre-and post- reading activities are included.**

* Books leveled according to Barbara Peterson's "Profiles of Books for Beginning Readers," on page 9 of the *Instant Readers Teacher's Guide.*

IDEA BANK

TIPS FOR CLASSROOM MANAGEMENT

IF children have demonstrated that they can share their ideas in a small-group environment, **THEN** assign the Group Talk activity.

LISTENING AND SPEAKING

Group Talk

TRAVELING THROUGH THE SEASONS

Remind children that the way people travel in a certain place depends on that place's climate and weather. For an example, have children look on page 27 and tell how Niels and Solveig travel to school. Talk about how skiing is a good way to travel in snowy weather. Why wouldn't travel by bus or boat be a good choice? Then organize children into small groups to talk about the seasons in your area and the different weather during each season. Have them discuss how travel and dress change from season to season.

After small-group discussions, gather children to share their ideas about ways to travel in your area during different seasons.

CHALLENGING THE TEXT

REAL-LIFE READING

Reading Transportation Signs

Use page 26 to point out the place where a sign would be on the front of the trolley. Ask children what is usually written on that part of a trolley or bus and how people use that information. (the place where the vehicle is going; to find the right vehicle) Discuss other information they have seen on buses and trains.

Partners might enjoy drawing a large trolley, bus, or train and adding environmental print to it. Then allow some children to wait at the "bus stop" (or "train platform"), while other children walk by with their vehicles. The children waiting at the stop can read the signs.

LISTENING/SPEAKING/ READING/ WRITING

WRITER'S MAGAZINE, pages 2–5

Informal Assessment

Note how children use their understanding of the story to contribute to the group discussions about how climate and weather affect travel.

ORAL LANGUAGE

Choral Reading

THIS IS THE WAY WE READ THE STORY

Read *This Is the Way We Go to School* aloud so children can hear and enjoy its rhythm and rhyme. Have children find the pairs of rhyming words on each page. Then read the story aloud as a group.

Then organize children into three groups. Begin as a group by reading the first sentence of the story: *One by one or two by two—Come along, it's fun to do!* Then have groups take turns reading either a sentence or a page until the last page of the story, when all groups can chime in to read the right-hand side of page 33: *Go by Copter? . . . We'll look for you.* **LISTENING/ SPEAKING**

KINESTHETIC

Creative Connection

MATERIALS
- **chart paper**
- **marker**

ACT IT OUT!

Work with children to list all the kinds of transportation covered in the story. Then organize children into small groups to play "Act It Out!" Each group chooses one kind of transportation from the list and pantomimes it for classmates to guess. Encourage children to be creative and to work together as they think of how to pantomime different forms of transportation. **KINESTHETIC**

PERSONAL JOURNAL

REFLECTING ON THE STORY **Have children think about what they have learned about transportation in other places from reading "This Is the Way We Go to School" as well as from their group's discussion. Have children write about a kind of transportation they would like to try.**

WRITER'S WORKSHOP

Sentences About a Picture

TIPS FOR CLASSROOM MANAGEMENT

IF children are familiar with the writing process approach, **THEN** present the writing assignment and have them use the Sentences About a Picture model on pages 10–11, of the *Language Handbook.*

IF at this time you want a short writing activity, **THEN** have children do the prewriting activity and refer to the chart to give oral descriptions of their pictures.

TECHNOLOGY

THE AMAZING WRITING MACHINE Primary Level Activity Disk Pack Grade 2
Have children enter their sentences in the Journals mode

KID PIX
Children may want to use this program to create their pictures.

Thinking as Writers

WRITING FORM: Sentences About a Picture Remind children that "This Is the Way We Go to School" shows pictures of children going to school and has sentences that tell the main ideas about those pictures. Then invite children to choose one of the pictures and read the sentence that tells about it. Explain to children that they will work independently to draw a picture of something they do at school and then write sentences about the picture.

Display Chart/Transparency 2, or write the model Sentences About a Picture on the board. Discuss what the sentences tell us that we might not learn from the picture alone.

CHART/TRANSPARENCY 2

WRITER'S CRAFT: Using *I* and Me Explain that good writers pay close attention to the way they use the words *I* and *me* in their writing. Remind children that in their writing they use the words *I* and *me* to tell about themselves and that *I* is always capitalized. Invite children to tell about how they travel to school, using *I* and *Me*.

PREWRITING

Invite children to tell about the things they usually do at school. Record children's responses on a chart similar to the following:

"Our School Day"

• Morning •	• Afternoon •
say Pledge of Allegiance	music
reading	writing
math	recess
gym	science

Encourage children to tell about their favorite parts of the day. Then have children draw a picture of themselves at school. Suggest that they look at the chart if they need ideas.

DRAFTING

Ask children to write sentences on a separate sheet of paper to tell about their pictures. Remind them to

- use their pictures for ideas.
- write a sentence that tells the main idea of the picture. Add more sentences, if needed, to explain the picture.
- write quickly to capture their ideas.

As children work through the stages of the writing process, have them save their drafts and revisions in their writer's folder.

RESPONDING AND REVISING

Work with groups of four to six children. Invite children to take turns showing their pictures and reading aloud their sentences. Encourage children to respond by answering questions like these:

- Do the sentences tell about the picture?
- Is there one sentence that tells the main idea about the picture?
- What do you like about the picture and the sentences?

PROOFREADING

Offer some tips to help children proofread. Help them focus on the following:

CAPITAL LETTERS Each sentence begins with a capital letter. A person's name begins with a capital letter. (See the Grammar Minilesson on page T39.)

END MARKS A sentence that tells about something ends with a period.

PUBLISHING

Have children make a clean copy of their sentences. Then offer publishing options like the following:

ART DISPLAY Children can glue their pictures and sentences onto large sheets of paper. They might want to keep their sentences together or cut them into strips and glue them around the picture like a frame.

Handwriting
Remind children that their handwriting must be neat and clear so that the person reading the sentences can understand them. If children need assistance, refer them to the Handwriting models in the *Language Handbook* or in the classroom.

AUTHOR'S CHAIR Children can share their pictures and sentences from the Author's Chair.

PORTFOLIO OPPORTUNITY

After children publish, make copies of their sentences and pictures and have them attach their Writing Self-Assessment Checklists to them. Have them place the sentences, pictures, and checklists in their portfolios.

LANGUAGE HANDBOOK

Sentences About a Picture, pages 10–11

Student Self-Assessment ✓

Children can use the Writing Self-Assessment Checklist in the *Portfolio Assessment Teacher's Guide.*

EVALUATING THE WRITTEN RESPONSE

When evaluating children's sentences, consider:

CONTENT	ORGANIZATION	STYLE
Do the sentences expand or explain the content of the picture?	Does each sentence tell a complete thought?	Is the sentence complete and not just a label?

EVALUATION BENCHMARKS

The child uses disconnected words or phrases that may or may not relate clearly to the picture.	= EMERGENT
The child uses descriptive words or phrases instead of complete sentences or thoughts to tell about the picture.	= BEGINNING
The child writes complete sentences that tell the main idea and specific details about the picture.	= PROFICIENT

Tested Skill

GRAMMAR

Sentences

Reading↔Writing Connection

Connect to the story. Have children leaf through "This Is the Way We Go To School" and find their favorite parts. Have children read the sentences aloud, and write them on the board. For example,

Michael and his friend Miguel see the rooftops from the El.

Then read each sentence aloud with children, and point out the capital letter and end mark.

Build oral language. Write sentence starters, such as *The children* and *A boy,* on the board, and ask children to say sentences about the story. Write their responses.

The children jog to school.
The children ski across the snow.
The girl rides a yellow school bus.
A boy rides a Skidoo to school.

Then read the sentences with children, and point out the capital letters and end marks.

Teach/Model

Discuss sentences. Use children's sentences as a springboard to discuss what a sentence is. Tell children that a **sentence** is a group of words that tells a complete thought. Erase the subject or predicate part of a sentence and ask, for example, "Is *The children* a complete thought?" Explain that *The children* does not tell about an action. A sentence must tell about someone or something and an action. Next, discuss the capital letter and the end mark in each of the children's sentences on the board.

Practice/Apply

Check understanding. Write on the board the word groups below from the story, omitting sentence capitalization and end punctuation. Read each one aloud, and ask children to identify which word groups are sentences. Ask volunteers to add the capital letters and periods. For groups of words that are not sentences, ask children to make them sentences.

we'll look for
palm trees help keep Ahmed cool
through the traffic of Nanjing
Mira takes time out to play

LANGUAGE HANDBOOK
Sentences, pages 36–37

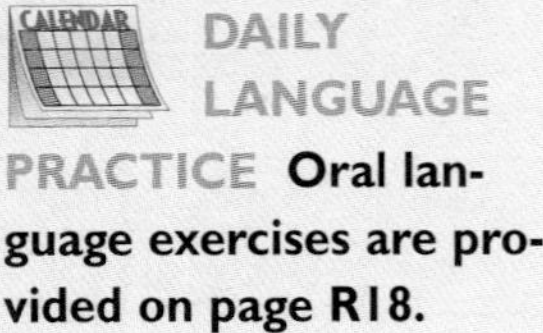

DAILY LANGUAGE PRACTICE **Oral language exercises are provided on page R18.**

Practice Activities

Animal Sentences

WRITING APPLICATION Have each child draw a picture of an animal that might be seen in a zoo. Tell children to write two or three sentences that tell about the animal, describing things like its color, habitat, and any unusual features. Invite children to share their sentences with classmates. Encourage children to say whether the sentences tell a complete thought and whether they are punctuated correctly.
VISUAL

Chain Stories

ORAL APPLICATION Have small groups of children work together to make chain stories. Each group sits in a circle and listens as you give a one-sentence story starter. Give each group a different starter, such as *One day, my family went to the park for a picnic.* Then children take turns adding one sentence at a time to the story. Groups can choose a Recorder to write down all the sentences. When everyone has had a chance to add at least one sentence, children can choose a group member to read their group's story aloud. **AUDITORY**

READING SENTENCES

ORAL APPLICATION Have pairs of children sit with a favorite book. Partners take turns reading aloud from the book. One partner reads, choosing to read a sentence or only a part of a sentence to the other child, who must say whether what the first child read is or is not a sentence.
VISUAL/AUDITORY

APPLY TO WRITING

You may want children to check the sentences they wrote about their pictures to see if the sentences are complete and are punctuated correctly

USAGE TIP Look in your writing to see if each sentence begins with a capital letter and ends with an end mark.

STUDENTS ACQUIRING ENGLISH

Work with a small group to help children with the names of punctuation marks and what each end mark signifies. Write sentences, emphasizing the end marks. When children have grasped the concept, you might want to write some more sentences, asking them to add the mark.

RETEACH

See page R4 for lessons in multiple modalities.

GRAMMAR PRACTICE BOOK
pages 13-14

Name ______________ This Is the Way We Go to School

A **sentence** is a group of words that tells a complete thought.

Read each group of words. Write the groups of words that are sentences. If a word group is not a sentence, add words to make it a sentence.

1. We go home together.
   We go home together.
2. after school
   Possible response: We eat snacks after school.
3. My sister runs home.
   My sister runs home.
4. I ride my bike.
   I ride my bike.
5. on his skates
   Possible response: He goes home on his skates.
6. We race to the corner.
   We race to the corner.

TRY THIS! Writing — Draw a picture that shows what you do on the way home from school. Write a sentence to go with your picture.

6 SENTENCES — OUT OF THE BLUE Practice Book

PRACTICE BOOK, page 6

5-DAY PLAN

Use in conjunction with Daily Language Practice.

Day 1 Complete page T56.	**Day 4** Choose a Practice Activity or *Grammar Practice Book* pages 13–14.
Day 2 Complete a Practice Activity on page T57.	**Day 5** Complete *Practice Book* page 6.
Day 3 Choose a Practice Activity or *Language Handbook* pages 36–37.	

2

SPELLING

5-Day Plan

Integrated Spelling Lesson 1: student book, pages 10–13; Teacher's Edition, pages T21–T26.

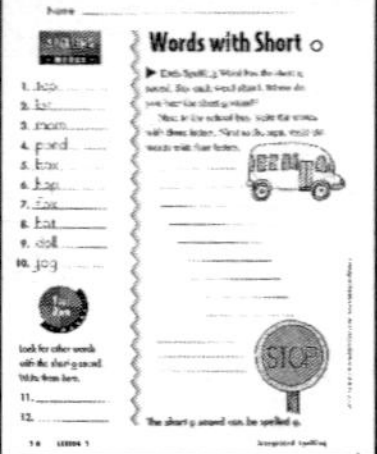

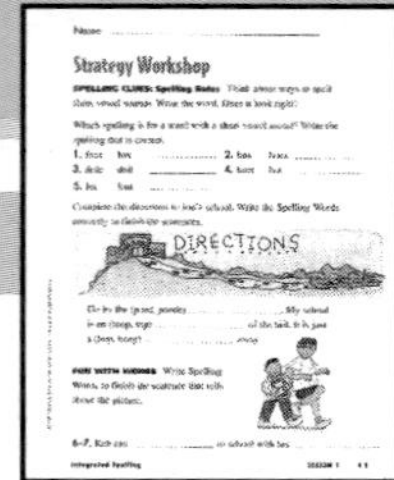

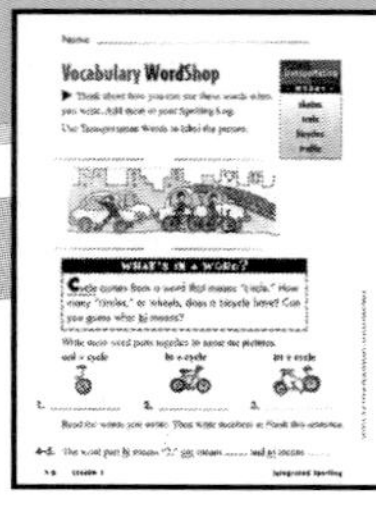

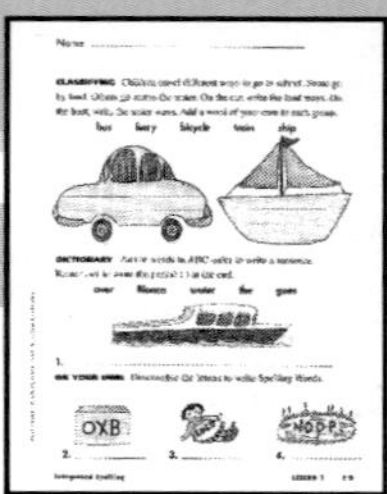

SPELLING WORDS

1. top
2. lot
3. mom
4. pond
5. box
6. hop ★
7. fox
8. hot
9. doll
10. jog ★

STUDENT'S PERSONAL WORDS

11. 13.
12. 14.

Additional story words are *rooftops* and *trolley.*

★ Words appearing in "This Is the Way We Go to School"

Words with Short *o*

Pretest

DAY 1 **Administer the pretest.** Say each word and use it in the sentence given below. Then repeat the word. Have pairs of children check their own pretests by referring to the word list.

OPEN SORT

DAY 2 **Have children classify words.** Have children classify the Spelling Words according to their similarities, noting that all the words have the *o* spelling for the short *o* sound. For instance, children might sort according to the number of letters, or they might pair rhyming words. Then have children tell their classmates about their categories.

CLOSED SORT

Sort by spelling pattern. Write the chart below on the board, and ask pairs of children to copy the chart. Ask children how many letters follow the *o* in *not* (one) and how many follow the *o* in *rock.* (two) Then have them write each Spelling Word where it belongs.

Words like *not*		Words like *rock*
top	lot	pond
mom	box	doll
hop	fox	
hot	jog	

Teach/Model

DAY 3 **Discuss the generalization.** Write the words *top* and *pond* on the board. Ask what vowel sound is heard in both. (the short *o* sound) Have volunteers circle the letter that spells the short *o* sound in both words. Point out that words like *top* end with one consonant, and words like *rock* end with two consonants. Both are one-syllable words. Help children form generalizations about words with short *o*—for example:

- **The letter *o* in one-syllable words can be followed by one or two consonants.**
- **The short *o* sound can be spelled *o* in one-syllable words.**

DAY 4 **Apply to writing.** If children wrote sentences in the Writer's Workshop, have them check their work to see if they spelled words with a short *o* correctly.

Posttest

DAY 5 **Assess children's progress.** The sentences below should be used as the posttest.

DICTATION SENTENCES

1. I rode to the top of the hill.
2. Kevin picked a lot of apples.
3. Ted's mom watched his game.
4. Frogs play in the pond.
5. Al keeps cards in a box.
6. Kim likes to hop.
7. There's a fox in the woods.
8. Is it hot outside?
9. I play with my doll.
10. Gus likes to jog.

This Is the Way We Go to School   Name ______

A. Read each sentence. Circle the word that is spelled right. Write it in the sentence.

lot hop jog pond hot

1. I am hot. (hot) hogt
2. We like to jog. jogg (jog)
3. I can hop. (hop) houp
4. We are a lot of fish. (lot) lote
5. I live in the pond too. ponde (pond)

B. Look at the mixed-up Spelling Words. Write each word correctly on the line. Then use the picture to tell a story.

top mom doll fox box

6. oxf fox
7. mmo mom
8. xbo box
9. pto top
10. lodl doll

OUT OF THE BLUE Practice Book   WORDS WITH SHORT o 7

PRACTICE BOOK, page 7

VOCABULARY WORKSHOP

Reviewing Key Words

To review how the vocabulary was used in the story, distribute copies of page R52 to children. Then write the Key Words on the board.

Have children read the sentences silently. Then read the sentences aloud with children. Ask them to choose the word that best completes each sentence and write the word.

I'll wear my new __shoes__ today.

I'll __start__ my day by walking to school.

It's rainy and windy, so I'll hold up my umbrella __against__ the rain.

I like to smell the fresh __air__.

On my walk, I see a big, rocky __mountain__.

__Sometimes__ I ride my bike to school.

Harcourt Brace School Publishers

Children can cut apart sentence strips and use them to retell the story. They may also want to glue the strips to sheets of paper and add illustrations to create their own books.

Extending Vocabulary

RHYMING WORDS

Write the following words from "This Is the Way We Go to School" on large self-stick notes and stick them to the board in random order: *grow, slow, past, fast, far, car, train, chain, sky, dry, line, fine.*

Put the *slow* word card under the *grow* word card and have a volunteer read the words aloud. Ask how the words are alike. (They rhyme.) Then work with children to pair the other rhyming words.

After all the words are paired, brainstorm other words that rhyme with each pair of words and add them to each list. Children may want to use the rhyming words to compose short poems.

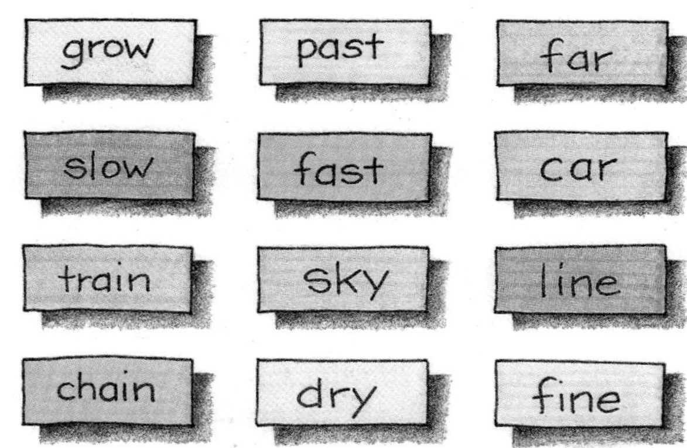

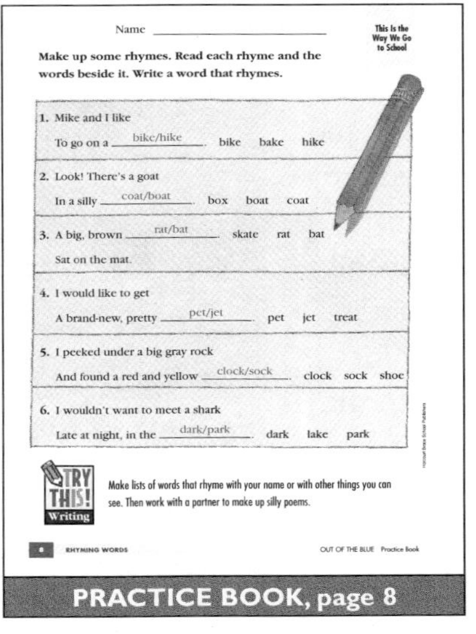

Name __________

This Is the Way We Go to School

Make up some rhymes. Read each rhyme and the words beside it. Write a word that rhymes.

1. Mike and I like
   To go on a __bike/hike__. bike bake hike
2. Look! There's a goat
   In a silly __coat/boat__. box boat coat
3. A big, brown __rat/bat__. skate rat bat
   Sat on the mat.
4. I would like to get
   A brand-new, pretty __pet/jet__. pet jet treat
5. I peeked under a big gray rock
   And found a red and yellow __clock/sock__. clock sock shoe
6. I wouldn't want to meet a shark
   Late at night, in the __dark/park__. dark lake park

TRY THIS! Writing — Make lists of words that rhyme with your name or with other things you can see. Then work with a partner to make up silly poems.

8 RHYMING WORDS — OUT OF THE BLUE Practice Book

Harcourt Brace School Publishers

PRACTICE BOOK, page 8

STUDENTS ACQUIRING ENGLISH

Help children list rhyming words with phonograms, such as *-arm* and *-ark.* This will help children become more aware of common English spellings as well as acquaint them with some sounds in English that may not be used in their primary languages.

TAKE-HOME/ KEEP-AT-HOME BOOK

New School, New Friends
Distribute the pages and have children make their own TAKE-HOME/ KEEP-AT-HOME BOOKS, which reinforce Key Words and known vocabulary. Have children read to partners and then take the book home to read.

Tested Skill

INTRODUCE: PHONICS AND DECODING

R-Controlled Vowel: /är/*ar*

OBJECTIVE: To understand the relationship between letters and sounds

Informal Assessment ✓

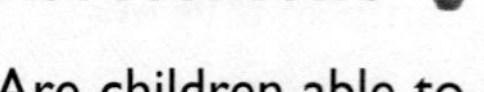

Are children able to

- ☑ read and write words that have the /är/ sound?
- ☑ recognize that /är/ is spelled *ar*?
- ☑ read words with /är/ in sentences?

Teach/Model

Connect to the story. Have children turn to page 22 and read this sentence aloud:

And the fastest way by far
is by school bus or by car!

Ask a volunteer to identify the two words in the sentence that rhyme (*far, car*) and to write the words on the board. Tell children that they will learn more about the sound that is alike in these words.

Phonemic awareness: Listen to the sound. Display page 4 of the *Big Book of Rhymes*. Read the rhyme aloud with children. Then read it again, and have children listen for words with the same vowel sound heard in *far* and *car*. Reread the rhyme and encourage children to join in, especially for words with the /är/ sound.

Big Book of Rhymes, page 4

Find and read words with /är/*ar*. As children locate words in the poem with the /är/ sound, list the words on the board:

star **dark** **spark**

Then have children study the list. Prompt them to make their own generalizations about words with the /är/ sound. Encourage them to name other words with the same sound to see whether their rules apply to these words, too. Then explain that the letters *ar* can stand for the vowel sound heard in *far* and *car*. Ask volunteers to circle *ar* in each word on the list. If children suggested listing the word *are* from the poem, you may want to discuss why this word doesn't follow the same spelling pattern.

Practice/Apply

Read the words in context. Write these sentences on the board:

Will the car be able to go that far?
It's getting dark.
It's hard to see.
Let's park by that barn.

Ask children to read each sentence and identify the words that have the same vowel sound as *far*. Add these words to the list.

Practice Activities

WORD BUILDING

PHONOGRAM / BLENDING ACTIVITY Have each child make a Word Builder by folding a piece of construction paper one inch up to make a pocket and stapling it.

Then distribute letter cards or *Word Builder Cards* and phonogram card *-ark* to children. Model adding *b* to the phonogram *-ark* to form the word *bark*. Say the word aloud, blending the sounds to form the word. Have children read the word. Then have children make and read more words with the phonogram *-ark*. VISUAL/AUDITORY/KINESTHETIC

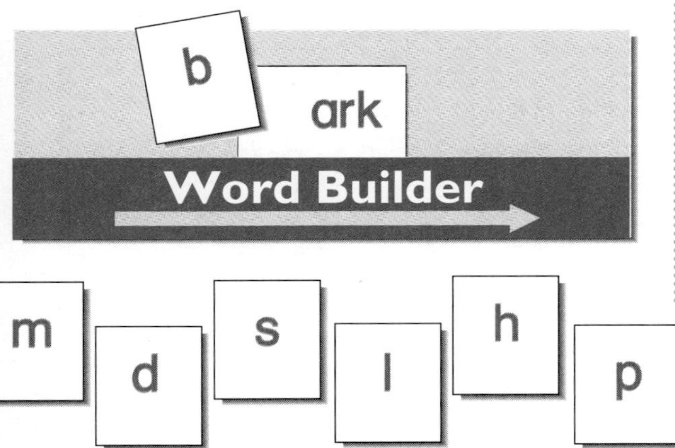

You're a Star!

PERFORMANCE ASSESSMENT Write *star* on the board, and have the word read aloud. Have children draw and decorate a star on a sheet of construction paper. Then read aloud the following words, one at a time, and ask children to hold up their star if the word has the same vowel sound as *star: bike, barn, read, smile, charm, dance, farm, sled, card, lamp, hard, sleep, yard, yarn, stop, sharp, bug, cart, part, nest, chart, fish, start, kite, smart.* Then write the *ar* words on the board. Ask children to write a sentence on each side of their star, using some of the *ar* words. VISUAL/AUDITORY

MEETING INDIVIDUAL NEEDS

STUDENTS ACQUIRING ENGLISH

Help children write three sentences that use /är/*ar* words. Invite them to read their sentences aloud.

RETEACH

See page R5 for lessons in multiple modalities.

CHALLENGE

Have children play a guessing game in which one child thinks of an /är/*ar* word and gives hints about the word. Other children try to guess the word.

PHONICS ACTIVITY BOOK, page 1

PHONICS PRACTICE BOOK, pages 133–134

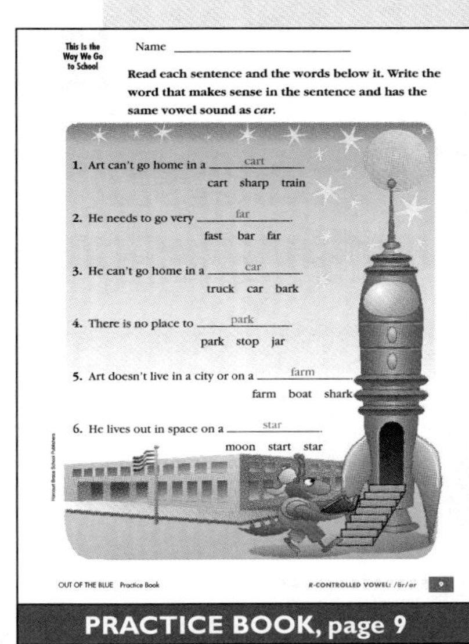

This Is the Way We Go to School

Name ____________

Read each sentence and the words below it. Write the word that makes sense in the sentence and has the same vowel sound as *car.*

1. Art can't go home in a __cart__. cart sharp train
2. He needs to go very __far__. fast bar far
3. He can't go home in a __car__. truck car bark
4. There is no place to __park__. park stop jar
5. Art doesn't live in a city or on a __farm__. farm boat shark
6. He lives out in space on a __star__. moon start star

OUT OF THE BLUE Practice Book — R-CONTROLLED VOWEL: /är/ar — 9

PRACTICE BOOK, page 9

Reading Trade Books FOR R-CONTROLLED VOWEL /ÄR/AR

A Carpenter
by Douglas Florian. Greenwillow, 1991.
EASY

Farm Noises
by Jane Miller. Simon & Schuster, 1989. AVERAGE

The Garden in the City
by Gerda Muller. Dutton, 1992.
CHALLENGE

PHONICS PRACTICE READER 11

INTRODUCE: COMPREHENSION STRATEGY

Sequence

OBJECTIVE: To identify the sequence of events in a story

Informal Assessment ✓

Are children able to

- ☑ identify events in a story?
- ☑ identify and use time-order words?
- ☑ list story events in order?

TECHNOLOGY

Bailey's Book House (Make-A-Story) Children can use this to create stories that show a strong sequence of events.

Teach/Model

Connect to the story. Ask children to reread pages 26–27 of the story. Then ask them to tell you, in order, who is named and how those people travel. Encourage children to discuss any patterns they notice in the way the story was written.

Model recognizing sequence. Tell children that the author of this story wrote it in a certain order. The first part of the story tells about children in the United States, and the rest of the story tells mostly about children in other countries. Explain that knowing the order of events in a story and the pattern of a story will help children to read and remember the story.

Tell children that authors sometimes use time-order words, like *first, next,* and *last night* to help the reader know the order of the events in a story. Then model recognizing sequence.

MODEL **After I read the pages about Ellen walking, the kids jogging and skating, and the kids traveling by bus and car, I realized that the story had a certain pattern. Before I looked at the next page, I thought it would be about a new way to travel—and I was right!**

Practice/Apply

Have children demonstrate understanding. Divide a large sheet of drawing paper in half. Then, in keeping with the school theme of the story, brainstorm a list of things children do at school every day. Record their responses in the left column of the chart. Then work together to put the activities in order, from morning to afternoon, as they happen in a typical school day. Use the right column of the chart to order the activities.

	In Order
go to lunch	read books
read books	recess
Art class	Art class
recess	go to lunch
Science centers	Science centers

When the ordered list is finished, talk about how putting the events in order makes the list easier to read and understand. Then have volunteers refer to the ordered list and retell the "story" of a typical school day, using time-order words to make it clear when events happen.

Practice Activities

FROM SEED TO PLANT

Display a plant and discuss how the plant grew from a seed. Ask children what they would need to plant a seed. Brainstorm all the necessary materials and the steps they would follow. Then children can work in pairs to draw the steps for planting a seed and for helping the seed grow. Suggest that children draw the steps on separate pieces of paper as they think of them. Then they can go back and put the steps in order, checking to make sure they haven't left out any steps.

You might want to provide planting materials. With them, children could follow the steps in order as an added check. They could then add steps or change the order. VISUAL/AUDITORY/ KINESTHETIC

What's the Story?

PERFORMANCE ASSESSMENT A great way for children to practice sequencing is to write story summaries. Remind children that order is important to any story. Have each child choose a favorite book and think about its characters, setting, and plot. Have children write summaries of their books, concentrating on putting the story events in order. Write *first, then, next, after, last,* and *finally* on the board and encourage children to use some of these words in their summaries. Have children share their completed summaries in small groups. VISUAL/AUDITORY

STUDENTS ACQUIRING ENGLISH

Review time-order words such as *first, next,* and *last*. Cut out the individual frames of a cartoon strip from the newspaper, and have children glue them onto construction paper in the correct order. Have them label each frame with a time-order word.

RETEACH

See page R6 for lessons in multiple modalities.

CHALLENGE

Have children work with a partner to read a folktale. Then have each pair retell the folktale for classmates, telling the events in the correct order. Allow time for children to practice storytelling.

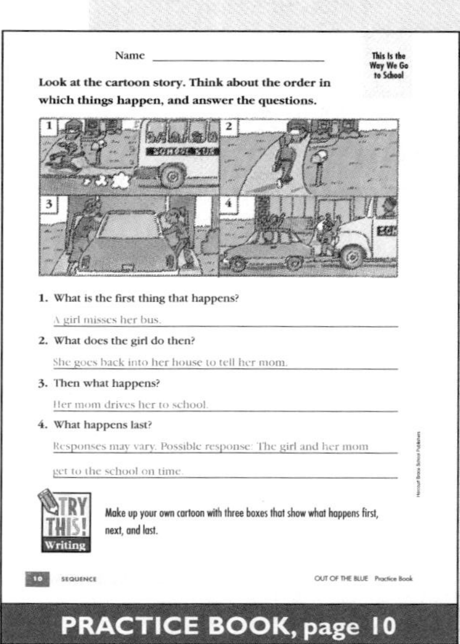

Name ______________

This Is the Way We Go to School

Look at the cartoon story. Think about the order in which things happen, and answer the questions.

1. What is the first thing that happens?
   A girl misses her bus.
2. What does the girl do then?
   She goes back into her house to tell her mom.
3. Then what happens?
   Her mom drives her to school.
4. What happens last?
   Responses may vary. Possible response: The girl and her mom get to the school on time.

TRY THIS! Writing — Make up your own cartoon with three boxes that show what happens first, next, and last.

10 SEQUENCE OUT OF THE BLUE Practice Book

PRACTICE BOOK, page 10

Reading Trade Books FOR SEQUENCE

***Anna in the Garden* by Diane Dawson Hearn. Silver Moon Press, 1994.** EASY

***Extra Cheese, Please! Mozzarella's Journey from Cow to Pizza* by Cris Peterson. Boyds Mills Press, 1994.** AVERAGE

***Make Me a Peanut Butter Sandwich (and a Glass of Milk)* by Ken Robbins. Scholastic, 1992.** AVERAGE

Integrated Curriculum

SOCIAL STUDIES

The World Around Me

TIPS FOR CLASSROOM MANAGEMENT

IF children do not know how to find information for Fact Finders, **THEN** take a trip to the school library. Point out the reference section, and help them find encyclopedias and other books to use in filling out their charts.

TECHNOLOGY

Thinkin' Things Collection 1: Flying Shapes; *Thinkin' Things* Collection 2: 2–3 D Blox

Imagination Express, Destination: Ocean

ART

What's in a Name?

MATERIALS
- construction paper
- crayons
- colored chalk
- glue
- scissors

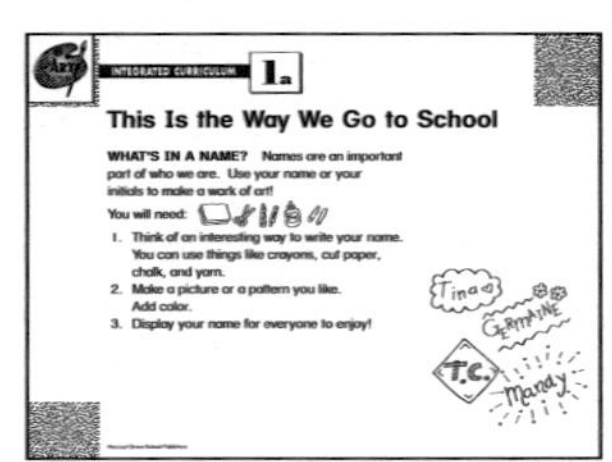

Curriculum Card 1a

Remind children that they learned some names of children in other countries from the story. Explain that names are an important part of who people are. Then have children put their imaginations to work to create art with their names. Encourage children to use colored chalk, torn pieces of construction paper, or any other materials they can think of to make their names or initials into works of art! Allow time for children to share their creations and display the finished products for all to see and enjoy. **LISTENING/SPEAKING/WRITING**

SOCIAL STUDIES

Fact Finders

MATERIALS
- drawing paper
- crayons or markers

Briefly review the places children read about in "This Is the Way We Go to School." If necessary, have children use pages 34–36 as a reference. Then have pairs of children copy the chart below onto a large sheet of drawing paper, omitting the column headings in parentheses. In the first column, children write the name of their state. In the second column, children write the name of one place from the story. Then children work together to find out the information they need to complete the chart. **SPEAKING/READING/WRITING**

	(State)	(Other Place)
Capital		
Flag		
Places of Interest		
Animals		
Other Information		

Reading Trade Books

CROSS-CURRICULAR READING

The Listening Walk by Paul Showers. HarperCollins, 1991. AVERAGE

On the Go by Ann Morris. Lothrop, Lee & Shepard, 1990. EASY

Window by Jeannie Baker. Greenwillow, 1991. EASY

MATH

Transportation Graphs

MATERIALS
- index cards
- crayons or markers
- butcher paper

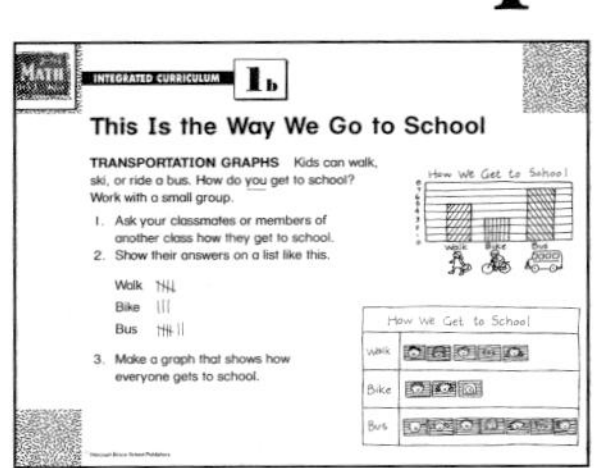

Curriculum Card 1b

Have children work in small groups to create a graph of how they, and perhaps other children, travel to school.

Explain how to tally information, and help groups who need it with organizing the information for their graphs. You might want to assign a bar graph to one group and a pictograph to another, and then compare how the two graphs present the same information. LISTENING/SPEAKING/READING/WRITING

Ways We Travel

How Many?

Bus	Car	Train	Walk
Ben	Terry	Maria	Chris
Tyrone	John	George	Carlos
Anna	Karla	Steven	Matt
Rita	Bobby		
Kim	Carrie		
Chen			
Demetri			
Alyssa			

SCIENCE

Rolling Experiments

MATERIALS
- toy cars and wheeled vehicles from home
- books, blocks, boxes, and boards
- paper
- pencils
- long pieces of string

COOPERATIVE LEARNING Have small groups experiment with things that roll. One or two group members can be Planners and set up the different tests; one child can be the Recorder, who writes down the results of each test. Another child can be the Measurer, who will measure the distances traveled in each test.

Encourage groups to experiment with the cars. Have children test which situations and materials will cause a toy car to roll the farthest. Suggest that children create varying degrees of steepness and try rolling their cars both up and down their hills. Groups can get together to discuss their results. LISTENING/SPEAKING/WRITING

MULTI-AGE CLASSROOMS

Older children might be able to help younger children as they do research for Fact Finders and as they develop ways to experiment in the Science activity.

Reading Trade Books

Trade Books That Connect to "This Is the Way We Go to School"

This Is the Way We Eat Our Lunch

by Edith Baer
illustrated by Steve Björkman

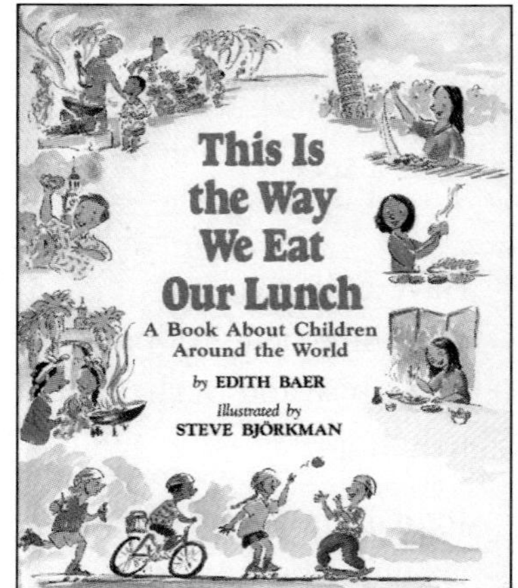

Have children compare the pattern of this book with the pattern of "This Is the Way We Go to School." Invite children to make up a rhyming verse about foods they like to eat, including the name of your town or city. Then reread the story as a group, adding the new verse.

How to Make an Apple Pie and See the World

by Marjorie Priceman

When children are familiar with the book, assign volunteers to point out on a world map each country as it is mentioned. You might wish to invite children who come from or who know about the countries mentioned in the book to serve as "tour guides" and share their knowledge with classmates.

On the Go

by Ann Morris
photographs by Ken Heyman

After reading, invite children to name their favorite ways to travel. Suggest they make a class book, perhaps titled "On the Go," in which they illustrate and write about ways they get around town.

TIPS FOR CLASSROOM MANAGEMENT

PARTNER
Have children work with partners to read *This Is the Way We Eat Our Lunch* and *How to Make an Apple Pie and See the World*. Encourage them to discuss how these books are like "This Is the Way We Go to School."

INDEPENDENT
Place *On the Go* and *Ruby the Copycat* in a Reading Center. Have children read the books and write their reactions to the stories in their journals.

READ ALOUD
Read *I Hate English!* and *Arthur's Teacher Trouble*. As you read aloud, pause to let children ask questions or talk about their own similar school experiences.

I Hate English!

by Ellen Levine
illustrated by Steve Björkman

Have children suggest ways to reread the story chorally. For example, half the children read paragraphs that end with the word *Chinese*; the other half read the ones that end with *English*.

Arthur's Teacher Trouble

by Marc Brown

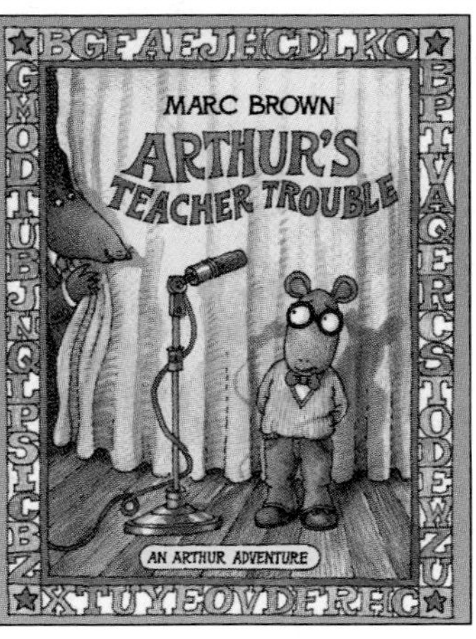

Invite children to give their opinions as to whether Arthur would have won the spellathon if he hadn't had Mr. Ratburn as a teacher. Then ask children what the members of the kindergarten class will think of Mr. Ratburn.

Ruby the Copycat

by Peggy Rathmann

Have children use the pictures to compare Ruby's and Angela's bows, sweaters, shirts, and flower-girl dresses. Then have children work with partners, one being an artist and the other a copycat. The artist draws a picture, step by step, while explaining to the copycat how to draw the same thing. The copycat can't look at the artist's picture. Afterward, partners compare pictures.

STUDENTS ACQUIRING ENGLISH

Invite children to tell whether they have ever felt like Mei Mei in *I Hate English!* Encourage them to talk about things in English that are confusing and some new things they've learned about the language.

Take a Look

PROJECT MANAGEMENT

STUDENTS ACQUIRING ENGLISH

As groups of children develop lists of safety rules, encourage them to add motions and gestures to go with each rule. This may help second-language learners connect words and meanings.

CLASSROOM MANAGEMENT

Have children make files for their work by folding and stapling large sheets of construction paper. Point out that they will need a safe place to keep their pages until they have made all the pages for their books.

Share Experiences of School

SELECTION CONNECTION

"This Is the Way We Go to School" focuses on the ways children around the world travel to school. Ask children to name story characters who travel to school in ways similar to theirs. Then ask what ways to travel that are different from theirs that they would like to try.

PROJECT CHECKLIST

During this stage, children should

- ☑ share memories of their first day of school and compare experiences.
- ☑ draw pictures or maps of how they get to school, and compare them with those of others who live nearby.
- ☑ work in groups to list rules for traveling safely to school.
- ☑ save their pictures or maps and lists of safety rules for their books.

When children have completed the checkpoint, have them think about the work and ideas they shared and record their thoughts in their Project Journals.

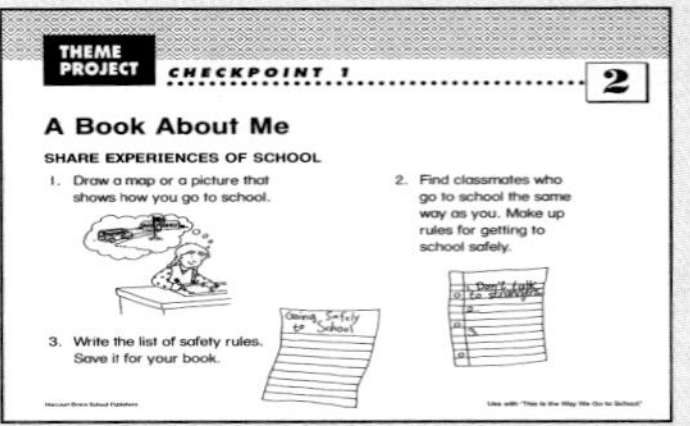
THEME PROJECT CHECKPOINT 1 2

A Book About Me

SHARE EXPERIENCES OF SCHOOL

1. Draw a map or a picture that shows how you go to school.
2. Find classmates who go to school the same way as you. Make up rules for getting to school safely.
3. Write the list of safety rules. Save it for your book.

Project Card 2

Project Card 2 can be found as a copying master on page R26.

PLANNING TIPS

As groups begin to work on their lists of safety rules, suggest that they

- choose a discussion Leader to call on volunteers, and a Recorder to take notes and keep track of answers.
- list everyone's ideas at first, and then vote to pick the best ones.
- have the Recorder read the final list out loud so everyone can make a copy.

Informal Assessment

As children complete this checkpoint, they will **solve problems** and **make cooperative decisions.** Children are thinking critically if they

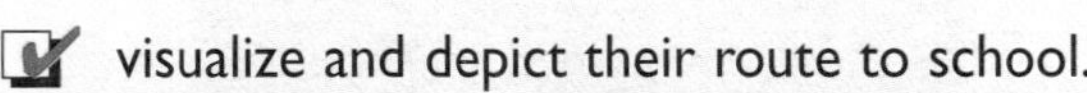

- ☑ visualize and depict their route to school.
- ☑ remember and share personal events.
- ☑ offer reasonable ideas for traveling safely.

Note that a more formal assessment rubric for this checkpoint is provided on page T225.

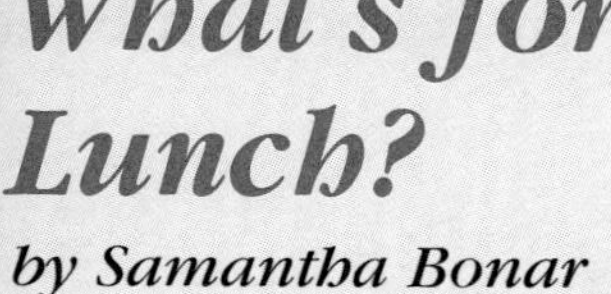

What's for Lunch?

by Samantha Bonar

SELECTION CONNECTION

Children have read "This Is the Way We Go to School," a story about how children in different parts of the world travel to school—walking; going by bus, car, trolley, boat; or on skis. As different as their means of transportation are, they have at least one thing in common—they all go to school. In a similar vein, children will read about typical lunches for children in other parts of the world.

SUMMARY

GENRE: Photo Essay

Most children eat lunch, but what they eat can be quite different. Children in Japan may eat cold rice with sesame seeds, sushi, vegetables, and fruit. Their lunches are packed in an *obento*. Australians enjoy meat pies, chiko rolls, and salt and vinegar potato crisps. Children in India munch on dry vegetables called Sukhi Bhaji with poori bread and hot mango pickles.

STUDENTS ACQUIRING ENGLISH

Help children create a picture chart of common foods they eat at home or bring for lunch. Help them write the name of each pictured food in English, in another language, or both. Display the chart and share the information with children.

Introducing the Photo Essay

PRIOR KNOWLEDGE

Tap children's prior knowledge by creating a "lunch food" web together. Ask children to supply names of lunch foods they eat. Use the food web to categorize foods into groups such as breads and cereals; fruits and vegetables; meats, eggs, and beans; and dairy products.

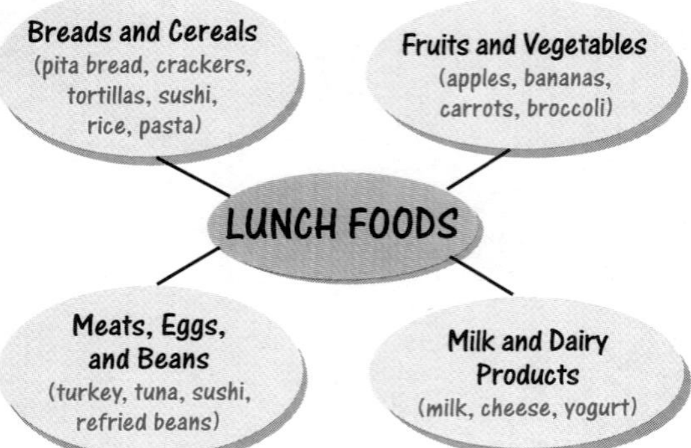

Reading a Photo Essay Point out to children that in this photo essay, both the words and the photographs give information. Ask children how they know which groups of words, or captions, go with which photos. Tell children to read all the words that go with one photo before moving on to another.

TIPS FOR CLASSROOM MANAGEMENT

SMALL GROUP

COOPERATIVE READING

Designate different children within a group to read certain passages. Have them practice reading their captions before they read them aloud in the group. Then children can discuss what they know about the foods mentioned and compare the foods in the article to foods they eat for lunch.

WHOLE CLASS

READ ALOUD

Children may benefit from listening as you read the captions aloud, since some of the words will be unfamiliar to them. Have children find each caption on the page as you read it. Encourage children to repeat the names of foods or lunch containers and then find them in the photos.

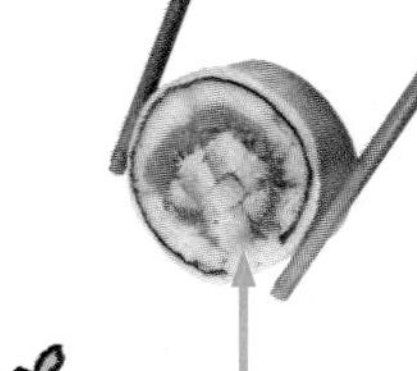

Lunch for Japanese kids isn't in the bag—it's in the obento!

What's for lunch? Cold rice with sesame seeds, fried goodies, vegetable salad, and fresh fruit.

Want a bite of sushi? This roll has avocado, rice, and fish eggs!

This chiko roll is like an egg roll.

Chips ahoy! Some kids like salt and vinegar crisps best.

Australian kids eat up meat pies—beef and sauce baked in a pastry crust.

43

Responding to the Photo Essay

When children have finished reading, have them talk about the experience of reading a photo essay. Ask them how reading photo captions is different from reading regular text. Then ask them to talk about what they learned from reading the photo essay.

IDEA BANK

Invite children to make their own photo or picture essay about food. First, have them browse through old magazines and newspapers and cut out photographs or pictures of interesting foods. Challenge children to write captions for the pictures. Then have them put the pages together to form a book. They can place their books in the class library or in a Reading Center.

REAL-LIFE CONNECTION

In Japan, lunch is carried in an *obento*. Have children compare the obento with other containers used to hold a lunch, such as paper bags, lunch boxes, and plastic containers. Ask children why some containers would be better for holding different foods than others.

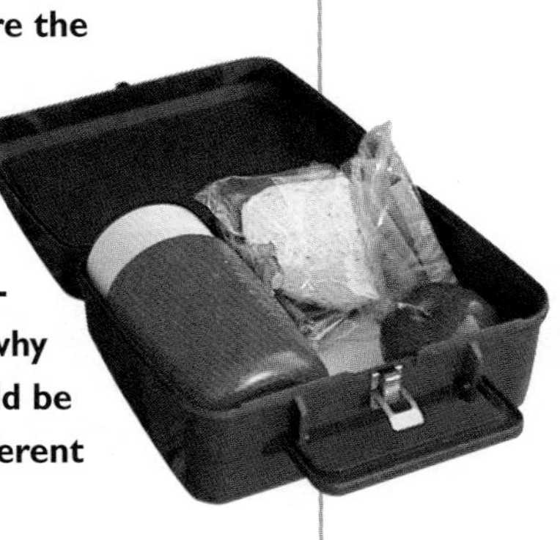

Integrating Language Arts

TIPS FOR CLASSROOM MANAGEMENT

IF some children share the same national backgrounds, THEN have them do the Writing activity together, featuring foods from their cultures.

IF some groups have trouble getting started with the Oral Language activity, THEN you might suggest a country to each group, show children where it is on a map or globe, and help them locate sources.

WRITING

Make a Menu

Have children create a week's worth of healthful lunch menus. Provide small groups with newspaper grocery ads to use for reference as they choose food items and for spelling the names of foods. Provide children with forms they can use for each day's menu. Then have children make their menus, including lots of fruits and vegetables. Children can draw pictures of their choices or cut out pictures from newspapers or magazines and glue them to their menus. Afterward, each group can post its menus around the room. Invite children to read the menus, choose their favorite lunches, and write a sentence about that lunch on a comment sheet.

READING/WRITING

ORAL LANGUAGE

Food Reports

COOPERATIVE LEARNING Arrange children in small groups to prepare and present oral reports about the foods of different countries. Assign Readers and a Recorder for each group. Make available a world map or globe. Suggest that children choose a country and find information in encyclopedias, magazines, and books about the kinds of foods that people in that country eat. The group's Readers can help locate information about the country and its foods and read it to group members. The Recorder takes down the information. Then, as a group, children decide what information to include in their reports. Children can select one child to present their report. Allow time for the Presenter to practice presenting the report. As each report is given, have children point out the country on a map or globe. LISTENING/SPEAKING/READING

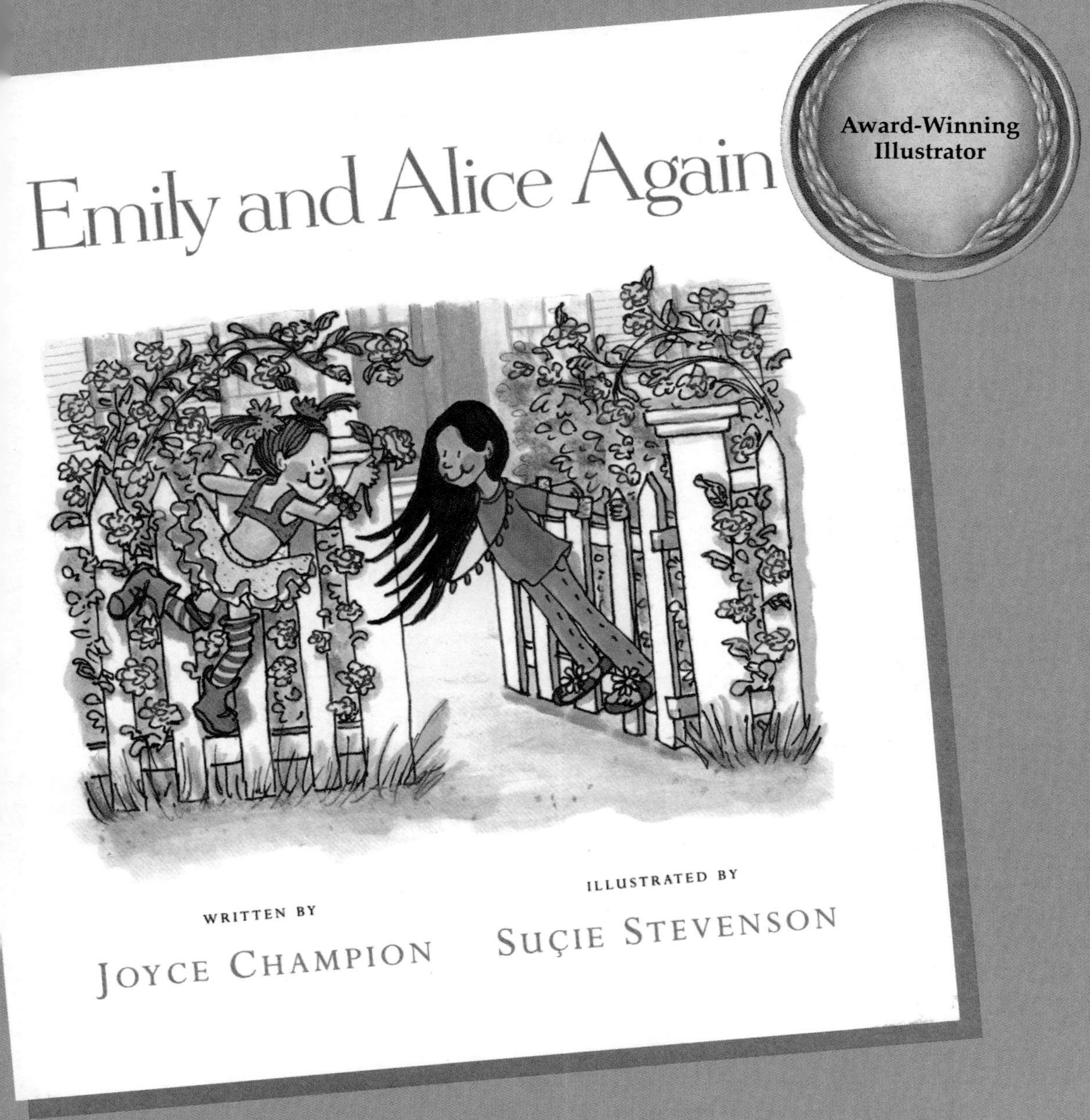

Emily and Alice Again

Award-Winning Illustrator

WRITTEN BY JOYCE CHAMPION

ILLUSTRATED BY SUÇIE STEVENSON

Joyce Champion

ABOUT THE AUTHOR AND THE ILLUSTRATOR

JOYCE CHAMPION has written two books about Emily and her best friend, Alice—*Emily and Alice* and *Emily and Alice Again.*

SUÇIE STEVENSON has illustrated numerous books for children, including *Emily and Alice* and *Emily and Alice Again* and the Henry and Mudge series by Cynthia Rylant.

For more information about the author and the illustrator, see pages T94–T95.

Suçie Stevenson

THEME: LEARNING ABOUT ONESELF

Celebrate Me!

In "Emily and Alice Again," children will read about a discovery that two best friends make when what they think they want and what they really want are two different things.

SELECTION SUMMARY

Genre: Realistic Fiction

Emily loves Alice's new sunglasses. Will Alice trade them for something? Emily offers Alice her stuffed animals and then her rock collection. Alice won't trade until Emily offers to trade her little sister, Nora, for the glasses. The trade is made. Everyone is happy until Emily hears how much fun Alice and Nora are having. Emily and Alice agree to trade back and decide to just borrow from then on.

SUGGESTED LESSON PLANNER

▶ ***Emily and Alice Again***

	DAY 1	DAY 2
PART 1 Reading Listening Speaking Viewing **Key Words** beautiful borrow sorry knew heard laugh idea enough	**BUILD BACKGROUND** T76 **VOCABULARY STRATEGIES** T76–T77 *Chart/Transparency 3* *Practice Book* pp. 13–14 **READING THE SELECTION** T78–T95 Options for Reading T78–T79 *Response Card 3* *Literature Cassette 1* **REVIEW PREDICTIONS/PURPOSE** T92 **APPRECIATING THE LITERATURE** T92 NOTE: Children may read the selection on Day 2.	**SUMMARIZE AND RETELL THE SELECTION** T93 *Practice Book* p. 15 ◆ **RESPONSE CORNER ACTIVITIES** T96 **CHECKING COMPREHENSION** T97 *End-of-Selection Test* 
PART 2 Writer's Workshop	**A PERSONAL STORY** Thinking as Writers T102 *Chart/Transparency 4*	Prewriting T102
Grammar	✓**NAMING PART OF A SENTENCE; JOINING NAMING PARTS** Teach the Concept T104 Daily Language Practice (1–2) R19	Daily Language Practice (3–4) R19 Practice Activity T105
Spelling	**WORDS WITH SHORT *e*** *get* *ten* *yes* *leg* *egg* *met* *mess* *set* *men* *yet* Pretest/Self-Check T106 *Integrated Spelling Teacher's Edition* pp. T27, T269	Open and Closed Sorts T106 *Integrated Spelling* p. 14 *Integrated Spelling Teacher's Edition* p. T28
PART 3 Phonics	**CONSONANT DIGRAPH: /f/*gh, ph*** Phonics-Vocabulary Connection T77	**CONSONANT DIGRAPH: /f/*gh, ph*** (Introduce) T108 *Big Book of Rhymes* p. 5 *Phonics Practice Book* p. 237
Skills and Strategies	◆ **INTEGRATED CURRICULUM** *Trading* **Social Studies** T112 **Math** T112 **Art** T113 **Science** T113 *Imagination Express, Destination: Ocean*	**COMPREHENSION SKILL** T110–T111 Story Elements (Introduce) *Practice Book* p. 21 *Imagination Express, Destination: Neighborhood; Destination: Castle*

	DAY 1	DAY 2
MEETING INDIVIDUAL NEEDS	Use the Extra Support note on page T80 and the Intervention Strategies note on page T84 to help **below-level readers.**	Use the Varying the Activity note on page T96 for **above-level readers.**

NOTE: An alternative lesson plan for **below-level readers** appears on *Intervention Strategies Manual* pp. 8–13. A lesson for **students acquiring English** appears on *Sheltered English/ESL Manual* pp. 6–9.

DAY 3	DAY 4	DAY 5
◆ **IDEA BANK ACTIVITIES** Listening and Speaking T100 Real-Life Reading: Reading an Address T100 Oral Language T101 Kinesthetic T101 *Writer's Magazine* pp. 6–9 School–Home Connection 2 R49 *Kid Pix*	**VOCABULARY WORKSHOP** T107 Reviewing Key Words Story Strips R53 Compound Words *Practice Book* pp. 18–19 *Take-Home/Keep-at-Home Book: The Case of the Missing Lunch* **READING TRADE BOOKS** T114–T115  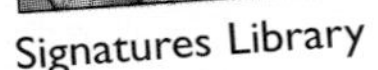 Signatures Library  Take-Home Book	**READING TRADE BOOKS** T109, T111, T113, T114–T115  Instant Reader™ Instant Reader™
Drafting T102 *Language Handbook* pp. 6–7 *The Amazing Writing Machine*	Responding and Revising T103	Proofreading and Publishing T103 *Kid Pix*
Daily Language Practice (5–6) R19 Practice Activity T105 *Language Handbook* pp. 38–41	Daily Language Practice (7–8) R19 Practice Activity T105 *Grammar Practice Book* pp. 15–18	Daily Language Practice (9–12) R19 *Practice Book* p. 16
Discuss the Generalization T106 *Integrated Spelling* p. 15 *Integrated Spelling Teacher's Edition* p. T29	Apply to Writing T106 *Integrated Spelling* pp. 16–17 *Integrated Spelling Teacher's Edition* pp. T30–T31	Posttest T106 *Practice Book* p. 17 *Integrated Spelling Teacher's Edition* p. T32
CONSONANT DIGRAPH: /f/*gh, ph* T108 *Phonics Practice Book* p. 238 *Phonics Practice Reader 12: The Phipp Family Photograph*	**CONSONANT DIGRAPH: /f/*gh, ph*** T109 *Practice Book* p. 20	**CONSONANT DIGRAPH: /f/*gh, ph*** T109 *Phonics Activity Book* pp. 4–5
PHONICS AND DECODING MINILESSON T83 Short Vowel: /e/*e* (Maintain) *Phonics Activity Book* p. 6 *Phonics Game Board Pattern Book* p. 3 *Phonics Practice Reader 1: How Odd* *Phonics Practice Book* pp. 33–37 *Practice Book* p. 22	**PHONICS AND DECODING MINILESSON** T87 ✓ R-Controlled Vowel: /är/*ar* (Review) *Phonics Game Board Pattern Book* p. 43 *Practice Book* p. 23 **GRAMMAR MINILESSON** T89 ✓ Sentences (Review) *Language Handbook* pp. 36–37	**COMPREHENSION MINILESSON** T89 ✓ Sequence (Review) *Practice Book* p. 24 Theme Project Checkpoint 2 T116
To help children build fluency, use the *Instant Readers™ The Drum* and *All Kinds of Rocks* on pages T98–T99.	Use the Students Acquiring English note on page T107 for **ESL readers.**	**Below-level** and **ESL readers** may read the *ESL/Title 1 Library* book *What Do You Like?*

✓ = Tested Skill
◆ = Optional activities that may be used to adjust pacing throughout the lesson
Titles in *italics* are optional materials.

BUILDING BACKGROUND AND CONCEPTS

PRIOR KNOWLEDGE

Discuss trading. Ask children if they have ever traded possessions with friends. Encourage volunteers to describe what things they traded and how they and their friends decided on what would make a fair trade in each case.

Play a trading game. Gather various objects such as pencils, erasers, books, and toys and distribute them among children. Then have children work in groups, trading their objects for other things they want. Once children have traded, ask:

- **How did you decide if a trade was fair?**
- **Were some things worth more than others?**

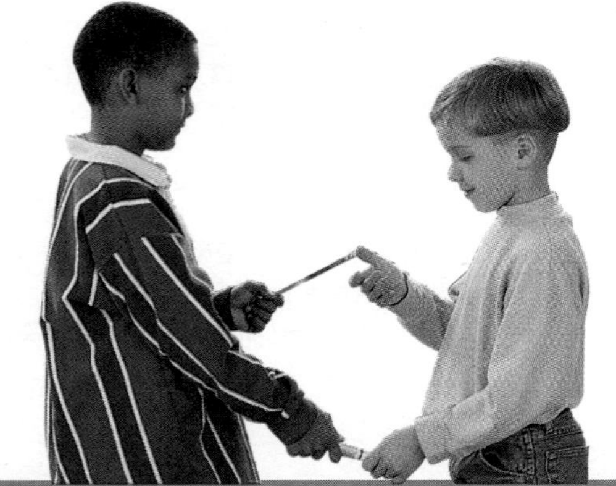

MEETING INDIVIDUAL NEEDS

Intervention Strategies

For children who may have difficulty reading "Emily and Alice Again," support is available in *Intervention Strategies Manual*, pages 8–13 and on pages T84 and T98–T99 in this lesson.

STUDENTS ACQUIRING ENGLISH

See *Sheltered English/ESL Manual*, pages 6–9.

VOCABULARY STRATEGIES

KEY WORDS DEFINED

beautiful very pretty
knew had the facts
idea a thought
borrow to use something that belongs to someone else and then return it to its owner
heard listened to
enough all that is needed or wanted
sorry feeling sad about something
laugh to make a sound that expresses happiness

SUPPORT WORDS

Display the words *collection, favorite, shriek, suspiciously,* and *thought*. Discuss their meanings and have children use them in sentences.

INTEGRATED SPELLING

SPELLING PRETEST: page T106
SPELLING GENERALIZATION: Words with Short *e*

"Because Alice's sunglasses make everything look pink, I like to have children experiment looking at things through different-colored pieces of acetate, colored plastic wrap, or sunglasses. I ask them to think about whether all the colors change and to try looking through two or more colors at the same time. At the end of the activity, I ask them whether they would like to see the world through another color all the time, and why or why not."

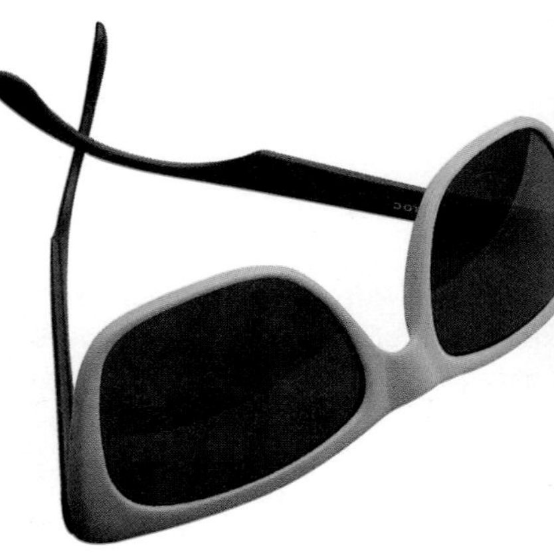

CUEING SYSTEMS

Have children read new vocabulary. Display Chart/Transparency 3, or write the words and sentences on the board. Have children read words they know.

Cover the word *beautiful* with a self-stick note and have children read the sentence. Ask them to suggest a word to complete the sentence. Show them the first letter of the word, and then show them the whole word. As children respond, ask:

> **Does your word make sense in the sentence?**
> **How did your ideas change when you saw the first letter of the word?**
> **What other parts of the word helped you read it?**

Have children continue to read the story, using the sounds for the letters and the sense of the story to help them figure out the underlined words.

CHART/TRANSPARENCY 3

beautiful	knew	idea	borrow
heard	enough	sorry	laugh

It looked like a beautiful sunny day. Sam knew it was his birthday, but he had no idea where his family was. He wanted to borrow a shirt from his brother.

He heard a loud noise outside. He thought he was brave enough to go see what it was.

When he looked outside, he was sorry he had felt afraid. He started to laugh. His family was outside waiting to surprise him for his birthday!

HANDS-ON ACTIVITY

Play a game with children. Have children write each Key Word on a word card. Have children hold up the word they think best goes with each clue.

After three slices of pie, you might say, "I've had _____." (enough)
You use this word when you see something pleasing to your eyes. (beautiful)
You do this after you hear something funny. (laugh)
You say this word when you feel bad about something you did. (sorry)
You do this when you use something that belongs to someone else. (borrow)
If you found out you can do it, you might say, "I ___ I could do it!" (knew)
You have this when you think of something new. (idea)
This is something you did with your ears yesterday. (heard)

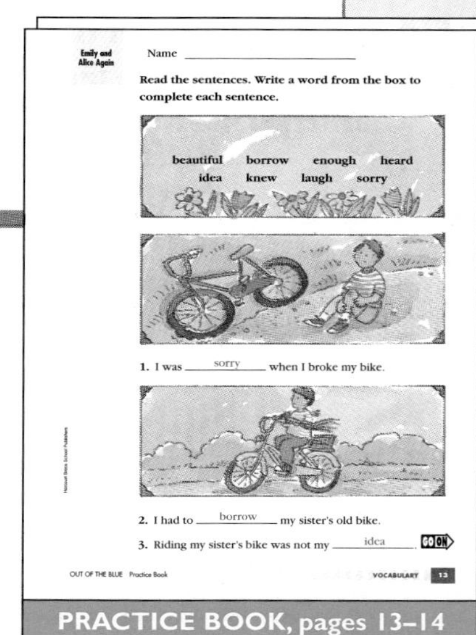

Emily and Alice Again

Name ______________________

Read the sentences. Write a word from the box to complete each sentence.

beautiful borrow enough heard
idea knew laugh sorry

1. I was ___sorry___ when I broke my bike.

2. I had to ___borrow___ my sister's old bike.

3. Riding my sister's bike was not my ___idea___.

PRACTICE BOOK, pages 13–14

PHONICS-VOCABULARY CONNECTION

WORD PLAY

Write *enough* and *laugh* in one column on the board. Read the words and ask how they are alike. Children may notice that the words end with the same sound and that the /f/ sound is spelled *gh* in both words. Repeat the process for the words *phone* and *photo,* writing them in a second column on the board.

Ask children to place the words *rough, pheasant, cough,* and *photograph* in the correct columns on the chart. Point out that *photograph* belongs under both columns.

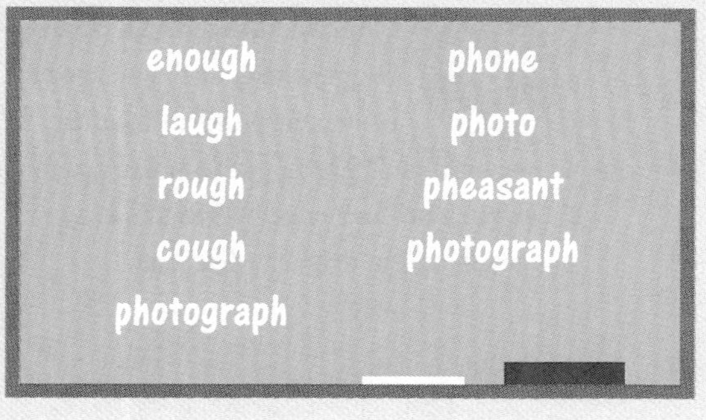

This concept of /f/*gh, ph* is further developed on pages T108–T109.

Strategic Reading

STRATEGY FOCUS: MAKING PREDICTIONS

Review with children some of the things good readers do when they read. Refer them to the classroom chart and review the responses already on it. Add any new responses.

What Good Readers Do
Try to remember story events in order
Try to guess what might happen next

Share with children the comprehension strategy that is the focus of this selection.

MODEL

Sometimes when I'm reading, I make a prediction, or a guess, about what will happen next. I think about what has happened so far in the story. When I read on, it's fun to find out how close my predictions are to what really happens in the story. Sometimes an author likes to surprise readers. In those cases, my predictions are far from what happens in the story.

Emily and Alice Again

Award-Winning Illustrator

WRITTEN BY JOYCE CHAMPION

ILLUSTRATED BY SUÇIE STEVENSON

44

TIPS FOR CLASSROOM MANAGEMENT

SMALL GROUP

STRATEGIC READING

Choose some or all of the suggestions and questions under Strategic Reading, pages T78–T93, to guide a literature discussion and model the STRATEGY FOCUS of Making Predictions.

COOPERATIVE READING

LITERATURE CIRCLES Small groups of children may enjoy reading "Emily and Alice Again" silently, stopping at given points to talk about what has happened so far. Provide copies of Reader Response Card 3 (Plot), page R23, to guide their discussion.

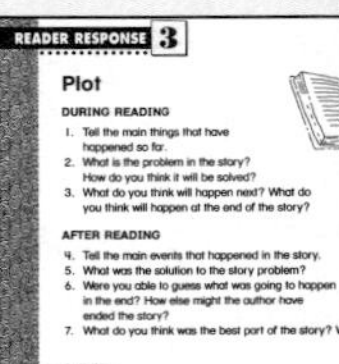

Response Card

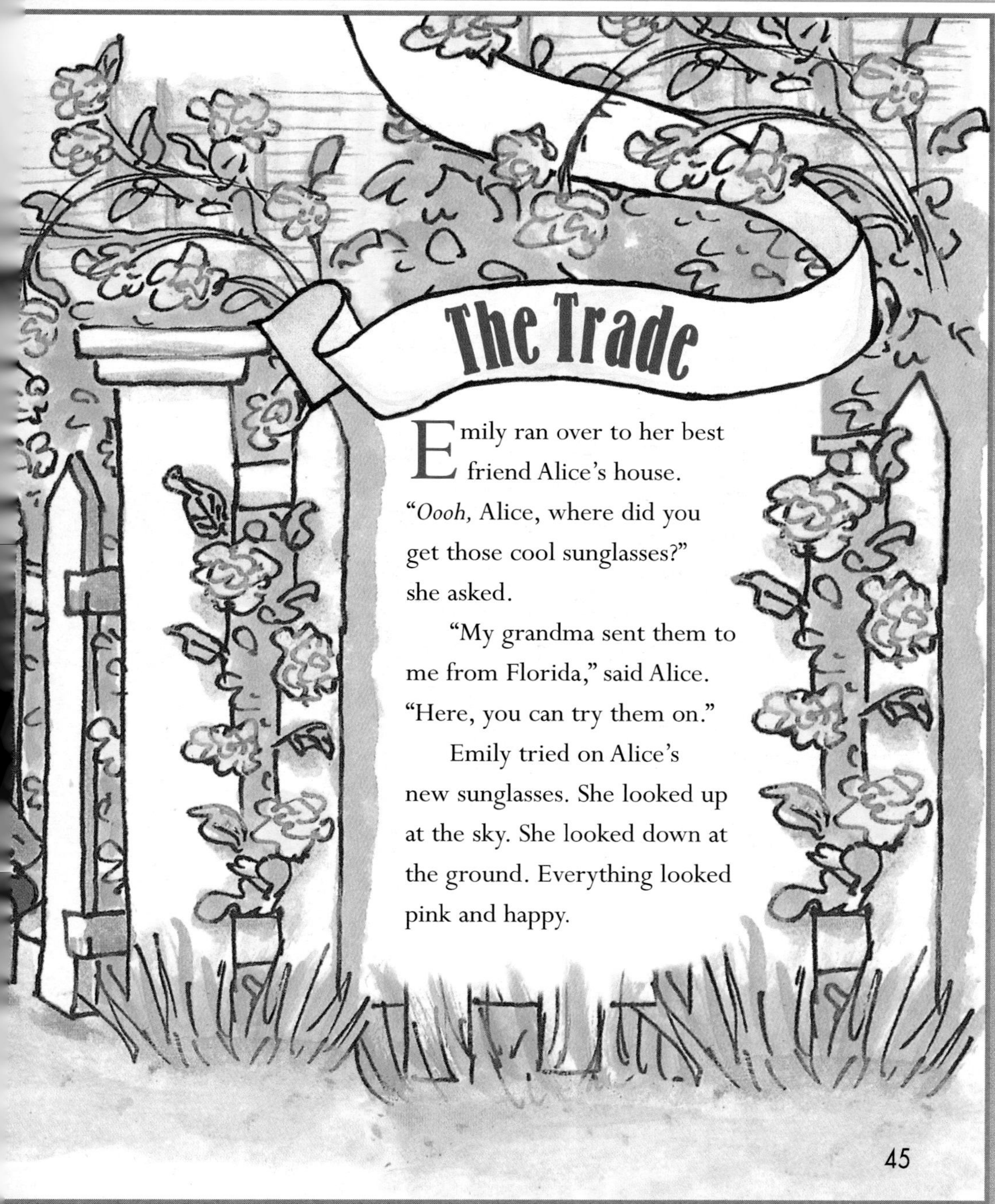

The Trade

Emily ran over to her best friend Alice's house. "*Oooh,* Alice, where did you get those cool sunglasses?" she asked.

"My grandma sent them to me from Florida," said Alice. "Here, you can try them on."

Emily tried on Alice's new sunglasses. She looked up at the sky. She looked down at the ground. Everything looked pink and happy.

45

PREVIEWING/ SETTING PURPOSES

Have children read the story title on page 44. Explain that the words in the banner on page 45 are a chapter title and that this selection is one chapter from a book. Have children flip through the illustrations on pages 44–47. Then have them use the pictures and the chapter title, "The Trade," to make predictions about the selection. Have them record their predictions in their personal journals. Then help children set their own purposes for reading.

MODELING A STRATEGY

STRATEGY FOCUS

PAGE 45 Ask children to read page 45 and then predict what Emily will want to do. If necessary, model your thinking: *I can tell that Emily really likes Alice's sunglasses, and I know that the selection is going to be about a trade. Maybe Emily will try to trade something for Alice's sunglasses.* MAKING PREDICTIONS

WHOLE CLASS

READ-ALOUD

Read "Emily and Alice Again" aloud as children follow along in their books. Comment and ask questions as you read. Invite children to respond to the story at each break you take in your reading.

INDEPENDENT READING

Have children read "Emily and Alice Again" silently. As they finish, have them write in their journals their reactions to how and what the girls traded. When all children have finished the story, have them use their journal entries to discuss it.

Strategic Reading

MODELING A STRATEGY

PAGES 46–47 Have children look at the pictures and then read the pages. After children have read, have them tell what they think Emily will do when she comes back. You may want to remind them to think about what happened when Emily said, "I'll be right back" at the end of page 46. **Think aloud:** *The last time Emily said, "I'll be right back," she came back with stuffed animals to trade. I think she's going to get something even better this time so that Alice will want to trade.* MAKING PREDICTIONS

"I *love* these sunglasses," said Emily. "I could wear them forever." At that moment she knew she had to have them.

Alice watched Emily suspiciously. "I want my sunglasses back now," she said.

Emily gave Alice her sunglasses. But she had a plan. "Don't move," she told Alice. "I'll be right back."

46

LISTENING CENTER

Some children may benefit from listening to the story and following along in their books. Record "Emily and Alice Again" on an audiocassette to put in the Listening Center for children to enjoy. (See Acknowledgments on pages R235–R236.)

EXTRA SUPPORT **Trying to figure out who is Emily and who is Alice may be confusing to children at the beginning of the story. Suggest that children use the pictures on pages 46 and 47 along with the text to figure out which girl in the illustrations is Alice and which is Emily.**

Emily ran to her house. She came back to Alice's holding two stuffed animals. "Want to trade Zippidy and Doodah for your new sunglasses?" she asked.

"Don't you have your own sunglasses?" asked Alice.

"I only have the plain round kind," answered Emily. "I don't have cool heart-shaped glasses like yours. I don't have sunglasses that make the world pink and happy. Let's trade."

Alice looked at Emily's bears and shook her head. "Sorry, Emily," she said. "No trade."

"I'll be right back," said Emily.

47

Student Self-Assessment

USING READING STRATEGIES

Invite children to tell what they do as they try to understand something in a story that confuses them:

- ☑ Do you try to read the confusing part again to see if it makes more sense the second time?
- ☑ Do you look at the pictures to see if they help explain what is happening?
- ☑ Do you look for clues in the story to help you figure out a new word?

MUSIC

SONG LYRICS The names of Emily's stuffed animals—Zippidy and Doodah—come from the song "Zip-a-dee-doo-dah," from Walt Disney's *Song of the South* (1943). The music is by Allie Wrubel and the lyrics by Ray Gilbert. You may want to sing the song with children.

AUTHOR'S CRAFT

During a rereading of the story, call children's attention to the pattern that the author has established at the end of pages 46, 47, and 48 when Emily says she'll be back. Talk about how the pattern adds to the story. Encourage children to speculate about why the author might have chosen to repeat the phrase.

Strategic Reading

APPLYING A STRATEGY

PAGES 48–49 Confirm with children their predictions about what Emily would do when she said, "I'll be right back." Then have children identify Emily's other ideas of what to trade for the sunglasses. Ask children what they think Emily's "best idea yet" will be. Encourage children to predict what will happen when Emily brings her little sister to Alice's house.

MAKING AND CONFIRMING PREDICTIONS

Emily returned to Alice's holding a box. "I'll trade you my favorite rocks," she said, "even all the sparkly ones, if I can have your sunglasses."

Alice looked at Emily's rock collection and shook her head. "Sorry, Emily," she said. "Still no trade."

"OK," said Emily, "wait here—because I'll be back."

48

SOCIAL STUDIES

TRADING The desire to trade goods first led explorers to venture from their homelands. As early as 2500 B.C., ancient Babylonians and Egyptians journeyed to search for people with whom to trade. Soon regular trade routes were established.

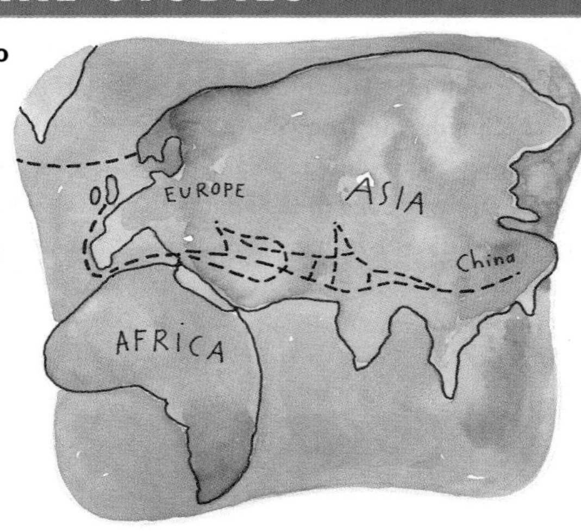

Emily ran to her house again. She *had* to find something to trade. She walked in circles around her room. Then she saw her little sister, Nora, in the doorway. This was her best idea yet!

Emily grabbed her sister's hand and ran back to Alice's.

49

MINILESSON

MAINTAIN: PHONICS AND DECODING

Short Vowel: /e/*e*

INFORMAL ASSESSMENT

As children read, notice how well they can decode words with the short e sound.

TEACH/MODEL

Ask children to find these words on page 49 as you list them on the board: *then, best, yet.* Read the words and ask children what vowel sound they hear in them. Remind children that the letter e can stand for the /e/ sound. Then have children list words that rhyme with *best, then,* and *yet.*

PRACTICE/APPLY

Display the following paragraph and ask children to read it aloud. Have volunteers circle the words that have the vowel sound they hear in *pet.*

Have you met my red hen? Her name is Beth. This is her nest. She has ten eggs. Beth is my best pet yet!

PHONICS ACTIVITY BOOK, page 6

For further reinforcement you might also like to use the game "Sounds Like *Hen,*" *Phonics Game Board Pattern Book,* page 3.

PHONICS PRACTICE READER 1

PHONICS PRACTICE BOOK, pages 33–37

ILLUSTRATOR'S CRAFT

Invite children to look more closely at the illustrations in the story. Have them talk about the details that the illustrator uses to make the characters look like real children. Encourage children to talk about other realistic details in the illustrations.

Name ______________ Emily and Alice Again

Read the sentences and the words on the nests. Write the word that makes sense in the sentence and has the same vowel sound as *jet.*

dress tent desk ten lets best pets

1. Penny loves all her ___pets___.
2. They are her ___best___ friends.
3. She has ___ten___ hens.
4. A lizard lives in her ___desk___.
5. A mouse is in the pocket of her ___dress___.
6. Penny ___lets___ her cat sleep on her bed.
7. Look who lives outside in a ___tent___!

22 SHORT VOWEL:/e/e — OUT OF THE BLUE Practice Book

PRACTICE BOOK, page 22

Strategic Reading

APPLYING A STRATEGY

PAGES 50–51 Ask children whether their predictions about what Emily would do when she and her sister got to Alice's house were correct. As children discuss the accuracy of their predictions, encourage children to talk about what parts of the story led them to make the predictions they did. When children have finished reading page 51, ask them to predict whether the girls' trade will work. **MAKING AND CONFIRMING PREDICTIONS**

50

CONVENTIONS OF PRINT

QUOTATION MARKS Ask two children to role-play the parts of Emily and Alice on page 51, reading only the words in quotation marks. Remind children that quotation marks are used to show the words that the characters say.

MEETING INDIVIDUAL NEEDS

Intervention Strategies

SUMMARIZING Have children repeat this sentence: *When I read, it helps me to think about what's happened so far.* Have children tell how using this strategy might help them understand what's happened in "Emily and Alice Again."

"Alice," she said, "I'll trade my favorite sister—my *only* sister—for your new sunglasses."

Alice looked at Nora. She looked at her chubby little legs and tiny red sneakers. Alice nodded. "OK, I'll trade!"

Alice gave Emily her new sunglasses. Emily gave Alice her only sister.

51

Informal Assessment

USING CUEING SYSTEMS

As children read, observe how they attempt to figure out new words.

- ☑ Do children suggest words that make sense?
- ☑ Do children pay attention to the letters that spell the word?
- ☑ Do children reread and self-correct if their substitutions do not make sense in the context?

PHONICS IN ACTION

Have children locate the words *only*, *chubby*, *tiny*, and *Emily* on page 51. Point out that the y in each of these words has the long e sound.

TINY
chubby
Only
EMILY

Strategic Reading

APPLYING A STRATEGY

PAGES 52–53 As children read these pages, encourage them to talk about how the illustrations help give them an idea of how Emily feels about the sunglasses. Ask children to find parts of the written story that appear in the illustrations. **RELATING PICTURES TO TEXT**

Emily ran home and put on her new sunglasses. Everything looked pink and happy. "I am a beautiful movie star," she said to the mirror. Then she ran out back.

52

CHALLENGE **Suggest that children look at a globe or an atlas to find a faraway island (or other place) they would like to visit. Then have them use reference books to find out about the place and decide whether they still would like to go there. Invite children to share what they learned about the place they chose.**

REAL-LIFE CONNECTION

Talk with children about Emily's imagining first that she is a movie star, and then that she's traveling on a cruise ship. Ask whether children have ever imagined things in the way that Emily is imagining them. Invite children to tell about pretend games they have played.

Emily lay on a beach chair. She looked up at the pink sun. She watched pink clouds float by. "I am on a big cruise ship," she said to the sky. "Soon I will be on a faraway island."

53

Tested Skill

MINILESSON

REVIEW: PHONICS AND DECODING

R-Controlled Vowel: /är/*ar*

INFORMAL ASSESSMENT

As children read, notice whether they can decode words with the vowel sound /är/ spelled *ar*.

TEACH/MODEL

Point out the words *star* and *faraway* on pages 52–53. Write them on the board and have children read them. Remind children that the letters *ar* can stand for the vowel sound heard in *star*. Ask a volunteer to underline the letters that spell the /är/ sound in both words. Have them brainstorm a list of words that rhyme with *star*.

PRACTICE/APPLY

Write the word *arm* on the board and have children copy it onto paper. As you give the instructions below, have children write each word. Ask a volunteer to read each new word.

arm

- Add ***h*** to the beginning. (harm)
- Add ***c*** to the beginning. (charm)
- Change the last letter to ***t***. (chart)
- Change the ***t*** to ***ge***. (charge)
- Change the ***ch*** to ***l***. (large)

For further reinforcement, children might also enjoy a game of "Star Bingo," *Phonics Game Board Pattern Book*, page 43.

A CLOSER LOOK

Talk with children about how the illustrator shows readers something like what Emily sees through Alice's pink sunglasses.

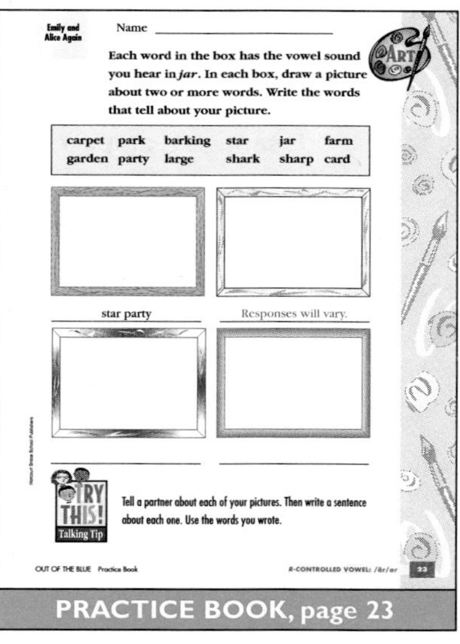

Emily and Alice Again

Name ______________________

Each word in the box has the vowel sound you hear in *jar*. In each box, draw a picture about two or more words. Write the words that tell about your picture.

carpet	park	barking	star	jar	farm
garden	party	large	shark	sharp	card

star party

Responses will vary.

TRY THIS! Talking Tip

Tell a partner about each of your pictures. Then write a sentence about each one. Use the words you wrote.

OUT OF THE BLUE Practice Book — R-CONTROLLED VOWEL: /är/ar — 23

PRACTICE BOOK, page 23

Strategic Reading

MODELING A STRATEGY

PAGES 54–57 Before children read the pages, ask them to look at the pictures and guess what is happening. If necessary, model the thinking children might use: *On pages 55 and 56, Emily doesn't look very happy. I wonder if she's getting lonely just sitting by herself. Alice and Nora seem to be having fun in the picture on page 54, but by page 57, it looks like Nora is pulling Alice's hair. On the same page, Emily is running over to Alice with the sunglasses in her hand. It looks like the girls are ready to trade back.*

Then have children read on to confirm their predictions. **MAKING AND CONFIRMING PREDICTIONS**

Emily heard giggles coming from Alice's backyard. She could see that Alice was teaching Nora how to do cartwheels. *I'm glad they're having fun,* she thought.

54

CONVENTIONS OF PRINT

ITALICS Have children read the last sentence on page 54 and the last sentence on page 55. Point out that these sentences tell what Emily is thinking and ask how the author showed that. Tell children that this kind of type is called italics and that it is used to set off certain words or sentences, such as a character's thoughts, from the rest of the text.

STUDENTS ACQUIRING ENGLISH Although the illustration helps somewhat, children who understand the words *cart* and *wheels* may still not know what a *cartwheel* is. You might ask volunteers who can do cartwheels to demonstrate. Talk about how a cartwheel looks like a cart's wheel that's turning.

Emily polished her sunglasses. She looked over at Alice's yard again. She watched Alice put on a puppet show for Nora. She watched Alice give Nora horseback rides. She heard Nora laugh and shriek. *They're REALLY having fun,* thought Emily.

55

Tested Skill

MINILESSON

REVIEW: GRAMMAR

Sentences

INFORMAL ASSESSMENT

Write word groups like these on the board:

he ran to school
Alice's new sunglasses.
Emily walked home.

Ask children to explain which of these are sentences and why.

TEACH/MODEL

Remind children that to be a sentence, a set of words must tell a complete thought, begin with a capital letter, and end with an end mark. Have children give examples of sentences and sets of words that are not sentences. Then work with them to change the nonsentences into sentences.

PRACTICE/APPLY

Copy the following sets of words onto the board. Ask children to read each line and tell whether or not it is a sentence. Have children add words to the groups that are not sentences to make them sentences. Ask children to write each sentence correctly.

my new sunglasses are blue
have gold stars
my old sunglasses
you can borrow my new sunglasses

LANGUAGE HANDBOOK
Sentences, pages 36–37

SOCIAL STUDIES

BARTERING People didn't always use money to trade for goods and services. Even though there were trading centers and traders who used coins, people in outlying areas would most likely barter, or trade things they made or grew for other things they would need. For example, someone with a chicken might trade a basket of eggs for yarn that someone else had spun.

Cooperative Reading

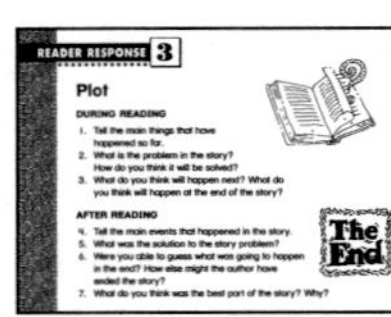
Response Card 3

As children discuss the questions on **Reader Response Card 3** (Plot), you might pose additional questions for them to consider:

1. **Do you think the girls are happy with their trade?**
2. **What do you think Emily's parents would say if they found out that Emily had traded Nora to Alice?**
3. **What was the most surprising thing that has happened in the story so far? Why was it surprising?**

Emily put her sunglasses on. She looked up at the sky. She looked down at the ground. The world was still pink. But it didn't seem quite so happy.

56

IDEA BANK

IDIOMATIC EXPRESSIONS **A person who always seems happy may be said to look at the world "through rose-colored glasses." Children may relate this expression to the way Emily feels about the sunglasses, especially after she first tries them on. Help children interpret another expression that might relate to the selection: "The grass is always greener on the other side of the fence."**

Emily yanked off the glasses and ran next door. "Alice," she said, "I think I've had enough fun with your cool sunglasses."

Alice tried to catch her breath. "I think I've had enough fun with your sister," she said.

57

Tested Skill

MINILESSON

REVIEW: COMPREHENSION

Sequence

INFORMAL ASSESSMENT

As children tell and write stories, note how well they put events in logical order.

TEACH/MODEL

Tell children a story with the events obviously in the wrong order.
For example:

They saw something strange on the sidewalk. (2) *Then it jumped up at them.* (4) *Two friends went for a walk.* (1) *At first, it didn't move.* (3) *They finally saw that it was a frog.* (5)

Talk with children about how little sense the story makes as you just read it. Talk about how important the order of events is to stories.

PRACTICE/APPLY

Have children write each sentence from your story on a sentence strip and work with partners to put their strips in an order that makes sense. When they have finished, have volunteers read the story aloud.

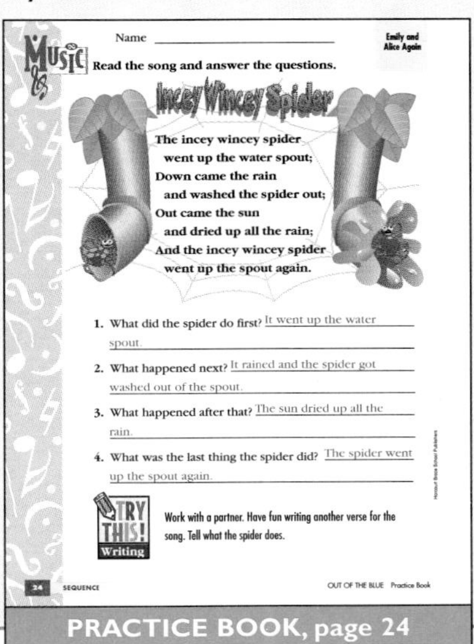

Name ____________

Emily and Alice Again

MUSIC

Read the song and answer the questions.

Incey Wincey Spider

The incey wincey spider
went up the water spout;
Down came the rain
and washed the spider out;
Out came the sun
and dried up all the rain;
And the incey wincey spider
went up the spout again.

1. What did the spider do first? It went up the water spout.
2. What happened next? It rained and the spider got washed out of the spout.
3. What happened after that? The sun dried up all the rain.
4. What was the last thing the spider did? The spider went up the spout again.

TRY THIS! Writing

Work with a partner. Have fun writing another verse for the song. Tell what the spider does.

24 SEQUENCE

OUT OF THE BLUE Practice Book

Harcourt Brace School Publishers

PRACTICE BOOK, page 24

ILLUSTRATOR'S CRAFT

An illustration may fill in details about a story that the words do not tell. Have children look at the picture on page 57. Then ask: ***What does this picture show that the words do not tell? How does the picture help explain why Alice wants to trade Nora back?***

REAL-LIFE CONNECTION

Some children may not have had the experience of trying to keep a younger brother or sister entertained. Allow those who have younger siblings to tell about times they may have tried to entertain the little ones.

Strategic Reading

APPLYING A STRATEGY

PAGES 58–59 Ask children to recall the predictions they made after page 57 about what Emily and Alice would do. Discuss how closely their predictions match what actually happened. Ask why children think the girls gave back what they traded. **MAKING AND CONFIRMING PREDICTIONS**

Returning to the Predictions/Purpose

Invite children to share the predictions they made before they read the story and compare them to what actually happened.

Appreciating the Literature

With the whole class or a small group, have an open discussion about the story.

- **What would you have traded to get the glasses? What do you think would have happened?**

Emily gave back Alice's sunglasses. Alice waved good-bye to Nora.

"Let's just *borrow* next time, OK?" asked Alice.

"Good idea," said Emily.

Alice smiled and put on her sunglasses.

58

WRITING

EXTEND THE STORY **Emily and Alice have decided that borrowing is better than trading. Encourage children to write some sentences detailing problems that could occur with borrowing things—and offering solutions.**

Emily smiled as she and Nora cartwheeled home.

59

Student Self-Assessment

FIX-UP STRATEGY: SOUNDING OUT WORDS

If children spend too much time trying to sound out words letter by letter, encourage them to look for parts of the word that they can read and have them use these word parts to figure out the whole word.

SUMMARIZE AND RETELL

Frame It

Use a story frame like the one shown to review the main story events. Then have children complete their own story frames on *Practice Book* page 15 and use them to retell the story to partners.

Who	What did Emily want?
Emily and Alice	Alice's sunglasses

What was the problem?	How did Emily try to solve it?
Alice didn't want what Emily had to trade.	Emily offered her baby sister. They traded.

Then what happened?	Ending
Emily missed Nora and Alice got tired of Nora.	Emily and Alice traded back.

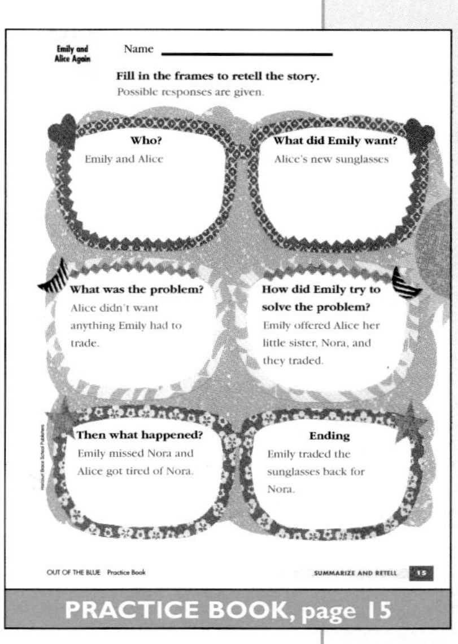

Emily and Alice Again Name ____________

Fill in the frames to retell the story.
Possible responses are given.

Who?
Emily and Alice

What did Emily want?
Alice's new sunglasses

What was the problem?
Alice didn't want anything Emily had to trade.

How did Emily try to solve the problem?
Emily offered Alice her little sister, Nora, and they traded.

Then what happened?
Emily missed Nora and Alice got tired of Nora.

Ending
Emily traded the sunglasses back for Nora.

OUT OF THE BLUE Practice Book SUMMARIZE AND RETELL 15

PRACTICE BOOK, page 15

About the Author

PAGES 60–61 Share with children the information about the author and illustrator on pages 60-61. Engage children in a discussion about why authors and illustrators use their experiences and people and/or pets they know in their work. Encourage children to share their ideas. You might want to ask them what they think would happen if an author or illustrator tried to show or tell about something he or she knew nothing about.

Joyce Champion's stories about Emily and Alice were inspired by her childhood wish to have a neighbor—and best friend—who was just like her. She finally got the neighbor, a girl who lived in an apartment next door. And although the girl was nothing like Joyce Champion, they became best friends. They still are.

JOYCE CHAMPION

Are Emily and Alice like any people you know?
Emily is like me. Alice is like my best friend when I was growing up. She lived in the apartment next door to my family.

Are you still friends with her?
Yes. She was even in my wedding.

Did you really trade your sunglasses for your little sister? Not really, but I did trade my mother for a doll.

You did? To Alice?
No. Another friend who had a neat doll was at my house. I traded, and my mother went along with it. My mother and my friend had such a good time that I made her trade back. *Joyce Champion*

60

ANOTHER BOOK BY JOYCE CHAMPION

***Emily and Alice*. Harcourt Brace, 1993.** AVERAGE

SUÇIE STEVENSON

Suçie Stevenson has been writing children's books and drawing pictures for them for many years. One way that this artist gets ideas for her art is to think about the big family she grew up in. When she made the pictures for this story, she used her memories of the things she and her sister used to do together.

Another way that Suçie Stevenson gets ideas for her art is to go to the beautiful seashore on Cape Cod in Massachusetts. She loves it there! That's where she lives with her two Labrador retrievers.

Suçie Stevenson

61

About the Illustrator

Suçie Stevenson has loved to draw ever since she was a little girl. "I am from a big family," she says. "I used to make birthday cards and other kinds of cards for my family."

She has fond memories of her family, especially her sister, who used to wrap the telephone cord around her toes while talking on the phone. Stevenson used memories like these as inspiration to illustrate *Emily and Alice Again.*

OTHER BOOKS ILLUSTRATED BY SUÇIE STEVENSON

Henry and Mudge and the Best Day of All **by Cynthia Rylant. Macmillan, 1995.** EASY

Henry and Mudge and the Wild Wind **by Cynthia Rylant. Bradbury, 1993.** EASY

RESPONSE CORNER ACTIVITIES

MAKE SUNGLASSES

COOL-LOOKING SHADES

PAGE 62 Read through the directions with children before they begin constructing their glasses. When children are at the point of decorating their glasses, encourage them to be creative and to make their "shades" as colorful as they can. **ART/DRAMA**

TRADE GOODS

LET'S TRADE!

PAGE 63 On "trading day," have children write their names on slips of paper or self-stick notes so others will know who made the bookmarks. Set up a display area where children can look at all the bookmarks. When they see a bookmark they like, they should approach the child who made it and offer to trade. When trading has ended, initiate a discussion about what children learned. **SOCIAL STUDIES**

RESPONSE CORNER

MAKE SUNGLASSES

Cool-Looking Shades

Just like Emily and Alice, everyone wants a pair of cool sunglasses to wear. You can make a pair!

1. Cut out two joined cups from an egg carton.
2. Cut a hole in the bottom of each cup.
3. Cut out a triangle between the two cups to fit over your nose.
4. Staple a pipe cleaner to each side of the glasses.
5. Decorate your glasses.

Then act out your favorite part of the story with a partner.

You will need:
egg carton
scissors
markers
decorations
glue
pipe cleaners
stapler

62

VARYING THE ACTIVITY

As an extension to the Cool-Looking Shades activity, challenge children to make up characters and scenes of their own to act out wearing their snazzy glasses.

TRADE GOODS

Let's Trade!

Did you ever trade something with a friend? Talk about how you know if a trade is fair. Then make a beautiful bookmark. Plan a trading day. Trade the bookmarks you have made. After trading, talk about what you learned.

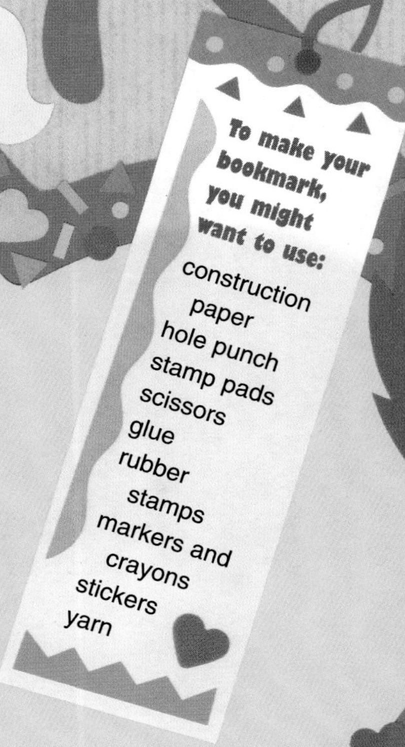

To make your bookmark, you might want to use:
construction paper
hole punch
stamp pads
scissors
glue
rubber stamps
markers and crayons
stickers
yarn

What Do You Think?

- What did Emily and Alice learn about trading?
- What part of the story did you like best? Why?

63

CHECKING COMPREHENSION

What Do You Think?

1. **What did Emily and Alice learn about trading?** (Responses may vary. Possible response: They learned that it's important to be sure that you want what you're trading for, and also not to give up something that you want to keep.) **DESCRIPTIVE RESPONSE**

2. **What part of the story did you like best? Why?** (Responses will vary. Try to get children to be as specific as possible as they talk about their favorite part of the story and why they liked it.) **PERSONAL RESPONSE**

An additional question for extending reading.

3. **What would you do if a friend were to ask you to trade something that is special to you?** (Responses will vary. Have children support their opinions.) **CREATIVE/CRITICAL ANALYSIS**

STUDENTS ACQUIRING ENGLISH **Try to pair children with English-proficient speakers as they role-play scenes from the story. Encourage children to try out new English words, and have them use gestures as they act out the scenes.**

Informal Assessment 

Observe children as they role-play scenes from the story.

- ☑ Do children act out their scenes in sequence?
- ☑ Do they switch roles and act out the scene again?
- ☑ In their dramatizations, do children show an understanding of the characters?

Intervention Strategies

Instant Readers™

Predictable and Patterned Little Books That Build Fluency

*** BOOK LEVEL: 9–10**

VOCABULARY:
beautiful, heard

PHONIC ELEMENT:
R-controlled vowel: /är/*ar*

SUMMARY:
In this traditional (East) Indian story, a boy gives up everything for what he really wants.

Informal Assessment ✓

Are children able to

- ☑ create new words using phonograms?
- ☑ write a sentence to describe?

Reading a New Book

INTRODUCING *THE DRUM*

Show children the cover of the book and read aloud the title. Explain that they will read a story about a boy who wants a drum. Share the illustrations, pointing out what the boy (Ram) gets and trades. Read aloud and point to the sound words with children.

READING THE STORY

Have children read the story independently to learn more about Ram and his drum.

WORKING WITH WORDS AND LETTERS

Use the story words *head, jar, drum*, and *stick* to help children with phonograms. Choose one or two words to work with, and have a volunteer make the story word with individual letter cards, *Word Builder Cards*, or magnetic letters. Provide beginning letters and give children an opportunity to form new words. Have children record the phonograms and words in their Word Banks.

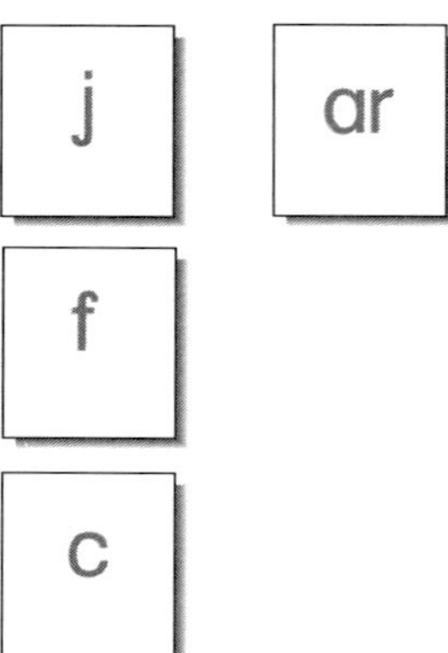

WRITING SENTENCES

Give children time to write a sentence or two about one part of the story they liked. Drawing pictures or looking at story pictures may assist them with their writing.

Additional activities are provided on pages 10-11 of the *Intervention Strategies Manual*.

* **BOOK LEVEL: 14–15**

VOCABULARY:
beautiful, enough

PHONIC ELEMENTS:
Digraph: /f/*gh*; *R*-controlled vowel: /är/*ar*; Short vowel: /e/*e*

SUMMARY:
Alec's amazing rock collection is featured in this rhyming story.

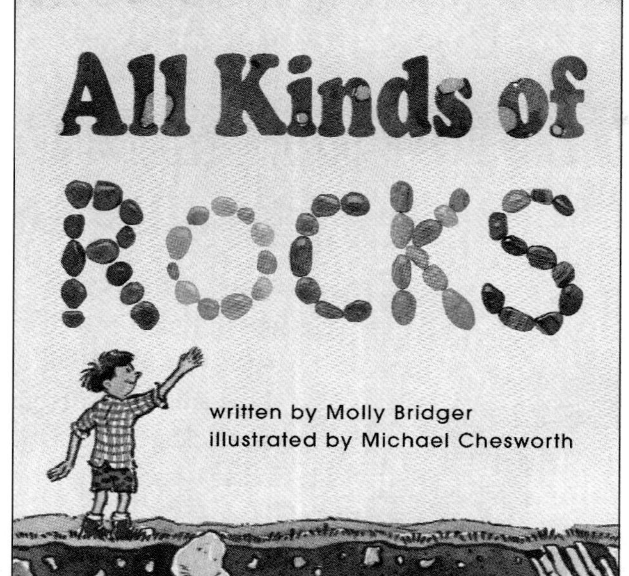

Reading a New Book

INTRODUCING *ALL KINDS OF ROCKS*

Discuss collections that people have and why they collect things. Explain that children will read a story about a boy who has his own collection. Share the cover and the first few pages to draw out that the book is about a boy who loves rocks. As the illustrations are shared, encourage children to describe the rocks.

READING THE STORY

Once children are familiar with the story concepts and the words used to describe them, have them read the story independently.

WORKING WITH WORDS AND LETTERS

To help children read and write words ending with the digraph *gh*, use the story words *enough, tough,* and *rough*. Construct a slip strip for the letters *ough* as shown below. Explain that with some words, the letters *ou* stand for a different sound.

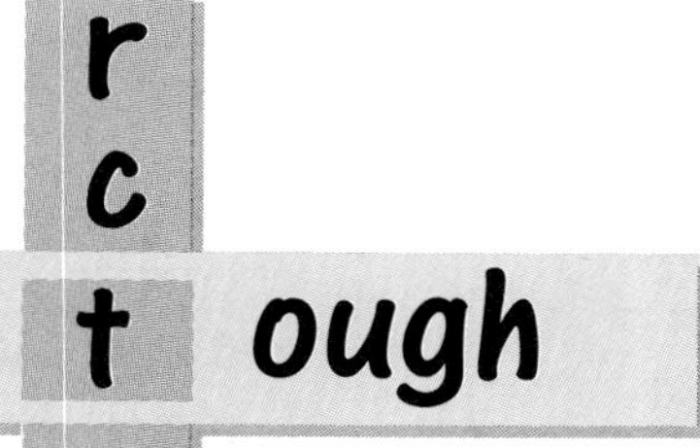

WRITING DESCRIPTIONS

Children may want to write a sentence or two in their personal journals about a collection they have or would like to have.

ESL/Title I Reading

What Do You Like? by Michael Grejniec

ESL/Title I Library

TECHNOLOGY

INSTANT READERS™

ELECTRONIC EDITION

***The Drum* and *All Kinds of Rocks* are available on CD-ROM. Pre- and post-reading activities are included.**

Working with "Emily and Alice Again"

GRAPHOPHONIC CUES While children are learning how to read fluently, help them explore and talk about the ways in which words work. When a child misreads a word, ask her or him to look at the beginning letter(s) and ending letter(s). Point out that the word may begin with a sound that he or she thought was correct. Assisting the child (once in a while) with this kind of strategy will help him or her do this independently.

* Books leveled according to Barbara Peterson's "Profiles of Books for Beginning Readers," on page 9 of the *Instant Readers Teacher's Guide.*

IDEA BANK

TIPS FOR CLASSROOM MANAGEMENT

IF children are interested in the Real-Life Reading activity, **THEN** you may want to extend it and have children write letters and "mail" them to each other. Children might also enjoy writing and "mailing" notes to siblings and to friends in other classes.

TECHNOLOGY

KID PIX
Encourage children to create a multimedia presentation of their book or movie review.

LISTENING AND SPEAKING

Group Talk

FRIENDSHIP ACTIVITIES

Invite groups of children to talk about the friendship between Alice and Emily. Point out that even though the friends made a trade that backfired, they solved this problem by cancelling their trade. From this discussion of friendship at work in the story, encourage children to talk about how they and their friends work out problems between themselves. Ask each group to generate a list of things friends can do to solve problems. Then allow time for groups to exchange ideas. CHALLENGING THE TEXT

Informal Assessment

Note how children use their understanding of the story and of friendship to participate in the discussion about friendship.

REAL-LIFE READING

Reading an Address

Remind children that in the story, Alice's grandmother sent her the sunglasses from Florida. Explain that her grandmother probably mailed her the glasses. Point out that the package must have had Alice's address written on it.

Write the address of the school on the board and ask a volunteer to read it aloud. Discuss the information it shows.

You may want to ask children to bring in envelopes from mail the family has received. Have children point out the parts of their own or classmates' addresses. Then have children write their addresses on index card "envelopes." Have them drop the "letters" into a "mail box," and allow children to take turns sorting and delivering the letters. READING/WRITING

ORAL LANGUAGE

Book/Movie Review

PICK OF THE LISTS

Explain to children that when you see a good movie or when you read a good book, you often want to tell others about it. When a person reviews a book or movie, the person tells a little bit about what happens and also tells why other people should read or see it.

Have children work independently to think of a good book or movie to recommend. Suggest that they make some notes about what they want to say about it. When children are ready, have them share their reviews with small groups. **LISTENING/SPEAKING**

Speakers

- ell what they liked about the tory.
- ell why they think other eople would like it.
- peak clearly.

Listeners

- ay attention to the speaker.
- sk questions if they want nore information.

KINESTHETIC

Creative Connection

MATERIALS
- sunglasses shapes cut from paper
- safety pins

SHADOW TAG

Take children outside to the playground or playing field on a sunny day. Choose several children to be "it." Use safety pins to attach the paper sunglasses to these children's clothing. Children who are "it" count to three and then chase the other children, trying to step on their shadows. A child "freezes" when his or her shadow has been stepped on. When everyone has been "frozen," choose different children to be "it" and play again. **KINESTHETIC**

PERSONAL JOURNAL

REFLECTING ON THE STORY Ask children to think about how they might feel if someone wanted them to give up a new toy. Suggest that they write in their personal journals about whether or not they would make the trade and why.

Which game do the steps go with? How do you know?

What's Inside?

PACKAGE

Emily and Alice have fun playing together with toys. Here's a toy you might have fun with. Read the package carefully, so you'll know what's inside.

BUILD UPS

Our Best Building Set Yet!

Has 120 pieces in six different colors.

Has directions.

You can build a plane, a house, a dinosaur, and much more!

For 6 years old and up.

WARNING! SMALL PARTS. Not safe for children under 3.

WRITER'S MAGAZINE, pages 6–9

TIPS FOR CLASSROOM MANAGEMENT

IF children are familiar with the writing process approach, **THEN** present the writing assignment and have them use the Personal Story model, pages 6-7 of the *Language Handbook.*

IF at this time you want a short writing activity, **THEN** have children do the prewriting activity and refer to their charts as they illustrate the steps in solving the problem.

WRITER'S WORKSHOP

A Personal Story

Thinking as Writers

WRITING FORM: Personal Story Discuss the problem Emily and Alice had and how the two friends solved the problem. Explain to children that they will write a personal story about something real that happened to them and a friend.

Display Chart/Transparency 4, or write the model Personal Story on the board. Discuss differences between the personal story and "Emily and Alice Again."

CHART/TRANSPARENCY 4

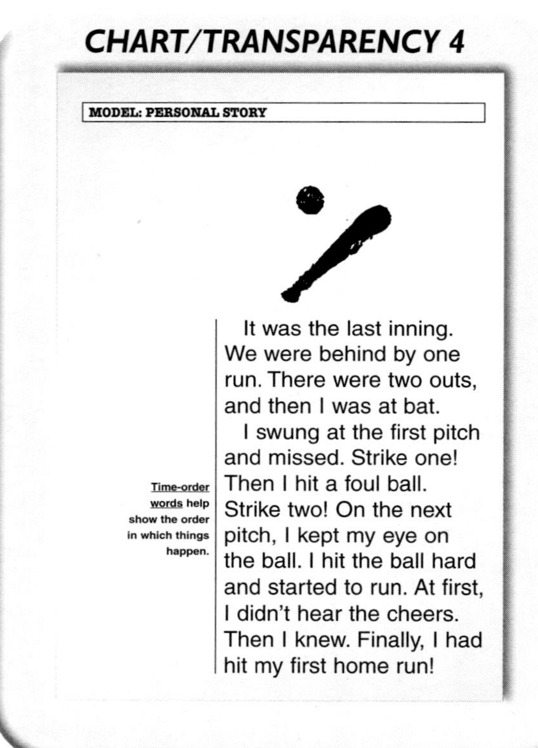

MODEL: PERSONAL STORY

It was the last inning. We were behind by one run. There were two outs, and then I was at bat.

I swung at the first pitch and missed. Strike one! Then I hit a foul ball. Strike two! On the next pitch, I kept my eye on the ball. I hit the ball hard and started to run. At first, I didn't hear the cheers. Then I knew. Finally, I had hit my first home run!

Time-order words help show the order in which things happen.

WRITER'S CRAFT: Time-Order Words Explain that good writers often use clue words like *first, next, after, then,* and *last* to help the reader understand the order of events in the story. Encourage children to look back at "Emily and Alice Again" and ask themselves this question: *Did the order in which things happened in the story make sense?*

PREWRITING

Brainstorm with children a list of problems they may have had with friends and ways the problems were resolved. Talk about a variety of solutions to each problem.

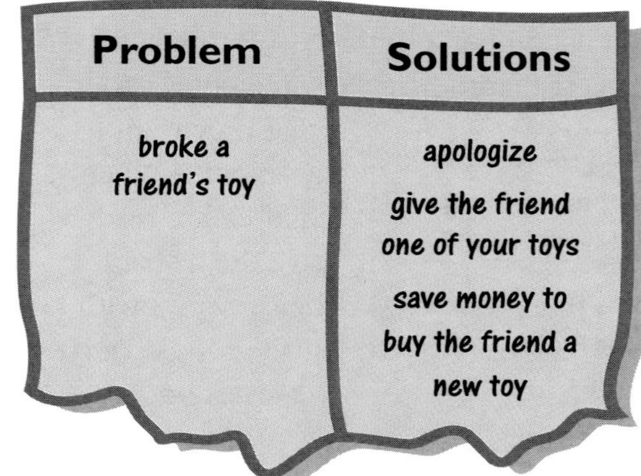

Give children a few minutes to talk over their topics with partners to decide what personal experience they will write about. Have children make their own problem-solution chart to help them choose a problem and solutions to write about.

DRAFTING

Then have children write their personal stories. As they write, remind them to

- use the information in their charts to tell about solving the problem.
- use words like *I* and *me.*
- write their story in the order in which things happened, using words like *first, next, then,* and *last.*
- tell about their feelings.

As children work through the stages of the writing process, have them save their drafts and revisions in their writer's folder.

RESPONDING AND REVISING

Work with small groups of children. Invite children to take turns reading aloud their stories. Suggest that the other children in the group answer these questions:

- What did you like best about the story?
- Does the story tell about a problem with a friend and how the problem was solved?
- Does the story tell what happened *first, next,* and *last?*

PROOFREADING

Offer some tips to help children proofread. Help them focus on the following:

CAPITAL LETTERS The word *I* is written as a capital letter. A person's name begins with a capital letter.

SENTENCES A sentence tells a complete thought. It begins with a capital letter, and a telling sentence ends with a period. (See the Grammar Minilesson on page T89.)

SPELLING Remind children to circle words they may have misspelled. On another sheet of paper, have them write each word several ways and choose the way that looks correct. (See also the Spelling lesson on page T106.)

PUBLISHING

Have children make a clean copy of their stories. Then offer publishing options like the following:

Handwriting
Remind children that their handwriting must be neat and clear so that the person reading the story can understand it. If children need assistance, refer them to the Handwriting models in the *Language Handbook* or in the classroom.

ACT IT OUT
Children can work in pairs to act out the situation in one child's story. As children prepare, suggest that they read the story together, decide who will play each character, and decide how they will present the story to classmates.

CLASS BOOK Children can share their stories and then put their finished products in a scrapbook about friends. Work as a group to think of a title and place it in the classroom library.

PORTFOLIO OPPORTUNITY

After children publish, make copies of their personal stories and have them attach their Writing Self-Assessment Checklists to them. Have children place the stories and checklists in their portfolios.

LANGUAGE HANDBOOK

Personal Story, pages 6–7

Student Self-Assessment ✓

Children can use the Writing Self-Assessment Checklist in the *Portfolio Assessment Teacher's Guide.*

EVALUATING THE WRITTEN RESPONSE

When evaluating children's personal stories, consider:

CONTENT	ORGANIZATION	STYLE
Is the story about a real experience with a friend?	**Are the story events in a logical order?**	**Are time-order words used to help show the sequence of events?**

EVALUATION BENCHMARKS

The child writes sentences about a friend but does not develop a story idea.	= **EMERGENT**
The child provides details but does not develop them into a story. The child makes an attempt to share personal feelings.	= **BEGINNING**
The child writes a story with a logical sequence of events and shares personal feelings.	= **PROFICIENT**

Tested Skill

GRAMMAR

Naming Part of a Sentence; Joining Naming Parts

TECHNOLOGY

Children may use *IMAGINATION EXPRESS, Destination: Neighborhood* to make a poster with their own sentences.

Reading↔Writing Connection

Connect to the story. Ask where Alice got her new sunglasses and encourage children to respond with a complete sentence. Then write this sentence on the board.

Alice's grandmother sent the sunglasses from Florida.

Reread the sentence with children and ask who sent the glasses. As children respond, underline the words *Alice's grandmother*. Explain that these words name the person who sent the glasses.

Build oral language. Ask children to say other sentences that tell something about the story. Write their sentences on the board and ask who or what did the action in each sentence. Have volunteers underline this part of each sentence.

Emily trades her little sister for sunglasses.
Alice and Nora played in the yard.
Emily felt pink and happy.

Teach/Model

Discuss naming parts of sentences. Help children conclude that the first part of a sentence usually tells who or what the sentence is about. Explain that this part of a sentence can be called the **naming part** of a sentence. Check understanding of the concept by asking questions about the sentences on the board.

Discuss joining naming parts. Write these sentences on the board:

Emily cartwheeled home.
Nora cartwheeled home.

Have children read the sentences and tell what the naming part of each sentence is. Point out the similarity of the two sentences and ask children if they can think of a way to say the same thing in only one sentence.

Write this new sentence on the board:

Emily and Nora cartwheeled home.

Ask what the naming part of the new sentence is. Be sure children understand that both girls' names are the naming part.

Practice/Apply

Check understanding. Have children rewrite pairs of sentences as one sentence.

Alice liked the sunglasses.
Emily liked the sunglasses.

Three dogs live on the farm.
Six cats live on the farm.

My brother got new sunglasses.
I got new sunglasses.

LANGUAGE HANDBOOK

Naming Part of a Sentence, pages 38–39; Joining Naming Parts, pages 40–41

DAILY LANGUAGE PRACTICE

See page R19 for oral language exercises.

Practice Activities

To Name, or Not to Name?

ORAL APPLICATION Write the following word groups on index cards or an overhead transparency. Have children take a card, read the words, and then tell whether or not the words could be the naming part of a sentence. (If you are using an overhead transparency, expose one word group at a time.) **VISUAL/AUDITORY**

went very fast
three happy children
sang three songs
all the animals in the zoo
Pablo and Carmen
wiggled their toes
ate too much

Make a Silly Sentence

WRITING APPLICATION Have children use the sentence parts from the previous activity or other fanciful phrases to make silly sentences. Have children put together two or more sentence parts to make complete sentences. Then children can illustrate their silliest sentence. **VISUAL**

A Sentence Game

WRITING APPLICATION Provide pairs of children with four strips of paper. Partners first write a sentence on each strip. Then have them identify the naming part of each sentence, cut it off of the strip, and mix up the pieces.

Have partners trade strips with another pair. Partners make four sentences with the sentence parts they have and then read their new sentences to the pair who wrote the original sentences. **VISUAL/AUDITORY/KINESTHETIC**

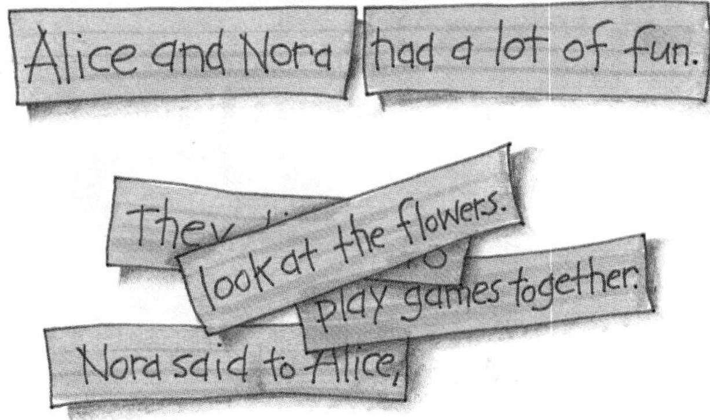

APPLY TO WRITING

Suggest that children use sentences they write in their personal stories to identify naming parts and to check whether they correctly joined naming parts of sentences.

USAGE TIP Look in your writing to see if you can join naming parts of sentences to make your writing sound better.

STUDENTS ACQUIRING ENGLISH

Have children practice making sentences in English. Use props and perform an action while you describe it in a complete sentence (for example, *I am bouncing the ball*). Give the prop to the child, who then performs the same action and repeats the sentence. For variety, have the child use his or her name or the name of the object as the sentence subject.

RETEACH

See R7 for lessons in multiple modalities.

GRAMMAR PRACTICE BOOK
pages 15-18

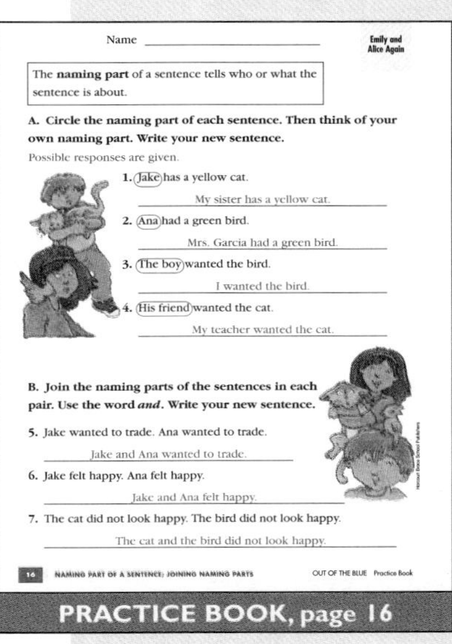

Name ______ Emily and Alice Again

The **naming part** of a sentence tells who or what the sentence is about.

A. Circle the naming part of each sentence. Then think of your own naming part. Write your new sentence.

Possible responses are given.

1. (Jake) has a yellow cat. My sister has a yellow cat.
2. (Ana) had a green bird. Mrs. Garcia had a green bird.
3. (The boy) wanted the bird. I wanted the bird.
4. (His friend) wanted the cat. My teacher wanted the cat.

B. Join the naming parts of the sentences in each pair. Use the word *and*. Write your new sentence.

5. Jake wanted to trade. Ana wanted to trade. Jake and Ana wanted to trade.
6. Jake felt happy. Ana felt happy. Jake and Ana felt happy.
7. The cat did not look happy. The bird did not look happy. The cat and the bird did not look happy.

16 NAMING PART OF A SENTENCE: JOINING NAMING PARTS OUT OF THE BLUE Practice Book

PRACTICE BOOK, page 16

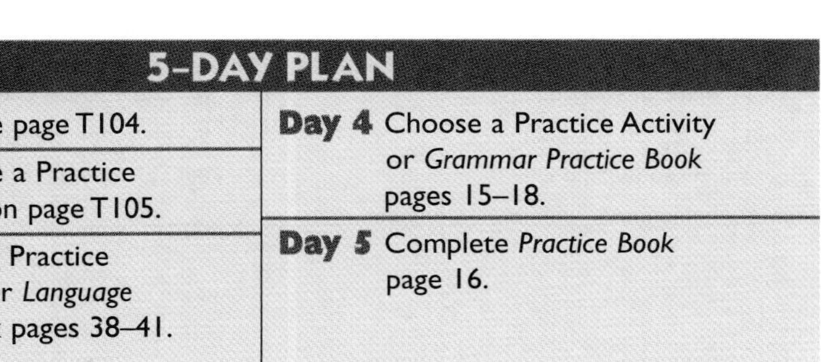

5-DAY PLAN

Day 1 Complete page T104.	**Day 4** Choose a Practice Activity or *Grammar Practice Book* pages 15–18.
Day 2 Complete a Practice Activity on page T105.	**Day 5** Complete *Practice Book* page 16.
Day 3 Choose a Practice Activity or *Language Handbook* pages 38–41.	

Use in conjunction with Daily Language Practice.

2

SPELLING

5-Day Plan

Integrated Spelling Lesson 2: student book, pages 14–17; Teacher's Edition, pages T27–T32.

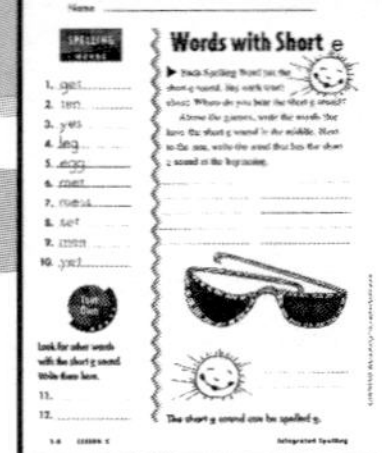

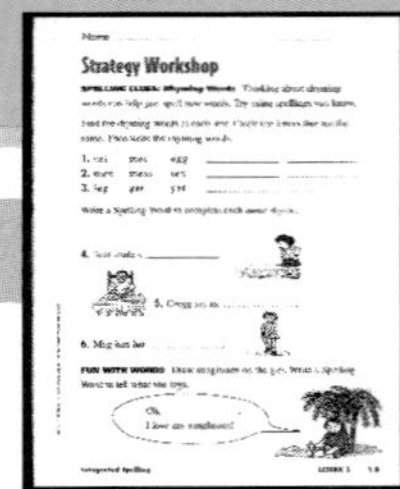

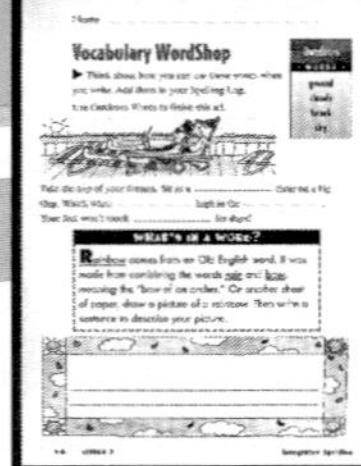

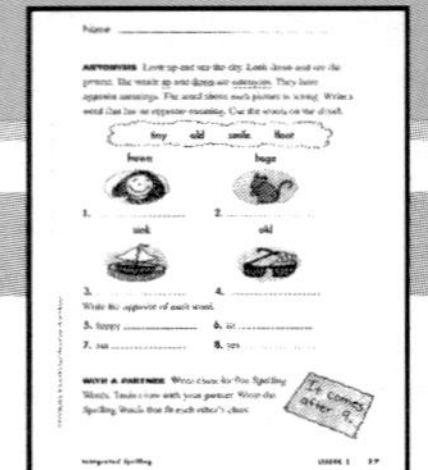

SPELLING WORDS

1. get ★
2. ten
3. yes
4. leg ★
5. egg
6. met
7. mess
8. set
9. men
10. yet ★

STUDENT'S PERSONAL WORDS

11. 13.
12. 14.

Additional story words are *best, let's, next, sent,* and *them.*

★Words appearing in "Emily and Alice Again"

Words with Short *e*

Pretest

DAY 1 **Administer the pretest.** Say each word, use it in the dictation sentence below, and repeat the word. Have partners check their own pretests by referring to the word list.

OPEN SORT

DAY 2 **Have children create categories.** Have children select their own methods for sorting the Spelling Words. For example, they may want to sort according to rhymes or number of letters. Encourage children to share their methods.

CLOSED SORT

Sort by location of vowel. Write these headings on the board and have children copy them onto sheets of paper. Have children write the Spelling Words under the appropriate heading.

Short e Sound at the Beginning	Short e Sound in the Middle	
egg	*get*	*mess*
	ten	*set*
	yes	*men*
	leg	*yet*
	met	

Teach/Model

DAY 3 **Discuss the generalization.** Write the words *end, bed,* and *lesson* on the board and have children read them. Ask what sound the letter *e* stands for in each word. Help children form generalizations about short *e* words—for example:

- **When a word (or syllable) has only one vowel, and that vowel is followed by a consonant, the vowel usually has a short sound.**
- **The /e/ sound can be spelled with the letter *e*.**

DAY 4 **Apply to writing.** If children wrote personal stories in the Writer's Workshop, have them check their work to see if they spelled words with short *e* correctly.

Posttest

DAY 5 **Assess children's progress.** The sentences below should be used as the posttest.

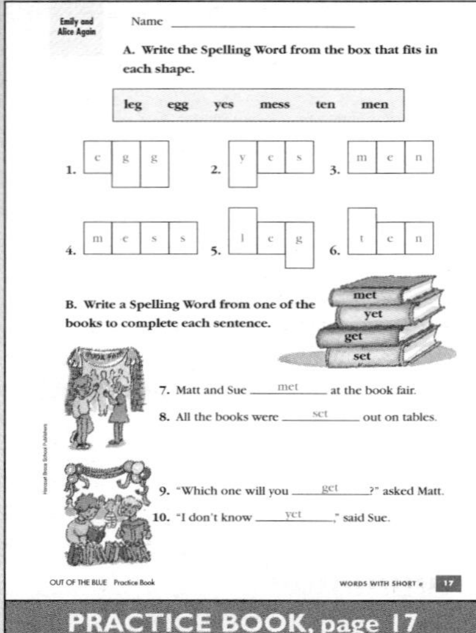

PRACTICE BOOK, page 17

DICTATION SENTENCES

1. I want to get a bike.
2. Ten balls are in the bag.
3. Yes, you can write this word.
4. Jill bumped her leg on the chair.
5. Lucy ate an egg sandwich.
6. I met a new friend today.
7. I spilled paint and made a mess.
8. Did you set the table for dinner?
9. Five men got off the bus.
10. This is your best story yet!

VOCABULARY WORKSHOP

Reviewing Key Words

To review how the vocabulary was used in the story, distribute copies of page R53. Write the Key Words on the board.

Have volunteers read each sentence aloud. As a group activity, have children choose the Key Word to complete each sentence. Have them write the word.

Alice had __beautiful__ new sunglasses.

Emily __knew__ that there must something she could trade for the glasses.

Trading Nora to Alice for the glasses was Emily's __idea__.

Soon Emily __heard__ Alice and Nora having fun.

Emily did not have anything to __laugh__ about.

Emily was __sorry__ she had traded away her sister.

Alice had had __enough__ fun with Nora.

Next time, Emily and Alice will only __borrow__ things.

Children may cut apart the sentences. They can use the sentence strips to retell the story of Emily and Alice, or they can glue the strips to paper and illustrate them to make their own storybook.

Extending Vocabulary

COMPOUND WORDS

Write the word *sunglasses* on the board and ask children to tell where or when they may have worn sunglasses. Underline each word of the compound, and explain that sometimes two words are put together to make one word called a **compound word.**

Write the following lists of words on the board.

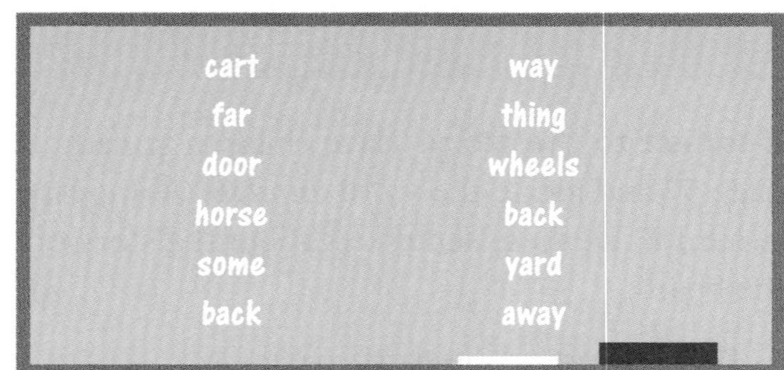

Have small groups of children look through "Emily and Alice Again" to find compound words formed by using one word from each list. Have them mark the spot with a self-stick note. When all groups are finished, ask one group at a time to read aloud a sentence from the story that contains one of the compound words and to draw a line on the board to connect the words of the compound. Encourage children to add compound words to the list.

Name ______________

Emily and Alice Again

Read the words in the box below the picture. See how many compound words you can make. Use the picture for ideas.

bird + house = birdhouse

house shine sun play bird place
some time fire light black day

18 COMPOUND WORDS

OUT OF THE BLUE Practice Book

PRACTICE BOOK, pages 18–19

STUDENTS ACQUIRING ENGLISH

Combining the meanings of two words to make a new word may be confusing for children who don't know the meanings of the individual words. It may be easier to teach the meanings of compound words as whole words. For example, children may understand *cupcake* as a "small cake" more easily than as "a cake that fits in a cup."

TAKE-HOME/ KEEP-AT-HOME BOOK

The Case of the Missing Lunch

Distribute the pages and have children make their own TAKE-HOME/KEEP-AT-HOME BOOKS, which reinforce Key Words and known vocabulary. Have children read to partners and then take the book home to read.

INTRODUCE: PHONICS AND DECODING

Consonant Digraph:
/f/*gh, ph*

OBJECTIVE: To understand the relationship between letters and sounds

Informal Assessment ✓

Are children able to

- ☑ identify a word that contains a digraph?
- ☑ identify digraphs that represent a specific sound?
- ☑ read words with digraphs?

Teach/Model

Connect to the story. Have children reread page 57 and locate the word *enough.* (It appears twice.) Write these sentences about the story on the board.

1. *I've had enough fun with the glasses.*
2. *Emily could hear Alice and Nora laugh.*

Underline the words *enough* and *laugh* on the board and have volunteers read each word. Discuss the sound children hear at the end of each word.

Next, write the words *phone* and *photo* on the board and have volunteers read each word. Ask what sound children hear at the beginning of each word. Tell children that they will learn more about the sound that is the same in these words.

Phonemic awareness: Listen to the sound. Display page 5 of the *Big Book of Rhymes.* Have children listen for words with the same sound heard at the beginning of *phone.* Reread the rhyme so that children can hear its rhyme and rhythm. Then have children read the rhyme with you, this time emphasizing words with the /f/ sound.

Big Book of Rhymes, page 5

Find and read words with /f/. In the rhyme, have children read and frame words with /f/ spelled *ph* or *gh.* As children frame the words, write them on the board under the appropriate columns.

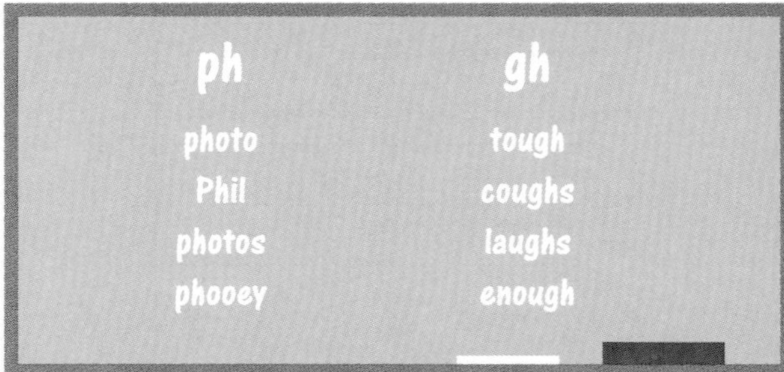

ph	gh
photo	tough
Phil	coughs
photos	laughs
phooey	enough

Ask children how the words in each column are similar. (They all have the /f/ sound.) Point out that *ph* at the beginning of a word stands for /f/ and that *gh* at the end of a word stands for /f/.

Practice/Apply

Read words in context. Write this rhyme on the board:

Yesterday Ralph made us laugh.
Then he took a photograph.
We tried not to giggle, but it was tough.
At last we yelled, "Ralph, that's enough."

Have children read each line. Then ask volunteers to circle the letters that stand for the /f/ sound. Have them tell what they have learned about the /f/ sound in words.

Practice Activities

Identifying Words

COOPERATIVE LEARNING Write the following on the board:

Organize children into teams. Set a time limit and have each team compile a list of words that contain each letter or digraph. They may look through books to find words. At the end of the time period, have each group read its words. Each correct word receives points as shown on the board. A team may not use the same word more than once, but a word may receive points for each spelling it contains: *fluffy* = 2 points, *photograph* = 6 points. A word in which the digraph does not represent the /f/ sound, such as *through*, receives no points. **VISUAL/AUDITORY**

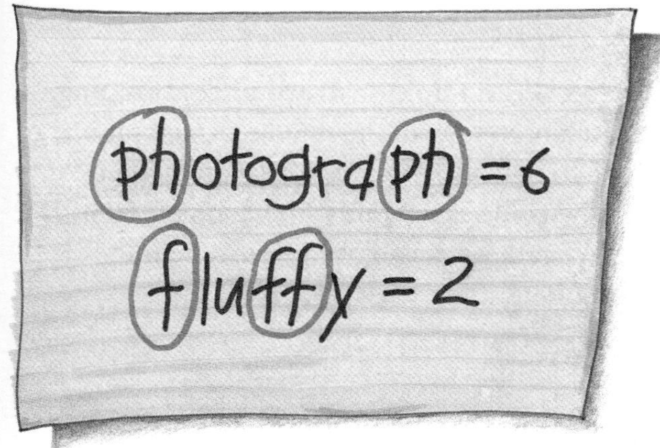

Sorting ph and gh Words

PERFORMANCE ASSESSMENT Write the words *laugh, laughing, sift, enough, rough, graph, phone, photograph, telephone,* and *photographer* on cards. Children can read the words and sort them into two piles, one for the *gh* digraph and one for the *ph* digraph. They should also identify one word that contains no digraph. (sift) Have children choose some words and write sentences using them. **VISUAL/KINESTHETIC**

"Phunny" Sentences

Have children brainstorm words with /f/*ph, gh*. Then have them create sentences using as many of the words as possible in one sentence. Groups of children might enjoy creating a silly story using the words. **VISUAL**

STUDENTS ACQUIRING ENGLISH

Make cards for words with various spellings for a sound and help children practice reading the words.

RETEACH

See page R8 for lessons in multiple modalities.

CHALLENGE

The words *laugh, rough,* and *tough* can be combined with a number of suffixes. Challenge children to make as many words as they can by adding suffixes to these base words, such as *roughly* and *toughness*.

PHONICS ACTIVITY BOOK pages 4–5

PHONICS PRACTICE BOOK, pages 237–238

Name ______________ Emily and Alice Again

Read the puzzle clues. Write the word from the box that goes with each clue and has the sound you hear at the beginning of *phone*.

photos cough laugh rough phone

1. l a u g h goes with a joke
2. p h o n e goes with talking
3. c o u g h goes with a cold
4. p h o t o s go with a camera
5. r o u g h goes with bumpy

20 CONSONANT DIGRAPH: /f/ gh, ph OUT OF THE BLUE Practice Book

PRACTICE BOOK, page 20

Reading Trade Books FOR CONSONANT DIGRAPH /f/ gh, ph

***Elmer* by David McKee. Lothrop, Lee & Shepard, 1989. AVERAGE**

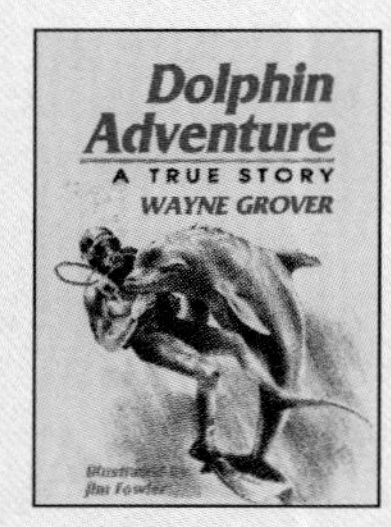

***Dolphin Adventure: A True Story* by Wayne Grover. Greenwillow, 1990. CHALLENGE**

PHONICS PRACTICE READER 12

INTRODUCE: COMPREHENSION

Story Elements (Characters)

OBJECTIVE: To identify major and minor characters and to use their words and actions to identify their traits

Teach/Model

Connect to the story. Have children turn to page 45 in "Emily and Alice Again," and ask them to tell the names of the two girls. Explain that Emily and Alice are the main characters of the story because they do most of the action. Then ask what other character is in the story. When children identify Nora, ask whether Nora is a main character. Explain that a character that has only a small part in a story is a minor character.

Model recognizing character traits. Ask children to turn to page 46 and read the first paragraph. Model using the information in the paragraph to figure out what kind of person the character Emily is.

MODEL

Emily says that she loves the sunglasses and that she could wear them forever. She just *has* to have those glasses. In this paragraph, the author has told me what Emily said and what she is thinking. I think Emily is the kind of person who makes up her mind right away about something. She doesn't stop to think things over.

Have volunteers read the last paragraph on the page. Discuss what Emily is going to do. Then ask what hints the author gave on the page that help readers figure out what kind of person Emily is. Point out that the author told what Emily said, how Emily felt, and what Emily was thinking. All this information makes Emily seem to be a real person.

Practice/Apply

Have children demonstrate understanding. Ask children to read the middle paragraph on page 46. Ask what Alice is like and whether or not she is the same kind of person that Emily is. Ask what hints the author gives to help the reader determine what Alice is like.

Informal Assessment

Are children able to

- identify the characters in a story?
- identify actions or words that indicate a character trait?
- tell what kind of person a character is?

Practice Activities

Identify Traits of Favorite Characters

Have children work individually or with a partner to name a favorite story character and to list some traits that character has. They may list characters from this book or from books they have read on their own. **VISUAL**

Create a Character

COOPERATIVE LEARNING Have partners write a dialogue they would put in this story or another story. Encourage them to act out the dialogue first and then to write it. Children should not worry about writing all the quotation marks and other punctuation correctly. Encourage children to reveal what their characters are like through their words. Have them role-play their dialogues. **VISUAL/AUDITORY**

Matching Characters and Their Traits

PERFORMANCE ASSESSMENT Write the following words on the board.

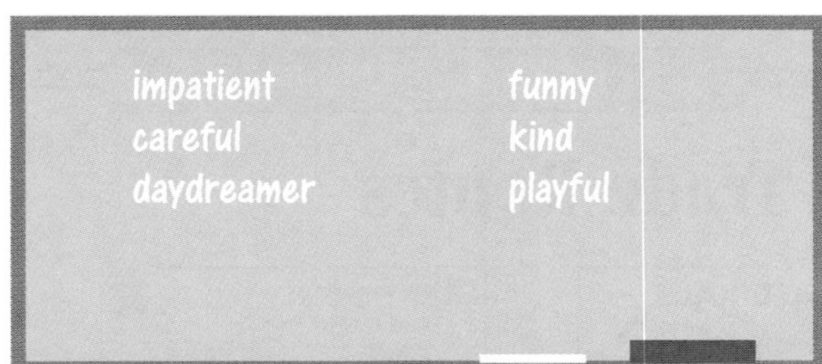

Have children write *Emily* and *Alice* as headings on a sheet of paper and list words from the board that describe them under the headings. Have them add their own words to the lists, too. Children should be ready to show where in the story the character exhibits the trait. Provide time for children to compare and discuss their completed lists. **VISUAL**

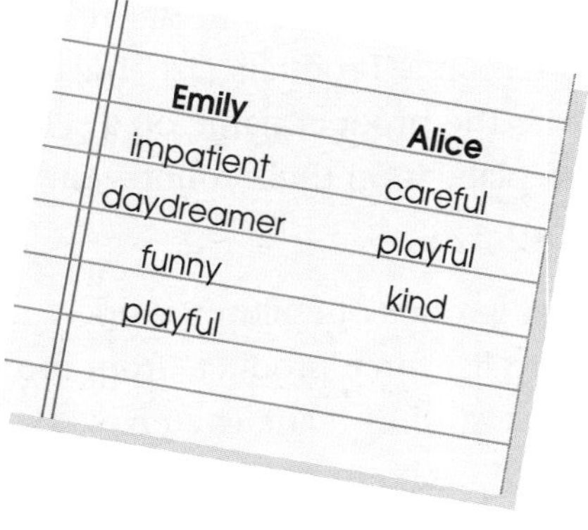

MEETING INDIVIDUAL NEEDS

STUDENTS ACQUIRING ENGLISH

Children may not know many words to describe character traits. Help them determine the meanings of words like *impatient, daydreamer, careful,* and *playful* and to use them to describe Emily, Alice, and Nora.

RETEACH

See page R9 for lessons in multiple modalities.

CHALLENGE

List some character traits, such as selfish, grouchy, generous, and forgetful. Ask children to choose one trait and to create a character who has that trait. Encourage children to write about their character, telling what the character does and says.

Emily and Alice Again

Name ______________________

Read the story and think about who it is about. Then fill in the web.

Mr. Budge likes to make people laugh. He wears funny clothes. His tie has fish with eyes that light up. His trick flower gets us wet. When Molly goes to Mr. Budge's house, she spends a long time on the porch. Mr. Budge tells all his favorite jokes. Mr. Budge likes to cook, too. He bakes cakes that look like rabbits. He hides little toys in his pudding. All the kids love to visit Mr. Budge.

Make a web. Make up a new character, and write about the character in the web. Then tell a story about your character to a partner.

OUT OF THE BLUE Practice Book — STORY ELEMENTS (Characters) 21

PRACTICE BOOK, page 21

Reading Trade Books FOR STORY ELEMENTS (CHARACTERS)

A Bargain for Frances **by Russell Hoban. HarperCollins, 1978.** **AVERAGE**

The Day I Had to Play With My Sister **by Crosby N. Bonsall. HarperCollins, 1988.** **EASY**

Integrated Curriculum

SOCIAL STUDIES

Trading

TIPS FOR CLASSROOM MANAGEMENT

IF children do not have experience with traveling, **THEN** provide them with plenty of travel brochures and suggest that they choose one of the advertised destinations for their poster in the Making a Poster activity.

TECHNOLOGY

Imagination Express, Destination: Ocean

SOCIAL STUDIES

Trade Routes

MATERIALS
- world map
- geography books or encyclopedias

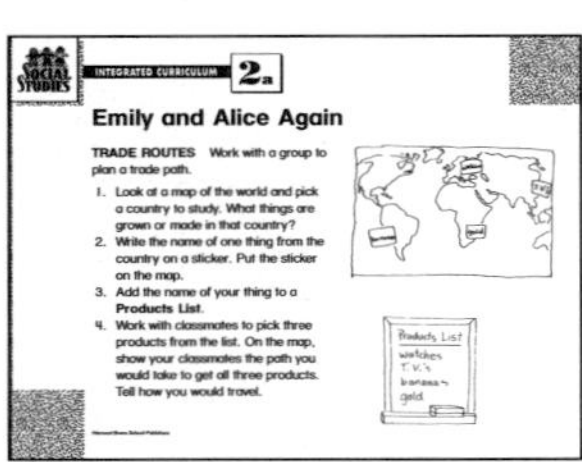
SOCIAL STUDIES INTEGRATED CURRICULUM 2a

Emily and Alice Again

TRADE ROUTES Work with a group to plan a trade path.

1. Look at a map of the world and pick a country to study. What things are grown or made in that country?
2. Write the name of one thing from the country on a sticker. Put the sticker on the map.
3. Add the name of your thing to a **Products List**.
4. Work with classmates to pick three products from the list. On the map, show your classmates the path you would take to get all three products. Tell how you would travel.

Curriculum Card 2a

Explain that long ago people explored the world looking for food or other goods to trade. Display a world map and have children select a country to research. Have them choose a product from the country and write it on a "Products List." Have children write the product name on a self-stick note and place it on their country on the world map.

Have small groups of children work together to list three products from the "Products List" they want. Then have the members of each group find on the map the three places they would have to visit to get their products. Ask groups to devise a route and transportation from one country to another. Provide time for each group to show classmates how its members might travel from one country to the next to acquire their goods.

LISTENING/SPEAKING/READING/WRITING

MATH

Trading Day

MATERIALS
- paper or index cards
- magazines
- scissors
- crayons or markers
- glue

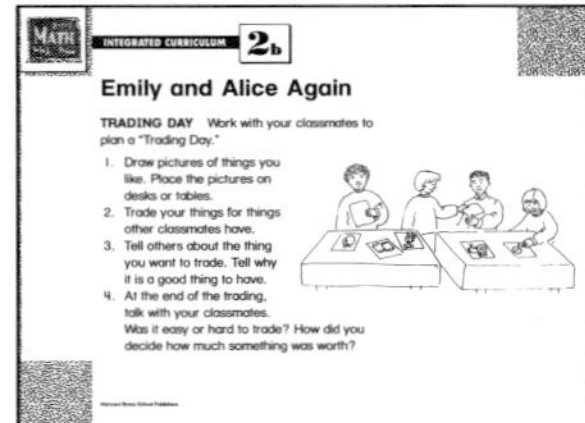
MATH INTEGRATED CURRICULUM 2b

Emily and Alice Again

TRADING DAY Work with your classmates to plan a "Trading Day."

1. Draw pictures of things you like. Place the pictures on desks or tables.
2. Trade your things for things other classmates have.
3. Tell others about the thing you want to trade. Tell why it is a good thing to have.
4. At the end of the trading, talk with your classmates. Was it easy or hard to trade? How did you decide how much something was worth?

Curriculum Card 2b

COOPERATIVE LEARNING Explain that when Emily was trying to find something that Alice would take for her sunglasses, the girls were "bartering." Explain that long ago, people traded or bartered things or services. Have a Trading Day during which children work in groups to barter. Have children make trading cards by cutting out magazine pictures or drawing pictures of things they like. Have groups of children take turns displaying their "items" on a tabletop while other children bring their trading cards and barter for items they want.

LISTENING/SPEAKING/WRITING

Reading Trade Books

CROSS-CURRICULAR READING

If You Made a Million by David M. Schwartz. Lothrop, Lee & Shepard, 1989. CHALLENGE

A New Coat for Anna by Harriet Ziefert. Knopf, 1988. AVERAGE

ART

Making a Poster

MATERIALS
- **large sheets of paper**
- **markers, crayons, or paints**

Remind children that Emily imagined that she was on a cruise ship when she was wearing the sunglasses. Suggest that children make posters advertising vacations. You may wish to display some travel posters or brochures to give children ideas. Their posters might be for cruises, for travel to a foreign country, or even to an imaginary location. Remind children that their posters should include information about how to sign up for the vacation, the destination, the cost, and other pertinent facts. **READING/WRITING**

SCIENCE

Observing the Sun

MATERIALS
- **binoculars or telescope**
- **mirror on a stand**

Explain to children that looking directly at the sun is harmful to people's eyes. Indeed, sunlight itself can be harmful, so many people wear sunglasses. So that children can see the sun, place the binoculars in a window directly facing the sun. Place the mirror in front of the eyepiece and adjust it so that it reflects the sun onto an opposite wall. Darken the room, if necessary. Children may see birds and clouds passing in front of the sun and will also observe how quickly the sun moves, or rather, how fast the earth is rotating. Show a child how to adjust the binoculars to keep them aligned with the sun. Discuss children's observations. Have children draw and write about their observations in a "Sun Log" booklet. **LISTENING/SPEAKING/READING/WRITING**

MULTI-AGE CLASSROOMS

For the Trade Routes activity, older children may want to make their own maps to show the route. They may also want to research seafaring explorers and share the information with their classmates.

Reading Trade Books

TIPS FOR CLASSROOM MANAGEMENT

PARTNERS
Have children work with partners to read the book. Have them decide how they will read the book together and where in the story they will stop to discuss it.

SMALL GROUP
Read the story in a small circle of children. As you read aloud, pause to let children read the phrase "Jimmy Lee did it."

For a comprehensive lesson plan, refer to the complete lesson for *Jimmy Lee Did It* on pages T226–T229.

Jimmy Lee Did It

by Pat Cummings

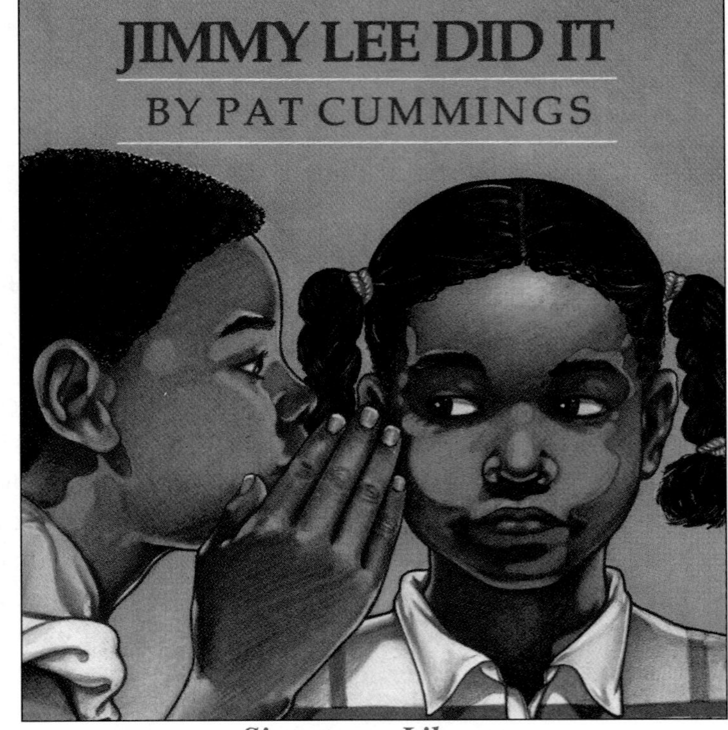

Signatures Library

READER'S CHALLENGE

Emily and Alice are friends who live next door to each other. They see each other almost every day. Do you think someone could have a friend that no one can see? Why might you want a friend you can't see?

READING STRATEGY: DRAWING CONCLUSIONS

As children read, ask why Arte's bed is unmade, why the comics are pulled apart, and why Angel's pancakes are gone. At the end of the story, ask what children conclude was the real cause of all those things.

LINK TO THE THEME

Children who are reading the book may want to discuss the following:

- What kinds of things does Jimmy Lee do?
- How are you like Jimmy Lee? How are you different?
- Who is really Jimmy Lee?
- Do you know anyone who is like the characters in the story? Explain your answer.

RESPONSE ACTIVITY: RETELLING THE STORY

Ask each child to draw a picture of what Jimmy Lee might look like. Then have the story reread, and invite different children to hold up their picture of Jimmy Lee. Put all the pictures in the Reading Center with the book.

Other Trade Books

Emily and Alice

by Joyce Champion
illustrated by Suçie Stevenson

Have children work in groups to act out one of the chapters in the book. Before they begin, have volunteers describe how Emily and Alice are different and how they are alike. Ask whether it is easy to be best friends.

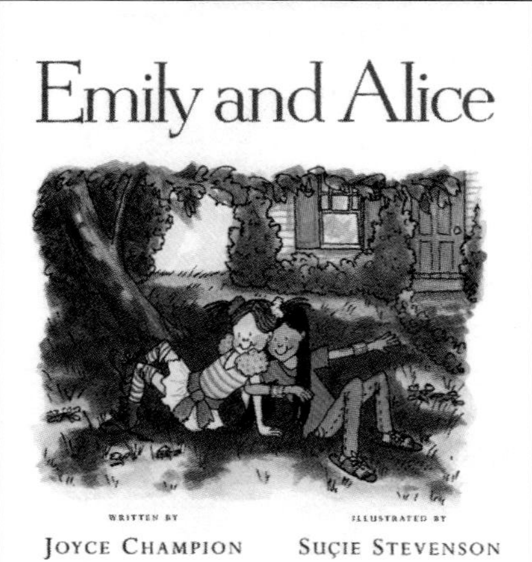

Chester's Way

by Kevin Henkes

Have children discuss what kinds of things three friends could do better than two friends. Have them make a list of "threes," such as three bears, three blind mice, three little pigs, and three billy goats gruff. Then have partners work together to design costumes or disguises for the three friends.

Pinky and Rex and the New Baby

by James Howe
illustrated by Melissa Sweet

Emily traded her little sister for something she wanted. Ask children what Rex almost gave up for her little brother. Have them tell what Rex was like at the beginning, in the middle, and at the end of the story.

MEETING INDIVIDUAL NEEDS

STUDENTS ACQUIRING ENGLISH

Invite children to use two or three words in their first language to describe themselves. Then have them find English words that mean the same, or almost the same, thing as they read the books.

MEETING INDIVIDUAL NEEDS

STUDENTS ACQUIRING ENGLISH

Encourage children to share words (and symbols) for family relationships in their primary languages. This way, although the English words may be new to them, they are offering something new to classmates.

MULTIPLE INTELLIGENCES

Children who are visually inclined may enjoy making a chart or other visual representation of the information on the group's list of titles of family members.

Draw and Write About Families

SELECTION CONNECTION

In "Emily and Alice Again," Emily trades her little sister for Alice's sunglasses. Both characters learned lessons from their trade. Ask children what each character learned.

PROJECT CHECKLIST

During this stage, children should

- work as a whole group to list titles that show family relationships. Encourage children to share special names they have for some of their relatives.
- draw pictures of special times they have spent with family members and write sentences about their drawings.
- save their work for their books.

When children have completed this checkpoint, have them think about the family relationships and the different names that came up in the group discussion and then write their thoughts in their Project Journals.

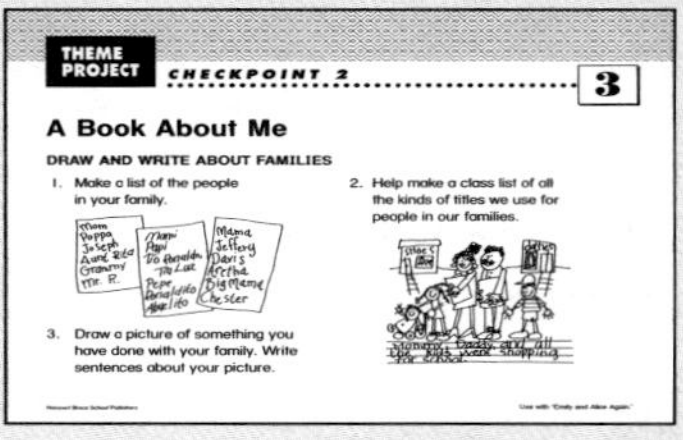

THEME PROJECT CHECKPOINT 2 — 3

A Book About Me

DRAW AND WRITE ABOUT FAMILIES

1. Make a list of the people in your family.
2. Help make a class list of all the kinds of titles we use for people in our families.
3. Draw a picture of something you have done with your family. Write sentences about your picture.

Project Card 3

Project Card 3 can be found as a copying master on page R27.

PLANNING TIPS

As children think of subjects for their drawings, suggest that they

- think of ways to make these pages of their books look attractive.
- use separate sheets of paper or different areas of one sheet to draw scenes showing different family members.
- use titles from the group list in the sentences they write about their pictures.

Informal Assessment

As children complete this checkpoint, they will **compare** titles classmates use to indicate family relationships and **make decisions** about what to draw and write on their book pages. Children are thinking critically if they

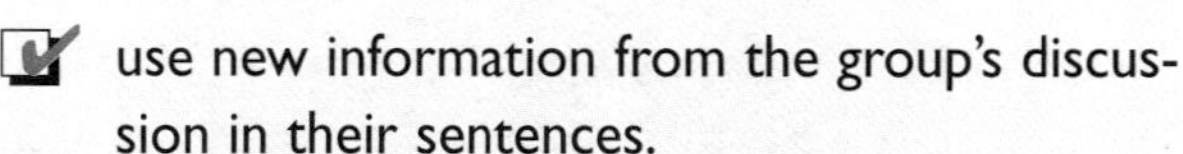

- use new information from the group's discussion in their sentences.

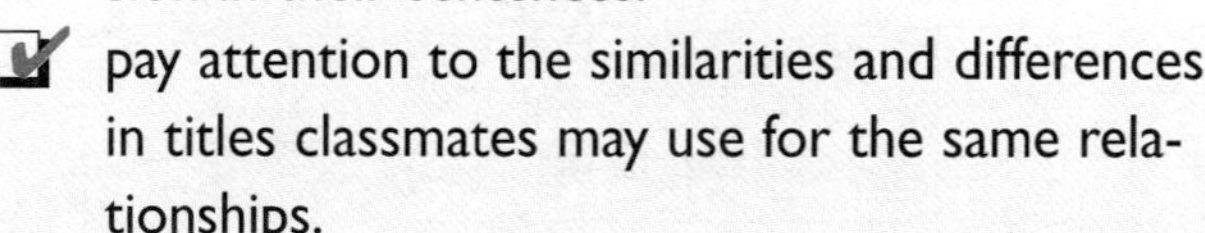

- pay attention to the similarities and differences in titles classmates may use for the same relationships.

Note that a more formal assessment rubric for this checkpoint is provided on page T225.

ART AND LITERATURE

Ronde des Enfants (circa 1900) • by Pablo Picasso (1881–1973)

ABOUT THE ARTIST

Pablo Picasso's talent for drawing was encouraged by his parents. By age fourteen he was an advanced student at the Barcelona Academy of Fine Arts in Barcelona, Spain. Four years later, Picasso moved to Paris, where his work was influenced by the artists he met. Picasso experimented with several styles. His Blue Period is characterized by paintings of somber subjects in shades of blue. This was followed by the Rose Period, in which he used brighter colors. Eventually, Picasso developed the style of Cubism, in which several viewpoints of a subject are shown at the same time.

ABOUT THE PAINTING

Picasso painted *Ronde des Enfants* shortly before he entered his Blue Period. It depicts three girls dancing in a circle. The rhythm of the dance is shown in the positioning of the girls' bodies, as well as in their flying hair and skirts. The brush strokes emphasize the circular motion of the *ronde,* which is danced in a circle to the singing of the dancers.

What are the children in this painting doing? Would you like to play with them? What might they be celebrating?

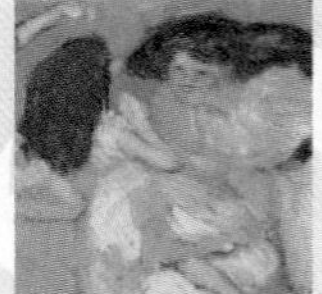

Ronde des Enfants
by Pablo Picasso

Pablo Picasso was a famous Spanish artist. He painted this picture when he was 19 years old. The title is French and means "children's dance." In this kind of dance, children move in a circle and sing. How does Picasso show you that these girls are moving?

64

65

Art and Literature

MAKING CONNECTIONS

Have children follow along as you read aloud the first paragraph on page 64. Encourage them to respond to the questions. Ask children what they sometimes do when they are very happy or are celebrating something. Talk about ways that celebrations are special times.

EXTENDING FINE ART

Hands-On Activity **Have children each draw a picture that shows a special celebration. Encourage them to fill the page with their drawings and to add details. You may want to display the drawings on a "Celebrate Us!" bulletin board.**

Brian Pinkney

ABOUT THE AUTHOR/ ILLUSTRATOR

BRIAN PINKNEY is the illustrator of several highly acclaimed picture books and has received such honors as Parents' Choice Picture Book Awards, the Golden Kite Award, the Coretta Scott King Honor Award, and an ALA Notable Book designation. *Max Found Two Sticks* is the first book he has both written and illustrated.

For more information about Brian Pinkney, see page T149.

THEME: LEARNING ABOUT ONESELF

Celebrate Me!

In "Max Found Two Sticks," children will further explore the theme by discovering the power of using their imaginations to create new and interesting uses for ordinary objects.

SELECTION SUMMARY

Genre: Realistic Fiction

Two sticks fall from a tree one day as Max sits on the front steps and watches the clouds. Since he doesn't feel like talking, he responds to people's questions by using the sticks to tap out the rhythms of things he sees and hears—the sound of pigeons startled into flight, rain beating against the window, church bells chiming, and a subway rumbling. When a real marching band comes around the corner, Max gets a surprise when a drummer throws him his extra pair of drumsticks.

SUGGESTED LESSON PLANNER

▶ ***Max Found Two Sticks***

	DAY 1	DAY 2
PART 1 Reading, Listening, Speaking, Viewing **Key Words** strong sound called appeared spare brought thanks	**BUILD BACKGROUND** T122 **VOCABULARY STRATEGIES** T122–T123 *Chart/Transparency 5* *Practice Book* pp. 25–26 **READING THE SELECTION** T124–T149 Options for Reading T124–T125 *Response Card 5* *Literature Cassette 1* **REVIEW PREDICTIONS/PURPOSE** T148 **APPRECIATING THE LITERATURE** T148 NOTE: Children may read the selection on Day 2.	**SUMMARIZE AND RETELL THE SELECTION** T149 *Practice Book* p. 27 ◆ **RESPONSE CORNER ACTIVITIES** T150 **CHECKING COMPREHENSION** T151 *End-of-Selection Test* 
PART 2 Writer's Workshop	**A STORY** Thinking as Writers T156 *Chart/Transparency 6*	Prewriting T156 Story Map R197
Grammar	✓**TELLING PART OF A SENTENCE AND JOINING TELLING PARTS** Teach the Concept T158 Daily Language Practice (1–2) R20	Daily Language Practice (3–4) R20 Practice Activity T159
Spelling	**WORDS WITH SHORT *a*** *an bad bat tap sat* *at hat dad as sad* Pretest/Self-Check T160 *Integrated Spelling Teacher's Edition* pp. T33, T270	Open and Closed Sorts T160 *Integrated Spelling* p. 18 *Integrated Spelling Teacher's Edition* p. T34
PART 3 Phonics	**CONSONANT DIGRAPHS: /ng/ng, /ngk/nk** Phonics-Vocabulary Connection T123	**CONSONANT DIGRAPHS: /ng/ng, /ngk/nk** (Introduce) T162 *Big Book of Rhymes* pp. 6–7 *Phonics Practice Book* p. 236
Skills and Strategies	◆ **INTEGRATED CURRICULUM** *Rhythm* **Music** T166 **Math** T166 **Art** T167 **Science** T167 *Thinkin' Things Collection 1: Toony Loon; Thinkin' Things Collection 2: Oranga Banga's Band and Toony's Tunes*	**STUDY SKILL** T164–T165 Test-Taking Strategies (Introduce) *Practice Book* p. 31
	To help children build fluency, use the *Instant Readers™ No Matter How You Play It* and *What a Catch!* on pages T152–T153.	Use the Extra Support note on page T150 to help **below-level readers** complete the Response Corner activity.

NOTE: An alternative lesson plan for **below-level readers** appears on *Intervention Strategies Manual* pp. 14–19. A lesson for **students acquiring English** appears on *Sheltered English/ESL Manual* pp. 10–13.

DAY 3	DAY 4	DAY 5
◆ **IDEA BANK ACTIVITIES** Listening and Speaking T154 Real-Life Reading: Reading Uniform Insignia T154 Oral Language T155 Kinesthetic T155 *Writer's Magazine* pp. 10–11 *Thinkin' Things Collection 1 (Oranga Banga); Thinkin' Things Collection 2 (Oranga Banga's Band* and *Toony's Tunes)* School–Home Connection 3 R50	**VOCABULARY WORKSHOP** T161 Reviewing Key Words Story Strips R54 Onomatopoeia (Sound Words) *Take-Home/Keep-at-Home Book: Run-Away Tire* **READING TRADE BOOKS** T168–T169  Signatures Library  Take-Home Book	**READING TRADE BOOKS** T163, T165, T167, T168–T169  Instant Reader™ Instant Reader™
Drafting T156 *Language Handbook* pp. 8–9 *The Amazing Writing Machine*	Responding and Revising T157	Proofreading and Publishing T157 *Kid Pix*
Daily Language Practice (5–6) R20 Practice Activity T159 *Language Handbook* pp. 42–45	Daily Language Practice (7–8) R20 Practice Activity T159 *Grammar Practice Book* pp. 19–22	Daily Language Practice (9–12) R20 *Practice Book* p. 28
Discuss the Generalization T160 *Integrated Spelling* p. 19 *Integrated Spelling Teacher's Edition* p. T35	Apply to Writing T160 *Integrated Spelling* pp. 20–21 *Integrated Spelling Teacher's Edition* pp. T36–T37	Posttest T160 *Practice Book* p. 29 *Integrated Spelling Teacher's Edition* p. T38
CONSONANT DIGRAPHS: /ng/ng, /ngk/nk T162 *Phonics Practice Reader 13: Frank's Gift for the King*	**CONSONANT DIGRAPHS: /ng/ng, /ngk/nk** T163 *Practice Book* p. 30 *Bailey's Book House* (Read-A-Rhyme)	**CONSONANT DIGRAPHS: /ng/ng, /ngk/nk** T163 *Phonics Activity Book* p. 7
PHONICS AND DECODING MINILESSON T127 Initial Clusters with *r* (Maintain) *Phonics Activity Book* p. 9 *Phonics Practice Book* pp. 189–190 *Phonics Game Board Pattern Book* pp. 24–26 *Practice Book* p. 32	**GRAMMAR MINILESSON** T135 ✓ Naming Part of a Sentence; Joining Naming Parts (Review) *Language Handbook* pp. 38–41 **COMPREHENSION MINILESSON** T143 ✓ Sequence (Review) *Practice Book* p. 34	**PHONICS AND DECODING MINILESSON** T141 Short Vowel: /a/a (Maintain) *Phonics Activity Book* p. 8 *Phonics Practice Reader 2: The Maps* *Phonics Practice Book* pp. 40–44 *Phonics Game Board Pattern Book* p. 1 *Practice Book* p. 33 Theme Project Checkpoint 3 T170
Above-level writers may complete the Writer's Workshop independently at their own pace.	Have children read "Balloon Tom Tom," pages 94–95, to connect a how-to piece with the fictional story they just completed.	**Below-level** and **ESL readers** may read the *ESL/Title I Library* book *Who Is Tapping at My Window?*

✓ = Tested Skill
◆ = Optional activities that may be used to adjust pacing throughout the lesson
Titles in *italics* are optional materials.

BUILDING BACKGROUND AND CONCEPTS

PRIOR KNOWLEDGE

Create rhythms. Hold up two sticks with rounded ends and have children suggest possible uses for them. List suggestions on the board. Invite volunteers to use the sticks to tap rhythms on their desks. Then tap a rhythm and have children use their pencils to imitate it.

Have children close their eyes as volunteers tap rhythms on other surfaces in the classroom (for example: metal file cabinet, chalkboard, floor). Challenge children to guess what is being tapped.

VOCABULARY STRATEGIES

KEY WORDS DEFINED

strong powerful
appeared came into sight
brought carried
sound a noise
spare extra
thanks an expression of gratitude
called shouted

SUPPORT WORDS

Display the words *conductor, copying, created, imitated, reply,* and *rhythm*. Discuss their meanings and have children use them in sentences.

INTEGRATED SPELLING

SPELLING PRETEST: page T160
SPELLING GENERALIZATION: Words with short *a*

Intervention Strategies

For children who may have difficulty reading "Max Found Two Sticks," support is available in *Intervention Strategies Manual,* pages 14–19, and on pages T135 and T152–T153 in this lesson.

STUDENTS ACQUIRING ENGLISH

See *Sheltered English/ESL Manual,* pages 10–13.

TIPS FOR TEACHERS

"I like to bring in different types of music to share with my class. It's fun to have my students listen to the music and determine the rhythm, or beat. Sometimes I have my students imitate the rhythms they hear. I will occasionally play slow, soothing music to relax the children and get them ready to listen. If children seem tired, playing music with a strong beat perks them up."

CUEING SYSTEMS

Have children read new vocabulary. Display Chart/Transparency 5, or write the words and sentences on the board. Have children read words they might know.

Cover the letters *ong* in *strong* with a self-stick note. Have children read the sentence and suggest words that make sense. As children respond, ask:

> **How does seeing the first three letters help you figure out the word? Does the word make sense in the sentence?**

Have children read the rest of the story, using sounds for letters and the sense of the story to help them figure out the underlined words.

HANDS-ON ACTIVITY

Play a game with children. Have children write the Key Words on cards for their Word Files. Then tell children to bring one of the cards with them, and have them sit in a circle on the floor. Invite children to pass the cards around the circle to the rhythm of a drumbeat. When the drumming stops, have children hold up the card they have if you give the appropriate clue.

Show me the word that . . .

- means "powerful." (*strong*)
- means "something you can hear." (*sound*)
- rhymes with *care*. (*spare*)
- means "shouted." (*called*)
- begins like *brother*. (*brought*)
- you might say when someone gives you a gift. (*thanks*)
- means "came into sight." (*appeared*)

CHART/TRANSPARENCY 5

strong	appeared	brought	sound
spare	thanks	called	

A strong wind was blowing around leaves when the mail carrier appeared. What had she brought me? I shook the box, but it didn't make a sound. Inside the box were a drum and three sticks. I'll save one of the sticks to have as a spare. "Thanks," I called, as the mail carrier walked on down the street.

PHONICS-VOCABULARY CONNECTION

WORD BUILDING

Distribute letter cards and Word Builders to children. Begin with *ank* in the Word Builder. Have children add letters to the beginning and end to make new words, such as *thank(s), bank, rank, sank, shrank, tank*, and *yank*. List the words on the board as children offer them. Repeat the procedure beginning with *ong* in the Word Builder, having children make words, such as *strong, gong, long, wrong,* and *song*.

The concept of /ng/*ng* and /ngk/*nk* is further developed on pages T162–T163.

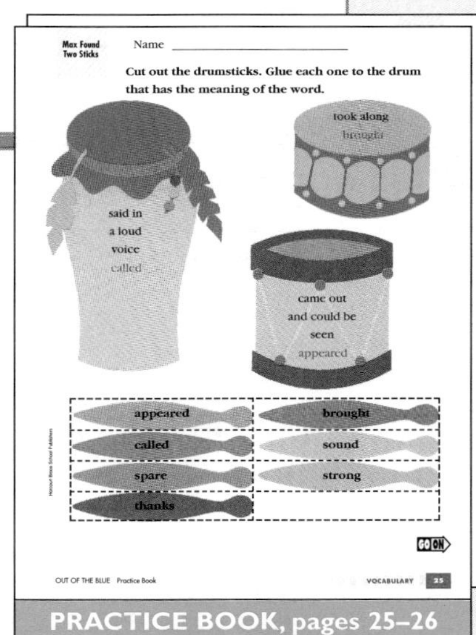

PRACTICE BOOK, pages 25–26

Strategic Reading

STRATEGY FOCUS: RELATING PICTURES TO TEXT

Review with children some of the things good readers do. Add new responses to the classroom chart.

What Good Readers Do
Put things in the order they happen
Guess what might happen next
Use pictures to help understand the story

Share with children the comprehension strategy which is the focus of this selection.

MODEL **I look carefully at the pictures as I read a story. The pictures tell me what the characters are like and how they are feeling. The author may not tell everything about the setting, but the pictures may show it clearly. If I'm not sure what a word means, sometimes I can find it in the pictures or else the pictures give clues that help me figure it out. I use the pictures as I read each page.**

66

TIPS FOR CLASSROOM MANAGEMENT

SMALL GROUP

CHART READING

Distribute a copy of the chart below. Ask children to fill in the chart as they read "Max Found Two Sticks." After children finish, they can refer to the chart as they retell and discuss the story.

What Max Uses	Sound Max Makes	What It Sounds Like
sticks on his thighs	pat. . . pat-tat. . . putter putter. . . pat-tat	flying pigeons

COOPERATIVE READING

PARTNER READING **Have partners pause at appropriate points and take turns being Max, using two pencils to tap the rhythms, as they read the story aloud. Make Reader Response Card 5 (Free Response), page R22, available for pairs to use.**

Response Card

MAX FOUND TWO STICKS

BY BRIAN PINKNEY

MAX FOUND TWO STICKS
BRIAN PINKNEY

Award-Winning Author

67

PREVIEWING/ SETTING PURPOSES

Have children locate and read the title on page 67. Then have them preview the pictures on pages 66–73. Ask children if they know who Max is. Then ask them to predict what the story will be about. Have children write their predictions in their personal journals. Then help them set their purposes for reading.

WHOLE CLASS

STRATEGIC READING

Choose some or all of the suggestions and questions under Strategic Reading, pages T124–T148, to guide a literature discussion and model the STRATEGY FOCUS of Relating Pictures to Text.

READ ALOUD

Read "Max Found Two Sticks" aloud as children follow along in their books. Invite discussion by having children predict and then confirm their predictions as the story unfolds. Encourage children to join in as you read the sounds Max makes.

Strategic Reading

MODELING A STRATEGY

STRATEGY FOCUS

PAGES 68–69 Before children read, have them look at the pictures and tell how they think Max is feeling. Encourage children to look at the pictures as they read the pages to see what they can find out. After children read, model how to use pictures to get additional information from the story. **Think aloud:** *On page 68, I read that Max didn't feel like talking to anyone. In the picture he looks bored or maybe sad. Perhaps that's why he doesn't feel like talking.*

Based on what children found out from the words and the pictures, have them tell what they think will happen next.
RELATING PICTURES TO TEXT

It was a day when Max didn't feel like talking to anyone. He just sat on his front steps and watched the clouds gather in the sky.

68

LISTENING CENTER

"Max Found Two Sticks" is available on *Literature Cassette 1*. Some children may benefit from listening to the story as they follow along in their books.

REAL-LIFE CONNECTION

Explain that body language can tell a lot about how a person is feeling. Invite children to imitate Max's expression and the way he is sitting. Then ask children to demonstrate body language for emotions such as nervousness, happiness, or pride.

A strong breeze shook the tree in front of his house, and Max saw two heavy twigs fall to the ground.

69

MINILESSON

MAINTAIN: PHONICS AND DECODING

Initial Clusters with *r*

INFORMAL ASSESSMENT

As children read, notice whether they can decode words that begin with an *r* cluster.

TEACH/MODEL

Have children reread page 69 and find words that begin with consonant clusters with *r*. Write the words on the board. *(breeze, tree, front, ground)* Have children underline the initial clusters. Remind children that when another consonant is blended with the letter *r* at the beginning of a word, both consonant sounds are heard. Ask children to name other words that begin with consonant clusters with *r*.

PRACTICE/APPLY

Say words that begin with consonant clusters with *r*. Tell children to pretend to beat a drum each time they hear a word that begins with *dr*. Have children name the initial clusters of the words that don't begin like *drum*. Some examples are: *trip, drip, print, drink, drop, brook, try, dry, dream,* and *dragon*.

PHONICS ACTIVITY BOOK, page 9

PHONICS PRACTICE BOOK, pages 189–190

For further reinforcement, you may want to use "Pick-Up Sticks," *Phonics Game Board Pattern Book*, pages 24–26.

ILLUSTRATOR'S CRAFT

Point out how the illustrator uses sweeping lines to show the whirling leaves and the breeze shaking the tree. Discuss other ways illustrators might show what the weather is like.

Name ______________ Max Found Two Sticks

Read the words in the box. Then read each clue. Write the word that tells what the thing is.

tree brother prize truck crow drum grape

1. You can win me. I am a prize.
2. You can bang on me. I am a drum.
3. You can hug me. I am your brother.
4. You can climb me. I am a tree.
5. You can drive me. I am a truck.
6. You can see me fly. I am a crow.
7. You can eat me. I am a grape.

32 INITIAL CLUSTERS WITH r — OUT OF THE BLUE Practice Book

PRACTICE BOOK, page 32

Strategic Reading

MODELING A STRATEGY

PAGES 70–71 After children read, model how to visualize what is happening and how to "hear" Max's rhythms by reading and demonstrating the sound words. **Think aloud:** *The author uses sound words so that I can "hear" the rhythms Max makes. The author also tells what the sounds sound like, such as surprised pigeons flying away. I close my eyes and picture the pigeons being surprised and try to "hear" the sound of their wings. I imagine a sound like many quick taps in a row. I wonder if that's what Max's taps really sounded like.* VISUALIZING

CONVENTIONS OF PRINT

ITALICS AND ELLIPSES Point out that the words *Pat . . . pat-tat* on page 70 are in italics to set them off from the rest of the text—in this case to show that the words imitate sounds. Point out that the ellipsis points indicate a pause in the rhythm Max is tapping. Encourage children to look for other ellipses and italics in the story.

Putter-putter . . . pat-tat.
His rhythm imitated the sound of the pigeons, startled into flight.

71

Student Self-Assessment

FIX-UP STRATEGY: USING CUEING SYSTEMS

Have a volunteer read the second sentence on page 70. Ask children what they might do if they weren't able to read the word *thighs*. Point out that there are several strategies that good readers could use.

- Children could reread the sentence and think of a word that begins with *th* and would make sense in the sentence.
- They could look at the picture to see if it shows what Max is tapping that begins with *th*.
- Children could also try to pick out a part of the word they know, such as *high*, and use this to help them sound out *thighs*.

EXPANDING VOCABULARY

Have children read the second sentence on page 71, and discuss the meaning of the word *startled*. Ask them to tell about times when they were startled. Encourage children to think of synonyms for *startled*, such as *surprised* or *scared*.

STARTLED
SURPRISED
SCARED

STUDENTS ACQUIRING ENGLISH

Read and discuss the meaning of the word *imitated*. Invite volunteers to make simple body movements, and have the rest of the group imitate the movements. Ask children how they think Max's rhythm imitated the sound of pigeons startled into flight.

Strategic Reading

MODELING A STRATEGY

STRATEGY FOCUS

PAGES 72–75 Before children read, have them look at the pictures and talk about what they think is happening in the story. After reading the pages, have children look at the pictures again and tell what they know about where the story takes place. **Think aloud:** *On page 75, I see a street with rows of houses. There do not seem to be any front yards. The children are playing on the sidewalk. I think that Max lives in the city.*

Based on what children know about where Max lives and what has happened so far, ask them to tell what other sounds they think Max will imitate.
RELATING PICTURES TO TEXT

VIEWING

Ask children why the illustrator has drawn extra lines above the drumsticks on page 72. (to show movement) **Ask whether the illustration would have been as effective if he had left out the lines. Why or why not?**

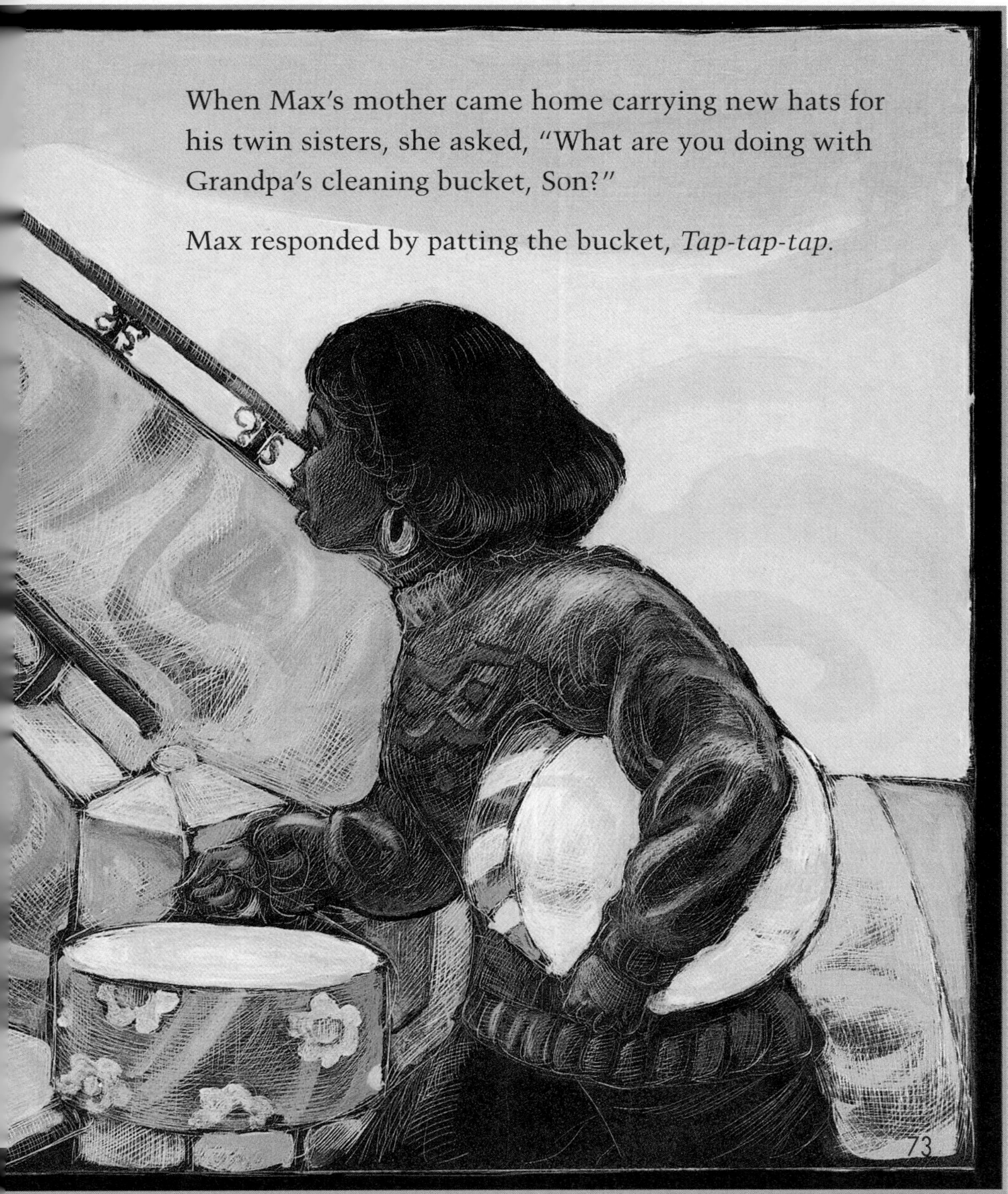

When Max's mother came home carrying new hats for his twin sisters, she asked, "What are you doing with Grandpa's cleaning bucket, Son?"

Max responded by patting the bucket, *Tap-tap-tap.*

73

EXPANDING VOCABULARY

Some children may not be familiar with the word *bucket*. Explain that in some parts of the country the word *pail* is used instead of *bucket*. Invite children to share other pairs of words that name the same thing, such as *purse/pocketbook* and *sneakers/ tennis shoes.*

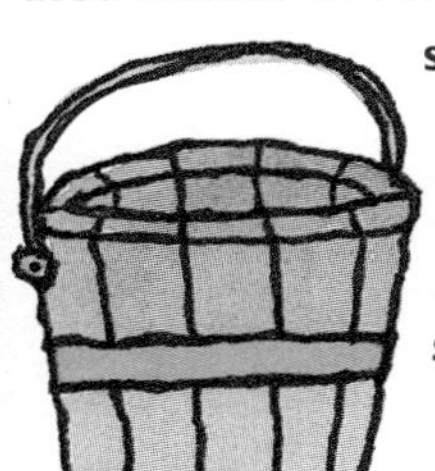

pail bucket

SOCIAL STUDIES

FACT FINDER

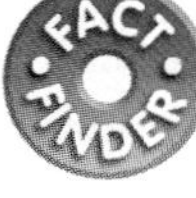

AFRICAN MUSIC Drums are important instruments in African music. Much African music consists of complex rhythms. The music is created by combining different patterns of beats played on drums and iron bells or produced by hand-clapping.

KIMBWALA
TANZANIA
1972

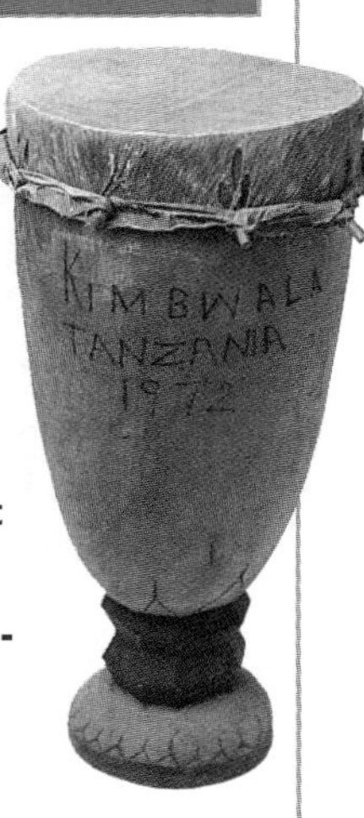

Critical Thinking Questions

1. **Think about how Max felt at the beginning of the story. How do you think he feels now? Why?** (Possible response: I think he feels happier now that he has a drum to play.) CRITICAL: UNDERSTANDING CHARACTERS' FEELINGS

2. **What do you think Max will do next? Why?** (Possible response: I think Max will keep playing his drum because he is having fun tapping out the things he hears around him.) CRITICAL: SPECULATING

74

IDEA BANK

Invite children to write a story describing an adventure Max might have. Suggest that they include sounds in nature, such as thunder, waves, birds chirping, and so on, in their writing. Encourage children to include sound effects as they read their stories aloud.

A CLOSER LOOK

Point out ways in which Brian Pinkney has shown that a light rain is falling, such as the children running with their hands over their heads and the small streaks in the art.

Tippy-tip . . . tat-tat. He created the rhythm of the light rain falling against the front windows.

75

Student Self-Assessment 

FIX-UP STRATEGY: READING ON

Choose a volunteer to read page 75 aloud. Ask children what they could do if the word *created* is unfamiliar. If necessary, explain that sometimes it's a good idea to skip an unknown word and read on, using the other words nearby as clues to figure out what the unknown word might be.

Encourage children to keep a list of words they come across in their reading that they don't know. Suggest that children write the definition beside each word after they have determined its meaning. Encourage children to use a dictionary to check their definitions.

EXPANDING VOCABULARY

Ask children what the word *light* means as used in the sentence on page 75. ("not a lot") **Point out that the word *light* has various meanings. Discuss the meaning of *light* as used in each of the following sentences:**

Light comes from the sun.

The suitcase is very light.

We will light the fire.

Strategic Reading

APPLYING A STRATEGY

PAGES 76–79 Ask children what Max is tapping. (hatboxes) Have them look back at page 73 and notice that Max's mother is bringing the hatboxes into the house. Explain that the author provided this clue in the art about something that would happen later in the story. Based on this, have children look carefully at the objects on page 76 and predict what they think Max will play on next. Then have children read on to confirm their predictions. **MAKING AND CONFIRMING PREDICTIONS**

AUTHOR'S CRAFT

Point out that the author uses words such as *Whatcha* and *doin'* in the dialogue to make the characters sound like real children. Call on volunteers to explain the meanings of the words. (*Whatcha* means "what are you," and *doin'* means "doing.")

Tested Skill

MINILESSON

REVIEW: GRAMMAR

Naming Part of a Sentence and Joining Naming Parts

INFORMAL ASSESSMENT

As children write, notice whether their sentences have naming parts and whether they can use *and* to join naming parts.

TEACH/MODEL

Remind children that the naming part of a sentence names who or what the sentence is about. Display the following, and invite children to circle the naming part in each sentence:

Max likes music.
His mom likes music.

Review how to use the word *and* to join naming parts of sentences with the same telling parts.

PRACTICE/APPLY

Display this sentence:

________ likes to _________.

Have children copy and complete the sentence on a strip of paper. Display the sentence strips, and work with children to combine pairs of sentences with the same telling parts.

LANGUAGE HANDBOOK
Naming Part of a Sentence, pages 38–39
Joining Naming Parts, pages 40–41

Intervention Strategies

USING CUEING SYSTEMS Have children repeat this sentence: *When I read and I get stuck on a word, it helps me sometimes to look at the first letter of the word and the picture on the page.* Have children share any words with which they might have had trouble and how they figured out the words.

Cooperative Reading

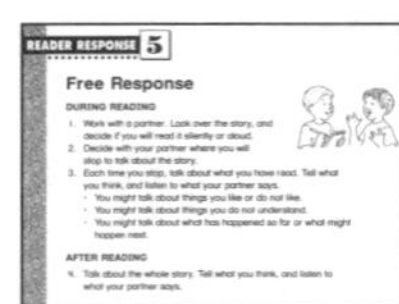
READER RESPONSE 5

Free Response

DURING READING

AFTER READING

Response Card 5

As children use **Reader Response Card 5** (Free Response), encourage them to talk about things they like about the story so far and things that they don't like. You may wish to use the following questions to generate discussion and assess the group's progress:

1. **What is your favorite part of the story so far?**
2. **What do you like about the art?**
3. **What would you change in the story?**

CROSS-CULTURAL VIEWPOINT

Point out that marching bands are often part of parades. Explain that parades are often held to celebrate a holiday or a special occasion. Ask children to name some holidays on which parades are held. (Fourth of July, Veterans Day) **Ask children from other cultures to share whether music or bands are used in any of their celebrations.**

Di-di-di-di. Dum-dum.
Max drummed the beat of the tom-toms in a marching band.

79

NOTES

Here's a place to list ideas or activities that you would like to use the next time you teach this lesson.

SOCIAL STUDIES

TOM-TOMS Tom-toms are drums that have small heads and are beaten with the hands. They date back to ancient times. The earliest tom-toms were made of animal skins stretched across the opening of a hollow log. Today, tom-toms are used as rhythm instruments in many rock and jazz bands.

Strategic Reading

APPLYING A STRATEGY

PAGES 80–83 After children have read page 80, ask them to recall their predictions about what Max would play on next. Encourage children to compare their predictions to what actually happened. Then, ask children to predict what Max will do next. **MAKING AND CONFIRMING PREDICTIONS**

"What are you up to with those soda bottles?" his dad asked as he brought out the garbage cans on his way to work.

Max answered on the bottles,
Dong . . . dang . . . dung.

Ding . . . dong . . . ding! His music joined the chiming of the bells in the church around the corner.

80

MUSIC

BELLS The first bells were made in Asia. Archaeologists have found bells that were used in China as early as 800 B.C. Among other uses, bells have been used in religious services, to celebrate important events, to announce a curfew, to warn of fires, and to remind citizens that their taxes were due!

Informal Assessment

RELATING PICTURES TO TEXT
As children read or reread the selection, observe whether they relate the pictures to the text when they come to something they don't understand.

- ☑ Do children look at the pictures before, during, and after they read the story?
- ☑ Do children use the pictures to help them figure out a word or a concept they don't understand?
- ☑ Do children point out pictures they especially enjoy?

SCIENCE CONNECTION

EXPERIMENT WITH SOUND Fill identical glass jars or bottles with varying amounts of colored water. Invite children to tap the jars with a wooden spoon and describe the sounds they make. Ask how the sounds are alike and how they are different. Invite children to experiment with the sounds by adding water to or removing water from the jars.

Critical Thinking Questions

1. **Why do you think the author used sound words in the story?** (Possible responses: He wanted to make it fun to read; he wanted to show how things in the city really sound.) CRITICAL: AUTHOR'S CRAFT/ DETERMINING AUTHOR'S PURPOSE
2. **Which sound words that the author used do you think sounded most like the real object?** (Responses will vary.) CRITICAL: AUTHOR'S CRAFT/ APPRECIATING LANGUAGE

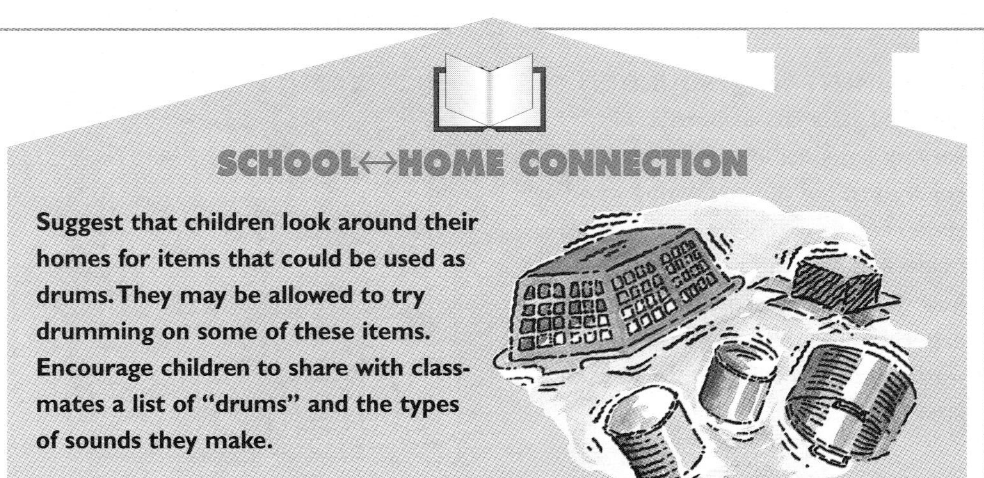

SCHOOL↔HOME CONNECTION

Suggest that children look around their homes for items that could be used as drums. They may be allowed to try drumming on some of these items. Encourage children to share with classmates a list of "drums" and the types of sounds they make.

Soon the twins came out to show off their new hats. "Hey, Max," they asked, "what are you doin' with those garbage cans?"

Max hammered out a reply on the cans, *Cling . . . clang . . . da-BANG!*

83

MINILESSON

MAINTAIN: PHONICS AND DECODING

Short Vowel: /a/*a*

INFORMAL ASSESSMENT

As children read, notice whether they can decode words with the short *a* sound.

TEACH/MODEL

Ask children what the twins were wearing, and write *hats* on the board. Have a volunteer underline the letter *a* and make the short *a* sound. Remind children that the vowel in CVC words is usually short. Have children name other short *a* words, list them on the board, and read the list aloud with children.

PRACTICE/APPLY

Give children one minute to write as many short *a* words as they can. When time is up, have children exchange papers with a partner. Tell children to award one point for each word with short *a*. Invite children to read aloud the lists.

PHONICS ACTIVITY BOOK, page 8

PHONICS PRACTICE READER 2

PHONICS PRACTICE BOOK, pages 40–44

For further reinforcement, you may want to use "That Sounds Like Cat," *Phonics Game Board Pattern Book*, page 1.

AUTHOR'S CRAFT

Point out the word *hammered*, and ask why the author may have used that word instead of *beat*. Explain that the author makes the story interesting by using colorful action words. Invite children to come up with some other action words that could be used in that sentence.

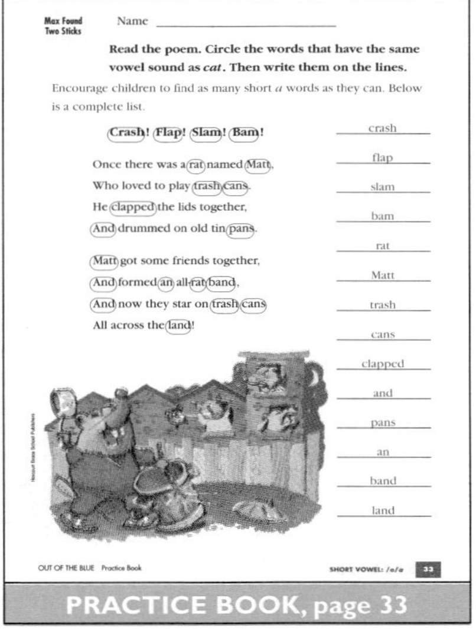

Max Found Two Sticks

Name ____________________

Read the poem. Circle the words that have the same vowel sound as *cat*. Then write them on the lines.

Encourage children to find as many short *a* words as they can. Below is a complete list.

Crash! Flap! Slam! Bam!

Once there was a rat named Matt,
Who loved to play trash cans.
He clapped the lids together,
And drummed on old tin pans.

Matt got some friends together,
And formed an all-rat band,
And now they star on trash cans
All across the land!

crash
flap
slam
bam
rat
Matt
trash
cans
clapped
and
pans
an
band
land

OUT OF THE BLUE Practice Book — SHORT VOWEL: /a/*a* — 33

PRACTICE BOOK, page 33

Strategic Reading

APPLYING A STRATEGY

STRATEGY FOCUS **PAGES 84–85** Tell children to read page 84 and then look at the picture. Have children tell how the picture helps them understand what kind of train the author is describing. Then ask how the train in the picture is similar to and different from trains with which children are familiar. If necessary, explain that in many large cities trains are a primary means of transportation. Sometimes these city trains go on tracks raised above the ground to avoid street traffic. **RELATING PICTURES TO TEXT**

A-cling-clang . . . DA-BANGGGG!
Max pounded out the sound of the wheels thundering down the tracks under the train on which his father worked as a conductor.

84

AUTHOR'S CRAFT

Ask children how the author tells the reader how loud the train and Max were. Point out that some of the sound words are written in capital letters to indicate that the sounds of the rhythms are getting louder and louder. Point out how the author also uses the words *thundering* to tell how loud the train sounded and *pounded* to tell how loudly Max was hitting.

Tested Skill

MINILESSON

REVIEW: COMPREHENSION

Sequence

INFORMAL ASSESSMENT
As children read and discuss the story, observe whether they can put events in the order in which they happened.

TEACH/MODEL
Remind children that remembering the order of events in a story will help them become better readers. Sometimes words give clues about the sequence of events. Have children look back at the story for words that help the reader know the sequence of events. *(when, After a while, Again, Soon)* Encourage children to look for sequence clues to help them better understand their reading.

PRACTICE/APPLY
Have children name things that have happened in the story so far. Write each response on a sentence strip that will fit in a pocket chart or can be taped to the board. Display the strips, and invite children to put them in the order in which the events in the story happened. Allow children to use their books to verify their responses. Encourage them to add events to the chart as they read the rest of the story.

Social Studies

Name ______________________

Max Found Two Sticks

Think about how the mole can get to the music store. Then read the directions. Write the numbers 1 to 5 to put the directions in order.

BUS STOP
BOOKS
JAM RD.
SOUTH ST.
MARKET PL.
CURVE ST.
SOUND AVE.
CROSS ST.
DRUM ST.

__4__ Go past the bakery.

__2__ Turn left at the bus stop.

__3__ Go straight. Cross three streets.

__1__ Turn right and go down the sidewalk.

__5__ Turn right at Drum Street. You've found it!

Harcourt Brace School Publishers

34 SEQUENCE OUT OF THE BLUE Practice Book

PRACTICE BOOK, page 34

Strategic Reading

APPLYING A STRATEGY

PAGES 86–87 Before children read, have them look at the pictures and talk about what Max is doing and what might be happening in the story. After children have read, have them review the illustrations to see what else they can learn about what happened.

1. **Why do you think all the people are on the steps or looking out the window on page 86?**
2. **Do you think the band is practicing or at a performance? How can you tell?**
3. **Do you think Max saw or heard the band first?**

RELATING PICTURES TO TEXT

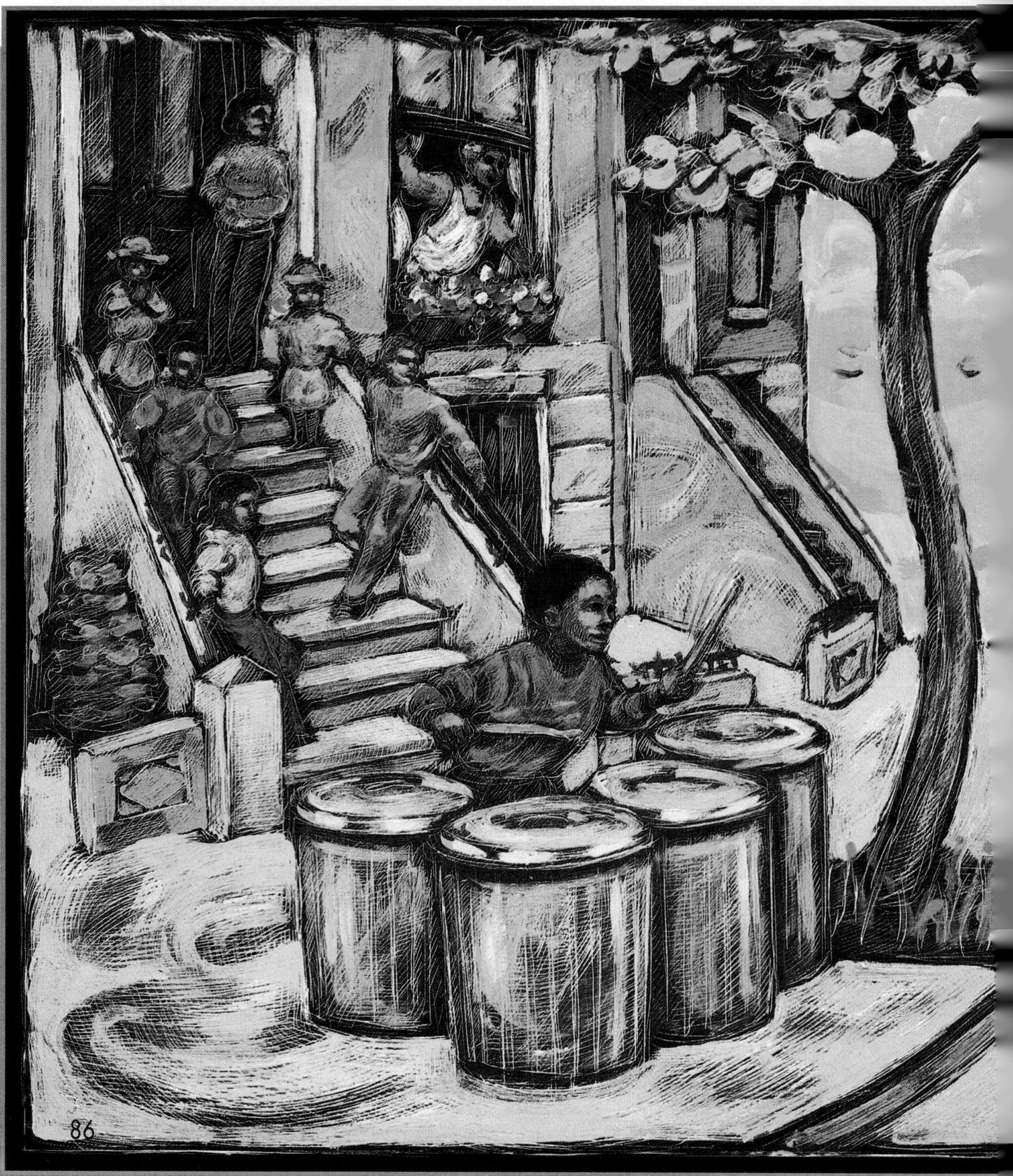

86

SOCIAL STUDIES

DRUMS Drums have not always been used only as musical instruments. For example, armies in ancient China beat huge drums to scare their enemies during wartime. People of many cultures have used drums to communicate with others who are long distances away.

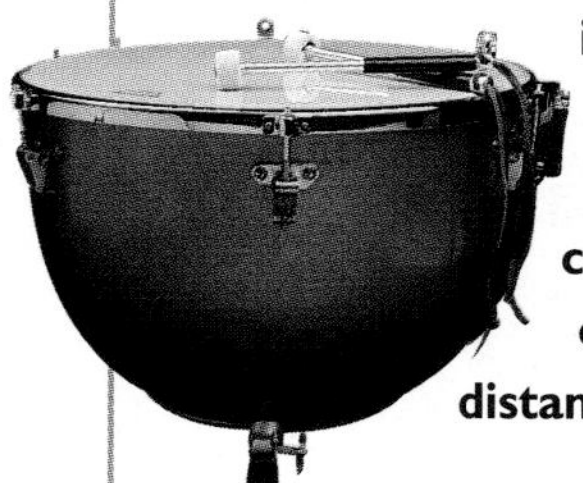

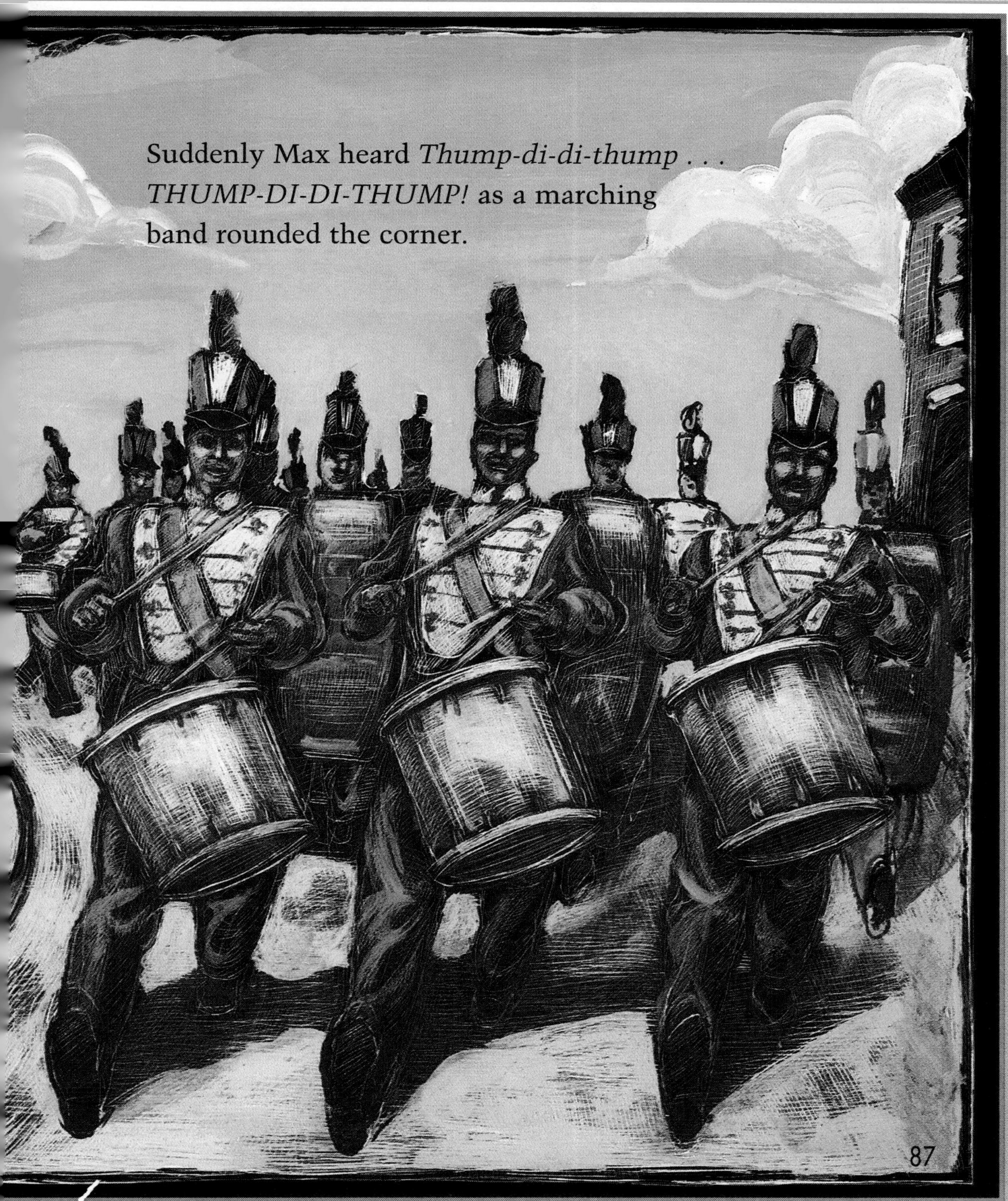

Suddenly Max heard *Thump-di-di-thump . . . THUMP-DI-DI-THUMP!* as a marching band rounded the corner.

87

Student Self-Assessment

FIX-UP STRATEGY: RELATING TO PERSONAL EXPERIENCES

Explain that good readers make connections between what they read and their personal lives. You may want to have children make and complete a diagram comparing themselves and Max.

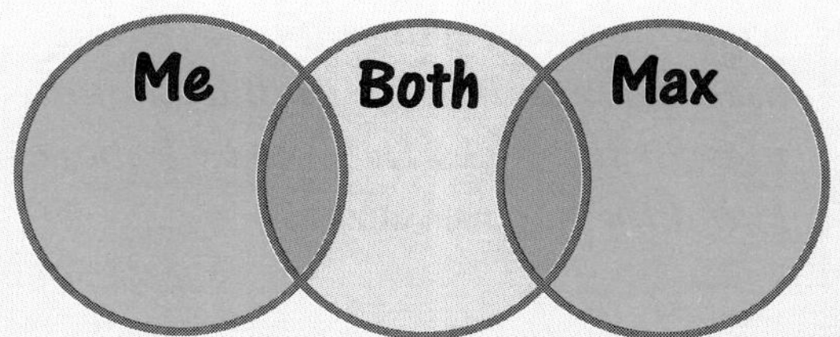

STUDENTS ACQUIRING ENGLISH Some children may not understand what *rounded the corner* means. Demonstrate the meaning by lining up and walking beside a row of classroom chairs, then turning at the last one as if turning a corner. If possible, take the group outside to round an actual corner.

WRITING

EXTEND THE STORY Now that Max has real drumsticks, what do you think he will do? Encourage children to write some sentences telling what they think will happen. Then invite children to illustrate their sentences, including picture clues in their illustrations.

Strategic Reading

MODELING A STRATEGY

PAGES 88–90 Before children read, have them look at the pictures and tell their own versions of what is happening. After children read, help them summarize how finding the two sticks changed the way Max felt. **Think aloud:** *At the beginning of the story, Max seemed bored and unhappy. Now he seems to be enjoying himself. He has used his imagination to find so many uses for the sticks. He is lucky to have found them!* SUMMARIZING

Max watched the drummers with amazement as they passed, copying their rhythms. The last drummer saw Max. Then with a nod and a wink, he tossed Max his spare set of sticks.

88

MUSIC CONNECTION

KINDS OF DRUMS **The drum was the first musical instrument. Although there are many types of drums, the three that are probably the best known today are the snare drum, the bass drum, and the timpani. The timpani, often called the kettledrum, is a huge drum that can produce definite musical notes. The snare drum and the bass drum are used mainly for rhythm.**

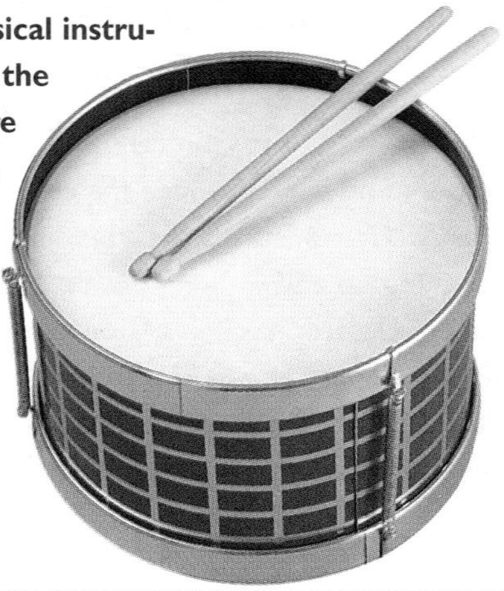

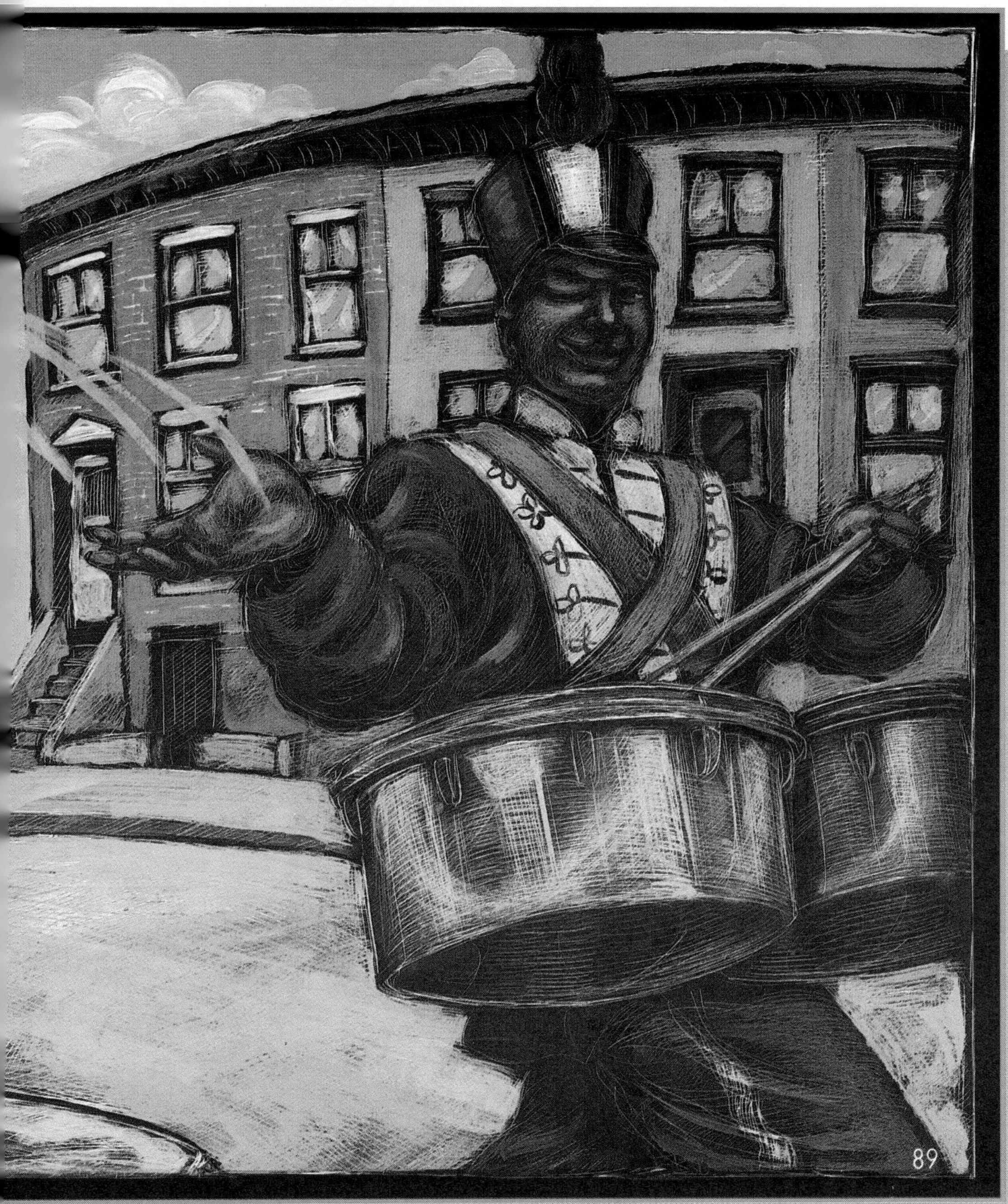

Student Self-Assessment

READING STRATEGIES

After children have read the story, provide time for them to share reading strategies they use to better understand a story. Encourage children to give specific examples of times they have used a strategy to understand a word or a story event. If you like, have them create "Good Reader Awards" from construction paper. Each award should include a child's name and a reading strategy that he or she uses effectively.

CHALLENGE **Invite children to look through the selection to find pictures that show movement. Challenge children to draw a picture of their own that shows movement. Encourage them to use techniques similar to those of the illustrator.**

Returning to the Predictions/Purpose

Before children read this story, they wrote about what they thought the story would be about. Invite them to share their predictions and compare them with what actually happened.

Appreciating the Literature

With the whole class or a small group, have an open discussion about the story.

- **Has this story changed the way you think about ordinary things, such as twigs, bottles, and boxes? Why or why not?**

AUTHOR'S CRAFT

Point out that this is the only page on which Max speaks. Ask how he responds to questions on the other pages of the story. (by tapping out rhythms) **Ask children whether they think this is a good way to end the story.**

BRIAN PINKNEY

What made you decide to write this book?
I wanted to write a book about drumming because I've been a drummer most of my life. I almost made music my career. But even though I had the idea, I didn't really have a story. I would jot down notes about a boy and how he liked to drum.

It took me about four years to finish the book. I decided to start with the pictures. I would draw a little, then write a little. Most of the words came to me when I was just waking up in the morning or when I was away from my studio.

91

About the Author/Illustrator

PAGE 91 Have children read page 91 to find out about how Brian Pinkney wrote the story. Tell them that authors often write stories about things that are important to them.

Brian Pinkney has illustrated several children's books, but "Max Found Two Sticks" is the first book he has both written and illustrated. Since he began playing the drums when he was eight years old, he probably has a lot in common with Max. He keeps a set of drumsticks in his studio and often taps out rhythms on the back of his chair.

OTHER BOOKS ILLUSTRATED BY BRIAN PINKNEY

The Ballad of Belle Dorcas **by William H. Hooks. Knopf, 1990.**
CHALLENGE

Where Does the Trail Lead? **by Burton Albert. Simon & Schuster, 1991.**
AVERAGE

SUMMARIZE AND RETELL

Story Flow

Work with children to complete the following flowchart. Then have children use the flowchart to retell "Max Found Two Sticks." See *Practice Book* page 27.

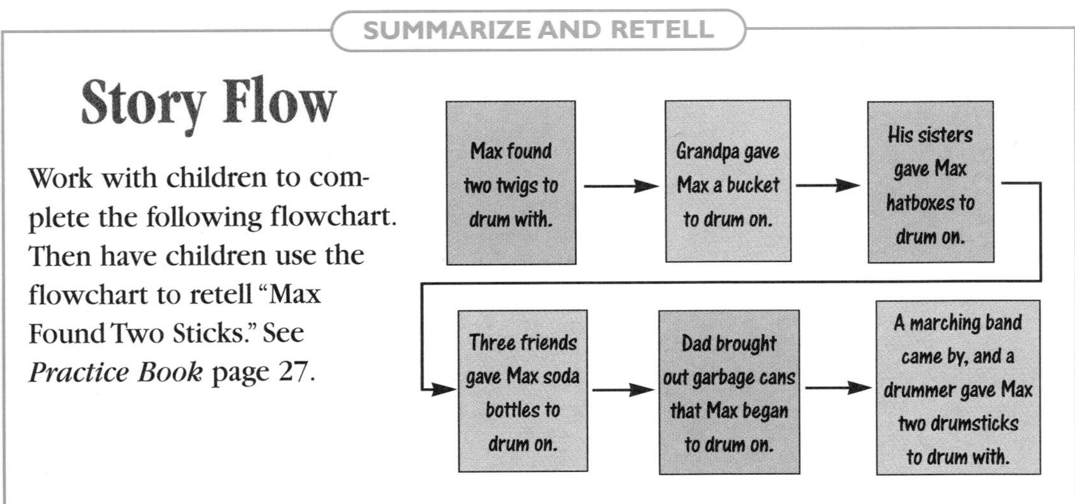

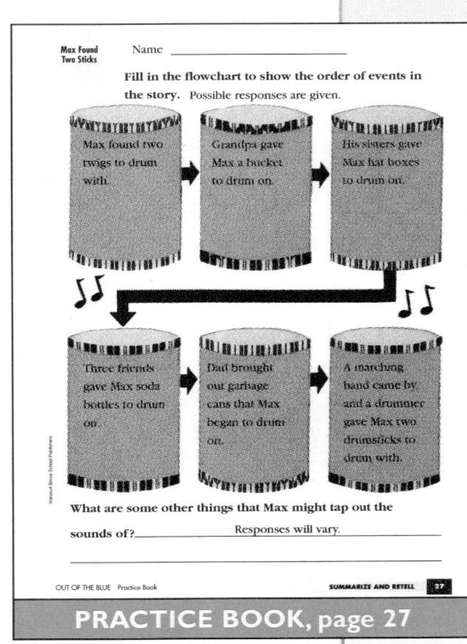

Max Found Two Sticks Name ______

Fill in the flowchart to show the order of events in the story. Possible responses are given.

Max found two twigs to drum with. → Grandpa gave Max a bucket to drum on. → His sisters gave Max hat boxes to drum on.

Three friends gave Max soda bottles to drum on. → Dad brought out garbage cans that Max began to drum on. → A marching band came by and a drummer gave Max two drumsticks to drum with.

What are some other things that Max might tap out the sounds of? Responses will vary.

OUT OF THE BLUE Practice Book SUMMARIZE AND RETELL 27

PRACTICE BOOK, page 27

RESPONSE CORNER ACTIVITIES

EXPERIMENT WITH RHYTHM

MAKE YOUR OWN MUSIC
PAGE 92 Let children experiment with making different sounds and rhythms created by actions, such as clapping hands. Encourage children to keep the actions and rhythms simple.
MUSIC

EXTEND THE STORY

WHAT WILL MAX DO WITH TWO . . . ?
PAGE 93 Set up a table with a variety of objects, such as plastic bottles, stones, buttons, pipe cleaners, and boxes. Invite partners to choose two items. Suggest that partners discuss what Max might do with the items before they write. Encourage both musical and nonmusical creations, such as a cardboard box maraca full of buttons or decorated plastic bottles used as flower vases.
WRITING

VARYING THE ACTIVITY

For children who need extra support with the What Will Max Do with Two . . . ? activity, have them choose two objects and retell "Max Found Two Sticks," using the two objects to make sounds. Children can use the story as a framework for their own stories.

EXTEND THE STORY

WHAT WILL MAX DO WITH TWO . . . ?

Max made music when he found two sticks. What will Max do with the next two things he finds?

Work with a partner. Together, choose two things Max might find next. Then write a story to tell what Max does with those two things.

WHAT DO YOU THINK?

- How does Max feel at the beginning of the story? How does he feel at the end?
- Have you ever done something just right on your first try? How did it feel?

93

CHECKING COMPREHENSION

What Do You Think?

1. **How does Max feel at the beginning of the story? How does he feel at the end?** (Possible response: At first, Max didn't want to talk to anyone; he seemed bored. At the end, Max was excited about the drummers and glad one of them gave him some drumsticks.) DESCRIPTIVE RESPONSE
2. **Have you ever done something just right on your first try? How did it feel?** (Responses will vary. Be sure children support their answers.) PERSONAL RESPONSE

An additional question for extending reading.

3. **Why do you think the drummer gave Max his spare set of sticks?** (Possible response: The drummer thought that since Max could play garbage cans with twigs, he probably would know how to use real drumsticks.) CRITICAL/CREATIVE ANALYSIS

MULTI-AGE CLASSROOMS

Pair children of different ages for What Will Max Do with Two . . . ? Older, more-advanced children can share writing skills and strategies with younger partners as they work together on their story. Then encourage readers and writers to partner-read or echo-read the story.

Informal Assessment

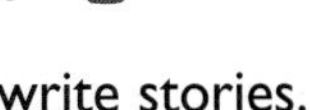

Observe pairs of children as they write stories.

- ☑ Does each child contribute story ideas?
- ☑ Do children include in their story the two items Max might find?
- ☑ Do children tell the story in a logical sequence?

Intervention Strategies

Instant Readers™

Predictable and Patterned Little Books That Build Fluency

*** BOOK LEVEL: 16–17**

VOCABULARY:
sound

PHONIC ELEMENTS:
Digraph: /ng/*ng*; Short vowel: /a/*a*; Initial clusters with *r*

SUMMARY:
Musical instruments and facts about them are presented.

Reading a New Book

INTRODUCING *NO MATTER HOW YOU PLAY IT*

With children, name and list some musical instruments. Have children describe them, how they are played, or the sounds they make. As you share the cover, talk about the title and what it may mean (that there are all kinds of music and everyone enjoys music). Compare the list generated earlier with the musical instruments described in the book, and examine the detailed pictures of the instruments and read the labels.

Informal Assessment ✓

Are children able to

- ☑ find word parts and bits in large, technical words?
- ☑ hear and identify the short *a* sound?

READING THE STORY

Have children read aloud the book to a partner to find out more about the instruments and how they are played. Suggest that children take turns reading aloud each spread.

WORKING WITH WORDS AND LETTERS

Pictures will assist children as they read the labels for the instruments. Further help may give them an opportunity to use additional strategies for these technical words. Have them read the labels aloud, clapping out the syllables. Ask them to look at the words carefully to see if they can find smaller words within each. Help them copy the words in their Word Banks and circle the smaller word bits in each.

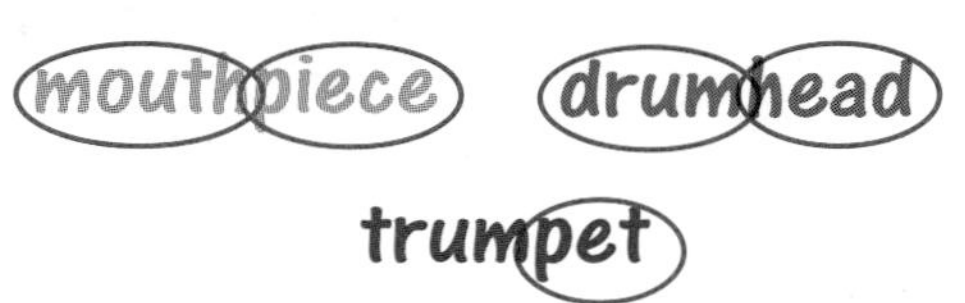

WRITING LABELS

Have children use the story format as a model to draw a picture of a tool, toy, or game that they enjoy using. Have them describe the object by labeling it with words that describe or tell about the working parts.

Additional activities are provided on pages 16–17 of the *Intervention Strategies Manual*.

* **BOOK LEVEL: 13–14**

VOCABULARY:
brought, strong

PHONIC ELEMENTS:
Digraphs: /ng/*ng*, /ngk/*nk*; Short vowel: /a/*a*; Initial clusters with *r*

SUMMARY:
A girl's persistence pays off during a fishing contest.

Reading a New Book

INTRODUCING *WHAT A CATCH!*

As illustrations are shared, make sure children follow the repetitive lines and story pattern. On each spread, have children point out what the girl is doing. Use past-tense verbs to get children ready to read.

READING THE STORY

Have children read the story independently to find out what the girl (Sam) catches.

WORKING WITH WORDS AND LETTERS

Review the sound for short *a* with children after they have read the story several times. Have children write on the board the words that contain short *a*. Help children draw conclusions about these words by pointing out the similarities (Each word has a consonant on either side of short *a*; no other vowels are next to the short *a*).

WRITING SUPERLATIVES

Have children use the superlatives in the story to write a sentence or a label about something they have done. Post writing and pictures of the superlatives on a bulletin board.

ESL/Title I Reading

Who Is Tapping At My Window?
by A. G. Deming

ESL/Title I Library

Working with "Max Found Two Sticks"

GRAPHOPHONIC AND SYNTACTIC CUES If children have trouble reading the story because of the lengthy sound words for Max's drum playing, mask out the words for the sounds. First, have children read aloud the sentences on the page to get the story meaning. If you think children can integrate the sound and story words, reveal all the text for a subsequent reading.

* Books leveled according to Barbara Peterson's "Profiles of Books for Beginning Readers," on page 9 of the *Instant Readers Teacher's Guide.*

IDEA BANK

TIPS FOR CLASSROOM MANAGEMENT

IF children have demonstrated the ability to share ideas in a small group, **THEN** assign the Group Talk activity.

IF children can follow written directions, **THEN** write out the directions for making the drum in the Creative Connection activity, and place the directions and materials in a learning center.

LISTENING AND SPEAKING

Group Talk

MAX'S RHYTHMS

Invite groups to study the pictures in the story and list other objects on which Max might have tapped rhythms, such as the stairs, the railings, and the sidewalk. Have children make up new parts of the story to include the new objects. Suggest that children include sound words like the author did.

After small-group discussions, gather children to share their stories. CHALLENGING THE TEXT

Informal Assessment

Notice how children use picture clues to recall and clarify the story when discussing it.

REAL-LIFE READING

Reading Uniform Insignia

Refer to the picture of Max's father on page 81. Point out and discuss the badges on his uniform jacket and hat. Ask children what Max's father's job is.

Brainstorm with children other workers who wear uniforms, such as police officers, firefighters, sports players, and transportation workers. If any school workers or parents wear a uniform with badges, invite them to the classroom and have children read their badges. Then ask groups of children to choose one group of workers and design the badges and insignia for their uniform. LISTENING/ SPEAKING/ READING/WRITING

TECHNOLOGY

In *Thinkin' Things Collection 1*, Oranga Banga challenges children to repeat a variety of percussion patterns. In *Thinkin' Things Collection 2*, children can use Oranga Banga's Band and Toony's Tunes to create music.

ORAL LANGUAGE

Rereading for Fluency

CHORAL READING

Organize children into five groups, and assign each group a part of the story that includes one of Max's rhythm "instruments." Allow time for groups to practice reading their assigned pages. Encourage them to read the pages as expressively as possible and to try to make rhythms that sound just as Max's did to accompany their reading. When groups are ready, have them come together to do a choral reading of the selection. Begin by reading the title and the first two pages aloud, and then have the groups read their assigned pages. Invite the whole group to read pages 87–90 together to finish the story. **LISTENING/SPEAKING/READING**

KINESTHETIC

Creative Connection

MATERIALS
- **drum-like containers, such as oatmeal boxes**
- **paper**
- **markers or crayons**
- **tape or glue**

MAKING DRUMS

Have children cut paper to fit around their containers. Then have them use crayons or markers to decorate the paper. Children should wrap the decorated paper around their "drum," attaching it with tape or glue. Encourage them to go back through the story and use their fingers or pencils to tap out on their drums the rhythms that Max tapped. Then suggest they create their own rhythms. **LISTENING/KINESTHETIC**

PERSONAL JOURNAL

REFLECTING ON THE STORY Ask children to write in their personal journals how the author's use of sound words contributed to their enjoyment of the story. Encourage children to list sound words from the story that they like and to make up some of their own.

Have you ever sent away for a cereal-box offer like this? What did you get?

Real-Life MAIL-IN OFFER Skills

It's in the Mail!

Max loves making music. So he'll be interested in this cereal-box offer. How about you?

Crunch-Ums

Make Music While You Crunch!
Crunch-Ums breakfast cereal offers these cool musical toys—

Single Drum 10 UPCs
Double Drum 15 UPCs
Flute 12 UPCs

You can make music for FREE! Just send the right number of UPCs from Crunch-Ums cereal. There is one UPC on every box. They look like this.

Mail your form and the UPCs to this address:
Crunch-Ums Toy Offer
300 Breakfast Blvd.
Cereal City, KS 66066

WRITER'S MAGAZINE, pages 10–11

WRITER'S WORKSHOP

A Story

TIPS FOR CLASSROOM MANAGEMENT

IF children are familiar with the writing process approach, **THEN** present the writing assignment and have them use the Story model on pages 8–9 of the *Language Handbook.*

IF at this time you want a short writing activity, **THEN** have children do the prewriting activity and refer to their story maps to tell their stories.

TECHNOLOGY

THE AMAZING WRITING MACHINE **Primary Level Activity Disk Pack Grade 2**
Have children enter their stories in the Stories mode.

KID PIX **Children can illustrate their stories by creating pictures of their own or using the stamps.**

ASSESSMENT WORKSHOP: ***Scoring Student Writing, Primary Level***

Thinking as Writers

WRITING FORM: Story Discuss what a dream is. Help children see that a dream can be something that a person or character wishes for or hopes could come true. Explain to children that they will work independently to write a make-believe story about a dream coming true.

Display Chart/Transparency 6, or write the model Story on the board. Encourage children to tell, in order, the things that happen in the story.

CHART/TRANSPARENCY 6

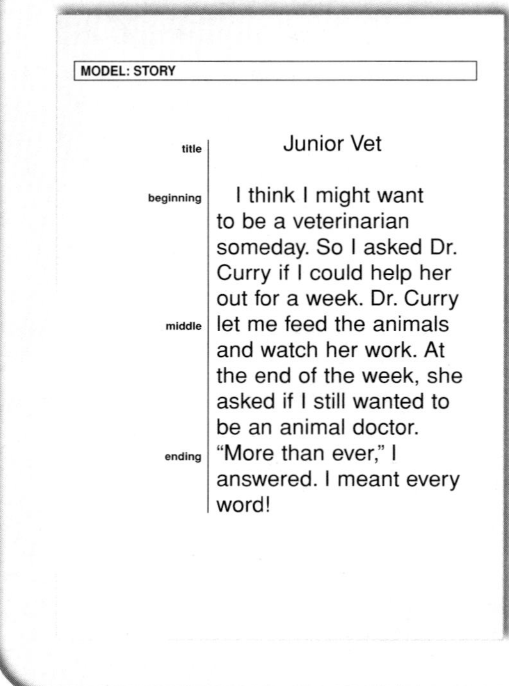
MODEL: STORY

title — Junior Vet

beginning — I think I might want to be a veterinarian someday. So I asked Dr. Curry if I could help her out for a week. Dr. Curry

middle — let me feed the animals and watch her work. At the end of the week, she asked if I still wanted to be an animal doctor.

ending — "More than ever," I answered. I meant every word!

WRITER'S CRAFT: Character Traits and Sequence of Events Discuss how good writers tell stories in a certain order to help readers understand the story. Also explain that good writers try to make their characters seem real. Have children look back at the story to find ways the writer shows how characters act, speak, and show their feelings.

PREWRITING

Have children work in small groups to brainstorm plot ideas about a dream coming true. Model how to complete a story map using one group's ideas. (See page R197 for a Story Map.) Then have children use a story map to organize ideas for their story's characters and what happens in the beginning, the middle, and the ending.

Who	Where	When
Maria and Chan Lee	the soccer field	next week

Beginning
Our team makes the championship finals.
Everyone is nervous.

Middle
We miss chances to score a goal.
The other team scores.
Maria plays harder than ever.

Ending
Chan Lee scores two goals.
Maria stops shots.
Our team wins the championship.

DRAFTING

As children write their stories, remind them to

- use their story maps to help them remember what to include.
- write a beginning, a middle, and an ending.
- think of an exciting title for the story.

As children work through the stages of the writing process, have them save their drafts and revisions in their writer's folder.

RESPONDING AND REVISING

Work with small groups. Read a child's story aloud and offer these guidelines so that children can give positive feedback to each other.

- As they listen, suggest that children close their eyes and try to imagine the story as a movie. They could then ask the writer for more details to make the images clearer.
- Do the characters seem real?
- Are the story events in an order that makes sense?

PROOFREADING

Offer some tips to help children proofread. Help them focus on the following:

CAPITAL LETTERS Each sentence begins with a capital letter.

NAMING PARTS OF A SENTENCE Each sentence has a naming part. Sometimes two naming parts can be joined with *and*. (See the Grammar Minilesson on page T135.)

PUBLISHING

Have children make a clean copy of their stories. Then offer publishing options like the following:

Handwriting
Remind children that their handwriting must be neat and clear so that the person reading the story can understand it. If children need assistance, refer them to the Handwriting models in the *Language Handbook* or in the classroom.

DREAM TEAMS
Children can work in small groups to present their stories. Groups can read the stories aloud using different voices and sound effects.

DREAM BOOKS
Children can staple several sheets of paper together to make a storybook. They can copy their stories into their books. Then they can decorate a construction-paper cover with a "dream design" by blowing through a straw onto spots of wet paint.

PORTFOLIO OPPORTUNITY

After children publish, make copies of their stories and have them attach their Writing Self-Assessment Checklists to them. Have them place the stories and checklists in their portfolios.

LANGUAGE HANDBOOK

Story, pages 8–9

Student Self-Assessment

Children can use the Writing Self-Assessment Checklist in the *Portfolio Assessment Teacher's Guide.*

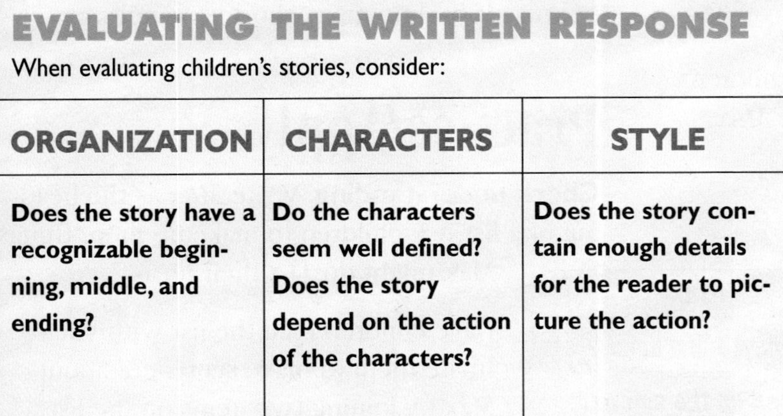

EVALUATING THE WRITTEN RESPONSE

When evaluating children's stories, consider:

ORGANIZATION	CHARACTERS	STYLE
Does the story have a recognizable beginning, middle, and ending?	Do the characters seem well defined? Does the story depend on the action of the characters?	Does the story contain enough details for the reader to picture the action?

EVALUATION BENCHMARKS

The child identifies characters but does not tell a story.	= EMERGENT
The child keeps to the story idea and makes an attempt to develop characterization, plot, and setting. The child uses details.	= BEGINNING
The child successfully writes a story. The story has interesting characters and follows a logical sequence.	= PROFICIENT

Tested Skill

GRAMMAR

Telling Part of a Sentence and Joining Telling Parts

Reading↔Writing Connection

Connect to the story. Have children tell who the main character in the story is. Ask them to tell two things Max did in the story. Write their ideas on the board, using simple sentences such as these:

Max patted a bucket.

Max played on the boxes.

Invite children to read the sentences aloud.

Build oral language. Write *Max* as the heading of a list, and have children tell about other things Max did. Record their responses.

Max
patted his thighs
tapped on bottles
hammered on trash cans
watched a marching band
caught some drumsticks

When the list is completed, encourage children to make sentences, beginning each with *Max*, and read them aloud.

Teach/Model

Discuss telling parts. Remind children that a sentence has two parts. Have them identify the naming part in each sentence on the board. *(Max)* Explain that each sentence also has another part—the telling part. Every sentence has a telling part that tells what someone or something is or does. Have children identify the telling part of each sentence on the board by telling what Max did. (patted a bucket; played on the boxes)

Show how to join telling parts. Tell children that two sentences with the same naming parts can be joined together into one sentence, using the word *and*. Show them how.

Max patted a bucket *and* played on the boxes.

Invite a volunteer to underline the telling part of the new sentence. (patted a bucket and played on the boxes) Work with children to combine more sentences about Max, using ideas from the list they made.

Tell children that writers sometimes join sentences when their writing sounds choppy because it has too many short sentences.

Practice/Apply

Check understanding. Write *Max* as the heading of a list. Ask children to make up more things Max might do. List their ideas.

Max
played in a band
tapped on the sidewalk
pounded on the steps
patted his shoes

Have children read the list with you. Invite them to make sentences about Max by joining two items on the list with *and*. Write the sentences on the board. Have volunteers underline the telling part of each sentence.

LANGUAGE HANDBOOK
Telling Part of a Sentence, pages 42–43; Joining Telling Parts, pages 44–45

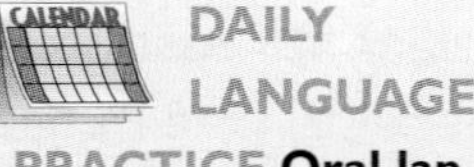

DAILY LANGUAGE PRACTICE Oral language exercises are provided on page R20.

Practice Activities

Stand Up, Sit Down

ORAL APPLICATION Remind children that sentences have two parts—a naming part and a telling part. Tell children to stand up when they hear you say a naming part and to sit down when they hear you say a telling part. For example, naming parts—*the dog, a big red car, Max, my little brother*; telling parts—*went to bed early, tapped on his thighs, jumped over the fence*, and *came down the street*. Invite volunteers to make up complete sentences. Have other children identify the naming and telling parts in each sentence. **AUDITORY/KINESTHETIC**

Silly Sentences

WRITING APPLICATION Write telling parts of sentences on strips of paper. Be sure you have two telling parts for each child, and that the telling parts are written in the present tense. Put the telling parts into a bag. Invite children to each pick two telling parts. Then have them form a silly sentence by adding a naming part and using the word *and* to join telling parts. Tell children to write their sentence on a sheet of paper and draw a picture to go with it. Compile the pages into a book for children to enjoy. **VISUAL/KINESTHETIC**

Be an Author

WRITING APPLICATION Duplicate the following story, and invite children to rewrite it to make it more interesting. Remind children to use *and* to join the telling parts of some of the sentences.

> Sam sat on the steps. Sam watched his friends play. It looked like everyone was having fun! Leah jumped rope. Leah laughed. Martin threw a ball. Martin ran. Two girls skipped down the street. Finally, they called for Sam to join them.

Have children read the original story aloud and then read their revised version. Have them compare the stories and decide which sounds better and why. **VISUAL**

APPLY TO WRITING

Suggest to children that they look back at their stories for telling parts that could be joined to vary the length of their sentences. Point out that this can make their writing more interesting.

USAGE TIP Look in your writing to see if you can join any telling parts to make it less choppy.

STUDENTS ACQUIRING ENGLISH

Have a volunteer pantomime two actions and say sentences about what he or she did, such as: *I jumped. I blinked my eyes.* Then have the child say a sentence, joining the telling parts: *I jumped and blinked my eyes.* Write each sentence and read it aloud with the group.

RETEACH

See page R10 for lessons in multiple modalities.

GRAMMAR PRACTICE BOOK
pages 19-22

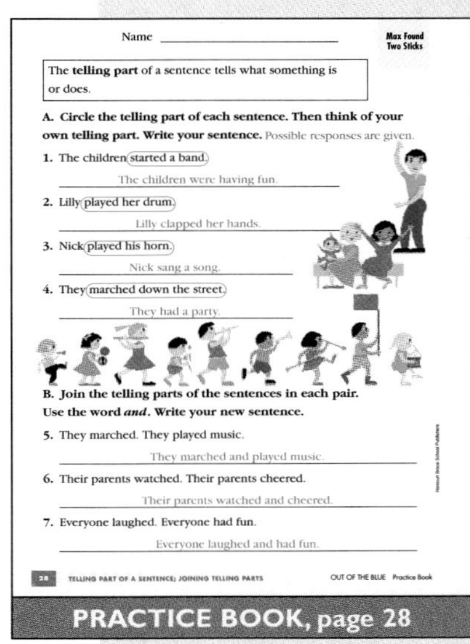

Name ____________ **Max Found Two Sticks**

The **telling part** of a sentence tells what something is or does.

A. Circle the telling part of each sentence. Then think of your own telling part. Write your sentence. Possible responses are given.

1. The children (started a band.)
   The children were having fun.
2. Lilly (played her drum.)
   Lilly clapped her hands.
3. Nick (played his horn.)
   Nick sang a song.
4. They (marched down the street.)
   They had a party.

B. Join the telling parts of the sentences in each pair. Use the word *and*. Write your new sentence.

5. They marched. They played music.
   They marched and played music.
6. Their parents watched. Their parents cheered.
   Their parents watched and cheered.
7. Everyone laughed. Everyone had fun.
   Everyone laughed and had fun.

28 TELLING PART OF A SENTENCE; JOINING TELLING PARTS OUT OF THE BLUE Practice Book

PRACTICE BOOK, page 28

Use in conjunction with Daily Language Practice.

5-DAY PLAN	
Day 1 Complete page T158.	**Day 4** Choose a Practice Activity or *Grammar Practice Book* pages 19–22.
Day 2 Complete a Practice Activity on page T159.	**Day 5** Complete *Practice Book* page 28.
Day 3 Choose a Practice Activity or *Language Handbook* pages 42–45.	

2

SPELLING

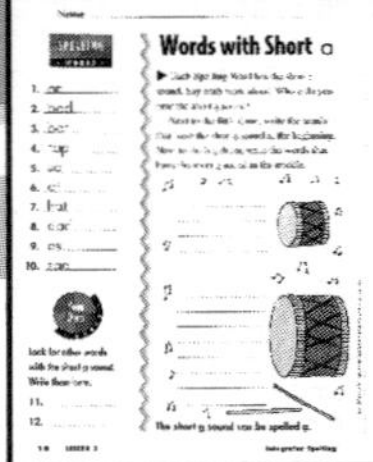
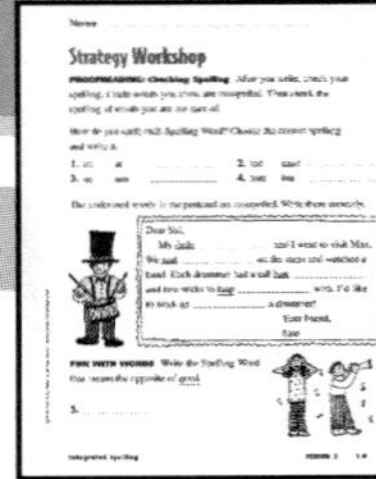

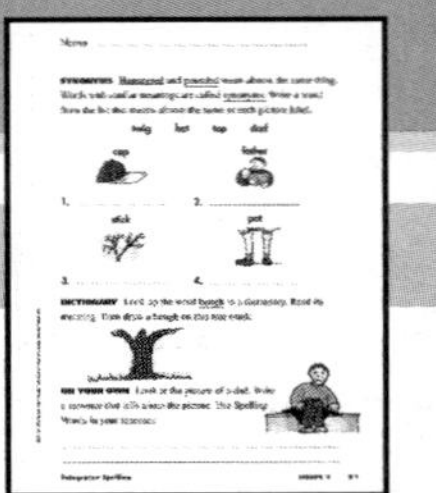

5-Day Plan

***Integrated Spelling* Lesson 3: student book, pages 18–21; Teacher's Edition, pages T33–T38.**

SPELLING WORDS

1. an
2. bad
3. bat
4. tap ★
5. sat ★
6. at
7. hat ★
8. dad ★
9. as ★
10. sad

STUDENT'S PERSONAL WORDS

11. 13.
12. 14.

Additional story words are: *asked, band, last, Max,* and *tracks.*

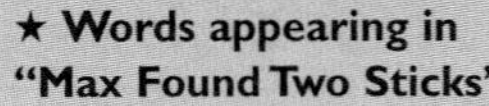

★ Words appearing in "Max Found Two Sticks"

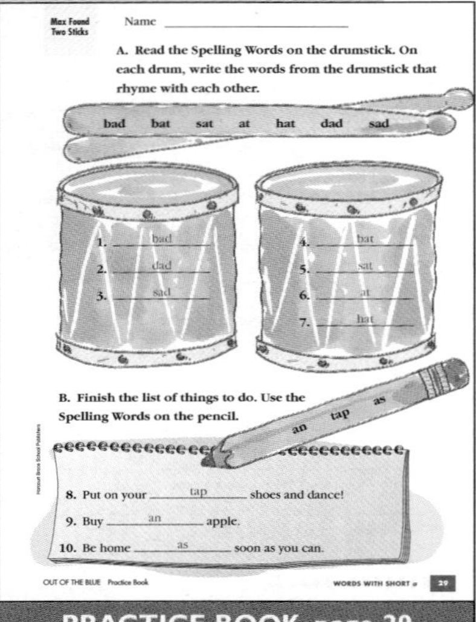

PRACTICE BOOK, page 29

Words with Short *a*

Pretest

DAY 1 **Administer the pretest.** Say each word and then use it in the dictation sentence provided below. Have pairs of children check their own pretests by referring to the word list.

OPEN SORT

DAY 2 **Have children create categories.** Have children select their own categories for sorting the Spelling Words. They may wish to sort them according to the beginning sound, the position of the *a*, or the number of letters. Have volunteers share their ideas.

CLOSED SORT

Sort by spelling pattern. On the board, write the headings from the chart below. Have children each make a similar chart and write each Spelling Word under the appropriate heading.

Words like am	Words like fat	
an	bad	hat
at	bat	dad
as	tap	sad
	sat	

Teach/Model

DAY 3 **Discuss the generalization.** Write the words *an* and *at* on the board, and ask what vowel sound is the same in both. (the /a/ sound) Tell children that when a word has a single vowel that comes at the beginning or between two consonants, that vowel is usually short. Write *an* and *bad* on the board and have a volunteer circle the *a* in each. Then ask children to look at each Spelling Word and tell whether it follows the generalization.

DAY 4 **Apply to writing.** Children should look for words with /a/ in their stories to see if they are spelled correctly.

Posttest

DAY 5 **Assess children's progress.** The sentences below should be used as the posttest.

DICTATION SENTENCES

1. I ate an apple.
2. My puppy was bad.
3. I hit the ball with my bat.
4. When I hear a song, I tap my feet.
5. The two boys sat together.
6. We had fun at the party.
7. My hat keeps my head warm.
8. Sometimes I help my dad.
9. He says I work as hard as he does.
10. That's a very sad book.

VOCABULARY WORKSHOP

Reviewing Key Words

To review how the vocabulary was used in the story, distribute copies of page R54 to children.

Then write the Key Words on the board. Have children choose, as a group, the word that best completes each sentence. Then have them read the sentence aloud and write the word.

A ___strong___ breeze shook the tree by Max's house.

It rained, and then the sun ___appeared___.

Max's dad ___brought___ out the trash cans.

Max made the ___sound___ of a train.

A drummer gave his ___spare___ sticks to Max.

Max said ___thanks___.

He ___called___ out so the drummer could hear him.

Then tell children to cut apart the sentence strips and arrange them in story order. Call on volunteers to act out sentences.

Extending Vocabulary

ONOMATOPOEIA (SOUND WORDS)

Write the heading *Sound Words* on the board, and list the following phrases in a column under the heading: *ding . . . dong . . . ding* and *thump-di-di-thump*. Remind children that these words were used in "Max Found Two Sticks," and tell them that the words imitate the sound associated with an object. Ask children what the sound words remind them of. (bells, drums) Write the heading *What Makes the Sound?* on the board, and write children's responses under it.

Ask children to brainstorm more sound words, and add them to the chart. (*buzz, tweet-tweet, vroom, hiss*) Ask children what makes each of these sounds, and fill in the second column of the chart. Encourage children to use sound words in their writing.

Sound Words	What Makes the Sound?
ding...dong...ding	bells
thump-di-di-thump	drums
buzz	
tweet-tweet	
vroom	
hiss	

STUDENTS ACQUIRING ENGLISH

Ask children to say sound words in their primary language, and have their classmates guess what makes each sound. Ask children to identify any words that are similar to those in English.

TAKE-HOME/ KEEP-AT-HOME BOOK

Run-Away Tire

Distribute the pages and have children make their own TAKE-HOME/ KEEP-AT-HOME-BOOKS, which reinforce Key Words and known vocabulary. Have children read to partners and then take the book home to read.

INTRODUCE: PHONICS AND DECODING

Consonant Digraphs: /ng/*ng*, /ngk/*nk*

OBJECTIVE: To understand the relationship between letters and sounds

Informal Assessment ✓

Are children able to

- ☑ identify words that end with the digraphs *ng* and *nk*?
- ☑ listen for words that end with the /ng/ and /ngk/ sounds?
- ☑ read words with the digraphs *ng* and *nk*?

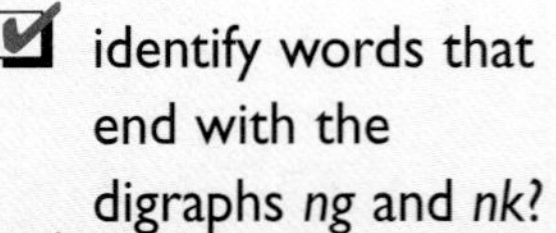

TECHNOLOGY

***Bailey's Book House* (Read-A-Rhyme)**

Teach/Model

Connect to the story. Have children reread page 88, and ask how they knew the drummer was friendly. (He nodded, winked, and tossed the sticks.) Write *wink* on the board and read it. Then write *strong* on the board, have children find the sound words in the story that end with the same sound as *strong,* and write them on the board. Read them with children.

dong ... dang ... dung
ding ... dong ... ding
cling ... clang ... da-BANG
a-cling-clang ... DA-BANGGGG

Tell children that they will learn more about the sounds at the end of *strong* and *wink.*

Phonemic awareness: Listen to the sounds. Display pages 6–7 in the *Big Book of Rhymes*.

Big Book of Rhymes, pages 6–7

Read the poem aloud, and have children listen for words with the same sound as at the end of *strong*. Reread the poem, and have them listen for the word with the same sound as at the end of *wink*. Then read the poem again, encouraging children to join in, especially for words with /ng/ and /ngk/.

Find and read words that end with *ng* and *nk*. In the poem, frame and read the words *belong* and *thinks*. Write belong and think on the board as headings on a chart. Ask how the words end. (ng, nk) Then invite children to add more words to the chart that end with ng and nk.

Practice/Apply

Read words in context. Write these sentences on the board:

Sing a song with me.
It will not take long.
Thank you for the ring.
The boat sank in the storm.
Did it belong to you?
I will take the money to the bank.

Have children read each sentence and make a list of the words with *ng* or *nk*. Have volunteers add the words to the chart.

Practice Activities

CREATE A WORD SEARCH PUZZLE

Have children name words that end with *ng* and *nk*, and write them on the board. Then give children a sheet of grid paper, and invite them to create a word search puzzle with the words. Tell children that the words may be written vertically, horizontally, and diagonally. Remind them to fill in any empty squares with other letters. Have children trade and solve one another's puzzles. **VISUAL/AUDITORY**

s	x	r	a	n	g
o	t	c	i	s	d
n	y	h	o	q	n
g	s	v	i	b	j
c	z	f	o	n	w
l	d	r	i	n	k

Wink or Ring

Read aloud the following words. Tell children to wink when they hear a word with the same ending sound as *wink* and to form a ring shape with their fingers when they hear a word that has the same ending sound as *ring*: *song, think, wrong, rink, spring, ink, ring, belong, strong, sting, rang, sank, long.* **AUDITORY/ KINESTHETIC**

LET YOUR FINGERS DO THE WALKING

PERFORMANCE ASSESSMENT Have partners go on an *ng, nk* hunt. Distribute old magazines and these clues to each pair:

- *something a king would like*
- *something pink*
- *something to drink*
- *something with wings*
- *something that grows in the spring*
- *a beautiful ring*
- *something that will sink*

Have partners read each clue and circle the words that contain the /ng/ or /ngk/ sound. Then tell children to cut out a picture to go with each clue. Have pairs share their pictures with classmates. **VISUAL/KINESTHETIC**

STUDENTS ACQUIRING ENGLISH

Write *swing, wing, blink, drink,* and *wink* on cards, and display them. Have a volunteer act out each word. Then have children find and say the word and use it in a sentence.

RETEACH

See page R11 for lessons in multiple modalities.

CHALLENGE

Invite partners to play Tic Tac Toe and to choose either *nk* or *ng* instead of *x* or *o*. Before a player can fill in a space, he or she must name a word that ends with *ng* or *nk*.

PHONICS ACTIVITY BOOK, page 7

PHONICS PRACTICE BOOK, pages 239–240

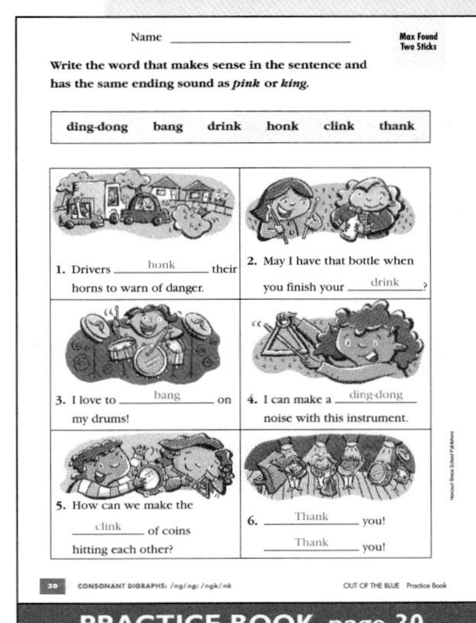

Name ______________ Max Found Two Sticks

Write the word that makes sense in the sentence and has the same ending sound as *pink* or *king*.

ding-dong bang drink honk clink thank

1. Drivers honk their horns to warn of danger.
2. May I have that bottle when you finish your drink?
3. I love to bang on my drums!
4. I can make a ding-dong noise with this instrument.
5. How can we make the clink of coins hitting each other?
6. Thank you! Thank you!

30 CONSONANT DIGRAPHS: /ng/ng; /ngk/nk OUT OF THE BLUE Practice Book

PRACTICE BOOK, page 30

Reading Trade Books FOR CONSONANT DIGRAPHS: /NG/ *NG*, /NGK/ *NK*

Arthur's Camp-Out
by Lillian Hoban. HarperCollins, 1993.
AVERAGE

Julian, Dream Doctor
by Ann Cameron. Random House, 1990.
AVERAGE

Lionel in the Spring
by Stephen Krensky. Dial, 1990.
EASY

PHONICS PRACTICE READER 13

INTRODUCE: STUDY SKILLS

Test-Taking Strategies

OBJECTIVE: To identify test-taking strategies to increase success

Informal Assessment ✓

Are children able to

- ☑ name good test-taking strategies?
- ☑ tell when to use each strategy?

Teach/Model

Discuss before, during, and after a test. Ask children why they think they need to take tests. Point out that it is important for children to do their best on tests and that there are certain things they can do to become better test takers. Explain that although what they do during the test is very important, what children do before a test and after a test is also important.

Ask children what they think they need to do before a test. Model a response:

MODEL **I need to know what the test is going to be about so that I can study the right things. I might study by myself and then later ask a friend or someone in my family to study with me. We can read the information and ask each other questions. I need to get plenty of sleep the night before the test so that I won't be tired when I take the test.**

Point out that during the test it is important to listen to and read the directions carefully and to answer the easy questions first. Tell children that after finishing a test, it is a good idea to check to see that they have answered all the questions, marked the correct answers, and made their answers as neat as possible.

Practice/Apply

Make a chart. On chart paper, make a chart of test-taking strategies, similar to the one below. Review with children the things they should do before, during, and after a test, and write them on the chart. Display it for children to add and refer to at test time.

Before the Test	During the Test	After the Test
1. Find out what the test will be about. 2. Study for the test. 3. Get plenty of sleep.	1. Follow directions. 2. Answer the easy questions first. 3. Keep your eyes on your own paper.	1. Check your answers. 2. Make sure your name is on your test. 3. Sit quietly.

TECHNOLOGY

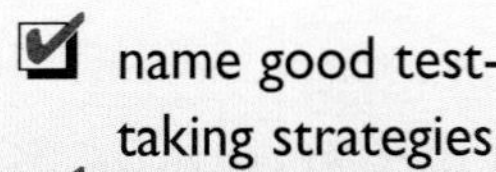

Children can use *Kid Pix* when creating their pennants in the Three Cheers for Tests! activity.

Practice Activities

Three Cheers for Tests!

Have children choose their favorite test-taking strategy from the chart or one that they make up. Ask them to write the strategy on a piece of construction paper shaped like a sports pennant and decorate it. Display the pennants at test time to cheer children on to success. VISUAL

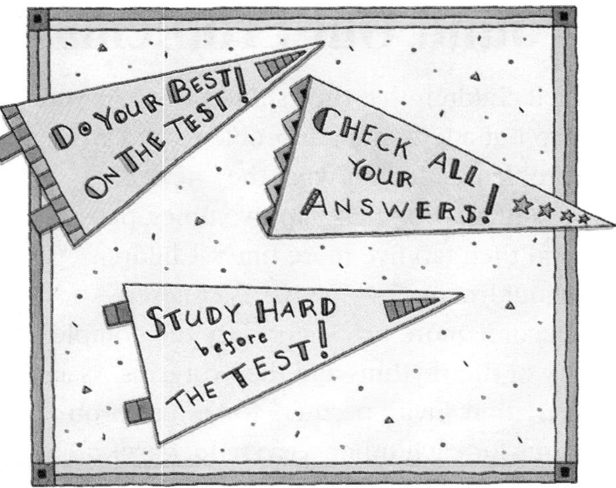

Test It Out!

Invite pairs of children to make up questions with yes or no answers for a test on "Max Found Two Sticks." Encourage children to make their questions fair and easy to answer if one has read the story. Then have pairs trade papers and use test-taking strategies to complete each other's test. Afterwards, have pairs check their tests and discuss the test-taking strategies they used. VISUAL

True or False?

PERFORMANCE ASSESSMENT Write the following on sentence strips:

- Stay up late the night before a test.
- Don't read the directions.
- Study before the test.
- Think about what you have learned.
- Think about something else while your teacher is giving directions.
- Check each answer to see if it is right.
- Do the hard questions first.
- Check to see that you answered all the questions.
- See how fast you can get done.

Have children sort the sentences into true statements and false statements. Encourage them to talk about each statement and discuss why it is true or false. Then have children rewrite the false statements to make them true. VISUAL/KINESTHETIC

MEETING INDIVIDUAL NEEDS

STUDENTS ACQUIRING ENGLISH

Have children add language-oriented items to the chart about what should be done during a test. For example, children might point out that it is important to ask the teacher to explain an unfamiliar word if it is necessary for understanding a test item.

RETEACH

See page R12 for lessons in multiple modalities.

CHALLENGE

Have partners each choose a favorite book and write test questions about it. Then have partners take each other's tests. Encourage children to discuss the strategies they used to answer the questions.

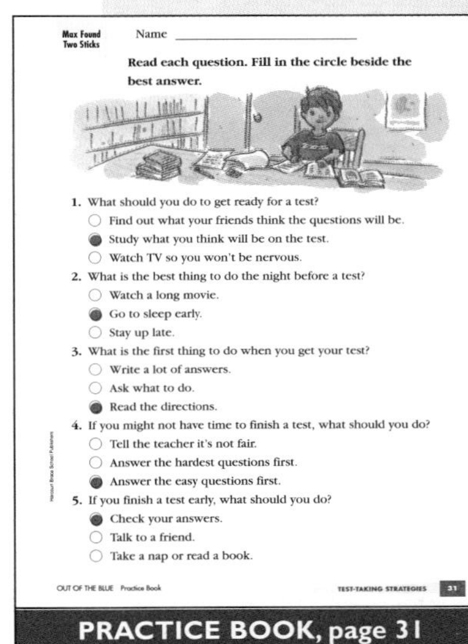

Max Found Two Sticks   Name ____________

Read each question. Fill in the circle beside the best answer.

1. What should you do to get ready for a test?
   - ○ Find out what your friends think the questions will be.
   - ● Study what you think will be on the test.
   - ○ Watch TV so you won't be nervous.
2. What is the best thing to do the night before a test?
   - ○ Watch a long movie.
   - ● Go to sleep early.
   - ○ Stay up late.
3. What is the first thing to do when you get your test?
   - ○ Write a lot of answers.
   - ○ Ask what to do.
   - ● Read the directions.
4. If you might not have time to finish a test, what should you do?
   - ○ Tell the teacher it's not fair.
   - ○ Answer the hardest questions first.
   - ● Answer the easy questions first.
5. If you finish a test early, what should you do?
   - ● Check your answers.
   - ○ Talk to a friend.
   - ○ Take a nap or read a book.

OUT OF THE BLUE Practice Book   TEST-TAKING STRATEGIES 31

PRACTICE BOOK, page 31

Reading Trade Books FOR TEST-TAKING STRATEGIES

Henry and Mudge Take the Big Test by Cynthia Rylant. Bradbury, 1991. EASY

Arthur Meets the President by Marc Brown. Little, Brown, 1991. CHALLENGE

Integrated Curriculum

MUSIC

Rhythm

TIPS FOR CLASSROOM MANAGEMENT

IF you think children will need help locating information about their family of instruments in the Here Comes the Band activity, **THEN** gather a set of books and other media for children to use.

TECHNOLOGY

Thinkin' Things Collection 1: Toony Loon; *Thinkin' Things Collection 2:* Oranga Banga's Band and Toony's Tunes

MUSIC

Here Comes the Band

MATERIALS
- books about instruments
- poster board
- markers

COOPERATIVE LEARNING Tell children that the instruments in a marching band belong to one of three families—brass, woodwind, or percussion. Organize children into groups, and assign a family of instruments to each group. Then have children research and compile a list of instruments that belong to their assigned family. Encourage children to use books and other media to find information about the instruments.

Have children copy their information onto a class chart titled *Instruments in a Marching Band*. When the chart is finished, invite the groups to tell about the instruments they have included in their section of the chart.
LISTENING/SPEAKING/ READING/ WRITING

MATH

Pound Out Problems

Tell children that they should listen as you tap out addition math problems and write a problem based on what they hear. For example, you might tap five times, pause, and then tap five more times. Children should write 5 + 5 = 10. As children become more proficient, vary the complexity of the rhythms and the problems. As a variation, invite partners to tap out problems for each other. LISTENING/WRITING

ART

Paper-Plate Maracas

MATERIALS
- paper plates
- crayons or markers
- dried beans, dried peas, or pebbles
- stapler

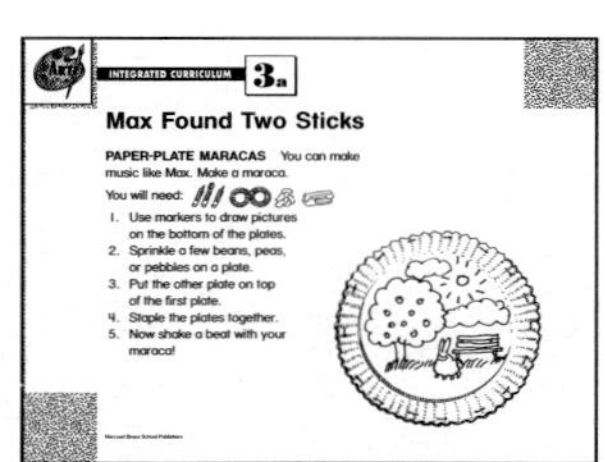
INTEGRATED CURRICULUM 3a

Max Found Two Sticks

PAPER-PLATE MARACAS You can make music like Max. Make a maraca.

You will need:

1. Use markers to draw pictures on the bottom of the plates.
2. Sprinkle a few beans, peas, or pebbles on a plate.
3. Put the other plate on top of the first plate.
4. Staple the plates together.
5. Now shake a beat with your maraca!

Curriculum Card 3a

Explain that a maraca is a percussion instrument sometimes made of a dried gourd with pebbles inside that rattle when the maraca is shaken. Invite children to make their own maracas. Display the following directions in an Art Center or have children use *Curriculum Card 3a*:

How to Make a Maraca
1. Decorate the bottom sides of two paper plates.
2. Put a few beans, peas, or pebbles on one of the plates.
3. Turn over the other plate and place it on top of the first.
4. Staple the plates together around outside edge.

Have children take turns shaking rhythms for their classmates to imitate.
LISTENING/READING

SCIENCE

Sounds Treasure Hunt

MATERIALS
- paper
- pencils
- prepared chart

INTEGRATED CURRICULUM 3b

Max Found Two Sticks

SOUNDS TREASURE HUNT Max heard sounds all around him. Go on a treasure hunt for sounds.

1. Make a chart like this:
2. Take a walk inside and outside your school. Listen carefully! On the chart, write the sounds you hear.
3. Talk to classmates about what you heard.
4. Work with a partner to think of words that sound like each thing you heard. Write the words on the chart.

Sounds Treasure Hunt

What I heard	How It Sounded
footsteps	thump thump
laughing	ha ha ha

Curriculum Card 3b

Invite children to go on a sounds treasure hunt inside and outside the school. Have children prepare a chart like the one below. Tell them to listen carefully as they walk and to write the sounds they hear on the left side of the chart.

SOUNDS TREASURE HUNT

What I Heard	How It Sounded
footsteps	click, click, click
laughing	Ha, Ha, Ha, Ha!
door slamming	Ka-bang
bird singing	twit-ter, twit-ter

Invite children to compare their lists when they get back to the classroom. Then, have children work in small groups to try to think of sound words that might be used to imitate the sounds on their lists. Have children write their sound words in the right-hand column of their chart. Encourage children to use their sound words in their writing. **LISTENING/SPEAKING/WRITING**

Reading Trade Books

CROSS-CURRICULAR READING

The Gum on the Drum **by Barbara Gregorich. School Zone, 1993.**
EASY

A Very Young Musician **by Jill Krementz. Simon & Schuster, 1991.**
CHALLENGE

MULTI-AGE CLASSROOMS

Older children can help younger children spell the sound words on their charts for the Sounds Treasure Hunt.

Reading Trade Books

TIPS FOR CLASSROOM MANAGEMENT

INDEPENDENT
Place *Puddle Jumper: How a Toy Is Made* in a Reading Center. Have children read the book and write a short report about the book that tells the steps for making a puddle jumper.

PARTNER
Have children work with partners to read the book. Have them decide how they will read the book together and where to pause to discuss what they've read.

SMALL GROUP
Read the story in a small circle of children. As you read aloud, pause to let children talk about the photographs and the steps for making a puddle jumper.

For a comprehensive lesson plan, refer to the complete lesson for *Puddle Jumper: How a Toy Is Made* on pages T230–T233.

Puddle Jumper: How a Toy Is Made

by Ann Morris

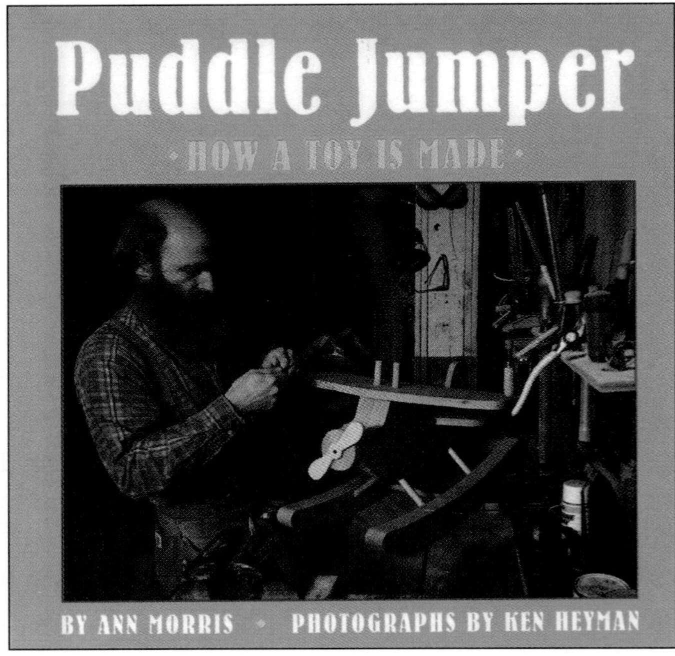

Signatures Library

READER'S CHALLENGE

Max made a toy out of sticks and other things he found on his street. If you could design a toy, what would it be? Who do you think makes up ideas for toys?

READING STRATEGY: SEQUENCING

As children read the book, have them list the steps Barry goes through to make the puddle jumper. Then have them use the list to retell the story.

LINK TO THE THEME

Children who are reading the book may want to discuss the following:

- What would you do for fun with a puddle jumper?
- How does Sarah help Barry?
- Do you think Barry likes his job? Why do you think as you do?

RESPONSE ACTIVITY: GIVING DIRECTIONS

Have children work in groups of two or three to make a plaything, such as a puppet or a simple toy. Then invite the groups to tell others the steps they followed to make the toy.

Other Trade Books

Galimoto

by Karen L. Williams
illustrated by Catherine Stock

In "Max Found Two Sticks," Max found something to use as a toy. Have children tell where Kondi found all the wire he needed and about all the things he made with it. Invite children to draw a picture of something that they might make with the wire. Encourage them to share their pictures.

William's Doll

by Charlotte Zolotow
illustrated by William Pène Du Bois

William wants a toy that may be unusual for a boy. Ask why Grandmother bought William the doll he wanted. Have children work in groups to make up a story about William and his doll. Encourage them to illustrate their story and make it into a book.

Musical Max

by Robert Kraus
illustrated by Jose Aruego and Ariane Dewey

In "Max Found Two Sticks," Max is a drummer. In *Musical Max*, another Max plays all kinds of instruments. Have children identify the musical instruments that are labeled in the story. Then ask children to identify the instruments in the orchestra at the end of the story.

MEETING INDIVIDUAL NEEDS

STUDENTS ACQUIRING ENGLISH

Galimoto **is a word for a toy vehicle, such as a car, in the Chichewa language, the official language of the African country of Malawi. Provide pictures of toys and corresponding word cards, and have children add the name of the toy in their primary language.**

PROJECT MANAGEMENT

- PROJECT LAUNCH
- CHECKPOINT 1
- CHECKPOINT 2
- CHECKPOINT 3
- CHECKPOINT 4
- PRESENTATIONS
- ASSESSMENT

Draw and Write About Goals

SELECTION CONNECTION

In "Max Found Two Sticks," a boy makes his own music using objects he finds. Talk with children about his creative solution, and ask volunteers to share something creative they have done that reminds them of Max.

PROJECT CHECKLIST

During this stage, children should

- think about their interests and how they might use them in a career.
- write steps they could take to reach a goal; draw pictures of themselves in the future.
- share their plans with a group and save the illustrated plans for their books.

When children have completed this checkpoint, have them reflect on some of their wishes for their futures in their Project Journals.

THEME PROJECT CHECKPOINT 3 4

A Book About Me

DRAW AND WRITE ABOUT GOALS

1. Think about your future.

2. Write about what you will do someday. Draw a picture, too.

3. Share it with your friends.

Project Card 4

Project Card 4 can be found as a copying master on page R28.

PLANNING TIPS

As children prepare to write and illustrate their plans for the future, suggest that they

- make a list of all their interests.
- choose one they think they'll still have when they're grown up.
- think of how they'll look when they're older.

Informal Assessment

As children complete this checkpoint, they will **think creatively** about their futures and **make inferences** about steps they might take to reach their goals. Children are thinking critically if they

- can identify goals for the future.
- identify steps to take to reach those goals.

Note that a more formal assessment rubric for this checkpoint is provided on page T225.

STUDENTS ACQUIRING ENGLISH

Make sure that children know the English words to describe their interests and goals. Pair children with fluent English-speakers to help them develop lists of steps to achieve a goal.

CHALLENGE

Invite children to read a book about an interest or a career and share what they learned with a group.

"Balloon Tom-Tom" from *Making Music*

by Eddie Herschel Oates

SELECTION CONNECTION

Children have read "Max Found Two Sticks," the story of a boy who finds two sticks that he uses as drumsticks. He uses various things for drums: a bucket, soda bottles, and garbage cans. Children will have the chance to make their own drums.

ABOUT THE AUTHOR

Eddie Herschel Oates is a teacher at Rhode Island School of Design. Each year his students make their own instruments and give a concert. He and his wife Susan live in Sandwich, Massachusetts.

ABOUT THE ILLUSTRATOR

Michael Koelsch took his first art class when he was eight years old. Later, he earned a B.F.A. in illustration at Art Center College of Design and was a top award winner in the 1991 and 1992 Society of Illustrators student competition. He lives in Huntington Beach, California.

SUMMARY

GENRE: Nonfiction

Step-by-step directions tell readers how to make a simple drum from a large balloon and a coffee can or other cylindrical container. They stretch a balloon over both ends of the container and secure it with a rubber band. Children can experiment with rhythm and sound by striking their drums in different ways.

EXTRA SUPPORT

Some children may need a demonstration of the steps for making the drums. While previewing the selection, run through the steps for making the drum, holding up the materials and showing children how to follow the directions.

Introducing the Selection

BUILDING BACKGROUND

Talk with children about how Max managed to drum without using an actual drum or real drumsticks. Ask children to look around the room for objects that could be used to make musical sounds. Call on volunteers to name the objects and then demonstrate how the objects can be used to make musical sounds.

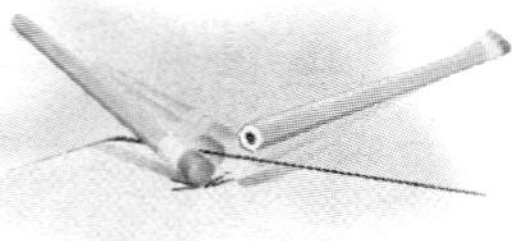

Reading a How-to Selection As children preview pages 94 and 95, direct their attention to the three main parts of the article: "Materials needed," "Putting it together," and the section at the end about how to play the drum. Ask children why they think the list of materials comes first. Explain that this article tells how they can make drums of their own. Read through the directions with the children. Then, if possible, distribute materials and encourage children to create a balloon tom-tom step-by-step.

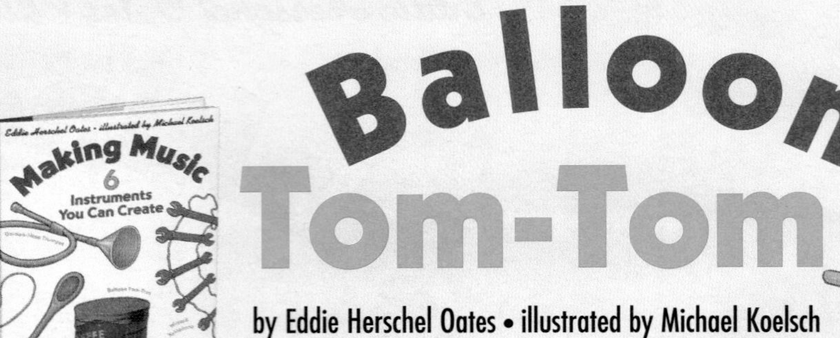

Balloon Tom-Tom

by Eddie Herschel Oates • illustrated by Michael Koelsch

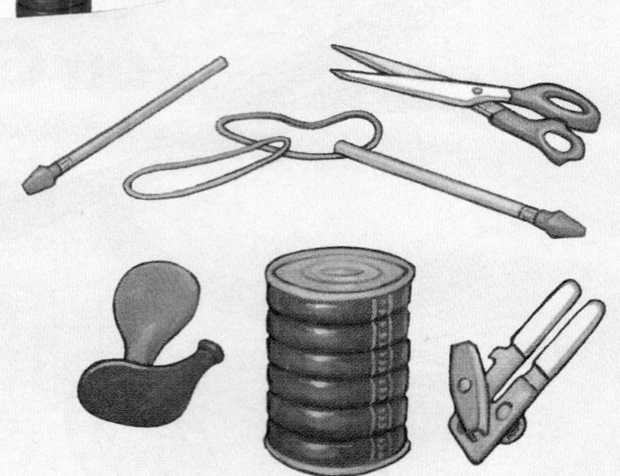

Materials needed:

EMPTY JUICE CAN, OATMEAL BOX, POTATO-CHIP CAN, or other cylindrical container
CAN OPENER
SCISSORS
2 LARGE BALLOONS
2 HEAVY RUBBER BANDS
2 PENCILS (with erasers)

Putting it together:

1. If your container is open at only one end, use scissors or a can opener to open the other end of the container. This is the drum body.

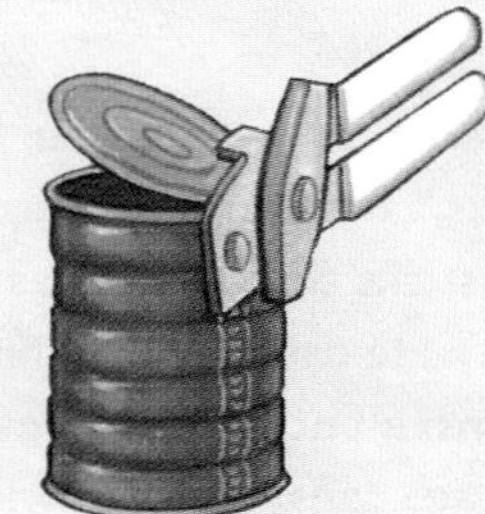

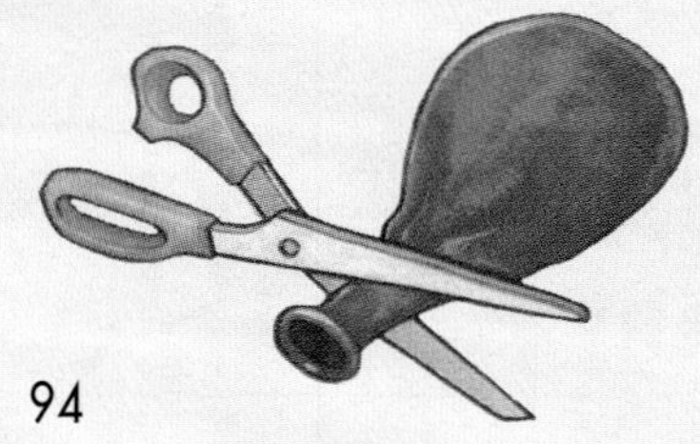

2. Cut the open end off a large balloon.

94

TIPS FOR CLASSROOM MANAGEMENT

SMALL GROUP

PARTNER READING

Children can each read the materials list silently. Then partners can take turns reading each step of the directions for making a drum. Partners can read aloud the last paragraph in unison.

WHOLE CLASS

READ ALOUD

To focus children on the materials and the steps for making a balloon tom-tom, read the selection aloud. As you read the materials list, children can point to the picture of each item as you name it. After you have read all of the directions, ask children whether they think they could follow the directions to make a drum.

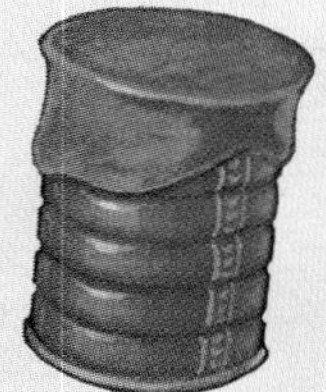

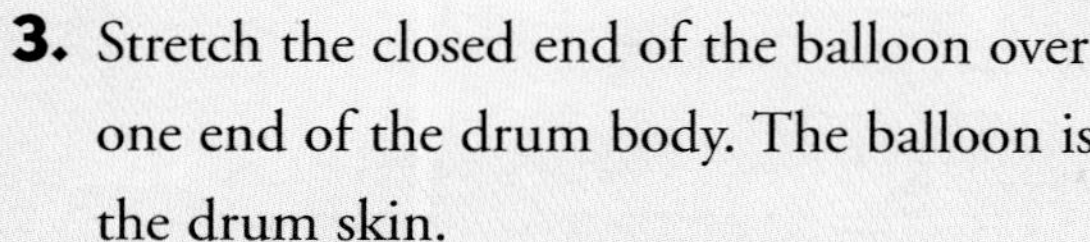

3. Stretch the closed end of the balloon over one end of the drum body. The balloon is the drum skin.

4. Hold the balloon in place with a heavy rubber band and smooth out all the wrinkles to make the skin tight.

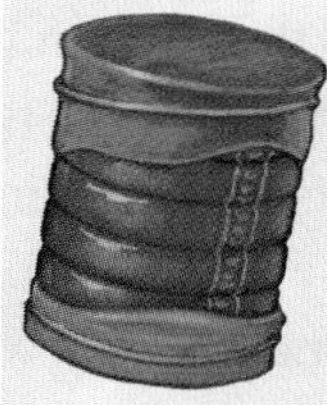

5. Repeat steps 2 to 4 on the other end of the drum body.

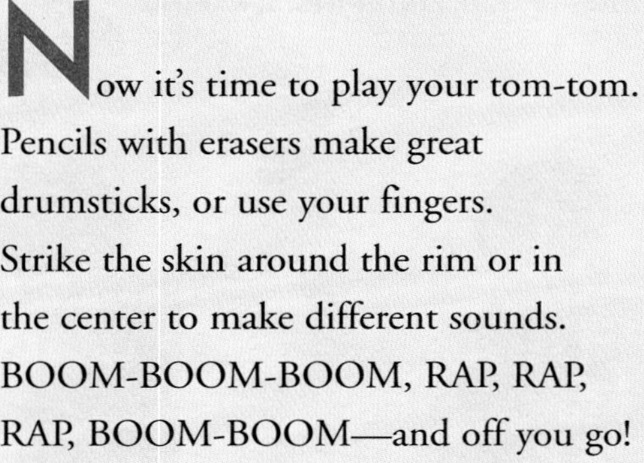

Now it's time to play your tom-tom. Pencils with erasers make great drumsticks, or use your fingers. Strike the skin around the rim or in the center to make different sounds. BOOM-BOOM-BOOM, RAP, RAP, RAP, BOOM-BOOM—and off you go!

95

Responding to the Selection

Ask children why they think it is important to read through a list of materials *and* all the directions before beginning to make something. Talk about how the pictures in the how-to article would help them if they were to make their own balloon tom-toms.

MULTICULTURAL CONNECTION

Ask children what else besides music they think drums might be used for. If necessary, explain that drums can also be used for communication. In northern Nigeria, for example, people use drums to send messages. These talking drums can be heard up to 18 miles away.

MUSIC CONNECTION

TAMBOURINES A tambourine is a simple drum. Provide one or more tambourines. Ask children how a tambourine is like and unlike a balloon tom-tom. Have volunteers hold a tambourine in one hand and tap the skin with their other hands, or find their own ways to make music with the tambourine. Children might play tambourines and balloon tom-toms as you play a tape of rhythmic music.

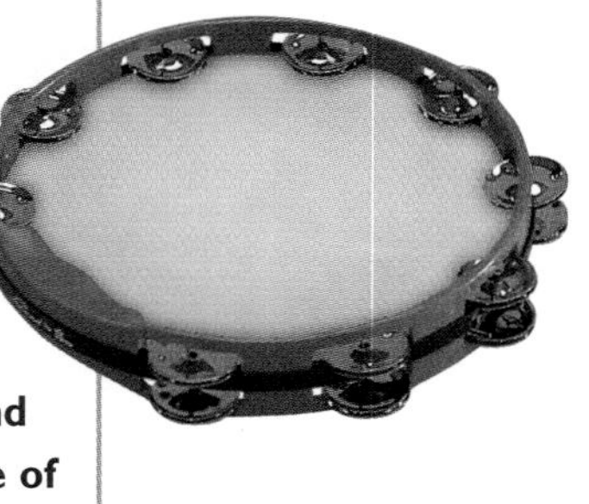

Integrating Language Arts

TIPS FOR CLASSROOM MANAGEMENT

IF children enjoy crafts and music, **THEN** they should complete the Kinesthetic activity.

IF children enjoy performing, **THEN** they should complete the Oral Language activity.

KINESTHETIC

Making Music

MATERIALS
- small, flat boxes of different sizes
- rubber bands of different sizes
- dry rice and beans
- containers such as small boxes, film containers, plastic food-storage containers, and empty soda cans

COOPERATIVE LEARNING Place the materials on a large table. Have pairs of children create musical instruments. For example, children can wrap rubber bands of different sizes around an open box to make a stringed instrument or put dry rice, beans, or paper clips in containers to make shakers. Then have children work in small groups to create rhythms with their instruments. **LISTENING/SPEAKING**

ORAL LANGUAGE

Hear the Beat

Have partners choose a favorite poem or song. One child reads the poem aloud or sings the song as the other child accompanies by beating out the rhythm on a balloon tom-tom or other instrument. Suggest that partners switch roles to perform another song or poem. Invite children to present their poems and songs, if they wish. Encourage aspiring musicians to think of different drum sounds or other musical sounds to add. **LISTENING/SPEAKING**

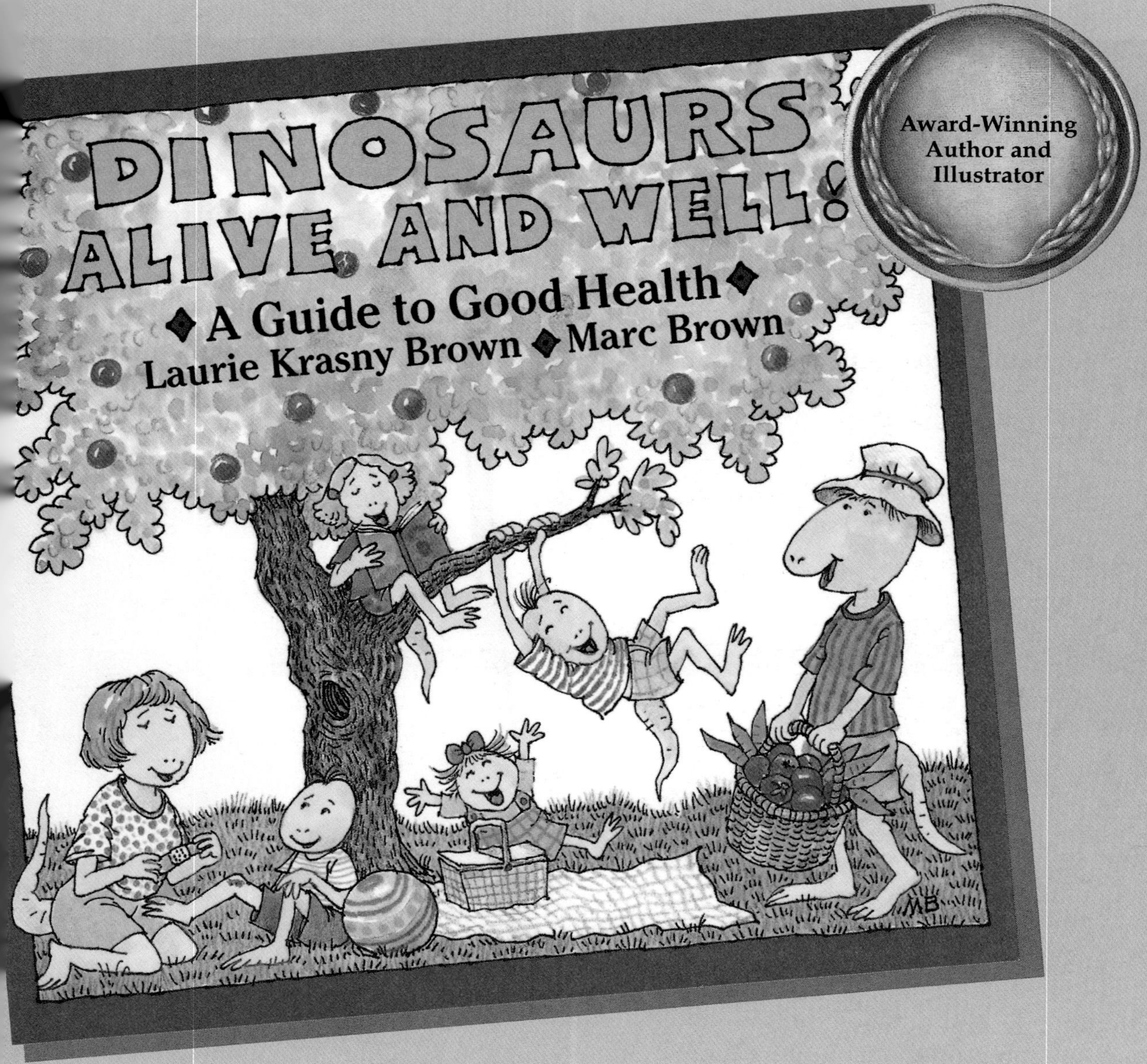

Award-Winning Author and Illustrator

Laurie Krasny Brown
Marc Brown

ABOUT THE AUTHOR AND THE ILLUSTRATOR

LAURIE KRASNY BROWN and **MARC BROWN** have collaborated on many of the books in the popular Dinosaurs series. One book in particular, *Dinosaurs Divorce: A Guide for Changing Families,* was cited as a *New York Times* Notable Book in 1986.

For more information about the author and the illustrator, see pages T200–T201.

THEME: LEARNING ABOUT ONESELF

Celebrate Me!

In "Dinosaurs Alive and Well!" children are encouraged to feel good about themselves and to take an active role in their own physical and emotional well-being . . . an important part of understanding—and celebrating—themselves!

SELECTION SUMMARY

Genre: Narrative Nonfiction

A lovable group of dinosaurs takes readers on an adventure that will help them establish good health habits that will last a lifetime. The story begins with this positive, healthy thought: "There's just one you. That makes you special." From there, the simple text, highlighted by colorful and lively illustrations, offers advice on exercise, relationships with friends and family, and ways of dealing with feelings.

SUGGESTED LESSON PLANNER

▶ ***Dinosaurs Alive and Well!***

	DAY 1	DAY 2
PART 1 Reading, Listening, Speaking, Viewing **Key Words** special many proud believe practice yourself remember wrong	**BUILD BACKGROUND** T178 **VOCABULARY STRATEGIES** T178–T179 *Chart/Transparency 7* *Practice Book* pp. 35–36 **READING THE SELECTION** T180–T201 Options for Reading T180–T181 *Response Card 6* *Literature Cassette 1* **REVIEW PREDICTIONS/PURPOSE** T198 **APPRECIATING THE LITERATURE** T198 NOTE: Children may read the selection on Day 2.	**SUMMARIZE AND RETELL THE SELECTION** T199 *Practice Book* p. 37 ◆ **RESPONSE CORNER ACTIVITIES** T202 **CHECKING COMPREHENSION** T203 *End-of-Selection Test* 
PART 2 Writer's Workshop	**HOW-TO SENTENCES** Thinking as Writers T208 *Chart/Transparency 8*	Prewriting T208
Grammar	✓ **WORD ORDER** Teach the Concept T210 Daily Language Practice (1–2) R21	Daily Language Practice (3–4) R21 Practice Activity T211
Spelling	**WORDS WITH SHORT *i*** *pin sit if fix is* *will hill six win this* Pretest/Self-Check T212 *Integrated Spelling Teacher's Edition* pp. T39, T271	Open and Closed Sorts T212 *Integrated Spelling* p. 22 *Integrated Spelling Teacher's Edition* p. T40
PART 3 Phonics	**CONSONANT DIGRAPH: /r/*wr*** Phonics-Vocabulary Connection T179	**CONSONANT DIGRAPHS: /r/*wr*; /n/*kn, gn*** (Introduce) T214 *Big Book of Rhymes* pp. 8–9 *Phonics Practice Book* pp. 237–239
Skills and Strategies	◆ **INTEGRATED CURRICULUM** *My World* **Social Studies** T218 **Art** T218 **Social Studies** T219 **Science** T219 *Imagination Express, Destination: Ocean; Destination: Rain Forest*	**COMPREHENSION SKILL** T216–T217 ✓ Main Idea and Details (Introduce) *Practice Book* p. 42
	Use the Students Acquiring English notes on pages T191, T192, and T194 to help **ESL readers.**	During the skills lessons, refer to the Challenge notes on pages T215 and T217 for **above-level readers.**

NOTE: An alternative lesson plan for **below-level readers** appears on *Intervention Strategies Manual* pp. 20–25. A lesson for **students acquiring English** appears on *Sheltered English/ESL Manual* pp. 14–17.

DAY 3	DAY 4	DAY 5
◆ **IDEA BANK ACTIVITIES** Listening and Speaking T206 Real-Life Reading: Reading Food Labels T206 Oral Language T207 Kinesthetic T207 *Writer's Magazine* pp. 12–15 School–Home Connection 4 R51	**VOCABULARY WORKSHOP** T213 Reviewing Key Words Story Strips R55 Antonyms *Practice Book* p. 40 *Take-Home/Keep-at-Home Book: The Best Machine* **READING TRADE BOOKS** T220–T221  Take-Home Book	**READING TRADE BOOKS** T215, T217, T219, T220–T221  Instant Reader™ Instant Reader™
Drafting T208 *Language Handbook* pp. 28–29 *The Amazing Writing Machine*	Responding and Revising T209	Proofreading and Publishing T209 *Kid Pix*
Daily Language Practice (5–6) R21 Practice Activity T211 *Language Handbook* pp. 46–47	Daily Language Practice (7–8) R21 Practice Activity T211 *Grammar Practice Book* pp. 23–24	Daily Language Practice (9–12) R21 *Practice Book* p. 38
Discuss the Generalization T212 *Integrated Spelling* p. 23 *Integrated Spelling Teacher's Edition* p. T41	Apply to Writing T212 *Integrated Spelling* pp. 24–25 *Integrated Spelling Teacher's Edition* pp. T42–T43	Posttest T212 *Practice Book* p. 39 *Integrated Spelling Teacher's Edition* p. T44
CONSONANT DIGRAPHS: /r/*wr*; /n/*kn, gn* T214 *Phonics Practice Reader 14: Knight Knocking-Knees*	**CONSONANT DIGRAPHS: /r/*wr*; /n/*kn, gn*** T215 *Practice Book* p. 41	**CONSONANT DIGRAPHS: /r/*wr*; /n/*kn, gn*** T215 *Phonics Activity Book* p. 10
GRAMMAR MINILESSON T197 ✓ Telling Part of a Sentence; Joining Telling Parts (Review) *Language Handbook* pp. 42–45 **PHONICS AND DECODING MINILESSON** T191 ✓ R-Controlled Vowel: /är/*ar* (Review) *Practice Book* p. 44 *Phonics Game Board Pattern Book* p. 43	**PHONICS AND DECODING MINILESSON** T185 Initial Clusters with *l* (Maintain) *Phonics Activity Book* p. 11 *Phonics Practice Reader 3: How to Spot a Swog* *Phonics Practice Book* pp. 191–192 *Practice Book* p. 43	**PHONICS AND DECODING MINILESSON** T195 Short Vowel: /i/*i* (Maintain) *Phonics Activity Book* p. 12 *Phonics Practice Reader 4: Jim and Jill* *Phonics Practice Book* pp. 45–49 *Practice Book* p. 45 Theme Project Checkpoint 4 T222

The Semantic Cues lesson on page T205 can be used to help **below-level readers** read strategically.

Use the Students Acquiring English note on page T213 to help **ESL readers** complete the Vocabulary Workshop.

To help children build fluency, use the *Instant Readers™ Get Ready to Race* and *Grandma J* on pages T204–T205.

✓ = Tested Skill
◆ = Optional activities that may be used to adjust pacing throughout the lesson
Titles in *italics* are optional materials.

Reading and Responding

BUILDING BACKGROUND AND CONCEPTS

PRIOR KNOWLEDGE

Discuss staying healthy. On a large sheet of butcher paper, begin a K-W-L chart as follows:

• STAYING HEALTHY AND HAPPY •

K—What I Know	W—What I Want to Know	L—What I Learned
Exercise makes me strong.		
It's fun to learn new things.		
I like to feel healthy and happy.		

Brainstorm with children what they already know about staying healthy and happy, including good eating and exercise habits. Record responses in the first column of the chart. Display the chart for future reference.

VOCABULARY STRATEGIES

KEY WORDS DEFINED

special very important
believe to trust
remember to keep in your memory
many a great number of
practice to do something many times
wrong not right
proud feeling good about yourself
yourself your own person or self

SUPPORT WORDS

Display the words *different, energy, exercise, healthy,* and *muscles.* Discuss their meanings and have them used in sentences.

INTEGRATED SPELLING

SPELLING PRETEST: page T212
SPELLING GENERALIZATION: Words with Short *i*

Intervention Strategies

For children who may have difficulty reading "Dinosaurs Alive and Well!" support is available in *Intervention Strategies Manual,* pages 20–25, and on pages T196 and T204–T205 in this lesson.

STUDENTS ACQUIRING ENGLISH

See *Sheltered English/ESL Manual* pages 14–17.

Q: How can children benefit from completing a K-W-L chart?

A: The K-W-L model is a classroom-tested strategy that helps children participate actively when they read nonfiction selections. Children first focus on what they already know, then determine what they want to know. After they have completed the selection, they record what they learned. Understanding and participating in the K-W-L model influences the way children read and makes them more aware of reading as a thinking, interactive process.

CUEING SYSTEMS

Have children read new vocabulary. Display Chart/Transparency 7, or write the words and sentences on the board. Have children read words they might know.

Cover the word *special.* Ask children to read the first two sentences and suggest a word that would make sense in the first sentence. As suggestions are made, uncover the letters *sp* and have children identify the sound. Ask:

Does the word make sense in the sentence?
Does the word begin with *sp*?

Have children read the rest of the story, using sounds for letters and the rest of the words in the sentence to help them figure out words they don't know.

CHART/TRANSPARENCY 7

special	**believe**	**remember**	**many**
practice	**wrong**	**proud**	**yourself**

Today was a very special day. I can't believe I won the spelling contest! We had to remember how to spell so many words. All that practice really helped.

My father said, "You didn't spell one word wrong. You should be proud of yourself!"

HANDS-ON ACTIVITY

Identify words and their definitions. Ask children to fold paper into eight sections. Have them copy a Key Word in each section. Have children follow these directions:

- Draw a green circle around the word that is the opposite of *right.* *(wrong)*
- Write *me* in blue next to the word that means "very important." *(special)*
- Draw a red star under the word that begins like *yarn.* *(yourself)*
- Draw two blue squares above the word that ends like *twelve.* *(believe)*
- Draw a yellow sun around the word that rhymes with *crowd.* *(proud)*
- Draw a brown line under the word that ends like *brother.* *(remember)*
- Draw a purple triangle around the word that means "a large number of." *(many)*
- Draw a red house around the word that tells how you get good at something. *(practice)*

PRACTICE BOOK, pages 35–36

PHONICS-VOCABULARY CONNECTION

WORD PLAY

Invite children to use letter cards and Word Builders to make words that begin with *wr.* Write the following word frames on the board: *__eck, __ong, __ap, __ench, __ist, __ite, __inkle.* Have children make the word endings in their Word Builder one at a time, and add the letters *wr* to the beginning of each word. Read the words with children, and ask them what they notice. Explain that when a word begins with *wr*, the *r* is heard and the *w* is silent.

The concept of /r/*wr* is further developed on pages T214–T215.

Strategic Reading

STRATEGY FOCUS:
SELF-QUESTIONING

Review with children some of the things good readers do. Encourage children to suggest new ideas and add them to the classroom chart.

What Good Readers Do
Think about the order in which things happen
Guess what might happen next
Ask themselves questions and read to find the answers

Share with children the comprehension strategy that is the focus of this selection.

MODEL **I ask myself questions before I read, while I read, and after I have finished reading a story. I ask myself questions about why characters act the way they do. I also ask myself questions about information I don't understand or about things that might happen later in a story. Asking myself questions helps me pay attention to what I've read and to learn from it.**

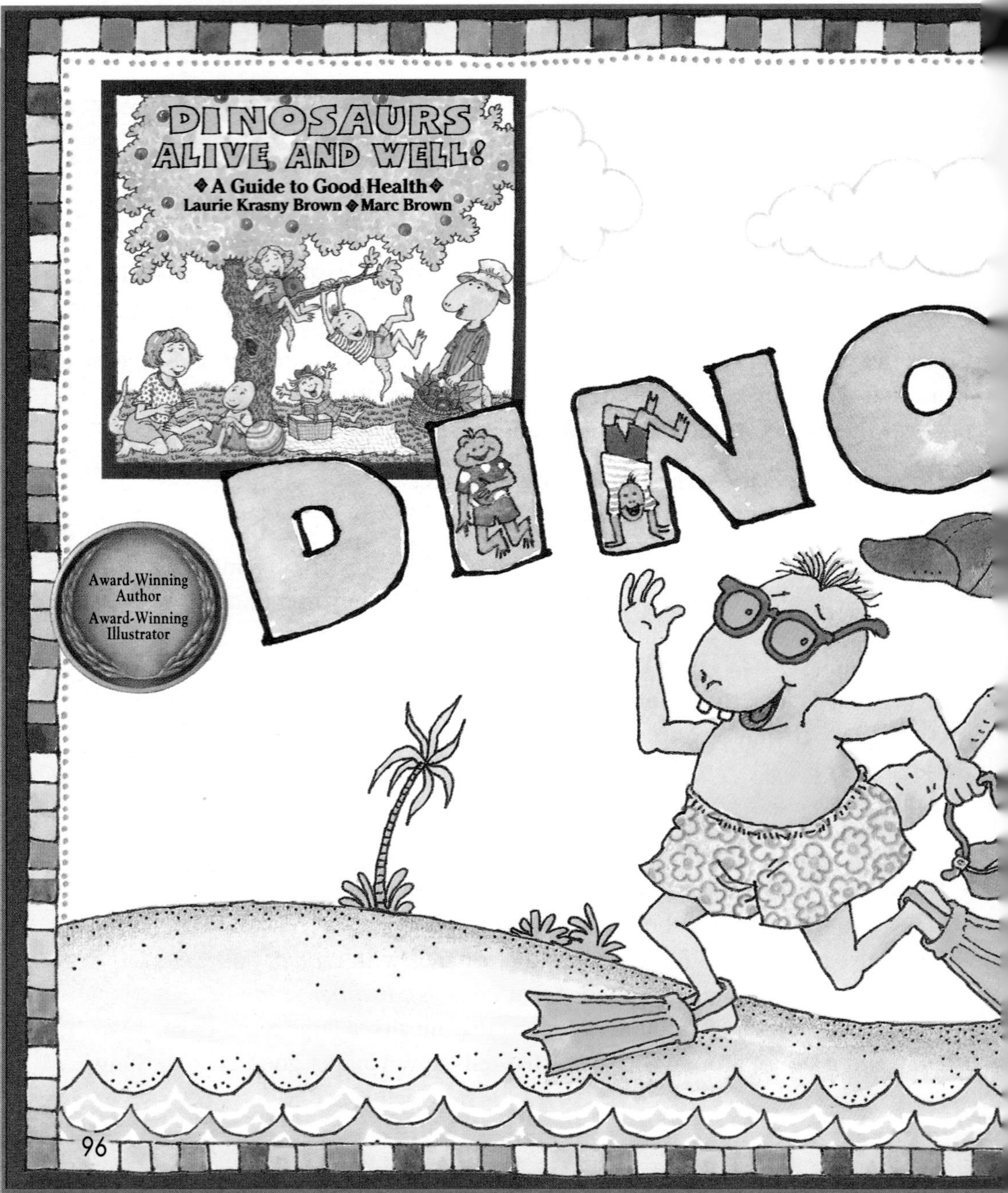

DINOSAURS ALIVE AND WELL!
A Guide to Good Health
Laurie Krasny Brown ◆ Marc Brown

Award-Winning Author
Award-Winning Illustrator

DINO

96

SMALL GROUP

STRATEGIC READING

Choose some or all of the suggestions and questions under Strategic Reading, pages T180–T199, to guide a literature discussion and model the STRATEGY FOCUS of Self-Questioning.

PARTNER READING

Have partners use Reader Response Card 6 (Written Conversation), page R24. They can read each section of the story, write a question about it, exchange papers, and answer one another's questions. Afterward have children use their questions to discuss the story.

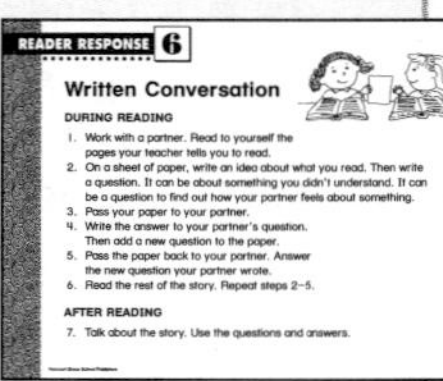

Response Card 6

PREVIEWING/SETTING PURPOSES

Have children read the title on pages 96 and 97 and talk about what they see. Then display the K-W-L chart you began in Building Background and Concepts. Direct children's attention to the second column of the chart, *What I Want to Know.* Encourage them to look at the pictures and preview the selection. Ask children what they think they will be reading about and what they would like to learn about staying healthy. Then help children set purposes for reading by filling in the second column of the K-W-L chart.

• STAYING HEALTHY AND HAPPY •

K—What I Know	W—What I Want to Know	L—What I Learned
Exercise makes me strong.	What are some fun exercises?	
It's fun to learn new things.	How can I exercise my mind?	
I like to feel healthy and happy.	What can I do to help myself feel happy?	

WHOLE CLASS

READ ALOUD

Work with children to read "Dinosaurs Alive and Well!" aloud. You may want to read the explanatory paragraphs and have children read the information in the speech balloons.

INDEPENDENT READING

Have children read "Dinosaurs Alive and Well!" silently. As they read, have them complete their K-W-L charts by answering their "What I Want to Know" questions and adding any new things they learn. When all children are finished, encourage them to share their responses in a discussion.

Strategic Reading

APPLYING A STRATEGY

PAGES 98–99 Have children look at the illustrations on pages 98 and 99 and talk about how each one relates to the main idea stated in the section title *Take Care of Yourself.* Encourage children to take time throughout the story to examine how the art highlights and explains the text. **RELATING PICTURES TO TEXT**

Take Care of Yourself

There's just one you.
That makes you special.
There's a lot you can do to take care of yourself and become the healthiest, happiest person you can be!

98

LISTENING CENTER

Children may benefit from listening to "Dinosaurs Alive and Well!" Record the story on an audiocassette. Put it in the Listening Center for children to enjoy as they follow along in their books.

(See Acknowledgments on pages R235–R236.)

PHONICS IN ACTION

Have children find the words *healthiest* and *happiest* on page 98. Ask children what these two words have in common (-est ending) and to which words the endings were added. (*healthy, happy*) Ask children to name other words they know like *healthiest* and *happiest*. (*funniest, fluffiest, silliest*)

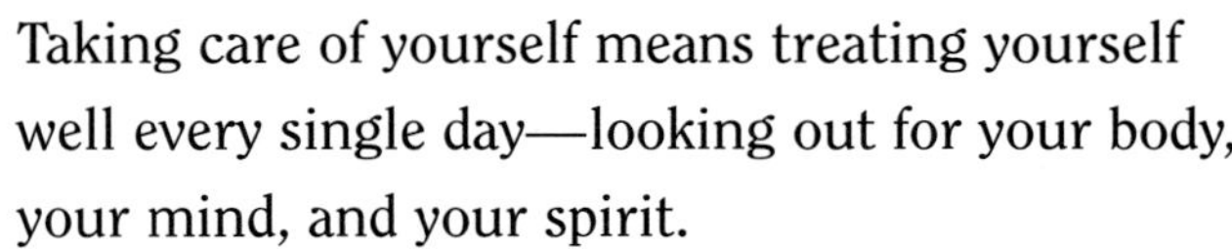

Taking care of yourself means treating yourself well every single day—looking out for your body, your mind, and your spirit.

99

Student Self-Assessment ✓

USING READING STRATEGIES

When children are reading in small groups, provide a time for them to talk about the good reading strategies they use and observe one another using. You may want to include some of their ideas on the What Good Readers Do chart.

CONVENTIONS OF PRINT

DASH Direct children's attention to the dash on page 99. Explain that sometimes an author uses a dash to set off an important part of a sentence. Explain that the writer may have wanted readers to pay special attention to the three ways people can take care of themselves.

ILLUSTRATOR'S CRAFT

Marc Brown often hides the names of his three children, Eliza, Tolon, and Tucker, and his wife, Laurie, in his illustrations. Children may enjoy searching for the names in "Dinosaurs Alive and Well!" as well as other stories by Marc Brown. Hint: See if children can find the names of Brown's sons on page 101. (on the boats)

Strategic Reading

MODELING A STRATEGY

PAGES 100–102 Have children read the title of this section, look through the pictures, and tell what they think this section is about. After children read, ask whether there was anything they didn't understand or anything they wonder about. Model self-questioning: *In the part about the heartbeat, I read that you can feel your pulse. I wonder how to do that. Then, as I read the part about why exercise is important, I asked myself:*

1. Do I exercise enough?
2. What kinds of exercises can I do?

SELF-QUESTIONING

Exercise Your Body

Exercising every day helps your body stay healthy. When you exercise, your body works harder, your heartbeat is stronger, and you can feel your pulse go faster. Even though it takes energy to exercise, getting exercise helps you feel *more* energetic.

100

HEALTH WORDS

BODY WORDS Write these words from pages 100–101 on chart paper: *heartbeat, pulse, energy, body, muscles.* Discuss how these words are related. Help children see that these words tell about the body. Challenge children to think of other "health words" to add to the list.

PHONICS IN ACTION

Have children find the words *harder, stronger, faster,* and *longer* on pages 100 and 101. Ask how these words are similar. Point out that they all have the *-er* ending and are used to compare two objects.

STRONGER

FASTER

Some exercises make you stronger. Muscles that get no exercise become weak and flabby. They may even shrink in size.

Other exercises help your body stay flexible.

And, the more you exercise, the longer you'll be able to play without getting tired.

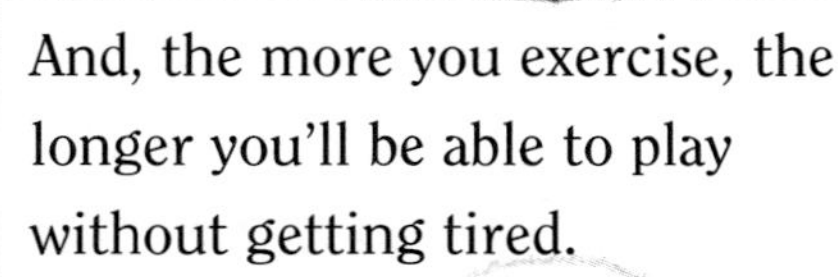

101

MINILESSON

MAINTAIN: PHONICS AND DECODING

Initial Clusters with *l*

INFORMAL ASSESSMENT

When children read, notice whether they can decode words that have initial consonant clusters with *l*.

TEACH/MODEL

Write these words from page 101 on the board: *play, flexible, flabby.* Ask children to read the words aloud and tell how the words are alike. If necessary, underline the *pl* and *fl* in each word. Help children see that each word begins with a consonant followed by the letter *l*. Remind children that when a word begins with a consonant and *l*, the sounds of both letters can be heard blended together.

PRACTICE/APPLY

Have children listen as you say each of the following words: *cloud, slice, pouch, flag, fort, blue, clown, comet, clap, plum, clever, fellow, flake, place, park,* and *blink.* Tell children to raise their hand if the word you say begins with a consonant followed by the letter *l*.

PHONICS ACTIVITY BOOK, page 11

PHONICS PRACTICE READER 3

PHONICS PRACTICE BOOK, pages 191–192

AUTHOR'S CRAFT

Draw children's attention to the right-hand frame at the top of page 101. Ask how these words are different from other words on the page. If necessary, point out that the words are in a speech balloon and are printed in a different type size. Ask how else the author and illustrator could have shown that someone is speaking. (use quotation marks)

Dinosaurs Alive and Well! Name ______

Read each question. Write the word that makes sense and makes the answer YES.

blue	glue	flower	slow	clock	flea	play

1. Is the sky _blue_? YES!
2. Does a _clock_ tick? YES!
3. Is a snail _slow_? YES!
4. Does a _flea_ bite? YES!
5. Can a kitten _play_? YES!
6. Does _glue_ stick? YES!
7. Does a _flower_ grow? YES!

OUT OF THE BLUE Practice Book INITIAL CLUSTERS WITH l 43

PRACTICE BOOK, page 43

Strategic Reading

MODELING A STRATEGY

PAGES 103–105 After children have read the section title, ask them to look through the pictures and formulate questions about what they think this part is about. For example, children may be confused by how they could exercise their minds. If necessary, model how you would use the self-questioning strategy. **Think aloud:** *I've always heard the word* exercise *used to mean exercising your body, doing activities like walking, playing, swimming, and skating. I wonder how a person could exercise his or her mind. I'll have to read to find out. Oh, I see. Exercising your mind means thinking and learning.*

Remind children to ask themselves questions as they read, and then read on to see how many they can answer.

SELF-QUESTIONING

There are many different games and sports. The only way to find out which ones you like is to try them!

Some sports take lots of practice. Try to remember: you don't have to be perfect at a sport to have fun.

Everyone's body is different. Don't worry about what yours can't do— be proud of what you *can* do!

102

SCIENCE

MUSCLES There are more than 650 muscles in the human body. These muscles are responsible for all of the body's movements. Every movement, whether it is the lifting of an arm or the beating of the heart, begins with the contraction of a muscle. Even a seemingly simple task, such as taking one step, involves about 200 muscles!

CROSS-CULTURAL VIEWPOINT

Point out that people in all times and places have engaged in games and sports, both for pleasure and for exercise. Invite children to share what they know about games and sports enjoyed by people in other countries.

Exercise Your Mind

Your body isn't all that needs exercise—so does your mind. Every time you pretend, make decisions, figure something out, or learn something new, you're exercising your mind. It doesn't happen only in school!

103

PHONICS IN ACTION

Have children complete this sentence, using what they read on page 102: "Some sports take lots of ______." If necessary, have children look back at the page to find the word. *(practice)* Ask what two letters stand for the beginning sound in *practice*. *(pr)* Challenge children to find two other words on pages 102 and 103 that begin like *practice*. *(proud, pretend)*

WRITING

DESCRIPTIVE WRITING

Invite children to think about ways they have exercised their minds recently. Have them write sentences describing what they did and why it was "exercise."

Critical Thinking Questions

1. Why do you think the author says that it's good to think for yourself? (Possible response: It's good to think for yourself because your ideas are unique and show what kind of person you are. Besides, your friends are not always right!) CRITICAL: DRAWING CONCLUSIONS

2. Why do you think your mind needs exercise? (Possible response: Exercising your mind will make you smarter. If you don't exercise your mind, you won't learn how to do new things and your life won't be as interesting.) CRITICAL: DRAWING CONCLUSIONS

104

FROM THE ILLUSTRATOR

Share this interesting quote from Marc Brown about the important collaboration between author and illustrator:

"When Laurie and I do a book together, we work in our separate studios—she on the text, I on the pictures. But we consult often, contributing ideas to every aspect of the book . . . changes in the text usually require changes in the illustrations, so it's important for us to be in touch every step of the way."

105

Informal Assessment ✓

USING CUEING SYSTEMS

During a rereading of the selection, observe how well children apply cueing systems to develop meanings.

- ☑ Do children read ahead to see what word might make sense in the context of the sentence?
- ☑ Do children reread and then self-correct?
- ☑ Do children make logical predictions and then verify them?

PHONICS IN ACTION

Ask children to find the words *good* and *too* on page 104 and to say the words aloud. Point out that oo can stand for two sounds, as in *good* and *too*.

IDEA BANK

Have children reread the last sentence on page 105: *Trying different activities helps you discover your own special talents.* Allow time for children to tell about their own talents and things they would like to learn. Be sure to join in, sharing information about your own talents and interests. Help children make a bulletin board highlighting everyone's talents.

Strategic Reading

MODELING A STRATEGY

PAGES 106–109 First, have children read the section title and preview the pictures in this part. Ask them what they think this part is about. After children read pages 106-109, have them use the sequence of illustrations for each emotion—mad, sad, scared, and glad—to tell the stories that are told only in the pictures.

Model one of the stories, if necessary: *The two characters are mad because they both want the same building block. The characters have a fight and then don't play together—one hammers a nail and the other paints. Then they decide to use the building block to build a tunnel they can both play with. They're not mad anymore.*

RELATING PICTURES TO TEXT

Deal with Your Feelings

Feelings aren't right or wrong—they just are. Sometimes we all feel . . .

mad

sad

scared

glad

106

HEALTH WORDS

FEELINGS WORDS Have children locate the feelings words on pages 106–107, and list them on chart paper. Brainstorm more feelings words with children, and add them to the list.

Feelings Words

mad	nervous
sad	proud
scared	angry
glad	cheerful
happy	

Letting out your feelings is healthier than keeping them to yourself.

107

Tested Skill

MINILESSON

REVIEW: PHONICS AND DECODING

R-Controlled Vowel: /är/*ar*

INFORMAL ASSESSMENT

When children read, notice whether they can decode words with the /är/ sound spelled *ar.*

TEACH/MODEL

Write on the board and have children complete this sentence from page 107: *"This test will be so ______."* Write *hard* on the board and underline *ar.* Remind children that when the letters *ar* are together in a word, the word will sometimes have the /är/ sound as in *hard.* Then have children suggest other words that contain the vowel sound in *hard.*

PRACTICE/APPLY

Have children write these word frames at the top of a sheet of paper.

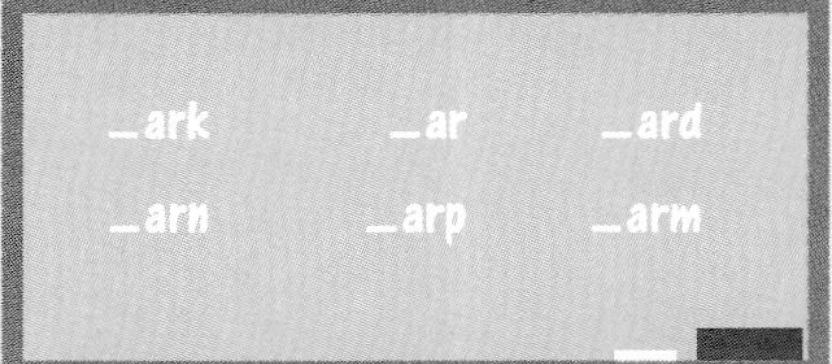

Encourage children to use consonant substitutions to make and list words. Suggest that children try consonant clusters, such as *sh, sp, st,* and *ch,* as well as single consonants.

For further reinforcement of /är/*ar,* children can play Star Bingo on *Phonics Game Board Pattern Book,* page 43.

MEETING INDIVIDUAL NEEDS

STUDENTS ACQUIRING ENGLISH **Children may be confused by two figurative phrases on page 107: *letting out your feelings* and *don't sit and stew.* Discuss with children what these sayings mean so that they will better understand the story.**

Name

Dinosaurs Alive and Well!

SCIENCE

Read each clue. Write the word that makes sense and has the same vowel sound as *star.*

school far
yard carton
park farm
some start
part box

1. I come from a dairy farm.
2. I start inside a cow.
3. Sometimes I travel far to a store.
4. Part of me is cream.
5. You can buy me in a carton.
6. You can drink me in your yard.
7. You might drink me in a park.

What am I? I am milk.

44 R-CONTROLLED VOWEL: /är/ar OUT OF THE BLUE Practice Book

PRACTICE BOOK, page 44

Cooperative Reading

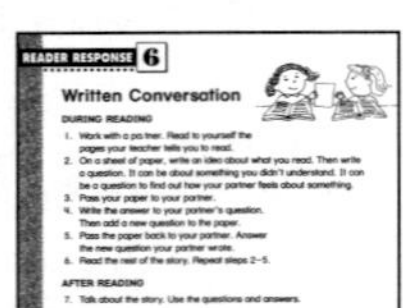

Response Card 6

As children use **Reader Response Card 6** (Written Conversation) while they read, you may wish to ask a question or two as a way of encouraging discussion and assessing the group's progress. Here are some ideas:

1. **What things do you like about the way the author has written the story? What don't you like?**
2. **How have the pictures helped you to understand the story?**
3. **What new things have you learned so far from the story?**
4. **What questions do you still have about what you're reading?**

Solving problems isn't always easy. But most problems can be solved if you look them right in the eye. And you'll usually feel better in the end.

mad

Try to think up fair ways to settle arguments.

108

STUDENTS ACQUIRING ENGLISH **Direct children's attention to this sentence:** ***But most problems can be solved if you look them right in the eye.*** **Explain that** ***right in the eye*** **means that when you have a problem, you can't just ignore it and hope that it will go away. You must face it and try to solve it.**

Student Self-Assessment

FIX-UP STRATEGY: REREADING

To help children recognize that they are using reading strategies, encourage them to keep a list of any parts of the story that they had to reread in order to understand words or ideas. Point out that children are using the rereading strategy, which good readers use to better understand what they are reading.

EXPANDING VOCABULARY

Have children find the word *courage* on page 109. Ask a volunteer to read the sentence aloud. Discuss what *courage* means ("the ability to face something unafraid"). If a dictionary is available, model how you would find the word and then read the definition aloud. Invite children to share times when they or someone they know showed courage.

REAL-LIFE CONNECTION

After children read *Deal with Your Feelings* (pages 106–109), encourage them to share times when they have felt mad, sad, scared, or glad, and to describe how they dealt with their feelings.

Strategic Reading

APPLYING A STRATEGY

PAGES 110–114 After children read the brief section *Take It Easy*, have them summarize what they have learned so far in the selection about taking care of your body and your mind.

Then point out the section title *Be a Friend, Have a Friend* and talk about what children might learn. Ask them to share any questions they have about friendship before they begin reading. They may want to add the questions to their K-W-L charts. Then have children read the pages and see how many questions are answered. Remind them to keep wondering and asking themselves questions as they read. **SELF-QUESTIONING**

STUDENTS ACQUIRING ENGLISH **Point out the figurative phrase *friends stick together.* Ask what children think the phrase means. If necessary, help them see that the phrase means that friends stay together and help each other when good—and even bad—things happen.**

Be a Friend, Have a Friend

There's nothing like a good friend to make you feel happy.

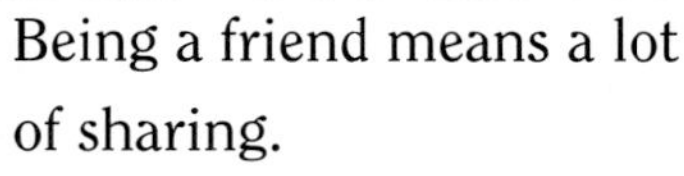

Being a friend means a lot of sharing.

Friends stick together through good and bad.

111

MINILESSON

MAINTAIN: PHONICS AND DECODING

Short Vowel: /i/*i*

INFORMAL ASSESSMENT
Observe whether children can decode words with short *i*.

TEACH/MODEL
Write these words from pages 110 and 111 on the board: *it, stick.* Have children read the words aloud and tell what vowel sound they have. Underline the letter *i*, and remind children that the letter *i* stands for the short *i* sound in *it* and *stick*.

PRACTICE/APPLY
Distribute copies of the Grid, page R205, and have children write nine short *i* words from the list above in random order in the boxes. To play "Three-in-a-Row Bingo," distribute nine game markers to each player. Read the short *i* words from the list in random order as children look for each word and cover its space with a marker.

PHONICS ACTIVITY BOOK, page 12

PHONICS PRACTICE READER 4

PHONICS PRACTICE BOOK, pages 45–49

MUSIC CONNECTION

LISTENING TO MUSIC **Many people find listening to music to be relaxing after a stressful day. Play some relaxing music for children, and have them close their eyes and listen for a while. Then discuss whether the music helped children feel calm and relaxed.**

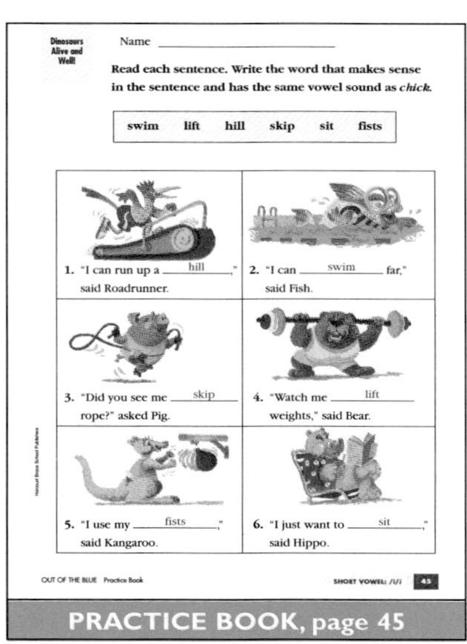

Dinosaurs Alive and Well!

Name ____________

Read each sentence. Write the word that makes sense in the sentence and has the same vowel sound as *chick*.

swim lift hill skip sit fists

1. "I can run up a hill." said Roadrunner.
2. "I can swim far," said Fish.
3. "Did you see me skip rope?" asked Pig.
4. "Watch me lift weights," said Bear.
5. "I use my fists," said Kangaroo.
6. "I just want to sit," said Hippo.

Harcourt Brace School Publishers

OUT OF THE BLUE Practice Book SHORT VOWEL: /i/i 45

PRACTICE BOOK, page 45

Critical Thinking Questions

1. **What makes you a good friend?** (Possible response: I am helpful, fun, loyal, and a good listener.) METACOGNITIVE: DETERMINING CHARACTER TRAITS
2. **What does *Be a Friend, Have a Friend* mean?** (Possible response: It means if you are a friend to others, they will be your friends, too.) CRITICAL: DRAWING CONCLUSIONS

Intervention Strategies

SELF-QUESTIONING Have children repeat this sentence: *When I read, it helps me to check to see whether I can answer any questions I asked myself before I began reading.* Have children tell how using this strategy can help them answer questions they wrote in the K-W-L chart, such as *What are some fun exercises?*

But sometimes even friends want to do something different or to be by themselves. That's okay, too.

113

Tested Skill

MINILESSON

REVIEW: GRAMMAR

Telling Part of a Sentence; Joining Telling Parts

INFORMAL ASSESSMENT

When children write, notice whether their sentences are complete and vary in structure.

TEACH/MODEL

Display the following sentences:

Friends play ball together.
Friends share their toys.
Friends help each other.

Have volunteers circle the naming part of each sentence (*Friends*) and underline the telling part of each sentence. Remind children that when the naming part of two sentences is the same, the telling parts can be combined into one sentence. Have volunteers combine two sentences from the board. Write the new sentence—for example:

Friends play ball together and share toys.

PRACTICE/APPLY

Have children write this sentence frame on a sheet of paper: *Friends* ________.

Identify *friends* as the naming part of the sentence. Have children write telling parts for the sentence and join some of their sentences.

LANGUAGE HANDBOOK
Telling Part of a Sentence, pages 42–43

Joining Telling Parts, pages 44–45

MULTICULTURAL CONNECTION

Many children are faced with having to "fit in." This is a great opportunity to talk about being a good friend—to a new child who joins your classroom or to a person from another country. Remind children to keep what they learned from this selection in mind when making new friends.

Strategic Reading

MODELING A STRATEGY

PAGE 115 After reading, model self-questioning: *How can I be part of the world of living things and be unique at the same time? Oh, I see. Everyone can be special and unique, but together we all make up the world of living things.*
SELF-QUESTIONING

Returning to the Predictions/Purpose

Display the K-W-L chart. Encourage children to compare their questions with what they learned. Then ask them how they might find the answers to questions that were not answered. See "Summarize and Retell" to complete the chart.

Appreciating the Literature

With the whole class or a small group, have an open discussion about the story.

- **Why is it important to be the best person you can be?**

114

IDEA BANK

Generate a bank of *friend* words. Write the word *friend*. Have children suggest as many words as they can that have to do with friends and friendship. When the list is complete, work as a group to categorize the words, choosing a label for each category, such as *Words That Describe Friends* and *Things Friends Do Together*.

SCHOOL↔HOME CONNECTION

Encourage children to keep a chart of things they do at home to stay healthy. The chart might include items such as *wash hands before eating, brush teeth,* and *eat fruits and vegetables*. Suggest that children check off what they do each day.

Now that you know how to take care of yourself, you can help take care of others, too. You're part of the world of living things, each one special and unique . . . just like you!

115

NOTES

Here's a place to list ideas or activities that you would like to use the next time you teach this lesson.

SUMMARIZE AND RETELL

What Did I Learn?

Display the K-W-L chart from earlier in the lesson. Review what children already knew about staying healthy and happy and what they wanted to learn. Then complete the *What I Learned* column. Invite children to each tell one thing they learned. Have children use the chart to summarize the selection. See *Practice Book* page 37.

• STAYING HEALTHY AND HAPPY •		
K—What I Know	W—What I Want to Know	L—What I Learned
Exercise makes me strong.	What are some fun exercises?	I can dance, jump rope, ice-skate, and play soccer.
It's fun to learn new things.	How can I exercise my mind?	I can try new things to find out what I like and what I do well.
I like to feel healthy and happy.	What can I do to help myself feel happy?	I can try to understand my own feelings. I can do things that make myself feel happy, like read a good book and play with my friends.

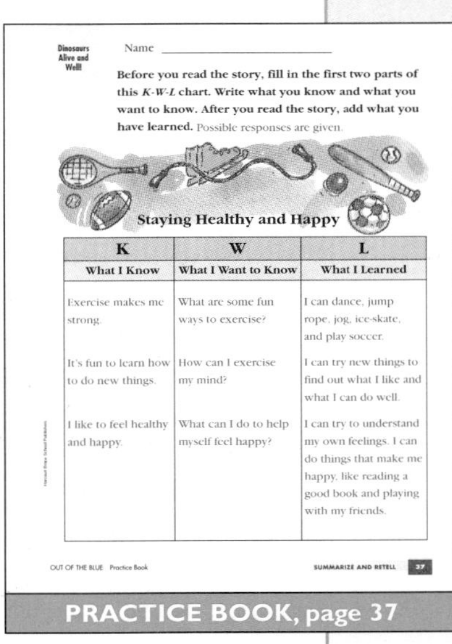

Dinosaurs Alive and Well!

Name ________________

Before you read the story, fill in the first two parts of this *K-W-L* chart. Write what you know and what you want to know. After you read the story, add what you have learned. Possible responses are given.

Staying Healthy and Happy

K	W	L
What I Know	What I Want to Know	What I Learned
Exercise makes me strong.	What are some fun ways to exercise?	I can dance, jump rope, jog, ice-skate, and play soccer.
It's fun to learn how to do new things.	How can I exercise my mind?	I can try new things to find out what I like and what I can do well.
I like to feel healthy and happy.	What can I do to help myself feel happy?	I can try to understand my own feelings. I can do things that make me happy, like reading a good book and playing with my friends.

OUT OF THE BLUE Practice Book SUMMARIZE AND RETELL 37

PRACTICE BOOK, page 37

About the Author

Have children read pages 116 and 117 to learn about Laurie Krasny Brown and Marc Brown. As enrichment, share with children any or all of the following information that you feel will be of interest to them.

Laurie Krasny Brown was on her way to becoming a concert pianist, but changed her mind in college when she decided to study child development, psychology, and education. From that point on, all of her jobs had something to do with education, including investigating what children learn from radio, film, television, and picture books.

According to Brown, "Somehow, I gradually realized that I wanted to be the person writing the books . . . I wanted to do the creating myself. Rather than finding out what children as audience members liked or disliked, I wanted to try making the materials for them to enjoy."

LAURIE KRASNY BROWN

Dear Reader,

I've written a lot of books, but *Dinosaurs Alive and Well!* is extra special to me. You see, I wrote the words and my husband, Marc Brown, drew the pictures.

Whenever I start to write a book, I read all I can on the subject. Next, I make a list of what I need to put in the book. Then, I write and rewrite.

When I am done, I get someone who knows a lot about what's in the book to read it. One expert who looked at this book said that being healthy is more than just taking care of your body. It's taking care of your spirit, too. I really liked that idea.

Your friend,

Laurie Krasny Brown

116

OTHER BOOKS BY LAURIE KRASNY BROWN AND MARC BROWN

Dinosaurs Divorce: A Guide for Changing Families. **Little, Brown, 1988. AVERAGE**

Dinosaurs to the Rescue: A Guide to Protecting Our Planet. **Little, Brown, 1992. AVERAGE**

Dinosaurs Travel: A Guide for Families on the Go. **Little, Brown, 1988. AVERAGE**

Dear Reader,

Many kids know my artwork from my Arthur books, but I like to do information books, too. I have done several books using these dinosaur characters. I chose to draw dinosaurs because they are powerful animals and I want my readers to feel powerful. I am proud of these books because I think they help kids feel good about themselves.

When I was young, I spent most of my time drawing. After my grandmother took me to an art museum, I became interested in painting. My three children are also interested in art. Today, when I'm not working, I like to spend time gardening. My wife, Laurie, and I grow flowers, fruits, and vegetables.

Your friend,

Marc Brown

117

About the Illustrator

Marc Brown has always been fascinated with art. As a child he loved looking at the great works of art—especially those by French artist Marc Chagall. As a matter of fact, it was that very artist who inspired Brown to change his name from Mark (with a *k*) to Marc (with a *c*)!

Marc Brown is an accomplished children's author as well as an illustrator. Many of Brown's story ideas come from things that happen within his own family. Like many good writers, Brown keeps his own variation of a personal journal close at hand: "My ideas have to germinate a long time before they come together in a book."

OTHER BOOKS BY MARC BROWN

***Arthur's Pet Business.* Little, Brown, 1990. AVERAGE**

***Arthur Meets the President.* Little, Brown, 1991. CHALLENGE**

***Arthur's Teacher Trouble.* Little, Brown, 1989. AVERAGE**

RESPONSE CORNER ACTIVITIES

CREATE AN EXERCISE ROUTINE

FUN FITNESS!

PAGE 118 Have small groups of children work together to prepare exercise routines. Provide a variety of rhythmic music, and invite each group to choose a song for its exercise routine. As groups practice and teach their exercise routines, join in the exercise fun! **PHYSICAL EDUCATION/ MUSIC**

PLAN A PUPPET PLAY

PASS ON THE NEWS WITH PUPPETS!

PAGE 119 Read and discuss the directions for making stick puppets. Then have small groups of children work together to plan their play and make their puppets. Have groups include a second health tip in their play, if necessary, so that all children are included. Finally, have each group present its puppet show for all to enjoy. **ART/DRAMA**

VARYING THE ACTIVITY

If space or physical restrictions prevent children from large motor skill exercising, have groups make up hand movements to go along with rhythmic music. Practice the movements until the group can do them in unison. Then invite another class to a performance.

PLAN A PUPPET PLAY

Pass on the News with Puppets!

The tips in "Dinosaurs Alive and Well!" are important to remember. Work with a small group. Choose a tip from the story that you think is important. Make puppets and plan a short play about the tip. Put on your puppet play for another class. Share what you learned about staying healthy.

To make dinosaur stick puppets:

1. Draw and cut out a dinosaur shape.
2. Tape the shape to a stick to make a handle.

What Do You Think?

- What are three things you can do to stay healthy?
- What have you learned about staying healthy that you did not know before?

119

CHECKING COMPREHENSION

What Do You Think?

1. **What are three things you can do to stay healthy?** (Possible response: exercise my body and my mind, discover my own special talents, make friends) **DESCRIPTIVE RESPONSE**
2. **What have you learned about staying healthy that you did not know before?** (Responses will vary, but should reflect information from the selection.) **PERSONAL RESPONSE**

An additional question for extending reading.

3. **Pretend that you have been asked to give a talk to your classmates about staying healthy. What would you tell your classmates?** (In their responses, children may want to cover all three aspects of staying healthy covered in the story: body, mind, and spirit.) **CRITICAL/ CREATIVE ANALYSIS**

MEETING INDIVIDUAL NEEDS

STUDENTS ACQUIRING ENGLISH **Have children work in a group that includes children proficient in English for the Pass on the News with Puppets! activity. They can plan the play along with the group and perform a part with limited lines. Work with children to practice their lines before they perform.**

Informal Assessment ✓

Observe children as they work in groups to plan their puppet shows.

- ☑ Do children focus on a health tip from the story?
- ☑ Do children show why the tip is important?
- ☑ Do all children participate in preparing for or presenting the puppet show?

Intervention Strategies

Instant Readers™

Predictable and Patterned Little Books That Build Fluency

*** BOOK LEVEL: 17–18**

VOCABULARY:
believe, practice, proud, remember, yourself

PHONIC ELEMENTS:
Digraph: /n/*kn*; *R*-controlled vowel: /är/*ar*; Initial clusters with *l*; Short vowel /i/*i*

SUMMARY:
Here's all you need to know about running a race.

Informal Assessment ✓

Are children able to

- ☑ hear and identify words with clusters with *l* or the short *i*?
- ☑ write a sentence about someone special?

Reading a New Book

INTRODUCING *GET READY TO RACE*

If children have ever participated in a running race, ask them how a runner prepares for the event. Draw out that there are certain things runners need to do to get ready for a race. Share the illustrations, asking children how the animals in the book get ready. Help children get ready to read by describing the pictures and asking questions.

READING THE STORY

Have children read aloud the story with a partner.

WORKING WITH WORDS AND LETTERS

Review short *i* by helping children locate story words in which the letter *i* stands for the short vowel. Have children write the words on small pieces of paper. On the reverse side of the papers, have them write their first names or initials. Collect all the papers in an envelope that is marked like the one below. Have children check and count the papers to determine how many short *i* words were found.

WRITING CAPTIONS

Distribute old magazines or catalogs, and have children cut out pictures of people who are engaged in an activity. Have each child glue the picture onto a sheet of paper and write a caption describing the activity or telling what the person is saying.

Additional activities are provided on pages 22–23 of the *Intervention Strategies Manual*.

* **BOOK LEVEL: 16–17**

VOCABULARY:
many, remembered, special, wrong

PHONIC ELEMENTS:
Digraph: /r/*wr*; Initial clusters with *l*; Short vowel: /i/*i*

SUMMARY:
When an accident leaves the neighborhood "grandma" bedridden, four children rally for their neighbor and friend.

Reading a New Book

INTRODUCING *GRANDMA J*

Introduce the main character of the story by sharing the illustrations with children. Ask what kind of person Grandma J appears to be. Explain that Grandma J isn't really the children's grandma, but she does things with them. With children, look at story pages 2–11 and then explain that something happens on pages 12 and 13 to signal a change in the friendship. Discuss the rest of the story pictures and the changes that are observed.

READING THE STORY

Have children read the story independently to gather story details about Grandma J.

WORKING WITH WORDS AND LETTERS

Help children locate the story word *plant*. Say the word slowly, emphasizing each sound. Write the word on the board and underline the letters *pl*. Have children say the sounds the letters stand for. Write the letters, and have children think of other words with the same beginning sounds. Help children list the words. Follow the same procedure for the story word *flower*.

WRITING SENTENCES

Have children write a sentence or two in their personal journals about someone special.

ESL/Title I Reading

Kitten for a Day
by Ezra Jack Keats

TECHNOLOGY

INSTANT READERS™

ELECTRONIC EDITION

***Get Ready To Race* and *Grandma J* are available on CD-ROM. Pre- and post-reading activities are included.**

Working with "Dinosaurs Alive and Well!"

SEMANTIC CUES Read aloud with children the subheadings in the story. Use self-stick notes to number them so that readers can see the organization. Ask individual children who are having difficulty to pick one section they would like to read. First, read along with the child and then have him or her read alone. Offer praise for efforts to use decoding strategies on unknown words.

* Books leveled according to Barbara Peterson's "Profiles of Books for Beginning Readers," on page 9 of the *Instant Readers Teacher's Guide.*

IDEA BANK

TIPS FOR CLASSROOM MANAGEMENT

IF children have not had much experience with small-group discussions, **THEN** you may want to do the Group Talk activity as a whole class to model discussion techniques.

IF children have difficulty finding and counting their pulses in the Creative Connection activity, **THEN** have them work with partners who are able to do it.

LISTENING AND SPEAKING

Group Talk

KEEPING HEALTHY

Write this sentence from the story on a large sheet of chart paper: *There's a lot you can do to take care of yourself and become the healthiest, happiest person you can be!* Have children read the sentence aloud. Organize children into groups of three or four, and have each group talk about the many things they do to keep themselves healthy. Encourage children to name things they do that the story does not mention.

After small-group discussions, gather children to share their ideas and insights. Record children's ideas on the chart paper, and display the chart for all to enjoy. Encourage children to continue adding to the chart. **CHALLENGING THE TEXT**

REAL-LIFE READING

Reading Food Labels

Call attention to the illustrations in the bottom left corner of page 99 and the top left corner of page 101. Ask what the dinosaurs are eating. Invite children to bring to school clean, empty food containers such as cans, boxes, and bags. Point out the information on the packaging, such as the manufacturer's name, the food name, the ingredients, and the nutrition information. Ask volunteers to read various parts of the labels.

Children might enjoy making a pantry using the containers. Have children take turns selecting food for meals or snacks. Encourage them to read the labels as they make their selections. **READING**

WRITER'S MAGAZINE, pages 12–15

ORAL LANGUAGE

Giving and Following Directions

BE A SPORT

Have children work with partners to choose a favorite game or sport that they could teach to their classmates. Have them work together to formulate directions for playing that game or sport. Discuss the important things children should include in their directions: what equipment is needed, how teams are organized, how to play the game, and so on. Some children might benefit from writing the directions before presenting them orally to a small group.

Encourage the rest of the group to listen carefully to the directions as they are given. After partners present their directions, you may wish to allow children to follow the directions and play the game.

Develop with children tips for giving directions similar to the following:

TIPS FOR GIVING DIRECTIONS

- ✔ Think about who is listening to the directions.
- ✔ Think about why you are giving the directions.
- ✔ Tell what to do, one step at a time, in the correct order.

LISTENING

Informal Assessment

When children are giving directions, notice whether the directions are logical and easy to follow.

KINESTHETIC

Creative Connection

CHECK YOUR PULSE

Demonstrate how to take your pulse. Gently press your first two fingers on the side of your neck until you find your pulse. Then have children do the same. Once they find their pulse, have them count and record the number of heartbeats they feel as you time them for twenty seconds.

Then have children do some light exercise such as toe-touches. Have children take their pulses again for twenty seconds after doing the exercises and record the results. Discuss the difference in pulse rates and why they might be different before and after exercising. Remind children that exercise helps the heart pump stronger and keeps them healthy. LISTENING/KINESTHETIC

MY JOURNAL

PERSONAL JOURNAL

REFLECTING ON THE STORY Have children think about what they have learned about keeping themselves healthy—inside and out—by reading "Dinosaurs Alive and Well!" Have them write about one change they would like to make in their daily routines to help themselves become healthier and happier.

WRITER'S WORKSHOP

How-to Sentences

Thinking as Writers

WRITING FORM: How-to Sentences Remind children that "Dinosaurs Alive and Well!" explained that people can take care of themselves by exercising their bodies. Explain to children that they will work in pairs to write sentences that tell how to do an exercise.

Display Chart/Transparency 8, or write the model How-to Sentences on the board. Ask children how these sentences are different from a story about someone planting seeds.

CHART/TRANSPARENCY 8

MODEL: HOW-TO SENTENCES

steps in order

Here's how you can plant some seeds. First, put some dirt into a cup. Next, put some seeds into the dirt. Cover the seeds with dirt. Last, water the seeds and put them in the light.

WRITER'S CRAFT: Steps in Order and Time-Order Words Explain that it is very important when telling how to do something to list directions in order. Remind children that good writers sometimes use time-order words such as *first, next, then,* and *last* to help readers follow the correct order.

PREWRITING

Have volunteers demonstrate exercises such as jumping jacks and jogging in place. List children's exercise ideas on the board. For one of the demonstrated exercises, give oral directions as a volunteer follows them.

Have children work with partners to talk about an exercise, including the steps that must be followed to do it. Suggest that they write the steps on a chart similar to the one below. If children forget a step or put the steps in the wrong order, they can cut them out and rearrange them in the right order, or renumber the steps.

DRAFTING

As children write their sentences, remind them to

- start with a sentence that tells what the exercise is.
- refer to their charts to list the steps in the right order.
- use words such as *first, next, then,* and *last* when describing how to do the exercise.

Have children save their drafts and revisions in their writer's folder.

TIPS FOR CLASSROOM MANAGEMENT

IF children are familiar with the writing process approach, **THEN** present the writing assignment and have them refer to the model How-to Sentences on Chart/Transparency 8.

IF at this time you want a short writing activity, **THEN** have children do the prewriting activity, rewrite the list, and place it in the Writing Center for children's reference during independent writing.

TECHNOLOGY

THE AMAZING WRITING MACHINE
Primary Level Activity Disk Pack Grade 2
Have children enter their sentences in the Essays mode.

KID PIX
Children can illustrate their sentences by creating pictures of their own or using the stamps.

RESPONDING AND REVISING

Have partners take turns reading their drafts to each other. Suggest that partners follow the directions to do the exercises. That way, children will see immediately if they have left out any steps or have put steps in the wrong order. Offer these guidelines:

- Does the first sentence tell what the exercise is?
- Do the sentences give the steps in the correct order?
- Could a person who does not know how to do the exercise learn how to do it by reading the sentences?

PROOFREADING

Offer some tips to help children proofread. Help them focus on the following:

END MARKS A telling sentence ends with a period.

TELLING PART OF A SENTENCE A sentence has a telling part that tells what someone or something does. (See the Grammar Minilesson on page T197.)

PUBLISHING

Have children make a clean copy of their sentences. Then offer publishing options like the following:

ILLUSTRATE THE STEPS Have children draw pictures to illustrate each step of their directions. Display the pictures and sentences in your hallway or in the gymnasium.

BE A TEACHER
Weather and location permitting, take your class outside for some exercise. Volunteers can read their directions aloud as classmates follow the directions.

Handwriting
Remind children that their handwriting must be neat and clear so that the person reading the sentences can understand them. If children need assistance, refer them to the Handwriting models in the *Language Handbook* or in the classroom.

PORTFOLIO OPPORTUNITY

After children publish, make copies of their how-to sentences and have them attach their Writing Self-Assessment Checklists to them. Have them place the sentences and checklists in their portfolios.

LANGUAGE HANDBOOK

How-to Paragraph, pages 28–29

Student Self-Assessment

Children can use the Writing Self-Assessment Checklist in the *Portfolio Assessment Teacher's Guide.*

EVALUATING THE WRITTEN RESPONSE

When evaluating children's how-to sentences, consider:

IDEAS	ORGANIZATION	STYLE
Do the sentences explain a process?	Are the steps in a logical order?	Are time-order words used to clearly show the order of the steps?

EVALUATION BENCHMARKS

The child does not phrase the directions as identifiable steps.	= EMERGENT
The child writes some of the steps in the correct order but does not include time-order words to help show the sequence of the steps.	= BEGINNING
The child writes the steps in the correct order and uses time-order words to relate the correct sequence of the steps.	= PROFICIENT

Tested Skill

GRAMMAR

Word Order

Reading↔Writing Connection

Connect to the story. Write each word from the following sentence on a separate index card: *Be proud of what you can do.* Tape the words to the board in random order, and ask a volunteer to read the words from left to right. Ask if the words make sense in this order. Have children place the cards in order to form a sentence. Talk about why this sentence sounds right.

Build oral language. Repeat the procedure by having children suggest other sentences to be written on word cards. Ask volunteers to arrange and rearrange the words to form sentences. They need not use all the cards.

Teach/Model

Discuss word order. Remind children that sentences make sense only if the words are in an order that makes sense. Work together to formulate rules about word order similar to the following: *The words in a sentence must be in an order that makes sense. If the words are mixed up, the sentence will not make sense.* Explain that the naming part of the sentence usually comes before the telling part. Then write the following mixed-up sentences on the board:

brush their teeth Dinosaurs
ate meat and vegetables Many dinosaurs

Invite volunteers to switch the naming parts of the sentences so that they make sense. Write the new sentences.

Practice/Apply

Check understanding. Write these words on the board: *are, up, words, not, These, mixed.* Have each child fold and cut a sheet of paper into six squares and write one of the words from the board in each square. Allow time for children to manipulate the word order to make a sentence. *(These words are not mixed up.)* Then have children follow a similar procedure with sentences they have written. Allow time for children to trade sets of words and to rearrange the words to make sentences.

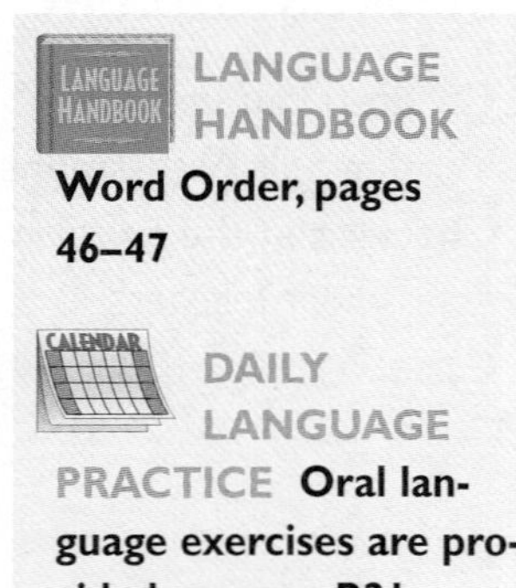

LANGUAGE HANDBOOK
Word Order, pages 46–47

DAILY LANGUAGE PRACTICE **Oral language exercises are provided on page R21.**

TECHNOLOGY
Bailey's Book House (Make-A-Story)

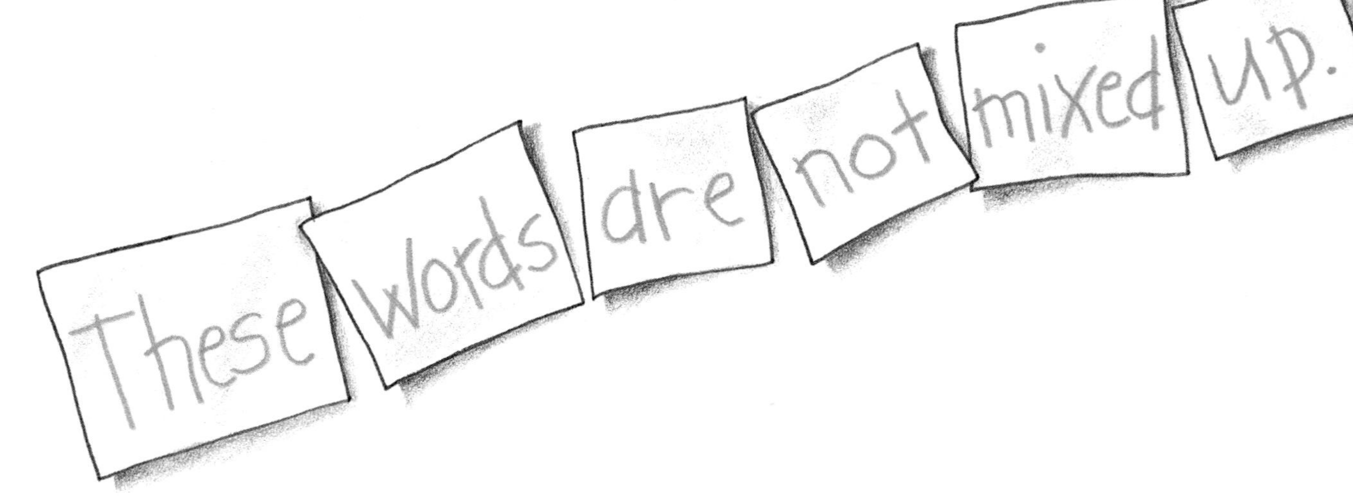

Practice Activities

WORD ORDER DETECTIVES

WRITING APPLICATION Write the following sentences on the board:

The table is under the cat.
The car is faster than the train.

Discuss how the word order in each sentence could be changed to give the sentence a completely different meaning, such as *The cat is under the table.* Have children each make up a sentence that takes on new meaning with a simple change in word order. Have them fold a sheet of drawing paper in half and illustrate the two meanings. VISUAL/AUDITORY

Friendship Pieces

WRITING APPLICATION Have children fold and cut a long sheet of light-colored construction paper in half horizontally. On each strip, have children write a five- or six-word sentence about friendship. Then have them cut each sentence between the words and place the pieces in separate envelopes, reconstruct the sentences, and read the sentences aloud.
VISUAL/KINESTHETIC

Sentence Circle

ORAL APPLICATION Have small groups of children sit in a circle to play a word order game. The first person gives a word that could appear at the beginning of a sentence. The next person adds a word to the sentence, and so on. When the sentence is complete, the last person says "Period." Have a group Recorder write down the sentences the group makes. AUDITORY

APPLY TO WRITING

You may want children to check their how-to sentences to be sure the words are in the correct order in each sentence.

STUDENTS ACQUIRING ENGLISH

The word order in many other languages is different from the common placement of words in English. Children can get a good idea of the correct English word order by listening to others speak, by speaking in English, and by reading in English.

RETEACH

See R13 for lessons in multiple modalities.

CHALLENGE

Put the cut-apart sentences together in one envelope. Children can put them back together.

GRAMMAR PRACTICE BOOK
pages 23–24

Name ______________ Dinosaurs Alive and Well!

The words in a sentence are in an order that makes sense.

Put the words from each group in order. Write the sentence you make. If the words are already in order, write sentence.

1. to exercise like We — We like to exercise.
2. I play outside with my friends. — sentence
3. swims Todd — Todd swims.
4. each other chase we — We chase each other.
5. plays Kim soccer — Kim plays soccer.
6. for you is good exercise — Exercise is good for you.

TRY THIS! Activity: Write a sentence about exercise. Cut the sentence apart so that each word is on a separate piece of paper. Let a partner put the words in order.

38 WORD ORDER — OUT OF THE BLUE Practice Book

PRACTICE BOOK, page 38

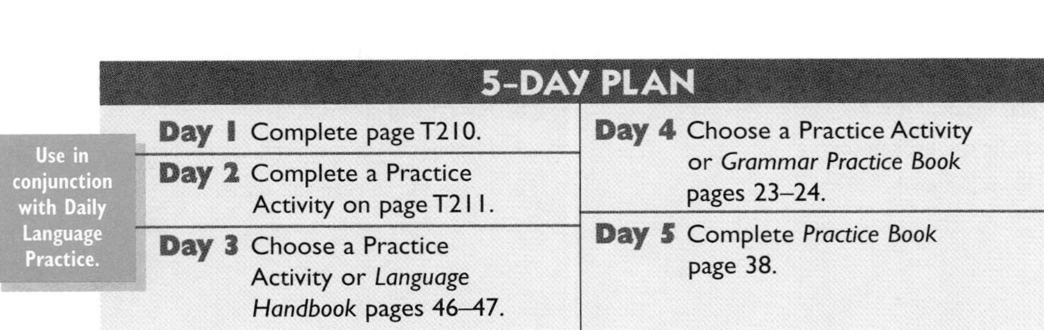

Use in conjunction with Daily Language Practice.

5-DAY PLAN	
Day 1 Complete page T210.	**Day 4** Choose a Practice Activity or *Grammar Practice Book* pages 23–24.
Day 2 Complete a Practice Activity on page T211.	**Day 5** Complete *Practice Book* page 38.
Day 3 Choose a Practice Activity or *Language Handbook* pages 46–47.	

2

SPELLING

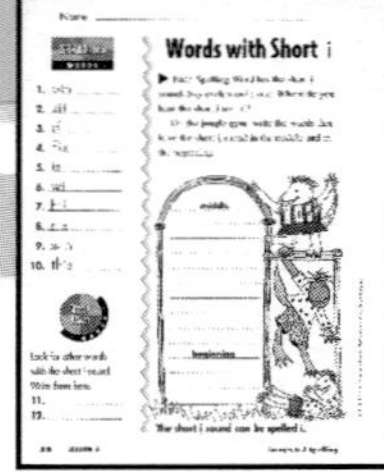
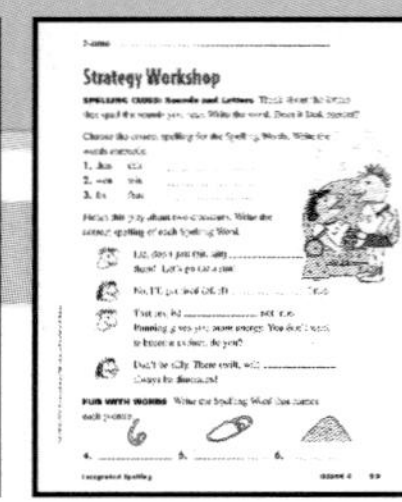

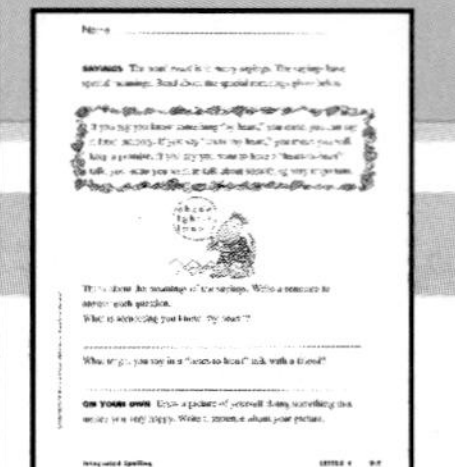

5-Day Plan

Integrated Spelling Lesson 4:
student book, pages 22–25;
Teacher's Edition, pages T39–T44.

SPELLING WORDS

1. pin
2. sit ★
3. if ★
4. fix
5. is ★
6. will
7. hill
8. six
9. win
10. this ★

STUDENT'S PERSONAL WORDS

11.
12.
13.
14.

Additional story words are *in, stick,* and *with.*

★Words appearing in "Dinosaurs Alive and Well!"

Words with Short *i*

Pretest

DAY 1 **Administer the pretest.** Say each word, use it in the dictation sentence below, and repeat the word. Have pairs of children check their own pretests by referring to the word list.

OPEN SORT

DAY 2 **Have children classify words.** Have groups of children classify the Spelling Words according to their similarities. For instance, groups can create lists of rhyming words; words with two, three, and four letters; or any other criteria they think of. Volunteers can share their sorting methods with their classmates.

CLOSED SORT

Sort by spelling pattern. Write on the board the headings from the chart below, and have partners make a similar chart. Have them write each Spelling Word in the column where it belongs. Then encourage children to add more words to their charts and to their Personal Words lists.

Words with the Short i Sound		
in the middle		at the beginning
pin	hill	if
sit	six	is
fix	win	
will	this	

Teach/Model

DAY 3 **Discuss the generalization.** Point out the words *pin* and *if* on the chart. Ask what vowel sound is the same in both. (the short *i* sound) Help children form generalizations about how the short *i* sound is spelled—for example:

- **The short *i* sound can be in the middle or at the beginning of a word.**
- **The short *i* sound can be spelled with the letter *i*.**

DAY 4 **Apply to writing.** Children should look for words with short *i* in their how-to sentences and their other writing to be sure they are spelled correctly.

Posttest

DAY 5 **Assess children's progress.** The sentences below should be used as the posttest.

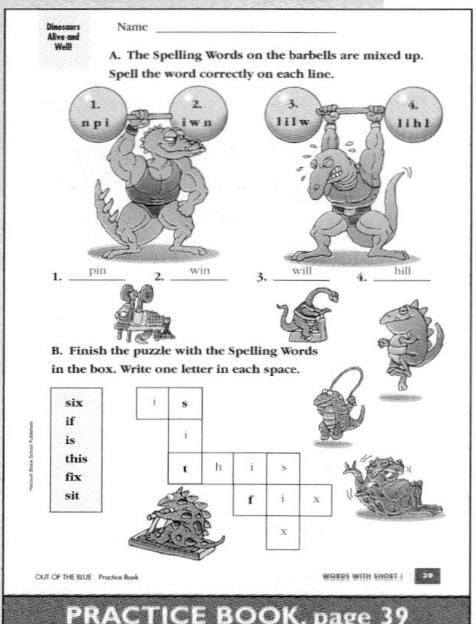

PRACTICE BOOK, page 39

DICTATION SENTENCES

1. That pin is very sharp.
2. Let's sit in the shade.
3. We'll play inside if it rains.
4. Can you fix the broken toy?
5. That clown is funny!
6. Our trip to the zoo will be fun.
7. We went up a big hill.
8. My cat had six kittens.
9. I hope we win the game today!
10. It was fun to read this book.

VOCABULARY WORKSHOP

Reviewing Key Words

To review how the vocabulary was used in the story, distribute copies of page R55 to children. Then write the Key Words on the board.

Have children choose, as a group activity, the word that best completes each sentence. Then have them write the word and read the sentence aloud.

Just being *you* makes you special.

You can do a lot to take care of yourself.

You can learn to play many different games and sports.

Some games and sports take lots of practice.

Just remember this: Think for yourself.

Be proud of all the things you can do.

You have to believe in yourself.

It's not wrong to feel sad or mad sometimes.

Then tell children to cut apart the sentences. Children can use the strips to retell the story or glue the strips to sheets of paper to create their own information booklet about being healthy.

Extending Vocabulary

ANTONYMS

Write the following story words on index cards, and place them in a pocket chart in any order:

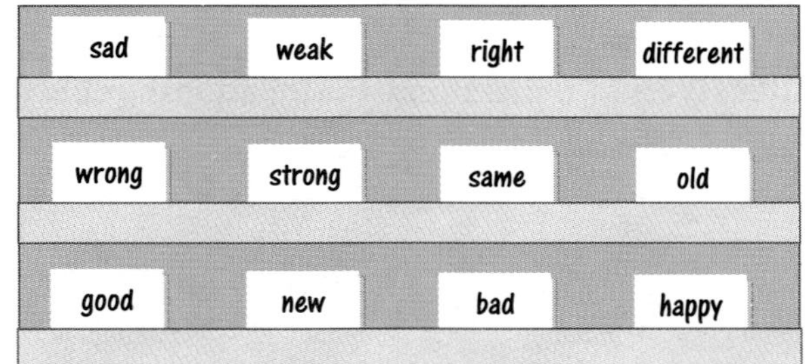

Point out the word *right* and ask children to find the word in the pocket chart that means the opposite of *right*. *(wrong)* If necessary, tell children that *right* and *wrong* have opposite meanings and that words with opposite meanings are called antonyms. Ask children to match each pair of antonyms.

Have volunteers add these four words to the pocket chart—*hard, weak, scared, different*. Have children tell what each word means and suggest words that have the opposite meaning. Make cards for the new words, and have a volunteer place each card next to its antonym.

Name ________ Dinosaurs Alive and Well!

Read the sentences. Each sentence has two words that are opposites. Write the opposites on the lines.

1. My best friend has the worst luck! best worst
2. She's over there, under the covers. over under
3. I hear you are sick. Please get well. sick well
4. My leg feels better, but it's still hard to go up and down the stairs. up down
5. How many more days and nights will I wear this cast? days nights
6. Close your eyes and open your hands! close open

TRY THIS! Game: Write opposites on cards. Turn them upside down. You and a partner can play a matching game with them.

40 ANTONYMS — OUT OF THE BLUE Practice Book

PRACTICE BOOK, page 40

STUDENTS ACQUIRING ENGLISH

Ask children to share antonym pairs in their primary language. Have children use the new words to tell about objects in the classroom that are big or little, things that make them feel happy or sad, or things that happen during the night or day. Then tell them the English equivalents of the words.

TAKE-HOME/ KEEP-AT-HOME BOOK

The Best Machine

Distribute the pages and have children make their own TAKE-HOME/ KEEP-AT-HOME BOOKS, which reinforce Key Words and known vocabulary. Have children read to partners and then take the book home to read.

INTRODUCE: PHONICS AND DECODING

Consonant Digraphs:
/r/wr; /n/kn, gn

OBJECTIVE: To understand the relationship between letters and sounds

Informal Assessment

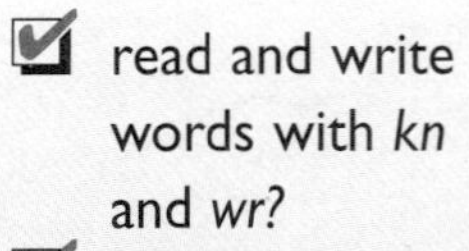

Are children able to

- read and write words with *kn* and *wr*?
- associate *kn* and *wr* with their sounds?

Teach/Model

Connect to the story. Have children turn to page 106 and read aloud the first sentence: *Feelings aren't right or wrong—they just are.* Point out the word *right.* Ask children to find another word in the sentence that begins with the same sound as *right,* and write it on the board. *(wrong)* Then have children turn to page 112 and read aloud the first part of the first sentence: *Give yourself time to get to know new friends.*

Point out the word *new.* Ask children to find another word in the sentence that begins with the same sound as *new*, and write it on the board. *(know)* Then write *gnat* on the board, say it, and ask children which sound it begins with. (/n/) Tell children that they will learn more about these beginning sounds.

Phonemic awareness: Listen to the sound. Display pages 8–9 in the *Big Book of Rhymes*. Read the rhyme aloud, and have children listen for words that begin with the same sound as *right* and *new*. Then reread the rhyme, encouraging children to join in.

Big Book of Rhymes, pages 8–9

Read words that begin with /r/ and /n/. Write these headings on the board: *wr, kn, gn*. In the rhyme, have children read and frame words that begin with these consonants, and list them.

wr	kn	gn
wrinkly	knew	gnu
wrapped	knees	gnarled
wrong	knotty	gnaw

Have children read aloud with you the words under *wr.* Ask what is alike about these words. (They begin with *wr,* which stands for the /r/ sound.) Ask children what they notice about the letter *w* in the words. (It is silent.) Follow a similar procedure with the *kn* and *gn* words. Then have volunteers circle the letters that stand for the beginning sound in each word.

Practice/Apply

Sort words by beginning sounds. Write the following words on the board: *knob, write, gnaw, kneel, walk, knot, knife, kite, wrap, wrist, wagon, wrote, gnat, kitten, wrinkle.*

Have each child fold a sheet of paper in four sections and write one of these words in each section: *web, king, run,* and *nine*. Have each word on the board read aloud, and have children write it in the correct section of their paper.

Practice Activities

KNOCK, KNOCK, WHO'S THERE?

Have available a collection of joke books that contain popular knock-knock jokes, such as *Old Turtle's 90 Knock-Knocks, Jokes, and Riddles* by Leonard Kessler (Greenwillow, 1991). Allow pairs of children to look through the books and choose knock-knock jokes to share with classmates. Children who are comfortable with the format might want to try their hand at writing some knock-knock jokes to share. **VISUAL/AUDITORY**

> Knock, Knock.
> Who's there?
> Boo.
> Boo who?
> Don't cry!

I KNEW A GNU

Provide the following list of homophones for children: *rap/wrap, not/knot, right/write, no/know, new/knew/gnu*. Talk about the meanings of any unfamiliar words. Then invite children to write silly sentences, using pairs of homophones. Have children illustrate their sentences and share them with the group. **VISUAL/AUDITORY**

THREE IN A ROW

PERFORMANCE ASSESSMENT Have partners play Digraph Tic-Tac-Toe. Distribute copies of the Grid, page R205, or have partners make their own Tic-Tac-Toe grid. The first player chooses a digraph, such as *kn,* and writes a word that begins that digraph in any square on the gameboard and reads the word aloud. The other player chooses a different digraph and writes a word on a square. Players alternate writing and reading words with the appropriate digraph until a player is able to draw a line through three squares in a row that contain words that begin with the digraph he or she chose. **VISUAL/AUDITORY**

knock	wrap	kneel
knot	wrong	wrist
knife		

MEETING INDIVIDUAL NEEDS

STUDENTS ACQUIRING ENGLISH

Help children write words with *wr, kn,* and *gn.* Have them cover up the silent letter, say the word, uncover the letter, and repeat it.

RETEACH

See page R14 for lessons in multiple modalities.

CHALLENGE

Have children use their maps to find and list place names that begin with *wr, kn,* and *gn.* Encourage children to share what they found out.

PHONICS ACTIVITY BOOK, page 10

PHONICS PRACTICE BOOK, pages 241–242

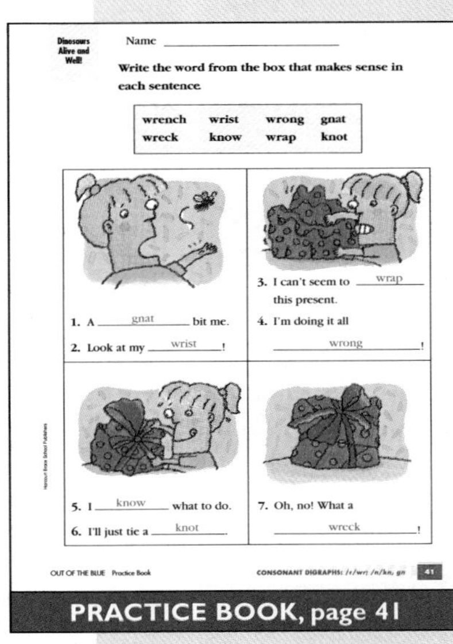
Dinosaurs Alive and Well!

Name ______________

Write the word from the box that makes sense in each sentence.

wrench	wrist	wrong	gnat
wreck	know	wrap	knot

1. A gnat bit me.
2. Look at my wrist!
3. I can't seem to wrap this present.
4. I'm doing it all wrong!
5. I know what to do.
6. I'll just tie a knot.
7. Oh, no! What a wreck!

OUT OF THE BLUE Practice Book — CONSONANT DIGRAPHS: /r/wr; /n/kn, gn — 41

PRACTICE BOOK, page 41

Reading Trade Books FOR CONSONANT DIGRAPHS

Don't Forget to Write **by Martina Selway. Ideals, 1992.**
AVERAGE

I Know a Place **by Karen Ackerman. Houghton Mifflin, 1992.**
EASY

Turtle Knows Your Name **retold by Ashley Bryan. Atheneum, 1989.**
AVERAGE

PHONICS PRACTICE READER 14

Tested Skill

INTRODUCE: COMPREHENSION

Main Idea and Details

OBJECTIVE: To identify the main idea of a nonfiction passage and the details that support it

Informal Assessment ✓

Are children able to

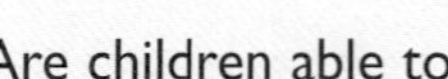

- ☑ formulate or identify the main idea?

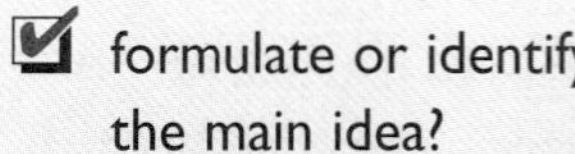

- ☑ generate details about a topic?

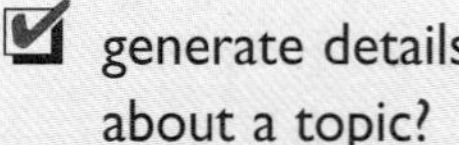

Teach/Model

Connect to the story. Have children look back at page 100. Invite a volunteer to read the title of the section and the paragraph aloud. Ask children what the paragraph is about. (exercising your body)

Discuss the main idea. Discuss with children how the title of the section helps them know what the page is about. Then ask children what one idea the paragraph is mostly about. If children cite the first sentence, point out that sometimes a sentence in the paragraph tells what the paragraph is about, or gives the main idea. The rest of the sentences give the details that explain the main idea.

Find details in a paragraph. Have children continue on page 100. Divide a large sheet of paper into two columns, and write one of these headings in each column: *Main Idea, Details.* Ask children what the main idea of the paragraph is. (Exercising every day helps your body stay healthy.) Write this sentence in the left-hand column of the chart. Then invite volunteers to add details from the paragraph to the chart. Conclude that in selections about real things, like this one, the main idea and details are usually stated clearly.

Work together to formulate a definition of *main idea,* or the "most important" idea. If necessary, explain that the main idea is often one sentence that tells about the whole paragraph. The details tell about smaller parts of the paragraph.

Practice/Apply

Have children identify the main idea. Write the following details on the board:

> Tyrannosaurus rex was longer than a large truck.
>
> It had a huge mouth with many sharp teeth.
>
> It hunted dinosaurs and anything else it could find.

Ask children to each write a main idea to go with the details. (Possible responses: *Tyrannosaurus rex was greatly feared by other dinosaurs.*)

Practice Activities

What's the Big Idea?

Have pairs of children look back at the stories that appear before "Dinosaurs Alive and Well!" to formulate a main idea for each one. Then have them write a sentence stating the main idea of each selection on a sentence strip. Have children share their sentence strips as the others guess which story the sentence describes. You may want to have children identify details that support the main idea for each story. VISUAL/ AUDITORY

Children travel to school in different ways depending on where they live.

Emily learns that her little sister means more to her than the sunglasses she likes.

Max enjoys playing the drums.

Let's Go into Detail

PERFORMANCE ASSESSMENT Display some objects—interesting enough so that children can generate an assortment of descriptive details about size, color, texture, and so on. Some possibilities are an interesting shell, a vase of flowers, a collection, a painting, or a photograph. Have small groups generate a list of details about several objects and write a main idea to go with each set of details. Display the main ideas and details with the objects. VISUAL/AUDITORY

STUDENTS ACQUIRING ENGLISH

Have children identify the main idea in a detailed illustration by writing a caption. Then ask them to name or point to details that support the main idea.

RETEACH

See page R15 for lessons in multiple modalities.

CHALLENGE

Suggest that children consider one of the objects displayed as a detail and think of other things that could go with it. Then have them write a main idea to go with the details.

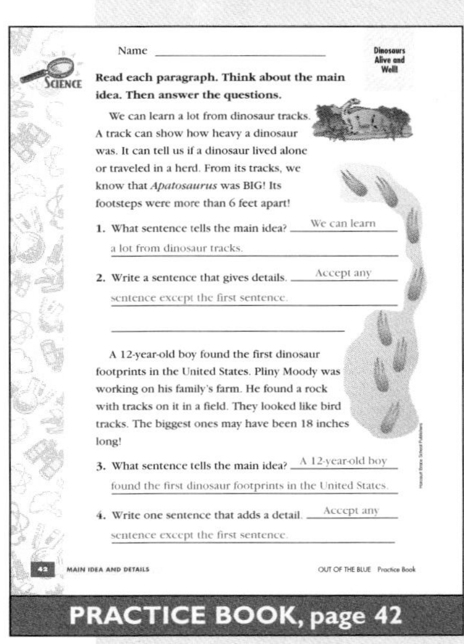

Name ____________

Dinosaurs Alive and Well!

SCIENCE

Read each paragraph. Think about the main idea. Then answer the questions.

We can learn a lot from dinosaur tracks. A track can show how heavy a dinosaur was. It can tell us if a dinosaur lived alone or traveled in a herd. From its tracks, we know that *Apatosaurus* was BIG! Its footsteps were more than 6 feet apart!

1. What sentence tells the main idea? We can learn a lot from dinosaur tracks.
2. Write a sentence that gives details. Accept any sentence except the first sentence.

A 12-year-old boy found the first dinosaur footprints in the United States. Pliny Moody was working on his family's farm. He found a rock with tracks on it in a field. They looked like bird tracks. The biggest ones may have been 18 inches long!

3. What sentence tells the main idea? A 12-year-old boy found the first dinosaur footprints in the United States.
4. Write one sentence that adds a detail. Accept any sentence except the first sentence.

42 MAIN IDEA AND DETAILS OUT OF THE BLUE Practice Book

PRACTICE BOOK, page 42

Reading Trade Books FOR MAIN IDEA AND DETAILS

The Dinosaur Who Lived in My Backyard **by B. G. Hennessy. Viking Penguin, 1988.** AVERAGE

Dinosaurs Walked Here and Other Stories Fossils Tell **by Patricia Lauber. Bradbury, 1987.** CHALLENGE

The Magic School Bus in the Time of Dinosaurs **by Joanna Cole. Scholastic, 1994.** CHALLENGE

Integrated Curriculum

SOCIAL STUDIES

My World

TIPS FOR CLASSROOM MANAGEMENT

IF children would like to know more about time capsules, **THEN** tell them about the ones that are often placed in the cornerstones of new buildings for people to find in the distant future.

IF you are not able to go on a Listening Walk, **THEN** have children close their eyes and imagine what sensations they might experience.

TECHNOLOGY

Children can use *Imagination Express, Destination: Ocean* and *Destination: Rain Forest* to learn more about the world.

SOCIAL STUDIES

"Me" Time Capsules

Encourage children to gather objects (photographs, keepsakes, etc.) for a time capsule that will be opened in the future. Remind children that everything in the capsule should tell something about themselves and their world. Have children make special boxes for their collections. When children have completed their "capsules," have them write a letter, with a return address, to the person who may find and open the box, telling about themselves and the objects in their collection. Display the collections and letters for all to enjoy! Some children may want to take their time capsules home to store. Others may want to leave them at school to be opened by next year's class. READING/WRITING

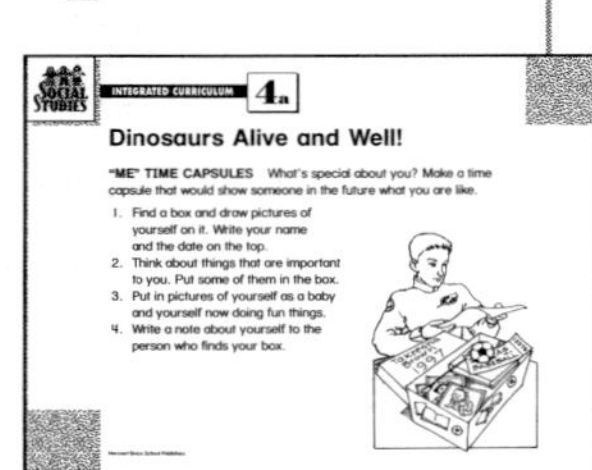

Curriculum Card 4a

ART

Tips for Healthy Seasons

COOPERATIVE LEARNING Display four long sheets of butcher paper. Organize children into four groups, and assign a season to each one: spring, summer, winter, fall. Have each group talk about things people do in your part of the world to keep healthy and safe during that season. Then have groups work together to plan and make a mural that represents their discussion. In their cooperative groups, children might assign the roles of Recorder (who takes notes on all the ideas presented) and Summarizer (who continually summarizes for the group what has been discussed and decided). When all the murals are complete, have groups share their creations. LISTENING/SPEAKING

Reading Trade Books

CROSS-CURRICULAR READING

I Like Me! by Nancy L. Carlson. Viking, 1988.
EASY

Oh, the Places You'll Go! by Dr. Seuss. Random House, 1990.
CHALLENGE

SOCIAL STUDIES

Let's Work Together

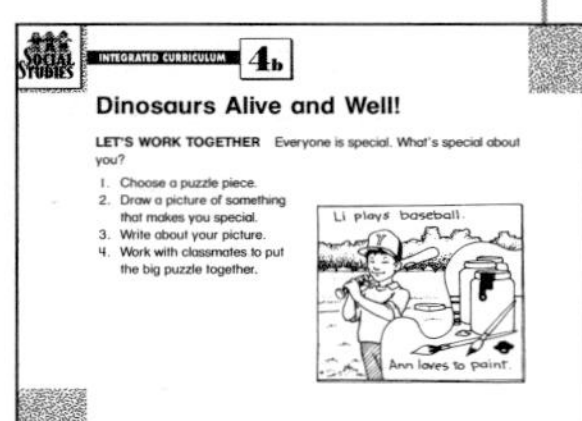
INTEGRATED CURRICULUM 4b

Dinosaurs Alive and Well!

LET'S WORK TOGETHER Everyone is special. What's special about you?

1. Choose a puzzle piece.
2. Draw a picture of something that makes you special.
3. Write about your picture.
4. Work with classmates to put the big puzzle together.

Curriculum Card 4b

Draw lines to divide a large piece of white tagboard into large puzzle pieces, one for each child. (Tip: Mark the back side of each puzzle piece so children are all working on the same side of the puzzle.) Have children each choose a puzzle piece and decorate it with pictures and words that tell something special about himself or herself. Then place all the pieces on a table and work as a group to assemble the class puzzle. WRITING

SCIENCE

Listening Walk

Read aloud *The Listening Walk* by Paul Showers (HarperCollins, 1991). Then take children on a listening walk. Encourage children to be very quiet and to use their senses—smell, touch, sight, and hearing—as they pay attention to their environment. When you return to the classroom, make a language-experience chart about the walk, recording everything children experienced. If time allows, work together to group the responses according to the senses. Then have children write a description of something they saw on the walk. Encourage children to refer to the chart for ideas. LISTENING/SPEAKING

Our Listening Walk

baby birds in a nest
a school bus
ducks in a pond
burning leaves
animal tracks
train whistle
dogs barking

MULTI-AGE CLASSROOMS

Expand upon the Science activity by encouraging children to write poems based on their experiences on the Listening Walk. Have them share their poems with classmates.

Reading Trade Books

Trade Books That Connect to "Dinosaurs Alive and Well!"

The Bionic Bunny Show

by Marc Brown and Laurene Krasny Brown

Invite children to tell what they learned from the story about how television programs are put together. Ask them to tell about actors and directors, special effects, scripts, and props.

Dinosaurs to the Rescue: A Guide to Protecting Our Planet

by Laurie Krasny Brown
illustrated by Marc Brown

In *Dinosaurs to the Rescue,* children will talk about how to take care of the earth. After reading, have children summarize things people can do to help protect the planet. Then have them work in groups to make posters emphasizing something that one person can do, such as recycle a paper bag as a basket liner.

Dinosaurs Travel: A Guide for Families on the Go

by Laurie Krasny Brown
illustrated by Marc Brown

Invite children to share their travel experiences—how they traveled and what they did. Have them compare their experiences with those in the book.

TIPS FOR CLASSROOM MANAGEMENT

SMALL GROUP

Read *Feelings* to a small group of children. As you read aloud, pause to let children give examples of times when they had these feelings or saw others display them.

INDEPENDENT

Place *Max* and *Tacky the Penguin* in a Reading Center. Have children read the stories and write their reactions in their personal journals. Encourage them to write about how they feel about Max and Tacky.

Feelings

by Aliki

After reading, have children talk about something they learned about themselves. Then ask what they learned about other people's feelings. Children may want to keep track of their feelings. Each day, they can mark a simple grid with a drawing of a smiley face or other kind of face to illustrate their feelings.

Max

by Rachel Isadora

Ask children whether they exercise on their own in addition to school physical education classes. Have them tell how warming up helped Max when he played ball. Invite volunteers to lead small groups in an exercise.

Tacky the Penguin

by Helen Lester
illustrated by Lynn Munsinger

Have children draw pictures of themselves showing a way in which they are unique and special. Invite children to show their pictures and tell about a time when they, like Tacky, were not afraid to be themselves.

STUDENTS ACQUIRING ENGLISH

Distribute cards with words like *sad, happy, angry,* and *brave.* Have each child act out the feeling on the card. Classmates can guess what the word is. Have volunteers add simple faces to the cards to illustrate the feelings. Display the cards on a Word Wall, and encourage children to add to it.

PROJECT MANAGEMENT

- PROJECT LAUNCH
- CHECKPOINT 1
- CHECKPOINT 2
- CHECKPOINT 3
- CHECKPOINT 4
- PRESENTATIONS
- ASSESSMENT

STUDENTS ACQUIRING ENGLISH

Suggest that children make a list of any new words and expressions they have learned while working on this project and put stars next to the new words they particularly like.

MULTIPLE INTELLIGENCES

Children who are **linguistically** inclined may be of help to others who are finishing their books. Children who are **logically** inclined might enjoy estimating how much they will grow by the end of the year and include their estimates to be verified later.

Take Measurements and Assemble Books

SELECTION CONNECTION

Ask children which piece of advice from "Dinosaurs Alive and Well!" was most useful to them and why they think so. Encourage volunteers to share new things they learned from reading the selection.

PROJECT CHECKLIST

During this stage, children should

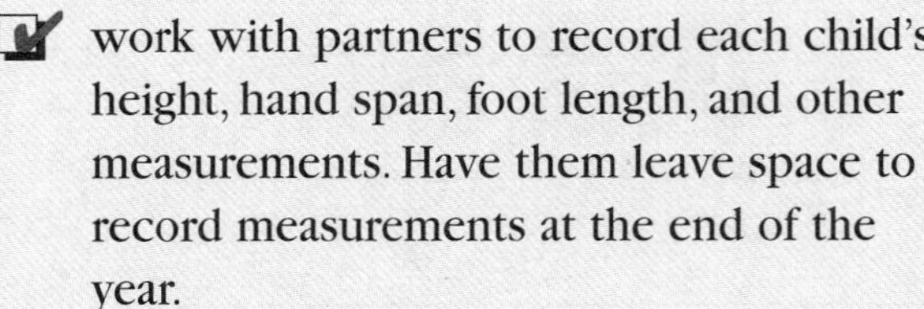

- work with partners to record each child's height, hand span, foot length, and other measurements. Have them leave space to record measurements at the end of the year.
- make fingerprint records.
- add these records to their books.
- put their books together.

When children have completed this checkpoint, have them read through the books they have made about themselves and write in their Project Journals their thoughts about the process and the information their books hold.

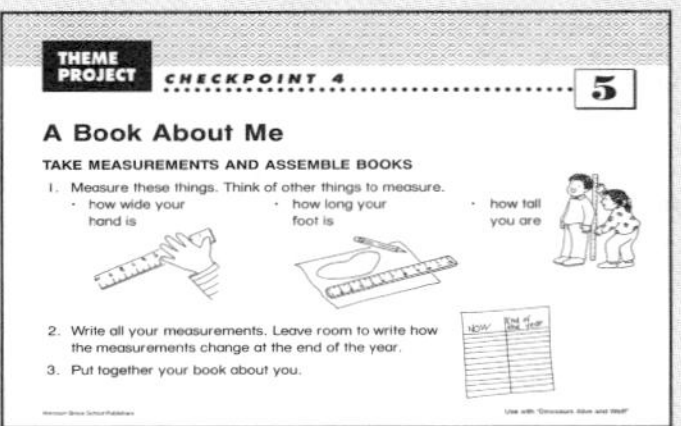

Project Card 5

Project Card 5 can be found as a copying master on page R29.

PLANNING TIPS

As children begin to collect and combine their book pages, suggest that they

- try putting the pages in different orders before binding them.
- find a partner to help them punch holes, tie yarn or ribbon, or staple.

Informal Assessment

As children complete this checkpoint, they will **make decisions** about how they want their books to look and **synthesize** the information about themselves. Children are thinking critically if they

- make accurate measurements.
- work cooperatively to put together and bind their books.
- show careful attention to detail.

Note that a more formal assessment rubric for this checkpoint is provided on page T225.

THEME
Wrap-Up

People may do some things differently, but each one of us has something special to share.

- **Max, Emily, and Alice all tried something new. What did each character learn about himself or herself?**
- **What advice might the dinosaurs in "Dinosaurs Alive and Well!" give to Emily and Alice? What might they say to Max? Explain your answers.**

Activity Corner

Think about something that you have learned. It could be a new thing that you have tried, like riding a bike. Draw a picture of yourself doing that thing. Write sentences that tell about your picture. Celebrate what you learned!

THEME 1
Wrap-Up

1. **Max, Emily, and Alice all tried something new. What did each character learn about himself or herself?** (Possible responses: Max learned that he had a special talent for playing the drums; Emily learned that she likes her little sister better than a pair of cool sunglasses; Alice got to know Emily's little sister and found out that it was hard work to take care of her.) **CRITICAL: ANALYZING CHARACTER TRAITS**

2. **What advice might the dinosaurs in "Dinosaurs Alive and Well!" give to Emily and Alice? What might they say to Max? Explain your answers.** (Possible responses: The dinosaurs might tell Emily and Alice that it's okay to try new things, and also to change one's mind if plans don't work out; the dinosaurs might tell Max that everyone is good at something and remind him that he discovered his own talent by trying something new.) **CRITICAL: SUMMARIZING**

ACTIVITY CORNER Encourage children to include as much detail in their pictures as they can. Then, as children write their sentences, remind them that the sentences can tell what's in the picture and also can add information that's not in the picture. You may want to review proper capitalization and punctuation of a sentence.

A Book About Me

THEME PROJECT PRESENTATIONS

Options

SHARING AMONG OURSELVES

- Have children exchange books with partners. For a different approach, collect children's books and pass them out randomly.
- After everyone has read a partner's book, ask children to share three new things that they learned about the person from reading the book.
- Have small groups of children arrange the group's books in alphabetical order by author's name. Then have representatives from each group work together to put all the books in alphabetical order.

SHARING WITH OTHERS

- Have a library committee create a Reading Center display of the books. Encourage children to borrow and read the books.
- Have groups of children think of ways to share their exhibit with other children in the school.
- Children can lend their books to another class as a way of introducing themselves to another group of children.

SCHOOL↔HOME CONNECTION

Help children plan a Grand Opening to celebrate the opening of their display.

- Have children write notes to their families and friends, inviting them to view the display and enjoy some refreshments.

Project Card 6

Project Card 6 can be found as a copying master on page R30.

Community Connections

As children think of ways to share their books within the school community, remind them to think of ways others in the community might be able to read their books.

- Arrange with the school or library to display the books for a week.
- As a whole group, compose a letter to a local newspaper, announcing the book exhibit.
- Groups of children can make posters to invite the school and community to view the exhibit. Other children can place the posters in such public areas as supermarket bulletin boards (with the help of a family member).
- Children could also lend their books to people at a nursing home, and then follow up with a visit to tell the residents about themselves and their books.

THEME PROJECT ASSESSMENT

SELF-ASSESSMENT

To assess children's perception of their own performance during this project, ask them to respond to the following questions orally or in writing:

- **Did you add your ideas when you were discussing in a group? Give an example of an idea you shared.**
- **What did you learn from this project? What helped you learn this?**

Children may also complete the Self-Evaluation Checklist in the *Out of the Blue Teacher's Edition.*

PEER ASSESSMENT

To assess children's ideas about how well their groups worked together, ask them to respond to the following questions orally or in writing:

- **Tell how children in your group talked about one another's work.**
- **Did everyone in the group have a chance to share his or her ideas? Why or why not?**
- **What did you learn from other people in your group?**

Children may also complete the Peer Evaluation Checklist in the *Out of the Blue Teacher's Edition.*

RUBRIC			
Performance Goals	Observable Characteristics		
	3	2	1
LAUNCH Web of interests and personal traits	• easily identifies interests and abilities	• seems unsure of interests and abilities	• is unable to identify interests and abilities
CHECKPOINT 1 Picture or map with route to school and a list of safety rules	• can visualize and depict route • suggests realistic rules for safety	• requires help visualizing route • some suggestions for safety rules are realistic	• cannot visualize or depict route • does not add to group safety discussion
CHECKPOINT 2 Labeled drawings of activities done with family members	• uses family titles in sentences describing drawing	• labels drawing without including family titles	• either does not draw or does not label drawing
CHECKPOINT 3 Illustrated list of steps to follow to reach a future goal	• has realistic plans and steps for achieving goals	• most plans and steps for achieving goals are realistic	• cannot identify goals or steps for achieving them
CHECKPOINT 4 Records of fingerprints and measurements; assembled books	• makes accurate measurements and records • makes a creative, attractive book	• has some difficulty measuring or keeping records • completes book; some parts are creative	• has great difficulty measuring and record-keeping • book shows a lack of creativity or effort
PRESENTATIONS Overall Project	• involvement in project was enthusiastic	• involvement in project was acceptable	• was not very involved in the project

Reading Trade Books
Signatures Library

Jimmy Lee Did It

by Pat Cummings

THEME: LEARNING ABOUT ONESELF

Celebrate Me!

One of the most wonderful inventions of childhood is an imaginary friend. Children will see how the imaginary Jimmy Lee makes life easier for Angel's mischievous older brother, Artie. Children may also realize that while imaginary friends might not be fun for everyone, a sense of humor can definitely help in dealing with life.

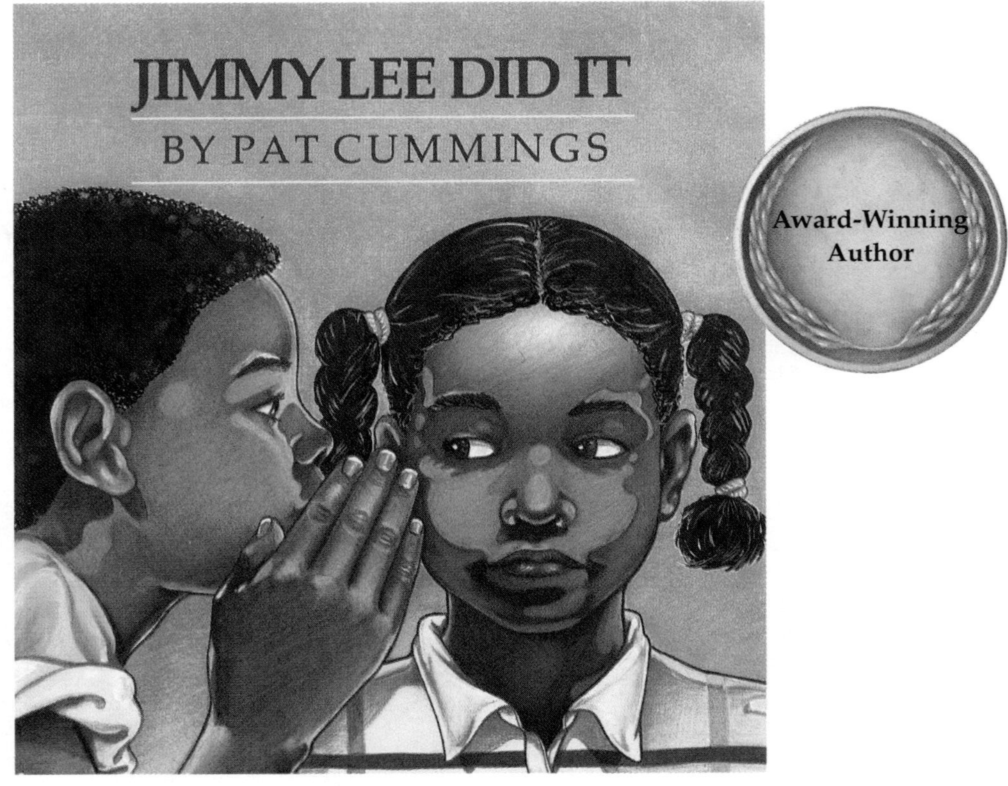

SUMMARY **Genre: Rhyming Story**

Strange things are happening, and Angel's brother, Artie, is being blamed for causing the trouble. Artie claims that the troublemaker is someone named Jimmy Lee, so Angel tries to catch him in the act. Although the words at the end of the story indicate that Angel doesn't figure out who Jimmy Lee is, the expression on her face shows she may be close to understanding that Jimmy Lee is Artie's imaginary friend.

ABOUT THE AUTHOR/ILLUSTRATOR

Pat Cummings grew up in a military family that moved often, so she always felt like the "new kid on the block." Her art was the one thing that helped her get involved in school activities and meet new people. Pat has won two Coretta Scott King Honor awards for illustration. *Jimmy Lee Did It* was her first book for children.

Building Background and Concepts

PRIOR KNOWLEDGE

Solving mysteries. Ask children to pretend to be detectives to solve the mystery of who has the toy. Have children sit in a circle, and ask two volunteers to sit in the middle with their eyes closed. Have the children in the circle pass a small toy or other object from one to another behind their backs. When you say *stop*, the children in the middle of the circle will open their eyes and guess who has the toy. Encourage the children in the middle to look for telltale clues, such as giggling or facial expressions.

Developing Concept Vocabulary

EXTENDING BACKGROUND KNOWLEDGE

Generate a discussion. Ask children to suggest words that come to mind when they think of the word *mystery*. Record their suggestions in a web similar to this one:

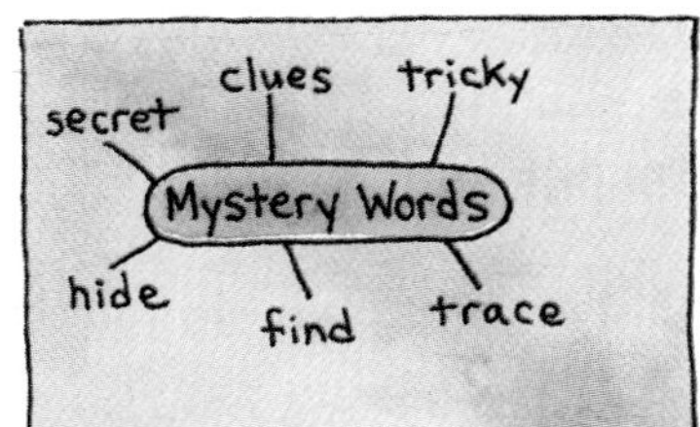

INTRODUCING THE BOOK

Display the book *Jimmy Lee Did It.* Read aloud the title and share the information about the author/illustrator.

SCHOOL↔HOME CONNECTION

Encourage children to work with a family member to play a detective game. Have children ask the family member to hide an object. Then children ask questions to find out clues. Some questions might be *What color is it? How big is it? What is it made of?*

STUDENTS ACQUIRING ENGLISH

Explain to children that a mystery is like a secret. Show pictures from the book to help children understand the concept. You may want to ask volunteers to demonstrate. Have one child hide somewhere in the classroom, and have another child find him or her.

SPELLING GENERALIZATION

Sound words
Integrated Spelling Lesson 5

OPTIONS FOR READING

Tips for Classroom Management

SMALL GROUP		WHOLE CLASS	
PARTNER	**READ ALOUD**	**INDEPENDENT**	**READ ALOUD**
Before partners read, have them page through the story and talk about what they think it is about. Then children can take turns reading pages in the story. Have children discuss what they think about Jimmy Lee after they finish reading.	Have children speculate about what Jimmy Lee will do, based on the title and the cover illustration. Then have children alternate reading the rhyming sentence pairs and use the illustrations to find clues to the identity of Jimmy Lee.	Place the book in the Reading Center for independent reading. As children read, ask them to write down who they think Jimmy Lee is. Have them use the illustrations for clues.	As you read each sentence pair, pause to allow children time to supply the last rhyming words. Then ask children to predict who Jimmy Lee is. Write the names on the board. After reading, have children decide from the list who Jimmy Lee is.

Response Options

PERSONAL RESPONSE

- Do you think Angel knows who Jimmy Lee is? Do you think Angel's parents know? Do you think the dog knows? Tell why or why not.
- Why do you think Angel wants to find Jimmy Lee?
- How would you capture Jimmy Lee?
- What kind of person do you think Angel is? Artie? Explain why you think as you do.
- Why doesn't Jimmy Lee get caught?

SMALL GROUP	WHOLE CLASS	INDEPENDENT
Reread the story. Ask children to find new clues in the illustrations that show who Jimmy Lee is.	Have children draw a matrix to solve the mystery. Horizontally, they list all the people in the story. Vertically, they list all the trouble Jimmy Lee causes. They put check marks below names to show who or what may have caused each problem.	Talk about other things that Jimmy Lee may have done without getting caught.
Reread the story in a whisper. How does this change the story? Then organize children into two groups to read the story chorally, each group alternating reading the rhyming pairs of sentences.	Have children use the illustrations to describe some of the things that Jimmy Lee does that are not described in the text.	Have children pretend to be Angel and tell what else she can do to catch Jimmy Lee.

Culminating Activities

HIDDEN OBJECTS

MATH Have each child make a grid with A, B, C, and D written vertically and 1, 2, 3, and 4 written horizontally. Next, each child "hides" an object by drawing it in one of the squares. Then, have partners take turns trying to guess where one another's objects are hidden by asking questions like *Is it in A4?*

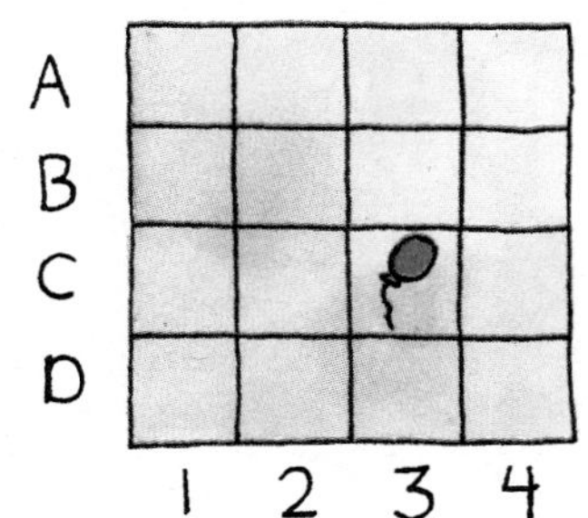

Guess My Secret

PROBLEM SOLVING Think of an object in the classroom, and have children take turns asking yes-and-no questions to guess what the secret object is. Try the game with animals, fruits, colors, sports, or subjects that the children have studied. You can vary the activity by hiding an object in a box or an envelope.

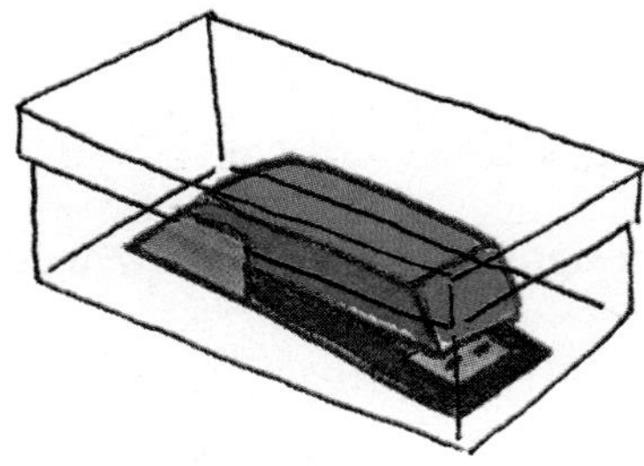

PASS IT ON

DRAMATIC PLAY Have children take turns whispering a secret, passing it on from one child to the next. The last child to hear the secret repeats it aloud. Is it the same secret? Talk about how the secret might have changed.

Rhyming Words and Riddles

LANGUAGE ARTS Ask children to think of other words that rhyme with those used in the story. Then challenge them to make up their own rhyming sentence pairs or riddles that rhyme, such as

I'm a very famous game.
What is my name?

I'm busy as a bee.
I live in a tree.

I'm round like a ball.
I'm orange in the Fall.

MULTI-AGE CLASSROOMS Have older children make up rhyming sentence pairs or riddles, and let younger children solve them. The older children may want to read their rhymes and leave out the rhyming words for the younger ones to supply.

STUDENTS ACQUIRING ENGLISH Suggest that children find words in their primary languages that rhyme. Encourage them to teach others to say the words. Then everyone can use the words to make up short rhymes.

CHALLENGE Motivate children who especially liked *Jimmy Lee Did It* to go to the school library to find other mysterious stories. Have children put together a collection of stories for their classmates.

Reading Trade Books
Signatures Library

EASY AVERAGE CHALLENGE

Puddle Jumper: How a Toy Is Made

written by Ann Morris

photographed by Ken Heyman

THEME: LEARNING ABOUT ONESELF

Celebrate Me!

Children get an inside look at a real toy workshop and learn how the woodworker's daughter, a child about their age, provides important help to her father in his work.

SUMMARY Genre: Photo Essay

Real photographs show how Sarah helps her father as he designs and builds a new wooden toy, called a Puddle Jumper, in his workshop.

ABOUT THE AUTHOR AND THE PHOTOGRAPHER

Ann Morris worked for many years as a teacher in New York City schools. Later, she became an editor for an educational book publisher and taught at Teachers College, Columbia University; New York University; and Bank Street College of Education. She is presently a writer of children's books.

Ken Heyman is an acclaimed photographer who studied under the famous anthropologist Margaret Mead. He later worked with her on two books. He has also photo-illustrated numerous books for adults and children.

Building Background and Concepts

PRIOR KNOWLEDGE

Show and tell about toys. Have children bring their favorite toys to share with classmates. Ask them to describe what the items are made of and how they think the toys were made and then demonstrate how the toys are used. List their descriptions on the board in a chart like the following:

How It Looks	How It Moves	Materials Used	Tools Used
brown	Karate-Kick leg	wood	saw
green	propeller spins	metal	screwdriver
smooth	rolls	plastic	glue
has a bell	batteries	fabric	needle + thread

STUDENTS ACQUIRING ENGLISH

Write words generated from the chart on word cards. Display picture cards that represent the words. Have children match the words with the toys children brought to school or with pictures of toys.

SPELLING GENERALIZATION

Sound words
Integrated Spelling Lesson 5

Developing Concept Vocabulary

EXTENDING BACKGROUND KNOWLEDGE

Categorizing toys. Have children use the chart on the board to categorize the toys they brought in. Use story language to help them by asking:

Which toys are made with wood?
Which toys can bounce?
Which toys are soft? Which are hard?
Which toys can be made with a saw?

Encourage children to create a display with their toys in the different categories.

INTRODUCING THE BOOK

Display the book *Puddle Jumper: How a Toy Is Made.* Read aloud the title and share the information about the author and the photographer.

SCHOOL↔HOME CONNECTION

Suggest that children work with adult family members to make a simple recipe at home, such as pudding, cookies, soup, or lemonade. Have them make a list of the ingredients and write the steps in sequence to make the recipe. Have them bring their recipes to school and share them with their classmates.

OPTIONS FOR READING

Tips for Classroom Management

SMALL GROUP		WHOLE CLASS	
PARTNER	**READ ALOUD**	**READ ALOUD**	**INDEPENDENT**
Have partners take turns reading pages in the story. Have them work together to figure out word meanings and share relevant background information. Then have them discuss their reactions to the book.	Ask children why they think the toy is called a Puddle Jumper. Have them take turns reading the passages aloud, and point to the pictures to help explain the vocabulary. If some children have experience with woodworking, ask them to provide additional information to their groups.	As you read the book, stop occasionally and ask children to predict the next step in making the Puddle Jumper. Write Barry's steps on the board in a numbered list. Also talk about picture clues that helped children understand the words.	Place the book in the Reading Center for independent reading. As children read the book, ask them to write down each step that Barry does. After they finish, ask them to talk about how the toy was made and how it works.

Response Options

PERSONAL RESPONSE

- What did you learn about working with wood? About building toys?
- What sounds are there in Barry's workshop? What smells?
- Would you like to help Barry? Tell why and how you would help.
- What are some things Barry does for safety?
- What kind of wooden toy would you like? Why?

SMALL GROUP	WHOLE CLASS	INDEPENDENT
Reread the book. Ask children to explain other steps in building the Puddle Jumper that are not described in the text.	Challenge children to count and name all the parts in the Puddle Jumper.	Have children draw and number a series of pictures to show the Puddle Jumper taking shape.
As you reread the book, list the vocabulary under headings such as these: **Materials** **Machines** **Tools** **Plane Parts**	Ask children to study the pictures and discuss the things they see and what they might be used for.	Invite children to design their own Puddle Jumper. How would they change Barry's Puddle Jumper and why?

Culminating Activities

PAPER ART

ART Provide children with books on folding and constructing paper hats, boats, and greeting cards or making origami figures. Then provide them with colored paper and markers. Have them follow the directions to create figures from folded paper. Emphasize the importance of following the steps in order. When children have finished, have them describe step-by-step how they made their figures.

Winging It!

SCIENCE Have children fold paper to make paper airplanes. Then have them observe their airplanes to see whose can fly the farthest, the highest, and the longest. Encourage children to record their observations.

DO AN INTERVIEW

ROLE-PLAY Have groups of three role-play an interview. Have them take turns being the interviewer, Sarah, and Sarah's dad. Encourage the group to work together to write interview questions before they begin.

Helping Hands

DRAMATIC PLAY Have children create new verses for the following action rhyme, sung to the tune of "Mary Had a Little Lamb":

This is the way I pound a nail,
pound a nail,
pound a nail,
This is the way I pound a nail,
When I help my dad.

New verses may include *saw a saw, paint the house*, or *drill a hole*.

MEETING INDIVIDUAL NEEDS

MULTI-AGE CLASSROOMS Ask older children to assist younger ones with the art projects and any research. Older children can also help them with the book's specialized vocabulary in *Puddle Jumper: How a Toy Is Made*.

STUDENTS ACQUIRING ENGLISH Suggest that children keep a list of new vocabulary words in their journals. Have them include a drawing or definition of each word to help them remember the new words.

CHALLENGE Encourage children to work in cooperative groups to design and build things from various materials on hand, such as construction sets, fabric, cardboard tubes, and craft sticks. Afterward, invite children to teach others how to make their creations.

End-of-Theme Assessment Tools

IF you want to measure a child's mastery of reading and language skills and strategies, **THEN** administer the multiple-choice diagnostic **Skills Assessment.**	**IF** you want information about a child's ability to apply thinking skills in a global and holistic manner, **THEN** administer the **Holistic Reading Assessment.**	**IF** you want a comprehensive view of a child's reading and writing development skills, **THEN** administer the **Integrated Performance Assessment.**

Name ______________________ **Date** ______________________

Teacher ______________________ **Grade** ______________________

I have looked at all the things in my portfolio.

1. This picture or writing tells about the thing I like best.

2. This is the work I have the most of.
   Here is my picture or writing about it

3. This is the work I would like to do next.
   Here is my picture or writing about it.

Organizing My Portfolio Checklist

We Belong Together

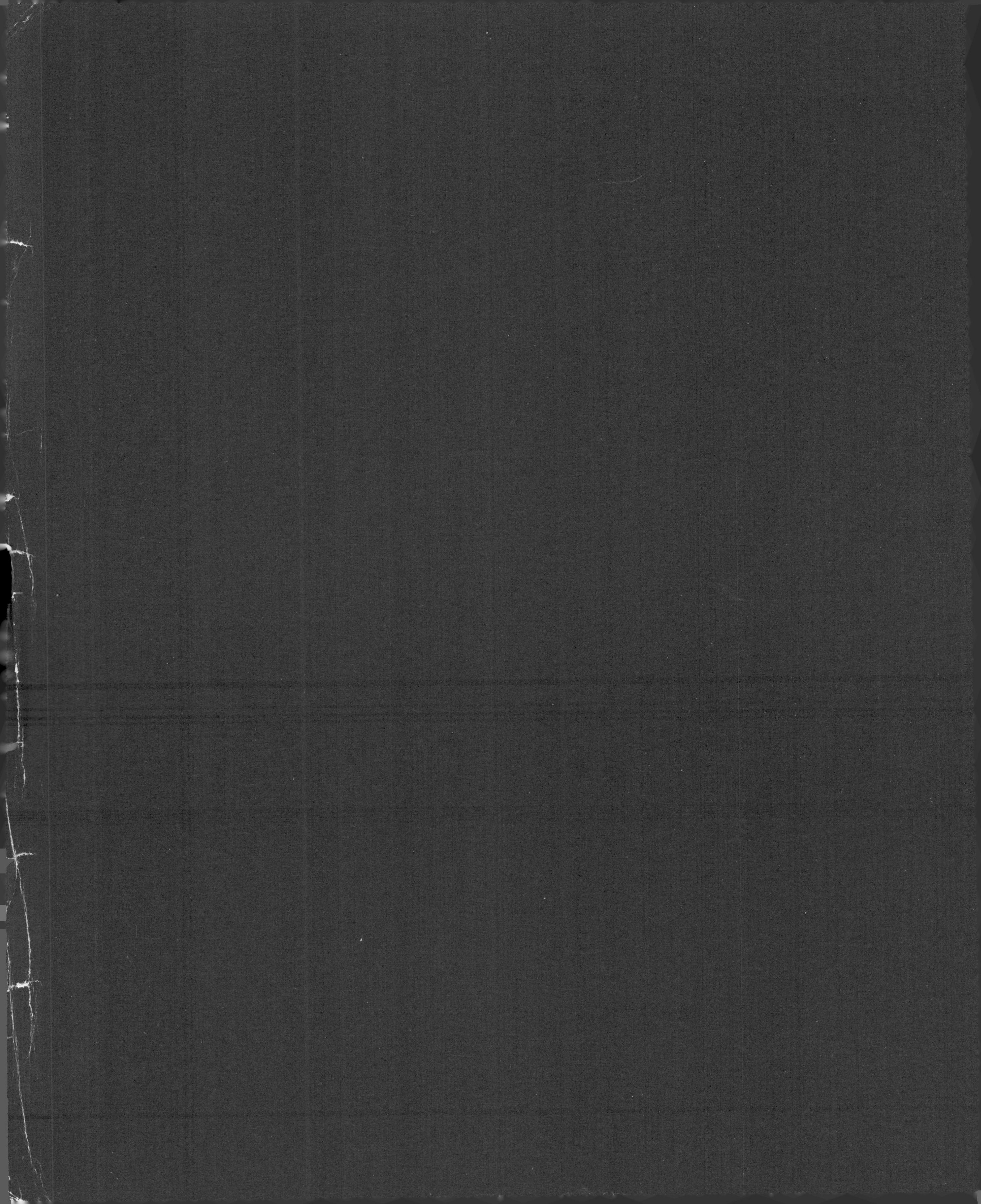

Theme 2

Friendship

WE BELONG TOGETHER

What would our lives be like without friends?

In this theme, friends are neighbors, pets, children, and grandmothers. What's important is that friends are there for each other.

Theme Overview

We Belong Together

Friendship

In this theme, children are exposed to relationships between friends and family members, as well as between people and animals. The selections explore the joys and the responsibilities of friendship.

MATTHEW and TILLY
by REBECCA C. JONES
illustrated by BETH PECK

Matthew and Tilly by Rebecca C. Jones T249–T296
"Sometimes, though, Matthew and Tilly got sick of each other."

Best friends Matthew and Tilly have an argument and refuse to play together. They both find that playing alone is no fun and make moves to patch things up between them.

Two Friends by Nikki Giovanni T274–T275
This poem shows that people can be different and still be good friends.

Hopscotch Around the World by Mary D. Lankford T297–T304
This nonfiction selection describes variations of hopscotch in Aruba and France, demonstrating similarities among children's games the world over.

ART AND LITERATURE: ***Two Young Girls at the Piano*** by Pierre Auguste Renoir T305–T306

Mr. Putter and Tabby Pour the Tea

by Cynthia Rylant T307–T354

"Mr. Putter was tired of living alone. Mr. Putter wanted a cat."

A person's best friend might be a pet, as shown in this warm-hearted story of a lonely man and the cat he adopts.

Six-Dinner Sid by Inga Moore T355–T398

"Unlike Aristotle Street, the people who lived on Pythagoras Place talked to their neighbors. So, right from the start, everyone knew about Sid's six dinners."

This amusing story illuminates a different kind of belonging — a cat's desire to belong to many families at once.

Rosie the Visiting Dog by Stephanie Calmenson T399–T402

Children will discover the special friendship an animal can offer to people who need to be cheered up.

Abuela by Arthur Dorros T403–T450

"That's just one of the things I love about Abuela. She likes adventures."

A girl and her grandmother take an imaginary journey over New York City in this fantasy bursting with family pride and love.

Flexible Grouping

MATTHEW AND TILLY T249–T296

	BELOW-LEVEL READERS	ABOVE-LEVEL READERS	ESL	BILINGUAL
1 READING AND RESPONDING Build Background and Concepts Vocabulary Strategies Strategic Reading Response Corner	**BEFORE** reading the selection, use the Previewing the Literature pages of the *Intervention Strategies Manual* (p. 26). **TEACHER-LED GROUP** **AFTER** reading the selection, have children read an *ESL/Title I Library* book while listening to the audiocassette. **COOPERATIVE GROUPS**	**AFTER** children read the selection, have partners write their version of what Matthew and Tilly might say to each other. (p. T268) **PAIRS** **AFTER** children read the selection, they can choose a *Signatures Library* book. **INDEPENDENT**	**AFTER** reading the selection, children can read an Instant Reader *I Have Another Language*. **INDEPENDENT** **AFTER** reading the selection, children can complete an activity from the *Intervention Strategies Manual.* (pp. 26–31) **TEACHER-LED GROUP**	**BEFORE** reading the anthology selection, choose the translation in the *Anthology Translation Booklet* and have children share it at home. **INDEPENDENT** **INSTEAD OF** Strategic Reading, share *Mateo y Tili* in CIELO ABIERTO and have children listen to the *Student Literature Cassette*. Share *The Rainbow Fish* from the *Multi-Language Library* with Chinese-speaking children. **TEACHER-LED GROUP**
2 INTEGRATING LANGUAGE ARTS Idea Bank Writer's Workshop Grammar Spelling Vocabulary Workshop	**AFTER** the Grammar lesson, have children read Phonics Practice Reader 4. **INDEPENDENT** **DURING** the Spelling lesson, use the *Integrated Spelling* Teacher's Edition Lesson 7 for additional support lessons. **TEACHER-LED GROUP**	**DURING** the Spelling lesson, children may use the Journal mode of *The Amazing Writing Machine* to enter and sort words as a tool for relating new words to words they know. **COOPERATIVE GROUPS** **WHILE** others work in groups, children can make the Take-Home/Keep-at-Home Book *Sisters Forever* and read it with a less-fluent partner. **PAIRS**	**WHILE** others work on Idea Bank activities, children may use *Imagination Express, Destination: Neighborhoods.* **INDEPENDENT** **DURING** the Vocabulary Workshop, review the rules for making contractions from *not.* (p. T287) **TEACHER-LED GROUP**	**DURING** the Writer's Workshop, use CIELO ABIERTO *Teacher's Handbook* page 70 to have children write a friendly letter. **TEACHER-LED GROUP** **INSTEAD OF** completing the Grammar lesson, refer to page 11 in *Mateo y Tili Teacher's Guide*. **TEACHER-LED GROUP**
3 LEARNING THROUGH THE LITERATURE Direct Skills Instruction Integrated Curriculum Reading Trade Books Theme Project	**AFTER** the Phonics and Decoding lesson, children can complete the *Phonics Activity Book* (p. 13). **TEACHER-LED GROUP** **WHILE** reading Trade Books, have children read a book and write in their personal journals about their favorite story parts. (p. T294) **INDEPENDENT**	**AFTER** the Phonics and Decoding lesson, have children write and illustrate poems that include the /ûr/ sound spelled *ur* and *er*. **COOPERATIVE GROUPS** **WHILE** reading Trade Books, have children tape-record short mysteries for classmates to solve (p. T291). **COOPERATIVE GROUPS**	**WHILE** others work in groups, have children make the Take-Home/Keep-at-Home Book *Sisters Forever* to read for homework. **TEACHER-LED GROUP** **WHILE** others work in centers, children can choose and complete a Trade Book activity. **COOPERATIVE GROUPS**	**WHILE** others work in groups, have children complete the ongoing cross-curricular project. See page 2 in *Mateo y Tili Teacher's Guide*. **COOPERATIVE GROUPS** **WHILE** others work in groups, help children to complete Drawing Conclusions on pages 22–23 in the CIELO ABIERTO *Teacher's Handbook*. **TEACHER-LED GROUP**

MR. PUTTER AND TABBY POUR THE TEA T307–T354

	BELOW-LEVEL READERS	ABOVE-LEVEL READERS	ESL	BILINGUAL
1 READING AND RESPONDING Build Background and Concepts Vocabulary Strategies Strategic Reading Response Corner	**BEFORE** reading the selection, use the Previewing the Literature pages of the *Intervention Strategies Manual* (p. 32). **TEACHER-LED GROUP** **AFTER** reading the selection, children can listen to it on Literature Cassette 1 while following along in their books. **COOPERATIVE GROUPS**	**BEFORE** reading the story, have children write their story predictions in their personal journals. **INDEPENDENT** **WHILE** others complete the Strategic Reading, have children complete the Science activity. (p. T350) **COOPERATIVE GROUPS**	**BEFORE** reading the selection, have children listen to it on Literature Cassette 1 while following along in their books. **COOPERATIVE GROUPS** **AFTER** reading the selection, help a group complete the Phonics and Decoding lesson in Intervention Strategies. (pp. T336–T337) **TEACHER-LED GROUP**	**AFTER** reading the anthology selection, choose the translation in the appropriate *Anthology Translation Booklet* and have children take it home to share. **INDEPENDENT** **INSTEAD OF** Strategic Reading, share with Spanish-speaking children *Stelaluna* in CIELO ABIERTO. **TEACHER-LED GROUP**
2 INTEGRATING LANGUAGE ARTS Idea Bank Writer's Workshop Grammar Spelling Vocabulary Workshop	**DURING** the Spelling lesson, pull out a needs-based group for *Integrated Spelling* Teacher's Edition, Lesson 8. **TEACHER-LED GROUP** **WHILE** others work in groups, have children complete the Take-Home/Keep-at-Home Book *The Perfect Pet* to read at home. **COOPERATIVE GROUPS**	**WHILE** working on the Writer's Workshop, children may use the *Language Handbook* (pp. 12–13) for a model of a friendly letter. **INDEPENDENT** **AFTER** the Writer's Workshop, children can use the Writing Self-Assessment Checklist and add it to their portfolios. **INDEPENDENT**	**WHILE** others work on Idea Bank activities, model and guide children to complete the *Writer's Magazine* (pp. 22–25). **TEACHER-LED GROUP** **WHILE** others work on the Vocabulary Workshop, have children share time words in their primary languages and pantomime things they do at different times. (p. T345) **COOPERATIVE GROUPS**	**DURING** the Writer's Workshop, use CIELO ABIERTO *Teacher's Handbook* page 75 to have children write a report. **TEACHER-LED GROUP** **INSTEAD OF** completing the Grammar lesson, refer to page 11 in *Stelaluna Teacher's Guide*. **TEACHER-LED GROUP**
3 LEARNING THROUGH THE LITERATURE Direct Skills Instruction Integrated Curriculum Reading Trade Books Theme Project	**WHILE** others work in centers, pull out a needs-based group for the Word Building activity. (p. T347) **TEACHER-LED GROUP**	**WHILE** others work in centers, have children choose and read a *Signatures Library* selection. **INDEPENDENT**	**AFTER** the Phonics and Decoding lesson, children can complete the *Phonics Activity Book*. (p. 15) **TEACHER-LED GROUP** **BEFORE** the Study Skills lesson, spend time introducing unfamiliar words found on forms and applications. **TEACHER-LED GROUP**	**WHILE** others work in groups, have children complete the ongoing cross-curricular project. See page 2 in *Stelaluna Teacher's Guide*. **COOPERATIVE GROUPS** **WHILE** others are sharing trade books, have children choose a book from the *Multi-Language Library* to take home to share with family members. **INDEPENDENT**

Flexible Grouping

SIX-DINNER SID T355–T398

	BELOW-LEVEL READERS	ABOVE-LEVEL READERS	ESL	BILINGUAL
1 READING AND RESPONDING Build Background and Concepts Vocabulary Strategies Strategic Reading Response Corner	**BEFORE** reading the selection, pull out a needs-based group for review of Key Words. (p.T359) **TEACHER-LED GROUP** **WHILE** reading the selection, have children read in pairs with an above-level partner. **PAIRS**	**AFTER** children read the selection, have them discuss how Sid's life differs in the six homes, and challenge them to imagine and write about Sid's life with one of the neighbors. (p.T368) **COOPERATIVE GROUPS** **AFTER** children read the selection, have them choose a *Signatures Library* book. **INDEPENDENT**	**BEFORE** children read the selection, do a "picture walk" through it. **TEACHER-LED GROUP** **AFTER** children read the selection, pull out a needs-based group for Intervention Strategies activities (pp.T380–T381) **TEACHER-LED GROUP**	**BEFORE** reading the anthology selection, choose the translation in the appropriate *Anthology Translation Booklet* and have children take it home to share. **INDEPENDENT** **INSTEAD OF** Strategic Reading, share with Spanish-speaking children *El gallo de bodas* in CIELO ABIERTO. **TEACHER-LED GROUP**
2 INTEGRATING LANGUAGE ARTS Idea Bank Writer's Workshop Grammar Spelling Vocabulary Workshop	**WHILE** doing the Writer's Workshop, children may use the *Language Handbook* (pp. 18–19) to model the use of a paragraph that describes. **INDEPENDENT** **WHILE** others work in groups, children can make their Take-Home/Keep-at-Home Book *The Big Sneeze* to read for homework. **INDEPENDENT**	**WHILE** others work on Idea Bank activities, children can write in their personal journals what it means to be a good neighbor. (p.T383) **INDEPENDENT** **DURING** the Integrating Language Arts section, have children complete the *Writer's Magazine* (pp. 26–27). **INDEPENDENT**	**WHILE** others complete Idea Bank activities, have children work on *Imagination Express, Destination: Neighborhoods.* **INDEPENDENT** **DURING** the Spelling lesson, use the Students Acquiring English note from *Integrated Spelling* Teacher's Edition Lesson 9. **TEACHER-LED GROUP**	**DURING** the Writer's Workshop, use CIELO ABIERTO *Teacher's Handbook* page 68 to have children write sentences about a picture. **TEACHER-LED GROUP** **INSTEAD OF** completing the Grammar lesson, refer to page 11 in *El gallo de bodas Teacher's Guide.* **TEACHER-LED GROUP**
3 LEARNING THROUGH THE LITERATURE Direct Skills Instruction Integrated Curriculum Reading Trade Books Theme Project	**AFTER** children review the Phonics and Decoding lesson, have them complete the reproducible Phonics page of the *Intervention Strategies Manual* (p. 43). **INDEPENDENT** **AFTER** children complete the Study Skills lesson, have pairs read a Trade Book that focuses on alphabetical order. **PAIRS**	**AFTER** the Phonics and Decoding lesson, have children complete the *Phonics Activity Book* (p.18). **INDEPENDENT** **WHILE** you work with others, partners can make up, define and illustrate more words that begin with the consonant clusters *str* and *scr.* (p.T391) **PAIRS**	**AFTER** the Study Skills lesson, have children read *Dr. Seuss's ABC,* a *Living Book.* **COOPERATIVE GROUPS** **WHILE** others work in centers, have children make the Take-Home/Keep-at-Home Book *The Big Sneeze* to read for homework. **TEACHER-LED GROUP**	**WHILE** others work in groups, have children complete the ongoing cross-curricular project. See page 2 in *El gallo de bodas Teacher's Guide.* **COOPERATIVE GROUPS** **WHILE** others work in groups, work with children to complete the Sequence lesson on pages 20–21 in the CIELO ABIERTO *Teacher's Handbook.* **TEACHER-LED GROUP**

ABUELA T403–T450

	BELOW-LEVEL READERS	ABOVE-LEVEL READERS	ESL	BILINGUAL
1 READING AND RESPONDING Build Concepts and Vocabulary Strategic Reading Response Corner	**BEFORE** reading the selection, use the Previewing the Literature pages of the *Intervention Strategies Manual* (p. 44). **TEACHER-LED GROUP** **AFTER** reading the selection, children can read the *Instant Reader One Quiet Afternoon.* **INDEPENDENT**	**AFTER** reading the selection, have children create a brochure for New York City using encyclopedias and reference books. Have them share their work with the class (p. T417). **COOPERATIVE GROUPS**	**BEFORE** reading the selection, use the Introducing the Literature pages of the *Sheltered English/ESL Manual* (pp. 30-33). **TEACHER-LED GROUP** **AFTER** reading the selection, children can read an *Instant Reader.* **INDEPENDENT**	**AFTER** reading the anthology selection, choose the translation in the appropriate *Anthology Translation Booklet* and have children take it home to share. **INDEPENDENT** **INSTEAD OF** Strategic Reading, share *Abuela* in CIELO ABIERTO with Spanish-speaking children. **TEACHER-LED GROUP**
2 INTEGRATING LANGUAGE ARTS Idea Bank Writer's Workshop Grammar Spelling Vocabulary Workshop	**AFTER** the Grammar lesson, guide children in completing a page in the *Practice Book.* (p. 78) **TEACHER-LED GROUP** **DURING** the Writer's Workshop, children may use the *Language Handbook* (pp. 14–15, 17) for a model of invitations and envelopes. **INDEPENDENT**	**AFTER** the Idea Bank activities, children can write descriptions of their neighborhoods using *Imagination Express, Destination: Neighborhood.* (p. T434) **COOPERATIVE GROUPS** **AFTER** the Writer's Workshop, children can complete the *Writer's Magazine.* (pp. 28–31) **COOPERATIVE GROUPS**	**AFTER** the Grammar lesson, make copies of a story page that contains proper nouns, and help children identify them. (p. T439) **TEACHER-LED GROUP**	**DURING** the Writer's Workshop, use CIELO ABIERTO *Teacher's Handbook* page 68 to have children write sentences about a picture. **TEACHER-LED GROUP** **INSTEAD OF** completing the Grammar lesson, refer to page 9 in *Abuela Teacher's Guide.* **TEACHER-LED GROUP**
3 LEARNING THROUGH THE LITERATURE Direct Skills Instruction Integrated Curriculum Reading Trade Books Theme Project	**DURING** the Study Skills lesson, children can use *Kid Pix* to add visuals to their glossaries and dictionaries. (p. T444) **COOPERATIVE GROUPS**	**WHILE** others work on the Comprehension lesson, have partners write sentences with words that are missing because of the "word washer" and have them guess at answers. (p. T443) **PAIRS** **WHILE** others work in centers, have children select and read a Trade Book. **INDEPENDENT**	**WHILE** others work on the Comprehension lesson, have children make the Take-Home/Keep-at-Home book *I Can Go Anyplace* to read at home. **TEACHER-LED GROUP** **WHILE** reading Trade Books, pair children with native speakers of English, and have them take turns reading and using context clues to figure out unfamiliar words. (p. T443) **PAIRS**	**WHILE** others work in groups, have children complete the ongoing cross-curricular project. See page 2 in *Abuela Teacher's Guide.* **COOPERATIVE GROUPS** **WHILE** others are sharing trade books, have children choose a book from the *Multi-Language Library* to take home to share with family members. **INDEPENDENT**

Ongoing Assessment Strategies

KIDS DO THE WORK

Children must feel that their portfolios truly belong to them before they can begin to analyze their work and take control of their own learning. To promote ownership, make portfolios accessible, and give children the responsibility for managing their portfolios. To foster responsibility, encourage children to

- design and decorate their portfolios, including the Contents page.
- keep up their reading and writing logs, recording reactions and comments about everything they read and write.
- file works-in-progress, including artwork, prewriting notes, and first drafts as well as finished work.
- organize and review the contents of their portfolios, especially before conferences.
- write a title on each piece of writing and then categorize the titles into sections, using cardboard, colored-paper dividers, or any other materials.

When children manage their own portfolios and remain in control of the information that is created, collected, and presented, they interpret their portfolios according to their own needs and interests and become aware of their development as readers and writers.

See the Organizing My Portfolio Checklist on page T234 and the SIGNATURES *Portfolio Assessment Teacher's Guide.*

MISCUE ANALYSIS/RUNNING RECORDS

You can use Running Records, a form of Miscue Analysis, to learn about an individual student's word recognition skills and strategies and reading behaviors. Ask the child to read aloud a short passage. As the child reads, record his or her miscues on a copy of the selection or tape-record the oral reading for later listening and analysis.

When the child is finished reading, check the child's comprehension by discussing the selection with the child or by asking the child to retell or tell you about what was read. Use both the miscues and the child's comprehension to gain information about a child's use of reading strategies to construct meaning.

Consider the following questions as you analyze a child's miscues:

- How many miscues did the child make?
- What types of miscues did the child make?
  —Are they meaning-based miscues?
  —Are they letter/sound–based miscues? What strategies did the child use to decode unfamiliar words?
- Does the child self-correct his or her own miscues?

End-of-Theme Formal Assessment Tools

SKILLS ASSESSMENT

Multiple-choice diagnostic tests that measure mastery of the following skills:

- Reading: vocabulary, *r*-controlled vowel (/ûr/*er, ur, ir, ear*), and making predictions
- Language: statements, questions, exclamations, commands, end marks, nouns, and names of special people, animals, and places

HOLISTIC READING ASSESSMENT

Reading passages with multiple-choice and open-ended questions to assess children's application of literal, inferential, and critical thinking in a global and holistic manner

INTEGRATED PERFORMANCE ASSESSMENT

Performance tasks to gain a comprehensive view of a child's reading and writing progress. Children read and respond to "Jamaica Tag-Along" by award-winning author Juanita Havill. Children demonstrate expressive writing in a friendly letter. One or both sections may be used.

WE BELONG TOGETHER

Having special people in your life can make you happy. Families, friends, pets, and others cheer you up when you're sad. They celebrate with you when you're happy. Whether your special ones are old or young, and whether they live with you or far away, they make the world a better place.

121

THEME 2

We Belong Together

DISCUSSING THE THEME

Invite children to read about the theme on page 121. Encourage them to tell about special people in their lives. Talk about what makes these people special. Then ask children how the theme title We Belong Together relates to the special people or pets in their lives.

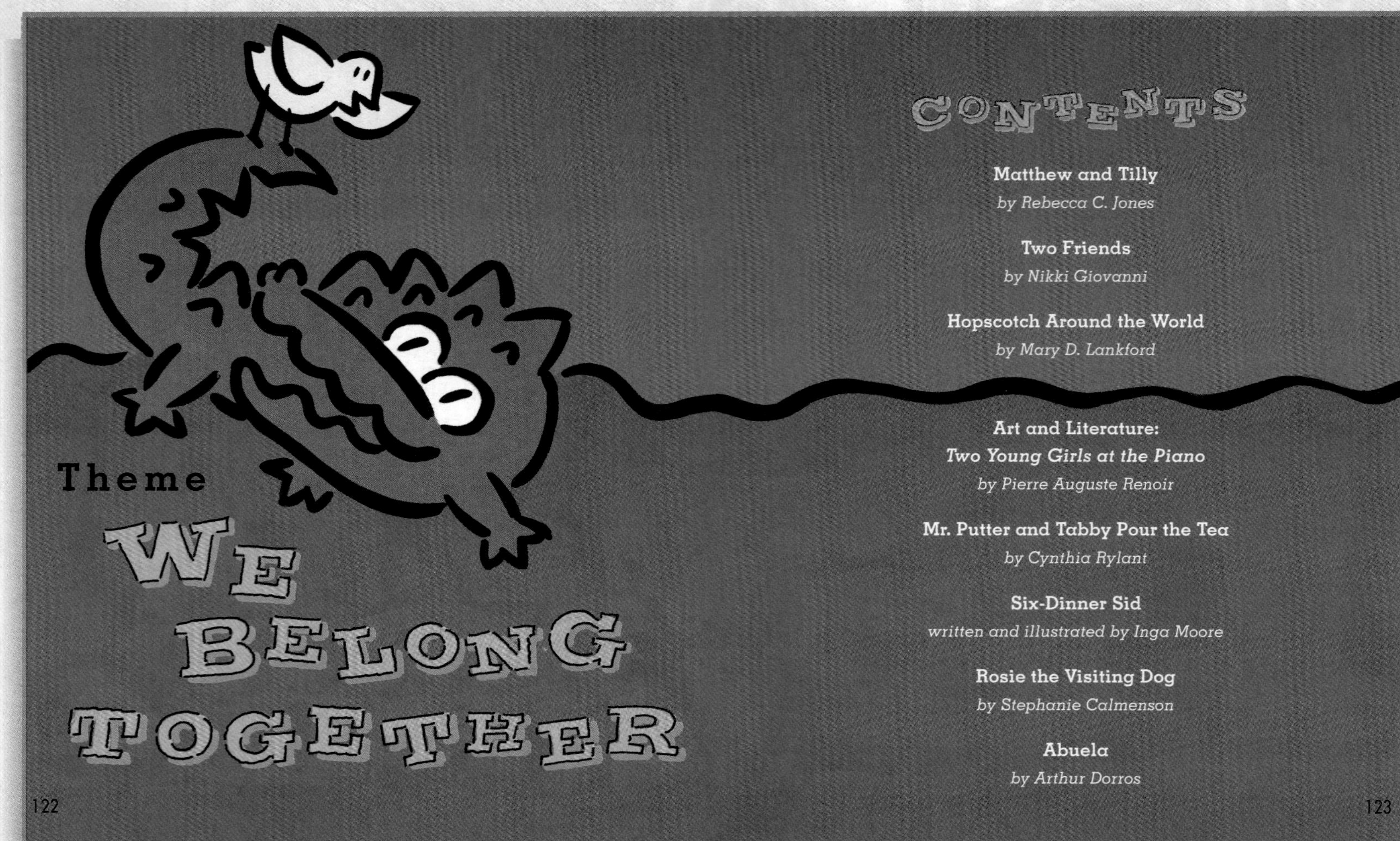

Previewing the Theme Literature

Read the table of contents on pages 122–123 with children. If they are familiar with any of the selections, poets, authors, or illustrators, ask them to tell what they know.

Brainstorm with children the characteristics of a special friend. Ask:

- **What makes a friend special?**
- **Can people still be friends if they live far away from one another?**

Ask children to recall stories they have read that tell about special friends—people or animals! Encourage them to describe the characters and tell how their friendships are special.

BOOKSHELF

There's a Dragon in My Sleeping Bag
by James Howe

Alex feels left out when his brother Simon spends time with a make-believe friend—a dragon. Then Alex discovers a make-believe friend, too!

Signatures Library
Award-Winning Author

Mary Ann
written and illustrated by Betsy James

When Amy's best friend moves away, Amy finds a new friend—an insect!

Signatures Library
SLJ Best Books

Chester's Way
by Kevin Henkes

Chester and Wilson like to do things their way. But things change when they meet Lilly.

ALA Notable Book

Angel Child, Dragon Child
by Michele Maria Surat

A new friend and the whole school help a girl bring her mother from Vietnam to America.

Notable Trade Book in Social Studies

Polka and Dot
by Dena Schutzer

A lonely bird flies near and far to find her best friend.

124 125

The Signatures Library

There's a Dragon in My Sleeping Bag **by James Howe, tells about Alex, who creates an imaginary friend, Calvin the camel, when he feels left out by his older brother's imaginary dragon, Dexter.**

Mary Ann, **written and illustrated by Betsy James, tells about Amy and Mary Ann, two best friends. When Mary Ann moves away, Amy finds a praying mantis and names it Mary Ann.**

Strategies for reading *There's a Dragon in My Sleeping Bag* appear with the "Matthew and Tilly" lesson on page T294. Strategies for *Mary Ann* appear with the "Six-Dinner Sid" lesson on page T396.

A comprehensive lesson plan for each book is available on pages T454–T461.

Related Reading

These trade books offer children further opportunities to work with the We Belong Together theme.

ESL / Title I Library

These easy-to-read library books connect to the theme We Belong Together: *Have You Seen My Cat?* by *Eric Carle*; *Bein' With You This Way* by *W. Nikola-Lisa*.

THEME PROJECT OVERVIEW

Make a Mail Center

THEME OVERVIEW

The selections in this theme show different aspects of friendship. One thing all good friendships have in common is communication. This project will demonstrate the different forms communication can take. Each lesson is followed by a Project Checkpoint that will help children complete the project, a classroom mail center.

PROJECT PLANNER

QUESTIONS: What happens at the post office? How can we set up a mail system in the classroom? (Problem Solving)

STAGES	GOALS
PROJECT LAUNCH (p.T247) 2–3 days	Discuss mail and the post office. • Compare ways people communicate. • Form project groups and create delivery addresses with ZIP codes in the classroom.
CHECKPOINT 1 (p.T296) 3–4 days	Research how the post office works. • Plan a post office tour or invite a postal worker in to speak to the class. • Prepare questions to ask the postal worker.
CHECKPOINT 2 (p.T354) 4–6 days	Create a classroom mail center. • Discuss setting up a mail center. • Make and decorate mailboxes for the center. • Follow plans to install the mail center.
CHECKPOINT 3 (p.T398) 3–4 days	Set up rules for the mail center. • Discuss and agree upon rules. • Make a list of rules.
CHECKPOINT 4 (p.T450) 4–6 days	Prepare material to place in the center. • Write messages, put them in envelopes, and mail them in the drop-off box. • Take turns sorting and delivering mail.
PROJECT PRESENTATIONS (p.T452) 3–4 days	Share the mail center. • Invite other classes in to see the center. • Explain how the center was created.

STUDENTS ACQUIRING ENGLISH

Have children draw a picture of the field trip or the postal worker's visit and write sentences about it. Have them write about something new that they learned.

MULTIPLE INTELLIGENCES

Invite children with strong verbal skills to write guidelines for working in a group.

INQUIRY PROJECT IDEAS

Some children may wish to investigate other forms of communication. They may research and share information on such topics as

- **the meaning of road signs and signals.**
- **signals used by sports officials.**
- **computer networks.**

PROJECT LAUNCH

LAUNCH OPTIONS

SIMON WRITES (SMALL GROUP)

Play a familiar game, such as "Simon Says," but have children use only written directions. Prepare, or have children prepare in advance, signs with appropriate directions, half of which are preceded by "Simon writes." As they play the game, children should follow only the "Simon writes" directions. The signs should be readable from a few feet away.

IT'S A SIGN! (WHOLE GROUP)

Take a walk with children to find and read different signs in the neighborhood. Ask children to remember at least one sign they found particularly interesting. Have children draw the sign and explain what made it interesting to them. Talk about what messages each sign gives.

WHOLE-GROUP DISCUSSION

Talk with children about all the types of messages that are expressed in writing. Ask children for examples of places where they see writing and what messages they see.

FORM PROJECT GROUPS

Provide letters, postcards, and magazines. Let children examine them as you point out information on the envelopes and labels (stamp, delivery and return addresses, ZIP code). Ask *How does this information help the post office?*

Help children form "geographic" groups by their locations in the classroom. Groups should

- develop their own classroom addresses, including ZIP codes.
- contribute to a classroom map that shows each group's area of the classroom and ZIP code.

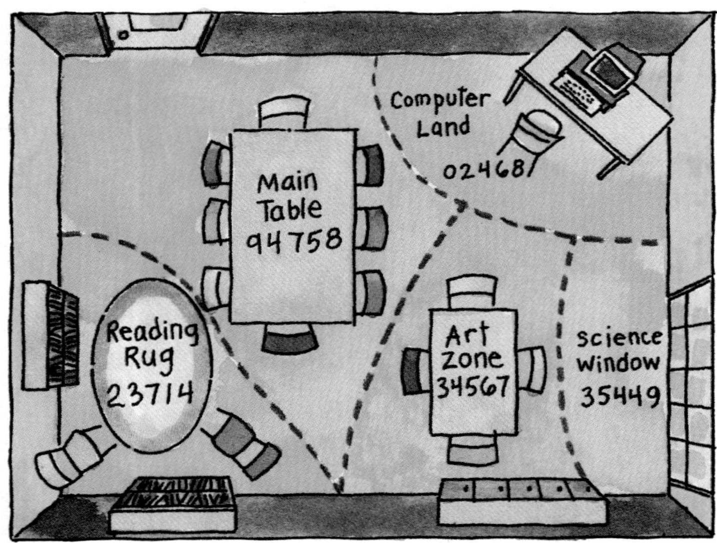

DID YOU KNOW?

- The first three digits of a ZIP code identify the major city post office that serves the area of the address. The next two digits identify a branch or station of the major post office.

Project Card 7 can be found as a copying master on page R87.

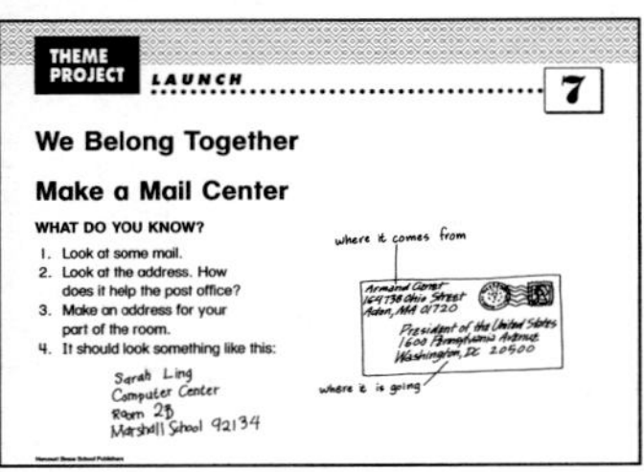
THEME PROJECT LAUNCH 7

We Belong Together

Make a Mail Center

WHAT DO YOU KNOW?

1. Look at some mail.
2. Look at the address. How does it help the post office?
3. Make an address for your part of the room.
4. It should look something like this:

Project Card 7

PROJECT MANAGEMENT

PROJECT LAUNCH

CHECKPOINT 1

CHECKPOINT 2

CHECKPOINT 3

CHECKPOINT 4

PRESENTATIONS

ASSESSMENT

ADDITIONAL RESOURCES

BOOKS

The Jolly Postman: Or Other People's Letters by Janet Ahlberg and Allan Ahlberg. Little, Brown, 1986.

The Post Office Book by Gail Gibbons. HarperCollins, 1982.

MAGAZINE ARTICLE

"Make Your Own Mail Pouch," *Sesame Street*, April 1995.

FORMAL ASSESSMENT

Prompts for self- and peer assessment and a rubric for teacher assessment are provided on page T453.

Planning a Literacy Event

Open House Begin planning an Open House as a culminating activity at the completion of the theme. Children who have completed the theme project will take turns explaining how their mail center works. Children can reinforce what they have learned by explaining it to others.

- Begin collecting, with community help, shoe boxes that will be adapted to use as classroom mailboxes.
- Set a date for the Open House.
- Advise other teachers of the nature of the project and the opportunities it will offer their classes.
- Appoint an educational committee whose responsibility will be to keep a journal, which can be used later as a reference source for a history of the project.

Enlisting Parents as Partners

Reading: The Key to Success During conferences, parents may ask for ideas to get their children reading. Offer these suggestions:

- ☑ Let your child distribute the household mail each day. Help him or her read handwritten addresses.
- ☑ Encourage family and friends to send mail to your child.
- ☑ Let your child see you enjoying reading every day.
- ☑ Read aloud to your child. Talk about what you read.

MAIL

There will be an
Open House
for Room 2B's
post office on
November 10.
Keep this date free!

MAIL

TECHNOLOGY

The *At Home in Our Schools* videocassette contains numerous ideas for family involvement projects.

Surfing the Internet? See Issues and Ideas on the Harcourt Brace Home Page: http://www.hbschool.com

The *Family Involvement Newsletter* for this theme contains further suggestions on this topic and other topics of interest to parents.

Notable Trade Book in Social Studies

MATTHEW and TILLY

by REBECCA C. JONES
illustrated by BETH PECK

THEME: FRIENDSHIP

We Belong Together

In "Matthew and Tilly," children will discover that friends belong together even though they don't always agree.

Linking Poetry to Fiction

Children read about two best friends.

SELECTION SUMMARY

Genre: Realistic Fiction

Matthew and Tilly are friends who live in a city neighborhood. They play and ride bikes together, sell lemonade together, and even rescue a kitten together. When they get into an argument over a crayon, Matthew goes inside to play store while Tilly draws a hopscotch game on the sidewalk. They soon learn that playing alone is no fun. They apologize and go off to play—together again.

Rebecca C. Jones

ABOUT THE AUTHOR AND THE ILLUSTRATOR

REBECCA C. JONES has been a reporter, a journalism instructor, and a writer. She has written numerous stories for children and young adults.

BETH PECK has illustrated several books. Her work has been presented in *Society of Illustrators Annual*.

For more information about the author and the illustrator, see pages T272–273.

Beth Peck

SUGGESTED LESSON PLANNER

▶ ***Matthew and Tilly***

	DAY 1	DAY 2
PART 1 Reading Listening Speaking Viewing **Key Words** purple wondered break herself piece	**BUILD BACKGROUND** T252 **VOCABULARY STRATEGIES** T252–T253 *Chart/Transparency 9* *Practice Book* p. 46 **READING THE SELECTION** T254–T273 Options for Reading T254–T255 *Response Card 3* *Literature Cassette 1* **REVIEW PREDICTIONS/PURPOSE** T270 **APPRECIATING THE LITERATURE** T270 NOTE: Children may read the selection on Day 2.	**SUMMARIZE AND RETELL THE SELECTION** T271 *Practice Book* p. 47 **READ POETRY** T274–T275 "Two Friends" ◆ **RESPONSE CORNER ACTIVITIES** T276 **CHECKING COMPREHENSION** T277 *End-of-Selection Test*
PART 2 Writer's Workshop	**A DIALOGUE** Thinking as Writers T282 *Chart/Transparency 10*	Prewriting T282
Grammar	✓**STATEMENTS AND QUESTIONS** Teach the Concept T284 Daily Language Practice (1–2) R80	Daily Language Practice (3–4) R80 Practice Activity T285
Spelling	**WORDS WITH SHORT *u*** *fun sun up nut duck* *us cut bus gum bun* Pretest/Self-Check T286 *Integrated Spelling Teacher's Edition* pp. T57, T274	Open and Closed Sorts T286 *Integrated Spelling* p. 34 *Integrated Spelling Teacher's Edition* p. T58
PART 3 Phonics	✓ ***R*-CONTROLLED VOWEL: /ûr/*er, ur*** Phonics-Vocabulary Connection T253	✓ ***R*-CONTROLLED VOWEL: /ûr/*er, ur*** (Introduce) T288 *Big Book of Rhymes* pp. 10–11 *Phonics Practice Book* pp. 135–136
Skills and Strategies	◆ **INTEGRATED CURRICULUM** *Neighborhoods* **Social Studies** T292 **Math** T292 **Science** T293 **Art** T293 *Imagination Express, Destination: Neighborhood*	**COMPREHENSION SKILL** T290–T291 ✓ Making Predictions (Introduce) *Practice Book* p. 52 *Living Book: The Berenstain Bears Get in a Fight*
	Use the Extra Support note on page T260 and the Intervention Strategies note on page T262 to help **below-level readers.**	During the Response Corner activities, use the Varying the Activity note on page T276 for **above-level readers.**

NOTE: An alternative lesson plan for **below-level readers** appears on *Intervention Strategies Manual* pp. 26–31. A lesson for **students acquiring English** appears on *Sheltered English/ESL Manual* pp. 18–21.

DAY 3

◆ **IDEA BANK ACTIVITIES**
Listening and Speaking T280
Real-Life Reading: Reading Store Signs T280
Oral Language T281
Kinesthetic T281
Writer's Magazine pp. 18–21

School–Home Connection 5 R110

Drafting T282
Language Handbook pp. 26–27
The Amazing Writing Machine

Daily Language Practice (5–6) R80
Practice Activity T285
Language Handbook pp. 48–51

Discuss the Generalization T286
Integrated Spelling p. 35
Integrated Spelling Teacher's Edition p. T59

✓ ***R*-CONTROLLED VOWEL: /ûr/*er, ur*** T288
Phonics Practice Reader 15: Desert Fire

GRAMMAR MINILESSON T259
✓ Word Order in Sentences (Review)
Language Handbook pp. 46–47

DAY 4

VOCABULARY WORKSHOP T287
Reviewing Key Words
Story Strips R114
Contractions with *not*
Practice Book p. 50
Take-Home/Keep-at-Home Book: Sisters Forever

READING TRADE BOOKS T294–T295

Signatures Library

Sisters Forever

Take-Home Book

Responding and Revising T283

Daily Language Practice (7–8) R80
Practice Activity T285
Grammar Practice Book pp. 25–28

Apply to Writing T286
Integrated Spelling pp. 36–37
Integrated Spelling Teacher's Edition pp. T60–T61

✓ ***R*-CONTROLLED VOWEL: /ûr/*er, ur*** T289
Practice Book p. 51

PHONICS AND DECODING MINILESSON T261
Short Vowel: /u/*u* (Maintain)
Phonics Activity Book p. 14
Phonics Game Board Pattern Book p. 5
Phonics Practice Reader 4: Jim and Jill
Phonics Practice Book pp. 52–56
Practice Book p. 53

DAY 5

READING TRADE BOOKS T289, T291, T293, T294–T295

Instant Reader™

Instant Reader™

Proofreading and Publishing T283
Kid Pix

Daily Language Practice (9–12) R80
Practice Book p. 48

Posttest T286
Practice Book p. 49
Integrated Spelling Teacher's Edition p. T62

✓ ***R*-CONTROLLED VOWEL: /ûr/*er, ur*** T289
Phonics Activity Book p. 13

COMPREHENSION MINILESSON T263
Story Elements (Plot) (Review)
Practice Book p. 54

Theme Project Checkpoint 1 T296

To help children build fluency, use the *Instant Readers™ I Have Another Language* and *Secret Show and Tell* on pages T278–T279.

Have children read "Hopscotch Around the World," pages 150–155, to make connections between fiction and nonfiction pieces.

During the Project Checkpoint, refer to the Students Acquiring English note on page T296 to help **ESL readers.**

✓ = Tested Skill
◆ = Optional activities that may be used to adjust pacing throughout the lesson
Titles in *italics* are optional materials.

1 Reading and Responding

BUILDING BACKGROUND AND CONCEPTS

PRIOR KNOWLEDGE

Discuss friendship. Write the word *Friends* on the board. Give children paper strips, and ask them to write words they think of when they hear the word *friends*. Invite children to share their ideas. Use double-sided tape to organize words around the main idea *Friends*. Encourage children to add to the web as they think of new ideas.

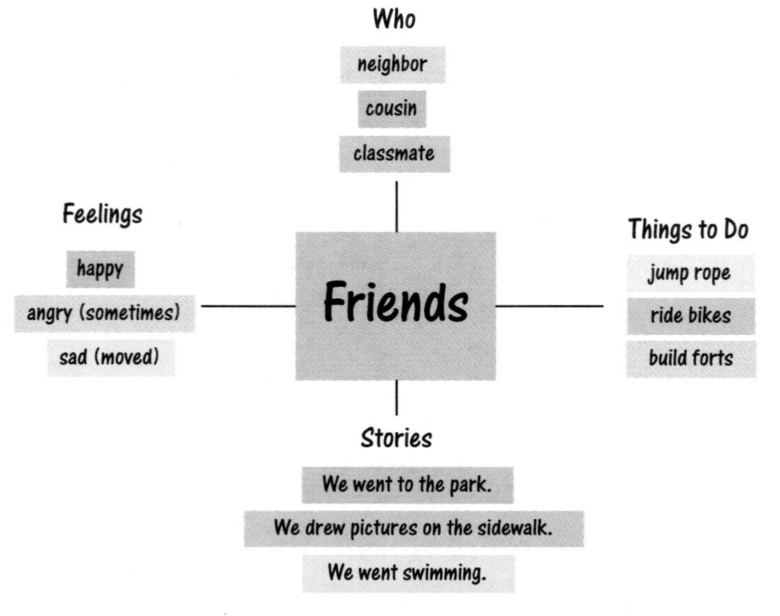

MEETING INDIVIDUAL NEEDS

Intervention Strategies

For children who may have difficulty reading "Matthew and Tilly," support is available in *Intervention Strategies Manual*, pages 26–31, and on pages T262 and T278–T279 in this lesson.

STUDENTS ACQUIRING ENGLISH

See *Sheltered English/ESL Manual*, pages 18–21.

VOCABULARY STRATEGIES

KEY WORDS DEFINED

purple a mixture of red and blue
break to crack into pieces
piece a part of a whole
wondered was curious about something
herself her and no one else

SUPPORT WORDS

Display the words *business, rescued, machines, cash register, probably*, and *customer*. Discuss their meanings and have them used in sentences.

INTEGRATED SPELLING

SPELLING PRETEST: page T286
SPELLING GENERALIZATION: Words with short *u*

TIPS FOR TEACHERS

"In my class, we have a Thoughtful Box and the kids just love it! When a student notices a classmate doing something thoughtful, such as being helpful or sharing, that student writes an anonymous note about the thoughtful act and puts it into the box. At the end of the day, we read the notes together. It really helps create an atmosphere of caring and belonging."

CUEING SYSTEMS

Have children read new vocabulary. Display Chart/Transparency 9, or write the Key Words and these sentences on the board.

Cover the letters *urple* in *purple* with a self-stick note. Have children read the sentence and suggest words that make sense. Uncover the word and ask:

How does seeing the first letter help you figure out the word?
Does the word make sense in the sentence?

Have children continue reading the story, using the sounds for letters and the sense of the story to help them figure out the underlined words.

HANDS-ON ACTIVITY

Children put together word-card puzzles. Distribute Puzzle Cards (page R202), or have children write the Key Words on cards. Then they should cut each word card into two pieces. Ask partners to exchange word-card puzzles and put each other's Key Words back together. Have children read the completed words and use them in sentences. Then have children add the words to their Word Files.

CHART/TRANSPARENCY 9

purple **break** **piece**

wondered **herself**

Clare had a lot of purple crayons and chalk. She tried not to break them. If she did, she saved every piece.

She used chalk to draw outside. Sometimes Clare drew numbers in squares on the sidewalk. When her friends saw what she had drawn, they wondered what game they could play. Clare liked to play by herself, but she was glad to let her friends play, too.

PHONICS-VOCABULARY CONNECTION

CLASSIFYING WORDS

Write the Key Words *purple* and *herself* on the board as headings of a chart. Read the words with children, and have them listen to each word for the sound at the end of *fur*. Ask children to brainstorm more /ûr/ words, and list their suggestions beside the chart. Then work with children to find only those words with /ûr/ spelled *ur* and *er*, and write them on the chart.

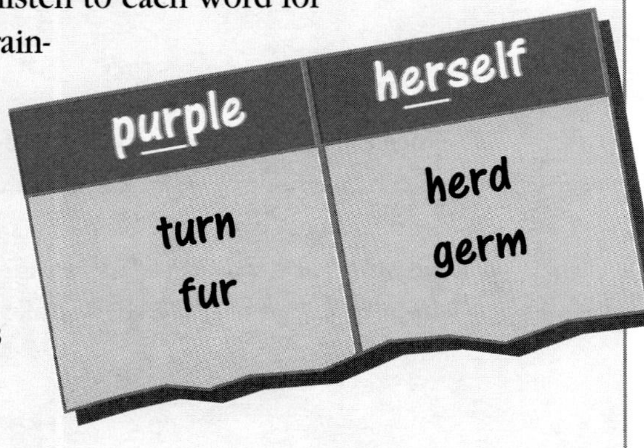

The concept of *r*-controlled vowel /ûr/*ur, er* is further developed on pages T288–T289.

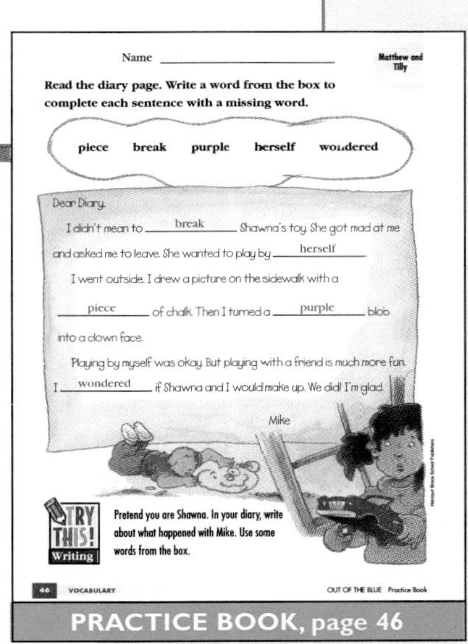
Name ____________ Matthew and Tilly

Read the diary page. Write a word from the box to complete each sentence with a missing word.

piece break purple herself wondered

Dear Diary,

I didn't mean to break Shawna's toy. She got mad at me and asked me to leave. She wanted to play by herself.

I went outside. I drew a picture on the sidewalk with a piece of chalk. Then I turned a purple blob into a clown face.

Playing by myself was okay. But playing with a friend is much more fun. I wondered if Shawna and I would make up. We did! I'm glad.

Mike

TRY THIS! Writing — Pretend you are Shawna. In your diary, write about what happened with Mike. Use some words from the box.

46 VOCABULARY OUT OF THE BLUE Practice Book

PRACTICE BOOK, page 46

Strategic Reading

STRATEGY FOCUS: MAKING PREDICTIONS

Review some things good readers do when they read. Encourage children to suggest new ideas and add them to their classroom chart.

What Good Readers Do
Keep in mind the order in which things happen
Notice things about the story's characters
Guess what might happen next

Share with children the comprehension strategy that is the focus of this selection.

MODEL **When I read, I think about what I know about the characters and what has happened in the story so far. I try to guess, or predict, what might happen next. Then I read on to find out if my prediction is right.**

MATTHEW AND TILLY

by REBECCA C. JONES
illustrated by BETH PECK

126

TIPS FOR CLASSROOM MANAGEMENT

SMALL GROUP

BUDDY READING

Pair children who need extra support with more fluent readers. Invite children to take turns reading pages of the story to each other. Encourage them to pause periodically to talk about the story.

COOPERATIVE READING

LITERATURE CIRCLES Have small groups read silently to page 137 and then to the end of the story. Invite the groups to discuss the main events, the problem, and solutions. Distribute Reader Response Card 3 (Plot), page R84, for discussion starters.

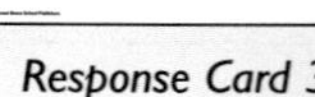
Response Card 3

MATTHEW and TILLY were friends.

127

PREVIEWING/ SETTING PURPOSES

Have children read the title on page 126 and preview the story illustrations. Ask children to predict who the story might be about and what they think Matthew and Tilly will do. Have children write their predictions in their journals. Then help children set purposes for reading.

APPLYING A STRATEGY

PAGES 127–131 Have children look at the illustrations on the pages. Then ask children what they think Matthew and Tilly are like. As children read the pages, have them think about whether Matthew and Tilly are like anyone they know. **RELATING TO PERSONAL EXPERIENCES**

WHOLE CLASS

STRATEGIC READING

Choose some or all of the suggestions under Strategic Reading, pages T254–T271, to guide a literature discussion and model the STRATEGY FOCUS of Making Predictions.

INDEPENDENT READING

Have children read "Matthew and Tilly" independently. As children finish, have them respond to the story in their journals. When all children have finished, encourage them to use their journal entries and the story pictures to help them summarize and discuss the story.

They rode bikes together,

128

LISTENING CENTER

You may want to prepare an audiocassette of "Matthew and Tilly" and place it in the Listening Center for children to enjoy individually or in small groups. Suggest that children follow along in their books as they listen to the tape. (See Acknowledgments on pages R235–R236.)

CONVENTIONS OF PRINT

HYPHENS Invite children to find the phrase *hide-and-seek* on page 129. Ask children what makes those words different from other words on the page. Explain that hyphens are sometimes used to join two or more words that work closely together to form one idea.

and they played hide-and-seek together.

129

NOTES

Here's a place to list ideas or activities that you would like to use the next time you teach this lesson.

IDEA BANK

WRITING A POEM **Invite children to write an acrostic poem using the word *FRIENDS*. Encourage children to refer to the Friends web from page T252, the story, and their personal experiences to write the poem. Children might like to customize their poem with a border or clip art using the software *Kid Pix 2*.**

F un to be with
R iding bikes
I nventing games to play
E ating ice cream
N icely playing together
D rawing on the sidewalk
S haring every day

Cooperative Reading

Have children summarize what they have read so far. Then ask them how they feel about Matthew and Tilly at this point in the story and why. **SUMMARIZING**

They sold lemonade together. When business was slow, they played sidewalk games together.

130

SOCIAL STUDIES CONNECTION

HOMES For children who are unfamiliar with city living, use the story pictures to help explain that many people live in big apartment buildings, often close to stores and businesses. Point out that each building has many apartments and that each apartment is a home.

And sometimes they ate ice-cream cones together.

131

Tested Skill

MINILESSON

REVIEW: GRAMMAR

Word Order in Sentences

INFORMAL ASSESSMENT

As children speak and write, notice whether they are using correct word order in their sentences.

TEACH/MODEL

Write this sentence on a sentence strip:

Matthew and Tilly play games.

Cut the sentence into individual words. Invite volunteers to manipulate the word cards to create a sentence that makes sense. Remind children that in order for a sentence to make sense, the words must be in a certain order.

Repeat with the following sets of words:

Tilly | numbers | the | boxes | draws | in | .

the | mixed | Matthew | lemonade | .

PRACTICE/APPLY

Have children write sentences on sentence strips, cut each sentence into separate words, mix up the words, and trade with a partner. Partners make a sentence. Encourage discussion of how meaning can change when word order is changed.

LANGUAGE HANDBOOK
Word Order, pages 46–47

CROSS-CULTURAL VIEWPOINT

Brainstorm with children other words they use for *friend,* such as *buddy* or *playmate.* Invite children to tell the words for *friend* in other languages, such as the Spanish *amigo* or the Japanese *tomodachi.* You may want to add their words to the web about friends on page T252.

ILLUSTRATOR'S CRAFT

Since the setting of "Matthew and Tilly" is a city neighborhood, Beth Peck based her illustrations on the Washington Heights neighborhood in New York City, where she once lived.

Strategic Reading

MODELING A STRATEGY

PAGES 132–133 After children read, help them make predictions. **Think aloud:** *I wonder what will happen next. The author has been talking about things Matthew and Tilly do together, but suddenly she says that sometimes Matthew and Tilly get sick of each other. Then she tells about a broken crayon. I can use these ideas from the story and what I know about how friends act to guess that they will get mad at each other.*

Ask children to predict what might happen. **MAKING PREDICTIONS**

Once they even rescued a lady's kitten from a tree together.
The lady gave them money for the bubble-gum machines.
So later they chewed gum together and remembered how brave they had been.

132

CONVENTIONS OF LANGUAGE

APOSTROPHES Write *lady's kitten* and *Tilly's purple crayon* on the board, and read the phrases with children. Cover the *'s* in *lady's* and *Tilly's*. Ask children to read the words. Then uncover the *'s* and have children read the words. Explain that *'s* shows ownership.

EXTRA SUPPORT Remind children that picture clues can be very helpful in figuring out unfamiliar words. If children have difficulty with *rescued,* direct their attention to the picture and ask what Matthew and Tilly are doing. If necessary, help them paraphrase the first sentence on page 132.

Sometimes, though, Matthew and Tilly got sick of each other. One day when they were coloring, Matthew broke Tilly's purple crayon. He didn't mean to, but he did.

133

MINILESSON

MAINTAIN: PHONICS AND DECODING

Short Vowel: /u/*u*

INFORMAL ASSESSMENT

When they are reading aloud, notice whether children are able to decode words that have the short vowel *u*.

TEACH/MODEL

Invite children to reread page 132, and ask them what Matthew and Tilly bought with the money. (gum) Write the word *gum* on the board. Ask a volunteer to underline the letter *u* and tell what sound the letter *u* stands for.

Next, write *bag* on the board. Ask a volunteer to read the word and then say a new word, replacing the /a/ sound with the /u/ sound. (bug) Write *bug* next to *bag*. Repeat with other words with short vowel sounds, such as *beg* (bug), *fin* (fun), and *hot* (hut).

PRACTICE/APPLY

Ask children to find another word with short *u* on page 132. (*bubble*) Begin a list of words with short *u* on chart paper, and have children brainstorm short *u* words.

PHONICS ACTIVITY BOOK, page 14

For further reinforcement, you may want to use "That Sounds Like Duck," *Phonics Game Board Pattern Book*, page 5.

PHONICS PRACTICE READER 4

PHONICS PRACTICE BOOK, pages 52–56

REAL-LIFE CONNECTION

Ask children to think about a time a favorite toy got broken or lost. What happened? How did they feel? Encourage children to share their experiences. Use these ideas to help them understand how Tilly feels when her crayon is broken.

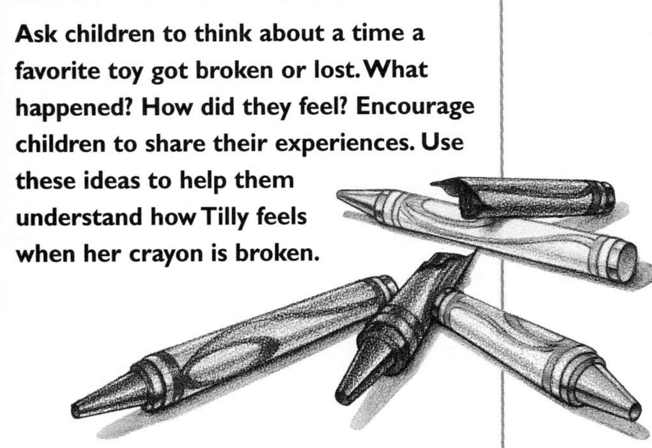

Matthew and Tilly   Name ____________

Read the poem. Circle the word in each line with the same vowel sound as *cub*. Then write the circled word that goes best with each clue.

Harvey heard a loud buzz.
His heart made a thump.
He was stung by a bee,
Which caused him to jump.
Harvey the duck
Got stuck in the mud.
He tried to get up,
But he fell with a thud.

1. Wet dirt — mud
2. A dull noise — thud, thump
3. A bee's sound — buzz
4. A kind of bird — duck
5. To be trapped — stuck
6. Not down — up
7. A way to move — jump
8. What a bee did — stung

OUT OF THE BLUE Practice Book   SHORT VOWEL: /u/u   53

PRACTICE BOOK, page 53

Strategic Reading

APPLYING A STRATEGY

PAGES 134–137 Have children use the pictures to describe how Matthew and Tilly feel. After children read the pages, have them revisit the predictions they made after reading page 133.

1. **Is this conversation between Matthew and Tilly what you expected would happen?**
2. **From what you have read and seen on these two pages, do you want to change your prediction?**

Allow time for children to confirm their previous predictions and to make new ones. Discuss how the information on page 135 may have affected their ideas about the plot. Then children can read on to confirm their new predictions.

MAKING AND CONFIRMING PREDICTIONS

134

MEETING INDIVIDUAL NEEDS

Intervention Strategies

MAKING PREDICTIONS Have children repeat this sentence: *While I'm reading, it helps me to check to see if my guesses are right or wrong.* Have children tell how using this strategy might help them understand the events in "Matthew and Tilly."

ILLUSTRATOR'S CRAFT

Point out that the author uses words to help the reader know Matthew and Tilly are angry. Talk about how the artist has drawn Matthew and Tilly to let the reader know they are angry.

"You broke my crayon," Tilly said in her crabbiest voice.

"It was an old crayon," Matthew said in his grouchiest voice. "It was ready to break."

"No, it wasn't," Tilly said. "It was a brand-new crayon, and you broke it. You always break everything."

"Stop being so picky," Matthew said. "You're always so picky and stinky and mean."

"Well, you're so stupid," Tilly said. "You're so stupid and stinky and mean."

135

MINILESSON

REVIEW: COMPREHENSION

Story Elements (Plot)

INFORMAL ASSESSMENT

As children read, notice whether they recognize the important actions and events that make up the story.

TEACH/MODEL

Ask children to tell what the story is mainly about up to page 135. Explain that most stories have a beginning, a middle, and an ending. Work with children to complete the first two sections of a story map like the one below for "Matthew and Tilly."

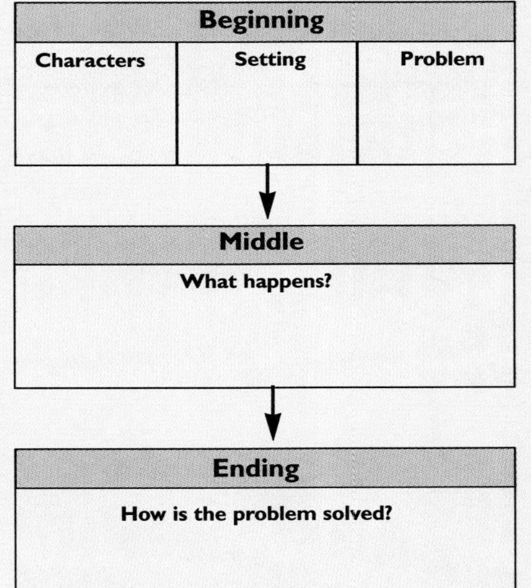

PRACTICE/APPLY

Have children suggest ways that the story would have been different if Matthew had not broken Tilly's crayon. Then ask children to create a new middle and ending for the story. Encourage them to include dialogue.

EXPANDING VOCABULARY

Have children reread the first four lines on page 135. Ask how Matthew and Tilly are feeling. Write these words on the board:

crabby	crabbiest
grouchy	grouchiest

Show children how the y was changed to *i* before *-est* was added, and discuss the meanings of the words.

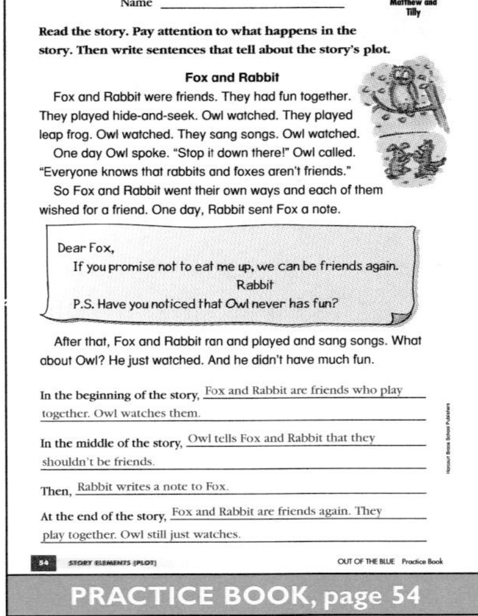

Name ____________ Matthew and Tilly

Read the story. Pay attention to what happens in the story. Then write sentences that tell about the story's plot.

Fox and Rabbit

Fox and Rabbit were friends. They had fun together. They played hide-and-seek. Owl watched. They played leap frog. Owl watched. They sang songs. Owl watched.

One day Owl spoke. "Stop it down there!" Owl called. "Everyone knows that rabbits and foxes aren't friends."

So Fox and Rabbit went their own ways and each of them wished for a friend. One day, Rabbit sent Fox a note.

Dear Fox,
If you promise not to eat me up, we can be friends again.
Rabbit
P.S. Have you noticed that Owl never has fun?

After that, Fox and Rabbit ran and played and sang songs. What about Owl? He just watched. And he didn't have much fun.

In the beginning of the story, Fox and Rabbit are friends who play together. Owl watches them.

In the middle of the story, Owl tells Fox and Rabbit that they shouldn't be friends.

Then, Rabbit writes a note to Fox.

At the end of the story, Fox and Rabbit are friends again. They play together. Owl still just watches.

54 STORY ELEMENTS (PLOT) OUT OF THE BLUE Practice Book

Harcourt Brace School Publishers

PRACTICE BOOK, page 54

Cooperative Reading

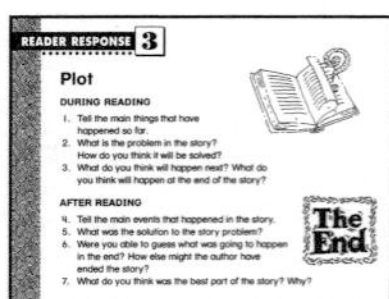
Response Card 3

This is a good point in the story for Literature Circles to answer questions 1–3 on **Reader Response Card 3** (Plot). Through these questions, children will summarize the part of the story they have read, identify the problem, and predict solutions.

After children have discussed the questions, you may want to ask additional questions about the plot.

1. **How has Matthew and Tilly's friendship changed?**
2. **Do you think Matthew and Tilly will be able to solve their problem? Why or why not?**

Matthew stomped up the stairs. By himself.

136

AUTHOR'S CRAFT

Sometimes an author places words in a special way to get across an idea. Point out that *By himself.* and *By herself.* aren't sentences. Discuss why the author might have written them that way. If necessary, explain that writing the words this way helps show how important these words are to the story.

STUDENTS ACQUIRING ENGLISH

Discuss with children the neighborhood sights in the picture on page 137. Provide the English names for some of these places and things.

Tilly found a piece of chalk and began drawing numbers and squares on the sidewalk. By herself.

137

Informal Assessment

USING CUEING SYSTEMS

During reading, or a rereading, of the selection, observe how well children are applying cueing systems to develop meaning.

- ☑ Do children suggest words that make sense in context and have appropriate sound/letter relationships?
- ☑ Do children make logical predictions and then verify them?
- ☑ Do children use picture clues to help them understand the characters and the plot in a story?

SCHOOL↔HOME CONNECTION

Children can walk around their own neighborhoods with an older family member, noting interesting sights and sharing information about the neighborhood. Encourage children to draw pictures and write about what they discovered, and to share their observations with classmates.

I love the park in my neighborhood, especially the slide!

Strategic Reading

MODELING A STRATEGY

PAGES 138–139 After children read, ask them what new problem Matthew and Tilly have. Discuss how knowing this new problem gives clues to what will happen next. Ask children what they think will happen next and why. If necessary, model your thinking: *I know that Matthew thinks his store is the best ever, but he is not happy because he has no customers. Tilly has the same problem. She is unhappy because she does not have anyone to play with. I think Matthew and Tilly will find a way to be friends again.* **MAKING AND CONFIRMING PREDICTIONS**

Upstairs, Matthew got out his cash register and some cans so he could play store. He piled the cans extra high, and he put prices on everything. This was the best store he had ever made. Probably because that picky and stinky and mean old Tilly wasn't around to mess it up.

But he didn't have a customer. And playing store wasn't much fun without a customer.

138

SOCIAL STUDIES WORDS

STORE WORDS Write *store* on the board. Ask children to find words on page 138 that relate to *store*. *(cash register, cans, prices, customer)* Invite children to add other words they know that relate to the word *store*. Help children organize the words into categories, such as equipment and products.

AUTHOR'S CRAFT

Have children reread pages 138–139, and discuss how each page follows the same pattern—the character sets up a game, but then the character isn't having fun because there is no one to play with. After children read, look back through the story with them to find other places where the story "repeats."

Tilly finished drawing the numbers and squares. She drew them really big, with lots of squiggly lines. This was the best sidewalk game she had ever drawn. Probably because that stupid and stinky and mean old Matthew wasn't around to mess it up.

But she didn't have anyone to play with. And a sidewalk game wasn't much fun without another player.

139

Student Self-Assessment

FIX-UP STRATEGY: VISUALIZING

Point out that good readers try to visualize, or picture in their minds, what is happening. As you reread page 138 aloud, ask children to picture in their minds what Matthew is doing. Discuss with children how picturing Matthew setting up the best store ever but then having no one to play with helps them understand how lonely Matthew feels.

CROSS-CULTURAL VIEWPOINT

Mention that various hopscotch games are played all around the world. For example, in Bolivia, children use the names of the days of the week in the squares rather than numbers. Encourage children to describe or demonstrate any other hopscotch games they know.

ITALY: 7, 8, 6, 9, 5, 10, 4, 11, 12, 3, 13, 2, 14, 1

	HONDURAS	
	cabeza (head)	
brazo (arm)	casa (house)	brazo (arm)
	tercera (third)	
	segunda (second)	
	primera (first)	

Strategic Reading

APPLYING A STRATEGY

PAGES 140–141 Have children look at the illustration, and ask what they think is happening. After children read, discuss how the story is changing. Point out that Matthew and Tilly are moving from a problem to a solution. Ask questions such as the following to help children think about this turning point in the story.

1. **Why was Matthew looking out the window?**
2. **Why was Tilly looking up at Matthew's window?**
3. **What did Tilly's smile mean to Matthew?**

Children can use their answers to help them draw conclusions about why Matthew said he was sorry.
DRAWING CONCLUSIONS

140

CHALLENGE **Have children write their version of what Matthew and Tilly might say to each other. Partners might use *Imagination Express, Destination: Neighborhood* to record in their own voices the dialogue between Matthew and Tilly.**

Matthew looked out the window and wondered what Tilly was doing. Tilly looked up at Matthew's window and wondered what he was doing.

She smiled, just a little. That was enough for Matthew.

"I'm sorry," he called.

"So am I," said Tilly.

141

Student Self-Assessment

READING STRATEGIES

Display the What Good Readers Do classroom chart. As children are reading, ask them to pause periodically and ask themselves if they are using the strategies good readers use. Have children ask themselves questions such as these:

- **Do I use the pictures to help me understand the words?**
- **Do I ask myself questions to be sure I understand the words?**
- **Do I use what I know to guess what might happen next?**

PHONICS IN ACTION

Point out the word *enough* on page 141. Tell children that the letters *gh* can stand for the sound heard at the end of *enough*.

Strategic Reading

APPLYING A STRATEGY
PAGES 142–143 Have children look at the pictures to see if they can tell what Matthew and Tilly are doing and how they feel. USING PICTURES CLUES

Returning to the Predictions/Purpose

Before children began to read, they wrote predictions about what they thought would happen in the story. Invite them to share what they wrote and compare it to what actually happened.

Appreciating the Literature

With the whole class or a small group, have an open discussion about the story.

- **How did this story make you feel? Why?**

WRITING

EXTEND THE STORY
Matthew and Tilly are friends again. What do you think they will do the next time they have an argument? Have children write a story about how Matthew and Tilly solve the problem.

Together again.

143

Student Self-Assessment 

FIX-UP STRATEGY: RETELLING
Mention to children that good readers sometimes retell a story to others in their own words. Point out that retelling the story helps the reader know how well he or she understood the story. Allow time for children to retell the story to a partner.

SUMMARIZE AND RETELL

Map the Story

the story map shown here on the , or use Story Map, page R197, to a transparency. Work with children to lete the story map. Then have chil- ıse the story map to retell "Matthew lly." See *Practice Book* page 47.

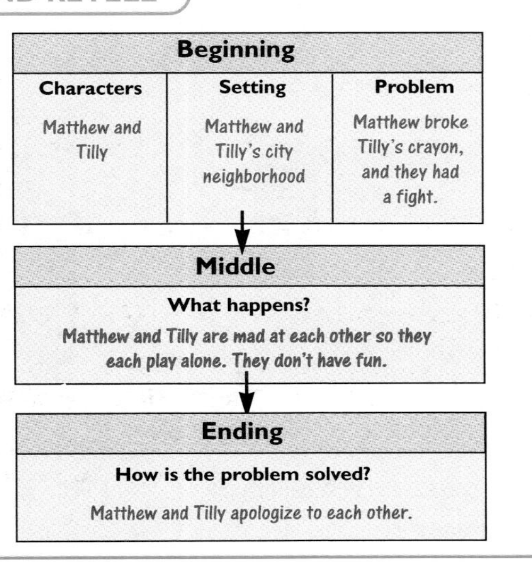

Beginning		
Characters	**Setting**	**Problem**
Matthew and Tilly	Matthew and Tilly's city neighborhood	Matthew broke Tilly's crayon, and they had a fight.

Middle
What happens?
Matthew and Tilly are mad at each other so they each play alone. They don't have fun.

Ending
How is the problem solved?
Matthew and Tilly apologize to each other.

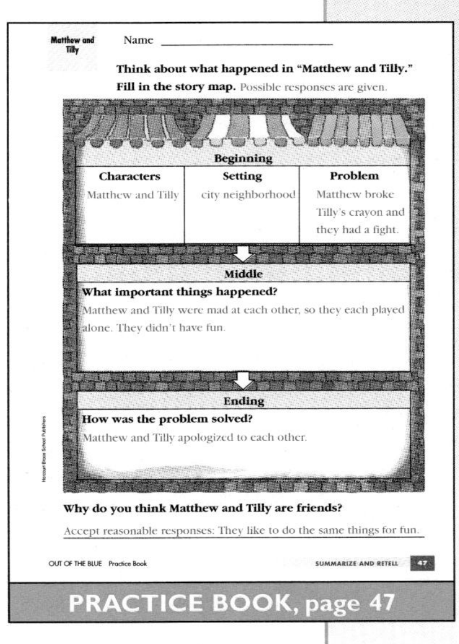

Matthew and Tilly Name ____________

Think about what happened in "Matthew and Tilly." Fill in the story map. Possible responses are given.

Beginning		
Characters	**Setting**	**Problem**
Matthew and Tilly	city neighborhood	Matthew broke Tilly's crayon and they had a fight.

Middle
What important things happened?
Matthew and Tilly were mad at each other, so they each played alone. They didn't have fun.

Ending
How was the problem solved?
Matthew and Tilly apologized to each other.

Why do you think Matthew and Tilly are friends?
Accept reasonable responses: They like to do the same things for fun.

OUT OF THE BLUE Practice Book SUMMARIZE AND RETELL 47

PRACTICE BOOK, page 47

About the Author

PAGES 144–145 Share with children the information on page 144 about the author and the illustrator. Talk about the author's and illustrator's use of their personal experiences to create stories and art.

Rebecca C. Jones grew up in the Chicago area. She is familiar with big-city life and the kind of neighborhood shown in "Matthew and Tilly." Over the years, Ms. Jones has held a variety of jobs, including newspaper reporter and editor and reporter for a TV station. She has taught college courses on writing. She has used all these experiences to help her write her stories.

Ms. Jones was frequently sick as a child, so she would make up characters to keep her company. Today, many of those characters can be found in the stories she writes.

Rebecca C. Jones

When Rebecca Jones was young, she had a friend named Larry. They used to argue all the time. That's what gave Rebecca Jones the idea for this story.

One time, she and Larry got lost when they took a walk. After a while, they found their way home. When they got to Rebecca Jones's house, there were police cars parked outside. They ran inside to see what all the excitement was about. They soon found out that their parents had called the police because *they* were missing.

Rebecca Jones moved when she was seven and never saw Larry again. She wishes that he could read this story and know that she wrote it about the two of them.

Beth Peck

Beth Peck decided to draw Matthew and Tilly in a place she knows very well. The pictures in the book are based on Beth's childhood home, a busy neighborhood in New York City. The book's apartment buildings, stores, signs, iron gates, sidewalks, and fire hydrants look a lot like what Beth Peck saw every day as a young girl.

144

OTHER BOOKS BY REBECCA C. JONES

Down at the Bottom of the Deep Dark Sea. **Macmillan, 1991. EASY**

Germy Blew the Bugle. **Knopf, 1990. AVERAGE**

About the Illustrator

Beth Peck likes to draw. She studied art all through school and continued to study art after graduating from college. For example, she spent time studying how to plan out a picture book, which helped her get a job designing books. As she looked at the artwork for the books she was designing, she realized that illustrating picture books was something she might like to do. She began sending out samples of her work and eventually was asked to illustrate some books.

Before Ms. Peck illustrates a book, she researches what she will need to know for the book. For example, she needed to find out more about a city neighborhood to illustrate "Matthew and Tilly" in a realistic way, so she paid a visit to her old neighborhood of Washington Heights in New York City. She uses her love of drawing to help readers imagine the stories authors tell.

ANOTHER BOOK ILLUSTRATED BY BETH PECK

The House on Maple Street **by Bonnie Pryor. William Morrow, 1992.** CHALLENGE

POEM

Two Friends

by Nikki Giovanni

INTRODUCING THE POEM "Two Friends" is a free-verse poem about the friendship between two best friends. As in "Matthew and Tilly," these friends like the same kinds of things. Ask children to read the title and look at the photograph on pages 146–147. Invite children to talk about what they see and to predict what the poem will tell about these two friends.

SHARING THE POEM Have children close their eyes and visualize what they see as you read the poem aloud. Then ask children to read each line and find items in the picture that are mentioned in the poem. Finally, invite partners to recite the poem together as "two friends."

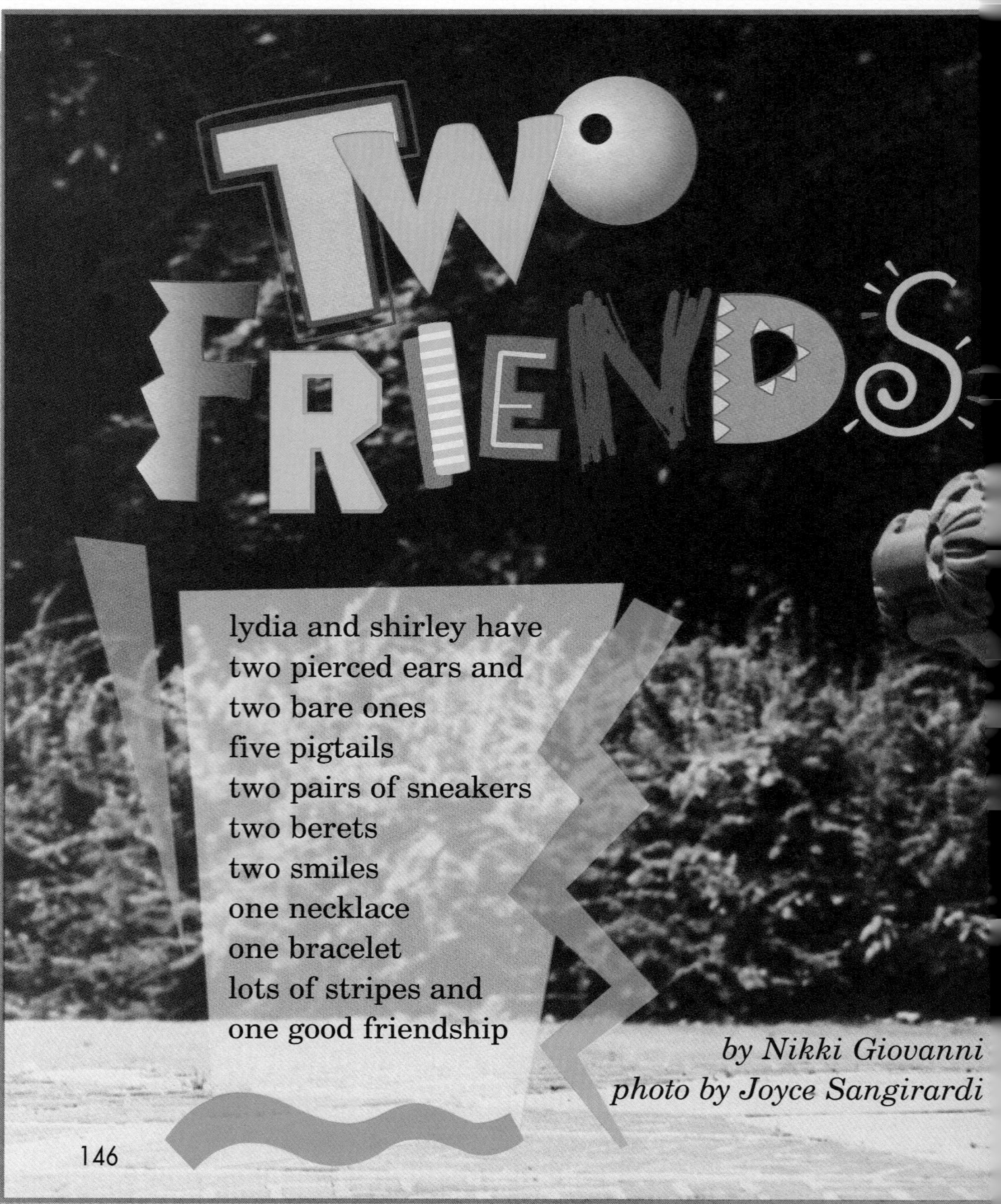

TWO FRIENDS

lydia and shirley have
two pierced ears and
two bare ones
five pigtails
two pairs of sneakers
two berets
two smiles
one necklace
one bracelet
lots of stripes and
one good friendship

by Nikki Giovanni
photo by Joyce Sangirardi

146

LISTENING CENTER

Children may enjoy listening to the poem "Two Friends" on *Literature Cassette 1* as they follow along in their books.

ABOUT THE POEM

Ask children what they notice about the way the words in the poem are written, including the names of the friends. (None of the words begin with capital letters.) **Ask children what reasons the poet may have had for not using capital letters in her poem.**

About the Poet

Nikki Giovanni has been writing poetry for twenty-five years. She has been honored by the Ford Foundation and by the National Council of the Arts. She believes children are an exciting audience to read to and to write for, and this is reflected in many of her poems. Giovanni hopes her poetry "reaches both the heart and the mind of a child who is a child and the adult who still nurtures the child within." Her poetry helps readers think about complex ideas such as friendship.

POET'S CRAFT

Explain that Nikki Giovanni used short phrases in her poem to express individual ideas. Point to each line, and ask children to think about the image, or picture, the words create. Then invite children to brainstorm other ideas they might add to the poem, such as "one pair of glasses." Ask children to read the poem again, adding their ideas.

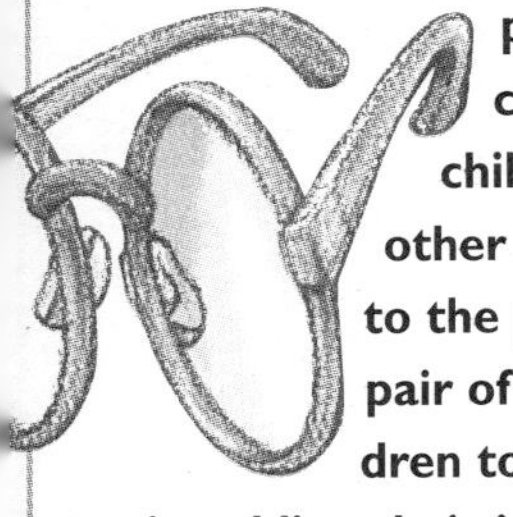

STUDENTS ACQUIRING ENGLISH **Children may need help with words such as *pierced, pigtails, sneakers, berets,* and *bracelet.* Help them find clues in the illustration to figure out these words. You may also want to have children find classmates that have pierced ears, pigtails, sneakers, and so on.**

RESPONSE CORNER ACTIVITIES

WRITE A CLASS BOOK

DO I HAVE A SURPRISE FOR YOU!

PAGE 148 Invite children to share fun surprises they have been given or have planned for others. As they draw and write about their surprises, remind them that a surprise means you don't let your partner know what you have planned until you are finished. **WRITING**

FOLLOW A RECIPE

"ALL SMILES"

PAGE 149 Plan this activity for snack time or after lunch. Provide a clean work table, along with materials and ingredients for each group of four children. Remind children to wash their hands before they begin.

After children make and enjoy their treats, they may want to share the recipe with their families. **COOPERATIVE LEARNING**

RESPONSE CORNER

WRITE A CLASS BOOK

Do I Have a Surprise for You!

Matthew and Tilly liked doing things together. What do you think they might do to surprise each other?

1. Work with a partner. One can be Matthew and one can be Tilly.
2. Plan a surprise for the other character. Draw and write about it.
3. Give hints to help your partner guess the surprise.
4. Show it to your partner.

Make a class book with everyone's pages.

148

VARYING THE ACTIVITY

Challenge children to expand upon what they wrote in the Do I Have a Surprise for You! activity. They could take their idea for a surprise and make it into a story about Matthew and Tilly or other characters.

FOLLOW A RECIPE

All Smiles"

Iake a smile you an eat!

When Matthew and 'illy were sharing and ıaving fun, they were all smiles." You and our friends can share treat that will ıake you all miles, too.

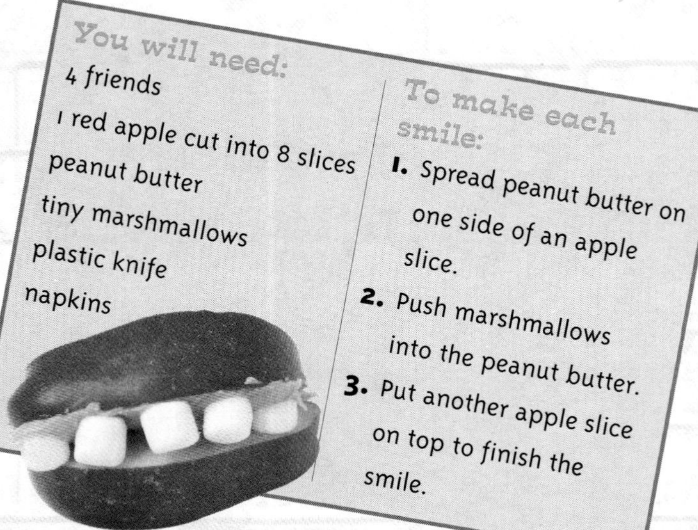

Vhat Do You Think?

What did Matthew and Tilly learn about friendship?
How are Matthew and Tilly like you and your friends?
How are they different?

149

CHECKING COMPREHENSION

What Do You Think?

1. **What did Matthew and Tilly learn about friendship?** (Possible response: Sometimes friends say mean things, but they can forgive one another and still be friends.) DESCRIPTIVE RESPONSE
2. **How are Matthew and Tilly like you and your friends? How are they different?** (Responses will vary.) PERSONAL RESPONSE

An additional question for extending reading.

3. **Would you like to be friends with Matthew and Tilly? Why or why not?** (Responses will vary but should reflect an understanding of the character traits of Matthew and Tilly.) CRITICAL/CREATIVE ANALYSIS

MEETING INDIVIDUAL NEEDS

STUDENTS ACQUIRING ENGLISH **Have children work with English-proficient partners on the Do I Have a Surprise for You! activity. Children acquiring English can write captions or short sentences for the class book in their first language and include them, along with translations, in the finished book. Encourage them to read the book aloud.**

Informal Assessment

Observe pairs of children as they discuss "Matthew and Tilly."

- ☑ Do they understand the main themes of the story?
- ☑ Do they compare the characters to people they know?
- ☑ Do they support their responses?

Intervention Strategies

Instant Readers™

Predictable and Patterned Little Books That Build Fluency

*** BOOK LEVEL: 14–15**

VOCABULARY:
herself, wonder

PHONIC ELEMENTS:
R*-controlled vowel: /ûr/*er, ur*; Short vowel: /u/*u

SUMMARY:
A hearing-impaired girl teaches her friend much more than sign language.

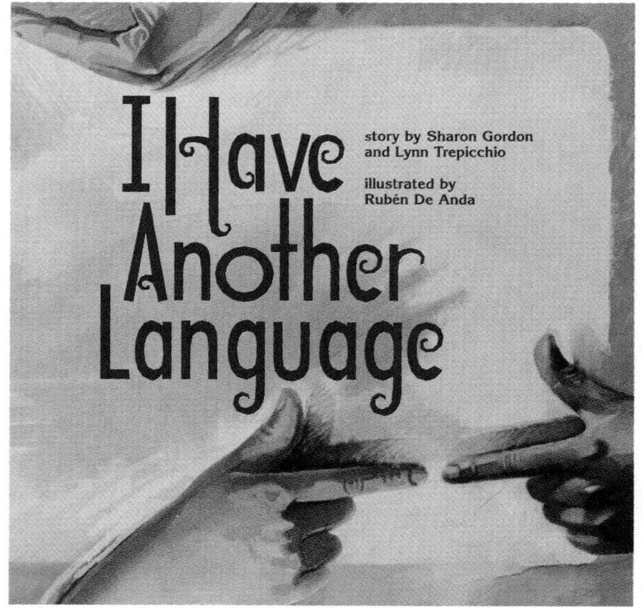

Informal Assessment ✓

Are children able to

- ☑ use a story to learn about the words and letters that make up a language?
- ☑ write messages and facts about something they have learned?

Reading a New Book

INTRODUCING *I HAVE ANOTHER LANGUAGE*

Ask children if they know about sign language and why it is used. Use the pictures of the signed words in the story to introduce the story of a girl and her friend. Have children look at the small pictures on the right-hand pages. Work with them to make the signs and read the captioned word or words under each picture. Explain that the words (and the signs) help tell the story about Karen and her friend.

READING THE STORY

Have children read aloud the story with a partner to find out about Karen and her special language.

WORKING WITH WORDS AND LETTERS

Because of the nature of this story, you may want to discuss it and then have children do their own research about sign language. As a basis for the discussion, you may want to explain that all the signed words in the story use one (relatively) simple gesture. Some words must be spelled out, letter by letter, using the Manual Alphabet. A good reference to use with children is *The Joy of Signing* by Lottie L. Riekehof (Gospel Publishing, 1989).

WRITING FACTS

Have children write one sentence that tells about something they have learned about sign language.

You can talk with sign language.

Additional activities are provided on pages 28–29 of the *Intervention Strategies Manual*.

* **BOOK LEVEL: 14–15**

VOCABULARY:
herself, wondered

PHONIC ELEMENTS:
R-controlled vowel: /ûr/ *ur*; Short vowel: /u/*u*

SUMMARY:
A secret show-and-tell is nearly spoiled, but who can resist blabbing about a new baby sister?

story by Cheryl Ryan
illustrations by Ethan Long

Reading a New Book

INTRODUCING *SECRET SHOW AND TELL*

Share the cover and read aloud the title of the story. Have children think about the secret and tell what it might be. Make a list of predictions on the board. Then share the rest of the illustrations, up to page 15. Have children describe the picture as if they were Josh, the main character in the story.

READING THE STORY

Have children read the story independently to find out if their predictions were correct.

WORKING WITH WORDS AND LETTERS

On the board, write the story word *Thursday.* Talk about the letters *ur* and how they stand for the /ûr/ sound. Help children locate another story word with the letters *ur* and add it to the board. Add other familiar words such as the ones below to the chart.

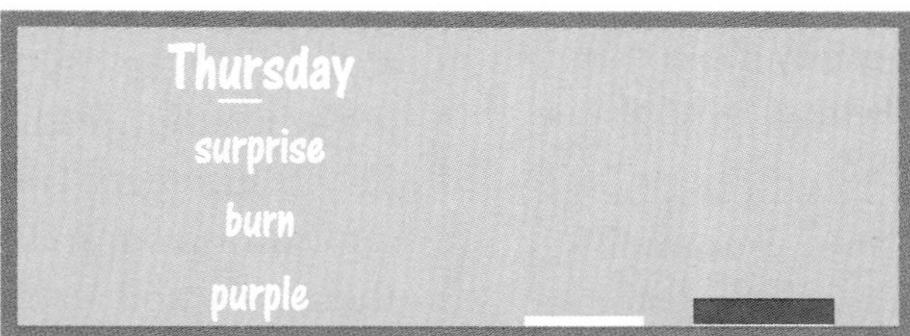

WRITING MESSAGES

Children may enjoy writing a message to a friend. If your classroom doesn't have a message board or a mailbox, have children write their messages and swap them during a specified time.

ESL/Title I Reading

Where's the Fish? by Taro Gomi

INSTANT READERS™

ELECTRONIC EDITION

I Have Another Language **and** ***Secret Show and Tell*** **are available on CD-ROM. Pre- and post-reading activities are included.**

Working with "Matthew and Tilly"

SEMANTIC CUES To help children focus on the story of Matthew and Tilly, have them read aloud story pages 135–141 with another child. Mask out the narrative and have children take turns reading only the dialogue of Matthew and Tilly. Remind them that Matthew and Tilly are angry at each other until page 141.

* Books leveled according to Barbara Peterson's "Profiles of Books for Beginning Readers," on page 9 of the *Instant Readers Teacher's Guide.*

IDEA BANK

TIPS FOR CLASSROOM MANAGEMENT

IF there aren't neighborhood stores near your school, **THEN** bring in magazines or photography books that include these types of photos.

IF children understand the basic rules of hopscotch, **THEN** organize them into small groups to play hopscotch in the Creative Connection activity.

Why did Karla call Tracy?

What is Tracy going to do? How do you know?

Real-Life Skills: TELEPHONE CONVERSATION

HELLO!

Good friends, like Matthew and Tilly, sometimes talk on the phone. Here's a telephone conversation between two friends.

Hi, Tracy. This is Karla. How are you?

Pretty good. What are you doing?

I want to sign up for the soccer team. Why don't you sign up too?

That sounds good— I really like soccer. But I'll have to talk to my mom about it. When are you going to sign up?

My dad's taking me over to the rec center in about an hour. Do you want to come?

Sure. Let me ask my mom. I'll call you back, OK?

Sure. I'll talk to you soon. Bye.

Bye.

18 Matthew and Tilly • Writer's Magazine

WRITER'S MAGAZINE, pages 18–21

LISTENING AND SPEAKING

Group Talk

BREAKING UP AND MAKING UP

Have volunteers describe Tilly and Matthew's argument and how they got back together. Invite children to tell how they felt when they read about Matthew and Tilly being angry. Then organize children into small groups. Have them think of other things Tilly and Matthew could have done to become friends again. Encourage groups to act out the situations, first quarreling, then getting back together. Have groups decide which of their ideas for making friends again would work best.

After small-group discussions, ask groups to share their ideas and insights with classmates. **CHALLENGING THE TEXT**

Informal Assessment

Note how children use their understanding of the story and personal experiences to contribute to the discussion about Matthew and Tilly's argument.

REAL-LIFE READING

Reading Store Signs

Use the illustrations on pages 128-131 to point out the signs associated with neighborhood stores. Ask volunteers to read the signs aloud. Talk with children about what other signs there might be in the stores.

You may wish to take children on a neighborhood walk to locate and read store signs. Then work with children to draw a city street scene like Matthew and Tilly's neighborhood, or a scene of your neighborhood, showing store signs. **READING**

ORAL LANGUAGE

Using the Telephone

MATERIALS
- toy telephones (optional)

DIAL A FRIEND

Have children pretend that they are calling Matthew or Tilly at home. Invite partners to choose a topic to talk about on the telephone and then practice what they will say. Before children have their phone conversations, discuss phone manners. Use the conversation to generate a list of telephone tips.

You may also want to discuss with children how to handle phone situations, such as how to call 911 in an emergency and how to answer the phone when parents are not home. LISTENING/SPEAKING/WRITING

SPEAKING TIPS

- Speak clearly.
- Speak slowly enough.
- Speak loudly enough.

LISTENING TIPS

- Pay attention.
- Be polite.
- Listen for important information.

WRITING MESSAGES

- Write down who called.
- Write the time the person called.
- Write why the person called.

KINESTHETIC

Creative Connection

MATERIALS
- chalk
- pebbles or other small objects

HOPSCOTCH

Have children look at the picture on page 130, and discuss the sidewalk game Matthew and Tilly are playing. Invite volunteers who know how to play hopscotch to demonstrate the game. Have them use chalk to draw the grid on the playground or use masking tape to make a grid on the classroom floor. Allow time for all children to each have a turn.

Then ask children to work in small groups to make up and write descriptions of different versions of hopscotch, including the rules of the games and hints for playing them successfully. Put the descriptions together in a class book. Place the book in the class library.

LISTENING/SPEAKING/WRITING/KINESTHETIC

PERSONAL JOURNAL

REFLECTING ON THE STORY Encourage children to think about what "Matthew and Tilly" teaches about friendship. Were they surprised when Matthew and Tilly argued? Ask children to use their personal journals to write what they learned from the story.

WRITER'S WORKSHOP

A Dialogue

TIPS FOR CLASSROOM MANAGEMENT

IF children are familiar with the writing process approach, **THEN** present the writing assignment and have them refer to the Dialogue model on Chart/Transparency 10.

IF at this time you want a short writing activity, **THEN** have children do the prewriting activity and place the chart in the Writing Center for children's reference during independent writing.

TECHNOLOGY

THE AMAZING WRITING MACHINE
Primary Level
Activity Disk Pack
Grade 2
Have children enter their dialogues in the Stories mode.

KID PIX
Children can illustrate their dialogues by creating pictures of their own or using the stamps.

Thinking as Writers

WRITING FORM: Dialogue Remind children that some parts of "Matthew and Tilly" include dialogue that tells what Matthew and Tilly said to each other. Look back through the story together to find examples. Explain to children that they will work with partners to write a dialogue about solving a problem.

Display Chart/Transparency 10, or write the model Dialogue on the board. Ask children to tell how the dialogue is different from a story and how it is the same.

CHART/TRANSPARENCY 10

MODEL: DIALOGUE

what one character says	TILLY: You broke my purple crayon!
what the other character says back	MATTHEW: I didn't mean to.
	TILLY: You always break everything.
	MATTHEW: It was an old crayon. It was ready to break.
	TILLY: No it wasn't.
	MATTHEW: I'm sorry I broke it.
	TILLY: I'm sorry I got so mad.

WRITER'S CRAFT: Characters and Plot Explain that one of the most important things a writer must do in planning a story is to think about the plot, or what happens in the story. In many stories, the events are the steps that the character takes to solve a problem. Authors also try to make their characters seem real by showing what they say and how they think and feel.

PREWRITING

Briefly review the problem Matthew and Tilly had in the story and how the two friends solved it. Copy the following chart on the board. Model how to complete it using "Matthew and Tilly."

Characters: (Matthew and Tilly)	
Problem: (They got mad at each other and argued when Matthew broke Tilly's crayon.)	**What the Characters Said:** ("You're picky and stinky and mean.")
Solution: (Matthew and Tilly apologized to each other.)	**What the Characters Said:** ("I'm sorry." "So am I.")

Then talk about other problems friends might have. Record children's ideas on the board.

Distribute blank copies of the chart. Pairs of children can choose a problem from the list on the board or make up one of their own and use the chart to plan their dialogues.

DRAFTING

As children write their dialogues, remind them to

- use their charts, the list, and their imagination for ideas.
- tell about the problem and how the characters solved the problem.
- think about the way people really talk.
- write freely to get their ideas down on paper.

As children work through the stages of the writing process, have them save their drafts and revisions in their writer's folder.

RESPONDING AND REVISING

Work with groups of four to six children. Have partners read aloud their dialogue, taking the parts of their characters. Encourage children to respond to each dialogue by answering questions like these:

- What did you like about the dialogue?
- Does the dialogue tell about how the characters tried to solve a problem?
- Are the characters interesting? Do they sound like real people?

PROOFREADING

Offer some tips to help children proofread. Help them focus on the following:

CAPITAL LETTERS The first word of a sentence begins with a capital letter.

WORD ORDER The words in a sentence are in an order that makes sense. (See the Grammar Minilesson on page T259.)

PUBLISHING

Have children make a clean copy of their dialogues. Then offer publishing options like the following:

SCRAPBOOK Help children add their finished products to a class book about solving problems. Display the book in the Reading Center or send it home with each child for a day or two.

Handwriting
Remind children that their handwriting must be neat and clear so that the person reading the dialogue can understand it. If children need assistance, refer them to the Handwriting models in the *Language Handbook* or in the classroom.

READERS THEATRE
Partners can read their dialogues for classmates. Help children prepare by suggesting that they decide who will play each character and then practice the dialogue.

PORTFOLIO OPPORTUNITY

After children publish, make copies of their dialogues and have them attach their Writing Self-Assessment Checklists to them. Have them place the dialogues and checklists in their portfolios.

LANGUAGE HANDBOOK

Play, pages 26–27

Student Self-Assessment ✓

Children can use the Writing Self-Assessment Checklist in the *Portfolio Assessment Teacher's Guide.*

EVALUATING THE WRITTEN RESPONSE

When evaluating children's dialogue, consider:

CONTENT	ORGANIZATION	STYLE
Does the dialogue describe a possible solution to a problem?	Are the characters identified clearly? Is it clear who is saying what in the dialogue?	Does each sentence in dialogue begin with a capital letter and end with the correct end mark?

EVALUATION BENCHMARKS

The child has difficulty indicating what characters say. The dialogue lacks organization and unity.	=	EMERGENT
The child makes an attempt to represent the different speakers clearly. Dialogue may not explain the problem and the solution.	=	BEGINNING
The child writes natural-sounding dialogue that tells about solving a problem. The dialogue expresses thoughts and emotions appropriate to the characters and the topic.	=	PROFICIENT

Tested Skill

GRAMMAR

Statements and Questions

Reading↔Writing Connection

Connect to the story. Have children look at the pictures on pages 142–143 and think about what Matthew and Tilly might be saying to each other. (Possible responses: *Do you want to play? Let's go get some ice cream. I'm not mad anymore.*) Ask volunteers to role-play the scenes, and write what they say on the board. Then ask children what they notice about the end marks of the sentences.

Build oral language. Write *Statements* and *Questions* as column heads on the board, and ask children to tell things they know about Matthew and Tilly. Record each sentence in the *Statements* column. Then have children ask questions about Matthew and Tilly, and record the questions in the *Questions* column.

Statements	Questions
Matthew and Tilly like each other.	Where does Matthew live?
They ride bikes.	Will they argue again?
They sell lemonade.	What other games do they play?
Matthew and Tilly fight sometimes.	Does Tilly have any brothers?

Teach/Model

Define statements and questions. Have volunteers read aloud the statements on the board. Ask children how these sentences are alike. (They tell something, begin with a capital letter, and end with a period.) Tell children that each of these sentences tells something and is called a **statement.** Invite volunteers to underline the initial capital letter and the period in each statement.

Then have a volunteer read aloud the list of questions. Ask children what is the same about these sentences. (They ask something, begin with a capital letter, and end with a question mark.) Explain that a sentence that asks something is called a **question.** Invite volunteers to underline the initial capital letter and the question mark in each question.

Practice/Apply

Check understanding. Write the following sentences on the board:

1. Will it rain tomorrow?
2. I hope not.
3. We are having a picnic.
4. What will we do if it rains?

Read each sentence aloud with children, and have them put up one finger if it is a statement or two fingers if it is a question. Then have partners write questions, exchange papers, and answer each other's questions with statements.

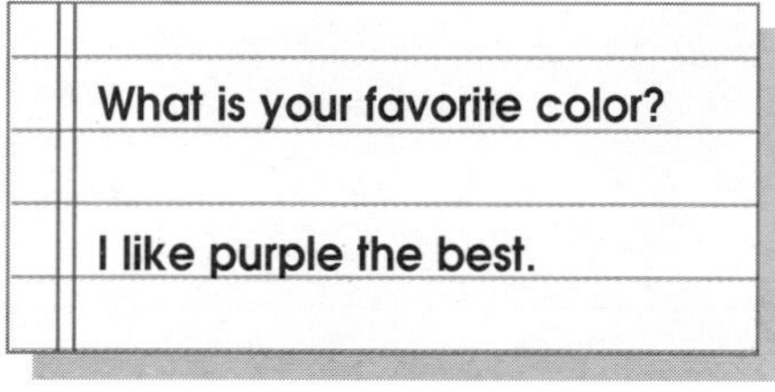

LANGUAGE HANDBOOK

Statements, pages 48–49
Questions, pages 50–51

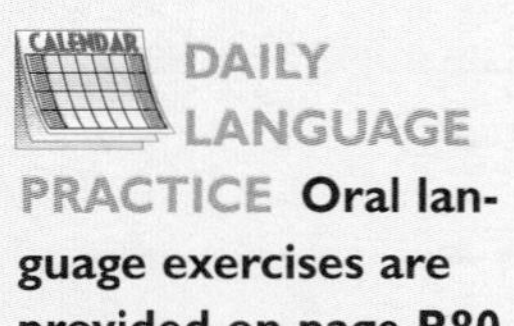
DAILY LANGUAGE PRACTICE Oral language exercises are provided on page R80.

TECHNOLOGY

THE AMAZING WRITING MACHINE Children can work with partners to write questions and answers.

Practice Activities

Clapping Game

ORAL APPLICATION Have children sit in a large circle to clap along and play a variation of "Who Stole the Cookies from the Cookie Jar?" Children may want to make up their own versions, using ideas from "Matthew and Tilly." VISUAL/KINESTHETIC

player 1: (name) broke the crayon from the crayon box.
player 2: Who me?
player 1: Yes you.
player 2: Couldn't be.
player 1: Then who?
player 2: (name) ate the ice cream from the ice cream shop.

Riddle Time

WRITING APPLICATION Organize children into small groups, and have each group choose an object in the classroom to write a riddle about. Children should write statements that give clues to the object without naming it. The riddles should end with a question like *What am I?* Then have groups share their riddles with their classmates. VISUAL

I have a face but no eyes.
I don't have legs.
My hands spin around
and around.
What am I? (clock)

Interview a Friend

WRITING APPLICATION Ask children to work with partners. Have each child write four questions to ask his or her partner. Have partners use their questions to interview one another. Some children may find it helpful to tape-record their interviews. Have partners draw a picture of themselves and their partners and attach it to their questions and answers. Children can share their interviews with their classmates. VISUAL/AUDITORY

APPLY TO WRITING

You may want children to look for statements and questions in their dialogues or other writing to see if they are written correctly.

STUDENTS ACQUIRING ENGLISH

Write these sentence starters on separate sentence strips: *Do you like _____? Yes, I like _____.* Have children work with a peer to complete the sentence starters. After they have made a few of each, children can mix up the strips and sort them as statements or questions.

RETEACH

See page R66 for lessons in multiple modalities.

GRAMMAR PRACTICE BOOK
pages 25-28

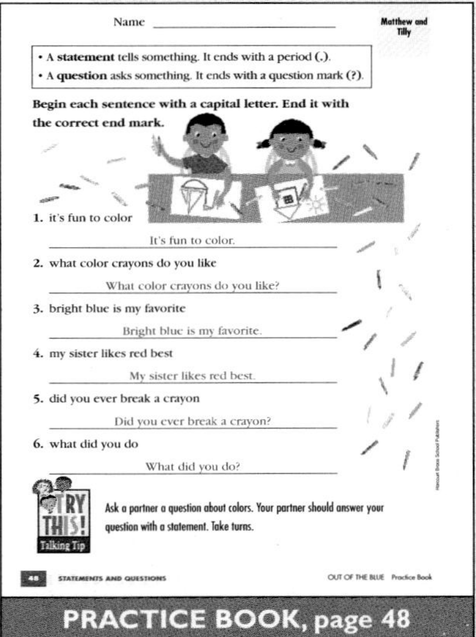

Name ____________ Matthew and Tilly

- A **statement** tells something. It ends with a period (.).
- A **question** asks something. It ends with a question mark (?).

Begin each sentence with a capital letter. End it with the correct end mark.

1. it's fun to color
   It's fun to color.
2. what color crayons do you like
   What color crayons do you like?
3. bright blue is my favorite
   Bright blue is my favorite.
4. my sister likes red best
   My sister likes red best.
5. did you ever break a crayon
   Did you ever break a crayon?
6. what did you do
   What did you do?

TRY THIS! Talking Tip — Ask a partner a question about colors. Your partner should answer your question with a statement. Take turns.

48 STATEMENTS AND QUESTIONS — OUT OF THE BLUE Practice Book

PRACTICE BOOK, page 48

5-DAY PLAN

Use in conjunction with Daily Language Practice.

Day 1 Complete page T284.	**Day 4** Choose a Practice Activity or *Grammar Practice Book* pages 25–28.
Day 2 Complete a Practice Activity on page T285.	**Day 5** Complete *Practice Book* page 48.
Day 3 Choose a Practice Activity or *Language Handbook* pages 48–51.	

SPELLING

5-Day Plan

Integrated Spelling Lesson 7: student book, pages 34–37; Teacher's Edition, pages T57–T62.

SPELLING WORDS

1. fun ★
2. sun
3. up ★
4. nut
5. duck
6. us
7. cut
8. bus
9. gum ★
10. bun

STUDENT'S PERSONAL WORDS

11. 13.
12. 14.

Additional story words are *but, numbers, much, customer,* and *just.*

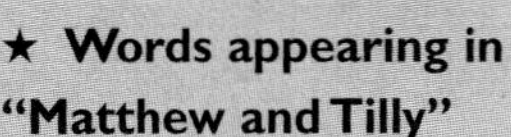

★ Words appearing in "Matthew and Tilly"

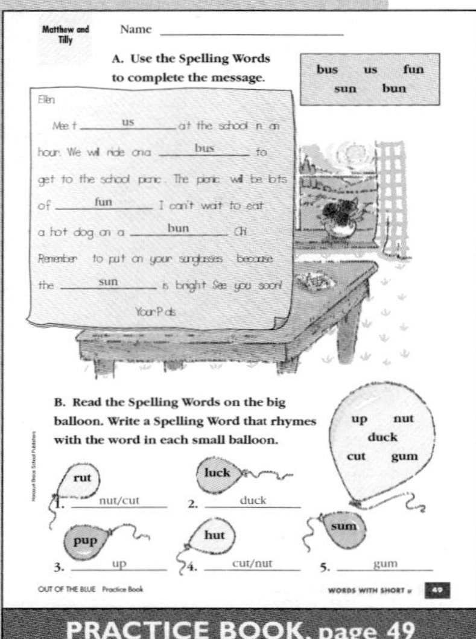

Matthew and Tilly Name

A. Use the Spelling Words to complete the message.

bus	us	fun
sun	bun	

Ellin,

Meet us at the school in an hour. We will ride on a bus to get to the school picnic. The picnic will be lots of fun. I can't wait to eat a hot dog on a bun. Oh! Remember to put on your sunglasses because the sun is bright. See you soon!

Your Pals

B. Read the Spelling Words on the big balloon. Write a Spelling Word that rhymes with the word in each small balloon.

up nut duck cut gum

1. rut — nut/cut
2. luck — duck
3. pup — up
4. hut — cut/nut
5. sum — gum

OUT OF THE BLUE Practice Book — WORDS WITH SHORT *u* 49

PRACTICE BOOK, page 49

Words with Short *u*

Pretest

DAY 1 **Administer the pretest.** Say each word, and then use it in the dictation sentence below. Help children self-check their pretests.

OPEN SORT

DAY 2 **Have children classify words.** Have children look for ways to sort the Spelling Words. For example, they may notice that some rhyme, or that some words have two letters and some words have three.

CLOSED SORT

Sort by letter position. Write the chart below on the board, and work with children to write each Spelling Word where it belongs.

u in the beginning	u in the middle	
up	fun	sun
us	nut	duck
	cut	bus
	gum	bun

Teach/Model

DAY 3 **Discuss the generalization.** Write the words *up* and *fun* on the board. Ask what vowel sound is the same in both words.(/u/) Have children circle the letter that stands for that vowel sound. Then ask children questions such as the following:

Where is the letter u in each of the words? (in the beginning, in the middle)
How many syllables does each word have? (one)

Help children form generalizations about words with short *u*—for example:

- **The short *u* sound can be at the beginning of a word or in the middle of a word.**
- **The short *u* sound can be spelled *u*.**

DAY 4 **Apply to writing.** Children should look for words with short *u* in their dialogues to see that they are spelled correctly.

Posttest

DAY 5 **Assess children's progress.** The sentences below should be used as the posttest.

DICTATION SENTENCES

1. It isn't much fun flying kites by yourself.
2. The sun was bright.
3. The kite went up into the sky.
4. A squirrel hid a nut near its nest.
5. A yellow duck swam in the pond.
6. My dad gave us ice-cream cones.
7. When she fell, she cut her knee.
8. Sometimes, I ride the city bus.
9. I chewed the gum.
10. He had a hot dog on a bun.

VOCABULARY WORKSHOP

Reviewing Key Words

To review how the vocabulary was used in the story, write on the board each Key Word and a page number where it appears in the story.

purple, page 133

break, page 135

piece, page 137

herself, page 137

wondered, page 141

Have children work in small groups. Each child selects a different Key Word and finds the word in the story. Next children take turns reading the Key Word and the story sentence that uses the word. Then have children use the Key Word in a sentence of their own.

As an alternative, sentence strips on page R114 can be used for reviewing vocabulary. Children can fill in the words, illustrate the sentences, and then arrange the sentences to create their own version of "Matthew and Tilly."

Extending Vocabulary

CONTRACTIONS WITH NOT

Have children turn to page 133 of "Matthew and Tilly," and read the last sentence. Ask what *didn't* means. Then explain that *didn't* is a contraction, a short way of writing *did not*. Point out the apostrophe in *didn't,* and explain that the apostrophe takes the place of a letter or letters that are left out when a contraction is written. Ask children which letter was left out when *did not* became *didn't*. Then work with children to brainstorm more contractions with *not*, and add them to the list.

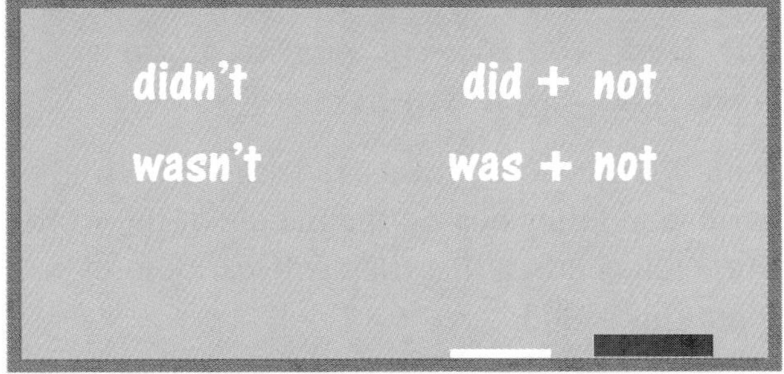

Explain that writers often use contractions when characters speak because that's the way people really talk. Then have partners role-play, using *did* and *was* in questions and *didn't* and *wasn't* in the answers.

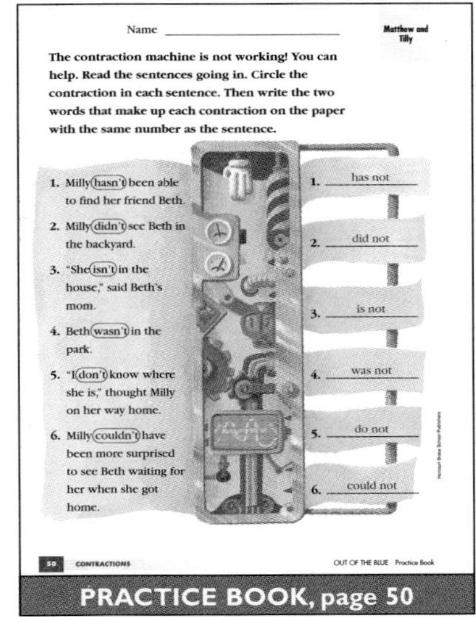
Name ______________ Matthew and Tilly

The contraction machine is not working! You can help. Read the sentences going in. Circle the contraction in each sentence. Then write the two words that make up each contraction on the paper with the same number as the sentence.

1. Milly hasn't been able to find her friend Beth.
2. Milly didn't see Beth in the backyard.
3. "She isn't in the house," said Beth's mom.
4. Beth wasn't in the park.
5. "I don't know where she is," thought Milly on her way home.
6. Milly couldn't have been more surprised to see Beth waiting for her when she got home.

1. has not
2. did not
3. is not
4. was not
5. do not
6. could not

50 CONTRACTIONS — OUT OF THE BLUE Practice Book

PRACTICE BOOK, page 50

STUDENTS ACQUIRING ENGLISH

Invite children to share examples from their first language in which two words are combined. Review the rules for making contractions with *not* in English, and then show children examples of *didn't* and *wasn't,* such as those in "Matthew and Tilly." Have children reread each sentence, substituting *did not* and *was not* for the contractions.

TAKE-HOME/ KEEP-AT-HOME BOOK

Sisters Forever

Distribute the pages and have children make their own TAKE-HOME/ KEEP-AT-HOME BOOKS, which reinforce Key Words and known vocabulary. Have children read to partners and then take the book home to read.

Tested Skill

INTRODUCE: PHONICS AND DECODING

R-Controlled Vowel: /ûr/er, ur

Objective: To understand the relationship between letters and sounds

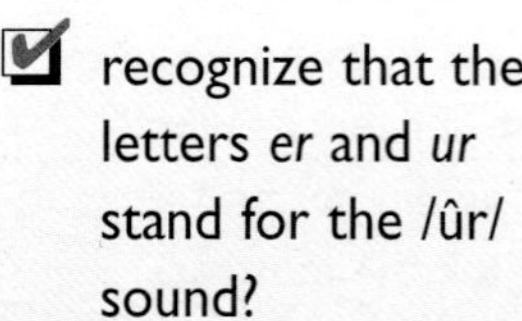

Informal Assessment ✓

Are children able to

- recognize that the letters *er* and *ur* stand for the /ûr/ sound?
- group /ûr/ words by spelling pattern?
- write and read /ûr/ *er, ur* words?

Teach/Model

Connect to the story. Have children read this sentence on page 133.

One day when they were coloring, Matthew broke Tilly's purple crayon.

Point out the word *purple,* and ask children what sound they hear in the middle of the word. (/ûr/) Tell children that they will learn more about this sound.

Phonemic awareness: Listen to the sound. Display pages 10–11 in the *Big Book of Rhymes*. Then read the rhyme to children, and have them listen for words with the same vowel sound heard in the first part of *purple.* Reread the rhyme, encouraging children to join in, especially for words with the /ûr/ sound.

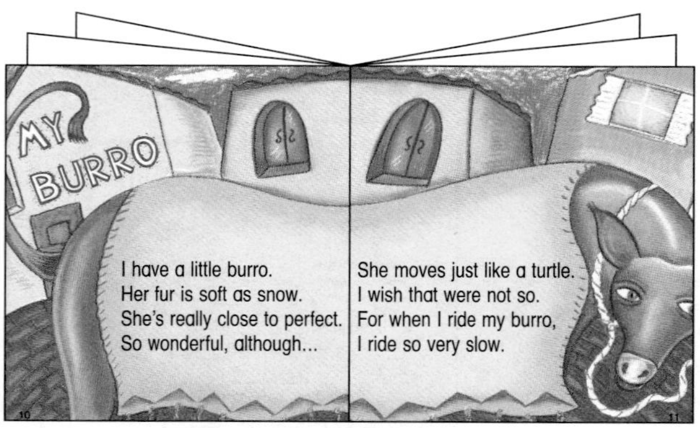

Big Book of Rhymes, pages 10-11

Find and read words with the /ûr/ sound. In the rhyme, have children frame and read words with the same vowel sound as at the beginning of *purple.* As children identify the words, write them on chart paper in appropriate columns.

ur	er
burro fur turtle	perfect

Read the words in the first column with children, and ask how they are alike. (They all have the /ûr/ sound; they all have the letters *ur*.) Ask children what vowel sound they hear at the beginning of *perfect* (/ûr/) and how this sound is spelled. (*er*) Explain that the letters *er* and *ur* often stand for the vowel sound heard in *fur* and in the first part of *perfect*.

Practice/Apply

Read words in context. Write these sentences on the board, omitting the underlining.

A nurse went on a perfect walk.

She brought her purse.

She saw a herd of furry cows.

Then she found a hermit crab by the curb.

Have children read each sentence and find the two words with the same vowel sound as *fur*. Have them add each word to the chart.

Practice Activities

Word Building

PHONOGRAM/BLENDING ACTIVITY Distribute individual letter cards or *Word Builder Cards*, phonogram card *-urry*, and Word Builders to children. Then model the following:

MODEL **I'm going to make a word that ends with *-urry*. I will make the word *furry*. Which letter should I add to make *furry*? Where should I put the letter?**

Demonstrate adding *f* to the phonogram card *-urry* and then blending to say the word. Have children do the same. Then ask children to make and read other words that have the phonogram *-urry* in them. *(blurry, curry, flurry, hurry, scurry)* VISUAL/AUDITORY/KINESTHETIC

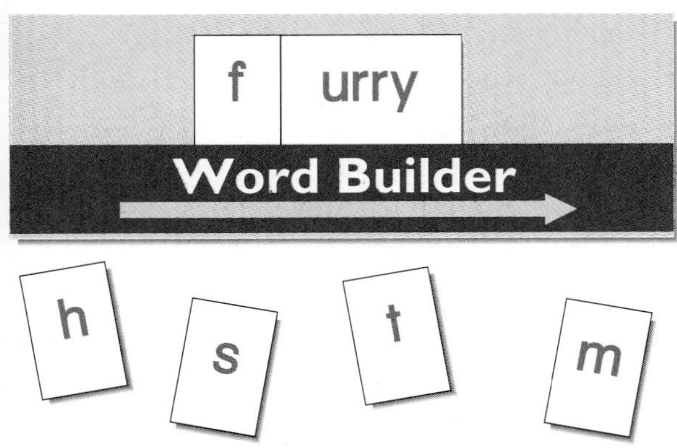

MATCHING GAME

PERFORMANCE ASSESSMENT Provide picture clues for words with the same vowel sound as *fur*, such as a person, a nurse, and a purse. Write labels on separate cards. Have children shuffle the cards and place them face down on the table. Children take turns turning the cards over and matching each label with its picture. Matched cards are set aside face up. When all cards are face up, children take turns reading the labels and identifying the letters that stand for the /ûr/ sound. Encourage children to use the words in sentences. VISUAL/AUDITORY

MEETING INDIVIDUAL NEEDS

STUDENTS ACQUIRING ENGLISH

Provide pictures of items whose names have /ûr/ *ur* such as *purse, nurse*, and *turkey*. Have children name each item. Label the picture, omitting *ur*. Have children complete each word and read the words. Repeat using *er* words.

RETEACH

See page R67 for lessons in multiple modalities.

CHALLENGE

Have children write poems using words with the /ûr/ sound spelled *ur* and *er*.

PHONICS ACTIVITY BOOK, page 13

PHONICS PRACTICE BOOK, pages 135–136

Matthew and Tilly

Name ____________

Read each sentence and the words below it. Circle the word that makes sense in the sentence and has the same vowel sound as *purse*. Write it on the line.

1. Janet heard a noise in her room.
   (her) herd mom
2. She turned on the light.
   hurt switched (turned)
3. It was coming from her mother's purse.
   basket (purse) fern
4. Look! A little ball of fur!
   perch (fur) yarn
5. The kitten began to purr.
   (purr) purse play
6. It was a perfect present.
   nice (perfect) curve

OUT OF THE BLUE Practice Book R-CONTROLLED VOWEL: /ûr/ er, ur 51

PRACTICE BOOK, page 51

Reading Trade Books FOR *R*-CONTROLLED VOWEL /ÛR/ *ER, UR*

The Wednesday Surprise
by Eve Bunting.
Clarion, 1989.
AVERAGE

A House for Hermit Crab
by Eric Carle.
Simon & Schuster, 1991.
EASY

PHONICS PRACTICE READER 15

INTRODUCE: COMPREHENSION STRATEGY

Making Predictions

OBJECTIVE: To understand that the author gives clues that help the reader guess what will happen next

Informal Assessment ✓

Are children able to

- ☑ use story clues and personal knowledge to make predictions?
- ☑ give reasons for their predictions?
- ☑ change their predictions when new clues are provided?

Teach/Model

Recall the story plot. Have children reread pages 133–135, and discuss with them the problem Matthew and Tilly had. Explain that as they read, they may have guessed what would happen next to Matthew and Tilly. Tell children that making a guess about what will happen next can help them understand the story better.

Model making predictions. Point out that the author and the illustrator provide clues in the story to help the reader guess, or **predict,** what will happen. Explain that children should use the clues in the words and the pictures and use things they already know to make a good prediction. Help children complete a chart like the following.

Making Predictions

I Know +	Clues I Read →	My Guess
Friends play together. Friends are nice to one another. Sometimes friends get mad at one another.	Matthew and Tilly are friends. They do lots of things together. Sometimes they get "sick of each other."	

Then model making a prediction.

MODEL

When I read the part of the story about the broken crayon, I could tell from the words and the pictures that Matthew and Tilly were mad at each other. I know that friends sometimes fight, but that they usually make up. So, I predicted Matthew and Tilly would make up.

Encourage children to share some of the predictions they made as they read. Ask them to tell about any predictions they changed and why.

Practice/Apply

Have children demonstrate understanding. Draw a chart like the one below on the board. Tell children that they will listen to a story about a boy who visits the library. Work with them to complete the first column of the chart. Then read the story aloud, telling children to listen for clues about what Steven does.

> Steven likes to visit the library. He always borrows a lot of books. He writes the titles of the books in a notebook to help him remember which books he has at home. Today his books are due, and he never returns books late.

Work with children to complete the second column of the chart. Tell them that Steven's books are due back at the library today. Ask them to predict what he will do. Work with them to complete the third column.

I Know +	I Read →	My Guess
I like to visit the library. You can borrow books. You have to return them at a certain time.	Steven writes titles in a notebook. He always returns his books on time.	Steven will return his books today.

Then distribute copies of a blank chart like the one above. Have children complete the chart for a book or story they are currently reading.

Practice Activities

HIDDEN ENDINGS

Organize children into small groups. Have each group member think of a very short story and write or draw on two separate cards what happened first and what happened next. A child shows her or his first card to the group. The group takes turns acting out what might happen next and telling why it might happen. Then the child shows the second card and tells why that would happen next. Continue until all children in the group have shared their stories.
VISUAL/AUDITORY/KINESTHETIC

Picture This

PERFORMANCE ASSESSMENT Provide wordless story books, such as *A Boy, a Dog, a Frog and a Friend* by Mercer and Marianna Mayer. Have partners take turns telling each other the story. Before turning each page, children guess what event will be pictured on the next page and give reasons for their guess. When they turn the page, they can discuss whether what happens is the same as or different from their prediction. VISUAL/AUDITORY

Reading Trade Books FOR MAKING PREDICTIONS

Fortunately by Remy Charlip. Macmillan, 1993. AVERAGE

A Boy, a Dog, a Frog and a Friend by Mercer and Marianna Mayer. Dial, 1971. EASY

The 13th Clue by Ann Jonas. Greenwillow, 1992. EASY

MEETING INDIVIDUAL NEEDS

STUDENTS ACQUIRING ENGLISH

Cut off the last frame of several comic strips that have a definite sequence. For each comic strip, discuss what is happening, and have children predict what the last frame will be. Then show them the last frame, and have children confirm their predictions.

RETEACH

See page R68 for lessons in multiple modalities.

CHALLENGE

Invite children to write or tape-record short mysteries for classmates to solve.

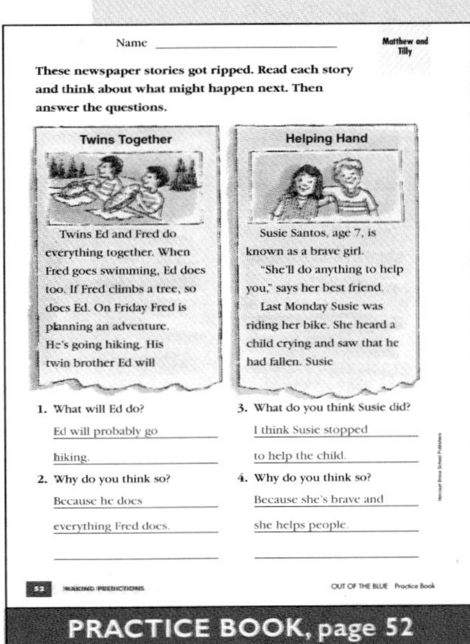

Name ______________________ Matthew and Tilly

These newspaper stories got ripped. Read each story and think about what might happen next. Then answer the questions.

Twins Together

Twins Ed and Fred do everything together. When Fred goes swimming, Ed does too. If Fred climbs a tree, so does Ed. On Friday Fred is planning an adventure. He's going hiking. His twin brother Ed will

Helping Hand

Susie Santos, age 7, is known as a brave girl.

"She'll do anything to help you," says her best friend.

Last Monday Susie was riding her bike. She heard a child crying and saw that he had fallen. Susie

1. What will Ed do?
Ed will probably go hiking.
2. Why do you think so?
Because he does everything Fred does.
3. What do you think Susie did?
I think Susie stopped to help the child.
4. Why do you think so?
Because she's brave and she helps people.

52 MAKING PREDICTIONS — OUT OF THE BLUE Practice Book

PRACTICE BOOK, page 52

Integrated Curriculum

SOCIAL STUDIES

Neighborhoods

TIPS FOR CLASSROOM MANAGEMENT

IF children are artistically inclined, **THEN** they may want to participate in the On the Map and Good Neighbor Award activities.

TECHNOLOGY

IMAGINATION EXPRESS, Destination: Neighborhood
Children can create stories about things that happen in a neighborhood.

SOCIAL STUDIES

On the Map

MATERIALS
- poster board
- sample maps
- craft sticks
- markers
- glue
- maps

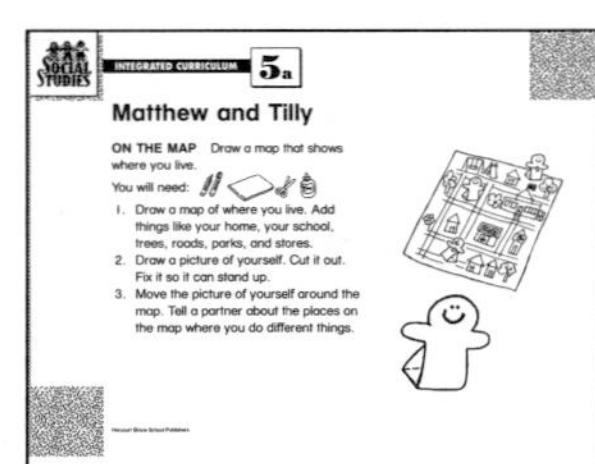

Curriculum Card 5a

Discuss Matthew and Tilly's neighborhood and compare it to children's neighborhoods. Show the sample maps and talk about how symbols are used.

Have children make a poster board map showing how they travel from their homes to school or someplace else they go often. Ask children to include pictures of neighborhood landmarks on their maps, such as a park or a store.

Then have children make stand-up figures of themselves from folded paper. Children can work in small groups, taking turns moving their stand-up figures from place to place on the map. Each child can talk about neighborhood sights as he or she moves the figure from place to place.
LISTENING/SPEAKING

MATH

Neighborhood Market

MATERIALS
- grocery store ads
- clean, empty food containers
- scissors
- toy cash register and play money (optional)

LEARNING CENTER
Remind children that Matthew set up a store when he was by himself. Talk with children about food stores they have seen.

- **How are the items organized?**
- **How does a customer know what to pay?**
- **How does a shopper know what to buy?**

Invite children to work in groups to set up a neighborhood store in the classroom, using pictures from sale ads and things like empty food boxes and egg cartons. Assign each group member a role: the Shopper looks through the flyers for items and cuts out the pictures; the Clerk organizes and prices the items; the Checker confirms that items are organized and that each item has a price; the Reporter explains why the group organized the items the way they did. Then allow time for children to shop at their store. LISTENING/SPEAKING

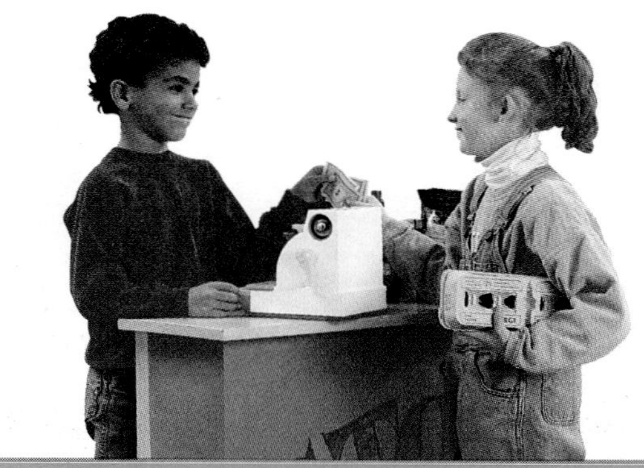

SCIENCE

Homes for Sale

MATERIALS
- realty ads from a local newspaper
- nature books showing animals and their homes
- large (4"x6") index cards
- markers, crayons, pencils

Remind children that Matthew and Tilly live in an apartment building. Talk with children about different types of homes for people. Then brainstorm a list of animals that live in the children's neighborhoods and what *their* homes might be like. Provide nature books for children to read to find out about animal homes. Ask children to select a favorite animal and create a newspaper ad for the animal's home, using the home ads in the newspaper as models. Glue the ads into a "realty supplement" for all to read and enjoy. **READING/WRITING**

ART

Good Neighbor Award

MATERIALS
- construction paper
- crayons or markers
- glue
- scissors
- collage materials

Curriculum Card 5b

As a group, brainstorm a list of ideas about what makes a good neighbor at school, such as sharing crayons, saying nice things to others, and helping. Post this list and add to it as new ideas arise.

Have children make a "good neighbor award" for a classmate. Randomly assign each child a partner. Tell children to keep their partner's identity secret until the award ceremony. Suggest that children maintain a list of "neighborly" things they see their partner do and then design a unique award to present to their "good neighbor." Have children refer to their lists and include on the award one or two reasons why their partner is a good neighbor. **LISTENING/SPEAKING/READING/WRITING**

Reading Trade Books

CROSS-CURRICULAR READING

The Whole World in Your Hands **by Melvin and Gilda Berger. Ideals, 1993. EASY**

Once Around the Block **by Kevin Henkes. Greenwillow, 1987. EASY**

A House Is a House for Me **by Mary Ann Hoberman. Puffin, 1993. AVERAGE**

MULTI-AGE CLASSROOMS

For the Science activity, have older children help younger children find information about animal homes. They may need to read the material to the younger children.

Reading Trade Books

TIPS FOR CLASSROOM MANAGEMENT

PARTNERS
Have children work with partners to read *There's a Dragon in My Sleeping Bag*. Encourage them to decide how they will read the book together and where they will stop to talk about the story.

SMALL GROUP
Read the story to a small circle of children. As you read aloud, pause to let children talk about how they think Alex feels each time Dexter is in his place, and how Simon feels when Calvin is in his place.

INDEPENDENT
Place the book in a Reading Center. Have children read the book and write about their favorite part in their personal journals.

For a comprehensive lesson plan, refer to the complete lesson for *There's a Dragon in My Sleeping Bag* on pages T454–T457.

There's a Dragon in My Sleeping Bag

by James Howe

Signatures Library

READER'S CHALLENGE

When Matthew and Tilly argued, each could go home and play. What happens when brothers or sisters don't want to play with one another? Do you think a brother or a sister could be a friend?

READING STRATEGY: SEQUENCE

As children read the book, ask them to predict what will happen when Alex meets Calvin the camel, when Dexter the dragon leaves, and when Calvin leaves. Then have children tell what Alex and Simon might do now that they are friends again.

LINK TO THE THEME

Children who are reading the book may want to discuss the following:

- **Why did Alex start seeing Calvin the camel?**
- **Why do you think each boy had his own make-believe friend?**
- **What do you think the two brothers learned about friendship?**

RESPONSE ACTIVITY: WRITING ABOUT THE STORY

Invite children to draw a picture of an imaginary friend and to name the friend. Then have them write sentences about what that friend might do, perhaps telling how their imaginary friend is helpful or fun.

Other Trade Books

Everett Anderson's Friend

by Lucille Clifton
illustrated by Ann Grifalconi

After reading, ask why Everett Anderson is disappointed at first with the new neighbors. Ask why he changed his mind. Have children work together to plan ways to read this rhyming story chorally.

A Weekend with Wendell

by Kevin Henkes

After reading, ask why Sophie changes her mind about Wendell and can't wait until he comes back. Tell children to think about a fun weekend they have had. Have them write a story about that special time, naming their story "A Weekend with . . ."

Rosie and Michael

by Judith Viorst
illustrated by Lorna Tomei

Have children write and illustrate sentences to include in an "A Good Friend Is . . ." book. Encourage them to draw pictures and to write about things good friends do even when they are angry with each other.

MEETING INDIVIDUAL NEEDS

EXTRA SUPPORT

Have children repeat and complete the sentence *My friend and I like to . . . .* Invite them to talk about things friends do together and to write sentences that tell about their friendly doings.

Trade Books

PROJECT MANAGEMENT

- PROJECT LAUNCH
- CHECKPOINT 1
- CHECKPOINT 2
- CHECKPOINT 3
- CHECKPOINT 4
- PRESENTATIONS
- ASSESSMENT

Learn About the Post Office

SELECTION CONNECTION

"Matthew and Tilly" is about two friends who quarrel and then feel lonely. Ask how Tilly communicated with Matthew to end their fight. (She smiled.) Then ask children how Tilly could have communicated with Matthew if he couldn't see her or hear her voice.

PROJECT CHECKLIST

During this stage, children should

- ☑ tour a post office or invite a postal worker in to speak to them.
- ☑ prepare questions to ask the postal worker.
- ☑ read books about the postal system.
- ☑ role-play jobs postal workers do.

When children have completed this checkpoint, have them write in their Project Journals what they learned about the postal system.

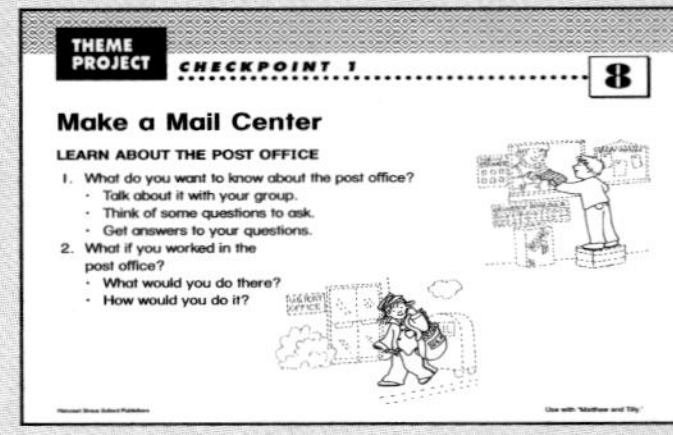
THEME PROJECT CHECKPOINT 1 — 8

Make a Mail Center

LEARN ABOUT THE POST OFFICE

1. What do you want to know about the post office?
   - Talk about it with your group.
   - Think of some questions to ask.
   - Get answers to your questions.
2. What if you worked in the post office?
   - What would you do there?
   - How would you do it?

Project Card 8

Project Card 8 can be found as a copying master on page R88.

PLANNING TIPS

As children prepare to learn more about the post office, suggest that groups

- brainstorm a list of questions.
- choose a Recorder to write down the questions and a Manager to assign questions to group members.
- plan to discuss and record the answers when the field trip, visit, or research is finished.

STUDENTS ACQUIRING ENGLISH

As the class tours the post office, pair children with partners who are proficient in English. Have children locate signs and work together to figure out new words.

MULTIPLE INTELLIGENCES

Children with strong visual/spatial abilities can design class stamps.

Informal Assessment

As children complete this checkpoint, they will gather information, **make decisions,** and **evaluate** and **apply** information. Children are thinking critically if they

- ☑ ask questions about the postal service.
- ☑ evaluate the information during class discussions.
- ☑ apply what they have learned by role-playing.

Note that a more formal assessment rubric for this checkpoint is provided on page T453.

Hopscotch Around the World

by Mary D. Lankford

SELECTION CONNECTION

In "Matthew and Tilly," one of the games the two friends play together is hopscotch. In "Hopscotch Around the World," children will read about two variations of this popular game—one from Aruba and one from France.

ABOUT THE AUTHOR

Mary D. Lankford grew up in Texas. She has enjoyed writing and has kept diaries and journals since she was very young. In the fourth grade, she knew she wanted to be a librarian. Today, she is Director of Library and Media Services for the Irving, Texas, Independent School District. She has four children and five grandchildren. Lankford's first book was a picture book called *Is It Dark? Is It Light?*

ABOUT THE ILLUSTRATOR

Karen Milone has illustrated other children's books including Stephanie S. Tolan's *Marcy Hooper and the Greatest Treasure in the World.* She makes her home in North Attleboro, Massachusetts.

SUMMARY

GENRE: Nonfiction

Hopscotch, or a variation of it, is played by children around the world. In Aruba, children play Pele (pā´lā), a variation of the game in which players use a stone puck and seven numbered boxes that form a double-T pattern. In France, children play Escargot (es•kär•gō´), named after a popular French food—escargots, or snails. The spiral pattern used in this hopscotch game resembles that of a snail's shell.

EXTRA SUPPORT

Directions for games are often detailed and can sometimes confuse young readers. Draw each hopscotch pattern on the board as children read about it. You or a child should point to the boxes or spaces as they are mentioned. You might want to have children "act out" a game before they play it.

Introducing the Selection

PRIOR KNOWLEDGE
Remind children that Matthew and Tilly liked to play hopscotch. Invite a volunteer to draw a hopscotch pattern on the board. Ask children what they know about playing hopscotch. Record children's information on an idea web like this one:

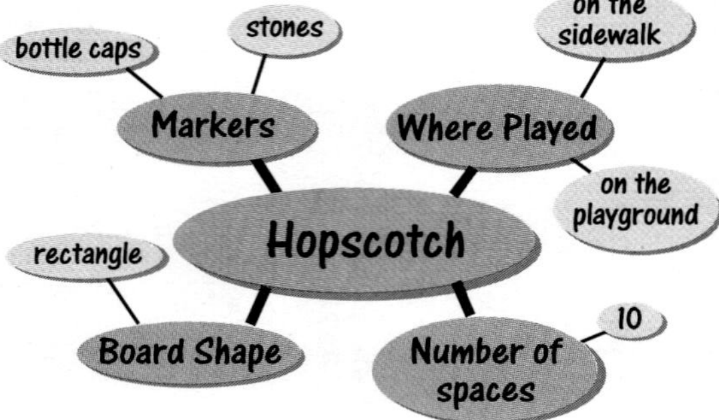

Reading Nonfiction Have children page through the first section of the selection. Ask what kinds of information they find on different pages. They might point out maps and diagrams on the first two pages and directions on the next pages. They might conclude that they will learn about places where different forms of hopscotch are played and then learn how to play them.

by
Mary D.
Lankford

PELE The island of Aruba in the Netherlands Antilles is just twenty miles north of the coast of Venezuela. Many of the trees on the island have been bent into unusual shapes by the strong winds that blow across the island. Because of these winds, an object that will not blow or roll away must be used as a puck. A stone or coin makes a good puck for the children of Aruba.

150

TIPS FOR CLASSROOM MANAGEMENT

SMALL GROUP

COOPERATIVE READING
Have children form small groups. Have groups choose one member to read the introductions and other group members to take turns reading game directions. When children have read about these hopscotch games, allow time for groups to try out the new games.

WHOLE CLASS

READ ALOUD
Read aloud as children follow along in their books. As you read the directions, pause after each step so that children can use the illustrations of hopscotch boards to visualize each step of the games. After reading, talk about these two forms of hopscotch. Compare the versions to each other as well as to versions that children play.

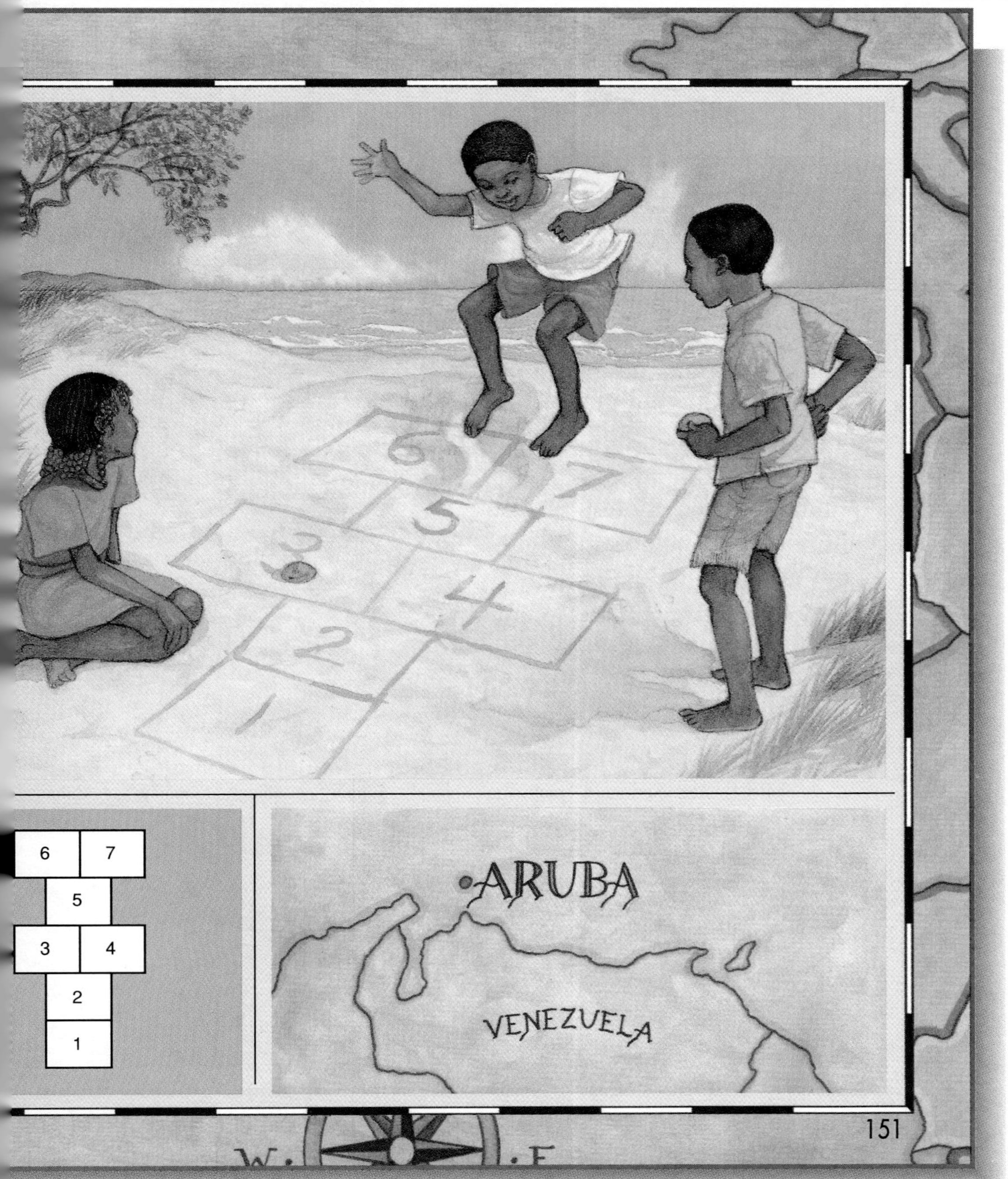

STUDENTS ACQUIRING ENGLISH

There are many directional words in the text that describe the countries and their locations. Work with children on the meanings of the words *north, south, east,* and *west,* as well as words such as *across, in, out, up, on,* and *through,* which can also be found in the selection.

SOCIAL STUDIES CONNECTION

ARUBA Ask children if they know what an island is. Define *island,* if necessary. As you talk about where Aruba is, point out South America, the country of Venezuela, and the approximate location of Aruba on a globe or world map. Ask children to find and name other islands in the same area as Aruba.

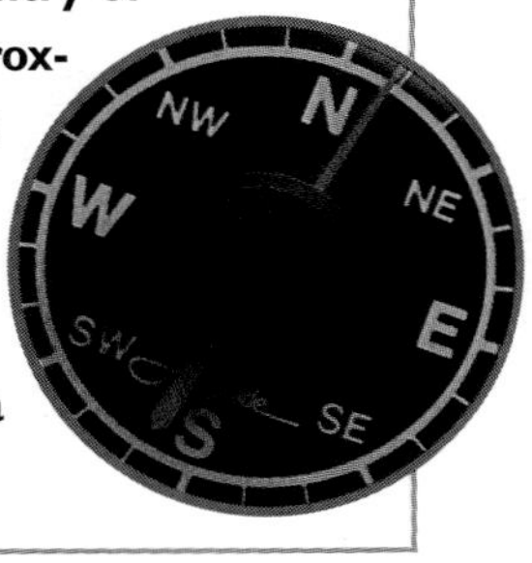

Critical Thinking Questions

1. **Why do you think hopscotch is played differently in different parts of the world?** (Possible responses: People in different places have different ideas. They might have different weather or different things to use to play a game.) **CRITICAL: SPECULATING**

2. **Why do you think hopscotch games around the world are as similar as they are, even though the places where they are played are far away from each other?** (Possible responses: Children like to hop; people in all places use numbers; sometimes people move from place to place, taking games and other activities with them and teaching them to the people they meet.) **METACOGNITIVE: SYNTHESIZING**

DIRECTIONS:

1. Throw the puck into box 1.
2. Hop into box 2. Then jump into boxes 3 and 4, putting one foot in each box.
3. Hop into box 5, and jump in boxes 6 and 7 just as you did for boxes 3 and 4.
4. Jump and turn, landing again in boxes 6 and 7, now facing the rest of the pattern.
5. Hop into box 5. Then jump into boxes 3 and 4, putting one foot in each box.
6. Hop into box 2, and pick up the puck from box 1. Hop out of the pattern without landing in box 1.

Step 1

Step 4

Step 6

152

EXPANDING VOCABULARY

Ask children what sport they'd be playing if they used a hard rubber disk called a *puck*. (ice hockey) **Ask a volunteer what the word *puck* means in this article.** (It means any type of stone, pebble, tile, or coin used in a hopscotch game.) **Ask children what they have used as a puck when they play hopscotch.**

7. Throw the puck into box 2, and repeat the entire pattern. If the puck lands in the wrong box or outside the pattern, you lose your turn.

8. Throw the puck into box 3. Hop into boxes 1 and 2 and then into box 4. Continue through the pattern and, on the way back, pick up the puck from box 3 while balancing on one foot in box 4. Never hop into a box with a puck in it.

9. If you step on a line, you also lose your turn, but your puck stays in place until you try again. Players cannot hop or jump into a box that holds either their own puck or that of another player.

10. The first player who completes the entire pattern wins the game.

Step 7

Step 8

153

Tested Skill

MINILESSON

PREVIEW: COMPREHENSION

Reading Directions

INFORMAL ASSESSMENT

Have children look at the directions for Pele on pages 152–153. Note whether children use the illustrations to help them understand how the game is played. Have children summarize the rules for playing the game.

TEACH/MODEL

Use the directions for Pele on pages 152–153 to model how to read and follow directions. Point out to children that these directions are numbered and that they have pictures as well as words to help readers understand how the game is played. Read each step of the directions aloud, modeling your thinking as you read:

MODEL **The first step says to throw the puck into box 1. The picture of the board shows me where the first box is. I'm ready to read the next step. Each time I read another step of the directions, I picture doing it in my mind before I read on. Whenever there is a picture that goes with a step, I use it to help me understand the game.**

PRACTICE/APPLY

Help children make the Pele hopscotch game with masking tape on the floor or with chalk on the playground. Then have partners play the game. Encourage them to refer to their books.

MATH CONNECTION

MEASUREMENT Have a child locate Aruba and France on a globe or world map. Take out a measuring tape—or use string. Measure the distance—or length of the string—between your location and Aruba; and between your location and France. Which is closer to where you live, Aruba or France?

Responding to the Selection

Have children share the new things they learned about hopscotch in other countries. How do the hopscotch games in the selection differ from the ones children have played? Talk about the way each game is presented.

- **Does the paragraph before the directions help the reader? How?**
- **How do the pictures, illustrations, and maps help?**
- **Why is it important to read the directions all the way through before trying to play the game?**

Finally, suggest that children compare their way of playing hopscotch with those in the article.

ESCARGOT Snails are a favorite food in France. The spiral shape of the shell of a snail (*escargot* in French) is the pattern used for one variation of hopscotch played there. Escargot is one of the few hopscotch games in which no puck is used. The game is also called La Marelle Ronde (round hopscotch).

FRANCE

DIRECTIONS:

1. Before you begin hopping, decide which foot you will hop on. If you decide on your left foot, you must hop in and out each time on that foot.
2. Hop through the snail.
3. Hop only once in each space. No player may touch a line when hopping.
4. In the center space, you may rest on both feet.
5. After resting, turn and hop back to the beginning. Repeat the pattern once more.
6. After you have hopped in and out twice, choose one space for your "house." Write your initials in this space. This becomes another rest space for you. No other player may hop into your house.
7. The game ends when it is impossible for anyone to hop into the center space or when all of the squares have initials in them. The player who "owns" the greatest number of squares wins.

154

SOCIAL STUDIES CONNECTION

THREE COUNTRIES When children have read the directions for Escargot, point out France on a world map or globe. Show children where Aruba, the United States, and France are in relation to one another. Invite children to name neighboring countries, tell which country is closer to the U.S., and name something all three countries share. (They have the Atlantic Ocean between them.)

CHECKING COMPREHENSION

What Do You Think?

1. **How are Pele and Escargot the same? How are they different?** (Possible responses: They are both games played on a shape drawn on the ground. In both games, players hop from space to space. The shapes of the games are different. Pele is played by throwing a puck while Escargot is not.) **DESCRIPTIVE RESPONSE**

2. **What did you find out about hopscotch that you didn't know before?** (Possible responses: There is more than one way to play hopscotch; hopscotch is played in different parts of the world; in each place where it is played, hopscotch has different names, shapes, and rules.) **PERSONAL RESPONSE**

3. **Why do you think children from such different parts of the world enjoy hopscotch?** (Possible responses: It's a fun game; it can be played almost anywhere; it doesn't need a lot of equipment.) **CRITICAL/CREATIVE RESPONSE**

STUDENTS ACQUIRING ENGLISH

Suggest that children acquiring English play another variation of hopscotch. Have each child write a number word or color word in his or her first language in a space on a hopscotch outline. Players teach one another the word from their languages, along with the English translation, before they play. This game would work best if words were all of a category (for example, color words, number words, or names of school objects).

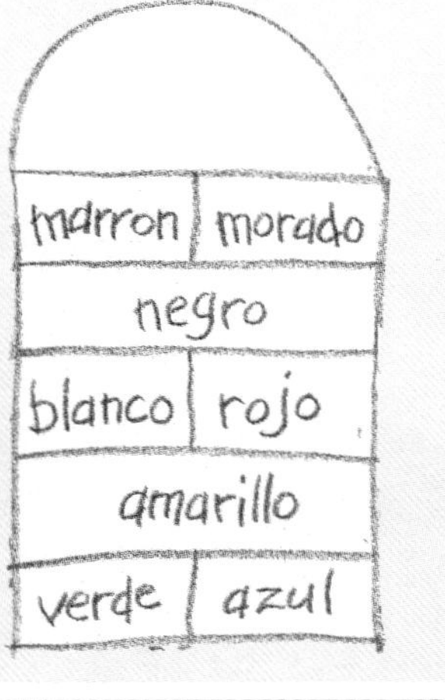

Integrating Language Arts

KINESTHETIC

Come On, Let's Play

MATERIALS
- chalk
- jump rope
- marbles
- jacks

COOPERATIVE LEARNING Gather the materials and place them in a game center or a central location. Invite children to use any of the materials you have gathered to play a sidewalk game with a group. Have them teach the game to a group and then play it. **KINESTHETIC**

WRITING

Hopscotch Fun!

COOPERATIVE LEARNING Partners or small groups can make up their own hopscotch patterns and write directions for a new kind of hopscotch game. Suggest children give their game a name. Have them display their hopscotch outlines and the directions for playing their new hopscotch games. Classmates can read the directions and try out the hopscotch variations.

READING/WRITING

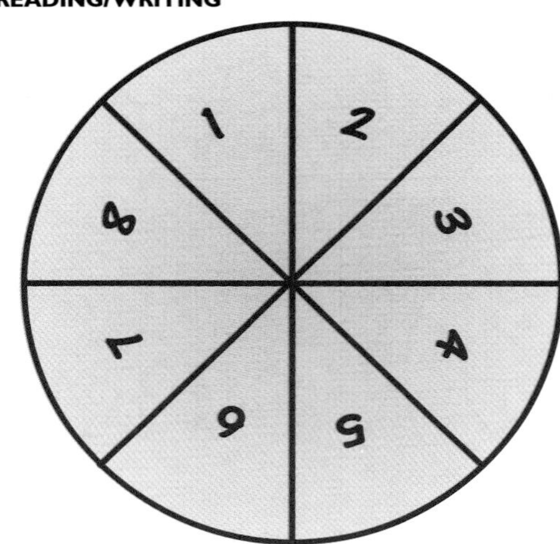

PIZZA HOPSCOTCH

TIPS FOR CLASSROOM MANAGEMENT

IF children have difficulty making up a game in the Writing activity, THEN suggest that they write the rules of a game that they know and that other children might not know.

ART AND LITERATURE

Two Young Girls at the Piano (1892) • by Pierre Auguste Renoir (1841–1919)

ABOUT THE ARTIST

French artist Pierre Renoir began his career at age thirteen, painting flowers on dishware. Eight years later he began to seriously study painting. Renoir joined other artists in developing a new and controversial way of painting. These artists tried to paint their impressions of a subject rather than a representative picture of it. Eventually they formed a loosely knit group known as Impressionists. Unlike artists before them who painted only in a studio, Impressionists took their canvases outdoors. They sought to show how light fell on a subject at different times of day and during different seasons of the year.

ABOUT THE PAINTING

Renoir created several versions of this painting. The first version, which varies only slightly from this one, hangs in the Louvre in Paris. The two girls in the painting appear in at least six Renoir works. In each painting, the girls wear the same dresses and their hair is combed the same way. One painting shows the girls picking and admiring flowers in a meadow. Another shows them reading a book.

ART AND LITERATURE

Matthew and Tilly learned that friends should be together. Do you think the girls in the painting like being together? What might a painting of you and a good friend show?

Two Young Girls at the Piano
by Pierre Auguste Renoir

Artist Pierre Renoir lived and painted in France. He liked to show ways that people are special. What do you think he wanted to show about the girls in this painting?

156

157

Art and Literature

MAKING CONNECTIONS

Ask children to read the first paragraph next to the painting on page 156. Discuss how this painting relates to the selections they have read so far. Talk about things that friends like to do together. Then discuss ways the artist shows that the girls are enjoying themselves. Emphasize the variety of ways that friends enjoy being together.

EXTENDING FINE ART

Hands-On Activity Tell children that they can have fun creating art together. Have children choose partners. Provide crayons and a sheet of drawing paper for each pair to share. Partners then think of an activity that they both enjoy. They take turns drawing themselves doing the activity. Encourage partners to create a background and add details to their drawing. Ask volunteers to share their drawings with classmates.

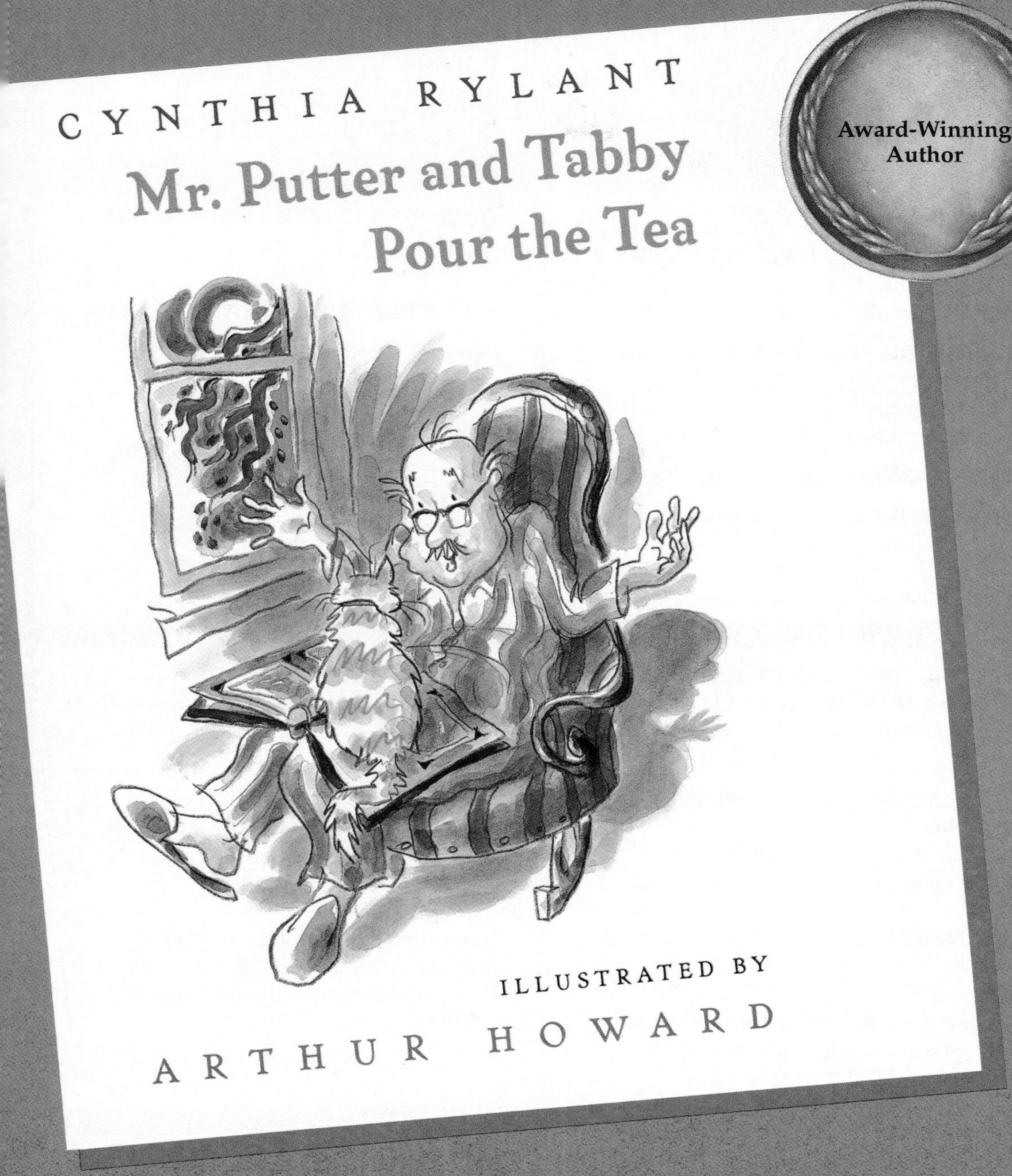

CYNTHIA RYLANT

Mr. Putter and Tabby Pour the Tea

Award-Winning Author

ILLUSTRATED BY

ARTHUR HOWARD

Cynthia Rylant

ABOUT THE AUTHOR AND THE ILLUSTRATOR

CYNTHIA RYLANT has received many awards for her writings, including the 1993 Newbery Medal for *Missing May.*

ARTHUR HOWARD has illustrated the Mr. Putter and Tabby series as well as many humor books for adults.

For more information about the author and the illustrator, see pages T332–T333.

Arthur Howard

THEME: FRIENDSHIP

We Belong Together

In "Mr. Putter and Tabby Pour the Tea," children will discover that people and pets can be perfect companions.

SELECTION SUMMARY

Genre: Realistic Fiction

Mr. Putter is tired of living alone and decides to get a cat. He goes to a pet store, but it sells only kittens. He then goes to an animal shelter where he sees a cat that is just like him—old, with creaky bones and thinning hair. He takes the cat home and names her Tabby. Together they share muffins, tea, tulips, long walks through the trees, opera, and the most perfect company of all—each other.

SUGGESTED LESSON PLANNER

▶ ***Mr. Putter and Tabby Pour the Tea***

	DAY 1	DAY 2
PART 1 Reading, Listening, Speaking, Viewing **Key Words** perfect enjoyed would wonderful loud without sure company	**BUILD BACKGROUND** T310 **VOCABULARY STRATEGIES** T310–T311 *Chart/Transparency 11* *Practice Book* pp. 55–56 **READING THE SELECTION** T312–T333 Options for Reading T312–T313 *Response Card 1* *Literature Cassette 1* **REVIEW PREDICTIONS/PURPOSE** T330 **APPRECIATING THE LITERATURE** T330 NOTE: Children may read the selection on Day 2.	**SUMMARIZE AND RETELL THE SELECTION** T331 *Practice Book* p. 57 ◆ **RESPONSE CORNER ACTIVITIES** T334 **CHECKING COMPREHENSION** T335 *End-of-Selection Test* 
PART 2 Writer's Workshop	**FRIENDLY LETTER AND ENVELOPE** Thinking as Writers T340 *Chart/Transparency 12*	Prewriting T340
Grammar	✓**EXCLAMATIONS AND COMMANDS; END MARKS** Teach the Concept T342 Daily Language Practice (1–2) R81	Daily Language Practice (3–4) R81 Practice Activity T343
Spelling	**WORDS WITH LONG *a* SPELLED *ay* AND *ai*** *may day say mail rain* *pay lay tail train away* Pretest/Self-Check T344 *Integrated Spelling Teacher's Edition* pp. T63, T275	Open and Closed Sorts T344 *Integrated Spelling* p. 38 *Integrated Spelling Teacher's Edition* p. T64
PART 3 Phonics	**VOWEL DIPHTHONG: /ou/*ou, ow*** Phonics-Vocabulary Connection T311	**VOWEL DIPHTHONG: /ou/*ou, ow*** (Introduce) T346 *Big Book of Rhymes* pp. 12–13 *Phonics Practice Book* pp. 143–146
Skills and Strategies	◆ **INTEGRATED CURRICULUM** *Pets and People* **Science** T350 **Art** T350 **Math** T351 **Music** T351	**STUDY SKILL** T348–T349 Form/Application (Introduce) *Practice Book* p. 61
 	Use the Extra Support note on page T315 and the Intervention Strategies note on page T317 to help **below-level readers.**	To help children build fluency, use the *Instant Readers™ Wolf Talk* and *The Missing Pet Mystery* on pages T336–T337.

NOTE: An alternative lesson plan for **below-level readers** appears on *Intervention Strategies Manual* pp. 32–37. A lesson for **students acquiring English** appears on *Sheltered English/ESL Manual* pp. 22–25.

DAY 3	DAY 4	DAY 5
◆ **IDEA BANK ACTIVITIES** Listening and Speaking T338 Real-Life Reading: Reading a Newspaper T338 Oral Language T339 Kinesthetic T339 *Writer's Magazine* pp. 22–25 School–Home Connection 6 R111	**VOCABULARY WORKSHOP** T345 Reviewing Key Words Story Strips R115 Time-Order Words *Take-Home/Keep-at-Home Book: The Perfect Pet* **READING TRADE BOOKS** T352–T353  Take-Home Book	**READING TRADE BOOKS** T347, T349, T351, T352–T353  Instant Reader™ Instant Reader™
Drafting T340 *Language Handbook* pp. 12–13, 17 *The Amazing Writing Machine*	Responding and Revising T340	Proofreading and Publishing T341 *Kid Pix*
Daily Language Practice (5–6) R81 Practice Activity T343 *Language Handbook* pp. 52–55	Daily Language Practice (7–8) R81 Practice Activity T343 *Grammar Practice Book* pp. 29–32	Daily Language Practice (9–12) R81 *Practice Book* p. 58
Discuss the Generalization T344 *Integrated Spelling* p. 39 *Integrated Spelling Teacher's Edition* p. T65	Apply to Writing T344 *Integrated Spelling* pp. 40–41 *Integrated Spelling Teacher's Edition* pp. T66–T67	Posttest T344 *Practice Book* p. 59 *Integrated Spelling Teacher's Edition* p. T68
VOWEL DIPHTHONG: /ou/*ou, ow* T346 *Bailey's Book House* (Read-A-Rhyme)	**VOWEL DIPHTHONG: /ou/*ou, ow*** T347 *Practice Book* p. 60	**VOWEL DIPHTHONG: /ou/*ou, ow*** T347 *Phonics Activity Book* p. 15
PHONICS AND DECODING MINILESSON T319 Long Vowel: /yōō/*u-e* (Maintain) *Phonics Activity Book* pp. 16–17 *Phonics Practice Reader 5: What Can You Do with a Tube?* *Phonics Practice Book* pp. 123–124 *Practice Book* p. 62	**COMPREHENSION MINILESSON** T321 ✓ Making Predictions (Review) *Practice Book* p. 63 **GRAMMAR MINILESSON** T325 ✓ Statements and Questions (Review) *Language Handbook* pp. 48–51	**PHONICS AND DECODING MINILESSON** T323 ✓ R-Controlled Vowel: /ûr/*er, ir* (Review) *Practice Book* p. 64 Theme Project Checkpoint 2 T354
Above-level writers may complete the Writer's Workshop independently at their own pace.	During the Vocabulary Workshop, refer to the Students Acquiring English note on page T345 for **ESL readers**.	**Below-level** and **ESL readers** may read the *ESL/Title I Library* book *Have You Seen My Cat?*

✓ = Tested Skill
◆ = Optional activities that may be used to adjust pacing throughout the lesson
Titles in *italics* are optional materials.

BUILDING BACKGROUND AND CONCEPTS

PRIOR KNOWLEDGE

Discuss pet cats. Ask children to tell about a cat they may have had or known about. Encourage them to give reasons why a cat might make a good pet.

Then introduce Prowler, an imaginary cat, using a stuffed toy, a puppet, or a stuffed sock decorated to look like a cat. Invite volunteers to use the toy cat to pantomime what they would do if Prowler were their new pet cat. Have the other children guess what the activity is—feeding the cat, playing with it, putting on its collar, or just holding and petting it—and list these ideas.

VOCABULARY STRATEGIES

KEY WORDS DEFINED

perfect just right

wonderful very good

sure positive; certain

enjoyed was pleased with

loud making a lot of noise

company person or people to spend time with

would past of *will*

without not having

SUPPORT WORDS

Display the words *delighted, opera, pour,* and *shelter*. Discuss their meanings and have children use them in sentences.

INTEGRATED SPELLING

SPELLING PRETEST: page T344

SPELLING GENERALIZATION: Words with long /ā/ spelled *ai* and *ay*

Intervention Strategies

For children who may have difficulty reading "Mr. Putter and Tabby Pour the Tea," support is available in *Intervention Strategies Manual,* pages 32–37, and on pages T317 and T336–T337 in this lesson.

STUDENTS ACQUIRING ENGLISH

See *Sheltered English ESL Manual,* pages 22–25.

"Integrating ESL children into the regular classroom can be a formidable task for a teacher who has little training in the field. I try always to keep in mind that children who are learning another language are like all children of this age—they are learning language and they need to feel good about themselves. When ESL children engage in puppetry and pantomime, they are actively participating in the same activities in which their peers are involved. These forms of expression provide 'safe' opportunities for ESL children to form relationships with their peers and to experience success in the classroom."

CUEING SYSTEMS

Have children read new vocabulary. Display Chart/Transparency 11, or write the words and story on the board. Encourage children to read the words they might know.

Cover the letters *fect* in *perfect*. Have children read the sentence and suggest the missing word. As children respond, uncover the rest of the word, one letter at a time, and ask:

How did seeing *per* help you?

Does the word make sense in the sentence?

Have children read the rest of the story, using word parts and the sense of the story to help them figure out the underlined words.

CHART/TRANSPARENCY 11

perfect	wonderful	sure
enjoyed	loud	company
would	without	

My cat Prowler is the perfect pet. We always have wonderful times together. Last week I gave him special treats for his birthday. I am sure he enjoyed them very much!

Sometimes I get loud, but he purrs quietly. We just like to keep each other company. What would I ever do without Prowler?

HANDS-ON ACTIVITY

Have children categorize words. Display the Key Words on construction paper cards and have children read them. Ask them to predict what a story that has these words might be about. Have children manipulate the cards to see how many ways they could categorize the words. Then call on volunteers to choose one or more words to use in a sentence. Invite children to try to use as many words as possible. Continue until all volunteers have responded. Then, have children write the Key Words on index cards and add them to their individual Word Files.

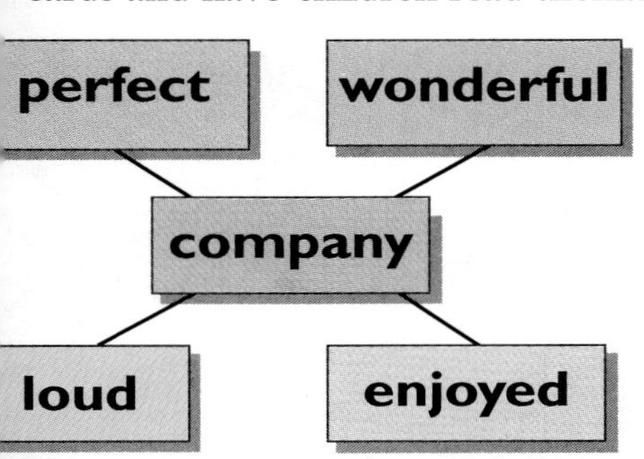

Mr. Putter and Tabby Pour the Tea

Name ____________

Cut out the words. Read the ads. Glue on the word that best completes each sentence.

PET WANTED

I am an old woman without a family.

I want a pet to keep me company.

My house is very quiet.

I would take very good care of a pet.

company	enjoyed	loud	perfect
sure	without	wonderful	would

PRACTICE BOOK, pages 55-56

PHONICS-VOCABULARY CONNECTION

WORD PLAY

Write the words *loud, without,* and *how* on the board. Read them aloud. Ask children how they are alike. (They all have the /ou/ sound.) Point out that in *loud* and *without* the /ou/ sound is spelled *ou*, but that in *how* it is spelled *ow*.

Have children use their Word Builders to create words by changing the beginning and ending letters of *loud* and changing the beginning letter of *how*. As children create new words, have them read them aloud.

The concept of vowel diphthong /ou/*ou, ow* is further developed on pages T346–T347.

Strategic Reading

STRATEGY FOCUS: RELATING PICTURES TO TEXT

Review with children some things good readers do when they read. Encourage children to suggest new ideas, and add them to their classroom chart.

What Good Readers Do
Guess what might happen next
Picture what is happening in their minds
Use pictures to help figure out what is happening

Share with children the comprehension strategy that is the focus of this selection:

MODEL **When I read a story, I look at the pictures carefully. Pictures can help me learn more about the story's characters, where the story takes place, and what has happened in the story so far. A picture can also show the meaning of a word.**

Mr. Putter and Tabby Pour the Tea

Award-Winning Author

BY
CYNTHIA RYLANT
ILLUSTRATED BY
ARTHUR HOWARD

158

SMALL GROUP

STRATEGIC READING

Choose some or all of the suggestions and questions under Strategic Reading, pages T312-T330, to guide a literature discussion and model the STRATEGY FOCUS of Relating Pictures to Text.

COOPERATIVE READING

STORY CIRCLES Have small groups take turns reading the story, stopping occasionally to use the During Reading questions on Reader Response Card 1 (Characters), page R85. Afterward, children can discuss the After Reading questions.

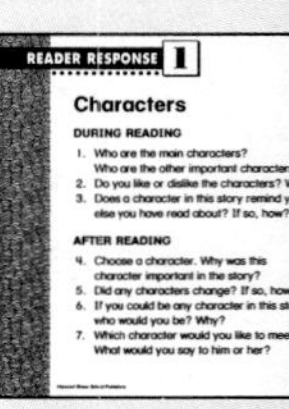

Response C

PREVIEWING/ SETTING PURPOSES

Have children read the story title on page 158, look through the illustrations on pages 158–163, and read the chapter title on page 161. Point out the picture of the man on page 160 and introduce him as Mr. Putter. Then have children predict what this story might be about and what they may find out about Mr. Putter. Have children write their predictions in their personal journals. Then help children set their purposes for reading.

WHOLE CLASS

INDEPENDENT READING

Have children read the entire story silently. As they finish, have them write their reactions to Mr. Putter and Tabby in their personal journals. When all children are finished, use their responses in a discussion about the characters and what happened in the story.

READ ALOUD

Read "Mr. Putter and Tabby Pour the Tea" aloud as children follow along in their books. Invite discussion by having children predict and then confirm their predictions as the story unfolds.

Strategic Reading

APPLYING A STRATEGY

PAGES 160–161 Before children read, have them look at the pictures on pages 160-161 and think about what is happening. As they read, encourage them to ask themselves questions like the following:

1. **What does Mr. Putter like to do?**
2. **How does he feel about doing these things by himself?**

SELF-QUESTIONING

LISTENING CENTER

"Mr. Putter and Tabby Pour the Tea" is available on *Literature Cassette 1*. Some children may benefit from listening to the story and following along in their books.

AUTHOR'S CRAFT

Point out that the author wrote "Mr. Putter and Tabby Pour the Tea" in three chapters. Ask why the author might have chosen to write the story in this way. Then have children find and read the titles of the chapters.

Mr. Putter

Before he got his fine cat, Tabby,
Mr. Putter lived all alone.

In the mornings he had no one to share his English muffins. In the afternoons he had no one to share his tea. And in the evenings there was no one Mr. Putter could tell his stories to. And he had the most wonderful stories to tell.

161

Student Self-Assessment 

FIX-UP STRATEGY: USING CONTEXT CLUES

Choose a volunteer to read page 161 aloud. Ask children what they would do if they did not know what *evenings* meant. Discuss their ideas. Then tell children that they can use the words around an unfamiliar word to figure it out. Explain that the author first talks about mornings and then talks about afternoons. If the reader knows that morning is the first part of the day and afternoon is the middle part, he or she can figure out that *evening* probably means "the end of the day." Encourage children to say the word a few times to help them remember it.

CONVENTIONS OF PRINT

TITLES **Call attention to the title of the chapter on page 161. Explain that *Mr.* is a title used with a man's name. Point out that titles of people begin with a capital letter. Most titles, like *Mr.*, end with a period.**

EXTRA SUPPORT **Ask children to reread the first sentence of the story and tell what information it gives. Help children see that the words *before he got his fine cat, Tabby* tell them that now Mr. Putter has a cat, but that first they are going to read about what Mr. Putter did before he got Tabby.**

Strategic Reading

MODELING A STRATEGY

PAGES 162–163 After children read the pages, have them look at the pictures again to see what else they can learn about Mr. Putter. Model your thinking: *I can tell by looking at the pictures on page 162 that Mr. Putter likes gardening. The picture on page 163 shows him lying in a hammock between two trees, so I can tell that his yard has some big trees. I read that Mr. Putter wants a cat. The picture on page 163 shows me the sort of cat Mr. Putter is thinking of.*

RELATING PICTURES TO TEXT

PLANT FOOD

All day long as Mr. Putter
clipped his roses
and fed his tulips
and watered his trees,
Mr. Putter wished for
some company.

162

PHONICS IN ACTION

Point out the words *watered* and *wished* on page 162, and *wanted* on page 163. Point out that the *-ed* ending is added to action words to show that something happened in the past. Talk about the different sounds the *-ed* ending makes in *wanted* and *wished.*

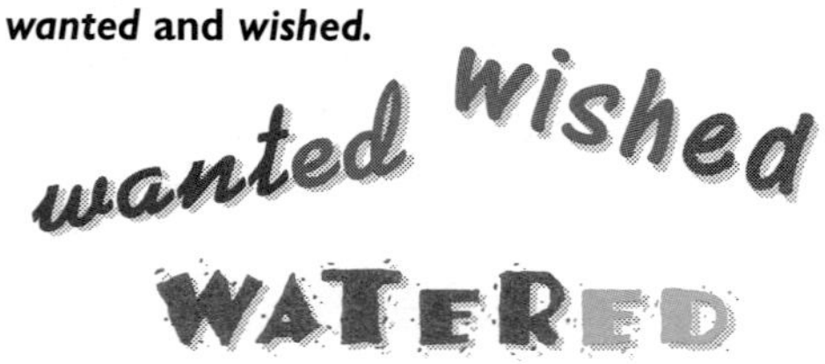

wanted wished

WATERED

AUTHOR'S CRAFT

Ask children what they think the word *putter* means. (Possible response: to work or be busy without really getting much done) **Ask them to speculate about why Cynthia Rylant might have chosen the name *Mr. Putter* for her character.**

He had warm muffins to eat.
He had good tea to pour.
And he had wonderful stories to tell.
Mr. Putter was tired of living alone.

Mr. Putter wanted a cat.

163

Student Self-Assessment 

FIX-UP STRATEGY: VOCABULARY JOURNALS
Have children make three columns on a page in a journal. In the first column, have children write a word from the story that causes them difficulty. In the middle column, have them write the sentence or phrase in which it appears. Then, in the third column, challenge them to write the word in a new sentence.

Intervention Strategies

MAKING PREDICTIONS Have children repeat this sentence: ***While I'm reading, it helps me to check to see if my guesses are right or wrong.*** Have children tell how using this strategy might help them understand the events in "Mr. Putter and Tabby Pour the Tea."

Strategic Reading

MODELING A STRATEGY

PAGES 164–167 Before children read, have them look at the pictures and talk about what Mr. Putter is doing and what they think will happen. After children have read, call attention to the pictures and discuss the following:

1. **Do these cats look like the cat Mr. Putter imagined?**
2. **How does Mr. Putter feel?**
3. **Do you think one of the kittens would be a good pet for Mr. Putter? Why or why not?**

RELATING PICTURES TO TEXT

Tabby

Mr. Putter went to the pet store. "Do you have cats?" he asked the pet store lady. "We have fourteen," she said. Mr. Putter was delighted. But when he looked into the cage, he was not.

164

SCHOOL↔HOME CONNECTION

Suggest that children draw a picture of their family's ideal pet. Encourage children to write the reasons for their choice. Completed work can be displayed in a Pet Corner.

"These are kittens," he said.
"I was hoping for a cat."
"Oh, no one wants cats, sir,"
said the pet store lady.
"They are not cute.
They are not peppy."

Mr. Putter himself had not been cute and peppy for a very long time. He said, "I want a cat."

165

MINILESSON

MAINTAIN: PHONICS AND DECODING

Long Vowel: /yo͞o/*u-e*

INFORMAL ASSESSMENT

As children read, notice whether they can decode words that have the /yo͞o/ sound spelled *u-e*.

TEACH/MODEL

Have children reread page 165. Ask volunteers to read the sentences *"They are not cute. They are not peppy."*

Ask children to tell why, according to the pet store lady, people like kittens better than cats. Write the sentence *Kittens are cute* on the board. Then circle the word *cute*. Ask a child to pronounce the word and name the vowel sound it contains. (/yo͞o/) Remind children that the /yo͞o/ sound can be spelled with the *u-e* pattern.

PRACTICE/APPLY

Write the following on the board:

Six Silly Things to Do

1. *Ride a mule to school.*
2. *Keep ice cubes in your desk.*
3. *Always use yellow paper.*
4. *Give your turtle a huge bowl of spaghetti.*
5. *Fuss and fume when it rains.*
6. *Say "Excuse me" to your goldfish.*

Have children read each sentence and circle the words with the same vowel sound they hear in *cute*.

PHONICS ACTIVITY BOOK, pages 16–17

PHONICS PRACTICE READER 5

PHONICS PRACTICE BOOK, pages 123–124

PHONICS IN ACTION

Have children find the word *sir* on page 165. Point out that the letters *ir* stand for the /ûr/ sound. Remind children that when they read "Matthew and Tilly," they learned that *er* and *ur* can also stand for the /ûr/ sound, as in *herself* and *purple*.

Name ________________

Mr. Putter and Tabby Pour the Tea

Here is a machine for making tea. Read the sentences that tell how it works. Finish each sentence with a word from the box that has the same vowel sound as *mule*.

hug tube fuss cubes cute huge
cup us cut fuse full tune

1. Push the ___huge___ button to turn on the machine.
2. Put water in the ___cute___ hat.
3. Pour the tea bags into the ___tube___.
4. Light the ___fuse___ to make it hot.
5. Whistle a ___tune___ while you wait for the tea.
6. Add as many ___cubes___ of sugar as you like.

62 LONG VOWEL: /yo͞o/u-e OUT OF THE BLUE Practice Book

PRACTICE BOOK, page 62

Critical Thinking Questions

1. **Do you think Mr. Putter made a good decision when he chose Tabby? Why or why not?** (Responses will vary. Children should support their answers.) CRITICAL: MAKING JUDGMENTS
2. **What do you think Mr. Putter and Tabby will do next?** (Possible response: Mr. Putter will take Tabby home, feed her, and show her around his house and yard.) CRITICAL: SPECULATING

"Then go to the shelter, sir,"
said the pet store lady.
"You are sure to find a cat."

Mr. Putter went to the shelter.

"Have you any cats?"
he asked the shelter man.
"We have a fat gray one,
a thin black one, and
an old yellow one," said the man.
"Did you say old?" asked Mr. Putter.

The shelter man brought
Mr. Putter the old yellow
cat. Its bones creaked,
its fur was thinning,
and it seemed a little
deaf. Mr. Putter creaked,
his hair was thinning,
and he was a little
deaf, too.

166

SOCIAL STUDIES CONNECTION

ANIMAL SHELTERS Point out that an animal shelter provides protection and a home for lost or unwanted animals until a new home can be found. Sometimes a shelter is called a humane society or an animal halfway house.

AUTHOR'S CRAFT

Call attention to the second block of text on page 166 and the way the author describes the cat and Mr. Putter. Ask children why the author may have chosen to repeat the description.

So he took the old yellow cat home.
He named her Tabby.
And that is how their life began.

167

Tested Skill

MINILESSON

REVIEW: COMPREHENSION

Making Predictions

INFORMAL ASSESSMENT

As children read, assess their ability to predict what will happen next by thinking about what has already happened.

TEACH/MODEL

Ask children whether they predicted that Mr. Putter would choose Tabby, and have them explain how they knew. Then model the thinking that children may have used to make this prediction:

MODEL **Mr. Putter seemed interested when he heard that one cat was old. Earlier, Mr. Putter had said that he did not want a peppy kitten, so I think he'll like the old cat. Then when he found out that the cat had creaky bones, thinning fur, and seemed a little deaf, Mr. Putter realized that the cat was a lot like him. That's why I thought Mr. Putter would choose the old cat.**

PRACTICE/APPLY

Ask children to predict whether Tabby and Mr. Putter will be happy together, or whether the story will tell about problems. Then encourage them to tell why they made the predictions they did. Have children read on to confirm their predictions.

STUDENTS ACQUIRING ENGLISH **Discuss the meaning of *its bones creaked.* Ask children what a door does when it creaks. If necessary, explain that the cat moves slowly because she is old. Make sure children understand that they can hear a door creak but cannot hear creaky bones, which just move slowly like a creaky door.**

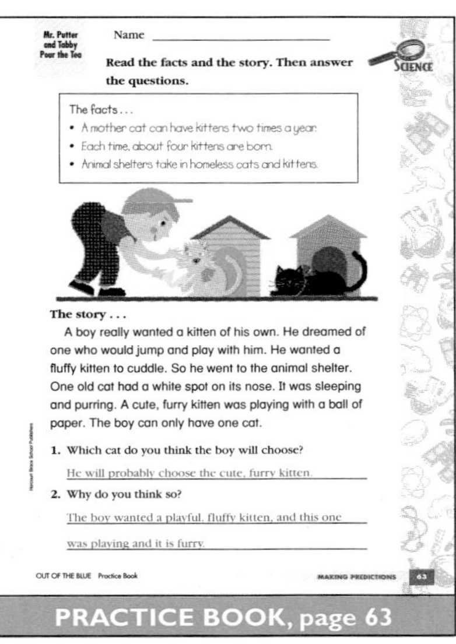

Mr. Putter and Tabby Pour the Tea

Name ____________

SCIENCE

Read the facts and the story. Then answer the questions.

The facts . . .

- A mother cat can have kittens two times a year.
- Each time, about four kittens are born.
- Animal shelters take in homeless cats and kittens.

The story . . .

A boy really wanted a kitten of his own. He dreamed of one who would jump and play with him. He wanted a fluffy kitten to cuddle. So he went to the animal shelter. One old cat had a white spot on its nose. It was sleeping and purring. A cute, furry kitten was playing with a ball of paper. The boy can only have one cat.

1. Which cat do you think the boy will choose?
He will probably choose the cute, furry kitten.
2. Why do you think so?
The boy wanted a playful, fluffy kitten, and this one was playing and it is furry.

OUT OF THE BLUE Practice Book — MAKING PREDICTIONS 63

PRACTICE BOOK, page 63

Strategic Reading

MODELING A STRATEGY

PAGES 168–171 Ask a volunteer to read the chapter title aloud. Then invite children to preview the illustrations on the pages. Have children predict what Mr. Putter and Tabby will do together. Provide a model if necessary. **Think aloud:** *On page 168 I see Mr. Putter clipping his roses while Tabby is in the flowers. On page 169, I see them eating together. I see a teapot and teacup on the tray. Maybe they will share tea. On pages 170 and 171, it looks as if they are doing everything together—talking, napping, and singing.* Then have children read to confirm their predictions. **MAKING AND CONFIRMING PREDICTIONS**

Mr. Putter and Tabby

Tabby loved Mr. Putter's tulips.
She was old,
and beautiful things
meant more to her.

She would rub past all
the yellow tulips.
Then she would roll past
all the red tulips.

Then she would take her
bath among all the pink
tulips. Mr. Putter clipped
roses while Tabby bathed.

168

SOCIAL STUDIES CONNECTION

FOODS FROM OTHER COUNTRIES

Ask children what both Mr. Putter and Tabby eat for breakfast. (an English muffin) **Ask what country they think English muffins came from originally.** (England) **Invite children to name other foods with a name that comes from the name of a country.** (French fries, French bread, French toast, Russian dressing, Swedish meatballs, Spanish rice, Irish stew, Hungarian goulash)

In the mornings
Mr. Putter and Tabby liked
to share an English muffin.
Mr. Putter ate his with jam.
Tabby ate hers with cream cheese.

In the afternoons
Mr. Putter and Tabby
liked to share tea.
Mr. Putter took his with sugar.
Tabby took hers with cream.

169

Tested Skill

MINILESSON

REVIEW: PHONICS AND DECODING

R-Controlled Vowel: /ûr/*er, ir*

INFORMAL ASSESSMENT

As children read, monitor how well they decode words in which *er* or *ir* stand for the *r*-controlled vowel sound /ûr/.

TEACH/MODEL

Suggest that children reread page 169. Ask whose English muffin had cream cheese on it. (Tabby's) Write on the board: *Tabby ate hers with cream cheese.* Then underline the word *hers.* Ask children what letters stand for the /ûr/ sound in *hers,* and circle *er.*

Next, write: *Tabby is a girl cat.* Ask children which word in the sentence has the same sound they hear in *hers.* Then underline *girl,* and ask a volunteer to circle the letters that stand for the /ûr/ sound.

PRACTICE/APPLY

Write the following sentences on the board, omitting the underlining:

1. **Tabby was the first cat Mr. Putter owned.**
2. **She was a perfect pet for Mr. Putter.**
3. **One morning Tabby saw a bird.**
4. **It perched on the fence.**
5. **Then it flew to a fern in the garden.**

Invite volunteers to read a sentence and underline a word in which the letters *er* or *ir* stand for the /ûr/ sound. Have the volunteers say the sentence and circle the letters *er* or *ir.*

Name ____________________

Mr. Putter and Tabby Pour the Tea

Look at the picture. Read the directions below the picture. Follow only the directions that have a word with the same vowel sound as *girl.*

1. Draw a bird in the birdbath.
2. Draw a girl and a boy on the first step.
3. Make her shirt red.
4. Make his pants red.
5. Put a kitten on the third step.
6. Draw the sun and clouds in the sky.
7. Put a squirrel on the grass.
8. Draw flowers in the dirt.
9. Draw a blue bow on the pot that holds the fern.

Children should draw a bird in the birdbath; a girl with a red shirt and boy on the first step; a kitten on the third step; a squirrel on the grass; flowers in the dirt; a blue bow on the pot holding the fern.

64 R-CONTROLLED VOWEL: /ûr/er, ir OUT OF THE BLUE Practice Book

PRACTICE BOOK, page 64

Cooperative Reading

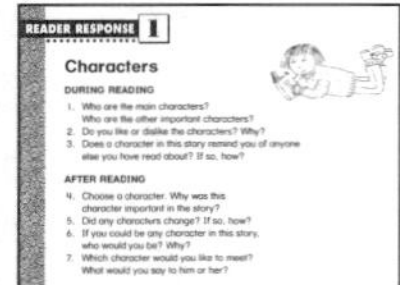
Response Card 1

As children discuss the questions on **Reader Response Card 1** (Characters), you might pose additional questions for them to consider:

1. **If you were getting a cat for a pet, how would it be like Tabby? How would it be different?**
2. **Do you like Mr. Putter? Do you like Tabby? Tell why you feel as you do.**

And in the evenings they sat by the window, and Mr. Putter told stories. He told the most wonderful stories. Each story made Tabby purr.

On summer days they warmed their old bones together in the sun. On fall days they took long walks through the trees.

170

SCIENCE CONNECTION

A CAT'S PURR Point out that on page 171 Tabby appears to be smiling. Ask children whether cats really smile. Explain that although cats don't smile, they can communicate happiness. As Tabby sits on Mr. Putter's shoulder, she rubs against his neck and purrs—her way of smiling.

EXPANDING VOCABULARY

Point out the word *purr* on page 170. Ask children how they say that word. Explain that sometimes authors use words that sound like the sound they describe. Ask children whether they know any other sound words. You may want to mention *bang, crash, snap*, and *meow*.

And on winter days they turned the opera up *very* loud.

171

Tested Skill

MINILESSON

REVIEW: GRAMMAR

Statements and Questions

INFORMAL ASSESSMENT

As children write, notice whether they use complete, well-formed statements and questions and punctuate them correctly.

TEACH/MODEL

Remind children that Mr. Putter wants a cat, but the pet store has only kittens. Ask children where Mr. Putter goes to find a cat. Then write these sentences on the board.

Mr. Putter goes to a shelter.
Does the shelter have any cats?

Review how the sentences are different. (The first one tells something—statement; the second one asks something—question.) Review how both sentences begin and end. Encourage children to dictate more statements and questions about the story.

PRACTICE/APPLY

Write the following sentences on the board. Ask children to rewrite them correctly. Afterward, discuss the sentences.

1. **mr. Putter does not want a kitten**
2. **he wants a cat**
3. **what does he like about Tabby?**
4. **why does Tabby like Mr. Putter.**
5. **mr. Putter tells wonderful stories**
6. **are they good friends?**

LANGUAGE HANDBOOK
Statements, pages 48–49
Questions, pages 50–51

MUSIC

FACT FINDER **OPERA Opera is a story told in song. Operas are usually sung in the language in which they were written, often Italian or German. Popular operas include *Hansel and Gretel* and *The Magic Flute*.**

Strategic Reading

APPLYING A STRATEGY

PAGES 172–173 After children have read the pages, ask them what the pictures tell about where Tabby likes to sleep and how much she likes being Mr. Putter's pet. **RELATING PICTURES TO TEXT**

After a while it seemed as if they had always lived together.

Tabby knew just what Mr. Putter was going to do next.

Mr. Putter knew just where Tabby was going to sleep next.

172

ILLUSTRATOR'S CRAFT

Discuss why the illustrator chose to show the picture of Tabby on the refrigerator door on page 172. Ask children to look ahead for other clues that show how Mr. Putter feels about Tabby that the illustrator has added. (page 174—mailbox; page 176—photograph of Mr. Putter and Tabby)

In the mornings each looked for the other as soon as they opened their eyes.

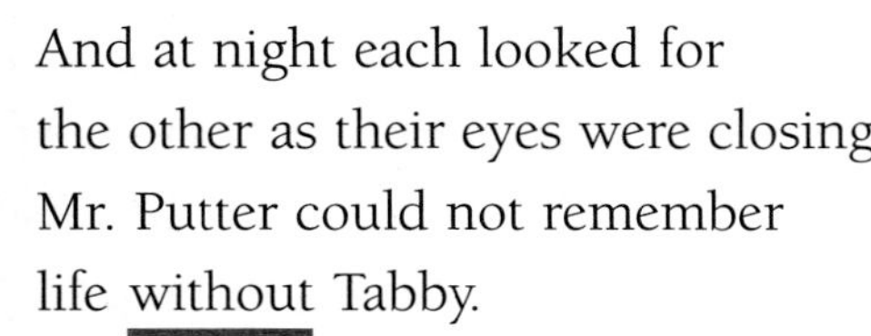

And at night each looked for the other as their eyes were closing. Mr. Putter could not remember life <u>without</u> Tabby.

173

Informal Assessment ✓

USING CUEING SYSTEMS

As children reread this selection or parts of the selection, observe how well they apply cueing systems to develop meaning.

- ☑ Do children suggest words that make sense in the context and have appropriate sound/letter relationships?
- ☑ Do children reread and then self-correct?

SCIENCE

A CAT'S NINE LIVES
Like many sayings, "A cat has nine lives" has a basis in fact. Certain qualities, such as an excellent sense of hearing and excellent balance, help cats survive. Cats can walk along narrow ledges without falling. If they do fall, they nearly always land on their feet.

Strategic Reading

APPLYING A STRATEGY

PAGES 174–177 Have children look at the pictures and talk about what Mr. Putter and Tabby are doing. After children have read, ask them to summarize the relationship between Mr. Putter and Tabby. **Think aloud:** *The story has been telling about things they do together every day and throughout the year. They must enjoy each other's company very much. They are friends.*

SUMMARIZING

IDEA BANK

Remind children that the story mentions Mr. Putter's tulips. Suggest that Mr. Putter may have attended events such as the annual tulip festival in Holland, Michigan, or the one in Pella, Iowa. If your town has a special festival, discuss it, and invite children to research it. Children who have attended such a festival might enjoy telling about it and sharing mementos.

Tabby could not remember
life without Mr. Putter.
They lived among their
tulips and trees.

175

MUSIC CONNECTION

MUSIC AND EMOTION Read a summary of an opera such as Mozart's *The Magic Flute*. Then play an excerpt from it. Encourage children to close their eyes as they listen. At the end of the excerpt, have them open their eyes and tell how the music made them feel: sad, afraid, joyful, excited. Encourage children to pantomime their feelings.

REAL-LIFE CONNECTION

What kinds of things do Mr. Putter and Tabby like to do together? Ask children if they have a friend or family member, or even a pet, that they especially enjoy being with. Encourage children to tell what kinds of activities they like to do with their special friends.

Returning to the Predictions/Purpose

Before children read, they wrote about what the story would be about and what they might learn about Mr. Putter. Invite them to share their work and compare their predictions with what actually happened.

Appreciating the Literature

With the whole class or a small group, have an open discussion about the story.

- **How do you think the author wanted you to feel about Mr. Putter and Tabby?**
- **Is that the way you feel? Why or why not?**

WRITING

EXTEND THE STORY Mr. Putter and Tabby seem to really belong together. What do you think Mr. Putter would advise other people who live alone to do? Encourage children to write a list of things Mr. Putter would say to a friend who is thinking of getting a pet.

EXPANDING VOCABULARY

Read aloud the last sentence of the story. Then write *company* and ask children what it means here. ("companionship; somebody who is with you")

Discuss these sentences with different meanings of *company:*

- **Mom works at a lumber company.**
- **We had company for dinner.**

each other.

177

NOTES

Here's a place to list ideas or activities that you would like to use the next time you teach this lesson.

SUMMARIZE AND RETELL

Map the Story

Work with children to complete the following story map.

Then have children use the story map to retell the story of "Mr. Putter and Tabby Pour the Tea." See *Practice Book* page 57.

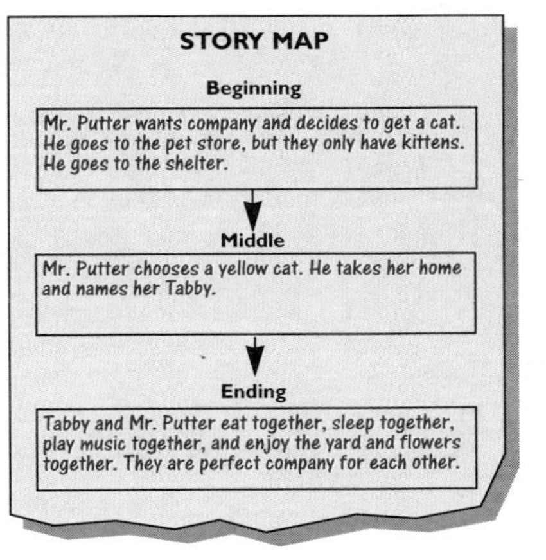

STORY MAP

Beginning

Mr. Putter wants company and decides to get a cat. He goes to the pet store, but they only have kittens. He goes to the shelter.

Middle

Mr. Putter chooses a yellow cat. He takes her home and names her Tabby.

Ending

Tabby and Mr. Putter eat together, sleep together, play music together, and enjoy the yard and flowers together. They are perfect company for each other.

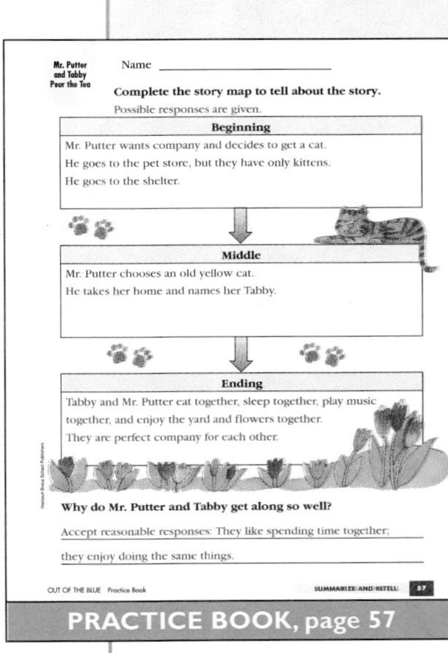

Mr. Putter and Tabby Pour the Tea

Name ______________

Complete the story map to tell about the story.

Possible responses are given.

Beginning

Mr. Putter wants company and decides to get a cat.
He goes to the pet store, but they have only kittens.
He goes to the shelter.

Middle

Mr. Putter chooses an old yellow cat.
He takes her home and names her Tabby.

Ending

Tabby and Mr. Putter eat together, sleep together, play music together, and enjoy the yard and flowers together.
They are perfect company for each other.

Why do Mr. Putter and Tabby get along so well?

Accept reasonable responses: They like spending time together; they enjoy doing the same things.

OUT OF THE BLUE Practice Book SUMMARIZE AND RETELL 57

PRACTICE BOOK, page 57

About the Author

PAGES 178–179 Have children read the information about the author and the illustrator. Talk about what Cynthia Rylant likes to write about and why Arthur Howard enjoys drawing. Also, children can find out about their pets.

Cynthia Rylant lived with her grandparents in West Virginia for the first eight years of her life. When she was growing up, she did not have many books to read, so she read comic books. Comic books gave her a love of stories. Roaming around country roads and a nearby town let her listen to people's conversations and to meet many animals. Rylant credits all these experiences with helping her become a writer.

Rylant now lives in Oregon, but she still visits her family in West Virginia a few times a year.

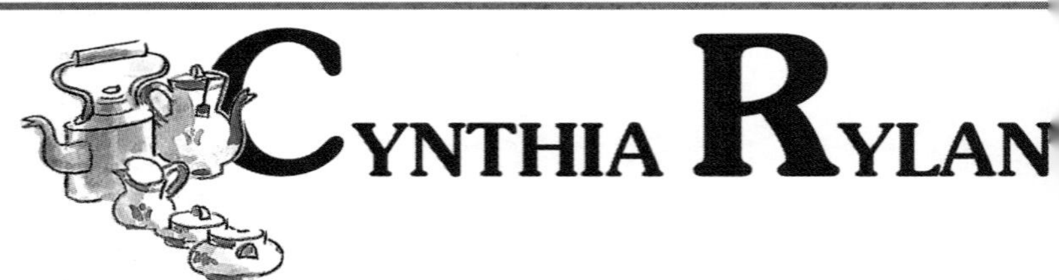

Dear friends and readers,

Hello! How do I introduce myself? I am the writer of many books about things like

having tea 

petting kittens 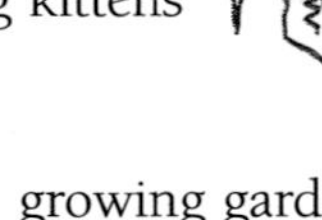

growing gardens

and all sorts of ordinary things.

I have a son who likes LOUD music and I have two good dogs and two sweet cats who like sunshine and food.

I think that life is full of beautiful things, beautiful small things and beautiful large things to celebrate. I celebrate them in my books. And I hope that you will celebrate with me.

Cynthia Rylant

178

OTHER MR. PUTTER BOOKS BY CYNTHIA RYLANT AND ARTHUR HOWARD

Mr. Putter and Tabby Bake the Cake. **Harcourt Brace, 1994.**
AVERAGE

Mr. Putter and Tabby Pick the Pears. **Harcourt Brace, 1995.**
AVERAGE

Mr. Putter and Tabby Walk the Dog. **Harcourt Brace, 1994.**
AVERAGE

ARTHUR HOWARD

Dear readers,

I had fun drawing the pictures for this story. What would Mr. Putter's house look like? What kind of car would he drive? Hmmm . . .

The house was easy. It's my brother's house in New York. With its pointy roof and big front porch with a porch swing, it was perfect for Mr. Putter.

The car was a little harder to find. Then one day, I saw the perfect car parked on the street. It was old, but not too old, and it looked slow-moving—kind of like Mr. Putter.

A lot of people ask me if I have a cat. I love cats, but I don't have one. I have a pet hermit crab named Buster, though.

Your friend,

Arthur Howard

179

About the Illustrator

Arthur Howard **has illustrated the Mr. Putter and Tabby series as well as many humor books for adults. Before Howard illustrates a book, he thinks a lot about what the characters are like, where they might like to live, and, in the case of Mr. Putter, what kind of car they might drive. He often spends a lot of time looking around his neighborhood and beyond to find just the right model for each object he wants to illustrate. He usually knows it when he sees it, as when he spotted a car that seemed old and slow-moving—just the kind that would suit Mr. Putter.**

Howard has appeared regularly on *Square One Television*, a production of the Children's Television Workshop. Howard plays a number of characters on the television series, including Superguy, Mr. District Attorney, and game-show host Monty Carlo.

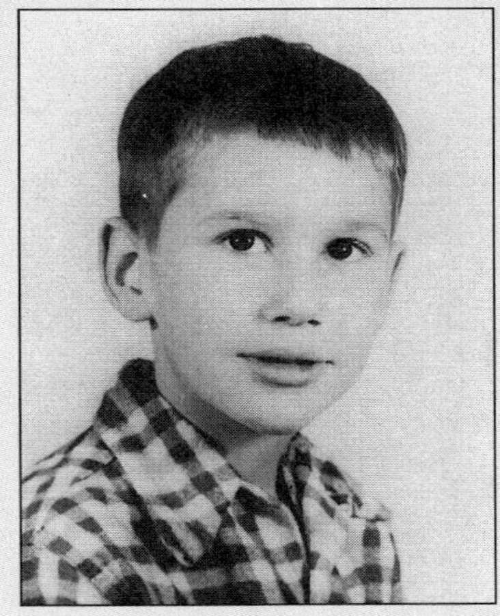

Arthur Howard in second grade

RESPONSE CORNER ACTIVITIES

MAKE A CARD

PERFECT COMPANY

PAGE 180 Discuss with children what makes someone "perfect company." Then read through the directions with children. In addition to drawing materials, you may want to provide glitter, ribbons, stickers, and other decorations for children's cards. Invite children to give the finished cards to their "perfect company." ART/WRITING

ADD TO A PHOTO ALBUM

MR. PUTTER'S FAMILY ALBUM

PAGE 181 To spark ideas, ask children to name things they do or would like to do with a special friend or pet. Then you can help children arrange their pictures of Mr. Putter and Tabby in a class album, perhaps using a loose-leaf binder. You may want to use photo-mounting corners to mount drawings, and give the binder a photo-album look. ART

Response Corner

MAKE A CARD

Perfect Company

Tabby was perfect company for Mr. Putter. Make a greeting card to give to the person or pet who is *your* perfect company.

To make your card:

1. Fold a piece of drawing paper in half.
2. On the top of the folded paper, draw the cover of your card.
3. Open the card and write a message to your perfect company. Write your name to show who made the card.

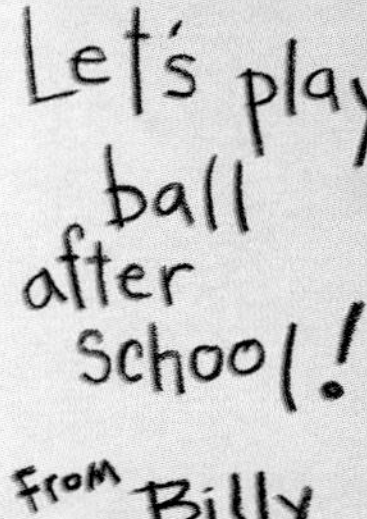

180

VARYING THE ACTIVITY

You may wish to extend the Mr. Putter's Family Album activity by having children write a new chapter about Mr. Putter and Tabby, based on their picture and caption. Encourage children to publish their stories, and then display them with the album for children to enjoy.

PORTFOLIO OPPORTUNITY

Children may wish to add their cards to their portfolios.

ADD TO A PHOTO ALBUM

Mr. Putter's Family Album

Tabby and Mr. Putter are a family. They do everything together. Mr. Putter even has an album full of photos of the two of them.

Draw a new picture for Mr. Putter's family album. Write a sentence to tell what Mr. Putter and Tabby are doing together. Add your drawing to a class album.

What Do You Think?

- How are Mr. Putter and Tabby alike?
- Why do you think Mr. Putter and Tabby make a good team?

181

CHECKING COMPREHENSION

What Do You Think?

1. **How are Mr. Putter and Tabby alike?** (They are both old and a little deaf, with creaky bones. They both like opera.) **DESCRIPTIVE RESPONSE**
2. **Why do you think Mr. Putter and Tabby make a good team?** (Responses will vary. Be sure children support their answers.) **PERSONAL RESPONSE**

An additional question for extending reading.

3. **Imagine that you meet Mr. Putter. What will you ask him or tell him?** (Accept reasonable responses. I will tell him about things I like to do. Then I will ask him what kind of cat he thinks I should get for a pet.) **CRITICAL/CREATIVE ANALYSIS**

STUDENTS ACQUIRING ENGLISH **Pair children with English-proficient partners for Mr. Putter's Family Album. Encourage children to draw pictures based on their own experiences if they are having difficulty thinking of one related to the story. Have children dictate their caption and then help each child read his or her sentence.**

Informal Assessment

Observe children as they make class photo album pages.

- ☑ Do children draw pictures that show both Mr. Putter and Tabby engaged in an activity?
- ☑ Do children write sentences to describe their pictures?
- ☑ Do children share stories about their pictures with a partner?

Intervention Strategies

Instant Readers™

Predictable and Patterned Little Books That Build Fluency

* **BOOK LEVEL: 19–20**

VOCABULARY:
company, loud

PHONIC ELEMENTS:
Vowel diphthong: /ou/ou, ow

PHONOGRAM:
-ound

SUMMARY:
How and why do wolves communicate with each other?

Informal Assessment ✓

Are children able to

- ☑ manipulate letters in a word to form new words?
- ☑ write questions and answers?

Reading a New Book

INTRODUCING WOLF TALK

Ask children to describe how their pets communicate with people when they are hungry, hurt, or need to go outside. Explain that animals that live in the wild communicate with each other. Share the cover and read aloud the title. Ask children how they think wolves talk to each other. As the pictures are described, ask children what they think the wolves are trying to say with their gestures. Try to use story words such as *stand, move, touch, leader,* and *pack* as the pictures are discussed.

READING THE STORY

Have children read the book with a partner to find out exactly what scientists think wolves say to each other.

WORKING WITH WORDS AND LETTERS

In a number of story words, the letters *ou* and *ow* stand for the same sound. Use individual Letter Cards, *Word Builder Cards,* or magnetic letters to write the word *loud*. Add the letter *c* to the word, and have a volunteer read the word. Manipulate the word as shown below, substituting and replacing diphthongs or beginning and ending sounds. Do the same with other story words such as *howl, down,* and *around*.

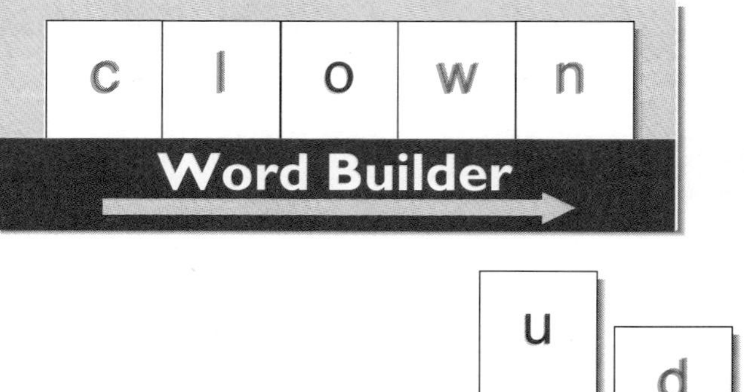

WRITING QUESTIONS AND ANSWERS

Have children use the facts they have learned from the story to write a question about the way wolves talk and an answer for the question.

Additional activities are provided on pages 34-35 of the *Intervention Strategies Manual*.

* **BOOK LEVEL: 16–17**

VOCABULARY:
loud, without, would

PHONIC ELEMENTS:
Vowel diphthong: /ou/ou, *ow*; *R*-controlled vowel: /ûr/*er*

PHONOGRAM:
-ound

SUMMARY:
A missing pet is recovered in this double mystery.

Reading a New Book

INTRODUCING THE MISSING PET MYSTERY

Explain to children what a mystery is if they do not know the concept (a question that cannot be answered or something that is unknown). Share the cover illustration, and ask children what they think the mystery is in this story. While sharing and discussing the pictures and the whereabouts of the pet, be sure to ask children what kind of pet is missing.

READING THE STORY

If children have not already caught on to the two mysteries in this story, tell them that this story will explain two things: what kind of pet is missing and where the pet is. As children read the story independently, have them look for clues to help them solve the mysteries.

WORKING WITH WORDS AND LETTERS

Throughout the story, some words tell where the story characters look for Bowser. With children, act out and write the words and phrases.

on the left
behind the washer
in the basket

WRITING MINIMYSTERIES

Have each child write on a sheet of paper a phrase or two to describe or give clues about an object or an animal. Then have them write the answer on the back of the paper.

ESL/Title I Reading

Have You Seen My Cat? by Eric Carle

ESL/Title I Library

Working with "Mr. Putter and Tabby Pour the Tea"

GRAPHOPHONIC CUES As readers learn more about sound-letter correspondences, they attempt to apply the strategy to new text. If a child attempts to read a word and cannot get past the initial letter/sound, try writing the word on the board one letter at a time so the child has an opportunity to analyze each letter. Always try to remind the child to put the word in the context of the sentence by prompting with questions like *Does that make sense?*

* Books leveled according to Barbara Peterson's "Profiles of Books for Beginning Readers," on page 9 of the *Instant Readers Teacher's Guide.*

IDEA BANK

TIPS FOR CLASSROOM MANAGEMENT

IF children are familiar with newspapers, THEN have them help others find appropriate items from newspapers to cut out for the Real-Life Reading activity.

IF children are hesitant about role-playing in the Oral Language activity, THEN work with children in small groups to develop scripts that can be read aloud.

LISTENING AND SPEAKING

Group Talk

FRIENDSHIP ACTIVITIES

Have children talk about what makes a good friend. Suggest that they find examples in the story in which Mr. Putter shows he is a good friend and in which Tabby shows she is a good friend. Organize children in small groups to share ideas about friendship, using parts of the story to show how each character is a good friend to the other.

After small-group discussions, gather children to share their ideas and insights. **CHALLENGING THE TEXT**

REAL-LIFE READING

Reading a Newspaper

MATERIALS
- newspapers
- scissors
- glue
- large sheets of paper

Point out that Mr. Putter is reading a newspaper on page 169. Discuss what is found in newspapers. Ask children to speculate about which part of the newspaper Mr. Putter is reading.

Provide newspapers for children to review, and point out things that can be found in almost all newspapers, such as comics, a weather forecast, headlines, and classified ads. Then ask children to work in groups to make a newspaper for Mr. Putter, choosing articles, pictures, and ads that he would enjoy. **READING**

ORAL LANGUAGE

Interviewing

LET'S TALK ABOUT PETS!

Have children work in pairs, with one child pretending to be a worker at an animal shelter and the other child pretending to be a customer, like Mr. Putter. Discuss questions workers and customers might ask, such as *Why do you want a pet? What kinds of things would you like to do with a pet? Do you have any small pets? How much time do you have to care for a pet?*

1. What would you name your pet?
2. Why do you want a pet?
3. How would you take care of your pet?
4. Do you have a favorite pet?

Work with children to develop tips for interviewing. Then let partners practice interviewing each other. Pairs of children may want to role-play their interview for their classmates. LISTENING/SPEAKING

TIPS FOR INTERVIEWING

- Ask questions that begin with *who, what, where, when, why*, and *how*.
- Listen carefully. Look at the person.
- Write short notes about important information.
- Thank the person for talking with you.

Informal Assessment

Evaluate children's ability to give and find out specific information as they interview each other.

KINESTHETIC

Creative Connection

MAKING SUN TEA

MATERIALS
- **large glass jar**
- **herbal tea bags**
- **disposable cups**
- **sugar or honey (optional)**

Mr. Putter and Tabby enjoyed sharing tea. Discuss that tea can be drunk hot with milk or sugar or lemon or drunk cold or iced, sometimes with lemon or sugar. Tell children that the water for tea has to be heated. Ask children to suggest ways to heat the water. If not suggested, explain that the heat from the sun can heat the water. Have children place several tea bags in the jar and fill it with water. Place the jar in the sun and leave it for several hours. Then discard the tea bags, sweeten the tea if you wish, and enjoy! LISTENING/SPEAKING/KINESTHETIC

PERSONAL JOURNAL

REFLECTING ON THE STORY Invite children to think about how Mr. Putter and Tabby become good friends. Have children write in their personal journals about their own wishes for what their perfect company would be like.

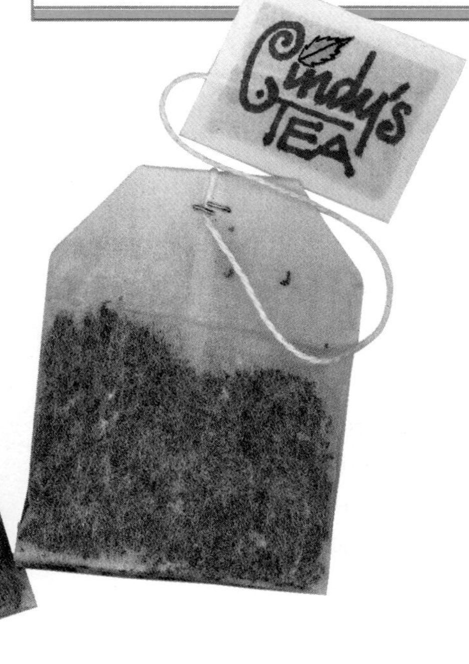

Which book would you like to read? Why?

Look at This! A display can tell about almost

Real-Life LIBRARY DISPLAY Skills

Here, Kitty Kitty

Mr. Putter and Tabby might want to look at this library display.

A CATalog of great CAT Books
Look for them right here—in your library!

The Best Pet Yet! written by C. J. Wylie

In the Jungle, In the City story by Stefania Washington

Amazing Cat Facts by Isabel Bustimanti

Kittens and Cats: A Look-and-Learn Book by Sasha Pfeifer

Cat Tricks written by Arlo Higgins Yee

22 Mr. Putter and Tabby Pour the Tea • Writer's Magazine

23

WRITER'S MAGAZINE, pages 22–25

WRITER'S WORKSHOP

Friendly Letter and Envelope

Thinking as Writers

WRITING FORM: Friendly Letter and Envelope Remind children that Mr. Putter adopted Tabby from an animal shelter. Explain to children that they will pretend to be Mr. Putter and write a letter to the man at the shelter, telling about life with Tabby.

Display Charts/Transparencies 12–13, or write the model Friendly Letter and an envelope on the board. Point out the parts of a friendly letter and discuss the return address and mailing address on the envelope.

CHART/TRANSPARENCY 12

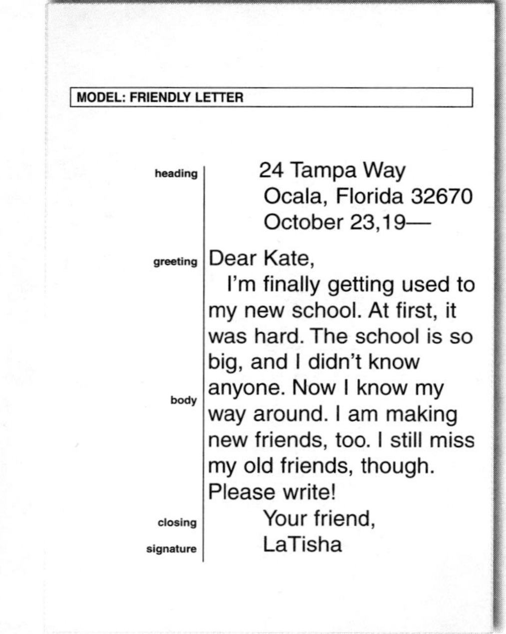
MODEL: FRIENDLY LETTER

heading: 24 Tampa Way
Ocala, Florida 32670
October 23,19—

greeting: Dear Kate,

body: I'm finally getting used to my new school. At first, it was hard. The school is so big, and I didn't know anyone. Now I know my way around. I am making new friends, too. I still miss my old friends, though. Please write!

closing: Your friend,

signature: LaTisha

WRITER'S CRAFT: Pattern of Question and Answer Explain that when someone writes a letter, he or she often includes questions that the reader can answer when he or she writes back. Invite children to think of questions they might ask Mr. Putter. Then invite other children to suggest what Mr. Putter might answer.

PREWRITING

Work with children to complete a web like the following about Mr. Putter's life with Tabby.

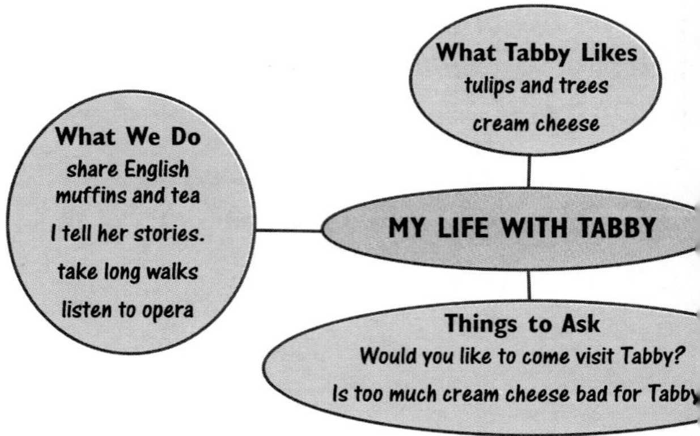

DRAFTING

Then have children work individually to write friendly letters that include some news and one or more questions. Remind children to

- pretend they are Mr. Putter.
- tell the shelter man all about life with Tabby. Use their webs for ideas.
- include the five parts of a letter: heading, greeting, body, closing, signature.
- include at least one question in the letter.

Have children save their drafts and revisions in their writer's folder.

RESPONDING AND REVISING

Work with small groups. Invite children to take turns reading their letters aloud. Offer these guidelines for giving positive feedback:

- Does the letter sound like Mr. Putter wrote it?
- Does the letter have a heading, a greeting, a body, a closing, and a signature?
- Does the letter tell about things Mr. Putter and Tabby do?
- Does the letter include a question for the reader to answer?

TIPS FOR CLASSROOM MANAGEMENT

IF children are familiar with the writing process approach, **THEN** present the writing assignment and have them use the Friendly Letter model on pages 12–13 and the Envelope model on page 17 of the *Language Handbook*.

IF at this time you want a short writing activity, **THEN** have children do the prewriting activity and place the web in the Writing Center for children's reference during independent writing.

TECHNOLOGY

THE AMAZING WRITING MACHINE
Primary Level Activity Disk Pack Grade 2
Have children enter their letters in the Letters mode.

KID PIX
Children can illustrate their letters and envelopes by creating pictures of their own or using the stamps.

PROOFREADING

Offer some tips to help children proofread. Help them focus on the following:

CAPITAL LETTERS The word *I* is written as a capital letter.

STATEMENTS AND QUESTIONS A statement tells something and ends with a period. A question asks something and ends with a question mark. (See the Grammar Minilesson on page T325.)

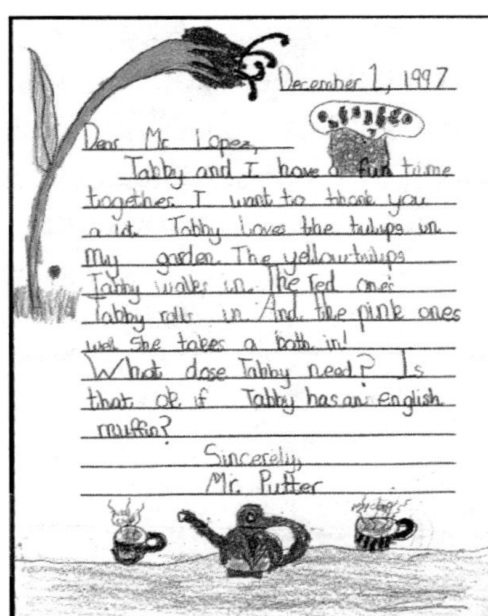

December 1, 1997

Dear Mr. Lopez,

Tabby and I have a fun time together. I want to thank you a lot. Tabby loves the tulips in my garden. The yellow tulips Tabby walks in. The red ones Tabby rolls in. And the pink ones well she takes a bath in! What dose Tabby need? Is that ok if Tabby has an english muffin?

Sincerely,
Mr. Putter

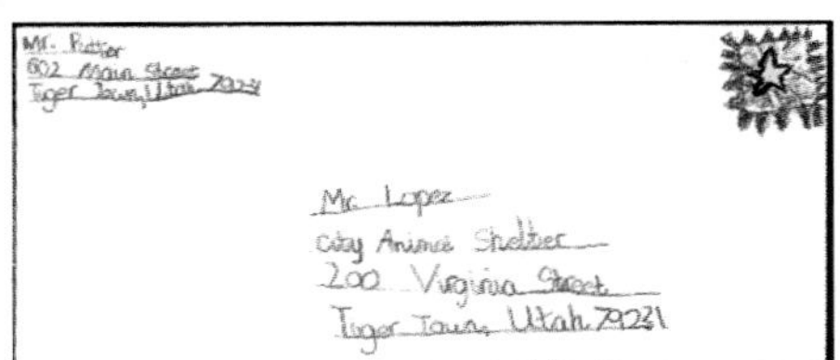

Mr. Putter
602 Main Street
Tiger Town, Utah

Mr. Lopez
City Animal Shelter
200 Virginia Street
Tiger Town, Utah 79231

PUBLISHING

Have children make a clean copy of their letters and address envelopes to an imaginary animal shelter. Then offer publishing options like the following:

> **Handwriting**
> Remind children that their handwriting must be neat and clear so that the person reading the letter and envelope can understand them. If children need assistance, refer them to the Handwriting models in the *Language Handbook* or in the classroom.

YOUR OWN STATIONERY Have children think about what type of person Mr. Putter is and what type of stationery he might use to write his letter. Have children design and create a piece of stationery for their letters. Have them copy their final drafts onto their stationery.

MAIL BAG Children can put their completed letters and envelopes in a bag. Volunteer mail carriers can take turns distributing the letters at random. Children may want to pretend to be the animal shelter employee and answer the letter.

PORTFOLIO OPPORTUNITY

After children publish, make copies of their letters and have them attach their Writing Self-Assessment Checklists to them. Have them place the letters, envelopes, and checklists in their portfolios.

LANGUAGE HANDBOOK

Friendly Letter, pages 12–13; Envelope, page 17

Student Self-Assessment ✓

Children can use the Writing Self-Assessment Checklist in the *Portfolio Assessment Teacher's Guide.*

EVALUATING THE WRITTEN RESPONSE

When evaluating children's friendly letters, consider:

ORGANIZATION	CONTENT	APPEARANCE
Do the letter and the envelope follow appropriate form?	Does the letter include interesting information? Does the letter include a question?	Is the letter neatly written and in the writer's best handwriting?

EVALUATION BENCHMARKS

The child has trouble following the form of a letter. The child does not offer much elaboration of personal feelings or details.	= EMERGENT
The child keeps to the topic and relates personal comments, but may not exhibit an awareness of the interests of the audience.	= BEGINNING
The child successfully follows the form of the letter. The child relates interesting information and offers questions the reader can respond to.	= PROFICIENT

Tested Skill

GRAMMAR

Exclamations and Commands; End Marks

LANGUAGE HANDBOOK

Exclamations and Commands, pages 52-53
End Marks, pages 54-55

DAILY LANGUAGE PRACTICE

Oral language exercises are provided on page R81.

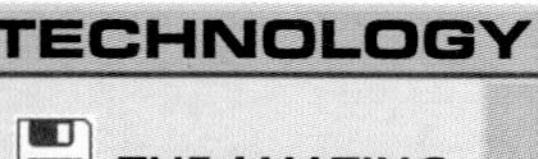

TECHNOLOGY

THE AMAZING WRITING MACHINE **Children can use the story feature in the program as they write their stories in the What Happens Next? activity.**

Reading↔Writing Connection

Connect to the story. Remind children that Mr. Putter likes Tabby a lot. When Mr. Putter talks about his cat, he probably shows strong feelings. For example:

What a great cat Tabby is!
She's terrific!

Write the sentences on the board, and ask children what they notice about the punctuation of the sentences.

Build oral language. Invite children to think of sentences they might say to show strong feelings about their real or made-up pet. Write their sentences on the board.

Next, ask what Mr. Putter might say to Tabby when it's tea time. Write the following sentences on the board:

Come here, Tabby.
Drink your tea now.

Invite children to make up sentences they might say to tell a pet what to do. Then talk about the punctuation of these sentences.

Teach/Model

Define exclamations and commands. Invite children to look again at the sentences on the board that show strong feeling. Explain that these sentences are called **exclamations** and end with an exclamation point.

Next, discuss the commands on the board. Explain that a sentence that tells someone to do something is called a **command** and usually ends with a period. It can end with an exclamation point if it shows strong feeling, such as *Don't touch the fire!* Then review statements and questions and their end marks. Ask volunteers to dictate statements, questions, exclamations, and commands. Write them on the board, and invite the volunteers to add the end marks.

Practice/Apply

Check understanding. Display these sentences, omitting the end marks. Ask volunteers to add the end marks, and explain why they used each mark.

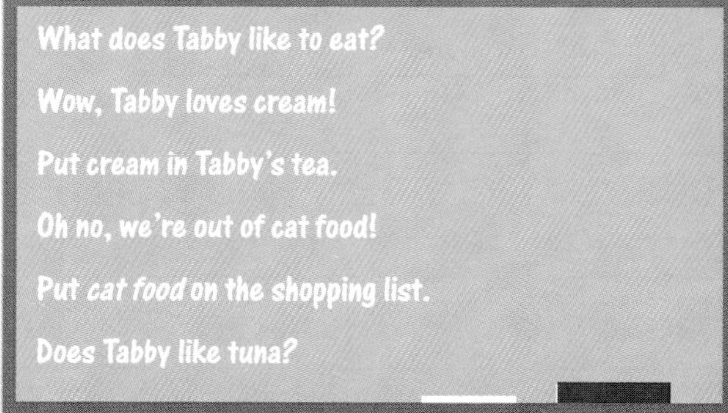

Practice Activities

Card Game

ORAL APPLICATION Have children write a large period, question mark, and exclamation point on separate cards. Read sentences like these, and have children hold up the card with the correct end mark. **VISUAL/AUDITORY**

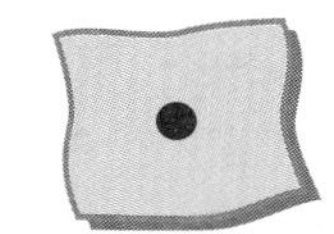

Mr. Putter lived alone.
Why did he go to the pet store?
The pet store lady had many kittens.

Why didn't Mr. Putter get a kitten?
Mr. Putter wanted a grown-up cat.
Explain why Mr. Putter wanted a cat.

Where did Mr. Putter get Tabby?
How happy Mr. Putter was with Tabby!

What Happens Next?

WRITING APPLICATION Form groups of three or four children, and give each a sentence. For example:

It was our best game ever!

What a surprise!

We had fun!

Each group will write a story that begins or ends with its sentence. One child will begin the story and then pass the paper to the next child. Have children use each of the four kinds of sentences in their stories. Afterward, a child from each group can read the group's story to their classmates. **VISUAL/AUDITORY**

Cartoon Caper

WRITING APPLICATION Find cartoons that show children or animals in action. Remove text from each cartoon balloon and show the cartoon pictures to children. Invite them to think of statements, questions, commands, and exclamations for each one, and name the correct end mark. Next, have each child draw and write a simple cartoon. Each cartoon should contain at least one statement, question, command, and exclamation. **VISUAL**

APPLY TO WRITING

Have children look for commands and exclamations in their friendly letters to check that they have correct end punctuation.

USAGE TIP Use an exclamation point if you want to show a strong feeling in your sentence, such as surprise or fear.

STUDENTS ACQUIRING ENGLISH

Play a game of "Simon Says" with children. Let them take turns leading the group. Afterward, ask children to dictate some of the commands they used. Write them on the board, and ask children to punctuate them. Encourage children to dictate questions, exclamations, and commands and follow the same procedure.

RETEACH

See R69 for lessons in multiple modalities.

GRAMMAR PRACTICE BOOK
pages 29–32

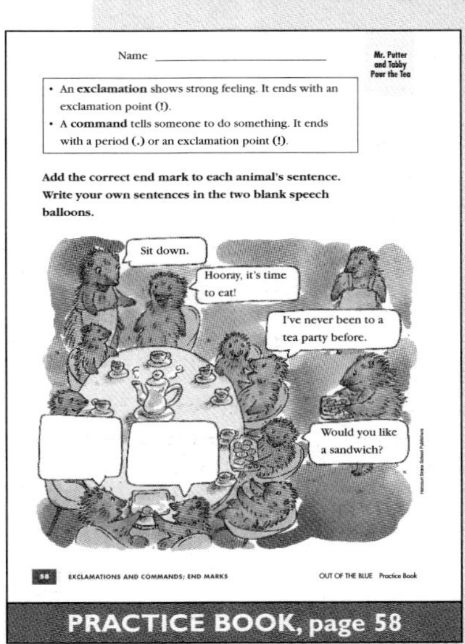

Name ______________

Mr. Putter and Tabby Pour the Tea

- An **exclamation** shows strong feeling. It ends with an exclamation point (!).
- A **command** tells someone to do something. It ends with a period (.) or an exclamation point (!).

Add the correct end mark to each animal's sentence. Write your own sentences in the two blank speech balloons.

Sit down.
Hooray, it's time to eat!
I've never been to a tea party before.
Would you like a sandwich?

58 EXCLAMATIONS AND COMMANDS; END MARKS — OUT OF THE BLUE Practice Book

PRACTICE BOOK, page 58

5-DAY PLAN	
Day 1 Complete page T342.	**Day 4** Choose a Practice Activity or *Grammar Practice Book* pages 29–32.
Day 2 Complete a Practice Activity on page T343.	**Day 5** Complete *Practice Book* page 58.
Day 3 Choose a Practice Activity or *Language Handbook* pages 52–55.	

Use in conjunction with Daily Language Practice.

2

SPELLING

5-Day Plan

Integrated Spelling Lesson 8:
student book, pages 38–41;
Teacher's Edition, pages T63–T68.

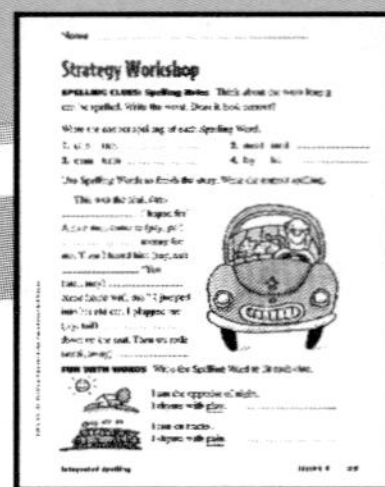
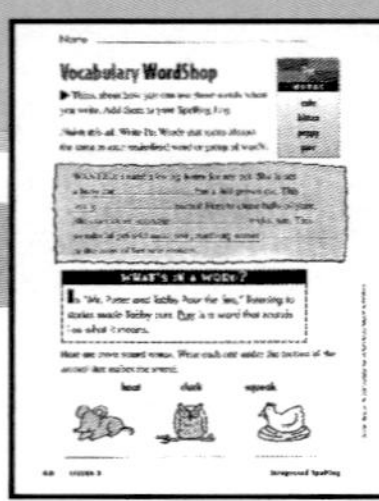
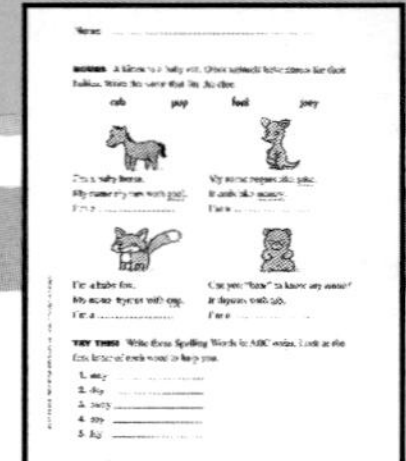

Words with Long *a* Spelled *ay* and *ai*

SPELLING WORDS

1. may
2. day ★
3. say ★
4. mail
5. rain
6. pay
7. lay
8. tail
9. train
10. away

STUDENT'S PERSONAL WORDS

11. 13.
12. 14.

Additional story words are *days* and *gray*.

★Words appearing in "Mr. Putter and Tabby"

Pretest

DAY 1 **Administer the pretest.** Say each word, and then use it in the dictation sentence below. Have partners check their own pretests by referring to the word list.

OPEN SORT

DAY 2 **Have children create categories.** Have children select their own criteria for sorting the Spelling Words. Suggest that they sort according to the number of letters, rhyming words, or some other category. Have volunteers share the methods they used.

CLOSED SORT

Sort by spelling pattern. Duplicate on the board the chart below, and have volunteers write each Spelling Word under the appropriate heading.

way	bait
may	mail
day	rain
say	tail
pay	train
lay	
away	

Teach/Model

DAY 3 **Discuss the generalization.** Write the words *may* and *rain* on the board, and have children read each word. Ask children what vowel sound they hear in both words. (the vowel sound /ā/) Ask which word has the long *a* sound at the end. Ask which word has the long *a* sound in the middle. Help children form generalizations about how the /ā/ sound is spelled—for example:

- **When the /ā/ sound, as in *may*, comes at the end of a word, it is often spelled *ay*.**
- **When the /ā/ sound, as in *rain*, comes in the middle of a word, it is often spelled *ai*.**

DAY 4 **Apply to writing.** Children should look in their friendly letters for words with long *a* spelled *ai* and *ay* to see if they are spelled correctly.

Posttest

DAY 5 **Assess children's progress.** Use the sentences below to administer the posttest.

DICTATION SENTENCES

1. I think it may snow later.
2. It was a cold day in winter.
3. I hear what you say.
4. Did you get a letter in the mail?
5. I think it will rain today.
6. I will pay for our lunch.
7. The cat lay in the sun.
8. The dog wagged its tail.
9. I saw a train go along the track.
10. Some birds go away in winter.

PRACTICE BOOK, page 59

VOCABULARY WORKSHOP

Reviewing Key Words

To review how the vocabulary was used in the story, distribute copies of page R115 to children. Then write the Key Words on the board.

Have children work as a group to choose the word that best completes each sentence. Then have a volunteer read the sentence aloud and write the word.

Mr. Putter had no one to listen to his wonderful stories.

He brought Tabby home for company.

Mr. Putter was sure that they would be happy.

He knew Tabby would be a good pet.

Sometimes they played loud music.

They enjoyed tea and muffins.

They were the most perfect company for each other.

Mr. Putter and Tabby wondered how they ever got along without each other.

Then have children cut apart the sentence strips. Children can use the strips to retell the story or glue the strips on to sheets of paper to create their own version of "Mr. Putter and Tabby Pour the Tea."

Extending Vocabulary

TIME-ORDER WORDS

List the following time-order words on the board: *morning, afternoon, evening, night; summer, fall, winter*. Explain that all these words are used in "Mr. Putter and Tabby Pour the Tea." Have children classify the words in a chart like the following:

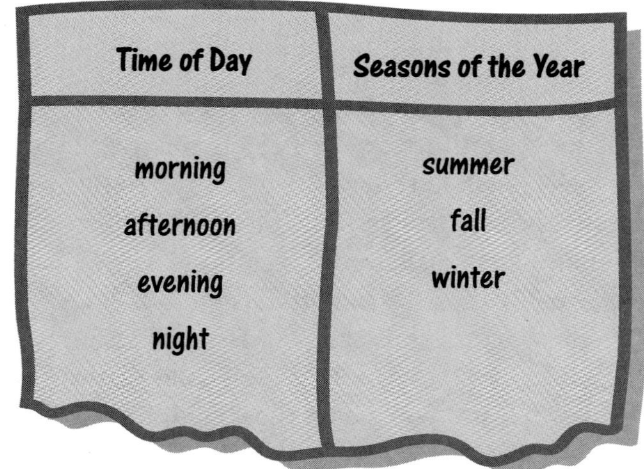

Time of Day	Seasons of the Year
morning	summer
afternoon	fall
evening	winter
night	

Explain that words like these show when things happen. They can use these words to make their own stories clearer. Ask children to add other words they can think of. (Possible responses: *spring, dawn, dusk, midnight*) Then have children copy and complete the following flowcharts to show the sequence and cyclical nature of these times.

STUDENTS ACQUIRING ENGLISH

Ask children to share time words for *morning, afternoon, evening, night, day, today,* and *tomorrow* in their primary language. Some children might enjoy pantomiming things they do in the morning, in the afternoon, in the evening, and at night.

TAKE-HOME/ KEEP-AT-HOME BOOK

The Perfect Pet
Distribute the pages, and have children make their own TAKE-HOME/ KEEP-AT-HOME BOOKS, which reinforce Key Words and known vocabulary. Have children read to partners and then take the book home to read.

INTRODUCE: PHONICS AND DECODING

Vowel Diphthong: /ou/*ou,ow*

OBJECTIVE: To understand the relationship between letters and sounds

Informal Assessment ✓

Are children able to

- group /ou/ words by spelling pattern?
- write and read /ou/ *ou, ow* words?
- make and read words that have a specific phonogram?

TECHNOLOGY

***Bailey's Book House* (Read-A-Rhyme)**

Teach/Model

Connect to the story. Ask children to recall the color of Mr. Putter's hat. (brown) Write *brown* on the board. Then ask how the opera music sounds when Mr. Putter turns it up. (loud) Write *loud* on the board. Read *brown* and *loud* with children, and ask how the words are alike. (They have the same vowel sound.) Tell children that they will learn more about the sound that is alike in these words.

Phonemic awareness: Listen to the sound. Display pages 12–13 in the *Big Book of Rhymes*. Have children listen for words with the same sound heard in *brown* and *loud* as you read the rhyme aloud. Then reread the rhyme and encourage children to join in.

Big Book of Rhymes, pages 12-13

Find and read /ou/ words. In the rhyme, have children frame and read words with the same vowel sound as *brown,* and write them on the board in appropriate columns.

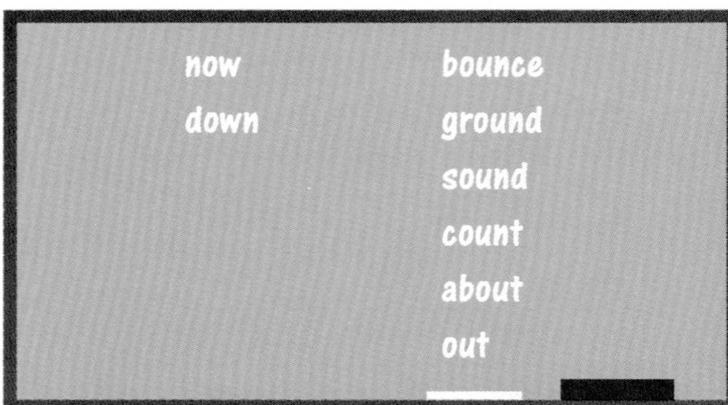

Point to the words under *now*. Ask how the words in the column are alike. (Both have the /ou/ sound; both have the letters *ow*.) Follow a similar procedure with the words in the second column. (All have the /ou/ sound; all have the letters *ou*.) Point out that the letters *ow* and *ou* can both be spellings for the /ou/ sound.

Practice/Apply

Read words in context. Display the following:

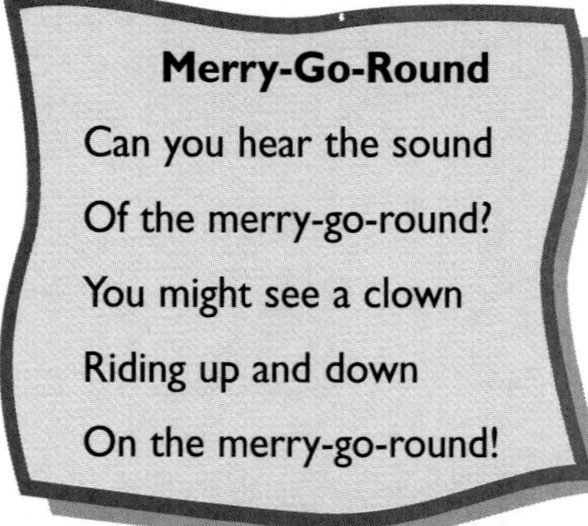

Have children find the words with the /ou/ sound and tell which spelling each has.

Practice Activities

Word Building

PHONOGRAM / BLENDING ACTIVITY Have small groups play "Phonogram Powwow." Distribute individual letter cards or *Word Builder Cards*, phonogram card *-ound,* and Word Builders to children. Have each player see how many words they can make. Encourage players to write down all the words. **VISUAL/AUDITORY/KINESTHETIC**

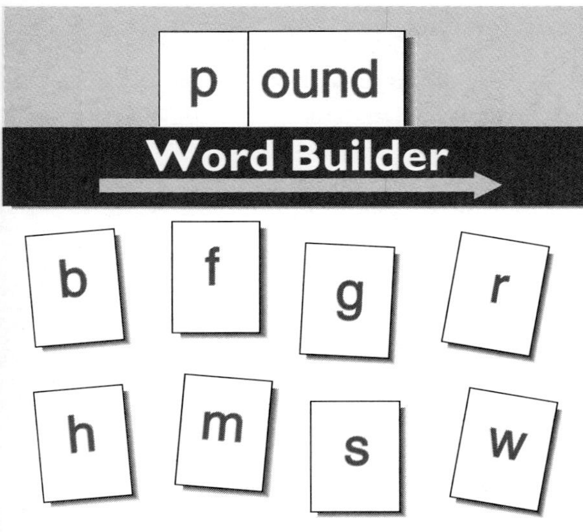

SORTING /OU/ WORDS

Write /ou/ words from the lesson on separate strips of paper. Have children sort the words into those spelled *ou* and those spelled *ow*. Then have children choose an *ou* word and an *ow* word and include them in sentences.
VISUAL/KINESTHETIC

Rhyme Climb

PERFORMANCE ASSESSMENT Have pairs of children draw five ladders and write these words on the bottom rungs: *sound, couch, brown, flower, cow*. Have children fill the other rungs of the ladders with words that rhyme with the words on the bottom rungs and have the same spellings. Then have children choose one word from each ladder, and write a sentence. You could put the ladders in a class book, and encourage children to refer to the book when writing sentences or rhymes. **VISUAL/AUDITORY**

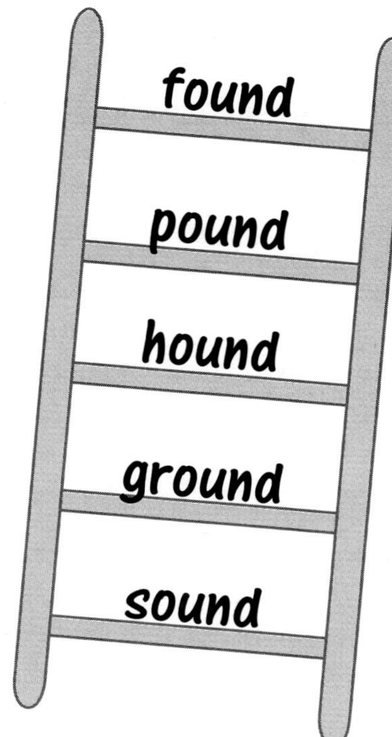

The Old Ladies Who Liked Cats
by Carol Greene.
HarperCollins, 1991.
AVERAGE

***Cloudy With a Chance of Meatballs* by Judith Barrett.**
Macmillan, 1982. CHALLENGE

STUDENTS ACQUIRING ENGLISH

Have children fold a sheet of paper and write *round* on one part and *brown* on the other. Then have them find objects that are round and objects that are brown. Children can write the names or draw the objects.

RETEACH

See page R70 for lessons in multiple modalities.

CHALLENGE

Have children write Hink Pinks for the /ou/ sound. For example, *noisy mob* (*loud crowd*).

PHONICS ACTIVITY BOOK, page 15

PHONICS PRACTICE BOOK, pages 143–146

Name ____________

Read the poem. Circle each word that has the same vowel sound as *cloud*. Then write the words on the chart where they belong. Add more words.

The little brown hound
I found down at the pound
Would run and sniff
Around the ground
With a barking sound
How he'd clown around—
My little brown dog
That I found at the pound.

Spelled Like *cow*	Spelled Like *cloud*
brown	hound
down	found
how	pound
clown	around
	ground
	sound

PRACTICE BOOK, page 60

Informal Assessment ✓

Are children able to

- ☑ recognize parts of a form?
- ☑ tell what information belongs on a particular form?
- ☑ complete a form/application?

INTRODUCE: STUDY SKILLS

Form/Application

OBJECTIVE: To read and fill out a form or an application

Teach/Model

Connect to the story. Ask children to reread page 166. Explain that before Mr. Putter could take Tabby home from the animal shelter, he probably had to fill out a form. The people who ran the shelter would keep the form so they would know who took Tabby home, when Tabby left the shelter, and where they could find Mr. Putter if they needed to contact him.

Discuss types of information to include on a form. Ask children what kind of information they think the shelter man would need to know about Mr. Putter. (Mr. Putter's name, where he lives, whether he can take good care of a pet, what kind of pet he wants)

Display and complete an application form. Display Chart/Transparency 14, or copy the information onto the board. Tell children that this form is like one Mr. Putter might have filled out. Model how to complete a form:

MODEL **When I fill out a form, I read it first to find out what kind of information it asks for. Then I fill it out neatly so it is easy for other people to read. I make sure I put the correct information in the right places.**

CHART/TRANSPARENCY 14

Felixville Animal Shelter
Application to Adopt a Pet

Name: Mr. Putter
Address: 234 Tulip Lane
Felixville, DE 40003
Telephone: 555-6298

What kind of pet do you want?
Mark an X in the correct space.
x cat ___ dog ___ other

Do you have any other pets? No

How will you take care of your pet?

I will keep my cat company, feed it, and give it a nice place to sleep.

Practice/Apply

Have children demonstrate understanding. Distribute a blank application form, page R203, to each child to complete as if he or she was adopting a pet. Have partners check each other's forms.

Form/Application

Felixville Animal Shelter
Application to Adopt a Pet

Name: ____
Address: ____
Telephone: ____

What kind of pet do you want?
Mark an **X** in the correct space.
___ cat ___ dog ___ other

Do you have any other pets? ____
How will you take care of your pet?

Practice Activities

GETTING A LIBRARY CARD

Arrange for children to visit your community's library, or invite a librarian to visit your class. The librarian can distribute library card application forms for children to fill out. You and the librarian can read the form with children and provide help as they fill out the forms. VISUAL/AUDITORY/KINESTHETIC

FORMS, FORMS, FORMS

COOPERATIVE LEARNING Ask children to think about forms and applications they may already have filled out, such as a registration form for summer camp, a permission slip for a field trip, or an order form for books. Have children collect forms from old magazines and newspapers or create their own. Have children fill out the forms and create a display on a bulletin board. VISUAL

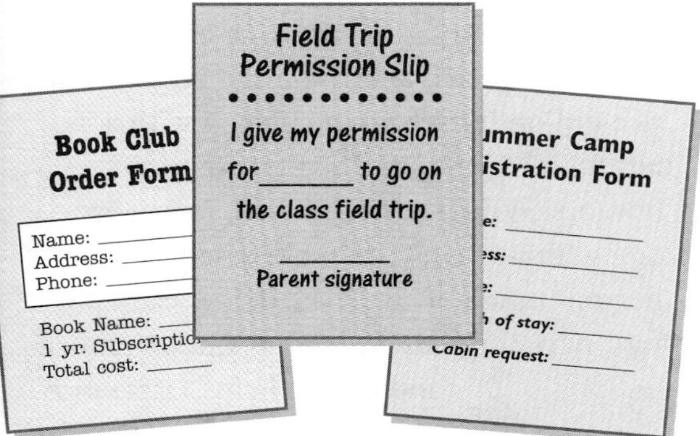

THAT'S AN ORDER!

PERFORMANCE ASSESSMENT Organize children into small groups, and give each group member a copy of a simple catalog order form, such as the one below. Each child should fill out the form. Then have group members talk about each part as children check their own work and ask each other any questions they have. VISUAL/AUDITORY/KINESTHETIC

• MACK'S GARDEN STORE •

Order Form for Spring Plants

Item	How Many	Cost of Each	Total Cost
Petunia	___	$0.75	___
Marigold	___	0.50	___
Zinnia	___	0.80	___
		Grand Total	$___

Name ______________________

Address ______________________

City __________ State ______ Zip ______

• Thank you for your business! •

STUDENTS ACQUIRING ENGLISH

You may want to spend additional time introducing unfamiliar words found in the forms and applications.

RETEACH

See page R71 for lessons in multiple modalities.

CHALLENGE

Ask children to work together to create a toy catalog, using pictures from sales circulars, magazines, and old catalogs. Then have them create an order form for the catalog. Duplicate the order form and let all children "order" from the catalog.

Mr. Putter and Tabby Pour the Tea — Name ______________

Read the form carefully. Then answer the questions.

Possible responses are given.

POPCORN PALACE VIDEO CLUB

Rent your favorite videos.

Name: ______________

Address: ______________

Phone Number: ______________

Account Number: ______ Club Number: ______

Name of Video	Date Needed	Number of Days: 1 or 2	Cost: $2 a Day
		Total Cost:	

1. Where would you see a form like this?
   in a store that rents videos
2. What would you use it for?
   to list videos you want to rent
3. How would you figure out how much each video costs to rent?
   add $2 for each movie for each day; multiply by two
4. Fill in the form for three movies you want to see.

OUT OF THE BLUE Practice Book — FORM/APPLICATION 61

PRACTICE BOOK, page 61

Reading Trade Books FOR FORM/APPLICATION

Linnea's Windowsill Garden by Christina Björk. Farrar, Straus & Giroux, 1988. CHALLENGE

Rufus M. by Eleanor Estes. Harcourt Brace, 1943. CHALLENGE

Integrated Curriculum

SOCIAL STUDIES

Pets and People

TIPS FOR CLASSROOM MANAGEMENT

IF children are musically inclined, **THEN** they may want to participate in the Create a Song activity.

SCIENCE

Give Me Shelter

MATERIALS
- poster board
- markers
- nonfiction books about animals

COOPERATIVE LEARNING Have children work in small groups to pretend that they are running an animal shelter, with each group responsible for one type of animal. Have each group choose an animal and find out its needs for food and shelter and any other important information. As they learn about their animal, ask group members to create a chart. When charts are completed, compare the needs of each animal. **READING/WRITING**

HAMSTERS	
Housing	Keep in cage with wire-mesh walls or in specially made plastic tank. Add wood chips or hay and cotton for hamsters to make a bed.
Food	Feed seeds and food pellets, 1 tablespoon a day. Give fresh water.
Care	Clean cage daily. Pet it.
Exercise	Provide an exercise wheel and climbing tubes.

ART

Animals Helping People

MATERIALS
- bulletin board covered with white drawing paper
- crayons or markers

Curriculum Card 6a

Cover a bulletin board with white paper. Tell children they will make a mural about animals who help people. Brainstorm a list of animal helpers. Discuss how children could show each animal on the mural, such as a girl on horseback, a chicken with a nestful of eggs, a nice dog guarding a house, sled dogs pulling a sled, seeing-eye dog with its owner, a monkey helping a person using a wheelchair. Below each picture, have the artist write the kind of animal and how it helps. **LISTENING/SPEAKING/WRITING**

MATH

Favorite Pets Bar Graph

MATERIALS
large sheet of butcher paper
crayons or markers
index cards

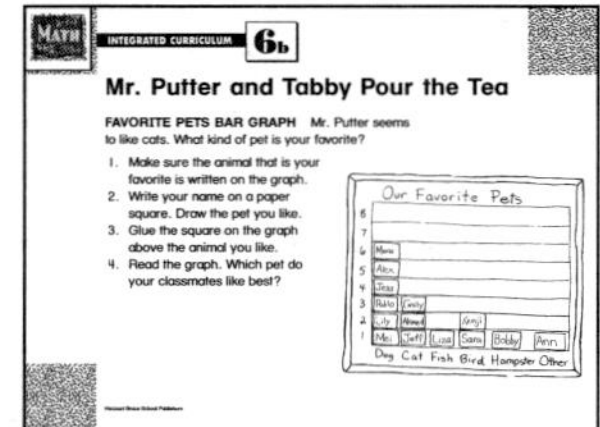
MATH
INTEGRATED CURRICULUM 6b

Mr. Putter and Tabby Pour the Tea

FAVORITE PETS BAR GRAPH Mr. Putter seems to like cats. What kind of pet is your favorite?

1. Make sure the animal that is your favorite is written on the graph.
2. Write your name on a paper square. Draw the pet you like.
3. Glue the square on the graph above the animal you like.
4. Read the graph. Which pet do your classmates like best?

Curriculum Card 6b

Explain that children will create a bar graph showing the kinds of pets they like best. Work with children to make a graph like the one below. Have children brainstorm likely pets, and write the animal types along the bottom. Have children write their name and draw their favorite pet on an index card and attach it above the name of the animal. Ask children to suggest a title, and write it at the top of the graph. Then, help children analyze the information. You might ask:

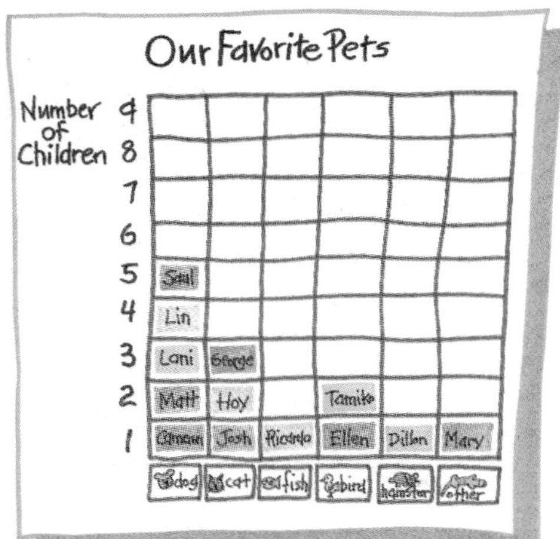

- **Which pet do most children like?**
- **Which pet do the same number of children like?**
- **How many more children like dogs than like cats?**

LISTENING/SPEAKING

MUSIC

Create a Song

MATERIALS
various instruments

COOPERATIVE LEARNING Remind children that Mr. Putter and Tabby spend winter days listening to opera music. Suggest that children work in small groups to create songs about Mr. Putter and Tabby. Encourage children to think about the ways Tabby and Mr. Putter move and to let the listener know that through the music. Some groups may want to describe a typical day for Mr. Putter and Tabby in their song. If instruments are unavailable, children can create their own by, for instance, placing beans or rice in containers and shaking them, snapping fingers, or tapping on a desk. Allow time for the groups to perform their songs. **LISTENING/SPEAKING/WRITING**

Reading Trade Books

CROSS-CURRICULAR READING

The Kids' Cat Book **by Tomie dePaola. Holiday House, 1979.**
AVERAGE

Let's Get a Pet **by Harriet Ziefert. Viking, 1993.**
EASY

MULTI-AGE CLASSROOMS

Creating a song is an activity in which children can create and perform at their own level. Some children may want to work alone, rather than in a group.

Reading Trade Books

Trade Books That Connect to "Mr. Putter and Tabby Pour the Tea"

TIPS FOR CLASSROOM MANAGEMENT

PARTNERS
Have children work with partners to read the Mr. Putter stories. Encourage them to talk about how each book adds to what they know about the characters from "Mr. Putter and Tabby Pour the Tea."

INDEPENDENT
Place *Night Noises* in a Reading Center. Have children read the story and draw a picture of the part they liked best.

READ ALOUD
Read *The Adventures of Taxi Dog* to a small group of children. As you read aloud, encourage children to join in with the rhyme.

Mr. Putter and Tabby Bake the Cake

by Cynthia Rylant
illustrated by Arthur Howard

After the book is read, ask how Mr. Putter learns to bake a cake. Invite children to bring cookie cutters, especially those in different shapes, to class. Tell them to choose cookie cutters, trace around them, and cut out and decorate the shapes to make the most beautiful cookies in the world.

Mr. Putter and Tabby Walk the Dog

by Cynthia Rylant
illustrated by Arthur Howard

Ask how Mr. Putter and Tabby change the dog from a nightmare into a dream dog. Then have children work in groups to act out the story.

Mr. Putter and Tabby Pick the Pears

by Cynthia Rylant
illustrated by Arthur Howard

Encourage children to think of other ways Mr. Putter and Tabby could solve their problem and pick pears. Have children speculate about other problems Mr. Putter and Tabby might have because of their old, creaky bones and then brainstorm ways they could solve them.

The Adventures of Taxi Dog

by Debra and Sal Barracca
illustrated by Mark Buehner

Ask volunteers to retell some of Maxi's adventures. Then invite children to plan ways to read the story chorally.

Mrs. Merriwether's Musical Cat

by Carol Purdy
illustrated by Petra Mathers

Organize children into two groups. Lead half the group in singing a song, and have the other half direct or "swish a tail" to the beat. Then have the two groups switch roles.

Night Noises

by Mem Fox
illustrated by Terry Denton

Have children suggest materials they could use or things they could do to make the "night noises." Then, during a rereading of the story, invite children to add their sound effects.

STUDENTS ACQUIRING ENGLISH

Children have a head start understanding the three Mr. Putter and Tabby books since they are already familiar with the characters and some of the vocabulary associated with them. Before children read, you may want to review with them what Mr. Putter and Tabby are like.

Trade Books

PROJECT MANAGEMENT

- PROJECT LAUNCH
- CHECKPOINT 1
- CHECKPOINT 2
- CHECKPOINT 3
- CHECKPOINT 4
- PRESENTATIONS
- ASSESSMENT

STUDENTS ACQUIRING ENGLISH

Pair children with English-proficient peers to discuss ideas for setting up the center. They can then share their insights with their groups.

MULTI-AGE CLASSROOMS

Encourage older children to help younger ones, both in thinking of questions about the postal service, and in the planning and organization of the mail center. If children are reading books and articles about the postal service, have older children do research and report back to their groups.

Plan the Mail Center

SELECTION CONNECTION

In "Mr. Putter and Tabby Pour the Tea," a man and a cat form a friendship. Encourage discussion about differences between communicating with animals and communicating with people.

PROJECT CHECKLIST

During this stage, children should

- ☑ work in small groups to discuss where and how to set up the center.
- ☑ share their ideas with the whole group and decide on the best plan.
- ☑ make and decorate their own mailboxes (from shoe boxes).
- ☑ organize the center according to the agreed-upon plan.

When children have completed this checkpoint, have them think about the work they did to create the mail center and record their thoughts in their Project Journals.

THEME PROJECT CHECKPOINT 2 9

Make a Mail Center

PLAN THE MAIL CENTER

1. Make your post office. Plan how it will work.
   - Where will the collection box be?
   - Where will you sort the mail?
   - How will you deliver it?
   - Where will you put your mailboxes?
2. Make your own mailbox.
   - Use a shoe box.
   - Put your name on it in big letters.
3. Finish your post office.

Project Card 9

Project Card 9 can be found as a copying master on page R89.

PLANNING TIPS

As children plan and set up the center, they should

- consider such points as where a drop-off box for mail should be placed, how mail will be sorted and delivered, where to place mailboxes, and what jobs need to be done.
- be considerate while deciding upon the best plan.
- create and decorate individual mailboxes.

Informal Assessment 

As children complete this checkpoint, they will **evaluate** information, **solve problems,** and **make decisions** about the classroom mail center. Children are thinking critically if they

- ☑ make judgments about suggestions.
- ☑ think about space and organization needs as they make decisions.
- ☑ use problem-solving skills to create workable mailboxes.

Note that a more formal assessment rubric for this checkpoint is provided on page T453.

THEME: FRIENDSHIP

We Belong Together

In "Six-Dinner Sid," children further explore the theme by discovering that people and pets can make changes in order to suit one another better.

SELECTION SUMMARY

Genre: Realistic Fiction

Sid is a cat who eats six dinners a day by living with six different families on Aristotle Street. For a time, Sid is able to keep this a secret because the neighbors on Aristotle Street don't talk to one another. One day, though, Sid gets a cough and ends up taking six trips to the vet. He is found out. The neighbors vow to put an end to his six-dinner ways. Sid then moves on to six houses on Pythagoras Place, where the neighbors are happy to feed Sid six dinners every day.

ABOUT THE AUTHOR/ ILLUSTRATOR

INGA MOORE has received several awards for her writing, including the Parents' Choice Award. One of her books was named a Notable Trade Book in Social Studies. The National Council of Teachers of English named *Six-Dinner Sid* a Notable Children's Book in the Language Arts.

For more information about the author and illustrator, see page T377.

SUGGESTED LESSON PLANNER

▶ ***Six-Dinner Sid***

	DAY 1	DAY 2
PART 1 Reading, Listening, Speaking, Viewing **Key Words** people different scratched neighbors discovered future caught	**BUILD BACKGROUND** T358 *Big Book of Rhymes* p. 19 **VOCABULARY STRATEGIES** T358–T359 *Chart/Transparency 15* *Practice Book* pp. 65–66 **READING THE SELECTION** T360–T377 Options for Reading T360–T361 *Response Card 1* **REVIEW PREDICTIONS/PURPOSE** T376 **APPRECIATING THE LITERATURE** T376 NOTE: Children may read the selection on Day 2.	**SUMMARIZE AND RETELL THE SELECTION** T377 *Practice Book* p. 67 ◆ **RESPONSE CORNER ACTIVITIES** T378 **CHECKING COMPREHENSION** T379 *End-of-Selection Test* 
PART 2 Writer's Workshop	**A PARAGRAPH THAT DESCRIBES** Thinking as Writers T384 *Chart/Transparency 16*	Prewriting T384
Grammar	**NOUNS** Teach the Concept T386 Daily Language Practice (1–2) R82	Daily Language Practice (3–4) R82 Practice Activity T387
Spelling	**WORDS WITH LONG *e* SPELLED *ee* AND *ea*** *need eat read keep team* *feel seat three sleep each* Pretest/Self-Check T388 *Integrated Spelling Teacher's Edition* pp. T69, T276	Open and Closed Sorts T388 *Integrated Spelling* p. 42 *Integrated Spelling Teacher's Edition* p. T70
PART 3 Phonics	**INITIAL CLUSTERS: *str, scr*** Phonics-Vocabulary Connection T359	**INITIAL CLUSTERS: *str, scr*** (Introduce) T390 *Big Book of Rhymes* p. 14 *Phonics Practice Book* pp. 197–198
Skills and Strategies	◆ **INTEGRATED CURRICULUM** *Cats* **Math** T394 **Science** T394 **Social Studies** T395 **Creative Dramatics** T395	**STUDY SKILL** T392–T393 ✓ Alphabetical Order (Introduce) *Practice Book* p. 71 *Living Book: Dr. Seuss's ABC*

A suggestion to help **below-level readers** use graphophonic cues while reading appears on page T381 of Intervention Strategies.

During the Response Corner activities, use the Varying the Activity note on page T378 for **above-level readers**.

NOTE: An alternative lesson plan for **below-level readers** appears on *Intervention Strategies Manual* pp. 38–43. A lesson for **students acquiring English** appears on *Sheltered English/ESL Manual* pp. 26–29.

DAY 3	DAY 4	DAY 5
◆ **IDEA BANK ACTIVITIES** Listening and Speaking T382 Real-Life Reading: Reading Street Signs T382 Oral Language T383 Kinesthetic T383 *Writer's Magazine* pp. 26–27 School–Home Connection 7 R112	**VOCABULARY WORKSHOP** T389 Reviewing Key Words Story Strips R116 Number Words *Take-Home/Keep-at-Home Book: The Big Sneeze* **READING TRADE BOOKS** T396–T397  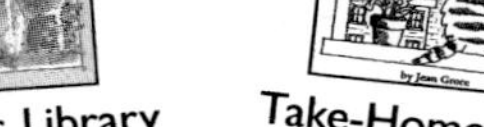 Signatures Library Take-Home Book	**READING TRADE BOOKS** T391, T393, T395, T396–T397  Instant Reader™ Instant Reader™
Drafting T384 *Language Handbook* pp. 18–19 *The Amazing Writing Machine*	Responding and Revising T385	Proofreading and Publishing T385 *Kid Pix*
Daily Language Practice (5–6) R82 Practice Activity T387 *Language Handbook* pp. 56–57	Daily Language Practice (7–8) R82 Practice Activity T387 *Grammar Practice Book* pp. 33–34	Daily Language Practice (9–12) R82 *Practice Book* p. 68
Discuss the Generalization T388 *Integrated Spelling* p. 43 *Integrated Spelling Teacher's Edition* p. T71	Apply to Writing T388 *Integrated Spelling* pp. 44–45 *Integrated Spelling Teacher's Edition* pp. T72–T73	Posttest T388 *Practice Book* p. 69 *Integrated Spelling Teacher's Edition* p. T74
INITIAL CLUSTERS: *str, scr* T390 *Phonics Practice Reader 17: Screech and Stripes*	**INITIAL CLUSTERS: *str, scr*** T391 *Practice Book* p. 70 *Bailey's Book House* (Read-A-Rhyme)	**INITIAL CLUSTERS: *str, scr*** T391 *Phonics Activity Book* p. 18
PHONICS AND DECODING MINILESSON T363 Consonant Digraphs: /sh/*sh*; /ch/*ch, tch* (Maintain) *Phonics Activity Book* pp. 19–20 *Phonics Practice Reader 6: Make a Wish* *Phonics Practice Book* pp. 226–229 *Practice Book* p. 72 **COMPREHENSION MINILESSON** T371 ✓ Sequence (Maintain)	**COMPREHENSION MINILESSON** T367 ✓ Making Predictions (Review) *Practice Book* p. 74 **GRAMMAR MINILESSON** T373 ✓ Exclamations, Commands, and End Marks (Review) *Language Handbook* pp. 52–55	**PHONICS AND DECODING MINILESSON** T365 Consonant Digraphs: /hw/*wh*; /th/*th* (Maintain) *Phonics Activity Book* pp. 21–22 *Phonics Practice Reader 6: Make a Wish* *Phonics Practice Book* pp. 230–234 *Practice Book* p. 73 Theme Project Checkpoint 3 T398
Have children read "Rosie the Visiting Dog," pages 202–203, to connect nonfiction with the selection they just read.	During the Vocabulary Workshop, refer to the Students Acquiring English note on page T389 to help **ESL readers**.	To help children build fluency, use the *Instant Readers™ My Big Surprise* and *Buddies* on pages T380–T381.

✓ = Tested Skill

◆ = Optional activities that may be used to adjust pacing throughout the lesson

Titles in *italics* are optional materials.

Reading and Responding

BUILDING BACKGROUND AND CONCEPTS

PRIOR KNOWLEDGE

Discuss what animals eat.

Display page 19 of the *Big Book of Rhymes*. Read "Brown Bear's Supper" with children, and then open a discussion about the eating habits of animals.

***Big Book of Rhymes* page 19**

Encourage children to discuss the differences between what animals in the wild eat and what pets eat. You might make an idea web on the board to record children's responses.

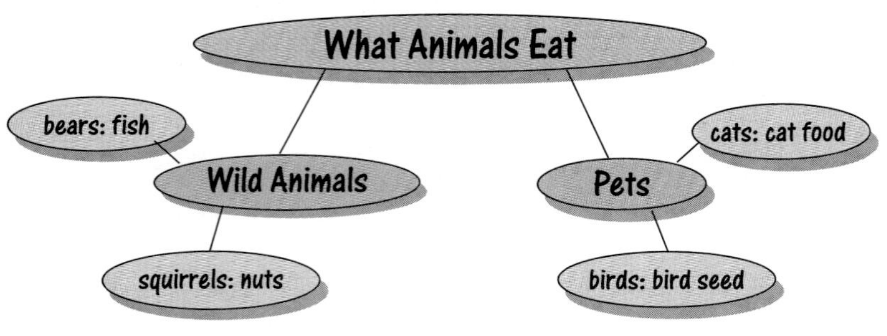

VOCABULARY STRATEGIES

KEY WORDS DEFINED

people more than one person
neighbors people who live near one another
future time that hasn't happened yet
different not the same
discovered found out
caught got
scratched rubbed or scraped with fingernails

SUPPORT WORDS

Display the words *airs, appointment, cough, medicine,* and *vet*. Discuss their meanings and have them used in sentences.

INTEGRATED SPELLING

SPELLING PRETEST: page T388
SPELLING GENERALIZATION: Words with long e spelled *ee* and *ea*

Intervention Strategies

For children who may have difficulty reading "Six-Dinner Sid," support is available in *Intervention Strategies Manual*, pages 38–43, and on pages T369 and T380–T381 in this lesson.

STUDENTS ACQUIRING ENGLISH

See *Sheltered English/ESL Manual* pages 26–29.

"A Drama Center can add to the reading of any story. For 'Six-Dinner Sid,' I set up large boxes to stand for numbers one through six Aristotle Street or Pythagoras Place. I also brought in a stuffed toy cat, a pet dish, a basket, and a big straw bag to use as a pet carrier. Costuming was easy: a white coat for the vet and glasses, coats, and purses for the owners. It's fun to have telephone props so children can act out the call the vet makes to the owners. The more real-life items I bring in, the more the children's enthusiasm grows."

CUEING SYSTEMS

Have children read new vocabulary. Display Chart/Transparency 15, or write the words and sentences on the board. Encourage children to read the words they know.

Ask a volunteer to read the first sentence aloud. When the child reaches the word *people*, encourage him or her to try sounding out the word, looking at the letters at the beginning and the end of the word. Ask:

> **Does the word make sense in the sentence?**
> **How did looking at the letters and sounding them out help?**

Have children read the rest of the story, using sounds for letters and the sense of the story to help them read the underlined words.

HANDS-ON ACTIVITY

Play a game with children. Have children write each Key Word on a small strip of paper that looks like a cat tail. Have partners practice reading the words and telling their meanings. Then display a large outline of a cat without a tail. Have children each choose one cat tail to play "Pin the Tail on the Cat." Let each child have a turn being blindfolded and spun around before trying to tape the tail to the right part of the cat outline. Then he or she reads the word and uses it in a sentence.

Finally, have children copy each word from their cat tails onto an index card to add to their Word Files.

caught

discovered

CHART/TRANSPARENCY 15

people	neighbors	future
different	discovered	caught
scratched		

Lots of <u>people</u> live on our street. The <u>neighbors</u> like to talk to each other. We talk about our days and about the <u>future</u>. Everyone gets along even though we are <u>different</u>.

One day I <u>discovered</u> a lost kitten on our street. Its paw was <u>caught</u> in a fence. Everyone gave it some food, and I <u>scratched</u> its soft head. We all love Ernie, our new neighborhood kitten.

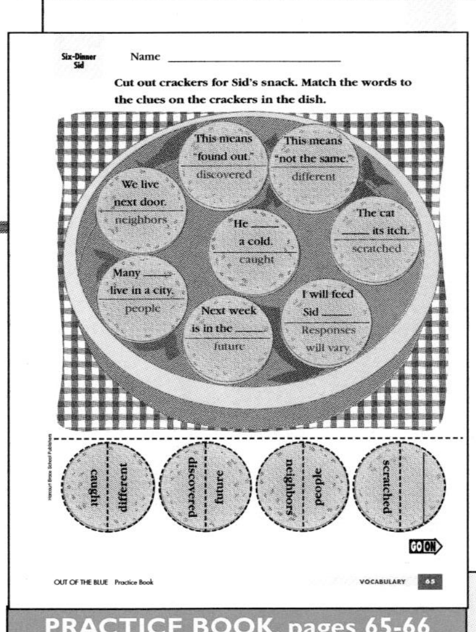

PRACTICE BOOK, pages 65-66

PHONICS-VOCABULARY CONNECTION

WORD PLAY

Begin the chart below on the board. Read the words *scratch* and *scream*. Ask how the words are alike. (They begin with *scr*.) Repeat the procedure with *stretch* and *strap*.

Then read the following words to children: *strike, strong, scrap, string, scrape, screech, stream, scrub, strawberry, street, scrawny, stripe, screen, strap.* Have a volunteer tell in which column each word belongs, and write the word on the chart.

The concept of initial clusters *scr* and *str* is further developed on pages T390–T391.

scratch	stretch
scream	strap

Strategic Reading

STRATEGY FOCUS: MAKING PREDICTIONS

Review with children some of the things good readers do while reading. Add new ideas to their classroom chart.

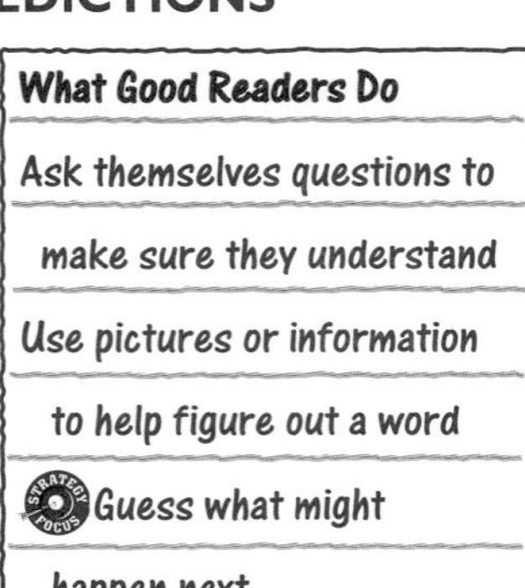
What Good Readers Do
Ask themselves questions to make sure they understand
Use pictures or information to help figure out a word
Guess what might happen next

Share with children the comprehension strategy that is the focus of this selection.

MODEL

As I'm reading, I make guesses about what will happen next. Sometimes my guesses are right! Other times, they're close to what really happens, and sometimes I'm surprised by what happens. It's fun to make guesses about what will happen in a story. It can help you pay better attention to what you're reading, and it gives you your own reasons for reading on.

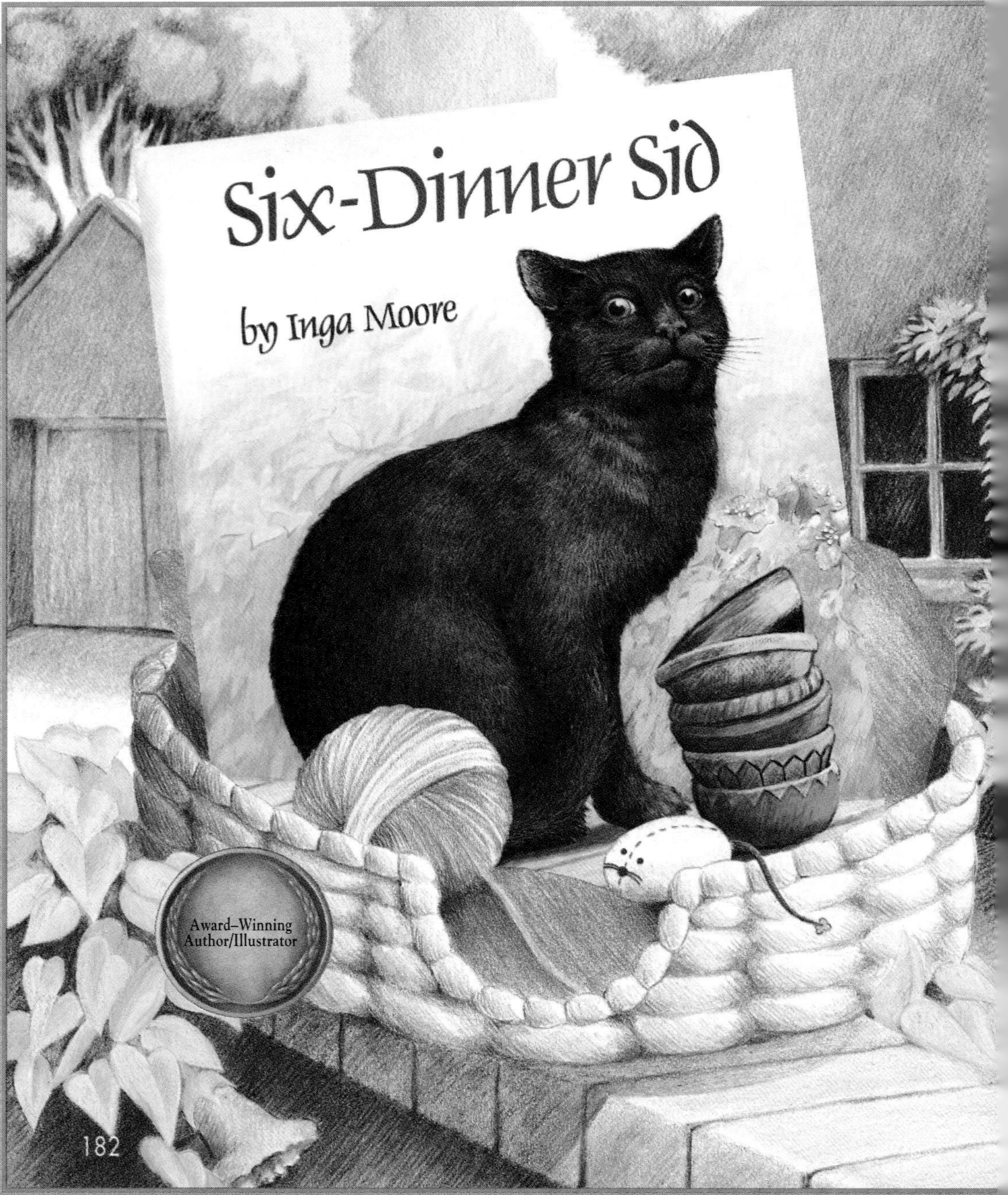

Six-Dinner Sid

by Inga Moore

Award-Winning Author/Illustrator

182

SMALL GROUP

STRATEGIC READING

Choose some or all of the suggestions under Strategic Reading, pages T360–T376, to guide a literature discussion and model the STRATEGY FOCUS of Making Predictions.

COOPERATIVE READING

PARTNER READING Have pairs of children use Reader Response Card 1 (Characters), page R85, as they read aloud "Six-Dinner Sid." Children can use the During Reading and After Reading questions to discuss the characters.

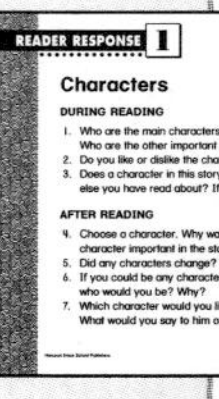

Response

Sid lived at number one Aristotle Street.

He also lived at number two, number three, number four, number five, and number six.

183

PREVIEWING/ SETTING PURPOSES

Have children read the story title on page 182 and look at the pictures on pages 182–183. Ask children who they think Sid is. Then ask them to predict what might happen in a story called "Six-Dinner Sid."

Have children write their predictions in their journals. Then help children set their purposes for reading.

MODELING A STRATEGY

PAGES 182–183 After children read these pages, ask them to predict what Sid will do. If necessary, model your thinking: *I think that Sid likes to eat six dinners, and I've read that he lives in six different houses. I bet Sid goes to all six houses for dinner.* **MAKING PREDICTIONS**

WHOLE CLASS

READ ALOUD

Before reading "Six-Dinner Sid," invite children to look carefully at the illustrations and describe what they see. Then read the story aloud as children follow along in their books. Stop at key points (for example, after pages 182–187, 188–191, 192–198) to discuss with children what is happening and why.

INDEPENDENT READING

Invite children to read "Six-Dinner Sid" silently. As children finish, have them write in their personal journals what they think about Sid. When all children are finished, use their responses to discuss what Sid is like and what happened in the story.

Strategic Reading

MODELING A STRATEGY

PAGES 184–185 Before children read, ask them to look at the pictures and think about the predictions they made for pages 182-183. Then have children read on to confirm their predictions. After children read these pages, have them predict what they think will happen next. Model your thinking: *Sid looks pretty full after all of his dinners. I think he'll stop eating and go take a nap.* **MAKING AND CONFIRMING PREDICTIONS**

Sid lived in six houses so that he could have six dinners. Each night he would slip out of number one, where he might have had chicken, into number two for fish . . .

184

LISTENING CENTER

You may want to record "Six-Dinner Sid" on an audiocassette. Some children may benefit from listening to the story and following along in their books. (See Acknowledgments on pages R235–R236.)

CONVENTIONS OF PRINT

ELLIPSES Call attention to the ellipses on pages 184–185. Explain that in this case, they are used to let the reader know to pause while reading. Read the text aloud, first without pausing at the ellipses, and then with pauses. Ask children to comment on the readings, telling which one they liked more and why.

on to number three for lamb

liver at number four

fish again at number five . . .

ending at number six with beef-and-kidney stew.

185

MINILESSON

MAINTAIN: PHONICS AND DECODING

Consonant Digraphs:/sh/*sh*; /ch/*ch, tch*

INFORMAL ASSESSMENT

As children read, notice whether they decode words with the consonant digraphs /sh/*sh* and /ch/*ch, tch*.

TEACH/MODEL

Have children locate *each* and *chicken* on page 184. Write the words on the board, and ask which letters stand for the /ch/ sound. Ask a volunteer to circle *ch*. Point out that after six meals, Sid would yawn and stretch. Write *stretch,* and ask a volunteer to circle the letters that stand for the /ch/ sound. (tch) Then write *fish*, and repeat the process for the /sh/ sound.

PRACTICE/APPLY

Write the following sentences on the board:

Sid will choose chicken.
Should Sid wish for fish?
Will Sid catch a mouse?
We'll watch and find out.

Read the sentences aloud. Have children identify words with the /ch/ and /sh/ sounds and the digraphs that stand for the sounds.

PHONICS ACTIVITY BOOK, pages 19–20

PHONICS PRACTICE READER 6

PHONICS PRACTICE BOOK, pages 226–230

CROSS-CULTURAL VIEWPOINT

Many cultures have specific ideas about cats and luck. In the United States, black cats like Sid have been thought to bring bad luck. In England, white cats, and in Canada, three-colored cats are considered unlucky. In Japan, some people believe a calico cat brings good luck. In China, the older and scruffier a cat is, the more good fortune it carries with it.

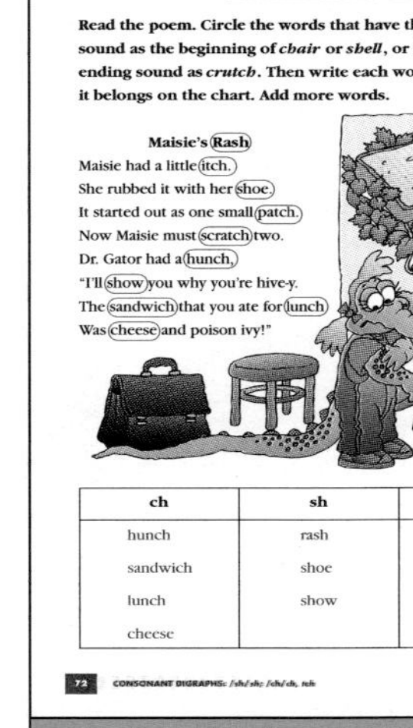

Name ____________________ Six-Dinner Sid

Read the poem. Circle the words that have the same sound as the beginning of *chair* or *shell*, or the same ending sound as *crutch*. Then write each word where it belongs on the chart. Add more words.

Maisie's Rash

Maisie had a little itch.
She rubbed it with her shoe.
It started out as one small patch.
Now Maisie must scratch two.
Dr. Gator had a hunch,
"I'll show you why you're hive-y.
The sandwich that you ate for lunch
Was cheese and poison ivy!"

ch	sh	tch
hunch	rash	itch
sandwich	shoe	patch
lunch	show	scratch
cheese		

Harcourt Brace School Publishers

72 CONSONANT DIGRAPHS: /sh/sh; /ch/ch, tch OUT OF THE BLUE Practice Book

PRACTICE BOOK, page 72

Strategic Reading

MODELING A STRATEGY

PAGES 186–187 Ask children to read page 186 and look closely at the illustrations. Talk with them about what new things they have learned about Sid and the neighbors. Ask them to make predictions that take this new information into account. Model your thinking: *We already know that Sid eats a dinner at every house on the street, but now we know that all the neighbors think Sid is their cat. I think the neighbors will find out about Sid and his six dinners.*

MAKING PREDICTIONS

Since the neighbors did not talk to each other on Aristotle Street, they did not know what Sid was up to. They all believed the cat they fed was theirs, and theirs alone.

186

SOCIAL STUDIES

ARISTOTLE Aristotle (384–322 B.C.) was an important Greek philosopher. His ideas and writings about logic, nature, metaphysics, ethics, and politics greatly influenced Arabic and Western thought.

STUDENTS ACQUIRING ENGLISH **Reread with children the first sentence on page 186, and point out the phrase *up to*. Explain that *up to* means "doing." Tell children that this phrase is most often used with the sense that someone who is "up to" something is most likely making mischief.**

MINILESSON

MAINTAIN: PHONICS AND DECODING

Consonant Digraphs: /hw/*wh*, /th/*th*

INFORMAL ASSESSMENT

As children read, notice how well they decode words containing the consonant digraphs *wh* and *th*.

TEACH/MODEL

Have children reread page 186. Ask volunteers to name words that contain the digraph *th (the, other, they, theirs)* and the digraph *wh (what)*. Write the words on the board. Ask volunteers to underline the letters that stand for the /th/ sound or the /hw/ sound in each word.

PRACTICE/APPLY

Write these questions on the board:

Where does Sid live?
What is Sid up to?
Why don't the neighbors know about Sid's secret?

Read aloud each question. Have children answer the question and include a word with the /th/ sound in their answer. Ask other children to name the word with the /th/ sound. List the words on the board. Then ask volunteers to circle the letters that stand for the /th/ or /hw/ sound in each word.

PHONICS ACTIVITY BOOK, pages 21–22

PHONICS PRACTICE READER 6

PHONICS PRACTICE BOOK, pages 232–235

A CLOSER LOOK

Allow time for children to study the illustrations. Ask what they can learn about the different characters from the illustrations. Encourage children to speculate about what each character may be thinking, using details in the illustrations to support their opinions.

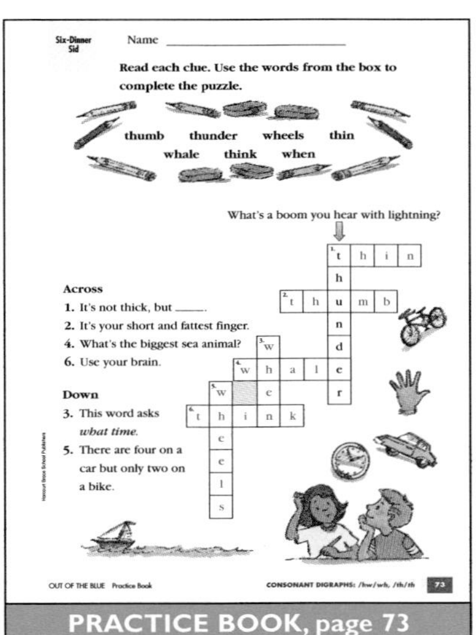

Six-Dinner Sid Name ____________

Read each clue. Use the words from the box to complete the puzzle.

thumb thunder wheels thin
whale think when

What's a boom you hear with lightning?

Across
1. It's not thick, but ____.
2. It's your short and fattest finger.
4. What's the biggest sea animal?
6. Use your brain.

Down
3. This word asks *what time.*
5. There are four on a car but only two on a bike.

Harcourt Brace School Publishers

OUT OF THE BLUE Practice Book CONSONANT DIGRAPHS: /hw/wh, /th/th 73

PRACTICE BOOK, page 73

Strategic Reading

MODELING A STRATEGY

PAGES 188–189 Help children analyze Sid's character. **Think aloud:** *What do we know about Sid? We know that he definitely likes to eat because he has six dinners every day. He has to work hard for those dinners, though. He has to remember six different names, and he has to act differently in each house where he eats. This gives us a picture of just how important food is to Sid.*

- **What else have you learned about Sid's character?**
- **What parts of the story gave you clues?**

MAKING INFERENCES

But Sid had to work hard for his dinners. It wasn't easy being six people's pet. He had six different names to remember and six different ways to behave.

When he was being Scaramouche, Sid put on swanky airs.

As Bob he had a job.

He was naughty as Mischief . . .

188

MEETING INDIVIDUAL NEEDS

STUDENTS ACQUIRING ENGLISH **Call attention to the phrase *put on swanky airs*. Explain that *swanky* means "fancy" and that people "put on airs" when they try to act as if they are better than others. Encourage children to pantomime *putting on swanky airs*.**

and silly as Sally.

As Sooty he smooched . . .

but as Schwartz he had to act rough and tough.

189

Tested Skill

MINILESSON

REVIEW: COMPREHENSION

Making Predictions

INFORMAL ASSESSMENT

As children read, assess their ability to combine personal experience with word and picture clues to make predictions.

TEACH/MODEL

Encourage children to discuss what's easy and what's hard about Sid's life. Then ask whether children think Sid will be able to go on fooling his six owners. Model your thinking:

MODEL

It's not easy to be a pet for six people. I think that one day, Sid will make a mistake and his owners will find out about one another.

PRACTICE/APPLY

Have children make their own predictions. Ask what they think will happen next in the story. Encourage them to tell why they make the predictions they do. Then have them read on to confirm their predictions.

Name ______________ Six-Dinner Sid

Finish the cartoons. Draw or write what you think will happen next.

Responses will vary. Perhaps three kittens sleep in the basket.

1. What do you think will happen next? ______________

2. Why do you think so? ______________

Responses will vary. Perhaps the kittens overturn the milk and lick it up.

3. What do you think will happen next? ______________

4. Why do you think so? ______________

TRY THIS! Talking Tip

Talk with a partner. Take turns making up the beginning of a story. Predict what will happen next in each other's stories.

74 MAKING PREDICTIONS OUT OF THE BLUE Practice Book

PRACTICE BOOK, page 74

PHONICS IN ACTION

Call attention to the words *rough* and *tough* on page 189. Point out that the *gh* at the end of the words can stand for the /f/ sound.

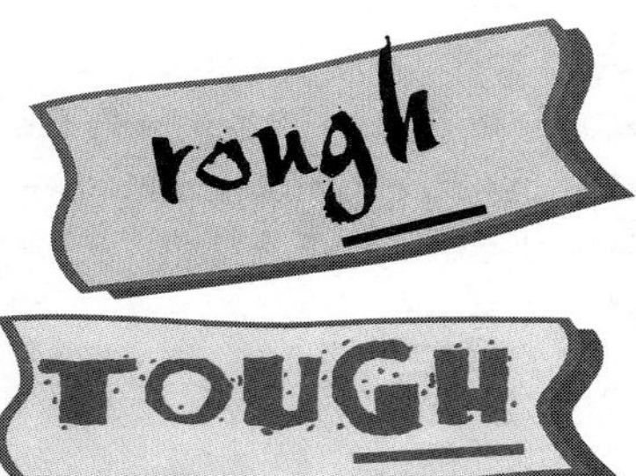

EXTRA SUPPORT **Invite children to use details in the illustrations to help them better understand the text. Encourage them to discuss what they see in each picture. Ask questions such as *What is Sid's job when he's "Bob"?* Remind children that none of Sid's six owners know about the others.**

Strategic Reading

APPLYING A STRATEGY

PAGES 190–191 Before reading the pages, have children look at the pictures and talk about what Sid is doing. After reading, help children use the illustrations to add meaning to the text. Encourage them to talk about the six different ways the neighbors scratch Sid and the different beds they make for him. Ask children to talk about how the illustrations help them know what each of the neighbors on Aristotle Street is like. Ask children to guess which neighbor made which bed for Sid and to tell why they think so. **RELATING PICTURES TO TEXT**

All this work sometimes wore Sid out. But he didn't care, as long as he had his six dinners. And, besides, he liked being . . .

scratched in six different places . . .

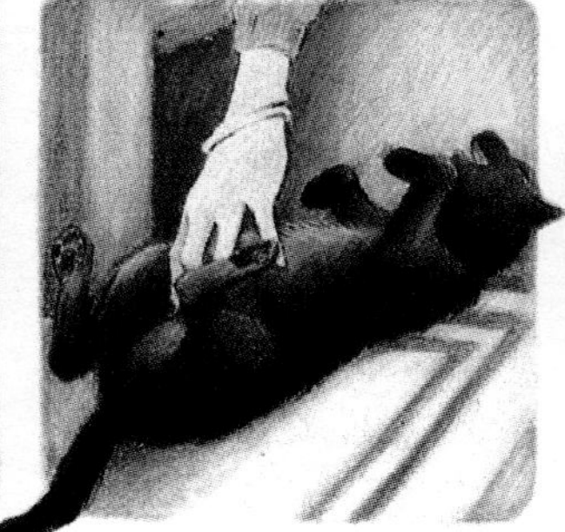

190

MEETING INDIVIDUAL NEEDS

STUDENTS ACQUIRING ENGLISH **Call attention to the phrase *wore Sid out* on page 190. Encourage children to look at the top picture for clues to the meaning of *wore Sid out.* (made Sid very tired)**

MEETING INDIVIDUAL NEEDS

CHALLENGE **Discuss with children how Sid's life differs in the six homes. Challenge interested children to each choose a different neighbor and write about Sid's life in that home, expanding on information in the story.**

and sleeping in six different beds.

191

Informal Assessment ✓

DRAWING CONCLUSIONS

During a rereading of this selection, observe how children use story clues and apply their knowledge to draw logical conclusions.

- ☑ Do children express an understanding of the story that incorporates factors not expressly stated in the text?
- ☑ Do children use their own knowledge to enhance their understanding of what they are reading?
- ☑ Do children use information in pictures and text, and do they make inferences about story events based on what they see?

MEETING INDIVIDUAL NEEDS

Intervention Strategies

USING PICTURE CLUES **Have children repeat this sentence:** ***When I read, it helps me to look at the pictures to understand what is happening.*** **Have children tell how looking at the pictures might help them understand how Sid feels about having six owners.**

WRITING

EXTEND THE STORY **Encourage children to discuss the illustrations on pages 190–191. Have them write captions for one or more of the illustrations. Invite volunteers to read their captions and ask classmates to guess which illustrations they match.**

Strategic Reading

APPLYING A STRATEGY

PAGES 192–195 Before children read, have them look at the pictures and predict what they think is happening to Sid. Then have them read the pages to confirm their predictions. After children read, have them compare the predictions they made earlier in the story with what has actually happened. Have children make new predictions about what will happen to Sid. As children share their ideas and predictions, ask:

- **How did Sid's cough and his six trips to the vet change his life?**
- **What do you think the vet said to Sid's owners?**
- **How has what you've read so far changed your ideas about what will happen next?**

MAKING AND CONFIRMING PREDICTIONS

In fact, life on Aristotle Street was just about perfect for Sid, until . . .

one cold, damp day, he caught a nasty cough.

192

EXPANDING VOCABULARY

Call attention to the word *vet* on page 193. Point out that it is a short form of the word *veterinarian*. Ask volunteers to tell what a vet is or does. Explain that there are special vets for pets, farm animals, and zoo animals. Ask children whether they would like to be a vet and for what kind of animals they would like to care.

veterinarian

The next thing he knew, he was being taken to the vet. Poor Sid, he was taken not once . . .

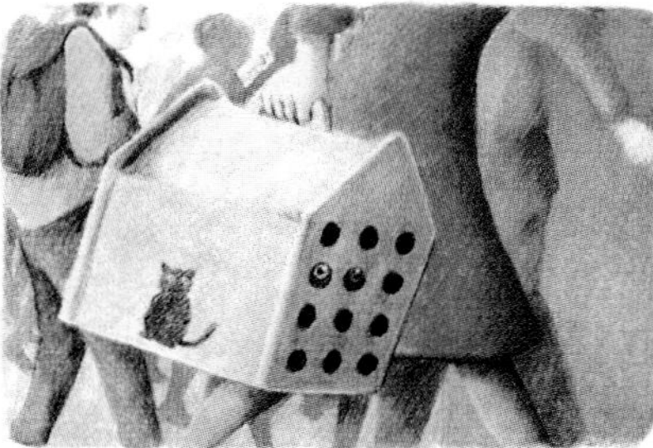

not twice . . .

but six times!

He went with six different people, in six different ways.

193

Tested Skill

MINILESSON

MAINTAIN: COMPREHENSION

Sequence

INFORMAL ASSESSMENT

As children discuss the story, notice whether they refer to story events in the correct order.

TEACH/MODEL

Talk with children about what happened in the story. Invite them to look back through the story for the signal words and phrases that helped them keep track of the order of events. (number words *one–six, on to, ending, next*) Talk with children about how the number words in the story helped them keep track of the characters and the places Sid went.

PRACTICE/APPLY

Review the order of events in "Six-Dinner Sid" with children. Then have small groups of children play a game. One child names a story event—for example, "Sid gets a nasty cough." Other children in the group name a story event that happened before the event named, and an event that happened after it.

Sid visits his six owners every day.

Sid gets a nasty cough.

Sid goes to the vet.

REAL-LIFE CONNECTION

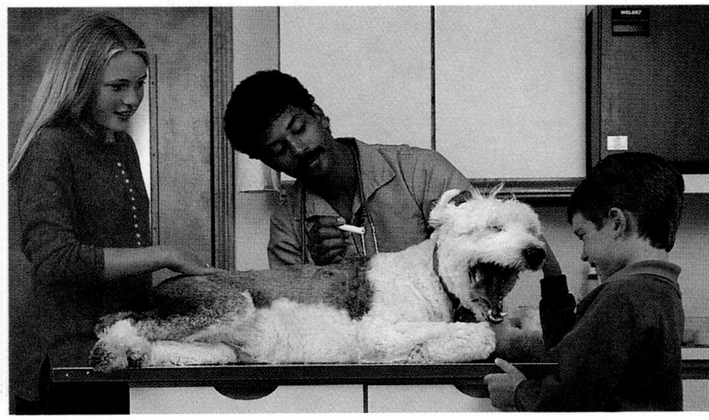

Invite children who have taken pets to the vet to talk about their experiences. Discuss the importance of taking pets to the vet for immunizations and regular checkups, as well as when they are ill.

Cooperative Reading

As children discuss the questions on **Reader Response Card 1** (Characters), you might pose additional questions for them to consider:

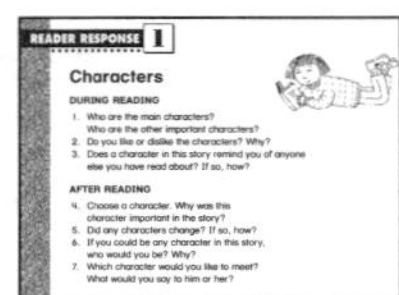

Response Card 1

- **What do you think Sid's owners will do after they speak with the vet on the phone?**
- **What do you think Sid will do?**

The vet said Sid's cough wasn't nearly as nasty as it sounded; but, to be on the safe side, he should have a spoonful of medicine.

Of course,
Sid didn't have just one spoonful of medicine.

He had six!

194

A CLOSER LOOK

Invite children to look at the series of illustrations of Sid being given six doses of medicine. Draw their attention to the changes in Sid's facial expression as he's given more and more medicine. Have children discuss how Sid feels in each of the six pictures and how they can tell. You may also want to discuss why it's not a good idea for animals or people to have more medicine than they should.

MULTI-AGE CLASSROOMS

Older children may want to find out more about veterinarians and report their findings to their classmates. Encourage them to find information about veterinarians in the school or local library.

Now, one black cat does look much like another; but nobody, not even a busy vet, could see the same cat six times without becoming suspicious. Sure enough, when he checked in his appointment book, the vet found six cats with a cough—all living on Aristotle Street!

So he called the owners at once . . .

195

Tested Skill

MINILESSON

REVIEW: GRAMMAR

Exclamations, Commands, and End Marks

INFORMAL ASSESSMENT

As children read and write, notice whether they use exclamations, commands, and appropriate end marks.

TEACH/MODEL

Ask children to reread pages 194 and 195 to locate the following exclamations:

He had six!; Sure enough . . . the vet found six cats with a cough—all living on Aristotle Street!

Ask volunteers to read the sentences aloud with feeling, and talk about what the exclamation mark means. Then write on the board the sentence *Sid, come here!*, and review the concept of commands. Finally, ask children what end mark they would put at the end of the following sentence: *Can you believe Sid did that?*

PRACTICE/APPLY

Write these sentences on the board. Have children write them and add the correct end marks.

I can't believe Sid eats six dinners a day
Eat your dinner, Sid
I'm so mad at you, Sid
Come here, Sid
What will we do now

LANGUAGE HANDBOOK

Exclamations and Commands, pages 52–53
End Marks, pages 54–55

EXPANDING VOCABULARY

Reread the first sentence on page 195, calling attention to the word *suspicious.* Invite children to speculate about the word's meaning, guiding them to realize that it means "doubtful; wondering about something." Then help children pronounce it correctly.

SCHOOL↔HOME CONNECTION

Encourage children to work with family members to make a list of the different kinds of pets people in their neighborhood have. Children can bring their lists to school to share with classmates.

Strategic Reading

APPLYING A STRATEGY

PAGES 196–198 After children read page 196, have them compare their predictions with what the owners actually decided to do to Sid. Then ask children to look at the pictures on pages 197-198 and predict how the story will end. Finally have children read the rest of the story. **MAKING AND CONFIRMING PREDICTIONS**

and, oh dear, Sid was found out!
When they discovered what he had been up to, Sid's owners said he had no business eating so many dinners.

They said, in the future, they would make sure he had only one dinner a day.

196

WRITING

EXTEND THE STORY Encourage children to speculate about how Sid's owners would make sure that he only had one dinner a day. Have them write a few sentences outlining a possible plan. Invite volunteers to share their work.

ILLUSTRATOR'S CRAFT

Direct children's attention to the facial expressions and body positions of the six people shown in the picture on this page. Ask what they think the illustrator wants to tell us about the characters and their feelings.

ANGRY HAPPY
ashamed sad

But Sid was a six-dinner-a-day cat. So he went to live at number one Pythagoras Place. He also went to live at numbers two, three, four, five, and six.

197

Student Self-Assessment 

USING READING STRATEGIES

When children are reading the story in small groups, provide a time for them to share any good reading strategies they use, such as guessing what will happen next and then reading on to find out, or skipping an unknown word and reading on.

SOCIAL STUDIES

PYTHAGORAS Like Aristotle, Pythagoras (580–500 B.C.) was a noted Greek philosopher. He was also a religious leader. Pythagoras made great contributions in the development of mathematics and astronomy, as well as music theory.

MULTICULTURAL CONNECTION

Invite children who speak a language other than English to teach their classmates to count to six in that language. If children also know how to write the words or characters, invite them to participate in making a chart of the numbers one through six in other languages.

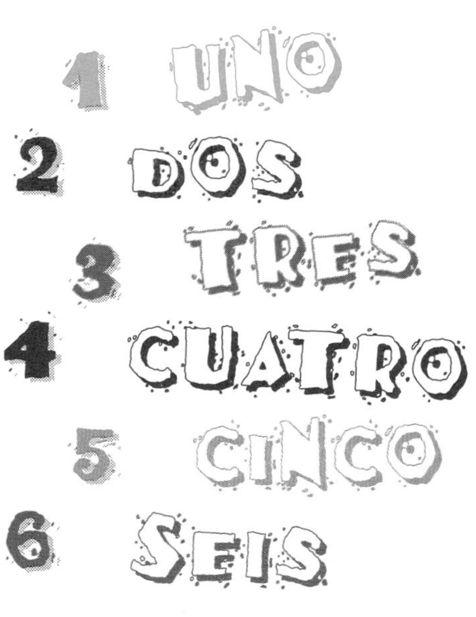

Strategic Reading

APPLYING A STRATEGY

PAGE 198 After children have read, have them compare their predictions with what actually happened. Emphasize that it's not important for readers to predict correctly every story event. **CONFIRMING PREDICTIONS**

Returning to the Predictions/Purpose

Before reading the story, children wrote what they thought would happen in the story. Invite them to share their predictions and compare them with what actually happened.

Appreciating the Literature

With the whole class or a small group, have an open discussion about the story.

Would you rather be a neighbor on Aristotle Street or Pythagoras Place? Why?

Unlike Aristotle Street, the people who lived on Pythagoras Place talked to their neighbors. So, right from the start, everyone knew about Sid's six dinners.

And, because everyone knew, nobody minded.

198

SOCIAL STUDIES

CATS IN JAPAN Cats were highly valued pets in seventeenth-century Japan. It was the custom to keep cats on silk leashes. After rats and mice seriously damaged grain supplies and nearly ruined the silk industry, the emperor ordered that all cats be allowed to run free in order to rid the country of its rodent problem.

A Note About Inga Moore

Dear Readers,

"MEEOWW!" That's my way of saying hello. Being the star of a book was hard work. To help Inga Moore write and draw Six-Dinner Sid, *I showed her how cats leap, stretch, and purr. She became a real cat expert.*

Did you know that Inga Moore was born in England and moved to Australia when she was seven? Now she lives in London, England.

When Inga Moore was young, she loved to ride horses. She wanted to be a vet. I'm glad that she became a writer and artist instead so that I could be in her book!

Hmmm. . . all of this writing has made me hungry. Dinner number one, here I come!

Sid

199

About the Author/Illustrator

PAGE 199 Have children read the letter from Sid on page 199. You might want to explain that although a cat couldn't really write a letter, the information about the author is true.

Inga Moore's first job as an illustrator was at an advertising agency. She found more pleasure in the illustrations she did for herself than in those from which she earned her living. In time, she left the agency and began illustrating books.

OTHER BOOKS BY INGA MOORE

A Big Day for Little Jack. **Candlewick Press, 1994. AVERAGE**

Little Dog Lost. **Macmillan, 1991. AVERAGE**

Oh, Little Jack. **Candlewick Press, 1994. AVERAGE**

The Truffle Hunter. **Kane-Miller, 1987. AVERAGE**

SUMMARIZE AND RETELL

The Tale of a Cat

Discuss the story with children, focusing on the characters of Sid and the neighbors on Aristotle Street. Work with children to fill in a flowchart like the one shown.

Then have children use the flowchart to retell the story of "Six-Dinner Sid." See *Practice Book* page 67.

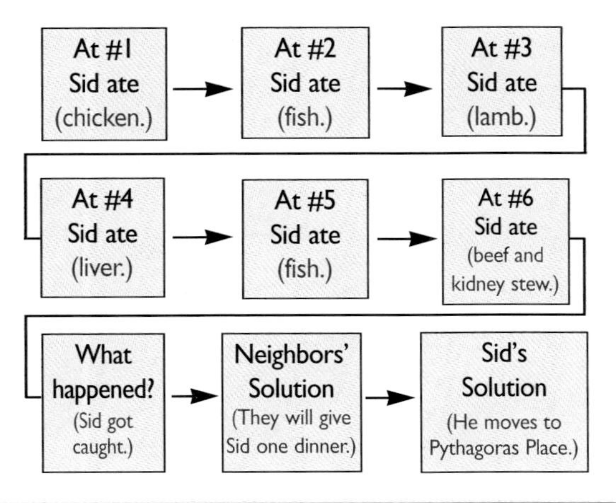

Six-Dinner Sid Name ____________

Complete the flowchart for the story.

Possible responses are given.

1. At house number one, Sid ate chicken.
2. At house number two, Sid ate fish.
3. At house number three, Sid ate lamb.
4. At house number four, Sid ate liver.
5. At house number five, Sid ate fish.
6. At house number six, Sid ate beef-and-kidney stew.

What happened? Sid got sick and was taken to the vet six times. He got caught.

Neighbors' Solution: The neighbors made sure Sid had only one dinner a day.

Sid's Solution: Sid went to a new neighborhood where he could have six dinners.

OUT OF THE BLUE Practice Book SUMMARIZE AND RETELL 67

PRACTICE BOOK, page 67

RESPONSE CORNER ACTIVITIES

MAKE A STORY STRIP

SIX SIDES TO SID

PAGE 200 Have children work in groups of six. Each member of the group should draw Sid doing something different or behaving in a different way. After group members finish, have them arrange all six pictures in an order that retells the original story—or a new story about Sid. **ART**

INTERVIEW A CHARACTER

IF SID COULD TALK

PAGE 201 Children may use materials such as cardboard tubes to make microphones and paper plates or face paints to make cat masks. Children can make up names for their shows. Suggest that in the interviews, "Sid" answer in character as a cat that is hungry, clever, silly, naughty, and so on, depending on the question. You may want to videotape the shows for everyone to watch. **LISTENING/SPEAKING**

Response Corner

MAKE A STORY STRIP

Six Sides to Sid

Work in groups of six to make a story strip that shows six different sides of Sid.

1. Think about what you liked most about Sid.
2. Draw and write about your idea.
3. When your group has finished, look at all the pictures.
4. Put the pictures in order. Tape them together to make your story strip.

200

VARYING THE ACTIVITY

Challenge children to expand their guest list for the If Sid Could Talk activity to include some of the neighbors from both neighborhoods and the vet. Children will need to work in larger groups to do this. The talk show host will work with others to prepare questions to ask the additional guests.

INTERVIEW A CHARACTER

If Sid Could Talk

You and a partner can make up a TV talk show about Sid. Decide who will be Sid and who will be the host. Plan what you both will say.

What Do You Think?

- How is Pythagoras Place different from Aristotle Street?
- If Sid were your pet, which one would you want him to act like—Scaramouche, Bob, Mischief, Sally, Sooty, or Schwartz? Tell why.

BEFORE THE SHOW...

If you are the TV talk show host

- plan the questions you will ask.
- think about what people would want to know about Sid.

If you are Sid

- read the questions.
- think about how a cat might answer.

201

CHECKING COMPREHENSION

What Do You Think?

1. **How is Pythagoras Place different from Aristotle Street?** (Accept reasonable responses: Sid's owners on Aristotle Street do not talk to each other; his owners on Pythagoras Place do.) DESCRIPTIVE RESPONSE
2. **If Sid were your pet, which one would you want him to act like—Scaramouche, Bob, Mischief, Sally, Sooty, or Schwartz? Tell why.** (Responses will vary. Be sure children support their answers.) PERSONAL RESPONSE

An additional question for extending reading:

3. **If Sid could talk, what would you ask him and why?** (Possible response: I'd ask him which pet cat he is most like—Scaramouche, Bob, Mischief, Sally, Sooty, or Schwartz—because I want to know the real Sid.) CRITICAL/CREATIVE ANALYSIS

STUDENTS ACQUIRING ENGLISH **Pair children with English-proficient partners for If Sid Could Talk. Suggest that children acquiring English role-play Sid, using words, pantomime, facial expressions, and gestures to answer questions.**

Informal Assessment

Observe pairs of children as they make up a TV talk show.

- Do children who role-play the talk show host write questions to ask Sid?
- Do children who role-play Sid answer the questions as Sid might?
- Do children respond appropriately to one another as they act out the talk show?

Intervention Strategies

Instant Readers™

Predictable and Patterned Little Books That Build Fluency

*** BOOK LEVEL: 14–15**

VOCABULARY:
caught, neighbors, scratched

PHONIC ELEMENTS:
Initial cluster: *scr*;
Digraphs: /sh/*sh*, /ch/*tch*, /hw/*wh*, /th/*th*

SUMMARY:
What a surprise for a dog that wants a little puppy to play with!

Informal Assessment ✓

Are children able to

- ☑ discuss strategies used to read?
- ☑ form new words, using known word parts?

Reading a New Book

INTRODUCING *MY BIG SURPRISE*

After children look at the cover, ask whom they think this story is about. Explain that in this story the dog tells about his boy (his owner) and the surprise he gets. With children, examine the pictures, focusing on where the boy and the dog go and what they see.

READING THE STORY

Have children read the story independently to find out about the puppy's surprise.

WORKING WITH WORDS AND LETTERS

Many of the story words contain the consonant digraphs *sh, tch, wh,* and *th*. Have children work together to manipulate individual letter cards, *Word Builder Cards,* or magnetic letters to form words. Encourage children to replace the digraphs with other letters to form other words.

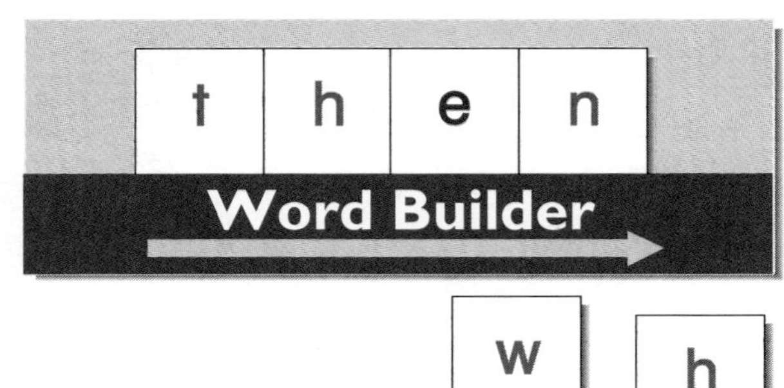

WRITING LETTERS

Have children write a couple of sentences in a letter from the dog to his boy. Ask children to consider what the dog would want to tell his boy.

Additional activities are provided on pages 40–41 of the *Intervention Strategies Manual*.

* **BOOK LEVEL: 18–19**

VOCABULARY:
different, neighborhood, scratched

PHONIC ELEMENTS:
Initial cluster: ***scr;***
Digraphs: /ch/*ch, tch,* /hw/*wh,* /th/*th*

SUMMARY:
Two critters learn to adjust to the addition of another friend.

Reading a New Book

INTRODUCING *BUDDIES*

Share the front and back covers of the story, and ask children what they think is happening. Talk about the title and what it means. As the illustrations are shared, talk about what the animals (Ben, Marty, and Andy) are doing and the problem they seem to have. Include in the discussion the expression *through thick and thin* and talk about what it means.

READING THE STORY

Have children read the story with a buddy to find out how the animals solve their problem.

WORKING WITH WORDS AND LETTERS

Have each child work with the same reading buddy to talk about one reading strategy he or she used to read or understand a new word in the story. Encourage children to focus on a specific word or phrase that gave them trouble and write the word or phrase. Partners can then share what they learned from the reading strategy discussed.

WRITING STORIES

Children can write a personal journal entry about how they solved a problem with a buddy.

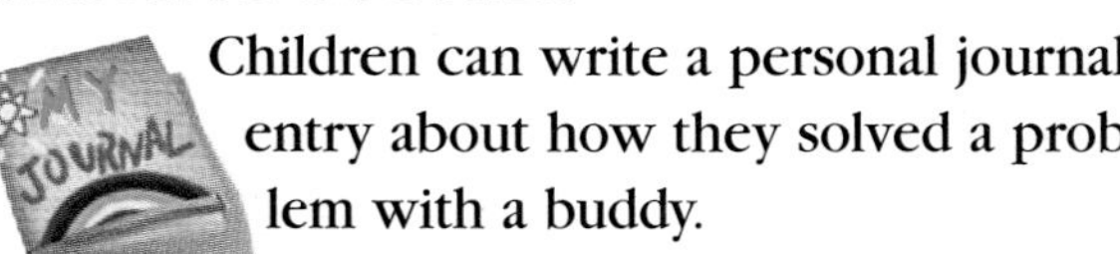

ESL/Title I Reading

Red Cat, White Cat by Peter Mandel

Working with "Six-Dinner Sid"

GRAPHOPHONIC CUES Keep a write-on, wipe-off board in the Reading Center so that children can write their names and any troublesome or unknown words they encounter in their reading. Underneath the word, write one or two smaller or similar words the children know to help them apply the decoding strategy.

Kyle: weigh
neighbor

INSTANT READERS™

ELECTRONIC EDITION

***My Big Surprise* and *Buddies* are available on CD-ROM. Pre- and post-reading activities are included.**

* Books leveled according to Barbara Peterson's "Profiles of Books for Beginning Readers," on page 9 of the *Instant Readers Teacher's Guide.*

IDEA BANK

TIPS FOR CLASSROOM MANAGEMENT

IF children have their own ideas about what makes a good neighbor, **THEN** assign the Group Talk activity.

IF children have difficulty naming streets in the Reading Street Signs activity, **THEN** take them on a short walk around the neighborhood to look at street signs before making a list of street names and their abbreviations.

LISTENING AND SPEAKING

Group Talk

GOOD NEIGHBORS

Have small groups of children share their ideas about what makes a good neighbor. They could begin by comparing the neighbors on Aristotle Street and Pythagoras Place. Have each group make a list of qualities they'd like their neighbors to have. They might also want to illustrate their lists.

After small-group discussions, gather children to share their ideas and insights.

CHALLENGING THE TEXT

REAL-LIFE READING

Reading Street Signs

Ask volunteers to tell the name of the street on which they live. Write the street names on the board without any abbreviations. If necessary, add names to the list to get a variety of kinds of streets. Point out the words for kinds of streets, such as *avenue*, *street*, and *road*. Tell children that in order to make addresses easier to write, they often include shortened forms, or abbreviations of street names. Fill in a chart like the one below. Point out the period at the end of each abbreviation.

LISTENING/SPEAKING/READING

Full Name	Short Name
Street	St.
Avenue	Ave.
Road	Rd.
Lane	Ln.
Boulevard	Blvd.
Place	Pl.
Drive	Dr.

What clues let you know that the quiz was written to be funny?

Are You an Awesome Pet Owner?

SID LOOKED FOR JUST THE RIGHT OWNERS SO HE COULD BE TAKEN CARE OF. HOW MUCH DO YOU KNOW ABOUT TAKING CARE OF PETS? THIS QUIZ WILL TELL YOU.

Silly PET QUIZ

1. What should your pet drink every day?
A. Fresh water.
B. Chocolate milk or lemonade for a tasty treat.
C. Carrot juice—it's full of vitamins.

2. You see your neighbor walking a new dog. What should you do?
A. Run right over and give it a big hug.
B. Jump out from behind a tree and yell "YAAH!"
C. Let the dog see you. Ask its owner if it's okay for you to pet the dog.

3. What should you do for your pet when it's cold outside?
A. Leave your pet outside for a long time.
B. Make sure your pet has a warm place to live.
C. Buy a down jacket specially made for your pet.

4. You forgot to feed your pet today. What should you do?
A. Wait. Your pet will ask for food if it's really hungry.
B. Give your pet something to eat.
C. Who needs food every day? It can wait until tomorrow.

from Kid City, March 1995

WRITER'S MAGAZINE, pages 26–27

ORAL LANGUAGE

Rereading for Fluency

A STORY JUST FOR YOU

Brainstorm with children ways to tell or dramatize a story. If children run out of ideas, you might suggest the following: act out the story with puppets, read it aloud with sound effects, or present it as a play. Discuss the best way to act out "Six-Dinner Sid" for different types of audiences:

- **How would a kindergarten class most enjoy the story?**
- **What would be a good way to share the story with teachers or other adults?**
- **How would you use the story to teach something about neighbors to other second graders?**

Have small groups of children choose an audience to which they would like to present "Six-Dinner Sid." Each group should plan and present its reading.
LISTENING/SPEAKING

Informal Assessment

Note how fluently children read as they present "Six-Dinner Sid."

KINESTHETIC

Creative Connection

MAKE A CAT TO PET

MATERIALS
- **poster board**
- **fabric scraps and collage materials with a variety of textures (net, velvet, felt, buttons, cardboard)**

Invite children to draw an outline of a cat on poster board and cut it out. Have them select a variety of fabric scraps and other textured materials and glue them to cover the cat like fur. When the collages are dry, encourage children to describe how their cats' "fur" feels. Have children "pet" several classmates' cats, describe their "fur," and compare how they feel. LISTENING/SPEAKING/KINESTHETIC

PERSONAL JOURNAL

REFLECTING ON THE STORY Invite children to draw and write in their personal journals about what it means to be a good neighbor.

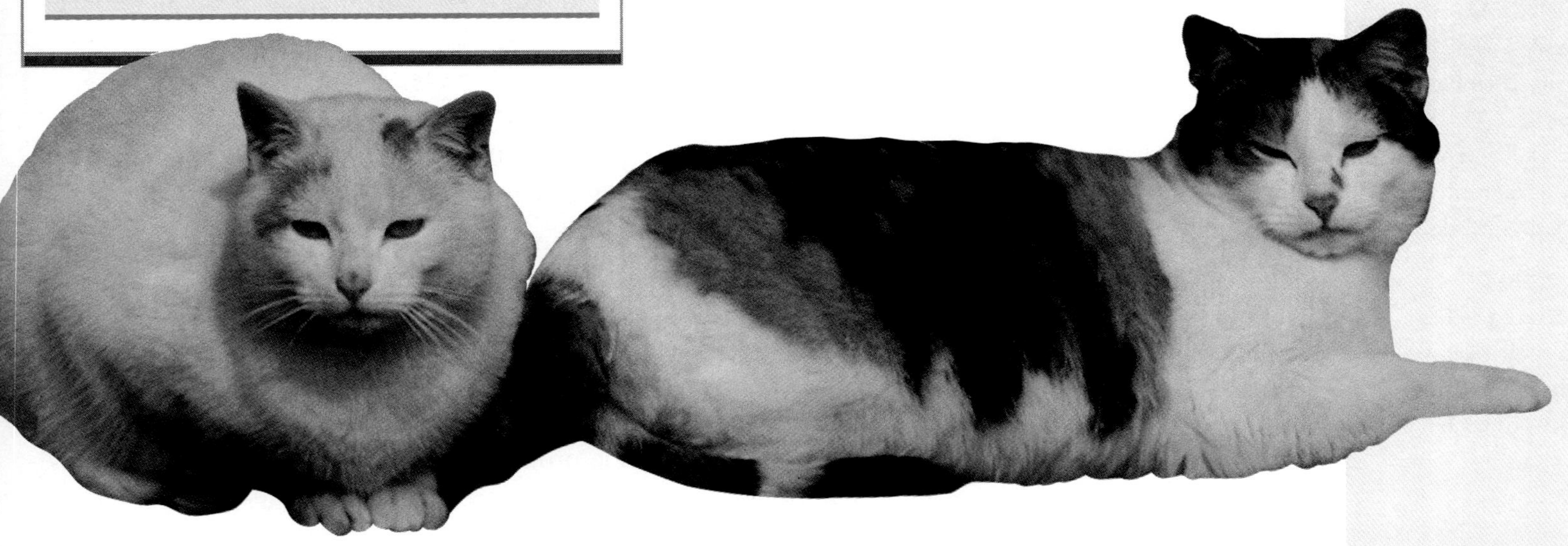

WRITER'S WORKSHOP

A Paragraph That Describes

TIPS FOR CLASSROOM MANAGEMENT

IF children are familiar with the writing process approach, **THEN** present the writing assignment and have them use the Paragraph That Describes model on pages 18–19 of the *Language Handbook.*

IF at this time you want a short writing activity, **THEN** have children do the prewriting activity and place the web in the Writing Center for children's reference during independent writing.

TECHNOLOGY

THE AMAZING WRITING MACHINE
Primary Level Activity Disk Pack Grade 2
Have children enter their paragraphs in the Essays mode.

KID PIX
Children can illustrate their paragraphs by creating pictures of their own or using the stamps.

Thinking as Writers

WRITING FORM: Paragraph That Describes
Remind children that "Six-Dinner Sid" tells them a lot about a very clever cat. Explain to children that they will work independently to write a paragraph that describes Sid or a pet they know.

Display Chart/Transparency 16, or write the model Paragraph That Describes on the board. Encourage children to discuss the differences between this paragraph and a story. Point out the paragraph indent.

CHART/TRANSPARENCY 16

MODEL: PARAGRAPH THAT DESCRIBES

topic sentence — My family went to visit Mammoth Cave in Kentucky.

describing words in detail sentences — It is a very big cave. It is cold and dark on the inside. When the lights are turned off, you can't even see your hands! The walls are wet and feel slimy. The whole cave has a damp smell.

WRITER'S CRAFT: Details and Exact Words
Explain that good writers use details and descriptive words to make their writing interesting. They choose words carefully to mean exactly what they intend. Good writers try to avoid saying *went* when what they mean is *galloped*. Point out that if a description is clearly written, readers should be able to picture exactly what is being described.

PREWRITING

Initiate a discussion about Sid the cat. Brainstorm words that describe him and add them to a web.

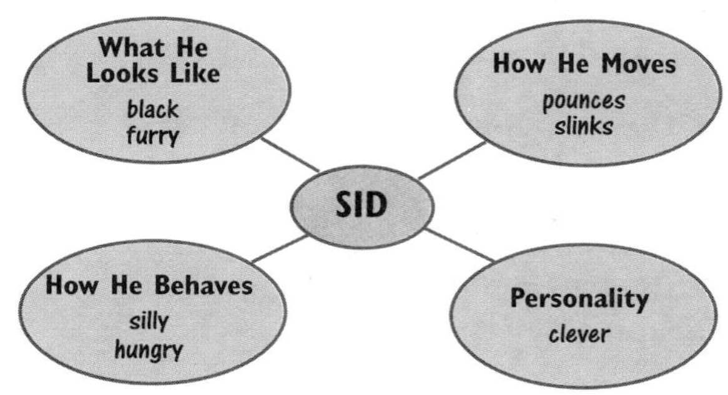

Have children decide whether they are going to describe Sid or a pet they know. Suggest that they draw a picture of their choice and then complete a web like the one above, describing that pet.

DRAFTING

As children write the drafts of their paragraphs, remind them to

- use their picture and web for ideas.
- write a sentence that tells the main idea.
- include words that tell how the pet looks, sounds, and acts.

As children work through the stages of the writing process, have them save their drafts and revisions in their writer's folder.

RESPONDING AND REVISING

Invite children to read their descriptions aloud to a partner or small group. Invite listeners to use the details and exact words to "see" Sid or the pet. Offer these guidelines for children to use as they listen and comment:

- What did you like about the paragraph?
- Does the paragraph include details and words that help you picture the pet?
- Does the paragraph include a sentence that tells what the paragraph is mainly about?

PROOFREADING

Offer some tips to help children proofread. Help them focus on the following:

INDENT The first word of a paragraph is indented.

EXCLAMATIONS, COMMANDS, AND END MARKS An exclamation shows strong feeling. It ends with an exclamation point. A command is a sentence that tells someone to do something. It ends with a period. (See the Grammar Minilesson on page T373.)

PUBLISHING

Have children make a clean copy of their paragraphs. Then offer publishing options like the following:

Handwriting
Remind children that their handwriting must be neat and clear so that the person reading the paragraph can understand it. If children need assistance, refer them to the Handwriting models in the *Language Handbook* or in the classroom.

PARTNER DRAWING Children can read their paragraphs aloud several times to a partner, who will draw a picture of the pet described. When the picture is completed, the partners can discuss what other information would have helped the illustrator make an even more accurate drawing.

PET SHOW Use copies of children's paragraphs to create an interactive bulletin board display. On the left, display the paragraphs, with a long piece of bright yarn attached to each one. On the right, display children's illustrations in random order. Have viewers match up descriptions with illustrations.

PORTFOLIO OPPORTUNITY

After children publish, make copies of their paragraphs and have them attach their Writing Self-Assessment Checklists to them. Have them place the paragraphs and checklists in their portfolios.

LANGUAGE HANDBOOK

Paragraph That Describes, pages 18–19

Student Self-Assessment ✓

Children can use the Writing Self-Assessment Checklist in the *Portfolio Assessment Teacher's Guide.*

EVALUATING THE WRITTEN RESPONSE

When evaluating children's paragraphs, consider:

CONTENT	ORGANIZATION	STYLE
Does the description tell about Sid or another pet and how it looks and acts?	Does the paragraph have a main idea supported by details?	Are descriptive words used in the paragraph?

EVALUATION BENCHMARKS

The child offers some describing words but does not create a fully detailed description.	= EMERGENT
The child provides good description, but the paragraph lacks cohesiveness.	= BEGINNING
The child uses specific describing words and helps create a vivid image. The paragraph contains a strong topic sentence and no extraneous details.	= PROFICIENT

Tested Skill

GRAMMAR

Nouns

Reading↔Writing Connection

Connect to the story. Have children name people, animals, places, and things from the story. Record their ideas on a chart like the following:

People	Animals	Places	Things
owners vet children	Sid cat	Aristotle Street number 1 Pythagoras Place	chair bed basket box stew meat

Build oral language. Invite children to make up sentences about more places Sid might go and the things he might do. Record on the chart the naming words that children use in their sentences.

Teach/Model

Discuss nouns. Point out that each of the words in the chart names something. Explain that we call a word that names a person, an animal, a place, or a thing a **noun.** Have children think of more nouns that relate to the story, and add them to the chart. Ask whether each noun names a person, an animal, a place, or a thing.

Practice/Apply

Check understanding. Write the following words on the board:

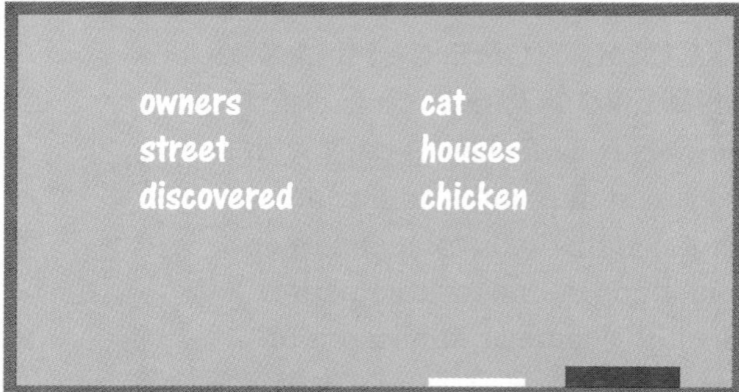

Have children identify the word that is not a noun and explain why it is not. (*Discovered* is a verb.) Then have them tell what each of the other words names: a person, an animal, a place, or a thing. Repeat with other sets of nouns and words that are not nouns.

LANGUAGE HANDBOOK
Nouns, pages 56–57

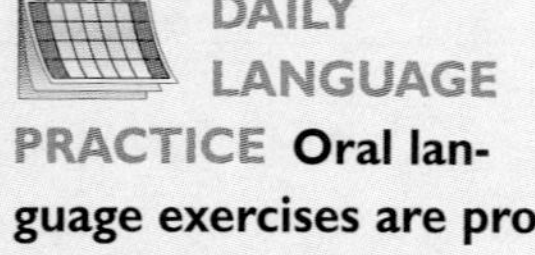

DAILY LANGUAGE PRACTICE **Oral language exercises are provided on page R82.**

Practice Activities

Quick Lists

WRITING APPLICATION Have small groups of children work together to make lists of nouns. Give each group a magazine picture of a place and an allotted time, such as five minutes. Encourage groups to write as many nouns as they can that could be found in the places in their pictures.

Invite groups to share their lists. Allow time for children to write some of their favorite nouns on index cards to add to their Word Files.

VISUAL/KINESTHETIC

Animal Sentences

WRITING APPLICATION Invite children to write a few sentences about an animal and its owner. Have them include where the animal lives, how the owner cares for it, and what it eats. Children can trade papers with a partner and underline all the nouns they find. Then they can trade back and check each other's work. **VISUAL**

Sing a Song of Nouns

ORAL APPLICATION Invite small groups to make up verses to a song that defines and gives examples of nouns. Use the tune of "If You're Happy and You Know It." Give each group the first line to one of four verses:

A word that names a person is a noun.
A word that names an animal is a noun.
A word that names a place is a noun.
A word that names a thing is a noun.

Children repeat the first line, and then make up the rest of the verse. Here is a sample first verse:

A word that names a person is a noun.
A word that names a person is a noun.
Teacher, brother, sister, cousin.
Neighbor, friend, and uncle, aunt.
A word that names a person is a noun.

When groups have finished composing their verses, have a sing-along, with each group singing its verse in turn. **AUDITORY**

APPLY TO WRITING

Suggest that children add nouns to their descriptive paragraphs and their other writing, as needed, to add details.

STUDENTS ACQUIRING ENGLISH

Use pictures from magazines to reinforce nouns that name people, animals, places, and things. Have children cut out pictures, label them, and add them to a chart with the headings *People, Animals, Places,* and *Things.*

RETEACH

See page R72 for lessons in multiple modalities.

GRAMMAR PRACTICE BOOK
pages 33–34

Name ______ Six-Dinner Sid

A **noun** names a person, a place, an animal, or a thing.

Use the nouns from the picture to finish the story. You can use some nouns more than once.

The hungry __cat__ walked into the __park__ and sat down on a __bench__. A __man__ walked by and did not look at the __cat__. Then a friendly __boy__ walked up.

"Hello. Would you like some __food__?" asked the __boy__. "Come with me. My __mother__ and I will feed you."

TRY THIS! Writing: Draw your own picture of a park. Write nouns to label people, animals, places, and things.

68 NOUNS — OUT OF THE BLUE Practice Book

PRACTICE BOOK, page 68

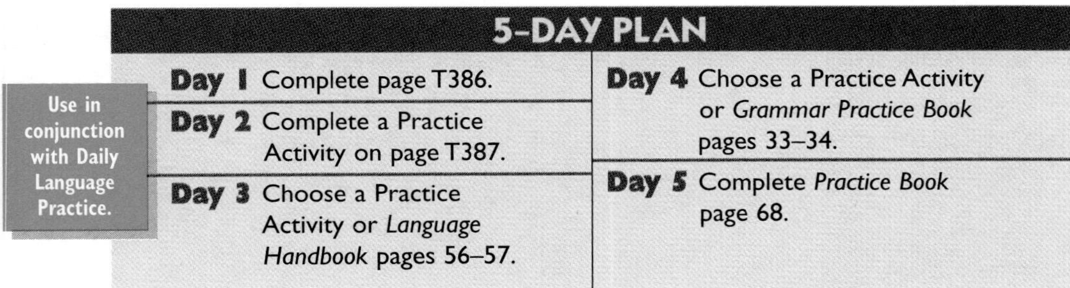
5-DAY PLAN

Use in conjunction with Daily Language Practice.

Day 1 Complete page T386.

Day 2 Complete a Practice Activity on page T387.

Day 3 Choose a Practice Activity or *Language Handbook* pages 56–57.

Day 4 Choose a Practice Activity or *Grammar Practice Book* pages 33–34.

Day 5 Complete *Practice Book* page 68.

SPELLING

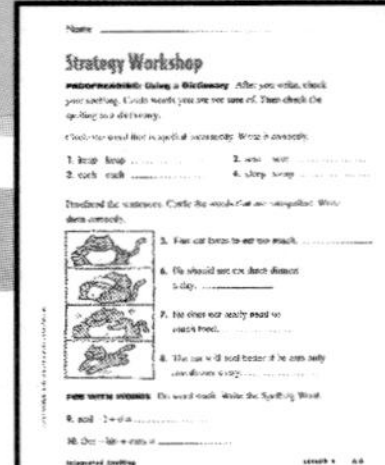

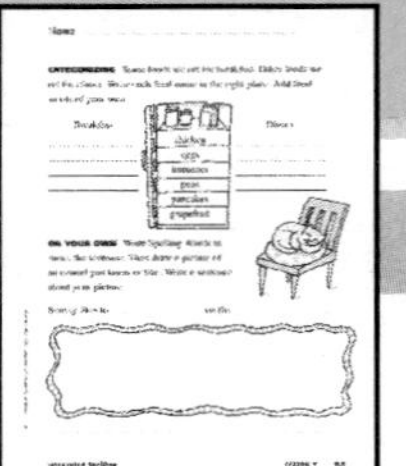

5-Day Plan

Integrated Spelling Lesson 9: student book, pages 42–45; Teacher's Edition, pages T69–T74.

SPELLING WORDS

1. need
2. eat ★
3. read
4. keep
5. team
6. feel
7. seat
8. three ★
9. sleep ★
10. each ★

STUDENT'S PERSONAL WORDS

11. 13.
12. 14.

Additional story words are *beef, easy,* and *street.*

★ Words appearing in "Six-Dinner Sid"

Words with Long *e* Spelled *ee* and *ea*

Pretest

DAY 1 **Administer the pretest.** Say each word, use it in the dictation sentence below, and repeat the word. Have pairs of children check their own pretests by referring to the word list.

OPEN SORT

DAY 2 **Have children classify words.** Have small groups create their own criteria by which to sort the Spelling Words. They might sort them into action words and nouns, by spelling pattern, or by some other attribute. Have groups share how they sorted.

CLOSED SORT

Sort by spelling pattern. Write on the board the headings from the chart below, and have volunteers write each Spelling Word under the appropriate heading. Ask children to name other words with the *ea* and *ee* spelling patterns.

Words like neat	Words like meet
eat	need
read	keep
team	feel
seat	three
each	sleep

Teach/Model

DAY 3 **Discuss the generalization.** Offer the following mnemonic device as a generalization:

When two vowels go walking, the first one does the talking.

Explain the rhyme, and tell children that it holds true for many words, including those in this lesson, but there are many exceptions. Write *eat* and *read* on the board, and ask a volunteer to explain whether these words follow the rhyme. The child should point out that these words do follow the rhyme because they have the long *e* sound, and the letter *e* comes before the *a*. Talk about how the generalization also works for words with *ee*.

DAY 4 **Apply to writing.** Children should look for words in which *ea* and *ee* stand for the long *e* sound in their descriptive paragraphs and other writing to see if they are spelled correctly.

Posttest

DAY 5 **Assess children's progress.** Use the sentences below as the posttest.

DICTATION SENTENCES

1. I need to do my homework.
2. When will we eat lunch?
3. Do you like to read books?
4. Keep this to remember me by.
5. Our team will play tomorrow.
6. I don't feel well today.
7. Sit in this seat.
8. We have three eggs left.
9. The baby will sleep soon.
10. Each of us packed a lunch.

Six-Dinner Sid Name

A. Write the Spelling Word that tells what the cat is doing in each picture. Then write the word that rhymes with it.

eat keep sleep seat

1. sleep 3. eat
2. keep 4. seat

B. Finish the puzzle with the Spelling Words in the box. Write one letter in each space.

each need read team three feel

OUT OF THE BLUE Practice Book WORDS LIKE *keep* AND *team* 69

PRACTICE BOOK, page 69

VOCABULARY WORKSHOP

Reviewing Key Words

To review how the Key Words were used in the story, distribute copies of page R116 to children. Then write the Key Words on the board.

Sid ate in six different houses.

He was fed and scratched in each one.

The neighbors didn't talk, so no one knew.

One day, Sid caught a cough.

When he went to the vet, his trick was discovered!

In the future, he'll still be Six-Dinner Sid.

Sid will live with other people on another street.

Have children, as a group, choose the word that best completes each sentence. Then have them read the sentence aloud and write the word.

Then tell children to cut apart the page to make sentence strips. Partners can mix up the strips and then work together to put them back in story order.

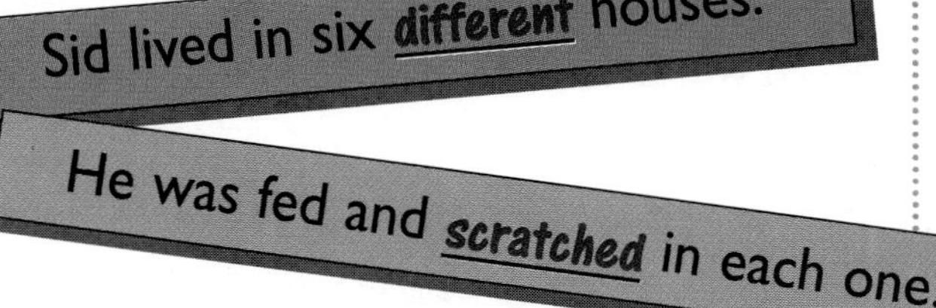

Extending Vocabulary

NUMBER WORDS

Have children reread pages 183–185 of "Six-Dinner Sid" to find words that name numbers. Then work with children to make a chart with numerals 0–19. Write each number word next to the numeral. Continue the chart with numerals 20–29, and ask children what they notice about the spelling of these number words. (They all begin with the word *twenty* plus the number words from *one* to *nine*; they have a hyphen.) Tell children that in their writing, number words instead of numerals should usually be used. Then have partners work together to practice writing number words. One partner says a number and the other partner writes the number words.

Numbers	Words	Numbers	Words
0	zero	20	twenty
1	one	21	twenty-one
2	two	22	twenty-two
3	three	23	twenty-three

STUDENTS ACQUIRING ENGLISH

Invite children to share number words from their primary language. Some children might know a counting song they'd like to share with classmates.

TAKE-HOME/ KEEP-AT-HOME BOOK

The Big Sneeze

Distribute the pages and have children make their own TAKE-HOME/ KEEP-AT-HOME BOOKS, which reinforce Key Words and known vocabulary. Children can read to partners and then take the book home to read.

INTRODUCE: PHONICS AND DECODING

Initial Clusters: str, scr

OBJECTIVE: To understand the relationship between letters and sounds

Informal Assessment ✓

Are children able to

- ☑ identify words with initial *str* and *scr* clusters?
- ☑ distinguish between words beginning with *str* and *scr*?
- ☑ read and write words beginning with *str* and *scr*?

TECHNOLOGY

Bailey's Book House **(Read-A-Rhyme)**

Teach/Model

Connect to the story. Ask children where the story began. (Aristotle Street) Write *street* on the board. Then ask children to reread page 190 of the story. Draw their attention to the word *scratched*, and write it on the board. Ask children what they notice about how the words *street* and *scratched* begin.

Phonemic awareness: Listen to the sound. Display page 14 in the *Big Book of Rhymes.* Have children listen for words with the same beginning consonant sounds as in *street* as you read the rhyme aloud. Have children listen again for words that begin like *scratched*. Then reread the rhyme. Encourage children to join in, especially for words that begin with *str* and *scr*.

Big Book of Rhymes, page 14

Find and read words with str and scr. Ask children to look in the rhyme for words that begin with the consonant clusters *str* and *scr*. As children name the words, write them on the board in appropriate columns.

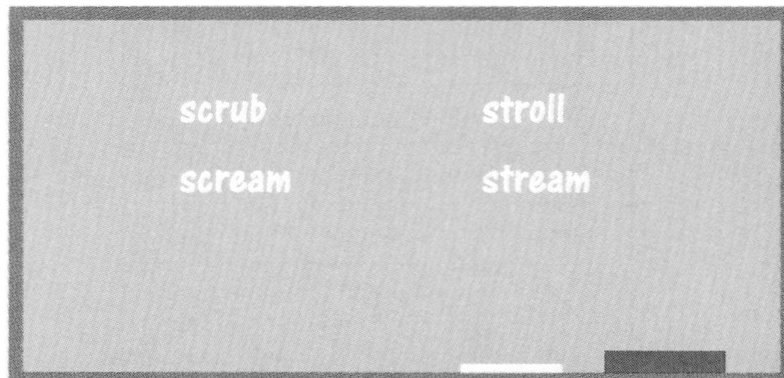

Talk about the words on the board. Encourage children to read the words *scrub* and *scream*, and identify the beginning sounds. Ask a volunteer to circle the letters that stand for the beginning sounds. Help children recognize that the beginning sounds are made by blending three letters' individual sounds—*s, c*, and *r*. Follow the same process for *stroll* and *stream*.

Practice/Apply

Read words in context. Write these sentences on the board:

Amy saw a scrap of paper hanging on a string.

How strange, she thought, and she stretched to reach it.

The writing on the strip looked like a code, but it was only scribbling.

Have children read each sentence and find two words beginning with *scr* or *str.* As children find words, have volunteers add them to the correct column on the board.

Practice Activities

Word Building

Have small groups use their Word Builders and letter cards or *Word Builder Cards* to play a game called "Screech or Strum." Using the letter cards, players make the initial consonant clusters *scr* and *str*. Then they take turns using the rest of their letter cards to make words with *scr* or *str*. After reading each word, players classify it as a *screech* or a *strum* by imitating one of those sounds. Have children create a list with the headings *screech* and *strum* and write each word under the appropriate heading. **VISUAL/AUDITORY/KINESTHETIC**

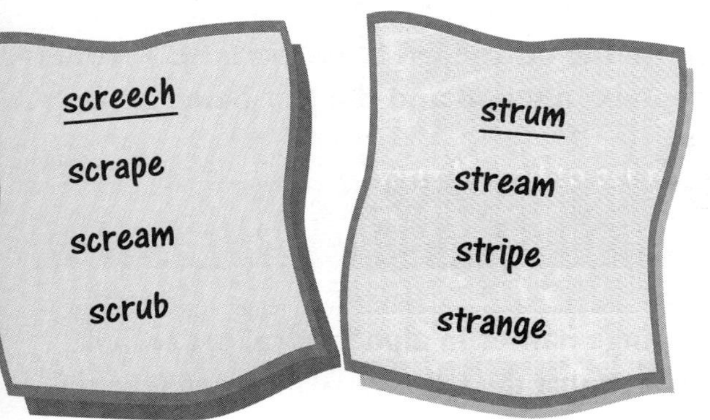

Titles with scr and str

PERFORMANCE ASSESSMENT Have partners work together to make up story titles that contain words with the initial consonant clusters *scr* and *str*. Challenge children to include one word that has each cluster. They might come up with such titles as "The Scratchy Strawberry" or "The Stray That Got Scraped." Have children write their title on a sheet of paper folded in half to resemble a book and a few sentences inside to tell about the story. **VISUAL/AUDITORY**

Strange Sentences

Have children write sentences containing the words beginning with *scr* and *str* that they listed in the Word Building activity. They can then read their sentences aloud to partners, who should raise their hand when they hear the initial consonant cluster *scr* or *str* and identify which one it is. **VISUAL/AUDITORY**

STUDENTS ACQUIRING ENGLISH

Display pictures that illustrate words like these: *stripes, strap, street, straw, screen, scratch, scribble.* Help children name and label each picture. Then use the pictures to review the initial consonant clusters *scr* and *str*.

RETEACH

See page R73 for lessons in multiple modalities.

CHALLENGE

Invite partners to make up nonsense words that begin with *str* and *scr*. They can define and illustrate their new words.

PHONICS PRACTICE BOOK, pages 197–198

PHONICS ACTIVITY BOOK, page 18

Name ________________ Six-Dinner Sid

Read the sentences. Write the word from the box that best completes each sentence.

scrub, scratched, straight, screen, scrape, stray, screeched, scraps, street, strong

1. Old Stripes was a __stray__ cat.
2. A nice family fed him __scraps__ of food.
3. Stripes just sat outside at their __screen__ door.
4. He __scratched__ when he was hungry.
5. Then he would go __straight__ to the food dish.
6. Once they tried to __scrub__ Stripes in the tub.
7. But he __screeched__ and ran out of the room.

TRY THIS! Learning Log — Make up tongue twisters using words that start with *str* and *scr*.
Steve strung the strawberries on strings.

70 INITIAL CLUSTERS: *scr, str* — OUT OF THE BLUE Practice Book

PRACTICE BOOK, page 70

Reading Trade Books FOR INITIAL CLUSTERS *str, scr*

***The House on Maple Street* by Bonnie Pryor. William Morrow, 1987.**
CHALLENGE

***Harry the Dirty Dog* by Gene Zion. HarperCollins, 1956.**
AVERAGE

PHONICS PRACTICE READER 17

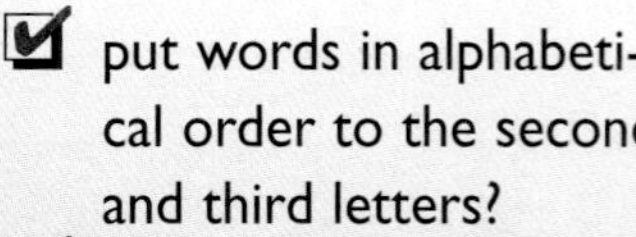

INTRODUCE: STUDY SKILLS

Alphabetical Order

OBJECTIVE: To alphabetize words to the second and third letters

Informal Assessment ✓

Are children able to

- ☑ put words in alphabetical order to the second and third letters?
- ☑ use alphabetical order to locate words in a dictionary?

Teach/Model

Connect to the story. Ask children to turn to page 195. Explain that the appointment book is one form of records that many doctors, including veterinarians, keep. Explain that doctors also keep records about their patients. The records are in ABC, or alphabetical, order so that they are easier to find.

Discuss alphabetical order. Ask children what they know about alphabetical order. Explain that alphabetical order means that words are placed in the order of the letters of the alphabet. Write these names of possible pets in a column on the board: *alligator, bird, cat*. Read them with children, and underline the first letter in each. Point out that these words are in alphabetical order. Demonstrate how if *alligator* were at the bottom of the list, the words would no longer be in alphabetical order.

Model using alphabetical order. Ask children to reread pages 188–189 and locate all the different names Sid has. List them on the board. (Sid, Scaramouche, Bob, Mischief, Sally, Sooty, Schwartz) Tell children that you want to put these names in alphabetical order. Explain that some names have the same first letter, so you will need to use the second letter to put them in alphabetical order, and if the second letter is the same, you'll have to refer to the third letter. Model alphabetizing the names:

MODEL

Bob **should be first because it begins with *B*, and *Mischief* comes next because M is the next letter in alphabetical order when looking at the first letter of all the names. I'll have to look at the second letter for the rest of the names because they all begin with *S*. *Sally* is next because *a* is the second letter, and *a* comes before *c*, which is the second letter in both *Scaramouche* and *Schwartz*. I'll have to look at the third letter for these two words. *Scaramouche* comes before *Schwartz* because *a* comes before *h*. The next name on the list is *Sid* because *Si* comes next after *Sc* and the last name is *Sooty*.**

Practice/Apply

Arrange names in alphabetical order. Tell children that the following names could be the names of Sid's owners:

Bernice Fancy	Tom Martin	Trent Franklin
Willie Brown	Betty Bridges	Karen Stone

Have partners copy the first names or the last names onto cards and put them in alphabetical order. Then children can make up their own names for the owners and alphabetize them.

Practice Activities

Sid's List

COOPERATIVE LEARNING Sid wants to make a list of items to buy at the grocery store. Have a small group work together to make a list of foods Sid would like and put the list in alphabetical order. Encourage children to use information from the story and their own knowledge about cats to think of items for the list. Then have groups share their lists. **VISUAL**

Alphabet Books

COOPERATIVE LEARNING Invite children to make letter books to donate to the school kindergarten or preschool program. Organize children into small groups. Have each group choose a letter and draw or cut out of magazines pictures with names that begin with that letter. Have the group glue each picture onto a sheet of paper, label the picture, and put the pages in alphabetical order. Ask each group to make a cover by cutting its letter's shape from sandpaper or textured fabric and gluing it onto heavy paper. **VISUAL/KINESTHETIC**

The Name Game

PERFORMANCE ASSESSMENT Organize children into groups of four or five. Provide a T-shirt outline cut from construction paper for each child. Have children write their first names on their shirts. Encourage groups to work together to arrange the shirts in alphabetical order as they pretend to hang them up to dry. Have children explain how they decided in which order to arrange the shirts. **VISUAL/KINESTHETIC**

STUDENTS ACQUIRING ENGLISH

You may wish to spend additional time reviewing the alphabet with these children. Encourage children to look at an alphabet chart or to sing an alphabet song to themselves if they need help alphabetizing words.

RETEACH

See page R74 for lessons in multiple modalities.

CHALLENGE

Provide local telephone directories, and challenge children to use alphabetical order to find their families' names in the phone book. For children whose families are not listed, have them look up the name of a friend.

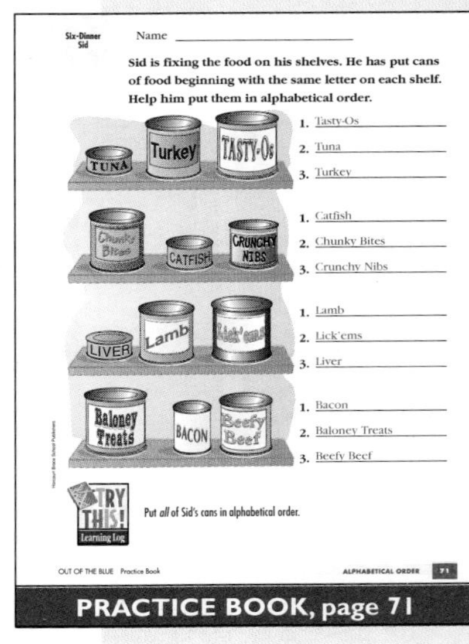

Six-Dinner Sid Name ____________

Sid is fixing the food on his shelves. He has put cans of food beginning with the same letter on each shelf. Help him put them in alphabetical order.

1. Tasty-Os
2. Tuna
3. Turkey

1. Catfish
2. Chunky Bites
3. Crunchy Nibs

1. Lamb
2. Lick'ems
3. Liver

1. Bacon
2. Baloney Treats
3. Beefy Beef

TRY THIS! Learning Log — Put *all* of Sid's cans in alphabetical order.

OUT OF THE BLUE Practice Book ALPHABETICAL ORDER 71

PRACTICE BOOK, page 71

FOR ALPHABETICAL ORDER

***Miss Hindy's Cats* by Helena C. Pittman. Carolrhoda, 1990.** AVERAGE

***Annie, Bea, and Chi Chi Dolores: A School Day Alphabet* by Donna Maurer. Orchard, 1993.** EASY

Integrated Curriculum

SCIENCE

Cats

TIPS FOR CLASSROOM MANAGEMENT

IF children have difficulty keeping track of the children who have and haven't answered their survey questions in the Take a Survey activity, **THEN** suggest that they record classmates' names as they ask their questions.

MATH

Measure with Whiskers

MATERIALS
- rulers
- construction paper
- stapler
- scissors

LEARNING CENTER Explain that cats use their whiskers to measure whether or not they can fit through a certain space. If a cat can get its head through a space without its whiskers touching the sides, it will be able to get its whole body through. Have children cut three narrow strips of construction paper in six-inch lengths. Have them staple the strips to make a set of whiskers.

Provide boxes with cutouts or blocks stacked to form openings for children to measure. Have children hold up the whiskers they made and see whether a cat with those whiskers could fit through that space. Have children record their findings and discuss them. LISTENING/SPEAKING/WRITING

SCIENCE

All in the Cat Family

MATERIALS
- poster board
- markers
- nonfiction books about the cat family

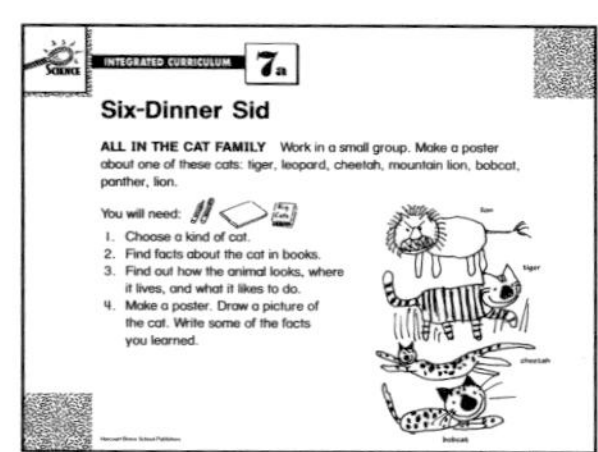
INTEGRATED CURRICULUM 7a

Six-Dinner Sid

ALL IN THE CAT FAMILY Work in a small group. Make a poster about one of these cats: tiger, leopard, cheetah, mountain lion, bobcat, panther, lion.

You will need:

1. Choose a kind of cat.
2. Find facts about the cat in books.
3. Find out how the animal looks, where it lives, and what it likes to do.
4. Make a poster. Draw a picture of the cat. Write some of the facts you learned.

Curriculum Card 7a

COOPERATIVE LEARNING Have children work in small groups to create a fact poster about a wild member of the cat family, such as a lion, a tiger, or a leopard. Each group can select a different cat to research in books you provide. As children learn about their cat, they can create a poster showing and telling how the cat looks, where it lives, and what its habits are. LISTENING/SPEAKING/READING/WRITING

SOCIAL STUDIES

Take a Survey

MATERIALS
- paper
- pencils or markers
- poster board

COOPERATIVE LEARNING Invite groups of three or four children to survey classmates or neighbors they know to find out how many people do and do not have cats. Partners may move around the classroom and ask classmates whether or not they have a cat. One child may ask the questions, and another may record the responses using a tally chart.

	Yes	No	Total Asked
Do you have a cat?	卌 卌	卌 卌 III	23

When groups are finished, encourage them to share their information and compile a class tally. LISTENING/SPEAKING/WRITING

CREATIVE DRAMATICS

Act Like a Cat

MATERIALS
- 1 extra-long pipe cleaner and 2 regular-length ones per child

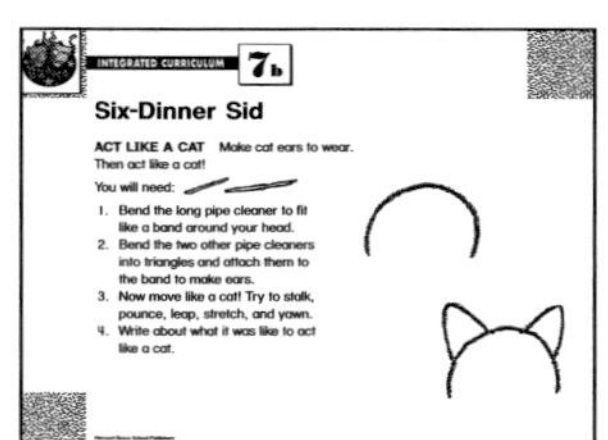
INTEGRATED CURRICULUM 7b

Six-Dinner Sid

ACT LIKE A CAT Make cat ears to wear. Then act like a cat!

You will need:

1. Bend the long pipe cleaner to fit like a band around your head.
2. Bend the two other pipe cleaners into triangles and attach them to the band to make ears.
3. Now move like a cat! Try to stalk, pounce, leap, stretch, and yawn.
4. Write about what it was like to act like a cat.

Curriculum Card 7b

Invite children to fashion cat ears by bending the long pipe cleaner to fit like a band around their head. They can bend the other two pipe cleaners into triangular shapes and attach them to the band to look like cat ears. Invite children to wear their cat ears and move like cats. Call out a movement, such as *stalk, pounce, leap, stretch, yawn*, or *wash*, and have children enact the movement. You may want to show a movie or video that includes cats so that children can observe them before imitating their movements. Have children write a few sentences describing how it feels to behave like a cat. Invite volunteers to share their writing.

LISTENING/SPEAKING/WRITING

Reading Trade Books

CROSS-CURRICULAR READING

Annie and the Wild Animals **by Jan Brett. Houghton Mifflin, 1993.** AVERAGE

Have You Seen My Cat? **by Eric Carle. Simon & Schuster, 1991.** EASY

How Big? How Fast? How Hungry? A Book About Cats **by B. Waverly. Raintree / Steck-Vaughn, 1990.** EASY

MULTI-AGE CLASSROOMS

In the Take a Survey activity, older children can help younger children mark their tally charts and also accompany them if they conduct the survey outside the classroom.

Reading Trade Books

TIPS FOR CLASSROOM MANAGEMENT

PARTNERS
Have partners read the book together. Before reading, they can decide how they will read the story and where they will pause to discuss what they've read.

SMALL GROUP
Read the book in a small circle of children. As you read aloud, pause to ask children to make and revise their predictions of what will happen next.

For a comprehensive lesson plan, refer to the complete lesson plan for *Mary Ann* on pages T458–T461.

Mary Ann

by Betsy James

Signatures Library

READER'S CHALLENGE
The neighbors on Aristotle Street all thought Sid was their own pet. How did they take care of him? Have you ever had an insect as a pet? How would you take care of it? What's different about caring for a cat and caring for an insect?

READING STRATEGY: MAKING PREDICTIONS

Have children predict what will happen at different points in the story. If children need prompting, use questions such as these:

- **What will Amy do now that Mary Ann has moved away?**
- **Do you think the eggs will hatch? Why or why not?**
- **Where are Amy and her family going? Why do you think so?**

LINK TO THE THEME

Children who are reading *Mary Ann* may want to discuss the following questions:

- **How can you tell that Amy and Mary Ann are friends?**
- **How is Mary Ann's move different from Sid's move?**

RESPONSE ACTIVITY: FINDING FACTS

Have partners choose an insect and read about it in a book or a magazine. Then encourage them to draw a picture of the insect and write what they learned about it. Display children's work.

Other Trade Books

Charlie Anderson

by Barbara Abercrombie
illustrated by Mark Graham

Ask children to tell about Charlie Anderson's two homes and whether they think both Charlie Anderson and the girls are lucky. Then have children make an illustrated chart by first drawing a line down the center of a sheet of paper. On one side, they should draw something Charlie might do with the girls, and on the other, something Anderson might do with his other family.

Everybody Cooks Rice

by Norah Dooley
illustrated by Peter J. Thornton

Ask children whether they like rice. Suggest that they collect the names and recipes for some of their families' favorite rice dishes. Invite each child to share a favorite rice dish for a page in a class book.

Switch Cat

by Garry Disher
illustrated by Andrew McLean

Help children recall Sid's different names and the ways he acted in each of the six houses on Aristotle Street. Ask children to tell about how the cats in *Switch Cat* were able to end up with their rightful owners. Encourage children to tell what they liked or didn't like about the story.

MEETING INDIVIDUAL NEEDS

STUDENTS ACQUIRING ENGLISH

Some children may want to follow along as a partner who is proficient in English reads aloud the story.

CHALLENGE

Have children choose one of the books and tell how the story is different from and similar to "Six-Dinner Sid."

Trade Books

PROJECT MANAGEMENT

- PROJECT LAUNCH
- CHECKPOINT 1
- CHECKPOINT 2
- CHECKPOINT 3
- CHECKPOINT 4
- PRESENTATIONS
- ASSESSMENT

Make Rules for the Center

SELECTION CONNECTION

"Six-Dinner Sid" moves to a new neighborhood so he can be sure of eating his six meals. The new neighbors talk to one another. Ask children to compare the neighborhoods and talk about the benefits of communicating with other people.

PROJECT CHECKLIST

During this stage, children should

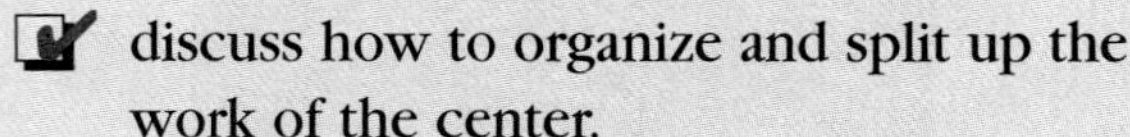
discuss how to organize and split up the work of the center.

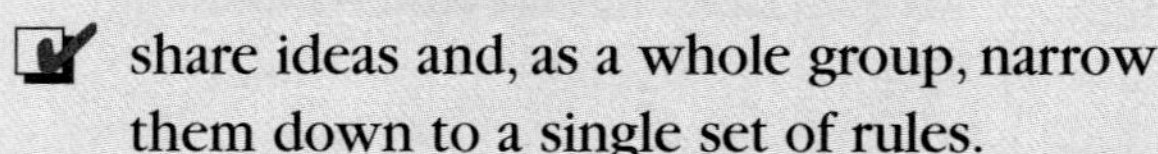
share ideas and, as a whole group, narrow them down to a single set of rules.

write the rules on chart paper and display them in the mail center.

THEME PROJECT CHECKPOINT 3 10

Make a Mail Center

MAKE RULES FOR THE CENTER

1. Make rules for your post office.
   - What can we mail?
   - When can we mail letters?
   - When can we check mailboxes?
   - Who will deliver mail each day?
2. Write down your rules.

Project Card 10

When children have completed this checkpoint, have them think about the rules they established for the center. Have them write in their Project Journals about how the rules will help the center run smoothly.

Project Card 10 can be found as a copying master on page R90.

PLANNING TIPS

As children prepare rules for the mail center, suggest that they

- think of how to solve problems like noise, crowding, and lack of cooperation.
- develop rules to take care of each problem.
- develop rules to make sure everyone is treated fairly.

Informal Assessment

As children complete this checkpoint, they will **make judgments, evaluate, solve problems,** and **make decisions** about the running of the mail center. Children are thinking critically if they

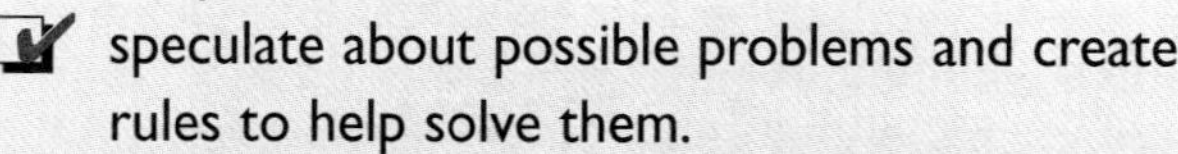
analyze ideas.

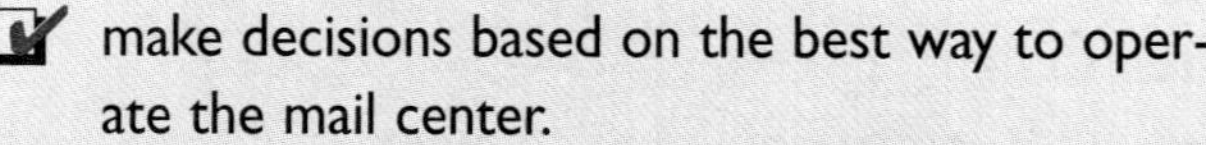
speculate about possible problems and create rules to help solve them.

make decisions based on the best way to operate the mail center.

STUDENTS ACQUIRING ENGLISH

Have children discuss with English-proficient peers possible solutions to potential mail center problems. Encourage them to share their ideas with the whole group.

EXTRA SUPPORT

Use the mail center yourself, both to receive and distribute mail. It can be a useful device for boosting some children's morale, especially those who might not get much mail from classmates.

Rosie the Visiting Dog

by Stephanie Calmenson

THEME CONNECTION

"Rosie the Visiting Dog" illustrates the importance of relationships between people and animals. Rosie makes people feel loved and accepted, and Rosie is loved in return. This article expands upon the theme of friendship by showing how an animal can be a special friend and companion.

ABOUT THE AUTHOR

Stephanie Calmenson is Rosie's owner. When she was a girl, she was never allowed to have a dog. When she grew up, she got Rosie. About Rosie, Calmenson says, "She turned out to be so sweet, I wanted to share her with as many people as I could. That is why we joined the visiting dog program." Calmenson takes Rosie to visit people in her New York neighborhood. Stephanie Calmenson is the author of many books for children, including *The Principal's New Clothes* and *Dinner at the Panda Palace*.

ABOUT THE PHOTOGRAPHER

Justin Sutcliffe, an award-winning photojournalist, has had his photographs published in many magazines, including *Time*, *Life*, and *People*. He says, "Photographing Rosie presented unusual challenges and opportunities."

SUMMARY

GENRE: Nonfiction

Rosie is a dog who has been specially trained. She and her owner visit people, such as the elderly or handicapped, and help cheer them up and make them feel better. Rosie has been taught to be a gentle, patient visitor. She makes friends quickly with people of all ages and brings them happiness.

STUDENTS ACQUIRING ENGLISH

Pair second-language learners with children who are native speakers of English. As the native English speaker reads each caption, his or her partner follows along and echo-reads each sentence. After children have read each caption, they can talk about the photograph it describes.

Introducing the Article

PRIOR KNOWLEDGE
Talk with children about dogs. Invite children whose families have dogs as pets to share information about their dogs. Then bring up the topic of working dogs. Make a chart like the one below and have children help you fill in roles that dogs that are pets play for their owners, as well as their ideas about working dogs.

Dogs as Pets	Work Dogs
playmates	guard dogs
companions	police dogs
show dogs	Seeing Eye dogs
watch dogs	sheep dogs
	hearing dogs for hearing impaired

Then ask a volunteer to read the title of the article. Ask children whether they think this article is about a pet or a working dog, and why.

Reading an Article Point out that the article is made of photographs and captions. Tell children that this article is about a real dog and the work she does.

Rosie the Visiting Dog

Meet Rosie. She is a special kind of pet. She visits people to make them feel better.

Rosie went to a special school to become a visiting dog. She learned a lot of things, like how to be patient and never grab at food.

She also learned to be gentle with those who might be rough with her, even though they don't mean to.

202

TIPS FOR CLASSROOM MANAGEMENT

SMALL GROUP

LITERATURE CIRCLES
Children can take turns reading each caption. After each caption is read, the child who read it should comment on it. Other children can then add ideas and comments of their own. After children finish reading, have them discuss their thoughts about and feelings for Rosie.

WHOLE CLASS

INDEPENDENT READING
Children may read the article independently. As they finish reading, have them write their reactions to Rosie in their journals. When everyone has finished the article, have children use what they wrote in their journals as a starting point to discuss what they have read.

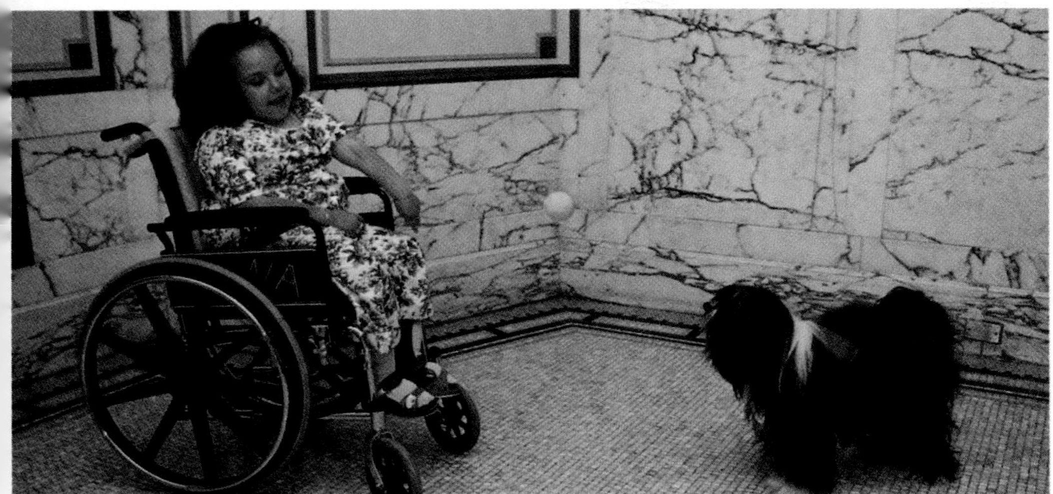

This girl is having fun playing fetch with Rosie.

Sometimes Rosie sits with people who are sad. Her friendship soon cheers them up.

This boy, who is blind, likes to brush Rosie's fur. He loves being with her. So do many other people. Rosie is a good visiting dog—and also a very good friend!

203

Responding to the Article

Lead children in a discussion of the article and how it relates to other stories they have been reading in this theme. You might want to ask how Rosie is like Tabby from "Mr. Putter and Tabby Pour the Tea," for example, or how Rosie and Sid from "Six-Dinner Sid" are alike. Encourage children to talk about the idea that people can have all different sorts of friendships.

SCIENCE

HELPING MONKEYS Dogs aren't the only animals that help people. Some capuchin (kə•po͞oʹsh ən) monkeys are trained to assist physically disabled people. These monkeys can serve food or beverages, get a book, put an audiocassette in a player, and replace a mouthstick that has fallen out of its owner's mouth. (A mouthstick is a tool used for typing on the computer, turning book pages, and using a phone.)

CHALLENGE Explain that this magazine article is also part of a book of the same title. Challenge interested readers to read the book *Rosie the Visiting Dog* and share new information they learn about Rosie with classmates.

Integrating Language Arts

TIPS FOR CLASSROOM MANAGEMENT

IF computers and a word-processing program are available, **THEN** have children write their letters for the Writing activity on a computer.

WRITING

Write a Letter

Do children know anyone who would benefit from a visit from Rosie? Could Rosie make that person feel better? Suggest that children write a letter to the person they chose, telling about Rosie and other dogs like her. Encourage children to make a neat copy of their letter, prepare an envelope, and then mail it to the person.

READING/WRITING

November 3

Dear Grammy,

I read a story about a visiting dog named Rosie. She visits people and helps cheer them up. I thought a visiting dog might help cheer you up. I'd like to visit you too.

Love,
Holly

ORAL LANGUAGE

Let's Talk!

Discuss each photograph with children. Invite children to speculate about who the people are, where they live, what they like to do, how they feel about Rosie, and so forth. Then tell children to work in pairs to tell "the rest of the story" about the people in the photographs. One child can be a person in a photo. The partner asks the first child questions about Rosie's visits and some other things that person does every day. Children can reverse roles and repeat the question-and-answer process.

LISTENING/SPEAKING

Abuela

by Arthur Dorros
illustrated by Elisa Kleven

ALA Notable Book

Notable Trade Book in Socal Studies

THEME: FRIENDSHIP

We Belong Together

In "Abuela," children will further explore the theme of relationships. Children will see what a girl and her grandmother "do" for fun.

SELECTION SUMMARY

Genre: Fantasy

A girl imagines that she and her grandmother fly over New York City. On this extraordinary adventure, they glide past parks, buildings, and streets, out over the sea, and into the clouds. Spanish words and phrases add another dimension to the text that describes this fantastic journey.

Arthur Dorros

ABOUT THE AUTHOR AND THE ILLUSTRATOR

ARTHUR DORROS is the author of many picture books. *Abuela* was named an ALA Notable Book for Children and a Notable Trade Book in Social Studies.

ELISA KLEVEN has both illustrated and written many books for children.

For more information about the author and the illustrator, see page T429.

Elisa Kleven

SUGGESTED LESSON PLANNER

▶ ***Abuela***

	DAY 1	DAY 2
PART 1 Reading, Listening, Speaking, Viewing **Key Words** cousin adventure touch country building says whole	**BUILD BACKGROUND** T406 **VOCABULARY STRATEGIES** T406–T407 *Chart/Transparency 17* *Practice Book* pp. 75–76 **READING THE SELECTION** T408–T429 Options for Reading T408–T409 *Response Card 2* *Literature Cassette 1* **REVIEW PREDICTIONS/PURPOSE** T426 **APPRECIATING THE LITERATURE** T426 NOTE: Children may read the selection on Day 2.	**SUMMARIZE AND RETELL THE SELECTION** T427 *Practice Book* p. 77 ◆ **RESPONSE CORNER ACTIVITIES** T430 **CHECKING COMPREHENSION** T431 *End-of-Selection Test* 
PART 2 Writer's Workshop	**AN INVITATION AND ENVELOPE** Thinking as Writers T436 *Chart/Transparency 18*	Prewriting T436
Grammar	✓ **NAMES OF SPECIAL PEOPLE, ANIMALS, AND PLACES** Teach the Concept T438 Daily Language Practice (1–2) R83	Daily Language Practice (3–4) R83 Practice Activity T439
Spelling	**WORDS WITH LONG *o* SPELLED *oa* AND *ow*** *boat row load low slow* *coat coast own road show* Pretest/Self-Check T440 *Integrated Spelling Teacher's Edition* pp. T75, T277	Open and Closed Sorts T440 *Integrated Spelling* p. 46 *Integrated Spelling Teacher's Edition* p. T76
PART 3 Phonics	**LONG VOWEL: /ō/*o, oa, o-e*** Phonics-Vocabulary Connection T407	**PHONICS AND DECODING MINILESSON** T413 ✓ R-Controlled Vowel: /ûr/*ear, ir, er, ur* (Review) *Phonics Activity Book* pp. 23–24 *Practice Book* p. 83
Skills and Strategies	◆ **INTEGRATED CURRICULUM** *The City* **Social Studies** T446 **Art** T446 **Math** T447 **Science** T447 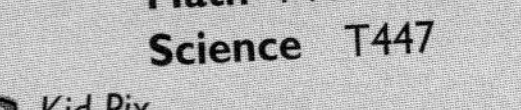 *Kid Pix* *Imagination Express, Destination: Neighborhood*	**COMPREHENSION SKILL** T442–T443 Context Clues (Introduce) *Practice Book* p. 81

Use the Students Acquiring English notes on pages T413, T421, and T424 to help **ESL readers**.

To help children build fluency, use the *Instant Readers™ One Quiet Afternoon* and *Country Family, City Family* on pages T432–T433.

NOTE: An alternative lesson plan for **below-level readers** appears on *Intervention Strategies Manual* pp. 44–49. A lesson for **students acquiring English** appears on *Sheltered English/ESL Manual* pp. 30–33.

DAY 3	DAY 4	DAY 5
◆ **IDEA BANK ACTIVITIES** Listening and Speaking T434 Real-Life Reading: Reading Company Names and Logos T434 Oral Language T435 Kinesthetic T435 *Writer's Magazine* pp. 28–31 *Imagination Express, Destination: Neighborhood* *Living Book: Just Grandma and Me* School–Home Connection 8 R113	**VOCABULARY WORKSHOP** T441 Reviewing Key Words Story Strips R117 Spanish Words Used in English *Practice Book* p. 80 *Take-Home/Keep-at-Home Book: I Can Go Anyplace* **READING TRADE BOOKS** T448–T449  Take-Home Book	**READING TRADE BOOKS** T443, T445, T447, T448–T449 
Drafting T436 *Language Handbook* pp. 14–15, 17 *The Amazing Writing Machine*	Responding and Revising T437	Proofreading and Publishing T437 *Kid Pix*
Daily Language Practice (5–6) R83 Practice Activity T439 *Language Handbook* pp. 58–61	Daily Language Practice (7–8) R83 Practice Activity T439 *Grammar Practice Book* pp. 35–38	Daily Language Practice (9–12) R83 *Practice Book* p. 78
Discuss the Generalization T440 *Integrated Spelling* p. 47 *Integrated Spelling Teacher's Edition* p. T77	Apply to Writing T440 *Integrated Spelling* pp. 48–49 *Integrated Spelling Teacher's Edition* pp. T78–T79	Posttest T440 *Practice Book* p. 79 *Integrated Spelling Teacher's Edition* p. T80
PHONICS AND DECODING MINILESSON T415 Long Vowel: /ā/*ay, ai, a-e* (Maintain) *Phonics Activity Book* pp. 25–26 *Phonics Game Board Pattern Book* pp. 32–33 *Phonics Practice Reader 7: A Great Place to Play* *Phonics Practice Book* pp. 65–76 *Practice Book* p. 84	**PHONICS AND DECODING MINILESSON** T423 Long Vowel: /ō/*o, oa* (Maintain) *Phonics Activity Book* p. 27 *Phonics Game Board Pattern Book* pp. 34, 35, 44 *Phonics Practice Reader 8: Jo Frog and Joan Toad* *Phonics Practice Book* pp. 77–91 *Practice Book* p. 85	
GRAMMAR MINILESSON T411 ✓ Nouns (Review) *Language Handbook* pp. 56–57	**STUDY SKILL** T444–T445 Reference Sources (Dictionary, Glossary) (Introduce) *Practice Book* p. 82 *Kid Pix*	Theme Project Checkpoint 4 T450

Above-level writers may complete the Writer's Workshop independently at their own pace.

During the Reference Sources lesson, refer to the Students Acquiring English note on page T445 to help **ESL readers**.

Below-level and **ESL readers** may read the *ESL/Title I Library* book *Bein' With You This Way.*

✓ = Tested Skill
◆ = Optional activities that may be used to adjust pacing throughout the lesson
Titles in *italics* are optional materials.

BUILDING BACKGROUND AND CONCEPTS

PRIOR KNOWLEDGE

Draw a neighborhood picture. Invite children to brainstorm a list of places in your community. Then have small groups choose one place and draw a picture of how that place might look from an airplane. Invite the groups to share their completed pictures with classmates. They can guess the place each group has drawn. Talk about how things look different from above than they do from the ground.

VOCABULARY STRATEGIES

KEY WORDS DEFINED

cousin son or daughter of an aunt or uncle

country a nation

says tells in words

adventure an exciting experience

building a place built for people to live or do things in

whole complete; all of

touch to put the hand or another part of the body on or against something

SUPPORT WORDS

Display the words *carried, factories, harbor, soared,* and *surrounds.* Discuss their meanings and have them used in sentences.

INTEGRATED SPELLING

SPELLING PRETEST: page T440

SPELLING GENERALIZATION: Words with long *o* spelled *oa* and *ow*

MEETING INDIVIDUAL NEEDS

Intervention Strategies

For children who may have difficulty reading "Abuela," support is available in *Intervention Strategies Manual,* pages 44–49, and on pages T420 and T432–T433 in this lesson.

STUDENTS ACQUIRING ENGLISH

See *Sheltered English/ESL Manual,* pages 30–33.

TIPS FOR TEACHERS

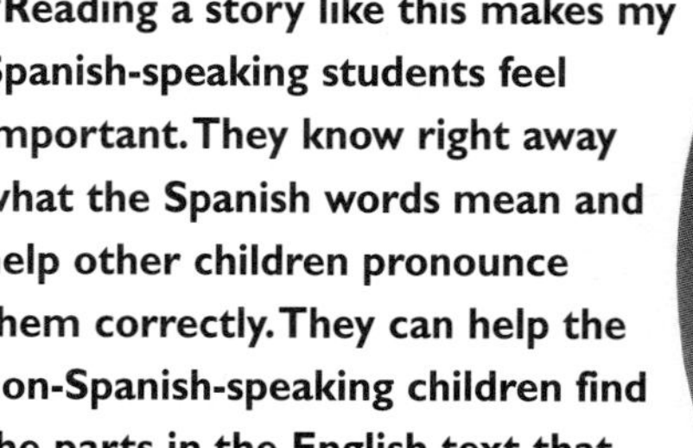

"Reading a story like this makes my Spanish-speaking students feel important. They know right away what the Spanish words mean and help other children pronounce them correctly. They can help the non-Spanish-speaking children find the parts in the English text that translate the Spanish parts."

CUEING SYSTEMS

Have children read new vocabulary. Display Chart/Transparency 17, or write the words and sentences on the board. Have children read the words they know.

Cover all the letters except the *c* in the words *cousin* and *country*. Have children read the first sentence and suggest the missing words. As children respond, ask:

> **What sound begins each word? Which letter stands for that sound? Do the words make sense in the sentence?**

Have children read the rest of the story silently. Encourage them to use the beginning sounds and sense of the story to help them figure out the underlined words.

CHART/TRANSPARENCY 17

cousin country says adventure
building whole touch

My cousin lives in another country far away. We like to write letters to each other. Sometimes she visits me. She says her visits are a great adventure. The last time she came here, we went to the top of a tall building. We were so high that we could see the whole city. We felt like we could even touch the sky.

HANDS-ON ACTIVITY

Play a game. Have children write the Key Words on cards and write their initials on the back. Then have them place the cards face up in different parts of the room. Explain that they will be picking up cards according to clues that you will read. Children don't have to pick up their own cards, just any card with the correct word on it. Children find and hold up words as you give these directions:

Show me the word that. . .

rhymes with *pole.* (*whole*)
tells what the United States is. (*country*)
names a member of a family. (*cousin*)
tells what I can do with my hand. (*touch*)
means "tells." (*says*)
is something exciting. (*adventure*)
names what a school is. (*building*)

PRACTICE BOOK, pages 75–76

PHONICS-VOCABULARY CONNECTION

WORD PLAY

Write the following words on the board and on word cards: *oak*, *soak*, *gold*, *whole*, *old*, *cloak*, *mole*, *told*, *pole*, *sold*. Read the words aloud, and ask what children notice about them. (All of the words have the long *o* sound; some of the words rhyme.)

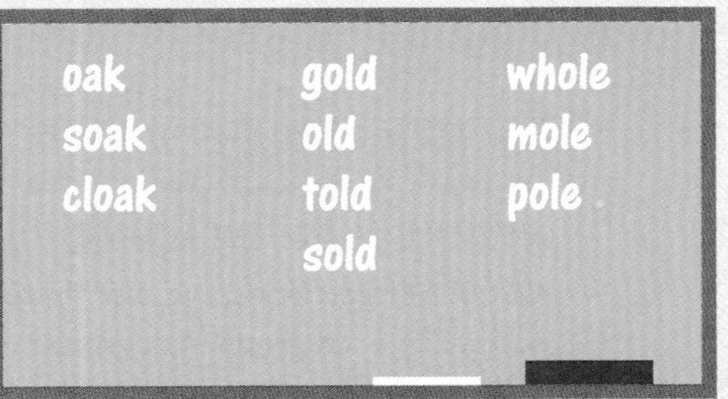

Invite children to classify the words, either using the cards or writing them on the board. Have them group together all the words that rhyme. Then ask children to look at the lists of rhyming words on the board and tell what they notice about each set of words. (They all have the same spellings for the long *o* sound.) Review with children these spellings for the long *o* sound: *oa*, *o*, *o-e*.

The concept of long *o* is reviewed on page T423.

Strategic Reading

STRATEGY FOCUS:
USING CONTEXT CLUES

Review with children some of the things good readers do. Add new responses to their classroom chart.

What Good Readers Do
Look for clues to story events in the pictures
Guess what might happen next
Use pictures and other words to help figure out something in the story

Share with children the comprehension strategy that is the focus of this selection.

MODEL

When I read, I use clues in the story to help me figure out something I don't understand. For example, if I don't know the word *mountain*, but the sentence says that someone climbs to the top of it, I would think that the word probably says "mountain." Sometimes I reread parts of the story to find clues that tell me about something I didn't understand the first time.

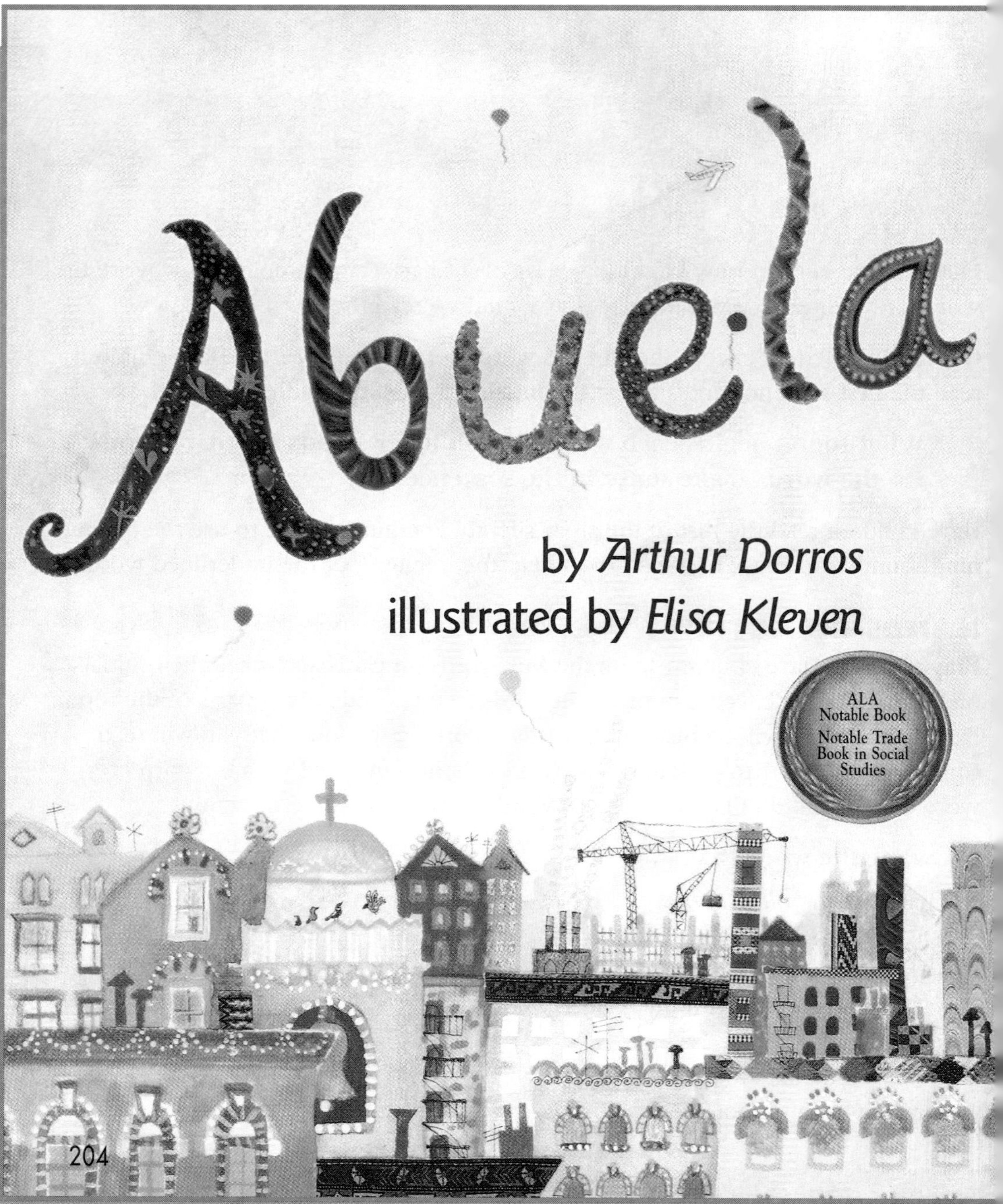

Abuela

by *Arthur Dorros*
illustrated by *Elisa Kleven*

ALA Notable Book
Notable Trade Book in Social Studies

204

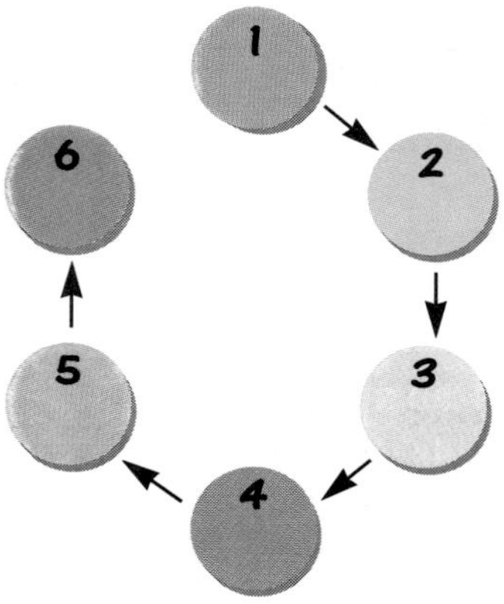

SMALL GROUP

STORY-MAP READING

Cut out large circles, and distribute several to each group. Ask groups to keep track of important story events as they read and write each event on a circle. Have them number the circles as they make them. Then have each group use its circles to make a circular story map. Groups can reread their story maps to review the story.

1 → 2 → 3 → 4 → 5 → 6

COOPERATIVE READING

PARTNER READING **Partners may take turns reading "Abuela" aloud. Tell partners to read to different stopping points, at which time each talks about the story. Suggest that children use Reader Response Card 2 (Setting), page R86, when they discuss the story.**

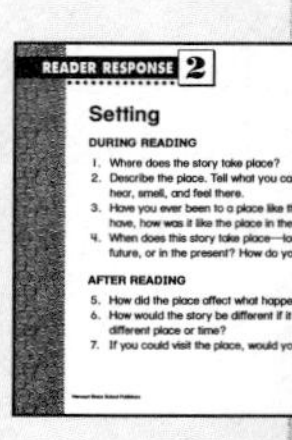

Response C

205

PREVIEWING/ SETTING PURPOSES

Help children read the title on page 204, and explain that *Abuela* is a Spanish word. Ask if children know what *abuela* means. Invite children to preview the first few pages of the story to see if they can figure out who Abuela is. (Rosalba's grandmother) Next, ask children to make predictions about the story and write their predictions in their journals. Then help children set their purposes for reading.

WHOLE CLASS

READ ALOUD

Read "Abuela" aloud as children follow along in their books. As you read each Spanish word or phrase, you may want to show children how to look up its meaning in the Spanish-English glossary on page 224.

STRATEGIC READING

Choose some or all of the suggestions and questions under Strategic Reading, pages T408–T428, to guide a literature discussion and model the STRATEGY FOCUS of Using Context Clues.

Strategic Reading

MODELING A STRATEGY

PAGES 206–207 Invite children to find Spanish words on the pages (*El parque es lindo; Tantos pájaros*), and ask them how they can figure out what those words mean. Model how children can use the sentences in English to figure out the meaning of the Spanish words and phrases with which they may not be familiar. **Think aloud:** El parque es lindo.... *I wonder what Abuela is saying. The next sentence says, "I know what she means." The one after that says, "I think the park is beautiful too."* Parque *sounds a little like* park. *I think* El parque es lindo *means "The park is beautiful."* USING CONTEXT CLUES

Abuela takes me on the bus.
We go all around the city.

Abuela is my grandma.
She is my mother's mother.
Abuela means "grandma" in Spanish.
Abuela speaks mostly Spanish because that's what people spoke where she grew up, before she came to this country.
Abuela and I are always going places.

Today we're going to the park.
"*El parque es lindo,*" says Abuela.
I know what she means.
I think the park is beautiful too.

"*Tantos pájaros,*" Abuela says as a flock of birds surrounds us.
So many birds.
They're picking up the bread we brought.

206

LISTENING CENTER

"Abuela" is available on *Literature Cassette 1*. Some children may benefit from listening to the story and following along in their books.

CONVENTIONS OF PRINT

ITALICS Call attention to the words in italics on page 206. Point out that these are Spanish words. Tell children that there will be other Spanish words in this story and that these words will always be in the same kind of type. Explain that this kind of type is called *italics* and that words from other languages are often printed in italics. Ask children to share how knowing this can help them read "Abuela."

Tested Skill

MINILESSON

REVIEW: GRAMMAR

Nouns

INFORMAL ASSESSMENT
As children speak, read, and write, notice whether they identify and use nouns correctly.

TEACH/MODEL
Remind children that a word that names a person, an animal, a place, or a thing is called a noun. Write the following sentences on the board:

The girl goes to the park.

The girl feeds bread to the birds.

Invite volunteers to circle the nouns in each sentence. *(girl, park; girl, bread, birds)*

Ask children to identify the noun that names a person *(girl)*, an animal *(bird)*, a place *(park)*, and a thing. *(bread)*

PRACTICE/APPLY
Write the words *person, animal, place*, and *thing* as headings for columns on the board. Invite children to find nouns on page 206 that fit each category. Call on volunteers to write the nouns in the appropriate column.

Have children write the same headings on a sheet of paper. Challenge them to fill in their charts by writing as many nouns as they can. Encourage children to share their lists with classmates.

LANGUAGE HANDBOOK
Nouns, pages 56–57

SOCIAL STUDIES CONNECTION

SPANISH-SPEAKING COUNTRIES
Remind children that the girl's grandmother comes from a place where the people speak Spanish. Display a world map and point out Spanish-speaking countries, such as Mexico, Panama, and Argentina. Invite children to trace the route Abuela might have taken from one of these countries to get to New York City.

Strategic Reading

APPLYING A STRATEGY

PAGES 208–209 Before children read, have them look at the pictures and tell what they think is happening. After children read page 209, ask them what is happening in the story and what clues in the words or pictures make them think as they do. You might want to use the following questions:

1. **What are Rosalba and Abuela doing? How do you know?**
2. **Which words or sentences let you know that Rosalba and Abuela are flying like birds?**
3. **Which parts of the story are real and which are made up? How can you tell?**

USING CONTEXT CLUES

208

EXPANDING VOCABULARY

SIMILES Ask children to read the first paragraph and identify the phrase that tells how Rosalba would move. (*Swooping like a bird*) Point out how this phrase compares Rosalba to a bird. Ask children to think of other phrases that make comparisons.

SCIENCE

BIRDS' FLIGHT When birds flap their wings, the parts of the wing closest to the bird's body move up and down. The outer parts of the wing move up and down, but also twist forward, which is how birds move forward through the air. Birds also overlap their feathers on downstrokes so air can't pass through, and twist them open on upstrokes.

What if they picked me up, and carried me high above the park?
What if I could fly?
Abuela would wonder where I was.
Swooping like a bird, I'd call to her.

Then she'd see me flying.
Rosalba the bird.
"*Rosalba el pájaro,*" she'd say.
"*Ven, Abuela.* Come, Abuela," I'd say.
"*Sí, quiero volar,*" Abuela would reply as she leaped into the sky with her skirt flapping in the wind.

209

Tested Skill

MINILESSON

REVIEW: PHONICS AND DECODING

R-Controlled Vowel: /ûr/*ear, ir, er, ur*

INFORMAL ASSESSMENT

As children read, notice whether they use the /ûr/ sound when called for in decoding words that contain *ear, ir, er,* or *ur*.

TEACH/MODEL

Write *Swooping like a bird, I'd call to her* on the board, and ask children what words have the same vowel sound as *fur.* (*bird, her*) Call on volunteers to circle the letters in the words that stand for the vowel sound. (*ir, er*) Write the words *heard* and *hurt* on the board, and ask children to tell which letters stand for the vowel sound. (*ear, ur*) Remind children that *ear, ir, er,* and *ur* can all stand for the vowel sound in *bird, heard, her,* and *hurt.*

PRACTICE/APPLY

Write these words on index cards: *girl, shirt, skirt, stir, heard, her, serve, perch, burn, hurt, curl, fur.* Place the cards in a pocket chart or on the chalk ledge.

Invite children to write a sentence using one of the words. Collect the sentences, and read them one at a time. Invite volunteers to name the word with the same vowel sound as *fur* in each sentence and find the corresponding word card.

PHONICS ACTIVITY BOOK, pages 23–24

STUDENTS ACQUIRING ENGLISH **Some children may not understand the meanings of the words *leaped* and *flapping*. Ask volunteers to demonstrate the words by leaping up and making flapping motions with their arms.**

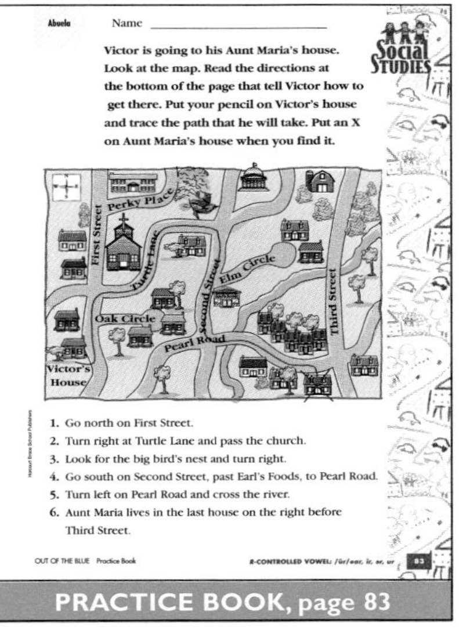

Abuela Name ____________

Victor is going to his Aunt Maria's house. Look at the map. Read the directions at the bottom of the page that tell Victor how to get there. Put your pencil on Victor's house and trace the path that he will take. Put an X on Aunt Maria's house when you find it.

1. Go north on First Street.
2. Turn right at Turtle Lane and pass the church.
3. Look for the big bird's nest and turn right.
4. Go south on Second Street, past Earl's Foods, to Pearl Road.
5. Turn left on Pearl Road and cross the river.
6. Aunt Maria lives in the last house on the right before Third Street.

OUT OF THE BLUE Practice Book R-CONTROLLED VOWEL: /ûr/ear, ir, er, ur 83

PRACTICE BOOK, page 83

Strategic Reading

APPLYING A STRATEGY

PAGES 210–211 Before children read, have them look at the pictures, and invite them to predict what Rosalba and her grandma will see as they fly. Encourage children to be creative as they share their ideas. Then ask children if they think the two characters will come down, and what might happen if they do. Then children can read on to confirm their predictions.

MAKING AND CONFIRMING PREDICTIONS

PHONICS IN ACTION

Have children find the contractions on page 211, and write them on the board. *(I'd, we'd, they'd)* **Invite volunteers to name the two words from which each contraction is made.**

MUSIC CONNECTION

SING A SONG **Sing the song "The Wheels on the Bus" with children. Sing all known verses, and then have children add verses of their own that relate to the story.**

We would fly all over the city.
"*Mira,*" Abuela would say, pointing.

And I'd look, as we soared over parks and streets, dogs and people.

We'd wave to the people waiting for the bus.
"*Buenos días,*" we'd say.
"*Buenos días.* Good morning," they'd call up to us.
We'd fly over factories and trains . . .

211

MINILESSON

MAINTAIN: PHONICS AND DECODING

Long Vowel: /ā/ *ay, ai, a-e*

INFORMAL ASSESSMENT

As children read, notice whether they decode words that contain *ay, ai,* or *a-e.*

TEACH/MODEL

Ask children to reread page 211 and tell what Rosalba and Grandma would do to the people waiting for the bus. (*wave*) Write *wave* and *waiting* on the board, and ask children how the words are alike. (They both have the long *a* sound and begin with *w*.) Ask a volunteer to circle the letters in each word that stand for the long *a* sound. Ask children to find a word on the page with long *a* spelled *ay*. (*say*)

PRACTICE/APPLY

Write these words on cake slices: *train, nail, wait, day, play, stay, bake, gave,* and *shake*. Have a volunteer sit with his or her back to the class. Another child takes a piece of cake and hides it. The first player guesses who ate the cake. Then the player with the slice reads the word on it and uses it in a sentence.

PHONICS ACTIVITY BOOK, pages 25–26

For further reinforcement, you may want to use "Snake's Day Dream" or "Word Sort—Long *a*," *Phonics Game Board Pattern Book*, pages 32–33.

PHONICS PRACTICE READER 7

PHONICS PRACTICE BOOK, pages 65–76

WRITING

EXTEND THE STORY Rosalba and her grandmother waved and called to the people who were waiting for the bus. Invite children to write what the people at the bus stop might have said to one another after seeing this unusual sight. Encourage children to share their written conversations with classmates.

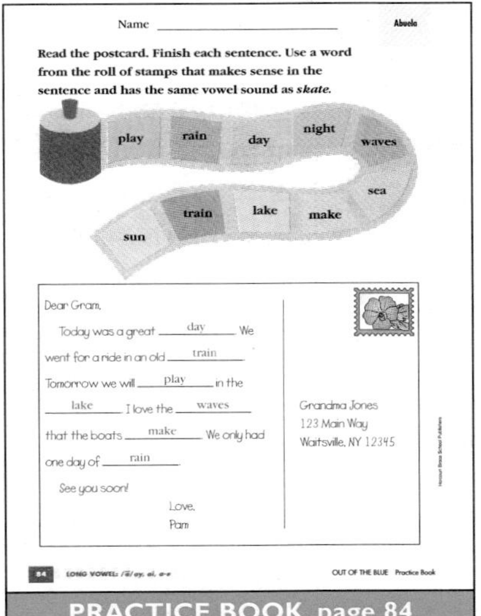

Name ______________ Abuela

Read the postcard. Finish each sentence. Use a word from the roll of stamps that makes sense in the sentence and has the same vowel sound as *skate*.

play rain day night waves sea make lake train sun

Dear Gram,

Today was a great __day__. We went for a ride in an old __train__. Tomorrow we will __play__ in the __lake__. I love the __waves__ that the boats __make__. We only had one day of __rain__.

See you soon!

Love,
Pam

Grandma Jones
123 Main Way
Waitsville, NY 12345

84 LONG VOWEL: /ā/ay, ai, a-e — OUT OF THE BLUE Practice Book

PRACTICE BOOK, page 84

Strategic Reading

APPLYING A STRATEGY

PAGES 212–213 Allow children a few moments to read page 213 and look at the illustration. Ask volunteers to tell what is happening at this point in the story. Then ask them what words or parts of the picture helped them figure it out. Encourage other children to share clues that helped them figure out what is happening. **USING CONTEXT CLUES**

ILLUSTRATOR'S CRAFT

Point out that the illustrator used scraps of material in her pictures. Invite children to find examples of this in the pictures on these pages. Encourage them to look at the patterns in the characters' clothing and in the rest of the picture. Talk about what the illustrator did with the patterns.

AUTHOR'S CRAFT

Discuss how Arthur Dorros has written about things that are real and things that are make-believe in this story. Ask children to pinpoint what the first make-believe event was. (pages 208–209: Rosalba flew like a bird.) **Talk about how the author mixed real things with make-believe ones.**

and glide close to the sea.
"*Cerca del mar,*" we'd say.
We'd almost touch the tops of waves.

Abuela's skirt would be a sail.
She could race with the sailboats.
I'll bet she'd win.

213

Student Self-Assessment

FIX-UP STRATEGIES: REREADING AND READING AHEAD

Ask children to reread the first paragraph on page 213 and tell how they figured out what *cerca del mar* might mean. Tell children that when they come to words they don't know, they can reread a sentence or two or read ahead a sentence or two to find clues.

CHALLENGE **Children can work in groups to create a travel brochure for New York City. Encourage them to use reference materials to find out about the city.**

SOCIAL STUDIES

NEW YORK CITY **New York is the largest city in the United States and the sixth largest in the world, with over 8 million people. New York has more parks, playgrounds, and other recreational areas than any other city in the United States.**

Strategic Reading

MODELING A STRATEGY

PAGES 214–217 Before reading, have children look carefully at the pictures and predict what this part of the story will be about. After reading the pages, children can look back at the pictures on pages 214–217. Model how the pictures illustrate what is happening in the story. **Think aloud:** *In the pictures on pages 214–215, it looks like a box attached to a hook is being lowered from the ship. The words tell me that there is fruit in the boxes, and that a crane is being used to load and unload the ship. The picture helped me understand what a crane is and how it works. It also helped me understand what happens when a ship is unloaded.* RELATING PICTURES TO TEXT

We'd fly to where the ships are docked,
and watch people unload fruits from the
land where Abuela grew up.
Mangos, bananas, papayas—those are
all Spanish words.
So are rodeo, patio, and burro.
Maybe we'd see a cousin of Abuela's
hooking boxes of fruit to a crane.
We saw her cousin Daniel once,
unloading and loading the ships.

214

SOCIAL STUDIES CONNECTION

TROPICAL FRUITS If possible, bring in a mango, a banana, and a papaya. Explain that these fruits cannot grow in the cold, and are raised mainly in the hot, wet parts of the world. Talk about how the fruits look, and allow interested children to taste them. Talk a bit with children about fruits or other plants that grow well in your area.

Informal Assessment ✓

USING CONTEXT CLUES

As children reread the selection, observe whether they use context clues when they come to words they don't know. Ask yourself these questions:

- ☑ Do children use clues in the sentence to help them figure out a word?
- ☑ Do children reread parts of the story to find clues to help them understand a word or idea?
- ☑ Do children read ahead to find clues to unknown words or phrases?

EXPANDING VOCABULARY

Ask a volunteer to tell classmates what cranes are and explain what they are used for. Invite children to name other pieces of heavy machinery, such as bulldozers, front-end loaders, and dump trucks, that help move or lift heavy things.

Cooperative Reading

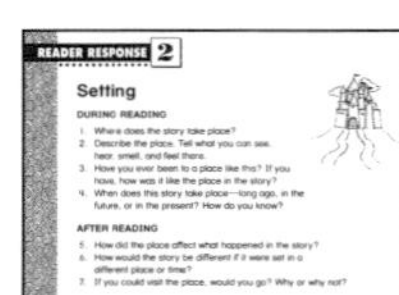
Response Card 2

Observe how children use **Reader Response Card 2** (Setting) as they discuss the sights and sounds of the characters' trip over New York City.

1. **How do children answer the questions about the setting during and after reading the story?**
2. **How well do they describe the places Rosalba and Abuela see?**
3. **Do they include details from the illustrations?**

Ask children why the setting is important to this story. Help them understand that the story would be quite different if it took place elsewhere. Talk about what the characters would see in a local place that is familiar to children.

Out past the boats in the harbor we'd
see the Statue of Liberty.
"*Me gusta,*" Abuela would say.
Abuela really likes her.
I do too.
We would circle around Liberty's head
and wave to the people visiting her.
That would remind Abuela of when she
first came to this country.

"*Vamos al aeropuerto,*" she'd say.
She'd take me to the airport where the
plane that first brought her landed.
"*Cuidado,*" Abuela would tell me.
We'd have to be careful as we went for
a short ride.

216

SOCIAL STUDIES

THE STATUE OF LIBERTY The Statue of Liberty was pledged to the people of the United States by the people of France in 1884. It is one of the largest statues ever built, standing about 151 feet high from its feet to the top of the torch.

MEETING INDIVIDUAL NEEDS

Intervention Strategies

USING PICTURE CLUES Have children repeat this sentence: *When I read, it helps me to look at the pictures to understand what is happening.* Have children tell how looking at the pictures will help them keep track of the places in New York City that Rosalba and Abuela visit.

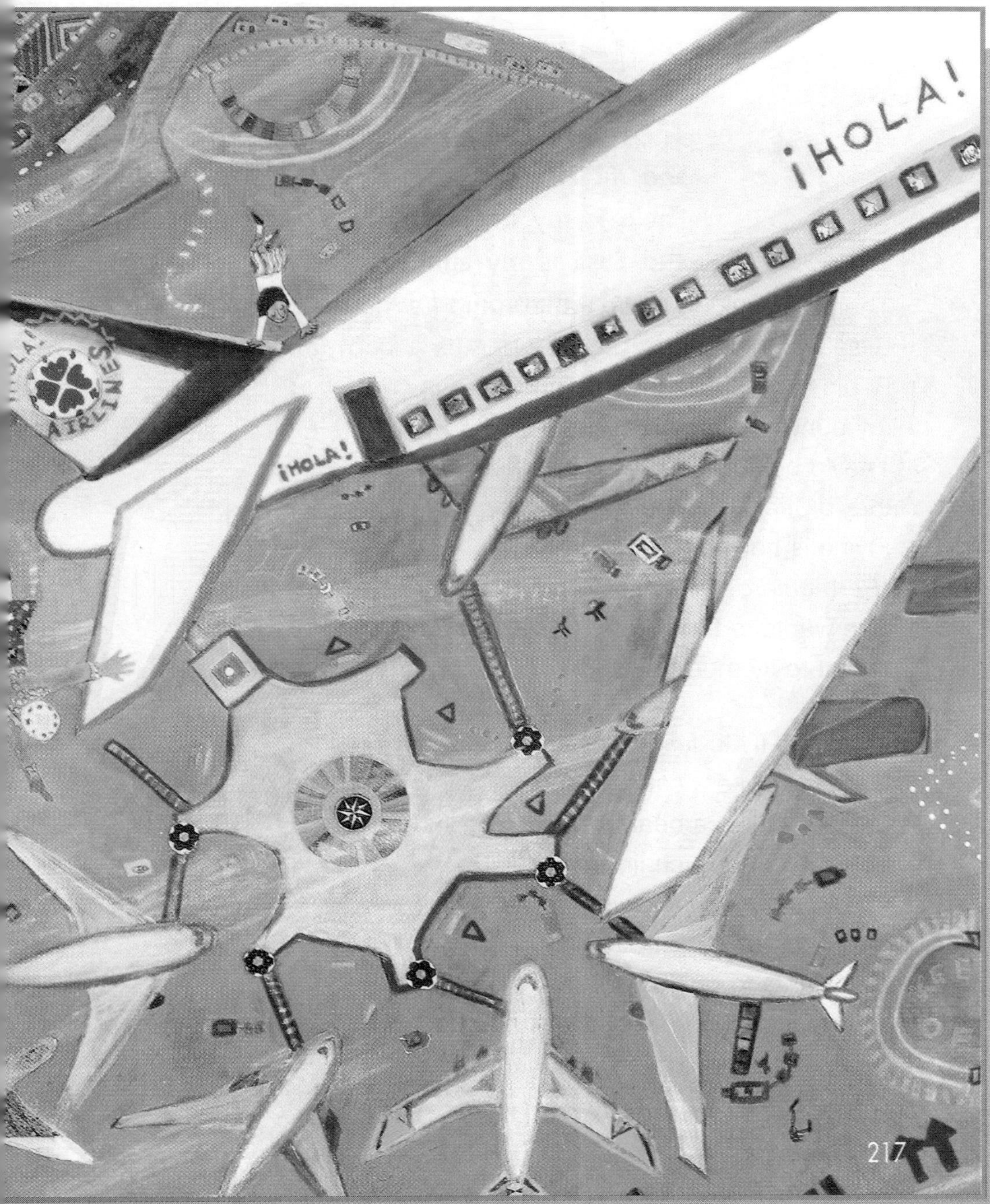

MULTICULTURAL CONNECTION

Remind children that Abuela first came to this country on an airplane. Invite children who have lived in or visited other countries to tell about different ways that they have traveled in those places.

STUDENTS ACQUIRING ENGLISH Some children may not understand the meaning of the phrase *circle around Liberty's head.* Demonstrate the concept by having a volunteer pretend to be the Statue of Liberty and another to use a paper airplane to circle around Liberty's head.

Strategic Reading

APPLYING A STRATEGY

PAGES 218–219 Ask children if they have ever looked up at clouds and seen cloud shapes that reminded them of other things. Then encourage them to take a few moments to try to picture in their minds what a cloud that resembles a cat would look like. Have them do the same for the other cloud shapes that are mentioned on page 218. **VISUALIZING**

Then we could fly to *tío* Pablo's and *tía* Elisa's store.
Pablo is my uncle, my *tío,* and Elisa is my aunt, my *tía.*
They'd be surprised when we flew in, but they'd offer us a cool *limonada.*
Flying is hot work.
"*Pero quiero volar más,*" Abuela would say.
She wants to fly more.
I want to fly more too.

We could fly to *las nubes,* the clouds.
One looks like a cat, *un gato.*
One looks like a bear, *un oso.*
One looks like a chair, *una silla.*
"*Descansemos un momento,*" Abuela would say.
She wants to rest a moment.
We would rest in our chair, and Abuela would hold me in her arms, with the whole sky our house, *nuestra casa.*

218

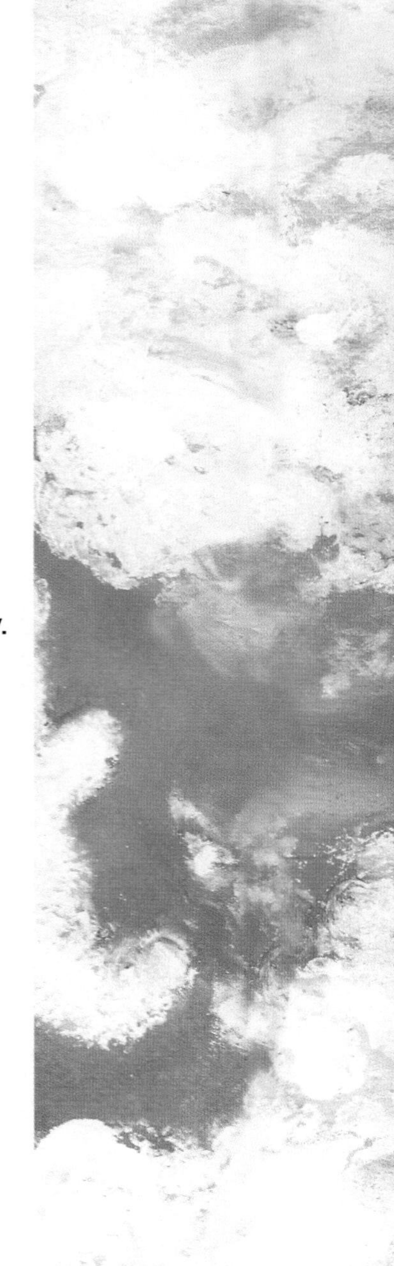

SCHOOL↔HOME CONNECTION

Invite children and their families to look at clouds from their homes, draw the shapes they see, and write about them. Ask children to share interesting observations with classmates.

219

MINILESSON

MAINTAIN: PHONICS AND DECODING

Long Vowel: /ō/ *o, oa*

INFORMAL ASSESSMENT

As children read, notice whether they use the sound of long *o* when decoding words that contain *o* and *oa*.

TEACH/MODEL

Write these sentences on the board:

They flew over the boats on the water.
Abuela would hold me in her arms.
Pablo is my uncle.

Read the sentences aloud, and ask children to name the words with the long *o* sound. *(over, boats, hold, Pablo)* Review the spellings for the long *o* sound in these words *(o, oa)*, and ask children to list more words with these spellings for long *o*.

PRACTICE/APPLY

Write the words *go, so, no, float, boat, coal, coat, foam, goal, goat, load, loaf, oak, road, roast, soak, soap, toad,* and *toast* on the board and on small slips of paper. Put them in a bag. Have children make a Bingo board and write one of the long *o* words in each space. Play long *o* Bingo.

For further reinforcement, you may want to use "Troll's Road" or "Words Sort—Long *o*," *Phonics Game Board Pattern Book*, pages 34, 35, and 44.

PHONICS ACTIVITY BOOK, page 27

PHONICS PRACTICE READER 8

PHONICS PRACTICE BOOK, pages 77–89

PHONICS IN ACTION

Have children find the words *clouds* and *house*. Ask how the words are alike. (They both have the /ou/ sound.) Remind children that *ou* stands for the vowel sound heard in *clouds* and *house*.

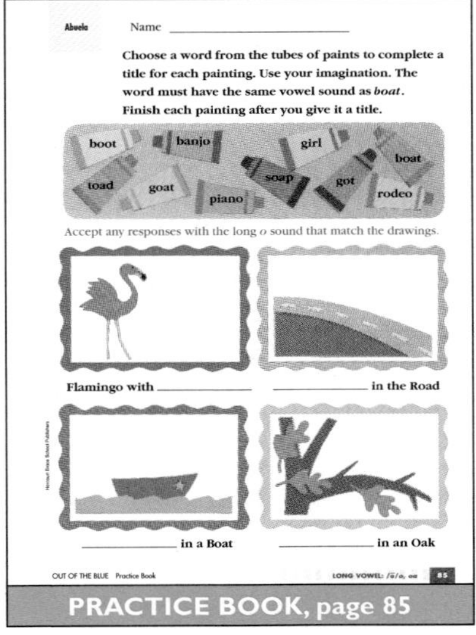

Abuela Name ______

Choose a word from the tubes of paints to complete a title for each painting. Use your imagination. The word must have the same vowel sound as *boat*. Finish each painting after you give it a title.

boot banjo girl boat toad goat piano soap got rodeo

Accept any responses with the long *o* sound that match the drawings.

Flamingo with ______

______ in the Road

______ in a Boat

______ in an Oak

OUT OF THE BLUE Practice Book LONG VOWEL: /ō/o, oa 85

PRACTICE BOOK, page 85

Strategic Reading

APPLYING A STRATEGY

PAGES 220–221 After children have read the pages, have them describe Rosalba and Abuela.

- **Why do the characters do the things they do?**
- **Would you like to know them? Tell why or why not.**

Then have children predict what Rosalba and Abuela will do next.

MAKING INFERENCES

We'd be as high as airplanes, balloons, and birds, and higher than the tall buildings downtown.
But we'd fly there too to look around.

We could find the building where my father works.

"*Hola, papá,*" I'd say as I waved.
And Abuela would do a flip for fun as we passed by the windows.

"*Mira,*" I hear Abuela say.
"Look," she's telling me.

I do look, and we are back in the park.

220

MEETING INDIVIDUAL NEEDS

STUDENTS ACQUIRING ENGLISH

Some children may not understand what "do a flip" means. Use a doll or toy figure to demonstrate. Then have children look at the small picture on page 220 to see how Abuela does a flip.

221

Student Self-Assessment 

USING READING STRATEGIES

As children read the story, allow time for them to think about the strategies they use when they come to unknown words or phrases. Encourage them to share how they figure out things they don't understand.

MULTI-AGE CLASSROOMS

Provide a large sheet of paper for children to use to make a map of Rosalba and Abuela's adventure. Older children can draw in the basic outlines of places and trace the route that the characters took. Younger children can draw pictures to fill in details.

REAL-LIFE CONNECTION

Some children may never have seen tall buildings or skyscrapers. Encourage them to look at the pictures and try to visualize how tall the buildings are. Have children name the tallest landmark in your area. Talk with them about whether the skyscrapers in New York and other cities are taller or shorter.

Strategic Reading

APPLYING A STRATEGY

PAGES 222–223 After children read, have them recall their predictions about what Rosalba and Abuela would do and then compare their ideas with what actually happened. **CONFIRMING PREDICTIONS**

Returning to the Predictions/Purpose

Before children read, they wrote about what they thought would happen in the story. Invite children to share predictions and compare them with what actually happened.

Appreciating the Literature

With the whole class or a small group, have an open discussion about the story.

- **Did you like that the story is about a make-believe trip over a real city? Why or why not?**

AUTHOR'S CRAFT

Discuss how the author makes the story more realistic by using Spanish words. Discuss ways that the story would have been different if he had not done this. Encourage children to share their ideas and opinions about this technique.

HOLA ADIOS
VAMOS

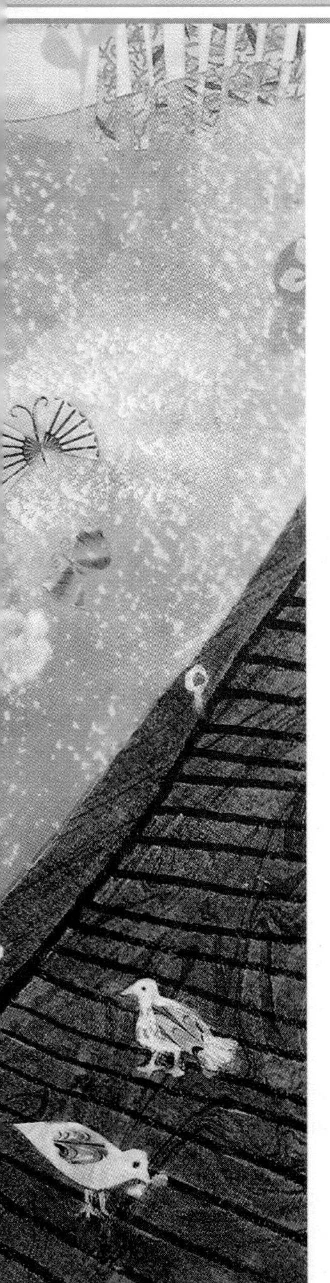

We are walking by the lake.
Abuela probably wants to go for a boat ride.
"*Vamos a otra aventura,*" she says.
She wants us to go for another adventure.
That's just one of the things I love about Abuela.
She likes adventures.

Abuela takes my hand.
"*Vamos,*" she says.
"Let's go."

223

NOTES

Here's a place to list ideas or activities that you would like to use the next time you teach this lesson.

SUMMARIZE AND RETELL

Web Your Ideas

Work with children to fill in the outer ovals of this web with things Rosalba and Abuela saw on their adventure. Children can use the web to retell the story. See *Practice Book* page 77.

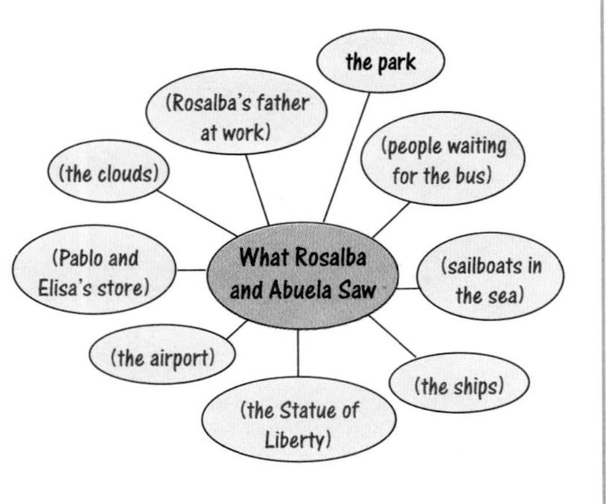

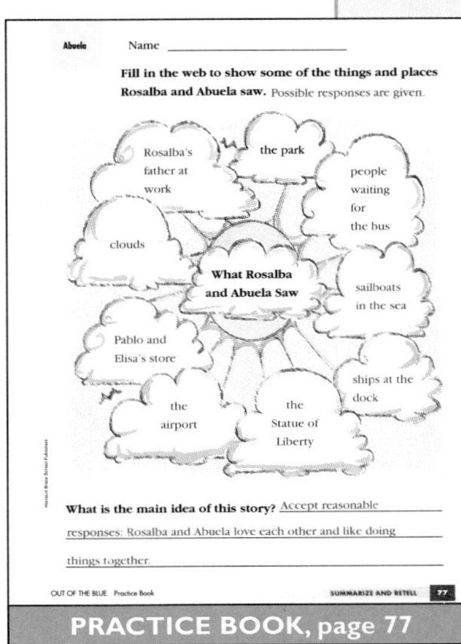
Abuela Name ______________

Fill in the web to show some of the things and places Rosalba and Abuela saw. Possible responses are given.

What is the main idea of this story? Accept reasonable responses: Rosalba and Abuela love each other and like doing things together.

OUT OF THE BLUE Practice Book SUMMARIZE AND RETELL 77

PRACTICE BOOK, page 77

Strategic Reading

PAGE 224 Have children examine the page, and briefly discuss how to use the story Glossary. Help children pronounce the Spanish words. See pages T444–T445 for a lesson about using glossaries and dictionaries.

Abuela (ah-BWEH-lah) Grandmother
Buenos días (BWEH-nohs DEE-ahs) Good day
Cerca del mar (SEHR-kah dehl mahr) Close to the sea
Cuidado (kwee-DAH-doh) Be careful
Descansemos un momento (dehs-kahn-SEH-mohs oon moh-MEHN-toh) Let's rest a moment
El parque es lindo (ehl PAHR-kay ehs LEEN-doh) The park is beautiful
Hola, papá (OH-lah, pah-PAH) Hello, papa
Las nubes (lahs NOO-behs) The clouds
Limonada (lee-moh-NAH-dah) Lemonade
Me gusta (meh GOO-stah) I like
Mira (MEE-rah) Look
Nuestra casa (NWEH-strah CAH-sah) Our house
Pero quiero volar más (PEH-roh key-EH-roh boh-LAR mahs) But I would like to fly more
Rosalba el pájaro (roh-SAHL-bah ehl PAH-hah-roh) Rosalba the bird
Sí, quiero volar (see, key-EH-roh boh-LAR) Yes, I want to fly
Tantos pájaros (TAHN-tohs PAH-hah-rohs) So many birds
Tía (TEE-ah) Aunt
Tío (TEE-oh) Uncle
Un gato (oon GAH-toh) A cat
Un oso (oon OH-soh) A bear
Una silla (OON-ah SEE-yah) A chair
Vamos (BAH-mohs) Let's go
Vamos al aeropuerto (BAH-mohs ahl ah-ehr-oh-PWEHR-toh) Let's go to the airport
Vamos a otra aventura (BAH-mohs ah OH-trah ah-behn-TOO-rah) Let's go on another adventure
Ven (behn) Come

The capitalized syllable is stressed in pronunciation.

224

CROSS-CULTURAL VIEWPOINT

Write the words *momento, limonada,* and *aventura* on the board, and pronounce each word. Invite children to name English words that look or sound like these words. Point out that when words in other languages are similar to English words, the words from both languages may mean the same thing.

Arthur Dorros

When I was little, I loved to listen to my grandmother's stories. I also thought about flying like a bird. I liked to go up on the roof of my apartment building in New York City. From there, I could see all the places that Rosalba sees when she flies.

When I got older, I married a woman whose family came from Latin America. All the Spanish names in the story belong to members of my wife's family.

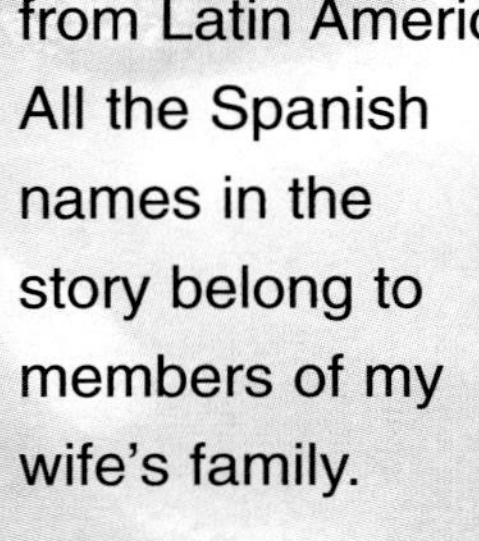

Elisa Kleven

Do you like to collect things? I collect scraps of everything, from wrapping paper to yarn. I have special boxes where I store all my scraps. When I do my artwork, first I draw the pictures. Then I fill them in with different scraps.

I enjoyed making the pictures for "Abuela." I even used some material from a blouse of mine to make Abuela's purse.

225

About the Author and the Illustrator

PAGE 225 Share with children the information about the author and the illustrator. Talk about how authors and illustrators use experiences they have had to create stories and art.

Arthur Dorros has experience in filmmaking, carpentry, and horticulture in addition to writing. When he lived in New York City, he taught children about writing and book illustration. Dorros is fascinated by people in the United States who maintain their ethnic roots by speaking their native languages and practicing their native customs. *Abuela* was inspired in part by this fascination.

Elisa Kleven was interested in book illustration even as a child. When she illustrates a book, she first draws the pictures and then fills them in, using media such as cloth and ribbon. She loves color and texture, and keeps bits of fabric, yarn, and wrapping paper on hand to use in her artwork.

OTHER BOOKS BY ARTHUR DORROS AND ELISA KLEVEN

Radio Man—Don Radio: A Story in English and Spanish **by Arthur Dorros. HarperCollins, 1993. CHALLENGE**

The Lion and the Little Red Bird **by Elisa Kleven. Dutton, 1992. CHALLENGE**

RESPONSE CORNER ACTIVITIES

DRAW A PICTURE

COME FLY WITH ME
PAGE 226 Ask children if they have ever looked down from a tall building or the window of a plane. Encourage those who have to describe the view for classmates. When children have finished their pictures, have them share their work with partners or in small groups. ART/WRITING

EXTEND THE STORY

ANOTHER ADVENTURE
PAGE 227 Invite children to brainstorm a list of things Rosalba and Abuela could come across on an adventure at sea. Provide a variety of materials for children to compile their stories into a class book, including a tape recorder so that they can take turns recording their stories. Place the book and cassette in the Reading Center or class library for children to read and enjoy. WRITING

VARYING THE ACTIVITY

Some children might enjoy the challenge of using the format of the story to write more story extensions, such as Rosalba and Abuela's adventures in space. They might want to create books with their stories, including collages for the illustrations, like those made by Elisa Kleven.

EXTEND THE STORY

Another Adventure

On their first adventure, Abuela and Rosalba went flying through the air. They are ready for a new adventure on a boat. Work with a partner. Write what they see and do. Choose a way to share your new story. You might make a book or record your story.

What Do You Think?

- How can you tell that Rosalba and Abuela like being together?
- Would you like to fly with Rosalba and Abuela? Why or why not?

227

CHECKING COMPREHENSION

What Do You Think?

1. **How can you tell that Rosalba and Abuela like being together?** (Possible response: They look happy in the pictures, and they do silly things together for fun.) DESCRIPTIVE RESPONSE
2. **Would you like to fly with Rosalba and Abuela? Why or why not?** (Responses will vary, but children should support their answers.) PERSONAL RESPONSE

An additional question for extending reading.

3. **Before reading this story, did you ever think about flying like a bird? What do you think about the idea now?** (Responses will vary.) CRITICAL/CREATIVE ANALYSIS

MEETING INDIVIDUAL NEEDS

STUDENTS ACQUIRING ENGLISH **For children whose first language is Spanish, suggest that they include Spanish words and phrases in their stories and translate them as Rosalba did in "Abuela." Suggest that children who speak other languages do the same in their stories, using words from their primary languages.**

Informal Assessment

Observe pairs of children as they write and record their story extensions.

- ☑ Do children write about what the characters see and do?
- ☑ Does the story follow a logical sequence?
- ☑ Do children share in making up and presenting their stories?

Intervention Strategies

Instant Readers™

Predictable and Patterned Little Books That Build Fluency

*** BOOK LEVEL: 19–20**

VOCABULARY:
touch, whole

PHONIC ELEMENTS:
R*-controlled vowel: /ûr/*ur*; Long vowel: /ā/*ay, a-e

SUMMARY:
Based on the song "Animal Fair," this romp is total pandemonium.

Informal Assessment ✓

Are children able to

- ☑ hear and identify the sounds contained in words?
- ☑ write a brief comparison?

Reading a New Book

INTRODUCING *ONE QUIET AFTERNOON*

Because this rhyme is based on a song, you may want to teach children the original words and music to "Animal Fair," which is in *Tom Glazer's Treasury of Songs for Students* (Doubleday, 1988). Learning the rhythm of the language will help children read the story. Share the story pictures, and have children describe what is happening.

READING THE STORY

This rhyme is perfect for a choral reading or sing-along.

WORKING WITH WORDS AND LETTERS

To help children with the letters that stand for the long *a* sound, use some of the story words. Have children locate words that have the long *a* sound in the story and write them in a chart as shown below. Invite children to add other words they know to the list. Discuss the letter combinations that stand for this sound.

ay	a-e	ai
day away	made cake	straight

WRITING RHYMES

Have children work with partners to create simple two-line rhymes, using words with the long *a* sound.

Additional activities are provided on pages 46–47 of the *Intervention Strategies Manual*.

* **BOOK LEVEL: 16–17**

VOCABULARY:
adventure, building, country, whole

PHONIC ELEMENTS:
R-controlled vowel: /ûr/*ir, er;* Long vowels: /ā/*a*, /ō/*o*

SUMMARY:
Life for a girl is nicely divided between two houses.

Reading a New Book

INTRODUCING *COUNTRY FAMILY CITY FAMILY*

As the illustrations are shared and discussed, draw out that the girl in the story divides her time between her mother's house in the country and her father's apartment in the city. Invite children to explain the similarities and differences of the two locations.

READING THE STORY

Have children read the story independently to find out how the girl feels about her two homes.

WORKING WITH WORDS AND LETTERS

Write the story words *city* and *country* in a chart. Point out that the letter *c* stands for two different sounds in these words. Discuss the sounds of hard and soft *c*. When children locate other story words or think of other words that begin with *c*, have them write the words in the appropriate column. Talk about how the words in each column are alike. Draw out that when the letter *c* is followed by the vowel *e* or *i*, it stands for the /s/ sound; when *c* is followed by *a*, *o*, or *u*, it stands for the /k/ sound.

sounds like k	car coin cut	sounds like s	city cent

WRITING COMPARISONS

Have children write a short comparison of two places they like to go. Make sure that the comparisons show how two things can be opposites.

ESL/Title I Reading

Bein' With You This Way by W. Nikola-Lisa

ESL/Title I Library

TECHNOLOGY

INSTANT READERS™

ELECTRONIC EDITION

***One Quiet Afternoon* and *Country Family, City Family* are available on CD-ROM. Pre- and post-reading activities are included.**

Working with "Abuela"

SYNTACTIC AND SEMANTIC CUES Assist children with the story by reading aloud (or having another child read aloud) the Spanish dialogue. Copy onto the board the girl's translation of the Spanish that follows. Have children find both the Spanish and the translation on the story page.

* Books leveled according to Barbara Peterson's "Profiles of Books for Beginning Readers," on page 9 of the *Instant Readers Teacher's Guide.*

2 Integrating Language Arts

IDEA BANK

TIPS FOR CLASSROOM MANAGEMENT

IF children need help getting started in the Group Talk activity in their discussion about the characters' relationship, **THEN** help them cite story events that show how the two characters get along.

TECHNOLOGY

IMAGINATION EXPRESS, Destination: Neighborhood

LIVING BOOK: Just Grandma and Me

LISTENING AND SPEAKING

Group Talk

SUCH GOOD FRIENDS

Encourage children to talk about Rosalba and Abuela's relationship. What do they enjoy doing together? What are some adventures they might have had before the one in the story? Invite children to tell about an older friend or relative they have fun with. Encourage children to share experiences they have had with this person. **CHALLENGING THE TEXT**

Informal Assessment

Note how children use their understanding of the story to formulate their ideas about Rosalba and Abuela's relationship.

REAL-LIFE READING

Reading Company Names and Logos

Call attention to the illustration of the airplane on page 217. Ask volunteers to tell what is written on the tail and side of the plane. Point out that *Hola* is a Spanish word that means *"hello."* Direct children's attention also to the airline logo.

Provide children with magazines, and have them find and cut out pictures that show objects or vehicles with a company name and/or logo. Gather the pictures in a folder. Help children recognize that this print is a form of advertising. Suggest that children work with family members for a day, or longer, to list the company names and logos they see on vehicles. **READING/WRITING**

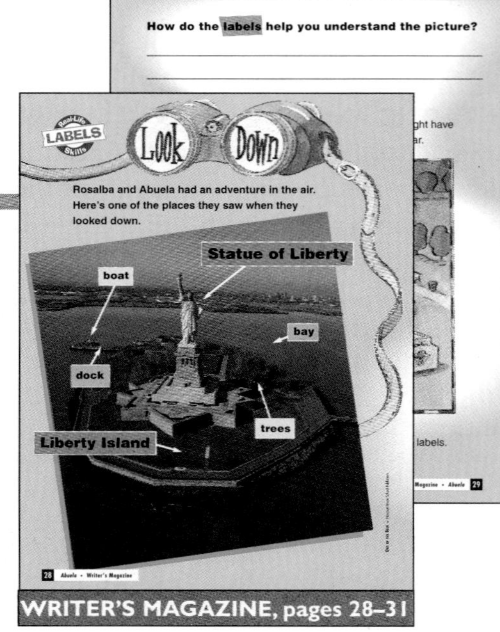

How do the **labels** help you understand the picture?

LABELS

Look Down

Rosalba and Abuela had an adventure in the air. Here's one of the places they saw when they looked down.

boat

Statue of Liberty

bay

dock

trees

Liberty Island

28 Abuela • Writer's Magazine

WRITER'S MAGAZINE, pages 28–31

ORAL LANGUAGE

Oral Description

TELL ALL ABOUT IT

Organize children into four groups. Write the words *park, streets, harbor*, and *airport* on index cards, and put them in a bag. Each group chooses a card and orally describes the named place. Tell children that each person in the group should give at least one part of the group's presentation. Encourage children to use the pictures in "Abuela," as well as the text, as they prepare their descriptions.

As an added twist, have groups prepare descriptions that do not name the place being described. As each group presents its description, encourage the listeners to visualize the place and guess what it is. Remind children to be courteous listeners and to wait until everyone in the group has spoken before they ask questions or make guesses. **LISTENING/SPEAKING**

KINESTHETIC

Creative Connection

MATERIALS
- origami paper or colored construction paper cut in squares

BUSY BIRDS

Tell children that they will experiment with folding paper to make bird shapes. Demonstrate how to fold a square of paper in half to make a triangle as children follow along. Then children can fold the top differently to make a variety of head shapes.

Invite children who know origami to show classmates other ways to make birds. Interested children could also use an origami reference book to make more animal shapes. **KINESTHETIC**

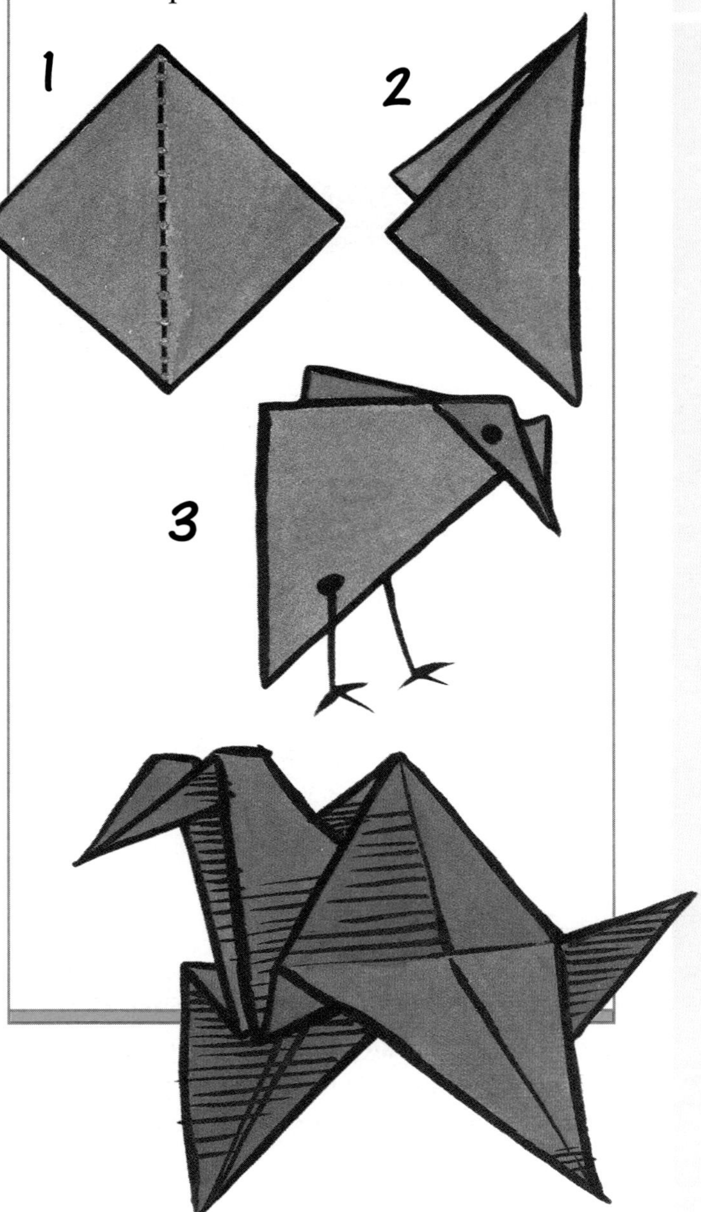

PERSONAL JOURNAL

REFLECTING ON THE STORY Children can use their personal journals to draw or write what "Abuela" made them think about. For example, they might have thought about what the relationship between Rosalba and Abuela taught them about friendship.

WRITER'S WORKSHOP

An Invitation and Envelope

TIPS FOR CLASSROOM MANAGEMENT

IF children are familiar with the writing process approach, **THEN** present the writing assignment and have them use the Invitation model on pages 14–15, and the Envelope model on page 17 of the *Language Handbook.*

IF at this time you want a short writing activity, **THEN** have children do the prewriting activity and place the chart in the Writing Center for children's reference during independent writing.

TECHNOLOGY

THE AMAZING WRITING MACHINE
Primary Level Activity Disk Pack Grade 2
Have children enter their invitations in the Letters mode.

KID PIX
Children can illustrate their invitations by creating pictures of their own or using the stamps.

Thinking as Writers

WRITING FORM: Invitation and Envelope Ask children to tell which of the sights Rosalba and her grandmother saw as they flew over New York City were their favorites. Then explain to children that they will write a letter inviting Abuela and Rosalba to fly over their town.

Display Charts/Transparencies 13 and 18, or write the model Invitation and an envelope on the board. Help children identify the four most important pieces of information to include in an invitation: *who, what, when, where*. Point out the parts of the addresses on the envelope.

CHART/TRANSPARENCY 18

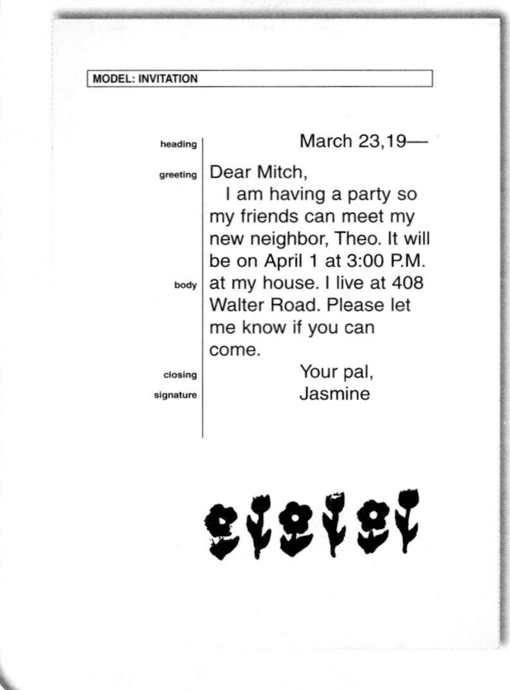

MODEL: INVITATION

heading March 23,19—

greeting Dear Mitch,

body I am having a party so my friends can meet my new neighbor, Theo. It will be on April 1 at 3:00 P.M. at my house. I live at 408 Walter Road. Please let me know if you can come.

closing Your pal,

signature Jasmine

WRITER'S CRAFT: Details Explain that good writers use details to make their writing clear and interesting. Ask children what details an invitation writer might want to include to help the reader know what kind of event she or he is invited to.

PREWRITING

Brainstorm with children the interesting things they could see if they flew over their own community. Record children's responses on chart paper or on the board. Then have each child copy the following headings onto a sheet of paper:

Who?	What?	When?	Where?

Have children use their chart to plan an invitation to Rosalba and Abuela.

DRAFTING

As children work independently to write their invitations and envelopes, remind them to

- use their charts to remember to tell who is invited, what the invitation is for, and when and where the event will take place.
- include a heading, greeting, body, closing, and signature.
- include details about one or two of the sights they might see.
- include a return address and mailing address on the envelope.

As children work through the stages of the writing process, have them save their drafts and revisions in their writer's folder.

RESPONDING AND REVISING

Work with groups of four to six children. Read aloud a child's invitation and offer these guidelines so that children can give positive feedback to each other:

- What in the invitation makes you want to say, "Yes, I'd love to come"?
- Does the invitation tell *who, what, when,* and *where*?
- Does the invitation letter include all five parts: heading, greeting, body, closing, and signature?

PROOFREADING

Offer some tips to help children proofread. Help them focus on the following:

END MARKS A statement ends with a period. A question ends with a question mark. A sentence that shows strong feeling ends with an exclamation point.

NOUNS A noun names a person, animal, place, or thing. (See the Grammar Minilesson on page T411.)

PUBLISHING

Have children make a clean copy of their invitations. Then offer publishing options like the following:

Handwriting
Remind children that their handwriting must be neat and clear so that the person reading the invitation can understand it. If children need assistance, refer them to the Handwriting models in the *Language Handbook* or in the classroom.

GROUP TALK
Children can form small groups and pretend to be a committee welcoming Rosalba and Abuela to their community. As part of their presentation, children can read their invitations and share any pictures they drew.

COMMUNITY INVITATION BOOK Children can combine their finished products into a class book called "Invitation to (*your community*)." Encourage children to draw pictures of the places mentioned in their invitations and add them, as well as any magazine or newspaper pictures they find, to the book.

PORTFOLIO OPPORTUNITY

After children publish, make copies of their invitations and have them attach their Writing Self-Assessment Checklists to them. Have them place the invitations, envelopes, and checklists in their portfolios.

LANGUAGE HANDBOOK

Invitation, pages 14–15; Envelope, page 17

Student Self-Assessment ✓

Children can use the Writing Self-Assessment Checklist in the *Portfolio Assessment Teacher's Guide.*

EVALUATING THE WRITTEN RESPONSE

When evaluating children's invitations and envelopes, consider:

CONTENT	ORGANIZATION	STYLE
Does the invitation include all the important information about *who, what, where,* and *when?*	Does the invitation follow the correct form, including the heading, greeting, body, closing, and signature?	Does the invitation include interesting details to appeal to the reader?

EVALUATION BENCHMARKS

The child has trouble following the form of an invitation. Some important information is omitted.	= EMERGENT
The child is able to follow the basic form of an invitation but may not include appropriate details.	= BEGINNING
The child clearly follows the form of an invitation. The child includes specific and helpful details about *who, what, when,* and *where.*	= PROFICIENT

Tested Skill

GRAMMAR

Names of Special People, Animals, and Places

Reading↔Writing Connection

Connect to the story. Write the following sentence on the board:

Rosalba and Abuela flew over the Statue of Liberty.

Ask a volunteer to read the sentence. Ask children which words name special people or places. (Rosalba, Abuela, Statue of Liberty) Then ask what else children notice about these words. (They begin with capital letters.)

Build oral language. Call on volunteers to come to the board and write their first and last names. Ask children what they notice about the way the names are written. Help them see that each name begins with a capital letter. Have children recall the names of people in "Abuela" and write them on the board. Point out that each special name begins with a capital letter.

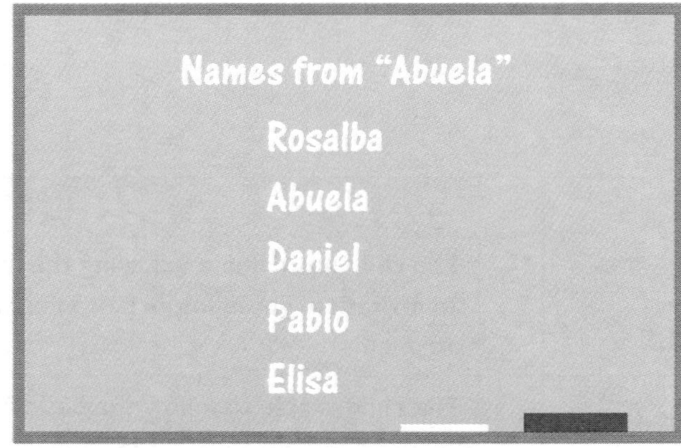

Teach/Model

List proper nouns. Tell children that titles of people and names of special people, animals, and places are called proper nouns and begin with a capital letter. Make a list on the board of common nouns, such as those shown here.

Ask children to suggest a proper noun to go with each common noun. Talk about how the words in the first and second columns are different. Explain again that the words in the second column are proper nouns and begin with capital letters. Ask children why they think capital letters are used in proper nouns.

Practice/Apply

Check understanding. Write this sentence on the board:

Mrs. Williams lives in San Francisco, California.

Ask children which word is a title and which words are the special names of people and places. (*Mrs.* is a title; *Williams, San Francisco,* and *California* are special names of people and places.) Encourage children to write sentences using proper nouns. Invite volunteers to read their sentences aloud, and have classmates identify the proper nouns.

LANGUAGE HANDBOOK

Special Names and Titles of People, pages 58–59
Names of Special Animals and Places, pages 60–61

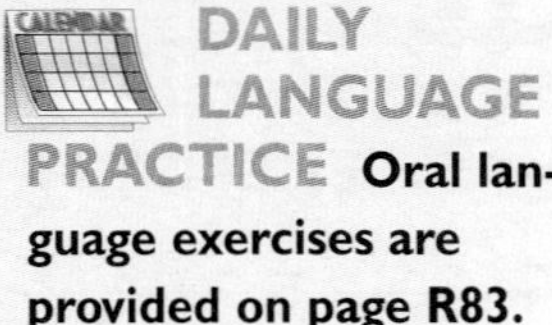

DAILY LANGUAGE PRACTICE Oral language exercises are provided on page R83.

Practice Activities

Word Boxes

WRITING APPLICATION Organize children into four groups, and give each group an empty box. Have groups cover their box with colored construction paper and write the headings *Names and Titles, Animals*, and *Places,* each on one side of the box. Then have each group brainstorm and write on their box as many proper nouns as they can think of for each category. Put the boxes in the Writing Center for children to refer to. **VISUAL/KINESTHETIC**

Yes or No

ORAL APPLICATION Distribute index cards to children, and have them write *yes* on one side and *no* on the other. Then read the following list of nouns aloud: *Mr. González; Charlie; suitcase; (the name of your town); the Golden Gate Bridge; Ms. Martin; picture; Abraham Lincoln.* Children hold up the *yes* side if the word is a proper noun and begins with a capital letter or the *no* side if the word is not a proper noun. **AUDITORY**

Up, Up, and Away

WRITING APPLICATION Tell children that they are going to write a story about an imaginary journey in a hot-air balloon. Give each child paper shaped like a hot-air balloon for the final drafts of their stories. As they write, encourage them to think of different kinds of words that begin with capital letters to use in their stories.

Then have children read their stories aloud to small groups. Encourage listeners to identify words that begin with capital letters and tell why each should be capitalized. **VISUAL/AUDITORY**

APPLY TO WRITING

Have children review their invitations and envelopes to see that they used capital letters where they should have.

STUDENTS ACQUIRING ENGLISH

Provide children with extra opportunities to practice recognizing proper nouns in their reading. Distribute copies of pages from stories children have read containing proper nouns. Have children find and circle the proper nouns.

RETEACH

See page R75 for lessons in multiple modalities.

GRAMMAR PRACTICE BOOK
pages 35–38

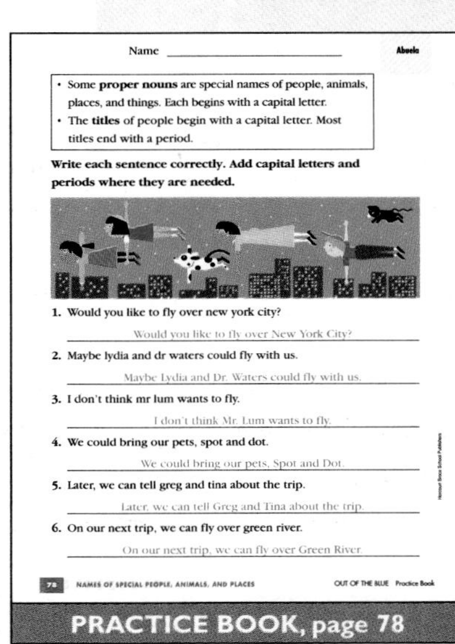

Name ______________ **Abuela**

- Some **proper nouns** are special names of people, animals, places, and things. Each begins with a capital letter.
- The **titles** of people begin with a capital letter. Most titles end with a period.

Write each sentence correctly. Add capital letters and periods where they are needed.

1. Would you like to fly over new york city?
   Would you like to fly over New York City?
2. Maybe lydia and dr waters could fly with us.
   Maybe Lydia and Dr. Waters could fly with us.
3. I don't think mr lum wants to fly.
   I don't think Mr. Lum wants to fly.
4. We could bring our pets, spot and dot.
   We could bring our pets, Spot and Dot.
5. Later, we can tell greg and tina about the trip.
   Later, we can tell Greg and Tina about the trip.
6. On our next trip, we can fly over green river.
   On our next trip, we can fly over Green River.

78 NAMES OF SPECIAL PEOPLE, ANIMALS, AND PLACES — OUT OF THE BLUE Practice Book

PRACTICE BOOK, page 78

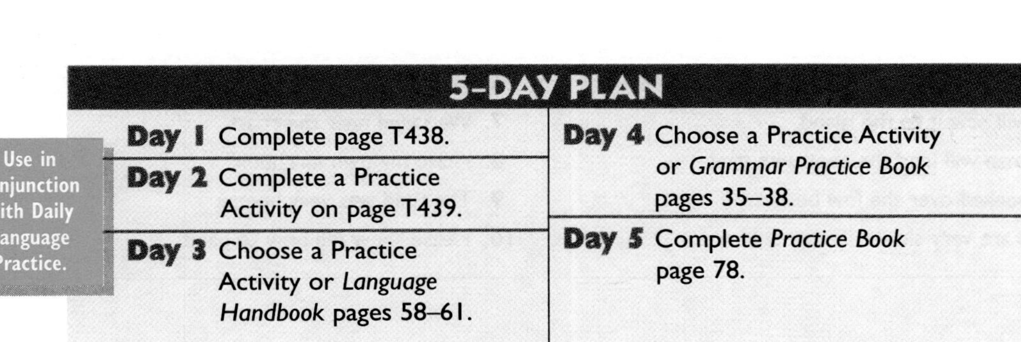

5-DAY PLAN

Use in conjunction with Daily Language Practice.

Day 1 Complete page T438.	**Day 4** Choose a Practice Activity or *Grammar Practice Book* pages 35–38.
Day 2 Complete a Practice Activity on page T439.	**Day 5** Complete *Practice Book* page 78.
Day 3 Choose a Practice Activity or *Language Handbook* pages 58–61.	

2

SPELLING

5-Day Plan

Integrated Spelling Lesson 10: student book, pages 46–49; Teacher's Edition, pages T75–T80.

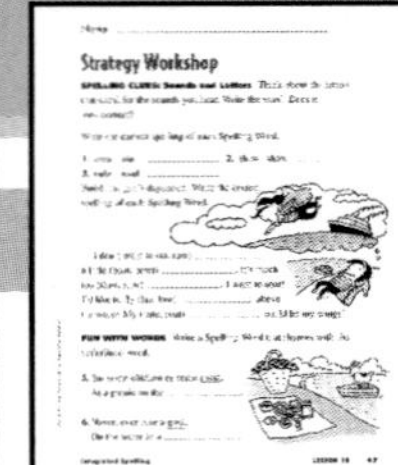

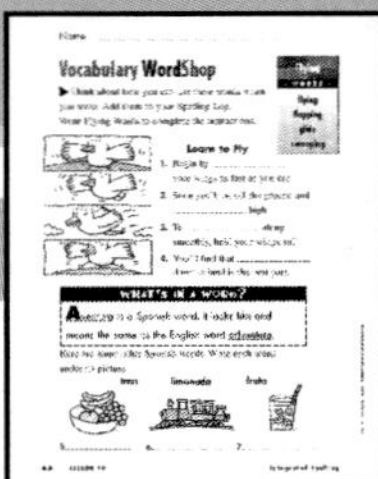

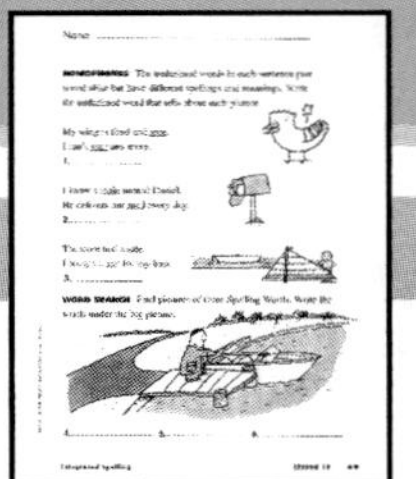

Words with Long *o* Spelled *oa* and *o*

SPELLING WORDS

1. boat ★
2. row
3. load ★
4. low
5. slow
6. coat
7. coast
8. own
9. road
10. show

STUDENT'S PERSONAL WORDS

11. 13.
12. 14.

An additional story word is *know*.

★ **Words appearing in "Abuela"**

Pretest

DAY 1 **Administer pretest.** Say each word, use it in the sentence provided below, and repeat the word. Have partners self-check their pretests by referring to the word list.

OPEN SORT

DAY 2 **Have children classify words.** Have children create their own categories to sort the Spelling Words. They may sort according to the position of the vowel sound in words, the spelling of the vowel sound, or other criteria. Volunteers can share their ideas.

CLOSED SORT

Sort by spelling pattern. Write headings on the board for a chart similar to the one below. Have children copy the chart and write each Spelling Word under the correct heading. Ask them to name other long *o* words spelled with *oa* and *ow*, and have them add them to their charts.

oa__		ow__	
boat	coast	row	own
load	road	low	show
coat		slow	

Teach/Model

DAY 3 **Discuss the generalization.** Write the following words on the board:

boat slow
road own

Ask children to read the words and name the vowel sound they hear in each. (long *o*) Call on volunteers to circle the letters that stand for the long *o* sound. Help children form generalizations about spelling words with the long *o* sound—for example:

- **Long *o* can be spelled with *oa* and *ow*.**

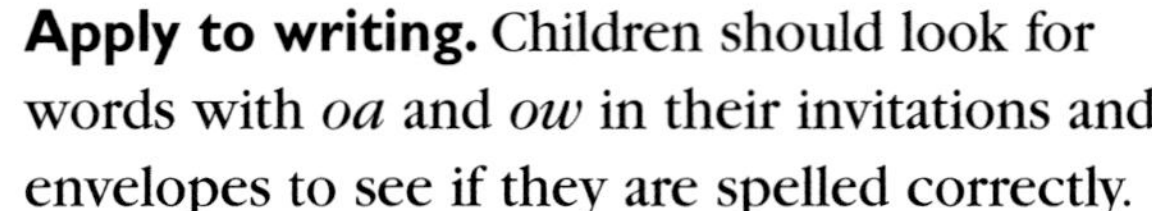

DAY 4 **Apply to writing.** Children should look for words with *oa* and *ow* in their invitations and envelopes to see if they are spelled correctly.

Posttest

DAY 5 **Assess children's progress.** Use the sentences below to administer the posttest.

Abuela Name ________

A. Write the Spelling Word that names each picture. Then write the word or words that rhyme with it.

low boat road load row coat slow show

1. boat
2. coat
3. row 4. slow
5. low 6. show
7. road
8. load

B. Write Spelling Words to finish what the people say.

We are near the coast.
I can see my own home.

OUT OF THE BLUE Practice Book WORDS LIKE boat AND show 79

PRACTICE BOOK, page 79

DICTATION SENTENCES

1. The boat is in the water.
2. We will row it to the island.
3. The man will load the boat with fruit.
4. We peeked over the low bushes.
5. Snails are very slow.
6. I wear my coat when it's chilly.
7. We sailed near the coast.
8. I have my own lunchbox.
9. The road was very bumpy.
10. Please show me how to paint.

VOCABULARY WORKSHOP

Reviewing Key Words

To review how the vocabulary was used in "Abuela," distribute copies of page R117 to children. Write the Key Words on the board.

Have children choose the word that best completes each sentence. Ask children to read the sentences to themselves and write the words in the spaces.

Abuela came here from another country.

Abuela says most things in Spanish.

Sometimes she feels like she can touch the sky.

Abuela's cousin loads and unloads ships.

Rosalba and Abuela pretend the whole sky is their house.

They fly by a very tall building.

Abuela is ready for another adventure.

Harcourt Brace School Publishers

Tell children to cut apart the sentence strips and find the page in the story that corresponds with each. Then have them arrange the strips in story order and use them to retell "Abuela."

Extending Vocabulary

SPANISH WORDS USED IN ENGLISH

Have children solve the following riddle:

I'm thinking of the Spanish word for yellow fruit that grows in bunches on trees.

Write the word *bananas* on the board. Then write *mangos* and *papayas* on the board, and remind children that these words all name fruits and come from Spanish.

Write *rodeo, patio*, and *burro* on the board, and discuss their meanings. Explain that when English- and Spanish-speaking people settled close to each other, in the southwestern U.S., for example, the English speakers started to use some of the Spanish words. Ask children to name other words that are the same or nearly the same in Spanish and English.

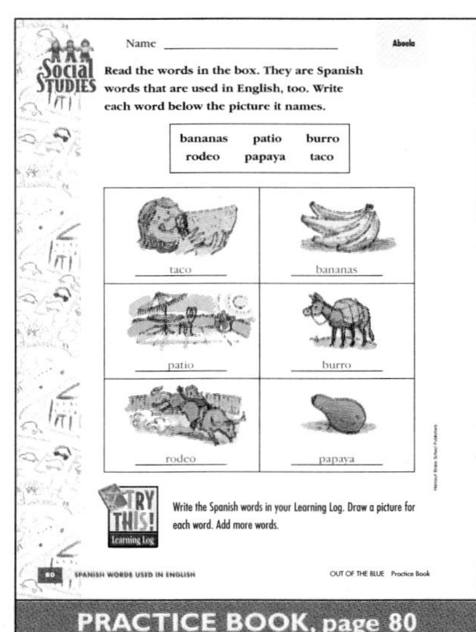
Name ______ Abuela

Social Studies

Read the words in the box. They are Spanish words that are used in English, too. Write each word below the picture it names.

bananas	patio	burro
rodeo	papaya	taco

taco	bananas
patio	burro
rodeo	papaya

TRY THIS! Learning Log

Write the Spanish words in your Learning Log. Draw a picture for each word. Add more words.

80 SPANISH WORDS USED IN ENGLISH OUT OF THE BLUE Practice Book

PRACTICE BOOK, page 80

CHALLENGE

Challenge children to make up stories of their own, using words that are the same in Spanish and English. They can also keep a Spanish-English page in their journals.

TAKE-HOME/ KEEP-AT-HOME BOOK

I Can Go Anyplace

Distribute the pages and have children make their own TAKE-HOME/ KEEP-AT-HOME BOOKS, which reinforce Key Words and known vocabulary. Children can read to partners and then take the book home to read.

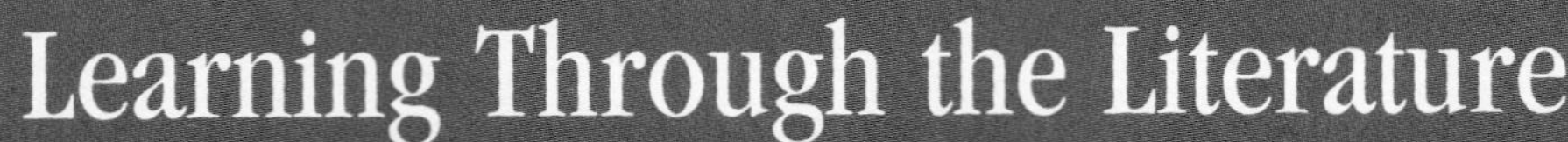

INTRODUCE: COMPREHENSION STRATEGY

Context Clues

OBJECTIVE: To use context clues to understand unfamiliar words or ideas

Informal Assessment ✓

Do children

- ☑ continue reading when they come to an unfamiliar word?
- ☑ use context clues to help them figure out unfamiliar words?

Teach/Model

Connect to the story. Ask volunteers to name a story word that was difficult for them to read. Turn to the page on which the word appears, and ask children to talk about the clues to the word's meaning that appear on that page.

Model using context clues. Ask children what they might do when they are reading and they come to a word they don't know. Explain that readers can use clues from the parts they do understand to figure out words they don't know. Write the following sentence on the board:

Rosalba was so tired that she yawned.

Model using context clues:

MODEL **What if I didn't know the underlined word in this sentence? How could I figure it out? I can read the whole sentence to see if the other words might give me clues. The word *tired* will help me. I yawn when I'm tired. The underlined word begins with *y* and ends with *d*. It must be *yawned*.**

Practice/Apply

Have children demonstrate understanding. Write the following sentences on the board:

The reply to my question was a loud "Yes!"

The choppy waves made it hard to tie the boat to the dock.

The mammoth football player had to duck to fit through the door.

Call on volunteers to tell what each underlined word means and how the other words in the sentence helped them figure out the word. If more than one word makes sense in the sentence, help children look for other clues, such as the sounds of letters, to figure out exactly which word is used in the sentence.

Practice Activities

Put It In Context

Write the following words from "Abuela" on the board and on index cards, and give one card to each pair of children:

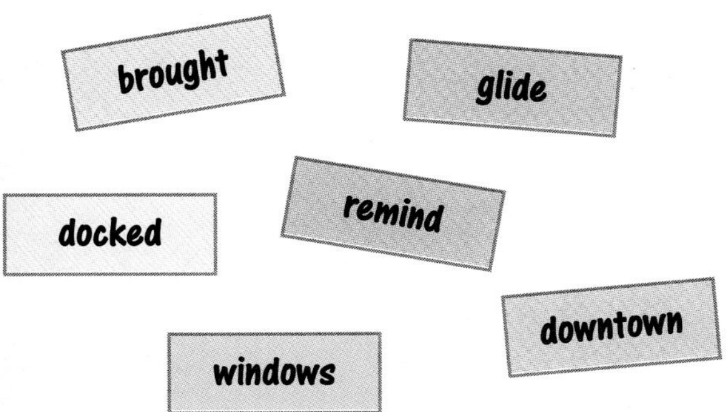

Tell partners to reread the story, looking for the word on their card. Have them use context clues to figure out the word's meaning and then write a sentence that will help classmates figure out the word. Have partners read their sentences to the group, leaving out the words on the cards. Challenge the rest of the group to figure out the missing words. Talk about the clues that helped children figure out the missing words.
VISUAL/AUDITORY

We brought food to the picnic.

There are many buildings downtown.

You remind me of my friend Josie.

The Word Washer

PERFORMANCE ASSESSMENT Duplicate the following story:

> Yesterday everything went wrong! On my way to school, I fell in a (1) _______ and got all wet. Then I broke my (2) _______, and I could hardly see! I spilled a jar of red (3) _______ during art class and broke the point off my (4) _______ in math. What an awful day!
>
> 1. puddle 2. glasses
>
> 3. paint 4. pencil

Tell children that when you got to school this morning some of the words in your story had disappeared. Then you learned that a mysterious creature called the "Word Washer" is going around the school washing away words from stories. Distribute copies of the story, and have children use context clues to figure out the words the "Word Washer" erased. Children can write their suggestions at the bottom of the page.
VISUAL/AUDITORY/KINESTHETIC

STUDENTS ACQUIRING ENGLISH

Pair children with native speakers of English to practice using context clues. Have partners take turns reading to each other, working together to try to figure out unfamiliar words.

RETEACH

See page R76 for lessons in multiple modalities.

CHALLENGE

Partners can write and exchange sentences that are missing words because of the "Word Washer."

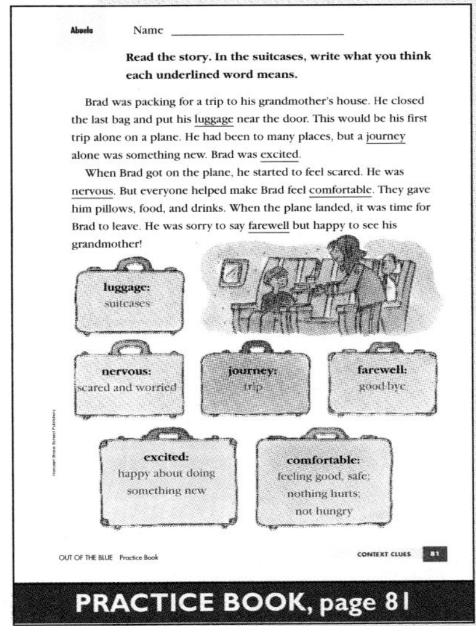

Abuela Name ______________

Read the story. In the suitcases, write what you think each underlined word means.

Brad was packing for a trip to his grandmother's house. He closed the last bag and put his luggage near the door. This would be his first trip alone on a plane. He had been to many places, but a journey alone was something new. Brad was excited.

When Brad got on the plane, he started to feel scared. He was nervous. But everyone helped make Brad feel comfortable. They gave him pillows, food, and drinks. When the plane landed, it was time for Brad to leave. He was sorry to say farewell but happy to see his grandmother!

luggage: suitcases

nervous: scared and worried

journey: trip

farewell: good-bye

excited: happy about doing something new

comfortable: feeling good, safe; nothing hurts; not hungry

OUT OF THE BLUE Practice Book CONTEXT CLUES 81

PRACTICE BOOK, page 81

FOR CONTEXT CLUES

***Grandmother and I* by Helen Buckley. Lothrop, Lee & Shepard, 1994. EASY**

***Sitti's Secrets* by Naomi Shihab Nye. Four Winds, 1994. CHALLENGE**

INTRODUCE: STUDY SKILLS

Reference Sources (Dictionary, Glossary)

OBJECTIVE: To locate information in a dictionary or glossary

Informal Assessment ✓

Are children able to

- ☑ arrange words in alphabetical order?
- ☑ locate words on a page?
- ☑ use guide words to help them locate words on a page?

Teach/Model

Discuss the function of glossaries and dictionaries. Ask children how they could figure out the Spanish words in "Abuela" if there were no clues in the story to help them. Remind them that the glossary on page 224 is a special dictionary for Spanish words and phrases from the story. Explain that words whose meanings can be found in a glossary or dictionary are called entry words. Ask children to look at the entry for the word *Abuela*. Ask them what information about the word follows it. Briefly explain how the pronunciation guide works. Do the same for another entry.

Point out that entry words on a dictionary or glossary page are always in alphabetical order. Provide dictionaries for children, or use the glossary pages in the Student Anthology. Have children all turn to the same page. Ask a volunteer to identify the first and last entry word on the page.

Then point out the guide words at the top of the page, and ask why they are there. (They are the first and last words on the page.) Explain that the guide word on the left-hand side of the page is the first entry word on the page, and the guide word on the right-hand side tells what the last entry word on the page is.

Practice/Apply

Have children use the dictionary and glossary. Tell children you will call out entry words for them to find in the dictionary. Encourage them to use alphabetical order and the guide words to help them. When a word has been located, have volunteers tell the page number, name the guide words, and read the definition.

Then have children turn to the glossary on page 224 and follow these directions:

- Point to the word *tía*. What does it mean? ("aunt")
- Point to the words that mean "Good day." (*Buenos días.*)
- Tell what *Cuidado* means. ("Be careful.")
- Point to the words that mean "so many birds." (*tantos pájaros*)
- What does *una silla* mean? (a chair)

Practice Activities

Make a Glossary

COOPERATIVE LEARNING Children can work in small groups to compile a glossary for a book. Provide each group with a different book that contains unfamiliar words. Have children find unknown words and list them on a sheet of paper. Then children can alphabetize the words. Provide dictionaries so that children can find definitions for the words. Then collect and display the books. Invite children to read the words in their glossary, and have classmates match the glossary with the appropriate book. If possible, insert the glossaries in the books and leave them in the class library. **VISUAL/AUDITORY**

Create a Dictionary Page

PERFORMANCE ASSESSMENT Duplicate a sheet of word cards with the following words: *bird, baby, banana, boat, city, cousin, bear, building.*

Tell children that they will use these words to make a dictionary or glossary page. Invite children to cut out the words and glue them in alphabetical order to another sheet of paper. Have them create definitions for each word and then write guide words at the top of the page. Encourage children to add pictures and example sentences to make their definitions as clear as possible. **VISUAL**

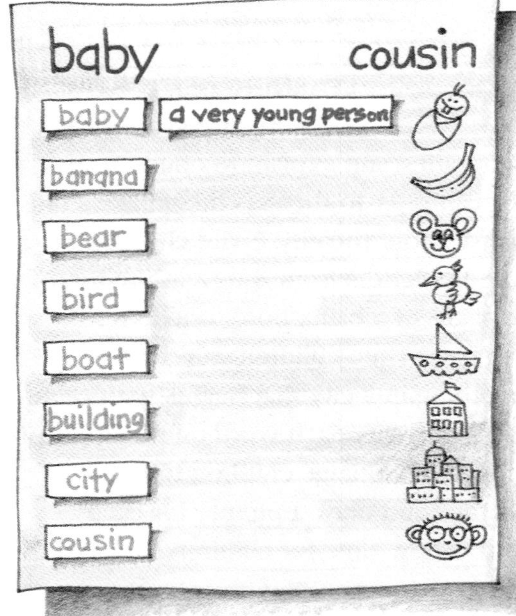

Reading Trade Books FOR REFERENCE SOURCES

"T" Is for "terrific," MAHJI'S ABC'S **by Mahji Hall. Open Hand, 1989.** **EASY**

MEETING INDIVIDUAL NEEDS

STUDENTS ACQUIRING ENGLISH

Provide an alphabet chart for children to use as a guide when looking up words in a dictionary or glossary.

RETEACH

See page R77 for lessons in multiple modalities.

CHALLENGE

Children can work in pairs to find unfamiliar words in favorite stories and look up each word in a dictionary. Encourage them to keep a log of words and their definitions.

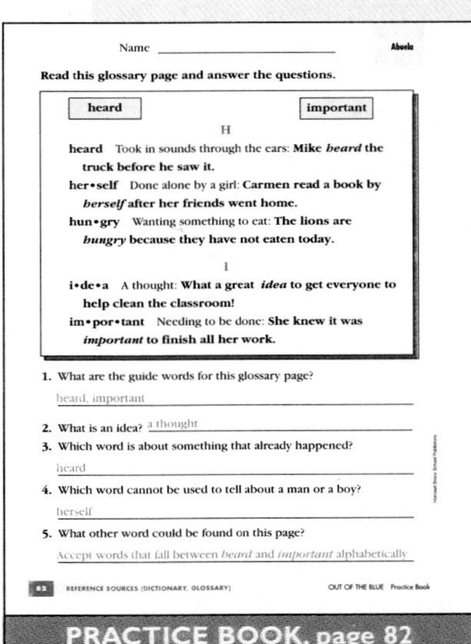

Name ______________ Abuela

Read this glossary page and answer the questions.

heard important

H

heard Took in sounds through the ears: **Mike *heard* the truck before he saw it.**

her•self Done alone by a girl: **Carmen read a book by *herself* after her friends went home.**

hun•gry Wanting something to eat: **The lions are *hungry* because they have not eaten today.**

I

i•de•a A thought: **What a great *idea* to get everyone to help clean the classroom!**

im•por•tant Needing to be done: **She knew it was *important* to finish all her work.**

1. What are the guide words for this glossary page? heard, important
2. What is an idea? a thought
3. Which word is about something that already happened? heard
4. Which word cannot be used to tell about a man or a boy? herself
5. What other word could be found on this page? Accept words that fall between *heard* and *important* alphabetically.

82 REFERENCE SOURCES (DICTIONARY, GLOSSARY) OUT OF THE BLUE Practice Book

PRACTICE BOOK, page 82

Integrated Curriculum

SOCIAL STUDIES

The City

TIPS FOR CLASSROOM MANAGEMENT

IF you don't wish to have children create whole alphabet books individually, **THEN** plan the activity as a class. Give each child a page to write and illustrate.

SOCIAL STUDIES

ABCs of the City

MATERIALS
- picture books about cities
- 26 pages stapled together in blank books
- markers or crayons
- pencils

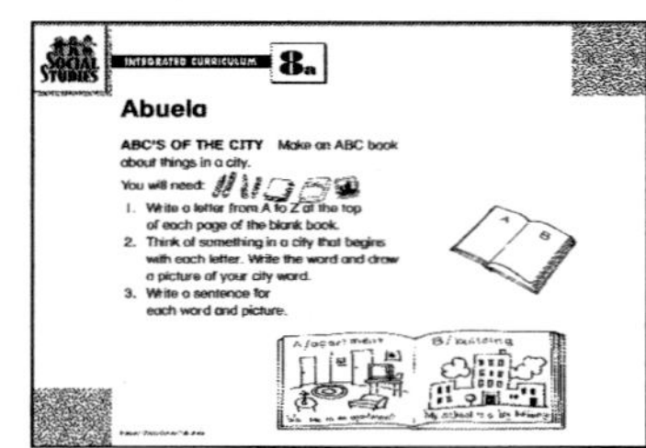
SOCIAL STUDIES INTEGRATED CURRICULUM 8a

Abuela

ABC'S OF THE CITY Make an ABC book about things in a city.

You will need:
1. Write a letter from A to Z at the top of each page of the blank book.
2. Think of something in a city that begins with each letter. Write the word and draw a picture of your city word.
3. Write a sentence for each word and picture.

Curriculum Card 8a

LEARNING CENTER Display a variety of picture books about cities, and explain to children that they can refer to them as they make a dictionary about the city. Invite children to write the letters from *A* to *Z* at the top of the pages of a blank book, one letter on each page. Then children can think of something in a city that begins with each letter and write each word on the appropriate page. Encourage children to write a sentence and draw a picture for each word. Allow time for children to share their books. READING/WRITING

ART

Design a City

MATERIALS
- large pieces of cardboard
- paper rolls
- small empty boxes
- corrugated paper
- fabric scraps
- pipe cleaners
- craft sticks
- cotton balls
- paint
- glue
- markers
- other materials useful for building a city

COOPERATIVE LEARNING Organize children into groups, and give each group a large piece of cardboard on which to build a model of a city. Place all the other materials in a central location. Each group will plan and build a model city, using the materials. Suggest that groups create buildings, streets, parks, schools, and stores for their cities. They might wish to bring toy cars, trucks, buses, people, and other objects from home to put in their cities. When cities are finished, invite each group to write sentences describing its city. Read the descriptions. Can children guess which city is being described? LISTENING/SPEAKING/READING/WRITING

TECHNOLOGY

Children can use *KID PIX* as they make their city dictionaries.

Imagination Express, Destination: Neighborhood

MATH

City Math

MATERIALS
- index cards
- pencils
- file box for the cards

Have children turn to pages 214–215 of "Abuela," and ask them to tell how many boxes of mangos, how many boxes of bananas, and how many boxes of papayas they see. Then model using this information to write a word problem. Provide index cards on which children can write their own word problems about things that might happen in a city. Write *City Math* on a card, and tape it to the top of a file box. Tell children to file their word problems in the box, and keep the box in a central location. Suggest that children choose and solve a problem from the box whenever they have spare time. READING/WRITING

There are 3 boxes of mangos on the dock. Each box has 22 mangos in it. How many mangos are there in all?

SCIENCE

Make It Fly

MATERIALS
- paper
- four paper clips per child

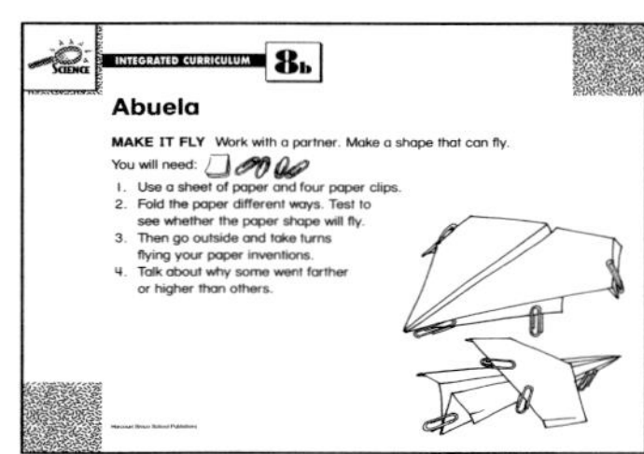

Curriculum Card 8b

Give pairs of children a sheet of paper and four paper clips each. Challenge pairs to use all the materials to make something that can fly. Suggest that they use scrap paper to try out their ideas before making their finished product. When children are finished, take them outside to take turns flying their creations. Observe and discuss why some of them went farther or higher than others. LISTENING/SPEAKING

Reading Trade Books

CROSS-CURRICULAR READING

City Sounds by Craig Brown. Greenwillow, 1992. EASY

The Inside-Outside Book of New York City by Roxie Munro. Puffin, 1994. EASY

MULTI-AGE CLASSROOMS

Have older children help younger children develop and solve City Math word problems.

CHALLENGE

Write *statue, traffic, subway, sirens, curb,* and *port* on the board. Expand on the Social Studies activity by having children find the meanings of these words and add them to their ABC books.

Reading Trade Books

Trade Books That Connect to "Abuela"

The Lion and the Little Red Bird

by Elisa Kleven

Talk with children about how the lion and the little red bird were able to understand each other without using language. Then have partners take turns trying to communicate with each other without using words or sounds.

Animal Tracks

by Arthur Dorros

Have children identify the tracks shown in the book. Ask them to choose one of the animals and then write an entry in the journal of a forest ranger. The journal entry can include the name of the animal, what it did, and a drawing of its footprint.

Ant Cities

by Arthur Dorros

Before reading, ask what children know about ants. Ask what they would like to know and write down their questions. After children have read, talk about the questions that were answered. Discuss the author's suggestion that ants build places to live and have workers just like people in a city do.

TIPS FOR CLASSROOM MANAGEMENT

SMALL GROUP
Read *The Lion and the Little Red Bird, The Armadillo from Amarillo,* and *Tar Beach* in small circles of children. As you read aloud, pause to let children talk about each part of the story.

PARTNER
Have children work with partners to read *Animal Tracks* and *Ant Cities.* Have them decide how they will read each book together.

INDEPENDENT
Place *Lunch with Milly* in a Reading Center. Have children read the book and write a letter to Milly in their personal journals.

MEETING INDIVIDUAL NEEDS

STUDENTS ACQUIRING ENGLISH

Ask children to tell about ways they celebrate events in their cultures. Invite them to name musical instruments or food from their cultures and identify the English word that has the same, or almost the same, meaning.

The Armadillo from Amarillo

by Lynne Cherry

Have children pretend to be an animal from their hometown or from a city in another country—a deer from Detroit, Michigan, or a llama from Lima, Peru. Help them locate their city on a world map, along with the state, country, and continent where it is found.

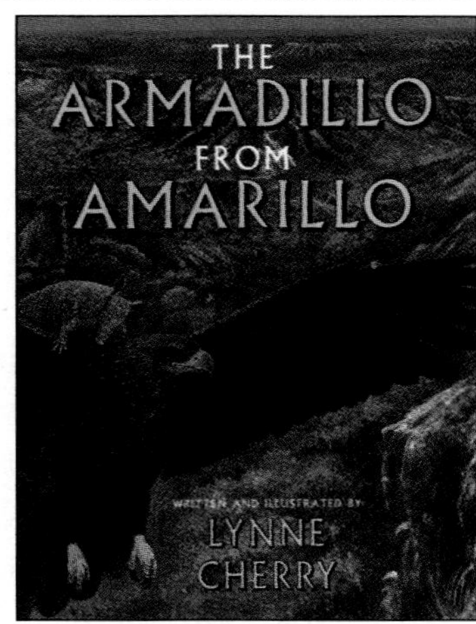

Lunch with Milly

by Jeanne Modesitt
illustrated by Robin Spowart

Ask children how the girl in *Lunch with Milly* used her imagination to persuade the animals to give her the ingredients for a dessert. Encourage children to use their imaginations to think of ways they could charm animals into giving them something.

Tar Beach

by Faith Ringgold

Ask children to tell how this story is like "Abuela." Then have them imagine that they are flying over a favorite place near where they live. Invite them to draw a picture and write about it.

Write and Send Mail

SELECTION CONNECTION

"Abuela" focuses on the fun Rosalba and her grandmother have together. Have children discuss how Rosalba and Abuela could communicate if Abuela had not come to this country.

PROJECT CHECKLIST

During this stage of the theme project, children should

- examine and discuss samples of written communication: notes, friendly letters, greeting cards, postcards, invitations, and thank-you notes.
- address envelopes to themselves, using group addresses and ZIP codes.
- pick a classmate's envelope, write to the classmate, and send the message.

When children have completed the checkpoint, have them write in their Project Journals about the kinds of communications they would like to send and receive.

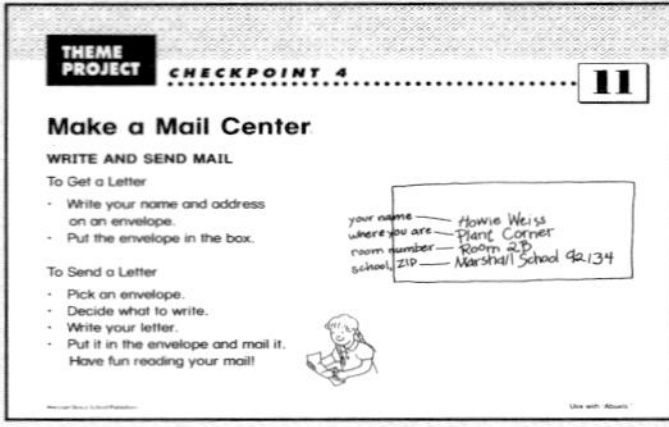

THEME PROJECT CHECKPOINT 4 **11**

Make a Mail Center

WRITE AND SEND MAIL

To Get a Letter

- Write your name and address on an envelope.
- Put the envelope in the box.

To Send a Letter

- Pick an envelope.
- Decide what to write.
- Write your letter.
- Put it in the envelope and mail it. Have fun reading your mail!

Project Card 11

Project Card 11 can be found as a copying master on page R91.

PLANNING TIPS

As children read samples of written communication, suggest that they

- study the parts of each message, such as the greeting and closing.
- notice the tone of the message; that is, formal or informal.
- experiment with different forms as they begin to send mail to classmates.

Informal Assessment

As children complete this checkpoint, they will **compare and contrast** forms of communication, **analyze** details in addresses, and **apply** what they learned as they create their own written communications. Children are thinking critically if they

- notice details in samples and write messages using what they have learned.
- make decisions about forms and formats to use for their messages.
- develop and send creative, original messages.

MEETING INDIVIDUAL NEEDS

STUDENTS ACQUIRING ENGLISH

Encourage children to include at least one new vocabulary word in their letters and notes. Have them keep a list of new words they've used.

MULTIPLE INTELLIGENCES

Children who are musically inclined might enjoy delivering singing messages to classmates.

HEME WRAP-UP

One of the most important lessons we can learn is how to be a good friend.

- How are the friendships between Matthew and Tilly and between Abuela and Rosalba alike? How are their friendships different?
- Do you think that Sid would be happy to find Mr. Putter and Tabby? Would Tabby be happy living on Aristotle Street or Pythagoras Place? Tell why you think as you do.

Activity Corner

All the stories in this theme are about people and pets that are special to someone. Think about someone who is special to you. What do you most want to tell that person? Write a note to tell your special someone how you feel.

THEME 2

Wrap-Up

1. **How are the friendships between Matthew and Tilly and between Abuela and Rosalba alike? How are their friendships different?** (Possible responses: Alike: The characters like to do different things together. Different: Matthew and Tilly are the same age, and Abuela and Rosalba are different ages; Abuela and Rosalba are in the same family, but Matthew and Tilly are not.) **CRITICAL: CLASSIFYING**

2. **Do you think that Sid would be happy to find Mr. Putter and Tabby? Would Tabby be happy living on Aristotle Street or Pythagoras Place? Tell why you think as you do.** (Responses will vary but could focus on these ideas: Sid might be happy with Mr. Putter and Tabby because he also likes to do the same things every day. He might not be happy, though, since he likes to be active and be with different people. Tabby probably wouldn't be happy on either street because she is more of a one-person cat.) **CRITICAL: MAKING JUDGMENTS**

ACTIVITY CORNER Suggest that children organize their thoughts about their special person before they begin writing. You may wish to model how to write a simple note.

Make a Mail Center

THEME PROJECT PRESENTATIONS

Options

EXTENDING INVITATIONS

- Have children invite other classes to see their mail center in action.
- Children can write and deliver the invitations to other classes.
- Have different groups take turns explaining and demonstrating how the system works.
- Children can offer to help other classes set up a mail center in their classrooms.

PEN PAL MAIL CENTER

- Have children make a videotaped presentation like the one they used to share their center with other classes in the school.
- Then have volunteers write to children in another school, inviting them to become your class's pen pals and telling them about the video.
- The pen pals can use information from the video to set up their own mail center.
- The two groups can write back and forth, using their mail systems for delivery.

SCHOOL↔HOME CONNECTION

Have children help plan a newsletter for their parents in which they report about the classroom mail center. The newsletter might include

- a report of the events leading up to the opening of the center.
- a drawing of the center or a flowchart showing how the system works.
- a survey reporting the reactions of several children to the experience.

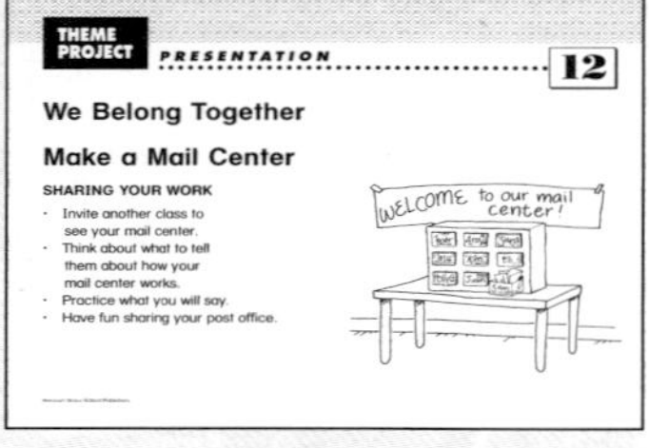

Project Card 12

Project Card 12 can be found as a copying master on page R92.

Community Connections

- As a group, write a letter to the post office expressing thanks for the tour or for the visit by a postal worker and explaining how your class applied what it learned to its own mail center.
- Have volunteer historians make a written, illustrated, and bound record of the project to be left for next year's class.
- Children can write letters to the children in next year's class to be delivered when they create their own mail center.

THEME PROJECT ASSESSMENT

SELF-ASSESSMENT

To assess children's perception of their own performance during this project, ask them to respond to the following questions orally or in writing:

- **What ideas did you share during group discussion?**
- **What did you do to finish your jobs?**
- **What did you learn from this project? How did you learn this?**

Children may also complete the Self-Evaluation Checklist in the *Out of the Blue Teacher's Edition.*

PEER ASSESSMENT

To assess children's perception of how well their groups worked together during this project, ask them to respond to the following questions.

- **Did each person in your group talk during discussions? Tell how they talked about others' work.**
- **What did you learn from other members of your group?**

Children may also complete the Peer Evaluation Checklist in the *Out of the Blue Teacher's Edition.*

RUBRIC

Performance Goals	Observable Characteristics 3	2	1
LAUNCH Classroom postal zones with ZIP codes	• easily synthesizes information to plan a classroom mail center	• can synthesize information, with help; offers ideas for classroom center	• has difficulty synthesizing information; does not offer ideas for classroom center
CHECKPOINT 1 Field trip to post office or Visit from postal worker or Group research	• is able to analyze new information during discussion • easily applies new information through role-play	• can analyze information during discussion fairly well • applies some new information through role-play	• cannot analyze information during discussion • cannot apply new information through role-play
CHECKPOINT 2 Class postal system plan	• is able to make reasonable judgments • easily applies information to create a mailbox	• is able to make fairly reasonable judgments • applies information to create a mailbox	• is unable to make reasonable judgments • has difficulty applying information to create a mailbox
CHECKPOINT 3 Class postal system rules	• can easily make good decisions about what to include	• can make somewhat reasonable decisions about what to include	• cannot make reasonable decisions about what to include
CHECKPOINT 4 Written communications	• analyzes information and applies it to create own letters	• with some help, can analyze and apply information to create own letters	• cannot analyze or apply information to create own letters without help
PRESENTATIONS Overall project	• participates cooperatively throughout • completes tasks on time	• usually participates cooperatively • completes tasks on time or a little late	• rarely participates cooperatively • completes tasks late or not at all

Reading Trade Books
Signatures Library

There's a Dragon in My Sleeping Bag

written by James Howe

illustrated by David S. Rose

THEME: FRIENDSHIP

We Belong Together

When a game of fantasy comes between two brothers, the boys realize the value of their friendship. Through the story, children learn about brotherly love and growing up.

SUMMARY Genre: Fantasy

Ever since Alex's older brother Simon invented the imaginary Dexter the Dragon, Alex hasn't had any fun. Simon now plays with Dexter instead of Alex. That's when Alex invents Calvin the Camel. But soon, Dexter and Calvin take over the boys' sleeping bags, chairs, swing, seesaw, and slide, and neither boy has any fun. Luckily, both Dexter and Calvin move to Boston and the brothers can play with each other again.

ABOUT THE AUTHOR AND THE ILLUSTRATOR

James Howe has written many popular books for children, including a series about Bunnicula, the vampire rabbit, and a series about two inseparable best friends, Pinky and Rex. He lives with his wife and daughter in New York.

David S. Rose has illustrated two other books written by James Howe. He has also written and illustrated his own children's books. He lives in a small town in Massachusetts with his family and their pets.

Building Background and Concepts

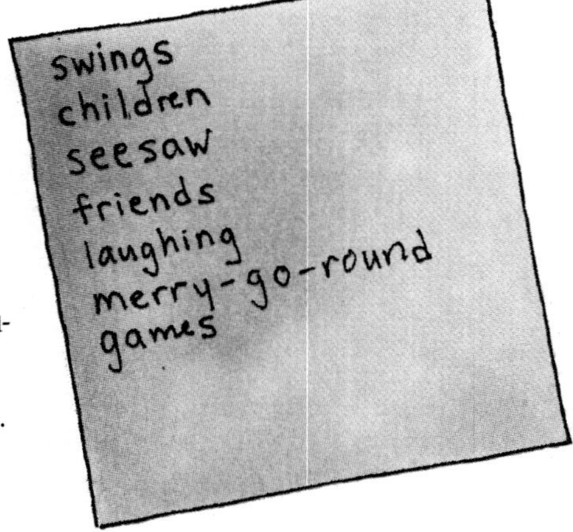

PRIOR KNOWLEDGE

Talk about playground sights and sounds. Have children pretend that they are at the playground. Ask them to share what they usually see and hear while playing. List children's responses.

Developing Concept Vocabulary

EXTENDING BACKGROUND KNOWLEDGE

Create a map. Review with children the playground list that was generated earlier. Then have them create and label a map of a playground or their own favorite place to play.

INTRODUCING THE BOOK

Display the book *There's a Dragon in My Sleeping Bag*. Read aloud the title and share the information about the author and the illustrator.

SCHOOL↔HOME CONNECTION

Have children create a make-believe "add-to" story with a family member. Have children begin the story and ask a family member to add to it. Have them keep taking turns adding to the story. Children can illustrate the story and bring it in to share with their classmates.

STUDENTS ACQUIRING ENGLISH

To help children understand the discussion of playgrounds, use illustrations from the book to show the swings, the slide, and the seesaw. Encourage them to record the new words in their journals, along with an illustration for each entry.

SPELLING GENERALIZATION

Words with o

Integrated Spelling Lesson 11

OPTIONS FOR READING

Tips for Classroom Management

SMALL GROUP		WHOLE CLASS	
PARTNER	**READ ALOUD**	**READ ALOUD**	**INDEPENDENT**
If some children have difficulty understanding the story, pair them with children who enjoy fantasy and can help explain the real and make-believe story events. Have partners take turns reading the story. Afterward, encourage them to discuss how they think each of the characters felt.	Have children preview some story illustrations and predict what the story will be about, based on their preview. Have each child read a page orally, then describe what they see in the illustrations. As children read, ask them whether they think Alex believes his brother.	Introduce the characters. Have children use the title and the cover illustrations to predict what the story is about. Read the story aloud and pause periodically to ask children how Alex feels about the dragon, his brother Simon, and Calvin the Camel.	Place the book in the Reading Center for independent reading. As children read the story, ask them to write down what they learn about Simon. For example, Simon has a great imagination, Simon is older than Alex, he is teasing Alex, and he misses playing with Alex.

Response Options

PERSONAL RESPONSE

- Do you think Alex believes in Dexter? In Calvin? Why or why not?
- What kind of person do you think Simon is? And Alex? Explain.
- Why do you think Dexter and Calvin go away?
- What did Simon learn in the story? What did Alex learn?
- Would you like an imaginary friend like Dexter or Calvin? Why or why not?

SMALL GROUP	WHOLE CLASS	INDEPENDENT
Have children reread the book, focusing on the relationship between the two brothers and how it changes.	Create a class chart. What conclusions can children draw? **What Dexter Did** | **What Calvin Did**	Have children pretend to be Alex. Ask what they would have done about the dragon.
In the story, the boys don't always say what they mean. As you reread the story, have children focus on the hidden meaning behind the words. Ask them to describe what is really happening in the story.	Ask children to role-play how the brothers feel about each other at different points in the story.	Have children complete the following chart for the story: **Things That Are Real** | **Things That Are Make-Believe**

Culminating Activities

ANIMAL FRIENDS

ART Encourage children to use their imagination to dream up an imaginary animal friend of their own. Have them draw their make-believe friend, including as many details as possible. Display the art on a bulletin board, and allow children to share their pictures with their classmates.

Play Acting

DRAMATIC PLAY Have groups of children collaborate on a short play about two or more siblings who don't get along. Encourage them to resolve the conflict. Have children perform the plays for their classmates.

GUESS THE ANIMAL

DRAMATIC PLAY Children may enjoy pantomiming different animals. Organize children into small groups. Then write the names of animals, such as *camel, elephant, monkey, giraffe, rabbit,* and *bird* on word cards. Have a volunteer from each group choose a card. Then have them pretend to be the animal, using only hand and body gestures. Have the other children guess the name of the animal.

Map It Out!

SOCIAL STUDIES Have children create and label a map of their homes. Encourage them to include rooms for family members and places where they like to play.

Dining Room | Kitchen | Bath-room | My Room | Ann's Room | Living Room | Play Room! | Mom and Dad's Room

MULTI-AGE CLASSROOMS Younger children often express their imaginative ideas easily. Have them help the older ones with ideas for the art and writing projects.

STUDENTS ACQUIRING ENGLISH Pair children with fluent readers who can help them figure out the meanings of new words and explain story events.

CHALLENGE Have children choose a paragraph or two from a realistic story and then rewrite it as a make-believe story.

Reading Trade Books
Signatures Library

Mary Ann

by Betsy James

THEME: FRIENDSHIP

We Belong Together

Children discover that sadness and loneliness can be overcome by new friendships. They will also learn that friendship itself can be found almost anywhere, even in nature.

SUMMARY Genre: Realistic Fiction

When her best friend, Mary Ann, moves away, Amy is sad and lonely until she finds a praying mantis. Amy names the mantis Mary Ann and cares for it in a terrarium until the insect lays her eggs and dies. Amy waits all winter for the eggs to hatch but nothing happens. Then she goes on a trip to visit her friend Mary Ann. When Amy returns home, the eggs have hatched and there are hundreds of Mary Anns!

ABOUT THE AUTHOR/ILLUSTRATOR

Betsy James is the daughter of a zoologist. Her father encouraged her to love nature and its creatures. *Mary Ann* was based on her childhood experiences. She now lives in New Mexico and has written several books for children and young adults. Her book *Long Night Dance* was named a VOYA Best Fantasy of 1990.

Building Background and Concepts

PRIOR KNOWLEDGE

Exploring the insect world. Have children express their thoughts and feelings about insects, spiders, worms, and other similar creatures. Encourage children to share any experiences they have had with insects, such as catching butterflies or fireflies. Ask children to imagine an insect as their friend. How does it compare with another pet they might have?

Developing Concept Vocabulary

EXTENDING BACKGROUND KNOWLEDGE

Gather group knowledge. Invite children to share what they know about insects. List their responses in a chart like the following:

Insect	What It Looks Like	Where It Lives	What It Eats
harvester ant	small; six legs	in the ground	seeds
grasshopper	long; wings	in the grass	leaves
caterpillar	long and green	in trees	leaves

INTRODUCING THE BOOK

Display the book *Mary Ann*. Read aloud the title and share the information about the author/illustrator.

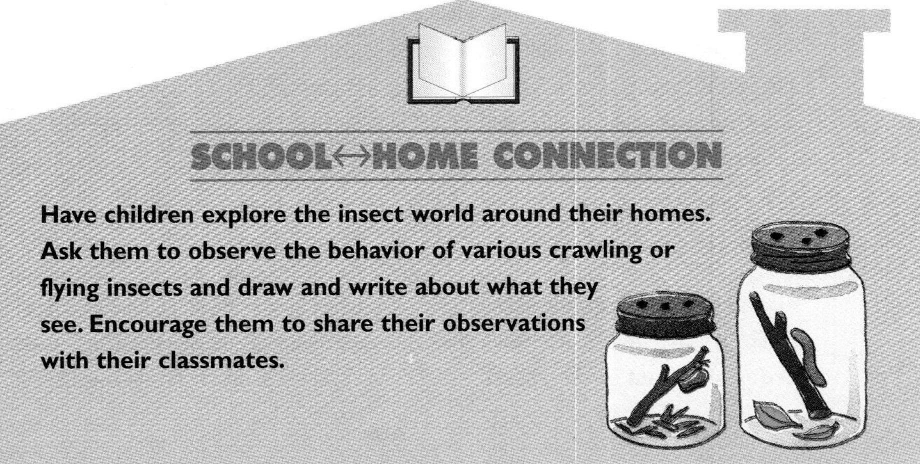

SCHOOL↔HOME CONNECTION

Have children explore the insect world around their homes. Ask them to observe the behavior of various crawling or flying insects and draw and write about what they see. Encourage them to share their observations with their classmates.

STUDENTS ACQUIRING ENGLISH

Write the names of various insects on word cards. Prepare another set of cards with pictures to match the words. Have children match the word cards to the picture cards. Encourage children to tell about different insects they have seen.

SPELLING GENERALIZATION

Words with o

Integrated Spelling Lesson 11

OPTIONS FOR READING

Tips for Classroom Management

SMALL GROUP		WHOLE CLASS	
PARTNER	**READ ALOUD**	**READ ALOUD**	**INDEPENDENT**
Have pairs of children take turns reading the story together. Encourage them to work together to figure out words they don't know. After children read the story, invite them to share their reactions, as well as experiences they have had with friends or insects.	Have children predict what the story will be about, based on the title and the cover. Then invite children to participate in the reading by having groups of three read the parts of Amy, her father, and her mother. Other children can take turns reading the narration.	As you or volunteers read the book, pause periodically to let children enjoy the illustrations. Ask them to predict whether Amy will get her wish for "hundreds and hundreds of Mary Anns." Can they predict where the family is going on its trip?	Place the book in the Reading Center for independent reading. As children read, have them write down what they learn about Amy from the illustrations, such as *she likes her cat because the cat is always with her* or *she likes to stay busy because she smiles when she is doing something.*

Response Options

PERSONAL RESPONSE

- Do you think Amy still misses her friend after she finds the praying mantis? Why or why not?
- Is it "fair" that Mary Ann moves away and the mantis dies? Explain.
- What kind of parents does Amy have? How do you know?
- What do you think happens to all the Mary Anns?
- Would you like a praying mantis for a friend? Why or why not?

SMALL GROUP	WHOLE CLASS	INDEPENDENT
Reread the book and allow time for children to observe and interpret details, such as the color green, the cat, and interesting details in the illustrations.	Have children make a list of all the things that Amy did for her praying mantis as they reread the story.	Have children draw their own pictures of a praying mantis.
Have children pretend to be Amy. Have them record ideas for a class chart. **How I Felt** **What I Did** **What I Found**	Have children work together to make a time line that shows the order of events in the story.	Challenge children to describe what happens next, either orally or in writing, to continue the story.

Culminating Activities

FRIENDSHIP TREE

LANGUAGE ARTS Have children think about qualities they like in a friend and write these qualities on small pieces of paper. Provide children with pieces of yarn to hang their word cards on a small tree or plant.

A Pet of Your Own

SCIENCE Allow children to share their experiences with pets and talk about the responsibilities of care and feeding. Ask children to think about pets they would like to have and explore the responsibilities involved in owning each type of animal. Then have small groups each make a poster that shows a pet, the kind of environment it needs, the food it eats, and its special requirements.

BUGS, BUGS, BUGS!

SCIENCE Take children outside to observe insects in their natural environment. Have them record their findings.

Pick Me!

LANGUAGE ARTS Have children pretend to be a pet that would like a new home. Have them write a newspaper ad that tells the kind of pet they are and the kind of home they are looking for. Then have them draw a picture of themselves to accompany the ad.

MULTI-AGE CLASSROOMS Ask older children to assist younger ones in locating books or magazine articles on animals and helping with vocabulary.

STUDENTS ACQUIRING ENGLISH Invite children whose first language is not English to share the names of various animals in their primary languages. If they have lived in another country, ask them to describe animals of that country.

CHALLENGE Suggest that children look for animal tracks when they are on a field trip or hiking on their own. Then have them try to identify the kinds of animals that made the tracks. Encourage them to make drawings of the tracks.

End-of-Theme Assessment Tools

IF you want to measure a child's mastery of reading and language skills and strategies, **THEN** administer the multiple-choice diagnostic **Skills Assessment.**	**IF** you want information about a child's ability to apply thinking skills in a global and holistic manner, **THEN** administer the **Holistic Reading Assessment.**	**IF** you want a comprehensive view of a child's reading and writing development skills, **THEN** administer the **Integrated Performance Assessment.**

Name ______________________ **Date** ______________________

Teacher ______________________ **Grade** ______________________

Theme Project Self-Assessment Checklist

WORKING IN A GROUP	☺	😐	☹
I shared my ideas.			
I listened to others.			
I worked well in my group.			
I did my job.			
I did my job on time.			

How I helped with the project:

THE FINAL PROJECT	☺	😐	☹
The project was neat, not messy.			
The project was put together the right way.			
The way we shared the project was good.			
The project was done on time.			

To make my next project even better, I could

THEME 3

Tell a Tricky Tale

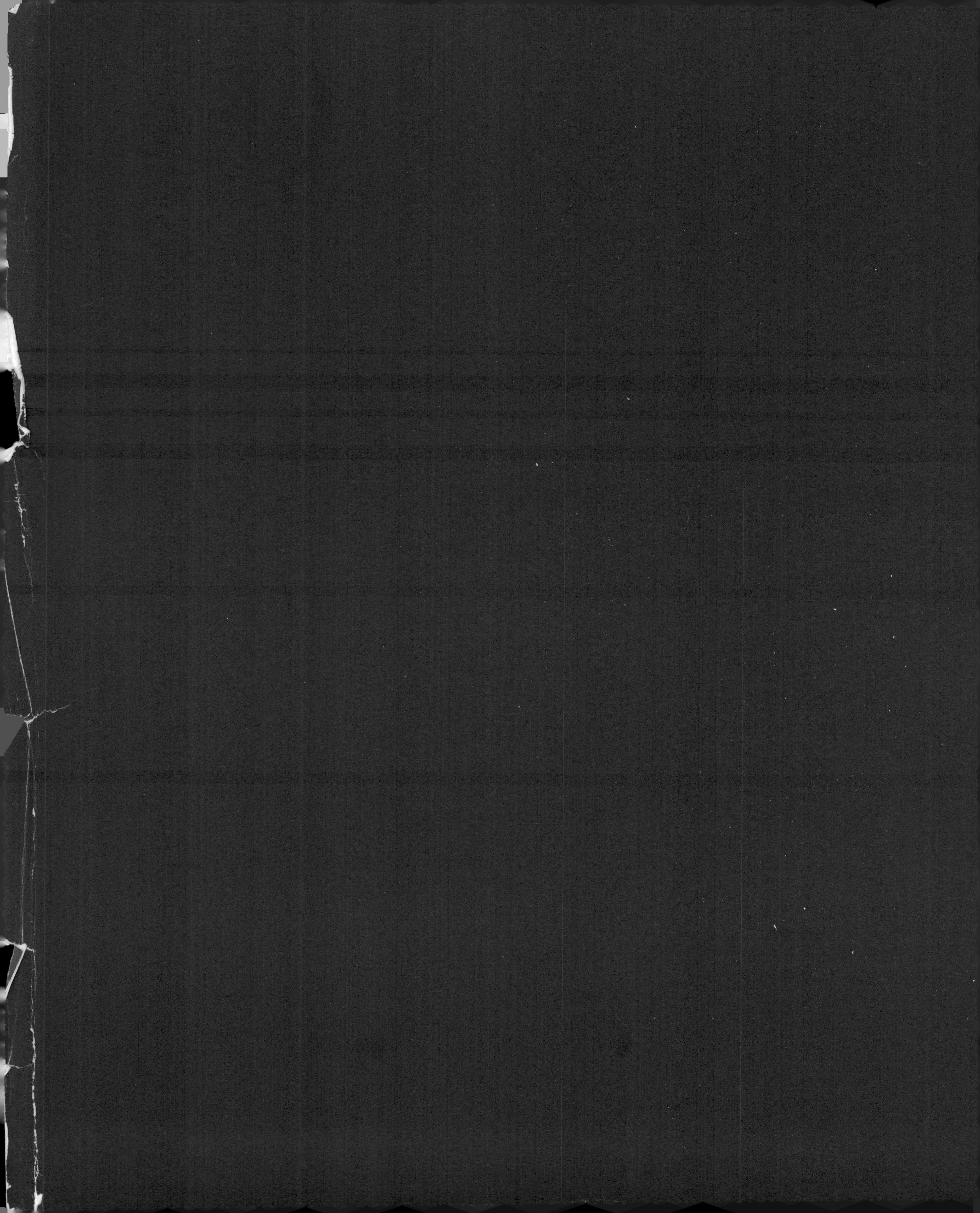

Communication

TELL A TRICKY TALE

Stories have been a form of communication for centuries.

In this theme, stories from Laos, the American Southwest, Africa, and Puerto Rico have something in common—smaller, more clever characters outwit larger, stronger animals.

Theme Overview

Tell a Tricky Tale

Communication

Long before people used written language, they communicated information and beliefs through storytelling. Stories about clever characters who play tricks on others appear in various forms in many cultures. Selections in this theme introduce readers to trickster tales.

Anansi and the Talking Melon

retold by Eric A. Kimmel T477–T528

"Anansi loved to eat melons, but he was much too lazy to grow them himself."

The character Anansi originated in West Africa and is also found in the Caribbean. In this tale, Anansi gets stuck inside a melon and then tricks the other animals into believing the melon can talk.

Anansi by Bert Simpson T506–T507

Anansi outsmarts a whole flock of crows in this poem, illustrating another exploit of this famous trickster.

Tricks Animals Play by Jan Nagel Clarkson T529–T536

Readers discover survival "tricks" of real animals in this nonfiction selection illustrated with fascinating photos.

Nine-in-One, Grr! Grr!

told by Blia Xiong T537–T588

"If Tiger has nine cubs each year, they will eat all of us. Soon there will be nothing but tigers in the land."

Clever Bird outwits forgetful Tiger to keep the tiger population in check in this tale from Laos.

ART AND LITERATURE: ***Storyteller Doll*** by Michelle Paisano T589–T590

Coyote by Gerald McDermott T591–T638

"Oh, if only I could fly," said Coyote. "I would be the greatest coyote in all the world!"

In this Zuni tale, trickster Coyote learns a lesson about bragging when he tries to fly like the birds.

Secret Messages by Gordon Penrose T639–T642

This selection gives readers directions to try out a surprising new way to communicate.

Rabbit and Tiger by F. C. Nicholson T643–T690

"My friends, when I am finished, Tiger will never show his striped face in Puerto Rico again!"

This play uses the theme of a smaller animal using its wits to get the better of a big, strong one.

Flexible Grouping

ANANSI AND THE TALKING MELON T477 – T528

	BELOW-LEVEL READERS	ABOVE-LEVEL READERS	ESL	BILINGUAL
1 READING AND RESPONDING Build Concepts and Vocabulary Strategic Reading Response Corner	**BEFORE** reading the selection, use the Previewing the Literature page of the *Intervention Strategies Manual* (p.50). **TEACHER-LED GROUP** **BEFORE** reading the selection, have children read the *Instant Reader Trickster* in pairs. **PAIRS**	**WHILE** others complete the strategic reading, have children choose and complete an Idea Bank activity. **COOPERATIVE GROUPS** **WHILE** others work in groups, have students read another book by Janet Stevens. **INDEPENDENT**	**AFTER** reading the selection, have children complete the reproducible page of the *Sheltered English/ESL Manual* (p. 35). **TEACHER-LED GROUP**	**AFTER** reading the anthology selection, choose the translation in the appropriate *Anthology Translation Booklet* and have children take it home to share. **INDEPENDENT** **INSTEAD OF** Strategic Reading, have Spanish-speaking children read *Estaba el Señor Don Gato* in CIELO ABIERTO. **TEACHER-LED GROUP**
2 INTEGRATING LANGUAGE ARTS Idea Bank Writer's Workshop Grammar Spelling Vocabulary Workshop	**WHILE** others work on Idea Bank activities, have children work with an above-level partner on the *Imagination Express, Destination: Rain Forest.* **PAIRS** **AFTER** the Writer's Workshop, children can enter their stories in *The Amazing Writing Machine.* **COOPERATIVE GROUPS**	**WHILE** others work on Idea Bank activities, children can complete the *Writer's Magazine* (pp. 34–35). **INDEPENDENT** **WHILE** doing the Writer's Workshop, children may use the *Language Handbook* (pp. 8–9) for a model of a story. **INDEPENDENT**	**BEFORE** the Writer's Workshop, use the Responding to the Literature page of the *Sheltered English/ESL Manual* (p. 37). **TEACHER-LED GROUP**	**DURING** the Writer's Workshop, use CIELO ABIERTO *Teacher's Handbook* page 74 to have children write a poem. **TEACHER-LED GROUP** **INSTEAD OF** completing the Grammar lesson, refer to page 11 in *Estaba el Señor Don Gato Teacher's Guide.* **TEACHER-LED GROUP**
3 LEARNING THROUGH THE LITERATURE Direct Skills Instruction Integrated Curriculum Reading Trade Books Theme Project	**WHILE** others work in groups, pull out a needs-based group for the Word Building activity on /ôr/. (p.T521) **TEACHER-LED GROUP** **WHILE** others work in groups, have children choose and read an *ESL/Title I Library* book. **INDEPENDENT**	**AFTER** the Practice Activities, have children add letters to the ends and beginnings of *or, ore,* and *our* to create more words. (p.T521) **INDEPENDENT** **AFTER** reading Trade Books, have children write a tale about a trickster like Anansi. (pp.T526–T527) **INDEPENDENT**	**AFTER** the Phonics and Decoding lessons, children can complete the *Phonics Activity Book* (pp. 28–29, 30). **COOPERATIVE GROUPS** **DURING** the Practice Activities, have children create a picture dictionary of common words that have the sound /ôr/ spelled *or, ore,* and *our.* (p.T521) **COOPERATIVE GROUPS**	**WHILE** others work in groups, have children complete the ongoing cross-curricular project. See page 2 in *Estaba el Señor Don Gato Teacher's Guide.* **COOPERATIVE GROUPS** **WHILE** others are reading trade books, have children choose and read a book from the *Multi-Language Library* and then take it home to share. **INDEPENDENT**

NINE-IN-ONE, GRR! GRR! T537 – T588

	BELOW-LEVEL READERS	ABOVE-LEVEL READERS	ESL	BILINGUAL
1 READING AND RESPONDING Build Background and Concepts Vocabulary Strategies Strategic Reading Response Corner	**BEFORE** reading the selection, use the Previewing the Literature page of the *Intervention Strategies Manual* (p. 56). **TEACHER-LED GROUP** **AFTER** reading the selection, children can reread with a partner. **PAIRS**	**AFTER** reading the selection, have children do some library research about the plants and land forms of Laos. (p.T545) **COOPERATIVE GROUPS** **AFTER** reading the story, children can choose and complete a Response Corner activity. **COOPERATIVE GROUPS**	**AFTER** children read the selection, have them choose and complete a Post-Reading Activity from Intervention Strategies. (pp.T570–T571) **TEACHER-LED GROUP**	**BEFORE** reading the anthology selection, choose the translation in the appropriate *Anthology Translation Booklet* and have children take it home to share. **INDEPENDENT** **INSTEAD OF** Strategic Reading, have Spanish-speaking children read *Dulce es la sal* in CIELO ABIERTO. Share *Shao and His Fire* with Hmong-speaking children and *Two Folk Tales from Southeast Asia,* with Vietnamese-speaking children, both books from the *Multi-Language Library.* **TEACHER-LED GROUP**
2 INTEGRATING LANGUAGE ARTS Idea Bank Writer's Workshop Grammar Spelling Vocabulary Workshop	**AFTER** the Grammar lesson, have children look for plural nouns with *-s* and *-es* as they read any of the *Living Books* on CD-ROM. (p.T576) **COOPERATIVE GROUPS** **DURING** the Vocabulary Workshop, help children draw a Venn diagram to compare the two parts of a simile. (p.T579) **TEACHER-LED GROUP**	**AFTER** completing the Writer's Workshop, have children write evaluations of their paragraphs for their portfolios. (p.T575) **INDEPENDENT**	**WHILE** others work on Practice Activities, give children sentences with plural nouns, and have them identify the plurals and their singular forms. (p. T577) **TEACHER-LED GROUP** **DURING** the Spelling lesson, use the Students Acquiring English note from *Integrated Spelling* Teacher's Edition Lesson 14. **TEACHER-LED GROUP**	**DURING** the Writer's Workshop, use the writing activity in the Activities for Responding to the Poem in *Dulce es la sal Teacher's Guide.* **TEACHER-LED GROUP** **INSTEAD OF** using the Vocabulary Workshop activities, use one of the Activities for Responding to the Poem in *Dulce es la sal Teacher's Guide.* **TEACHER-LED GROUP**
3 LEARNING THROUGH THE LITERATURE Direct Skills Instruction Integrated Curriculum Reading Trade Books Theme Project	**WHILE** reviewing the Phonics and Decoding lesson, have children complete the reproducible Phonics page of the *Intervention Strategies Manual* (p. 61). **INDEPENDENT**	**WHILE** others work in centers, children can practice reading a Trade Book aloud and then record it. **PAIRS**	**WHILE** others work on the Phonics and Decoding lesson, help a group complete the Word Building activity on the *-oy* phonogram. (p.T581) **TEACHER-LED GROUP**	**WHILE** others are reading trade books, have children choose and read a book from the *Multi-Language Library.* **INDEPENDENT**

Flexible Grouping

COYOTE T591–T638

	BELOW-LEVEL READERS	ABOVE-LEVEL READERS	ESL	BILINGUAL
1 READING AND RESPONDING Build Background and Concepts Vocabulary Strategies Strategic Reading Response Corner	**BEFORE** reading the selection, use the Previewing the Literature page of the *Intervention Strategies Manual* (p. 62). **TEACHER-LED GROUP** **AFTER** reading the selection, have children preview the Take-Home/Keep-at-Home Book *Leo's Trip to the City* to read for homework. **INDEPENDENT**	**BEFORE** reading the selection, children can make predictions in their personal journals. **INDEPENDENT** **WHILE** others read *Instant Readers,* have children complete the Writing to Extend the Story activity. (p. T610) **INDEPENDENT**	**AFTER** reading the selection, children can read the *Instant Reader The Fox and the Crow.* **INDEPENDENT** **AFTER** children read the selection, pull out a needs-based group for review of Key Words. (p. T594) **TEACHER-LED GROUP**	**AFTER** reading the anthology selection, choose the translation in the appropriate *Anthology Translation Booklet* and have children take it home to share. **INDEPENDENT** **INSTEAD OF** Strategic Reading, have Spanish-speaking children read *Coyote* in CIELO ABIERTO and then listen to it on the *Student Literature Cassette.* **TEACHER-LED GROUP**
2 INTEGRATING LANGUAGE ARTS Idea Bank Writer's Workshop Grammar Spelling Vocabulary Workshop	**WHILE** others work on Idea Bank activities, children can complete the *Writer's Magazine* (pp. 40–43). **TEACHER-LED GROUP** **WHILE** doing the Writer's Workshop, children may use the *Language Handbook* (pp. 8–9) for a model of a story. **INDEPENDENT**	**WHILE** you work with others, children can choose and complete an Idea Bank activity. **COOPERATIVE GROUPS** **AFTER** the Writer's Workshop, have children enter their stories in *The Amazing Writing Machine.* (p. T624) **COOPERATIVE GROUPS**	**BEFORE** the Writer's Workshop, pull out a needs-based group for a review of plural nouns. **TEACHER-LED GROUP** **DURING** the Spelling lesson, use the Students Acquiring English note in *Integrated Spelling* Teacher's Edition Lesson 15. **TEACHER-LED GROUP**	**DURING** the Writer's Workshop, use CIELO ABIERTO *Teacher's Handbook* page 71 to have children write a description. **TEACHER-LED GROUP** **INSTEAD OF** completing the Grammar lesson, refer to page 9 in *Coyote Teacher's Guide.* **TEACHER-LED GROUP**
3 LEARNING THROUGH THE LITERATURE Direct Skills Instruction Integrated Curriculum Reading Trade Books Theme Project	**WHILE** others work in centers, pull out a needs-based group for the Word Building activity using phonograms. (p. T631) **TEACHER-LED GROUP**	**WHILE** others are reading library books, children can complete the Theme Project Checkpoint. (p. T638) **COOPERATIVE GROUPS**	**WHILE** others work on Practice Activities, help children complete the *Phonics Activity Book* (p. 35). **TEACHER-LED GROUP** **WHILE** others work in groups, have children choose and read a selection from the *ESL/Title I Library.* **INDEPENDENT**	**WHILE** others work in groups, have children complete the ongoing cross-curricular project. See page 2 in *Coyote Teacher's Guide.* **COOPERATIVE GROUPS** **WHILE** others are working in groups, have children choose and read a book from the *Multi-Language Library.* **INDEPENDENT**

RABBIT AND TIGER T643–T690

	BELOW-LEVEL READERS	ABOVE-LEVEL READERS	ESL	BILINGUAL
1 READING AND RESPONDING Build Background and Concepts Vocabulary Strategies Strategic Reading Response Corner	**WHILE** reading the selection, use the Guided Reading page from the *Intervention Strategies Manual* (p. 69). **TEACHER-LED GROUP** **AFTER** reading the selection, have children research tigers by using encyclopedias and reference books. (p. T659) **COOPERATIVE GROUPS**	**AFTER** reading the selection, have children speculate about where Tiger will go after leaving Puerto Rico and describe his new life. (p. T666) **COOPERATIVE GROUPS** **AFTER** reading the selection, have children write an imaginary agreement between Rabbit and Tiger for their portfolios. (p. T657) **INDEPENDENT**	**AFTER** reading the selection, children can choose and complete an activity from Intervention Strategies. (pp. T672–T673) **COOPERATIVE GROUPS**	**BEFORE** reading the anthology selection, choose the translation in the appropriate *Anthology Translation Booklet* and have children take it home to share. **INDEPENDENT** **INSTEAD OF** Strategic Reading, have Spanish-speaking children read a play from *Escenas y alegrías* in CIELO ABIERTO. Share *The Tiger and the Frog* with Vietnamese-speaking children. **TEACHER-LED GROUP**
2 INTEGRATING LANGUAGE ARTS Idea Bank Writer's Workshop Grammar Spelling Vocabulary Workshop	**AFTER** the Spelling lesson, pull out a needs-based group for *Integrated Spelling* Lesson 16. **TEACHER-LED GROUP** **WHILE** you work with others, children can make the Take-Home/Keep-at-Home Book with an above-level partner. **PAIRS**	**WHILE** doing the Writer's Workshop, children may use the *Language Handbook* (pp. 26–27) for a model of a play format. **INDEPENDENT** **AFTER** the Writer's Workshop, children can enter their plays in *The Amazing Writing Machine*. **COOPERATIVE GROUPS**	**WHILE** others work on Grammar activities, write *he, she,* and *they* on the board, and have children stand up one or two at a time for others to label with a pronoun. (p. T679) **TEACHER-LED GROUP**	**INSTEAD OF** the Idea Bank activities, use one of the Responding to the Script activities in *Escenas y alegrías Teacher's Guide*. **TEACHER-LED GROUP**
3 LEARNING THROUGH THE LITERATURE Direct Skills Instruction Integrated Curriculum Reading Trade Books Theme Project	**WHILE** children review the Phonics lesson, use the Phonics and Decoding lesson and the reproducible Phonics page of the *Intervention Strategies Manual* (pp. 72–73). **INDEPENDENT** **WHILE** others work in groups, have children read *Phonics Practice Reader* 22. **INDEPENDENT**	**WHILE** others complete Trade Book activities, have children write a book report for a Trade Book they read. (pp. T688–T689) **INDEPENDENT**	**AFTER** the Phonics and Decoding lesson, children can complete the *Phonics Activity Book* (pp. 37–38). **TEACHER-LED GROUP** **WHILE** others work on Practice Activities for charts, have children make a chart of words in English and counterparts from their first languages. (p. T685) **TEACHER-LED GROUP**	**WHILE** others are reading trade books, have children choose a book from the *Multi-Language Library* to read and then take home to share with family members. **INDEPENDENT**

Ongoing Assessment Strategies

PORTFOLIOS

CONFERENCING WITH KIDS

Portfolio conferences provide you with an opportunity to learn about a child's reading and writing interests, attitudes, habits, and ability to use language strategies and conventions. Children benefit from the portfolio conference because it promotes reflection and self-assessment of their reading and writing. This helps them gain confidence in their own ideas and empowers them to take responsibility for their own progress and growth.

Try to hold a conference with each child during each marking period, scheduling conferences when children are organizing or reviewing their portfolios, revising and editing papers, writing in their journals, or reading silently. Before each conference, have children organize their portfolios to encourage self-reflection and analysis before the conference even begins.

When conducting conferences, remember these tips:

- Allow children to do most of the talking. Ask open-ended questions that call for explanations and examples.
- Avoid making judgments or being evaluative. Think of the conference as a time for the child to reflect about his or her own reading and writing.
- Help children assume responsibility for their development by urging them to discuss and articulate their progress.
- Collaborate with the child on a list of goals.
- Take notes during the conference, and review them together at the end.
- Put the notes and list of goals into the portfolio so they can be reviewed at the next conference.

See the SIGNATURES *Portfolio Assessment Teacher's Guide.*

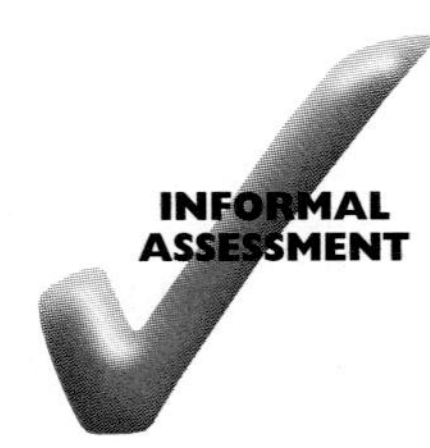

RUBRICS

Rubrics are tools that provide criteria to describe performance at varying levels of proficiency and provide a consistent way of assessing children's work. A rubric may be as simple as a checklist, in which a teacher indicates whether a child did or did not display a behavior, or it may be a set of scores or levels of attainment in which each score or level has its own set of performance criteria. One of the most important reasons for using rubrics is that they can help teachers score children's work more accurately and fairly.

Rubrics can also help children. When a teacher shares a scoring rubric, it provides children with

- an opportunity to focus on the criteria for excellence before they attempt the task.
- a listing of concrete qualities their work should exhibit—thereby giving them a better chance to produce those qualities.
- an understanding of how their work has been evaluated.

As the use of performance assessment spreads, rubrics that provide criteria describing performance at various levels of proficiency are becoming more commonplace—whether they are provided for teachers or written by teachers. Assessment then becomes a systematic rather than an intuitive process for both the teacher and the student.

End-of-Theme Formal Assessment Tools

SKILLS ASSESSMENT

Multiple-choice diagnostic tests that measure mastery of the following skills:

- Reading: vocabulary, *r*-controlled vowel (/ôr/*ore, or, our, oor, oar*), and alphabetical order
- Language: names of days, months, and holidays; plural nouns with *s* and *es;* irregular plurals; and pronouns

HOLISTIC READING ASSESSMENT

Reading passages with multiple-choice and open-ended questions to assess children's application of literal, inferential, and critical thinking in a global and holistic manner

INTEGRATED PERFORMANCE ASSESSMENT

Performance tasks to gain a comprehensive view of a child's reading and writing progress. Children read and respond to "I Win!" from *That Tricky Coyote,* retold by award-winning author Gretchen Will Mayo. Children demonstrate expressive writing in folktale form. One or both sections may be used.

THEME 3

Tell a Tricky Tale

DISCUSSING THE THEME

Invite children to read about the theme on page 229. Ask them to name some favorite fairy tales, fables, and folktales. Explain that some stories have been told and retold many times over the years. Many storytellers add their own ideas and twists, which change the tales a little. For example, there are many different versions of the classic tale "The Three Little Pigs." Ask children what they think the tricky tales in this theme will be about.

TELL A TRICKY TALE

230

231

Previewing the Theme Literature

Read the table of contents on pages 230–231 with children. If they are familiar with any of the selections, poets, authors, or illustrators, ask them to share what they know.

As children scan the table of contents, encourage them to predict how some of the titles might relate to the theme Tell a Tricky Tale.

Discuss stories children have read in which characters are tricked. Have volunteers describe the characters and tell how they tricked another character or were tricked themselves.

The Signatures Library

Two of Everything, retold and illustrated by Lily Toy Hong, is a Chinese folktale that tells about a poor farmer and his wife who find a large pot that duplicates anything that is put inside it. They soon find, however, that even their troubles begin to double!

The Rooster Who Went to His Uncle's Wedding by Alma Flor Ada, is a cumulative folktale from Latin America that tells how a rooster enlists his friend the sun to help him clean his beak.

Strategies for reading *Two of Everything* appear with the "Nine-in-One, Grr! Grr!" lesson on page T586. Strategies for *The Rooster Who Went to His Uncle's Wedding* appear with the "Rabbit and Tiger" lesson on page T688.

Comprehensive lesson plans are available on pages T694–T701.

Related Reading

These trade books offer children further opportunities to work with the Tell a Tricky Tale theme.

ESL / Title I Library

These easy-to-read library books connect to the theme Tell a Tricky Tale: *Buzz Said the Bee* by *Wendy C. Lewison*; *Hello, House!* by *Linda Hayward.*

THEME PROJECT OVERVIEW

Create and Present Stories

THEME OVERVIEW

The selections in this theme all have one thing in common—a trickster character. In this project, children will explore different storytelling styles and formats and then create their own tales. Each lesson is followed by a Project Checkpoint that will help children complete the project.

PROJECT PLANNER

QUESTION: How can we use our imaginations to create and present stories? (Invention)

STAGES	GOALS
 **PROJECT LAUNCH** (p.T475) 2-3 days	**Make a list of ways to tell a story.** • Name and share favorite stories. • List ways to tell a story.
 **CHECKPOINT 1** (p.T528) 3-4 days	**Explore storytelling techniques.** • Learn about different storytelling techniques. • Explore visual and oral devices used to tell stories. • Learn movements from a guest storyteller that they can use to tell a story.
 **CHECKPOINT 2** (p.T588) 2-3 days	**Choose a story idea.** • Brainstorm a list of stories to tell. • Choose favorite ideas and form story groups.
 **CHECKPOINT 3** (p.T638) 4-6 days	**Create a story.** • Plan and record their stories. • Divide tasks, keeping in mind group members' interests and abilities.
 **CHECKPOINT 4** (p.T690) 4-6 days	**Create a unique way to share the group's story.** • Develop ways to make their stories come alive. • Plan a Story Festival and practice their stories.
 **PROJECT PRESENTATIONS** (p.T692) 3-4 days	**Perform and display their work.** • Tell their stories. • Videotape the performance. • Lend their videotape to the school or public library.

STUDENTS ACQUIRING ENGLISH

Encourage children to use body language, facial expressions, and gestures to express things they have trouble verbalizing in English. Help them find ways to contribute to their groups' stories.

EXTRA SUPPORT

Enrich the class library with easy-to-read versions of folktales and encourage children to read them independently. Choose traditional tales for read-aloud time.

INQUIRY PROJECT IDEAS

Children may also wish to investigate other aspects of storytelling. They may research and share information about such topics as

- **sign language.**
- **a favorite story writer.**
- **stories that have been passed down in their cultures.**

PROJECT LAUNCH

LAUNCH OPTIONS	
AND THEN . . . (PAIRS) Give each child a comic strip from the newspaper. Tell them to study the comics and then tell the stories to partners.	**PICTURE READING** (SMALL GROUPS) Cut out magazine and newspaper pictures that show people involved in different situations. Have groups study one of the photographs and discuss as a group what they think is happening in it. Encourage different interpretations.

WHOLE-GROUP DISCUSSION

Ask children about their favorite kinds of stories. Ask them to think of a story they enjoyed recently. Talk about what children liked about a story and about its characters or plot. If possible, plan for children to bring in their favorite books, tapes, or videos and share them over a span of a few days.

FORM PROJECT GROUPS

Encourage children to notice different forms of stories and different ways stories can be told. Ask children to brainstorm a list of as many ways to share a story as they can.

Kinds of Stories	Ways to Share Stories
adventure	in a book
fairy tales	on a video or on TV
realistic	at the movies
fantasy	songs
rhyming	telling someone
stories without words	putting on a play
	tape recording

Project Card 13 can be found as a copying master on page R150.

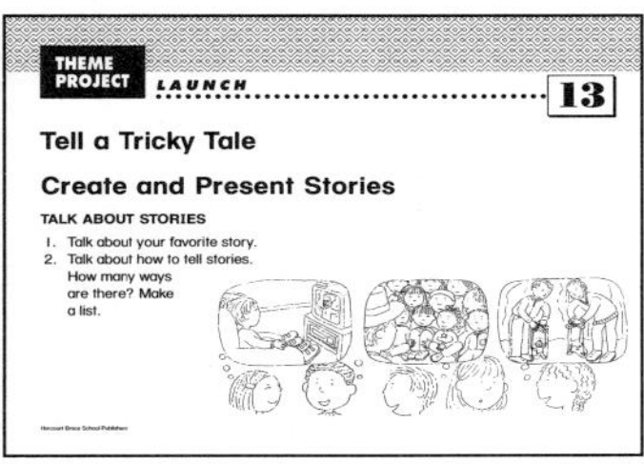
THEME PROJECT LAUNCH 13

Tell a Tricky Tale

Create and Present Stories

TALK ABOUT STORIES

1. Talk about your favorite story.
2. Talk about how to tell stories. How many ways are there? Make a list.

Project Card 13

DID YOU KNOW?

- The development of video cameras began in the 1930s. They were first developed to record live television broadcasts. They produced black-and-white images.
- Color video was developed in the 1950s.
- By the 1980s, videotape recorders were small enough to be combined with a video camera in one unit, the camcorder.

PROJECT MANAGEMENT

ADDITIONAL RESOURCES

BOOKS

Life Story by Virginia Lee Burton. Houghton Mifflin, 1962.

Sing, Pierrot, Sing: A Picture Book in Mime by Tomie dePaola. Harcourt Brace, 1983.

The Tapestry Cats by Ann Turnbull. Little, Brown, 1992.

FORMAL ASSESSMENT

Prompts for self- and peer assessment and a rubric for teacher assessment are provided on page T693.

Planning a Literacy Event

Story Festival Begin planning a Story Festival as a culminating activity to be held at the completion of the theme. Children who complete the theme project will present their stories at this event, and an adult will videotape their presentations. Children invite everyone who attends to join them for the cast party that follows. They prepare simple refreshments to be enjoyed as everyone views the videotape.

- Set a date for the Story Festival.
- Have children prepare a program for this event, including introductions by each group.
- Children can design and prepare invitations for family members and other interested adults.
- Appoint a publicity committee to generate interest for the event.

Enlisting Parents as Partners

Reading: The Key to Success During conferences, parents may ask for ideas to get their children reading. Offer these suggestions:

- ☑ Read aloud to your child regularly. Let your child learn that reading together can be a special time for the two of you.
- ☑ Try practicing beforehand so your reading is smooth and animated. This will help your child learn how to read more naturally, too.
- ☑ Ask your child to read along, but remember to have some "free" sessions when your child can just relax and listen. Listening is valuable language experience, too!

TECHNOLOGY

The *At Home in Our Schools* videocassette contains numerous ideas for family involvement projects.

Surfing the Internet? See Issues and Ideas on the Harcourt Brace Home Page: http://www.hbschool.com

The *Family Involvement Newsletter* for this theme contains further suggestions on this topic and other topics of interest to parents.

Anansi and the Talking Melon

retold by Eric A. Kimmel

illustrated by Janet Stevens

Children's Choice

Linking Poetry to Fiction

Children experience the clever nature of Anansi the spider.

Anansi

Anansi has a mango tree,
He loves the fruit so ripe.
He cannot reach the mangoes
But he longs to have a bite.

Anansi tells his friend the crow,
"You're beautiful to me."
Old crow calls her friends
So they can hear his flattery.

The crows fly to the mango tree,
They bend the branches down.
Anansi sees them swing and sway
And mangoes hit the ground.

Bert Simpson

Illustrated by Mercedes McDonald

THEME: COMMUNICATION

Tell a Tricky Tale

In "Anansi and the Talking Melon," children will meet a troublemaking spider that is a well-known African folktale trickster.

SELECTION SUMMARY

Genre: Folktale

Anansi the spider bores his way into one of Elephant's melons and plays a trick by speaking to Elephant from inside the melon. Elephant and his gullible friends show the "talking" melon to the king. The melon insults him, so the angry king throws it and smashes it. Released, Anansi begins to eat some bananas and says teasingly to Elephant, *"We bananas should have warned you. Talking melons are nothing but trouble!"*

Eric A. Kimmel

ABOUT THE AUTHOR AND THE ILLUSTRATOR

ERIC A. KIMMEL, a native of Brooklyn, New York, grew up hearing the stories of his grandmother, an immigrant to the United States from Eastern Europe.

JANET STEVENS is not only an illustrator of children's books, but an author as well.

For more information about the author and the illustrator, see pages T504–T505.

Janet Stevens

SUGGESTED LESSON PLANNER

▶ *Anansi and the Talking Melon*

	DAY 1	DAY 2
PART 1 Reading Listening Speaking Viewing **Key Words** lazy angry used hungry thorn full course bore squeezed	**BUILD BACKGROUND** T480 **VOCABULARY STRATEGIES** T480–T481 *Chart/Transparency 19* *Practice Book* pp. 86–87 **READING THE SELECTION** T482–T505 Options for Reading T482–T483 *Response Card 1* **REVIEW PREDICTIONS/PURPOSE** T502 **APPRECIATING THE LITERATURE** T502 NOTE: Children may read the selection on Day 2.	**SUMMARIZE AND RETELL THE SELECTION** T503 *Practice Book* p. 88 **READ POETRY** T506–T507 "Anansi" ◆ **RESPONSE CORNER ACTIVITIES** T508–T509 **CHECKING COMPREHENSION** T509 *End-of-Selection Test* 
PART 2 Writer's Workshop	**A STORY** Thinking as Writers T514 *Chart/Transparency 6*	Prewriting T514
Grammar	✓ **NAMES OF DAYS, MONTHS, AND HOLIDAYS** Teach the Concept T516 Daily Language Practice (1–2) R142	Daily Language Practice (3–4) R142 Practice Activity T517 *Trudy's Time & Place House* (Calendar Clock)
Spelling	**WORDS WITH *a-e* AND *i-e*** *take game gave life five late nice make fine time* Pretest/Self-Check T518 *Integrated Spelling Teacher's Edition* pp. T93, T280	Open and Closed Sorts T518 *Integrated Spelling* p. 58 *Integrated Spelling Teacher's Edition* p. T94
PART 3 Phonics	✓ ***R*-CONTROLLED VOWEL: /ôr/*or, ore, our*** Phonics-Vocabulary Connection T481	✓ ***R*-CONTROLLED VOWEL: /ôr/*or, ore, our*** (Introduce) T520 *Big Book of Rhymes* p. 15 *Phonics Practice Book* p. 147 *Bailey's Book House* (Read-A-Rhyme)
Skills and Strategies	◆ **INTEGRATED CURRICULUM** *Africa* **Social Studies** T524 **Music** T524 **Science** T525 **Health** T525 *Imagination Express, Destination: Rain Forest*	**PHONICS AND DECODING MINILESSON** T485 Long Vowel: /ō/*o-e, ow* (Maintain) *Phonics Activity Book* p. 31 *Phonics Practice Book* pp. 77–89 *Practice Book* p. 93
MEETING INDIVIDUAL NEEDS	Use the Students Acquiring English notes on pages T489, T490, T493, and T501 to help **ESL readers.**	During the Response Corner activities, refer to the Varying the Activity note on page T508 for **below-level readers**.

NOTE: An alternative lesson plan for **below-level readers** appears on *Intervention Strategies Manual* pp. 50–55. A lesson for **students acquiring English** appears on *Sheltered English/ESL Manual* pp. 34–37.

DAY 3	DAY 4	DAY 5
◆ **IDEA BANK ACTIVITIES** Listening and Speaking T512 Real-Life Reading: Reading Seed Packets T512 Oral Language T513 Kinesthetic T513 *Writer's Magazine* pp. 34–35 *Imagination Express, Destination: Rain Forest* School–Home Connection 9 R172	**VOCABULARY WORKSHOP** T519 Reviewing Key Words Story Strips R176 Dialogue Words *Take-Home/Keep-at-Home Book: Cloud Weaver* **READING TRADE BOOKS** T526–T527  Take-Home Book	**READING TRADE BOOKS** T521, T523, T525, T526–T527 
Drafting T514 *Language Handbook* pp. 8–9 *The Amazing Writing Machine*	Responding and Revising T515	Proofreading and Publishing T515 *Kid Pix*
Daily Language Practice (5–6) R142 Practice Activity T517 *Language Handbook* pp. 62–65	Daily Language Practice (7–8) R142 Practice Activity T517 *Grammar Practice Book* pp. 39–42	Daily Language Practice (9–12) R142 *Practice Book* p. 89
Discuss the Generalization T518 *Integrated Spelling* p. 59 *Integrated Spelling Teacher's Edition* p. T95	Apply to Writing T518 *Integrated Spelling* pp. 60–61 *Integrated Spelling Teacher's Edition* pp. T96–T97	Posttest T518 *Practice Book* p. 90 *Integrated Spelling Teacher's Edition* p. T98
✓ ***R*-CONTROLLED VOWEL: /ôr/*or, ore, our*** T521 *Phonics Practice Reader 18: Mort's Country Store and More* *Phonics Activity Book* pp. 28–29 *Practice Book* p. 91	**SHORT VOWEL: /u/*ou*** (Introduce) T522 *Big Book of Rhymes* pp. 16–17 *Phonics Practice Book* pp. 63–64 *The Amazing Writing Machine*	**SHORT VOWEL: /u/*ou*** T523 *Phonics Practice Reader 19: What Can I Touch?* *Phonics Activity Book* p. 30 *Practice Book* p. 92
GRAMMAR MINILESSON T493 ✓ Names of Special People, Animals, and Places (Review) *Language Handbook* pp. 58–61	**STUDY SKILLS MINILESSON** T495 ✓ Alphabetical Order (Review) *Practice Book* p. 94	**PHONICS AND DECODING MINILESSON** T501 ✓ R-Controlled Vowel: /är/*ar* (Maintain) Theme Project Checkpoint 1 T528
During the phonics skill lesson, refer to the Challenge note on page T521 for **above-level readers**.	Have children read "Tricks Animals Play," pages 262–267, to connect nonfiction about animal tricks with the selection.	To help students build fluency, use the *Instant Readers™ Trickster* and *Hiding in Plain Sight* on pages T510–T511.

✓ = Tested Skill
◆ = Optional activities that may be used to adjust pacing throughout the lesson
Titles in *italics* are optional materials.

1 Reading and Responding

BUILDING BACKGROUND AND CONCEPTS

PRIOR KNOWLEDGE

Discuss spiders. Ask children what comes to mind when they hear the word *spider*. List their responses on the board. Ask them to imagine what a spider might say if it could talk. Have children take turns role-playing a talking spider. Encourage other children to ask the "spider" questions—for example: "*What do you eat? Where do you sleep? Are you afraid of anything?*"

EXTRA SUPPORT

Discuss whether a talking spider is real or make-believe. Encourage children to list some things that might be included in a selection about real spiders and one about a make-believe spider.

Real Spiders	Make-Believe Spiders
spin webs	talk
eat insects	wear clothes
have eight legs	eat sandwiches

Intervention Strategies

For children who may have difficulty reading "Anansi and the Talking Melon," support is available in *Intervention Strategies Manual*, pages 50–55 and on pages T496 and T510–T511 in this lesson.

STUDENTS ACQUIRING ENGLISH

See *Sheltered English/ESL Manual* pages 34–37.

VOCABULARY STRATEGIES

KEY WORDS DEFINED

lazy not willing to work
hungry wanting food
(of) course naturally
angry mad
thorn a sticker on a plant
bore make a hole
used made use of
full having had enough to eat
squeezed pressed

SUPPORT WORDS

Display the words *exclaimed, impatient, insult, replied,* and *ridiculous.* Discuss their meanings and have them used in sentences.

INTEGRATED SPELLING

SPELLING PRETEST: page T518
SPELLING GENERALIZATION: Words with *a-e* and *i-e*

"One method of building background for a story that I find particularly helpful is to read a short nonfiction account or watch an informative video about a person, place, or thing important to the story. I ask the children to list facts they learn and then compare this information with what they read in the story. Not only is this a good way to expand prior knowledge, but it also helps children discover and appreciate the difference between fiction and nonfiction."

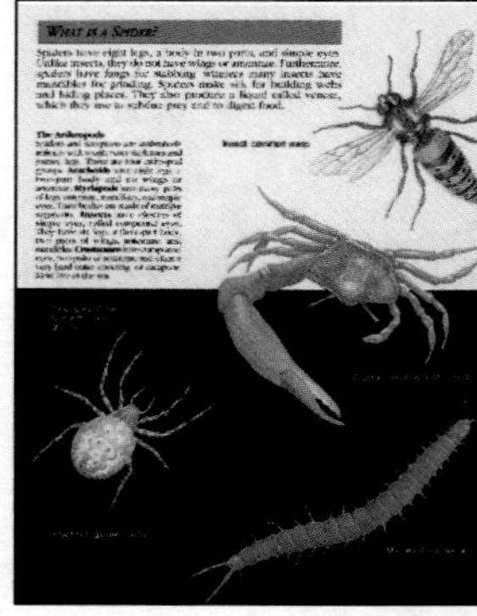

CUEING SYSTEMS

Use the chart to teach new vocabulary. Display Chart/Transparency 19, or write the words and sentences on the board. Encourage children to read words they might know.

Cover all but the letter *l* in the word *lazy* with a self-stick note. Ask children to suggest words that would make sense in the sentence and list them on the board. Then have them read the second and third sentences, and encourage them to revise their list. Ask:

Does the word make sense in the sentence?
Does it make sense with the rest of the sentences?
Does it begin with the letter *l*?

Have children read the rest of the story, using sounds for letters and the sense of the story to help them figure out the underlined words.

CHART/TRANSPARENCY 19

lazy	hungry	course	angry	thorn
bore	used	full	squeezed	

Deep in the jungle lived a lazy monkey. One day the monkey was hungry. Of course, she didn't feel like swinging over to the banana tree.

Just then an angry elephant came by. He had a thorn stuck in his trunk. It must have been really sharp to bore a hole through an elephant's skin.

The monkey felt sorry for the elephant. She got the thorn out for him. The happy elephant used his trunk to get bananas for the monkey.

The monkey got so full eating bananas that she almost got stuck in the tree! Finally, she squeezed between the branches and went home.

HANDS-ON ACTIVITY

Play a Key Word card game. Have each child write the Key Words on word cards. Then have children form groups of four to play "Go Fish." Children combine their sets and shuffle; then one child gives four cards to each player in the group. The rest of the cards become a draw pile. Children lay any matching pairs of word cards down, and then take turns asking other players questions like "Do you have *hungry*?" If so, the second player gives the card to the first, who lays the matching pair down and uses the word in a sentence. If not, the first player takes a card from the draw pile.

THORN thorn bore bore

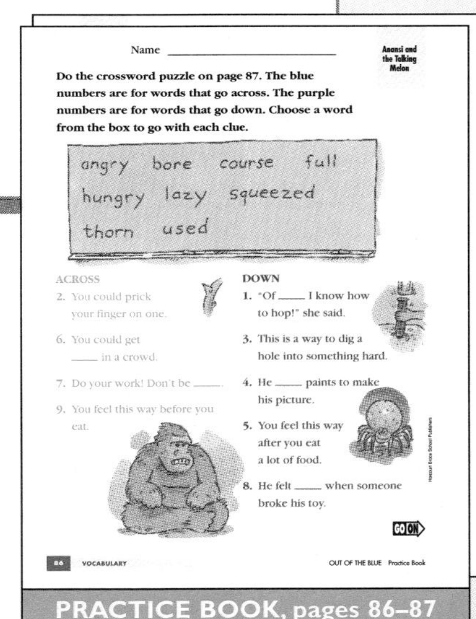
Name ______

Anansi and the Talking Melon

Do the crossword puzzle on page 87. The blue numbers are for words that go across. The purple numbers are for words that go down. Choose a word from the box to go with each clue.

angry bore course full
hungry lazy squeezed
thorn used

ACROSS
2. You could prick your finger on one.
6. You could get ____ in a crowd.
7. Do your work! Don't be ____.
9. You feel this way before you eat.

DOWN
1. "Of ____ I know how to hop!" she said.
3. This is a way to dig a hole into something hard.
4. He ____ paints to make his picture.
5. You feel this way after you eat a lot of food.
8. He felt ____ when someone broke his toy.

86 VOCABULARY OUT OF THE BLUE Practice Book

PRACTICE BOOK, pages 86–87

PHONICS-VOCABULARY CONNECTION

WORD TOWER

Invite children to build a word tower. At the bottom in a rectangular "brick" is the word *thorn.* On top children should add as many words as they can that rhyme with *thorn* and that are spelled with *or.* Each word should be inside a brick. Ask children to build a second tower with the word *bore* at its base. Compare the heights of the towers. Then have children repeat with *four.* The concept of the *r*-controlled vowel /ôr/*ore, or, our* is further developed on pages T520–T521.

Strategic Reading

STRATEGY FOCUS: VISUALIZING

Review with children some of the things good readers do when they read. Encourage children to suggest new ideas and add them to their classroom chart.

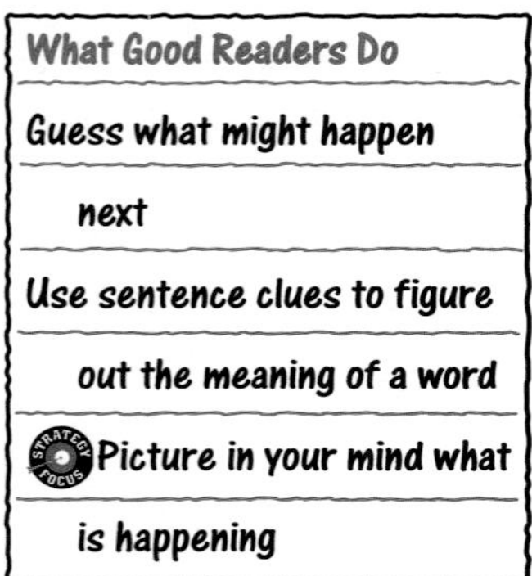
What Good Readers Do
Guess what might happen next
Use sentence clues to figure out the meaning of a word
Picture in your mind what is happening

Share with children the comprehension strategy that is the focus of this selection.

MODEL

The pictures in a book often can help me better understand the story. But not everything that happens in a story can be shown in the pictures. So when I read, I try to picture in my mind what is happening. I imagine what each character looks like and how each character acts. Doing this helps me understand why characters act the way they do and what is going on.

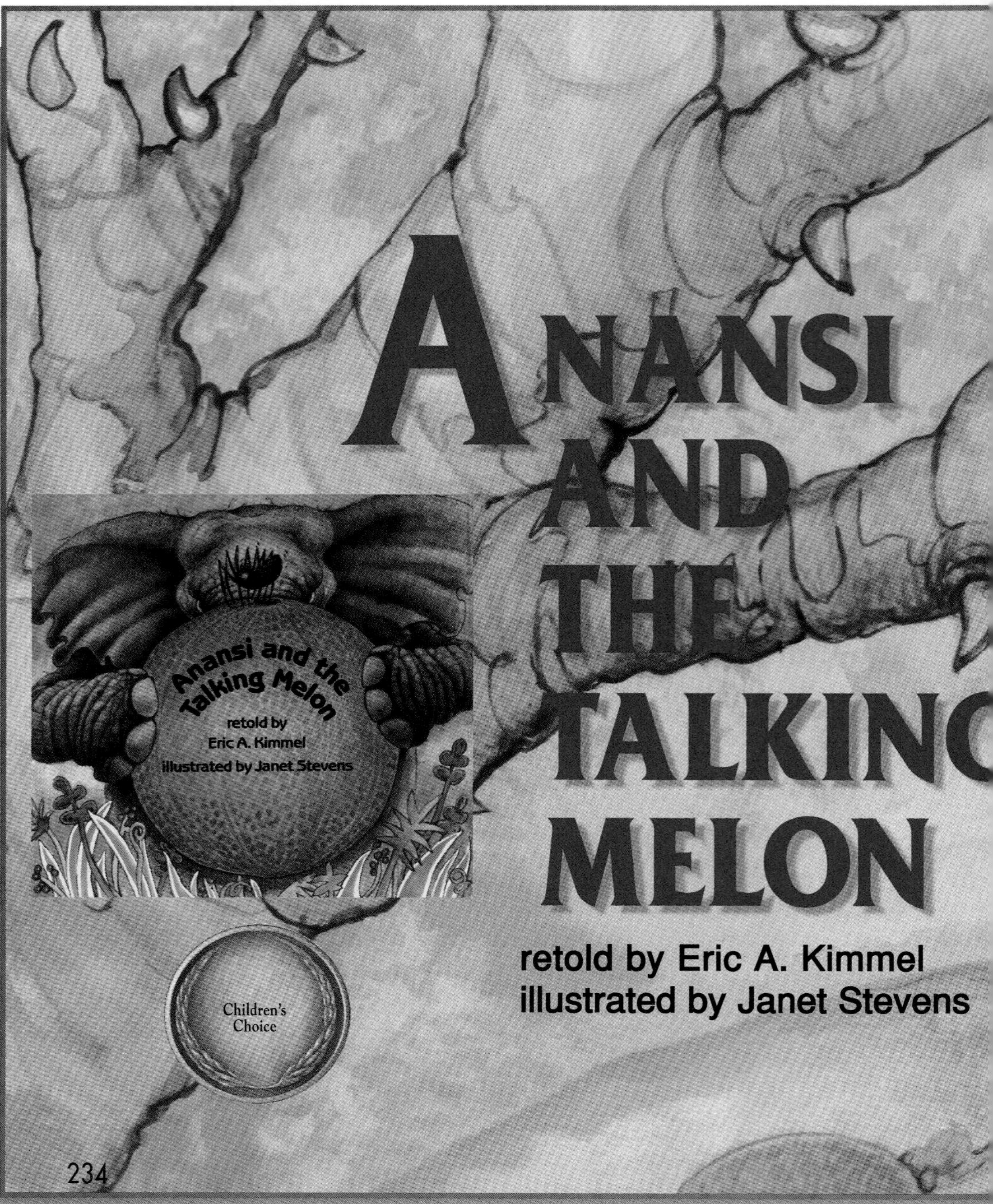

Anansi and the Talking Melon

Anansi and the Talking Melon
retold by Eric A. Kimmel
illustrated by Janet Stevens

Children's Choice

retold by Eric A. Kimmel
illustrated by Janet Stevens

234

TIPS FOR CLASSROOM MANAGEMENT

SMALL GROUP

COOPERATIVE READING

LITERATURE CIRCLES Invite the children to form small circles, and take turns reading the story aloud. Ask them to use the During Reading questions on Reader Response Card 1 (Characters), found on page R147, to discuss the characters as they read, and the After Reading questions when they have finished.

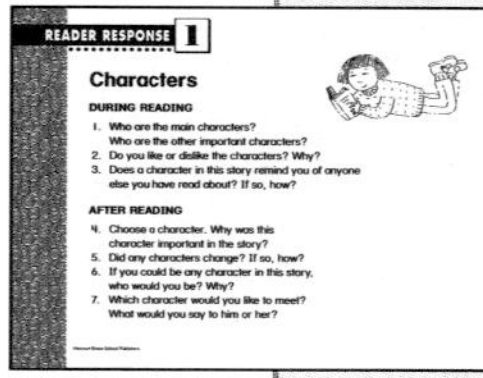
Response Card 1

PARTNER READING

Have children work in pairs to read "Anansi and the Talking Melon." Suggest that one child read all the lines of speech and the other child read the narrator's words. After every few pages, have children stop to discuss what they have read.

One fine morning Anansi the Spider sat high up in a thorn tree looking down into Elephant's garden. Elephant was hoeing his melon patch. The ripe melons seemed to call out to Anansi, "Look how juicy and sweet we are! Come eat us!"

235

PREVIEWING/ SETTING PURPOSES

Have children read the story title on page 234 and look at the picture. Pronounce the name *Anansi* (uh NAHN see) and explain that it is an African name. In the story it is the name of a spider. Then have children preview the pictures on pages 234–239. After children have previewed the pictures, ask them to predict what the story will be about and whether a melon will really talk. Have children write their predictions in their personal journals. Then help children set their purposes for reading.

MODELING A STRATEGY

PAGES 234–235 Before children read, talk about what the elephant and the spider are doing. After children have read, ask them to predict what Anansi will do about the melons. **Think aloud:** *I think Anansi is hungry because he's imagining the juicy, sweet melons. I think he'll ask Elephant for a melon to eat.* MAKING PREDICTIONS

WHOLE CLASS

STRATEGIC READING

Choose some or all of the suggestions and questions under Strategic Reading, pages T482–T502, to guide a literature discussion and to model the STRATEGY FOCUS of Visualizing.

INDEPENDENT READING

Have children read the entire story silently. As they read, they can fill in a web with Anansi's characteristics.

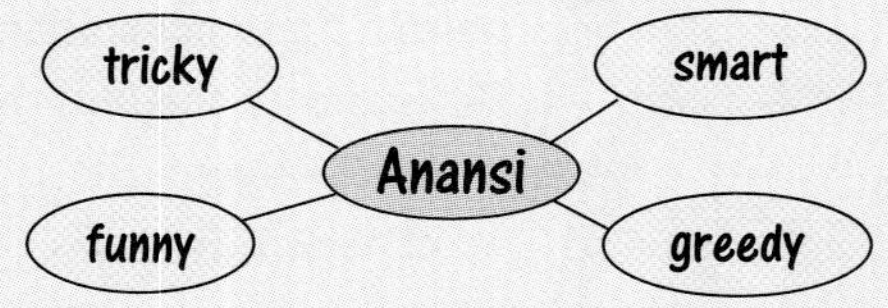

After children have finished, have them use their webs to discuss Anansi and what he does.

Strategic Reading

MODELING A STRATEGY

PAGES 236–237 Have children look at the pictures and then read to confirm their predictions. After children have read, talk about what Anansi did. Tell them that picturing in their minds what's happening in the story will help them understand the parts of the story not shown in the illustrations. Have children close their eyes as you read the part beginning with *Here was the moment Anansi had been waiting for.* Ask them to imagine what Anansi is doing inside the melon and how he looks. Model your thinking: *I can picture Anansi squeezing through the little hole and popping through into the melon. Then I think he just starts filling his mouth with one bite after another until he's round like a ball and can hardly move.*

Encourage children to discuss what they imagined. **VISUALIZING**

Anansi loved to eat melons, but he was much too lazy to grow them himself. So he sat up in the thorn tree, watching and waiting, while the sun rose high in the sky and the day grew warm. By the time noon came, it was too hot to work. Elephant put down his hoe and went inside his house to take a nap.

Here was the moment Anansi had been waiting for. He broke off a thorn and dropped down into the melon patch. He used the thorn to bore a hole in the biggest, ripest melon.

Anansi squeezed inside and started eating. He ate and ate until he was as round as a berry.

"I'm full," Anansi said at last. "Elephant will be coming back soon. It is time to go."

236

A CLOSER LOOK

Note to children that the illustration spanning pages 236–237 is part of a melon drawn from the perspective, or viewpoint, of a small spider. Discuss why the illustrator may have chosen this view.

EXTRA SUPPORT **Have children reread the first paragraph on page 236. Ask who becomes too hot to work. Ask what Anansi is waiting for. Help children understand that Anansi is waiting for Elephant to leave so that he can eat one of Elephant's melons. Help them infer that Anansi is something of a schemer.**

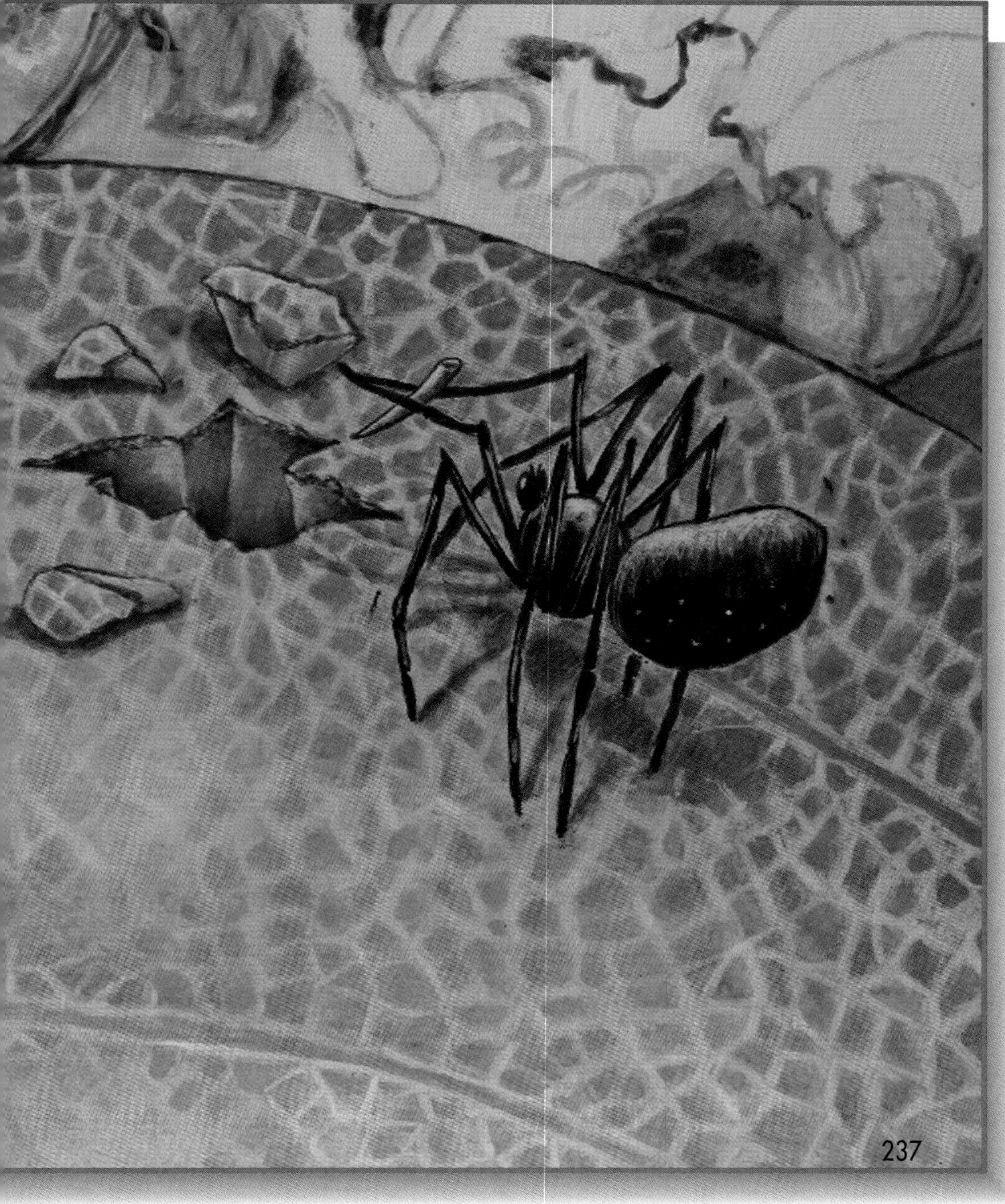

MINILESSON

MAINTAIN: PHONICS AND DECODING

Long Vowel: /ō/*o-e, ow*

INFORMAL ASSESSMENT

As children read, note how well they decode words in which the long *o* sound is spelled *o-e* or *ow*.

TEACH/MODEL

Have children turn to page 236. Help them locate words on the page in which the long *o* sound is spelled *o-e* or *ow* (*grow, rose, broke, hole*) and write the words on the board. Remind children that the letters *o-e* and *ow* can stand for the long *o* sound. Have volunteers underline *o-e* and *ow* in the words.

PRACTICE/APPLY

Write the following sentences on the board:

1. The sun rose high in the sky.
2. Elephant went home to take a nap.
3. Elephant must show his melon to the king.
4. The king has his own melons.
5. Do you know how to grow a talking melon?

Read each sentence to children. Have them give a "thumbs up" when they hear a long *o* word. Invite a volunteer to underline the word in which *o-e* or *ow* stands for the long *o* sound, and circle the *o-e* or *ow*.

PHONICS ACTIVITY BOOK, page 31

PHONICS PRACTICE BOOK, pages 77–89

CROSS-CULTURAL VIEWPOINT

The character Anansi appears in many folktales of the Ashanti, a West African people living in Ghana, and related Akan peoples. Anansi is a trickster, a cultural hero, and sometimes even a buffoon. In some stories, he is referred to as Kwaku (Uncle) Anansi. In some stories from the West Indies, a character called "Aunt Nancy" derives from Anansi.

Anansi and the Talking Melon

Name ______________________

Read this cereal box. Then fill out the contest form.

Prizes
bunch of roses
toy tow truck
smoke alarm
chrome race car
glow-in-the-dark ring
snow globe
break-the-code kit

Eat Home-Grown Crunchies!

If you chose this cereal, you know the best way to stay fit. Crunchies are low in fat and high in whole grains. It's not a joke! We hope Crunchies gets your vote. Crunchies—the snack that helps you grow!

CONTEST!

Circle the words on this box (but not on this form) that have the long *o* sound you hear in *rope*. How many words did you circle? 18

Now answer these questions.

1. What is Crunchies high in? whole grains
2. What is Crunchies low in? fat
3. What will Crunchies help you do? grow

Which prize would you like? (See side of box.) Responses will vary.

Name: Information will vary.
Address: ______
City: ______ State: ______ Zip: ______

Harcourt Brace School Publishers

OUT OF THE BLUE Practice Book — LONG VOWEL: /ō/o-e, ow — 93

PRACTICE BOOK, page 93

Strategic Reading

APPLYING A STRATEGY

PAGES 238–239 Have children look at the pictures and talk about what Anansi is doing. After they have read, ask them to make predictions about what Anansi will do to keep from being bored. Discuss what they know about the kind of character Anansi is that might help them make more accurate predictions. Then have children read on to confirm their predictions. **MAKING AND CONFIRMING PREDICTIONS**

But when he tried to squeeze through the hole, Anansi had a surprise. He didn't fit! The hole was big enough for a thin spider, but much too small for a fat one.

"I'm stuck!" Anansi cried. "I can't get out. I will have to wait until I am thin again."

238

PHONICS IN ACTION

Remind children that they learned the consonant digraph sounds /sh/, /ch/, /hw/, and /th/. Invite them to find examples of words with these sounds on pages 238–239. *(when, thin, much, wish, something)*

MUSIC CONNECTION

SING A SONG Review and sing the song "The Itsy Bitsy Spider." If you wish, have children make up new words to the song to relate it to the story. For example: "The itsy bitsy spider bored a little hole. Into the melon the hungry spider goes."

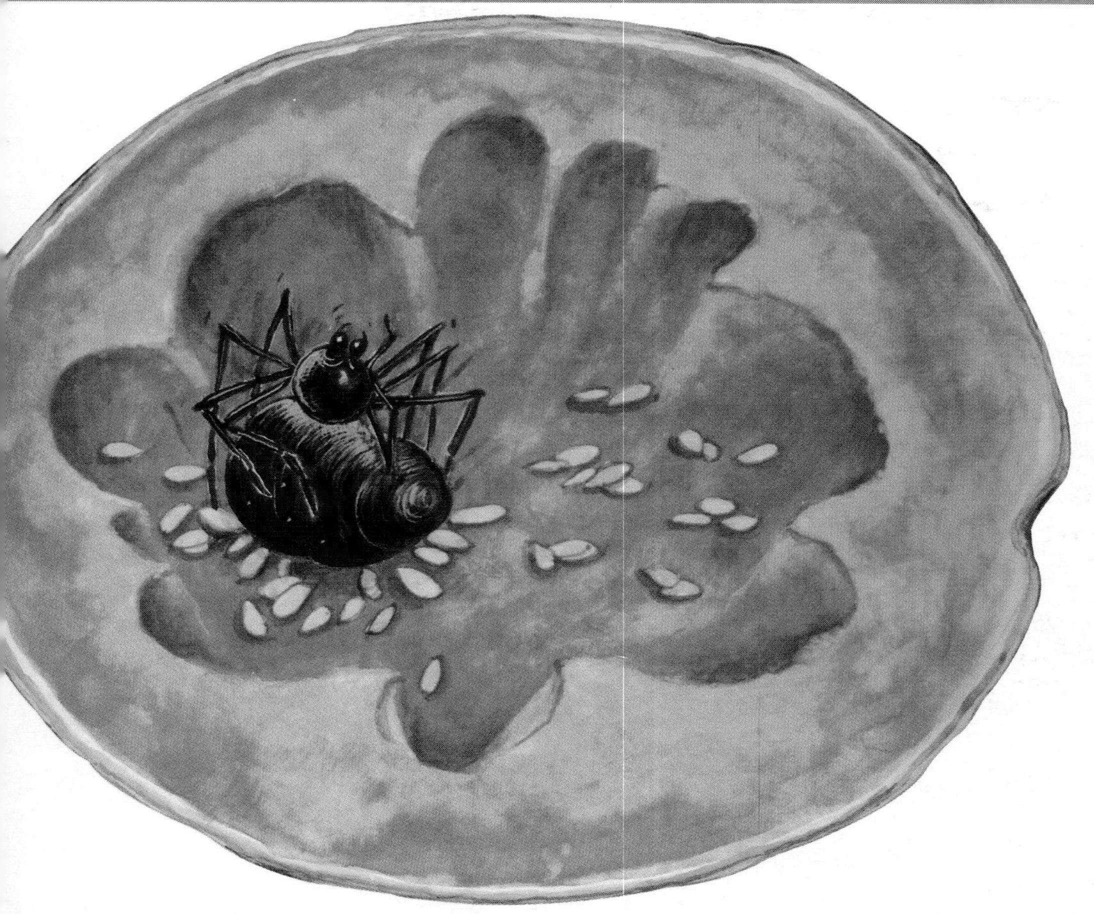

Anansi sat down on a pile of melon seeds and waited to get thin. Time passed slowly.

"I'm bored," Anansi said. "I wish I had something to do."

239

Informal Assessment

USING CUEING SYSTEMS

To determine whether children are applying cueing systems to figure out the word *bored*, ask them questions like the following:

- What letter and sound does the word begin with?
- What word would make sense in the sentence?
- Does the word still make sense after reading the next sentence, *I wish I had something to do?*

ILLUSTRATOR'S CRAFT

Ask children what is happening in the picture. Discuss how the illustrator shows what is happening inside the melon. Children may be interested to know that this kind of illustration is called a cutaway view. Encourage interested children to draw their own cutaway views of simple objects, such as apples.

SCHOOL↔HOME CONNECTION

Children and their families can visit the produce department of a grocery store to see various kinds of melons. Families may wish to sample one or two kinds of melon. Suggest that children draw cutaway pictures of the melons, label them, and describe how they tasted.

Strategic Reading

MODELING A STRATEGY

PAGES 240–241 Ask children to look at the pictures and to talk about what they think is happening in this part of the story. As children read, encourage them to picture in their minds what each character is doing, how their voices sound, and the expressions on their faces.

After children have read, discuss how they pictured Anansi and Elephant. You may want to reread the page aloud, modeling the strategy: *I picture Elephant returning to the garden walking slowly and calmly. I picture Anansi inside the melon, laughing to himself about his tricky plan. When the melon talks, I picture Elephant's eyes opening wide and him jumping up high because he's so surprised.* **VISUALIZING**

Just then he heard Elephant returning to the garden. Anansi had an idea. "When Elephant gets closer, I will say something. Elephant will think the melon is talking. What fun!"

Elephant walked over to the melon patch. "Look at this fine melon. How big and ripe it is!" he said, picking it up.

240

PHONICS IN ACTION

Have children find the word *heard* on page 240. Write the word on the board, and circle the letters *ear*. Remind children that the letters *ear* can stand for the /ûr/ sound.

HEARD

earn

"Ouch!" cried Anansi.
Elephant jumped.
"Aah! Who said that?"

241

NOTES

Here's a place to list ideas or activities that you would like to use the next time you teach this lesson.

STUDENTS ACQUIRING ENGLISH Discuss the exclamations *ouch* and *aah*. Children might enjoy repeating these words after you as Anansi and Elephant might have said them. Then ask children to share words from their first languages that are used in the same way that *aah* and *ouch* are used in English.

Strategic Reading

MODELING A STRATEGY

PAGES 242–244 Before children read these pages, have them preview the pictures and guess what Elephant is going to do next. **Think aloud:** *I know Elephant has been surprised by hearing a voice coming from the melon. I see him holding the melon up to his ear and then running with it toward another animal—a hippo. I think he's going to tell someone else that the melon talks.*

After children finish the pages, ask them to predict what the rest of the message will be. Have them read on to confirm their predictions. **MAKING AND CONFIRMING PREDICTIONS**

"I did. The melon," Anansi said.

"I didn't know melons could talk," said Elephant.

"Of course we do. We talk all the time. The trouble is, you never listen."

"I can't believe my ears!" Elephant exclaimed. "A talking melon! Who could believe it? I must show this to the king."

242

STUDENTS ACQUIRING ENGLISH **Assess whether children are having difficulty with the referents for the pronouns *I* and *we* on this page. Help them understand that Anansi is first speaking only about the melon he is inside of. (*"I did. The melon."*) In his next response, he is speaking for all the melons. (*"Of course we do. We talk all the time."*)**

Elephant ran down the road, carrying the melon with Anansi inside. Along the way, he ran into Hippo.

"Where are you going with that melon?" Hippo asked.

"I'm taking it to the king," Elephant told him.

"What for? The king has hundreds of melons."

"He doesn't have one like this," Elephant said. "This is a talking melon."

Hippo didn't believe Elephant. "A talking melon? What an idea! That's as ridiculous as . . ."

243

Student Self-Assessment 

FIX-UP STRATEGY: VISUALIZING

Ask children if they are trying to picture the story in their minds. Ask them what they think Anansi is doing inside the melon pictured on page 242. One picture that may come to mind is that he is laughing quietly at Elephant. Discuss how picturing Anansi in this situation helps a reader understand this character.

CONVENTIONS OF PRINT

ELLIPSES Point out the ellipsis points at the end of page 243. Explain that three small dots means the speaker is not yet finished. They also make the reader want to turn the page to find out what is spoken next.

A CLOSER LOOK

Ask children what Hippo is doing in the illustration on page 243. Discuss how the animals in the story not only speak but also act like humans.

Strategic Reading

MODELING A STRATEGY

PAGES 245–247 Have children preview the pictures and predict what Anansi will do in this part of the story. **Think aloud:** *Hippo and Elephant are showing the melon to another animal. Then that animal gets angry, just as Hippo did. I think Anansi says something rude to him, too.*

Then have children read on to find out what happens. MAKING AND CONFIRMING PREDICTIONS

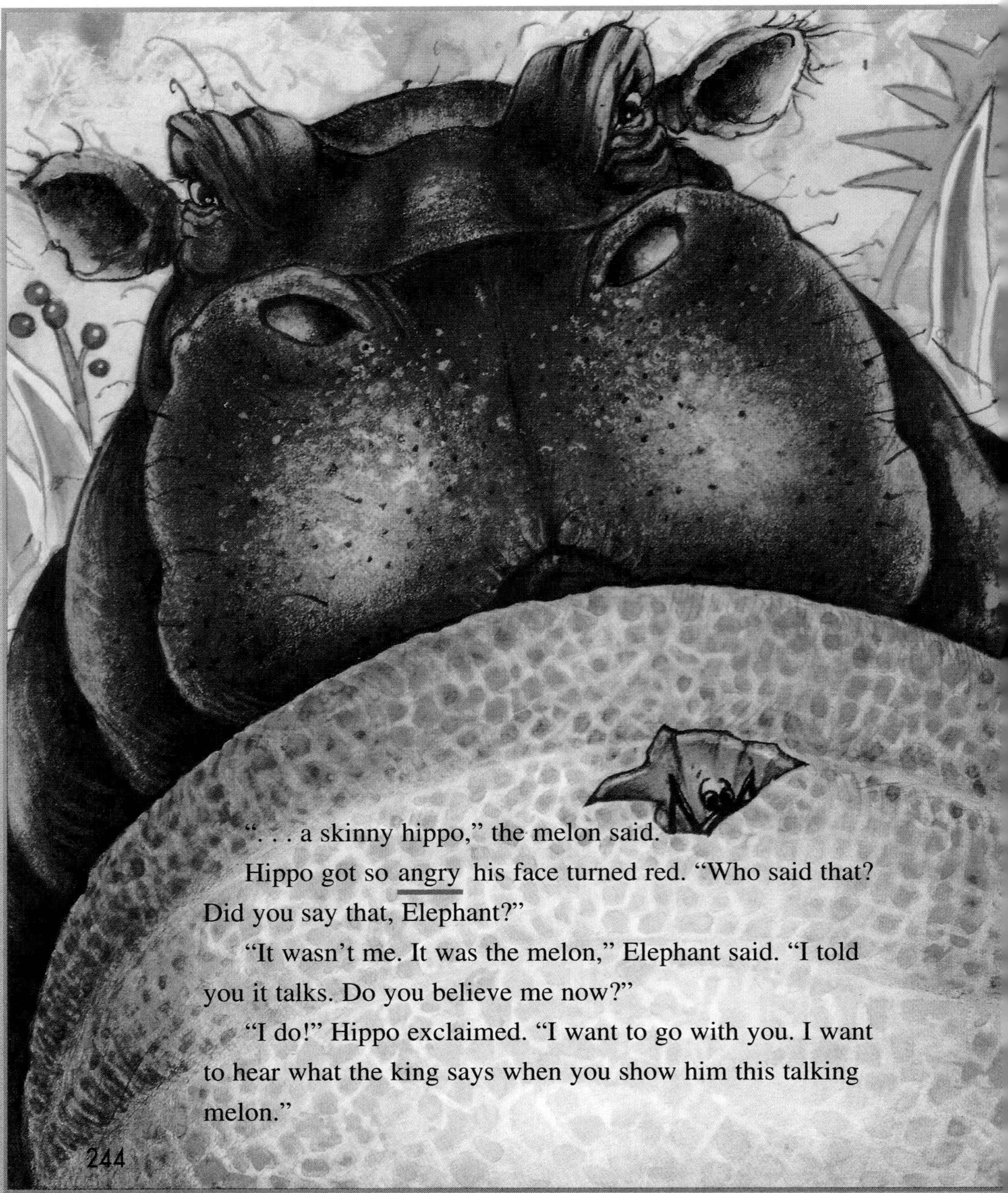

". . . a skinny hippo," the melon said.

Hippo got so angry his face turned red. "Who said that? Did you say that, Elephant?"

"It wasn't me. It was the melon," Elephant said. "I told you it talks. Do you believe me now?"

"I do!" Hippo exclaimed. "I want to go with you. I want to hear what the king says when you show him this talking melon."

244

PHONICS IN ACTION

Ask children to find the word *say* on page 244. Write the word on the board, and circle *ay*. Then ask them to find the word *exclaimed*. Write the word on the board, and circle *ai*. Remind children that *ay* and *ai* can both be spellings of the long *a* sound.

play say EXCLAIMED RAIN

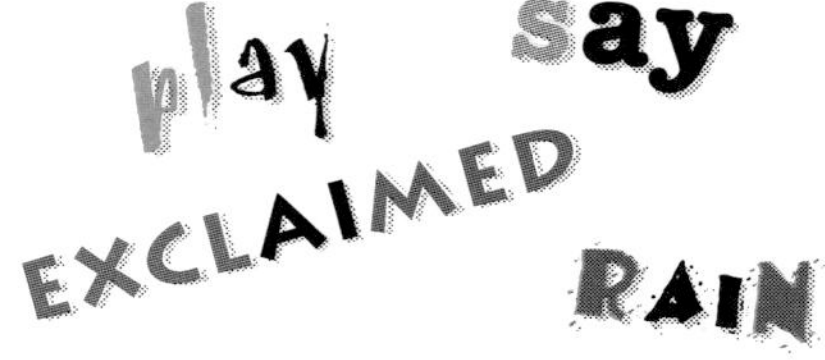

"Come along, then," said Elephant. So Elephant and Hippo went down the road together, carrying the melon.

By and by, they ran into Warthog. "Where are you taking that melon?" Warthog asked them.

"We're taking it to the king," Elephant and Hippo told him.

"What for? The king has hundreds of melons," Warthog said.

"He doesn't have one like this," Hippo replied. "This melon talks. I heard it."

Warthog started to laugh. "A talking melon? Why, that's as ridiculous as . . ."

245

Tested Skill

MINILESSON

REVIEW: GRAMMAR

Names of Special People, Animals, and Places

INFORMAL ASSESSMENT

As children read, note whether they recognize proper nouns. As children write about the story, note whether they capitalize the names of the animals.

TEACH/MODEL

Have children locate the names *Elephant, Hippo,* and *Warthog* on page 245. Then write this sentence on the board: *An elephant and a hippo stood near a warthog.* Ask what is different about the spellings of the animals' names in this sentence from the ones in the story. (The names in the story are capitalized because they are the names of special animals.) Remind children that the names of people and the names of certain animals and places are capitalized and are called **proper nouns**.

PRACTICE/APPLY

Write the following sentences on the board without capitalizing the proper nouns. Have children write the sentences correctly.

1. *Stories of Anansi were first told in Africa.*
2. *The rhinoceros is Juan's favorite animal.*
3. *Another famous spider frightened Miss Muffet.*

LANGUAGE HANDBOOK **Special Names and Titles of People, pages 58–59**

Names of Special Animals and Places, pages 60–61

AUTHOR'S CRAFT

Ask children which lines on page 245 sound familiar. If necessary, ask them to compare the text with that on page 243 to find words and actions that are similar. Discuss how children can use this pattern in the story to predict what will happen next.

STUDENTS ACQUIRING ENGLISH **You may need to explain that the phrase *by and by* is an expression meaning "after a while."**

Cooperative Reading

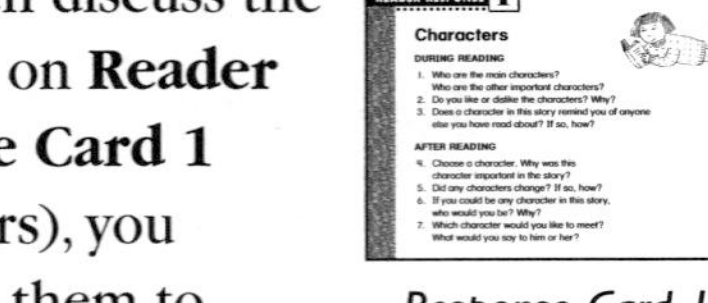

Response Card 1

As children discuss the questions on **Reader Response Card 1** (Characters), you might ask them to also consider these questions:

1. **What makes Anansi different from the other animals in the story?**
2. **How are the other animals like each other?**

". . . a handsome warthog," said the melon.

Warthog got so angry he shook all over. "Who said that? Did you say that, Elephant? Did you say that, Hippo?"

"Of course not!" Hippo and Elephant told him. "The melon talks. Do you believe us now?"

246

IDEA BANK

Anansi refers to the ridiculousness of *a skinny hippo* (page 244) and *a handsome warthog* (page 246), implying that hippos are fat and warthogs are ugly. Such ridiculous descriptions, which are called oxymorons, might be fun for children to construct themselves. Have them make a list of ridiculous descriptions of other animals. Examples might include: *a quick turtle, a loud mouse, a crying hyena.*

WRITING

ADD TO THE STORY

Have children write the dialogue that may have occurred when Elephant, Hippo, and Warthog met Ostrich, Rhino, and Turtle. Remind them of the pattern of dialogue the author used on pages 243 and 245.

"I do!" cried Warthog. "Let me go with you. I want to see what the king does when you show him this talking melon."

So Warthog, Elephant, and Hippo went down the road together, carrying the melon.

Along the way, they met Ostrich, Rhino, and Turtle. They didn't believe the melon could talk either until they heard it for themselves. Then they wanted to come along too.

247

Tested Skill

MINILESSON

REVIEW: STUDY SKILLS

Alphabetical Order

INFORMAL ASSESSMENT

As children use encylopedias or dictionaries, notice whether they use alphabetical order to locate words and information easily.

TEACH/MODEL

Have children locate the animals' names on page 247. List them on the board: *Warthog, Elephant, Hippo, Ostrich, Rhino,* and *Turtle.* Ask children how to put these words in alphabetical order, and rewrite the list in order. (Elephant, Hippo, Ostrich, Rhino, Turtle, Warthog) Then work with children to add these animal names to the list: *rabbit, owl, wallaby,* and *toucan.* If necessary, review that children must look at the second letters when the first letter is the same, and the third letters when the first two letters are the same.

PRACTICE/APPLY

Write these lists of words from the story on the board:

1. thorn, tree, talking, tried
2. bore, berry, believe, broke
3. spider, squeezed, surprise, small
4. hippo, hundreds, handsome, him
5. patched, prodded, picked, placed

Have partners choose a group of words and write them in alphabetical order. Ask them to circle the letters that they used to alphabetize the words.

EXPANDING VOCABULARY

Point out the word *Warthog* and explain that it is a compound word. Help children identify the two smaller words, *wart* and *hog*, and discuss whether this is an appropriate name for the animal pictured.

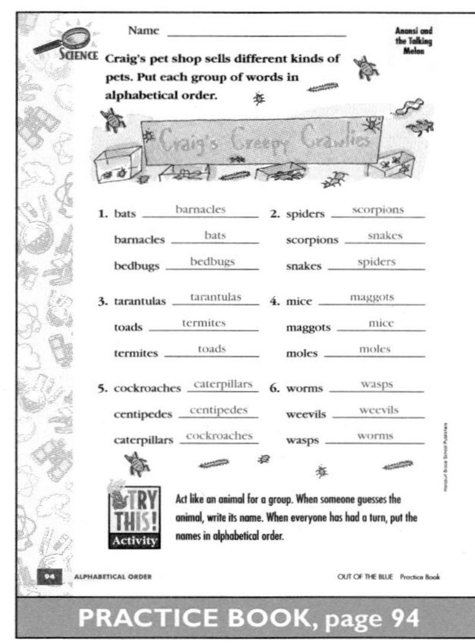

Name ________ Anansi and the Talking Melon

SCIENCE Craig's pet shop sells different kinds of pets. Put each group of words in alphabetical order.

Craig's Creepy Crawlies

1. bats barnacles / barnacles bats / bedbugs bedbugs
2. spiders scorpions / scorpions snakes / snakes spiders
3. tarantulas tarantulas / toads termites / termites toads
4. mice maggots / maggots mice / moles moles
5. cockroaches caterpillars / centipedes centipedes / caterpillars cockroaches
6. worms wasps / weevils weevils / wasps worms

TRY THIS! Activity: Act like an animal for a group. When someone guesses the animal, write its name. When everyone has had a turn, put the names in alphabetical order.

94 ALPHABETICAL ORDER OUT OF THE BLUE Practice Book

PRACTICE BOOK, page 94

Strategic Reading

APPLYING A STRATEGY

PAGES 248–249 Ask children to look at the pictures before, during, and after reading the pages. Ask questions like these about the pictures and the words:

1. **What kind of animal is the king and how do you know?**
2. **What does the king think of the melon? Why do you think so?**

RELATING PICTURES TO TEXT

SCIENCE

FACT FINDER

AFRICAN ANIMALS

The elephant and the rhinoceros have been illustrated accurately as African animals. Unlike the Indian elephant, the African elephant has larger tusks and ears. Unlike two species of one-horned Asian rhinoceroses, African rhinoceroses have two horns.

Intervention Strategies

SUMMARIZING Have children repeat this sentence: *When I read, it helps me to think about what's happened so far.* Have children tell how using this strategy might help them understand what's happened in "Anansi and the Talking Melon."

The animals came before the king. Elephant bowed low as he placed the melon at the king's feet.

The king looked down. "Why did you bring me a melon?" he asked Elephant. "I have hundreds of melons growing in my garden."

"You don't have one like this," Elephant said. "This melon talks."

Student Self-Assessment

MAKING PREDICTIONS

Allow time for children to discuss in pairs or small groups whether they are making and checking predictions as they read. They might ask one another if they were able to guess

- that Anansi would make a funny remark about warthogs to Warthog.
- that Warthog's response would be the same as Hippo's.
- what Ostrich, Rhino, and Turtle would think of the talking melon.
- what the king will say about the melon.

IDEA BANK

VISUALIZE A SCENE **To reinforce the strategy of visualizing, ask children to close their eyes as you read this page. Then have them draw pictures of what they imagined as you read.**

Strategic Reading

MODELING A STRATEGY

PAGES 250–253 Have children summarize what has happened so far in the story. Provide a model, if necessary: *Anansi crawled into a melon and tricked Elephant into believing the melon could talk. Then Anansi tricked Hippo, Warthog, and other animals in the same way.*

Then have children read to find out what the king does. SUMMARIZING

"A talking melon? I don't believe it. Say something, Melon." The king prodded the melon with his foot.

The melon said nothing.

"Melon," the king said in a slightly louder voice, "there is no reason to be shy. Say whatever you like. I only want to hear you talk."

The melon still said nothing. The king grew impatient.

"Melon, if you can talk, I want you to say something. I command you to speak."

The melon did not make a sound.

The king gave up. "Oh, this is a stupid melon!" he said.

250

A CLOSER LOOK

Invite children to compare the illustrations on pages 244, 246, and 251. Then ask what the reader can see in each picture that the animal character cannot see. Discuss how the illustrator hides Anansi from the other animals' view.

Just then the melon spoke. "Stupid, am I? Why do you say that? I'm not the one who talks to melons!"

251

Student Self-Assessment

FIX-UP STRATEGY: USING CONTEXT CLUES

Ask children what the king did to the melon first. If children have difficulty understanding the word *prodded*, tell them they have two clues to its meaning: the rest of the sentence (*with his foot*) and the illustration.

IDEA BANK

Invite volunteers to pretend to be Anansi. Have each "Anansi" get together with a partner and answer one another's questions about things Anansi likes to do and other tricks he is planning.

Critical Thinking Questions

1. **What could have happened to Anansi when the king threw the melon after he insulted the king?** (Possible responses: He could have been injured; the melon may have rolled away with him still inside.) **CRITICAL: SPECULATING**
2. **Why do you think Anansi was rude to the king even though Anansi could have been hurt?** (Possible response: Anansi is not the kind of character who thinks about what can happen before he does something.) **CRITICAL: DETERMINING CHARACTERS' TRAITS**
3. **What do you think Anansi will do next?** (Responses will vary. Children should use what they know about Anansi to think of an answer.) **CRITICAL: SPECULATING**

The animals had never seen the king so angry. "How dare this melon insult me!" he shouted. The king picked up the melon and hurled it as far as he could.

252

PHONICS IN ACTION

Ask children to find the word on page 252 in which the letters *ur* spell the /ûr/ sound. (*hurled*) Challenge them to find another word with the same letters and sound on page 253. (*burst*) Remind children that *ur* is just one of the spellings that can stand for the /ûr/ sound.

burst

hurled

The melon bounced and rolled all the way to Elephant's house. KPOM! It smacked into the thorn tree and burst into pieces. Anansi picked himself up from among the bits of melon rind.

253

Tested Skill

MINILESSON

MAINTAIN: PHONICS AND DECODING

R-Controlled Vowel: /är/*ar*

INFORMAL ASSESSMENT

As children read, note how well they decode words with the *r*-controlled vowel sound /är/ spelled *ar*.

TEACH/MODEL

Ask children what the king did with the melon once he picked it up. Write this sentence on the board, and read it aloud:

The king hurled the melon as far as he could.

Ask children which word has the same vowel sound as *star*. (far) Ask them which letters stand for the /är/ sound in *far*, and circle *ar*. Remind children that the letters *ar* can stand for the /är/ sound, as in *far*.

PRACTICE/APPLY

Display the following sentences, and read them with children.

1. Anansi saw a melon in Elephant's garden.
2. He bored a hole through the hard rind.
3. It was dark inside the melon.
4. Anansi started to eat part of the melon.
5. Then he heard Elephant marching back.

Have children make a list of the /är/ words and then use each one in a new sentence about the story.

MEETING INDIVIDUAL NEEDS

STUDENTS ACQUIRING ENGLISH You may need to pronounce and explain the word *KPOM* to children. Explain that it is a word the author made up to tell the sound that the melon made when it hit a tree. Ask fluent speakers to share some other English words that might have been used here: *BANG*, *SPLAT*, or *CRASH*.

SCIENCE

SPIDER FACTS

- Spiders eat insects, which they catch in webs or else stalk and capture.
- All spiders have poison glands that they use when capturing prey.
- Spiders can hear well.
- A few spiders can make sounds.
- Most spiders are not harmful to people.

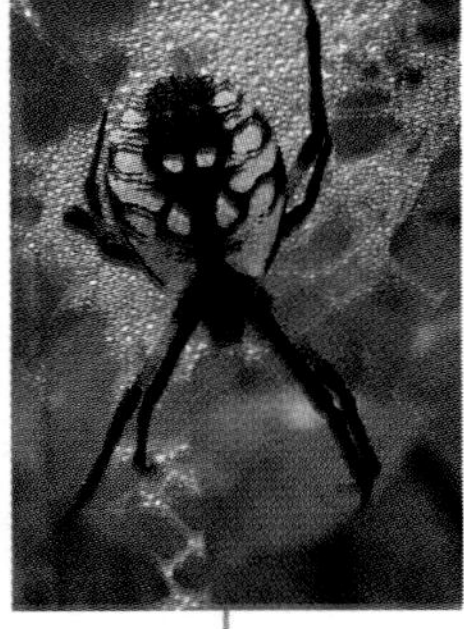

Strategic Reading

APPLYING A STRATEGY

PAGES 254–255 After reading, have children speculate about what the elephant might do about the "talking" bananas. Ask whether children think the elephant learned a lesson from the "talking" melon episode. **MAKING PREDICTIONS**

Returning to the Predictions/Purpose

Before children read, they wrote predictions about the story and about the talking melon. Invite them to share their predictions and compare them to what actually happened.

Appreciating the Literature

With the whole class or a small group, have an open discussion about the story.

- **What do you know about Anansi that lets you know he won't stop playing tricks?**

All the excitement had made him thin. And now that he was thin again, he was hungry. Anansi climbed the banana tree. He settled himself in the middle of a big bunch of bananas and started eating.

254

SCIENCE CONNECTION

SPIDERS Although Anansi was not helpful in the story, spiders in real life can be helpful to people. Discuss how spiders are helpful (eat insects such as mosquitoes and flies). Discuss how spiders trap insects in their webs.

FROM THE AUTHOR

"I think stories have a lot to teach us. The problem of the world, as I see it, is that we spend too much time listening to dull, ugly stories (which we call 'history' or 'current events') and too little time listening to the ageless, beautiful ones, which we dismiss as 'fairy tales.' It is a foolish person indeed who thinks the former have more truth than the latter."

—Eric A. Kimmel

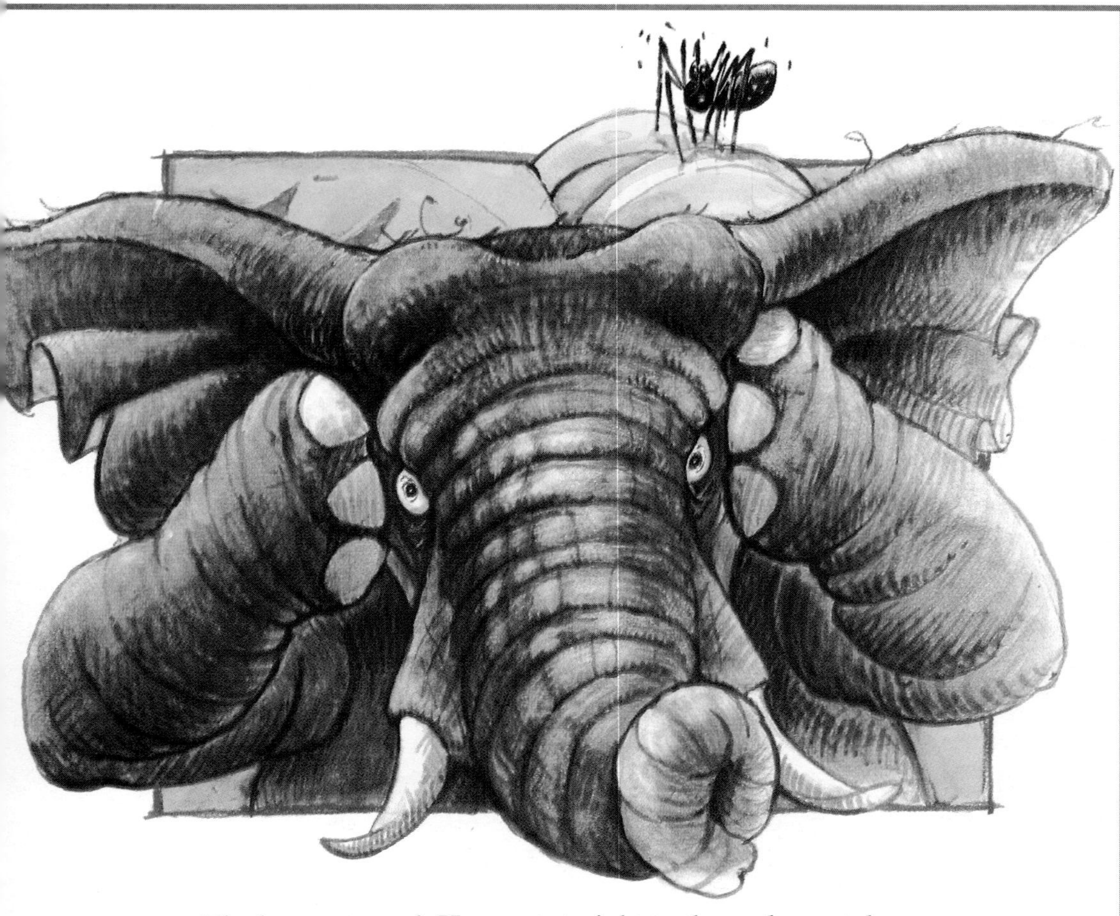

Elephant returned. He went straight to the melon patch.

"You melons got me in trouble with the king!" Elephant said. "From now on, you can talk all you like. I'm not going to listen to a word you say!"

"Good for you, Elephant!" Anansi called from the bananas. "We bananas should have warned you. Talking melons are nothing but trouble."

255

SUMMARIZE AND RETELL

What's the Effect?

Work with children to complete the following cause-and-effect chart. Then have groups use the chart to retell the story of Anansi. See *Practice Book* page 88.

CAUSE	EFFECT
1. Anansi was hungry.	1. Anansi bored a hole in a melon, climbed in, and began eating.
2. Anansi ate too much.	2. Anansi got too big and couldn't get out of the melon.
3. Anansi gets bored inside the melon.	3. He decides to play a trick on Elephant and the other animals.
4. Anansi makes the animals think the melon can talk.	4. The animals are amazed. They bring it to the king.
5. Anansi is rude to the king.	5. The king throws the melon.
6. The melon breaks open.	6. Anansi is free.

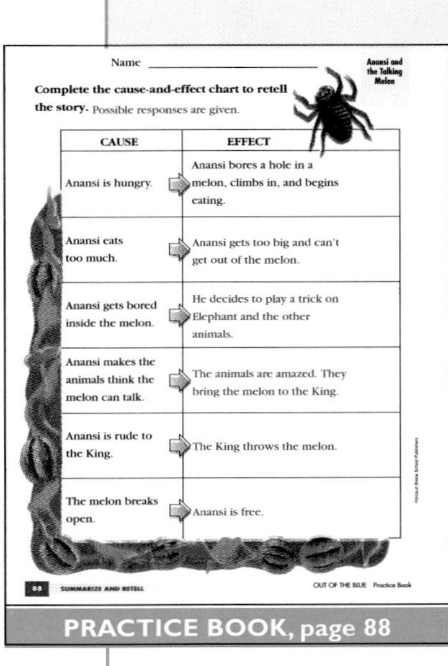

Name ______________________

Anansi and the Talking Melon

Complete the cause-and-effect chart to retell the story. Possible responses are given.

CAUSE	EFFECT
Anansi is hungry.	Anansi bores a hole in a melon, climbs in, and begins eating.
Anansi eats too much.	Anansi gets too big and can't get out of the melon.
Anansi gets bored inside the melon.	He decides to play a trick on Elephant and the other animals.
Anansi makes the animals think the melon can talk.	The animals are amazed. They bring the melon to the King.
Anansi is rude to the King.	The King throws the melon.
The melon breaks open.	Anansi is free.

88 SUMMARIZE AND RETELL OUT OF THE BLUE Practice Book

PRACTICE BOOK, page 88

About the Author

PAGES 256–257 Have children read the information about the author and the illustrator on pages 256–257. Talk about how authors and illustrators get enjoyment out of what they do.

Eric A. Kimmel fulfilled a lifelong dream when he moved to Oregon several years ago. He admits that sometimes it's hard to sit and write when he could be outside riding a horse through the beautiful countryside. But he also truly gets pleasure from writing, especially for children.

Some people think his stories are too "adult" for children, but Mr. Kimmel believes that such people don't really understand children. When he reads his stories to children, they enjoy them!

Eric A. Kimmel

Anansi and the Talking Melon is a trickster tale that Eric Kimmel has retold. Anansi stories first came from West Africa. They have been passed along to the islands of the Caribbean, to Central America, and to the United States. Each Anansi story teaches a lesson. In some stories, Anansi is a spider. In others, he is a man. But he is always a trickster!

When Eric Kimmel writes, he gets some of his ideas from the mountains, ocean, and deserts near his home on the West Coast. He says that if his wishes come true, he will spend his days on a ranch riding horse and writing books.

256

OTHER BOOKS BY ERIC A. KIMMEL

***Three Sacks of Truth: A Story from France*. Holiday House, 1993.** CHALLENGE

***The Three Princes: A Story from the Middle East*. Holiday House, 1994.** CHALLENGE

***The Four Gallant Sisters*. Henry Holt, 1992.** CHALLENGE

Janet Stevens

Janet Stevens has always liked art. When she was little, she thought her sister and brother were better at things than she was. Then she found out that she was good at art and that made her feel happy.

Can you tell that Janet Stevens loves animals? She is well-known for the funny animals she draws in her books. She probably had fun drawing Anansi and all the animals he tricks!

Janet Stevens is married and has two children. She likes to go camping, skiing, and bike-riding with her family.

257

About the Illustrator

Janet Stevens began her career in art by designing fabrics. She first became interested in illustrating children's books when she went to a workshop. Although her first attempts at illustrating books were not successful, her interest continued. She went to a second workshop—this one with renowned children's book writer and illustrator Tomie de Paola, who encouraged her not to give up. Stevens has gone on to illustrate other authors' books for children, as well as classic children's tales that she has retold.

OTHER BOOKS BY JANET STEVENS

How the Manx Cat Lost Its Tail. **Harcourt Brace, 1990.** AVERAGE

Coyote Steals the Blanket. **Holiday House, 1993.** AVERAGE

Tops & Bottoms. **Harcourt Brace, 1995.** AVERAGE

POEM

Anansi

by Bert Simpson

INTRODUCING THE POEM Ask children what they already know about Anansi. Then have children look at the picture on pages 258–259. Ask them to predict what the poem will be about.

SHARING THE POEM Read the poem aloud. Ask children to explain how Anansi tricks the crows. Point out that he uses flattery. Ask volunteers what the word *flattery* means. ("praise given without meaning it")

Then work with children to plan a finger-play to accompany different lines of the poem (for example, eyes opening wide for the line *"You're beautiful to me"* and hands fluttering in the air for the line *The crows fly to the mango tree*). Invite children to read the poem aloud and use their gestures.

If possible, bring in a mango for children to see and taste. Explain that mangoes are as popular in tropical countries as apples and oranges are in the United States.

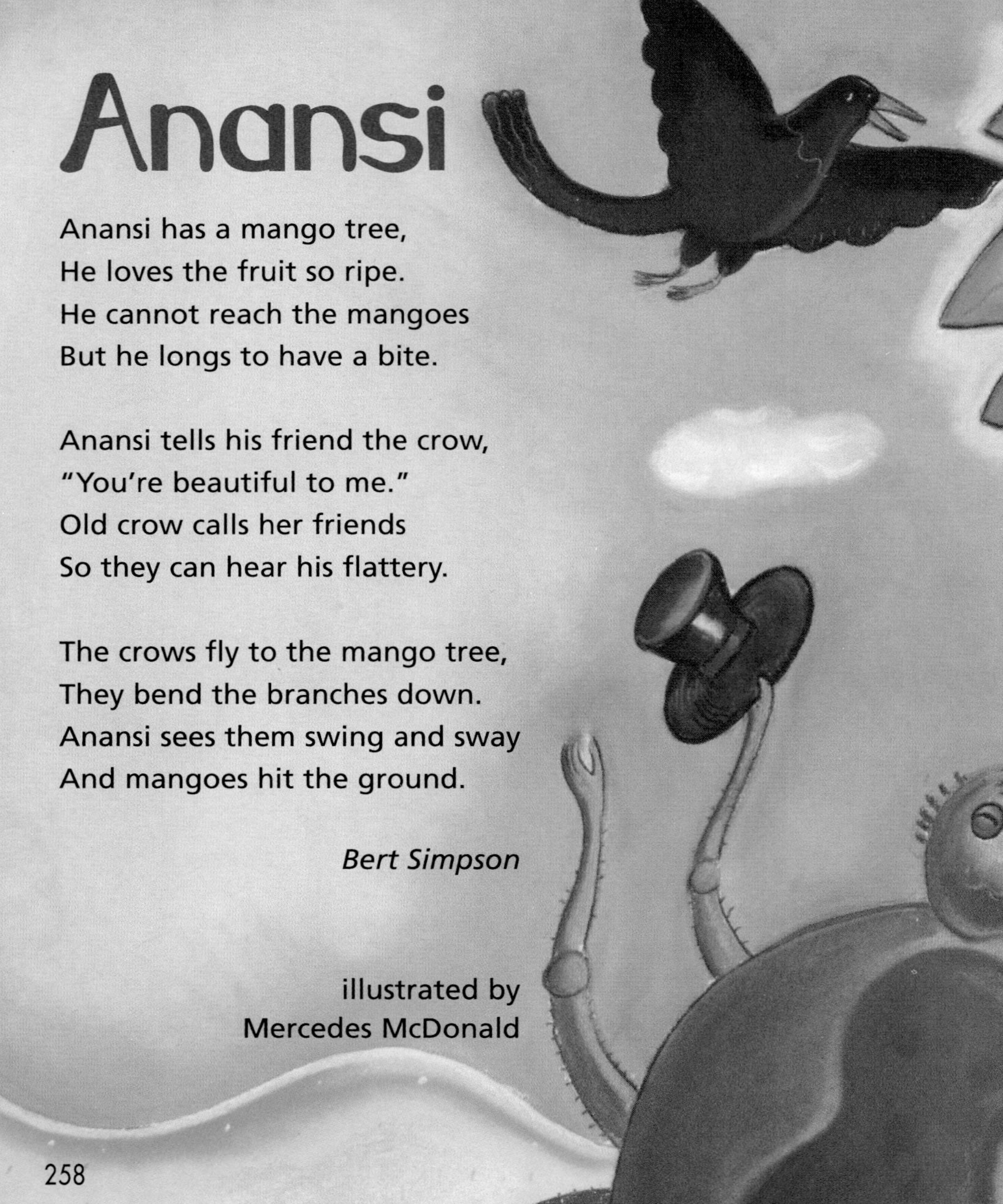

Anansi

Anansi has a mango tree,
He loves the fruit so ripe.
He cannot reach the mangoes
But he longs to have a bite.

Anansi tells his friend the crow,
"You're beautiful to me."
Old crow calls her friends
So they can hear his flattery.

The crows fly to the mango tree,
They bend the branches down.
Anansi sees them swing and sway
And mangoes hit the ground.

Bert Simpson

illustrated by
Mercedes McDonald

258

POET'S CRAFT

Explain that Bert Simpson used word families to create rhyme in the poem. Ask children which lines of the poem seem to rhyme. (the second and fourth lines of each stanza) Explain that *ripe* and *bite* share the long *i* vowel sound but don't actually rhyme. The words *down* and *ground* share the /ou/ sound but don't rhyme exactly either. The poet has used words with similar sounds so that the lines seem to rhyme when the poem is read aloud.

MULTICULTURAL CONNECTION

Anansi stories originated in Africa. They were taken to the West Indies and to parts of the United States, where the stories now differ widely from those told in Africa. Some students brought Anansi tales from the West Indies and told them to their teacher, Bert Simpson.

259

About the Poet

Bert Simpson wrote the poem after listening to Anansi stories told to him by his first-, second-, and third-grade students. Simpson enjoyed listening to stories about the famous trickster. Simpson's poem was set to music by Raffi, a songwriter well known to educators as a children's entertainer. Simpson and Raffi have collaborated on a number of songs. Simpson is an elementary school teacher in Toronto.

MORE POETRY

***Shake My Sillies Out* by Bert and Bonnie Simpson. Crown, 1987.**

LISTENING CENTER

"Anansi" is available on *Literature Cassette 1*. Some children may benefit from listening to the poem and following along in their books.

RESPONSE CORNER ACTIVITIES

ACT OUT A STORY

ANIMAL MASKS
PAGE 260 Suggest that children review the pictures in the story to get ideas for their animal mask. Then have them read the directions and make their masks. In addition to the materials listed, you may want to provide fake fur, fringe, buttons, and other decorations. Have groups act out "Anansi and the Talking Melon" or their own story, using their masks. **ART/DRAMA**

MAKE A POSTER

I'M SORRY!
PAGE 261 Invite children to brainstorm additional poster information they might include, such as special games or music. Also discuss things Anansi might need or want others to bring to a party.

Display the finished posters. Then you may want to hold an Anansi party based on children's poster ideas. **ART/WRITING**

RESPONSE CORNER

ACT OUT A STORY

Animal Masks

Work in a group. Make an animal mask. Each person in your group can make a mask for a different character from the story.

You will need:
poster board
markers or crayons
tape
scissors
craft stick

1. Draw the animal's face on poster board.
2. Cut out holes for your eyes and your mouth.
3. Color and decorate your mask.
4. Tape a craft stick to the back of your mask to make a handle.

Use your masks to act out the Anansi story you just read. Or act out an Anansi story of your own.

260

VARYING THE ACTIVITY

For children who need extra support with this activity, first discuss and make a list of the characters in the story. Then have children look back at the pictures to see how each character looked. Ask questions such as: *What kind of expression should the character have on its face? What one word could you use to describe the character?*

Then encourage children to select a character and make a mask based on the discussion.

MAKE A POSTER

I'm Sorry!

Pretend that Anansi is sorry he played tricks on the other animals. He decides to have a party to show them he's sorry. Make a poster that Anansi could use to tell the animals about his party.

Then, share your poster with your classmates.

To make your poster:

- Make up a time and a place for Anansi's party.
- Think about food and games for the party.
- Remember, Anansi is a lazy spider. Think of things he might ask the other animals to bring.

What Do You Think?

What lesson do you think the animals should have learned?
What did you like about the story? What didn't you like? Why?

261

CHECKING COMPREHENSION

What Do You Think?

1. **What lesson do you think the animals should have learned?** (Possible response: Don't believe everything you hear.) DESCRIPTIVE RESPONSE
2. **What did you like about the story? What didn't you like? Why?** (Responses will vary. Children should support their answers.) PERSONAL RESPONSE

An additional question for extending reading.

3. **What do you think Elephant will do next? Why do you think that?** (Accept reasonable responses.) CRITICAL/CREATIVE ANALYSIS

MEETING INDIVIDUAL NEEDS

MULTI-AGE CLASSROOMS

Group children of different ages together for the Animal Masks activity. As children act out the story, encourage the more-skilled readers to take the more difficult roles and to help the less-skilled readers practice their parts. Suggest that children take turns being the Narrator.

Informal Assessment

Observe groups of children as they act out the story.

- ☑ Do children include the main events in their rendition?
- ☑ Do children tell the story in a logical order?
- ☑ Do all children participate in acting out the story?

Intervention Strategies

Instant Readers™

Predictable and Patterned Little Books That Build Fluency

*** BOOK LEVEL: 16–17**

VOCABULARY:
angry, course, lazy

PHONIC ELEMENTS:
R*-controlled vowel: /ôr/*ore, our*; /är/*ar*; Long vowel: /ō/*ow

PHONOGRAM:
-ore

SUMMARY:
Coyote meets his match in this play.

Informal Assessment

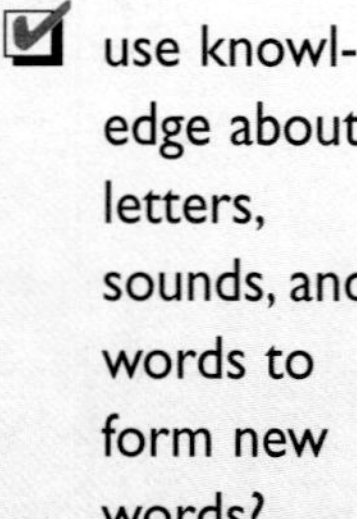

Are children able to

- use knowledge about letters, sounds, and words to form new words?
- attend to and recreate sentence structure?

Reading a New Book

INTRODUCING *TRICKSTER*

After children have looked at the cover and the title page, talk about the genre of this story (a play). With children, read the cast of characters on page 2. Talk about how a play is read aloud and performed before the text is previewed.

READING THE STORY

Assign the seven roles in the play. Make sure that children look for the small picture of the character they are reading.

WORKING WITH WORDS AND LETTERS

Have children work with the phonogram *-ore* and the story words *snore* and *more*. Have them use individual letter cards, *Word Builder Cards,* or magnetic letters to form new words. Then have children experiment with the same sound in the letters *-our*. Have children compare the words they formed.

ore	our
snore	four
more	pour
shore	course

WRITING DIALOGUE

Have children work in a group to write a new ending for the play. Encourage them to use the script format from the play.

Additional activities are provided on pages 52–53 of the *Intervention Strategies Manual*.

* **BOOK LEVEL: 17–18**

VOCABULARY:
hungry, lazy, uses

PHONIC ELEMENTS:
R*-controlled vowels: /ôr/*or*, /är/*ar*; Long vowel: /ō/*o-e

SUMMARY:
Some animals are so clever they know how to fool both predators and admirers.

Reading a New Book

INTRODUCING *HIDING IN PLAIN SIGHT*

To introduce the concept of camouflage, share the cover illustration with children and talk about what they see. If they cannot see the animal hiding in the art, tell them that there is one. Ask them why some animals use camouflage. As the story pictures are shared, talk about the kinds of camouflage (color, texture, habitat, and so on) shown in the pictures.

READING THE STORY

Have children read the story independently to learn more about camouflage.

WORKING WITH WORDS AND LETTERS

Have children work with a partner to choose a story sentence to study. Give partners strips of paper to copy the sentences onto, and then have them cut apart the words and reassemble the sentences. As an extra activity, have them use the words to construct another sentence.

WRITING DESCRIPTIONS

Have children use the story pictures to write two sentences about their favorite animal in hiding. Make sure the writing includes a description of the way the animal looks.

ESL/Title I Reading

Five Little Monkeys Sitting in a Tree by Eileen Christelow

Working with "Anansi and the Talking Melon"

SYNTACTIC CUES Reading fluency can be impaired when children pay too much attention to individual sounds and letters. Try framing text phrases or copying sentences from the story onto a transparency and having children read a chunk of text at a time. Track the print, pausing only for necessary punctuation marks.

* Books leveled according to Barbara Peterson's "Profiles of Books for Beginning Readers," on page 9 of the *Instant Readers Teacher's Guide.*

IDEA BANK

TIPS FOR CLASSROOM MANAGEMENT

IF children have difficulty understanding the ending of the story, **THEN** assign them to small groups to discuss the questions in the Group Talk activity.

IF children have difficulty pantomiming the story in the Creative Connection activity, **THEN** allow them to role-play, speaking out loud.

TECHNOLOGY

IMAGINATION EXPRESS: Destination, Rain Forest allows children to select scenery, choose and animate characters, record conversations, and write stories using the background of a rain forest.

LISTENING AND SPEAKING

Group Talk

STORY ENDINGS

Encourage children to talk about the ending of the story. If they have difficulty getting started, suggest that they discuss these questions:

- **Did you like the ending? Why or why not?**
- **How else might the author have ended the story?**

After small-group discussions, gather children to share their thoughts.
CHALLENGING THE TEXT

REAL-LIFE READING

Reading Seed Packets

Remind children that Elephant grew melons in his garden. Ask what Elephant planted to grow the melons. (melon seeds) Display some seed packets (melon seeds, if possible). Have small groups examine the packets, and ask children to tell what the seed packets have in common. (name of plant, picture of plant, planting instructions)

Then have children use the seed packets as models to create a seed packet for an imaginary plant. READING/WRITING

Informal Assessment

Use children's comments in the Group Talk discussion to assess whether they understood the ending of the story.

ORAL LANGUAGE

Puppet Theater

PAPER-BAG PUPPETS

Put on a class puppet presentation of "Anansi and the Talking Melon." Children can make puppets out of small brown paper bags for the characters Anansi, Elephant, Hippo, Warthog, Rhino, Turtle, Ostrich, and the king. In addition, one puppet, made from a bigger bag, should be the melon that is put over Anansi when the spider is inside. A group of children may read the narrator's words as a chorus.

Allow time for children to prepare and practice. Remind children that during the presentation they should speak clearly and loudly enough to be heard by the audience.

LISTENING/SPEAKING/READING

KINESTHETIC

Creative Connection

ANANSI CHARADES

Invite children to pantomime events from "Anansi and the Talking Melon" and have their classmates guess the event. Possible actions:

- Elephant hoeing in his garden
- Anansi boring a hole in the melon
- Anansi squeezing into the melon
- Elephant jumping in surprise when he hears the melon talk
- each of the animals getting angry when the melon insults it
- the king prodding the melon
- the king throwing the melon

KINESTHETIC

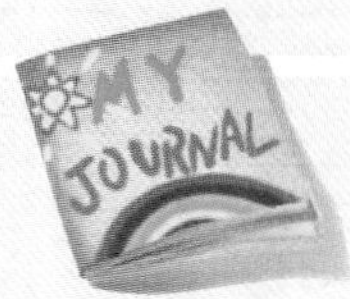

PERSONAL JOURNAL

REFLECTING ON THE STORY **Have children use their personal journals to tell what they think of the way Anansi acts. Would they like to have Anansi as a friend?**

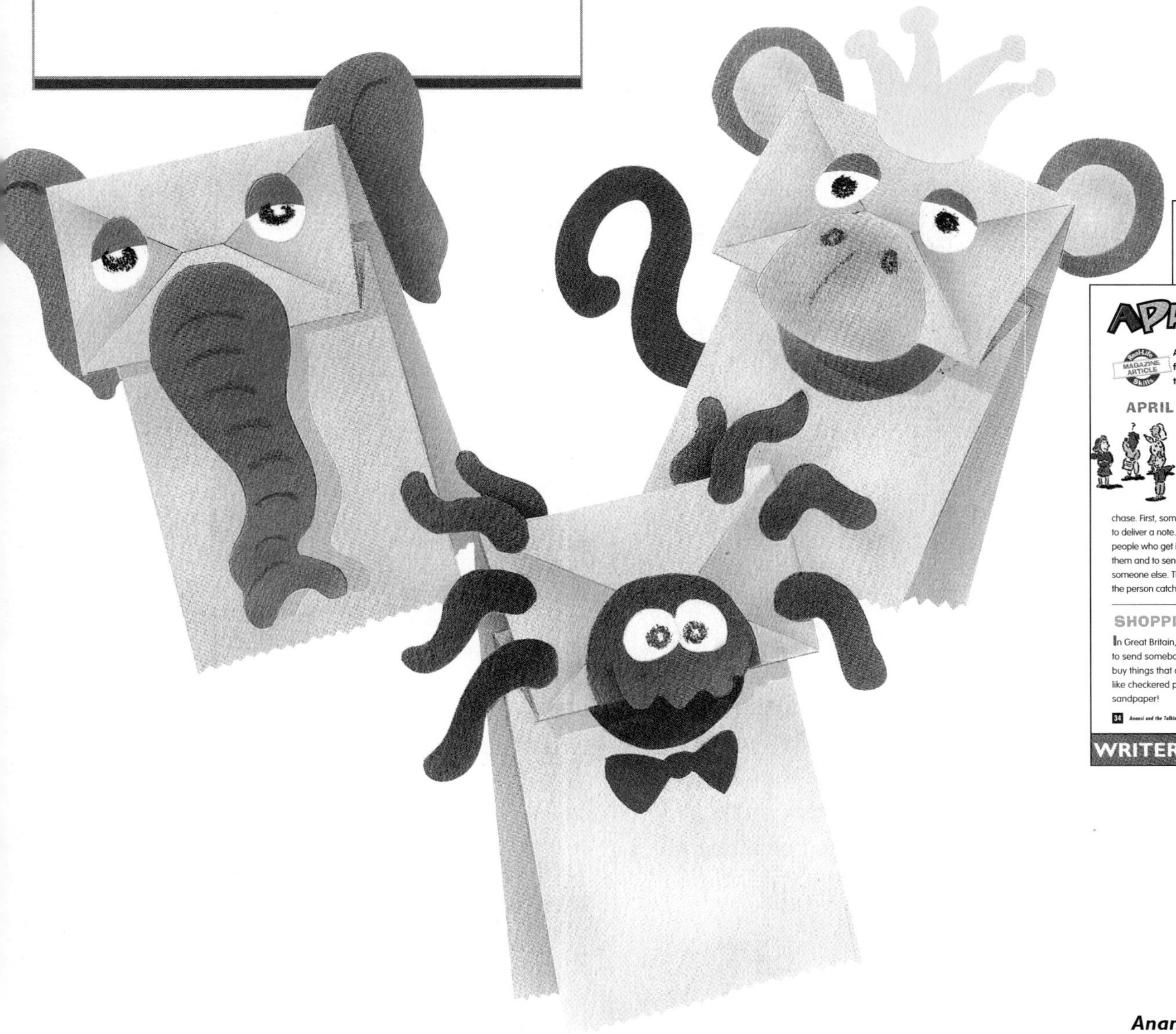

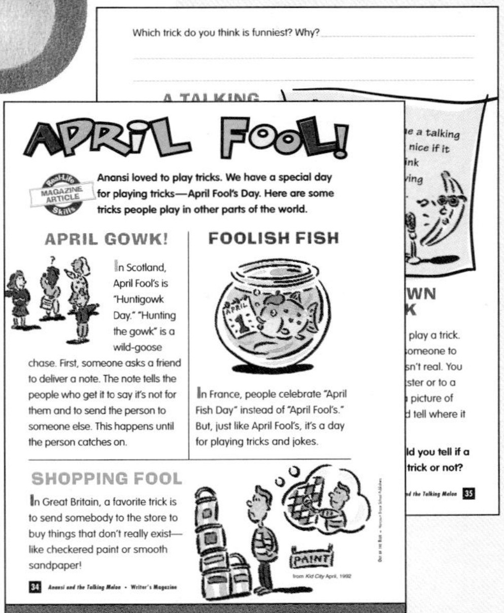

Which trick do you think is funniest? Why?

APRIL FOOL!

Anansi loved to play tricks. We have a special day for playing tricks—April Fool's Day. Here are some tricks people play in other parts of the world.

APRIL GOWK!

In Scotland, April Fool's is "Huntigowk Day." "Hunting the gowk" is a wild-goose chase. First, someone asks a friend to deliver a note. The note tells the people who get it to say it's not for them and to send the person to someone else. This happens until the person catches on.

FOOLISH FISH

In France, people celebrate "April Fish Day" instead of "April Fool's." But, just like April Fool's, it's a day for playing tricks and jokes.

SHOPPING FOOL

In Great Britain, a favorite trick is to send somebody to the store to buy things that don't really exist—like checkered paint or smooth sandpaper!

from Kid City April, 1992

34 Anansi and the Talking Melon • Writer's Magazine

WRITER'S MAGAZINE, pages 34–35

WRITER'S WORKSHOP

A Story

Thinking as Writers

WRITING FORM: Story Remind children that "Anansi and the Talking Melon" is a make-believe story. Have children retell "Anansi and the Talking Melon." Then explain to children that they will work with a partner to create a new story about Anansi.

Display Chart/Transparency 6, or write the model Story on the board. Discuss the beginning, middle, and ending of a story.

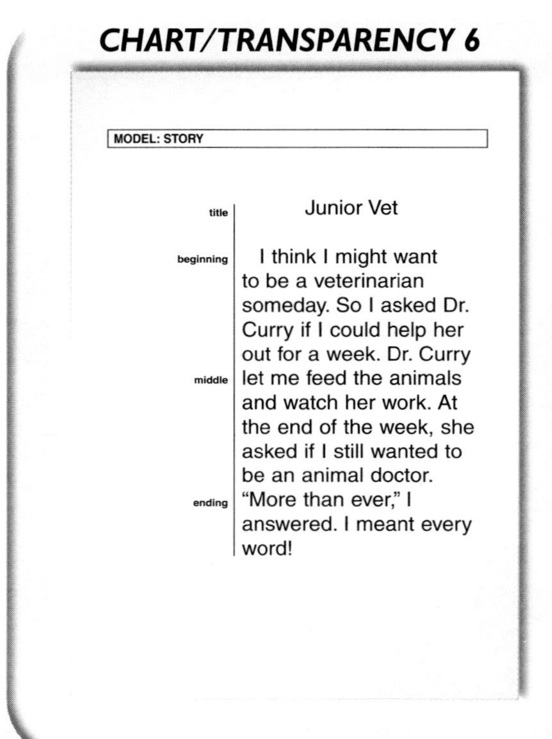

CHART/TRANSPARENCY 6

MODEL: STORY

title — Junior Vet

beginning — I think I might want to be a veterinarian someday. So I asked Dr. Curry if I could help her out for a week. Dr. Curry

middle — let me feed the animals and watch her work. At the end of the week, she asked if I still wanted to be an animal doctor.

ending — "More than ever," I answered. I meant every word!

WRITER'S CRAFT: Writing a Good Beginning Explain that, when planning a story, a writer decides who the characters are and where the story takes place. Help children discover that the beginning of a story is important because it should make readers want to keep reading. Have children discuss the beginning of "Anansi and the Talking Melon."

PREWRITING

Before children begin writing, brainstorm plot ideas with them. Suggest that they think about what might happen next now that the bananas are "talking," or about another trick Anansi might play. Then ask partners to discuss how their stories might begin. Suggest that children plan their stories, using a story map.

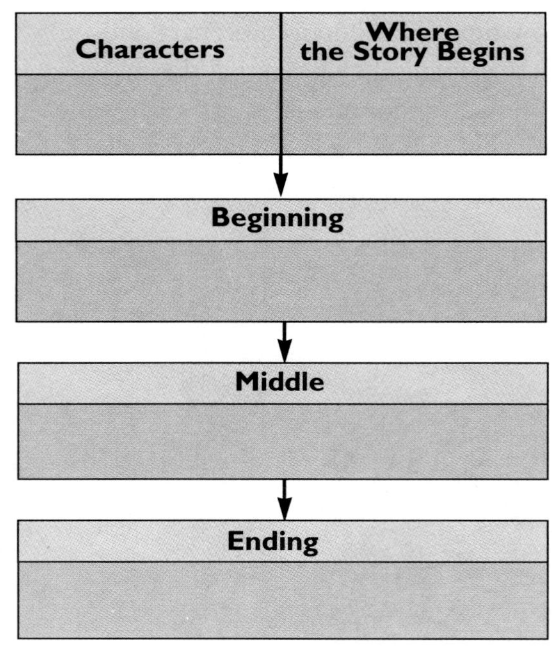

Have children first list events within each section in any order. Then ask them to number the events in order.

DRAFTING

As partners work on their stories, remind them to

- use their story maps for ideas.
- write a beginning that gets readers' attention.
- tell what happens in the beginning, the middle, and the ending.
- write a title that tells what their story is about.

Have children save their drafts and revisions in their writer's folder.

TIPS FOR CLASSROOM MANAGEMENT

IF children are familiar with the writing process approach, **THEN** present the writing assignment and have them use the Story model on pages 8–9 of the *Language Handbook.*

IF at this time you want a short writing activity, **THEN** have children do the prewriting activity and refer to their story maps to give an oral story about Anansi.

RESPONDING AND REVISING

Work with small groups to help partners revise their stories. Read aloud one pair's story and have children discuss ways to make the story better. Guide them with the questions below:

- What is Anansi like in this story?
- Does the beginning make you want to hear more of the story?
- Does the story have a beginning, a middle, and an ending?

PROOFREADING

Suggest some tips to help children proofread. Help them focus on the following:

NAMES OF SPECIAL PEOPLE, ANIMALS, AND PLACES Names of special people, animals, and places begin with a capital letter. (See the Grammar Minilesson on page T493.)

SPELLING Remind children to circle words in their stories that may be misspelled. Have them verify the spellings of these words by using a dictionary or asking someone. (See also the Spelling lesson on page T518.)

PUBLISHING

Have children make a clean copy of their stories. Then offer publishing options like the following:

Handwriting
Remind children that their handwriting must be neat and clear so that the person reading the story can understand it. If children need assistance, refer them to the Handwriting models in the *Language Handbook* or in the classroom.

PICK A STORY
Display a construction-paper banana tree on a bulletin board or a wall. Use double-sided tape to attach children's stories to the tree. Suggest that readers pick a story from the banana tree to find out what happens to Anansi.

WEAVE A TALE Decorate the Author's Chair with yarn to resemble a spider's web. Have children read their stories from Anansi's "web."

PORTFOLIO OPPORTUNITY

After children publish, make copies of their stories and have them attach their Writing Self-Assessment Checklists to them. Have them place the stories and checklists in their portfolios.

LANGUAGE HANDBOOK

Story, pages 8–9

Student Self-Assessment ✓

Children can use the Writing Self-Assessment Checklist in the *Portfolio Assessment Teacher's Guide.*

EVALUATING THE WRITTEN RESPONSE

When evaluating children's stories, consider:

CONTENT	ORGANIZATION	STYLE
Is the story about Anansi and a talking banana or other talking thing?	**Does the story have a beginning, a middle, and an ending?**	**Does the story's beginning catch the reader's interest?**

EVALUATION BENCHMARKS

The child has difficulty creating a story. The child might relate only a single event. There is no plot.	= EMERGENT
The child writes a story but has difficulty placing story events in order.	= BEGINNING
The child successfully writes a story. The story has a good beginning, a middle, and an ending.	= PROFICIENT

GRAMMAR

Names of Days, Months, and Holidays

Reading↔Writing Connection

Connect to the story. Have children describe what kind of character Anansi is. List some words on the board that describe him. Then, using the descriptive words as clues, discuss what Anansi's favorite holidays might be. Write responses on the board. (Possible responses: April Fool's Day or Halloween)

Build oral language. Ask children to name their favorite day of the week, month, and holiday. List their responses.

Days	Months	Holidays
Wednesday	July	Fourth of July
Friday	October	Halloween
Saturday	December	Christmas
		Kwanzaa

Teach/Model

Discuss days, months, and holidays. Ask children what they notice about each of the words on the chart. Have volunteers circle the capital letter at the beginning of each word. Tell children that the names of the days of the week, months, and holidays are proper nouns and they always begin with capital letters.

Practice/Apply

Check understanding. Write the following sentences on the board, omitting the underlining. Have volunteers identify each word that should be capitalized by erasing the first letter of the word and replacing it with a capital letter.

On a <u>sunday</u> in the month of <u>may</u>, we celebrate <u>mother's day</u>.
On a hot day in <u>june</u>, we honor our fathers with <u>father's day</u>.

As words are capitalized, ask children why the word should begin with a capital letter.

LANGUAGE HANDBOOK
Names of Days and Months, pages 62–63

Holidays, pages 64–65

DAILY LANGUAGE PRACTICE **Oral language exercises are provided on page R142.**

Trudy's Time & Place House (Calendar Clock)

Practice Activities

CAPITALIZATION CARDS

ORAL APPLICATION Have each child make two identifier cards: one labeled *A–Z,* and the other labeled *a–z.* Read a series of words, some naming days, months, and holidays, and others naming common time words (for example, *day, month, year, today, tomorrow, birthday,* and *minute*). As you read each word, children should hold up the appropriate card to show whether it should begin with a capital letter *(A–Z)* or a lowercase letter *(a–z).* VISUAL/AUDITORY

Calendar Kids

WRITING APPLICATION Have small groups of children make calendars, beginning with next month. Each group could be responsible for two or three months of the year. Children should write the name of the month across the top and the days of the week below the month, and should then add important holidays. Ask them to illustrate each month with pictures representing things they do at that time of year, especially on listed holidays. Post the monthly calendars in sequence on a bulletin board. VISUAL

Greetings!

WRITING APPLICATION Have children make greeting cards to give to their relatives for various holidays throughout the year. Encourage them to write rhyming verses for their cards. Ask them to include the name of the holiday on the card. VISUAL

APPLY TO WRITING

You may want children to check the stories they wrote and their other writing to be sure they capitalized the names of the days, months, and holidays.

STUDENTS ACQUIRING ENGLISH

Ask if the days of the week, months, and holidays are capitalized in children's first languages. If they are, suggest that this would be a good way to remember to capitalize them in English.

RETEACH

See page R128 for lessons in multiple modalities.

GRAMMAR PRACTICE BOOK
pages 39-42

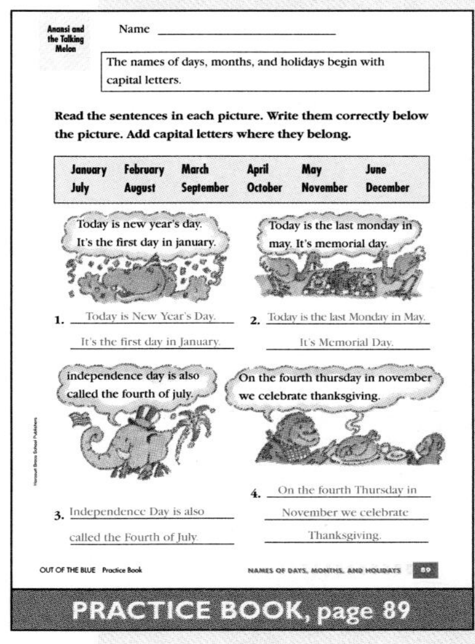

Anansi and the Talking Melon

Name ____________

The names of days, months, and holidays begin with capital letters.

Read the sentences in each picture. Write them correctly below the picture. Add capital letters where they belong.

January	February	March	April	May	June
July	August	September	October	November	December

Today is new year's day. It's the first day in january.

Today is the last monday in may. It's memorial day.

1. Today is New Year's Day. It's the first day in January.

2. Today is the last Monday in May. It's Memorial Day.

independence day is also called the fourth of july.

On the fourth thursday in november we celebrate thanksgiving.

3. Independence Day is also called the Fourth of July.

4. On the fourth Thursday in November we celebrate Thanksgiving.

OUT OF THE BLUE Practice Book — NAMES OF DAYS, MONTHS, AND HOLIDAYS 89

PRACTICE BOOK, page 89

5-DAY PLAN

Use in conjunction with Daily Language Practice.

Day 1 Complete page T516.	**Day 4** Choose a Practice Activity or *Grammar Practice Book* pages 39–42.
Day 2 Complete a Practice Activity on page T517.	**Day 5** Complete *Practice Book* page 89.
Day 3 Choose a Practice Activity or *Language Handbook* pages 62–65.	

SPELLING

5-Day Plan

Integrated Spelling Lesson 13: student book, pages 58–61; Teacher's Edition, pages T93–T98.

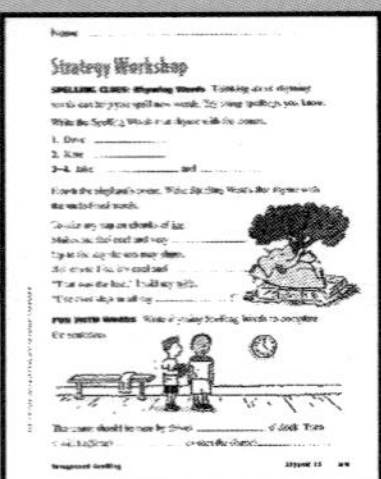

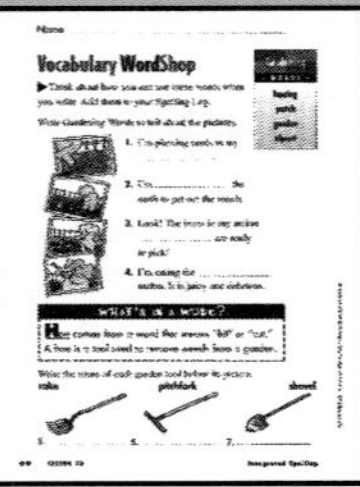

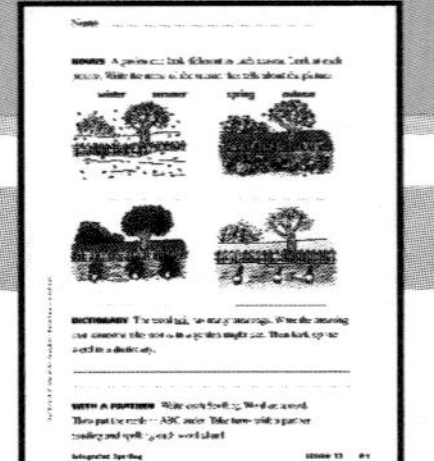

SPELLING WORDS

1. take ★
2. gave ★
3. five
4. nice
5. fine ★
6. game
7. life
8. late
9. make ★
10. time ★

STUDENT'S PERSONAL WORDS

11. 13.
12. 14.

Additional story words are *ate, came, face, pile, ripe,* and *while.*

★Words appearing in "Anansi and the Talking Melon"

Words with *a-e* and *i-e*

Pretest

DAY 1 **Administer the pretest.** Say each word, use it in the dictation sentence below, and repeat the word. Have pairs of children check their own pretests by referring to the word list.

OPEN SORT

DAY 2 **Have children classify words.** Ask children to classify the Spelling Words according to certain criteria, such as beginning letter, number of letters, or vowel sound. Invite volunteers to share their lists.

CLOSED SORT

Sort by spelling pattern. Write on the board the headings from the chart below, and have volunteers write each Spelling Word under the correct heading.

same	like
take	five
gave	nice
game	fine
late	life
make	time

Teach/Model

DAY 3 **Discuss the generalization.** Write the words *same* and *like* on the board. Explain that these words both have a long vowel sound. Have children identify the vowel sound and circle the letters which stand for the vowel sound in each word. (/ā/*a-e*, /ī/*i-e*) Help children form generalizations about how the /ā/ and /ī/ sounds are spelled—for example:

- **The long *a* sound may be spelled *a-e.***
- **The long *i* sound may be spelled *i-e.***

DAY 4 **Apply to writing.** Children should look for words with /ā/ and /ī/ in their Anansi stories and other writing to be sure those words are spelled correctly.

Posttest

DAY 5 **Assess children's progress.** The sentences below should be used as the posttest.

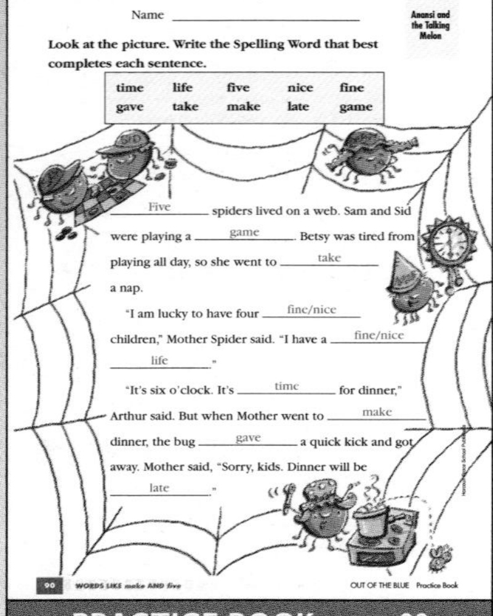

Name ____________ Anansi and the Talking Melon

Look at the picture. Write the Spelling Word that best completes each sentence.

time	life	five	nice	fine
gave	take	make	late	game

Five spiders lived on a web. Sam and Sid were playing a game. Betsy was tired from playing all day, so she went to take a nap.

"I am lucky to have four fine/nice children," Mother Spider said. "I have a fine/nice life."

"It's six o'clock. It's time for dinner," Arthur said. But when Mother went to make dinner, the bug gave a quick kick and got away. Mother said, "Sorry, kids. Dinner will be late."

90 WORDS LIKE *make* AND *five* OUT OF THE BLUE Practice Book

PRACTICE BOOK, page 90

DICTATION SENTENCES

1. The tired baby must take a nap.
2. My dad gave me a gift.
3. I have five fingers on my hand.
4. Thank you for the nice present.
5. It is a fine day for a picnic.
6. Did your team win the game?
7. The life of a pet cat is easy.
8. Don't be late for dinner!
9. A jet can make a loud sound.
10. It is time to go to bed.

VOCABULARY WORKSHOP

Reviewing Key Words

To review how the vocabulary was used in the story, distribute copies of page R176 to children. Then write the Key Words on the board.

Have children choose the word that best completes each sentence. Then have volunteers read the completed sentence aloud as children write the word.

Anansi was a ___lazy___ spider who didn't want to work.

One day, he was ___hungry___ and needed to eat.

He wanted to ___bore___ a hole in a melon.

Anansi broke a sharp ___thorn___ off a tree.

He ___used___ it to make a hole in the rind.

Then he ___squeezed___ himself through the tiny hole.

He ate melon until he was ___full___.

Of ___course___, that is only one tricky thing he did.

Anansi made the king ___angry___.

Tell children to cut apart the sentences to make sentence strips. Children can use the strips to retell the story or glue the strips to a sheet of paper to create a newspaper article with a picture, reporting what Anansi did.

Extending Vocabulary

DIALOGUE WORDS

Display these story sentences and have children read them:

"Ouch!" cried Anansi.
"Why did you bring me a melon?" he asked Elephant.

Then list the following dialogue words on chart paper:

said	cried	exclaimed
asked	told	replied
shouted	called	

Explain that these words describe the ways in which the animals spoke to each other in "Anansi and the Talking Melon." Explain that dialogue words can change the tone of a sentence completely. For example, *whispered* would give a sentence a much different meaning than *shouted*.

Write the following sentences, with blanks, on the board:

1. ***Elephant ________, "I'm going to show my melon to the king."***
2. ***Hippo ________, "Come along, then."***
3. ***"Where are you taking that melon?" Warthog ________.***
4. ***"I can't get out!" Anansi ________.***
5. ***The king ________, "I command you to speak."***

Invite volunteers to use a dialogue word to complete a sentence, write the word in the blank, and then read the sentence as the dialogue word indicates. Display the list of dialogue words in the Writing Center and ask children to add to it.

STUDENTS ACQUIRING ENGLISH

Children may need extra help differentiating between the various dialogue words. Have children identify dialogue words in their primary languages and tell how different words change how things are said. Then use gestures and facial expressions to show the meaning of the English dialogue words.

TAKE-HOME/ KEEP-AT-HOME BOOK

Cloud Weaver

Distribute the pages and have children make their own TAKE-HOME/ KEEP-AT-HOME BOOKS, which reinforce Key Words and known vocabulary. Have children read to partners and then take the book home to read.

Tested Skill

INTRODUCE: PHONICS AND DECODING

R-Controlled Vowel: /ôr/*or, ore, our*

OBJECTIVE: To understand the relationship between letters and sounds

Informal Assessment ✓

Are children able to

- ☑ identify words that contain a specific phonogram?
- ☑ make and read *or, ore,* and *our* words?
- ☑ understand that *or, ore,* and *our* can be spellings of the /ôr/ sound?

Teach/Model

Connect to the story. Ask children to recall how Anansi got into the melon. (He used a thorn to bore a hole.) Write that sentence on the board, followed by this one: *Of course, Anansi was up to no good!*

Have the sentences read. Then underline the words *thorn, bore,* and *course,* saying them aloud as you do. Ask how the words are alike. (They have the same vowel sound.) Tell children that they will learn more about this sound.

Phonemic awareness: Listen to the sound. Display page 15 in the *Big Book of Rhymes.* Have children listen for words with the same vowel sound heard in *thorn, bore,* and *course* as you read aloud the rhyme. Then have children read aloud the rhyme with you, emphasizing the words with the /ôr/ sound.

Big Book of Rhymes, page 15

Find and read words with the /ôr/ sound. Have children look at the rhyme and identify words with the same vowel sound as *thorn.* As children identify words, write them on the board in appropriate columns.

thorn	bore	course
for	shore	four
or	more	pour

Point to the words under *thorn,* and ask how they are alike. (Both have the letters *or*; they have the /ôr/ sound.) Tell children that the letters *or* often stand for the vowel sound heard in *thorn.* Follow a similar procedure with *bore* and *course.* Have volunteers circle the letters *or, ore,* and *our* in the words.

Practice/Apply

Read words in context. Write the following sentences on the board:

1. *I'll make more popcorn shortly.*
2. *Rain poured down during the storm.*
3. *Go to the store for more juice.*

Have children read each sentence and circle the words with the /ôr/ sound. Then ask them to write each word in the appropriate column on the board.

TECHNOLOGY

Bailey's Book **House (Read-A-Rhyme)**

Practice Activities

SPORTS SCORES

Provide today's sports section from the newspaper. Have children look at the sports section and write sentences telling about the events, including and underlining words with or, our, and ore. Provide the following sample sentences: Oregon scored four more than Idaho. The Comets performed poorly on their home court. Encourage children to share their sentences. **VISUAL/KINESTHETIC**

Four for /ôr/ Words

Have children listen to the following words, and hold up four fingers each time they hear a word with the same vowel sound as *thorn*: *door, more, bear, soar, star, store, corn, here, four, fair, torn.* **AUDITORY**

Word Building

PERFORMANCE ASSESSMENT Have partners use their Word Builder and letter cards to create families of rhyming words. Have partners use their letter cards to form *or*, *our*, and *ore*. Then have them take turns placing letters and letter clusters in front of each spelling of the /ôr/ sound to see how many words they can make. Encourage partners to keep a list of the words they make. Then have children choose some of the words to use in sentences. **VISUAL/AUDITORY/KINESTHETIC**

STUDENTS ACQUIRING ENGLISH

Help children create a picture dictionary of common words with the sound /ôr/ spelled *or, ore,* and *our*.

RETEACH

See page R129 for lessons in multiple modalities.

CHALLENGE

Have children add letters to the ends as well as to the beginnings of the word families *or, ore,* and *our*. Ask children to list all the words they form.

PHONICS ACTIVITY BOOK, pages 28-29

PHONICS PRACTICE BOOK, page 147

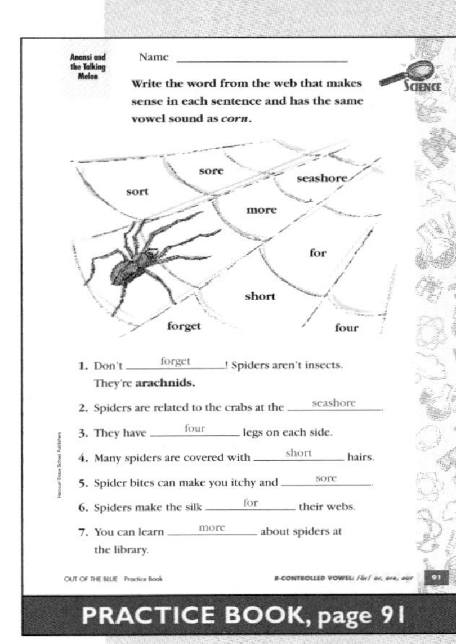

Anansi and the Talking Melon

Name ______

Write the word from the web that makes sense in each sentence and has the same vowel sound as *corn*.

sort, sore, seashore, more, for, short, forget, four

1. Don't forget! Spiders aren't insects. They're **arachnids.**
2. Spiders are related to the crabs at the seashore.
3. They have four legs on each side.
4. Many spiders are covered with short hairs.
5. Spider bites can make you itchy and sore.
6. Spiders make the silk for their webs.
7. You can learn more about spiders at the library.

PRACTICE BOOK, page 91

Reading Trade Books FOR R-CONTROLLED VOWEL /ôr/

***And to Think That I Saw It on Mulberry Street* by Dr. Seuss. Random House, 1937.** AVERAGE

***The Lady and the Spider* by Faith McNulty. HarperCollins, 1986.** AVERAGE

***Storm in the Night* by Mary Stolz. HarperCollins, 1988.** CHALLENGE

PHONICS PRACTICE READER 18

INTRODUCE: PHONICS AND DECODING

Short Vowel: /u/*ou*

OBJECTIVE: To understand the relationship between letters and sounds

Informal Assessment

Are children able to

- read words in which the letters *ou* stand for the short *u* sound?
- hear the /u/ sound spelled *ou* in words?
- distinguish between words with /u/*ou* and /ou/*ou*?

TECHNOLOGY

THE AMAZING WRITING MACHINE **Children may use a word processing program to write their stories with words with the /u/ sound.**

Teach/Model

Connect to the story. Display these sentences about the story and read them with children:

> Anansi made a hole in the melon big enough for a spider.
> Anansi told Elephant that talking melons are nothing but trouble.

Underline *enough* and *trouble*, and ask what is alike about the words. (the letters *ou*; the short *u* sound) Tell children that they will learn more about this vowel sound.

Phonemic awareness: Listen to the sound. Display pages 16–17 in the *Big Book of Rhymes*. Have children listen for words with the same vowel sound heard in *enough* as you read the rhyme aloud. Reread the rhyme, and have children read it with you, emphasizing words with the /u/ sound. Then invite three groups of children to each read a verse.

Big Book of Rhymes, pages 16-17

Find and read words with /u/*ou*. Have children identify and frame words in the poem with the same vowel sound as *trouble*. (*tough, rough, cousin, trouble*) List the words on the board. Call on volunteers to read the words and tell how they are alike (all have the short *u* sound), and circle the letters that stand for the short *u* sound in each. (*ou*)

Practice/Apply

Read words in context. Write the following paragraph on the board:

> Having one puppy is a lot of work. Having two is double trouble. It's tough to get them to sleep at the same time. They are a couple of chewing machines. They chew one sock, but that is not enough. They chew the other one too!

Have children read the paragraph and identify words with the short *u* sound spelled *ou*. Then have them extend the story, including the words *young, touch*, and *rough*.

Practice Activities

TOUCHDOWN!

Write *Touchdown!* on the board. Have a volunteer underline the letters that stand for the short *u* sound. Demonstrate for children the arm signal used by football officials to rule a touchdown (arms raised straight overhead).

Tell children to make the touchdown signal every time you read a word that has the short *u* sound they hear in *cup* and *trouble*.

Then read aloud the following words: *enough, spider, young, rough, bread, double, much, trouble, tough, ouch, touch, hungry*. **AUDITORY/ KINESTHETIC**

SHORT U ADS

Write the following words on the board: *double, trouble, tough, touch, enough, young, rough*. Encourage children to use some of these words to write an ad for a new product for kids. Invite children to illustrate their ads. Then allow time for children to present their ads to their classmates. **VISUAL/AUDITORY**

A STORY OF SHORT U

PERFORMANCE ASSESSMENT Have children form small groups. Ask each group to think of six words in which *ou* stands for the short *u* sound. Have each group write a story using those six words. Groups should assign a Leader to lead the discussion and a Recorder to write the story. Allow groups to share their stories with classmates. Have the audience listen for /u/*ou* words. **VISUAL/AUDITORY**

STUDENTS ACQUIRING ENGLISH

Help children make word cards for the following words: *cousin, enough, young, rough, double, trouble, tough,* and *touch*. As you read a word, have a child locate the card with that word and read it.

RETEACH

See page R130 for lessons in multiple modalities.

CHALLENGE

Have children use a dictionary and other books to find more /u/*ou* words to add to their Word Files.

PHONICS ACTIVITY BOOK, page 30

PHONICS PRACTICE BOOK, pages 63–64

Reading Trade Books FOR SHORT VOWEL /U/OU

***Donkey Trouble* by Ed Young. Atheneum, 1995.**
CHALLENGE

***The Trouble with Tyrannosaurus Rex* by Lorinda Bryan Cauley. Harcourt Brace, 1988.**
CHALLENGE

PHONICS PRACTICE READER 19

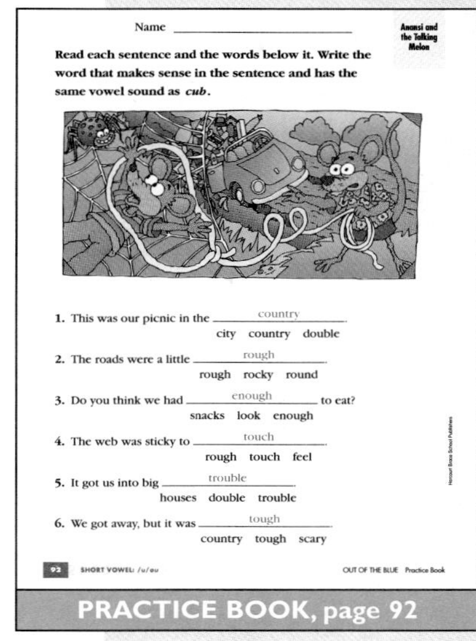

Name ______________ Anansi and the Talking Melon

Read each sentence and the words below it. Write the word that makes sense in the sentence and has the same vowel sound as *cub*.

1. This was our picnic in the country. city country double
2. The roads were a little rough. rough rocky round
3. Do you think we had enough to eat? snacks look enough
4. The web was sticky to touch. rough touch feel
5. It got us into big trouble. houses double trouble
6. We got away, but it was tough. country tough scary

92 SHORT VOWEL: /u/ou OUT OF THE BLUE Practice Book

PRACTICE BOOK, page 92

Integrated Curriculum

SOCIAL STUDIES

Africa

TIPS FOR CLASSROOM MANAGEMENT

IF children need help understanding how far away Africa is in the Traveling Stories activity, **THEN** use a globe to show them where it is located compared to other places with which children may be more familiar.

TECHNOLOGY

Imagination Express, Destination: Rain Forest

SOCIAL STUDIES

Traveling Stories

MATERIALS
- map of the world
- yarn
- tape

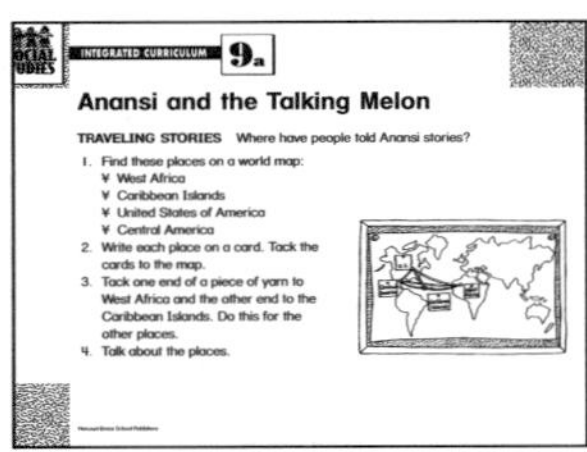

INTEGRATED CURRICULUM 9a

Anansi and the Talking Melon

TRAVELING STORIES Where have people told Anansi stories?

1. Find these places on a world map:
   - West Africa
   - Caribbean Islands
   - United States of America
   - Central America
2. Write each place on a card. Tack the cards to the map.
3. Tack one end of a piece of yarn to West Africa and the other end to the Caribbean Islands. Do this for the other places.
4. Talk about the places.

Curriculum Card 9a

Review with children the information on page 256 about the appearance of Anansi stories in the Caribbean and elsewhere. Discuss how children think such stories may have spread from land to land.

Help children identify West Africa, some Caribbean islands, Central America, and the United States on a map.

Have children cut pieces of yarn and attach one end of each piece to West Africa and piece to West Africa and the other end to one of the areas mentioned above. Have children make cards to label each area. They may wish to tag each piece of yarn with the number of miles it represents and attach the title "The Travels of Anansi."

READING/WRITING

MUSIC

The Sounds of Africa

MATERIALS
- tape player
- tapes of African music
- African instruments (optional)

Play different kinds of African music. If possible, display African instruments and allow children to play them.

Have children discuss and then choose which music best fits the story of "Anansi and the Talking Melon." Or, they may wish to choose individual pieces of music or instruments to represent the different characters, as in the operetta *Peter and the Wolf*. Then work with children to play music as they read aloud or pantomime "Anansi and the Talking Melon." LISTENING/SPEAKING

Reading Trade Books

CROSS-CURRICULAR READING

Beat the Story-Drum, Pum-Pum by Ashley Bryan. Atheneum, 1980.
CHALLENGE

SCIENCE

On Safari

MATERIALS
- books and magazines about African animals
- butcher paper
- markers

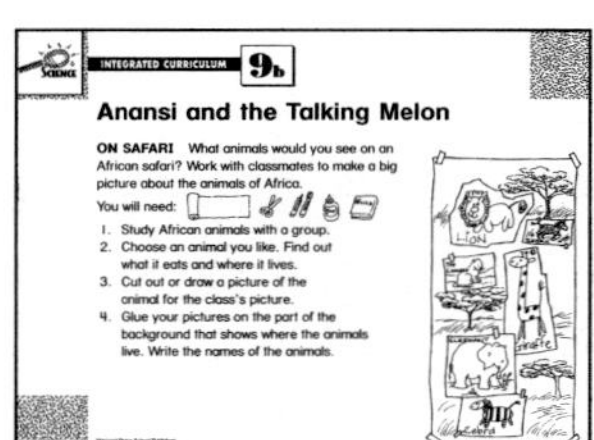
INTEGRATED CURRICULUM 9b

Anansi and the Talking Melon

ON SAFARI What animals would you see on an African safari? Work with classmates to make a big picture about the animals of Africa.

You will need:

1. Study African animals with a group.
2. Choose an animal you like. Find out what it eats and where it lives.
3. Cut out or draw a picture of the animal for the class's picture.
4. Glue your pictures on the part of the background that shows where the animals live. Write the names of the animals.

Curriculum Card 9b

COOPERATIVE LEARNING Have children work in small groups to complete a classroom mural about the animals of Africa on butcher paper. Each group can choose animals from a certain area—for example, rain forest animals or grassland animals—and research what the animals look like and where they live. Then children may draw or cut out magazine pictures of the animals as assigned by their group and design the background for the pictures. In the meantime, one representative from each group should meet with others to plan the mural and allot space on the paper. Once the background is drawn and the animals are drawn or glued onto it, children can label the animals. READING/WRITING

HEALTH

Fruit Stand

Anansi may be a troublemaker, but he knows how to eat well. The melon and bananas he eats in "Anansi and the Talking Melon" belong to the fruit group on the food pyramid. Nutritionists say we should eat two to four servings from this group each day.

Most children will be familiar with the fruits in the story "Anansi and the Talking Melon." Have children list other fruits they like to eat. Then have them research, if possible, which of their favorite fruits also grow in Africa. Each child may cut out pictures of or, if possible, bring in the kinds of fruit he or she likes best. Ask children to create a fruit stand with labels to display the fruit. Then you may want to help children make a fruit salad to enjoy. READING/WRITING

MULTI-AGE CLASSROOMS

The broad social studies topic of Africa is a rich source of learning and activities for all levels. Older children may do progressively more in-depth research regarding the Ashanti and other peoples, their traditions, their folktales, and their ways of life. Younger children may enjoy finding out about African animals and foods.

Reading Trade Books

Trade Books That Connect to "Anansi and the Talking Melon"

Anansi and the Moss-Covered Rock

by Eric A. Kimmel
illustrated by Janet Stevens

After reading, ask volunteers to retell in their own words how Anansi was tricked so that the animals could get back their belongings. Children can perform the story as Readers Theatre.

Anansi Goes Fishing

by Eric A. Kimmel
illustrated by Janet Stevens

After children have read the book, ask them to tell how Anansi was tricked and to summarize how spider webs came to be. Have children make a spider web by tracing one with glue and adding glitter. They may wish to add pictures of Anansi and Turtle.

Nanny Goat and the Seven Little Kids

retold by Eric A. Kimmel
illustrated by Janet Stevens

Ask children to identify the familiar "bad-guy" character in this story. Ask them to tell about other tales in which a wolf is the "bad guy." Invite children to share what they know about wolves, and discuss whether wolves are as bad as some folktales portray them.

TIPS FOR CLASSROOM MANAGEMENT

PARTNERS
Have children work with partners to read the books about Anansi (including Ananse in *A Story, A Story*). Have them discuss who gets tricked in each tale, Anansi or someone else.

SMALL GROUP
Read *Nanny Goat and the Seven Little Kids* aloud in a small circle of children. Pause every so often to let children ask questions or talk about what you've read.

Other Trade Books

Anansi the Spider

by Gerald McDermott

Explain that Anansi is a favorite character in African folktales. After reading aloud *Anansi the Spider*, help children make a chart to identify the names of Anansi's sons and how they helped rescue him. Then ask a volunteer to explain why the moon, according to this tale, is in the sky.

Traveling to Tondo

retold by Verna Aardema
illustrated by Will Hillenbrand

After children have read the book, have them draw pictures of the characters and put them on craft sticks to make stick puppets. Then have narrators read the story while other children use their puppets to act it out.

A Story, A Story

by Gail E. Haley

Ananse is not only tricky, but also very clever. Have children discuss how Ananse uses these skills to catch the leopard, the hornet, and the fairy in *A Story, A Story*.

STUDENTS ACQUIRING ENGLISH

Some children may want to read with a partner who is proficient in English and who will read aloud.

CHALLENGE

Encourage children to write a tale about a trickster. The trickster could be Anansi or a character they create. Have them share their tale with classmates.

PROJECT MANAGEMENT

Explore Storytelling Techniques

SELECTION CONNECTION

"Anansi and the Talking Melon" shows what a pest Anansi the spider can be. Ask children what they think of Anansi as a character and why he is successful at tricking others.

PROJECT CHECKLIST

During this stage, children should

- have an opportunity to hear and view storytelling techniques.
- look at stories told with pictures: comic strips, wordless books, and flip-books.
- listen to songs that tell stories, such as "There Was an Old Lady Who Swallowed a Fly."
- learn simple movements from a guest storyteller that they could use to tell a story.

NOTE: Before children work on this Project Checkpoint, contact a storyteller to visit the class. If you are so inclined, *you* could dress in a simple costume and be the storyteller.

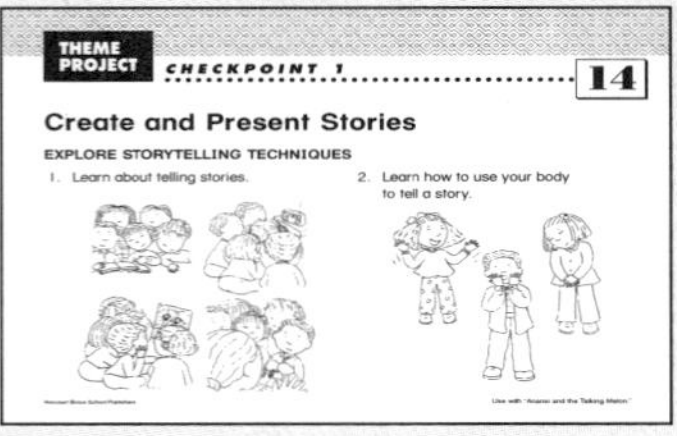

Project Card 14

When children have completed the checkpoint, have them think about the different forms stories can take. Encourage them to compare the merits of each type of story format in their Project Journals.

Project Card 14 can be found as a copying master on page R151.

PLANNING TIPS

As children begin to gather information, suggest that they

- have one group member act as a Recorder for the information they gather.
- use a separate page for notes about each technique or way to present a story that they find.
- save the notes for later use.

STUDENTS ACQUIRING ENGLISH

Pair children with fluent English-speakers when it's time to write. Have partners take turns reading stories or parts of stories aloud to each other.

MULTI-AGE CLASSROOMS

Storytelling creates a bond between older and younger children. Encourage older children to introduce younger ones to favorite stories and to read aloud from books younger children may not be ready to read.

Informal Assessment

As children complete this checkpoint, they will **compare and contrast** story formats and **evaluate** and **classify** information. Children are thinking critically if they

- are able to distinguish between different types of story formats.
- demonstrate an understanding of how different forms of presenting a story might affect the story's impact on an audience.
- evaluate and classify storytelling techniques and formats.

Note that a more formal assessment rubric for this checkpoint is provided on page T693.

Tricks Animals Play

by Jan Nagel Clarkson

THEME CONNECTION

Children have already read fictional selections about animals that play tricks on others. Now they will read a nonfiction selection called "Tricks Animals Play" about real animals that "play tricks" on their enemies to protect and defend themselves.

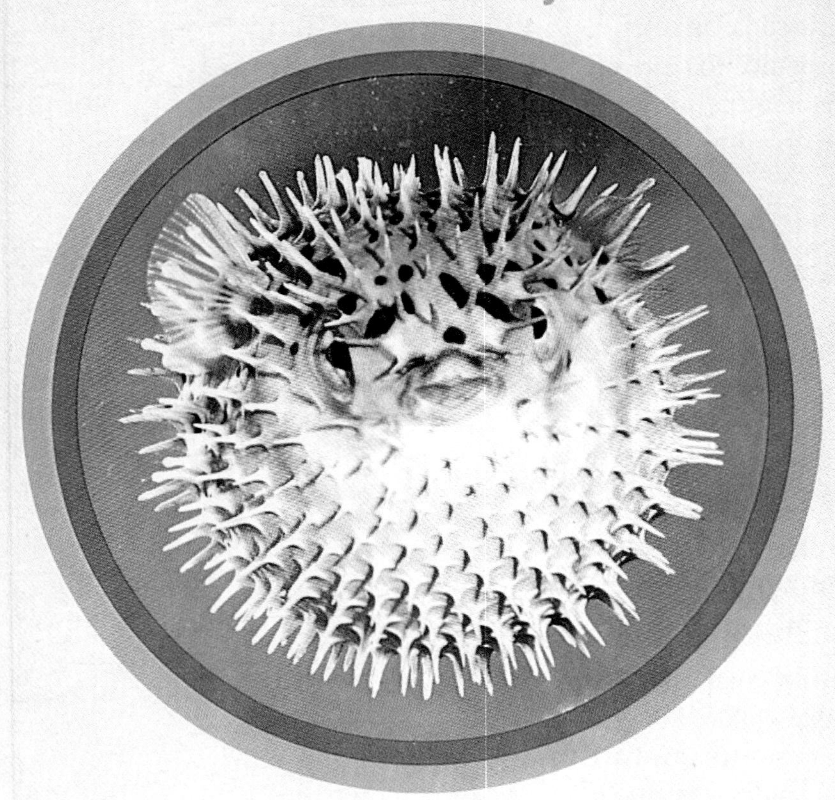

SUMMARY

GENRE: Nonfiction

Some animals have natural defenses against their enemies that seem like tricks to us. Opossums either hiss or play dead. The porcupine fish and bearded lizard puff up their bodies to make themselves look bigger and more threatening. Other animals, such as the dead-leaf mantis, the ring-necked snake, the bark katydid, and the crayfish, use bright colors to ward off enemies.

CHALLENGE

Encourage children to become "animal experts." Assign each child one of the animals in the selection. Provide books and other reference materials with information about the animals. Have children read about their animals and then share what they learned with a group.

Introducing the Selection

BUILDING BACKGROUND

To experience how some animals change their appearance to scare off enemies, have children try the following:

> **Pretend to be a very small animal. Scrunch down into a tiny ball, wrapping your arms around your legs. Listen for a signal given by the teacher to alert the "animals" that an enemy is approaching. Try to become as big as possible by standing and stretching out arms and legs and making scary faces or sounds to frighten away the enemy.**

Tell children that they will be reading about animals with ways to trick the animals that hunt them.

Reading Nonfiction Point out that the story and poem that children read about Anansi are made-up stories that have little to do with real spiders. As children preview "Tricks Animals Play," talk about the differences between the Anansi stories and this piece. Point out the title in large type and the headings of each section in smaller type.

262

Opossum

TIPS FOR CLASSROOM MANAGEMENT

SMALL GROUP

COOPERATIVE READING

Have groups of three form Reading Circles. Each child reads one of the three subtitles and the section of the selection below it. Suggest that children read their sections silently before reading aloud. After each section is read, group members ask the reader questions about that section of the piece.

WHOLE CLASS

READ ALOUD

Ask children to listen and follow along as you read the selection aloud. After reading each section, invite children to ask one another questions about what you've just read. Encourage them to point out interesting details in the photographs.

Tricks Animals Play

BY JAN NAGEL CLARKSON

The Opossum Plays Dead

HISS! The opossum tries to scare an enemy. If the enemy does not go away, the opossum falls down and plays dead. When it lies very still, it is playing possum. Then an enemy may leave it alone. This is a trick that protects the opossum. Other animals have unusual ways to get food and to keep from being eaten.

263

EXPANDING VOCABULARY

Point out the first word in the first paragraph—"HISS!" The sound of the word *hiss* is something like the sound the opossum might make. Ask children to name other animals that make hissing sounds.

SCIENCE

OPOSSUMS Like a kangaroo, an opossum is a marsupial, a mammal that has a pouch. Although the opossum gives birth to live young, the young are very small. After they are born, they spend several months in their mother's pouch nursing and growing. Opossums are nocturnal, or active at night.

Critical Thinking Questions

1. **How does puffing up protect some animals from predators?** (Possible responses: It makes an animal look bigger and scarier. This may scare away an enemy.) CRITICAL: DRAWING CONCLUSIONS
2. **Why don't all animals use tricks to scare off enemies?** (Possible responses: Some animals have other ways of protecting themselves, like hiding, running away, or fighting. Some animals protect themselves with sharp claws or sharp teeth.) CRITICAL: SPECULATING

Porcupine Fish

264

SCIENCE CONNECTION

PORCUPINES When a porcupine is in danger, it arches its back and makes its thousands of quills stand up along its back and tail. If a predator gets too close, the porcupine smacks its tail against the other animal. Its barbed quills stick into the skin of the other animal, causing great pain. Ask children to compare the porcupine and the porcupine fish.

Intervention Strategies

SELF-QUESTIONING Have children repeat this sentence: *When I read, it helps me to check to see if I can answer any questions I asked myself before I began reading.* Have children tell how using this strategy might help them understand information presented in "Tricks Animals Play."

These Animals Puff Up Like Balloons

◀ A porcupine fish gulps water when there is danger. It puffs up, and sharp spines stick out all over its body. Do you think another fish will try to swallow a puffed-up porcupine fish?

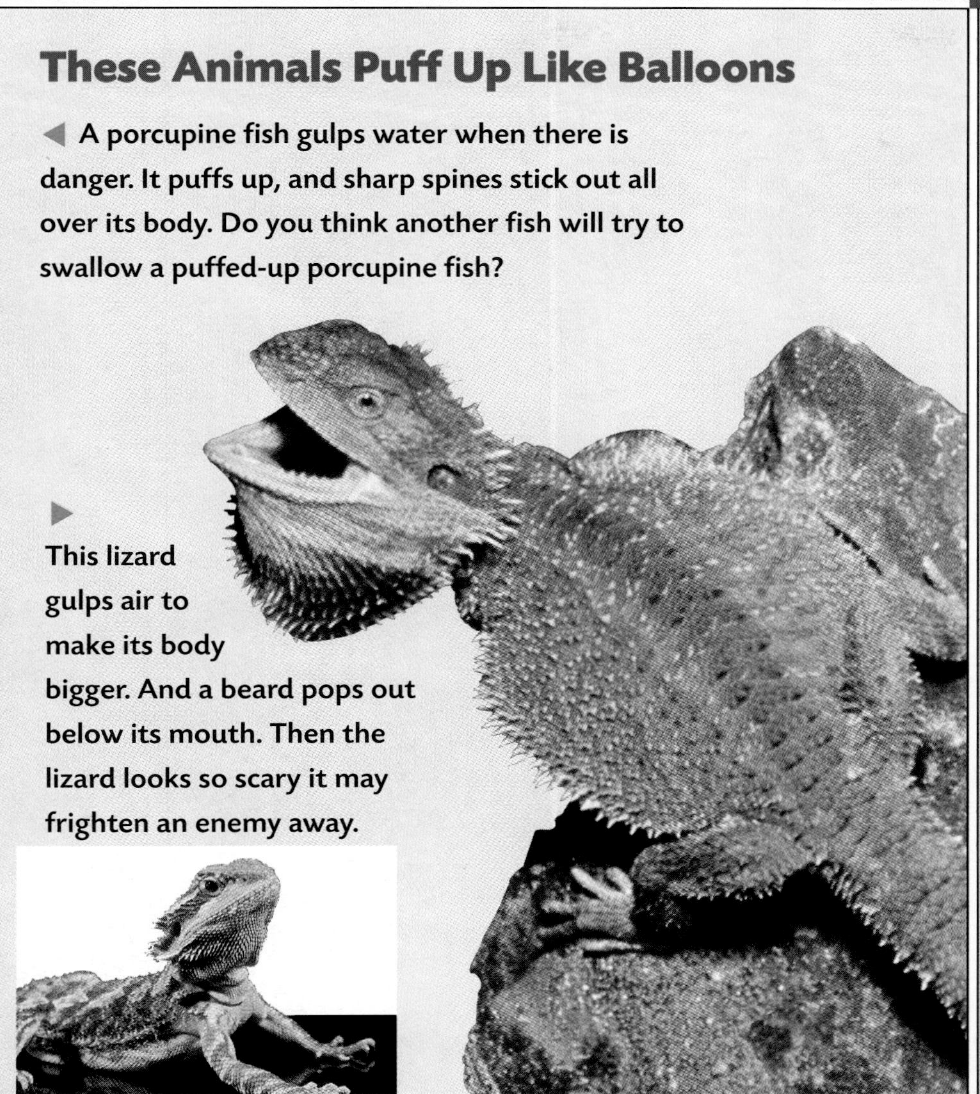

▶ This lizard gulps air to make its body bigger. And a beard pops out below its mouth. Then the lizard looks so scary it may frighten an enemy away.

Bearded Lizard

265

Tested Skill

MINILESSON

REVIEW: COMPREHENSION

Main Idea and Details

INFORMAL ASSESSMENT

Ask children to study the photographs on pages 264 and 265. Ask them first to say in one sentence the most important thing that these photos show. Then ask children to share details from the pictures that back up the main-idea statement they made.

TEACH/MODEL

Ask children to reread the information about the porcupine fish and the bearded lizard on page 265. Ask children to say a sentence that tells the most important way that both of these animals protect themselves. Then ask for details from the text and the photos. If necessary, model your thinking: *Both the porcupine fish and the bearded lizard puff themselves up when they are in danger. That sentence tells how both animals act when an enemy is near. Then I could give details: the porcupine fish swallows water to puff itself up and to make spikes stick out all over its body. The bearded lizard gulps air and makes itself bigger and makes a spiky beard pop out under its neck.*

PRACTICE/APPLY

Have children look for the details and the main idea on pages 262–263 and 266–267. Have children tell about the information on the pages. As children make statements, ask whether their statement is a main idea or a detail that tells about the main idea.

SCIENCE

THE RINGED PLOVER All different sorts of animals have "tricks" that can fool predators. A bird called the ringed plover will act as if it has a broken wing in order to lead a dangerous animal away from its nest of chicks or eggs on the ground. Just when the other animal thinks it can catch the injured bird, the ringed plover flies away.

Responding to the Selection

Ask children how the animals in this article and their tricks are different from Anansi and his tricks. Then ask children to think about how the information in the selection is presented—in three parts about different kinds of animal "tricks." Encourage them to talk about how the organization of the selection helped them understand the information it presents. Then invite them to share what they learned from the selection.

266

Dead-Leaf Mantis

STUDENTS ACQUIRING ENGLISH

This selection has many words that name specific body parts of animals. As children encounter the names of animal parts — *spine, mouth, beard, wing, tail*, or *claw*, — have them point to that body part in the photograph and repeat its name. Then share with children body parts named in the selection that people also have — *spine, mouth*.

Some Animals Scare Their Enemies With Bright Colors

◀ A red light at the street corner tells you to STOP! The red wings of this mantis seem to say STOP too. Scientists think some animals use bright colors to protect themselves. These bright colors may help scare away their enemies.

◀ The ring-necked snake curls up, and the enemy sees the orange tail.

◀ The bark katydid lifts its wings to show the red color on its back.

◀ As the crayfish gets ready to fight, it shows the red part of its claws.

267

CHECKING COMPREHENSION

What Do You Think?

1. **What did you learn about the ways in which animals protect themselves?** (Possible responses: Some animals trick their enemies by playing dead; some puff up and look scary; some scare their enemies with their bright colors.) **DESCRIPTIVE RESPONSE**

2. **What else would you like to learn about the ways animals protect themselves?** (Responses will vary. Encourage children to explore further ways that animals protect themselves.) **PERSONAL RESPONSE**

3. **Think about what you have learned about animals from reading this selection. How has it changed the way you think about and look at animals?** (Possible response: I will notice more details about how animals look, and I will think about why they act in certain ways.) **CREATIVE/CRITICAL RESPONSE**

SCIENCE

ANIMAL CAMOUFLAGE

Some animals protect themselves by disguise, or camouflage. If they are the same color as their backgrounds, their enemies will have difficulty seeing them. The furry white coats of the polar bear, Arctic fox, and snowshoe hare blend in with their snowy habitats. Some animals such as the silk moth and leaf-fish look just like dead leaves, and the walking stick looks like a twig!

Integrating Language Arts

TIPS FOR CLASSROOM MANAGEMENT

IF children's descriptions of their imaginary animals from the Writing activity are lacking in detail, THEN have children take some time to read about real animals and go back to fill in details about the imaginary animals they have created.

KINESTHETIC

It's Camouflaged

MATERIALS

- different colored toothpicks, the same number of each color

COOPERATIVE LEARNING Play a game with children about animal camouflage. Before you begin, scatter different colored toothpicks in the grass or on a shaggy carpet. Include toothpicks that are the same color as the background, for example, green to match the grass. Scatter the same number of each color. Then tell children that they are animals looking for food. Give them a short amount of time to collect as many toothpicks as they can find.

Then work with children to count the toothpicks of each color that were found by the group. Talk about why some colors were easier to find. Then talk about how this relates to the colors of some kinds of animals. **LISTENING-SPEAKING**

WRITING

Imaginary Animals

Have children each make a large drawing of an imaginary animal and cut it out. Have children then write a description of the animal—its name, what it looks like, where it lives, what it eats, and how it protects itself. Reserve an area in the room for children to display their animals and descriptions for all to enjoy. **READING/ WRITING**

THEME: COMMUNICATION

Tell a Tricky Tale

In "Nine-in-One, Grr! Grr!," children will read about a bird who tricks a tiger into having fewer cubs.

SELECTION SUMMARY

Genre: Folktale

Lonely Tiger climbs a mountain to ask the great Shao how many cubs she will have. As long as she remembers his words, she will have nine cubs each year, he tells her. After hearing Tiger sing *Nine-in-one, Grr! Grr!*, Bird asks Shao about Tiger's song and is worried by the idea of so many tigers in the world. Bird quickly finds Tiger and convinces her that she was singing *One-in-nine, Grr! Grr!,* and saves the world from too many tigers.

ABOUT THE AUTHORS AND THE ILLUSTRATOR

BLIA XIONG, who first heard this tale as a child in Laos, lives in the United States now. *Nine-in-One, Grr! Grr!* was named an ALA Notable Book for Children.

CATHY SPAGNOLI, a professional storyteller, was interested in Asian folktales when she first met Blia Xiong and heard "Nine-in-One, Grr! Grr!" These authors work together to share the tales they collect.

NANCY HOM, the illustrator, used watercolors and colored pencils to illustrate this story, copying the style of Hmong story cloths.

For more information about the authors and the illustrator, see pages T566–T567.

SUGGESTED LESSON PLANNER

▶ ***Nine-in-One, Grr! Grr!***

	DAY 1	DAY 2
PART 1 Reading, Listening, Speaking, Viewing **Key Words** change decided explained lonely noise terrible important coins sighed	**BUILD BACKGROUND** T540 **VOCABULARY STRATEGIES** T540–T541 *Chart/Transparency 20* *Practice Book* pp. 95–96 **READING THE SELECTION** T542–T567 Options for Reading T542–T543 *Response Card 4* *Literature Cassette 1* **REVIEW PREDICTIONS/PURPOSE** T564 **APPRECIATING THE LITERATURE** T564 NOTE: Students may read the selection on Day 2.	**SUMMARIZE AND RETELL THE SELECTION** T565 *Practice Book* p. 97 ◆ **RESPONSE CORNER ACTIVITIES** T568–T569 **CHECKING COMPREHENSION** T569 *End-of-Selection Test* 
PART 2 Writer's Workshop	**A PARAGRAPH THAT GIVES INFORMATION** Thinking as Writers T574 *Chart/Transparency 21*	Prewriting T574
Grammar	✓ **PLURAL NOUNS WITH *s* AND *es*** Teach the Concept T576 Daily Language Practice (1–2) R143	Daily Language Practice (3–4) R143 Practice Activity T577
Spelling	**CONSONANT CLUSTERS** *last dry tree fly from* *flag fast try grass blow* Pretest/Self-Check T578 *Integrated Spelling Teacher's Edition* pp. T99, T281	Open and Closed Sorts T578 *Integrated Spelling* p. 62 *Integrated Spelling Teacher's Edition* p. T100
PART 3 Phonics	**VOWEL DIPHTHONG: /oi/*oi, oy*** Phonics-Vocabulary Connection T541	**VOWEL DIPHTHONG: /oi/*oi, oy*** (Introduce) T580 *Big Book of Rhymes* p. 18 *Phonics Practice Book* pp. 151–154
Skills and Strategies	◆ **INTEGRATED CURRICULUM** Wild Animals **Science** T584 **Math** T584 **Music** T585 **Art** T585 *Imagination Express, Destination: Rain Forest*	**COMPREHENSION SKILL** T582–T583 Referents (Introduce) *Practice Book* p. 102

Use the Intervention Strategies notes on pp. T551 and T560 and the Extra Support notes on pp. T547 and T556 for **below-level readers**.

To help students build fluency, use the *Instant Readers™ You'll Roar* and *How Moon Tricked Sun* on pages T570–T571.

NOTE: An alternative lesson plan for **below-level readers** appears on *Intervention Strategies Manual* pp. 56–61. A lesson for **students acquiring English** appears on *Sheltered English/ESL Manual* pp. 38–41.

DAY 3	DAY 4	DAY 5
◆ **IDEA BANK ACTIVITIES** Listening and Speaking T572 Real-Life Reading: Reading Music Recording Covers T572 Oral Language T573 Kinesthetic T573 *Writer's Magazine* pp. 36–39 School–Home Connection 10 R173	**VOCABULARY WORKSHOP** T579 Reviewing Key Words Story Strips R177 Similes *Practice Book* p. 100 *Take-Home/Keep-at-Home Book: Why Elephants Never Forget* **READING TRADE BOOKS** T586–T587  Signatures Library  Take-Home Book	**READING TRADE BOOKS** T581, T583, T585, T586–T587  Instant Reader™
Drafting T574 *Language Handbook* pp. 22–23 *The Amazing Writing Machine*	Responding and Revising T575	Proofreading and Publishing T575 *The New Kid Pix*
Daily Language Practice (5–6) R143 Practice Activity T577 *Language Handbook* pp. 68–71	Daily Language Practice (7–8) R143 Practice Activity T577 *Grammar Practice Book* pp. 45–48	Daily Language Practice (9–12) R143 *Practice Book* p. 98
Discuss the Generalization T578 *Integrated Spelling* p. 63 *Integrated Spelling Teacher's Edition* p. T101	Apply to Writing T578 *Integrated Spelling* pp. 64–65 *Integrated Spelling Teacher's Edition* pp. T102–T103	Posttest T578 *Practice Book* p. 99 *Integrated Spelling Teacher's Edition* p. T104
VOWEL DIPHTHONG: /oi/*oi, oy* T580 *Phonics Practice Reader 20: Roy Floyd's Shoes*	**VOWEL DIPHTHONG: /oi/*oi, oy*** T581 *Practice Book* p. 101 *Bailey's Book House* (Read-A-Rhyme)	**VOWEL DIPHTHONG: /oi/*oi, oy*** T581 *Phonics Activity Book* pp. 32–33
COMPREHENSION MINILESSON T545 Story Elements (Setting) (Review)	**COMPREHENSION MINILESSON** T549 ✓ Making Predictions (Review) **GRAMMAR MINILESSON** T547 ✓ Names of Special People, Animals, and Places (Review) *Language Handbook* pp. 58–61	**PHONICS AND DECODING MINILESSON** T555 ✓ R-Controlled Vowel: /ôr/*or, oor, oar* (Review) *Phonics Activity Book* p. 34 *Practice Book* p. 103 Theme Project Checkpoint 2 T588
Above-level writers may complete the Writer's Workshop independently at their own pace.	During the Vocabulary Workshop, refer to the Extra Support note on page T579 to help **below-level readers**.	**Below-level readers** and **ESL students** read the *ESL/Title I Library* book *Buzz, Said the Bee.*

✓ = Tested Skill
◆ = Optional activities that may be used to adjust pacing throughout the lesson
Titles in *italics* are optional materials.

Reading and Responding

BUILDING BACKGROUND AND CONCEPTS

PRIOR KNOWLEDGE

Discuss and sing songs. Ask children if they have ever made up a song or a rhyme to remember something. Talk about the song we use to sing the alphabet and how it helps us remember the names of the letters and their order in the alphabet.

Have children work in small groups to think of something they would like to remember, and make up a song or rhyme that would help them remember it. When groups have memorized their rhyme or song, they can teach it to classmates.

VOCABULARY STRATEGIES

KEY WORDS DEFINED

change make different
lonely sad about being alone
important necessary to know
decided made up one's mind
noise loud sounds
coins metal pieces of money
explained told about something
terrible awful
sighed sadly let out a long breath

SUPPORT WORDS

Display the words *decorations, except, gently, memory, respectfully,* and *squawked*. Discuss their meanings and have them used in sentences.

INTEGRATED SPELLING

SPELLING PRETEST: page T578
SPELLING GENERALIZATION: Consonant Clusters

MEETING INDIVIDUAL NEEDS

Intervention Strategies

For children who may have difficulty reading "Nine-in-One, Grr! Grr!," support is available in *Intervention Strategies Manual*, pages 56–61, and on pages T551, T560, and T570–T571 in this lesson.

STUDENTS ACQUIRING ENGLISH

See *Sheltered English/ESL Manual*, pages 38–41.

TIPS FOR TEACHERS

"The rhythmic nature of this story and its repetition help make children want to join in as it is being read. I like to have children take turns singing Tiger's song in their most convincing "tiger" voices. Other children make up voices for the Eu bird and for Shao. It's also fun to do a choral reading when children are familiar with the story."

CUEING SYSTEMS

Have children read new vocabulary. Display Chart/Transparency 20, or write the words and sentences on the board. Have children read words they might know.

Cover the word *lonely* with a self-stick note. Have children read the first two sentences and suggest words that make sense. Point out the word *felt* as a clue. Write their suggestions on the board. Then uncover the word one letter at a time:

Does the word begin with *l* ?

Does the word tell about someone's feelings?

Have children continue to read the story, using the sounds for letters and context clues to help them figure out the underlined words.

HANDS-ON ACTIVITY

Play a game. Have children write the Key Words on a sheet of paper and follow these directions:

- Draw a box around the word for things not staying the same. (*change*)
- Draw a line under the word that means "awful." (*terrible*)
- Put an *X* on the word that tells how someone alone might feel. (*lonely*)
- Draw a pocket around the word for metal things in a pocket. (*coins*)
- Draw ears next to the word that tells about something loud. (*noise*)
- Draw a star by the word that tells about how we feel when we do a good job. (*important*)
- Circle words for what someone did. (*decided, explained, sighed*)

Help children self-check their answers and add them to their Word Files.

CHART/TRANSPARENCY 20

change	lonely	important
decided	noise	coins
explained	terrible	sighed

"Something had to change. I felt too lonely. It's important to have someone to talk to. I decided to buy a pet.

The animals at the pet store sure made a lot of noise! I picked out a cute kitten. When I tried to pay for her, I saw that I didn't have enough money. I only needed a few more coins.

The clerk explained that I could not take the kitten until I paid for it. I felt terrible! The kitten sighed as I handed her back to the clerk. The next day I would buy her.

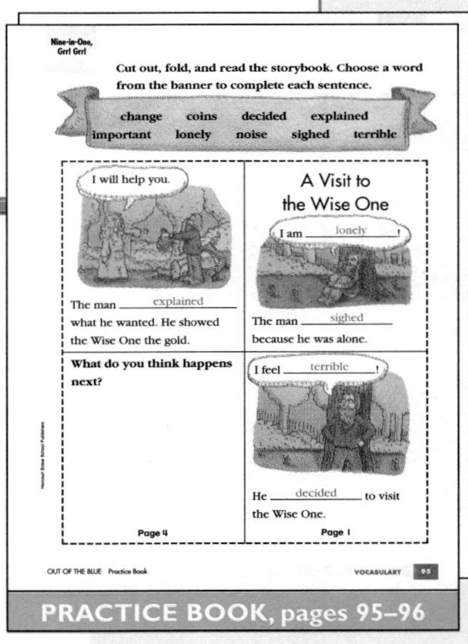
Nine-in-One, Grr! Grr!

Cut out, fold, and read the storybook. Choose a word from the banner to complete each sentence.

change coins decided explained important lonely noise sighed terrible

I will help you.

A Visit to the Wise One

I am lonely!

The man explained what he wanted. He showed the Wise One the gold.

The man sighed because he was alone.

What do you think happens next?

I feel terrible!

He decided to visit the Wise One.

Page 4

Page 1

OUT OF THE BLUE Practice Book

VOCABULARY

PRACTICE BOOK, pages 95–96

PHONICS-VOCABULARY CONNECTION

WORD PLAY

Write the words *coins* and *noise* on the board. Read them to children and let them listen to the vowel sound. Then have children choose an animal noise to make. As you read the following list of words, have children make their animal noises if they hear the same vowel sound as in *noise* and *coins*.

The concept of */oi/oi, oy* is further developed on pages T580–T581.

bears	joy
boys	chase
mouse	join
rope	phone
choice	toys
raise	mope
voice	enjoy

Strategic Reading

STRATEGY FOCUS: REREADING

Review with the children some of the things good readers do when they read. Add new suggestions to the classroom chart.

What Good Readers Do
Use the other words in a sentence to figure out what words mean
Try to picture in their minds what is happening
Go back and read again to understand something better

Share with children the comprehension strategy that is the focus of this selection.

MODEL **Sometimes when I'm reading, I think, "That doesn't make sense. What am I missing?" So, I back up a little and read the same part of the story again, slowly and carefully. Most of the time, reading part of the story again helps me understand what I didn't understand the first time.**

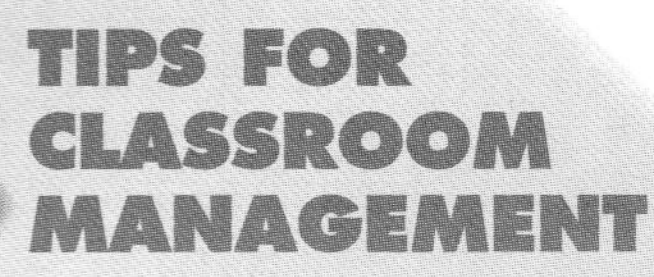

SMALL GROUP

STRATEGIC READING

Choose some or all of the suggestions and questions under Strategic Reading, pages T542–T564, to guide a literature discussion and model the STRATEGY FOCUS of Rereading.

COOPERATIVE READING

LITERATURE CIRCLES Distribute Reader Response Card 4 (Author's Craft), page R148. As small groups of children read the story silently, have them pause from time to time to discuss the questions.

Response

PREVIEWING/ SETTING PURPOSES

Read the title to children. Point out that this story was told by one author and written down by another. Then invite children to page from the beginning of the story to page 271. Ask them who will say "Nine-in-one, grr! grr!" and why. Have them write their predictions in their personal journals. Then help children set their purposes for reading.

MODELING A STRATEGY

PAGES 268–269 After they have read page 269, talk with children about anything on the page that was difficult to understand the first time they read it. Read the first sentence slowly, pointing out, if necessary, that the story must take place long, long ago because the tiger is the very first tiger. Then reread other sentences, pausing so children can make sense of each part. After this rereading, ask volunteers to tell what Tiger's problem is. **REREADING**

WHOLE CLASS

DRAMATIC READING

Invite children to read "Nine-in-One, Grr! Grr!" to themselves, and then read the story together. You might have groups of two or three children read the parts of Shao, Tiger, and the Eu bird, and other small groups or pairs of children read narrative passages.

READ ALOUD

Introduce the story by telling children that it has been told by Hmong people for years and years, but this is the first time it was written in English. Read the story aloud as children follow along in their books. Encourage them to help you put a melody to Tiger's song and to read along with you.

Strategic Reading

MODELING A STRATEGY

PAGES 270–271 As children read these pages, encourage them to form pictures in their minds of the place where the story is happening. Then ask them to say what parts of the text on page 270 helped them form their mental images. **Think aloud:** *When I read the words* past plants curved like rooster tail feathers, *I picture big ferns that bend over, just like a rooster's tail. The words* over rocks shaped like sleeping dragons *make me think of rocks that are really huge and bumpy.* VISUALIZING

Tiger decided to visit the great god Shao, who lived in the sky, who was kind and gentle and knew everything. Surely Shao could tell her how many cubs she would have.

Tiger set out on the road that led to the sky. She climbed through forests of striped bamboo and wild banana trees, past plants curved like rooster tail feathers, and over rocks shaped like sleeping dragons.

270

LISTENING CENTER

"Nine-in-One, Grr! Grr!" is available on *Literature Cassette 1*. Some children may benefit from listening to the story and following along in their books.

SOCIAL STUDIES CONNECTION

GEOGRAPHY Ask children to compare the plants, animals, and terrain they are reading about with the landscape where they live. If some children have been to a place with a landscape like the one described in the story, invite them to tell more about it.

MINILESSON

REVIEW: COMPREHENSION

Story Elements (Setting)

INFORMAL ASSESSMENT

As children read and discuss the story, assess their ability to describe the setting.

TEACH/MODEL

Remind children that paying attention to the setting of a story will help them to enjoy the story and to picture the action as it happens. Ask children to find some sentences in the story that describe the setting. For example:

- *She climbed through forests of striped bamboo and wild banana trees, past plants curved like rooster tail feathers, and over rocks shaped like sleeping dragons.* (page 270)
- *Beyond the wall was a garden where children played happily under a plum tree.* (page 272)
- *This was the land of the great Shao, a peaceful land without sickness or death.* (page 272)

PRACTICE/APPLY

Have children write a few sentences describing the setting of the story. Encourage them to use the illustrations as a source of information. Then have them trade papers with a partner and add to one another's descriptions.

CHALLENGE **Invite interested children to do some library research about the plants and landforms of Laos, where this story was first told. Encourage them to find books with pictures that they can share with classmates.**

Strategic Reading

APPLYING A STRATEGY

PAGES 272–273 As children read pages 272–273, remind them to look at the illustrations as well as the words. When they have finished reading, ask how the pictures helped them understand what Shao and his home are like and how Tiger feels and acts when she is talking to Shao. **RELATING PICTURES TO TEXT**

At last Tiger came to a stone wall. Beyond the wall was a garden where children played happily under a plum tree. A large house stood nearby, its colorful decorations shining in the sun. This was the land of the great Shao, a peaceful land without sickness or death.

272

PHONICS IN ACTION

CONSONANT DIGRAPHS Have children find the words *where, children, shining, this,* and *without*. Remind children that each of the letter pairs —*wh, ch, sh,* and *th*—stands for its own sound.

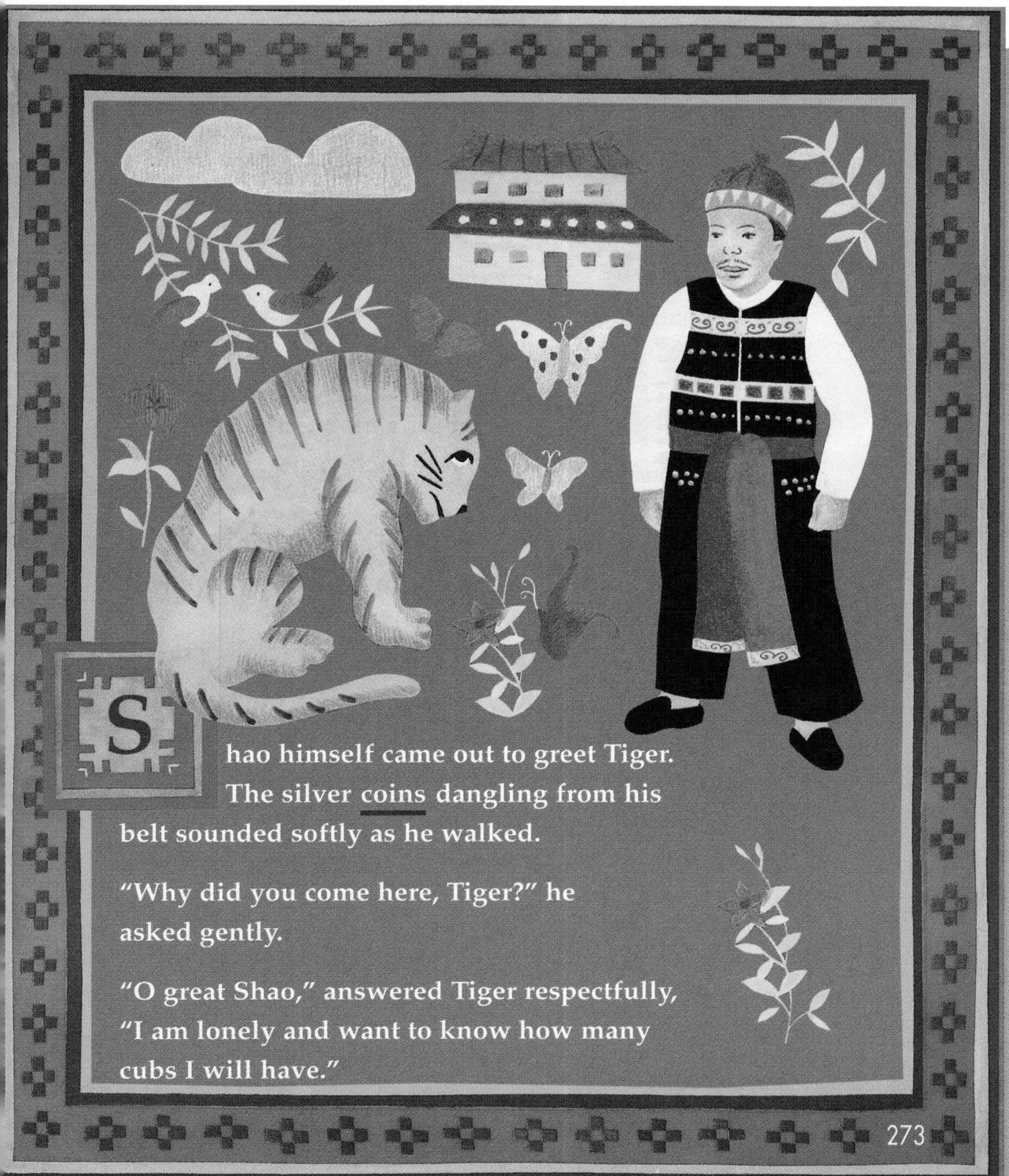

Shao himself came out to greet Tiger. The silver coins dangling from his belt sounded softly as he walked.

"Why did you come here, Tiger?" he asked gently.

"O great Shao," answered Tiger respectfully, "I am lonely and want to know how many cubs I will have."

273

Tested Skill

MINILESSON

REVIEW: GRAMMAR

Names of Special People, Animals, and Places

INFORMAL ASSESSMENT

To assess whether children recognize proper nouns, ask them to find the proper nouns on pages 272 and 273. (*Shao, Tiger*)

TEACH/MODEL

Remind children that proper nouns name special people, animals, places, and things and always begin with a capital letter. Make a list on the board as children name proper nouns in the story. (*Shao, Tiger, Bird*) Ask children how they can tell that these words are proper nouns. (They begin with capital letters and are characters' names.)

PRACTICE/APPLY

Display the paragraph. Have volunteers underline all the nouns and put two lines under the proper nouns.

> *Tiger went to tell her friend Lion what the great Shao said. Along the path Tiger stopped to rest in Xam Nua, a town in Laos. When Tiger woke up, Lion was there! So Tiger told Lion about her cubs.*

LANGUAGE HANDBOOK

Special Names and Titles of People, pages 58–59

Names of Special Animals and Places, pages 60–61

CHALLENGE **Challenge pairs of children to write sentences about the story in which the proper nouns are not capitalized. Then have them exchange papers and capitalize the proper nouns.**

EXTRA SUPPORT **The vowel sound heard in *Shao* and spelled *ao* is not found in the English language. It may be helpful for children to practice saying the word with rhyming English words. For example, *grow, flow, toe, Shao.***

Strategic Reading

MODELING A STRATEGY

PAGES 274–275 Have children look at the illustration and predict what Shao will tell Tiger about how many cubs she will have. After children have read, ask them what they could do if they were confused by Shao's warning to Tiger. Remind them that rereading can be helpful. Read the last paragraph on page 274 aloud, pausing to model your thinking. **Think aloud:** "You must remember carefully what I said. The words alone tell you how many cubs you will have." *Shao is warning Tiger that she has to remember what he said in order to know how many cubs she will have. Then Shao says that he can't help her anymore if she forgets what he says. It does make more sense the second time.* REREADING

hao was silent for a moment. Then he replied, "Nine each year."

"How wonderful," purred Tiger. "Thank you so much, great Shao." And she turned to leave with her good news.

"One moment, Tiger," said Shao. "You must remember carefully what I said. The words alone tell you how many cubs you will have. Do not forget them, for if you do, I cannot help you."

274

REAL-LIFE CONNECTION

Ask children if they've ever had to remember something important. Encourage volunteers to share the tricks they use to help them remember things.

A CLOSER LOOK

Have children look at the illustration on page 275. Ask how the artist showed that Tiger received Shao's message. Talk about how the artist used pictures to show what a character is thinking.

Tested Skill

MINILESSON

MAINTAIN: COMPREHENSION STRATEGY

Making Predictions

INFORMAL ASSESSMENT

As children read this and other selections, note whether they base predictions on information from the story and from their own experiences.

TEACH/MODEL

Remind children that one way to involve themselves in the stories they read is to predict what will happen at different points in a story, and then read on to find out how close their predictions are to what actually happens. Ask volunteers to share predictions they made before they began reading, and discuss any new predictions they have made about the story up to page 275.

PRACTICE/APPLY

Ask children to revise their original predictions about the story based on reading pages 268–275. Point out that Shao's warning to Tiger about not forgetting his words allows at least two possibilities for how the story will unfold:

Tiger will remember Shao's words and have nine cubs each year.

Tiger will forget Shao's words.

Have children predict whether Tiger will remember Shao's words and write their new predictions in their journals.

SCIENCE

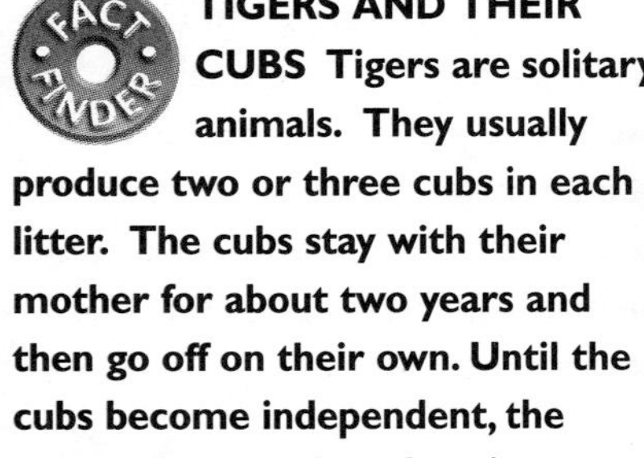

TIGERS AND THEIR CUBS **Tigers are solitary animals. They usually produce two or three cubs in each litter. The cubs stay with their mother for about two years and then go off on their own. Until the cubs become independent, the tigress does not breed again.**

Strategic Reading

APPLYING A STRATEGY

PAGES 276–279 Emphasize that Shao has warned Tiger how important it is to remember his words, and that Tiger is afraid of forgetting. Talk with children about how this new information affects the predictions they made earlier in their reading. If they haven't already done so, invite children to revise their predictions, and to share their reasons for changing them. **MAKING AND CONFIRMING PREDICTIONS**

At first Tiger was happy as she followed the road back to earth. But soon, she began to worry.

"Oh dear," she said to herself. "My memory is so bad. How will I ever remember those important words of Shao?" She thought and she thought. At last, she had an idea. "I'll make up a little song to sing. Then I won't forget." So Tiger began to sing:

Nine-in-one, Grr! Grr!
Nine-in-one, Grr! Grr!

276

MUSIC CONNECTION

CREATE A SONG Invite children to make up a tune for Tiger's song and sing it a few times. Encourage them to add lines to the song that might help Tiger remember it better. For example: *Nine-in-One, Grr! Grr! Nine cubs each year, Grr! Grr! Good news to hear, Grr! Grr!*

AUTHOR'S CRAFT

Talk about the words *grr, grr* in Tiger's song. Even though they are not true onomatopoeia, you can use them as a springboard for a discussion of onomatopoeia, or words whose sounds suggest their meanings. Invite children to list onomatopoeic words.

Student Self-Assessment

FIX-UP STRATEGY: USING CONTEXT CLUES

Ask children to tell what they could do if they did not know the word *memory*. Point out context clues such as the word *remember* and the phrase *won't forget* that might help them figure it out. Encourage children to share other strategies that have helped them as they read the story.

WRITING

WRITE DESCRIPTIVE PARAGRAPHS Have children use the illustrations and the passages that describe the landscape of the story to write paragraphs of their own about the setting of the story.

MEETING INDIVIDUAL NEEDS

Intervention Strategies

USING BACKGROUND KNOWLEDGE

Have children repeat this sentence: *When I read, it helps me to keep thinking about what I already know about things in the story to help me decide what's going to happen.* Have children tell what they know about trying to remember something important that helped them understand why Tiger made up her song.

Cooperative Reading

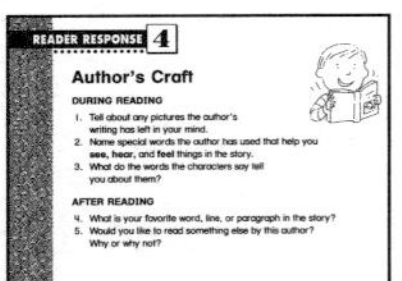

Response Card 4

As children read about Tiger making her way down the mountain, remind them to pause and discuss the questions on **Reader Response Card 4** (Author's Craft). You might suggest that children make a chart of words the author used that helped children "see" things in the story, "hear" things in the story, and "feel" things in the story.

See	Hear	Feel

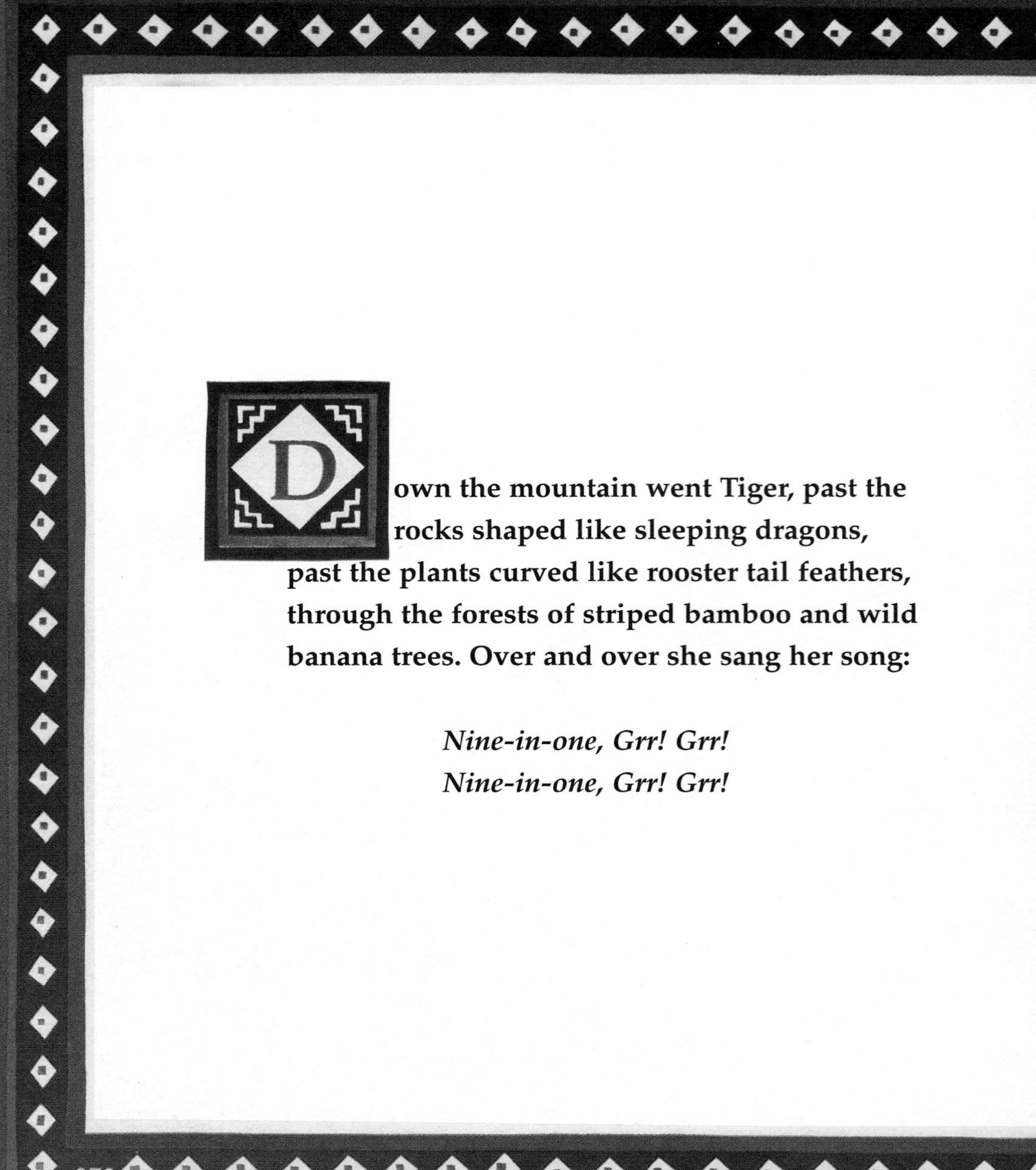

Down the mountain went Tiger, past the rocks shaped like sleeping dragons, past the plants curved like rooster tail feathers, through the forests of striped bamboo and wild banana trees. Over and over she sang her song:

Nine-in-one, Grr! Grr!
Nine-in-one, Grr! Grr!

278

AUTHOR'S CRAFT

Ask children to turn back to page 270 and compare the description of Tiger's journey up the mountain with the description of her trip down it on page 278. As children compare the descriptions, encourage them to discuss how the order of the things described in the two passages helps children envision Tiger's trips up and down the mountain.

A CLOSER LOOK

Have children compare the illustrations of Tiger's trip up the mountain (page 271) and her trip down the mountain (pages 277 and 279). Encourage children to notice differences in the animals and plants that the illustrator chose to put in each picture.

Strategic Reading

APPLYING A STRATEGY

PAGES 280–281 Have children compare the author's words with the illustrator's picture.

1. **What things that the author describes does the illustrator also show?**
2. **What parts of the author's description are left to your imagination as you read?**
3. **How can you tell that Bird is listening to Tiger?**
4. **What do you think the next picture will show? Why?**

RELATING PICTURES TO TEXT

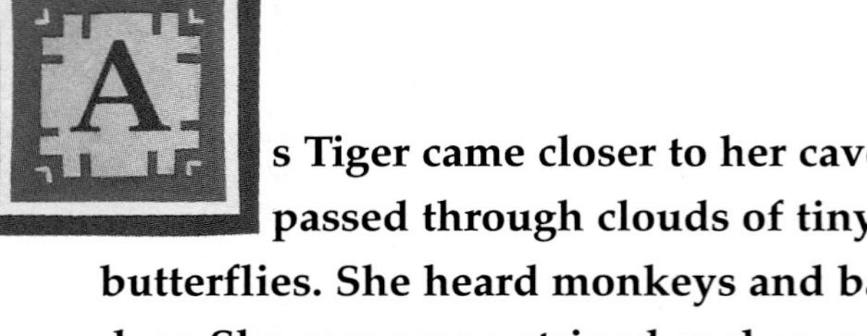

As Tiger came closer to her cave, she passed through clouds of tiny white butterflies. She heard monkeys and barking deer. She saw green-striped snakes, quails and pheasants. None of the animals listened to her song—except one big, clever, black bird, the Eu bird.

"Hmm," said Bird to herself. "I wonder why Tiger is coming down the mountain singing that song and grinning from ear to ear. I'd better find out." So Bird soared up the ladder which was a shortcut to Shao's home.

280

SOCIAL STUDIES

LAOS The story's setting resembles Laos, the storyteller's homeland. Laos has thickly forested mountains that rise as high as 9,248 feet. Two-thirds of Laos is covered with forests. The tropical rain forests in the north are made up of broadleaf evergreens; the monsoon forests in the south contain a mixture of evergreen and deciduous trees, including bamboo and wild banana, along with a tall, coarse grass called *tranh*.

Tested Skill

MINILESSON

REVIEW: PHONICS AND DECODING

R-Controlled Vowel: /ôr/*or, oor, oar*

INFORMAL ASSESSMENT

As children read, note whether they can decode words that have the *r*-controlled vowel /ôr/, spelled *or, oor,* and *oar*.

TEACH/MODEL

Have children reread page 280. Remind children that the ladder was a shortcut. Write *shortcut* on the board. Ask which word on the page tells how Bird moved up the ladder. (soared) Write *soared* next to *shortcut*. Talk about the vowel sounds children hear as they say these words. Then write *poor*.

shortcut **soared** **poor**

Have children read the words. Remind children that *or* can stand for the /ôr/ sound heard in *for*. Explain that *oar* and *oor* can also stand for the /ôr/ sound. Ask volunteers to underline the letters that stand for the vowel sound in each word.

PRACTICE/APPLY

Read riddles like the ones below whose answers are words with the vowel 3/ôr/. Then ask volunteers to write the words under *shortcut, soared,* or *poor*.

1. A cat meows, but a lion (roars).
2. People use this to eat food. (fork)
3. You open it to go in a house. (door)
4. This is the opposite of ceiling. (floor)

PHONICS ACTIVITY BOOK, page 34

WRITING

WRITING ABOUT A PLACE Invite children to write a paragraph that tells about a place they know well. Encourage them to use words that will help their readers see or feel what the place is like. Allow time for children to share their descriptions.

Nine-in-One, Grr! Grr! Name ____________

Read the little tiger's questions and the words in the tree. Write the word that makes sense in the sentence and has the same vowel sound as *corn*.

morning born
fly doors
floors roar
soar late
horns

YES.

1. Do you remember the day I was born?
2. Do lions roar, too?
3. Can people open doors?
4. Have you heard the horns of people's cars?
5. Does the sun come up every morning?
6. Do birds like to soar through the sky?
7. Do houses have floors?

OUT OF THE BLUE Practice Book R-CONTROLLED VOWEL: /ôr/or, oor, oar 103

PRACTICE BOOK, page 103

Strategic Reading

APPLYING A STRATEGY

PAGES 282–285 At this point in the story, it may be helpful for children to summarize the main events and put them in the order in which they happened. Doing so will help them keep track of what's happening in the story and make predictions about Bird's plan now that she knows what Tiger's song means. SUMMARIZING

"O wise Shao," asked Bird politely, "why is Tiger singing over and over:

Nine-in-one, Grr! Grr!
Nine-in-one, Grr! Grr!"

And Shao explained that he had just told Tiger she would have nine cubs each year.

282

EXTRA SUPPORT Help children determine the main events in the story and talk about what has happened so far. You may wish to help children write the events on sentence strips and then put them in order. Encourage them to predict the story's outcome.

Tiger wanted cubs.
She went to see Shao.
Shao said she would have nine cubs.
Tiger made up a song.
Bird heard Tiger's song.

SCHOOL↔HOME CONNECTION

Invite children to make up a song about the members of their family. If a child is one of three children, the song might begin: "One of three, that's me!" Encourage children to work with family members as they make up their songs. Invite them to share their songs with classmates.

Critical Thinking Questions

1. **How do you know that Bird is upset by what Shao tells her?** (Possible responses: She says "That's terrible!" and asks Shao to change what he said; the pictures show her jumping up; she looks upset.) CRITICAL: UNDERSTANDING CHARACTERS' FEELINGS
2. **What did you learn about Bird from reading this page?** (Possible responses: Bird is smart; Bird is afraid there will be too many tigers; Bird has a plan.) CRITICAL: ANALYZING CHARACTERS
3. **What do you think Bird means when she says, "Then I know what I must do"?** (Responses will vary. Children should support their answers.) CRITICAL: SPECULATING

"That's terrible!" squawked Bird. "If Tiger has nine cubs each year, they will eat all of us. Soon there will be nothing but tigers in the land. You must change what you said, O Shao!"

"I cannot take back my words," sighed Shao. "I promised Tiger that she would have nine cubs every year as long as she remembered my words."

"As long as she remembered your words," repeated Bird thoughtfully. "Then I know what I must do, O great Shao."

284

EXPANDING VOCABULARY

Have children read the first and last paragraphs on page 284. Point out the words *O Shao* and *O great Shao*. Ask if children knew that the letter O could be a word. Explain that the word O is used before a name to show respect. Bird uses O to show respect for the great and wise Shao.

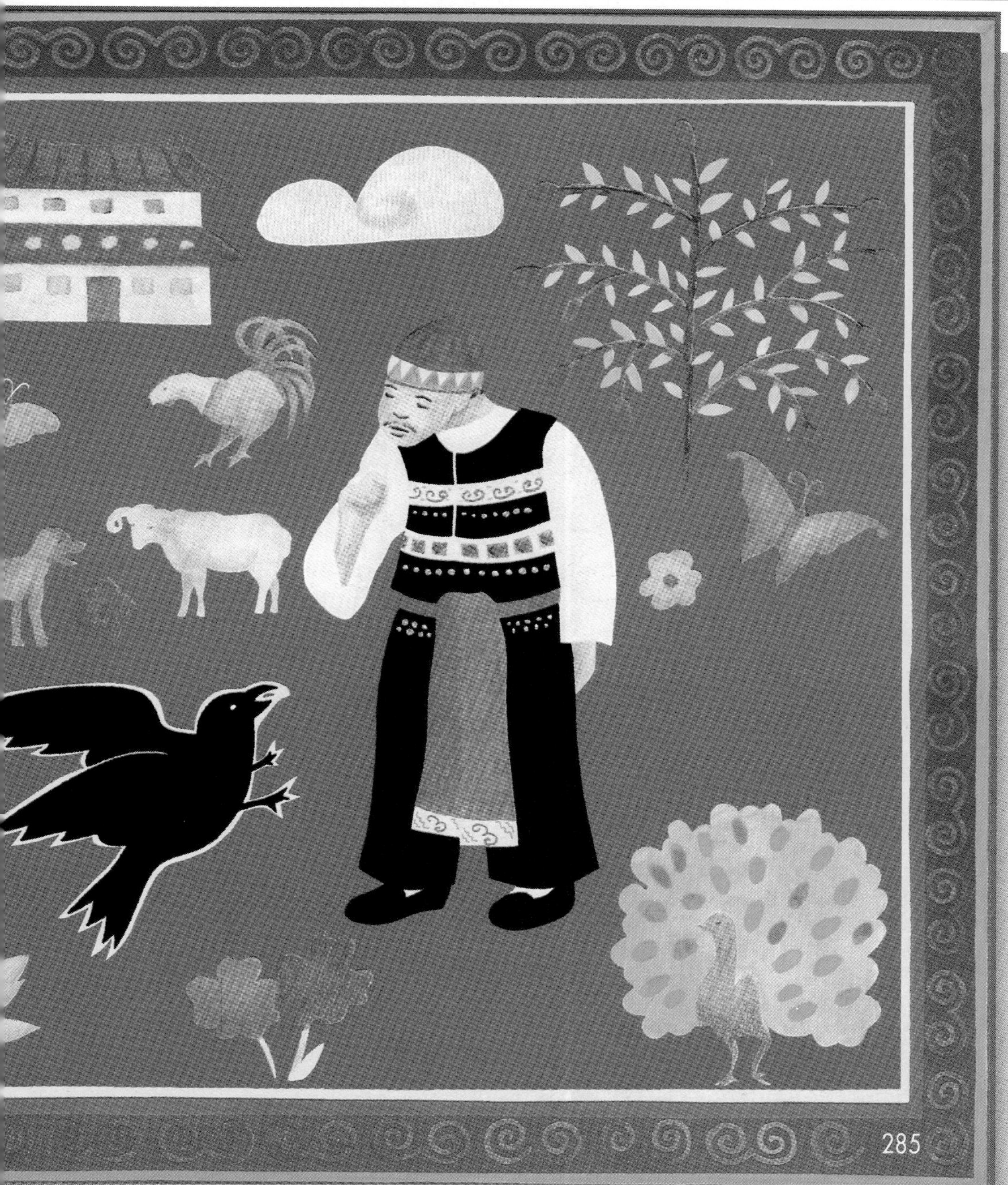

Informal Assessment

DRAWING CONCLUSIONS

During reading, or a rereading of the selection, observe how children use information in the story and their own experiences to draw conclusions about the plot.

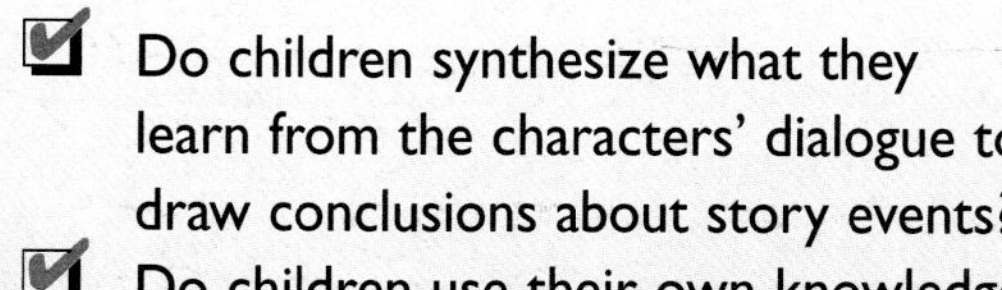

- Do children synthesize what they learn from the characters' dialogue to draw conclusions about story events?
- Do children use their own knowledge to put themselves in Bird's and Tiger's places as they draw conclusions about the story?

STUDENTS ACQUIRING ENGLISH **Children may encounter difficulties with the verbs *squawked, sighed,* and *repeated*. Explain that *squawked* and *sighed* give information about how a character said something. Point out the phrases *as long as she remembered my words* and *As long as she remembered your words* to help children understand the word *repeated*. Then have children work with another child who can read the dialogue expressively in order to demonstrate the meanings of the words.**

Strategic Reading

MODELING A STRATEGY

PAGES 286–287 After children have read these pages, invite them to make predictions about what Bird's plan could be. Encourage them to share clues from the story that helped them make their predictions. If necessary, model your thinking: *I read that Bird went to find Tiger. Bird landed in a tree near Tiger, but Tiger didn't see her. I think Bird is sneaking up on Tiger to surprise her. I think Tiger will start chasing Bird and forget her song.* Then have children read on to confirm their predictions. **MAKING AND CONFIRMING PREDICTIONS**

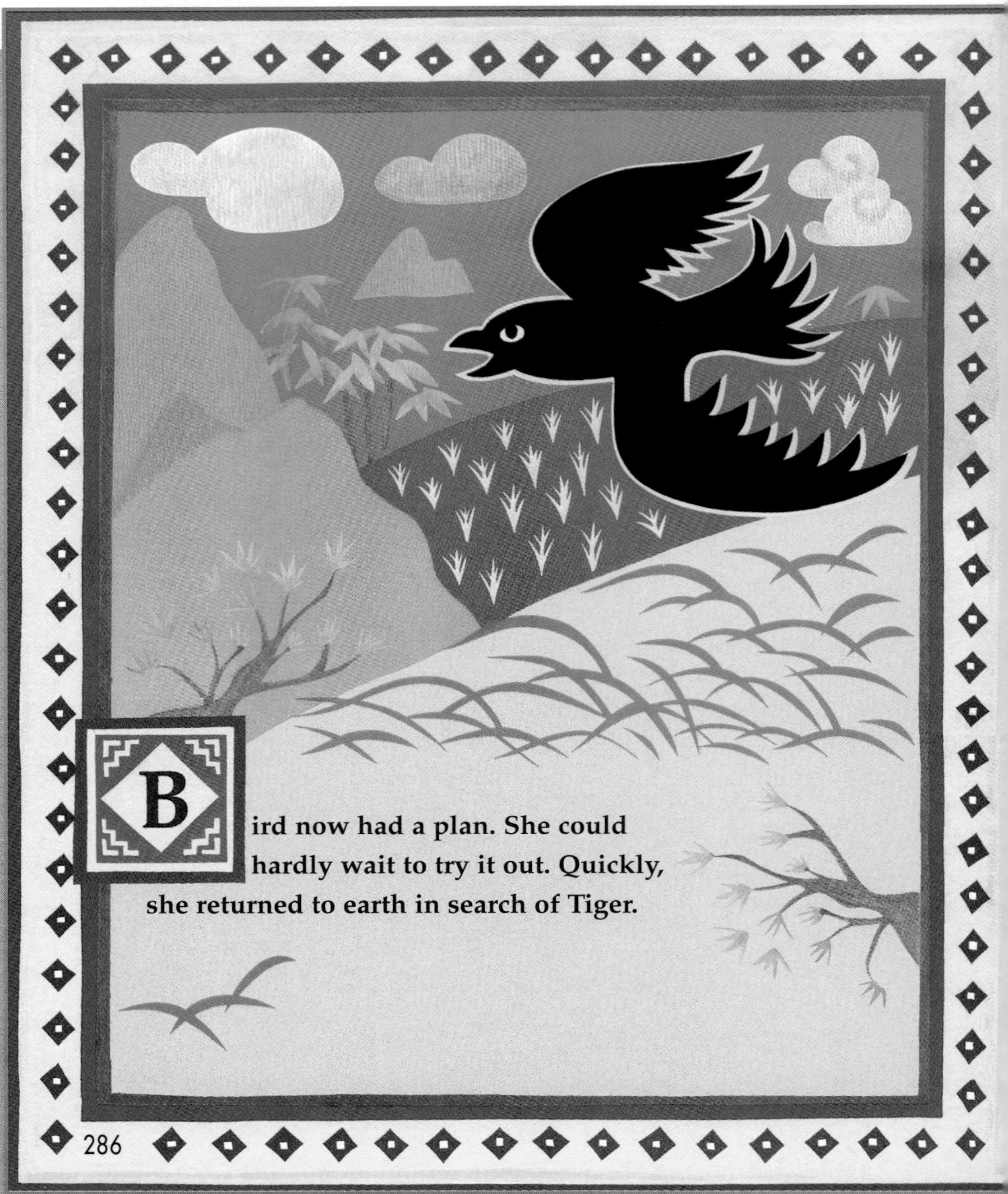

Bird now had a plan. She could hardly wait to try it out. Quickly, she returned to earth in search of Tiger.

286

Intervention Strategies

SUMMARIZING Have children repeat this sentence: *When I read, it helps me to think about what's happened so far.* Have children tell how using this strategy might help them understand what has happened in "Nine-in-One, Grr! Grr!" and what might happen next.

Bird reached her favorite tree as old grandmother sun was setting, just in time to hear Tiger coming closer and closer and still singing:

Nine-in-one, Grr! Grr!
Nine-in-one, Grr! Grr!

Tiger was concentrating so hard on her song that she didn't even see Bird landing in the tree above her.

287

Student Self-Assessment

FIX-UP STRATEGY: USING PRIOR KNOWLEDGE

As children read the story, remind them that it helps to think about what's happening to the characters in terms of things that have happened to themselves. Encourage children working in small groups to talk about:

- ☑ a time when they were told news that they didn't like, as when Shao tells Bird that Tiger will have nine cubs each year.
- ☑ a time when they were concentrating on something and missed something else that happened close by, as when Tiger doesn't notice Bird because she is concentrating on her song.

AUTHOR'S CRAFT

Ask children to reread the first sentence on page 287. Talk about the author's calling the sun "old grandmother sun." Ask children to talk about how the author's words give them more to think about than if she had written just "the sun."

Strategic Reading

APPLYING A STRATEGY

PAGES 288–290 Ask children to read the song on page 289 and the song on page 287 and then to reread the song on page 289. Ask how the song changed and how that affects Tiger. **REREADING**

EXPANDING VOCABULARY

Have volunteers read the sentences containing the words *furiously* and *innocently* on page 288 and *sweetly* on page 289. Invite children to tell what the words mean, providing help as needed. Point out that these words help give a picture of how the characters are speaking or acting. Encourage volunteers to read and act out these pages.

A CLOSER LOOK

Have children look at the picture of Tiger's thoughts on page 289 and to look back at the picture of Tiger's thoughts on page 275. Encourage children to talk about how the illustrations have changed just as the song has been changed (thanks to Bird).

Informal Assessment

USING CUEING SYSTEMS

Observe how children apply cueing systems as they read and construct meaning.

- Do children use story and picture clues to understand what they're reading?
- Do children read a whole sentence and think about what word might make sense in that context?
- Do children reread and self-correct?

IDEA BANK

PLAYING "TELEPHONE" Children can experiment with ways messages can change by playing "Telephone." The first player whispers a message to a neighbor, who whispers it to the next person, and so on. The last player tells what he or she heard, and the group compares the final message to the first player's message.

Strategic Reading

APPLYING A STRATEGY

PAGES 290–291 Encourage children to talk about the predictions they made about Bird's plan. Ask them how close their predictions were to what Bird did. **CONFIRMING PREDICTIONS**

Returning to the Predictions/Purpose

Before children read the story, they wrote predictions about who would say "Nine-in-one, Grr! Grr!" and why. Invite children to discuss their predictions in light of what actually happened.

Appreciating the Literature

With the whole class or a small group, have an open discussion about the story.

- **Do you think Tiger would still be happy at the end of the story if she knew Bird had tricked her? Tell why or why not.**

So Tiger returned to her cave, singing happily:

One-in-nine, Grr! Grr!
One-in-nine, Grr! Grr!

And that is why, the Hmong people say, we don't have too many tigers on the earth today!

290

SOCIAL STUDIES

THE HMONG PEOPLE Explain that the Hmong are one of many groups of people who are from the country of Laos. The Hmong people live primarily in the mountains. The author of this story, Blia Xiong, is one of many Hmong who have left Laos to live in the United States.

CONVENTIONS OF PRINT

ARTISTIC LETTERS Point out the large letter *S* at the beginning of page 290. Ask if children noticed a large letter like this one at the beginning of each page. Ask why these big letters might have been used.

291

NOTES

Here's a place to list ideas or activities that you would like to use the next time you teach this lesson.

SUMMARIZE AND RETELL

Follow the Path

Display a story path like the one shown and work with children to fill in story events. When children have filled in their own story paths, have them work with partners to retell the story. See *Practice Book* page 97.

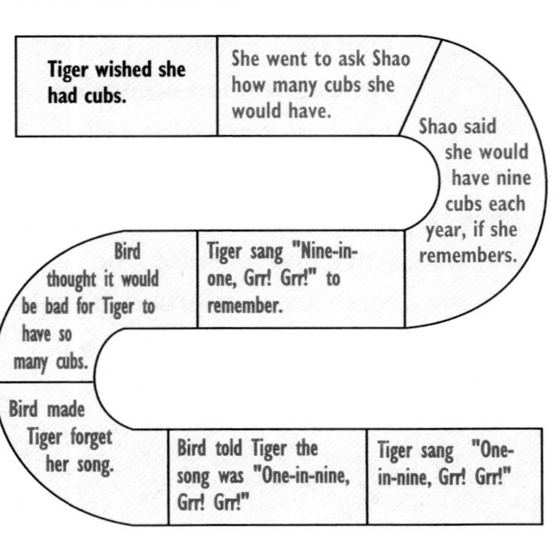

Nine-in-One, Grr! Grr!

Name ______________________

Fill in the story path to show the order of events in "Nine-in-One, Grr! Grr!" Possible responses are given.

Tiger wished that she had cubs of her own. → She went to ask Shao how many cubs she would have in the future. → Shao told her she would have nine cubs each year, if she remembers. → Tiger sang the song "Nine-in-one, Grr! Grr!" to help her remember. → Bird thought that it would be terrible for Tiger to have so many cubs. → Bird made a lot of noise, and Tiger forgot her song. → Bird told Tiger that her song was "One-in-nine." → Tiger began singing, "One-in-nine, Grr! Grr!"

Harcourt Brace School Publishers

OUT OF THE BLUE Practice Book SUMMARIZE AND RETELL 97

PRACTICE BOOK, page 97

About the Author

PAGES 292–293 Read with children the information on pages 292–293 about the storyteller and the illustrator. Invite children to talk about what Blia Xiong may have been like as a child and how the stories she heard when she was young became important when she grew up. Also discuss how Nancy Hom's pictures help show the setting (Laos) and what the Hmong people are like.

Blia Xiong was among the first Hmong refugees to settle in the United States. She has helped many Laotian people adjust to life in the United States. Laotian Americans greatly missed the traditions of their former land, so Xiong helped form the Hmong Association to preserve and pass on their music, dance, crafts, and stories.

"Nine-in-One, Grr! Grr!" is a favorite story of Xiong's. "I still have pictures in my mind of my mother telling this funny story."

Blia Xiong

Blia Xiong's (BLEE-AH SHONG) mother first told her *Nine-in-One, Grr! Grr!* when she was very young.

Blia Xiong's family are Hmong (MONG) people who came from the mountains of Laos, a small country near China. Many of the stories she heard when she was young had been told by her family for years.

In 1976, Xiong came to the United States from Laos to get away from the war there. Many other Hmong people from her country came, too. Xiong wanted to help them keep some of their old ways, so she helped start a special club. There, they taught their children music, dance, crafts, and stories like this one from Laos.

292

SOCIAL STUDIES

HMONG STORY CLOTHS
Hmong women embroider and appliqué tapestries, called pa' ndau (pan•DOW), through which they show things, such as everyday events, unusual events, and folktales. The Hmong people are very proud of their culture, and this is one way that it is shared and preserved.

Nancy Hom

The pictures Nancy Hom made for this story look like Hmong story cloths. The Hmong people use needle and thread to stitch these beautiful cloths. Each one tells a story.

Nancy Hom used silk screen, watercolors, and colored pencils to make the pictures for this story. Silk screen is done by rubbing different colors of ink through silk onto material or paper.

Nancy Hom was born in the southern part of China and moved to the United States when she was five. Her Chinese background is very important to her. Nancy Hom is married and has a daughter.

293

About the Illustrator

Nancy Hom used silk screen, watercolor, and colored pencils to illustrate this story. She modeled her pictures after embroidered Hmong story cloths. Needlework is highly treasured among the Hmong.

OTHER BOOKS ILLUSTRATED BY NANCY HOM

The Little Weaver of Thai-Yen Village by Tran-Khan-Tuyet. Children's Book Press, 1987.
CHALLENGE

Judge Rabbit and the Tree Spirit by Cathy Spagnoli. Children's Book Press, 1991.
CHALLENGE

RESPONSE CORNER ACTIVITIES

TELL A STORY WITH PICTURES

MAKE A STORY CLOTH

PAGE 294 Invite children to look at the story's illustrations for ideas about animals to choose for their stories. Help partners brainstorm questions that their animal might want to ask Shao. Encourage them to figure out how both partners can share in the storytelling. You may want to help children put together their story cloths into one large class story cloth. **ART/SPEAKING**

PLAY A MEMORY GAME

HOW GOOD IS YOUR MEMORY?

PAGE 295 Discuss the game's directions with groups and model a few rounds before they begin playing. You might suggest that they sing, add gestures, or speak in different voices for each item mentioned to help the group remember once the list grows long. **SPEAKING**

RESPONSE CORNER

TELL A STORY WITH PICTURES

MAKE A STORY CLOTH

The Hmong people sometimes use story cloths to tell a story. A storyteller sews pictur onto a large piece of cloth. The storyteller points to the pictures while telling the story. The pictures in "Nine-in-One, Grr! Grr!" look like a story cloth.

Work with a partner.

1. Choose another animal fr the story to visit Shao to a a question. Make up a sto
2. Make a picture that show one thing that happens in your story. Make it look li a story cloth.
3. Practice telling your story using the picture.
4. Share your story.

294

VARYING THE ACTIVITY

For children who need help with the memory game, suggest that they draw little sketches for each new item mentioned by group members. They can use their sketches when it is their turn to continue the story.

PLAY A MEMORY GAME

How Good Is Your Memory?

In the story, Bird had a good memory but Tiger did not. Test your memory as you play this game.

1. Sit in a circle.
2. The first person says, "On my way to see Shao, I saw a ________ " and names something, such as *tiger*.
3. The next person repeats what was said and adds another thing. That person might say, "On my way to see Shao, I saw a tiger and a mountain."
4. See how long your group's list can get!

What Do You Think?

- Why did Bird make Tiger forget her song?
- Do you think Bird was right to do what she did? Why or why not?

295

CHECKING COMPREHENSION

What Do You Think?

1. **Why did Bird make Tiger forget her song?** (Possible response: Bird didn't want Tiger to have nine cubs every year because then there would be too many tigers, and tigers eat other animals.) **DESCRIPTIVE RESPONSE**
2. **Do you think Bird was right to do what she did? Why or why not?** (Accept reasonable responses. Children should support their opinions.) **PERSONAL RESPONSE**

Another question to extend reading:

3. **How would the world be different if tigers really did have nine cubs every year?** (Accept reasonable responses. Possible response: There would be a lot more tigers and not as many other kinds of animals.) **CRITICAL/CREATIVE ANALYSIS**

MEETING INDIVIDUAL NEEDS

STUDENTS ACQUIRING ENGLISH **You might want to pair second-language learners with partners whose first language is English for the story cloth activity. The native English speaker can help his or her partner find the right words for the story.**

Informal Assessment

Observe pairs of children as they use their "story cloths" to tell their stories.

- ☑ Do children tell a story based on what they drew?
- ☑ Do children use their pictures as they share their stories?
- ☑ Do both partners participate in the telling of the story?

Intervention Strategies

Instant Readers™

Predictable and Patterned Little Books That Build Fluency

*** BOOK LEVEL: 14–15**

VOCABULARY:
important, noise

PHONIC ELEMENTS:
Vowel diphthong: /oi/oy; *R*-controlled vowel: /ôr/or, *oar*

PHONOGRAM:
-oy

SUMMARY:
There is lots of language play in this book of animal riddles and jokes.

Informal Assessment ✓

Are children able to

- ☑ discuss reading strategies?
- ☑ examine words to understand them?

Reading a New Book

INTRODUCING *YOU'LL ROAR*

Have children share jokes and riddles that they know. Talk about what makes a good joke and discuss the format of a joke. Share the book cover and title on page 2.

READING THE STORY

Children can read aloud the book with a partner, taking turns reading the questions and answers.

WORKING WITH WORDS AND LETTERS

Play a word game with children. Give each child one or two story words, and ask him or her to look for and write other words that are contained in the story word. The story word *hamusement* is a great word to manipulate.

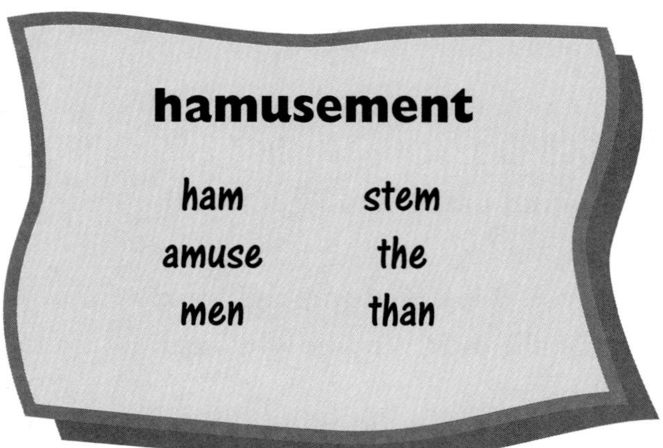

WRITING JOKES AND RIDDLES

Children can write their own jokes and riddles and try them out on each other. Encourage them to listen carefully to the words they use in the sentences.

Additional activities are provided on pages 58-59 of the *Intervention Strategies Manual*.

* **BOOK LEVEL: 20+**

VOCABULARY:
important, sighed

PHONIC ELEMENTS:
Vowel diphthong: /oi/oy; R-controlled vowel: /ôr/or, oar

PHONOGRAM:
-oy

SUMMARY:
A traditional legend about sibling rivalry is retold.

Reading a New Book

INTRODUCING *HOW MOON TRICKED SUN*

Share the illustrations with children, explaining that this story is based upon traditional legends from around the world. It tells why the sun and the moon take turns crossing the sky. Use the pictures to describe what happens when Sun stays in the sky and doesn't allow Moon to have a turn.

READING THE STORY

Once children understand the purpose of a legend (to explain a natural occurrence), have them read the story independently.

WORKING WITH WORDS AND LETTERS

Have children reread the story and focus on the words that describe Moon and Sun. Have them use blue and orange markers to record the words in a chart in their Word Banks.

Moon	Sun
sad	mean
clever	angry

WRITING SENTENCES

Give children an opportunity to write a few sentences to explain a natural occurrence, such as why the sky is blue, where tornadoes come from, or what causes rain.

ESL/Title I Reading

Buzz, Said the Bee by Wendy C. Lewison

ESL/Title I Library

Working with "Nine-in-One, Grr! Grr!"

SYNTACTIC CUES Have two children work together to help each other with difficult story vocabulary. Have each copy one or two sentences onto a write-on, wipe-off board and teach his or her partner to read them fluently. Then children switch roles. Teaching others to work through the text helps readers feel more confident with what they already know about reading and language.

* Books leveled according to Barbara Peterson's "Profiles of Books for Beginning Readers," on page 9 of the *Instant Readers Teacher's Guide*.

IDEA BANK

TIPS FOR CLASSROOM MANAGEMENT

IF children need help imagining the story with the roles of Tiger and Bird reversed for the Group Talk activity, **THEN** read page 289 aloud, replacing *Bird* with *Tiger* and vice versa.

IF children are not reading their parts with emotion in the Readers Theatre activity, **THEN** point out the words in the story that describe how the characters speak or move, and model them for children, if necessary.

PICTURE THIS!

BABIES, BABIES, BABIES

Tiger wanted to know how many babies she would have. Here are some other animal mothers and their babies.

Is this mother gorilla telling her baby a secret?

A cheetah and her cubs look out for food—and danger.

This rabbit and her babies enjoy a cozy nest of grass.

An owl mother and her babies are "all eyes."

WRITER'S MAGAZINE, pages 36–39

LISTENING AND SPEAKING

Group Talk

TRADING PLACES

Invite children to think about how the story might have been different if the roles of Tiger and Bird had been reversed. Have them draw or write about whether Tiger would have been upset if she found out that Bird would have nine babies every year and why. Then organize children into small groups, and have them share their ideas.

After small-group discussions, gather children to share their ideas and insights.
CHALLENGING THE TEXT

Informal Assessment

Note whether children understand the characters' traits as they discuss how the story would change if the characters' roles were reversed.

REAL-LIFE READING

Reading Music Recording Covers

Point out that Tiger would be less apt to forget her song if she'd had a recording of it, or had written down the lyrics.

Provide an array of records, CDs, and cassettes. Give children time to look at the boxes or album covers, and ask volunteers to find titles that you name. Then point out other information that comes with these recordings' packaging, such as the performers' names or the name of the band, the names of the songs, and sometimes the words to the songs. LISTENING/SPEAKING/READING

ORAL LANGUAGE

Rereading for Fluency

READERS THEATRE

Have children work in groups of four to prepare and present dramatic readings of "Nine-in-One, Grr! Grr!" Each group chooses a Narrator, Tiger, Shao, and Bird. Explain to children that they can pantomime actions such as climbing or flying up and down the mountain. Encourage children reading the parts of Tiger, Shao, and Bird to pay attention to the speaker tags, such as *asked Bird politely,* and to read expressively and clearly. **LISTENING/SPEAKING/READING**

KINESTHETIC

Creative Connection

MATERIALS
- poster board
- scissors
- hole punch
- yarn, various colors
- crayons or markers

IT'S A STITCH!

The pictures in the story were modeled after Hmong story cloths that are hand-stitched. Invite children to make their own stitchery pictures. Have children draw a large simple outline and facial features of something related to the story, such as a tiger or a bird, on a piece of poster board. Then have them cut out the shape, leaving a 1/2-inch margin around their drawing. Have them use a hole punch to make holes about 1/2 inch apart along the lines of their drawings. Then, using different colored yarns, they can fill in their pictures by stitching the yarn through the holes. **KINESTHETIC**

PERSONAL JOURNAL

REFLECTING ON THE STORY **Ask children to think about what they liked most about the story, as well as anything they didn't like about it, and write about their opinions in their personal journals.**

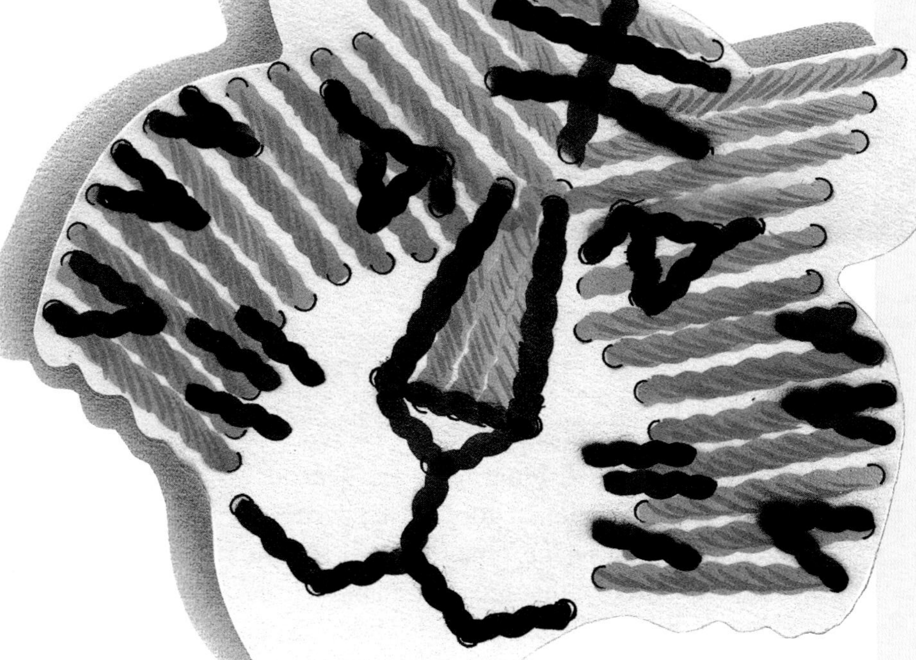

WRITER'S WORKSHOP

A Paragraph That Gives Information

TIPS FOR CLASSROOM MANAGEMENT

IF children are familiar with the writing process approach, **THEN** present the writing assignment and have them use the Paragraph That Gives Information model on pages 22–23 of the *Language Handbook*.

IF at this time you want a short writing activity, **THEN** have children do the prewriting activity and place the chart in the Writing Center for children's reference during independent writing.

TECHNOLOGY

THE AMAZING WRITING MACHINE Primary Level Activity Disk Pack Grade 2
Have children enter their paragraph in the Journals mode.

KID PIX
Children can illustrate their paragraphs by creating pictures of their own or using the stamps.

Thinking as Writers

WRITING FORM: Paragraph That Gives Information Explain to children that a paragraph that gives information tells facts and details about a person, animal, place, or thing. Ask children to recall the animals in "Nine-in-One, Grr! Grr!" Explain to children that they are going to write a paragraph that gives information about one of the animals in the story.

Display Chart/Transparency 21, or write the model Paragraph That Gives Information on the board. Help children find the main idea. Then discuss the detail sentences and the indent.

CHART/TRANSPARENCY 21

MODEL: PARAGRAPH THAT GIVES INFORMATION

topic sentence — Many African American people celebrate Kwanzaa. It is a celebration of the
detail sentences — customs and history of African American people. It is a gathering time for families, like Thanksgiving.
The holiday is celebrated for seven days. It begins the day after Christmas. On each night of Kwanzaa, a candle is lit. Each candle stands for a rule to help people live their lives.

WRITER'S CRAFT: Main Idea and Details Tell children that when a good writer writes a paragraph that gives information, he or she often includes a sentence that tells the main idea. It tells what the whole paragraph is about. Explain that the writer also adds details that tell more about the main idea.

PREWRITING

Invite children to draw a picture of an animal from the story that interests them. Encourage them to draw details that show what it looks like, where it lives, and what it eats. Then have children

- talk about their drawings in small groups.
- ask each other questions to clarify the information.
- organize their writing ideas in a chart.

Draw a chart like the one below and model how to complete it. Ask children to help by sharing information they know about tigers.

Interesting Animal: Tiger	
What it looks like:	big cat, orange with black stripes
Where it lives:	rain forest
What it eats:	meat
What sound it makes:	Grr!
How it moves:	runs and leaps

Have children complete similar charts for their animals. Provide reference books and children's science magazines for them to use.

DRAFTING

As children write their paragraphs, remind them to

- use their charts, pictures, and the information they learned from the group.
- write a sentence that tells the main idea and names the animal that the paragraph is about.
- add detail sentences that tell things like what the animal looks like, where it lives, and what it eats.

Have children save their drafts and revisions in their writer's folder.

RESPONDING AND REVISING

Work with groups of four to six children. Invite children to take turns reading aloud their paragraphs. Encourage children to discuss ways to make the paragraph better. Offer these guidelines:

- Does the paragraph have a sentence that tells the main idea?
- Does the paragraph give information like what the animal looks like, where it lives, and what it eats?
- What is the most interesting thing you learned about the animal?

PROOFREADING

Offer some tips to help children proofread. Help them focus on the following:

INDENT The first word of a paragraph is indented.

SPELLING Have children circle words that may be misspelled. On another sheet of paper, have them write each word several ways and choose the way that looks correct. (See also the Spelling lesson on page T578.)

PUBLISHING

Have children make a clean copy of their paragraphs. Then offer publishing options like the following:

ANIMAL MIX AND MATCH Group children together according to which animal they wrote about. Have them display their animal drawings and read their informational paragraphs to each other and then compare their paragraphs. Then regroup children so that each group has paragraphs about different animals.

Handwriting
Remind children that their handwriting must be neat and clear so that the person reading the paragraph can understand it. If children need assistance, refer them to the Handwriting models in the *Language Handbook* or in the classroom.

ANIMAL GUIDE BOOK Collate the drawings and paragraphs into a class "Animal Guide Book." Place it in your classroom library so children can use it as a reference.

PORTFOLIO OPPORTUNITY

After children publish, make copies of their paragraphs and have them attach their Writing Self-Assessment Checklists to them. Have them place the paragraphs and checklists in their portfolios.

LANGUAGE HANDBOOK

Paragraph That Gives Information, pages 22–23

Student Self-Assessment

Children can use the Writing Self-Assessment Checklist in the *Portfolio Assessment Teacher's Guide*.

EVALUATING THE WRITTEN RESPONSE

When evaluating children's paragraphs, consider:

CONTENT	ORGANIZATION	STYLE
Does the paragraph give information about an animal?	**Does the paragraph have a main idea and supporting details?**	**Does each statement end with a period?**

EVALUATION BENCHMARKS

The child has difficulty writing a sentence that tells the main idea.	= **EMERGENT**
The child writes a paragraph, but the details do not all support the main idea.	= **BEGINNING**
The child successfully writes an informational paragraph. The paragraph has a main idea and supporting details.	= **PROFICIENT**

Tested Skill

GRAMMAR

Plural Nouns with *s* and *es*

Reading↔Writing Connection

Connect to the story. Talk about Tiger and her curiosity about the family she would have. Write the following phrases on the board and ask children which one tells what Shao told Tiger.

nine cubs every year
one cub every nine years

Point out the words *cub, cubs, year,* and *years.* Talk about the pairs of words, and ask children to explain the difference between *cub* and *cubs* and between *year* and *years*. Encourage children to share what they know about nouns that name one and nouns that name more than one.

Build oral language. Invite children to brainstorm lists of nouns, either singular or plural, from the story and elsewhere. Record their responses in a chart on the board. Read the words aloud, asking children whether the words name one or more than one. Then have volunteers use the words in sentences about the story.

ONE	MORE THAN ONE
cub	cubs
tiger	tigers
coin	coins
fox	foxes
peach	peaches
class	classes
wish	wishes

Teach/Model

Discuss singular and plural nouns. Ask children what they notice about the words in the *More Than One* column of the chart. (They tell about more than one; they end with *s or es*.) Help children form generalizations about the words—for example:

- **Add *s* to most nouns to name more than one.**
- **Add *es* to some nouns to name more than one.**

Elaborate on the generalization about adding *es* by explaining that *es* is added to words ending with *s, x, ch*, or *sh* to name more than one.

Practice/Apply

Check understanding. Write the following sentences on the board, leaving extra space between words.

- Will Tiger have nine cub?
- In nine year, she'll have one cub.
- Tiger ate three box of apple.
- Fox are hiding near these tree.

Read each sentence aloud and ask why it doesn't sound right. (Some nouns should be plural.) Then have volunteers correct the sentences by adding *s* or *es* to words that should be plural.

LANGUAGE HANDBOOK

Plural Nouns with *s*, pages 68–69
Plural Nouns with *es*, pages 70–71

DAILY LANGUAGE PRACTICE

Oral language exercises are provided on page R143.

TECHNOLOGY

LIVING BOOKS
Suggest that children look for plural nouns with *s* and *es* as they read *The Tortoise and the Hare* and other *Living Books.*

Practice Activities

Which Ending?

ORAL APPLICATION Write the following list of singular nouns on the board: *inch, step, box, glass, lion, bear, brush, clock, desk, lunch, bush, branch.* Have children write *s* on one side of a slip of paper and *es* on the other side. As you read the words from the list, children should hold up the *s* or *es* side of their papers to show how they think the plural form is spelled. Ask volunteers to spell the plural form, and use the word in a sentence. **VISUAL/AUDITORY/KINESTHETIC**

Can You Hit It?

ORAL APPLICATION Gather some clean, empty cans and write either *s* or *es* on each can. Line up the cans on a table or wall and provide children with beanbags. Organize children into small teams. Children take turns tossing beanbags at the cans. A team scores a point if a child knocks over a can and can name a plural noun with the ending on the can. **VISUAL/AUDITORY/KINESTHETIC**

Musical Nouns

ORAL/WRITING APPLICATION In advance, write singular nouns on slips of paper, fold them, and put them in a container. Have children sit in a circle. Invite a volunteer to choose a slip from the container. Children pass the paper around the circle while you play music. When the music stops, the child holding the paper goes to the board, reads the word, writes its plural form, and uses the word in an oral sentence. That child picks another word to bring back to the circle. The music begins again, and the game continues. **VISUAL/AUDITORY/KINESTHETIC**

APPLY TO WRITING

Suggest that children look through their informational paragraphs and other writing to make sure they wrote plural nouns ending with *s* and *es* correctly.

MEETING INDIVIDUAL NEEDS

STUDENTS ACQUIRING ENGLISH

Some children may be confused by the idea that the plurals of most nouns can be formed by simply adding *s* or *es* to a singular noun. Give them sentences with plural nouns. Have them identify the plurals as well as their singular forms.

RETEACH

See page R131 for lessons in multiple modalities.

GRAMMAR PRACTICE BOOK
pages 45–48

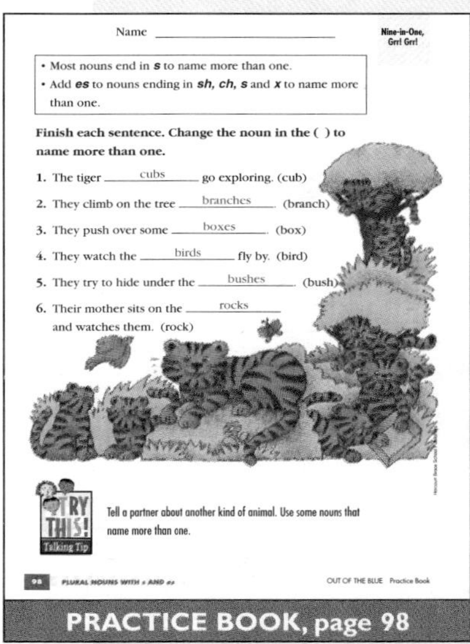

Name ____________ Nine-in-One, Grr! Grr!

- Most nouns end in ***s*** to name more than one.
- Add ***es*** to nouns ending in ***sh, ch, s*** and ***x*** to name more than one.

Finish each sentence. Change the noun in the ( ) to name more than one.

1. The tiger cubs go exploring. (cub)
2. They climb on the tree branches. (branch)
3. They push over some boxes. (box)
4. They watch the birds fly by. (bird)
5. They try to hide under the bushes. (bush)
6. Their mother sits on the rocks and watches them. (rock)

TRY THIS! Talking Tip: Tell a partner about another kind of animal. Use some nouns that name more than one.

98 PLURAL NOUNS WITH *s* AND *es* OUT OF THE BLUE Practice Book

PRACTICE BOOK, page 98

5-DAY PLAN

Use in conjunction with Daily Language Practice.

Day 1	Complete page T576.
Day 2	Complete a Practice Activity on page T577.
Day 3	Choose a Practice Activity or *Language Handbook* pages 68–71.
Day 4	Choose a Practice Activity or *Grammar Practice Book* pages 45–48.
Day 5	Complete *Practice Book* page 98.

SPELLING

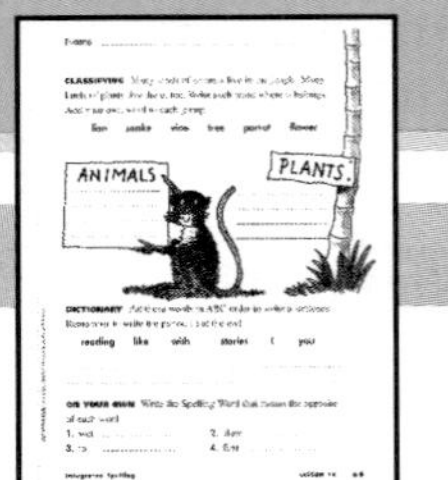

5-Day Plan

Integrated Spelling Lesson 14:
student book, pages 62–65;
Teacher's Edition, pages T99–T104.

Consonant Clusters

SPELLING WORDS

1. last ★
2. dry
3. tree★
4. fly
5. from ★
6. flag
7. fast
8. try★
9. grass
10. blow

STUDENT'S PERSONAL WORDS

11. 13.
12. 14.

Additional story words are *black, climb, clouds, great, green, just,* and *must.*

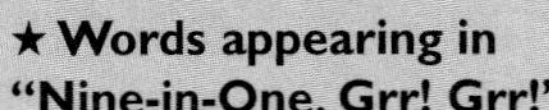

★ Words appearing in "Nine-in-One, Grr! Grr!"

Pretest

DAY 1 **Administer the pretest.** Say each word, use it in the dictation sentence provided, and repeat it. Have pairs of children check their own pretests by referring to the word list.

OPEN SORT

DAY 2 **Have children classify words.** Encourage children to think of ways to sort the Spelling Words. Suggest that they sort according to vowel sounds, spelling patterns, rhyming patterns, or other criteria. Have children share their sorting methods and talk about why they chose them.

CLOSED SORT

Sort by spelling pattern. Write on the board the headings from the chart below. Ask children to find other Spelling Words that belong with the headings, and then write each Spelling Word under its correct heading. Ask children to name other words with these consonant clusters.

freeze	flip	past
dry	fly	last
tree	flag	fast
from	blow	
try		
grass		

Teach/Model

DAY 3 **Discuss the generalization.** Tell children that when one consonant follows another, the sounds of the consonants usually blend together. Both consonant sounds are heard. Write *from* and *flag* on the board and use *fr* and *fl* as examples. Explain that if children have trouble remembering the order in which the consonants appear, they should say the word slowly to themselves to hear which letter comes first.

Tell children that most of the Spelling Words in this list begin with a consonant cluster. Ask them to find the words which do not. *(fast, last)* Ask children where they see the consonant cluster in these words.

DAY 4 **Apply to writing.** Children should look for words with consonant clusters in their informational paragraphs to be sure they are spelled correctly.

Posttest

DAY 5 **Assess children's progress.** The sentences below should be used as the posttest.

DICTATION SENTENCES

1. At last, I know how to swim!
2. The hot sun made the clothes dry.
3. Nancy climbed a big tree.
4. That bird will fly away.
5. How do you go from here to your house?
6. The flag waved in the wind.
7. Bill goes fast on his bike.
8. She will try to bake a cake.
9. The grass is growing tall.
10. The wind might blow away the paper.

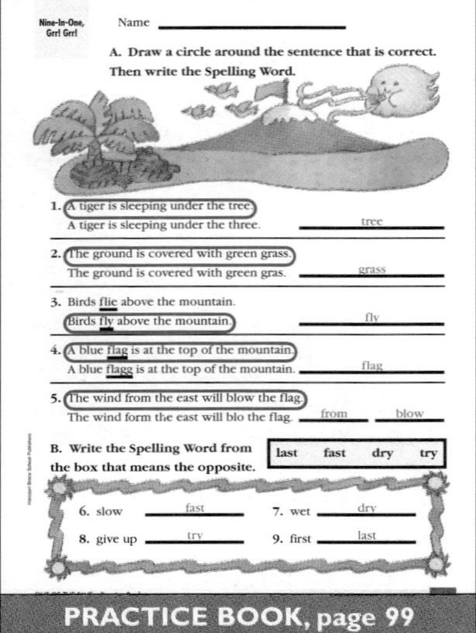
Nine-in-One, Grr! Grr! Name

A. Draw a circle around the sentence that is correct. Then write the Spelling Word.

1. A tiger is sleeping under the tree. / A tiger is sleeping under the three. — tree
2. The ground is covered with green grass. / The ground is covered with green gras. — grass
3. Birds flie above the mountain. / Birds fly above the mountain. — fly
4. A blue flag is at the top of the mountain. / A blue flagg is at the top of the mountain. — flag
5. The wind from the east will blow the flag. / The wind form the east will blo the flag. — from, blow

B. Write the Spelling Word from the box that means the opposite.

last fast dry try

6. slow — fast
7. wet — dry
8. give up — try
9. first — last

PRACTICE BOOK, page 99

VOCABULARY WORKSHOP

Reviewing Key Words

To review how the vocabulary was used in the story, distribute copies of page R177 to children. Then write the Key Words on the board.

Have children choose, as a group, the word that best completes each sentence. Then have volunteers read the completed sentence aloud.

Shao wore silver __coins__ on his belt.

He __decided__ to help Tiger.

She was sad and __lonely__.

Shao told her some __important__ words.

Shao __explained__ to Bird what he had said to Tiger.

He could not __change__ his promise.

Bird thought that this was __terrible__.

Shao __sighed__ as if he were sad.

The __noise__ of Bird's wings made Tiger forget her song.

Tell children to cut apart the sentences to make sentence strips. Children can use the strips to retell the story or use the sentences in new stories that they make up about Tiger, Bird, or other characters.

Extending Vocabulary

SIMILES

Tell children that a **simile** is a phrase that compares things and uses *like* or *as*. Writers sometimes use similes that help readers imagine story events, or form pictures in their minds. Have children reread page 270, and help them find two similes. Write them on the board.

plants curved like rooster tail feathers

rocks shaped like sleeping dragons

Ask children to tell what things are being compared in each simile. Then ask if the similes help them to imagine what the plants and the rocks look like. Add the following similes to the list and discuss them.

as fluffy as cotton
as quick as lightning
sleeping like a baby
as hungry as a shark

Invite children to add more similes, and put the list in the Writing Center for them to use.

Name ________ Nine-in-One, Grr! Grr!

Finish the simile in each sentence. To get ideas, look at the one that has been done.

1. The tiger's teeth looked like __big white knives__
2. It was as big as __Accept reasonable responses.__
3. Its roar was as loud as ________
4. Its eyes were shiny, like ________
5. All night, it walked in the forest, as quiet as ________
6. All day, it slept in a tree, snoring like ________

TRY THIS! Word Play
Use similes to describe a friend. For example:
His eyes sparkle like . . .
Her hair is as dark as . . .

100 SIMILES OUT OF THE BLUE Practice Book

PRACTICE BOOK, page 100

EXTRA SUPPORT

It may be confusing to children that similes compare things whose similarities are not immediately apparent. Work with them to draw a Venn diagram (page R201) comparing the two parts of a simile. Encourage them to list ways in which the two things are alike in the middle of the diagram.

TAKE-HOME/ KEEP-AT-HOME BOOK

Why Elephants Never Forget

Distribute the pages and have children make their own TAKE-HOME/ KEEP-AT-HOME BOOKS, which reinforce Key Words and known vocabulary. Have children read their books to partners and then take the books home to read.

INTRODUCE: PHONICS AND DECODING

Vowel Diphthong: /oi/*oi, oy*

OBJECTIVE: To understand the relationship between letters and sounds

Informal Assessment ✓

Are children able to

- ☑ identify words that contain vowel diphthong /oi/?
- ☑ generate a list of /oi/ words, spelled with *oi* and *oy*?
- ☑ form and read words that have the phonogram *-oy*?

TECHNOLOGY

Bailey's Book House **(Read-A-Rhyme)**

Teach/Model

Connect to the story. Ask children what dangled from Shao's belt. (coins) Remind them that Bird made noise to make Tiger forget her song. Write *noise* and *coins* on the board. Read the words aloud and ask how they are alike. (They have the letters *oi;* they have the same vowel sound.) Tell children that they will learn more about the sound that is alike in these words.

Phonemic awareness: Listen to the sound. Display page 18 of the *Big Book of Rhymes.* Read the rhyme aloud, and have children listen for words that have the same vowel sound as *coins* and *noise.* Then reread the poem, encouraging children to join in, especially for words with the vowel sound /oi/.

Big Book of Rhymes, page 18

Find and read words with the /oi/ sound. Have children read and frame words in the rhyme that have the vowel sound they hear in *coins.* As children frame words in the rhyme, ask what letters in each word stand for /oi/. Create columns for each spelling of the /oi/ sound in the words children name.

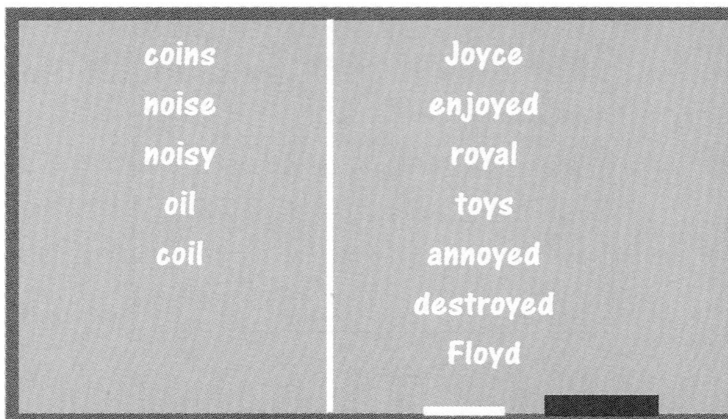

Review the chart with children, and invite them to add more words to each column.

Practice/Apply

Read words in context. Display the following tongue twisters:

toy boat
noisy nose
old oil
boy's coat

Ask volunteers to read each phrase. Then challenge children to try to say each tongue twister over and over. Have children make up their own tongue twisters using words with the /oi/ sound and share them with one another.

Practice Activities

WORD BUILDING

PHONOGRAM / BLENDING ACTIVITY Distribute individual letter cards or *Word Builder Cards*, phonogram card *-oy*, and Word Builders to children. Model using a letter card and the phonogram card *-oy* to build a word.

MODEL **I'm going to make a word with *-oy*. I will make the word *toy*. Which letter should I add to make *toy*? Where should I put the letter?**

Demonstrate adding *t* and then blending the sounds to say the word. Have children blend the sounds to say *toy*.

Invite children to make and read as many words as they can with the *-oy* phonogram. Encourage children to keep lists of the words they make.
VISUAL/AUDITORY/KINESTHETIC

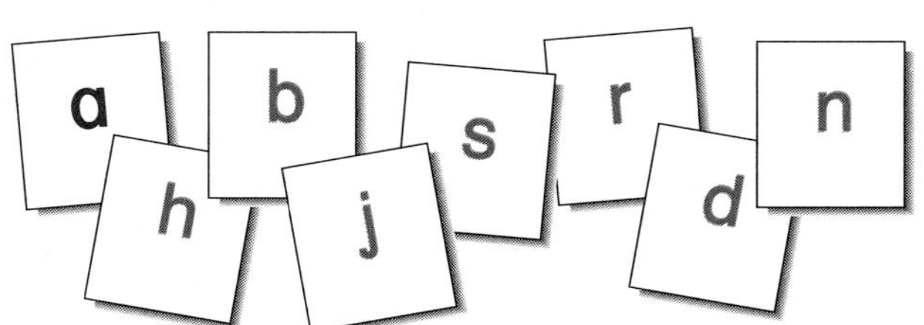

Flip a Coin

PERFORMANCE ASSESSMENT Cut twenty large paper "coins" for each group of several children. Have each group work together to generate a list of ten /oi/ words, write each word on two coins, and place the coins face down in five rows of four.

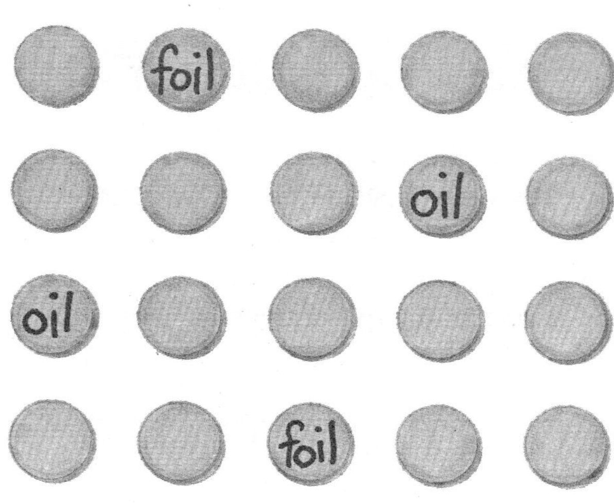

Explain that group members will take turns turning over two coins to try to make a word match. If a match is made, the child keeps the coins, uses the word in a sentence, and gets another turn. If a match is not made, the child replaces the coins face down in the same spot, and play passes to the next child. **VISUAL/KINESTHETIC**

Too Much Noise **by Ann McGovern. Houghton Mifflin, 1992.**
AVERAGE

Three Stalks of Corn **by Leo Politi. Macmillan, 1993.**
CHALLENGE

PHONICS PRACTICE READER 20

STUDENTS ACQUIRING ENGLISH

Display pictures or objects for these words: *coin, foil, point, toy, boy*. As you display each one, have a child identify the object. Label the pictures or objects and read aloud the words together.

RETEACH

See page R132 for lessons in multiple modalities.

CHALLENGE

Suggest that children write a story or a poem which includes as many /oi/ words as possible. Have children share their writing.

PHONICS ACTIVITY BOOK, pages 32–33

PHONICS PRACTICE BOOK, pages 151–154

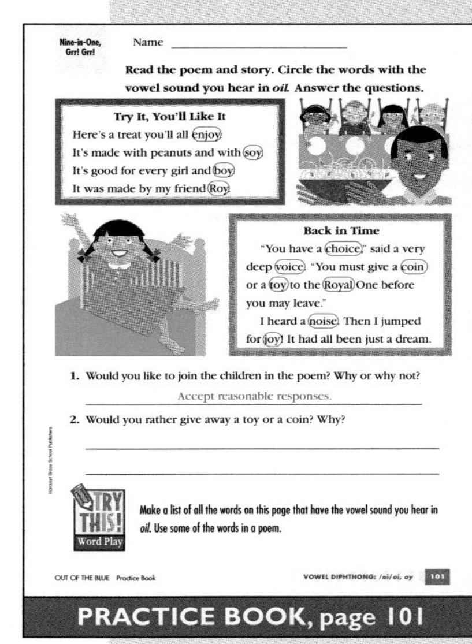
Nine-in-One, Grr! Grr! Name ____________

Read the poem and story. Circle the words with the vowel sound you hear in *oil*. Answer the questions.

Try It, You'll Like It
Here's a treat you'll all enjoy
It's made with peanuts and with soy
It's good for every girl and boy
It was made by my friend Roy

Back in Time
"You have a choice," said a very deep voice. "You must give a coin or a toy to the Royal One before you may leave."
I heard a noise. Then I jumped for joy! It had all been just a dream.

1. Would you like to join the children in the poem? Why or why not?
Accept reasonable responses.
2. Would you rather give away a toy or a coin? Why?

TRY THIS! Word Play
Make a list of all the words on this page that have the vowel sound you hear in *oil*. Use some of the words in a poem.

OUT OF THE BLUE Practice Book   VOWEL DIPHTHONG: /oi/oi, oy 101

PRACTICE BOOK, page 101

INTRODUCE: COMPREHENSION STRATEGY

Referents

OBJECTIVE: To understand the meaning and use of referents

Informal Assessment ✓

Are children able to

 identify pronouns?

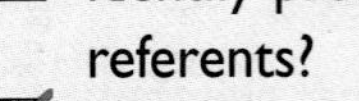 identify pronoun referents?

☑ write sentences using pronouns and referents?

Teach/Model

Connect to the story. Remind children that when they read "Nine-in-One, Grr! Grr!," they encountered words such as *she, he*, and *it*. Have children turn to page 276. Ask a volunteer to read aloud the first two sentences:

At first Tiger was happy as she followed the road back to earth. But soon, she began to worry.

Ask children which character the sentences are about. (Tiger)

Discuss referents. Write the pronoun *she* on the board and ask which word in the sentences it replaces. *(Tiger)* Then have a volunteer read aloud both sentences using *Tiger* in place of *she*. Help children understand the following:

- **The sentences mean the same thing either way, but they sound better and are easier to read when the word *Tiger* is not continually repeated.**
- **Children will understand the story better if they know to whom or to what words like *he, she, it, they, I,* and *me* refer.**

Then have children page through the story to find more examples of the use of referents.

Practice/Apply

Have children demonstrate understanding. Have children identify the words that have been replaced by each pronoun in the following story sentences. Ask a volunteer to reread the sentence, substituting a character's name or another noun for the pronoun.

Page 273: "O great Shao," answered Tiger respectfully, "I am lonely and want to know how many cubs I will have."

Page 282: And Shao explained that he had just told Tiger she would have nine cubs each year.

Page 286: Bird now had a plan. She could hardly wait to try it out.

Practice Activities

Get Past Bird

Copy and distribute a game board similar to the one shown. Working in groups of four, have children decorate the board to resemble the story's setting. The object of the game is to go from Start to Finish without landing on the space marked BIRD. Children play the game by taking turns rolling a number cube, moving a marker, and following the directions on the space. If they land on a space with a pronoun, children must use the pronoun in a sentence (or two) in which the referent is apparent. If successful, they move ahead two spaces; if not, they stay on the same space until their next turn. Play then passes to the next child. The first to pass the BIRD space is the winner. **VISUAL/AUDITORY/KINESTHETIC**

Name That Pronoun!

PERFORMANCE ASSESSMENT Prepare two sets of cards by writing pronouns on one set of cards and nouns on another set. Place the sets face down next to each other. Partners or small groups take turns choosing a card from each set, reading the pronoun and the noun, and saying whether the pronoun can be used in place of the noun. (Example: *it, book*—the pronoun can be used in place of the noun; *it, sister*—the pronoun cannot be used in place of the noun.) If the pronoun can replace the noun, children make up sentences to prove it. **VISUAL/AUDITORY/KINESTHETIC**

STUDENTS ACQUIRING ENGLISH

Children whose first language is one of the Romance languages may have difficulty with the pronouns *she, he,* and *it.* Provide extra practice for children to use *it* for objects and animals, rather than the *he* or *she* they would use in their first language.

RETEACH

See page R133 for lessons in multiple modalities.

CHALLENGE

Have partners each write a story in which no pronouns are used. Then they can exchange stories and edit them, using pronouns to refer to nouns and improve the story's flow.

***Baby Rattlesnake* by Te Ata, adapted by Lynn Moroney. Children's Book Press, 1989. AVERAGE**

***The Bigness Contest* by Florence Parry Heide. Little, Brown, 1994. AVERAGE**

***Crictor* by Tomi Ungerer. HarperCollins, 1958. CHALLENGE**

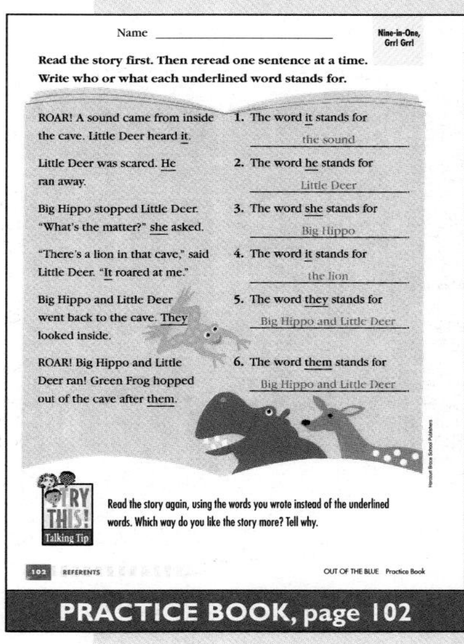

Name ______________ Nine-in-One, Grr! Grr!

Read the story first. Then reread one sentence at a time. Write who or what each underlined word stands for.

ROAR! A sound came from inside the cave. Little Deer heard it.

Little Deer was scared. He ran away.

Big Hippo stopped Little Deer. "What's the matter?" she asked.

"There's a lion in that cave," said Little Deer. "It roared at me."

Big Hippo and Little Deer went back to the cave. They looked inside.

ROAR! Big Hippo and Little Deer ran! Green Frog hopped out of the cave after them.

1. The word it stands for the sound
2. The word he stands for Little Deer
3. The word she stands for Big Hippo
4. The word it stands for the lion
5. The word they stands for Big Hippo and Little Deer
6. The word them stands for Big Hippo and Little Deer

TRY THIS! Talking Tip

Read the story again, using the words you wrote instead of the underlined words. Which way do you like the story more? Tell why.

Harcourt Brace School Publishers

102 REFERENTS OUT OF THE BLUE Practice Book

PRACTICE BOOK, page 102

Integrated Curriculum

SCIENCE

Wild Animals

TIPS FOR CLASSROOM MANAGEMENT

IF you don't have space in your classroom to string the time lines for the A Line Tells the Time activity, **THEN** have children put their pages together into a book.

SCIENCE

Be an Animal!

MATERIALS
- globe
- children's atlas
- animal reference books
- children's encyclopedia

LEARNING CENTER Help children locate Asia on a globe. Point out that the story takes place and mentions many animals that live in Asia. Invite children to skim the pages of "Nine-in-One, Grr! Grr!" for different animals. Then direct their attention to the research materials. Invite each child to choose an animal that lives in Asia, read about it, and take notes on it. Once the research is finished, encourage each child to pretend to act like the animal he or she chose while other children interview him or her, asking questions such as these:

- **Do you live in a forest?**
- **What kind of food do you like to eat?**

LISTENING/SPEAKING/READING/WRITING

MATH

How Many Tigers?

MATERIALS
- chart paper
- tape
- Tiger Cutouts, page R204

Help children solve the following word problem:

If Tiger had nine cubs a year for three years, how many cubs would she have?

Explain that a graph or a chart can make a math problem like this one easier to figure out. Make the outline of a chart like the one below. Distribute copies of page R204, and have children cut out the tigers on the page. Go through the chart step-by-step, having volunteers add a cutout tiger for each cub. Extend the chart to show nine years. Children will see the difference between nine-in-one and one-in-nine quite easily. Have children make up other word problems that can be answered using the chart. READING/WRITING

Years	Nine-in-One	One-in-Nine
1		
2		
3		

MUSIC

She'll Be Walking Up the Mountain . . .

MATERIALS
- crayons or markers
- paper

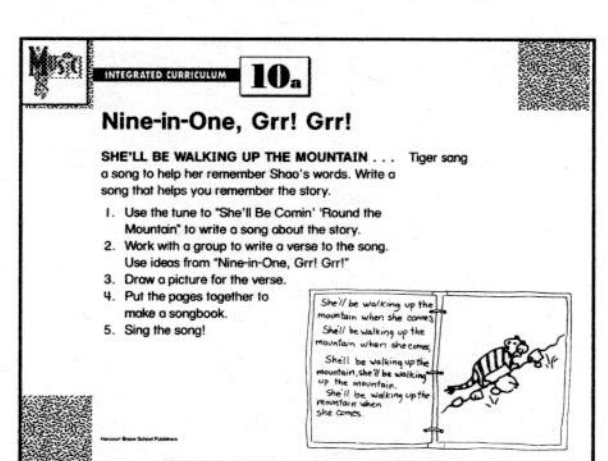
INTEGRATED CURRICULUM 10a

Nine-in-One, Grr! Grr!

SHE'LL BE WALKING UP THE MOUNTAIN . . . Tiger sang a song to help her remember Shao's words. Write a song that helps you remember the story.

1. Use the tune to "She'll Be Comin' 'Round the Mountain" to write a song about the story.
2. Work with a group to write a verse to the song. Use ideas from "Nine-in-One, Grr! Grr!"
3. Draw a picture for the verse.
4. Put the pages together to make a songbook.
5. Sing the song!

Curriculum Card 10a

COOPERATIVE LEARNING Suggest that children compose a song about the story, using the tune to "She'll Be Comin' Round the Mountain." Each verse should mention an important point in the story. For example, the first verse could be:

She'll be walking up the mountain when she comes,
She'll be walking up the mountain when she comes,
She'll be walking up the mountain, she'll be walking up the mountain,
She'll be walking up the mountain when she comes.

Have small groups of children work together to write and illustrate additional verses. Verses might include *She'll be asking Shao a question when she comes* and *She'll be happy with Shao's answer when she comes*. Bind the pages together to make a class songbook. **LISTENING/SPEAKING/ READING/ WRITING**

ART

A Line Tells the Time

MATERIALS
- clothespins or clips
- clothesline
- string or thread
- paper
- markers

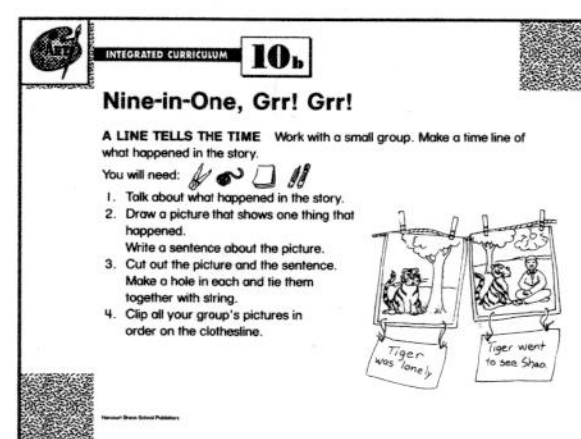
INTEGRATED CURRICULUM 10b

Nine-in-One, Grr! Grr!

A LINE TELLS THE TIME Work with a small group. Make a time line of what happened in the story.

You will need:

1. Talk about what happened in the story.
2. Draw a picture that shows one thing that happened. Write a sentence about the picture.
3. Cut out the picture and the sentence. Make a hole in each and tie them together with string.
4. Clip all your group's pictures in order on the clothesline.

Curriculum Card 10b

Challenge children to make a three-dimensional time line of story events. First, have small groups of children discuss the major story events. Suggest that groups assign each member one event to illustrate. Have children write captions for each picture. When complete, have children cut out their pictures and captions. Help them make a small hole in each piece and tie each caption to its corresponding picture. Then help children clip the pieces in story order to a clothesline. **READING/WRITING**

Amazing Cats by Alexandra Parsons. Knopf, 1991. **AVERAGE**

Imagine by Alison Lester. Houghton Mifflin, 1990. **AVERAGE**

MULTI-AGE CLASSROOMS

Challenge children to make up and solve more word problems appropriate to their level of math understanding like the one in the Math activity.

Reading Trade Books

TIPS FOR CLASSROOM MANAGEMENT

SMALL GROUP
Read the story in a small circle of children. As you read aloud, pause to let children talk about what things they would enjoy having two of, and what things they wouldn't want to see two of.

INDEPENDENT
Place the book in the Reading Center. Have children read the book and write their thoughts about the story in their personal journals.

For a comprehensive lesson plan, refer to the complete lesson for *Two of Everything* on pages T694–T697.

Two of Everything

by Lily Toy Hong

Signatures Library

READER'S CHALLENGE

Tiger had to remember Shao's words if they were to come true. Characters in folktales often have to do something to get their wish. What clue does the title *Two of Everything* give you about the story? Will the characters want "two of everything"?

READING STRATEGY: MAKING PREDICTIONS

As children read, have them predict what will happen when the man finds the brass pot and when the woman discovers what it does. As they read along, encourage children to use new information from the story to modify their predictions. Have them share, as well, their reasons for changing their predictions.

LINK TO THE THEME

Children who are reading the book may want to discuss the following:

- **What was the trickiest part of the story?**
- **How is this story like the other tricky tales you've read? How is it different?**
- **How would you have used the pot that makes two of everything?**

RESPONSE ACTIVITY: WRITING ABOUT THE STORY

On one half of a sheet of paper, have children draw a picture showing two of something that they would like to have. On the other half, have them write a short paragraph explaining why. Put the pages into a class book entitled "Two of Everything."

Other Trade Books

The Chinese Mirror

by Mirra Ginsburg
illustrated by Margot Zemach

Hold up a mirror and ask how a mirror might seem to play tricks. As children read the book, help them make a list of the people who looked in the mirror and who they saw in it. Ask why children think the people didn't recognize themselves in the mirror.

The Story of the Milky Way

by Joseph Bruchac and Gayle Ross
illustrated by Virginia A. Stroud

Ask if children know what the Milky Way is. Point out that there are many stories that tell about how things in nature came to be. Ask children to retell the story of cornmeal turned into stars. Suggest they make their own picture of the Milky Way, using cornmeal, sand, or glitter.

Why Mosquitoes Buzz in People's Ears

by Verna Aardema
illustrated by Leo and Diane Dillon

Ask whether children have ever wondered where mosquitoes come from or why they are so pesky. After reading, help children complete a cause-and-effect chart to show the chain of events that began when Iguana didn't want to listen to Mosquito's tales.

MEETING INDIVIDUAL NEEDS

STUDENTS ACQUIRING ENGLISH

List words for animal sounds, such as *buzz*, *bow-wow*, and *hee-haw*. Invite children to tell the words they use for each sound in their first language. Discuss similarities and differences.

Trade Books

PROJECT MANAGEMENT

STUDENTS ACQUIRING ENGLISH

Invite children to summarize favorite stories from their native cultures. Have them write and then read aloud brief summaries of the stories.

MULTIPLE INTELLIGENCES

Children with strong verbal/linguistic inclinations might enjoy writing stories on their own as well as in groups. Encourage them to help their groups write and develop the stories, and to share their strengths.

Choose a Story Idea

SELECTION CONNECTION

"Nine-in-One, Grr! Grr!" is about a tiger who tries to remember important information by singing it, only to be distracted by a clever bird. Ask children to share stories about remembering or forgetting something.

PROJECT CHECKLIST

During this stage, children should

- ☑ brainstorm a list of stories to tell. These stories can be retellings of tales they know, or they can be original ideas.
- ☑ choose story ideas they would like to develop and form story groups.

Project Card 15

When children have completed the checkpoint, have them think about the story ideas and write their thoughts about them in their Project Journals.

Project Card 15 can be found as a copying master on page R152.

PLANNING TIPS

After children have brainstormed a list of story ideas, help them narrow the list by referring to questions like these.

- **Is the story simple and easy to follow?**
- **Is it a story you can present in different ways?**
- **Which story idea does your group like best?**
- **Which idea would be the most fun for an audience?**

Informal Assessment

As children complete this checkpoint, they will **compare and contrast** story ideas, **evaluate ideas,** and **make decisions.** Children are thinking critically if they

- ☑ compare and contrast stories and story types.
- ☑ apply their knowledge of stories to develop ideas for new stories.
- ☑ have creative suggestions for retelling a familiar story or a new story.

Note that a more formal assessment rubric for this checkpoint is provided on page T693.

ART AND LITERATURE

Storyteller Doll (circa 1986) • by Michelle Paisano

ABOUT THE ARTIST

Michelle Paisano, a young artist from Laguna Pueblo in New Mexico, now lives and works in Albuquerque. She is one of many Pueblo artists who create clay pots and figures in the tradition of their ancestors. The ancient practice of making storyteller dolls was revived in the 1960s by Pueblo artist Helen Cordero. She grew up among people who shared a rich oral tradition. Important aspects of their history and culture were passed from one generation to the next in the form of stories. Helen Cordero made her first doll in memory of her grandfather, who was a storyteller.

ABOUT THE FIGURE

In Paisano's *Storyteller Doll,* the large doll—the mother—is surrounded by nine distinctly different children, several of whom are holding toys. Each of the child figures is smiling happily. In the storyteller tradition, dolls shown with their mouths open, as is the case with this figure, are said to be singing.

Art and Literature

MAKING CONNECTIONS

Ask a volunteer to read aloud the first paragraph on page 296. Tell children that the Pueblo people are a group of Native Americans from the southwestern United States who live in villages called pueblos. Ask children how they might use a doll like this to tell a story. Discuss how using a doll or a puppet can make storytelling fun.

EXTENDING THE FINE ART

Hands-On Activity Provide each child with a paper lunch bag. Have children use the bag, crayons, and scraps of paper and yarn to create a hand puppet. Encourage them to decorate it like a storyteller doll. When children have finished their puppets, invite volunteers to use them to tell a favorite story to classmates.

ALA
Notable Book

COYOTE

A TRICKSTER TALE FROM THE AMERICAN SOUTHWEST

Gerald McDermott

THEME: COMMUNICATION

Tell a Tricky Tale

In "Coyote," a trickster tale from the American Southwest, children will discover how Coyote is outsmarted by crows.

SELECTION SUMMARY

Genre: Folktale

Blue Coyote wants to be the greatest coyote in the world, so he asks the crows to help him fly. Each crow sticks a feather from its left wing into him. Coyote flies, but he is off balance and falls to the ground. Next, the crows stick feathers from their right wings into him. Coyote flies much better now. But he becomes rude and boastful, so the crows take back their feathers in midflight. Coyote falls into the canyon so fast that his tail burns. Then, he trips and rolls in the dirt. To this day, Coyote is the color of dust and has a burnt black tip on his tail.

Gerald McDermott

ABOUT THE AUTHOR/ ILLUSTRATOR

GERALD MCDERMOTT has written and illustrated several stories based on tales told by Native Americans. He uses gouache and black ink to create vivid illustrations for his books.

Coyote is an ALA Notable Book for Children. Another book by McDermott, *Arrow to the Sun,* won the 1975 Caldecott Medal, and *Anansi the Spider* was a Caldecott Honor book in 1973.

For more information about the author/illustrator, see page T617.

SUGGESTED LESSON PLANNER

▶ *Coyote*

	DAY 1	DAY 2
PART 1 Reading Listening Speaking Viewing **Key Words** foolish balance feather foot spread	**BUILD BACKGROUND** T594 **VOCABULARY STRATEGIES** T594–T595 *Chart/Transparency 22* *Practice Book* p. 104 **READING THE SELECTION** T596–T617 Options for Reading T596–T597 *Response Card 2* **REVIEW PREDICTIONS/PURPOSE** T616 **APPRECIATING THE LITERATURE** T616 NOTE: Children may read the selection on Day 2.	**SUMMARIZE AND RETELL THE SELECTION** T616 *Practice Book* p. 105 ◆ **RESPONSE CORNER ACTIVITIES** T618 **CHECKING COMPREHENSION** T619 *End-of-Selection Test* 
PART 2 Writer's Workshop	**A STORY** Thinking as Writers T624 *Chart/Transparency 6*	Prewriting T624
Grammar	✓ **IRREGULAR PLURALS** Teach the Concept T626 Daily Language Practice (1–2) R144	Daily Language Practice (3–4) R144 Practice Activity T627
Spelling	**WORDS WITH *o-e* AND *u-e*** *use, nose, hole, tune, note, bone, those, cute, woke, mule* Pretest/Self-Check T628 *Integrated Spelling Teacher's Edition* pp. T105, T282	Open and Closed Sorts T628 *Integrated Spelling* p. 66 *Integrated Spelling Teacher's Edition* p. T106
PART 3 Phonics	**VOWEL VARIANT: /o͞o/oo, ou** Phonics-Vocabulary Connection T595	**VOWEL VARIANT: /o͞o/oo, ou** (Introduce) T630 *Big Book of Rhymes* p. 19 *Phonics Practice Book* pp. 155–156
Skills and Strategies	◆ **INTEGRATED CURRICULUM** *The Southwest* **Social Studies** T634 **Science** T634 **Art** T635 **Math** T635	**STUDY SKILL** T632–T633 Library Skills (Introduce) *Practice Book* p. 111 *Living Book: The Tortoise and the Hare*

Day 1	Day 2
Use the Extra Support note on page T603 and the Intervention Strategies note on page T613 to help **below-level readers**.	During the Library Skills lesson, refer to the Challenge note on page T633 for **above-level readers**.

NOTE: An alternative lesson plan for **below-level readers** appears on *Intervention Strategies Manual* pp. 62–67. A lesson for **students acquiring English** appears on *Sheltered English/ESL Manual* pp. 42–45.

DAY 3

◆ **IDEA BANK ACTIVITIES**
Listening and Speaking T622
Real-Life Reading: Reading Song Lyrics T622
Oral Language T623
Kinesthetic T623
Writer's Magazine pp. 40–43

School–Home Connection 11 R174

Drafting T624
Language Handbook pp. 8–9
The Amazing Writing Machine

Daily Language Practice (5–6) R144
Practice Activity T627
Language Handbook pp. 72–73

Discuss the Generalization T628
Integrated Spelling p. 67
Integrated Spelling Teacher's Edition p. T107

VOWEL VARIANT: /o͞o/oo, ou T630
Phonics Practice Reader 21: The Good Crook

GRAMMAR MINILESSON T601
✓ Plural Nouns with *-s, -es* (Review)
Language Handbook pp. 68–71

PHONICS AND DECODING MINILESSON T603
Initial Clusters: *spr, shr* (Review)
Phonics Activity Book p. 36
Phonics Practice Book pp. 199–200
Practice Book p. 112

Use the Semantic Cues activity on page T621 to help **below-level** and **ESL readers** understand the selection.

DAY 4

VOCABULARY WORKSHOP T629
Reviewing Key Words
Story Strips R178
Synonyms
Practice Book pp. 108–109
Take-Home/Keep-at-Home Book: Leo's Trip to the City

READING TRADE BOOKS T636–T637

Take-Home Book

Responding and Revising T625

Daily Language Practice (7–8) R144
Practice Activity T627
Grammar Practice Book pp. 49–50

Apply to Writing T628
Integrated Spelling pp. 68–69
Integrated Spelling Teacher's Edition pp. T108–T109

VOWEL VARIANT: /o͞o/oo, ou T631
Practice Book p. 110
Bailey's Book House (Read-A-Rhyme)

PHONICS AND DECODING MINILESSON T609
Long Vowel: /ī/*i-e, igh* (Maintain)
Phonics Activity Book p. 39
Phonics Practice Reader 9: When I Get a Bike
Practice Book p. 114

Have children read "Dr. Zed's Science Surprises," pages 322–323, to connect nonfiction about tricks with "Coyote."

DAY 5

READING TRADE BOOKS T631, T633, T635, T636–T637

Proofreading and Publishing T625
Kid Pix

Daily Language Practice (9–12) R144
Practice Book p. 106

Posttest T628
Practice Book p. 107
Integrated Spelling Teacher's Edition p. T110

VOWEL VARIANT: /o͞o/oo, ou T631
Phonics Activity Book p. 35

PHONICS AND DECODING MINILESSON T607
✓ R-Controlled Vowel: /ôr/*or, ore, our, oor, oar* (Review)
Phonics Practice Book pp. 147–148
Practice Book p. 113

Theme Project Checkpoint 3 T638

To help children build fluency, use the *Instant Readers™ The Fox and the Crow* and *White Crow* on pages T620–T621.

✓ = Tested Skill
◆ = Optional activities that may be used to adjust pacing throughout the lesson
Titles in *italics* are optional materials.

1 Reading and Responding

BUILDING BACKGROUND AND CONCEPTS

PRIOR KNOWLEDGE

Discuss animal characters' traits. Write the phrase *a nose for trouble* on the board, and ask children what it means. Have them give examples of animals that might have *a nose for trouble.* Talk about what might happen to an animal that gets into trouble.

Distribute pictures of animals, such as an elephant, a lion, a coyote, a fox, a dog, a cat, a horse, and a parrot. Have the child holding the picture tell what kind of trouble that animal might get into if it had *a nose for trouble.*

Intervention Strategies

For children who may have difficulty reading "Coyote," support is available in *Intervention Strategies Manual*, pages 62–67, and on pages T613 and T620–T621 in this lesson.

STUDENTS ACQUIRING ENGLISH

See *Sheltered English/ESL Manual*, pages 42–45.

VOCABULARY STRATEGIES

KEY WORDS DEFINED

foolish not having good sense
feather a part of what covers a bird's body
spread to stretch out
balance a steady position
foot the part of the leg on which one walks

SUPPORT WORDS

Display the words *Badger, canyon, chanting, cringed, winced,* and *Woodpecker*. Discuss their meanings and have children use them in sentences.

INTEGRATED SPELLING

SPELLING PRETEST: page T628
SPELLING GENERALIZATION: Words with *o-e* and *u-e*

SCIENCE

Coyotes

In cartoons, the coyote never catches the roadrunner, but in real life the coyote is faster. However, coyotes prefer to eat rabbits. Coyotes live in burrows or holes. They have up to six pups. Both parents help raise the pups until they are old enough to be on their own.

CONTEXT CLUES

Have children read new vocabulary. Display Chart/Transparency 22, or write the words and story on the board. Have children read the words they know.

Then ask children to read the first two sentences. Model how to use context clues to figure out *foolish*.

MODEL **Sometimes I can use other words in a story to help me understand an unfamiliar word. Both *foolish* and *silly* are used to describe the dog. They must mean almost the same thing. I know that when people act silly, they don't make much sense. I think *foolish* also means "not making sense."**

Have children read the rest of the story, looking at other words to help them understand the meaning of the underlined words.

HANDS-ON ACTIVITY

Play a word-recognition game.

Have partners work together. On strips of paper, each partner writes the Key Words. The strips of paper are "feathers." Have partners mix up their ten feathers and turn them face down. Partners take turns turning over two feathers at a time. If a player matches words, he or she uses the word in a sentence and keeps both feathers.

CHART/TRANSPARENCY 22

foolish feather spread

balance foot

The foolish dog wanted to fly.

"I'll teach that silly dog a lesson," said the bird. She took a feather from her wing and put it in the dog's tail. "Now jump," she told him.

He spread out his legs like wings and jumped. He started to fly! When he lost his balance, some birds pulled on his ears to help him.

Even so, he fell to the ground with a thump. Each foot was pushed close to his body. That is why some dogs have long ears and short legs.

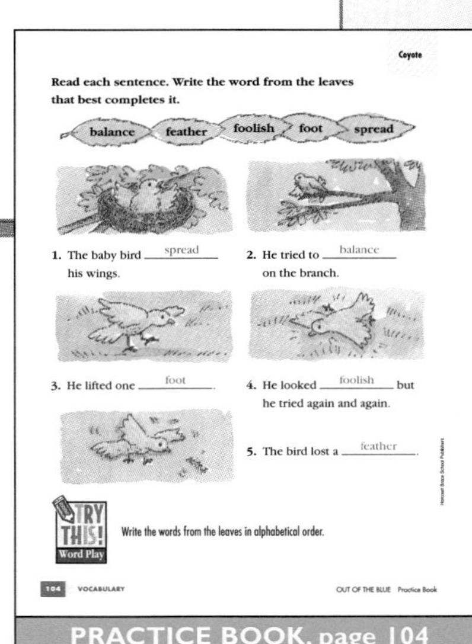

Coyote

Read each sentence. Write the word from the leaves that best completes it.

balance feather foolish foot spread

1. The baby bird spread his wings.
2. He tried to balance on the branch.
3. He lifted one foot.
4. He looked foolish but he tried again and again.
5. The bird lost a feather.

TRY THIS! Word Play: Write the words from the leaves in alphabetical order.

104 VOCABULARY — OUT OF THE BLUE Practice Book

PRACTICE BOOK, page 104

PHONICS-VOCABULARY CONNECTION

WORD PLAY

Write the following words on the board: *look, book, could, hook, took, would, football, should, good-bye, woodpecker, good, hood*. Say them aloud with children. Ask children how all the words are alike.

Ask volunteers to make up silly sentences, using as many of the words as possible, such as

Could that book be made of wood?

The concept of the vowel variant /o͝o/ is further developed on pages T630–T631.

Strategic Reading

STRATEGY FOCUS:
RELATING PICTURES TO TEXT

Review with children some of the things good readers do when they read. Add new responses to their classroom chart.

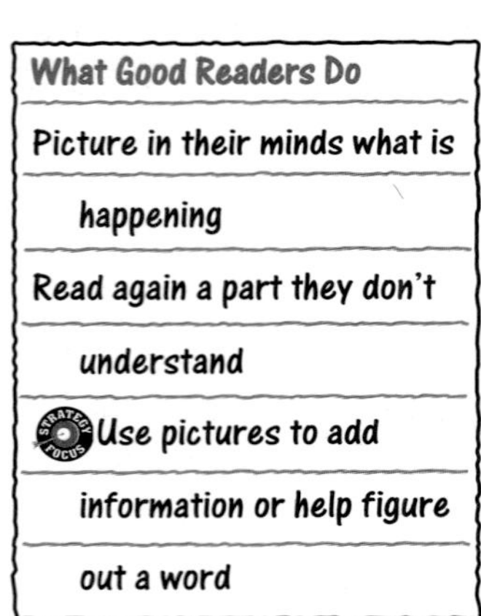

What Good Readers Do
Picture in their minds what is happening
Read again a part they don't understand
Use pictures to add information or help figure out a word

Share with children the comprehension strategy that is the focus of this selection.

MODEL

I look at the pictures to find out who the characters are and what they are like. I also find out what is happening in the story by following along with the pictures. If I come to a word I don't know as I am reading, I look at the picture to see if it helps me understand what the word means.

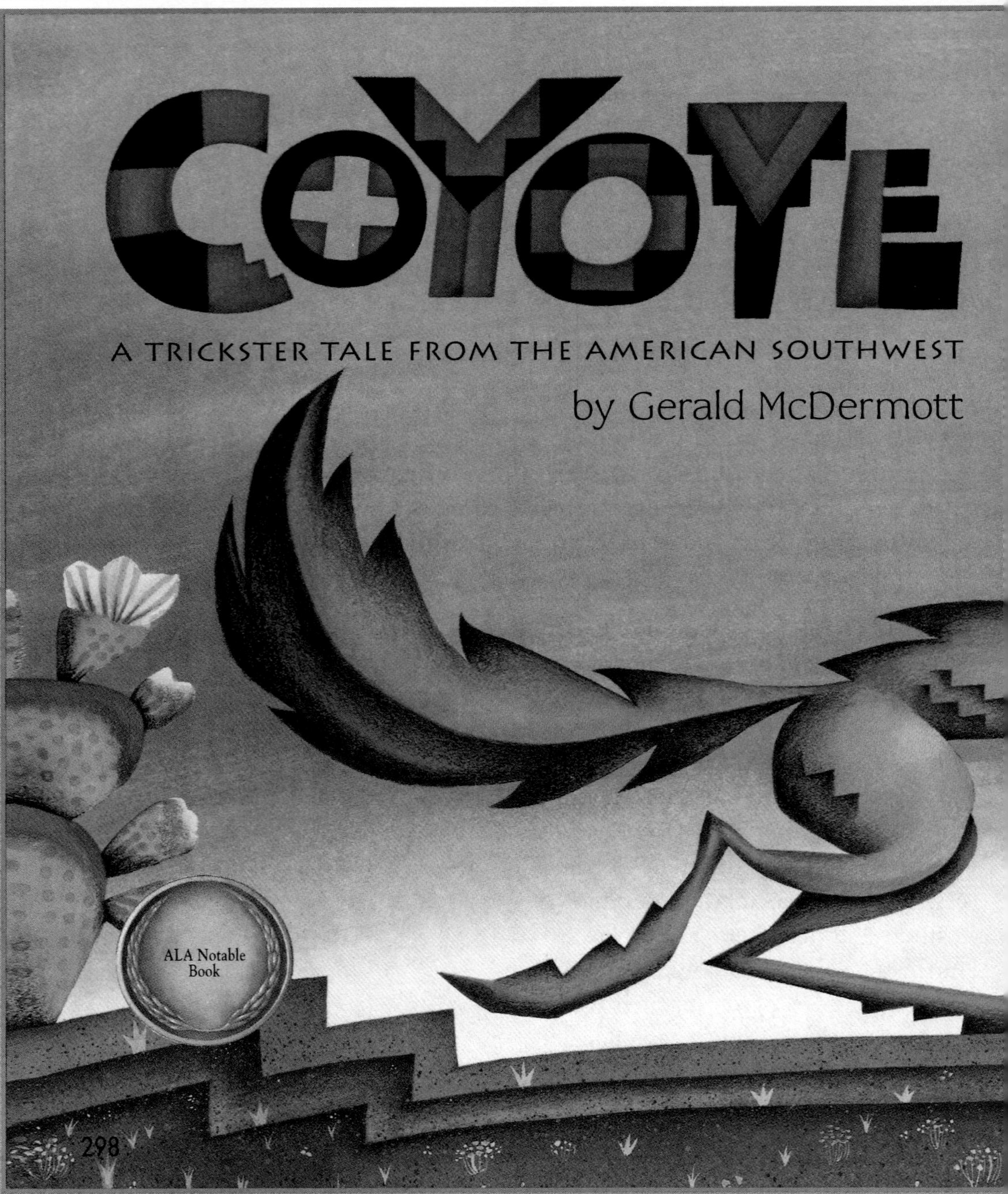

COYOTE
A TRICKSTER TALE FROM THE AMERICAN SOUTHWEST
by Gerald McDermott
ALA Notable Book
298

TIPS FOR CLASSROOM MANAGEMENT

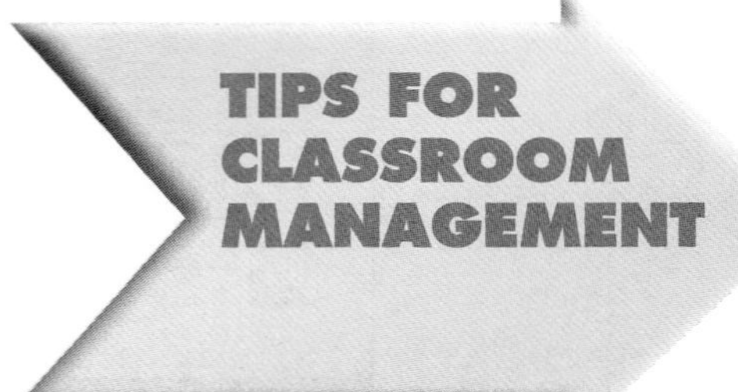

SMALL GROUP

INTERACTIVE READING

Walk children through the story, encouraging them to give thorough descriptions of the illustrations. Write sentences on sentence strips about the pictures. Read the sentences aloud with children. Then, as volunteers read the story aloud, children should tape the sentence strips to the board in story order.

COOPERATIVE READING

BUDDY READING Pair children who need extra support with more-fluent readers. Suggest that they take turns reading sections and then stop to talk about the story. They can use Reader Response Card 2 (Setting), page R149. After reading, discuss how a different setting might have changed the story.

READER RESPONSE 2
Setting

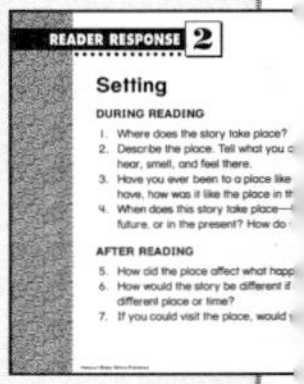

Response C

Coyote.
Blue Coyote.
He was going along, following his nose.
He had a nose for trouble.

299

PREVIEWING/SETTING PURPOSES

Have children read the title on page 298. Suggest that children look at the pictures on pages 298–303 and predict what Coyote will do in the story. Ask them to write their predictions in their personal journals. Then help children set their purposes for reading.

MODELING A STRATEGY

PAGES 298–301 Before children read, have them look at the pictures. Remind them that the pictures can give a lot of information about the characters. **Think aloud:** *Coyote doesn't look like a mean coyote. But he looks like he doesn't get along with the other animals. I wonder why not.* RELATING PICTURES TO TEXT

WHOLE CLASS

STRATEGIC READING

Choose some or all of the suggestions and questions under Strategic Reading, pages T596–T616, to guide a literature discussion and model the STRATEGY FOCUS of Relating Pictures to Text.

READ ALOUD

Read "Coyote" aloud as children follow along in their books. Invite discussion by having children look at the illustrations to predict what might happen next. Have them confirm their predictions as the story unfolds.

Strategic Reading

MODELING A STRATEGY

PAGES 300–301 After children read the pages, have them look at the pictures again and talk about other things they learned about Coyote and what happened to him. If necessary, model your thinking: *The picture shows flames coming from Coyote's head, so his fur really caught on fire. The picture shows me the trouble Coyote found with Snake—Snake wrapped himself tightly around Coyote.* **RELATING PICTURES TO TEXT**

Coyote stuck his nose into Badger's hole but got bitten.

Coyote wanted to have a flaming red head like Woodpecker, but his fur caught fire.

300

LISTENING CENTER

You may want to record "Coyote" on an audiocassette for children to listen to. Encourage them to follow along in their books as they listen.
(See Acknowledgments on pages R235–R236.)

MUSIC CONNECTION

NATIVE AMERICAN MUSIC You may wish to play a recording of music from the Southwest Native American tradition to set the mood as children read the story.

Coyote went looking for Snake but only found trouble.

Coyote was always in trouble.

301

Student Self-Assessment

USING READING STRATEGIES

When children are reading aloud in groups, suggest that they stop occasionally to discuss the good reading strategies they use and that they notice one another using.

SCIENCE

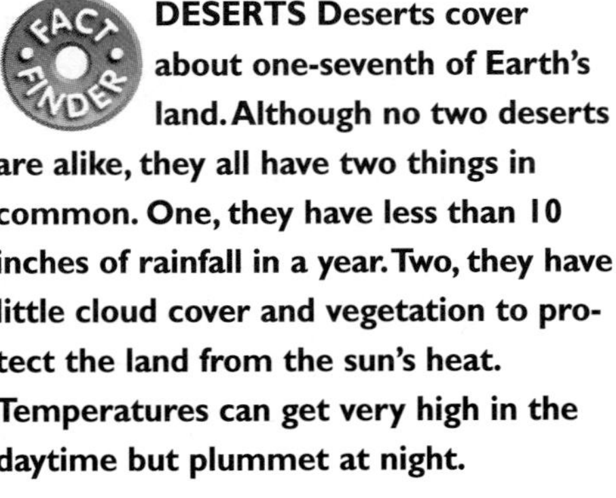

DESERTS Deserts cover about one-seventh of Earth's land. Although no two deserts are alike, they all have two things in common. One, they have less than 10 inches of rainfall in a year. Two, they have little cloud cover and vegetation to protect the land from the sun's heat. Temperatures can get very high in the daytime but plummet at night.

A CLOSER LOOK

Ask children to study the illustrations and to suggest where the story is from and which people first told it. If necessary, point out the design on the snake and the headdress on the crows, and identify them as Native American designs. Also help children identify elements of a desert, such as a cactus and a mesa.

Strategic Reading

MODELING A STRATEGY

PAGES 302–305 Before children read, have them look at the pictures and predict what Coyote might want from the crows. **Think aloud:** *Coyote was snooping in Badger's hole, and he wanted a red head like Woodpecker. Now he sees the crows lined up and then flying. I think Coyote wants something from the crows. Maybe he wants to try flying.*

MAKING PREDICTIONS

Coyote came to a place where
earth meets sky.
He heard laughing and singing.
He went up to take a look.

Coyote saw a flock of crows.
They were chanting.
They were dancing.

302

EXPANDING VOCABULARY

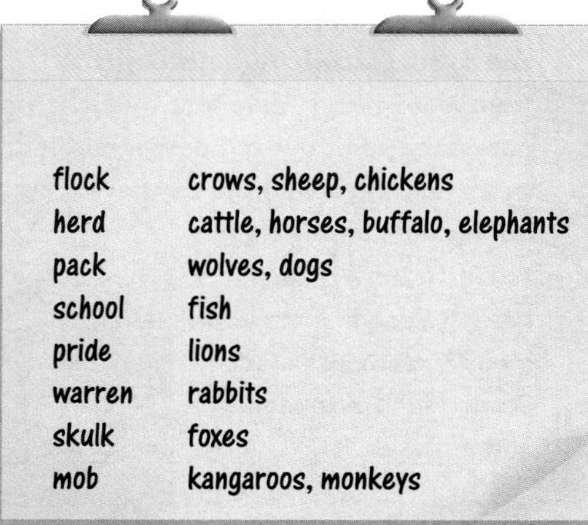

flock	crows, sheep, chickens
herd	cattle, horses, buffalo, elephants
pack	wolves, dogs
school	fish
pride	lions
warren	rabbits
skulk	foxes
mob	kangaroos, monkeys

Reread the sentence *Coyote saw a flock of crows* with children. Ask them what they think the word *flock* means. (group) **Invite children to name other animals whose group name is *flock*.** (sheep, chickens) **Help children create a chart of group names for animals.**

Tested Skill

MINILESSON

REVIEW: GRAMMAR

Plural Nouns with *-s, -es*

INFORMAL ASSESSMENT

As children write, notice whether they use *-s* or *-es* correctly to show plurals.

TEACH/MODEL

Write *crow* and *crows* on the board, and ask how *crow* was changed to show more than one. Have children brainstorm more words that form the plural with *s*. Then ask what the crows wore on their heads. Write *headdress* under *crow* and *headdresses* under *crows*. Have children tell how the plural forms of *crow* and *headdress* are different. Remind children that *-es* is added to words that end in the letters *s, sh, ch,* and *x*.

PRACTICE/APPLY

Write nouns on one set of cards and *s* or *es* on another set. Place the two sets of cards face down. Player 1 picks a card from the noun pile, reads the word, and says whether it needs *-s* or *-es* to make it plural. Player 1 then picks a card from the plural endings pile. If correct, Player 1 keeps the two cards. If incorrect, Player 1 puts both cards face down to be used in subsequent rounds. Then play passes to Player 2.

LANGUAGE HANDBOOK

Plural Nouns with *s*, pages 68–69

Plural Nouns with *es*, pages 70–71

REAL-LIFE CONNECTION

Ask children what they think the phrase *where earth meets sky* on page 302 means. Encourage volunteers to talk about a time they were on or in such a high place that they seemed able to touch the sky.

Cooperative Reading

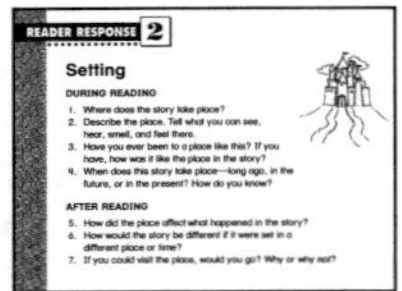
READER RESPONSE 2

Setting

Response Card 2

As children read in small groups, have them discuss how the setting has been important to the story so far. They may want to use the During Reading questions on **Reader Response Card 2** (Setting) for discussion starters.

Then the birds spread their wings. They flew through the air and circled the canyon.

"Oh, if only I could fly," said Coyote. "I would be the greatest coyote in all the world!"

304

AUTHOR'S CRAFT

Call attention to the way the author described the birds' flight: *They flew through the air and circled the canyon.* Point out how he illustrated the birds' circular flight.

SOCIAL STUDIES

FACT FINDER

ZUNI INDIANS "Coyote" is a tale from the Zuni tradition. The Zuni people are one of several tribes of Pueblo Indians. Many live in the Pueblo village of Zuni in northwestern New Mexico. Pueblo Indians are known for their multilevel apartment-type houses made from stone or adobe. *Pueblo* is a Spanish word that means *town*.

Coyote called to the crows.
"Let me join you," he said.

"This foolish coyote wants to be like us,"
Old Man Crow said to his flock.
"Let's have some fun with him."

305

MINILESSON

REVIEW: PHONICS AND DECODING

Initial Clusters: *spr, shr*

INFORMAL ASSESSMENT

As children read, notice whether they can decode words that begin with *spr* and *shr*.

TEACH/MODEL

Have children reread the first sentence on page 304. Ask what the birds did with their wings. *(spread)* Write *spread, spring,* and *spray* on the board, and ask children what they notice about the words. Circle the *spr* in each word. Follow a similar procedure with the words *shrug, shrink,* and *shrub*.

PRACTICE/APPLY

Display the following sentences, read them, and have volunteers identify the words with initial clusters.

The shrew ran under the shrub.

This spring I will spray water on the lawn.

I shrieked when I shrank my pants.

Stand on the springboard and spread your arms.

PHONICS ACTIVITY BOOK, page 36

PHONICS PRACTICE BOOK, pages 199–200

EXTRA SUPPORT **Have children reread the sentences on page 305. Then ask what Old Man Crow probably means when he says, "Let's have some fun with him." Point out that this might be an important clue to what will happen in the story. Invite volunteers to speculate how the crows feel about Coyote joining them.**

Name ____________ Coyote

SCIENCE

Complete each sentence with the word that makes sense and begins with *shr* or *spr*. Then answer the riddle at the bottom of the page.

1. I bring ___sprinkles___ of rain.
   showers spruce sprinkles
2. I also ___spray___ the earth with sunshine.
   paint spray shrill
3. Small green buds pop out on trees and ___shrubs___.
   shrubs bushes sprint
4. The grass begins to ___sprout___.
   shred grow sprout
5. I ___spread___ flowers everywhere.
   spread plant sprang
6. I come after the winter snows ___shrink___ and melt away.
   sprint sparkle shrink

What am I?
I am ___Spring___!

112 INITIAL CLUSTERS: spr, shr — OUT OF THE BLUE Practice Book

PRACTICE BOOK, page 112

Strategic Reading

APPLYING A STRATEGY

PAGES 306–309 Before children read, have them look at the pictures on pages 306–307 to confirm the predictions they made about what Coyote wants from the crows. Ask children how they think the crows feel about Coyote joining them. Then have children predict what will happen after Coyote gets his feathers and read on to confirm their predictions.

MAKING AND CONFIRMING PREDICTIONS

SCHOOL↔HOME CONNECTION

Suggest that children work with family members to compile examples of coyotes in cartoons on television and in newspapers and stories. Have children discuss their findings. They may wish to research whether the behavior of coyotes in stories is similar to that of real coyotes.

ILLUSTRATOR'S CRAFT

Old Man Crow's pendant was drawn to look like traditional Zuni jewelry. Point out the triangular shape which represents thunderclouds and the vertical lines which represent rain.

Old Man Crow plucked a feather from his left wing. He told his flock to do the same. They stuck the feathers in Coyote. Coyote winced. His nose twitched.

The crows chuckled.

"You are ready to fly," said Old Man Crow.

Student Self-Assessment 

FIX-UP STRATEGY: USING VOCABULARY JOURNALS

Have children write in a journal interesting words from the story. Tell them to write what they think the words mean and then check a dictionary to see if they are correct. Help children pronounce the words correctly. Then suggest that they use the words during the school day or at home and write in their journals how they used the words.

EXPANDING VOCABULARY

Have children reread page 307. Then call on volunteers to demonstrate a wince, a twitching nose, and a chuckle. Together, read the page again. Have everyone wince when *winced* is read, twitch when *twitched* is read, and chuckle when *chuckled* is read. Ask how those words help describe exactly what is happening in the story.

PHONICS IN ACTION

Have children locate the words *twitched* and *chuckled* on page 307. Write the words on the board, and remind them that both *tch* and *ch* can stand for the sound heard at the beginning of *chuckled*.

twitched

chuckled

Critical Thinking Questions

1. **How do you think Coyote feels about flying now?** (Possible response: I think he got scared when he fell to the ground. He wants to be the greatest coyote, though, so I think he'll try again.) **CRITICAL: UNDERSTANDING CHARACTERS' FEELINGS**
2. **What do you think the crows will do next?** (Responses will vary. Children should support their answers.) **CRITICAL: SPECULATING**

The birds began their slow, steady chant. They hopped from one foot to the other. Coyote joined in the dance. Even though he got out of step and sang out of tune, he was very proud of himself.

308

SCIENCE

BIRD'S SKELETON
A bird doesn't weigh much because many of its bones are hollow. Having a lightweight skeleton makes it easier for crows and other birds to take off from the ground and stay in the air. Birds also have very strong chest muscles that let them flap their wings quickly.

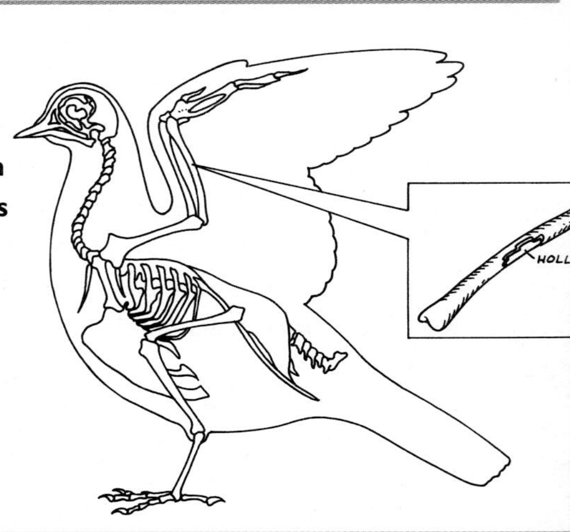

The crows spread their wings and soared into the sky. Coyote followed. His flight was jerky. He tilted to one side. Since his feathers were only from the left wing of each bird, he was off balance.

He fell to the ground. "Wait!" he cried out. "Don't leave me behind!"

309

Tested Skill

MINILESSON

REVIEW: PHONICS AND DECODING

R-controlled Vowel: /ôr/*or*, *ore, our, oor, oar*

INFORMAL ASSESSMENT

As children read, notice if they can decode words in which the /ôr/ sound is spelled with *or, ore, our, oor*, and *oar*.

TEACH/MODEL

Have children read the first sentence on page 309. Write *soared* on the board, and ask for words that have the same vowel sound as *soared.* *(board, born, roar, corn, pour, door, snore, bore,* and *sore)* Circle the letters that stand for the vowel sound in each word, and remind children that *or, ore, our, oor,* and *oar* can all stand for the /ôr/ sound

PRACTICE/APPLY

Ask the following Hink Pinks, explaining that each answer should have the same vowel sound as *soar.* Write the answers on the board. Have children circle the letters that stand for the vowel sound.

1. **What do you call an entry-way with an ache?** *(sore door)*
2. **What do you call a place that sells beds?** *(snore store)*
3. **What do you say when you want another glass of milk?** *(pour more)*

PHONICS PRACTICE BOOK, pages 147–148

CROSS-CULTURAL VIEWPOINT

Tricksters and trickery are common elements in folktales. The spider is often a trickster in African and Caribbean tales, and the coyote is a trickster in Mexican and Native American tales. Encourage children to share trickster tales from other cultures.

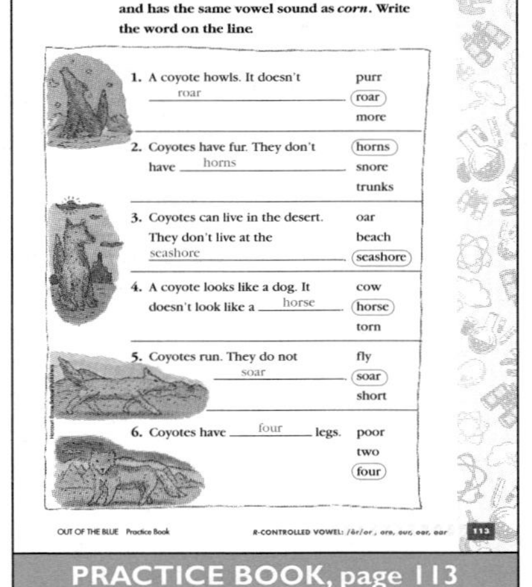
Coyote Name ______

Read these facts about coyotes. Then circle the word that makes sense in each sentence and has the same vowel sound as *corn*. Write the word on the line.

SCIENCE

1. A coyote howls. It doesn't roar. — purr / (roar) / more
2. Coyotes have fur. They don't have horns. — (horns) / snore / trunks
3. Coyotes can live in the desert. They don't live at the seashore. — oar / beach / (seashore)
4. A coyote looks like a dog. It doesn't look like a horse. — cow / (horse) / torn
5. Coyotes run. They do not soar. — fly / (soar) / short
6. Coyotes have four legs. — poor / two / (four)

OUT OF THE BLUE Practice Book R-CONTROLLED VOWEL: /ôr/or, ore, our, oor, oar 113

PRACTICE BOOK, page 113

Strategic Reading

MODELING A STRATEGY

PAGES 310–311 Have children find the word *cringed* on page 311. Suggest that they read the sentence and look at the picture to figure out what it means. If necessary, model your thinking: *Coyote cringed as feathers were stuck in his fur. I think that hurt. The picture shows him putting his arms up a little, making a face, and closing his eyes. I think that* cringed *must mean that he backed away from the feathers because he didn't like what was happening.*

RELATING PICTURES TO TEXT

The birds returned and gathered round Coyote. "We must balance him," said Old Man Crow.

310

PHONICS IN ACTION

Have children reread page 311, noticing the words *feather* and *each*. Point out that the letters *ea* can stand for short e as in *feather* or, more commonly, for long e as in *each*.

feather	each
weather	peach
bread	reach
thread	eat
spread	treat
read	read

MINILESSON

MAINTAIN: PHONICS AND DECODING

Long Vowel: /ī/ *i-e, igh*

INFORMAL ASSESSMENT
As children read, notice whether they have difficulty reading long *i* words that contain *i-e* and *igh*.

TEACH/MODEL
Have children read the first sentence on page 311. Write the word *right* on the board, and remind children that *igh* can stand for the long *i* sound. Write *like,* and remind children that *i-e* can also stand for the long *i* sound.

PRACTICE/APPLY
Write *right* on the board. Then call on volunteers to do the following:

Change *r* to *f*. Read the word. *(fight)*
Change *f* to *s*. Read the word. *(sight)*
Erase the *t*. Read the word. *(sigh)*
Change *gh* to *de*. Read the word. *(side)*
Change *s* to *r*. Read the word. *(ride)*
Add *p* before *r*. Read the word. *(pride)*
Change *d* to *c*. Read the word. *(price)*

PHONICS ACTIVITY BOOK, page 39

PHONICS PRACTICE READER 9

CONVENTIONS OF PRINT

ITALICS Ask children to find the word on page 311 that is in slanted type. Ask children why they think the author wanted to make the word *right* stand out. Point out that the author probably wanted readers to notice that this time, Old Man Crow was pulling a feather from his right wing, not his left wing as he had done before.

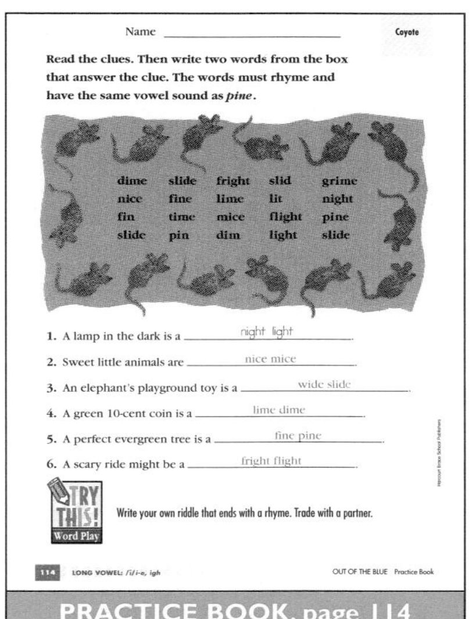
Name ______________ Coyote

Read the clues. Then write two words from the box that answer the clue. The words must rhyme and have the same vowel sound as *pine*.

dime	slide	fright	slid	grime
nice	fine	lime	lit	night
fin	time	mice	flight	pine
slide	pin	dim	light	slide

1. A lamp in the dark is a night light.
2. Sweet little animals are nice mice.
3. An elephant's playground toy is a wide slide.
4. A green 10-cent coin is a lime dime.
5. A perfect evergreen tree is a fine pine.
6. A scary ride might be a fright flight.

TRY THIS! Word Play — Write your own riddle that ends with a rhyme. Trade with a partner.

114 LONG VOWEL: /ī/ *i-e, igh* — OUT OF THE BLUE Practice Book

PRACTICE BOOK, page 114

Strategic Reading

APPLYING A STRATEGY

PAGES 312–315 Before children read, ask them to look at the pictures and talk about what is happening to Coyote. After children have read the pages, ask them what the pictures tell them about Coyote's feelings. RELATING PICTURES TO TEXT

WRITING

EXTEND THE STORY Have children look at the pictures on pages 312–313 and write in two thought balloons what Coyote might be thinking and what the crows might be thinking.

Coyote had become rude and boastful.
He danced out of step.
He sang off-key.
The crows were no longer having fun.

313

Informal Assessment

USING CUEING SYSTEMS

As children read or reread this story, observe how well they apply cueing systems to develop meaning. Ask yourself these questions:

- Do children make word substitutions that make sense?
- Do children use picture clues to figure out words?
- Do children read an entire sentence and think about what word might make sense in that context?

MEETING INDIVIDUAL NEEDS

STUDENTS ACQUIRING ENGLISH **Help children understand that to sing *out of tune* and to sing *off-key* have the same meaning. Music is written in a certain key, such as the key of G. Any notes that don't fit in that key—that is, sound "sour"—are *off-key*.**

Cooperative Reading

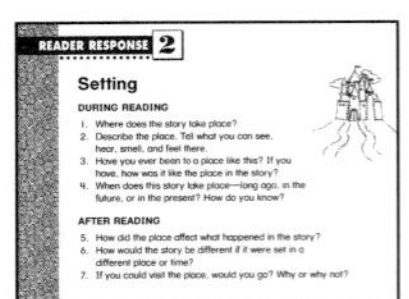
READER RESPONSE 2

Setting

DURING READING

1. Where does the story take place?
2. Describe the place. Tell what you can see, hear, smell, and feel there.
3. Have you ever been to a place like this? If you have, how was it like the place in the story?
4. When does this story take place—long ago, in the future, or in the present? How do you know?

AFTER READING

5. How did the place affect what happened in the story?
6. How would the story be different if it were set in a different place or time?
7. If you could visit the place, would you go? Why or why not?

Response Card 2

As children discuss the questions on **Reader Response Card 2** (Setting), ask how the setting makes them feel. The following are additional questions for them to consider:

1. **Why is it important that "Coyote" takes place in the hot desert, over a canyon?**
2. **How might this story be different if it took place in a forest?**

The birds again began their slow, steady chant.
Coyote hopped along, flapping his feathered legs and singing sour notes.
The dancers spread their wings and leapt into the air.

Soon the crows were flying high over the canyon.
Coyote struggled to keep up.

"Carry me!" he demanded.

314

PHONICS IN ACTION

Ask children to listen as you say the phrase *flying high*. Ask what sound they hear in both words. (long *i*) Point out that *y* and *igh* can both stand for the long *i* sound.

The crows circled Coyote but didn't carry him. Instead, they took back their feathers, one by one.

Coyote sank through the air.

He fell straight down.

315

NOTES

Here's a place to list ideas or activities that you would like to use the next time you teach this lesson.

Intervention Strategies

SUMMARIZING Have children repeat this sentence: ***When I read, it helps me to think about what's happened so far.*** Have children tell how using this strategy might help them understand what's happening in "Coyote."

Strategic Reading

APPLYING A STRATEGY

PAGES 316–318 Before children read, have them look at the pictures and tell how they think the story will end. After children have read the pages, ask them to summarize what happened after Coyote asked the crows to help him fly.
SUMMARIZING

"Wooooooooooo!" he howled.

Coyote fell so fast, his tail caught fire.
He fell into a pool on the mesa.

Coyote crawled out of the water.
He heard laughter and saw the crows flying away.

316

MULTICULTURAL CONNECTION

Tell children that in many stories Coyote is more than a trickster and a funny character. Although he often gets in trouble and disobeys the rules, he can be brave and helpful to other characters. In Pueblo stories, Coyote often teaches people about the world.

AUTHOR'S CRAFT

Have children reread the first sentence on page 316, and discuss the way that Coyote's howl is written. Ask children why they think the author wrote the word like this. Volunteers may want to imitate the sound.

Coyote ran after them.

He tripped and fell,
tumbling in the dirt.

317

SOCIAL STUDIES CONNECTION

LANDFORMS Have children look at the picture of the mesa on page 316 to determine that *mesa* means "a flat-topped hill with straight, steep sides." Tell children that canyons also have steep sides but are deep, long, and narrow because they were formed by rivers. Explain that mesas and canyons are found in the American Southwest, so they are often mentioned in stories set in the Southwest.

Returning to the Predictions/Purpose

Remind children that before they started reading, they wrote about what Coyote would do. Invite them to share their predictions and compare them with what actually happened.

Appreciating the Literature

With the whole class or a small group, have an open discussion about the story.

- **What did you think of Coyote at the beginning of the story?**
- **What did you think of him at the end?**

Coyote went home soaked and covered with dust.
To this day, he is the color of dust.
To this day, his tail has a burnt, black tip.

To this day, Coyote still follows his nose.
He has a nose for trouble.
He always finds it.

318

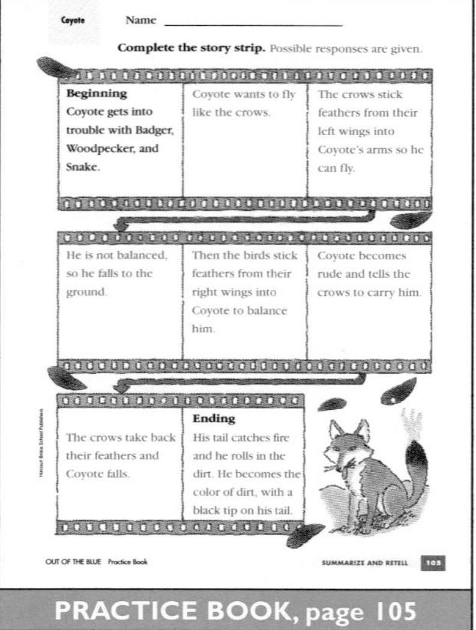
Coyote Name ____________

Complete the story strip. Possible responses are given.

Beginning Coyote gets into trouble with Badger, Woodpecker, and Snake.	Coyote wants to fly like the crows.	The crows stick feathers from their left wings into Coyote's arms so he can fly.
He is not balanced, so he falls to the ground.	Then the birds stick feathers from their right wings into Coyote to balance him.	Coyote becomes rude and tells the crows to carry him.
The crows take back their feathers and Coyote falls.	**Ending** His tail catches fire and he rolls in the dirt. He becomes the color of dirt, with a black tip on his tail.	

OUT OF THE BLUE Practice Book SUMMARIZE AND RETELL 105

PRACTICE BOOK, page 105

SUMMARIZE AND RETELL

Put It in Order

Work with children to complete a story organizer like the one shown. Then have children use the story organizer to retell the story of "Coyote." See *Practice Book* page 105.

1. Beginning	2.	3.
Coyote gets into trouble with Badger, Woodpecker, and Snake.	Coyote wants to fly like the crows.	The crows stick feathers from their left wings into Coyote so he can fly.
4. He is not balanced, so he falls to the ground.	**5.** Then the crows stick feathers from their right wings into Coyote to balance him.	**6.** Coyote becomes rude and tells the crows to carry him.
7. The crows take back their feathers, and Coyote falls.	**8. Ending** His tail catches fire, and he rolls in the dirt. He becomes the color of dirt and has a black tip on his tail.	

Gerald McDermott

I have liked folktales since I was a child, especially stories about journeys and heroes. I have spent a lot of time with Native Americans, and their folktales are among my favorites. There are many Native American tales about the trickster, Coyote. This story of Coyote comes from the Pueblo of Zuni. In the Zuni tradition, each of the world's directions has a certain color. The color of the West, where Coyote comes from, is blue. So I made Coyote blue.

Once I have chosen a tale I want to tell, I spend a lot of time talking through the story. I walk around my house saying it out loud over and over. Then, as I write the story, I see the pictures in my mind. I see a dreamscape that comes from my imagination.

319

About the Author/Illustrator

PAGE 319 Share with children the information on page 319. Discuss how and why Gerald McDermott created "Coyote."

Gerald McDermott was four when he took his first art class, part of a Saturday morning program at the Detroit Institute of Art. In the mornings, students would study art. In the afternoons, they were free to roam through the galleries. He says, "The freedom to wander through the halls of the museum, to be surrounded by beautiful art, had a profound effect on me. . . . By the time I was nine years old, I had decided that I was going to be an artist."

McDermott's artwork grows out of stories, often folklore or mythology. Before he begins his illustrations, he studies the art of the people from whom the story came. "Coyote" is a tale from the Pueblo of Zuni, so McDermott studied Pueblo art and culture. Pueblo colors and shapes can be seen in "Coyote."

After children have read about Gerald McDermott, they may enjoy viewing the videotape *Get to Know Gerald McDermott* (Harcourt Brace, 1996).

TWO OTHER BOOKS IN MCDERMOTT'S TRICKSTER SERIES

Raven: A Trickster Tale from the Pacific Northwest. **Harcourt Brace, 1993. AVERAGE**

Zomo the Rabbit: A Trickster Tale from West Africa. **Harcourt Brace, 1992. AVERAGE**

RESPONSE CORNER ACTIVITIES

MAKE A MASK

ZUNI HAND MASKS

PAGE 320 Talk about why making your handprint is like signing your name. Encourage children to add designs to their masks like the ones in the illustrations or from reference books that show Zuni designs or illustrations. Then encourage children to act out the story. **ART/READING**

MAKE A FACT SHEET

FACT AND FICTION

PAGE 321 Help children understand that in this activity they will combine an animal fact with a story idea about why it is so. Invite children to browse through books for animal facts to write about, such as why kangaroos have pouches or why zebras have stripes. In addition to the example on page 321, you might offer this:

Why Kangaroos Have Pouches

Kangaroos have pouches because one day long ago, a kangaroo wanted to move. She packed up her belongings, but she almost packed up her baby and put him in the moving van, too. Today kangaroos have pouches so that they'll always have a place to put their joeys as they move from place to place around Australia. **READING/WRITING**

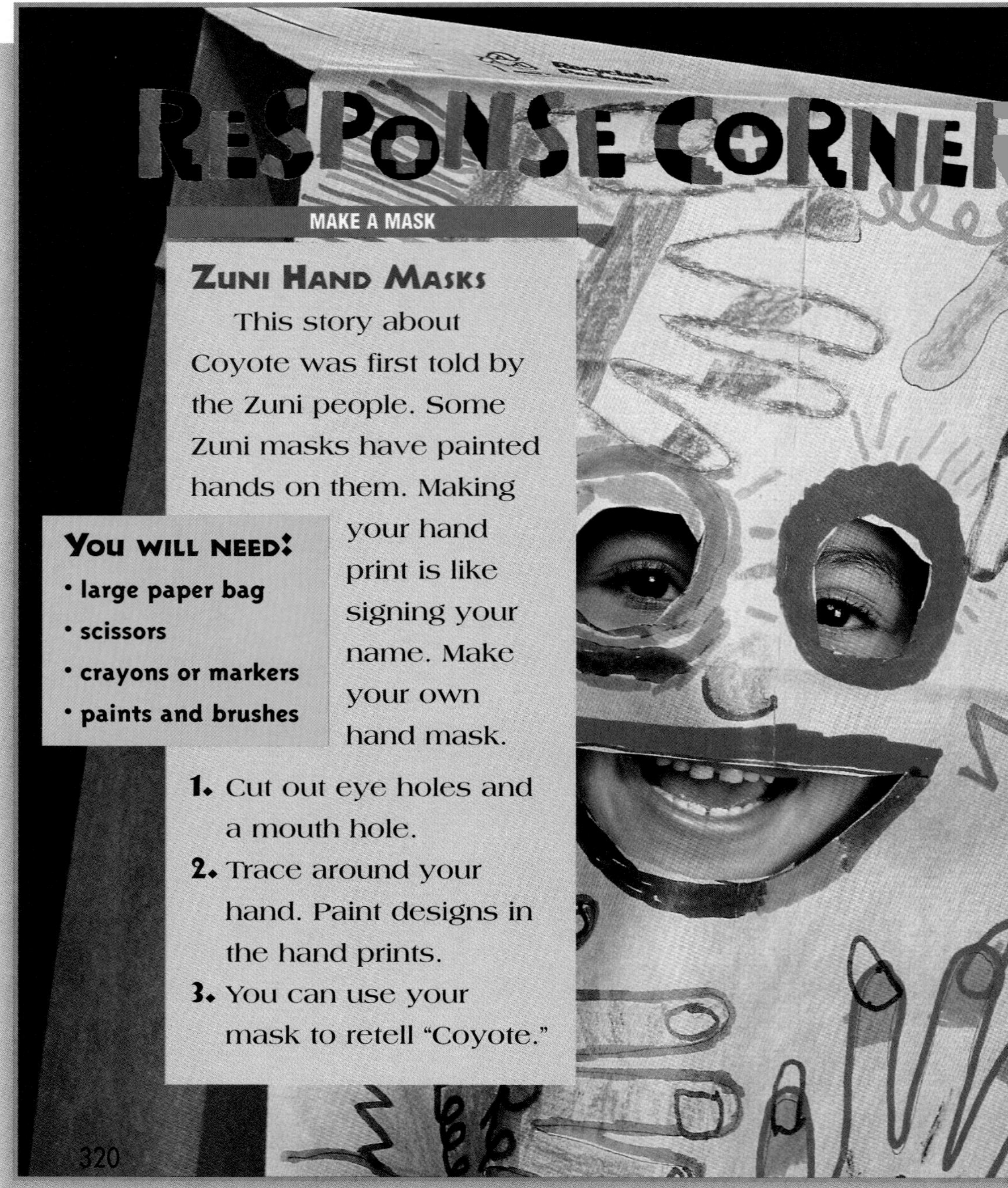

VARYING THE ACTIVITY

To extend the Fact and Fiction activity, you may want to have children use their ideas to write full-length stories similar to folktales that explain why something in nature is the way it is. Encourage children to publish and share their stories.

MAKE A FACT SHEET

Fact and Fiction

This story about Coyote tells why coyotes are the color of dust and why their tails have black tips. Think of why another animal looks or acts the way it does.

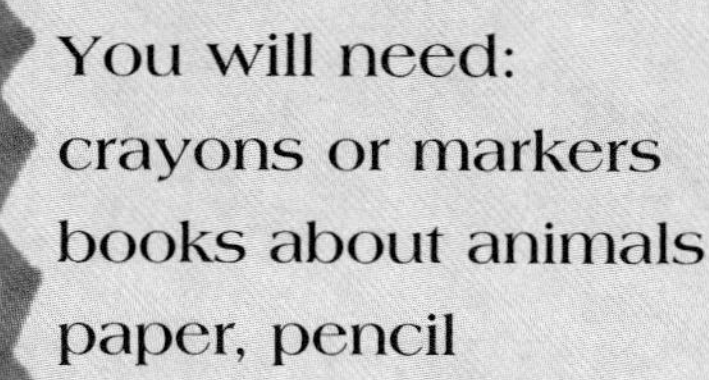

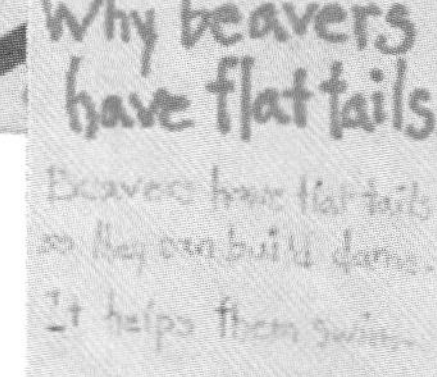

1. On one side of a sheet of paper, draw a picture of the animal.
2. On the other side, write one fact about the animal and your ideas about why it is so.
3. Put everyone's fact sheets together to make a class book.

What Do You Think?

- How did Coyote come to be the color of dust and have a black tip on his tail?
- Do you like Coyote? Tell why or why not.

321

CHECKING COMPREHENSION

What Do You Think?

1. **How did Coyote come to be the color of dust and have a black tip on his tail?** (Possible response: When the crows helped Coyote fly, he became rude, so they took away the feathers they had given him. He then fell so fast that his tail caught fire. That made the tip of his tail black. Then Coyote tripped in the dust, which made him a dusty gray color.) DESCRIPTIVE RESPONSE
2. **Do you like Coyote? Tell why or why not.** (Responses will vary.) PERSONAL RESPONSE

An additional question for extending reading.

- **Do you think Coyote tricked the crows, or do you think the crows tricked Coyote? Give reasons for your answer.** (Possible responses: I think the crows tricked Coyote because even though they let him fly, they later took away his feathers; I think Coyote tricked the crows, because they did teach him to fly, just as he wanted.) CRITICAL/CREATIVE ANALYSIS

PORTFOLIO OPPORTUNITY

Children may wish to add their fact sheets to their portfolios.

Informal Assessment

Observe children as they draw and write their fact sheets.

- ☑ Do children refer to books or other sources to get or check facts about animals?
- ☑ Do children include at least one fact about their animals?
- ☑ Do children write reasons why the animal is the way it is?

Intervention Strategies

Instant Readers™

Predictable and Patterned Little Books That Build Fluency

*** BOOK LEVEL: 20+**

VOCABULARY:
balance, feather, foolish, spread

PHONIC ELEMENTS:
Vowel variant: /o͞o/*oo*; Initial cluster: *spr*; R-controlled vowel: /ôr/*ore, our*; Long vowel: /ī/*igh*

PHONOGRAM:
-ook

SUMMARY:
In this adaptation of Aesop's fable, Crow's pride gets him in trouble.

Informal Assessment ✓

Are children able to

- ☑ identify words that begin with initial clusters?
- ☑ focus on story characters?

Reading a New Book

INTRODUCING *THE FOX AND THE CROW*

As illustrations are shared, have children describe what the crow and the fox are doing. Also discuss Fox's trickiness and Crow's pride in his appearance.

READING THE STORY

Have children read the story independently to find out if Fox gets the cheese he wants from Crow.

WORKING WITH WORDS AND LETTERS

Ask children to locate all the story words that contain the letters *oo,* and form them with individual letter cards, *Word Builder Cards,* or magnetic letters. Discuss the sounds that the letters *oo* stand for in each word. Then encourage children to explore with the words, substituting initial and final letters as shown below.

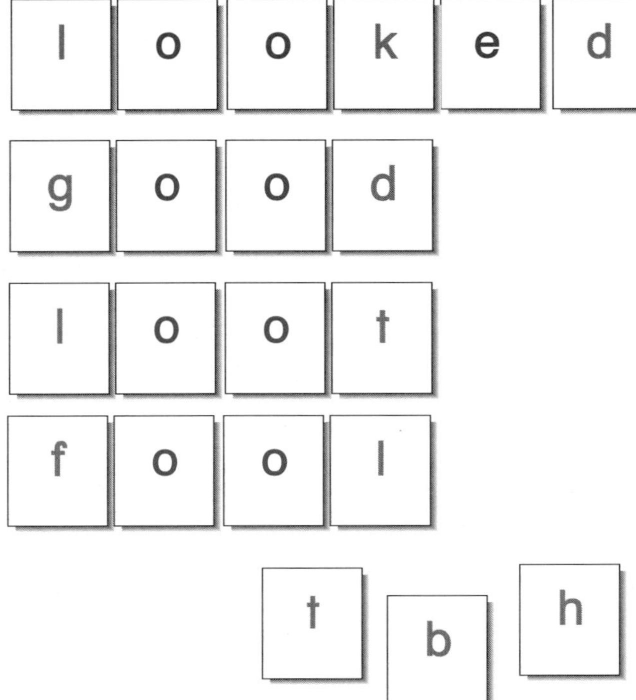

WRITING STORY INNOVATIONS

Have children work in a small group to write another story about two other animals. Encourage them to think and write about the characteristics usually associated with the animal.

Additional activities are provided on pages 64–65 of the *Intervention Strategies Manual*.

*** BOOK LEVEL: 19–20**

VOCABULARY:
feather, foot, spread

PHONIC ELEMENTS:
Vowel variant: /o͞o/oo; Initial cluster: *spr*; R-controlled vowel: /ôr/*or, ore*; Long vowel: /ī/*i-e, igh*

PHONOGRAM:
-ook

SUMMARY:
Here's what happens when two proud crows have an encounter.

Reading a New Book

INTRODUCING *WHITE CROW*

If children have ever seen a black crow, discuss the beautiful iridescent rainbow sheen on the crow's feathers. Explain that this story explains why the black crow's feathers look this way. As children look at the front and back covers, have them think about the title and the mirror-like images of the black and white crows.

READING THE STORY

After looking at and discussing the story pictures, have children read the story independently.

WORKING WITH WORDS AND LETTERS

As children reread the story, have them write the words that begin with two- or three-letter initial clusters. Have them read the list to a partner and discuss what happens when one of the letters in the initial cluster is removed.

WRITING DEFINITIONS

Children may feel differently about crows after reading this story. Suggest that they write a definition of *beautiful* in one or two sentences. Ask them how their definitions might differ from those of the two Crows.

ESL/Title I Reading

Rosie's Walk by Pat Hutchins

Working with "Coyote"

SEMANTIC CUES Find in a local library or video rental store a videotape of Warner Brothers' Coyote and Roadrunner animated short films. Show the videotape and discuss with children Coyote's trickiness and troublesome ideas. With children list some adjectives that describe Coyote. Have children find these adjectives (and more) in the story.

* Books leveled according to Barbara Peterson's "Profiles of Books for Beginning Readers," on page 9 of the *Instant Readers Teacher's Guide.*

IDEA BANK

TIPS FOR CLASSROOM MANAGEMENT

IF children need help thinking of alternative endings, THEN help children focus by asking them questions such as the following: ***What might the crows have done if Coyote had been polite and kind? What could a flying Coyote do that would be different?***

LISTENING AND SPEAKING

Group Talk

OTHER STORY ENDINGS

Have children talk about how the ending might have been different if Coyote had not become rude and boastful: Would he have become the best coyote in the world? Maybe the ending would have been different if he had been able to outsmart the crows and keep his wings. Organize children in groups of two or three and have each group suggest another ending for the story.

After small-group discussions, gather children to share their story endings.
CHALLENGING THE TEXT

REAL-LIFE READING

Reading Song Lyrics

Remind children that Coyote tried singing like the crows but was off-key. Maybe he was making up the words to the song, too. Ask children what might have helped Coyote sing better. Display a sheet of music (or a page from a book of songs) for a familiar song on an overhead projector. Explain that the lines of music show the sounds a singer's voice should make. Underneath the musical notes are the words to the song. Point out that sometimes the words are broken up to fit the music.

Ask volunteers to read the words of the song aloud. Then encourage the group to sing the song. **READING**

What did you find out from reading the catalog page?

Real-Life Skills FACT CARD

How can you tell a real coyote? Would it be blue with feathers? One way to find out is to look at facts and pictures about coyotes. What do you learn from this fact card?

COYOTE CROSSING

COYOTE

COYOTE

HOW TALL:
about 2 feet (to the top of the head)
HOW LONG:
about 3 to 4 feet long
WEIGHT:
25 to 40 pounds
COLOR:
light yellow, gray, or brown
SOUNDS IT MAKES:
howl, growl, whine, woof, yelp, bark
WHAT IT EATS:
small animals, insects, berries, beans
NUMBER OF BABIES:
6 to 10 pups

40 Coyote • Writer's Magazine

WRITER'S MAGAZINE, pages 40–43

ORAL LANGUAGE

Telling a Story

OUR STORIES

Have children create a story to tell. They may wish to use the characters from "Coyote" and put them in a different situation, make up another trickster tale with different animals, or use a similar plot with different animals.

With children, make a list of storytelling tips similar to the following:

TIPS FOR STORYTELLING

1. Say the words clearly.
2. Speak loudly. Pretend you are talking to the person in the back of the room.
3. Look at your audience.
4. Think about how your voice should sound: loud or soft, excited or scary.

Have children practice, and then allow time for volunteers to tell their stories to the class. LISTENING/SPEAKING/WRITING

Informal Assessment

Note how children use their imaginations and their knowledge of story structures to create and tell their own stories.

KINESTHETIC

Creative Connection

DANCING

Remind children that in the story the crows danced in a line, hopping from one foot to the other. Have children work in groups to make up dances. Suggest that they use their bodies as instruments to provide the rhythm for their dances. They might hum, sing, clap their hands, stamp their feet, snap their fingers, or slap their thighs. Allow time for groups to practice and to present their dances. KINESTHETIC

PERSONAL JOURNAL

REFLECTING ON THE STORY After children read and discuss how Coyote's boastfulness turns the crows against him, have them write in their personal journals about what it means to be boastful.

WRITER'S WORKSHOP

A Story

TIPS FOR CLASSROOM MANAGEMENT

IF children are familiar with the writing process approach, **THEN** present the writing assignment and have them use the Story model on pages 8–9 of the *Language Handbook.*

IF at this time you want a short writing activity, **THEN** have children do the prewriting activity and refer to their story maps to present an oral telling of a story.

TECHNOLOGY

THE AMAZING WRITING MACHINE Primary Level Activity Disk Pack Grade 2
Have children enter their stories in the Stories mode.

KID PIX
Children can illustrate their stories by creating pictures of their own or using the stamps.

ASSESSMENT WORKSHOP *Scoring Student Writing, Primary Level*

Thinking as Writers

WRITING FORM: Story Remind children that "Anansi and the Talking Melon," "Nine-in-One, Grr! Grr!," and "Coyote" are stories about tricks. Invite children to discuss tricks they have heard or read about. Then explain to children that they will work with a partner to write a story about a trickster.

Display Chart/Transparency 6, or write the model Story on the board. Ask children to tell what they remember about the beginning, middle, and ending of a story.

CHART/TRANSPARENCY 6

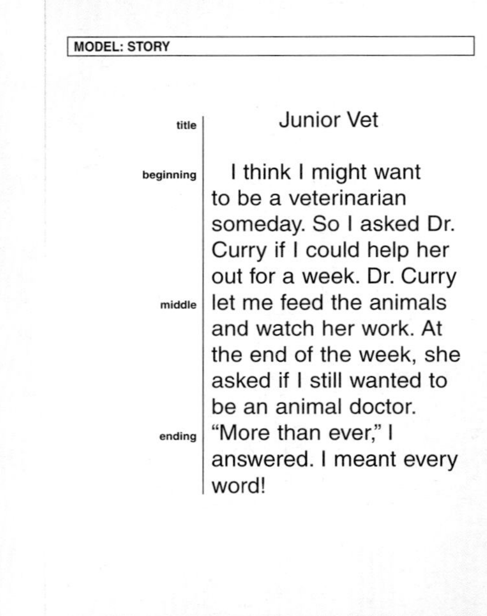

MODEL: STORY

title — Junior Vet

beginning — I think I might want to be a veterinarian someday. So I asked Dr. Curry if I could help her out for a week. Dr. Curry

middle — let me feed the animals and watch her work. At the end of the week, she asked if I still wanted to be an animal doctor.

ending — "More than ever," I answered. I meant every word!

WRITER'S CRAFT: Writing a Good Ending Explain that when a writer plans a story, he or she decides what will happen at the beginning, middle, and ending. A good ending can be a surprise or it can "wrap things up." Discuss how the events in "Coyote" lead up to the ending. Then ask children to discuss other possible good endings for "Coyote."

PREWRITING

Explain that many trickster tales have animal characters. Have partners choose who will be their trickster—one that they have read about or one they make up. Have children decide what the story will be about. It can be like a trickster tale that they have read or something new. Provide children with copies of a story map. Suggest that they may want to work backward—deciding on a good ending first and then planning the events that could lead to that ending. Their completed maps may look like the following:

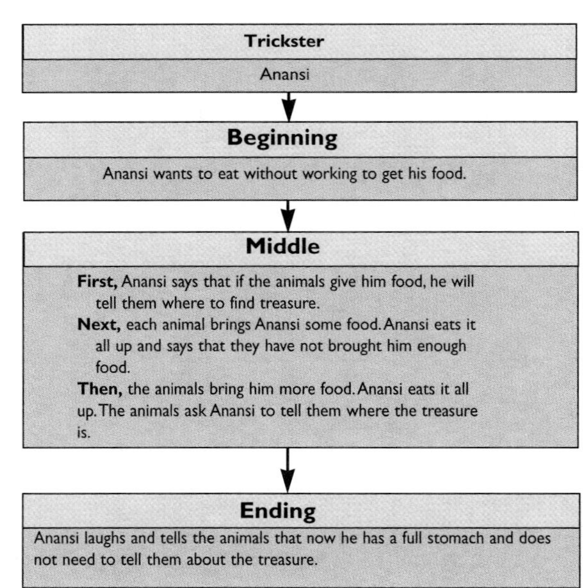

DRAFTING

As partners write their stories, remind them to

- use their story maps and the trickster tales they've read for ideas.
- tell what happens when their character plays a trick.
- tell what happens in the beginning, the middle, and the ending.
- write an interesting ending.

Have children save their drafts and revisions in their writer's folder.

RESPONDING AND REVISING

Work with two pairs of children. Have one pair read aloud their story, and have children discuss ways to make the story better. Offer these guidelines to help the group discuss each story:

- Does each event in the story follow another in a way that makes sense?
- Was the ending interesting or surprising?
- Was the trickster tricky?

PROOFREADING

As children proofread their stories, help them focus on the following:

NAMES OF SPECIAL PEOPLE, ANIMALS, AND PLACES Names of special people, animals, and places begin with a capital letter.

PLURAL NOUNS WITH -*S* AND -*ES* Some nouns end with *-s* or *-es* to name more than one. (See the Grammar Minilesson on page T601.)

PUBLISHING

Have children make a clean copy of their stories. Then offer publishing options like the following:

Handwriting
Remind children that their handwriting must be neat and clear so that the person reading the story can understand it. If children need assistance, refer them to the Handwriting models in the *Language Handbook* or in the classroom.

STORY SCREENS
Help children fold a piece of poster board into three equal parts to form a screen. They can write the beginning, middle, and ending of their story on the parts and draw pictures to go with each part. Invite them to stand the story on a table for others to read.

TELL TRICKY TALES Have children read their stories to younger children during story time. Offer these suggestions:

- Practice reading your story aloud.
- Draw pictures to go with your story. Hold them up so your audience can see them.
- Use your voice in different ways for different characters.

PORTFOLIO OPPORTUNITY
After children publish, make copies of their stories and have them attach their Writing Self-Assessment Checklists to them. Have them place the stories and checklists in their portfolios.

LANGUAGE HANDBOOK
Story, pages 8–9

Student Self-Assessment

Children can use the Writing Self-Assessment Checklist in the *Portfolio Assessment Teacher's Guide*.

EVALUATING THE WRITTEN RESPONSE

When evaluating children's stories, consider:

CONTENT	ORGANIZATION	STYLE
Does the story tell about a trick someone played?	Do the story events follow a logical sequence?	Are plural nouns used and spelled correctly?

EVALUATION BENCHMARKS

The child does not place story events in logical order. There is no clear ending.	= EMERGENT
The child places events in the correct order, but the ending leaves questions in the reader's mind.	= BEGINNING
The child successfully puts story events in the correct order. There is a good ending that tells what finally happened.	= PROFICIENT

Tested Skill

GRAMMAR

Irregular Plurals

LANGUAGE HANDBOOK
Other Plural Nouns, pages 72–73

DAILY LANGUAGE PRACTICE **Oral language exercises are provided on page R144.**

Reading ↔ Writing Connection

Connect to the literature. Remind children that when Coyote saw the crows, they were dancing and chanting. Have children talk about what the crows might have been doing in their dance. Record the ideas, such as *hopped from one foot to the other, flapped their wings*, and *bobbed their heads*.

Build oral language. Then make a list of singular nouns, and ask children to tell what the plural form is. For example:

foot	(feet)
wing	(wings)
head	(heads)

Explain that to make most nouns name more than one, *-s* or *-es* is added. Ask children what they notice about the words *foot* and *feet*. Then encourage children to say sentences, using the words from the list.

Teach/Model

Discuss irregular plural nouns. Explain that the spelling of some nouns, like *foot*, change when they name more than one. Write the following pairs of sentences on the board:

1. The man ate lunch.
   The men ate lunch.
2. Many children played a game.
   The child had fun.

Have a volunteer read each pair of sentences and identify the sentence that contains a noun that names more than one. List the words below. Help children supply the plural forms:

man	(men)
child	(children)
woman	(women)
tooth	(teeth)
foot	(feet)
mouse	(mice)
goose	(geese)

Practice/Apply

Check understanding. Display the following sentences:

The <u>man</u> stood on the hill.
The <u>woman</u> sat on the rocks.
The coyote ate with his sharp <u>tooth</u>.
The <u>child</u> saw the coyote.
Its <u>foot</u> didn't make a sound.

Have children read each sentence aloud. Ask them to identify the underlined word and to tell the plural form of that word. Call on volunteers to replace the underlined word in each sentence with the plural noun.

Practice Activities

SENTENCE SWITCH

WRITING APPLICATION Make the following sentence strips, omitting the answers and leaving enough room so the plural noun can be written above the underlined word. Give every child one sentence.

In the morning, I brush my <u>tooth</u>. *(teeth)*

The <u>man</u> went to work. *(men)*

The <u>woman</u> called a meeting. *(women)*

The <u>child</u> sang a song. *(children)*

They clapped their hands and stamped their <u>foot</u>. *(feet)*

Tell each child to read his or her sentence and then reread it, changing the underlined noun to name more than one. Then have children exchange sentence strips and read their new sentences. VISUAL

I Went Walking

ORAL APPLICATION Have children work in small groups to write *man, woman, child, tooth,* and *foot* on cards. The leader in the group holds up a card, such as *tooth*, while a player says a sentence with the plural form of the word, such as *I went walking, and I saw a tiger with large teeth.* Then the leader holds up a card for the next player. VISUAL/AUDITORY

Plural Book

WRITING APPLICATION Give each child several sheets of paper. On each sheet, have them illustrate one or more items listed below. Then have them write one sentence to describe each picture, being sure to use the correct form of the noun.

foot	feet
man	woman
tooth	teeth
child	children

Staple the finished pages together. VISUAL

APPLY TO WRITING

Have children look for plural nouns in their stories or other writing to see if they are spelled correctly.

USAGE TIP Have children think about words that mean more than one: *Do I add* s *or* es *to that noun, or do I change its spelling?*

MEETING INDIVIDUAL NEEDS

STUDENTS ACQUIRING ENGLISH

Display a variety of pictures. Work with children by discussing the singular and plural forms of each picture name.

RETEACH

See page R134 for lessons in multiple modalities.

GRAMMAR PRACTICE BOOK
pages 49-50

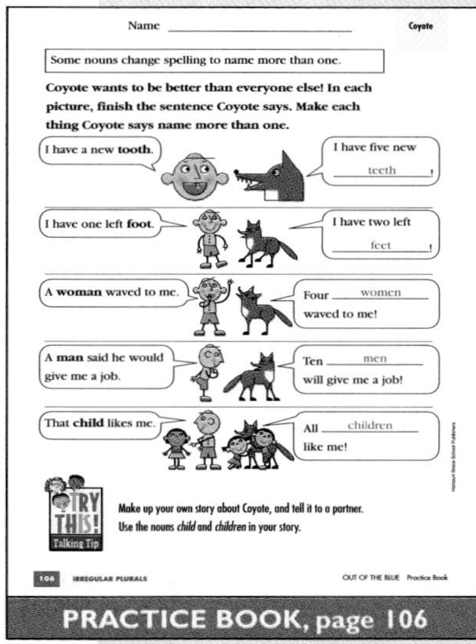

Name ______________ Coyote

Some nouns change spelling to name more than one.

Coyote wants to be better than everyone else! In each picture, finish the sentence Coyote says. Make each thing Coyote says name more than one.

I have a new **tooth**. — I have five new teeth!

I have one left **foot**. — I have two left feet!

A **woman** waved to me. — Four women waved to me!

A **man** said he would give me a job. — Ten men will give me a job!

That **child** likes me. — All children like me!

TRY THIS! Talking Tip — Make up your own story about Coyote, and tell it to a partner. Use the nouns *child* and *children* in your story.

106 IRREGULAR PLURALS — OUT OF THE BLUE Practice Book

PRACTICE BOOK, page 106

5-DAY PLAN

Use in conjunction with Daily Language Practice.

Day 1 Complete page T626.	**Day 4** Choose a Practice Activity or *Grammar Practice Book* pages 49–50.
Day 2 Complete a Practice Activity on page T627.	**Day 5** Complete *Practice Book* page 106.
Day 3 Choose a Practice Activity or *Language Handbook* pages 72–73.	

SPELLING

5-Day Plan

Integrated Spelling Lesson 15:
student book, pages 66–69;
Teacher's Edition, pages T105–T110.

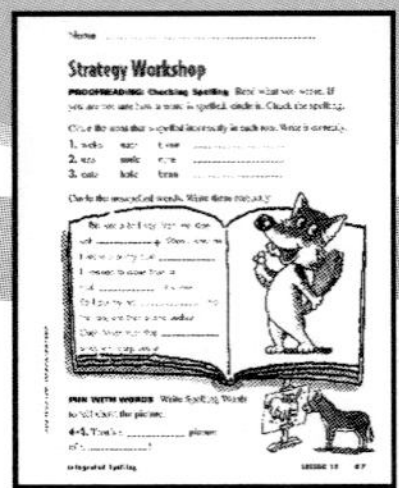

Words with *o-e* and *u-e*

SPELLING WORDS

1. use
2. nose ★
3. hole ★
4. tune ★
5. note ★
6. bone
7. those
8. cute
9. woke
10. mule

STUDENT'S PERSONAL WORDS

11. 13.
12. 14.

Additional story words are *home* and *rude*.

★ Words appearing in "Coyote"

Pretest

DAY 1 **Administer the pretest.** Say each word and then use it in the dictation sentence provided below. Have pairs of children check their own pretests by referring to the word list.

OPEN SORT

DAY 2 **Have children create categories.** Have children select their own categories for sorting the Spelling Words. Suggest that they sort according to vowel sound or use some other method, such as meaning, nouns, words that describe, or action words. Have volunteers share their methods.

CLOSED SORT

Sort by spelling pattern. Write on the board the headings from the chart below. Call on volunteers to write each Spelling Word under the appropriate heading.

Home	Huge
nose	use
hole	tune
note	cute
bone	mule
those	
woke	

Teach/Model

DAY 3 **Discuss the generalization.** Write the words *note* and *woke* on the board. Ask what vowel sound is the same in both. (the vowel sound /ō/) Have a volunteer circle the *o* and the final *e* in each word. Point out the vowel-consonant-*e* pattern. Then repeat this with the words *cute* and *mule*. Help children form generalizations about how *o-e* and *u-e* words are spelled—for example:

- **A vowel followed by a consonant and a silent *e* can have a long vowel sound.**

DAY 4 **Apply to writing.** Children should look in their stories for words with *o-e* and *u-e* to see if they are spelled correctly.

Posttest

DAY 5 **Assess children's progress.** The sentences below should be used as the posttest.

DICTATION SENTENCES

1. What should I use to hit the nail?
2. The bear stuck its nose in a honey pot.
3. The rabbit hid in its hole.
4. We like to sing a tune.
5. Please sing the right note.
6. The dog chews on a bone.
7. Where did you get all those crayons?
8. That is a cute bunny.
9. I woke up when my alarm went off.
10. I rode on a mule.

Coyote Name ______________

A. Write a Spelling Word to match each picture.

nose hole bone note mule

1. bone
2. mule
3. hole
4. note
5. nose

B. The Spelling Words on the cactus plants are mixed up. Write each word correctly.

netu kewo shote uect esu

6. tune 7. woke 8. those 9. cute 10. use

OUT OF THE BLUE Practice Book — WORDS LIKE *note* AND *cute* 107

PRACTICE BOOK, page 107

VOCABULARY WORKSHOP

Reviewing Key Words

To review how the vocabulary was used in "Coyote," distribute copies of page R178 to children. Then write the Key Words on the board.

Read the sentences aloud to children. Have them choose, as a group activity, the word that best completes each sentence. Then have them read the sentence aloud and write the word.

Each crow stuck a feather in Coyote.

They began to dance, first on one foot, then on the other.

The crows spread their wings and flew.

Coyote flew, too, but he lost his balance.

Did the foolish Coyote learn to fly?

Then have children cut apart the sentence strips. Children can use the strips to retell the story or glue the strips to sheets of paper and illustrate them to create their own versions of "Coyote."

Extending Vocabulary

SYNONYMS

Write these story sentences on the board:

(page 313) ***He sang off-key.***

(page 314) ***Coyote hopped along, flapping his feathered legs and singing sour notes.***

Have children read the sentences and identify the words that tell about Coyote's singing and mean almost the same thing. *(off-key, sour notes)* Explain that words that have almost the same meaning are called **synonyms.**

Display the following words, and have partners look through the story to find another word that has almost the same meaning. You may wish to give the page references as clues.

flew (page 309, *soared*)
winced (page 311, *cringed*)
laughed (page 307, *chuckled*; page 311, *cackled*)
started (page 308, *began*)
fell (page 315, *sank*)
rolling (page 317, *tumbling*)

Discuss why authors might use synonyms in their stories. Then tell children that they can use synonyms to make their own writing interesting.

TAKE-HOME/ KEEP-AT-HOME BOOK

Leo's Trip to the City

Distribute the pages, and have children make their own TAKE-HOME/ KEEP-AT-HOME BOOKS, which reinforce Key Words and known vocabulary. Have children read to partners and then take the book home to read.

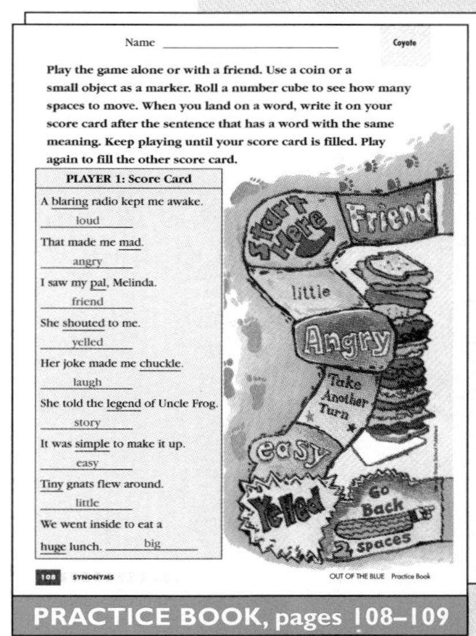
Name ____ Coyote

Play the game alone or with a friend. Use a coin or a small object as a marker. Roll a number cube to see how many spaces to move. When you land on a word, write it on your score card after the sentence that has a word with the same meaning. Keep playing until your score card is filled. Play again to fill the other score card.

PLAYER 1: Score Card

A blaring radio kept me awake. loud
That made me mad. angry
I saw my pal, Melinda. friend
She shouted to me. yelled
Her joke made me chuckle. laugh
She told the legend of Uncle Frog. story
It was simple to make it up. easy
Tiny gnats flew around. little
We went inside to eat a huge lunch. big

108 SYNONYMS OUT OF THE BLUE Practice Book

PRACTICE BOOK, pages 108–109

INTRODUCE: PHONICS AND DECODING

Vowel Variant: /o͝o/*oo, ou*

OBJECTIVE: To understand the relationship between letters and sounds

Informal Assessment

Are children able to

- ☑ make and read words that contain a specific phonogram?
- ☑ group /o͝o/ words by spelling pattern?
- ☑ write sentences, using /o͝o/ words?

TECHNOLOGY

***Bailey's Book* House (Read-A-Rhyme)**

Teach/Model

Connect to the story. Display this sentence:

Coyote took a look at the woodpecker's foot.

Ask children what they notice about this sentence. If necessary, circle the words *took, look, woodpecker*, and *foot*, and talk about how the words are alike. Then display:

If I could fly, I would be the best coyote in the world.

Circle *could* and *would,* and talk about how they are alike. Tell children that they will learn more about the sound that is alike in these words.

Phonemic awareness: Listen to the sound. Display page 19 in the *Big Book of Rhymes*. Have children listen for words with the same sound they hear in *took, foot*, and *could* as you read the rhyme aloud. Then reread the rhyme. Encourage children to join in, especially for words with the /o͝o/ sound.

Big Book of Rhymes, page 19

Find and read words with /o͝o/. In the rhyme, have children read and frame words with the same vowel sound as *book*. As children frame the words, write them on the board in appropriate columns.

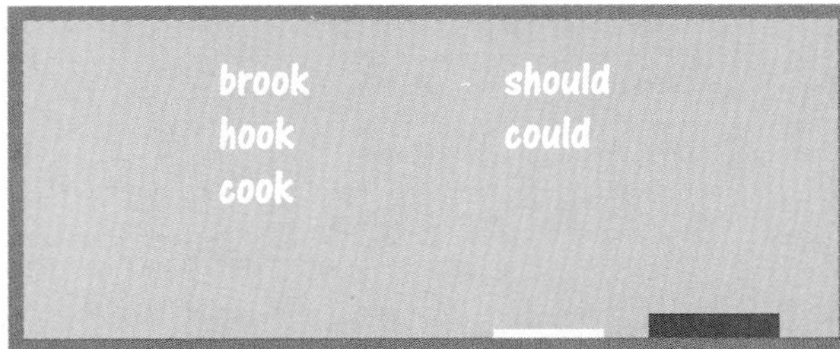

Point to the words under *brook*. Ask how the words are alike. (All have the /o͝o/ sound; they rhyme.) Follow a similar procedure with *should* and *could*. (All have the /o͝o/ sound; they rhyme.) Have volunteers circle the letters *oo* and *ou* in the words. Point out that the letters *oo* and *ou* stand for the vowel sound heard in *brook* and *should*.

Practice/Apply

Read words in context. Write the following words on the board:

could	**look**	**stood**
should	**book**	**wood**
would	**took**	

Have each child choose five words and write a sentence, using each word. Then have children exchange sentences with a partner and read their partner's sentences aloud.

Practice Activities

WORD BUILDING

PHONOGRAM/BLENDING GAME Have small groups use individual letter cards or *Word Builder Cards*, phonogram card *-ook*, and Word Builders to play a game. Have each player display the phonogram *-ook*. Players use their cards to see how many words they can make by combining them with *-ook*. Ask players to write down all the words they make. Score one point for each new word. VISUAL/AUDITORY/KINESTHETIC

Sound Pairs

Make a set of cards for words with the /o͝o/ sound. Have children play in small groups. Give each child five cards, and place the remaining cards face down in a pile. The first player lays down a card. The next player reads the word and lays down a card with the matching spelling for /o͝o/. If a player is unable to lay down a card, he or she picks up a card from the pile. The winner is the first one to lay down all his or her cards. VISUAL/AUDITORY

Sorting /o͝o/ Words

PERFORMANCE ASSESSMENT Have children work in groups of two or three, and assign each group a phonogram, such as *-ook, -ood*, or *-ould*. Tell each group to list as many words as they can that contain their phonogram and then use some of the words in a story about Coyote. Compile the stories into a class book. VISUAL/AUDITORY

Reading Trade Books FOR /o͝o/ oo, ou

Who Took the Farmer's Hat?
by Joan L. Nödset.
HarperCollins, 1963.
EASY

Green Eggs and Ham
by Dr. Seuss.
Random House, 1960.
AVERAGE

PHONICS PRACTICE READER 21

MEETING INDIVIDUAL NEEDS

STUDENTS ACQUIRING ENGLISH

Display the following sentences, along with a book, a safe hook, and a piece of wood.

I read a book.
I took the hook.
Could I touch wood?

Read each sentence aloud, and have children identify the /o͝o/ words. Have volunteers act out the sentences, using the real objects.

RETEACH

See page R135 for lessons in multiple modalities.

CHALLENGE

Have children write tongue twisters, using /o͝o/ words.

PHONICS ACTIVITY BOOK, page 35

PHONICS PRACTICE BOOK, pages 155–156

Name ______________ Coyote

Read the story. Finish each sentence with the word that makes sense in the sentence and has the same vowel sound as *book*.

Coyote told his friends he ___would___ bake something.
might stood would

"I'll ___look___ in my
peek look wood

___cook___ book," he said.
cook car hood

"I know, I'll make a fish pie. Yum yum."

So Coyote went to the ___brook___.
lake brook cookie

He caught four big fish on his ___hook___.
line book hook

He ___took___ the fish home,
could ran took

but he just ___couldn't___ wait.
couldn't didn't looked

"That fish pie ___would___
may stood would

have been ___good___," he said.
tasty wood good

"I am a wonderful ___cook___!"
cook baker took

110 VOWEL VARIANT: /o͝o/oo, ou OUT OF THE BLUE Practice Book

PRACTICE BOOK, page 110

INTRODUCE: STUDY SKILLS

Library Skills

OBJECTIVE: To understand how to find a book in the library

Informal Assessment ✓

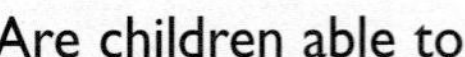

Are children able to

- ☑ tell the difference between fiction and nonfiction?
- ☑ decide whether they should look in the fiction or nonfiction section of the library for a specific title?
- ☑ understand that fiction books are put in alphabetical order by the author's last name?

Teach/Model

Explain fiction and nonfiction. Explain that the library has two kinds of books—fiction and nonfiction. **Fiction** books are stories made up by the authors, even though some stories seem very real. **Nonfiction** books give information about real people, places, animals, and things.

Explain how to find books. Explain that fiction books are kept in one section of the library and nonfiction books are kept in another section. Tell children that the library has a card catalog or a computer that will help them find the books they want to see. Suggest that if they want to know whether the library has the book *Coyote*, they should look under the letter *C* for *Coyote* or under the first letter of the author's last name, *M* for *McDermott*. The book can be found in the fiction section with books written by other authors whose last names begin with *M*. Invite children to tell about how they find books in the library.

Practice/Apply

Check children's understanding. Ask children to tell whether the following books can be found in the fiction or the nonfiction section of the library:

- a tale about a spider who tricks an elephant (fiction)
- a book about the Zuni Indians (nonfiction)
- a book about how to build an airplane (nonfiction)
- a book about a wolf and about three little pigs who build houses (fiction)

Then write the following titles and authors on the board. Ask children what to look for in the card catalog or computer to find each book.

Anansi and the Talking Melon by Eric A. Kimmel

Matthew and Tilly by Rebecca C. Jones

Practice Activities

Book Tracker

Tell children that their job is to track down "wild" books. Write titles such as the following, without the answers, on cards or paper decorated with paw prints:

Borreguita and the Coyote by Verna Aardema (B,A, fiction)

The Three Little Wolves and the Big Bad Pig by Eugene Trivizas (T,T, fiction)

Guinea Pigs by Mark Evans (G,E, nonfiction)

The Iguana Brothers by Tony Johnston (I, J, fiction)

How to Draw Wild Animals by Anne Simpson (H, S, nonfiction)

Distribute the cards. Have children tell the letter of the title and author's name they could use to help track down their book. Also have them tell whether they think the book is fiction or nonfiction. You may wish to have children find their books in the library. VISUAL

LIBRARY SCAVENGER HUNT

PERFORMANCE ASSESSMENT Arrange a time for children to visit the library. Prepare for the visit by writing book titles or descriptions of books on slips of paper. Make one or two slips for each child, fold the slips, and place them in a bag. At the library, have children draw a slip from the bag and locate an appropriate book. Observe children as they search for the books, and evaluate their library skills. VISUAL/KINESTHETIC

Find another book by Gerald McDermott.

Find another book about a coyote.

Find Coyote Steals the Blanket by Janet Stevens.

STUDENTS ACQUIRING ENGLISH

Some children will benefit from seeing actual books and studying the illustrations to determine whether the book is fiction or nonfiction, instead of classifying a book by its title alone.

RETEACH

See page R136 for lessons in multiple modalities.

CHALLENGE

Have children organize a personal or classroom library selection of books related to a specific theme, such as pets. They should determine which books are fiction and which are nonfiction and how the books should be arranged in the library.

Reading Trade Books FOR LIBRARY SKILLS

Check It Out!: The Book About Libraries **by Gail Gibbons. Harcourt Brace, 1988.** AVERAGE

I Took My Frog to the Library **by Eric A. Kimmel. Viking, 1990.** EASY

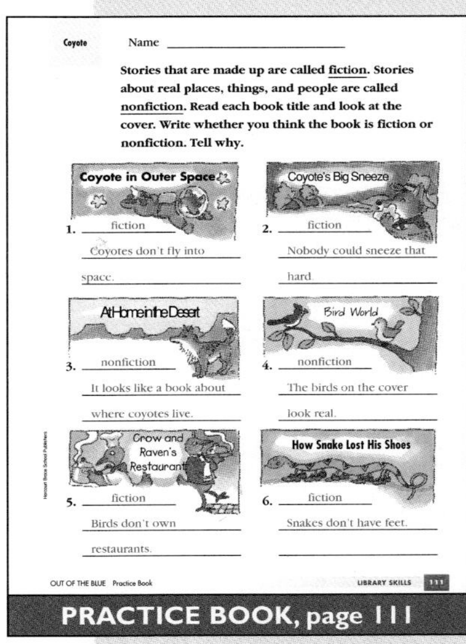

Coyote Name ____________

Stories that are made up are called fiction. Stories about real places, things, and people are called nonfiction. Read each book title and look at the cover. Write whether you think the book is fiction or nonfiction. Tell why.

1. Coyote in Outer Space — fiction — Coyotes don't fly into space.
2. Coyote's Big Sneeze — fiction — Nobody could sneeze that hard.
3. At Home in the Desert — nonfiction — It looks like a book about where coyotes live.
4. Bird World — nonfiction — The birds on the cover look real.
5. Crow and Raven's Restaurant — fiction — Birds don't own restaurants.
6. How Snake Lost His Shoes — fiction — Snakes don't have feet.

OUT OF THE BLUE Practice Book LIBRARY SKILLS 111

PRACTICE BOOK, page 111

Integrated Curriculum

SOCIAL STUDIES

The Southwest

TIPS FOR CLASSROOM MANAGEMENT

IF children are having difficulty thinking of a topic to research, **THEN** brainstorm a list of questions and topics as a group, and have children choose from the list.

SOCIAL STUDIES

Who Are the Zuni?

MATERIALS
- books on Native Americans from the Southwest

COOPERATIVE LEARNING
Tell children that "Coyote" is from the Zuni tradition. Explain that the Zuni Indians live in the Southwest. Have children work in groups of two or three to research the Zunis or another group of Native Americans from the Southwest. Suggest that they focus their attention on one aspect of the culture, such as traditional homes, clothes, or art. Some children might be interested in showing on a map where the Native American groups being researched live.

Then have children present their information in oral reports.
LISTENING/SPEAKING/READING/WRITING

SCIENCE

Who Lives in the Desert?

MATERIALS
- books about the desert
- butcher paper or mural paper
- paints or markers
- construction paper
- scissors
- glue

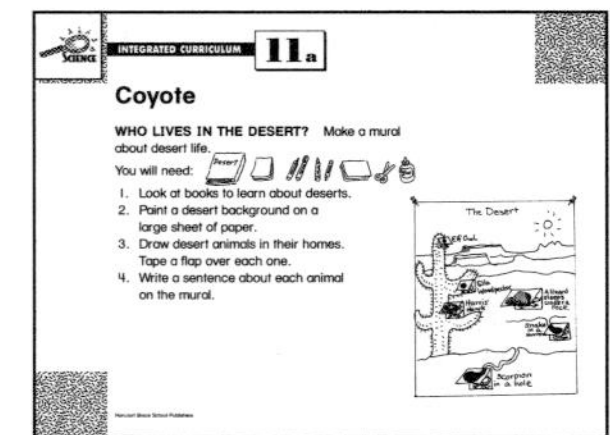
SCIENCE INTEGRATED CURRICULUM 11a

Coyote

WHO LIVES IN THE DESERT? Make a mural about desert life.

You will need:

1. Look at books to learn about deserts.
2. Paint a desert background on a large sheet of paper.
3. Draw desert animals in their homes. Tape a flap over each one.
4. Write a sentence about each animal on the mural.

The Desert

Scorpion in a hole

Curriculum Card 11a

COOPERATIVE LEARNING
Have children use "Coyote" and other sources to identify characteristics of the desert areas of the Southwest. Have children use this information to paint the background for a mural of the desert.

Have children work in small groups to research desert animals, such as reptiles, coyotes, and birds. Tell them to create "lift-the-flap" homes for their animals to show that most desert animals are nocturnal. One child can research and record information, one can draw the animal, and another can write a sentence about the animal. Children may want to give "tours" of the desert for other classes. LISTENING/SPEAKING/READING/WRITING

ART

Wearable Art

MATERIALS
- **paper**
- **crayons or markers**
- **modeling clay in a variety of colors**
- **string or yarn**

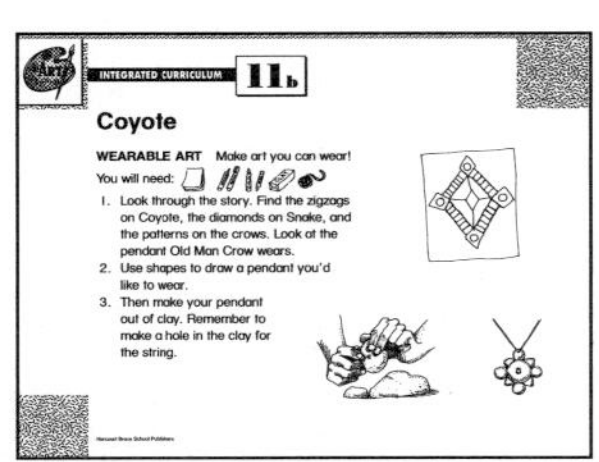
Curriculum Card 11b

Have children look at the illustrations in "Coyote" to observe the various geometric designs, such as the zigzag on Coyote, the diamonds on Snake, and the patterns on the crows. Then call attention to Old Man Crow's pendant on page 306. Explain that the triangular shape stands for a thundercloud and that the vertical lines stand for rain. Encourage children to sketch a design for their own pendants, using geometric designs. Once children are happy with their designs, suggest that they make their pendants, using colored clay. Poke a hole through the top of each pendant for a string. **LISTENING**

MATH

Count the Legs

MATERIALS
- **strips of paper**

LEARNING CENTER Place the paper strips in a center. Have each child draw a row of two to fifteen crows on a strip and write the words *How Many Legs?* On the back of their strips, children should write a number sentence for the answer. Example: 2 + 2 + 2 + 2 = 8. Some children might want to draw a row of crows plus a coyote; their number sentences should include the coyote also. Example: 2 + 2 + 2 + 2 + 4 = 12. Tell children to show their strips to classmates and ask them to figure out how many legs. **LISTENING/SPEAKING/WRITING**

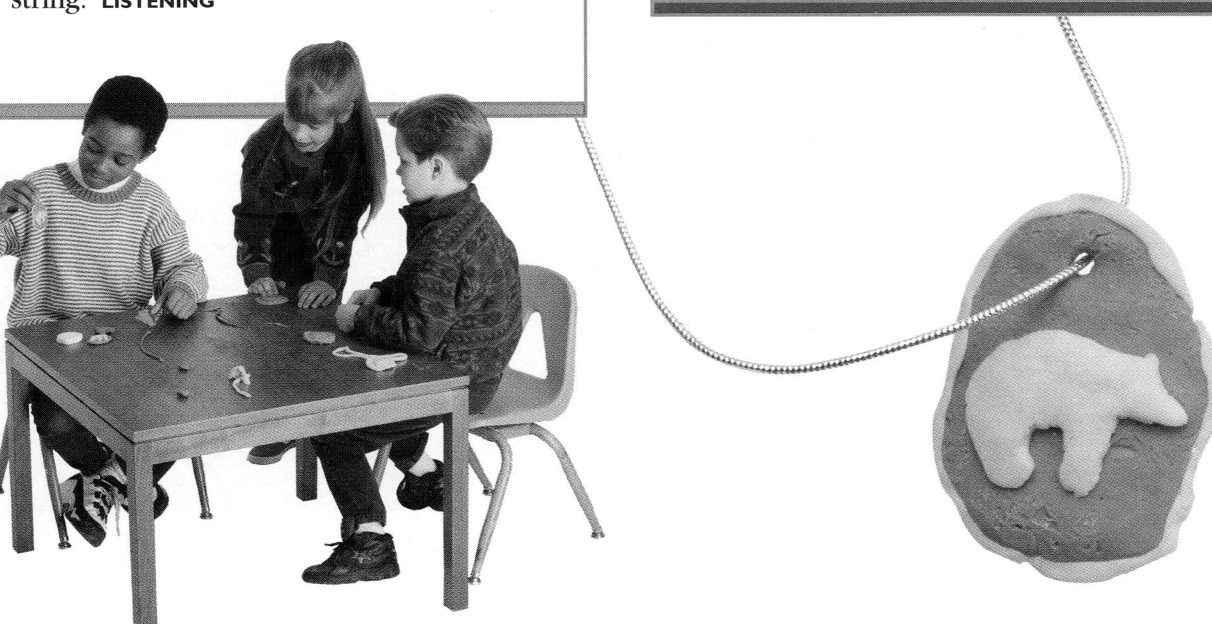

Reading Trade Books

CROSS-CURRICULAR READING

Borreguita and the Coyote: A Tale from Ayutla, Mexico. **Retold by Verna Aardema. Knopf, 1991.**
AVERAGE

The Iguana Brothers **by Tony Johnston. Scholastic, 1995.**
CHALLENGE

Rainbow Crow **by Nancy Van Laan. Knopf, 1989.**
AVERAGE

MULTI-AGE CLASSROOMS

Children who have already mastered the arithmetic in the Math activity may enjoy doing the same activity using multiplication instead of addition.

Reading Trade Books

Trade Books That Connect to "Coyote"

Papagayo: The Mischief Maker

by Gerald McDermott

Like Coyote, Papagayo the Parrot seems to have a nose for trouble. Ask children to retell how Papagayo helped the night creatures. Then have them compare the story and the artwork in "Coyote" with *Papagayo: The Mischief Maker*.

Raven: A Trickster Tale from the Pacific Northwest

by Gerald McDermott

"Coyote" explains how coyotes got their color. Introduce Raven by saying that at one time all the world was dark and that it took a trickster like Raven to bring light. After children read the tale, have them work in small groups to reread it and act it out.

Zomo the Rabbit: A Trickster Tale from West Africa

by Gerald McDermott

In this book, children will read about Zomo the Rabbit, who is very clever but wants wisdom. Have partners take turns rereading the parts about the different tasks Zomo has to do and how he does them.

TIPS FOR CLASSROOM MANAGEMENT

PARTNERS

Have children work with partners to read *Papagayo, Raven,* and *Zomo the Rabbit*. Have them talk about how each tale is similar to and different from "Coyote."

INDEPENDENT

Place *Coyote Steals the Blanket, How the Ostrich Got Its Long Neck,* and *Rainbow Crow* in the Reading Center. Have children read the books and write a review of one of the books in their personal journals.

Coyote Steals the Blanket

by Janet Stevens

Ask children to tell what happens when Coyote takes a blanket from the middle of nowhere. Have children use colored construction paper, scissors, and glue to make their own beautiful blankets. Tell them to make Coyote and Hummingbird, too, and to act out the story.

How the Ostrich Got Its Long Neck

by Verna Aardema
illustrated by Marcia Brown

Ask children to retell in their own words how Ostrich got its long neck. Ask them to tell why they think a long neck is good for an ostrich. Suggest that children pretend they are ostriches with long necks.

Rainbow Crow

by Nancy Van Laan
illustrated by Beatriz Vidal

Have partners work together to draw before-and-after pictures of Rainbow Crow. The before picture should show Rainbow Crow with beautiful, colorful feathers. The after picture should show a blackened Rainbow Crow. Partners can take turns holding up the appropriate picture and rereading parts of the story aloud.

CHALLENGE

Have children locate other books that tie to the theme Tell a Tricky Tale and to the message in "Coyote." Ask each child to decide how to share the content of one of the books.

Trade Books

PROJECT MANAGEMENT

- PROJECT LAUNCH
- CHECKPOINT 1
- CHECKPOINT 2
- CHECKPOINT 3
- CHECKPOINT 4
- PRESENTATIONS
- ASSESSMENT

Create a Story

SELECTION CONNECTION

Coyote is a trickster character who gets tricked himself in this story. Have children compare and contrast the tricky characters they have read about so far, including Coyote.

PROJECT CHECKLIST

During this stage, children should

- ☑ plan how to tell their stories, asking themselves what techniques to incorporate into their presentations.
- ☑ take on responsibilities according to their personal talents or skills.
- ☑ write their stories or use a graphic organizer to plan them.
- ☑ practice their stories.

THEME PROJECT CHECKPOINT 3 16

Create and Present Stories

CREATE A STORY

1. Share ideas about your story.
2. Think how to tell your story. Do you want to sing part of it, act it out, do a puppet show, or do something different?
3. Pick a job to do.
4. Write or plan your story.

Project Card 16

When children have completed the checkpoint, have them think about their plans for stories and write their ideas in their Project Journals.

Project Card 16 can be found as a copying master on page R153.

PLANNING TIPS

As children plan their stories, provide examples of graphic organizers. Suggest that they

- study the organizers to find ones that will help them plan their story.
- hold a group vote to choose the best one.
- pick a Recorder to fill in the organizer during group discussions.

STUDENTS ACQUIRING ENGLISH

Some children might feel more comfortable contributing to group efforts by doing a task that may not involve much reading or writing.

MULTIPLE INTELLIGENCES

Children with strong interpersonal skills can be recruited to act as Directors or Producers to coordinate the group's planning and presentation efforts. Encourage them to help group members cooperate.

Informal Assessment ✓

As children complete this checkpoint, they will **evaluate** and **make decisions** about ideas and **think creatively.** Children are thinking critically if they

- ☑ can examine the merits of different storytelling techniques.
- ☑ properly apply chosen techniques to their stories.
- ☑ evaluate their own skills to choose ways to contribute to the group's story.

Note that a more formal assessment rubric for this checkpoint is provided on page T693.

Secret Messages

from *Dr. Zed's Science Surprises*

by Gordon Penrose

THEME CONNECTION

The theme of Tell a Tricky Tale is applied to real life in these simple activities. Children can perform these "tricks" to send secret messages.

SUMMARY

GENRE: Experiments

Science can appear to play tricks in these activities from *Dr. Zed's Science Surprises*. In one experiment, readers use everyday materials—a cotton swab, lemon juice, salt, and a pencil—and follow four easy steps to write and read secret messages. The other activity requires only pencil and paper to write a message and a mirror to read it.

EXTRA SUPPORT

Some children may need someone to demonstrate the steps of the first experiment one step at a time. Either you or another child can help guide these children through the steps of the process.

Introducing the Selection

BUILDING BACKGROUND

In advance, write this on a sheet of paper: "Time for a science surprise." Fold the paper and tape it to your door. Then, on a separate sheet of thin see-through paper, print the following message:

1, 2, 3, 4
Find a note on the door.

Hold up the paper and show children the note. Ask why they can't read it. Then ask if they can think of an easy way to read the secret message. After they have figured out how to read the message and they find the other note on the door, explain the "science surprise"—ways to write secret messages.

Reading an Experiment Remind children that in this theme, the stories have been about tricks. Tell them that Dr. Zed's first experiment is a tricky way to send secret messages. You might also point out that this selection is not a made-up story, but real ways children can learn to send "tricky" messages.

TIPS FOR CLASSROOM MANAGEMENT

SMALL GROUP

PARTNER READING
Pair a child who needs extra support with a more-fluent reader. Have the more-fluent reader read each step of the first activity aloud. Have the other child "echo," or read back, that step. Encourage children to try this message-writing activity.

WHOLE CLASS

INDEPENDENT READING
Have children read the first science experiment on their own. Answer any questions children may have or allow other children to address questions. You may wish to make the materials available for those who want to do the experiment.

Secret Messages

Send secret messages to a special friend!

HERE'S HOW:

1 Dip a toothpick or cotton swab in lemon juice and draw or print your message on plain paper.

2 Pour salt on the paper to completely cover the message.

3 When the paper is totally dry, brush away the salt.

4 To see the message, rub a pencil or crayon back and forth across the paper several times.

IF YOU WANT TO READ THIS SECRET MESSAGE FROM DR. ZED, HOLD IT UP TO A MIRROR.

In the mirror
On your wall
Here's a message
For you all:

You can use mirror writing to send a secret message of your own. Simply write from right to left across the page, printing the letters of each word backwards.

323

Responding to the Selection

Have children share what they found surprising about the experiments. Then ask:

1. **When doing a science experiment, what are two important things to remember?** (Possible responses: You need the right materials, and you should follow the directions in order.) DESCRIPTIVE RESPONSE
2. **Why do you think the steps in the first activity are numbered?** (Possible response: Steps must be done in a certain order for the experiment to work.) PERSONAL RESPONSE

STUDENTS ACQUIRING ENGLISH

Write these abbreviated steps on a chart.

1. Dip a cotton swab in lemon juice. Write.
2. Pour salt on your message. Let the paper dry.
3. Brush the salt away.
4. Rub a pencil back and forth over your message.

Point to each sentence as a child demonstrates the instruction. Have children repeat each instruction as it is demonstrated.

Integrating Language Arts

TIPS FOR CLASSROOM MANAGEMENT

IF children need to practice reading for fluency, THEN they might benefit from the Oral Language activity.

ORAL LANGUAGE

Give Directions

Have children give oral directions for the secret message science experiment on an audiotape or videotape. Children should practice reading the directions aloud before taping. If they make an audiotape, they may wish to make drawings to accompany the oral directions. If they make a videotape, they can record someone actually doing the experiment. Children could also give directions on audiotape or videotape for the mirror-writing activity.

LISTENING/SPEAKING/READING

WRITING

Hide and Seek

Have children take turns hiding a small object in the room and writing directions for finding it, using one of the "secret message" tricks they just read about. They can exchange papers with a classmate, decode the message, and look for the object. READING/WRITING

THEME: COMMUNICATION

Tell a Tricky Tale

In "Rabbit and Tiger," children discover that a small, smart rabbit can outwit a fierce tiger. This time, a trickster's pranks are for the good of others.

SELECTION SUMMARY

Genre: Play

When animals in the Puerto Rican jungle have "tiger trouble," they call on Rabbit for help. Rabbit makes a deal with Tiger. If Rabbit is able to ride Tiger before sunset, Tiger must leave Puerto Rico forever. Through a series of tricks, Rabbit achieves his goal. In the end, Tiger leaves Puerto Rico but hopes to get even with that trickster Rabbit someday.

ABOUT THE AUTHOR AND THE ILLUSTRATOR

F. C. NICHOLSON writes for both children and adults. "Rabbit and Tiger" originally appeared in *Plays, The Drama Magazine for Young People,* and her nonfiction has been published in *Highlights for Children, Odyssey,* and *The Dolphin Log.*

RICHARD BERNAL has illustrated several children's books, including *The Ants Go Marching One by One* and *London Bridge Is Falling Down.*

For more information about the author and the illustrator, see pages T668–T669.

SUGGESTED LESSON PLANNER

▶ ***Rabbit and Tiger***

	DAY 1	DAY 2
PART  Reading Listening Speaking Viewing **Key Words** group fiercest kind scares mind jungle lies few bargain	**BUILD BACKGROUND** T646 **VOCABULARY STRATEGIES** T646–T647 *Chart/Transparency 23* *Practice Book* pp. 115–116 **READING THE SELECTION** T648–T669 Options for Reading T648–T649 *Response Card 1* *Literature Cassette 1* **REVIEW PREDICTIONS/PURPOSE** T666 **APPRECIATING THE LITERATURE** T666 NOTE: Students may read the selection on Day 2.	**SUMMARIZE AND RETELL THE SELECTION** T667 *Practice Book* p. 117 ◆ **RESPONSE CORNER ACTIVITIES** T670 **CHECKING COMPREHENSION** T671 *End-of-Selection Test* 
PART 2 Writer's Workshop	**A PLAY** Thinking as Writers T676 *Chart/Transparency 24*	Prewriting T676
Grammar	✓ **PRONOUNS** Teach the Concept T678 Daily Language Practice (1–2) R145	Daily Language Practice (3–4) R145 Practice Activity T679
Spelling	**FINAL DOUBLE CONSONANTS** *fall all ball less add* *pass dress miss call glass* Pretest/Self-Check T680 *Integrated Spelling Teacher's Edition* pp. T111, T283	Open and Closed Sorts T680 *Integrated Spelling* p. 70 *Integrated Spelling Teacher's Edition* p. T112
PART 3 Phonics	**LONG VOWEL:** */ī/i, y, ie* Phonics-Vocabulary Connection T647	**LONG VOWEL:** */ī/i, y, ie* (Introduce) T682 *Big Book of Rhymes* p. 20 *Phonics Practice Book* pp. 92–99
Skills and Strategies	◆ **INTEGRATED CURRICULUM** *Rain Forest* **Social Studies** T686 **Art** T686 **Music** T687 **Math** T687 *Trudy's Time & Place House (Symbol Sandbox, Earth Scout)* *Imagination Express, Destination: Rain Forest*	**STUDY SKILL** T684–T685 Graphic Aids (Introduce) *Practice Book* pp. 123–124 *Thinkin' Things Collection 1 (Fripple Shop); Collection 2 (Frippletration)*

Use the Intervention Strategies note on page T652 and the Extra Support notes on pages T658 and T661 to help **below-level readers.**

To help children build fluency, use the *Instant Readers™ Molly's Hard Bargain* and *Pretend You're a Tiger* on pages T672–T673.

NOTE: An alternative lesson plan for **below-level readers** appears on *Intervention Strategies Manual* pp. 68–73. A lesson for **students acquiring English** appears on *Sheltered English/ESL Manual* pp. 46–49.

DAY 3	DAY 4	DAY 5
◆ **IDEA BANK ACTIVITIES** Listening and Speaking T674 Real-Life Reading: Reading Playbills T674 Oral Language T675 Kinesthetic T675 *Writer's Magazine* pp. 44–47 School–Home Connection 12 R175	**VOCABULARY WORKSHOP** T681 Reviewing Key Words Story Strips R179 Homophones *Practice Book* pp. 120–121 *Take-Home/Keep-at-Home Book: Rosie Flamingo* **READING TRADE BOOKS** T688–T689  Signatures Library  Take-Home Book	**READING TRADE BOOKS** T683, T685, T687, T688–T689  Instant Reader™ Instant Reader™
Drafting T676 *Language Handbook* pp. 26–27 *The Amazing Writing Machine*	Responding and Revising T677	Proofreading and Publishing T677 *Kid Pix*
Daily Language Practice (5–6) R145 Practice Activity T679 *Language Handbook* p. 74	Daily Language Practice (7–8) R145 Practice Activity T679 *Grammar Practice Book* pp. 51–52	Daily Language Practice (9–12) R145 *Practice Book* p. 118
Discuss the Generalization T680 *Integrated Spelling* p. 71 *Integrated Spelling Teacher's Edition* p. T113	Apply to Writing T680 *Integrated Spelling* pp. 72–73 *Integrated Spelling Teacher's Edition* pp. T114–T115	Posttest T680 *Practice Book* p. 119 *Integrated Spelling Teacher's Edition* p. T116
LONG VOWEL: /ī/*i, y, ie* T682 *Phonics Practice Reader 22: I Spy* *Phonics Practice Book* pp. 100–106	**LONG VOWEL: /ī/*i, y, ie*** 683 *Practice Book* p. 122 *Bailey's Book House* (Read-A-Rhyme)	**LONG VOWEL: /ī/*i, y, ie*** T683 *Phonics Activity Book* pp. 37–38
STUDY SKILLS MINILESSON T651 ✓ Alphabetical Order (Review) *Practice Book* p. 125	**PHONICS AND DECODING MINILESSON** T655 ✓ R-Controlled Vowel: /ûr/*er, ir, ur, ear* (Maintain) *Phonics Practice Book* pp. 135–139	**GRAMMAR MINILESSON** T657 ✓ Irregular Plural Nouns (Review) *Language Handbook* pp. 72–73 Theme Project Checkpoint 4 T690

Above-level writers may complete the Writer's Workshop independently at their own pace.

During the Vocabulary Workshop, refer to the Students Acquiring English note on page T681 for **ESL readers**.

Below-level and **ESL readers** may read the *ESL/Title I Library* book *Hello, House!*

✓ = Tested Skill
◆ = Optional activities that may be used to adjust pacing throughout the lesson
Titles in *italics* are optional materials.

1 Reading and Responding

BUILDING BACKGROUND AND CONCEPTS

PRIOR KNOWLEDGE

Discuss and pantomime animal characters. Make the following chart on the board, and read the name of each animal. Invite children to tell what they know about the animals. Encourage them to volunteer words to describe traits of each animal, and add them to the chart.

Tiger	Rabbit	Mouse	Monkey	Turtle	Toucan
big teeth hunter	big ears shy	tiny quick	silly long tail	slow hard shell	bird big colorful beak

After discussing the animals, invite volunteers to each pantomime one of the animals. Other children can guess which animal is being acted out.

VOCABULARY STRATEGIES

KEY WORDS DEFINED

group a number of people or things together

scares makes afraid

lies rests in a stretched-out position

fiercest wildest; most dangerous

mind to care about

few not many

kind type; sort

jungle land thickly covered with trees, vines, and other plants

bargain an agreement; a deal

SUPPORT WORDS

Display the words *ancestor, bullying, deserves, island,* and *trickster*. Discuss their meanings and have children use them in sentences.

INTEGRATED SPELLING

SPELLING PRETEST: page T680

SPELLING GENERALIZATION: Final double consonants

Intervention Strategies

For children who may have difficulty reading "Rabbit and Tiger," support is available in *Intervention Strategies Manual,* pages 68–73, and on pages T652 and T672–T673 in this lesson.

STUDENTS ACQUIRING ENGLISH

See *Sheltered English/ESL Manual,* pages 46–49.

FACT FINDER

SOCIAL STUDIES

Tricksters in Literature

Rabbit is a trickster character in folktales around the world. Always clever, cunning, and witty, Rabbit typically outsmarts larger, fiercer animals. In the Deep South of the United States, stories have been told about Brer (Brother) Rabbit. A similar character known in Cuba as *Hermano Rabito*, in Panama and Colombia as *Tío Conejo*, and in Brazil as *O Coelho* plays tricks on and is occasionally tricked by other animals. Rabbit appears in Native American tales as a character who warns people of dangers and helps them escape these dangers. In stories from Japan, China, and Korea, Rabbit lives in the moon and protects the life force.

CUEING SYSTEMS

Have children read new vocabulary. Display Chart/Transparency 23, or write the words and sentences on the board. Encourage children to read words they might know.

Cover the word *group* with a self-stick note, and have children read the rest of the sentence. Ask children to suggest words that make sense in the sentence, and write them on the board. Uncover the word one letter at a time and ask:

> **Does your word begin with the letter *g*?**
> **Does the word make sense in the sentence?**

Have children read the rest of the story, using word parts and the sense of the story to help them figure out the meanings of the underlined words.

HANDS-ON ACTIVITY

Play a vocabulary game. Distribute copies of Rabbit and Tiger Cutouts, page R204, to children. Tell them to write a Key Word on each cutout. Have partners place their cutouts face down. One player says *Rabbit* or *Tiger*. The other player turns over a cutout in the shape of that animal. If the player reads the word and tells what it means, she or he keeps the cutout. If the word is not read or defined correctly, the cutout is turned back over. Then have children add the words to their Word Files.

CHART/TRANSPARENCY 23

group	scares	lies
fiercest	mind	few
kind	jungle	bargain

Bird, Mouse, and Monkey stood together in a group.

"Snake scares me," said Mouse. "Even when he lies down, his eyes are open."

"Snake is not the fiercest animal," said Bird. "Tiger is."

"I don't mind Tiger so much," said Mouse. "I'm too small a meal for him."

"I run a few steps when I hear him coming," said Monkey.

"He's one kind of cat we should all stay away from," said Bird.

"It's hard to stay away from Tiger in the jungle," said Mouse. "I'll make a bargain with you. When I hear Tiger, I'll tell you, and when you hear Snake, you tell me."

Rabbit and Tiger

First, color the picture on page 116. Then cut out the words and clues. Glue each word in the box that has the right clue. You can turn your pieces over and do a puzzle, or use the cards to play "Concentration" with a partner.

the scariest; the most fierce fiercest	A person who is tired does this on a couch or bed. lies	a kind of deal bargain
means "not many" few	You and your friends make a ____. group	This place is filled with trees and animals. jungle
This word is always about thinking. mind	This is what a mean tiger does to people. scares	Things or animals that go together are the same ____. kind

bargain	**few**	**mind**	**group**	**jungle**
kind	**lies**	**fiercest**	**scares**	

GO ON

OUT OF THE BLUE Practice Book VOCABULARY 115

PRACTICE BOOK, pages 115–116

PHONICS-VOCABULARY CONNECTION

WORD PLAY

Distribute word cards to small groups. Each set of cards should contain some or all of these rhyming words: *lies, ties, tries, flies, fries, pies, skies, mind, kind, find, grind, rind, wind*. Groups can use the cards to make rhyming sentences. Invite groups to share their favorites, writing them on the board for others to read. The concept of long vowel /ī/*i, y, ie* is further developed on pages T682–T683.

Strategic Reading

STRATEGY FOCUS: REREADING

Review with children some of the things good readers do when they read. Encourage children to suggest new ideas to add to the classroom chart.

What Good Readers Do
Picture what is happening in their minds
Guess what might happen next
Reread if they don't understand something

Share with children the comprehension strategy that is the focus of this selection.

MODEL

Sometimes while reading, I come to a part of the story and I think: What is going on here? I must have missed something. When that happens, I start at the top of my page or turn back a page and read that part again. It's amazing how many times I understand it better after I read it again.

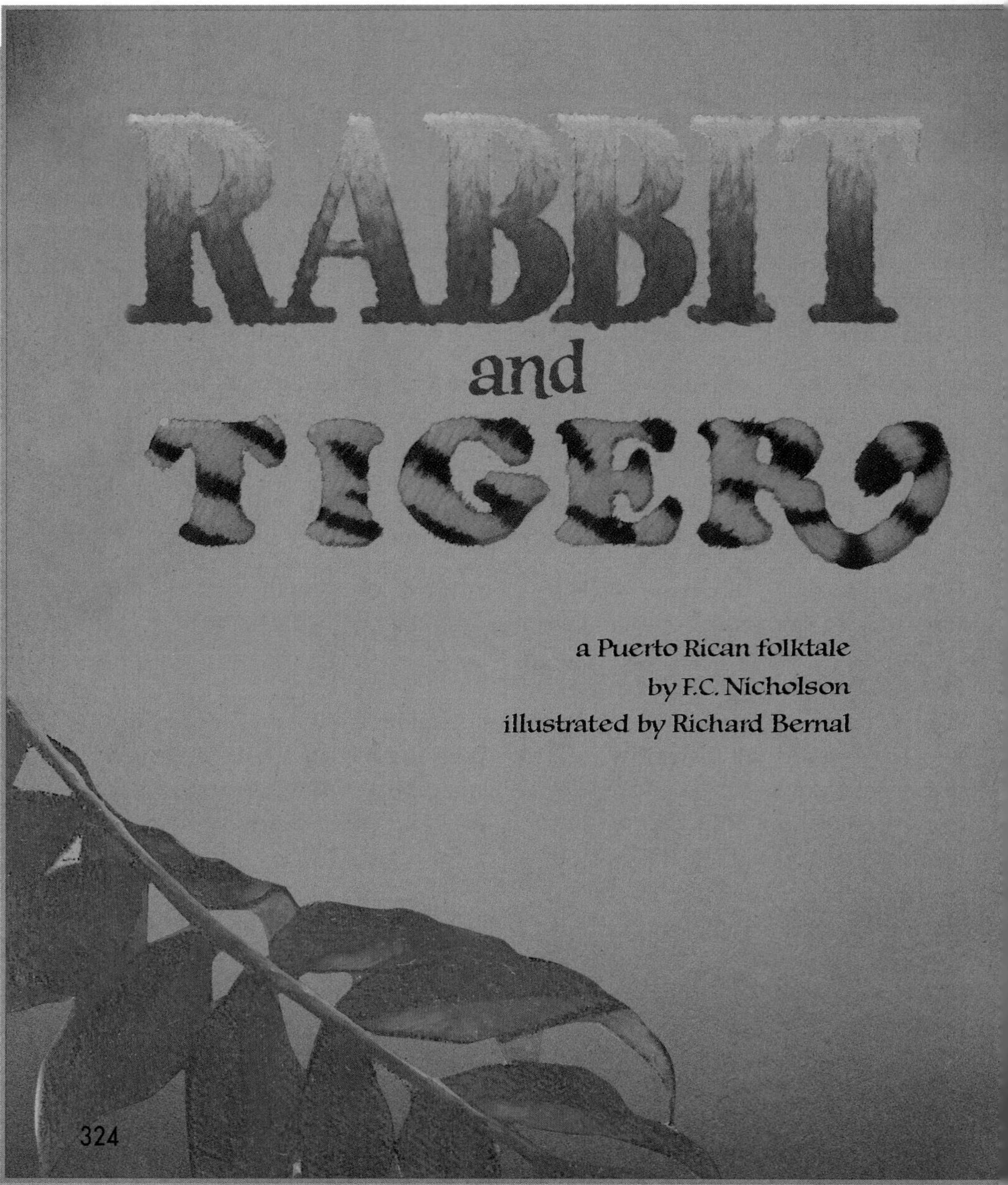

RABBIT and TIGER

a Puerto Rican folktale

by F.C. Nicholson

illustrated by Richard Bernal

324

SMALL GROUP

COOPERATIVE READING

DRAMA CIRCLES Children can read the play aloud in small groups, with each group member reading the part of one character. One child can be the storyteller and read all nonspeaking parts. Children can use Reader Response Card 1 (Characters), page R147, to discuss the play.

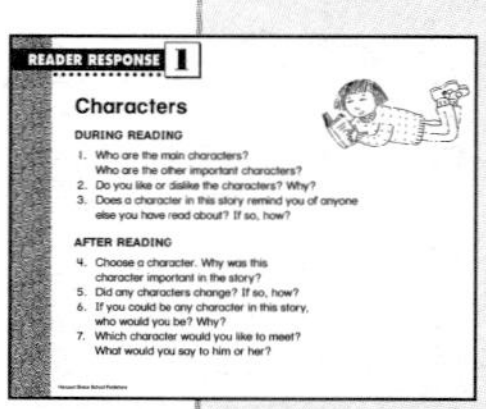

Response Card 1

STRATEGIC READING

Choose some or all of the suggestions and questions under Strategic Reading, pages T648–T667, to guide a literature discussion and model the STRATEGY FOCUS of Rereading.

CHARACTERS

RABBIT

TIGER

MOUSE

TOUCAN

MONKEY

TURTLE

325

PREVIEWING/ SETTING PURPOSES

Tell children that they will be reading a story in the form of a play. Explain that when stories are to be acted out in movies, on TV, or on a stage, they are written in a form to help actors and others working on the play to perform actions for an audience. Invite children to scan the first few pages of the play. Discuss some of the ways the play is set up differently from other stories.

- **What is the title of the play? Who are the characters?**
- **What do you notice about the way the story begins?**
- **How is the play different from other stories you've read?**

Talk with children about the illustrations and the characters, and allow time for them to record in their journals their predictions about what will happen in the play. Then help children set their purposes for reading.

WHOLE CLASS

READ ALOUD

To help familiarize children with the format of a play and the idea that plays are written to be performed, begin reading the play aloud with expression, using different voices for the characters. Then ask volunteers to read the parts of the different characters.

INDEPENDENT READING

Have children read "Rabbit and Tiger" silently. As children finish, have them write in their personal journals what they think of the way Rabbit treated Tiger. When all children are finished, have them refer to their responses as they discuss what happened in the play.

Strategic Reading

MODELING A STRATEGY

PAGES 326–327 Ask children to look at the pictures. Talk about what the animals are doing, how they might be feeling, and why they feel as they do. Have children predict what is happening and then read to confirm their predictions.

After children have read, have them compare their predictions with what actually happened. Then have them make a new prediction about what the characters will do about Tiger. Model your thinking: *The animals are upset about Tiger scaring them. Since they are smaller and weaker than Tiger, I think they'll set a trap to catch him. Then they can put him where he won't bother them.* MAKING AND CONFIRMING PREDICTIONS

326

LISTENING CENTER

"Rabbit and Tiger" is available on *Literature Cassette 1*. Some children may benefit from listening to the play and following along in their books.

CONVENTIONS OF PRINT

PLAY FORMAT Point out more distinctions between a play and a narrative. Call attention to the words *Scene 1, time,* and *setting*. Explain that the words in brown in slanted type, or italics, tell about the time, the place, and things the characters do, and that the words in regular type tell what they say.

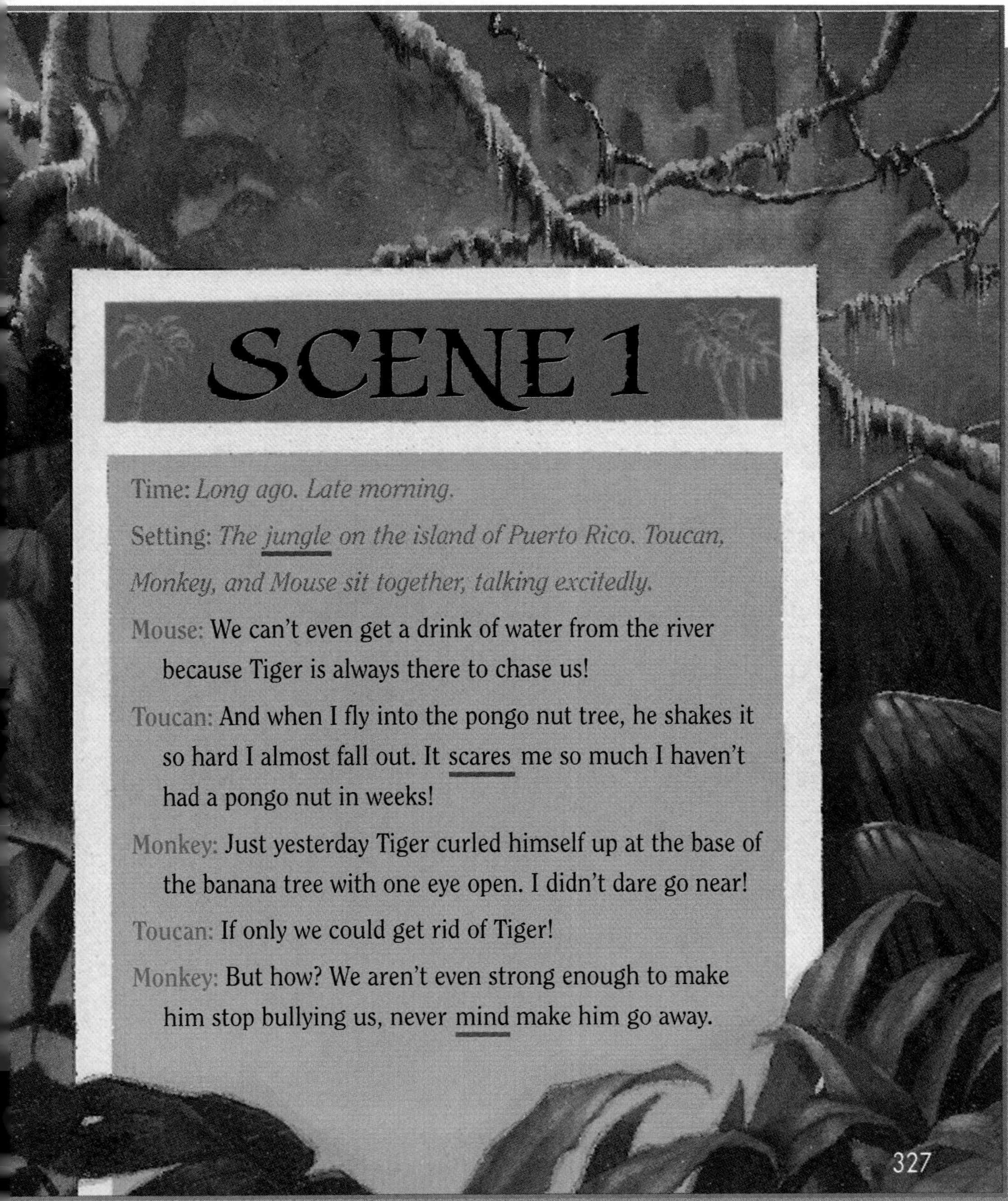

SCENE 1

Time: *Long ago. Late morning.*

Setting: *The jungle on the island of Puerto Rico. Toucan, Monkey, and Mouse sit together, talking excitedly.*

Mouse: We can't even get a drink of water from the river because Tiger is always there to chase us!

Toucan: And when I fly into the pongo nut tree, he shakes it so hard I almost fall out. It scares me so much I haven't had a pongo nut in weeks!

Monkey: Just yesterday Tiger curled himself up at the base of the banana tree with one eye open. I didn't dare go near!

Toucan: If only we could get rid of Tiger!

Monkey: But how? We aren't even strong enough to make him stop bullying us, never mind make him go away.

327

Tested Skill

MINILESSON

REVIEW: STUDY SKILLS

Alphabetical Order

INFORMAL ASSESSMENT

When children are using a dictionary or glossary, monitor whether they understand alphabetical order.

TEACH/MODEL

Ask children where they might find information about the real-life animals from the play. Help them recognize that reference books would be good sources. Remind children that in many reference books, subjects appear in alphabetical order.

Ask children to name the animals in the story. When you have listed the animals' names (Mouse, Rabbit, Tiger, Toucan, Monkey, Turtle), invite children to alphabetize the list with you. Remind them of the rules for alphabetizing words that begin with the same letter and with the same first and second letters.

PRACTICE/APPLY

Have partners write each of the following words on a self-stick note. Then they can work together to put the words in alphabetical order.

rabbit	tree	miss	stand	find
happy	fine	see	time	big
map	juice	tiger	treat	silly

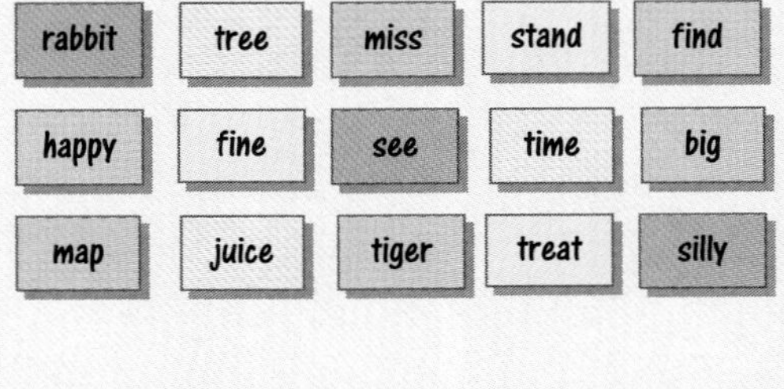

SOCIAL STUDIES CONNECTION

PUERTO RICO Help children locate Puerto Rico on a map or a globe. Explain that it is an island that is part of the United States and Spanish is the primary language.

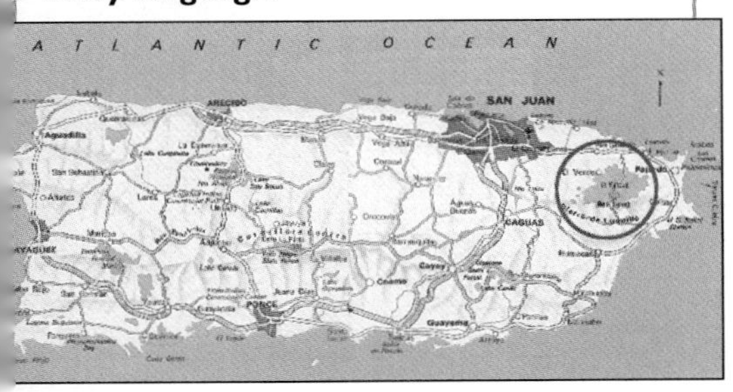

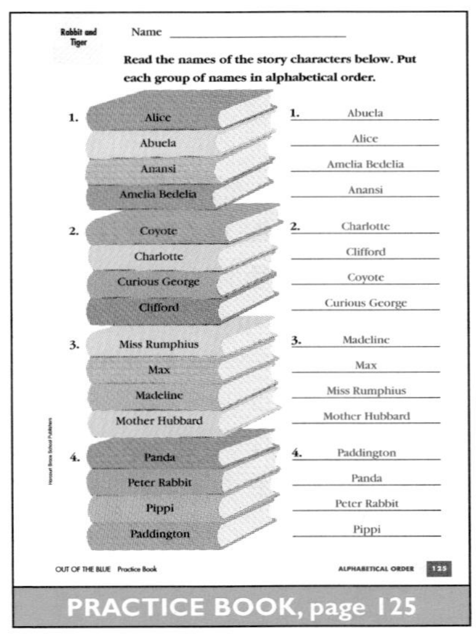

Rabbit and Tiger

Name ______________

Read the names of the story characters below. Put each group of names in alphabetical order.

1. Alice, Abuela, Anansi, Amelia Bedelia — 1. Abuela, Alice, Amelia Bedelia, Anansi
2. Coyote, Charlotte, Curious George, Clifford — 2. Charlotte, Clifford, Coyote, Curious George
3. Miss Rumphius, Max, Madeline, Mother Hubbard — 3. Madeline, Max, Miss Rumphius, Mother Hubbard
4. Panda, Peter Rabbit, Pippi, Paddington — 4. Paddington, Panda, Peter Rabbit, Pippi

OUT OF THE BLUE Practice Book — ALPHABETICAL ORDER 125

PRACTICE BOOK, page 125

Strategic Reading

MODELING A STRATEGY

PAGES 328–329 After children have read, have them compare the predictions they made about what the characters will do with what actually happened. Then encourage them to use what they know about Rabbit to predict whether he will manage to find a way to make Tiger leave Puerto Rico and how he might do it. **Think aloud:** *Mouse says that Rabbit is the smartest animal he knows. When the animals ask Rabbit to get rid of Tiger, he seems to have an idea about how to do it. I think Rabbit will find a way to trick Tiger into leaving. He might dress up like a large animal and scare Tiger away.*

MAKING PREDICTIONS

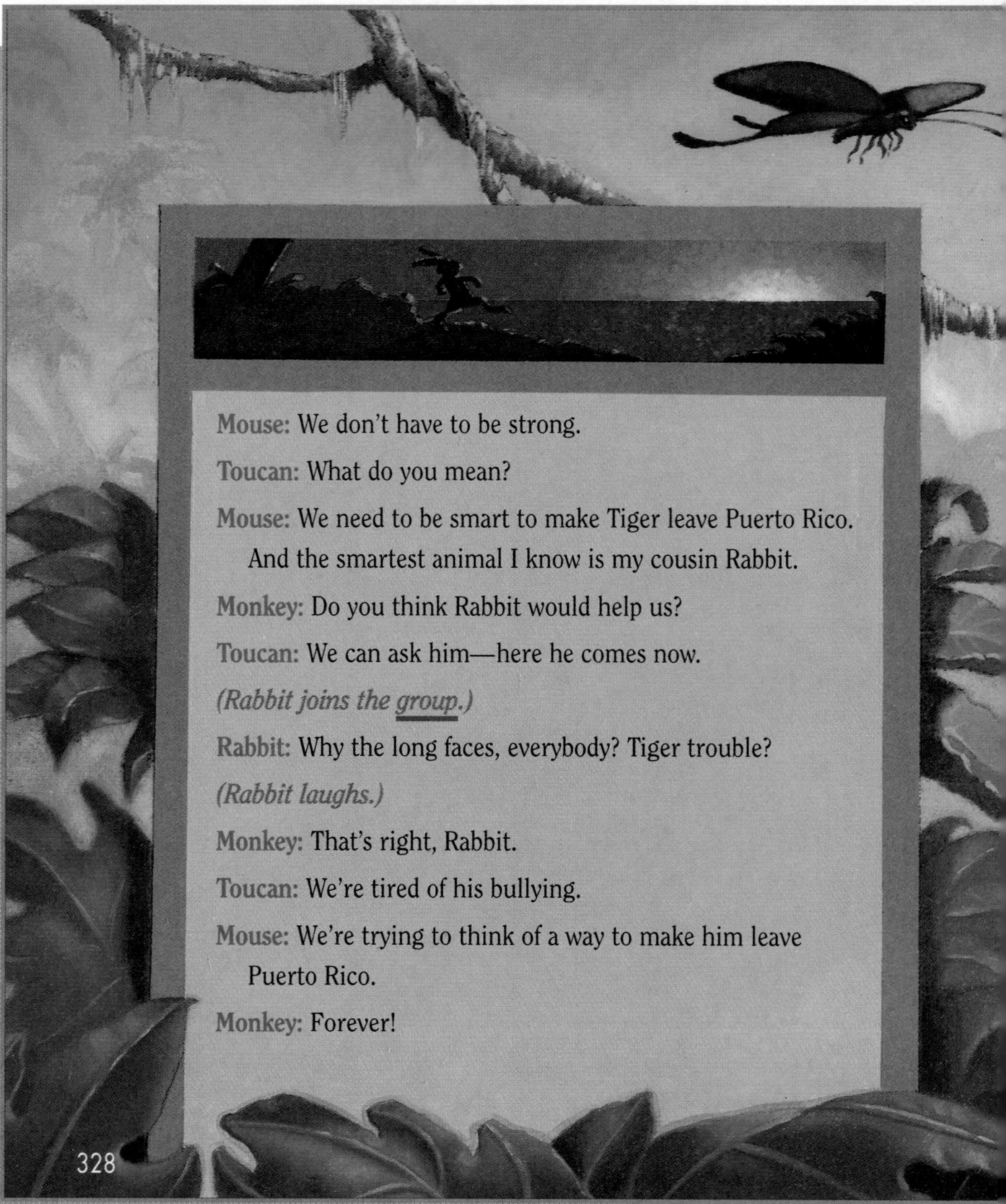

Mouse: We don't have to be strong.

Toucan: What do you mean?

Mouse: We need to be smart to make Tiger leave Puerto Rico. And the smartest animal I know is my cousin Rabbit.

Monkey: Do you think Rabbit would help us?

Toucan: We can ask him—here he comes now.

(Rabbit joins the group.)

Rabbit: Why the long faces, everybody? Tiger trouble?

(Rabbit laughs.)

Monkey: That's right, Rabbit.

Toucan: We're tired of his bullying.

Mouse: We're trying to think of a way to make him leave Puerto Rico.

Monkey: Forever!

328

Intervention Strategies

REREADING Have children repeat this sentence: *When I read, I reread some parts of the story to see if I can figure out what is happening.* Have children tell if rereading has helped them understand parts of "Rabbit and Tiger."

STUDENTS ACQUIRING ENGLISH Call attention to the phrase *long faces.* Explain that it means "sad faces." Encourage children to use facial expressions to show what *long faces* means.

Informal Assessment

USING CUEING SYSTEMS

During a rereading of the selection or parts of it, observe how children apply cueing systems to develop meaning.

- ☑ Do children suggest word substitutions that make sense in the context of the sentence and with the letters in the word?
- ☑ Do children reread and then self-correct?
- ☑ Do children read an entire sentence and then think about what word might make sense in that context?

PHONICS IN ACTION

Write on the board the words *leave* and *great*. Underline the letters *ea* in each word. Point out that *ea* represents different sounds in these words—the long *e* sound in *leave* and the long *a* sound in *great*.

leave

great

Strategic Reading

MODELING A STRATEGY

PAGES 330–333 Have children look at the pictures and talk about what they think this part of the story is about. Then stop for a moment to discuss with children ways that reading a play is different from reading a story. Point out that readers can lose track of which character is speaking, or they might forget to read the stage directions, which tell about the characters' movements and give other important information. Model rereading as a way to clarify information: *What could I do if I didn't know who Monkey is talking about when he says, "Listen! Here he comes!" I could go back one page. When I do that, I see that the animals are talking about Tiger. Tiger could be the* he. *When I read on, I see that Tiger walks in. So Monkey* was *talking about Tiger.* REREADING

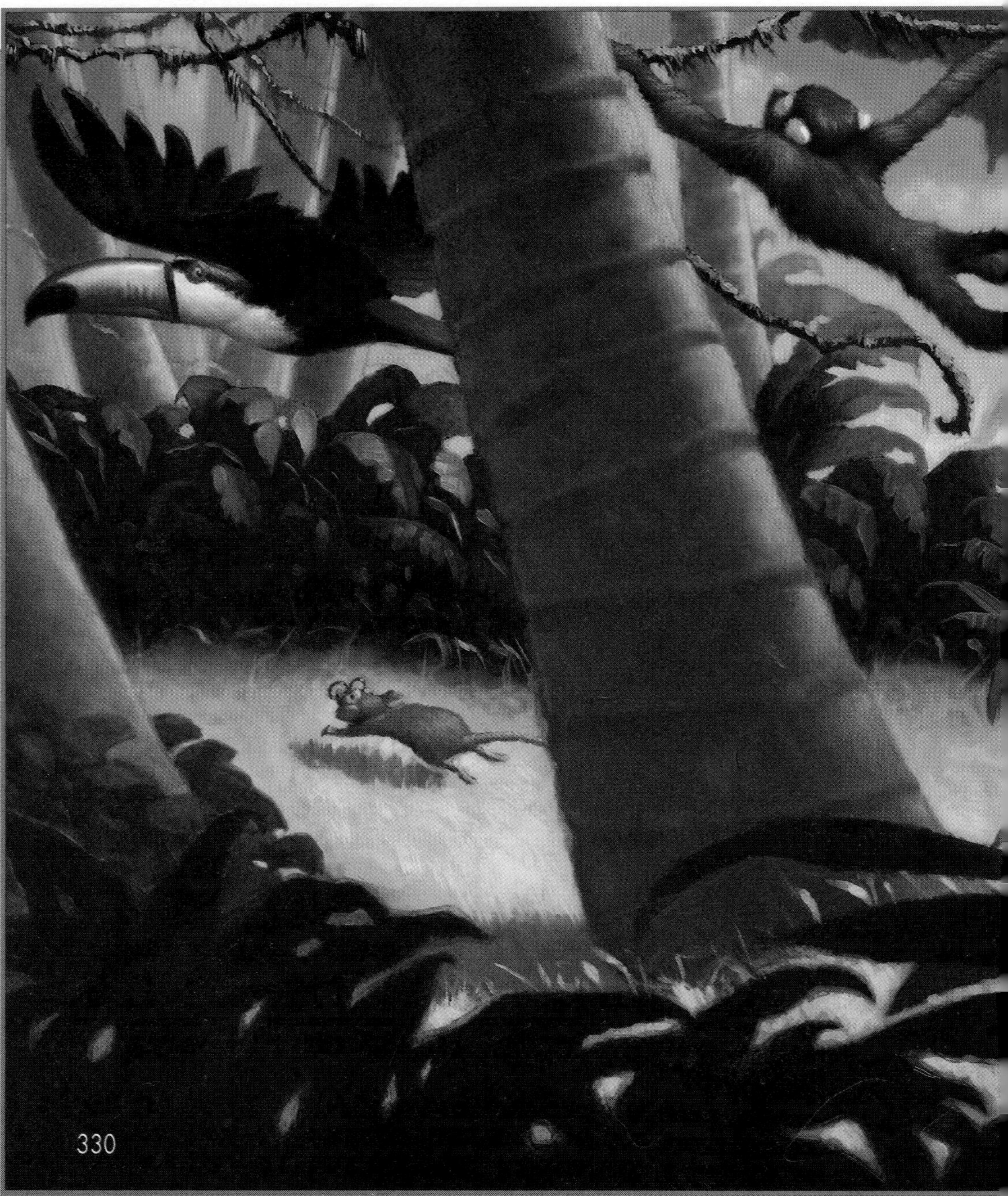

330

SOCIAL STUDIES

CARIBBEAN NATIONAL FOREST About 25 percent of the island of Puerto Rico is covered by forests. The jungle that is the setting of this play could be the Caribbean National Forest, a tropical rain forest preserve in Sierra de Luquillo. The forest covers 45 square miles (116 sq km).

SOCIAL STUDIES

PUERTO RICAN HISTORY The island of Puerto Rico was originally named Borinquén by the Taino Indians. After Christopher Columbus visited in 1493, it was renamed San Juan Bautista. The present name, meaning "rich port," was adopted after Ponce de León established a settlement in 1508.

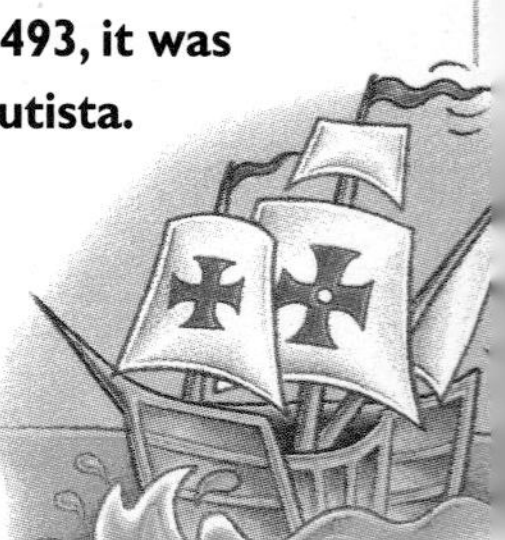

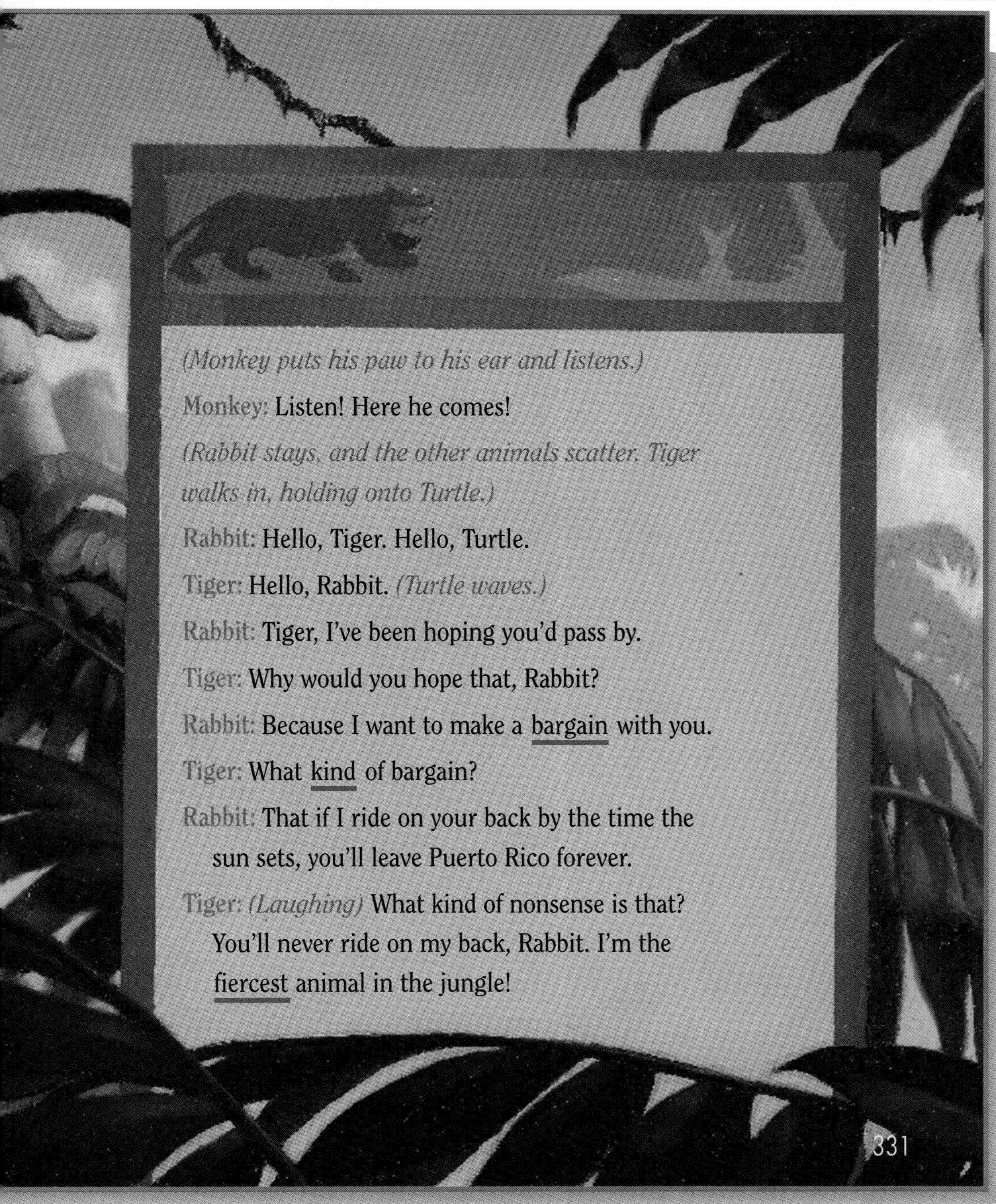

Tested Skill

MINILESSON

MAINTAIN: PHONICS AND DECODING

R-Controlled Vowel: /ûr/ *er, ir, ur, ear*

INFORMAL ASSESSMENT

As children read, notice whether they can decode words in which the letters *er, ir, ur*, or *ear* stand for the *r*-controlled vowel sound /ûr/.

TEACH/MODEL

Have children reread page 331 and tell who Tiger is carrying. (Turtle) Write the word *turtle*, and ask a volunteer to mark the letters that stand for the /ûr/ sound. Repeat the process for the words *perfect, earth*, and *bird*, beginning a new column for each spelling of the sound. Remind children that the letters *er, ir, ur*, and *ear* can stand for the /ûr/ sound as heard in *turtle*.

PRACTICE/APPLY

Write the following sentences on the board:

Many ferns grow in the rain forest.
They make perfect hiding places.
Rabbit said he would take a turn.
He was the first to try.
What did Rabbit learn?

Invite volunteers to read a sentence and underline a word that contains the /ûr/ sound as in *heard* and *turtle*. Then ask them to read the sentence aloud, name the word that contains the /ûr/ sound, and write it on the lists on the board.

PHONICS PRACTICE BOOK, pages 135–139

REAL-LIFE CONNECTION

Discuss the bargain that Rabbit made with Tiger. Invite children to share any bargains they may have made. Ask them to mention the person with whom they made the bargain, and to tell what each side agreed to.

CROSS-CULTURAL VIEWPOINT

SAYING "HELLO" Invite children who speak other languages to share the words used to say "hello" or other greetings. You can share the words for "hello" in the following languages:

bon jour (bohn zhōōr)—French
JAMBO SANA (jämbō sänä)—SWAHILI
GUTEN TAG (gōōten täg)—GERMAN
buon giorno (bwhon jor´nō)—*Italian*
kon´ ichi wa (kōnēchē wä)—**Japanese**

Cooperative Reading

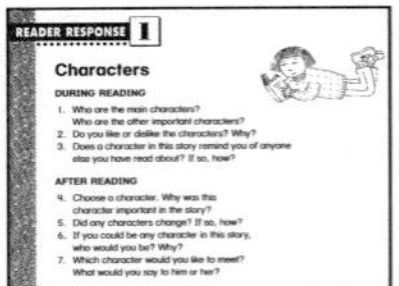
READER RESPONSE 1

Characters

DURING READING

1. Who are the main characters?
   Who are the other important characters?
2. Do you like or dislike the characters? Why?
3. Does a character in this story remind you of anyone else you have read about? If so, how?

AFTER READING

4. Choose a character. Why was this character important in the story?
5. Did any characters change? If so, how?
6. If you could be any character in this story, who would you be? Why?
7. Which character would you like to meet? What would you say to him or her?

Response Card 1

Remind children to pause from time to time and discuss the During Reading questions on **Reader Response Card 1** (Characters), page R147. You may want to ask the following questions to help children focus on the characters:

1. **What is the bargain that Rabbit and Tiger make?**
2. **Do you think they will both stick to the bargain? Why or why not?**

332

IDEA BANK

Invite children to help you create a Jungle Reading Center. Cover the area with green paper, and have children make pictures of rain forest plant and animal life. Arrange the reading area, and add plants and a tape recorder to play sounds of the rain forest.

ART CONNECTION

PAINT SCENERY As children reread and act out the play, invite them to create various backgrounds for their dramatizations. Small groups could create tropical murals. Groups could also draw scenes on blank transparencies and project the images as they act out the play.

Turtle: And the meanest.

Tiger: You be quiet, Turtle. I don't like back talk from my lunch!

(Tiger turns to Rabbit.)

All right, Rabbit. But if you don't ride on my back, I get to eat you up!

Rabbit: Agreed! Give me your paw on that!

(They shake hands.)

My, my, that's a mighty fine Turtle you've got there, Tiger. Not half as fine as the one I saw at the bottom of the stream, but . . .

Tiger: At the bottom of the stream?

Rabbit: Oh, yes. It must be the ancestor of all turtles. Why, it makes Old Man Alligator look puny.

(Tiger looks at Turtle's size and then lets Turtle go.)

333

Tested Skill

MINILESSON

REVIEW: GRAMMAR

Irregular Plural Nouns

INFORMAL ASSESSMENT

As children speak and write, notice whether they use the correct forms of irregular plural nouns.

TEACH/MODEL

Have children reread page 333. Call their attention to the name *Old Man Alligator.* Ask children what word is used to tell about more than one alligator. *(alligators)* Then ask how to tell about more than one man. If necessary, remind children that the spelling of *man* is changed to *men* to mean "more than one man." Remind children that the spelling of some other nouns also changes to tell about more than one.

PRACTICE/APPLY

Write the following words on the board in two columns:

tooth	**feet**
child	**women**
woman	**teeth**
foot	**children**

Have children write the lists, read a word from the left-hand column, and draw a line to match it with its plural form in the right-hand column.

LANGUAGE HANDBOOK

Other Plural Nouns, pages 72–73

EXPANDING VOCABULARY

Call attention to the word *puny*. Help children pronounce the word, and ask what they think the word might mean in this sentence. If necessary, tell them it means "small and weak." You might wish to ask children to make a list of synonyms for the word, or have volunteers use the word in sentences.

WRITING

EXTEND THE STORY Ask children to reread the part where Rabbit and Tiger shake paws to seal their bargain. Tell them that people can also write down an agreement and then sign their names to it. Have partners write an agreement for the deal between Rabbit and Tiger and add paw prints as signatures.

Strategic Reading

MODELING A STRATEGY

PAGES 334–335 Ask children to look at the pictures and to predict what they think happens to Tiger. Then have them read to confirm their predictions. After children have read, ask them how Tiger can fool Rabbit if Tiger says his plan out loud. If children are not able to answer the question, suggest that they reread part of page 334. If necessary, model your thinking. **Think aloud:** *I'll read the page again. Oh, I understand now. Earlier it says, "They hurry off." So Tiger is alone when he talks about his plan.*

REREADING

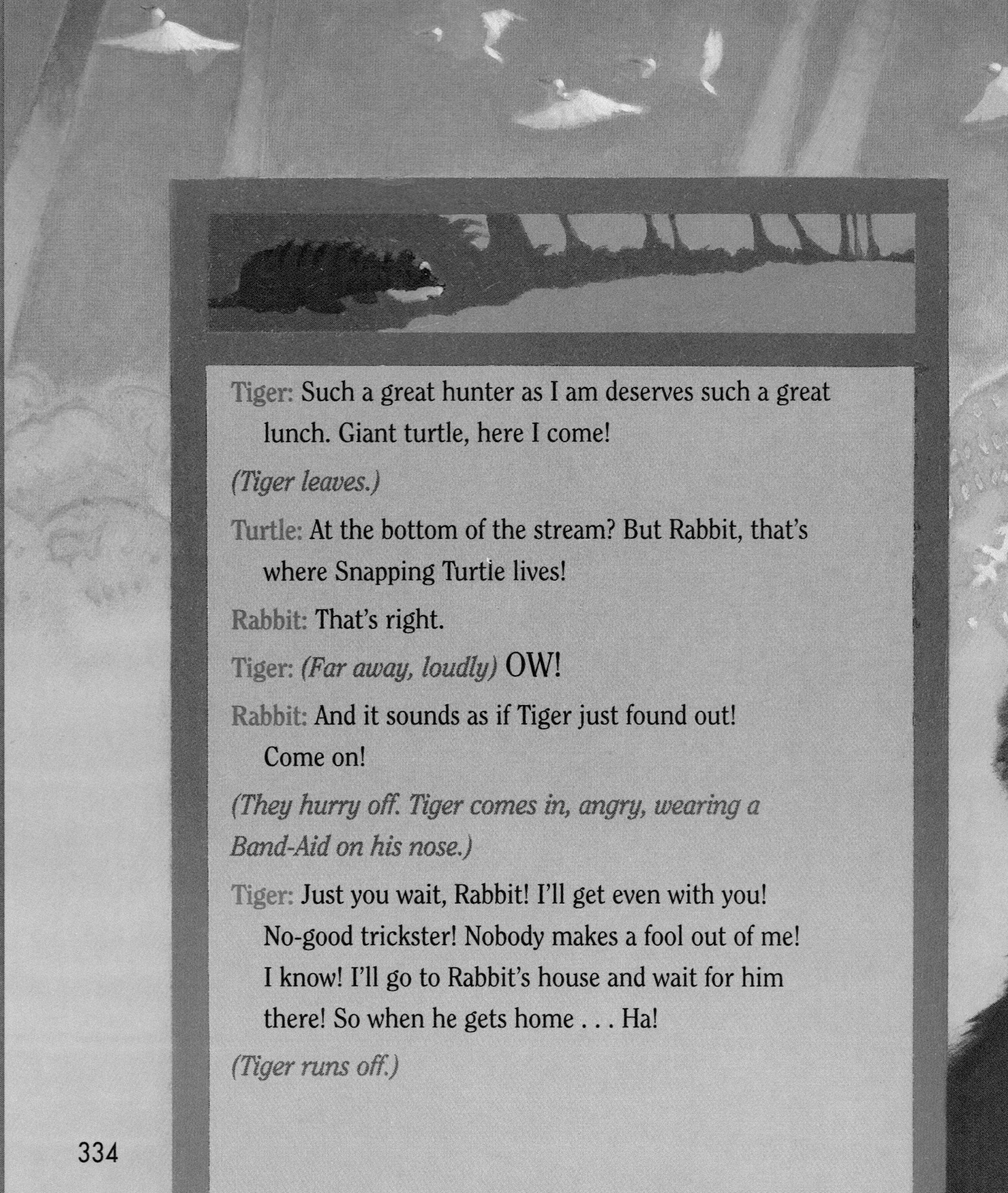

Tiger: Such a great hunter as I am deserves such a great lunch. Giant turtle, here I come!

(Tiger leaves.)

Turtle: At the bottom of the stream? But Rabbit, that's where Snapping Turtle lives!

Rabbit: That's right.

Tiger: *(Far away, loudly)* OW!

Rabbit: And it sounds as if Tiger just found out! Come on!

(They hurry off. Tiger comes in, angry, wearing a Band-Aid on his nose.)

Tiger: Just you wait, Rabbit! I'll get even with you! No-good trickster! Nobody makes a fool out of me! I know! I'll go to Rabbit's house and wait for him there! So when he gets home . . . Ha!

(Tiger runs off.)

334

MEETING INDIVIDUAL NEEDS

EXTRA SUPPORT Help children use clues from the text and illustrations to realize that Snapping Turtle nipped Tiger's nose. After children read the last sentence on the page, encourage them to discuss their ideas about what Tiger might be planning for Rabbit, and whether Tiger will be able to trick Rabbit.

335

Student Self-Assessment 

FIX-UP STRATEGY: DRAWING CONCLUSIONS

Ask children to reread page 334. Invite a volunteer to summarize story events up to this point. Then ask children to explain how they knew that Snapping Turtle nipped Tiger. Although an author doesn't always give readers all the details, the author often provides enough clues for readers to be able to figure out what happened. Make sure children realize that the clues on these pages were Tiger saying "Ow!" and then wearing a bandage on his nose.

WRITING

EXTEND THE STORY **Brainstorm with children what Rabbit might say to Tiger in a get-well card. Suggest that children fold a sheet of construction paper in half and use it to create a get-well card for Tiger.**

SCIENCE CONNECTION

TIGERS **Explain to children that tigers are in danger of becoming extinct. Help children research tigers. Small groups can use the facts they find to create a "Save the Tigers" poster.**

Strategic Reading

APPLYING A STRATEGY

PAGES 336–339 Have children read the pages silently. Then invite volunteers to act out the parts of Rabbit and Tiger on these pages. Before the others begin acting out the scene, have another child act as the narrator and read the information about the scene change. Then discuss with children how reading this part again helped them understand the story better. **REREADING**

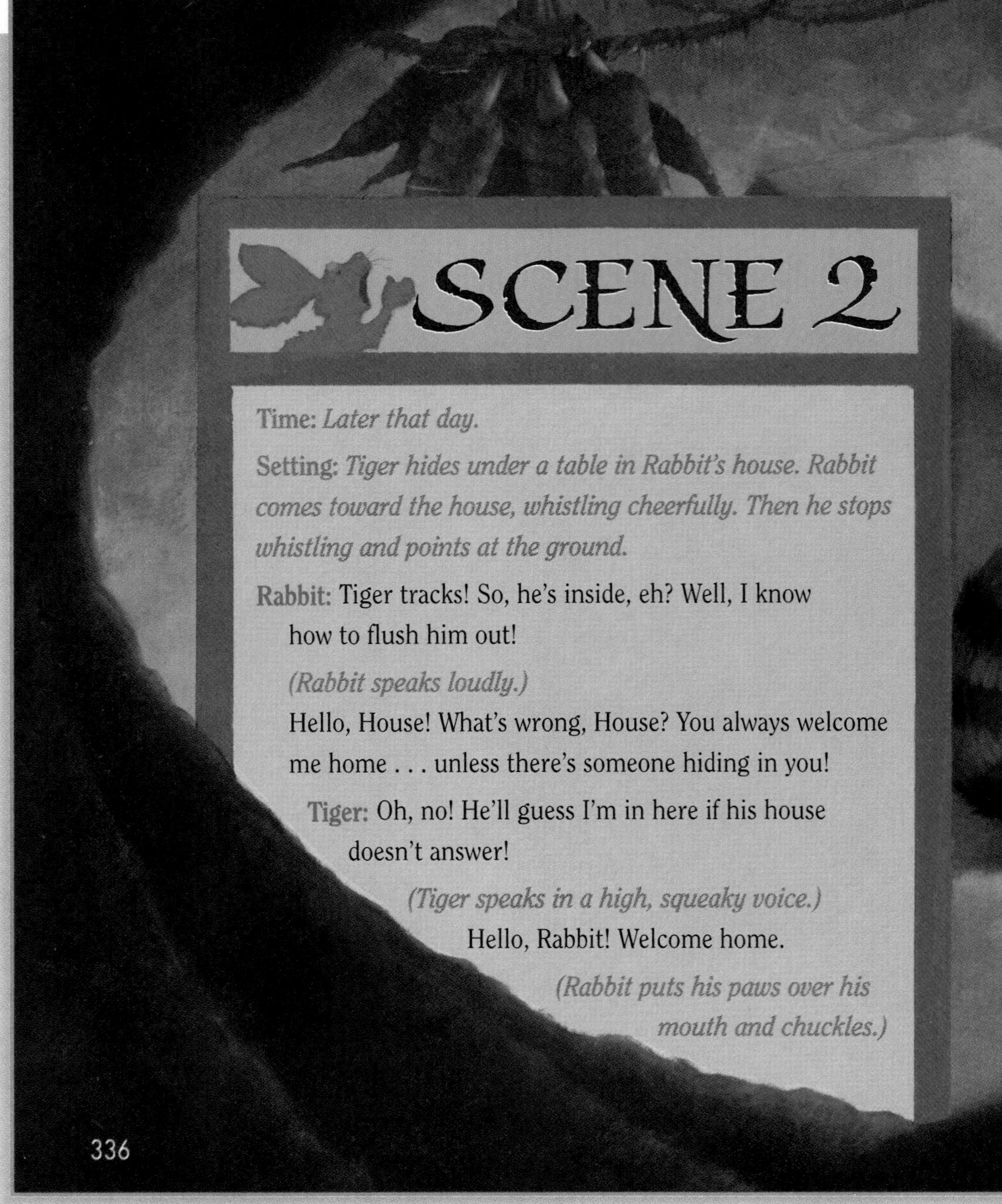

SCIENCE CONNECTION

ANIMAL TRACKS Point out that the tracks Tiger left behind were a clue for Rabbit. On index cards, draw familiar animal tracks, such as deer, dog, and bird tracks. Show each card to children and challenge them to name the animal that made the track. Encourage them to explain how they recognized the animal it belonged to.

Rabbit: Did you say something, House? I couldn't quite hear you!

Tiger: *(In a squeaky voice)* Hello, Rabbit!

Rabbit: What, House? What did you say?

Tiger: *(Loudly, in his Tiger voice)* Hello, Rabbit!

Rabbit: Hello yourself, you silly Tiger! You'll have to do more than hide under a table to catch me!

(Rabbit bounces off, laughing.)

Tiger: *(Crawling out from under the table)* Oh, that Rabbit! He makes me so mad! I'll catch him if it's the last thing I do!

337

Student Self-Assessment

FIX-UP STRATEGY: USING CONTEXT CLUES

Ask a volunteer to reread the last sentence on page 336. Ask children what they would do if they did not know what the word *chuckles* means. Point out that the beginning of the sentence tells us that Rabbit puts his paws over his mouth. We also know that Rabbit is trying to trick Tiger and probably thinks it's funny that Tiger answers and tries to disguise his voice. Children may conclude from these clues that the word *chuckles* means "laughs."

EXTRA SUPPORT **Help children understand that Rabbit's house does not really talk to him. Rabbit is just pretending it does so he can trick Tiger into talking. In that way, Rabbit will know that Tiger is really in his house.**

PHONICS IN ACTION

Call attention to the compound words *something* and *yourself on* page 337. Ask children to name the two words that make up each compound. Remind children that a good way to figure out long words while reading is to look for smaller words they know within the long word.

some + thing = something

YOUR + SELF = YOURSELF

Critical Thinking Questions

1. **How do you think Tiger feels in this part of the play? Why?** (Possible response: He is very angry because Rabbit has tricked him twice.) **CRITICAL: UNDERSTANDING CHARACTERS' FEELINGS**
2. **What do you think Rabbit's next trick is going to be?** (Responses will vary. Children should support their answers with information from the text.) **CRITICAL: SPECULATING**

338

SCIENCE

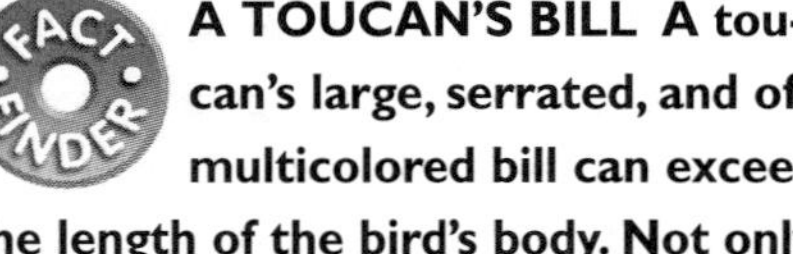

A TOUCAN'S BILL A toucan's large, serrated, and often multicolored bill can exceed the length of the bird's body. Not only is the bill used for feeding, it is also used in courtship displays.

ILLUSTRATOR'S CRAFT

Draw children's attention to Tiger's shadow in the illustration. Explore with them why the illustrator might have included the shadow and how it helps contribute to the mood of the scene. You might also want to have children look at the other illustrations and discuss how the artist helps give them a sense of what life in a rain forest is like.

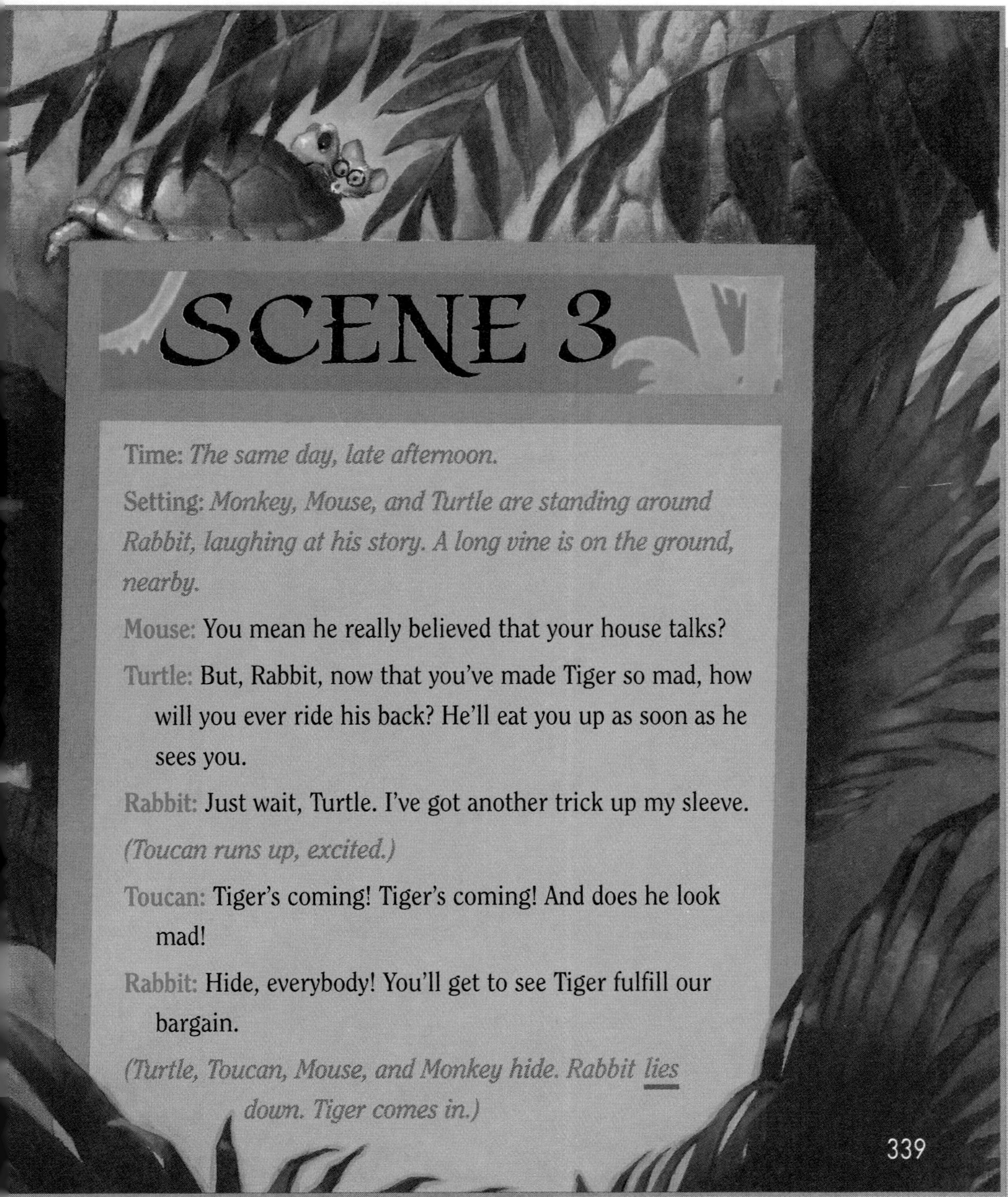

SCENE 3

Time: *The same day, late afternoon.*

Setting: *Monkey, Mouse, and Turtle are standing around Rabbit, laughing at his story. A long vine is on the ground, nearby.*

Mouse: You mean he really believed that your house talks?

Turtle: But, Rabbit, now that you've made Tiger so mad, how will you ever ride his back? He'll eat you up as soon as he sees you.

Rabbit: Just wait, Turtle. I've got another trick up my sleeve.

(Toucan runs up, excited.)

Toucan: Tiger's coming! Tiger's coming! And does he look mad!

Rabbit: Hide, everybody! You'll get to see Tiger fulfill our bargain.

(Turtle, Toucan, Mouse, and Monkey hide. Rabbit lies down. Tiger comes in.)

339

MEETING INDIVIDUAL NEEDS

STUDENTS ACQUIRING ENGLISH Call attention to the phrase *another trick up my sleeve.* Explain that it means "something else to try." To help children understand, you may wish to pantomime a magician's card trick to show the origin of the phrase.

MUSIC CONNECTION

A JUMP-ROPE RHYME At a time when the children are outside, provide jump ropes and teach children this jump-rope rhyme.

Rabbit's tricky, Tiger's mad,
Turtle's safe and very glad.
Rabbit's plans are right
on track.
How many stripes on
Tiger's back?
(Hot pepper!) 1, 2, 3, 4, . . .

Some children may enjoy creating their own jump-rope rhymes based on the play.

Strategic Reading

APPLYING A STRATEGY

PAGES 340–341 When children have read enough to get ideas about Rabbit's plan, have them predict how Rabbit's plan will work and also whether Tiger will give Rabbit a ride before the sun sets. Then have children read on to confirm their predictions. **MAKING AND CONFIRMING PREDICTIONS**

340

SCHOOL↔HOME CONNECTION

Have children ask family members to share stories that feature rabbit characters. Encourage children to share these stories with classmates.

SCIENCE CONNECTION

RABBIT CARE **Invite a pet owner or pet-store worker to bring in a rabbit and talk about how to care for a rabbit, as well as typical rabbit behavior. Then, help children compare the real rabbit with rabbit characters they know. Cut out two large rabbit shapes. Label one *Rabbit Facts* and the other *Rabbit Stories*. As children share their ideas, record their responses on the shapes.**

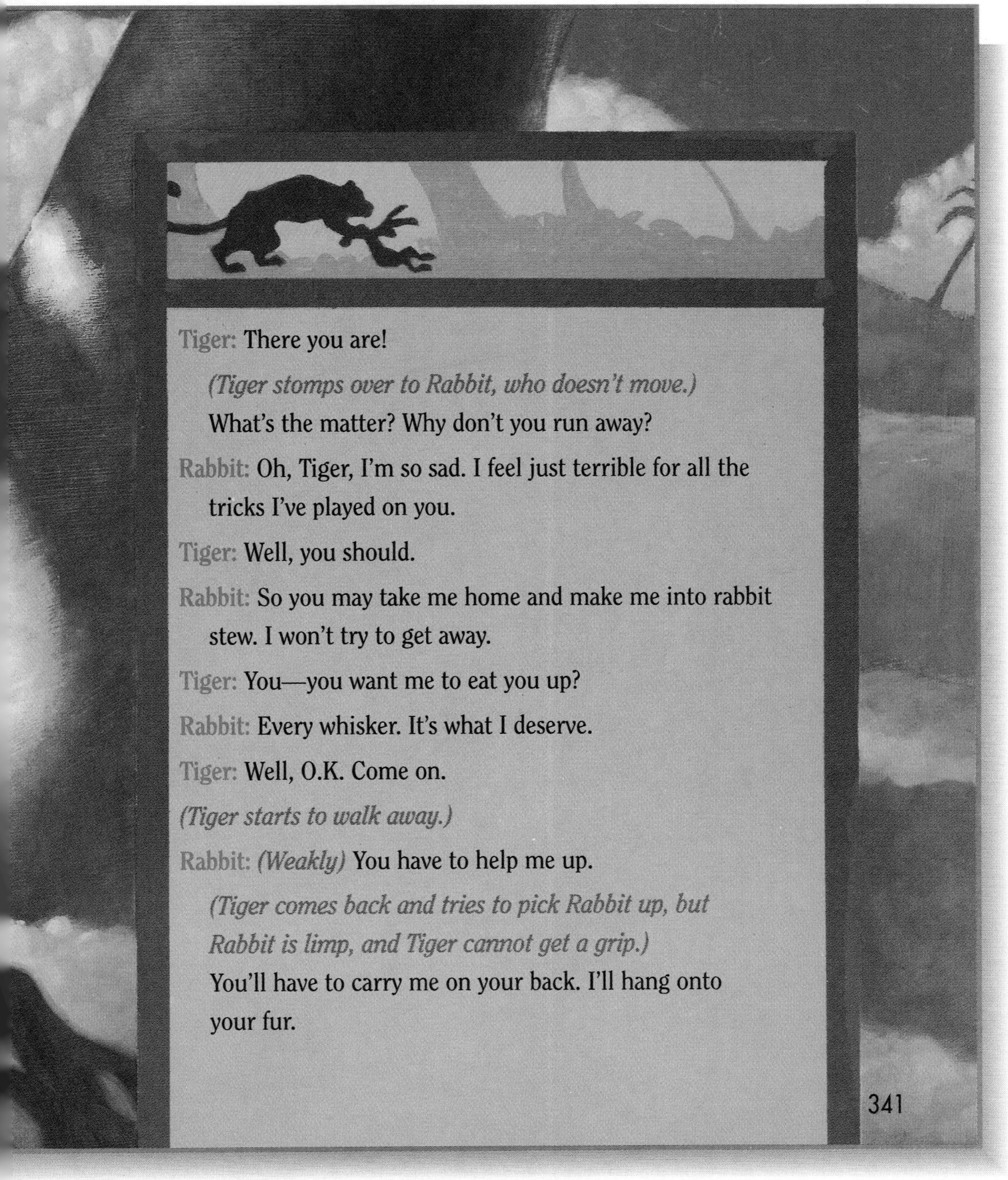

Tiger: There you are!

(Tiger stomps over to Rabbit, who doesn't move.)

What's the matter? Why don't you run away?

Rabbit: Oh, Tiger, I'm so sad. I feel just terrible for all the tricks I've played on you.

Tiger: Well, you should.

Rabbit: So you may take me home and make me into rabbit stew. I won't try to get away.

Tiger: You—you want me to eat you up?

Rabbit: Every whisker. It's what I deserve.

Tiger: Well, O.K. Come on.

(Tiger starts to walk away.)

Rabbit: *(Weakly)* You have to help me up.

(Tiger comes back and tries to pick Rabbit up, but Rabbit is limp, and Tiger cannot get a grip.)

You'll have to carry me on your back. I'll hang onto your fur.

341

MATH CONNECTION

ESTIMATING WEIGHT **Wild rabbits weigh from two to five pounds. Show children a few items of different weights, such as a 5-lb. bag of flour, a 10-lb. sack of potatoes, and a 2-lb. bag of rice. Mask the weights of the items. Invite children to pick up the items and tell which one they think is closest to a rabbit's weight of two pounds and then five pounds. Then uncover the weights and talk about children's estimates.**

Strategic Reading

APPLYING A STRATEGY

PAGES 342–343 Rabbit gets to ride Tiger, but how does he do it? Point out that rereading is also a good way to be more clear about the details in a story. Have children scan pages 342–343 and then tell a partner or small group exactly how Rabbit makes his plan work. **REREADING**

Returning to the Predictions/Purpose

Before children read, they wrote their predictions about the play. Invite them to share their predictions and compare them to what actually happened.

Appreciating the Literature

With the whole class or a small group, have an open discussion about the play.

- **What did you like most about the play? Why?**

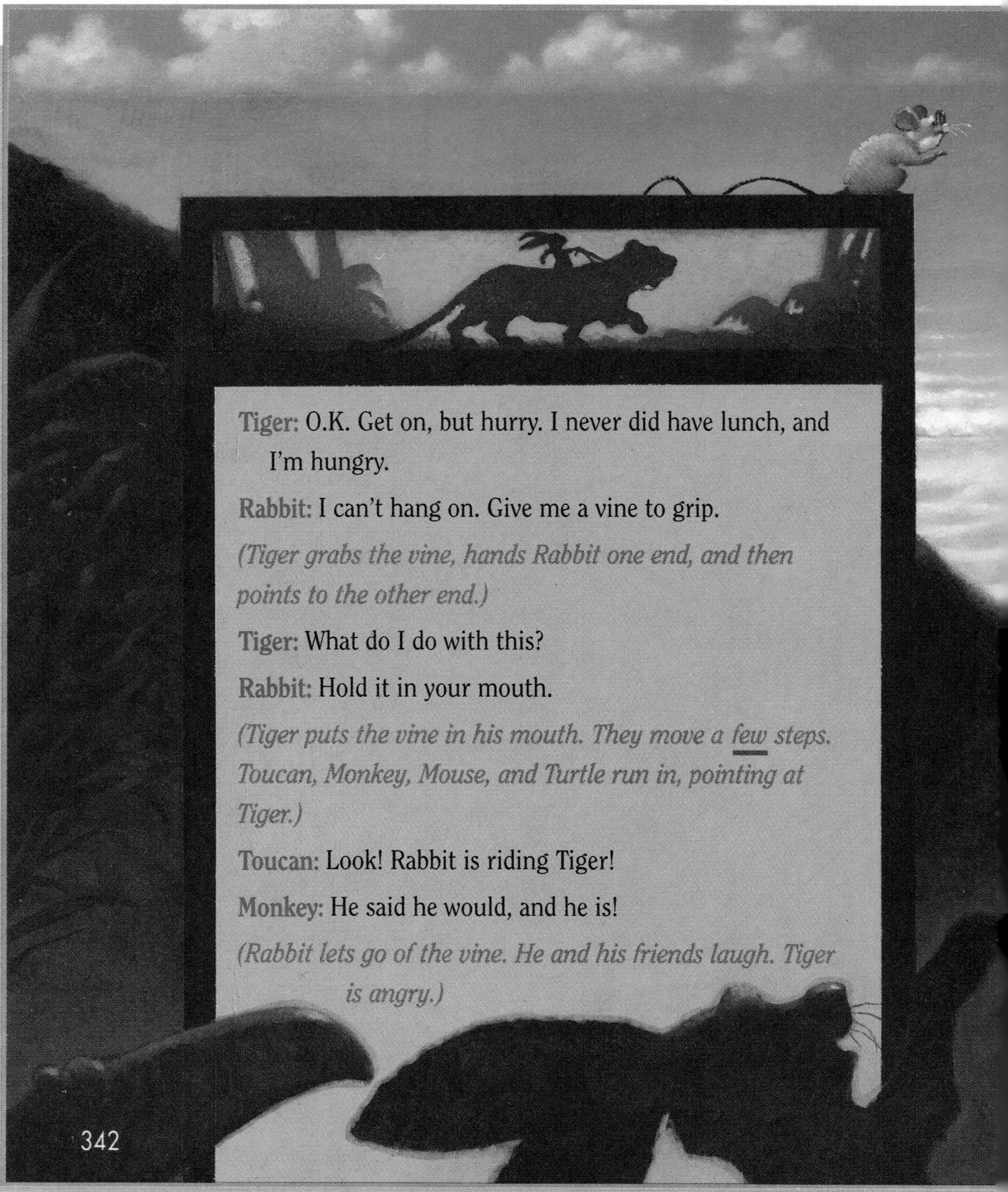

Tiger: O.K. Get on, but hurry. I never did have lunch, and I'm hungry.

Rabbit: I can't hang on. Give me a vine to grip.

(Tiger grabs the vine, hands Rabbit one end, and then points to the other end.)

Tiger: What do I do with this?

Rabbit: Hold it in your mouth.

(Tiger puts the vine in his mouth. They move a few steps. Toucan, Monkey, Mouse, and Turtle run in, pointing at Tiger.)

Toucan: Look! Rabbit is riding Tiger!

Monkey: He said he would, and he is!

(Rabbit lets go of the vine. He and his friends laugh. Tiger is angry.)

342

CHALLENGE **As children look at a world map, have them speculate about where Tiger will go after he leaves Puerto Rico. Encourage them to describe what Tiger's life might be like in his new home.**

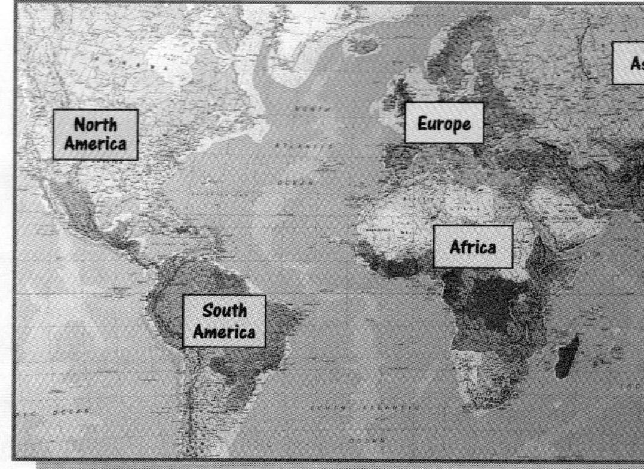

Rabbit: You gave your word, Tiger! We shook paws on it!

Tiger: You tricked me!

Rabbit: Trick or no, a bargain's a bargain. Now, do you want to walk down to the beach on your own, or shall we carry you?

Tiger: I'm going. I'm going!

(Tiger shakes his paw at Rabbit.)

But someday, trickster! Someday!

Rabbit: Goodbye, Tiger. I hope you're a fine swimmer!

THE END

343

NOTES

Here's a place to list ideas or activities that you would like to use the next time you teach this lesson.

SUMMARIZE AND RETELL

Map It

Discuss the setting, characters, problem, and solution of the play. Record children's ideas on a story map like the one shown. Then invite children to summarize the story of "Rabbit and Tiger." See *Practice Book* page 117.

STORY MAP

Title	Setting	Characters
Rabbit and Tiger	A jungle in Puerto Rico, long ago	Rabbit, Tiger, Mouse, Toucan, Turtle, Monkey

Problem

Tiger is scaring the other animals.

Solution

Rabbit makes a deal with Tiger and then tricks Tiger. Tiger must leave Puerto Rico.

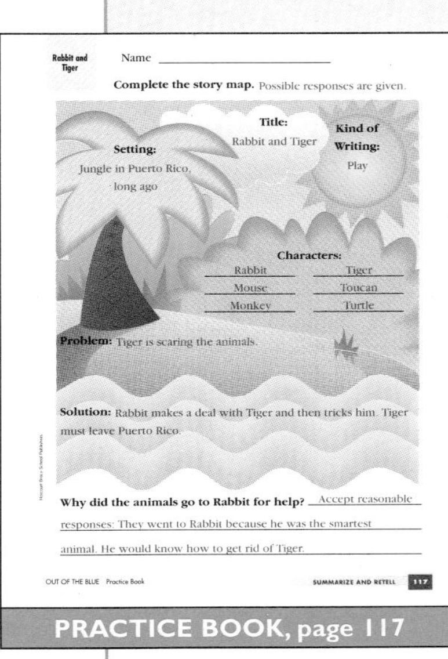
Rabbit and Tiger

Name ______

Complete the story map. Possible responses are given.

Title: Rabbit and Tiger

Setting: Jungle in Puerto Rico, long ago

Kind of Writing: Play

Characters: Rabbit, Tiger, Mouse, Toucan, Monkey, Turtle

Problem: Tiger is scaring the animals.

Solution: Rabbit makes a deal with Tiger and then tricks him. Tiger must leave Puerto Rico.

Why did the animals go to Rabbit for help? Accept reasonable responses: They went to Rabbit because he was the smartest animal. He would know how to get rid of Tiger.

OUT OF THE BLUE Practice Book SUMMARIZE AND RETELL 117

PRACTICE BOOK, page 117

About the Author

PAGES 344–345 Have children read about F. C. Nicholson and Richard Bernal. Discuss children's reactions to the play and the illustrations.

F. C. Nicholson decided to make "Rabbit and Tiger" into a play after hearing the folktale from a friend and then seeing it as a book. She remembers acting out the plays in her reading books when she was in school. Even then, she liked the idea that plays involve many readers rather than one reader sitting alone and reading. She remembers also, "I was always the narrator, and I guess I still am."

Nicholson lives near Boston, Massachusetts, with her cats.

F.C. NICHOLSON

"Rabbit and Tiger" is a folktale that F. C. Nicholson heard from a friend. Then she saw it in a book and turned it into a play. Ms. Nicholson says, "I liked the story because the smaller, weaker animal comes out on top."

"I read a lot when I was little," she says. "I could read before I went to school. I liked reading stories, and I liked telling them, too. That led me to writing them."

F. C. Nicholson Facts

- The F in her name is for Frances. She is named after her mom.
- She loves animals. She has six cats.
- Of course, she likes to read.
- She likes the outdoors, especially the sea.

F. C. Nicholson

344

RICHARD BERNAL

I was born in Chicago, Illinois. In the second grade, I liked to draw cartoons. I kept drawing all through elementary school, high school, and then in Art School.

Now I live in St. Louis, Missouri with my lovely wife Catherine and my dog Atticus. I enjoy jogging, hiking, and reading. I also like movies, music, and cartoons. Do you like to go to the zoo? I do! Sometimes when I'm there I draw, and sometimes I just enjoy looking at the animals—animals such as rabbits and tigers!

R. Bernal

345

About the Illustrator

Richard Bernal's interest in art began in second grade, when he started drawing cartoons. He still enjoys cartoons, but of all the illustrating he does, Bernal says, "Children's books are the most fun to do."

One thing he enjoys about working on children's books is the interactive process of submitting sketches; getting comments from art directors, editors, and others involved in producing the book; and revising the sketches until they really show what's happening in a story. When that process is complete, he paints the pictures. The illustrations for this play are a testament to Richard Bernal's ability to bring a story to life.

RESPONSE CORNER ACTIVITIES

PERFORM A PUPPET PLAY

PUPPET SHOW!

PAGE 346 Help children decide who in each group will play each character. Read the puppet-making directions with them. When groups present the puppet show, you might want to have each group perform one scene or section of the play. Groups might enjoy making backdrops to show the setting for their scenes. **ART/READING**

WRITE A STORY

THE BIG COVER-UP

PAGE 347 Discuss some ways Tiger might hide from the other animals—for example, by disguising himself as a tree, putting on a toucan beak, or painting his yellow stripes white to look like a zebra. Then, group members may want to work together on one drawing of Tiger or each member may do his or her own drawing. Have groups look at their drawing(s) together and use the ideas to plan their group story. **WRITING**

RESPONSE

PERFORM A PUPPET PLAY

Puppet Show!

Plan a puppet show for the play "Rabbit and Tiger." Work in a group to make paper-bag puppets. Use the puppets to put on the play.

You will need:

small paper bag
construction paper
scissors
glue
crayons or markers

- Draw your animal's paws, eyes, ears, or beak on construction paper. Cut them out.
- Glue the parts onto the bag.
- After you make your puppets, practice the play. You can perform your puppet play for another class.

346

VARYING THE ACTIVITY

Before forming groups to put on puppet plays, you may wish to review with some children the play format. Go over a section of the play with them to make sure they understand which characters say which parts, what parts of the play describe characters' actions or emotions, and other aspects of a play format.

CORNER

WRITE A STORY

The Big Cover-Up

What will happen if Tiger doesn't leave the island? Make up a way for Tiger to hide from the other animals. Write a story to tell what happens.

1. Make a painting or drawing of Tiger. Put a disguise on him so he looks like someone or something else.
2. Write a group story about what happens when Tiger tries to fool the other animals.
3. Share your picture and story with classmates.

What Do You Think?

- What kind of character is Rabbit?
- How would you have felt at the end of the story if you were Tiger?

347

CHECKING COMPREHENSION

What Do You Think?

1. **What kind of character is Rabbit?** (Accept reasonable responses: He is smart, funny, clever, and good at tricking Tiger.) DESCRIPTIVE RESPONSE
2. **How would you have felt at the end of the story if you were Tiger?** (Responses will vary, but children should support their answers.) PERSONAL RESPONSE

An additional question for extending reading.

3. **Imagine someone bullying you or your friends like Tiger bullied the other animals. What would you do?** (Accept reasonable responses.) CRITICAL/CREATIVE ANALYSIS

MEETING INDIVIDUAL NEEDS

MULTI-AGE CLASSROOMS

Group children of different ages together as they work on The Big Cover-Up. Encourage older children to share writing strategies they have learned with the group. Suggest that they work with younger, less-skilled readers to read the completed stories.

Informal Assessment

Observe children as they write their group stories.

- ☑ Do children base the stories on their drawings?
- ☑ Do they tell the story in a logical sequence?
- ☑ Do they take turns contributing to their group's story?

Intervention Strategies

Instant Readers™

Predictable and Patterned Little Books That Build Fluency

*** BOOK LEVEL: 18–19**

VOCABULARY:
bargain, mind

PHONIC ELEMENTS:
Long vowel: /ī/*i-e*;
R*-controlled vowel: /ûr/*ur, er

PHONOGRAM:
-ind

SUMMARY:
Molly's brother learns the hard way not to mess with his little sister.

Informal Assessment

Are children able to

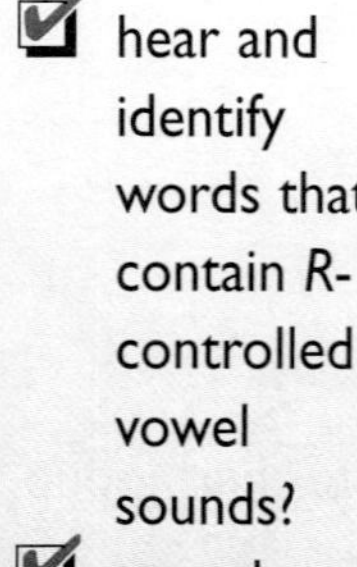
hear and identify words that contain *R*-controlled vowel sounds?

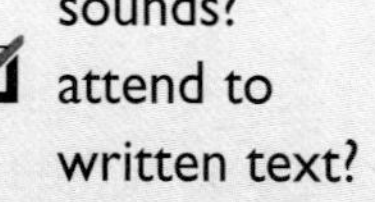
attend to written text?

Reading a New Book

INTRODUCING *MOLLY'S HARD BARGAIN*

Talk with children about the concepts of bargain and hard bargain. Share the illustrations and discuss the two main characters in the story, Molly and her big brother, Brian. The pictures may remind those children who have siblings of some common situations in their homes.

READING THE STORY

Once children grasp the concept of bargain, have them read the story independently to find out what kind of bargain Molly makes.

WORKING WITH WORDS AND LETTERS

Give children an opportunity to reread the story to find words that contain *R*-controlled vowel sounds, such as *bargain* and *turn*. Have children write the words on the board and underline the letters that stand for the *R*-controlled vowel sounds.

turn
her
Thursday

WRITING SECRET MESSAGES

Bring a mirror to class, and have children take turns writing while looking in the mirror. As children enjoy this activity, they will explore letter sequence with reverse writing.

Additional activities are provided on pages 70–71 of the *Intervention Strategies Manual*.

* **BOOK LEVEL: 20+**

VOCABULARY:
fierce, jungle, lie, mind

PHONIC ELEMENTS:
Long vowel: /ī/i-e, i;
***R*-controlled vowel: /ûr/ur**

PHONOGRAM:
-ind

SUMMARY:
Facts about tigers are presented.

Reading a New Book

INTRODUCING *PRETEND YOU'RE A TIGER*

As children look at the cover and the story illustrations, have them describe the ways a tiger looks and behaves. Ask questions of the children to draw out some of the story vocabulary about the characteristics of tigers and their habitat.

READING THE STORY

Have children read the story independently to learn more about tigers.

WORKING WITH WORDS AND LETTERS

Have children create a tiger description by using the letters from the word *tiger,* as shown in the sample below. If children have trouble finding a word for some of the letters, suggest that they write phrases.

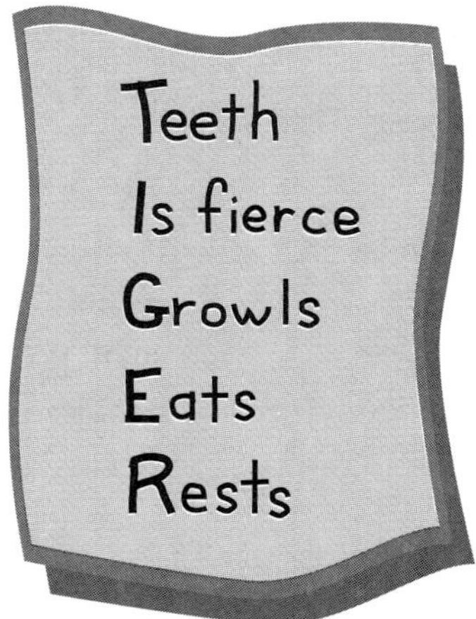

WRITING DESCRIPTIONS

Suggest that children write a brief description of their favorite animal.

ESL/Title I Reading

Hello, House!
by Linda Hayward

ESL/Title I Library

TECHNOLOGY

INSTANT READERS™

ELECTRONIC EDITION

***Molly's Hard Bargain* and *Pretend You're a Tiger* are available on CD-ROM. Pre- and post-reading activities are included.**

Working with "Rabbit and Tiger"

SEMANTIC CUES For a Readers Theatre, have children place self-stick notes next to their speaking parts. Suggest that children work with a buddy to rehearse their parts in one section of the play. Buddy-readers can read aloud together to gain fluency.

* Books leveled according to Barbara Peterson's "Profiles of Books for Beginning Readers," on page 9 of the *Instant Readers Teacher's Guide.*

IDEA BANK

TIPS FOR CLASSROOM MANAGEMENT

IF you do not have playbills of your own to show children for the Reading Playbills activity, **THEN** you could contact a local theater group or library to find samples.

IF your class is a multi-age one, **THEN** you might suggest that older children extend the Under the Forest Canopy activity by researching the plants and animals that live in the different levels of a rain forest.

LISTENING AND SPEAKING

Group Talk

TIGER TROUBLE

Invite children to think about the "tiger trouble" in the play. Help children form small groups and discuss ways that the problem could have been solved without forcing Tiger to leave Puerto Rico. Encourage children to be creative as they suggest possibilities and then discuss how well they think each idea would work.

After the small-group discussions, gather children to share their ideas and insights. **CHALLENGING THE TEXT**

Informal Assessment

Observe whether children's proposed solutions reflect an understanding of the story problem.

REAL-LIFE READING

Reading Playbills

Tell children that when people go to a play, they usually receive a booklet called a playbill. Playbills contain information about the theater, the play, the author, the director, the actors, costume designers, stage managers, musicians, and all the other people who worked on the production.

Provide children with sample playbills to browse through. Then have them make a playbill for a possible performance of "Rabbit and Tiger." Assign pairs of children a subject: the front cover, story summary, the theater, cast of characters, director, costume designer, and so on. Each pair should draw and write a page of the playbill. Then the whole group can assemble the playbill. **LISTENING/ READING/WRITING**

Hello, Is Your House Home?

Rabbit tricked Tiger into thinking a house could talk. But what happens if you call your friend's house, and no one is home?

Hi! This is Rabbit's house. You can leave a message, and maybe I'll call you back.

WHERE DID ALL THE TIGERS GO?

There aren't any tigers in Puerto Rico. In fact, there are only a few places in the world where tigers live in the wild. And even in those places, there aren't many tigers. This map shows where you can find tigers.

RUSSIA, Siberian Tiger, MONGOLIA, CHINA, South China Tiger, Bengal Tiger, INDIA, Indo-Chinese Tiger, Sumatran Tiger, SUMATRA, KEY Tigers

WRITER'S MAGAZINE, pages 44–47

ORAL LANGUAGE

Rereading for Fluency

READERS THEATRE/DRAMA

Have children work in small groups to reread the play aloud. Once they have grasped the play format, they can each take a part and read the play straight through, concentrating on reading with expression. Encourage children to add simple actions to enhance performance. LISTENING/READING

KINESTHETIC

MATERIALS
- bedsheet
- markers or paint
- reference books about rain forests

Creative Connection

UNDER THE FOREST CANOPY

Explain to children that there are so many trees in a rain forest that the tops of the trees make a cover over the forest called a canopy. Many animals live in and under the canopy. Spread out the bedsheet and let children use markers or paint to decorate it, coloring in treetops and rain forest animals. Invite small groups of children to take turns holding up the canopy while others pretend to be characters from the story, such as Toucan or Monkey, or other rain forest animals. Encourage children to make the sounds and movements of the animals. LISTENING/KINESTHETIC

PERSONAL JOURNAL

REFLECTING ON THE STORY **Invite children to write about the experience of reading a play. Ask them to write about what they liked as well as what they didn't like about reading/performing a play.**

WRITER'S WORKSHOP

A Play

TIPS FOR CLASSROOM MANAGEMENT

IF children are familiar with the writing process approach, **THEN** present the writing assignment and have them use the Play model on pages 26–27 of the *Language Handbook*.

IF at this time you want a short writing activity, **THEN** have children complete the Prewriting Chart and use it to practice an oral version of the play.

TECHNOLOGY

THE AMAZING WRITING MACHINE
Primary Level
Activity Disk Pack
Grade 2
Have children enter their plays in the Stories mode.

KID PIX
Children can illustrate their plays by creating pictures of their own or using the stamps.

Thinking as Writers

WRITING FORM: Play Remind children that "Rabbit and Tiger" is a play. Talk about which characters in the play seem most real and why. Then explain to children that they will work in small groups to create a new story about the characters from "Rabbit and Tiger" and write it as a play.

Display Chart/Transparency 24, or write the model Play on the board. Discuss the main parts of a play. Ask children to tell how a play is different from a story and how it is the same.

CHART/TRANSPARENCY 24

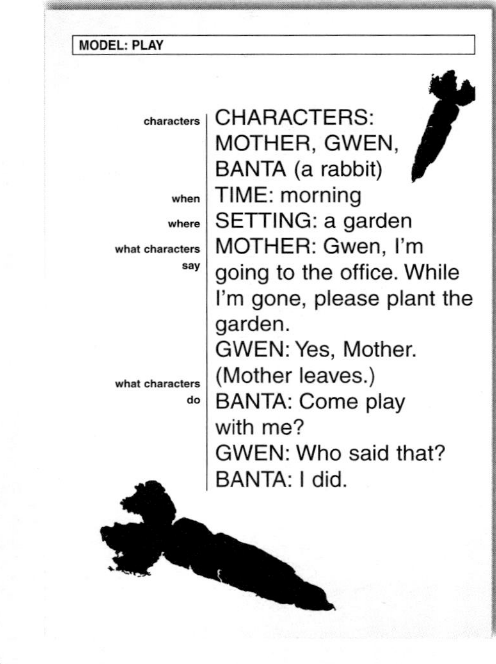
MODEL: PLAY

characters — CHARACTERS: MOTHER, GWEN, BANTA (a rabbit)
when — TIME: morning
where — SETTING: a garden
what characters say — MOTHER: Gwen, I'm going to the office. While I'm gone, please plant the garden.
GWEN: Yes, Mother.
what characters do — (Mother leaves.)
BANTA: Come play with me?
GWEN: Who said that?
BANTA: I did.

WRITER'S CRAFT: Character Traits and Dialogue Explain that playwrights make characters come alive through what they say and do. The words and actions of a character can show whether a character is shy, brave, or tricky. Have children look at the play to find dialogue and actions that show characters' traits.

PREWRITING

MATERIALS
- paper plates
- craft sticks
- tape
- glue
- collage materials such as fabric and paper scraps, yarn, feathers, foil, buttons, beads

Provide groups with materials to make stick puppets of the animals from "Rabbit and Tiger." Have children decorate a paper plate with collage materials to look like each character they choose and then tape a craft stick to the back of the plate.

Encourage the groups to play with their puppets to try out ideas for other adventures the characters might have. Then model how to complete a chart like the following, using "Rabbit and Tiger."

Time: *Long ago*
Setting: *The jungle of Puerto Rico*
Characters: *Rabbit, Tiger, Mouse, Toucan, Monkey, Turtle*
What will happen? *Rabbit will trick Tiger into leaving Puerto Rico.*
What will the characters say? *Mouse, Toucan, and Monkey will tell how scared of Tiger they are. Rabbit will tell them he knows how to trick Tiger.*

Distribute copies of the chart and have children work with their group to plan their play.

DRAFTING

As children work in groups to write their plays, remind them to

- use their chart, their puppets, and their imagination for ideas.
- include a time and a setting.
- write what each character says.
- think of a title for their play.

Have them save their drafts and revisions in their writer's folder.

RESPONDING AND REVISING

Work with one group at a time, using these questions to help children think about how to revise their plays:

- Is the play about what happened to the characters from "Rabbit and Tiger"?
- Does the play tell the exact words the characters say?
- Can you tell what the characters are like by what they say and do?

PROOFREADING

Suggest some tips as groups proofread their plays. Help children focus on the following:

NAMES OF SPECIAL PEOPLE, ANIMALS, AND PLACES Names of special people, animals, and places begin with a capital letter.

IRREGULAR PLURAL NOUNS Some nouns change spelling to name more than one. (See the Grammar Minilesson on page T657.)

PUBLISHING

Have children make a clean copy of their plays. Then offer publishing options like the following:

PLAY BOOKS
Children can make their own play books. Help them staple the book pages at the top between pieces of plain colored cloth. Then children can use markers to make the cloth resemble a theater curtain. Invite children to read and enjoy their plays as the "curtain" goes up.

Handwriting
Remind children that their handwriting must be neat and clear so that the person reading the play can understand it. If children need assistance, refer them to the Handwriting models in the *Language Handbook* or in the classroom.

SHOWTIME Have children construct a puppet stage by covering a table with an old sheet or curtain. Groups can perform their plays, using their stick puppets.

PORTFOLIO OPPORTUNITY

After children publish, make copies of their plays and have them attach their Writing Self-Assessment Checklists to them. Have them place the plays and checklists in their portfolios.

LANGUAGE HANDBOOK
Play, pages 26–27

Student Self-Assessment ✓

Children can use the Writing Self-Assessment Checklist in the *Portfolio Assessment Teacher's Guide.*

EVALUATING THE WRITTEN RESPONSE

When evaluating children's plays, consider:

CONTENT	ORGANIZATION	CHARACTERS
Does the play tell about another adventure of the characters from "Rabbit and Tiger"?	Does the play include a time and a setting? Does each character have a part in the play?	Does the dialogue reflect the characters' personality traits?

EVALUATION BENCHMARKS

The child has difficulty writing a play. The time and setting are missing, and there is no real dialogue.	= EMERGENT
The child writes a play, but the dialogue is stilted.	= BEGINNING
The child successfully writes a play. The characters come alive through what they say and do.	= PROFICIENT

Tested Skill

GRAMMAR

Pronouns

Reading↔Writing Connection

Connect to the story. Write these lines of Tiger's on the board:

Oh that Rabbit! He makes me so mad! I'll catch him if it's the last thing I do!

Read the lines aloud and then ask children which character said them. Then draw attention to the pronoun *He* in the second sentence. Ask who Tiger is talking about and how children know. Talk about who Tiger means when he uses the word *I* and when he uses the word *him*. Each time, ask children how they know.

Build oral language. Have children reread the information about the author and illustrator on pages 344 and 345. Ask them to tell what they learned about these people and their work on the play. Record sentences in which children use pronouns as they discuss the author, illustrator, and the play. (*he, they, it, I, she*) Read the sentences with children. Call attention to the pronouns. Ask children to whom or to what each pronoun refers.

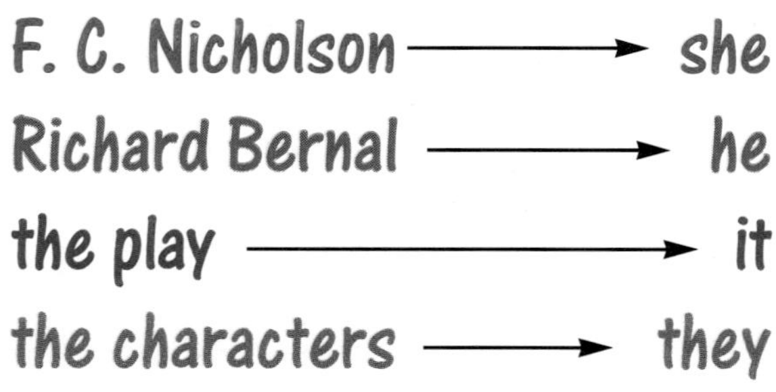

Teach/Model

Discuss pronouns. Tell children that the words *I, she, he, it, you,* and *they* are pronouns. Explain that these words can take the place of nouns. Pronouns can be used to shorten and to vary sentences. Then display the following story, and work with children to substitute pronouns for some of the nouns to make it sound less repetitious.

Rabbit walked into the jungle. Rabbit saw Toucan, Mouse, and Monkey. Toucan, Mouse, and Monkey were afraid of Tiger. Tiger even slept by the banana tree so that Monkey couldn't go near the banana tree!

You might also discuss the use of the pronouns *I* and *you*.

Practice/Apply

Check understanding. Write the following words on the board, and ask children to suggest pronouns that could stand for them.

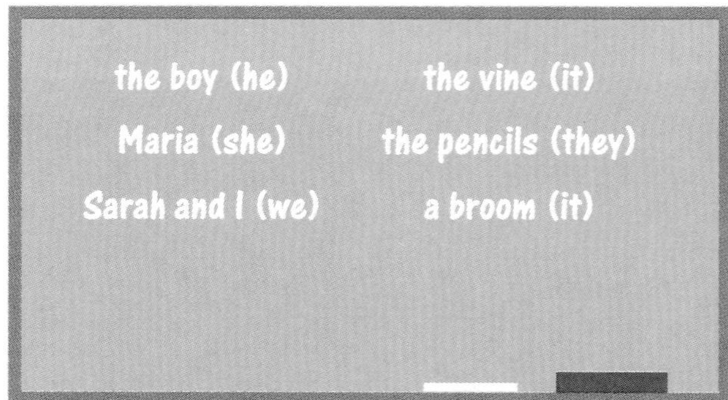

Ask volunteers to choose a noun or noun phrase and use it in a sentence. Then ask another volunteer to repeat the sentence, replacing the noun with a pronoun.

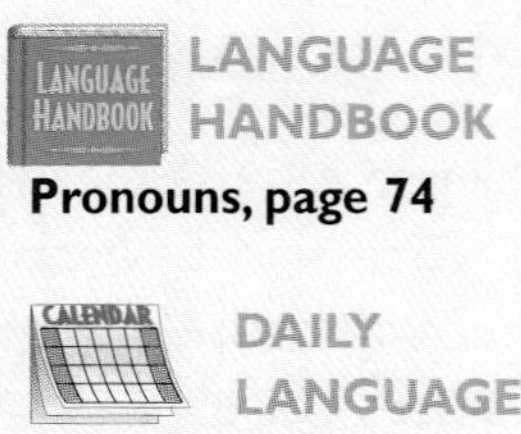

LANGUAGE HANDBOOK
Pronouns, page 74

DAILY LANGUAGE PRACTICE **Oral language exercises are provided on page R145.**

TECHNOLOGY

Children can practice using pronouns with *Bailey's Book House* (Make-A-Story).

Practice Activities

BAG OF NOUN TRICKS

WRITING APPLICATION On slips of paper, write nouns that can be replaced by the pronouns *I, he, she, it*, or *they*. Invite children to pick a slip of paper from the bag. Have them write a sentence using the noun and then write a second sentence using a pronoun in place of the noun or nouns. **VISUAL/KINESTHETIC**

Clapping Game

ORAL APPLICATION Invite children to play a clapping game in which they name nouns and the pronouns that can take their place. Help them establish a rhythm (for example, patting their laps twice and then clapping once). One player names a noun during the pats and that the others name the pronoun that replaces the noun during the clap. Children can take turns being the one to say the noun. **AUDITORY/ KINESTHETIC**

Search the Newspaper

WRITING APPLICATION Cut short articles or sections of articles from a children's magazine or newspaper. Write the pronouns *I, he, she, it*, and *they* for children to use as a reference. Have partners work together to find and circle the pronouns in their article. When they finish, invite each pair to share pronouns they found and to name the noun or nouns they took the place of. **VISUAL/AUDITORY/KINESTHETIC**

APPLY TO WRITING

If children have written plays in the Writer's Workshop, have them review their work to see whether they have used pronouns in place of nouns to vary their sentences.

5-DAY PLAN

Use in conjunction with Daily Language Practice.

Day 1 Complete page T678.	**Day 4** Choose a Practice Activity or *Grammar Practice Book* pages 51–52.
Day 2 Complete a Practice Activity on page T679.	**Day 5** Complete *Practice Book* page 118.
Day 3 Choose a Practice Activity or *Language Handbook* page 74.	

STUDENTS ACQUIRING ENGLISH

Write the words *he*, *she*, and *they* on the board. Form small groups. Have children stand up one or two at a time, and ask other children to tell which of the words on the board would be used to talk about that child or group of children.

RETEACH

See page R137 for lessons in multiple modalities.

CHALLENGE

Children can play a game in which one partner says a sentence that uses a pronoun. The other player says the same sentence, substituting a noun for the pronoun.

GRAMMAR PRACTICE BOOK
pages 51-52

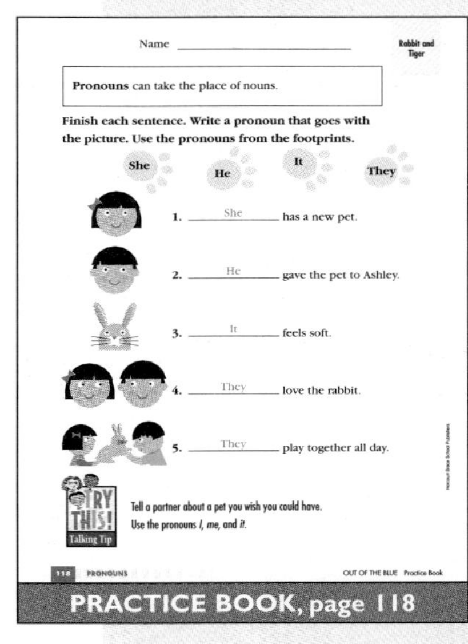
Name ______________ Rabbit and Tiger

Pronouns can take the place of nouns.

Finish each sentence. Write a pronoun that goes with the picture. Use the pronouns from the footprints.

She He It They

1. ___She___ has a new pet.
2. ___He___ gave the pet to Ashley.
3. ___It___ feels soft.
4. ___They___ love the rabbit.
5. ___They___ play together all day.

TRY THIS! Talking Tip

Tell a partner about a pet you wish you could have. Use the pronouns *I, me*, and *it*.

118 PRONOUNS OUT OF THE BLUE Practice Book

PRACTICE BOOK, page 118

2

SPELLING

5-Day Plan

Integrated Spelling Lesson 16:
student book, pages 70–73;
Teacher's Edition, pages T111–T116.

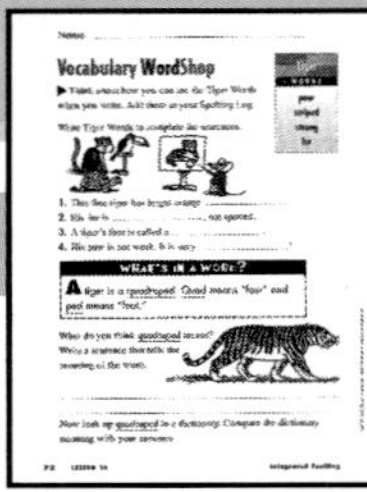

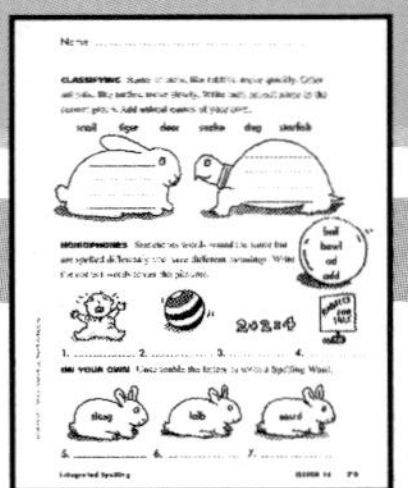

SPELLING WORDS

1. fall ★
2. all★
3. ball
4. less
5. add
6. pass ★
7. dress
8. miss
9. call
10. glass

STUDENT'S PERSONAL WORDS

11. 13.
12. 14.

Additional story words are *guess, off, shall, unless, well,* and *will.*

★Words appearing in "Rabbit and Tiger"

Final Double Consonants

Pretest

DAY 1 **Administer the pretest.** Say each word, and then use it in the dictation sentence below. Help pairs of children check their own pretests by referring to the word list.

OPEN SORT

DAY 2 **Have children classify words.** Have children classify the Spelling Words according to similarities they find, such as the vowel sound in each word or the last letter in each word. Encourage them to compare their lists.

CLOSED SORT

Sort by spelling pattern. Duplicate the chart below on the board, and ask partners to copy the chart and write each Spelling Word where it belongs.

tall	boss	Which word is left?
fall all ball call	less pass dress miss glass	add

Teach/Model

DAY 3 **Discuss the generalization.** Write the words *less* and *pass* on the board. Ask how the words are alike. (Both have *ss* at the end.) Repeat with *fall* and *all*. Then write *add*, and ask how all five words are alike. (All have two consonants that are the same at the end.) Help children form generalizations about final double consonants—for example:

- **Words ending in a short vowel sound followed by /s/ (/d/) can be spelled with the vowel plus *ss (dd)*.**
- **Words that rhyme with *all* can end with the letters *all*.**
- **Some one-syllable words with a short vowel sound have a double consonant at the end.**

DAY 4 **Apply to writing.** Children should look for words with final double consonants in their plays to see if they are spelled correctly.

Posttest

DAY 5 **Assess children's progress.** The sentences below should be used as the posttest.

Rabbit and Tiger Name ____________

A. Write words from the box to finish what the animals say.

call	all
fall	ball

Watch out, because all the coconuts will fall!

Playing ball is really fun!

Maybe we should call a doctor.

B. Write a Spelling Word from the boat to match each clue.

glass, miss, pass, dress, less, add

1. not more l e s s
2. cup g l a s s
3. put on d r e s s
4. go by p a s s
5. plus a d d
6. not get m i s s

OUT OF THE BLUE Practice Book FINAL DOUBLE CONSONANTS 119

PRACTICE BOOK, page 119

DICTATION SENTENCES

1. Don't fall out of the tree.
2. All our friends will be at the party.
3. Let's play ball before we eat.
4. The more we sleep, the less tired we'll be.
5. I can add the numbers.
6. Please pass the butter.
7. Sally wore her blue dress.
8. You won't want to miss the party.
9. Go outside and call your brother.
10. May I have a glass of milk?

VOCABULARY WORKSHOP

Reviewing Key Words

To review how the Key Words were used in the play, distribute copies of page R179 to children. Then write the Key Words on the board.

Have children choose, as a group, the word that best completes each sentence. Then have them read the sentence aloud and write the word.

Life was good in the big, green jungle.

There were a few problems.

But one group of friends had a big problem.

"Tiger scares me," said Mouse.

"What kind of animal is he?" Toucan asked.

"He is the fiercest one," said Monkey.

"Never mind Tiger," said Rabbit.

"He just lies around and growls."

"I'll make a bargain with him. Then he'll leave us alone."

Have children glue the sentence strips in order on a piece of construction paper. Invite them to make a story fan by rereading the first sentence and folding it forward, rereading the second sentence and folding it backward, and so forth until they have reread all the sentences.

Extending Vocabulary

HOMOPHONES

Write Rabbit's words from page 331 on the board and read them with children: *That if I ride on your back by the time the sun sets, you'll leave Puerto Rico forever.*

Underline *I, by*, and *sun*. Ask children to name words that sound like these words, but are spelled differently. List the words on the board:

I	**eye**
by	**buy**
sun	**son**

Have the words read, and ask how they are alike and different. (sound alike; spelled differently, different meanings) Discuss the meanings of the homophones. Mention that many words sound like other words but have different spellings and meanings.

Have children locate the story words listed below and spell the other word of the homophone pair. List the homophones on the board and have them used in sentences.

page 327:	one (won)
page 331:	here (hear)
page 331:	to (two, too)
page 333:	there (they're, their)

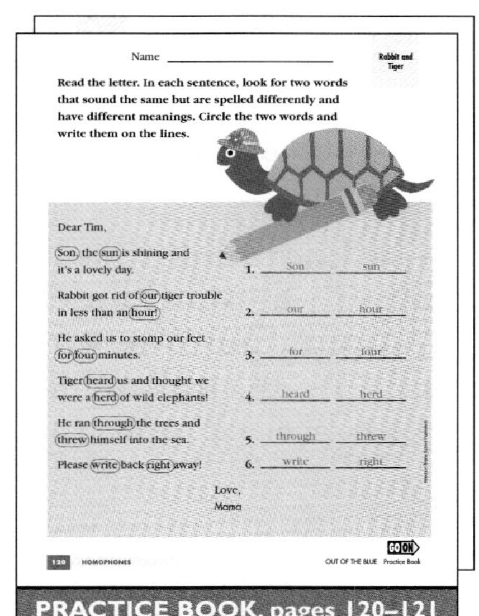
Name ______

Rabbit and Tiger

Read the letter. In each sentence, look for two words that sound the same but are spelled differently and have different meanings. Circle the two words and write them on the lines.

Dear Tim,

Son the sun is shining and it's a lovely day. 1. Son sun

Rabbit got rid of our tiger trouble in less than an hour! 2. our hour

He asked us to stomp our feet for four minutes. 3. for four

Tiger heard us and thought we were a herd of wild elephants! 4. heard herd

He ran through the trees and threw himself into the sea. 5. through threw

Please write back right away! 6. write right

Love,
Mama

120 HOMOPHONES — OUT OF THE BLUE Practice Book

PRACTICE BOOK, pages 120–121

STUDENTS ACQUIRING ENGLISH

Some children may find it helpful to develop their own illustrated list of homophones and reminders. Work with them to help them create mnemonic tricks that work for them.

TAKE-HOME/ KEEP-AT-HOME BOOK

Rosie Flamingo

Distribute the pages and have children make their own TAKE-HOME/ KEEP-AT-HOME BOOKS, which reinforce Key Words and known vocabulary. Have children read to partners and then take the book home to read.

LANGUAGE HANDBOOK

Troublesome Words, pages 100–101

INTRODUCE: PHONICS AND DECODING

Long Vowel: /ī/*i, y, ie*

OBJECTIVE: To understand the relationship between letters and sounds

Informal Assessment ✓

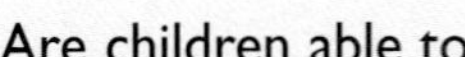

Are children able to

- ☑ read long *i* words in sentences?
- ☑ group long *i* words by spelling patterns?
- ☑ make and read words that have a specific phonogram?

Teach/Model

Connect to the story. Have children pretend to be Toucan, and ask: *How do you get into the pongo nut tree?* Write on the board *I fly*. Ask children what vowel sound they hear in the word *fly*. Underline the *y*. Then ask what vowel sound they hear in *I*. (the same as in *fly*) Then ask children to reread page 339 of the story. Ask: *What does Rabbit do?* Write *Rabbit lies down,* and underline the *ie* in *lies*. Tell children that they will learn more about the vowel sound that is alike in these words.

Phonemic awareness: Listen to the sound. Display page 20 of the *Big Book of Rhymes*. Have children listen for words with the same vowel sound heard in *I, fly,* and *lies* as you read the poem aloud. Then reread the poem. Encourage children to join in, especially for words with the /ī/ sound.

Big Book of Rhymes, page 20

Find and read long *i* words. Write *I, fly,* and *lies* as headings on the board. Then ask children to read the poem and find all the words with the long *i* sound. As children name words, have volunteers write them on the board in the appropriate columns.

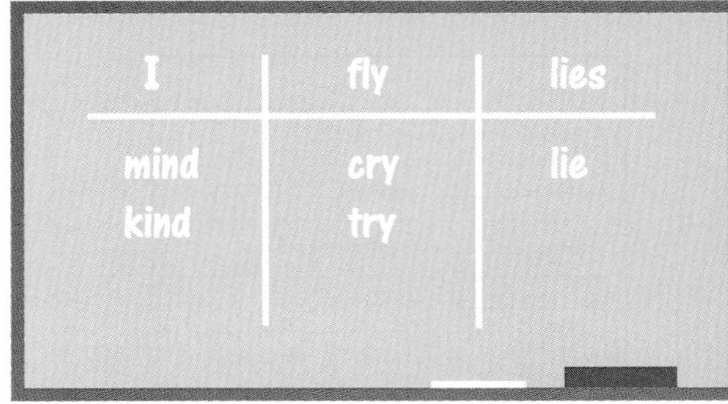

Point to the words under *I*, and ask how they are alike. (They rhyme; all have the long *i* sound; all have the letter *i*.) Follow a similar procedure with the second and third columns. Then ask children to suggest more words with the long *i* sound to add to the lists. Point out that *i, y,* and *ie* can all be spellings of the long *i* sound.

Practice/Apply

Read words in context. Write the sentences below on the board. Then have children read each sentence and find the words with the long *i* sound. Ask volunteers to add each word to the appropriate column on the board.

This cat can stand on its hind legs.
The dog sits in the sun by the window.
My pet bird has red feathers.
Why won't your parents let you have a pet?

Practice Activities

WORD BUILDING

PHONOGRAM / BLENDING ACTIVITY Distribute individual letter cards or *Word Builder Cards,* phonogram card *-ind,* and Word Builders to children. Then model making words.

MODEL **I'm going to make a word with *-ind*. What words have we already seen with *-ind*? Which letter should I use to make the word *mind*? Which should I use to make *kind*?**

Demonstrate adding the letter *m* and blending sounds to say the word. Have children blend the sounds to say *mind* along with you. Repeat for the word *kind*. Then have children make and read other words with the phonogram *-ind* in them. VISUAL/AUDITORY/KINESTHETIC

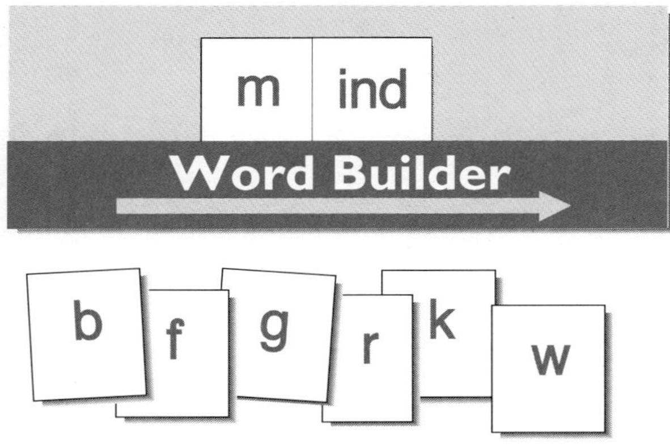

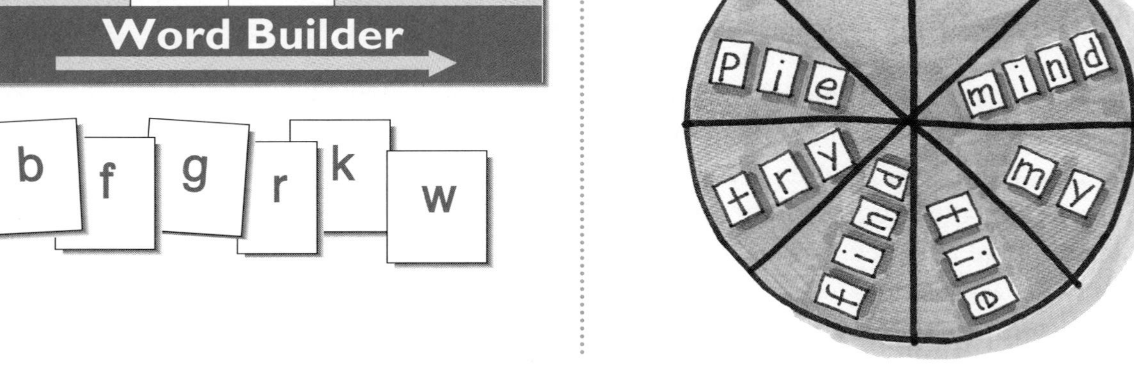

Long i Headlines

PERFORMANCE ASSESSMENT Partners can work together to write newspaper headlines using words that contain the long *i* sound. Challenge them to use all three of the spellings *i, ie,* and *y* in one headline. For example, they might generate "New Find! Fossil Lies in Dry River!" VISUAL/AUDITORY

Long i Pie

Draw a large circle divided into wedges and encourage small groups to use letter cards to play a game called "Long *i* Pie." Players take turns making a word that contains the long *i* sound spelled *i, ie,* or *y*. As they complete each word, players lay down their letter cards on the pie until all the spaces are filled. VISUAL/KINESTHETIC

Reading Trade Books FOR LONG VOWEL /ī/ i, y, ie

I Know an Old Lady Who Swallowed a Fly **retold by Nadine Bernard Westcott. Little, Brown, 1980.** EASY

Where the Wild Things Are **by Maurice Sendak. HarperCollins, 1988.** CHALLENGE

PHONICS PRACTICE READER 22

MEETING INDIVIDUAL NEEDS

STUDENTS ACQUIRING ENGLISH

Have children choose five of the long *i* words they learned in this lesson, draw a picture to illustrate each one, and label it.

RETEACH

See page R138 for lessons in multiple modalities.

CHALLENGE

Invite partners to play a variation on the game "I Spy" using items whose names contain the long *i* sound.

PHONICS ACTIVITY BOOK, pages 37–38

PHONICS PRACTICE BOOK, pages 92–106

Name ____________ Rabbit and Tiger

Read the poem and write a word to finish it. Circle the words with the same vowel sound as *tie*. Then write each word where it belongs in the chart. Add more words. Use a word from the chart to finish the rhyme.

Would it be sly
For me to try
To fly on over
And eat your pie?
My wings make a noise.
When I buzz on by
Why don't you love me?
I won't make you cry
Oh, don't try to swat me!
I'm just a fly!

i	ie	y	
I	pie	fly	sly
I'm		by	sky
		why	my
		try	cry

Harcourt Brace School Publishers

122 LONG VOWEL: /ī/ i, ie, y OUT OF THE BLUE Practice Book

PRACTICE BOOK, page 122

INTRODUCE: STUDY SKILLS

Graphic Aids (Chart)

OBJECTIVE: To understand how to make and read a chart

Informal Assessment ✓

Are children able to

- ☑ suggest information to be included in the chart?
- ☑ put information in the proper place on a chart?
- ☑ use information as it is presented on a chart?

TECHNOLOGY

For more practice with logic and discrimination skills, children can use the Fripple Shop in *Thinkin' Things Collection 1* and Frippletration in *Thinkin' Things Collection 2*.

Teach/Model

Connect to the story. Invite children to suppose that someone asked them how many tricks were attempted in the play and how many of those tricks were successful. Ask for their ideas about what they could do to be sure their answer was complete.

Discuss charts. Explain that people use charts to organize information. A chart can show a lot of information at the same time, and it makes it easier to compare pieces of information.

Model charting information. Display Chart/Transparency 25 or copy the chart headings on the board. Have children look through the play and tell about each trick. Encourage them to name the tricks in order. As children provide story events, record the information on the chart. After you have recorded information about one of the tricks, ask children to tell you where on the chart you should write a piece of information.

Discuss the chart. Spend a few moments discussing the chart. Invite children to talk about what they notice about the chart.

CHART/TRANSPARENCY 25

Trick	Who Played It?	Did It Work?
Rabbit gets Tiger to drop Turtle.	Rabbit	yes
Tiger tries to surprise Rabbit.	Tiger	no
Rabbit fools Tiger into thinking his house talks.	Rabbit	yes
Rabbit pretends to be sad so Tiger will carry him.	Rabbit	yes

Practice/Apply

Have children demonstrate understanding. Ask questions like these to check children's understanding:

1. **Which character played more tricks? Did the tricks work?**
2. **Did any of Tiger's tricks work?**
3. **How does the chart help you answer questions about the play?**

Practice Activities

Make a Baby Animal Chart

Have small groups of children work together to make a chart that lists animals and what their babies are called. Provide an assortment of reference materials for children to use. Remind groups to make a heading for each section of their charts. Help children find the names of several animals and their babies, such as tiger/cub, elephant/calf, frog/tadpole, kangaroo/joey, goat/kid, goose/gosling. Invite groups to share their charts with classmates. **VISUAL/AUDITORY**

CHART ANIMAL CHARACTERS

PERFORMANCE ASSESSMENT Have children in small groups work together to make up a chart about the characters in "Rabbit and Tiger." Have them list the animals in a column along the left-hand side of a sheet of paper. Group members can work together to make up headings for their charts and then fill them in. Chart headings might include *Number of Legs, Body Covering, Colors, How It Moves*.

After children have filled in their charts, display the charts and discuss the information each one contains about the animals in the play. **VISUAL/AUDITORY/KINESTHETIC**

	Number of legs	Body Covering	Color	How it Moves
Rabbit	4	fur	gray, white	hops crawls
Tiger				
Mouse				
Toucan				
Monkey				
Turtle				

STUDENTS ACQUIRING ENGLISH

Some children might find it helpful to make charts of words in both English and their primary language.

RETEACH

See page R139 for lessons in multiple modalities.

CHALLENGE

Provide children with lists of other animals. Help them use reference books to find out more about the animals. Then have them make a chart with the information they find.

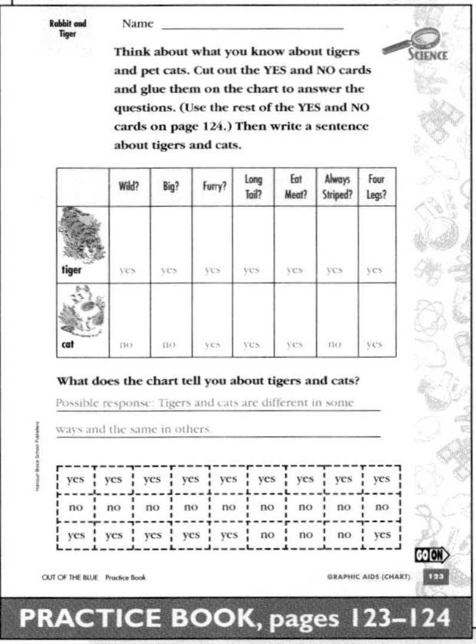

Rabbit and Tiger

Name ____________

Think about what you know about tigers and pet cats. Cut out the YES and NO cards and glue them on the chart to answer the questions. (Use the rest of the YES and NO cards on page 124.) Then write a sentence about tigers and cats.

SCIENCE

	Wild?	Big?	Furry?	Long Tail?	Eat Meat?	Always Striped?	Four Legs?
tiger	yes	yes	yes	yes	yes	yes	yes
cat	no	no	yes	yes	yes	no	yes

What does the chart tell you about tigers and cats?

Possible response: Tigers and cats are different in some ways and the same in others.

yes	yes	yes	yes	yes	yes	yes	yes	yes
no	no	no	no	no	no	no	no	no
yes	yes	yes	yes	yes	no	no	no	yes

GO ON

Harcourt Brace School Publishers

OUT OF THE BLUE Practice Book GRAPHIC AIDS (CHART) 123

PRACTICE BOOK, pages 123–124

Reading Trade Books FOR CHARTS

Anno's Math Games **by Mitsumasa Anno. Philomel, 1987. CHALLENGE**

The Magic School Bus Lost in the Solar System **by Joanna Cole. Scholastic, 1990. CHALLENGE**

Integrated Curriculum

SCIENCE

Rain Forest

TIPS FOR CLASSROOM MANAGEMENT

IF children are familiar with measuring in inches and feet, **THEN** suggest that they measure objects in the math activity twice, once using their "foot" measures, and again using rulers. Children can then compare their measurements.

TECHNOLOGY

Trudy's Time & Place House (Symbol Sandbox, Earth Scout)

Imagination Express, Destination: Rain Forest

SOCIAL STUDIES

Map the Jungle

MATERIALS
- butcher paper
- crayons or markers
- books about the rain forest

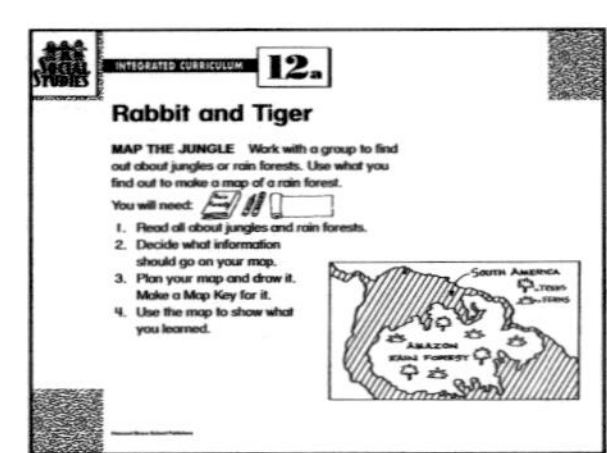
Curriculum Card 12a

COOPERATIVE LEARNING Invite small groups of children to work together to make a map of the jungle, also known as the rain forest. One child may serve as the Materials Manager and gather the supplies. Another child can serve as the Writer and add labels, such as *canopy* or *river*, and a map key to the group's map. A child who is artistic might be the Artist and do the majority of the drawings on the map. Invite groups to share their completed maps. LISTENING/SPEAKING/READING/WRITING

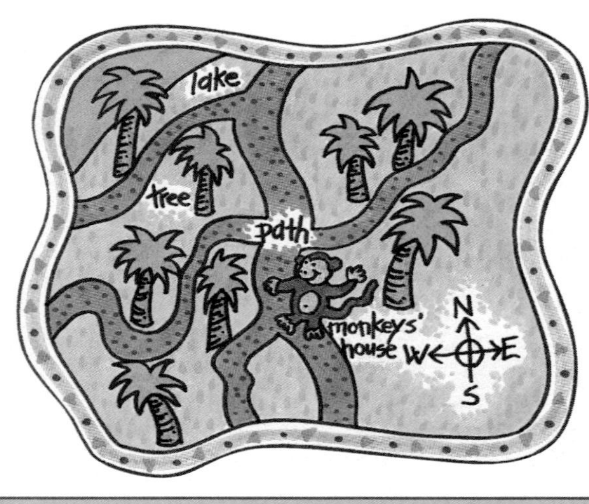

ART

Draw the Outdoors

Children can connect with the illustrations in the play as they think about and then make drawings of beautiful outdoor places that they have visited or that they see every day. Invite children to look through the play's illustrations and notice the details that the artist included to give a good picture of what rain forests are like. Children should try to include the same sorts of details in their drawings. When their drawings are finished, encourage children to write a few sentences about the place they chose, telling why they find it beautiful. Children might also enjoy framing their pictures with construction-paper frames and displaying them. LISTENING/SPEAKING/WRITING

MUSIC

Tiger Hunt

Some children may be familiar with the echo song "Going on a Bear Hunt." Invite them to sing and add motions to a variation of the song, called "Going on a Tiger Hunt." **LISTENING/SPEAKING**

CHORUS:
Going on a tiger hunt. (slap knees)
I'm not afraid. (point to self)
I have my trusty dog. (pat imaginary dog)
And all my friends are by my side. (stretch out arms)

FIRST VERSE:
There's some long grass. (shade eyes)
Can't go over it.
Can't go under it.
We'll have to go through it.
Swish, swish, swish. (Rub hands together to make a swishing sound.)

Repeat the pattern of the first verse using the locations, such as deep river, tall tree, huge rock, dark cave.

LAST VERSE:
There's a tiger!
Run! (run in place)
Shut the door! (pretend to slam a door)
Whew! (wipe sweat from brow)

MATH

Measure Your Tracks

MATERIALS
- construction paper
- scissors
- objects to measure

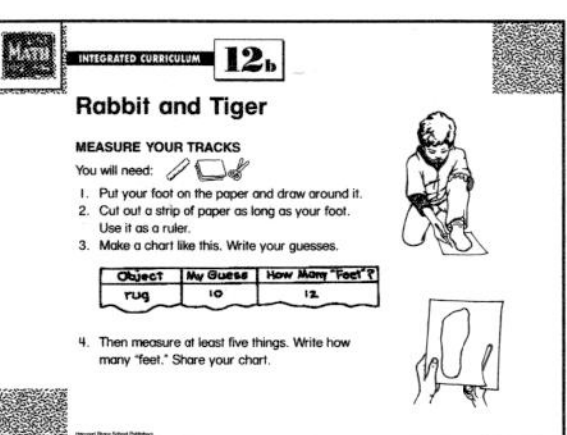
MATH
INTEGRATED CURRICULUM 12b

Rabbit and Tiger

MEASURE YOUR TRACKS

You will need:

1. Put your foot on the paper and draw around it.
2. Cut out a strip of paper as long as your foot. Use it as a ruler.
3. Make a chart like this. Write your guesses.

Object	My Guess	How Many "Feet"?
rug	10	12

4. Then measure at least five things. Write how many "feet." Share your chart.

Curriculum Card 12b

Have children mark off the length of one of their feet on a sheet of construction paper. They can then cut a strip of construction paper the length of their foot and use it to measure objects.

Before children begin, have them choose five objects in the classroom and estimate how many of their own "feet" long or wide each object is. Then, children can measure the objects with their construction-paper strips and check to see how close their estimates were to the length or width of an object. **LISTENING/ SPEAKING/WRITING**

Reading Trade Books

CROSS-CURRICULAR READING

The Great Kapok Tree **by Lynne Cherry. Harcourt Brace, 1990.** **CHALLENGE**

Stop That Noise! **by Paul Geraghty. Crown, 1992.** **AVERAGE**

MULTI-AGE CLASSROOMS

Encourage older children to take on leadership roles in the social studies activity. They could use reference materials to help their groups find and include more information on their maps.

Reading Trade Books

TIPS FOR CLASSROOM MANAGEMENT

READ ALOUD
As you read *The Rooster Who Went to His Uncle's Wedding* aloud, encourage children to chime in during the repetitive parts of the story.

PARTNERS
Have partners read the book together. They can figure out how they will divide the reading and where to pause to talk about the story.

SMALL GROUP
Have children read the book in a small group. Have them pass the book to another person each time the Rooster tries to find someone else to help him.

For a comprehensive lesson plan, refer to the complete lesson for *The Rooster Who Went to His Uncle's Wedding* on pages T698–T701.

The Rooster Who Went to His Uncle's Wedding

by Alma Flor Ada

Signatures Library

READER'S CHALLENGE

In "Rabbit and Tiger," Rabbit helps the other animals with their "Tiger troubles." In this story, Rooster gets his beak dirty on his way to his uncle's wedding. Will anyone help him clean his beak?

READING STRATEGY: RECOGNIZING TEXT PATTERNS

Once children have read enough of this cumulative tale to understand the repetitive pattern, have them predict what will happen next based on this pattern. After reading, have children suggest parts that could be added to the story to continue the pattern.

LINK TO THE THEME

Children reading the book may want to discuss these questions:

- In what ways is Rooster a tricky character? How is he different from other tricky characters you've read about?
- What is the same and what is different about this story and the other tricky tales you've read?

RESPONSE ACTIVITY: RETELLING THE STORY

Have children look at the illustrations and choose a character they would like to paint. Have them make a large, brightly colored painting or drawing of the character. Be sure that each character has been drawn by at least one child. Then have children retell the story, holding up their illustration of the character as they tell their part.

Other Trade Books

Borreguita and the Coyote

by Verna Aardema
illustrated by Petra Mathers

Rabbit was clever, not only to have avoided being eaten by Tiger but to have tricked Tiger into letting Rabbit ride him. Introduce *Borreguita and the Coyote* as a story from Mexico about a clever lamb. After reading, have children tell how Borreguita continually outsmarts the coyote who wants to eat her.

One Fine Day

by Nonny Hogrogian

After reading this cumulative tale, choose volunteers to be each of the characters in the story. Have the children stand in a row and tell what their characters wanted, beginning with the fox: "I am the fox. I was thirsty, so I drank the milk."

Who's in Rabbit's House?

by Verna Aardema
illustrated by Leo and Diane Dillon

Show children the illustrations in *Who's in Rabbit's House?* and point out that they show this story being acted out as a play. After children have read the story, help them turn the story into a play and act it out.

STUDENTS ACQUIRING ENGLISH

Encourage children who are learning English to keep word logs of interesting words they read in these folktales.

CHALLENGE

Have children write a book report about one of the books listed on these pages and present their reports dressed up as the main character.

Plan and Practice Story Presentations

SELECTION CONNECTION

In "Rabbit and Tiger," a clever rabbit tricks a threatening tiger into leaving an island. Ask children to explain what the tricksters they've read about have in common.

PROJECT CHECKLIST

During this stage, children should

- ☑ work on special features that will make their stories come alive when they present them.
- ☑ make invitations and programs for a Story Festival.
- ☑ practice their stories and, if possible, have a dress rehearsal.

Project Card 17

When children have completed the checkpoint, have them think about the upcoming Story Festival and write their thoughts in their Project Journals.

Project Card 17 can be found as a copying master on page R154.

PLANNING TIPS

As children refine their stories and add details to their presentations, they should

- search through costumes and props from other school productions.
- use book illustrations as a resource for costumes, masks, puppets, or props.
- think about how their characters should move and speak during their presentations.

CLASSROOM MANAGEMENT

Give each group a large "story box." They can use the box to store materials and work-in-progress, as well as completed props, scenery, and costumes. Have them label the box with their story's title.

MULTI-AGE CLASSROOMS

Have older children help younger children review their parts for the group's presentation. Encourage them to take leadership roles and help their groups stay organized.

Informal Assessment

As children complete this checkpoint, they will further **evaluate** and refine their story presentations, **analyze** their presentations, and **make decisions.** Children are thinking critically if they

- ☑ add unique features or devices to their stories.
- ☑ evaluate their work and make improvements, if needed.
- ☑ know when their presentations are ready.

Note that a more formal assessment rubric for this checkpoint is provided on page T693.

The stories you've just read have been passed on for many, many years. And they have some of the trickiest characters you'll ever find!

- Which characters in these stories learned a lesson? What lessons did the characters learn?
- In two of the stories, the clever characters are birds. In two of the stories, a tiger is tricked. How else are the stories alike?

Activity Corner

Who is the trickiest character in the stories in this theme? Is it Coyote, or the crows that fooled him? Is it the Eu bird, Rabbit, or is it Anansi? Draw a picture of the character you think is the trickiest one. Write a sentence that tells why.

THEME 3

Wrap-Up

1. **Which characters in these stories learned a lesson? What lessons did the characters learn?** (Possible responses might include: In "Coyote," Coyote learned that he shouldn't pretend to be something he isn't; In "Rabbit and Tiger," Tiger learned that smaller animals could trick him.) CRITICAL: SUMMARIZING
2. **In two of the stories, the clever characters are birds. In two of the stories, a tiger is tricked. What are some other ways that the stories are alike?** (Responses will vary but might include some of these ideas: The animals in all four stories talk; in two stories, "Nine-in-One, Grr! Grr!" and "Coyote," some fact about nature is explained.) CRITICAL: CLASSIFYING

ACTIVITY CORNER Encourage children to be specific as they write about why the character they chose is the trickiest. If necessary, review proper capitalization and punctuation of a sentence.

Create and Present Stories

THEME PROJECT PRESENTATIONS

Options

STORY FESTIVAL

- Have children complete preparations for the Story Festival.
- Before the day of the festival, have groups present their stories to the whole group and decide how to best put the presentations together.
- Distribute invitations to other classes, family members, and school personnel.
- Plan to serve refreshments.

VIDEOTAPING THE STORY FESTIVAL

- Arrange with a family member or community volunteer to videotape the Story Festival presentations.
- Share the videotape with other children.

SCHOOL↔HOME CONNECTION

Have children plan a cast party to celebrate the completion of the project. Children can invite everyone who was involved in the presentations, or who viewed them. They can prepare simple refreshments to be enjoyed as everyone views the videotape.

Project Card 18

Project Card 18 can be found as a copying master on page R155.

Community Connections

By sharing their stories with others, children demonstrate how cooperation between persons with different talents can produce inspiring results.

- Arrange with the school or public library to circulate the videotape.
- Children can prepare a flyer that describes the video and gives background on the stories.
- Have children decide what to do with the tape: leave it for next year's class, donate it to the school or public library, or lend it out to interested schoolmates.

THEME PROJECT ASSESSMENT

SELF-ASSESSMENT

To assess children's perception of their own performance during this project, ask them to respond to the following questions orally or in writing:

- **Why did you choose the group you worked with?**
- **What were your jobs in creating the stories?**
- **What was your favorite part of working on this project?**

Children may also complete the Self-Evaluation Checklist in the *Out of the Blue* Teacher's Edition.

PEER ASSESSMENT

To assess their group's effectiveness in working cooperatively during this project, ask children to respond to the following questions orally or in writing:

- **Did each person in your group help make decisions about your story and presentation? Describe how your group came to its decisions.**
- **Did everyone in the group have a chance to share his or her ideas? Why or why not?**

Children may also complete the Peer Evaluation Checklist in the *Out of the Blue* Teacher's Edition.

RUBRIC

Performance Goals	Observable Characteristics		
	3	2	1
LAUNCH Lists of ways to tell stories	• can classify stories and storytelling techniques	• can classify stories and techniques with guidance	• is not able to classify stories and storytelling techniques
CHECKPOINT 1 Comparison of storytelling techniques	• can analyze and compare techniques	• analyzes/compares techniques with effort	• is unable to analyze and compare techniques
CHECKPOINT 2 Develop story ideas	• adds known stories and new ideas to list • evaluates ideas appropriately	• adds known stories and some new ideas • usually evaluates ideas appropriately	• does not suggest ideas for list • cannot appropriately evaluate ideas
CHECKPOINT 3 Create a story	• recalls all or most storytelling techniques • contributions help make the story complete, well organized and interesting	• recalls many or most storytelling techniques • contributions help make the story organized and complete	• recalls few storytelling techniques • does not contribute ideas or suggestions for the story
CHECKPOINT 4 Presentation refinement and plans for Story Festival	• evaluates work appropriately	• usually evaluates work appropriately	• rarely evaluates work appropriately
PRESENTATIONS Overall project	• work is creative • work is well organized	• work is fairly creative • work is fairly well organized	• work often lacks creativity • work is disorganized

Two of Everything

retold and illustrated by Lily Toy Hong

THEME: COMMUNICATION

Tell a Tricky Tale

In this folktale, Mr. and Mrs. Haktak run into a problem communicated through many folktales from around the world—something wonderful happens, but there's a catch. Children will see that because Mr. and Mrs. Haktak are clever, they do not get tricked by their magical brass pot and are able to enjoy their good fortune.

Reading Trade Books
Signatures Library

SUMMARY Genre: Folktale

Mr. and Mrs. Haktak were poor farmers who barely grew enough food for themselves. But one day, Mr. Haktak found a magical brass pot in the garden. Whatever was put in the pot was doubled! So they doubled their gold coins but also doubled their troubles. Mrs. Haktak fell into the pot and two Mrs. Haktaks came out! The same thing happened to Mr. Haktak. Because the pot doubled everything, the two couples had enough money to buy double of everything and they became the best of friends.

ABOUT THE AUTHOR/ILLUSTRATOR

Lily Toy Hong grew up in a large Chinese American family. Ever since she was a young girl she knew she wanted to write and illustrate children's books. Hong lives in Utah where she hopes that one day she will find a magical old pot in her backyard.

Building Background and Concepts

PRIOR KNOWLEDGE

Exploring doubling. Provide small groups each with a box or bag and many small objects, such as building blocks, paper clips, or crayons. One group member puts one object into the container. Another group member adds an object and then removes both of them for the group to count. A Recorder writes down the amount. Group members guess what the amount will be when two objects are doubled and write down their predictions. Then group members put in two objects and add two more, and so on. Afterward, gather all groups and discuss what they found out.

Number of Objects	Guess	Actual Number
1	2	2
2	6	4

Developing Concept Vocabulary

EXTENDING BACKGROUND KNOWLEDGE

Generate a discussion. Talk about the doubling activity, and relate it to the story by asking:

What happened when you put one object into the container?
Two objects? Four objects?
What would be good about having a magical container that really doubled things?
What problems might the container cause?

INTRODUCING THE BOOK

Display the book *Two of Everything*. Read aloud the title and share the information about the author/illustrator.

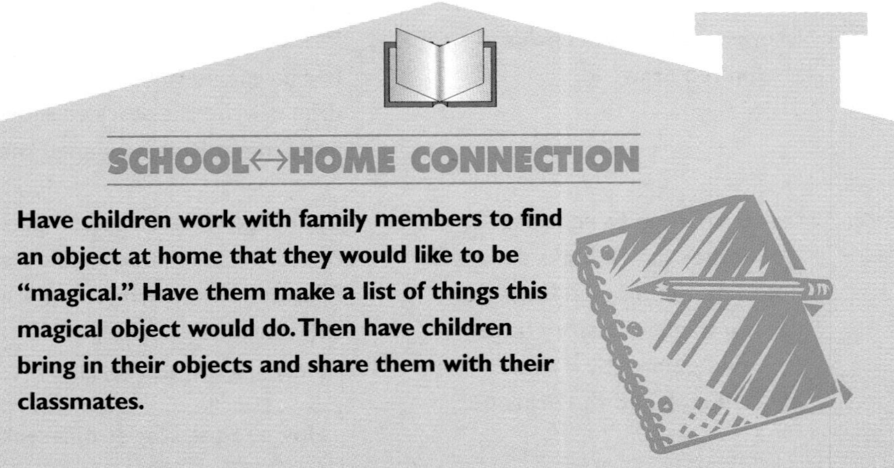

SCHOOL↔HOME CONNECTION

Have children work with family members to find an object at home that they would like to be "magical." Have them make a list of things this magical object would do. Then have children bring in their objects and share them with their classmates.

STUDENTS ACQUIRING ENGLISH

Have children read aloud and sound out the new words. As they read, have children use picture and context clues to help them understand the new words. Children who are of Chinese descent may want to explain cultural concepts in the story, such as bartering, rice bowls, silk embroideries, and bamboo furniture.

SPELLING GENERALIZATION

Food words
Integrated Spelling Lesson 17

OPTIONS FOR READING

Tips for Classroom Management

SMALL GROUP		WHOLE CLASS	
PARTNER	**READ ALOUD**	**READ ALOUD**	**INDEPENDENT**
Have partners decide how they will read the story. For example, one child could read the part of Mrs. Haktak, and one could read the part of Mr. Haktak. They could both share the narrative part. Afterward, have them discuss the Haktaks' problems and solutions.	Have children use the title and the cover illustration and preview some of the pictures to predict what the story is about. Then have children take turns reading the story aloud, pausing to notice details in the illustrations.	Have children predict what the story will be about, based on the title and the cover illustration. Then read the story aloud, stopping at the point where Mr. Haktak finds the brass pot. Ask children to predict what will happen next. Will good or bad things happen to the Haktaks?	Place the book in the Reading Center for independent reading. As children read the story, ask them to think about the characters of Mr. and Mrs. Haktak. Have children write in their journals whether they think good things or bad things will happen to Mr. and Mrs. Haktak.

Response Options

PERSONAL RESPONSE

- Do you think Mr. and Mrs. Haktak are greedy? Why or why not?
- What would you do with the magical brass pot?
- What do you think the village people think of the Haktaks? Why?
- Where do you think the old brass pot has come from?
- Do you think the Haktaks use the brass pot wisely? Why or why not?

SMALL GROUP	WHOLE CLASS	INDEPENDENT
Reread the book, and then have children role-play how the Haktaks solved their problems.	Ask children to list all the things that the Haktaks did with the brass pot. What conclusions can children draw?	Suppose Mr. Haktak had not dropped his purse in the pot and Mrs. Haktak had not dropped her hairpin in the pot. Have children rewrite the story to show what might have happened then.
Have children pretend to be Mr. or Mrs. Haktak. Ask what else children would do with the old brass pot.	Ask children to consider whether the Haktaks deserved to find the magical brass pot. How might the story have ended differently if someone else had found the brass pot?	Challenge children to compare this Chinese folktale with other folktales. Have them complete the chart. How are the stories alike? How are the stories different?

Culminating Activities

WISHFUL THINKING

LANGUAGE ARTS Have children add their wishes to the following rhyme:

Old brass pot, old brass pot,
I wished for a _____,
and that I got.

Two by Two

MATH Have children work with a partner with whom they have something in common and use statements like the following to tell how they are alike:

This pair has two red shirts.
This pair has two pairs of sneakers.
This pair has two pairs of jeans.
This pair has two hair ribbons.

PLAY CONCENTRATION

MATH Have children play a memory game. Provide groups of children with two sets of picture cards. One set should be identical to the other. Have children place all the cards face down. Then have them take turns turning two cards face up to try to find a match.

Puppet Play

LANGUAGE ARTS Have small groups of children draw and cut out the characters from the story and tape them to craft sticks to make stick puppets. They can decorate a box or a bag to be the magic brass pot. Then have children put on a puppet play of the story.

MULTI-AGE CLASSROOMS **Invite the older children to read other folktales to the younger ones. Have them help children recognize the themes and morals of folktales they read.**

STUDENTS ACQUIRING ENGLISH **Allow children who have difficulty with the vocabulary to retell the story in their own words, using the illustrations to help them.**

CHALLENGE **Ask children to write a modern version of "Two of Everything." Who are the characters? What would they find? What would they put into the container to be doubled? Encourage children to share their stories with their classmates.**

Reading Trade Books
Signatures Library

The Rooster Who Went to His Uncle's Wedding

by Alma Flor Ada

illustrated by Kathleen Kuchera

THEME: COMMUNICATION

Tell a Tricky Tale

This folktale begins simply and becomes more and more complex, as past events are retold each time a new event is added. From this story in the oral tradition, children can appreciate humor, language, and the art of storytelling.

SUMMARY Genre: Cumulative Tale

On his way to his uncle's wedding, the rooster gets mud on his beak. He asked the grass to clean his beak so he could go to the wedding, but it refused. He asked a lamb to eat the grass, but it refused. He asked a dog to bite the lamb, but it refused. And on it went until the sun agreed to help the rooster. The sun starts a chain of events that ends with the grass cleaning the rooster's beak so that he can finally go to the wedding.

ABOUT THE AUTHOR AND THE ILLUSTRATOR

Alma Flor Ada first heard this Cuban folktale from her grandmother, a gifted storyteller. Ada has published children's books in Latin America, Spain, and the United States and won the Christopher Award for her book *The Gold Coin*. Today, she lives on a mountain top in California.

Kathleen Kuchera is an illustrator from a family of artists: her father is an art director, her brother is a printer, and her sister is a sculptor and painter. Kuchera grew up in Rochester, New York, and now lives in Manhattan where she illustrates books. She likes to spend her time boxing with a speed bag, running, and vacationing in Maine.

Building Background and Concepts

PRIOR KNOWLEDGE

Experiencing repeated story events. Introduce the concept of "cumulative" stories by leading children in building their own shopping list: *I went to the store and bought a banana.* The next child would then buy a banana and something else, and so on.

I bought a banana.
I bought a banana and an apple.
I bought a banana, an apple, and some milk.

Developing Concept Vocabulary

EXTENDING BACKGROUND KNOWLEDGE

Create a cumulative story. Have children use story language and a cumulative story format to create a group story. Have them imagine walking down a country road in the summer. *I walked down the farm road and I saw a _____.* What do they see? Some examples may include: *rooster, lamb, dog, cow grazing, field, grass, corn, barn, pig,* and *horse*. Have children write their responses on a time-line path you have drawn on the board.

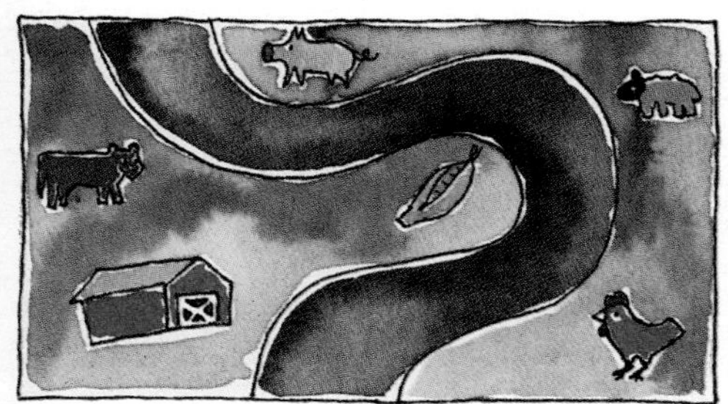

INTRODUCING THE BOOK

Display the book *The Rooster Who Went to His Uncle's Wedding.* Read aloud the title and share the information about the author and the illustrator.

SCHOOL↔HOME CONNECTION

Suggest that children work with family members to make up a cumulative story about a trip to a wedding or another family event. Encourage them to write the story and bring it to school to share with their classmates.

STUDENTS ACQUIRING ENGLISH

Ask children if they have heard this folktale or a variation of it before. If so, invite them to tell their version of the story. Have them share any other folktales from their home country.

SPELLING GENERALIZATION

Food words

See *Integrated Spelling* Lesson 17

OPTIONS FOR READING

Tips for Classroom Management

SMALL GROUP		WHOLE CLASS	
READ ALOUD	**PARTNER**	**INDEPENDENT**	**READ ALOUD**
Page through the first few illustrations, and have children predict what the story is about. Have children read the story aloud and use the illustrations to describe the sights and sounds the rooster encounters. Ask them to predict whether the rooster will get his beak cleaned.	Have partners take turns reading passages of the text. Encourage them to help each other understand story events. After they finish reading, have them discuss their reactions to the book. Should the rooster have eaten the corn?	Have children use the title and a preview of some story illustrations to respond to the question *What will happen to the rooster?* Have children write responses in their journals. Place the book in the Reading Center for independent reading.	Have children predict what the story is about, based on the title and the cover illustrations. Read the story aloud, stopping at the point where the rooster finds the corn. Ask children to predict what will happen next. Stop again later to ask them why no one helps the rooster.

Response Options

PERSONAL RESPONSE

- Do you think the grass, lamb, dog, stick, fire, and water should help the rooster? Why or why not?
- What would you do if you were the rooster?
- How would you describe the rooster's personality?
- Who do you think helps the rooster more—the sun or the grass? Explain.
- What did you learn from this story?

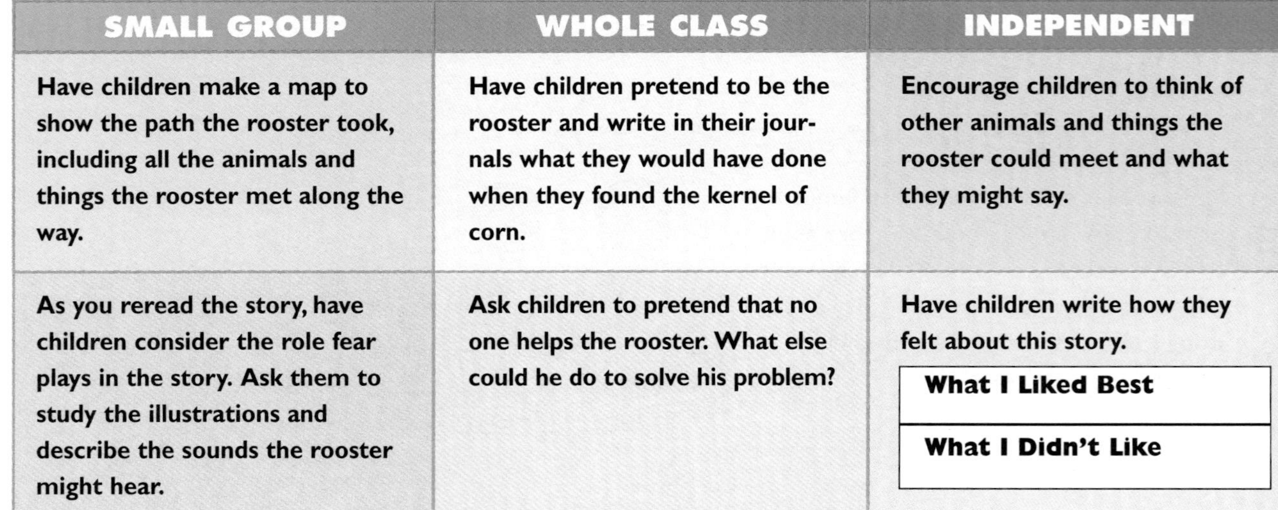

SMALL GROUP	WHOLE CLASS	INDEPENDENT
Have children make a map to show the path the rooster took, including all the animals and things the rooster met along the way.	Have children pretend to be the rooster and write in their journals what they would have done when they found the kernel of corn.	Encourage children to think of other animals and things the rooster could meet and what they might say.
As you reread the story, have children consider the role fear plays in the story. Ask them to study the illustrations and describe the sounds the rooster might hear.	Ask children to pretend that no one helps the rooster. What else could he do to solve his problem?	Have children write how they felt about this story. **What I Liked Best** **What I Didn't Like**

Culminating Activities

LATIN LANDS

SOCIAL STUDIES Provide children with books about countries with Latin cultures, such as Cuba, Mexico, Spain, and places in Central and South America. Have them choose a country they would like to visit. Then have them plan an itinerary for places they would like to go and things they would like to see.

GUESS HOW MANY

MATH Fill a jar with popcorn kernels, and ask children to estimate how many kernels are in the jar. Have them write their name and their estimate on a small slip of paper and place them in a bag. Invite volunteers to count the kernels and to check to see who had the best estimates.

Speaking Spanish

LANGUAGE ARTS List the following words from the story on the board: *rooster, beak, grass, lamb, dog, stick, fire, water, sun*. Then teach them the Spanish version of each word: *gallo, pico, hierba, oveja, perro, palo, fuego, agua, sol*. Encourage Spanish-speaking children to help with pronunciations.

dog	perro
grass	hierba
sun	sol

The Rooster Who Went to . . .

LANGUAGE ARTS Have small groups of children create their own cumulative stories about another rooster's adventures. Perhaps the rooster could go to school or to the store. Encourage children to share their finished versions.

MULTI-AGE CLASSROOMS

Older children can help the younger ones use the resource materials in the activities. They may also help them by sharing any relevant background information.

STUDENTS ACQUIRING ENGLISH

Encourage children to find a picture and tell about a special event in their home country. Have them share them with their classmates.

CHALLENGE

Some children may be interested in learning more about Cuba, since this is a Cuban folktale. Invite them to share what they learned with their classmates.

End-of-Theme Assessment Tools

IF you want to measure a child's mastery of reading and language skills and strategies, **THEN** administer the multiple-choice diagnostic **Skills Assessment.**	**IF** you want information about a child's ability to apply thinking skills in a global and holistic manner, **THEN** administer the **Holistic Reading Assessment.**	**IF** you want a comprehensive view of a child's reading and writing development skills, **THEN** administer the **Integrated Performance Assessment.**

Name ______________________ **Project** ________________ **Date** ____________

Here were our jobs for the project:

Name	**Job to Do**

Theme Project Peer Assessment Checklist

WORKING AS A GROUP

	☺	😐	☹
We each had jobs.			
We all helped.			
We shared ideas.			
We listened to each other.			
Together, we followed the rules.			

THE FINAL PROJECT

	☺	😐	☹
Our project was neat, not messy.			
Our project was put together the right way.			
The way we shared the project was good.			
Our project was done on time.			

To make our next project even better, we could

THEME 1 RESOURCES

Theme ONE
RESOURCES

Resources

Theme 1

Tested Skill

RETEACH: GRAMMAR

Sentences

OBJECTIVES: To understand that a sentence is a group of words that tells a complete thought; a sentence begins with a capital letter and ends with an end mark

Focus

Share the following information with children:

> **A sentence is a group of words that tells a complete thought. Each sentence begins with a capital letter and ends with a period or another end mark. Knowing about sentences helps you to understand what you read and to write sentences that make sense.**

Choose a Teaching Model

VERBAL/LINGUISTIC MODEL Display on chart paper the phrase in the center circle as shown:

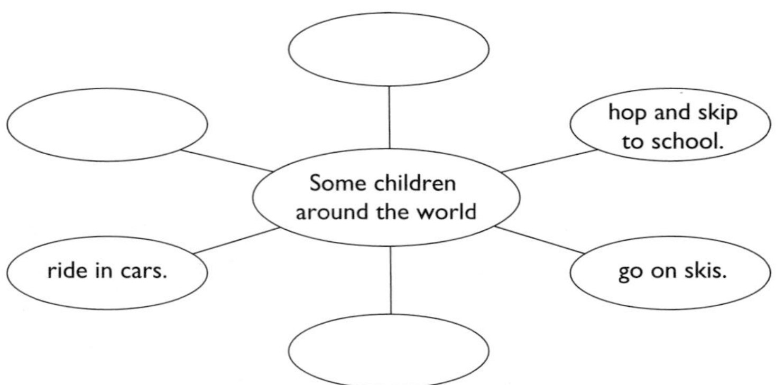

Read aloud the phrase to children. Invite a volunteer to tell whether the words make a sentence. Next, have children tell what could be added to the phrase to make it a sentence. Encourage them to use examples from the story. Write their suggestions around the center circle to create a web. Invite volunteers to match phrases in the web to make complete sentences as you write them on the board. Circle the capital letter and period in each sentence. Then follow the suggestions in **Summarize/Reinforce.**

VISUAL/SPATIAL MODEL Write the following phrases on sentence strips. Display the phrases and read them aloud with children.

the fluffy brown puppy	crawled up a leaf
the huge jet airplane	told me a funny bedtime story
two furry caterpillars	did a trick for her treat
my grandfather	whistled loudly
the teapot on the stove	left a white trail in the sky

Ask whether these phrases are sentences. Have children tell why they are not. Next, give children a sheet of drawing paper. Suggest that they match one phrase from the left-hand column with one from the right-hand column to make a complete sentence. Have children write their sentences at the bottom of the sheet of paper, using a capital letter and end punctuation, and illustrate their sentences. Then follow the suggestions in **Summarize/Reinforce.**

KINESTHETIC/MOTOR MODEL Form teams of four or five children. Have one person on each team pantomime the way he or she travels to school. The mode of transportation can be real or imagined. Other team members must guess what mode of transportation the child is showing. When the right answer is given, have each team member write a sentence telling how the "mime" gets to school. Team members can take turns pantomiming their own modes of transportation. Then follow the suggestions in **Summarize/Reinforce.**

Summarize/Reinforce

Check children's understanding of the lesson by having them say sentences about their favorite school activities. Summarize by telling children that a sentence is a group of words that tells a complete thought. It begins with a capital letter and ends with a period or another end mark. To reinforce this lesson, give children sentence strips and have them "label" the room by writing sentences about different items and places. These sentence strips can be taped on or near the items named.

Tested Skill

R-Controlled Vowel: /är/*ar*

OBJECTIVE: To understand the relationship between letters and sounds

Focus

Share the following information with children:

> **The letters *ar* can stand for the sound /är/ as heard in *far* and *car*. Knowing these two letters and the sound they stand for when they appear in the order *a-r* can help you figure out new words as you read.**

Choose a Teaching Model

LOGICAL/MATHEMATICAL MODEL Write the following words and sentences on the board. Then explain the following fill-in-the-blanks game to children. As you come to each blank in a sentence, children are to first use words with the /är/ sounds. Read each sentence and set of words aloud. Read the sentence again, and have children tell which word(s) to use first. Ask volunteers to fill in the blanks.

Example: Ellen likes parks and gardens but not trees.

1. **Liz likes to** (start) **jogging, not to** (stop) **jogging.** start, stop
2. **Pete likes** (large) **buildings, not** (small) **or** (brick) **buildings.** small, large, brick
3. **Jack likes to collect** (sharp), **pointed rocks, not** (smooth) **ones.** smooth, sharp
4. **Jane likes to spend time in** (barns) **and** (farms) **, not** (houses)**.** barns, houses, farms
5. **Niels likes to study the** (stars), **not the** (trees). trees, stars

Then follow the suggestions in **Summarize/Reinforce.**

INTERPERSONAL MODEL List the following words on the board. Have children work with a small group to read the words aloud and discuss their meanings.

smart **charming** **snarls**
sparkles **partner**

Encourage children to decide which words they would use to describe people they like and which they would like others to use to describe them. Draw this chart on the board, and have children write the words in the appropriate columns.

People I Like	Me
partner	smart
sparkles	sparkles

Ask children to explain the reasons for their choices. Invite them to add other /är/ words that they could use to describe people in a positive way. Then follow the suggestions in **Summarize/Reinforce.**

AUDITORY MODEL Make word cards for the following words. Display the cards, and read each word aloud with children. Have them wave each time they hear a word with the /är/ sound.

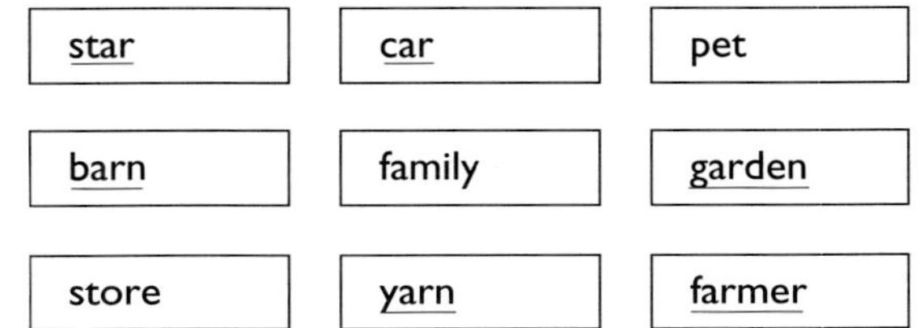

Then follow the suggestions in **Summarize/Reinforce.**

Summarize/Reinforce

Check children's understanding of the lesson by having them name the letter combination that can stand for the /är/ sound. *(ar)* Summarize by explaining that knowing that these letters can stand for this sound will help them read and write new words. To reinforce this lesson, have children identify examples of words that use the letter combination *ar* to stand for the /är/ sound. Encourage them to watch for these letters on street signs, in stores, and in other places they pass during a day. Have them report to the class any other words they find in which *ar* stands for the /är/ sound. Remind them to use the strategies from this lesson to help them read and write words with this letter combination standing for the /är/ sound.

Sequence

OBJECTIVE: To identify the sequence of events in a story

Focus

Share the following information with children:

Events in stories happen in a certain order. Time-order words, such as *first, next, then,* and *last,* are clues that make the order of the events clearer. Noticing the order of events in a story often makes it easier for you to remember it and to predict what might happen next.

Choose a Teaching Model

VERBAL/LINGUISTIC MODEL Write the following paragraph on the board, and read it aloud. Read it again slowly as children find and circle words that indicate time order, or the order of events.

Oh, no! It was almost time for the school bus, and Vida had so much to do! First, she put on her socks and shoes. Next, she put her books in her backpack and then put it on. After that, she grabbed her lunch bag and ran outside. She was just in time. The bus was coming down the street.

Have children use the same time-order words to summarize what happened to Vida, and then tell their own going-to-school stories. Then follow the suggestions in **Summarize/Reinforce.**

VISUAL/SPATIAL MODEL Prepare for this activity by making word cards for the words *First, Next, Last, Before,* and *After.* Write the following story sentences on the board, and display the word cards in random order. Ask volunteers to select the correct word to complete each sentence, and to hold the word card in place as the rest of the children read the completed sentence.

1. (Before) I eat breakfast, I get ready for school.
2. (First), I get dressed.
3. (Next), I comb my hair.
4. (Last), I make sure I have everything I need to take to school.
5. (After) breakfast, I brush my teeth.

Then follow the suggestions in **Summarize/Reinforce.**

KINESTHETIC/MOTOR MODEL Tell children that they will act out walking to school but that they must follow exactly the directions you give them. Start by walking in place as you say, "First we have to walk out the front door and to the end of the sidewalk." Once children are walking in place, stop walking and give oral instructions only, as follows:

- **First, walk five steps. Then stop to pet the dog.**
- **After you walk five more steps, hop once.**
- **Jump over a puddle before you walk five more steps.**
- **Turn to the right, and then walk five steps. Next, stop and look in a store window. Last, walk five more steps.**
- **Finally, wave to your friends. Then run up the steps.**

After a little practice, invite children to give their classmates directions, using time-order words. Then follow the suggestions in **Summarize/Reinforce.**

Summarize/Reinforce

Check children's understanding of the lesson by asking why writers use time-order words in stories. (to show the order of events) Summarize by telling children that events in a story happen in a certain order and that paying attention to time-order words can help them understand a story better. To reinforce this lesson, have children tell a story they know, using time-order words. Remind children to use the strategies from this lesson to help them follow the order of events in stories and understand what they read.

Naming Part of a Sentence; Joining Naming Parts

OBJECTIVES: To understand that the naming part of a sentence tells who or what the sentence is about; to understand that two or more sentences can be joined if those named in the naming parts are doing the same thing

Focus

Share the following information with children:

Every sentence has a naming part that names who or what the sentence is about. Sometimes sentences can be joined if those named in the naming parts are doing the same thing. Knowing about the naming part of a sentence helps you to understand sentences you read and to write sentences that make sense.

Choose a Teaching Model

VISUAL/SPATIAL MODEL On a bulletin board, attach sentence strips showing the action part of sentences. Provide strips with naming parts. Have children match each naming part with the rest of the sentence. See the completed bulletin board below:

Who Did It?	
Jack and Jill	went up a hill.
Cinderella and the Prince	got married.
Jack	climbed a beanstalk.
The Big Bad Wolf	tricked Red Riding Hood.
Humpty Dumpty	took a great fall.

Point out that the first two sentences name more than one person in the naming part. Use this same bulletin board model for sentences about other stories children have read. Then follow the suggestions in **Summarize/Reinforce.**

INTERPERSONAL MODEL Display or duplicate the following survey:

	Foods We Like			
apples				
carrots				
bananas				
green beans				
strawberries				
green peas				

Remind children that good friends like Emily and Alice often have a lot in common. Have children work in small groups and appoint a leader. Read the survey aloud to the class. Then have group leaders poll their members and write their names in the boxes next to the foods they like. When the survey is complete, have each group write sentences telling who likes each food, underlining the naming part. The naming parts of the sentences may tell about one or more people, depending on the results of the survey. Then follow the suggestions in **Summarize/ Reinforce.**

AUDITORY MODEL Read aloud the sentences for the bulletin board in the Visual Model. Ask children to listen for the naming part in each sentence. Reread each sentence, and ask a volunteer to identify the naming part. Next, have children listen to the following sentence endings and suggest naming parts to tell who or what the sentence is about.

- Jack **jumped over the candlestick.**
- Mary **had a little lamb.**
- Little Jack Horner **sat in a corner.**
- The Big Bad Wolf **huffed and puffed and blew the house down.**
- Old Mother Hubbard **went to the cupboard.**

Then follow the suggestions in **Summarize/Reinforce.**

Summarize/Reinforce

Check children's understanding of the lesson by having them say a sentence about one or more of their family members and identify the naming part of the sentence. Summarize by telling children that the naming part of a sentence tells who or what the sentence is about. To reinforce this lesson, have children compose sentences about other stories they have read and identify the naming part of each sentence. Remind them to use the strategies from this lesson to help them write clear, complete sentences and to understand the sentences they read.

Consonant Digraph: /f/*gh, ph*

OBJECTIVE: To understand the relationship between letters and sounds

Focus

Share the following information with children:

> **Two consonants appearing together in a word can stand for one sound. The letter combinations *gh* and *ph* can stand for the /f/ sound heard in *laugh* and *phone.***

Choose a Teaching Model

MUSICAL/RHYTHMIC MODEL Write the following chart on the board or on chart paper. Discuss the meanings of the words, and have children read the words aloud.

gh	ph
laugh cough rough tough enough	phone photo photograph graph trophy

Have children, sitting so that all can see the chart, play a clapping game that Emily and Alice might play. Have them clap at a steady beat and read a word at each third beat. When the group has hit a steady rhythm, point to random words to read. Then pause to tell children that you will point to either *gh* or *ph.* A player must say a word with that letter combination, continuing the rhythm of the game. Anyone who says a word from the wrong list drops out of the semicircle for a turn. Continue playing long enough to go around the group at least twice. Then follow the suggestions in **Summarize/Reinforce.**

KINESTHETIC/TACTILE MODEL Display the chart from the Musical/Rhythmic Model, and have children read the words. Briefly discuss their meanings. Then provide pairs or small groups of children with sets of cards that have the words from the chart written on them. As you point to a word on the chart, children must find that word in their pile of word cards. Children say the word, and then a volunteer uses the word in a sentence. Continue until all children have volunteered at least one sentence. Then follow the suggestions in **Summarize/ Reinforce.**

AUDITORY MODEL This exercise will familiarize children with words outside their reading vocabulary in which *ph* or *gh* stands for the /f/ sound. Tell children that in the words you are about to dictate the sound /f/ is spelled with either *gh* or *ph.* They must tell whether they hear that sound at the beginning, middle, or end of the word, or in more than one place. Read these words in random order. Have children respond as a group.

- **phrase, pheasant, photocopy, phonics**
- **gopher, trophy, alphabet, telephone, geography, nephew**
- **cough, laugh, tough, rough**
- **photograph, phosphate**

Ask children if they have heard any of these words before or if they know what any of the words mean. Suggest that children choose at least one word that interests them, write it on a card, and then find out as much as they can about it. Have them add their new word to their Word Files. Then follow the suggestions in **Summarize/Reinforce.**

Summarize/Reinforce

Check children's understanding of the lesson by asking them to name three letters or letter combinations that stand for /f/. (*f* or *ff, gh, ph*) Summarize by stating that sometimes two consonants can stand for one sound. To reinforce this lesson, have children look through magazines and newspapers to find words that contain *gh* and *ph.* Remind children to use the strategies from this lesson to help them read and pronounce new words that contain the letter combinations *gh* and *ph.*

Story Elements (Characters)

OBJECTIVE: To identify major and minor characters and to use their words and actions to identify their traits

Focus

Share the following information with children:

> **The people, and sometimes animals, in a story are called characters. The characters who do most of the action are main characters, and the characters who have small parts in the story are minor characters. Paying attention to what the characters do and say, and to what is said about them, helps readers understand and enjoy a story.**

Choose a Teaching Model

VERBAL/LINGUISTIC MODEL Review the character traits of the two main characters in "Emily and Alice Again." Build a web to show what each character is like. Add children's suggestions to the web.

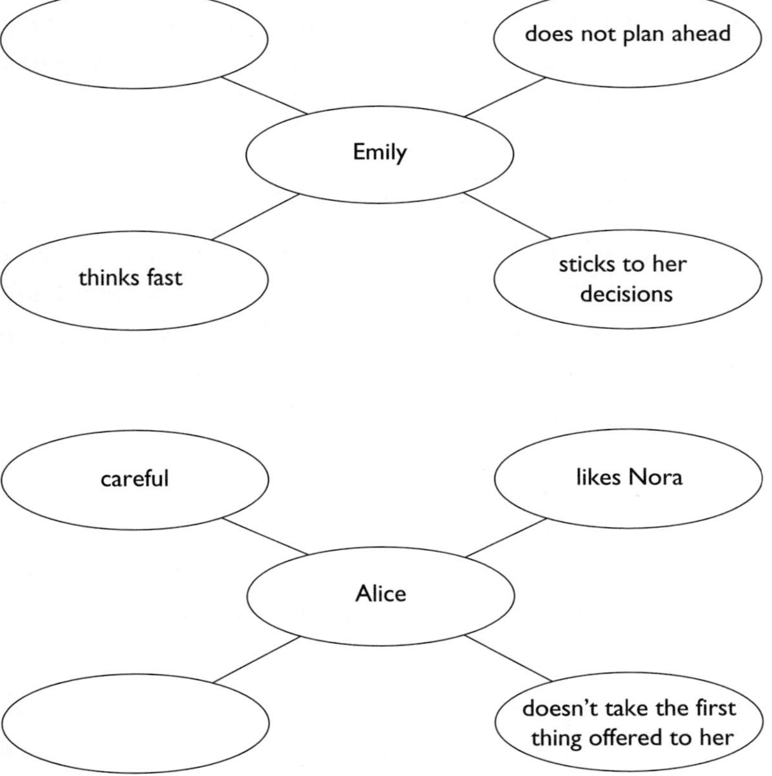

Encourage discussion about ways that Emily and Alice are alike and ways they are different. Ask children to speculate about how the two girls came to be such good friends. Then follow the suggestions in **Summarize/Reinforce.**

VISUAL/SPATIAL MODEL Have children work with a partner to examine the drawings in "Emily and Alice Again," watching for Emily's changing moods. Without rereading the text, they can find pictures that show where Emily begins to feel left out of the fun with Nora and sad about the trade she made with Alice. They can draw a time line to show the order in which Emily's feelings changed, using words or pictures to show how she feels at different points in the story. Then follow the suggestions in **Summarize/Reinforce.**

INTERPERSONAL MODEL Have children work in groups of three to discuss and compare the three characters in "Emily and Alice Again:" Emily, Alice, and Nora. Distribute copies of the Character Cutout on page R206. Children can label the cutouts with each character's name. Each child in the group takes one cutout and, as the group discusses the character, writes words to describe her. Ask individuals to tell which of the three characters is most like each of them, and in what ways. Then follow the suggestions in **Summarize/Reinforce.**

Summarize/Reinforce

Check children's understanding of the lesson by asking what the people in stories are called. Summarize by telling children that readers learn about characters in a story through what the characters say and do and what is said about them. To reinforce this lesson, have children identify the characters in a story they know. Remind them to use the strategies from this lesson to help them identify the traits of characters in stories they read and in plays and movies they watch.

Telling Part of a Sentence; Joining Telling Parts

OBJECTIVES: **To understand that the telling part of a sentence tells what someone or something is or does; to understand that sentences with different telling parts can be joined if the naming parts are the same**

Focus

Share the following information with children:

Every sentence has a telling part that tells what someone or something is or does. Two or more sentences with different telling parts can be joined if the naming parts are the same. Knowing about the telling part of a sentence helps you to understand sentences you read and to write sentences that make sense.

Choose a Teaching Model

VERBAL/LINGUISTIC MODEL On a bulletin board, attach sentence strips showing the naming part of sentences. Provide strips with telling parts. Have children match each telling part with the correct naming part. See the completed bulletin board below:

What Do They Do?	
A mail carrier	delivers mail.
A police officer	gives tickets for speeding.
A teacher	helps students learn.
A dentist	fills cavities in teeth.
A plumber	unclogs drains.

Invite children to add something else each person does to each sentence; for example: *A mail carrier delivers mail and drives a mail truck.* Suggest that children write sentences on sentence strips, cutting apart the naming and telling parts for classmates to match. Then follow the suggestions in **Summarize/Reinforce.**

MUSICAL/RHYTHMIC MODEL Gather objects to use as rhythm instruments, such as rulers, pencils, spoons, and small boxes. Choose an object, and tap a simple rhythm with it. Then ask children to clap the same rhythm. Invite a volunteer to make up a sentence about what you did to make the rhythm. Write the sentence on the board; for example, *Mrs. Smith tapped the ruler on her desk.* Choose another instrument and create another rhythm, and repeat the procedure. Encourage children to use a different telling word, such as *patted, hit, pounded*, or *hammered*. Write the new sentence on the board. Invite a volunteer to combine the two sentences by using the word *and* to join the telling parts. Continue, inviting volunteers to create rhythms. Then follow the suggestions in **Summarize/Reinforce.**

INTRAPERSONAL MODEL Remind children that Max found something fun to do when he felt like being alone. Ask children to reflect on times when they feel like being alone. Have them make a list of the things they like to do. Then encourage them to complete the following sentence frame to make sentences with activities on their list: *When I am alone, I* ____ *and* ____. Invite children to share their sentences, if they wish. Then follow the suggestions in **Summarize/Reinforce.**

Summarize/Reinforce

Check children's understanding by having them each say a complete sentence about something they do when they get home from school, and identify the telling part. Summarize by explaining that the telling part of a sentence tells what someone or something is or does. The telling part of a sentence can tell more than one thing that someone or something is or does. To reinforce this lesson, ask children to write sentences about their favorite part of "Max Found Two Sticks" and to identify the telling parts. Remind children to use the strategies from this lesson to help them express their ideas in complete sentences.

Consonant Digraphs:/ng/*ng*, /ngk/*nk*

OBJECTIVE: To understand the relationship between letters and sounds

Focus

Share the following information with children:

> **Sometimes the sounds of two consonants that appear together in a word blend together to form one sound. The letters *ng* stand for the sound at the end of the word *sing*. The letters *nk* stand for the sound at the end of the word *thank*.**

Choose a Teaching Model

VERBAL/LINGUISTIC MODEL Give half the children cards with the word endings *ng* or *nk* printed on them. Give the other half of the children cards with these word beginnings printed on them: *thi, si, ba, ra, ri, wi, cli, cla.* Have children circulate to find partners with whom they can make a real word. (All the word beginnings work with both endings.) When children have chosen a partner, have them sit down together with the partner and make up a sentence about Max, using their word. After a few minutes, stop the game and ask the pairs to stand up, show and say their word, and tell their sentence. Then follow the suggestions in **Summarize/Reinforce.**

thi	si	ba	ra	ri
wi	cli	cla	ng	nk

MUSICAL/RHYTHMIC MODEL Write the following story words as column heads on the board: *ring, bang, clink*, and *thank*.

ring	*bang*	*clink*	*thank*

Ask children to suggest words that rhyme with each word. List all their suggestions in the appropriate columns. Then challenge children to collaborate on making a rhyming story or rap, using words from the lists. As children suggest lines, write them down. Encourage children to revise the rhyme as a group. When it meets the group's approval and children have learned it by heart, have the group recite it for classmates. Then follow the suggestions in **Summarize/Reinforce.**

KINESTHETIC/MOTOR MODEL Prepare word cards with the following story words: *ding, dong, dang, cling, clang,* and *bang.* Read them aloud with children, underlining the *ng* ending in each and emphasizing the ending sound. Then have children work in pairs to use two, three, or four of the words in a rhythm they create, just as Max created rhythms in the story. If possible, assemble bells, sticks, kitchen pots, and empty boxes for children to strike as part of their rhythms. Allow time for pairs to share their rhythms with classmates. Then follow the suggestions in **Summarize/Reinforce.**

Summarize/Reinforce

Check children's understanding by having them tell what sounds the letter combinations *ng* and *nk* stand for. To summarize, explain that the sounds of two consonants can blend together to form the sounds at the end of the words *king* and *bank*. To reinforce this lesson, have children work in pairs to list words that end with *ng* and *nk*. Then ask them to read their lists aloud. Remind children to use the strategies from this lesson to help them read and pronounce words that end with the consonant digraphs *ng* and *nk*.

Test-Taking Strategies

OBJECTIVE: To identify test-taking strategies to increase success

Focus

Share the following information with children:

> **Tests measure what you have learned. Before, during, and after a test, taking certain steps will help you do your best.**

Choose a Teaching Model

LOGICAL/MATHEMATICAL Remind children that tests help them and their teachers know how well they understand what was taught. Ask children to share what they do to prepare for a test. Write their suggestions on tagboard sentence strips. Add any of the following that children don't mention:

- *Learn what the test will be about.*
- *Study by myself or with someone.*
- *Get plenty of sleep.*
- *Read the directions carefully.*
- *Answer easy questions first.*
- *Make sure all questions have been answered.*
- *Check answers.*

Write the following headings on chart paper, spacing them evenly: *Before a Test, During a Test,* and *After a Test.* Then read the sentences aloud with children. After reading each sentence, ask a volunteer to place the strip near the words that tell when to follow this step. After the strips have been placed, tape the sentence strips below appropriate headings to make a chart.

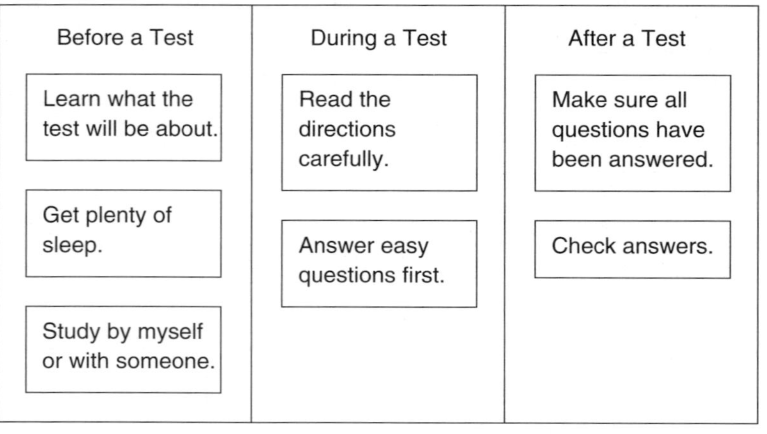

Before a Test	During a Test	After a Test
Learn what the test will be about.	Read the directions carefully.	Make sure all questions have been answered.
Get plenty of sleep.	Answer easy questions first.	Check answers.
Study by myself or with someone.		

Keep the chart posted where all can see, add to, and refer to throughout the year. Then follow the suggestions in **Summarize/Reinforce.**

INTRAPERSONAL MODEL Write this sample test item on the board or on a transparency:

> **Decide which word makes the most sense in the blank. Write the whole sentence on a sheet of paper.**
>
> **hats sticks bells**
>
> **Max made rhythms with the two _____.**

Let children read the item silently. Then have them follow the directions. After they have finished, discuss the steps each child took to answer the question. Encourage children to share their thinking and the steps they took to follow the directions and to arrive at a correct response. Provide similar examples of test questions for children to complete. Then follow the suggestions in **Summarize/Reinforce.**

AUDITORY MODEL Form children into groups of four or five. Ask whether any of them, like Max, love sounds. Explain that they will record their voices today. Have groups write a list of steps to remember when taking a test. Then have children take turns reading the steps aloud into a tape recorder. Play the tapes created by groups for the class. As children hear each new step, have volunteers say when to do it: before, during, or after a test. Then follow the suggestions in **Summarize/Reinforce.**

Summarize/Reinforce

Check children's understanding of the lesson by discussing the steps to take before, during, and after a test. Summarize by explaining that following these steps will help them prepare for and take tests. To reinforce this lesson, have each child choose and write down one test-taking step and read it aloud. Ask other children to tell when that rule is most important—before, during, or after a test.

Word Order

OBJECTIVE: To understand that for a sentence to make sense, the words in that sentence must be in a certain order

Focus

Share the following information with children:

> **The words in a sentence should be in an order that makes sense. Knowing how to put the words of a sentence in order helps you express your ideas in a way that makes sense to others.**

Choose a Teaching Model

VERBAL/LINGUISTIC MODEL Have children work in small groups. Each group will need a large sheet of paper and a Recorder, and each child will need a sentence strip. Have each group brainstorm a list of sentences that tell how to be a good friend as the Recorder writes the sentences on the paper. Next, invite each group member to choose one sentence from the list and write it on a sentence strip. Tell children to cut apart the words in their sentences, mix up the order, and paper-clip the mixed-up words together. Have children in one group switch clipped word bundles with children in another group. Invite children to arrange the words in each bundle into a sentence that makes sense. Then follow the suggestions in **Summarize/ Reinforce.**

KINESTHETIC/MOTOR MODEL Invite volunteers to perform various exercises for the class. For example, a child might do five sit-ups. Ask the rest of the class to make up a sentence about what the child did—for example, *Maria did five sit-ups.* Write the sentences on sentence strips. Distribute the strips, and have children cut apart the words in each sentence and clip them together. Have children trade clipped word bundles, arrange the words into a sentence, and perform the activity mentioned in the sentence. Then follow the suggestions in **Summarize/Reinforce.**

AUDITORY MODEL Have the children write on a card the word *sentence.* Then explain that you are going to read some sentences with words in order and some with words that are not in order. Children should hold up their *sentence* cards when they hear sentences that make sense. You might use sentences such as these:

> **Many foods are good for you.**
> **Bones milk strong builds.**
> **Spinach is rich in iron.**
> **You bread energy gives.**
> **Have vitamin C oranges.**
> **Carrots are good for your eyes.**

Then follow the suggestions in **Summarize/Reinforce.**

Summarize/Reinforce

Check children's understanding of this lesson by asking them why words in a sentence must be in order. Summarize by explaining that the words in a sentence must be in an order that makes the meaning of the sentence clear. To reinforce this lesson, have children write three sentences telling about things they can do to stay healthy. Have children exchange their sentences with a classmate and discuss whether their messages are clear.

Consonant Digraphs: /r/ *wr*; /n/*kn*, *gn*

OBJECTIVE: To understand the relationship between letters and sounds

Focus

Share the following information with children:

> **Sometimes two consonants that appear together in a word stand for only one sound. The letters *wr* can stand for the /r/ sound you hear at the beginning of the word *wrong*. The letters *kn* and *gn* can stand for the /n/ sound you hear at the beginning of the words *knee* and *gnat*.**

Choose a Teaching Model

VISUAL/SPATIAL MODEL Write the following words on the board or on a transparency: *knob, write, knight, knot, know, knee, knife, knock, wrap, knit, wrist,* and *gnat.* Read them aloud, and underline the two consonants that stand for the beginning sound in each. Discuss the meanings of the words. Have children choose a word from the list and then draw a picture representing that word. Ask them to label the back of the picture with the chosen word. Allow time for children to see whether classmates can identify the word from the drawing. Then follow the suggestions in **Summarize/Reinforce.**

KINESTHETIC/MOTOR MODEL Explain to children that they will get a chance to exercise their bodies and their minds. Write the following words on slips of paper, and place them in a bag: *knob, write, kneel, knot, know, knee, knock, wrap, knit, wrist, gnat,* and *wrinkle.* Tell children that all the words in the bag begin with *kn, gn,* or *wr,* and review the sounds that the letter combinations make. Invite each child to draw a slip from the bag and pantomime the word for other children to guess. You may wish to list the words on the board as a reference for children. When a word is guessed, ask the actor to write or to find the word on the board and to underline the two consonants that make its beginning sound. Then follow the suggestions in **Summarize/Reinforce.**

INTRAPERSONAL MODEL Distribute copies of these sentence starters. Read them aloud, and make sure children understand all the words.

> If someone says I'm wrong, I feel ______.
> Someday I want to know how to ______.
> I like to gnaw on ______.

Ask volunteers to tell which word in each sentence begins with two consonants that stand for one sound. Give children time to complete each sentence on their own. Be sure children understand that there are no "right" or "wrong" answers. Invite children to discuss in small groups how they completed the sentences. Then follow the suggestions in **Summarize/Reinforce.**

Summarize/Reinforce

Check children's understanding of the lesson by writing the following words on the board and asking children to read them aloud: *wrong, write, know, kneel, gnaw,* and *gnat.* Summarize by explaining that sometimes two consonants stand for one sound. To reinforce this lesson, ask volunteers to underline the consonants that stand for the beginning sound in each of the words on the board. Remind children to use the strategies from this lesson to help them read and pronounce words with the consonant combinations *wr, kn,* and *gn.*

Main Idea and Details

OBJECTIVE: To identify the main idea of a nonfiction passage and the details that support it

Focus

Share the following information with children:

> **The most important idea of a paragraph or story is called the main idea. Sometimes readers can find the main idea in one sentence. Other sentences give more information, or details, about the main idea.**

Choose a Teaching Model

VERBAL/LINGUISTIC MODEL Work with a group to write on chart paper a story about an experience they shared or a pastime in which they are all interested. To begin the story, write a first sentence that states the main idea—for example, *Our visit to the zoo taught us a lot about animals.* Have volunteers add detail sentences to the story. Make sure the details support the main idea. Invite children to illustrate the story when it is finished. Then follow the suggestions in **Summarize/Reinforce.**

LOGICAL/MATHEMATICAL MODEL Write the following paragraph on the board, and read it aloud.

> **There's nothing like a good friend to make you happy. Being a friend means a lot of sharing. Friends stick together in good times and bad. I like to listen to the radio. Friends like to do things together.**

Have children identify the main idea of the paragraph. Ask them to find the sentence that doesn't belong with the rest. Have volunteers explain why the sentence doesn't fit. Make sure that children understand that the detail does not tell about the main idea. Ask a volunteer to cross that sentence out. Have children think of a new sentence to replace the one that was crossed out, and write it on the board. Then follow the suggestions in **Summarize/Reinforce.**

AUDITORY MODEL Ask children to listen carefully while you read page 107 of "Dinosaurs Alive and Well!" aloud. Have a volunteer identify the main idea of the passage. (Letting out your feelings is healthier than keeping them to yourself.) Then reread the excerpt several times, and have children listen for details that support the main idea. Draw on the board the outline of the web below. Have volunteers add to the web on the board details that support the main idea.

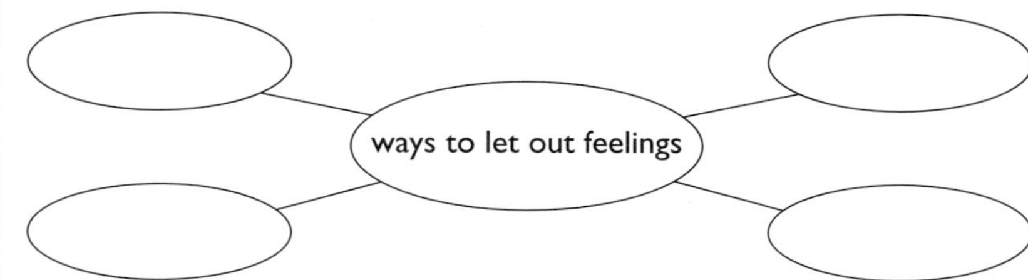

Then follow the suggestions in **Summarize/Reinforce.**

Summarize/Reinforce

Check children's understanding of the lesson by asking them to explain what a main-idea sentence does and what detail sentences do in a paragraph. Summarize by telling children that the main idea of a paragraph or story is its most important idea and that details tell more about the main idea. To reinforce this lesson, have children look through children's magazines and identify the main idea and details in articles they find. Remind children to use strategies from this lesson to help them identify main ideas and details as they read.

Daily Language Practice

Use Daily Language Practice as a quick and easy way to help children sharpen their proofreading skills as they check two or more sentences each day for errors in grammar, usage, mechanics, and spelling.

Daily Language Practice . . .

- is a set of proofreading activities of twelve sentences, one set for each major lesson in *Out of the Blue.*
- provides practice and reinforcement of language skills presented in each lesson.
- reinforces spelling and vocabulary in the context of sentences.

How to Use Daily Language Practice

1. Each day, write two exercises on the board or on a transparency (a copying master is provided) for children to proofread and correct. Corrected exercises are shown.
2. Have children correct the exercises and explain why each correction is needed.

SENTENCES OF THE DAY

❶

❷

Daily Language Practice

"This Is the Way We Go to School"

Capitalization and punctuation of sentences; writing *I*; spelling

1. Sometimes i jag all the way to school.
2. i wear my new red shoes

1. Sometimes I jog all the way to school.
2. I wear my new red shoes.

3. the train goes to the toop of the mountain.
4. we like the fresh air

3. The train goes to the top of the mountain.
4. We like the fresh air.

5. It is hot when i start to walk home
6. I see fish in the pand i pass on my way

5. It is hot when I start to walk home.
6. I see fish in the pond I pass on my way.

7. i hadd fun after school.
8. a lat of my friends came over to skate.

7. I had fun after school.
8. A lot of my friends came over to skate.

9. Do you see my mim
10. she is sitting against the school fence

9. Do you see my mom?
10. She is sitting against the school fence.

11. i like to take my rag dool to school.
12. she makes me happy

11. I like to take my rag doll to school.
12. She makes me happy.

Key Words are underlined. Spelling Words are printed in red.

Daily Language Practice

"Emily and Alice Again"

Capitalization and punctuation of sentences; writing *I*; spelling

1. i mat Jeff at the beach
2. he was wearing yellow sunglasses

1. I met Jeff at the beach.
2. He was wearing yellow sunglasses.

3. May i borrow your red sunglasses
4. Yas, that is a good idea

3. May I borrow your red sunglasses?
4. Yes, that is a good idea.

5. have you seen Betsy's funny sunglasses yit
6. they will make you laugh

5. Have you seen Betsy's funny sunglasses yet?
6. They will make you laugh.

7. Tom seet his sunglasses down on the ground
8. he is sorry he did not pick them up

7. Tom set his sunglasses down on the ground.
8. He is sorry he did not pick them up.

9. did you git your sunglasses
10. i knew you would look beautiful in them

9. Did you get your sunglasses?
10. I knew you would look beautiful in them.

11. we heard Molly has tin pairs of sunglasses
12. she has enough to last forever

11. We heard Molly has ten pairs of sunglasses.
12. She has enough to last forever.

Key Words are underlined. Spelling Words are printed in red.

Daily Language Practice

"Max Found Two Sticks"

Capitalization and punctuation of sentences; writing *I*; *I* and *me*; spelling

1. What is that sound me hear
2. someone appered at my window

1. What is that sound I hear?
2. Someone appeared at my window.

3. do you hear a hissing sound.
4. i am glad that our dod has a spare tire

3. Do you hear a hissing sound?
4. I am glad that our dad has a spare tire.

5. did Matt hear the telephone ring
6. Jan called him just aas he got home

5. Did Matt hear the telephone ring?
6. Jan called him just as he got home.

7. four strong min were building a house
8. the hammering made ane interesting noise

7. Four strong men were building a house.
8. The hammering made an interesting noise.

9. our Aunt Pat brought Ann a drum
10. Ann said thaks and sot down to play

9. Our Aunt Pat brought Ann a drum.
10. Ann said thanks and sat down to play.

11. Al heard a lat of bells ringing
12. he took off his het and went inside

11. Al heard a lot of bells ringing.
12. He took off his hat and went inside.

Key Words are underlined. Spelling Words are printed in red.

Daily Language Practice

"Dinosaurs Alive and Well!"

Capitalization and punctuation of statements and questions; writing *I*; *I* and *me*; word order; spelling

1. sometimes i am scared of the dark
2. i wull try to be brave about it

1. Sometimes I am scared of the dark.
2. I will try to be brave about it.

3. many things take practice
4. it helps ef you believe in yourself.

3. Many things take practice.
4. It helps if you believe in yourself.

5. i want to wen the spelling bee
6. Me will not about it worry

5. I want to win the spelling bee.
6. I will not worry about it.

7. i put the blocks in the wrong place
8. five or sax of them fell over

7. I put the blocks in the wrong place.
8. Five or six of them fell over.

9. Jill was the happiest girl in class the
10. she was proud of thus story

9. Jill was the happiest girl in the class.
10. She was proud of this story.

11. do you remember my neighbor Bill
12. he is my special friend

11. Do you remember my neighbor Bill?
12. He is my special friend.

Key Words are underlined. Spelling Words are printed in red.

READER RESPONSE 

Free Response

DURING READING

1. Work with a partner. Look over the story, and decide if you will read it silently or aloud.
2. Decide with your partner where you will stop to talk about the story.
3. Each time you stop, talk about what you have read. Tell what you think, and listen to what your partner says.
    - You might talk about things you like or do not like.
    - You might talk about things you do not understand.
    - You might talk about what has happened so far or what might happen next.

AFTER READING

4. Talk about the whole story. Tell what you think, and listen to what your partner says.

READER RESPONSE 3

Plot

DURING READING

1. Tell the main things that have happened so far.
2. What is the problem in the story? How do you think it will be solved?
3. What do you think will happen next? What do you think will happen at the end of the story?

AFTER READING

4. Tell the main events that happened in the story.
5. What was the solution to the story problem?
6. Were you able to guess what was going to happen in the end? How else might the author have ended the story?
7. What do you think was the best part of the story? Why?

READER RESPONSE 6

Written Conversation

DURING READING

1. Work with a partner. Read to yourself the pages your teacher tells you to read.
2. On a sheet of paper, write an idea about what you read. Then write a question. It can be about something you didn't understand. It can be a question to find out how your partner feels about something.
3. Pass your paper to your partner.
4. Write the answer to your partner's question. Then add a new question to the paper.
5. Pass the paper back to your partner. Answer the new question your partner wrote.
6. Read the rest of the story. Repeat steps 2–5.

AFTER READING

7. Talk about the story. Use the questions and answers.

THEME PROJECT

LAUNCH 1

Celebrate Me!

A Book About Me

SOMETHING TO THINK ABOUT

1. Think of what you like . . .
   to make   to eat   to look at
2. Talk with a group that likes one of the same things you do. Find out how all the group members are different.
3. Write your name. Draw a wheel around it and write down all the things you like.

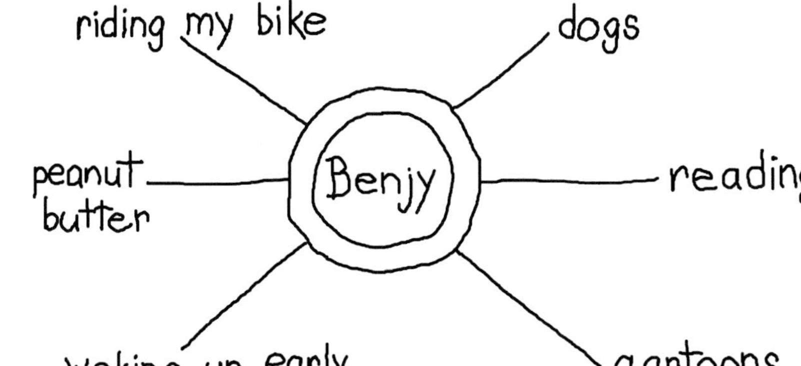

Harcourt Brace School Publishers

THEME PROJECT

CHECKPOINT 1

A Book About Me

SHARE EXPERIENCES OF SCHOOL

1. Draw a map or a picture that shows how you go to school.

2. Find classmates who go to school the same way as you. Make up rules for getting to school safely.

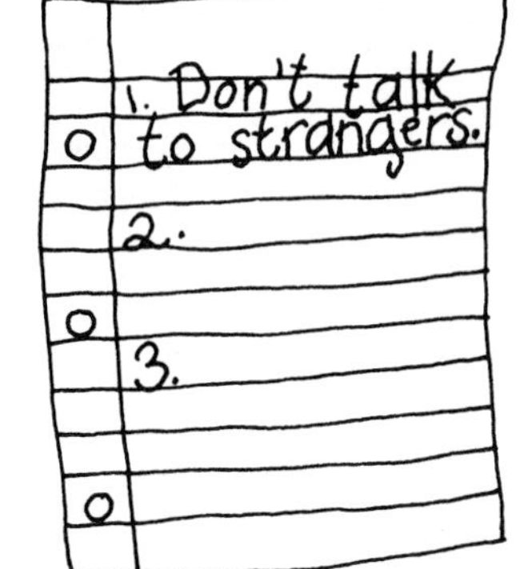

3. Write the list of safety rules. Save it for your book.

Harcourt Brace School Publishers

Use with "This Is the Way We Go to School."

THEME PROJECT

CHECKPOINT 2 **3**

A Book About Me

DRAW AND WRITE ABOUT FAMILIES

1. Make a list of the people in your family.

2. Help make a class list of all the kinds of titles we use for people in our families.

3. Draw a picture of something you have done with your family. Write sentences about your picture.

Harcourt Brace School Publishers

Use with "Emily and Alice Again."

THEME PROJECT

CHECKPOINT 3

A Book About Me

DRAW AND WRITE ABOUT GOALS

1. Think about your future.

2. Write about what you will do someday. Draw a picture, too.

3. Share it with your friends.

Harcourt Brace School Publishers

Use with "Max Found Two Sticks."

THEME PROJECT

CHECKPOINT 4

A Book About Me

TAKE MEASUREMENTS AND ASSEMBLE BOOKS

1. Measure these things. Think of other things to measure.
   - how wide your hand is
   - how long your foot is
   - how tall you are

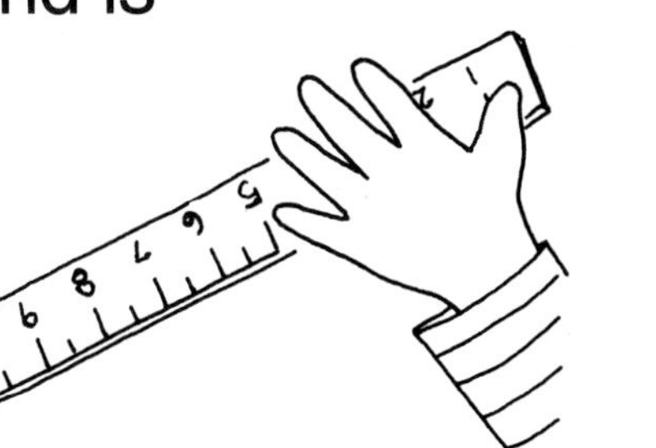

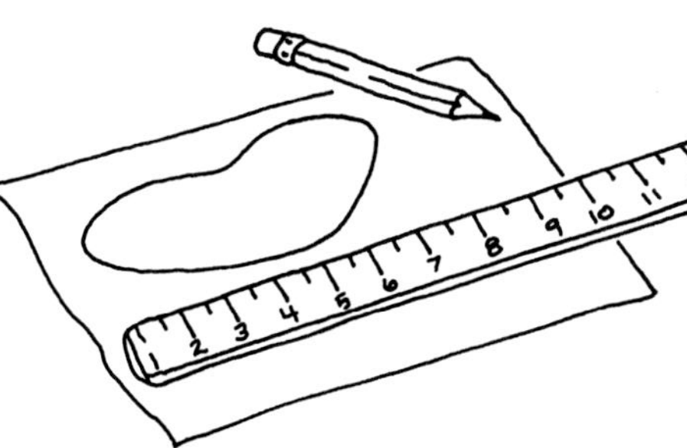

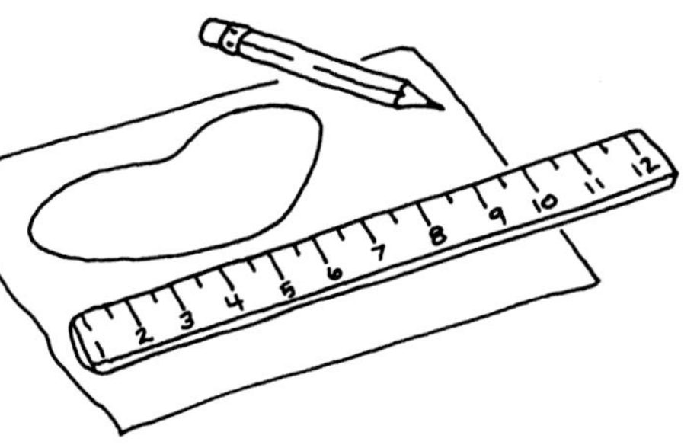

2. Write all your measurements. Leave room to write how the measurements change at the end of the year.
3. Put together your book about you.

Use with "Dinosaurs Alive and Well!"

THEME PROJECT

PRESENTATION **6**

Celebrate Me!

A Book About Me

SHARE YOUR BOOKS

1. Share your book about you with friends.

2. Plan a Grand Opening in the library.

This Is the Way We Go to School

WHAT'S IN A NAME? Names are an important part of who we are. Use your name or your initials to make a work of art!

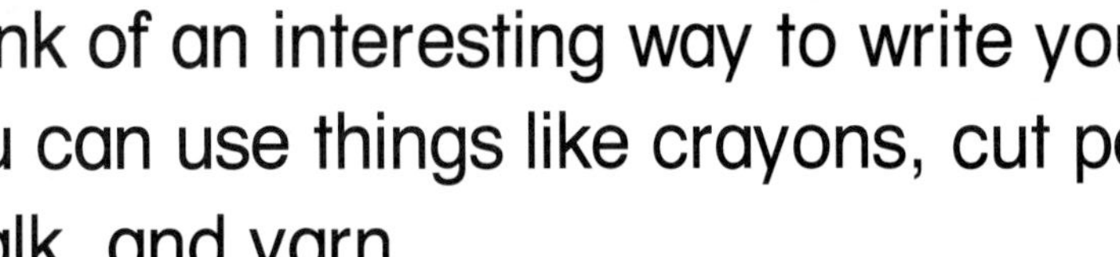

You will need:        

1. Think of an interesting way to write your name. You can use things like crayons, cut paper, chalk, and yarn.
2. Make a picture or a pattern you like. Add color.
3. Display your name for everyone to enjoy!

1b

This Is the Way We Go to School

TRANSPORTATION GRAPHS Kids can walk, ski, or ride a bus. How do you get to school? Work with a small group.

1. Ask your classmates or members of another class how they get to school.
2. Show their answers on a list like this.

Walk 𝍸
Bike |||
Bus 𝍸||

3. Make a graph that shows how everyone gets to school.

INTEGRATED CURRICULUM **2a**

Emily and Alice Again

TRADE ROUTES Work with a group to plan a trade path.

1. Look at a map of the world and pick a country to study. What things are grown or made in that country?
2. Write the name of one thing from the country on a sticker. Put the sticker on the map.
3. Add the name of your thing to a **Products List**.
4. Work with classmates to pick three products from the list. On the map, show your classmates the path you would take to get all three products. Tell how you would travel.

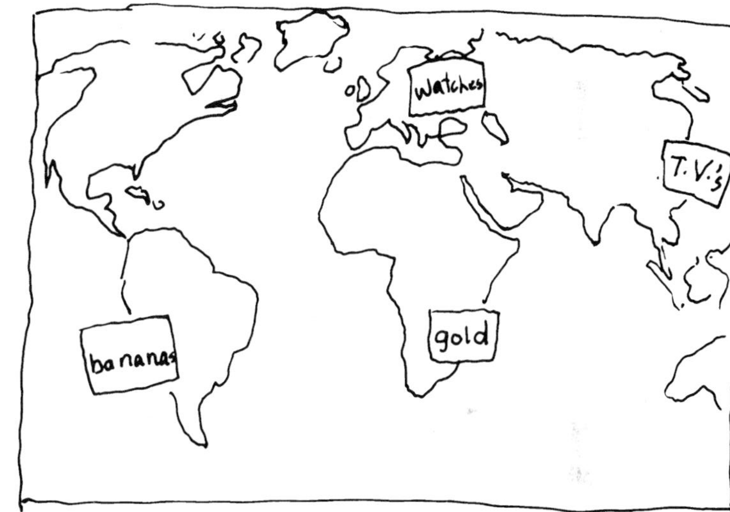

INTEGRATED CURRICULUM **2b**

Emily and Alice Again

TRADING DAY Work with your classmates to plan a "Trading Day."

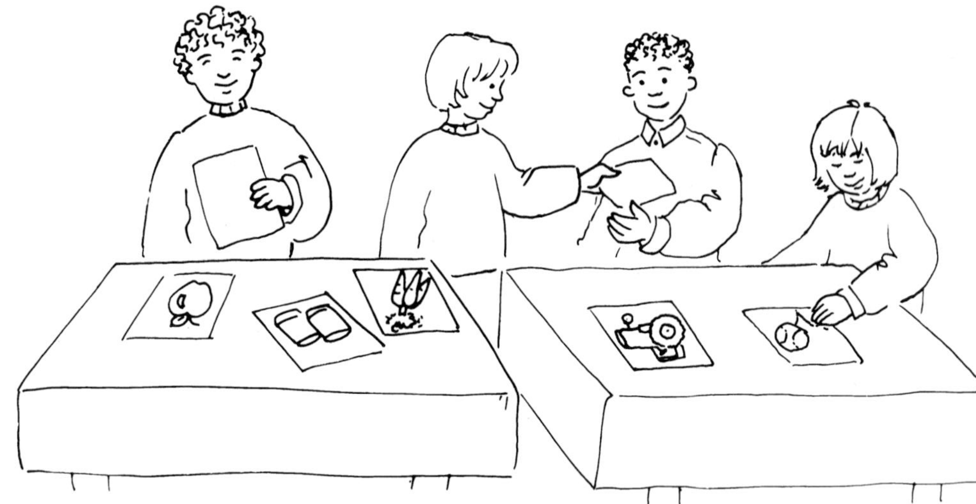

1. Draw pictures of things you like. Place the pictures on desks or tables.
2. Trade your things for things other classmates have.
3. Tell others about the thing you want to trade. Tell why it is a good thing to have.
4. At the end of the trading, talk with your classmates. Was it easy or hard to trade? How did you decide how much something was worth?

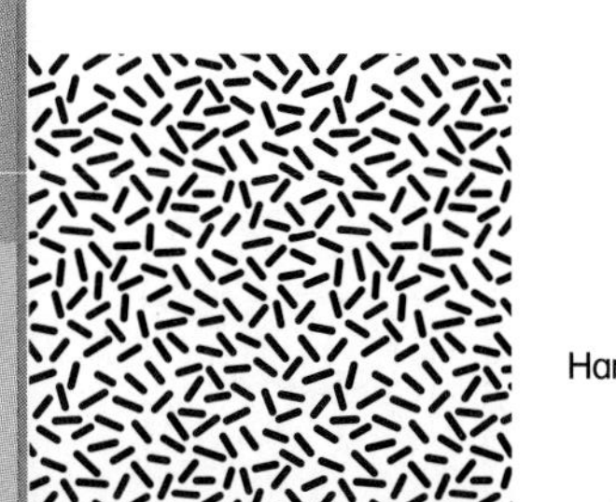

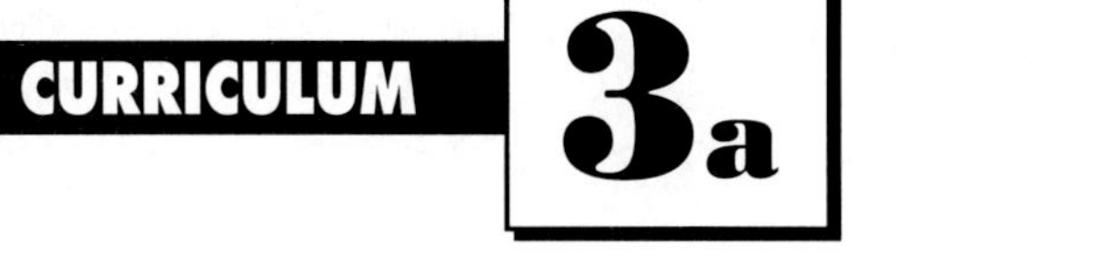

INTEGRATED CURRICULUM **3a**

Max Found Two Sticks

PAPER-PLATE MARACAS You can make music like Max. Make a maraca.

You will need: 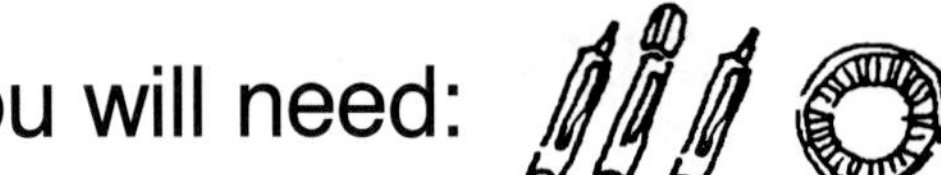  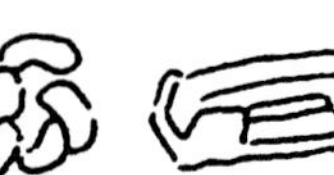 

1. Use markers to draw pictures on the bottom of the plates.
2. Sprinkle a few beans, peas, or pebbles on a plate.
3. Put the other plate on top of the first plate.
4. Staple the plates together.
5. Now shake a beat with your maraca!

SCIENCE

INTEGRATED CURRICULUM **3b**

Max Found Two Sticks

SOUNDS TREASURE HUNT Max heard sounds all around him. Go on a treasure hunt for sounds.

1. Make a chart like this:
2. Take a walk inside and outside your school. Listen carefully! On the chart, write the sounds you hear.
3. Talk to classmates about what you heard.
4. Work with a partner to think of words that sound like each thing you heard. Write the words on the chart.

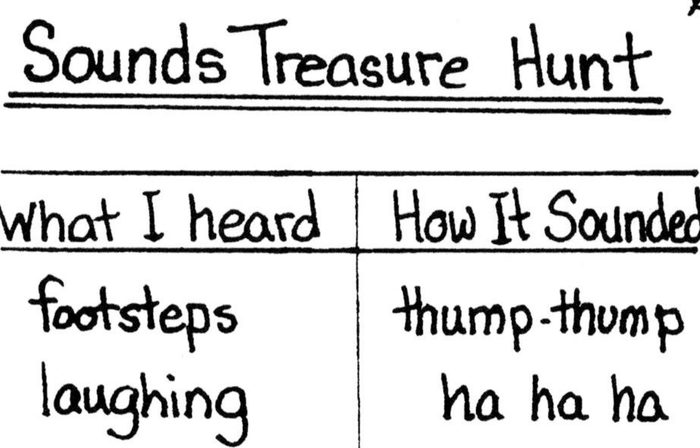

Sounds Treasure Hunt

What I heard	How It Sounded
footsteps	thump-thump
laughing	ha ha ha

INTEGRATED CURRICULUM **4a**

Dinosaurs Alive and Well!

"ME" TIME CAPSULES What's special about you? Make a time capsule that would show someone in the future what you are like.

1. Find a box and draw pictures of yourself on it. Write your name and the date on the top.
2. Think about things that are important to you. Put some of them in the box.
3. Put in pictures of yourself as a baby and yourself now doing fun things.
4. Write a note about yourself to the person who finds your box.

INTEGRATED CURRICULUM

Dinosaurs Alive and Well!

LET'S WORK TOGETHER Everyone is special. What's special about you?

1. Choose a puzzle piece.
2. Draw a picture of something that makes you special.
3. Write about your picture.
4. Work with classmates to put the big puzzle together.

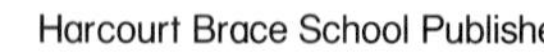

Writing Models

MODEL: SENTENCES ABOUT A PICTURE

capital letter	Dad likes to paint the
end mark	flowers in the garden.

Harcourt Brace School Publishers

MODEL: PERSONAL STORY

Time-order words help show the order in which things happen.

It was the last inning. We were behind by one run. There were two outs, and then I was at bat.

I swung at the first pitch and missed. Strike one! Then I hit a foul ball. Strike two! On the next pitch, I kept my eye on the ball. I hit the ball hard and started to run. At first, I didn't hear the cheers. Then I knew. Finally, I had hit my first home run!

MODEL: STORY

title	Junior Vet
beginning	I think I might want to be a veterinarian someday. So I asked Dr. Curry if I could help her out for a week. Dr. Curry
middle	let me feed the animals and watch her work. At the end of the week, she asked if I still wanted to be an animal doctor.
ending	"More than ever," I answered. I meant every word!

Writing Models

MODEL: HOW-TO SENTENCES

steps in order

Here's how you can plant some seeds. First, put some dirt into a cup. Next, put some seeds into the dirt. Cover the seeds with dirt. Last, water the seeds and put them in the light.

Additional Reading

Out of the Blue

The following list is a compilation of the Reading Trade Books selected for the lesson plans.

THEME: CELEBRATE ME!

***Anna in the Garden* by Diane Dawson Hearn. Silver Moon, 1994. EASY**
Anna plants and cares for seeds that later bloom into a beautiful garden.

***Arthur Meets the President* by Marc Brown. Little, Brown, 1991. CHALLENGE**
Arthur wins an essay contest and is asked to read his essay to the President during a special ceremony at the White House. *Children's Choice*

***Arthur's Camp-Out* by Lillian Hoban. HarperCollins, 1993. AVERAGE**
Arthur's camp-out doesn't turn out quite the way he imagined, but he has many memorable adventures that are sure to please young readers!

***Arthur's Pet Business* by Marc Brown. Little, Brown, 1990. AVERAGE**
Arthur's determination to prove he is responsible enough to have a puppy brings him a menagerie of animals to care for.

***Arthur's Teacher Trouble* by Marc Brown. Little, Brown, 1987. AVERAGE**
Schoolwork can be demanding for Arthur, especially when he is selected to be in a spellathon.

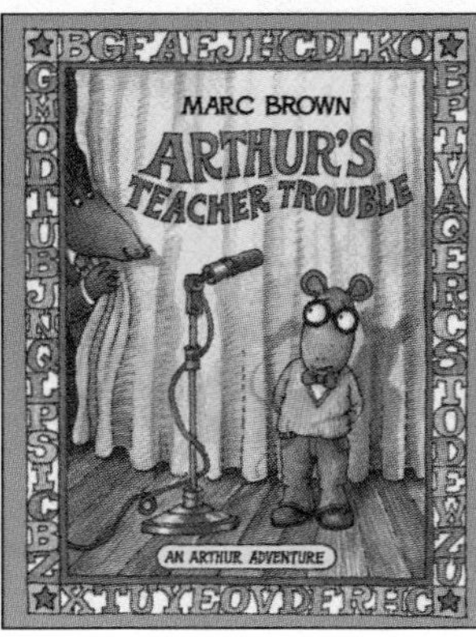

***The Ballad of Belle Dorcas* by William H. Hooks. Knopf, 1990. CHALLENGE**
Belle Dorcas falls in love with a slave named Joshua and uses magic to keep him. *Notable Trade Book in Social Studies; Notable Trade Book for the Language Arts*

***A Bargain for Frances* by Russell Hoban. HarperCollins, 1978. AVERAGE**
Frances finds a clever way to undo a trade even though she has agreed "no backsies."

***The Bionic Bunny Show* by Marc Brown and Laurene Krasny Brown. Little, Brown, 1985. AVERAGE**
Young readers learn how a television show is produced as they read about Wilbur, the rabbit who represents the Bionic Bunny. *ALA Notable Book;* SLJ *Best Books*

***A Carpenter* by Douglas Florian. Greenwillow, 1991. EASY**
This miniature essay follows a carpenter in his daily work as he measures, cuts, and builds with wood.

***Chester's Way* by Kevin Henkes. Greenwillow, 1988. AVERAGE**
Chester and Wilson prefer to do things their way. But things change when they meet Lilly. *ALA Notable Book*

The Day I Had to Play with My Sister **by Crosby N. Bonsall. HarperCollins, 1988. EASY**
A big brother's attempts to teach his little sister to play hide-and-seek prove to be frustrating.

The Dinosaur Who Lived in My Backyard **by B. G. Hennessy. Viking Penguin, 1988. AVERAGE**
A young boy imagines what it was like long ago when a dinosaur lived in his backyard.

Dinosaurs Divorce: A Guide for Changing Families **by Laurene Krasny Brown and Marc Brown. Little, Brown, 1988. AVERAGE**
This book provides positive ways for children to deal with changes in the family structure, such as the separation of parents. SLJ *Best Books*

Dinosaurs to the Rescue: A Guide to Protecting Our Planet **by Laurie Krasny Brown and Marc Brown. Little, Brown, 1992. AVERAGE**
This book provides tips for saving electricity, paper, and plastic, as well as for reusing and recycling common objects and materials.

Dinosaurs Travel: A Guide for Families on the Go **by Laurie Krasny Brown and Marc Brown. Little, Brown, 1988. AVERAGE**
This book provides travel tips for families to ensure their successful departure and safe return home.

Dinosaurs Walked Here and Other Stories Fossils Tell **by Patricia Lauber. Bradbury, 1987. CHALLENGE**
This book discusses how fossilized remains of plants and animals reveal the characteristics of the prehistoric world. Included are beautiful full-color photographs, paintings, and maps. *Outstanding Science Trade Book; ALA Notable Book; SLJ Best Books*

Dolphin Adventure: A True Story **by Wayne Grover. Greenwillow, 1990. CHALLENGE**
This is a true story of the author's encounter with a dolphin family and how he was able to rescue its baby. *Outstanding Science Trade Book*

Don't Forget to Write **by Martina Selway. Ideals, 1992. AVERAGE**
In a letter, Rosie expresses her changing feelings about her visit to her grandfather's farm.

Elmer **by David McKee. Lothrop, Lee & Shepard, 1989. AVERAGE**
A patchwork elephant wants to look like other elephants until experience teaches him to celebrate his difference. *Notable Trade Book in Social Studies*

Emily and Alice **by Joyce Champion. Harcourt Brace, 1993. AVERAGE**
Two girls learn that being best friends isn't always easy.

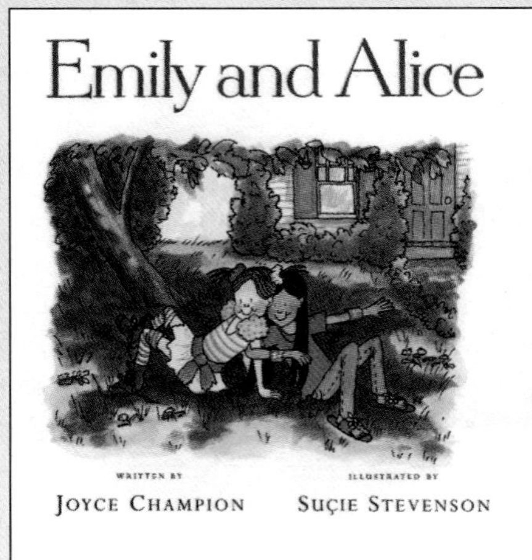

Extra Cheese, Please! Mozzarella's Journey from Cow to Pizza **by Cris Peterson. Boyds Mills Press, 1994. AVERAGE**
When Annabelle gives birth to her calf, she also begins to produce milk. The milk is processed into cheese, which is used to prepare the perfect pizza.

Farm Noises **by Jane Miller. Simon & Schuster, 1989. AVERAGE**
This book discusses the distinctive sounds made by animals, birds, and machines that may be heard on farms.

Feelings **by Aliki. William Morrow, 1986. AVERAGE**
In this book, the wide range of feelings that we all share is explored.

Galimoto **by Karen L. Williams. William Morrow, 1991. CHALLENGE**
A young boy collects wire to make a *galimoto*—a toy car. *Notable Trade Book in Social Studies; Notable Trade Book for the Language Arts*

The Garden in the City **by Gerda Muller. Dutton, 1992. CHALLENGE**
A family moves to the city and plants a garden together outside their new home. *Outstanding Science Trade Book*

The Gum on the Drum **by Barbara Gregorich. School Zone, 1992. EASY**
A drum-playing bear encounters silly adventures when he tries to hum with gum in his mouth.

Henry and Mudge and the Best Day of All **by Cynthia Rylant. Macmillan, 1995. EASY**
Henry and his dog, Mudge, celebrate Henry's birthday and make it the best day ever.

Henry and Mudge and the Wild Wind **by Cynthia Rylant. Bradbury, 1993. EASY**
Henry and his dog, Mudge, try to keep busy inside the house during a thunderstorm.

Henry and Mudge Take the Big Test **by Cynthia Rylant. Bradbury, 1991. EASY**
Henry's dog, Mudge, goes to obedience school. Will Mudge pass the test?

How to Make an Apple Pie and See the World **by Marjorie Priceman. Knopf, 1994. CHALLENGE**
When the market is closed, a baker travels around the world to obtain the exact ingredients to make an apple pie. *ALA Notable Book*

I Hate English! **by Ellen Levine. Scholastic, 1989. AVERAGE**
When her family moves from Hong Kong to New York City, Mei Mei has difficulty adjusting to school and learning English. *ALA Notable Book*

I Know a Place **by Karen Ackerman. Houghton Mifflin, 1992. EASY**
A girl describes a place where all the rooms have warmth, comfort, and love . . . a place that turns out to be home!

I Like Me! **by Nancy L. Carlson. Viking Penguin, 1988. EASY**
A little pig with a positive self-image expresses all that she likes about herself. She proves that sometimes the best friend you can have is yourself. *Children's Choice*

If You Made a Million **by David M. Schwartz. Lothrop, Lee & Shepard, 1989. CHALLENGE**
Marvelosissimo the Mathematical Magician, several young assistants, and four animals provide entertaining explanations of our different denominations of money. *ALA Notable Book; SLJ Best Books; Children's Choice*

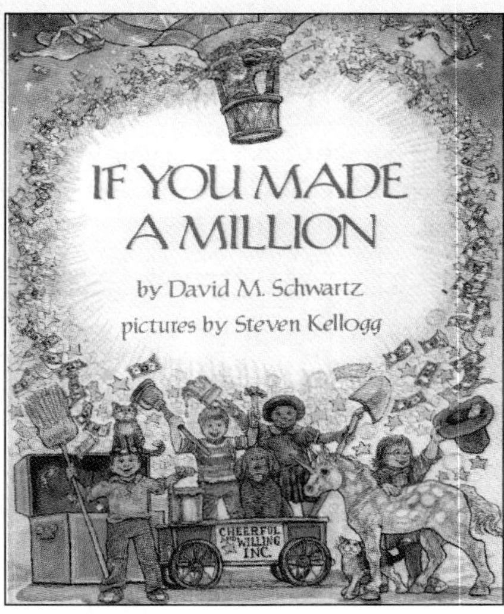

Julian, Dream Doctor **by Ann Cameron. Random House, 1990. AVERAGE**
Julian wants to get his dad something he's always dreamed about for his thirty-fifth birthday. But Dad's dream is not only unusual—it's also scary!

Lionel in the Spring **by Stephen Krensky. Dial, 1990. EASY**
Does Lionel really want to go through all the work to grow a garden? Why is it so difficult for him to get rid of things? Find out how Lionel faces these challenges and more.

The Listening Walk **by Paul Showers. HarperCollins, 1991. AVERAGE**
A young girl and her father set out on a quiet walk to listen to all the sounds around them.

The Magic School Bus in the Time of the Dinosaurs **by Joanna Cole. Scholastic, 1994. CHALLENGE**
Travel through time and learn fascinating information about dinosaurs. Find out when they lived and how they disappeared.

Make Me a Peanut Butter Sandwich (and a Glass of Milk) **by Ken Robbins. Scholastic, 1992. AVERAGE**
This book explores the process of making America's most popular snack, from baking the bread and milking the cows to making the peanut butter.

Max **by Rachel Isadora. Macmillan, 1976. EASY**
A young boy discovers that dancing is a good warm-up exercise for playing his favorite sport, baseball.

Musical Max **by Robert Kraus. Simon & Schuster, 1992. EASY**
Max loves to play his music, but the neighbors are bothered by the noise. When he stops playing, however, the neighbors miss the music.

A New Coat for Anna **by Harriet Ziefert. Knopf, 1988. AVERAGE**
Although there is no money to spare, Anna's mother finds a way to provide Anna with a badly needed winter coat. *ALA Notable Book; Notable Trade Book in Social Studies*

Oh, the Places You'll Go! **by Dr. Seuss. Random House, 1990. CHALLENGE**
Through colorful characters and scenes, Dr. Seuss provides children with positive messages about confidence, problem-solving, and self-esteem.

On the Go **by Ann Morris. Lothrop, Lee & Shepard, 1990. EASY**
This book shows how people travel in countries around the world—on foot and on things with wheels powered by animals or motors.

Pinky and Rex and the New Baby **by James Howe. Macmillan, 1993. AVERAGE**
Pinky feels left out when her best friend, Rex, spends more time with a new baby brother.

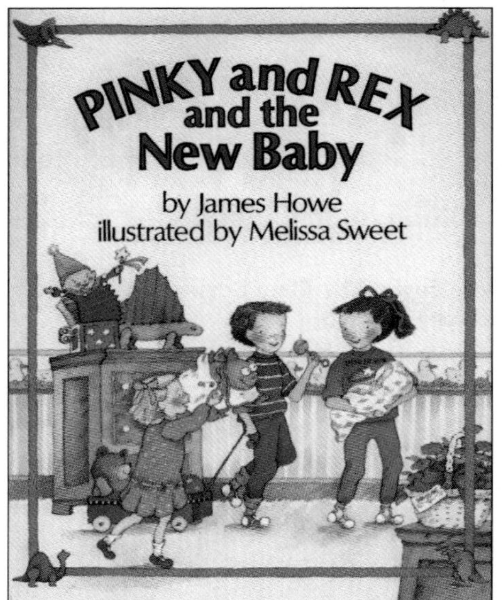

Ruby the Copycat **by Peggy Rathmann. Scholastic, 1991. AVERAGE**
Ruby discovers that being different is what makes her special. *Children's Choice*

Tacky the Penguin **by Helen Lester. Houghton Mifflin, 1988. AVERAGE**
A penguin proves that even an odd bird such as himself can be special. *California Young Reader Medal*

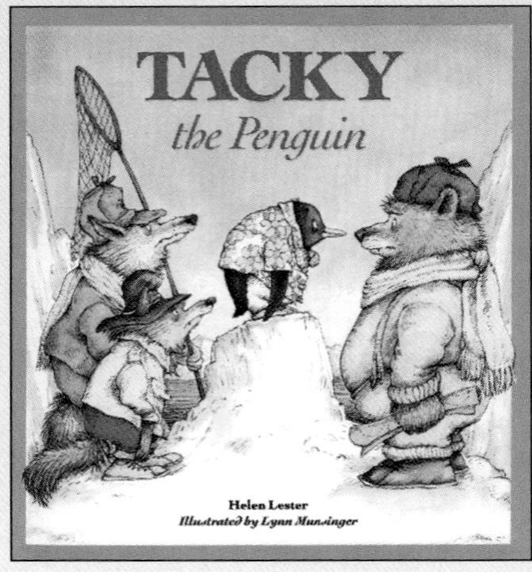

This Is the Way We Eat Our Lunch **by Edith Baer. Scholastic, 1995. AVERAGE**
This selection takes the reader around the world to find out what children in other countries eat for lunch.

Turtle Knows Your Name **retold by Ashley Bryan. Atheneum, 1989. AVERAGE**
A boy with a very long name is challenged by his grandmother to find out her real name.

***A Very Young Musician* by Jill Krementz. Simon & Schuster, 1991. CHALLENGE**

A ten-year-old boy makes new friends and meets many world-famous musicians as he learns to play the trumpet.

***Where Does the Trail Lead?* by Burton Albert. Simon & Schuster, 1991. AVERAGE**

A boy goes on an adventure when he explores a trail that leads to the beach.

***William's Doll* by Charlotte Zolotow. HarperCollins, 1972. EASY**

William is teased when he tells everyone he wants a toy doll.

***Window* by Jeannie Baker. Greenwillow, 1991. EASY**

Events and changes in a boy's life, from babyhood to his present youth, are captured through wordless scenes observed from the window of his room. SLJ *Best Books; Notable Trade Book in Social Studies*

SCHOOL ↔ HOME CONNECTION 1

FAMILY INVOLVEMENT ACTIVITIES

Your child is reading "This Is the Way We Go to School," a story that takes children on a travel adventure to other parts of the United States and other nations around the world. As they read this rhyming story, children learn how people in other places travel to and from school.

I have tried some of the activities.

Student: ______________________

Family Member: ______________________

Comments/Suggestions: ______________________

____

____

You may want to do some of these activities with your child.

ON THE GO!

Our class has been doing a lot of activities centered around the idea of travel. For the next few days, you might ask members of your family to keep a list of all of the places they go and how they travel to each place. You might also want to compare the forms of transportation. Which are the easiest to use? Which are the best for the environment? Which are the fastest?

PASSPORTS TO FUN

Talk about friends and family in other states or countries. For starters, make a list of the people and places, and help your child find the locations on a map or globe. Then share what you know about the place—the language, places to visit, weather, and so on. Be sure to share, too, any photographs or other pictures you may have.

WORDS, WORDS, WORDS

Have your child cut out the Key Words on the page. Help your child experiment with the word cards by sorting them into categories.

- Help your child make a Word File. You can use an old recipe box or other container. It would be helpful to have divider cards in the box with the letters of the alphabet on them. After your child has finished sorting the words, he or she can file the words alphabetically to keep for later use.

On your next visit to the library, you can look for *This Is the Way We Eat Our Lunch: A Book About Children Around the World* (Scholastic, 1995), another book by Edith Baer and Steven Björkman, the author and the illustrator of *This Is the Way We Go to School.*

start	shoes	against	air	sometimes	mountain

SCHOOL ↔ HOME CONNECTION 2

FAMILY INVOLVEMENT ACTIVITIES

Your child is reading a selection from "Emily and Alice Again" by Joyce Champion. In the story, Emily tries on Alice's new sunglasses and then wants them for herself. But Alice refuses to trade for them until Emily offers her little sister, Nora. Soon Alice and Nora are having a noisy good time, but Emily is sitting alone. Finally, Emily offers to trade back the sunglasses, and an exhausted Alice accepts. The girls decide that from now on they will stick to borrowing.

I have tried some of the activities.

Student: ______________________________

Family Member: ______________________________

Comments/Suggestions: ______________________________

____

____

You may want to do some of these activities with your child.

THE TRADE

Ask your child to use his or her own words to tell you the story from "Emily and Alice Again." Does your child think the girls made a good trade? Would he or she have traded something for the sunglasses? What would your child have done if he or she were Alice?

WORD SEARCH

Have your child cut out the Key Words on the page. Touch one word at a time and ask your child to read it. Mix up the words and turn them face down. Have your child turn over one word and use it in a sentence. Then turn over one yourself and use it in a sentence. Continue taking turns until all the words have been turned face up. Have your child add these words to his or her Word File.

beautiful
borrow
enough
heard
idea
knew
laugh
sorry

Harcourt Brace School Publishers

SCHOOL ↔ HOME CONNECTION 3

FAMILY INVOLVEMENT ACTIVITIES

Your child is reading "Max Found Two Sticks" by Brian Pinkney. In the story, a boy named Max uses sticks to tap out rhythms of things he hears around him—the sound of pigeons startled into flight, rain tapping against the windows, church bells chiming, tom-toms in a marching band, and the subway rumbling. When a real marching band comes around the corner, Max gets a surprise when one of the drummers throws him his extra pair of drumsticks.

I have tried some of the activities.

Student: ____________________

Family Member: ____________________

Comments/Suggestions: ____________________

____

____

You may want to do some of these activities with your child.

THE BEAT GOES ON

Invite your child to retell the story in his or her own words. Then imagine that Max is there with you. What kinds of rhythms might he tap? Would he hear some interesting sounds? Have your child find something that can be used for drumsticks. Then sit quietly with your child, perhaps outside, and listen to the sounds around you. Challenge your child to imitate sounds by tapping rhythms with the sticks. Can you guess the sound that is being tapped? Take turns with the sticks.

THE WAY I FEEL

Ask your child to describe how Max felt at the beginning of the story. (He didn't feel like talking to anyone; he seemed bored.) What happened to change the way he felt? Then have your child tell about times when he or she didn't feel like talking to anyone and what happened to change those feelings. Discuss things your child enjoys doing. Then make a list or write a book about fun things to do on a boring day.

DISAPPEARING WORDS

Have your child cut out the Key Words on this page. Place the words face up on one side of a table. Say a Key Word and have your child find it, use it in a sentence, and place it on the other side of the table. When all the words have been identified and moved, have your child close his or her eyes. Remove a word and challenge your child to name the word that has "disappeared." Continue until you have removed all the words. Have your child add these words to his or her Word File.

thanks	strong	spare	sound	called	brought	appeared

Harcourt Brace School Publishers

SCHOOL ↔ HOME CONNECTION 4

FAMILY INVOLVEMENT ACTIVITIES

Your child is reading "Dinosaurs Alive and Well!" It is a story about a lovable group of dinosaurs that demonstrate for children some good health habits that will last a lifetime. The story begins with this thought: "There's just one you. That makes you special." The lively pictures and words give advice on exercise, relationships with friends and family, and ways of dealing with feelings. Children are encouraged to feel good about themselves and to take an active role in their own well-being . . . an important part of understanding—and celebrating—themselves!

I have tried some of the activities.

Student: ______________________________

Family Member: ______________________________

Comments/Suggestions: ______________________________

____

____

You may want to do some of these activities with your child.

The selection your child is reading is from the book *Dinosaurs Alive and Well!* by Laurie Krasny Brown and Marc Brown. During your next visit to the library, you might check out this book as well as these others by the same author and illustrator: *Dinosaurs to the Rescue! A Guide to Protecting Our Planet* (Little, Brown & Co., 1992) and *Dinosaurs Travel: A Guide for Families on the Go* (Little, Brown & Co., 1988).

believe

many

practice

proud

remember

special

wrong

yourself

WORDS, WORDS, WORDS

Have your child cut out the Key Words. Help your child experiment with them.

- Sort some of the cards into different categories.
- Take out your child's Word File. See how some of these new words can be used with other words to make sentences.

Harcourt Brace School Publishers

I'll wear my new ______________ today.

I'll ______________ my day by walking to school.

It's rainy and windy, so I'll hold up my umbrella ______________ the rain.

I like to smell the fresh ______________.

On my walk, I see a big, rocky ______________.

______________ I ride my bike to school.

Alice had ______________ new sunglasses.

Emily ______________ that there must something she could trade for the glasses.

Trading Nora to Alice for the glasses was Emily's ______________.

Soon Emily ______________ Alice and Nora having fun.

Emily did not have anything to ______________ about.

Emily was ______________ she had traded away her sister.

Alice had had ______________ fun with Nora.

Next time, Emily and Alice will only ______________ things.

A ______________ breeze shook the tree by Max's house.

It rained, and then the sun ______________.

Max's dad ______________ out the trash cans.

Max made the ______________ of a train.

A drummer gave his ______________ sticks to Max.

Max said ______________.

He ______________ out so the drummer could hear him.

Just being *you* makes you ______________.

You can do a lot to take care of ______________.

You can learn to play ______________ different games and sports.

Some games and sports take lots of ______________.

Just ______________ this: Think for yourself.

Be ______________ of all the things you can do.

You have to ______________ in yourself.

It's not ______________ to feel sad or mad sometimes.

ABOUT THE STUDENT ANTHOLOGY

Reading Trade Books

Signatures Library

Other Theme-Related Books

Multimedia Resources

Community Resources

FAVORITE ACTIVITIES

Your own ideas for customizing the theme:

MATERIALS:

STEPS:

MATERIALS:

STEPS:

MATERIALS:

STEPS:

GRAPH-A-BOOK

Dear Family Members,

As a book is read at home, have the student graph his or her response. The student should write the title of the book and the author's name on the numbered line and then color the corresponding bar on the graph to evaluate the book. Ask the student to give a reason for his or her rating.

Book Titles and Authors' Names

1. ______________________________
2. ______________________________
3. ______________________________
4. ______________________________
5. ______________________________
6. ______________________________

Graph

	Would Not Recommend	OK	Good	GREAT!
Book 1				
Book 2				
Book 3				
Book 4				
Book 5				
Book 6				

Please return the graph to school when completed. Thank you.

Signature ______________________________

Harcourt Brace School Publishers

Duplicate the page and send it home with students to be completed with family members.

NEWS FROM:

Dear Family,

Special Announcements

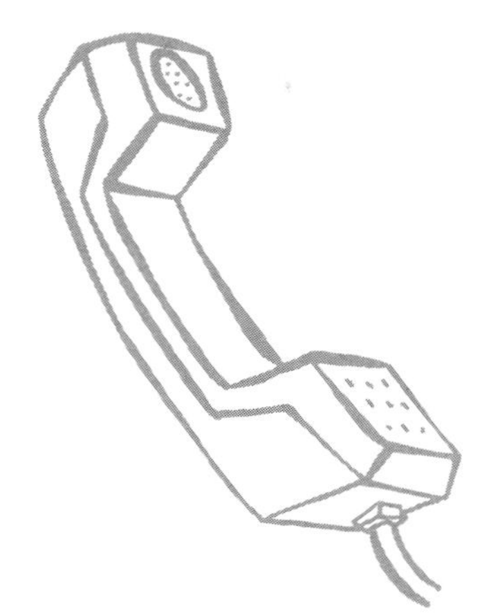

Spotlight on . . .

Something to Try at Home

From Your Child . . .

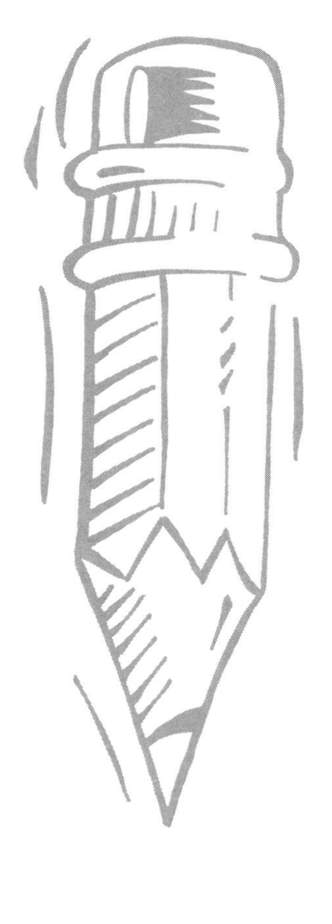

Book Corner

We have been very busy lately!

Harcourt Brace School Publishers

Complete the newsletter with news items from your class. Duplicate the page, and send it home to family members.

CREATE YOUR OWN SCHOOL-TO-HOME NEWSLETTER

Insert your school name or newsletter title to head your newsletter.

Personal note to parents

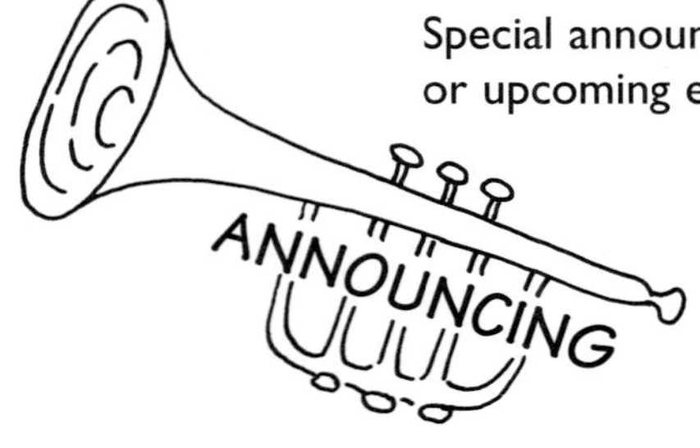

Special announcements or upcoming events

Reminder of upcoming meetings, conferences, or field trips

Classroom projects

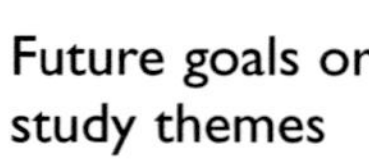

Future goals or study themes

List of recommended books for reading

Current events from the classroom, school, or community

Focus on a certain subject area, or parent self-help information

Call for volunteers or materials

Student column

Harcourt Brace School Publishers

Use any of these clip-art graphics to create a classroom newsletter to send home.

Harcourt Brace School Publishers

because: ______________________________

____

____

____

____

____

Signed: ______________________________

Theme TWO
RESOURCES

Resources

Theme 2

Tested Skill

RETEACH: GRAMMAR

Statements and Questions

OBJECTIVES: To understand that a sentence that tells something is called a statement and that it begins with a capital letter and ends with a period; to understand that a sentence that asks something is called a question and that it begins with a capital letter and ends with a question mark

Focus

Share the following information with children:

> **A statement is a sentence that tells something. It begins with a capital letter and ends with a period. A question is a sentence that asks something. It begins with a capital letter and ends with a question mark. Knowing about statements and questions helps you understand what you read and helps readers understand what you write.**

Choose a Teaching Model

VERBAL/LINGUISTIC MODEL Have groups of three children work together. Invite two of the children in each group to plan and act out an argument about something. Suggest that the third person serve as the mediator for the argument, asking questions that require the arguers to respond in complete sentences; for example, *Who had the crayon first? Which other color could you use while Martin uses this one?* Have groups record some of their questions and responses to share with the class. Then follow the suggestions in **Summarize/Reinforce.**

VISUAL/SPATIAL MODEL Suggest that because Matthew and Tilly were such good friends, they probably enjoyed sharing jokes. Then invite children to write and illustrate a class joke book. First, they should each recall or make up a joke that begins with a question. You may wish to provide a joke book for children to use for reference. Then, have children write the joke on a sheet of paper and draw a picture to illustrate it. Afterward, staple the jokes together, adding a construction-paper cover to make a class joke book. Invite volunteers to read aloud jokes from the book. Then follow the suggestions in **Summarize/Reinforce.**

AUDITORY MODEL Have each child prepare a period card and a question mark card. Then ask children to hold up the period card when they hear a statement and to hold up the question mark card when they hear a question. You may wish to use these sentences:

> **Matthew and Tilly were friends.**
> **They took a kitten from a tree together.**
> **Did Matthew and Tilly ever fight?**
> **Tilly drew numbers and squares on the sidewalk.**
> **Are Matthew and Tilly happy playing by themselves?**

Invite children to say questions or statements about the story. Have the rest of the class hold up the appropriate card. Then follow the suggestions in **Summarize/Reinforce.**

Summarize/Reinforce

Check children's understanding of the lesson by having them tell when they might use statements and when they might use questions. (Possible responses: when giving directions, when answering questions, when telling a story; when meeting a new person, when not understanding some information) Summarize by telling children that a statement is a sentence that tells something. It begins with a capital letter and ends with a period. A question is a sentence that asks something. It begins with a capital letter and ends with a question mark. To reinforce this lesson, have children look for statements and questions in stories they have read. Remind them to use the strategies from this lesson to help them read and write sentences.

Tested Skill

R-Controlled Vowel: /ûr/*er, ur*

OBJECTIVE: To understand the relationship between letters and sounds

Focus

Share the following information with children:

> **The letters *er* and *ur* can stand for the vowel sound you hear in *fern* and *turn*. Remembering these letter groups and the sound they stand for will help you figure out new words as you read.**

Choose a Teaching Model

VERBAL/LINGUISTIC MODEL Write these words and questions on the board, and read the words aloud with children. Ask volunteers to underline in each word the letters that make the vowel sound heard in *fern* and *turn*. Then have children answer the questions with words from the list.

clerk   turkey   herd   purple   fur

1. What color can also be called violet?
2. Who uses the cash register in a store?
3. What does a dog have that helps keep it warm?
4. What bird goes gobble-gobble?
5. What do you call a group of cows that travel together?

Have children brainstorm other *er* and *ur* words and make up questions that these words can answer. Have volunteers read their questions aloud. Write on the board the *er* and *ur* words that answer each new question. Have a volunteer circle the letters that make the /ûr/ sound in each word. Then follow the suggestions in **Summarize/Reinforce.**

MUSICAL/RHYTHMIC MODEL Prepare word cards for the words shown, and place them in a bag. Have children draw a word out of the bag, find a partner who has a rhyming word, and make up a short song or rhyme using the two words. Encourage children to find out the meanings of any unknown words before using them in a song.

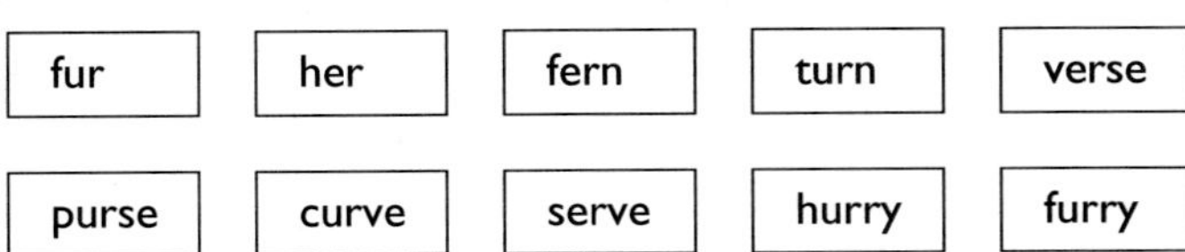

Invite pairs to share their songs with classmates. Then follow the suggestions in **Summarize/Reinforce.**

KINESTHETIC/MOTOR MODEL Write the following words on chart paper. Read them aloud with the children, emphasizing the vowel sound /ûr/ and pointing to the letters that stand for that sound in each word.

fur, curl, blur, herd, fern, turn, purple, herself, curtain, nurse, hurt, hurry, burst, turtle, her, gerbil, serve, purse, surprise

Take children and the list of words to an area where children can play a hopscotch game. As they land on each space on the grid, they choose a word from the list that uses the letters on their space for the /ûr/ sound. They say the word and use it in a sentence. Circle each word as it is used, and have children try to choose a new word each time. Then follow the suggestions in **Summarize/Reinforce.**

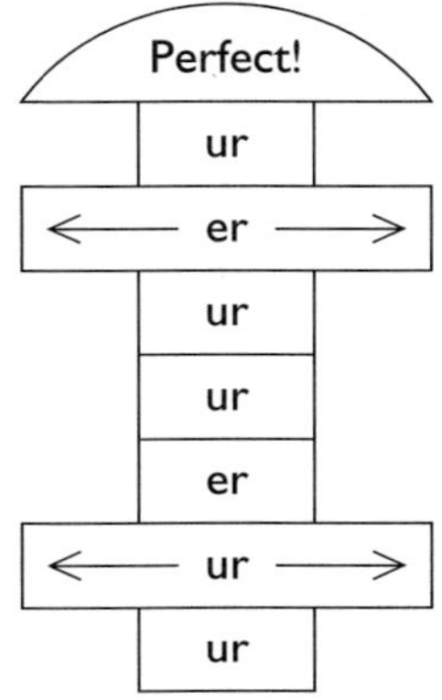

Summarize/Reinforce

Check children's understanding of the lesson by having them name two letter groups that can stand for the vowel sound heard in *fur.* Explain that knowing the sound that these letter groups make will help them read new words. To reinforce this lesson, have children find words in their reading that use *er* and *ur* to stand for the /ûr/ sound. Remind children to use the strategies from this lesson to help them read and write words with *er* and *ur* for /ûr/.

Making Predictions

OBJECTIVE: To understand that an author gives clues that help the reader guess what will happen next

Focus

Share the following information with children:

> **Readers often make guesses, or predictions, about what might happen next in a story. To do that, they use what they know and clues the writer gives them. Making predictions can help you understand a story and can make it more fun to read.**

Choose a Teaching Model

VERBAL/LINGUISTIC Locate and read aloud a variation of a familiar tale such as "The Three Little Pigs" or "The Three Bears." Many of these books have events and endings that are unexpected or funny. Pause periodically, and invite children to guess what will happen next. Ask children to share parts of the story they used as clues for their predictions. Then follow the suggestions in **Summarize/Reinforce.**

VISUAL/SPATIAL Invite children to think of a short story they could tell in pictures. Have children draw and label four or five separate pictures that tell a story, or draw their stories in a comic-strip format. When they have finished, invite children to mix up their drawings (or cut apart frames of a comic-strip story), exchange sets of drawings with partners, and try to put their partners' stories in order. Encourage partners to talk about the clues that helped them order each other's stories. Then follow the suggestions in **Summarize/Reinforce.**

AUDITORY MODEL Read aloud this story, omitting the last paragraph. Ask children to predict the outcome of the story and tell which clues led them to make the predictions they made.

Jay awoke with a start and reached for the clock by his bed.

"Oh, no!" he exclaimed. "I'm late for school!"

He wondered why no one else in his house was up yet. Quickly, he got dressed, poured some cereal for himself, and ate as fast as he could. Still, no one else was up.

Jay grabbed his jacket and ran out of the house. That was strange. His friends were not at the bus stop. What was happening?

Jay stood at the bus stop in front of his friend's house for a long time, but no familiar yellow bus came by.

Finally, his friend Anita called from her window, "Hey, Jay! Don't you know that today is Saturday?"

Read the ending, and then read the entire story again, stopping a few times during the reading. As you read, have partners record their predictions and the clues in the story on a chart like the one below. Discuss why the ending was predictable, taking story clues and children's experiences into account. Then follow the suggestions in **Summarize/Reinforce.**

Predictions	Clues

Summarize/Reinforce

Check children's understanding by having them explain what leads them to make predictions when they read a story. Summarize by telling children that trying to predict what will happen next in the story can help them understand and enjoy the story. To reinforce this lesson, have children tell about predictions they made as they read other stories or watched television shows. Remind children to use the strategies from this lesson to help them understand and enjoy stories.

Tested Skill

Exclamations, Commands, and End Marks

OBJECTIVES: To understand that a sentence that shows strong feeling is called an exclamation and ends with an exclamation point; to understand that a sentence that tells someone to do something is called a command and usually ends with a period

Focus

Share the following information with children:

> **An exclamation is a sentence that shows strong feeling. It begins with a capital letter and ends with an exclamation point. A command is a sentence that tells someone to do something. It begins with a capital letter and usually ends with a period. Knowing about exclamations and commands helps you write more clearly.**

Choose a Teaching Model

KINESTHETIC/MOTOR MODEL Using chalk, draw several hopscotch patterns on the sidewalk or playground. In each square, place a period, an exclamation point, or a question mark. Invite children to take turns throwing a marker into one of the boxes. After throwing the marker, a player hops to the end, skipping the square with the marker, and turns around. On the way back, the player picks up the marker and says a sentence that ends with the punctuation mark in that square. Then follow the suggestions in **Summarize/Reinforce.**

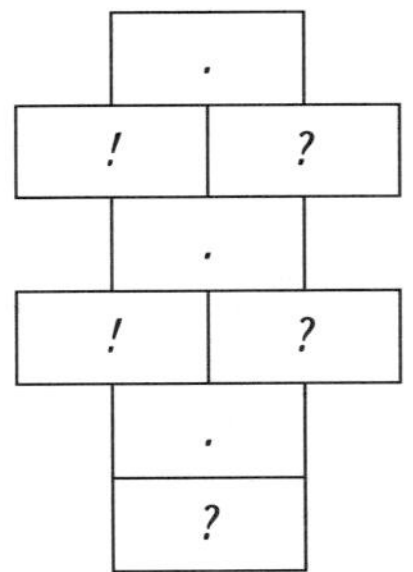

INTERPERSONAL MODEL Have children work in small groups. Provide each group with twenty-four index cards and a copy of a game board similar to the one shown:

Start
End
cards
spinner

Groups use twelve cards to write three of each: statements, questions, commands, and exclamations, omitting the end marks. They use the other cards to make four of each: periods, question marks, and exclamation points. To play, children draw a card from each pile. If the sentence card they choose goes with the punctuation mark, they spin the spinner and move that many spaces. They continue until a player reaches the end. Then follow the suggestions in **Summarize/Reinforce.**

AUDITORY MODEL Without letting children see them, write the following sentences on chart paper:

1. feed the cat
2. please pass the muffins
3. planting flowers is fun
4. this dinner is great
5. what do you like to do with your good friend
6. do you like to ride your bikes

Read each sentence with little or no inflection in your voice. Mention that different sentences are read in different ways. Explain that end punctuation helps readers know how to read a sentence properly. Show the chart and invite volunteers to change the first letter of each sentence to a capital and add the correct end mark. After they finish, children can read the sentences with the correct inflection. Then follow the suggestions in **Summarize/Reinforce.**

Summarize/Reinforce

Check children's understanding of the lesson by having them tell when they might use exclamations and commands. Summarize by telling children that an exclamation is a sentence that shows strong feeling. It begins with a capital letter and ends with an exclamation point. A command is a sentence that tells someone to do something. It begins with a capital letter and usually ends with a period. Remind children as well that periods appear at the end of statements, and questions always end with question marks. To reinforce this lesson, have pairs of children read a few pages of a story to find examples of statements, questions, commands, and exclamations.

Vowel Diphthong: /ou/*ou, ow*

OBJECTIVE: To understand the relationship between letters and sounds

Focus

Share the following information with children:

> **The letters *ou* and the letters *ow* can stand for the vowel sound you hear in *loud* and *brown.* Knowing the sounds different letters can stand for helps you read new words.**

Choose a Teaching Model

VERBAL/LINGUISTIC MODEL Copy this chart on the board, and ask children to recall words in which either *ou* or *ow* represents the /ou/ sound. Write their suggestions in the correct columns.

cl**ou**d	c**ow**
loud	now

Next, ask volunteers to use the words on the list in sentences that tell about Mr. Putter and Tabby. Check off each word as it is used. When all the words that can be used in sentences about the story have been checked off, follow the suggestions in **Summarize/Reinforce.**

MUSICAL/RHYTHMIC MODEL On the board, write these words in different sizes, as shown:

LOUD!	Soft now.
PROUD	cow
CLOUD	town
POUCH	brown
COUCH	owl
MOUSE	chow

Have children read the words and underline the letter pairs that stand for the /ou/ sound. Then use a ruler or a pointer to point to the first word three times, at regular intervals. Have children say "Meow" and clap loudly each time you point. Similarly, point three times to the phrase *Soft now,* and have children say "Meow" and clap softly to your beat. Then challenge them to match their loud and soft rhythm to your motions as you point to words in random order, but rhythmically. When you point to a word in the left-hand column, children should clap and meow loudly. For words in the right-hand column, they clap and meow softly. After a time, end the activity and ask children what is the same about the words in both columns (They have the same vowel sound.), and what is different about the two columns of words (Words on the left have /ou/ spelled *ou;* words on the right have /ou/ spelled *ow*.) Then follow the suggestions in **Summarize/Reinforce.**

VISUAL/SPATIAL MODEL Sketch a cat figure on the board.

Emphasize the /ou/ sound in *how* as you tell children that they will learn how to draw Tabby. Have them draw the cat in the air as you trace the head and body, the ears, and the tail. Then write the word *how* inside the shape. Invite children to identify other words with the same vowel sound, and ask each child who contributes a correct word to come to the board, draw a cat, and write the word inside or across the cat. Give spelling advice as needed. After two or three examples of each spelling—*ou* and *ow*—are on the board, have volunteers color in the cats with the *ou* spelling and circle the cats with the *ow* spelling. Then follow the suggestions in **Summarize/Reinforce.**

Summarize/Reinforce

Check children's understanding by having them tell two letter pairs that stand for the vowel sound in *loud*. Summarize by explaining that the letter pairs *ou* and *ow* can both stand for /ou/. To reinforce this lesson, have children use words with /ou/ in sentences. Remind children to use the strategies from this lesson to help them read unfamiliar words.

Form/Application

OBJECTIVE: To read and fill out a form or an application

Focus

Share the following information with children:

> **There are many reasons for people to have to fill out forms and applications. A form is a quick way to gather the same information from different people. People fill out forms to get library cards, to order things from a catalog, or to sign up for a team. Knowing how to read and fill out forms can help you do many important things in your life.**

Choose a Teaching Model

LOGICAL/MATHEMATICAL MODEL Copy this form on the board. Tell children that the form is for children who want to join a soccer league. Have children read and discuss the form and suggest why these facts would be useful to the soccer league's organizers.

Name ______________________
Address ______________________
Phone Number ______________________
Age _____ Height _____ Weight _____
Doctor's Notes ______________________
____

Then follow the suggestions in **Summarize/Reinforce.**

INTRAPERSONAL MODEL Write this form on the board and fill it in as Mr. Putter might have answered. Next, have children copy the form and fill it in with their own personal favorites. Give assistance as requested.

My Favorites

Animal ____(Tabby)____
Breakfast food ____(English muffin)____
Afternoon snack ____(tea)____
Kind of music ____(opera)____
Flowers ____(tulips)____

After children have completed their forms, encourage them to compare answers. Then follow the suggestions in **Summarize/ Reinforce.**

INTERPERSONAL MODEL Tell children that Mr. Putter has to go away for a few days and, sadly, he can't take Tabby with him. Of course, he wants someone to take good care of Tabby while he's gone. Have children work in small groups to discuss what information Mr. Putter might need to know about people applying for a cat-sitting job and to create an application for him to give them. As needed, help children get their applications on paper. Suggest that groups trade and fill out each other's applications. Then follow the suggestions in **Summarize/Reinforce.**

Summarize/Reinforce

Check children's understanding by having them tell what they have learned about filling out forms and applications. Summarize by explaining that it is important to read forms carefully before filling them out in order to understand what information is needed and where it should go. To reinforce this lesson, let children fill out forms to "apply" for jobs such as passing out papers, watering plants, and straightening the bookshelves. These can be very simple, including only name, job applied for, dates job will be done, and why the applicant would do a good job. Remind children to use the strategies from this lesson when they fill out forms in their everyday lives.

Nouns

OBJECTIVE: To understand that words that name people, places, animals, and things are called nouns

Focus

Share the following information with children:

> **A word that names a person, a place, an animal, or a thing is called a noun. Knowing how to use nouns helps you add details to your writing, which will make your ideas clearer.**

Choose a Teaching Model

VERBAL/LINGUISTIC MODEL On a large sheet of butcher paper, draw simple outlines of a person's head, a cat, the United States, and a tree as chart headings. Have children identify each outline and label it as a person, a place, an animal, or a thing. Then invite volunteers to give examples of nouns that fit each category and add them the chart. Display the chart and invite children to say sentences using the nouns. Then follow the suggestions in **Summarize/Reinforce.**

LOGICAL/MATHEMATICAL MODEL Ask children to name some things that show that Sid is a smart cat. Comment that a smart cat like Sid would enjoy playing the game "Noun A & Q." To prepare to play, draw a chart like the one shown. Write answers to questions about nouns on index cards, and tape them under the correct category headings. Sample answers follow:

a cat who ate six dinners
the street Sid first lived on
the first U.S. president
the capital of our state

NOUN A & Q			
People	Places	Animals	Things
		a cat who ate six dinners	

Invite children to choose an answer from the chart and reply by asking the correct question. For example, the correct response to the answer *a cat who ate six dinners* is "Who is Sid?" Remind children that all their responses will include nouns. Then follow the suggestions in **Summarize/Reinforce.**

VISUAL/SPATIAL MODEL Make several sets of word cards, using nouns such as these:

ski

baseball cap

nurse

bumble bee

playground

Invite small groups of children to play a game with the cards. Place a set of cards face down for each group. Have children take turns selecting a card and drawing a picture to illustrate the noun on the card. As the child draws, group members must try to guess what the word is. No spoken or written words may be used while children are drawing. When someone guesses correctly, one child uses the word in a sentence and tells whether it names a person, an animal, a place, or a thing. Continue the game until all team members have had a chance to draw. Then follow the suggestions in **Summarize/Reinforce.**

Summarize/Reinforce

Check children's understanding of the lesson by having them give examples of items that can be found in their houses whose names are nouns. Summarize by telling children that a noun is a word that names a person, an animal, a place, or a thing. To reinforce the lesson, have children turn to a previously read story and find as many nouns as possible. Have them write the nouns under the headings *People, Animals, Places*, and *Things.* Remind children to use the strategies from this lesson to help them in their reading and writing.

Initial Clusters: *str, scr*

OBJECTIVE: To understand the relationship between letters and sounds

Focus

Share the following information with children:

> **When words begin with groups of two or more consonants, often the sounds of the consonants are blended together. The word *straw* begins with the letters *str*. The word *scratch* begins with the letters *scr*. Knowing the sounds that groups of consonants can stand for will help you read many new words.**

Choose a Teaching Model

VERBAL/LINGUISTIC MODEL Place the following words in a box or bag.

strawberry	stray	string	strong
strip	street	stretch	screen
scream	scribble	scratch	scrap
scram	scrape		

Begin a story about Sid with a sentence such as "Sid was a cat who had to scrounge for a meal." Have pairs of children draw a word card from the bag and use the word in a sentence that continues the story. Record the sentences on sentence strips, underlining the *str* and *scr* beginnings of words. Bind the sentence strips together in order with yarn or metal rings. Make them available for all children to read. Then follow the suggestions in **Summarize/Reinforce.**

VISUAL/SPATIAL MODEL Use a red marker to draw a strawberry on chart paper and label it. Then using a blue marker, make a scribble and label it. Write the following words on self-stick notes and affix them in random order to the chart paper:

stray, string, strong, strip, street, stretch, scream, scratch, scrap, scram, scrape, screen

Read the words aloud with children. As each word is read, ask a volunteer to place it under the picture whose label begins with the same consonant cluster. Then follow the suggestions in **Summarize/Reinforce.**

AUDITORY MODEL Give each child two index cards. Have children draw a picture of a strawberry on one card and write *str* under the picture, then draw a scribble on the other card and write *scr* under it. Then read the following words in random order to children, and ask them to listen for the sounds they hear at the beginning of the words *strawberry* and *scribble.*

strong	string	stick	shower
streams	scrap	scrape	squirt
spout	squirrel	stretch	
stew	slam	screen	

If children hear the same beginning sound as they hear in *strawberry*, they raise the picture of the strawberry. If they hear the sounds they hear at the beginning of *scribble*, they raise the scribble card. If they hear a different sound at the beginning of the word, they sit still. Then follow the suggestions in **Summarize/Reinforce.**

Summarize/Reinforce

Check children's understanding of the lesson by having them identify the letter combinations that can stand for the sounds they hear at the beginning of *stripe, scribble, string,* and *scrap.* Summarize by explaining that when a word begins with *scr* or *str,* the sounds of all three consonants blend together. To reinforce this lesson, have children name words that begin with *scr* and *str.* Remind children to use the strategies from this lesson to help them read and write words that begin with *scr* and *str*.

Alphabetical Order

OBJECTIVE: To arrange words in alphabetical order to the second and third letters

Focus

Share the following information with children:

> **Putting words in alphabetical order means listing them in the order in which their first letters appear in the alphabet. Knowing alphabetical order helps you find a word in an alphabetical list and helps you order lists of your own alphabetically.**

Choose a Teaching Model

MUSICAL/RHYTHMIC MODEL Arrange children's chairs in groups of four, one chair for each child. Make a name tag for each child. Have children march around the groups of chairs as they listen to music. When the music stops, children sit in the nearest chair. Each random group of four then forms a line, putting themselves in alphabetical order by first name. Each group then says their names aloud in alphabetical order. Send one child from each group to a different group and begin the game again. Make sure that at least once during the game children whose names begin with the same letter are in the same group, providing help as needed to alphabetize to the second or third letter. Then follow the suggestions in **Summarize/ Reinforce.**

LOGICAL/MATHEMATICAL MODEL Assemble objects from around the classroom. Be sure to include a few objects whose names begin with the same letter and even the same two letters. Have children identify the objects. Then write the name of each object on a word card and place the card in front of the object. Have children work in two teams. One team works on putting the cards in alphabetical order while the other tries to put the objects in alphabetical order. The two teams get together to arrange the labels and the objects together in alphabetical order. If there is extra time, have children find other objects to identify and place in the correct location in the alphabetical line. Then follow the suggestions in **Summarize/Reinforce.**

INTERPERSONAL MODEL Divide the class into groups of six to represent the six dinners that Sid ate every day. Give every child a paper plate for one of Sid's meals and have him or her find any word from the story and write it on the plate. Add a few more plates with words that begin with the same letters as the words children chose from the story. Have children work together to arrange the words in alphabetical order, displaying their plates on a desk or table. Give each group a chance to read its set of words in alphabetical order to classmates. Then follow the suggestions in **Summarize/Reinforce.**

Summarize/Reinforce

Check children's understanding of the lesson by having small groups put sets of five or six words in alphabetical order. Summarize by explaining that words are alphabetized by their first letters. Remind children that if the first letters are the same they must look at the second letter of each word, and so on. Whether they are looking at the first, second, or third letters of a set of words, the word whose letter comes first in the alphabet comes first in an alphabetical list. To reinforce this lesson, have children work in small groups to list their last names in alphabetical order. Remind children to use the strategies from this lesson to help them put words in alphabetical order and to find words in alphabetical lists.

Names of Special People, Animals, and Places

OBJECTIVES: To understand that proper nouns are the names of certain people, animals, and places that begin with a capital letter; to understand that special titles for people begin with a capital letter and usually end with a period

Focus

Share the following information with children:

> **Some proper nouns are the names of people. People's names begin with a capital letter. Special titles for people also begin with a capital letter. Most titles are followed by a period. Other proper nouns are the names of special animals and places. These names begin with a capital letter. Knowing about proper nouns helps you better understand what you read. Being able to use proper nouns helps you write your ideas more clearly.**

Choose a Teaching Model

VERBAL/LINGUISTIC MODEL Write the following headings across the top of a large sheet of butcher paper:

Special Names of		
People	Animals	Places

Have small groups of children brainstorm as many special names as they can for each heading. Encourage each group to appoint a Recorder to record the responses on chart paper. Finally, have groups share their responses as you record them on the class chart. Then follow the suggestions in **Summarize/Reinforce.**

VISUAL/SPATIAL MODEL Remind children that Abuela and Rosalba flew above their city and watched the happenings below. Tell children that even though they can't fly, there is a way they can "see" the sights in a large area: with a map. On a large sheet of butcher paper, make a simple map of your school neighborhood. Invite children to label the items on the map. Remind them to use capital letters for the special names. Then have children each write a simple set of directions based on the map. Check to see that the proper nouns in their directions begin with capital letters. Then follow the suggestions in **Summarize/Reinforce.**

KINESTHETIC/MOTOR MODEL Write the following categories on word cards: *girls, boys, teachers, pets, cities or towns,* and *countries*. Have children sit in a circle, and put the stack of category cards face down in the center. One child stands in the center with a ball and takes a category card. The child then tosses the ball to someone in the circle and reads the category on the card. The child that catches the ball gives an example of a special name that fits the category and tosses the ball back. The center child then tosses the ball to the next person in the circle, who gives another example. Any child who cannot think of an example can say "Pass." Play continues until several examples have been given. Next, a new volunteer takes the center position and chooses another category card. Then follow the suggestions in **Summarize/Reinforce.**

Summarize/Reinforce

Check children's understanding of the lesson by having them write the names of adults they know, such as teachers, parents, doctors, and dentists. Summarize by telling children that proper nouns are the names of special people, animals, and places, and they always begin with a capital letter. Titles for people also begin with a capital letter. Most titles are followed by a period, such as *Mrs.* and *Dr.* To reinforce this lesson, have children look for proper nouns and titles in stories they have read. Remind children to use the strategies from this lesson to help them understand what they read and to help them write more exactly.

Context Clues

OBJECTIVE: To use context clues to understand unfamiliar words

Focus

Share the following information with children:

> **As they read, even good readers sometimes come across words they do not know. Sometimes it's possible to figure out an unknown word by using clues from the words and sentences around it. Knowing how to use clues to figure out the meanings of unknown words helps readers learn new words and understand what they read.**

Choose a Teaching Model

LOGICAL/MATHEMATICAL MODEL Write these sentences on the board, underlining one word in each as shown. Next to the sentences, draw a chart with the headings *New Word* and *Clues*.

1. **Abuela likes spicy foods better than bland foods.**
2. **The children needed three more planks of wood to finish making their treehouse.**
3. **The two friends had a spat, but soon their little fight was over.**

Read, or have children read, the sentences. Point out that the three underlined words are fairly easy to read, but children might not know what they mean. Have children reread the sentences for clues to the meanings of the new words. Have children fill in the chart as they identify context clues. Then follow the suggestions in **Summarize/Reinforce.**

KINESTHETIC/MOTOR MODEL Create sentence strips like these:

Slither like a snake in the grass.
Flail your arms like a skater who is trying not to fall.
Pretend you are a bird and preen your feathers.
Prance in a circle like a circus pony.
Sway back and forth like a tree in the wind.

Read each sentence aloud as you display it. Have children use clues in the rest of the sentence to move as the sentence instructs. Then talk about the clues in the sentences that helped children know how to move. Mix up the sentence cards and have children act them out again. Then follow the suggestions in **Summarize/Reinforce.**

AUDITORY MODEL Make up word cards, one for each child, with familiar nouns from "Abuela," such as the following:

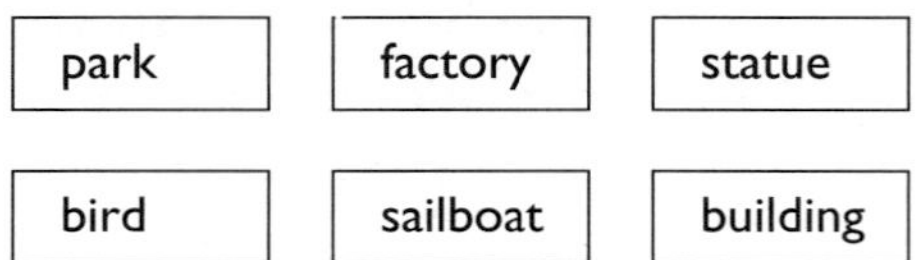

Distribute one card to each child, and ask a child to make up a sentence that uses the word. The child says the sentence, but instead of saying the word, he or she says "mumble." The rest of the children guess the missing word. The child who made up the sentence gives clues in different sentences until the others guess the word. Then follow the suggestions in **Summarize/Reinforce.**

Summarize/Reinforce

Check children's understanding of the lesson by having them define the word *fantasy* in this sentence: *"Abuela" is a fantasy story about a girl flying with her grandmother.* Summarize by telling children that one way to figure out the meaning of an unknown word is to look for clues in the words and sentences around the word. To reinforce this lesson, have children identify words from stories they've read that they have identified in this way. Remind children to use the strategies from this lesson to help them figure out the meanings of new words as they read.

Reference Sources (Dictionary, Glossary)

OBJECTIVE: To locate information in a dictionary or glossary

Focus

Share the following information with children:

> **Readers sometimes come across words that they don't know and can't figure out from clues in the story. When this happens, they can use a dictionary or a glossary to find out what the word means. Words in dictionaries and glossaries are in alphabetical, or ABC, order. Knowing how to find words in a dictionary or a glossary helps you discover meaning of any word you want to know.**

Choose a Teaching Model

VERBAL/LINGUISTIC MODEL Use the Student Anthology Glossary or a dictionary as a source for a list of questions like the following:

1. *What are the guide words on page 356?*
2. *What does the word ancestor mean?*
3. *Tell me what page the word memory is on.*
4. *What are the guide words on the same page as the word snowflake?*

Then distribute copies of the list and have small groups of children go on a word hunt to answer the questions. When groups have found the answers, have them make up two or three questions of their own to trade with another group. Then follow the suggestions in **Summarize/Reinforce.**

VISUAL/SPATIAL MODEL Draw a rectangle on the board or on a transparency. Explain to children that the drawing represents a page of the Glossary in their Student Anthologies. Ask a volunteer to show where the guide words would appear in the glossary. Announce the number of a page and have children see how quickly they can find the page and read aloud the guide words on that page. Ask volunteers to take turns reading an entry word from that page, pointing to the place on the displayed page that is about where the word is on the glossary page. Have the child read the word directly above and directly below the chosen word. Then follow the suggestions in **Summarize/Reinforce.**

INTRAPERSONAL MODEL Have children turn to the glossary at the end of "Abuela." Read the entries with children, making sure they know how each word is pronounced. Call out glossary words one at a time, having volunteers read aloud the meaning of each word. Ask them to tell how they found the words. If some children just read down the list until they found the word, and others looked for it alphabetically, encourage discussion of which method was quicker. Then follow the suggestions in **Summarize/Reinforce.**

Summarize/Reinforce

Check children's understanding of the lesson by having them tell what guide words and entry words are, and in what order words appear in a dictionary or glossary. Summarize by telling children of the importance of using dictionaries and glossaries to learn the meanings of new words and how to say them. To reinforce this lesson, encourage children to find words they don't understand and look them up in a dictionary or in the glossary of a book if it has one. Remind children to use the strategies from this lesson to help them learn more words.

Daily Language Practice

Use Daily Language Practice as a quick and easy way to help children sharpen their proofreading skills as they check two or more sentences each day for errors in grammar, usage, mechanics, and spelling.

Daily Language Practice . . .

- **is a set of proofreading activities of twelve sentences, one set for each major lesson in *Out of the Blue.***
- **provides practice and reinforcement of language skills presented in each lesson.**
- **reinforces spelling and vocabulary in the context of sentences.**

How to Use Daily Language Practice

1. **Each day, write two exercises on the board or on a transparency (a copying master is provided) for children to proofread and correct. Corrected exercises are shown.**

2. **Have children correct the exercises and explain why each correction is needed.**

SENTENCES OF THE DAY

Daily Language Practice

"Matthew and Tilly"

Capitalization and punctuation of statements and questions; writing *I*; word order; *I* and *me*; spelling

1. Sunny was sitting by her self on the buse
2. i asked if me could sit with her.

1. Sunny was sitting by herself on the bus.
2. I asked if I could sit with her.

3. would you like a piece of gom
4. i wondered if you would share some

3. Would you like a piece of gum?
4. I wondered if you would share some.

5. did the purple crayon break
6. i will help you it pick ap.

5. Did the purple crayon break?
6. I will help you pick it up.

7. the sune is shining
8. we play can outside today

7. The sun is shining.
8. We can play outside today.

9. it is fon to play games together
10. Me like being your friend

9. It is fun to play games together.
10. I like being your friend.

11. it es time to go home
12. Who wants to ride with os

11. It is time to go home.
12. Who wants to ride with us?

Key Words are underlined. Spelling Words are printed in red.

Daily Language Practice

"Mr. Putter and Tabby Pour the Tea"

Capitalization and punctuation of statements, questions, exclamations, and commands; *I* and *me;* spelling

1. Mai we get a dog to keep us company
2. would you take good care of a pet

1. May we get a dog to keep us company?
2. Would you take good care of a pet?

3. Spot is the perfect dag for us
4. look at him wag his tayl

3. Spot is the perfect dog for us.
4. Look at him wag his tail.

5. what a loud bark Spot has
6. it is sure to keep strangers awai

5. What a loud bark Spot has!
6. It is sure to keep strangers away.

7. Gail enjoyed helping Fay trane our dog
8. he can sit without any trouble

7. Gail enjoyed helping Fay train our dog.
8. He can sit without any trouble.

9. me take my dog for a walk each da
10. we see my friends and their dogs.

9. I take my dog for a walk each day.
10. We see my friends and their dogs.

11. spot had a wonderful time at the park
12. Then it started to rane

11. Spot had a wonderful time at the park.
12. Then it started to rain.

Key Words are underlined. Spelling Words are printed in red.

Daily Language Practice

"Six-Dinner Sid"

Capitalization and punctuation of statements, questions, exclamations, and commands; writing *I*; spelling

1. our cat likes to sleap next door
2. he thinks our neighbors are nice people

1. Our cat likes to sleep next door.
2. He thinks our neighbors are nice people.

3. this kitty caught a cold
4. he doesn't feal very well.

3. This kitty caught a cold.
4. He doesn't feel very well.

5. we discovered thre more kittens
6. how different each one is

5. We discovered three more kittens.
6. How different each one is!

7. the kittens like to ron and play
8. They will be big cats in the future

7. The kittens like to run and play.
8. They will be big cats in the future.

9. Can i keap this kitten
10. she likes to be scratched under the chin

9. Can I keep this kitten?
10. She likes to be scratched under the chin.

11. does the cat want to eet now
12. give him some chicken stew cat food

11. Does the cat want to eat now?
12. Give him some chicken stew cat food.

Key Words are underlined. Spelling Words are printed in red.

Daily Language Practice

"Abuela"

Writing special names and titles of people; writing names of special animals and places; capitalization and punctuation of statements and questions; *I* and *me;* spelling

1. joan and her grandma are going to the coost
2. grandma says it will be an adventure

1. Joan and her grandma are going to the coast.
2. Grandma says it will be an adventure.

3. will your friend sho you the whole building
4. she will be glad to take I around

3. Will your friend show you the whole building?
4. She will be glad to take me around.

5. sarah and her friend walk to the park
6. they have to cross the rood to get there

5. Sarah and her friend walk to the park.
6. They have to cross the road to get there.

7. grandma's doctor has a bird of his owne named tweety
8. dr. clark let me touch the bird

7. Grandma's doctor has a bird of his own named Tweety.
8. Dr. Clark let me touch the bird.

9. mrs franks and Grandma went downtown.
10. grandma bought a pretty yellow cote

9. Mrs. Franks and Grandma went downtown.
10. Grandma bought a pretty yellow coat.

11. my cousin tina knows how to row a bowt.
12. tina lives in the country of mexico

11. My cousin Tina knows how to row a boat.
12. Tina lives in the country of Mexico.

Key Words are underlined. Spelling Words are printed in red.

READER RESPONSE 

Plot

DURING READING

1. Tell the main things that have happened so far.
2. What is the problem in the story? How do you think it will be solved?
3. What do you think will happen next? What do you think will happen at the end of the story?

AFTER READING

4. Tell the main events that happened in the story.
5. What was the solution to the story problem?
6. Were you able to guess what was going to happen in the end? How else might the author have ended the story?
7. What do you think was the best part of the story? Why?

READER RESPONSE 1

Characters

DURING READING

1. Who are the main characters?
   Who are the other important characters?
2. Do you like or dislike the characters? Why?
3. Does a character in this story remind you of anyone else you have read about? If so, how?

AFTER READING

4. Choose a character. Why was this character important in the story?
5. Did any characters change? If so, how?
6. If you could be any character in this story, who would you be? Why?
7. Which character would you like to meet? What would you say to him or her?

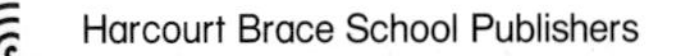

READER RESPONSE 

2

Setting

DURING READING

1. Where does the story take place?
2. Describe the place. Tell what you can see, hear, smell, and feel there.
3. Have you ever been to a place like this? If you have, how was it like the place in the story?
4. When does this story take place—long ago, in the future, or in the present? How do you know?

AFTER READING

5. How did the place affect what happened in the story?
6. How would the story be different if it were set in a different place or time?
7. If you could visit the place, would you go? Why or why not?

READER RESPONSE 1

Characters

DURING READING

1. Who are the main characters?
   Who are the other important characters?
2. Do you like or dislike the characters? Why?
3. Does a character in this story remind you of anyone else you have read about? If so, how?

AFTER READING

4. Choose a character. Why was this character important in the story?
5. Did any characters change? If so, how?
6. If you could be any character in this story, who would you be? Why?
7. Which character would you like to meet? What would you say to him or her?

READER RESPONSE 2

Setting

DURING READING

1. Where does the story take place?
2. Describe the place. Tell what you can see, hear, smell, and feel there.
3. Have you ever been to a place like this? If you have, how was it like the place in the story?
4. When does this story take place—long ago, in the future, or in the present? How do you know?

AFTER READING

5. How did the place affect what happened in the story?
6. How would the story be different if it were set in a different place or time?
7. If you could visit the place, would you go? Why or why not?

THEME PROJECT

LAUNCH

7

We Belong Together

Make a Mail Center

WHAT DO YOU KNOW?

1. Look at some mail.
2. Look at the address. How does it help the post office?
3. Make an address for your part of the room.
4. It should look something like this:

Harcourt Brace School Publishers

THEME PROJECT

CHECKPOINT 1

8

Make a Mail Center

LEARN ABOUT THE POST OFFICE

1. What do you want to know about the post office?
   - Talk about it with your group.
   - Think of some questions to ask.
   - Get answers to your questions.
2. What if you worked in the post office?
   - What would you do there?
   - How would you do it?

Harcourt Brace School Publishers

Use with “Matthew and Tilly.”

THEME PROJECT

CHECKPOINT 2

9

Make a Mail Center

PLAN THE MAIL CENTER

1. Make your post office. Plan how it will work.
   - Where will the collection box be?
   - Where will you sort the mail?
   - How will you deliver it?
   - Where will you put your mailboxes?
2. Make your own mailbox.
   - Use a shoe box.
   - Put your name on it in big letters.
3. Finish your post office.

Use with "Mr. Putter and Tabby Pour the Tea."

CHECKPOINT 3

10

Make a Mail Center

MAKE RULES FOR THE CENTER

1. Make rules for your post office.
   - What can we mail?
   - When can we mail letters?
   - When can we check mailboxes?
   - Who will deliver mail each day?
2. Write down your rules.

Harcourt Brace School Publishers

Use with "Six-Dinner Sid."

THEME PROJECT

CHECKPOINT 4

11

Make a Mail Center

WRITE AND SEND MAIL

To Get a Letter

- Write your name and address on an envelope.
- Put the envelope in the box.

To Send a Letter

- Pick an envelope.
- Decide what to write.
- Write your letter.
- Put it in the envelope and mail it. Have fun reading your mail!

Use with "Abuela."

PRESENTATION 12

We Belong Together

Make a Mail Center

SHARING YOUR WORK

- Invite another class to see your mail center.
- Think about what to tell them about how your mail center works.
- Practice what you will say.
- Have fun sharing your post office.

Harcourt Brace School Publishers

SOCIAL STUDIES

INTEGRATED CURRICULUM 

Matthew and Tilly

ON THE MAP Draw a map that shows where you live.

You will need: 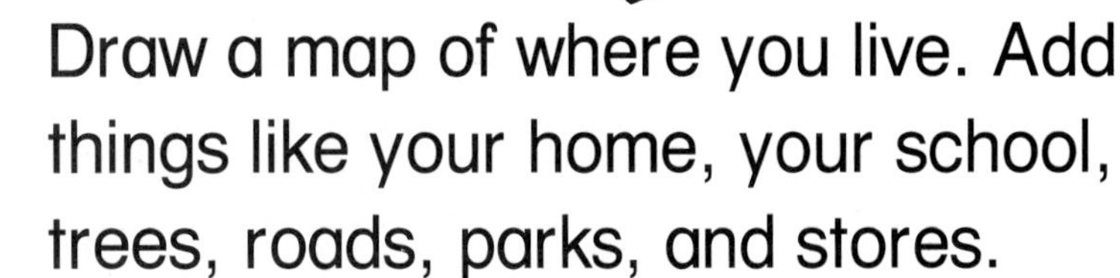     

1. Draw a map of where you live. Add things like your home, your school, trees, roads, parks, and stores.
2. Draw a picture of yourself. Cut it out. Fix it so it can stand up.
3. Move the picture of yourself around the map. Tell a partner about the places on the map where you do different things.

INTEGRATED CURRICULUM  

Matthew and Tilly

GOOD NEIGHBOR AWARD Who in your class is a good neighbor? Work together to make a list of what the good neighbors in class do. Then make a Good Neighbor Award for a classmate.

You will need:     

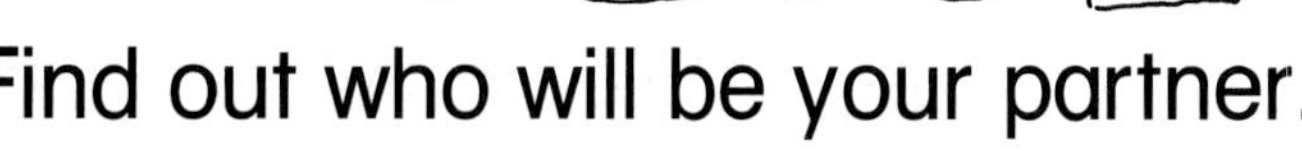

1. Find out who will be your partner. Remember: it's a secret!
2. Write a list of nice things you see your secret partner do.
3. Make a Good Neighbor Award for your partner.
4. Give the award to your partner.

Harcourt Brace School Publishers

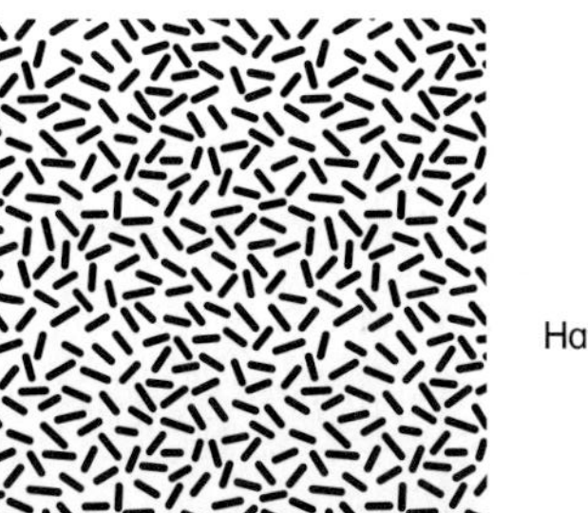

INTEGRATED CURRICULUM

Mr. Putter and Tabby Pour the Tea

ANIMALS HELPING PEOPLE Animals help people in all kinds of ways. Make a mural that shows how animals help people do things.

1. Make a list of ways animals help people.
2. Pick an animal helper to draw on the mural.
3. Show the animal helping.
4. Below each picture, write how the animal helps.

Mr. Putter and Tabby Pour the Tea

FAVORITE PETS BAR GRAPH Mr. Putter seems to like cats. What kind of pet is your favorite?

1. Make sure the animal that is your favorite is written on the graph.
2. Write your name on a paper square.
3. Glue the square on the graph above the animal you like.
4. Read the graph. Which pet do your classmates like best?

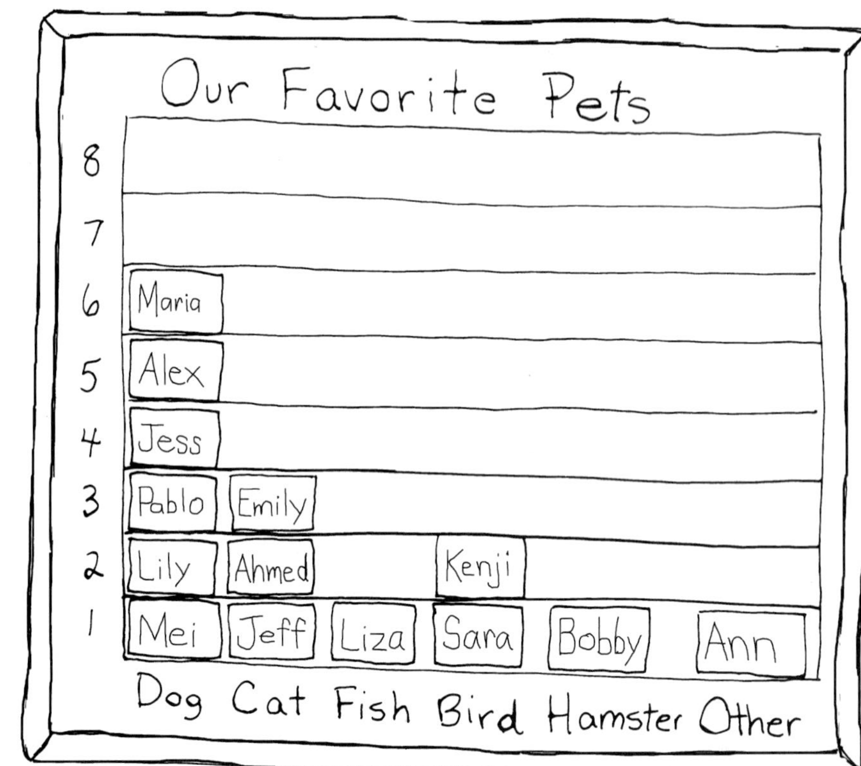

INTEGRATED CURRICULUM **7a**

Six-Dinner Sid

ALL IN THE CAT FAMILY Work in a small group. Make a poster about one of these cats: tiger, leopard, cheetah, mountain lion, bobcat, panther, lion.

You will need:    

1. Choose a kind of cat.
2. Find facts about the cat in books.
3. Find out how the animal looks, where it lives, and what it likes to do.
4. Make a poster. Draw a picture of the cat. Write some of the facts you learned.

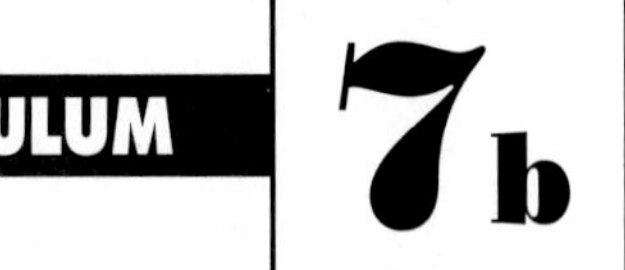

INTEGRATED CURRICULUM **7b**

Six-Dinner Sid

ACT LIKE A CAT Make cat ears to wear. Then act like a cat!

You will need:  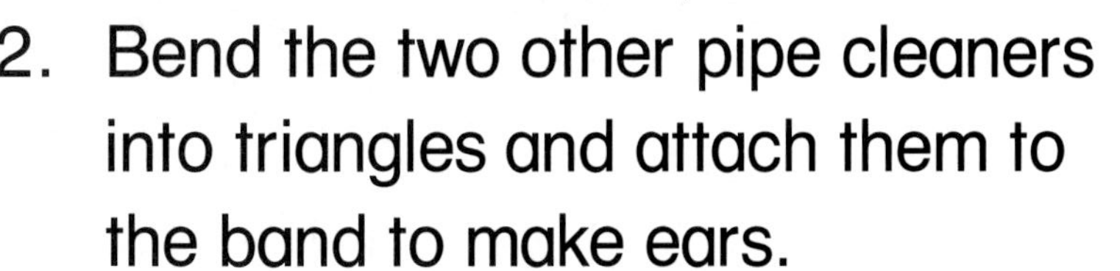

1. Bend the long pipe cleaner to fit like a band around your head.
2. Bend the two other pipe cleaners into triangles and attach them to the band to make ears.
3. Now move like a cat! Try to stalk, pounce, leap, stretch, and yawn.
4. Write about what it was like to act like a cat.

INTEGRATED CURRICULUM **8a**

Abuela

ABC'S OF THE CITY Make an ABC book about things in a city.

You will need: 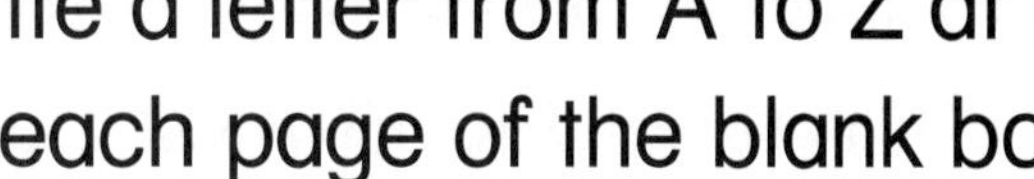            

1. Write a letter from A to Z at the top of each page of the blank book.
2. Think of something in a city that begins with each letter. Write the word and draw a picture of your city word.
3. Write a sentence for each word and picture.

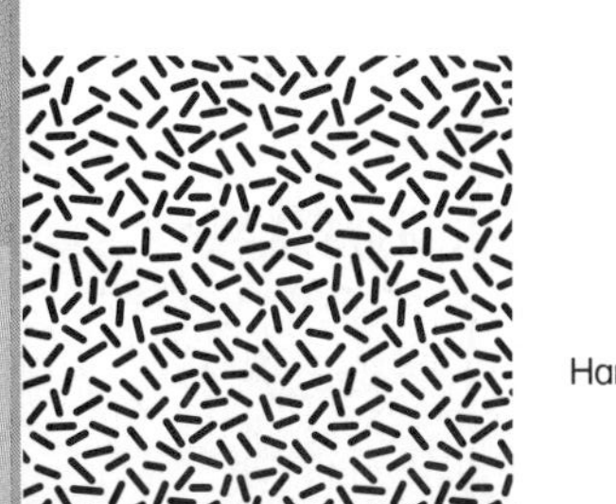

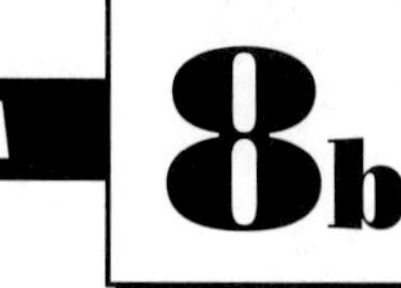

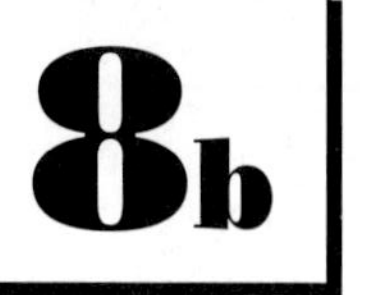

INTEGRATED CURRICULUM **8b**

Abuela

MAKE IT FLY Work with a partner. Make a shape that can fly.

You will need:  

1. Use a sheet of paper and four paper clips.
2. Fold the paper different ways. Test to see whether the paper shape will fly.
3. Then go outside and take turns flying your paper inventions.
4. Talk about why some went farther or higher than others.

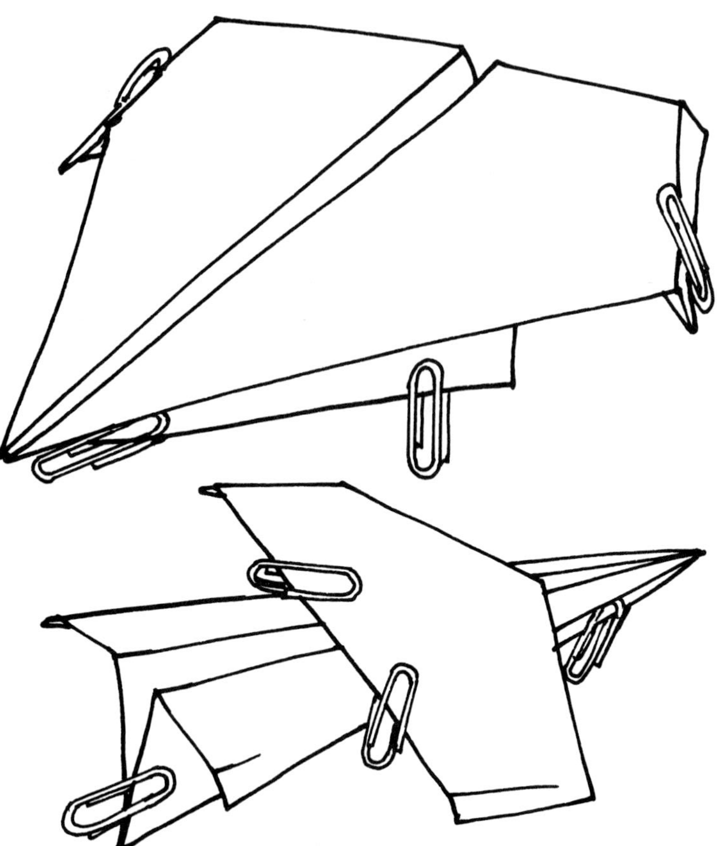

MODEL: DIALOGUE

what one character says	TILLY: You broke my purple crayon!
what the other character says back	MATTHEW: I didn't mean to.
	TILLY: You always break everything.
	MATTHEW: It was an old crayon. It was ready to break.
	TILLY: No it wasn't.
	MATTHEW: I'm sorry I broke it.
	TILLY: I'm sorry I got so mad.

MODEL: FRIENDLY LETTER

heading	24 Tampa Way Ocala, Florida 32670 October 23,19––
greeting	Dear Kate,
body	I'm finally getting used to my new school. At first, it was hard. The school is so big, and I didn't know anyone. Now I know my way around. I am making new friends, too. I still miss my old friends, though. Please write!
closing	Your friend,
signature	LaTisha

MODEL: ENVELOPE

return address

Kayla Wicker
162 Magnolia Street
Pomona, California 93944

mailing address

Sharon Johnson
2909 Buck Run Drive
Richmond, Virginia 23261

MODEL: PARAGRAPH THAT DESCRIBES

topic sentence	My family went to visit Mammoth Cave in Kentucky.
describing words in detail sentences	It is a very big cave. It is cold and dark on the inside. When the lights are turned off, you can't even see your hands! The walls are wet and feel slimy. The whole cave has a damp smell.

MODEL: INVITATION

heading	March 23,19—
greeting	Dear Mitch,
body	I am having a party so my friends can meet my new neighbor, Theo. It will be on April 1 at 3:00 P.M. at my house. I live at 408 Walter Road. Please let me know if you can come.
closing	Your pal,
signature	Jasmine

Additional Reading
Out of the Blue

The following list is a compilation of the Reading Trade Books selected for the lesson plans.

THEME: WE BELONG TOGETHER

The Adventures of Taxi Dog **by Debra and Sal Barracca. Dial, 1990. AVERAGE**
A stray dog is found by a taxi driver, who takes the dog with him everywhere he goes. *Parents' Choice*

Animal Tracks **by Arthur Dorros. Scholastic, 1991. EASY**
This book identifies tracks made along a stream and in a city park, including those made by a deer, bear, rabbit, and cat.

Annie and the Wild Animals **by Jan Brett. Houghton Mifflin, 1993. AVERAGE**
During midwinter in the north country, Annie's cat, Taffy, disappears. In her search, Annie makes friends with the wild animals she meets. *Children's Choice*

Annie, Bea, and ChiChi Dolores: A School Day Alphabet **by Donna Maurer. Orchard, 1993. EASY**
Three animal friends follow the alphabet through an exciting adventure. Children will love this book!

Ant Cities **by Arthur Dorros. HarperCollins, 1987. AVERAGE**
This book contains facts about ants and the ant cities they build and live in. *Outstanding Science Trade Book*

The Armadillo from Amarillo **by Lynne Cherry. Harcourt Brace, 1994. CHALLENGE**
An armadillo travels on an eagle's back to find out where he is in the city, state, country, continent, and world.

A Big Day for Little Jack **by Inga Moore. Candlewick, 1994. AVERAGE**
A young rabbit asks different family members to accompany him to his very first party. When they don't go, he discovers that he can have fun on his own.

A Boy, a Dog, a Frog and a Friend **by Mercer and Marianna Mayer. Dial, 1971. EASY**
In this wordless book, a boy, a dog, and a frog fish at the pond. They manage to catch a new friend to make them a foursome.

Charlie Anderson **by Barbara Abercrombie. Macmillan, 1990. EASY**
Two sisters find out that their cat, Charlie, stays with another family during the evenings. *Children's Choice; Irma Simonton Black Award*

City Sounds **by Craig Brown. Greenwillow, 1992. EASY**
Farmer Brown hears city sounds when he goes to the city to pick up an important package.

Cloudy With a Chance of Meatballs **by Judi Barrett. Macmillan, 1982. CHALLENGE**
The people from Chewandswallow depend on the weather for their food, which falls from the sky three times a day. *Children's Choice*; New York Times *Best Illustrated Book*

Down at the Bottom of the Deep Dark Sea **by Rebecca C. Jones. Macmillan, 1991. EASY**
Andrew hates water and intends to stay away from the ocean, but he changes his mind when he needs water for the sand city he is building.

Everett Anderson's Friend **by Lucille Clifton. Henry Holt, 1992. EASY**
Everett Anderson is disappointed when he finds out that his new neighbors are girls . . . until he gets to know one of them.

Everybody Cooks Rice **by Norah Dooley. Carolrhoda, 1991. CHALLENGE**
As Carrie goes from house to house searching for her brother to come home for dinner, she learns that people from many countries have rice with their meals.

Fortunately **by Remy Charlip. Macmillan, 1993. AVERAGE**
The story starts out with a birthday invitation to a boy. Unfortunately, the party is in Florida and the boy lives in New York. Children will have fun guessing what comes next.

Germy Blew the Bugle **by Rebecca C. Jones. Knopf, 1990. AVERAGE**
"Germy Blew It" thinks he's found a financial windfall with his latest scheme—a school newspaper. Germy has a lot of lessons to learn about the newspaper business or he may "blow it" again.

Grandmother and I **by Helen Buckley. Lothrop, Lee & Shepard, 1994. EASY**
A child thinks about her grandmother's lap being just right for those times when storms are coming or the cat is missing.

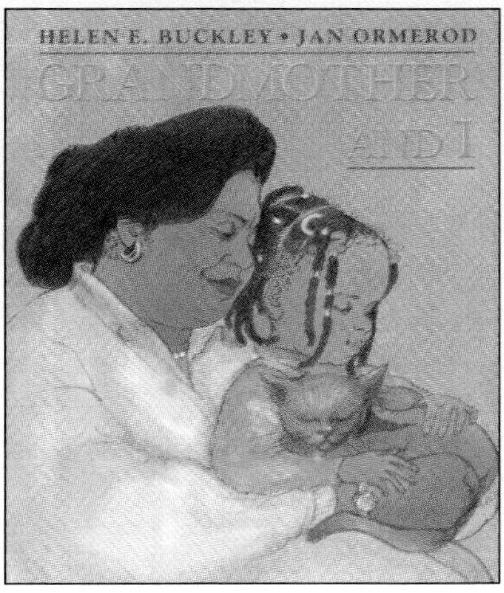

Harry the Dirty Dog **by Gene Zion. HarperCollins, 1956. AVERAGE**
A dog's owners fail to recognize their runaway dog when it returns completely covered with dirt.

Have You Seen My Cat? **by Eric Carle. Simon & Schuster, 1991. EASY**
In a worldwide search for his cat, a young boy explains to a series of strangers that a panther, a bobcat, a cheetah, a jaguar, a lion, a tiger, a puma, and a Persian are not his cat. Will he find his cat?

A House for Hermit Crab **by Eric Carle. Simon & Schuster, 1991. EASY**
Hermit Crab outgrows his shell and is on the lookout for a new home. *Outstanding Science Trade Book; Teachers' Choice*

A House Is a House for Me **by Mary Ann Hoberman. Puffin, 1993. AVERAGE**
This nonfiction book gets the young reader thinking about all kinds of homes. The information is presented in rhyme, and the text has a rhythmic flow that will keep readers moving along. *American Book Award*

The House on Maple Street **by Bonnie Pryor. William Morrow, 1987. CHALLENGE**
During the course of 300 years, many people have passed by or lived on the spot now occupied by a house numbered 107 Maple Street. *Notable Trade Book in Social Studies; Outstanding Science Trade Book*

How Big? How Fast? How Hungry? A Book About Cats **by B. Waverly. Raintree/Steck-Vaughn, 1990. EASY**
Wild members of the cat family are compared with the domestic cat in terms of how much they weigh, how fast they can run, and how much they eat.

The Inside-Outside Book of New York City **by Roxie Munro. Puffin, 1994. EASY**
New York City landmarks are presented in photographs and informative text. New York Times *Best Illustrated Book*

The Kids' Cat Book **by Tomie de Paola. Holiday House, 1979. AVERAGE**
Patrick learns a lot about cats and even goes home with a free kitten after visiting cat expert Granny Twinkle.

Let's Get a Pet **by Harriet Ziefert. Viking Penguin, 1993. EASY**
Sensible ideas and practical questions help young children decide on the perfect pet for themselves and their families. *Outstanding Science Trade Book*

Linnea's Windowsill Garden **by Christina Bjork. Farrar, Straus & Giroux, 1988. CHALLENGE**
Linnea presents information about plants in a lively and humorous style. *ALA Notable Book; Notable Trade Book for the Language Arts*

The Lion and the Little Red Bird **by Elisa Kleven. Dutton, 1992. CHALLENGE**
A little red bird and a lion become friends even though no words are spoken between them.

Little Dog Lost **by Inga Moore. Macmillan, 1991. AVERAGE**
When Liz and Tom move to the country, their dog, Pip, gets lost. Liz and Tom make new friends on their search.

Lunch with Milly **by Jeanne Modesitt. BridgeWater Books, 1995. AVERAGE**
Milly tells her friend to use her imagination to gather ingredients for a strawberry dessert.

Miss Hindy's Cats **by Helena C. Pittman. Carolrhoda, 1990. AVERAGE**
Miss Hindy acquires one cat after another and gives them names beginning with A through Z.

Mr. Putter and Tabby Bake the Cake **by Cynthia Rylant. Harcourt Brace, 1994. AVERAGE**
Mr. Putter plans to bake the perfect cake for his neighbor, Mrs. Teaberry.

Mr. Putter and Tabby Pick the Pears **by Cynthia Rylant. Harcourt Brace, 1995. AVERAGE**
Mr. Putter and Tabby have an unusual plan for making pear jelly.

Mr. Putter and Tabby Walk the Dog **by Cynthia Rylant. Harcourt Brace, 1994. AVERAGE**
Mr. Putter and Tabby take care of their neighbor's dog, with disastrous consequences.

Mrs. Merriwether's Musical Cat **by Carol Purdy. G. P. Putnam's Sons, 1994. AVERAGE**
Beethoven, a cat with musical talent, inspires students to play well. Then the cat mysteriously disappears. SLJ *Best Books*

Night Noises **by Mem Fox. Harcourt Brace, 1989. AVERAGE**
Old Lily Laceby dozes by the fire with her faithful dog at her feet as strange night noises herald a surprising awakening. *Notable Trade Book for the Language Arts*

Oh, Little Jack **by Inga Moore. Candlewick, 1992. AVERAGE**
Little Jack Rabbit is upset because he is too small to perform the same tasks as his family members. Then his grandfather surprises Jack with something that is just the right size.

The Old Ladies Who Liked Cats **by Carol Greene. HarperCollins, 1991. AVERAGE**
When the ladies of a town are told NOT to let their cats out at night, the result is an upset in the local ecology. The balance returns, thanks to the ladies' wise advice, when the cats are once again let out at night. *Children's Choice; Notable Trade Book in Social Studies*

Once Around the Block **by Kevin Henkes. Greenwillow, 1987. EASY**
Annie is bored, so she takes a walk around the block. Annie and the reader are in for some delightful surprises.

Radio Man—Don Radio: A Story in English and Spanish **by Arthur Dorros. HarperCollins, 1993. CHALLENGE**
Diego relies on his radio to provide him with companionship and to help connect him to all the different places in which he lives. The selection is written in both English and Spanish.

Richard Scarry's Biggest Word Book Ever! **by Richard Scarry. Random House, 1985. AVERAGE**
In this book, a child can discover all the words he or she wants to know.

Rosie and Michael **by Judith Viorst. Macmillan, 1988. AVERAGE**
Although Rosie and Michael tease and pull tricks on each other, they always remain good friends.

Rufus M. **by Eleanor Estes. Harcourt Brace, 1943. CHALLENGE**
A very determined boy persuades the librarian to let him apply for a library card. *Newbery Honor*

Sitti's Secrets **by Naomi Shihab Nye. Four Winds, 1994. CHALLENGE**
A young girl describes a visit to her grandmother in a Palestinian village on the West Bank. *Notable Trade Book in Social Studies, SLJ Best Books*

Switch Cat **by Garry Disher. Ticknor & Fields, 1995. AVERAGE**
There's some confusion as to which cat belongs to which girl. Eventually, everything works out.

"T" is for "terrific," MAHJI'S ABC'S **by Mahji Hall. Open Hand, 1989. EASY**
This book takes the reader on an adventure from *A* to *Z*.

Tar Beach **by Faith Ringgold. Crown, 1991. AVERAGE**
A young girl lies on the tar beach of a city rooftop and is lifted by the stars to fly over the city. *Caldecott Honor; ALA Notable Book; Coretta Scott King Award*

The 13th Clue **by Ann Jonas. Greenwillow, 1992. EASY**
A diary entry sets up this mystery, which readers follow picture clues to unravel. SLJ *Best Books*

Tonight Is Carnaval **by Arthur Dorros. Dutton, 1991. AVERAGE**
A family in South America eagerly prepares for the celebration of Carnaval. *Notable Trade Book in Social Studies*

The Truffle Hunter **by Inga Moore. Kane-Miller, 1987. AVERAGE**
The owners of Martine the pig are disgusted because Martine can't find truffles in the forest. Then a wild boar teaches Martine all she needs to know about truffles.

The Wednesday Surprise **by Eve Bunting. Clarion, 1989. AVERAGE**
Anna and her grandma are planning a surprise for Anna's dad's birthday. *ALA Notable Book;* SLJ *Best Books; Teachers' Choice*

A Weekend with Wendell **by Kevin Henkes. Greenwillow, 1986. AVERAGE**
Sophie discovers that having Wendell at the house for the weekend isn't so bad after all. *Children's Choice*

The Whole World in Your Hands **by Melvin and Gilda Berger. Ideals, 1993. EASY**
Children look at maps of places they are familiar with, such as a home, a neighborhood, and a town. Then they look at maps of a state, a country, and the world.

SCHOOL ↔ HOME CONNECTION 5

FAMILY INVOLVEMENT ACTIVITIES

Your child is reading "Matthew and Tilly" by Rebecca C. Jones. Matthew and Tilly are friends who live in a city neighborhood. Together they play games and do projects such as selling lemonade. They even work together to help others. As often happens with friends, Matthew and Tilly have an argument. Then they spend time by themselves until they are ready to apologize and get back together.

I have tried some of the activities.

Student: ______________________

Family Member: ______________________

Comments/Suggestions: ______________________

____

____

You may want to do some of these activities with your child.

WHAT IS A FRIEND?

Invite your child to use his or her own words to tell you about Matthew and Tilly's friendship. Then take turns completing the sentence, "A friend is ________ ."

WRITE TO A FRIEND

Suggest your child write a letter to a good friend. This might be a cousin, a grandparent, a neighbor, or a classmate. Encourage your child to include drawings. Help him or her with spelling or with addressing the envelope, if necessary.

WHAT BELONGS TOGETHER?

Matthew and Tilly belong together because they are friends. Go on a treasure hunt and make a list of things that belong together, such as a key and a lock. As you list items, talk about why they belong together.

WORD GUESS

You and your child can play a word game with friends or family members. Help your child cut out the Key Words on the page. Each player chooses a word, without showing other players which word he or she has chosen. The first player silently acts out the meaning of the word, and the other players try to guess the word. The player who guesses the word uses it in a sentence. The game continues until all words have been guessed. Have your child put the words in his or her Word File.

wondered	herself	piece	break	purple

SCHOOL ↔ HOME CONNECTION 6

FAMILY INVOLVEMENT ACTIVITIES

Your child is reading "Mr. Putter and Tabby Pour the Tea" by Cynthia Rylant. In the story, Mr. Putter is tired of living alone and decides he wants a cat. He goes to a pet store but finds only kittens there. He then goes to an animal shelter, where he finds a cat that is just like him—old, with creaky bones and thinning hair. He takes the cat home and names her Tabby. Together they share muffins, tea, long walks, opera, and the most perfect company of all—each other.

I have tried some of the activities.

Student: ____________________

Family Member: ____________________

Comments/Suggestions: ____________________

You may want to do some of these activities with your child.

LIBRARY TIME

Cynthia Rylant has written other Mr. Putter and Tabby books. She has also written books about Henry and his dog, Mudge. You may want to help your child find these books at your library. Share the stories.

PERFECT COMPANY

Have your child cut out the Key Words and use them to make up a story about a time he or she shared with some perfect company. Ask your child to write the story on a separate sheet of paper, laying down the word cards to show where they belong. He or she can draw a picture to go with the story and share it with your family. Then have your child put the words in his or her Word File.

company

enjoyed

loud

perfect

sure

without

wonderful

would

Harcourt Brace School Publishers

SCHOOL ↔ HOME CONNECTION 7

FAMILY INVOLVEMENT ACTIVITIES

Your child is reading "Six-Dinner Sid," a story about a cat who lives at six houses so that he can eat six dinners a day. Each owner thinks that Sid belongs only to him or her. Then Sid gets a cough and is taken to the vet—six times! The vet figures out that he is the same cat and tells the owners. Then the owners vow to put an end to his six-dinner-a-day ways. So Sid moves to a street where no one minds if he lives at six houses and eats six dinners a day.

I have tried some of the activities.

Student: ______________________

Family Member: ______________________

Comments/Suggestions: ______________________

____

____

You may want to do some of these activities with your child.

SIX-________ SID

Invite your child to retell the story. Can your child think of another thing that Sid could do at each of the six houses in the story? Take turns sharing new adventures for Sid. For example, the new story could be about "Six-Bath Sid" or "Six-Nap Sid."

LIBRARY TIME

Inga Moore has written other books about people and animals. You may want to help your child find these books at the library and share the stories. You may also want to look for other stories about cats.

WORDS AT WORK

Help your child cut out the Key Words on the page and use them to make up a story. Turn the cards face down. Have your child choose a word card and make up a sentence using the word. Take turns until all the cards are used and the story is told. Then have your child put the words in his or her Word File.

scratched	people	neighbors	future	discovered	different	caught

Harcourt Brace School Publishers

SCHOOL ↔ HOME CONNECTION 8

FAMILY INVOLVEMENT ACTIVITIES

Your child is reading "Abuela," by Arthur Dorros. In this story, a girl named Rosalba imagines that she and her grandmother fly over different parts of New York City. They fly over parks and streets, dogs and people. They glide over the sea and fly high into the clouds. Spanish words are woven into this story about a fantastic journey.

I have tried some of the activities.

Student: ______________________

Family Member: ______________________

Comments/Suggestions: ______________________

____

____

You may want to do some of these activities with your child.

LET'S FLY AWAY

Invite your child to retell the story "Abuela" in his or her own words. Then make a list of things you might see in your community if you took a trip like Abuela and Rosalba's. Talk about how things would look from the sky. You could play a game of "Twenty Questions." Think of a place you might see on your trip. Then have your child ask questions to figure out the place you are thinking of. The questions can be answered only with "yes" or "no." Take turns thinking of places and asking the questions.

FRIENDS OF ALL AGES

Rosalba loves her grandmother and enjoys doing things with her. Tell your child about an older relative or friend who is important to you. Talk about some good times you and this person have shared. Tell your child about the things that are special about your relationship with this person. Encourage your child to name people who are important to him or her.

ADVENTURES WITH WORDS

Help your child cut out the Key Words on this page, and place them face up in various places in your home. Then tell your child to pretend to fly above the rooms looking for the words. Have your child read each word he or she finds and use it in a sentence. Mix up the words and "hide" them again to repeat the game. Have your child put the new words in the Word File.

adventure	building	country	cousin	says	touch	whole

Tilly's favorite crayon was ______________.

Matthew did not want to ______________ it.

Tilly kept the biggest ______________ of the crayon.

She liked to color by ______________ sometimes.

Tilly ______________ if she would be an artist.

Harcourt Brace School Publishers

Mr. Putter had no one to listen to his _____________ stories.

He brought Tabby home for _____________.

Mr. Putter was _____________ that they would be happy.

He knew Tabby _____________ be a good pet.

Sometimes they played _____________ music.

They _____________ tea and muffins.

They were the most _____________ company for each other.

Mr. Putter and Tabby wondered how they ever got along _____________ each other.

Harcourt Brace School Publishers

Sid ate in six ____________ houses.

He was fed and ____________ in each one.

The ____________ didn't talk, so no one knew.

One day, Sid ____________ a cough.

When he went to the vet, his trick was ____________!

In the ____________, he'll still be Six-Dinner Sid.

Sid will live with other ____________ on another street.

Abuela came here from another ____________.

Abuela ____________ most things in Spanish.

Sometimes she feels like she can ____________ the sky.

Abuela's ____________ loads and unloads ships.

Rosalba and Abuela pretend the ____________ sky is their house.

They fly by a very tall ____________.

Abuela is ready for another ____________.

Harcourt Brace School Publishers

Notes on the Theme

ABOUT THE STUDENT ANTHOLOGY

Reading Trade Books

Signatures Library

Other Theme-Related Books

Multimedia Resources

Community Resources

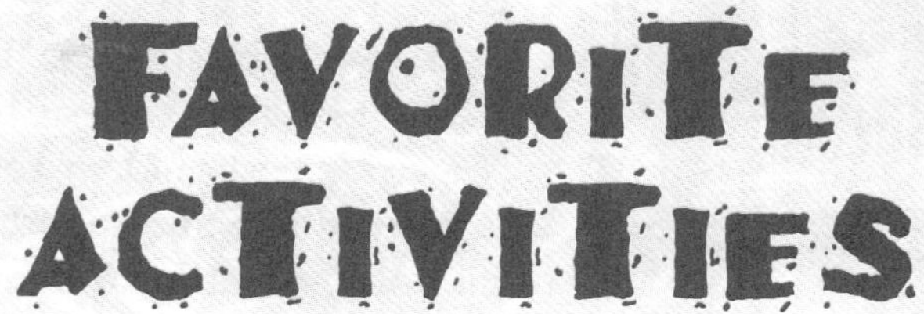

Your own ideas for customizing the theme:

MATERIALS:

STEPS:

MATERIALS:

STEPS:

MATERIALS:

STEPS:

GRAPH-A-BOOK

Dear Family Members,

As a book is read at home, have the student graph his or her response. The student should write the title of the book and the author's name on the numbered line and then color the corresponding bar on the graph to evaluate the book. Ask the student to give a reason for his or her rating.

Book Titles and Authors' Names

1. ____________________
2. ____________________
3. ____________________
4. ____________________
5. ____________________
6. ____________________

Graph

	Would Not Recommend	OK	Good	GREAT!
Book 1				
Book 2				
Book 3				
Book 4				
Book 5				
Book 6				

Please return the graph to school when completed. Thank you.

Signature ____________________

Harcourt Brace School Publishers

Duplicate the page and send it home with students to be completed with family members.

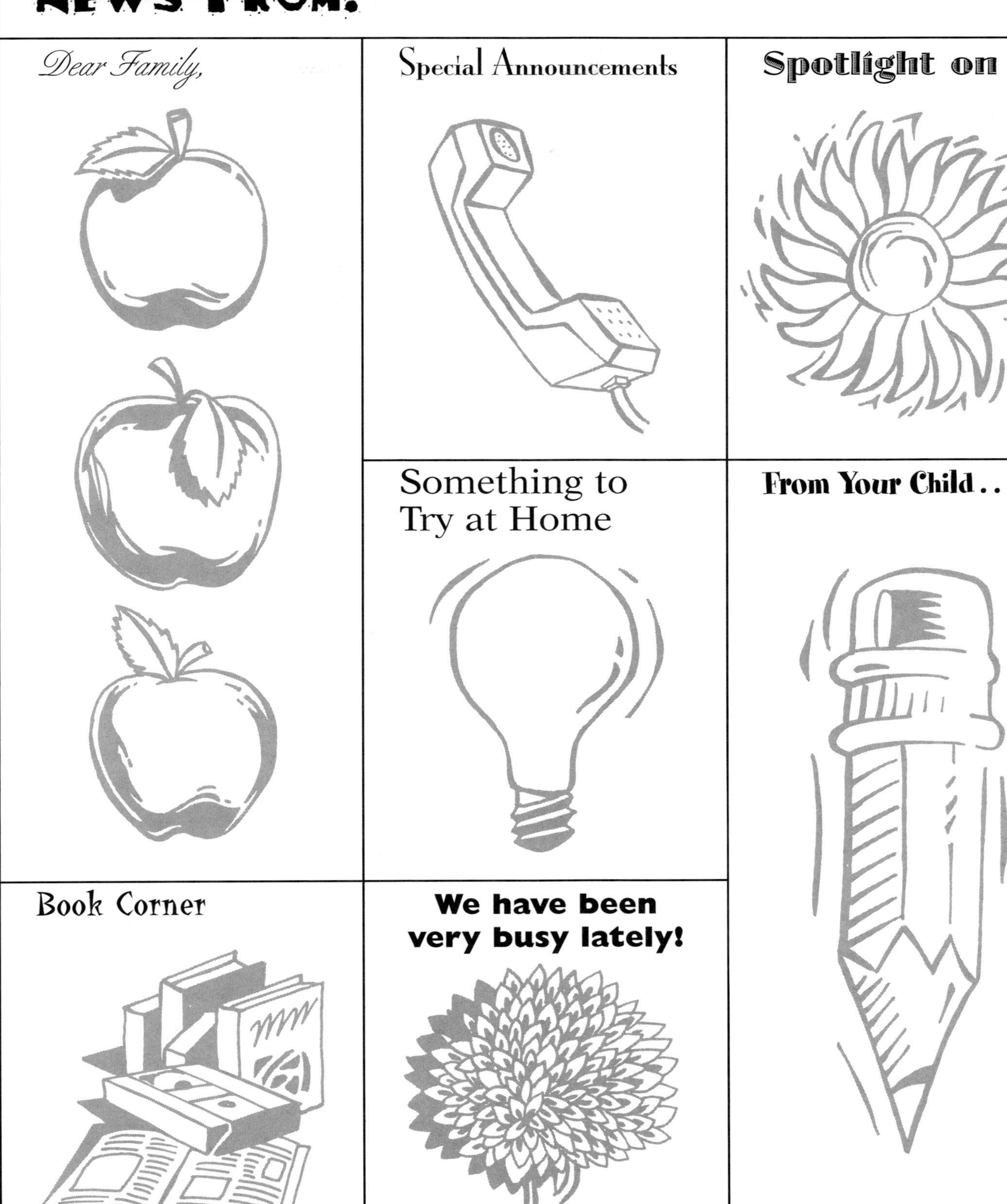

Complete the newsletter with news items from your class. Duplicate the page, and send it home to family members.

CREATE YOUR OWN SCHOOL-TO-HOME NEWSLETTER

Insert your school name or newsletter title to head your newsletter.

Personal note to parents

Special announcements or upcoming events

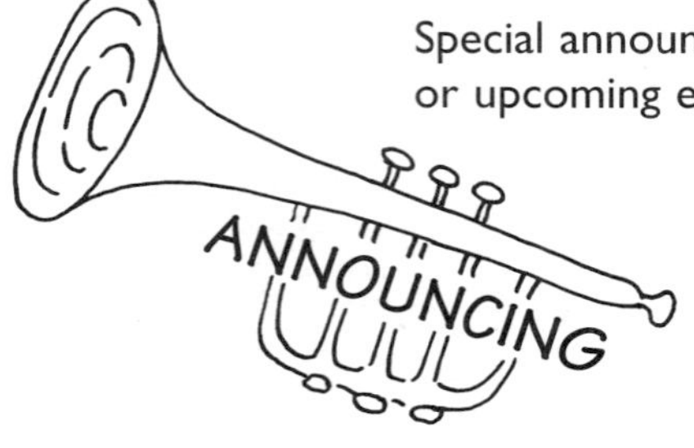

Reminder of upcoming meetings, conferences, or field trips

Classroom projects

Future goals or study themes

List of recommended books for reading

Current events from the classroom, school, or community

Focus on a certain subject area, or parent self-help information

Call for volunteers or materials

Student column

Harcourt Brace School Publishers

Use any of these clip-art graphics to create a classroom newsletter to send home.

Harcourt Brace School Publishers

because: ______________________________

____

____

____

____

____

Signed: ______________________________

Harcourt Brace School Publishers

Theme THREE
RESOURCES

Resources

Theme 3

Tested Skill

RETEACH: GRAMMAR

Names of Days, Months, and Holidays

OBJECTIVE: **To understand that the names of the days of the week, the months of the year, and holidays are proper nouns and begin with a capital letter**

Focus

Share the following information with children:

> **The names of days, months, and holidays are proper nouns. They begin with a capital letter. Knowing that these names are proper nouns will help you use them correctly in your writing.**

Choose a Teaching Model

VERBAL/LINGUISTIC MODEL Write the names of the days, the months, and five holidays on word cards. Next, make a chart similar to the one shown:

Days	Months	Holidays

Put the cards into a hat. Invite a volunteer to choose a card from the hat and tape it under the correct heading on the chart. Have volunteers do the same with the rest of the cards. Then have each child choose five names from the chart and write a sentence using each proper noun. Children exchange sentences with a partner and check to see that capital letters are used correctly. Then follow the suggestions in **Summarize/Reinforce.**

KINESTHETIC/MOTOR MODEL Use the word cards from the Verbal/Linguistic Model. Place the cards in a hat and invite a volunteer to choose a card. The child identifies the word on the card as "day," "month," or "holiday" and pantomimes something that is usually done on that day, month, or holiday. Volunteers try to guess what day, month, or holiday is being pantomimed. Whoever guesses correctly chooses the next card. Then follow the suggestions in **Summarize/Reinforce.**

AUDITORY MODEL Say sentences containing proper nouns, such as the following. Ask children to clap their hands when they hear a proper noun.

- **We started school on Tuesday this year.**
- **My favorite holiday is the Fourth of July.**
- **My father's birthday is in March.**

As a variation, say the beginning of each sentence, and have children complete it with the name of a day, month, or holiday. Then follow the suggestions in **Summarize/Reinforce.**

Summarize/Reinforce

Check children's understanding of the lesson by having them write the names of their favorite day, month, and holiday on separate word cards. Use these word cards to graph the results. Summarize by telling children that the names of days, months, and holidays are proper nouns and that they begin with a capital letter. To reinforce the lesson, provide children with a blank calendar page and a real calendar. Have children write the names of the days, the month, and the holidays for their birthday month. Remind children to use the strategies from this lesson when they want to include the names of days, months, and holidays in their writing.

R-Controlled Vowel /ôr/ *ore, or, our*

OBJECTIVE: To understand the relationship between letters and sounds

Focus

Share the following information with children:

> **The letters *ore, or,* and *our* can stand for the /ôr/ sound. The letters *ore* stand for the sound you hear in the word *bore*. The letters *or* stand for the sound you hear in the word *born*. The letters *our* stand for the sound you hear in the word *course*. Remembering these letter groups and the sound they stand for can help you figure out new words as you read.**

Choose a Teaching Model

VERBAL/LINGUISTIC MODEL Prepare word cards for the following words: *store, chore, score, fort, thorn, horn, four, course*. Write the following headings on the board:

ore	or	our

Say each word aloud, display its card, and have children repeat the word after you. Then have a volunteer write the word on the chart under the appropriate heading. Then follow the suggestions in **Summarize/Reinforce.**

MUSICAL/RHYTHMIC MODEL Write some or all of the following words on the board. Have volunteers read the words aloud and tell what they mean.

horse	course	store	chore
score	shore	sore	more
for	four	bore	core
pour	born	worn	torn
thorn	corn	horn	

Then form groups of four children. Challenge the groups to make up songs about Anansi using as many of the words from the list as possible. Invite groups to share their songs with the rest of the class. Then follow the suggestions in **Summarize/Reinforce.**

KINESTHETIC/MOTOR MODEL Write the following sentences on sentence strips. Distribute them to five children.

Anansi wants some ______ melon.

Hippo has a ______ stuck in his foot.

Hippo lives with his ______ sisters.

Lazy Anansi won't do his ______.

Anansi was ______ in the jungle.

Then write the words missing from the sentences (*more, four, chores, born,* and *thorn*) on self-stick notes, and distribute them to other children. Have a child holding a sentence strip stand up and read the sentence aloud and then ask, "Who can complete my sentence?" Have each child holding a word read his or her word silently and decide if the word completes the sentence. If it does, have him or her join the first child, place the word in the blank, and read the completed sentence. Then follow the suggestions in **Summarize/Reinforce.**

Summarize/Reinforce

Check children's understanding of the lesson by having them name letter combinations that can stand for the /ôr/ sound. Summarize by explaining that knowing the sound that *ore, or,* and *our* can stand for will help them read new words. To reinforce this lesson, have children find words in other stories that contain these letters standing for the /ôr/ sound. Remind children to use the strategies from this lesson to help them read and write words with the /ôr/ sound.

Short Vowel /u/ *ou*

OBJECTIVE: To understand the relationship between letters and sounds

Focus

Share the following information with children:

> **The vowels *ou* can stand for the short /u/ sound you hear in the words *touch* and *double*. Knowing the sound that this vowel combination can stand for will help you figure out new words as you read.**

Choose a Teaching Model

LOGICAL/MATHEMATICAL MODEL Put a large cup and a box side by side. Draw a cup on the box. Then draw a circle around the cup and a diagonal line across it. Write the following words on cards: *young, cousin, four, double, country, couple, count, touch, out*. Have a volunteer read a word on a card and decide whether the *ou* in the word sounds like the short *u* in cup. If so, have the child place the word card in the cup. If the *ou* stands for a different sound, the child places the card in the box. After all words are read and placed appropriately, other volunteers can remove the words from the cup and read them aloud. Then follow the suggestions in **Summarize/ Reinforce.**

VISUAL/SPATIAL MODEL Place word cards from the Logical/Mathematical Model around the classroom in various locations that are readily seen by children. Play "I Spy," starting with a meaning clue such as "I spy a word that names my aunt's child. What's the word?" If other clues are needed, give clues related either to meaning or to sound, such as "The word begins like *come*." As each word is identified, have children point to it. Then follow the suggestions in **Summarize/Reinforce.**

KINESTHETIC/TACTILE MODEL Write the vowel combination *ou* on eight self-stick notes and give the notes to eight children. Then write the following word lists on chart paper. Leave a blank line for the *ou* in each word.

c___ple	t___ch
d___ble	tr___ble
c___ntry	y___ng
c___sin	en___gh

Have each child who holds a note place it on one of the blanks and then read the word. Ask a volunteer to use the word in a sentence. Then follow the suggestions in **Summarize/ Reinforce.**

Summarize/Reinforce

Check children's understanding of the lesson by having them tell the vowel combination that stands for the short *u* sound in words such as *trouble* and *touch*. Summarize by explaining that in some words the vowel combination *ou* can stand for the short *u* sound. To reinforce this lesson, have children look for *ou* words in newspapers or magazines and tell which sound the *ou* stands for in each word they find. Remind children to use the strategies from this lesson to help them read and write words in which the vowel combination *ou* stands for the short *u* sound.

Plural Nouns with *s* and *es*

OBJECTIVES: To understand that most nouns end with the letter *s* to name more than one; to understand that nouns ending with *s, x, ch,* and *sh* end with *es* to name more than one

Focus

Share the following information with children:

> **Some nouns name more than one person, place, animal, or thing. Add the letter *s* to most nouns to name more than one. When a noun ends with *s, x, ch*, or *sh,* add *es* to name more than one. Knowing when to add *s* and *es* to form plural nouns will help you read and write new words.**

Choose a Teaching Model

VERBAL/LINGUISTIC MODEL Display the following words on chart paper: *zebra, stripe, bunch, grass, lion, stick, tail, tree, trick, patch, box*, and *wish*. Invite volunteers to write the plural form next to each word. Then have children write a story using at least six of the plural nouns from the list. Suggest that they write about an animal that likes to play tricks. Then follow the suggestions in **Summarize/Reinforce.**

VISUAL/SPATIAL MODEL Remind children that in "Nine-in-One, Grr! Grr!" Tiger was hoping to have nine baby tigers each year. Discuss children's interest in baby animals. Have children work in small groups to make animal counting books for the kindergarten children in your school. Give each group ten sheets of plain paper. Have the group brainstorm a list of animals. Only animals whose names form their plurals by adding *s* or *es* should be included in the book. Have children number the pages from 1 to 10 and then illustrate each page by drawing the appropriate number of animals. Encourage them to label each page with the number and name of the animal, such as *3 lions, 4 foxes*. Add construction paper covers and staple the pages of each group's book together. Then follow the suggestions in **Summarize/Reinforce.**

KINESTHETIC/TACTILE MODEL Write the numbers 2 through 12 and the words *dish, beach, box, hat, radish, watch, lunch, dress, class, fox,* and *pencil* on slips of paper. Put the words in one container and the numbers in another. Invite a volunteer to choose a piece of paper from each container and say a sentence using both the number and the word. Then the child writes the plural form on the board, circling the *s* or *es* that was added. Continue until all words and numbers have been chosen. Then follow the suggestions in **Summarize/Reinforce.**

Summarize/Reinforce

Check children's understanding of the lesson by having them write the plural forms of the following words: *pen, glass, peach, bus*, and *crutch.* Summarize by telling children that some nouns name more than one, and that *s* should be added to most nouns to make them name more than one. However, when a noun ends with *s, x, ch,* or *sh,* the letters *es* should be added to name more than one. To reinforce this lesson, have children find examples of plural nouns ending in *s* and *es* in the stories they have read.

Vowel Diphthong: /oi/*oi, oy*

OBJECTIVE: To understand the relationship between letters and sounds

Focus

Share the following information with children:

> **The letters *oi* and *oy* stand for the /oi/ sound you hear in the words *noise* and *toy*. Knowing the different letters that stand for a sound helps you read many new words.**

Choose a Teaching Model

MUSICAL/RHYTHMIC MODEL Write the following sentences on sentence strips:

I can use my voice.

I can make noise.

Have children read the sentences. Discuss sounds that can be made with the voice—singing, humming, yodeling, speaking, yelling—and sounds that are considered noise—objects falling, doors slamming, and pencils tapping. Call on volunteers to choose one of the sentence strips, read it, and make a sound to go with the chosen sentence. Remind children of Tiger's song, and encourage them to make up songs of their own. Then follow the suggestions in **Summarize/Reinforce.**

VISUAL/SPATIAL MODEL Draw the outlines of a boy and a pointing hand on the board. Have children copy them on sheets of drawing paper and label them as shown.

boy

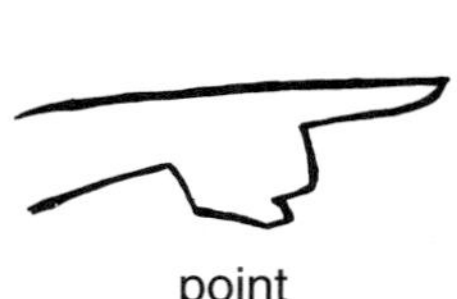
point

Children can then find words in books, newspapers, or magazines that use either *oi* or *oy* to stand for the /oi/ sound and write each word on or next to the appropriate shape. Then follow the suggestions in **Summarize/Reinforce.**

KINESTHETIC/MOTOR MODEL Ask children to think of words with the /oi/ sound that name things that can be pointed out in the classroom, acted out, or shown by facial expressions, such as *boy, toy, coin, soil, pointer, enjoy, voice, point, join,* and *noise.* Write the words on word cards as they are suggested. Then have a child select a word card and, without letting others see the word, use gestures and facial expressions to communicate the /oi/ word. Display the words when they have been acted out, or return them to the set to be used for another turn. Then follow the suggestions in **Summarize/Reinforce.**

Summarize/Reinforce

Check children's understanding of the lesson by having them tell the letter combinations that stand for the /oi/ sound. Summarize by explaining that the letters *oi* and *oy* can stand for the /oi/ sound. To reinforce this lesson, have children suggest /oi/ words as examples. Remind children to use the strategies from this lesson to help them read unfamiliar words.

Referents

OBJECTIVE: To understand the meaning and use of referents

Focus

Share the following information with children:

> **Some words take the place of other words. The word *she* can take the place of the name of a girl or a woman. The word *he* can take the place of the name of a boy or a man. The word *it* can take the place of the name of one animal or one thing. The word *they* can take the place of the name of more than one person, animal, or thing.**

Choose a Teaching Model

LOGICAL/MATHEMATICAL MODEL Write on the board a riddle, such as this one, to describe yourself, and have children work it out with you.

> **She sits at a table with six children. When you look at the windows, she is on your right. She is wearing a blue dress.**

Point out the use of *she* to stand for the mystery person. Review other words that can be used to stand for one or more mystery persons or objects in the classroom, and write them on the board.

he she they it I

Next, have children work with partners to write riddles about people and objects in the classroom. Remind children to use the pronouns listed on the board. Partners can read their riddles for others to try to solve. Then follow the suggestions in **Summarize/Reinforce.**

KINESTHETIC/TACTILE MODEL Have each child make word cards for the pronouns *he, she, they, it,* and *I.* Read each of the following sentences aloud, writing the underlined noun on the board. Have children hold up the card with the pronoun that can be used in place of the noun.

Tiger was told Tiger would have nine cubs a year.
Bird overheard Tiger singing about nine cubs, and Bird was afraid.
Bird perched on the tree and waited for Tiger.

Make up and dictate six or more sentences. Then follow the suggestions in **Summarize/Reinforce.**

AUDITORY MODEL Help children play a memory game in which no one loses. Write this list of pronouns on the board or on chart paper: *she, it, he, they.* Explain that you will say two sentences. The second sentence will include a word or words from the first sentence that can be replaced with a word from the list. Do the first one with children to help them see what they should do.

- **The children played the tape. The children like music.** (They like music.)
- **Janet was angry. Janet hid the toys.**
- **Robert is going to the zoo. Robert wants to see the tigers.**
- **All the animals ran from Tiger. All the animals were afraid.**
- **Anna has joined the basketball team. Anna plays very well.**
- **Paco bumped into the book. Suddenly the book fell.**

Then follow the suggestions in **Summarize/Reinforce.**

Summarize/Reinforce

Check children's understanding of the lesson by having them use the pronouns *he, she, it,* and *they* to retell the story of "Nine-in-One, Grr! Grr!" Summarize by explaining that writers use these words carefully to help readers know who the words refer to. To reinforce this lesson, have children play a "Who or What" game based on familiar facts. Use statements and questions such as *He shoots a basketball into the basket. Who is he?* (a basketball player). Remind children to use the strategies from this lesson to help them understand who the words *he, she, I, it,* and *they* refer to as they read and write.

Irregular Plurals

OBJECTIVE: To understand that the spelling of the base word for some nouns is changed to name more than one

Focus

Share the following information with children:

> **The spelling of some nouns changes when it names more than one. Knowing about these nouns helps you read and write new words.**

Choose a Teaching Model

VERBAL/LINGUISTIC MODEL Prepare a bulletin board showing the following words on index cards:

foot
tooth
woman
man
child

Write the words *feet, teeth, women, men,* and *children* on other index cards, and put them in a pile near the bulletin board. Children can take turns matching the singular and plural nouns. Next ask them to choose a pair and use the words in a sentence. Then follow the suggestions in **Summarize/Reinforce.**

VISUAL/SPATIAL MODEL Write the following words on the board: *foot, feet, tooth, teeth, woman, women, man, men, child,* and *children.* Have children work in pairs to write each word on a separate word card. Next, children use the word cards to play "Concentration," matching the singular and plural forms of the nouns. Have pairs place their word cards facedown and take turns choosing two cards. If the cards match, the child keeps them. If they do not, the child replaces them. Then follow the suggestions in **Summarize/Reinforce.**

AUDITORY MODEL Use the words displayed on the bulletin board in the Verbal/Linguistic Model to play the game "Twenty Questions." Choose one word without telling children what it is. Volunteers take turns asking *yes* and *no* questions to discover the word you chose. When a child guesses correctly, he or she writes the plural form on the board. Then follow the suggestions in **Summarize/Reinforce.**

Summarize/Reinforce

Check children's understanding of the lesson by having them create sentences using the plural form of the words listed in the Verbal/Linguistic Model. Summarize by telling children that the spellings of some nouns change to name more than one. To reinforce this lesson give each child a word card from the Visual/Spatial Model, making sure that all the cards are distributed. Tell children not to show their cards to anyone else. When you say "GO," children make a match by finding the person who is holding the card with the singular or plural form of the noun on their card. Remind children to use the strategies from this lesson to help them read and write nouns whose spellings change when they name more than one.

Vowel Variant: /o͝o/*oo, ou*

OBJECTIVE: To understand the relationship between letters and sounds

Focus

Share the following information with children:

> **In some words, the letters *oo* or *ou* stand for the vowel sound you hear in *foot* and *could*.**

Choose a Teaching Model

VISUAL/SPATIAL MODEL Display this sentence:

Flying would be good.

Have children read the sentence aloud with you and tell which words have the /o͝o/ sound. Underline the *ou* in *would* and circle the *oo* in *good*. Repeat with the following sentences, having volunteers underline each word that has the /o͝o/ sound spelled *ou* and circle each word that has the /o͝o/ sound spelled *oo*.

I should look for the book.

The cook could make good snacks.

Jeff would like a coat with a hood.

He took as much as he could.

Then follow the suggestions in **Summarize/Reinforce.**

KINESTHETIC/TACTILE MODEL Organize children into groups of four. Give each child two index cards. Child 1 writes the word *cook* and *brook*, one word to a card. Child 2 writes *would* and *should*, child 3 *look* and *took*, and child 4 *good* and *could*. Have children combine the cards, turn them face down, and then play "Coyote Concentration." Each child turns over two word cards. If the words rhyme, the child keeps the cards and takes another turn. If they don't rhyme, the child turns the cards face down again, and play passes to the next player. Then follow the suggestions in **Summarize/Reinforce.**

could	would	good	should
look	took	cook	brook

AUDITORY MODEL Display a chart like the one below, underlining the letters that spell the /o͝o/ sound.

Words like book and could	
book	could

Read the headings aloud. Then slowly read these sets of words.

1. **brake, bright, brook**
2. **could, kind, can**
3. **shout, should, shine**
4. **like, late, look**
5. **bike, bake, book**
6. **kite, cook, cake**
7. **take, took, tight**
8. **wild, would, wait**

Have children raise their hands each time they hear a word that has the vowel sound heard in *book* and *could*. Write each /o͝o/ word in the appropriate column on the chart. After the chart is completed, read the words with children. Then follow the suggestions in **Summarize/Reinforce.**

Summarize/Reinforce

Check children's understanding of the lesson by having them tell the letter combinations that can stand for the /o͝o/ sound in such words as *look* and *should*. Summarize by telling children that knowing the letters that stand for the /o͝o/ sound will help them read many words with those letter combinations. To reinforce this lesson, have children identify other examples of words in their reading that have the /o͝o/ sound. Remind children to use the strategies from this lesson to help them read and write new words.

Library Skills

OBJECTIVE: To understand how to find a book in the library

Focus

Share the following information with children:

> **A library has two kinds of books—fiction and nonfiction. Fiction books are stories made up by authors. These books are kept together in one place in the library and are arranged in alphabetical order by the authors' last names. Nonfiction books are about real people, places, and things. These books are kept in another part of the library and are grouped by their subjects. You can use the card catalog or the computer to help you find books you want.**

Choose a Teaching Model

LOGICAL/MATHEMATICAL MODEL Choose fiction and nonfiction books from the classroom or school library. Give two or three books of each type to partners, along with two index cards or slips of paper for each book. Before partners begin work, model the process by displaying one book of each type and writing information about the books on the board. Point out each book's title, the author's name, and talk about the kind of book each is and what readers might expect to find if they were to read it. Tell children to write for each book the title on one card and the author on a second card. Then tell them to circle the first letter of the first word in the title other than *A, An,* or *The.* Have them circle the author's last name. Ask them to flip through the book and decide whether it is fiction or nonfiction, and then add that information to each card. When children have written the needed information on the cards, have them arrange both sets of cards in alphabetical order. Then follow the suggestions in **Summarize/Reinforce.**

KINESTHETIC/MOTOR MODEL Organize children into two teams. Give each team a list of books to find in the school library. Be sure each list includes fiction and nonfiction titles. Tell team members to work together to find the books, using the card catalog. If possible, you may want to guide one team while the school media specialist guides the other team. Once the books have been collected, have team members explain how they found the books listed in the card catalog or the computer. Then follow the suggestions in **Summarize/Reinforce.**

INTRAPERSONAL MODEL Have children think about the books they like to read. Are their favorite books funny? Are they colorful? Do they tell about real people and events? Are they fiction or nonfiction? Take children to the school library and let each of them find two books that they think they would enjoy. Have them show their books to the class, tell what appeals to them about the books, and how they found them in the library. Then follow the suggestions in **Summarize/Reinforce.**

Summarize/Reinforce

Check children's understanding of the lesson by giving each child a book and asking how he or she would find that book in the library. Summarize by explaining that libraries group books into fiction and nonfiction sections to help readers find more easily the books they want. The card catalog or computer lists the titles and authors for all the books in the library. To reinforce this lesson, schedule regular book-finding sessions in the library to enhance lessons in content areas. Remind children to use the strategies from this lesson to help them locate different kinds of books in a library.

Pronouns

OBJECTIVE: To understand that a pronoun can take the place of a noun

Focus

Share the following information with children:

> **A pronoun is a word that takes the place of a noun. Writers use pronouns so they don't have to use the same nouns over and over again. Knowing how to use pronouns can help you make your writing more interesting.**

Choose a Teaching Model

VERBAL/LINGUISTIC MODEL Write the following paragraph on chart paper:

> **Rabbit was very clever. Rabbit helped his friends. Rabbit got rid of Tiger. Rabbit tricked Tiger, and Rabbit rode on Tiger's back.**

Invite a volunteer to read aloud the paragraph. Point out that the paragraph could be made more appealing by replacing several of the nouns with pronouns. Ask children to rewrite the paragraph using a pronoun to avoid repeating the word *Rabbit*. Children can share and compare their revised versions of the paragraph. Then follow the suggestions in **Summarize/ Reinforce.**

KINESTHETIC/TACTILE MODEL Duplicate a blank "Bingo" card with a free space in the middle. Have children fill in the boxes with the pronouns *I, he, she, it,* and *they* in random order.

she	he	they	it	I
I	they	it	she	he
they	it	FREE	he	I
it	they	he	I	she
he	she	I	it	they

Make a variety of word cards that have different referents for the pronouns, such as *Mary and Arthur, the puppy, your name* (for the pronoun *I*), *George, Ann,* and *tree*. Take a card from the stack, and read it aloud, having children use a marker to cover a pronoun that could replace the noun or nouns. Explain that when the card with the words *your name* is read, children should think of themselves, so the pronoun would be *I*. The first player to cover five spaces in a row says "BINGO." Continue for several rounds. Then follow the suggestions in **Summarize/ Reinforce.**

AUDITORY MODEL Have children play "Guess Who?" Think of a few sentences to describe yourself, a child, a pair of children, or a thing familiar to children. Say the sentences aloud without the name of the object or person: for example, *She is a wonderful artist. She sits in the first row. She loves to ride her bike to school, and she is the tallest person in the class. Guess who she is.* Children should guess the person and then tell which pronoun you used. Continue with several more examples. Invite children to think of descriptions to share. Then follow the suggestions in **Summarize/Reinforce.**

Summarize/Reinforce

Check children's understanding of the lesson by asking them to give examples of sentences using *I, he, she, it,* and *they*. Summarize by explaining that a pronoun is a word that takes the place of a noun. To reinforce the lesson, have children look for pronouns in stories or newspapers. Have them read the words surrounding each pronoun to determine which noun the pronoun replaces. Remind children to use the strategies from this lesson to help them use pronouns in place of nouns when they write.

Long Vowel: /ī/ *i, y, ie*

OBJECTIVE: To understand the relationship between letters and sounds

Focus

Share the following information with children:

> **The vowels *i* and *y* and the vowel combination *ie* can stand for the long *i* sound you hear in the words *child, fly,* and *lie*. Knowing the different letters that stand for a sound helps you read many new words.**

Choose a Teaching Model

VERBAL/LINGUISTIC MODEL Display the following words and sentences:

fly   lies   tie   try   wild   behind

Tiger is __________ a tree.
He __________ there every day.
Rabbit will __________ to trick him.
Toucan will not __________ into the tree.
Tiger is too __________.
Can we __________ him up?

Ask volunteers to complete each sentence by writing the word that makes sense. Have volunteers read aloud the completed sentences. Point out that each added word contains the long *i* sound. Then follow the suggestions in **Summarize/Reinforce.**

MUSICAL/RHYTHMIC MODEL Write the following headings on the board and challenge children to suggest and write at least four rhyming words in each column.

kind	why	
behind	my	fry
bind	by	hi
find	bye	lie
mind	cry	pie
rind	die	pry
wind	fly	tie

Explain that you will list only words that use *i, y,* or *ie* to stand for the long *i* sound; if a suggested word uses a variant spelling (as in *buy* or *high*) or a word with *i-e* (as in *lined*), let the child know that it's a good rhyme, but the word does not fit the pattern for this activity. Next, invite children to make up raps using the rhyming words. If possible, their raps should refer to "Rabbit and Tiger" or to another story they have read. Then follow the suggestions in **Summarize/Reinforce.**

KINESTHETIC/TACTILE MODEL Display these words:

fly	tie	wild	why
kind	by	pie	try
hi	fry	find	child
cry	mind	lie	my

Children can work in small groups to make one word card for each word, then label three other cards *i, y,* and *ie*. Have children put the *i, y,* and *ie* cards in a row on a tabletop and arrange the word cards under them to show which letter or letter combination they use for the long *i* sound.

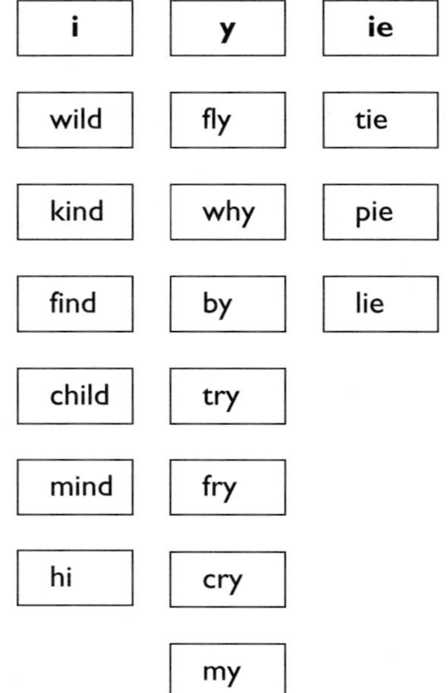

i	y	ie
wild	fly	tie
kind	why	pie
find	by	lie
child	try	
mind	fry	
hi	cry	
	my	

Then follow the suggestions in **Summarize/Reinforce.**

Summarize/Reinforce

Check children's understanding of the lesson by having them name letters or letter combinations that can stand for the long *i* sound in such words as *child, fly,* and *lie*. Summarize by explaining that knowing which letters can stand for this sound will help them read new words. To reinforce the lesson, have children write original sentences using the words *mind, try,* and *pie*. Remind children to use the strategies from this lesson to help them read unfamiliar words.

Graphic Aids (Chart)

OBJECTIVE: To understand how to read a chart

Focus

Share the following information with children:

When people want to show important facts and details, they often make a chart. A chart is a way of organizing information. Knowing how to read charts will help you find information quickly and remember it. You can make charts to help others understand information you have gathered.

Choose a Teaching Model

LOGICAL/MATHEMATICAL MODEL Invite children to discuss the trickster characters they have been reading about. List the following chart headings and questions on the board or on a transparency:

	Anansi	Bird	Coyote	Rabbit
Which story was the character in?				
Who was the character trying to trick?				
Who won?				
Which character did you like best?				

Help children complete the chart. Remind them that they can look back at the stories if they need to. Discuss where each piece of information should be placed in the chart. When the chart is complete, use the chart to discuss how the stories are alike and how they are different. Then follow the suggestions in **Summarize/Reinforce.**

VISUAL/SPATIAL MODEL Provide newspapers, magazines, catalogs, and other consumable print materials. Have children find and cut out charts, such as the charts of sizes and prices found in clothing catalogs. Display the charts on a bulletin board, and encourage discussion of the different kinds of information that can be presented in charts. Then follow the suggestions in **Summarize/Reinforce.**

INTERPERSONAL MODEL Organize children into four teams, one for each season of the year. Explain that each team will fill in details about their season in a chart. Before the teams begin work, the whole group will decide what the column headings will be. Draw this chart on the board.

Season	Weather	Sports	
spring			
summer			
fall			
winter			

Have children suggest and choose headings for two or more columns, such as *holidays, school activities, birthdays,* and so on. Then have team members work together to list details about their season for each column. Have them write the information for each column on a separate sheet of paper. When all the information has been gathered, assemble the individual sheets and create a large chart across one wall of the classroom. Then follow the suggestions in **Summarize/Reinforce.**

Summarize/Reinforce

Check children's understanding of the lesson by having them identify types of information that might be organized in charts. Summarize by explaining that authors use charts to help readers organize and find information quickly, and remember it. To reinforce this lesson, have children make charts comparing two story characters. Remind children to use the strategies from this lesson to help them make and read charts.

Daily Language Practice

Use Daily Language Practice as a quick and easy way to help children sharpen their proofreading skills as they check two or more sentences each day for errors in grammar, usage, mechanics, and spelling.

Daily Language Practice . . .

- is a set of proofreading activities of twelve sentences, one set for each major lesson in *Out of the Blue.*
- provides practice and reinforcement of language skills presented in each lesson.
- reinforces spelling and vocabulary in the context of sentences.

How to Use Daily Language Practice

1. Each day, write two exercises on the board or on a transparency (a copying master is provided) for children to proofread and correct. Corrected exercises are shown.
2. Have children correct the exercises and explain why each correction is needed.

SENTENCES OF THE DAY

2

Daily Language Practice

"Anansi and the Talking Melon"

Capitalization and punctuation of statements, questions, and exclamations; writing *I*; writing names of special animals and places; writing names of days, months, and holidays; spelling

1. Many tales about anansi come from africa
2. some have been around for a long tiem.

1. Many tales about Anansi come from Africa.
2. Some have been around for a long time.

3. what fun Anansi has
4. Of course, his tricks mak his friends angry

3. What fun Anansi has!
4. Of course, his tricks make his friends angry.

5. anansi was hungry, but he was also lazy
6. he used tricks to taik food and get full?

5. Anansi was hungry, but he was also lazy.
6. He used tricks to take food and get full.

7. he used a thorn to bore holes in fiiv melons
8. can you believe it's only tuesday.

7. He used a thorn to bore holes in five melons.
8. Can you believe it's only Tuesday?

9. i grew some fin melons in my garden.
10. i squeezed them to find a ripe one

9. I grew some fine melons in my garden.
10. I squeezed them to find a ripe one.

11. Do you play tricks on april fool's day?
12. I play only nic ones

11. Do you play tricks on April Fool's Day?
12. I play only nice ones.

Key Words are underlined. Spelling Words are printed in red.

Daily Language Practice

"Nine-in-One, Grr! Grr!"

Capitalization and punctuation of statements and questions; writing names of days, months, and holidays; plurals; spelling

1. tiger decided to tery a new food on monday
2. will she change her mind

1. Tiger decided to try a new food on Monday.
2. Will she change her mind?

3. Tiger sighed because she was lonely
4. she heard the wind balow through the dry gras.

3. Tiger sighed because she was lonely.
4. She heard the wind blow through the dry grass.

5. Tiger had a cub last year on november 30
6. she put up a falg to tell the others?

5. Tiger had a cub last year on November 30.
6. She put up a flag to tell the others.

7. new year's day was very important.
8. On that dai the cub ran fash.

7. New Year's Day was very important.
8. On that day the cub ran fast.

9. monkey heard a terrible noise in the turee
10. Tiger explained that it was five bird

9. Monkey heard a terrible noise in the tree.
10. Tiger explained that it was five birds.

11. Bird will fy down form the tree
12. she will bring two coin and three peachs.

11. Bird will fly down from the tree.
12. She will bring two coins and three peaches.

Key Words are underlined. Spelling Words are printed in red.

Daily Language Practice

"Coyote"

Capitalization and punctuation of statements and questions; writing names of special animals; writing *I*; plurals; irregular plurals; spelling

1. can you balance on two rail, Coyote
2. i will try to sing a tun instead

1. Can you balance on two rails, Coyote?
2. I will try to sing a tune instead.

3. i heard two crash
4. Coyote made thos sounds

3. I heard two crashes.
4. Coyote made those sounds.

5. the crows put a feather on coyote's noes.
6. now fly away, foolish Coyote

5. The crows put a feather on Coyote's nose.
6. Now fly away, foolish Coyote.

7. Coyote wook up next to two sheeps.
8. He saw a bird spread its winges and tak off

7. Coyote woke up next to two sheep.
8. He saw a bird spread its wings and take off.

9. the bird hopped on one foot
10. Coyote wanted to yuse two foots.

9. The bird hopped on one foot.
10. Coyote wanted to use two feet.

11. four class read a story about Coyote.
12. all the childs thought it was cuute.

11. Four classes read a story about Coyote.
12. All the children thought it was cute.

Key Words are underlined. Spelling Words are printed in red.

Daily Language Practice

"Rabbit and Tiger"

Capitalization and punctuation of statements, questions, exclamations, and commands; plurals; irregular plurals; pronouns; spelling

1. Tiger is the fiercest of al the animal
2. They has sharp claws on al four of his paw.

1. Tiger is the fiercest of all the animals.
2. He has sharp claws on all four of his paws.

3. tiger scares a group of jungle animal
4. She cawl him to make a bargain

3. Tiger scares a group of jungle animals.
4. They call him to make a bargain.

5. never mind Tiger's lovely striped fur
6. try to pas by his sharp tooths.

5. Never mind Tiger's lovely striped fur.
6. Try to pass by his sharp teeth.

7. Tiger lies outside a glast door
8. A few man and woman see him.

7. Tiger lies outside a glass door.
8. A few men and women see him.

9. What kind of animal knows how to ad
10. how smart Rabbit is

9. What kind of animal knows how to add?
10. How smart Rabbit is!

11. Mouse gave his childs three box.
12. Now the mouses have a dres and some dishes.

11. Mouse gave his children three boxes.
12. Now the mice have a dress and some dishes.

Key Words are underlined. Spelling Words are printed in red.

Daily Language Practice

Review Sentences

Capitalization and punctuation of statements, questions, exclamations, and commands; writing *I*; *I* and *me*; word order; writing special names and titles of people; writing names of special animals and places; writing names of days, months, and holidays; plurals; irregular plurals; pronouns; spelling

1. are you proud of your self
2. Yese, sometimes he am?

1. Are you proud of yourself?
2. Yes, sometimes I am.

3. Tury to remember that you special are
4. i like the sound of your foots walking

3. Try to remember that you are special.
4. I like the sound of your feet walking.

5. What a wonderful tim I had with you
6. me really enjoyed new york.

5. What a wonderful time I had with you!
6. I really enjoyed New York.

7. mr jones and I were neighbors.
8. we wile call each other on friday

7. Mr. Jones and I were neighbors.
8. We will call each other on Friday.

9. what dai is the most funn for Coyote
10. april fool's day is important to him.

9. What day is the most fun for Coyote?
10. April Fool's Day is important to him.

11. the wind will balow in january.
12. many foolish animal will cold be.

11. The wind will blow in January.
12. Many foolish animals will be cold.

Key Words are underlined. Spelling Words are printed in red.

READER RESPONSE 1

Characters

DURING READING

1. Who are the main characters?
   Who are the other important characters?
2. Do you like or dislike the characters? Why?
3. Does a character in this story remind you of anyone else you have read about? If so, how?

AFTER READING

4. Choose a character. Why was this character important in the story?
5. Did any characters change? If so, how?
6. If you could be any character in this story, who would you be? Why?
7. Which character would you like to meet? What would you say to him or her?

READER RESPONSE 

Author's Craft

DURING READING

1. Tell about any pictures the author's writing has left in your mind.
2. Name special words the author has used that help you **see, hear,** and **feel** things in the story.
3. What do the words the characters say tell you about them?

AFTER READING

4. What is your favorite word, line, or paragraph in the story?
5. Would you like to read something else by this author? Why or why not?

READER RESPONSE 2

Setting

DURING READING

1. Where does the story take place?
2. Describe the place. Tell what you can see, hear, smell, and feel there.
3. Have you ever been to a place like this? If you have, how was it like the place in the story?
4. When does this story take place—long ago, in the future, or in the present? How do you know?

AFTER READING

5. How did the place affect what happened in the story?
6. How would the story be different if it were set in a different place or time?
7. If you could visit the place, would you go? Why or why not?

LAUNCH

13

Tell a Tricky Tale

Create and Present Stories

TALK ABOUT STORIES

1. Talk about your favorite story.
2. Talk about how to tell stories. How many ways are there? Make a list.

CHECKPOINT 1 14

Create and Present Stories

EXPLORE STORYTELLING TECHNIQUES

1. Learn about telling stories.

2. Learn how to use your body to tell a story.

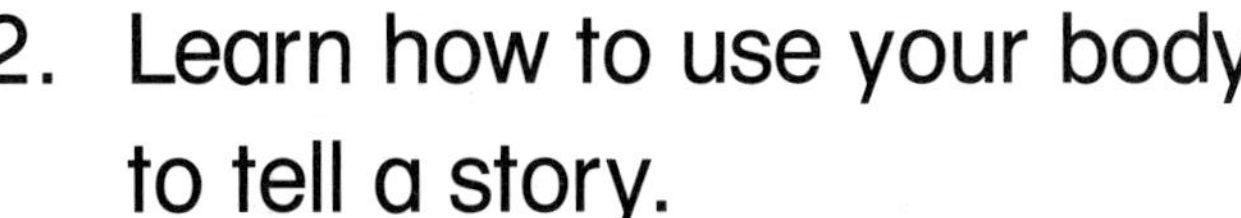

Harcourt Brace School Publishers

Use with "Anansi and the Talking Melon."

THEME PROJECT

CHECKPOINT 2 **15**

Create and Present Stories

CHOOSE A STORY IDEA

1. Make a list of good story ideas.
2. Pick one you like best.
3. Join a group that also likes that idea.

Harcourt Brace School Publishers

Use with "Nine-in-One, Grr! Grr!"

THEME PROJECT

CHECKPOINT 3

16

Create and Present Stories

CREATE A STORY

1. Share ideas about your story.
2. Think how to tell your story. Do you want to sing part of it, act it out, do a puppet show, or do something different?
3. Pick a job to do.
4. Write or plan your story.

Use with "Coyote."

CHECKPOINT 4 **17**

Create and Present Stories

PLAN AND PRACTICE STORY PRESENTATIONS

1. Plan things to make your story special.
2. Make invitations for your Story Festival.
3. Practice your story. Have a rehearsal.

Harcourt Brace School Publishers

Use with "Rabbit and Tiger."

THEME PROJECT

PRESENTATION

18

Tell a Tricky Tale

Create and Present Stories

STORY FESTIVAL

1. Get ready for the show.
2. Tell your story with your group.
3. Listen to the other stories.

Harcourt Brace School Publishers

INTEGRATED CURRICULUM

Anansi and the Talking Melon

TRAVELING STORIES Where have people told Anansi stories?

1. Find these places on a world map:
   - West Africa
   - Caribbean Islands
   - United States of America
   - Central America
2. Write each place on a card. Tack the cards to the map.
3. Tack one end of a piece of yarn to West Africa and the other end to the Caribbean Islands. Do this for the other places.
4. Talk about the places.

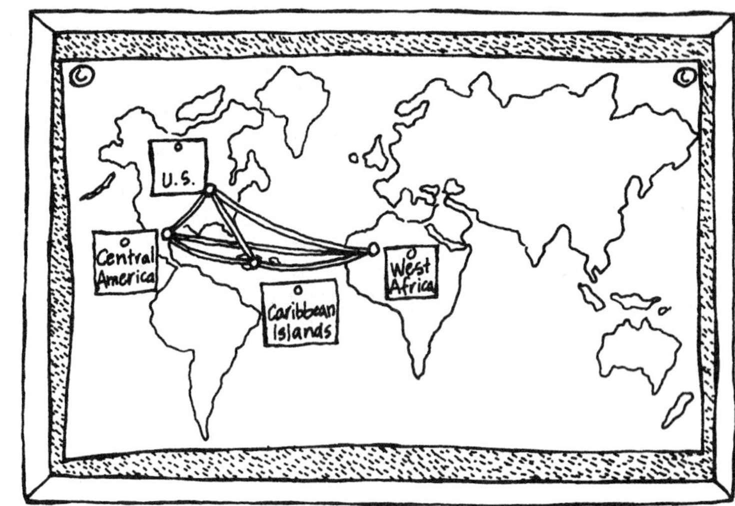

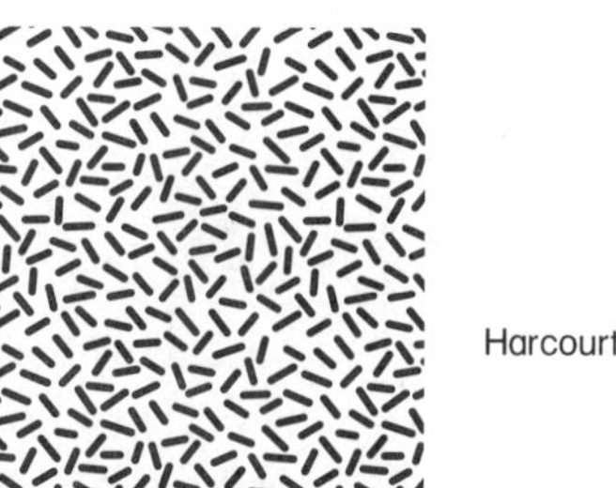

Harcourt Brace School Publishers

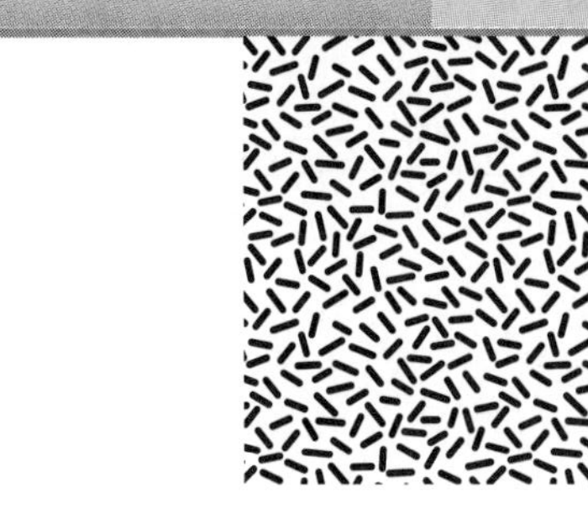

INTEGRATED CURRICULUM 

SCIENCE

Anansi and the Talking Melon

ON SAFARI What animals would you see on an African safari? Work with classmates to make a big picture about the animals of Africa.

You will need:  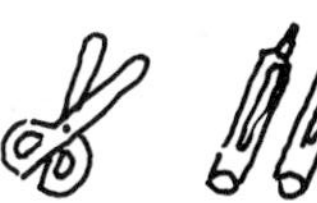        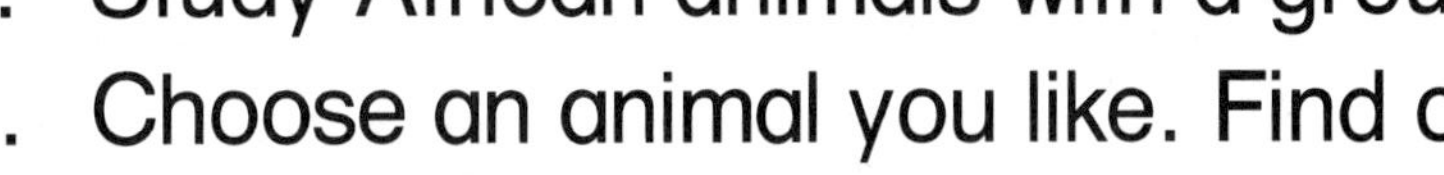

1. Study African animals with a group.
2. Choose an animal you like. Find out what it eats and where it lives.
3. Cut out or draw a picture of the animal for the class's picture.
4. Glue your pictures on the part of the background that shows where the animals live. Write the names of the animals.

INTEGRATED CURRICULUM

Nine-in-One, Grr! Grr!

SHE'LL BE WALKING UP THE MOUNTAIN . . . Tiger sang a song to help her remember Shao's words. Write a song that helps you remember the story.

1. Use the tune to "She'll Be Comin' 'Round the Mountain" to write a song about the story.
2. Work with a group to write a verse to the song. Use ideas from "Nine-in-One, Grr! Grr!"
3. Draw a picture for the verse.
4. Put the pages together to make a songbook.
5. Sing the song!

INTEGRATED CURRICULUM **10b**

Nine-in-One, Grr! Grr!

A LINE TELLS THE TIME Work with a small group. Make a time line of what happened in the story.

You will need:     

1. Talk about what happened in the story.
2. Draw a picture that shows one thing that happened. Write a sentence about the picture.
3. Cut out the picture and the sentence. Make a hole in each and tie them together with string.
4. Clip all your group's pictures in order on the clothesline.

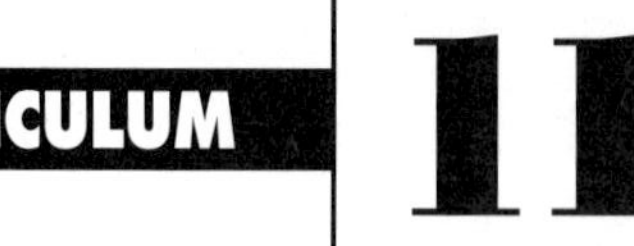

INTEGRATED CURRICULUM **11a**

Coyote

WHO LIVES IN THE DESERT? Make a mural about desert life.

You will need:

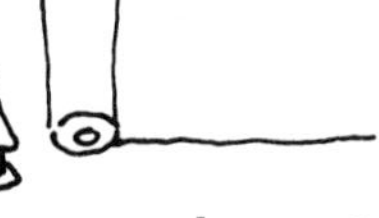

1. Look at books to learn about deserts.
2. Paint a desert background on a large sheet of paper.
3. Draw desert animals in their homes. Tape a flap over each one.
4. Write a sentence about each animal on the mural.

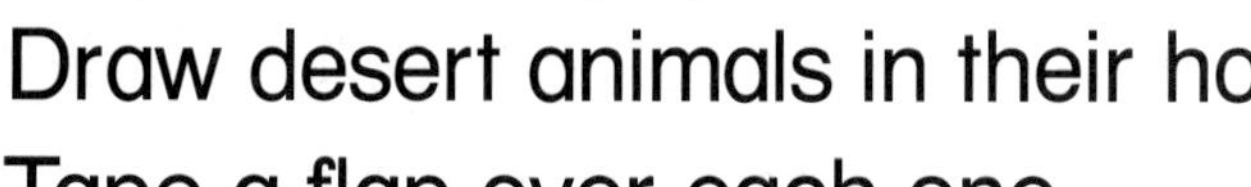
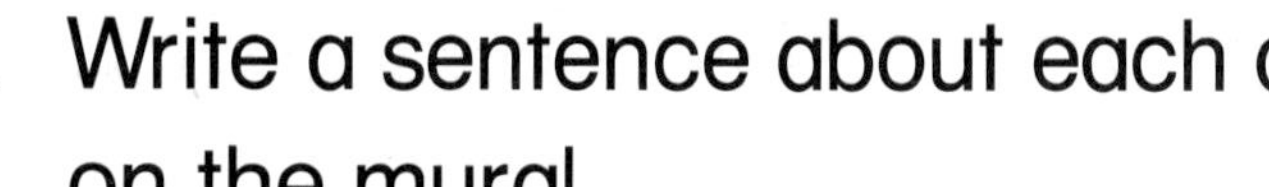

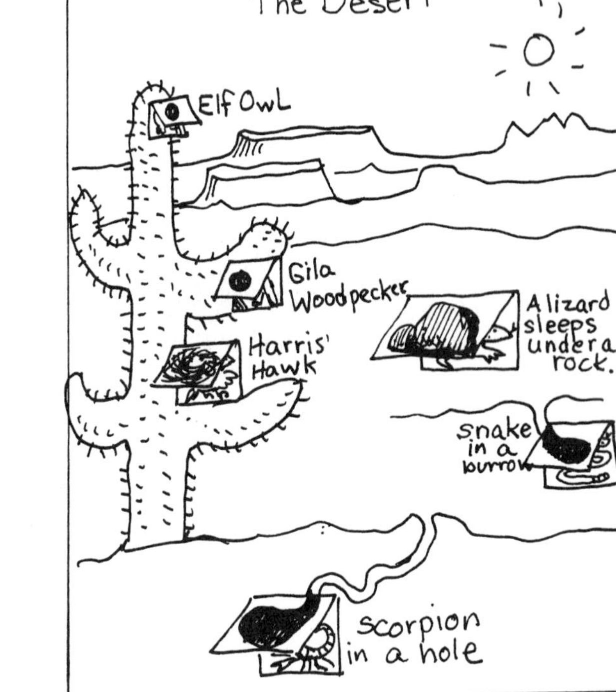

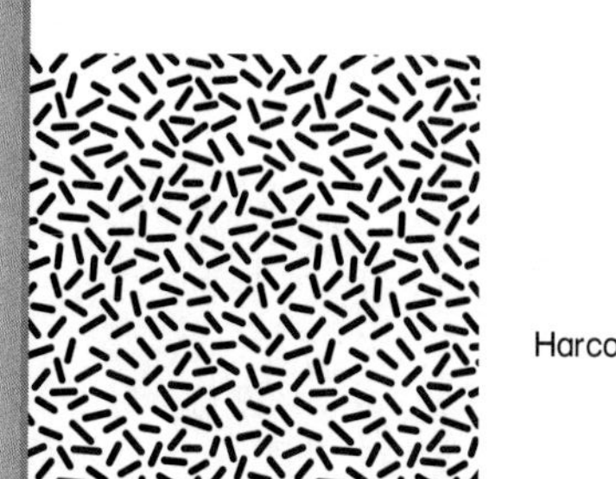

INTEGRATED CURRICULUM **11b**

Coyote

WEARABLE ART Make art you can wear!

You will need:         

1. Look through the story. Find the zigzags on Coyote, the diamonds on Snake, and the patterns on the crows. Look at the pendant Old Man Crow wears.
2. Use shapes to draw a pendant you'd like to wear.
3. Then make your pendant out of clay. Remember to make a hole in the clay for the string.

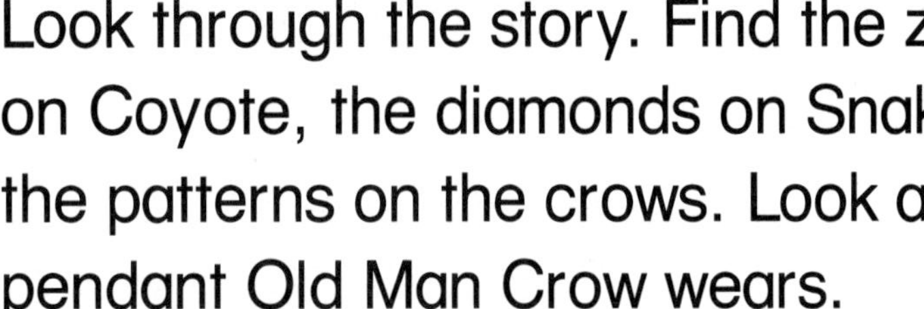

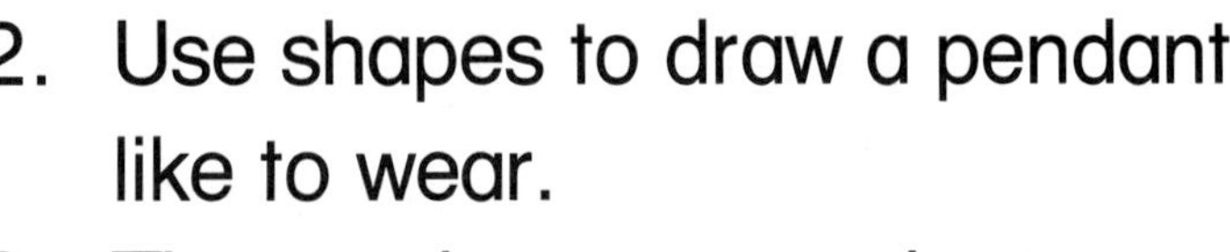

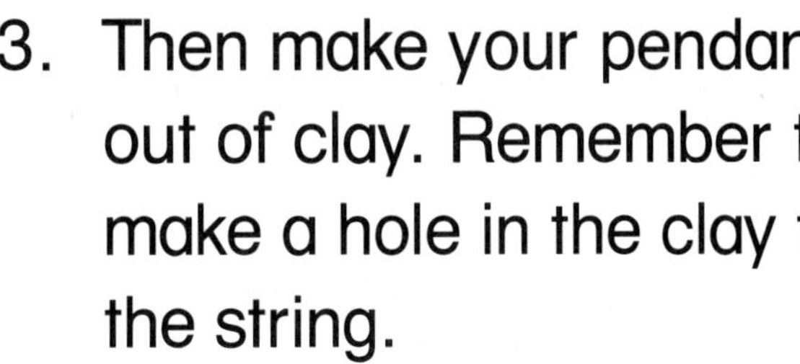

INTEGRATED CURRICULUM

Rabbit and Tiger

MAP THE JUNGLE Work with a group to find out about jungles or rain forests. Use what you find out to make a map of a rain forest.

You will need: 

1. Read all about jungles and rain forests.
2. Decide what information should go on your map.
3. Plan your map and draw it. Make a Map Key for it.
4. Use the map to show what you learned.

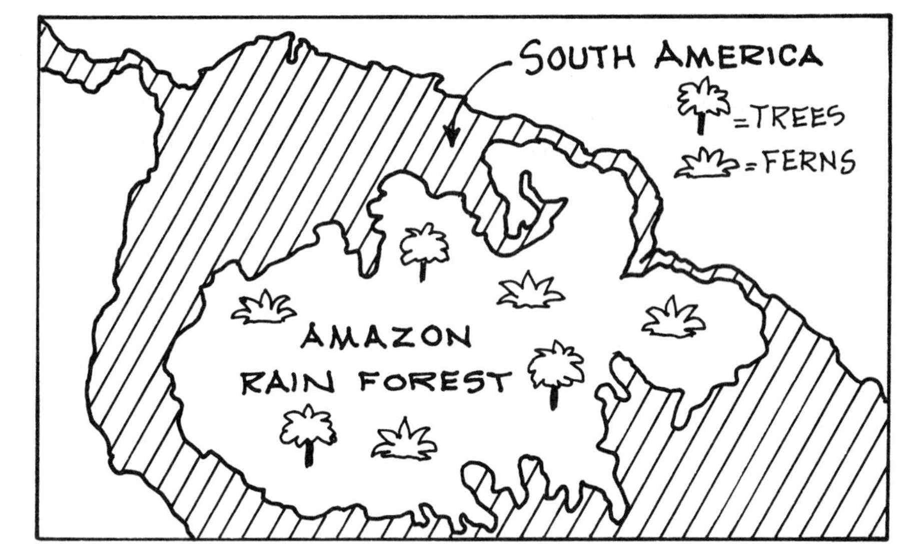

INTEGRATED CURRICULUM 12b

Rabbit and Tiger

MEASURE YOUR TRACKS

You will need:   

1. Put your foot on the paper and draw around it.
2. Cut out a strip of paper as long as your foot. Use it as a ruler.
3. Make a chart like this. Write your guesses.

Object	My Guess	How Many "Feet"?
rug	10	12

4. Then measure at least five things. Write how many "feet." Share your chart.

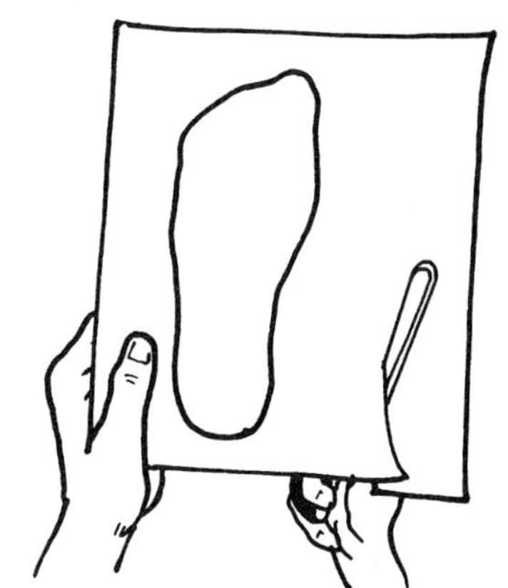

Harcourt Brace School Publishers

MODEL: STORY

title	Junior Vet
beginning	I think I might want to be a veterinarian someday. So I asked Dr. Curry if I could help her out for a week.
middle	Dr. Curry let me feed the animals and watch her work. At the end of the week, she asked if I still wanted to be an animal doctor.
ending	"More than ever," I answered. I meant every word!

MODEL: PARAGRAPH THAT GIVES INFORMATION

topic sentence

detail sentences

Many African American people celebrate Kwanzaa. It is a celebration of the customs and history of African American people. It is a gathering time for families, like Thanksgiving.

The holiday is celebrated for seven days. It begins the day after Christmas. On each night of Kwanzaa, a candle is lit. Each candle stands for a rule to help people live their lives.

MODEL: PLAY

characters	CHARACTERS: MOTHER, GWEN, BANTA (a rabbit)
when	TIME: morning
where	SETTING: a garden
what characters say	MOTHER: Gwen, I'm going to the office. While I'm gone, please plant the garden.
	GWEN: Yes, Mother.
what characters do	(Mother leaves.)
	BANTA: Come play with me?
	GWEN: Who said that?
	BANTA: I did.

Additional Reading

Out of the Blue

The following list is a compilation of the Reading Trade Books selected for the lesson plans.

THEME: TELL A TRICKY TALE

***Amazing Cats* by Alexandra Parsons. Knopf, 1990. AVERAGE**
One of the Eyewitness Juniors series, this engaging book offers many facts about wild and tame cats.

***Anansi and the Moss-Covered Rock* by Eric Kimmel. Holiday House, 1988. AVERAGE**
Anansi finds a strange rock and takes advantage of its powers to steal from the other animals until the bush deer outsmarts him.

***Anansi Goes Fishing* retold by Eric Kimmel. Holiday House, 1992. AVERAGE**
Turtle tricks Anansi into doing all the hard work during their fishing trip. *Children's Choice*

***Anansi the Spider: A Tale from the Ashanti* retold by Gerald McDermott. Henry Holt, 1972. EASY**
When Anansi travels far from home and falls into trouble, his six sons rescue him. *Caldecott Honor; Lewis Carroll Shelf Award*

***And to Think That I Saw It on Mulberry Street* by Dr. Seuss, Random House, 1989. AVERAGE**
This delightful classic tells the story of a young boy who imagines the most fantastic parade on his way home from school. *Lewis Carroll Shelf Award*

***Anno's Math Games* by Mitsumasa Anno. Philomel, 1987. CHALLENGE**
Anno proves that math is not just numbers, but also logical thinking, and does it so entertainingly that what children learn is math, but what they experience are games. *ALA Notable Book*

***Baby Rattlesnake* by Te Ata, adapted by Lynn Moroney. Children's Book Press, 1989. AVERAGE**
Willful Baby Rattlesnake throws tantrums to get his rattle before he's ready, but he misuses it and learns a lesson.

***Beat the Story-Drum, Pum-Pum* by Ashley Bryan. Atheneum, 1987. CHALLENGE**
These stories are retold from the Hausa and other African people. *Coretta Scott King Award*

***The Bigness Contest* by Florence Parry Heide. Little, Brown, 1994. AVERAGE**
Beasley thinks he's too big to win anything. After several failed attempts he enters the Bigness Contest.

***Borreguita and the Coyote: A Tale from Ayutla, Mexico* retold by Verna Aardema. Knopf, 1991. AVERAGE**

Borreguita, a little ewe lamb, cleverly avoids the coyote. SLJ *Best Books; Notable Trade Book in Social Studies*

***Check It Out: The Book About Libraries* by Gail Gibbons. Harcourt Brace, 1988. EASY**

Simple text and colorful pictures take the reader on a tour of the local library.

***The Chinese Mirror* edited by Mirra Ginsburg. Harcourt Brace, 1988. EASY**

A man returns from a trip with a small mirror that creates confusion when each person in his family looks into it.

***Coyote Steals the Blanket* retold by Janet Stevens. Holiday House, 1993. AVERAGE**

Coyote goes where he wants and takes what he pleases. SLJ *Best Books; Children's Choice*

***Crictor* by Tomi Ungerer. HarperCollins, 1958. CHALLENGE**

A pet boa constrictor thwarts a burglar and becomes a hero.

***Donkey Trouble* by Ed Young. Atheneum, 1995. CHALLENGE**

On the way to the market with their donkey, a kind man and his grandson find it impossible to please everyone they meet.

***The Four Gallant Sisters* adapted by Eric A. Kimmel. Henry Holt, 1992. CHALLENGE**

Disguised as men, four sisters are faced with challenges to prove their skill, courage, and wisdom.

***The Great Kapok Tree: A Tale of the Amazon Rain Forest* by Lynne Cherry. Harcourt Brace, 1990. CHALLENGE**

The many animals who live in the kapok tree in the Brazilian rain forest convince a man with an ax not to cut down their home. *Outstanding Science Trade Book; Teachers' Choice*

***Green Eggs and Ham* by Dr. Seuss. Random House, 1960. AVERAGE**

After repeated attempts, Sam finally persuades his friend to try green eggs and ham.

***How the Manx Cat Lost Its Tail* by Janet Stevens. Harcourt Brace, 1990. AVERAGE**

This story retells how the Manx cat lost its tail in the door of Noah's ark.

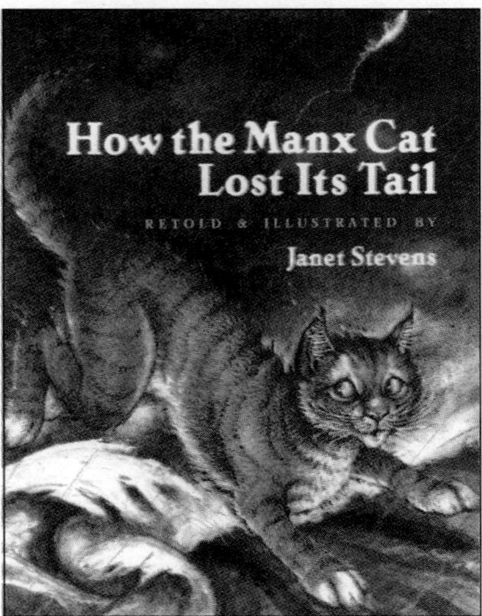

***How the Ostrich Got Its Long Neck* retold by Verna Aardema. Scholastic, 1995. EASY**

When Ostrich tries to help, she gets caught in Crocodile's mouth and pulls to be free, getting a long neck in the process.

***I Know an Old Lady Who Swallowed a Fly* retold by Nadine Bernard Westcott. Little, Brown, 1980. EASY**

We don't know why the old lady swallowed the fly, spider, bird, cat, dog, goat, and cow in this musical circular story, but this humorous rhyme is a perennial favorite.

I Took My Frog to the Library **by Eric A. Kimmel. Viking Penguin, 1990. EASY**
Each day, a young girl brings a different pet when she visits the library, and the results are disastrous.

The Iguana Brothers **by Tony Johnston. Scholastic, 1995. CHALLENGE**
The two iguana brothers, Tom and Dom, share ideas about life and discover that brothers can be friends.

Imagine **by Alison Lester. Houghton Mifflin, 1990. AVERAGE**
A girl and a boy visit different ecosystems around the world and learn about the animals in each one.

The Journey of the Red-Eyed Tree Frog **by Tanis Jordan. Green Tiger, 1992. AVERAGE**
A red-eyed tree frog, threatened by the destruction of the Amazon rain forest, journeys through the jungle to find safety and seek the wisdom of an oracle.

Judge Rabbit and the Tree Spirit **told by Lina Mao Wall, adapted by Cathy Spagnoli. Children's Book Press, 1991. CHALLENGE**
In this Cambodian folktale, a witty rabbit helps a man and his wife outsmart a troublesome tree spirit.

The Lady and the Spider **by Faith McNulty. HarperCollins, 1986. AVERAGE**
A spider has made her home among the green hills and valleys of a lettuce leaf. . . . How is the spider to know that the lady intends to eat that very lettuce for lunch one day? *Parents' Choice*

The Little Weaver of Thai-Yen Village **by Tran-Khan-Tuyet. Children's Book Press, 1987. CHALLENGE**
A young Vietnamese girl loses her family and is brought to the United States.

Lord of the Dance: An African Retelling **by Veronique Tadjo. J.B. Lippincott, 1989. EASY**
Poetry and art tell a story from the Ivory Coast of Africa. *Notable Trade Book in Social Studies*

The Magic School Bus Lost in the Solar System **by Joanna Cole. Scholastic, 1990. CHALLENGE**
Ms. Frizzle's class trip to the planetarium winds up with an exploration of the solar system. *SLJ Best Books; Notable Trade Book for the Language Arts*

Nanny Goat and the Seven Little Kids retold **by Eric Kimmel. Holiday House, 1990. AVERAGE**
When the big, bad wolf tricks the nanny goat's kids, he eats them and their mother—but Nanny Goat has a plan.

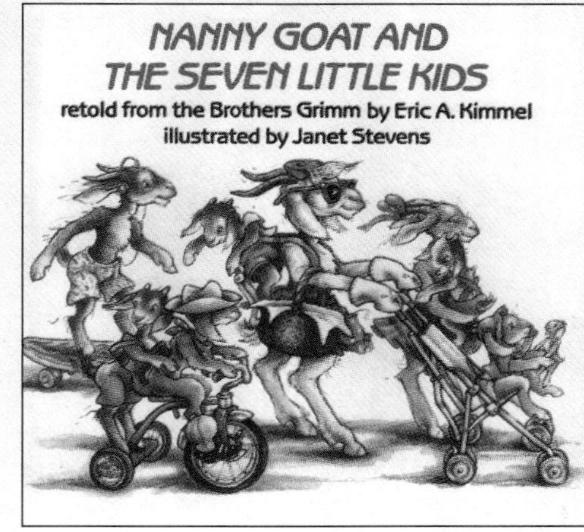

One Fine Day **by Nonny Hogrogian. Macmillan, 1974. EASY**
This cumulative tale follows the adventures of a fox as he tries to get milk for the old woman in order to get his tail back.

Papagayo: The Mischief Maker **by Gerald McDermott. Harcourt Brace, 1992. AVERAGE**
Papagayo the parrot stays up with the night creatures and helps them scare off the moon-dog.

Rainbow Crow **retold by Nancy Van Laan. Knopf, 1989. AVERAGE**
When the colorful crow carries fire to her people to keep them warm, she burns her beautiful feathers black.

Raven: A Trickster Tale from the Pacific Northwest **by Gerald McDermott. Harcourt Brace, 1993. AVERAGE**
Raven changes his shape in order to steal the sun from the Sky Chief and bring light into the dark world. *Caldecott Honor; ALA Notable Book;* Boston Globe-Horn Book *Honor*

Stop That Noise! **by Paul Geraghty. Crown, 1992. AVERAGE**
A tree mouse comes to appreciate the noises of the other forest animals after hearing the noise of a machine destroying the forest.

Storm in the Night **by Mary Stolz. HarperCollins, 1988. CHALLENGE**
During a power outage, a young boy listens to his grandfather tell him a story of his past youth. *Notable Trade Book in Social Studies*

A Story, A Story **retold by Gail E. Haley. Macmillan, 1970. AVERAGE**
Anansi the spider wants to buy the Sky God's stories. To do so, he catches the leopard, the hornet, and the fairy. *Caldecott Medal;* Boston Globe-Horn Book *Award*

The Story of the Milky Way **by Joseph Bruchac and Gayle Ross. Dial, 1995. AVERAGE**
When an old man and woman find that their cornmeal is gone, their grandson wants to find out where it went.

The Three Princes: A Tale from the Middle East **by Eric A. Kimmel. Holiday House, 1994. CHALLENGE**
A princess promises to marry the prince who finds the most precious treasure. *ALA Notable Book*

Three Sacks of Truth: A Story from France **adapted by Eric A. Kimmel. Holiday House, 1993. CHALLENGE**
With some special help, Petit Jean outsmarts a dishonest king and wins the hand of a princess. *Irma Simonton Black Award*

Three Stalks of Corn **by Leo Politi. Macmillan, 1993. CHALLENGE**
Angelica learns more about her grandmother's love for plants when her grandmother explains the origins of corn and why it is cherished.

Too Much Noise **by Anne McGovern. Houghton Mifflin, 1992. AVERAGE**
Peter complains that he can't sleep because his house is too noisy.

Tops & Bottoms **adapted by Janet Stevens. Harcourt Brace, 1995. AVERAGE**
A rabbit tricks a bear into giving him food from the bear's garden.

Traveling to Tondo **retold by Verna Aardema. Knopf, 1991. AVERAGE**
Bowane, the civet cat, travels to Tondo to get married. *ALA Notable Book; Notable Trade Book in Social Studies*

The Trouble with Tyrannosaurus Rex **by Lorinda Bryan Cauley. Harcourt Brace, 1988. CHALLENGE**
Ankylosaurus and Duckbill devise a plan with the other peaceful dinosaurs in their neighborhood to outwit and humiliate Tyrannosaurus Rex before he eats them.

Where the Wild Things Are **by Maurice Sendak. HarperCollins, 1963. CHALLENGE**
When Max is sent to his room for wild behavior, his imagination provides a romp with other wild things.

Who Took the Farmer's Hat? **by Joan L. Nodset. HarperCollins, 1963. EASY**
The wind took the farmer's hat, and no matter how hard he looks, he can't find it again.

Who's in Rabbit's House? **by Verna Aardema. Dial, 1979. CHALLENGE**
In this Masai tale, Rabbit can't get back into her house because the Long One is hiding inside. Rabbit's friends try to help her, but an unexpected source gives her the solution.

Why Mosquitoes Buzz in People's Ears **by Verna Aardema. Dial, 1975. AVERAGE**
Iguana doesn't want to listen to Mosquito's stories, so he puts sticks in his ears. This creates a chain of events. *Caldecott Medal; Children's Choice*

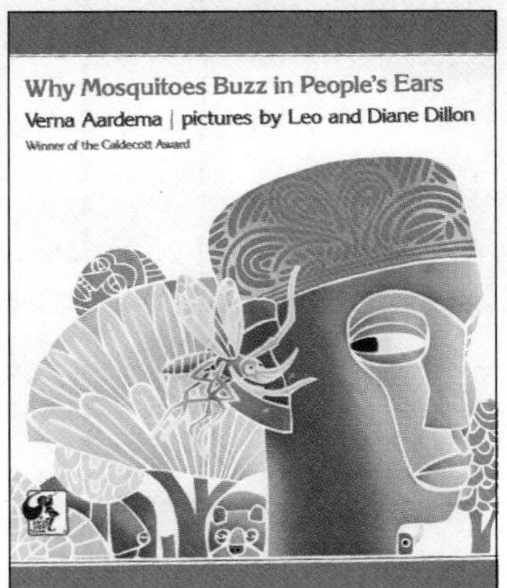

Zomo the Rabbit: A Trickster Tale from West Africa **by Gerald McDermott. Harcourt Brace, 1992. AVERAGE**
Zomo the rabbit asks the Sky God for wisdom. He earns it after doing three impossible tasks.

SCHOOL ↔ HOME CONNECTION 9

FAMILY INVOLVEMENT ACTIVITIES

Your child is reading an African folktale called "Anansi and the Talking Melon." In the story, Anansi is a lazy, tricky spider who bores his way into one of Elephant's melons. He eats so much that he is too fat to get out of the hole he made. Thinking he has a melon that can talk, Elephant goes to show it to the king. The animals he meets are also taken in by the talking melon. The melon insults the gorilla king, who throws and smashes it. After he gets out, Anansi begins to eat some bananas. Soon Anansi tricks Elephant again by pretending that the bananas talk!

I have tried some of the activities.

Student: ______________________________

Family Member: ______________________________

Comments/Suggestions: ______________________________

____

You may want to do some of these activities with your child.

TELL A TALE OF ANANSI

Encourage your child to make up a story about what Anansi might do if he lived in your home. Your child may want to write the story, illustrate it, and read it to family members.

THE WORD SPIDER

Have your child cut out the Key Words. Draw a small circle on a sheet of paper. Say a clue for one of the words, for example, "I'm thinking of a word that means *mad*." If your child does not find the correct word, draw a spider leg from the circle, and give another clue. (Other possible clues are: The word has the long e sound; the word rhymes with *me*; the word begins with *a*.) Your child should try to guess all the words before you add eight legs to the spider. Then have your child add the words to the Word File.

angry

bore

course

full

hungry

lazy

squeezed

thorn

used

Harcourt Brace School Publishers

SCHOOL ↔ HOME CONNECTION 10

FAMILY INVOLVEMENT ACTIVITIES

Your child is reading "Nine-in-One, Grr! Grr!" told by Blia Xiong and adapted by Cathy Spagnoli. In the story, Tiger asks the great Shao how many cubs she will have. He tells her that she will have nine cubs each year if she remembers his words. So she sings, "Nine-in-one, Grr! Grr!" When Bird learns of this, she is afraid that so many tigers will eat the rest of the animals. So she tricks Tiger into singing "One-in-nine, Grr! Grr!" and this saves the animals.

I have tried some of the activities.

Student: ______________________

Family Member: ______________________

Comments/Suggestions: ______________________

____

____

You may want to do some of these activities with your child.

A GRR-EAT STORY

Invite your child to tell you the story in his or her own words. Can you or your child think of another way Bird could have tricked Tiger? Make up a new ending for the story together.

LIBRARY TIME

Most libraries offer picture-book versions of folktales from many lands. You may want to share some with your child.

AN IMPORTANT EVENT

Help your child cut out the Key Words on the page. Ask him or her to make up a story that uses all the words. When the story is finished, suggest that your child draw pictures to go with it. Read the story with your family. Then have your child put the words in his or her Word File.

change
coins
decided
explained
important
lonely
noise
sighed
terrible

Harcourt Brace School Publishers

SCHOOL ↔ HOME CONNECTION 11

FAMILY INVOLVEMENT ACTIVITIES

Your child is reading "Coyote," a trickster tale. Coyote wants to learn to fly, so he asks the crows to help him. The crows stick feathers from their wings into him. Soon he thinks he can fly as well as they can. When the crows no longer enjoy the rude Coyote, they take back their feathers. Coyote falls so fast his tail starts to burn. Then he trips and rolls in the dirt. This tale explains why coyotes are the color of dust and have a black tip on their tails.

I have tried some of the activities.

Student: ______________________________

Family Member: __________________________

Comments/Suggestions: ____________________

____

____

You may want to do some of these activities with your child.

TRICKSTER TALES

Remember old tales about clever animals, like Brer Rabbit? Perhaps you and your child enjoy the cartoons in which the roadrunner always escapes the coyote. Ask your child to retell the story "Coyote." Then share a story you remember about a clever animal. With your child, make up another adventure with Coyote and the crows. For example, what might happen if Coyote wanted to race with the crows, or if he bragged to other coyotes about being able to fly?

LIBRARY TIME

Gerald McDermott has written more tales from other cultures, many of them Native American. You may wish to help your child find other stories by McDermott or other trickster tales at the library. Read the stories with your child.

IF I COULD FLY

Have your child cut out the Key Words on the page. Work together to think of an invention that would make it possible for a person to fly. The words on the cards might give some ideas for inventions. Ask your child to write about the invention. Then read the word cards, and ask your child to find them in the writing. Together, consider where you might add any words that weren't used. Then have your child put the words in the Word File.

balance	feather	foolish	foot	spread

Harcourt Brace School Publishers

SCHOOL ↔ HOME CONNECTION 12

FAMILY INVOLVEMENT ACTIVITIES

Your child is reading a play called "Rabbit and Tiger." In this tale, set in Puerto Rico, small animals who are being frightened by Tiger call on Rabbit for help. Rabbit makes a deal with Tiger: if Rabbit can ride Tiger by sunset, Tiger will leave Puerto Rico forever. Rabbit plays a series of funny tricks on Tiger—and wins! Tiger must leave the island, but vows to get back at Rabbit someday.

I have tried some of the activities.

Student: ______________________________

Family Member: ______________________________

Comments/Suggestions: ______________________________

____

____

You may want to do some of these activities with your child.

TIGER TROUBLE

Invite your child to tell the story from more than one point of view. Have your child first pretend to be Tiger and tell Tiger's version of what happened. Then, have your child tell the story from another character's point of view.

WORDS UP YOUR SLEEVE

Rabbit always has another trick up his sleeve. Help your child have fun while reading and defining the Key Words on this page. Have your child cut out the words and put them in his or her sleeves. Have your child pull a word from a sleeve, read it, and tell what it means or how it was used in the story. Then have him or her add the words to the Word File.

bargain

few

fiercest

group

jungle

kind

lies

mind

scares

Harcourt Brace School Publishers

Anansi was a ______________ spider who didn't want to work.

One day, he was ______________ and needed to eat.

He wanted to ______________ a hole in a melon.

Anansi broke a sharp ______________ off a tree.

He ______________ it to make a hole in the rind.

Then he ______________ himself through the tiny hole.

He ate melon until he was ______________.

Of ______________, that is only one tricky thing he did.

Anansi made the king ______________.

Shao wore silver ______________ on his belt.

He ______________ to help Tiger.

She was sad and ______________.

Shao told her some ______________ words.

Shao ______________ to Bird what he had said to Tiger.

He could not ______________ his promise.

Bird thought that this was ______________.

Shao ______________ as if he were sad.

The ______________ of Bird's wings made Tiger forget her song.

Each crow stuck a ______________ in Coyote.

They began to dance, first on one ______________, then on the other.

The crows ______________ their wings and flew.

Coyote flew, too, but he lost his ______________.

Did the ______________ Coyote learn to fly?

Life was good in the big, green ____________.

There were a ____________ problems.

But one ____________ of friends had a big problem.

"Tiger ____________ me," said Mouse.

"What ____________ of animal is he?" Toucan asked.

"He is the ____________ one," said Monkey.

"Never ____________ Tiger," said Rabbit.

"He just ____________ around and growls."

"I'll make a ____________ with him. Then he'll leave us alone."

Notes on the Theme

ABOUT THE STUDENT ANTHOLOGY

Reading Trade Books

Signatures Library

Other Theme-Related Books

Multimedia Resources

Community Resources

FAVORITE ACTIVITIES

Your own ideas for customizing the theme:

MATERIALS:

STEPS:

MATERIALS:

STEPS:

MATERIALS:

STEPS:

NEWS FROM:

Dear Family,

Special Announcements

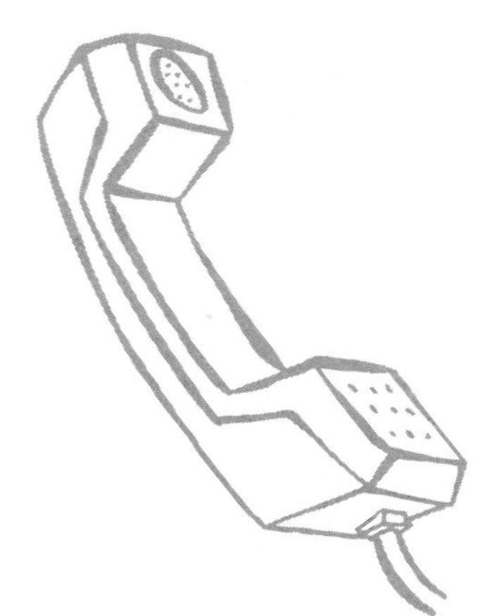

Spotlight on . . .

Something to Try at Home

From Your Child . . .

Book Corner

We have been very busy lately!

Harcourt Brace School Publishers

Complete the newsletter with news items from your class. Duplicate the page, and send it home to family members.

CREATE YOUR OWN SCHOOL-TO-HOME NEWSLETTER

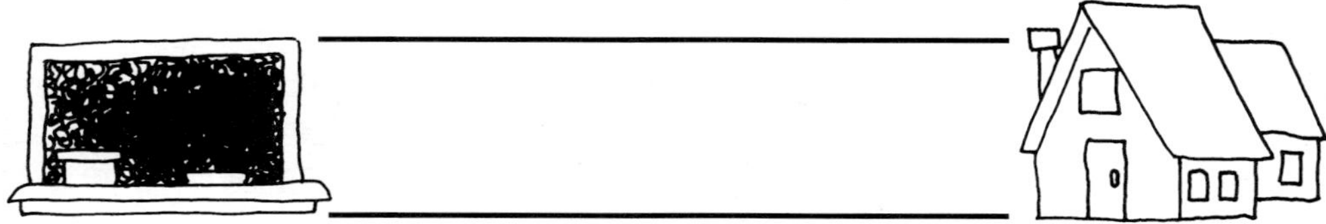

Insert your school name or newsletter title to head your newsletter.

Personal note to parents

List of recommended books for reading

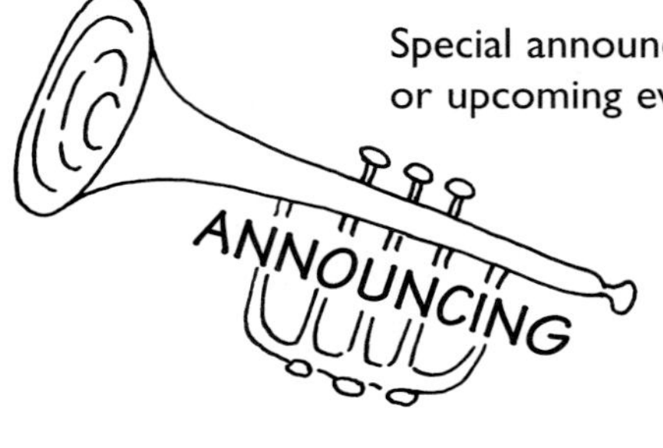

Special announcements or upcoming events

Current events from the classroom, school, or community

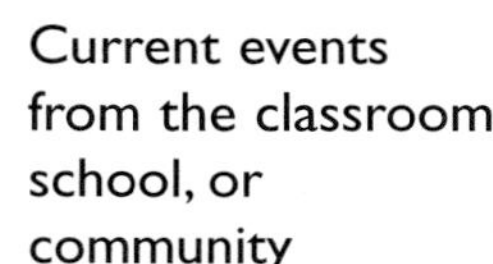

Reminder of upcoming meetings, conferences, or field trips

Focus on a certain subject area, or parent self-help information

Classroom projects

Call for volunteers or materials

Future goals or study themes

Student column

Use any of these clip-art graphics to create a classroom newsletter to send home.

GRAPH-A-BOOK

Dear Family Members,

As a book is read at home, have the student graph his or her response. The student should write the title of the book and the author's name on the numbered line and then color the corresponding bar on the graph to evaluate the book. Ask the student to give a reason for his or her rating.

Book Titles and Authors' Names

1. ______________________________
2. ______________________________
3. ______________________________
4. ______________________________
5. ______________________________
6. ______________________________

Graph

Book 1				
Book 2				
Book 3				
Book 4				
Book 5				
Book 6				
	Would Not Recommend	OK	Good	GREAT!

Please return the graph to school when completed. Thank you.

Signature ______________________________

Harcourt Brace School Publishers

Duplicate the page and send it home with students to be completed with family members.

Harcourt Brace School Publishers

because: ______________________________

____

____

____

____

____

Signed: ______________________________

Additional Resources

Additional Resources

Introducing the Glossary

Explain to children that a glossary is often included in a book so that readers can look up words used in the book. After reading and discussing the introductory material on page 349, you may want to choose a word, such as different, *and model using alphabetical order and guide words to look it up. Have children read the definition and tell how the example sentence and the illustration help the reader understand the definition.*

Select several other words in the glossary, with and without accompanying illustrations, and have children practice looking them up. Point out that one vocabulary strategy is to use a dictionary or a glossary to find the meanings of new words. You may want to discuss similarities and differences between a dictionary and a glossary. Then have children compare this glossary with a dictionary you use in the classroom.

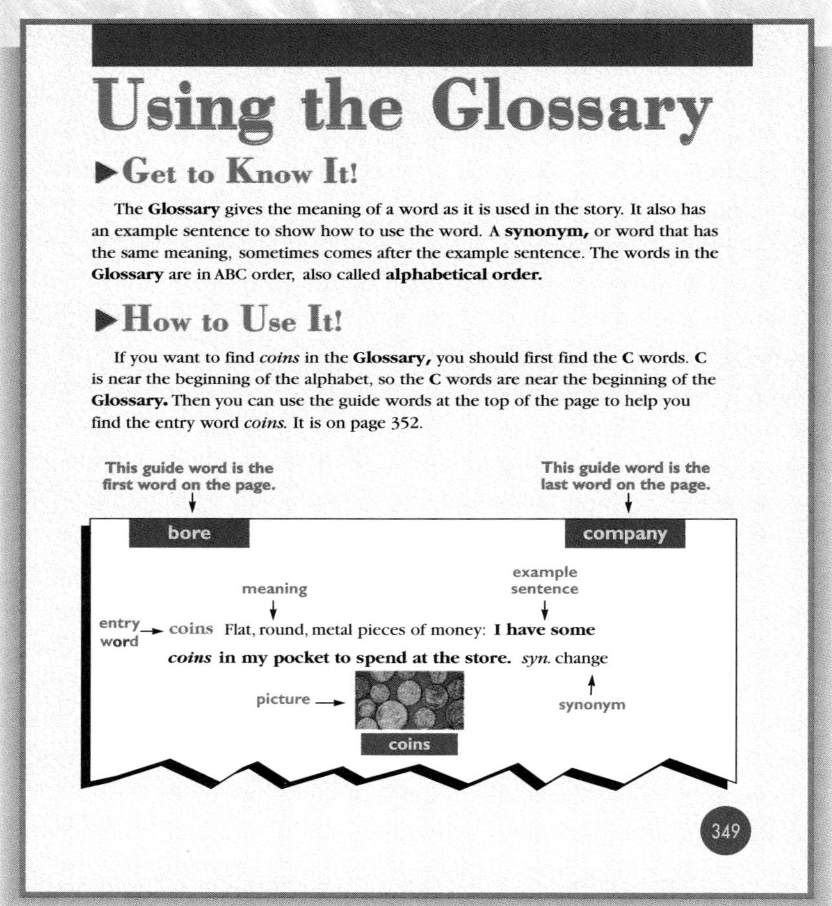

Using the Glossary

▶Get to Know It!

The **Glossary** gives the meaning of a word as it is used in the story. It also has an example sentence to show how to use the word. A **synonym,** or word that has the same meaning, sometimes comes after the example sentence. The words in the **Glossary** are in ABC order, also called **alphabetical order.**

▶How to Use It!

If you want to find *coins* in the **Glossary,** you should first find the **C** words. **C** is near the beginning of the alphabet, so the **C** words are near the beginning of the **Glossary.** Then you can use the guide words at the top of the page to help you find the entry word *coins.* It is on page 352.

A

angry

ad•ven•ture A new and exciting thing to do: **It would be a great *adventure* to go to the moon.**

a•gainst To be safe from: **We were dressed in coats *against* the cold wind.**

air The open space above the Earth: **A jet flew through the *air*.**

an•gry Mad: **Did he get *angry* when someone broke his toy?**

ap•peared Came out; could be seen: **The stars *appeared* after the sun went down.**

B

balance

bal•ance Steady; not tilting from side to side: **Susie lost her *balance* and fell down.**

bar•gain A deal: **Rosa made a *bargain* with her brother that she would fix his bike if he would let her ride it.**

beau•ti•ful Nice to look at: **Did you see the *beautiful* painting of flowers?** *syns.* pretty, lovely

be•lieve To trust; to think something is true: **I *believe* that I can learn to swim.**

bore

bore To dig into: **You can *bore* a hole through wood with a drill.**

bor•row To use someone's things for a while: **I need to *borrow* a pencil because I forgot mine.**

break To crack into pieces: **Let's *break* the candy into three pieces.**

brought Took along: **I *brought* a sandwich to school for my lunch.**

building

build•ing A place people make to live, work, or play in: **I watched workers put up a new office *building*.**

C

called Said in a loud voice to someone far away: **Tim *called* out "Hello!" to his friend down the street.** *syns.* yelled, shouted

coins

caught Got: **Tony *caught* a cold from his sister.**

change To become different: **Watch the light *change* from red to green.**

coins Flat, round, metal pieces of money: **I have some *coins* in my pocket to spend at the store.** *syn.* change

com•pa•ny Other people or animals to spend time with: **We had *company* at our house for dinner.**

coun•try The land where we live: **The United States is a *country* that has fifty states.** *syn.* nation

course Yes: **Of *course* I can help you pick up the toys!**

cous•in A child of an aunt or an uncle: **My *cousin* lives with her dad, my Uncle Fred.**

D

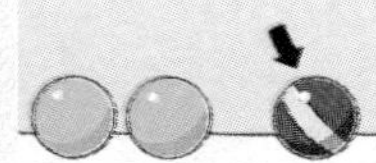

different

de•cid•ed Made a choice: **Jamal *decided* to go to the park instead of the zoo.**

dif•fer•ent Not the same: **A lion is *different* from a tiger.**

dis•cov•ered Found out: **Kathy was surprised when she *discovered* that Tanya likes to play baseball, too.**

E

en•joyed Liked: **Adriana *enjoyed* the song and wanted to hear it again.**

e•nough As much as is needed or wanted: **I have *enough* money to buy three packets of seeds.**

ex•plained Told about: **My dad *explained* how to make a kite.**

F

feather

feath•er Something that covers a bird's body: **The bird lost a blue *feather* from its wing.**

few Not many: **Chen only ate a *few* grapes, so he was still hungry.** *syn.* some

fierc•est Meanest: **The lion is the *fiercest* animal in the zoo.** *syn.* scariest

fiercest

fool•ish Silly; not wise: **The *foolish* clown tried to drive a car that had no wheels.**

foot The end part of the leg: **Clare put her *foot* into her shoe.**

full Not hungry; filled with food: **I ate until I was *full* and couldn't eat any more.**

fu•ture The time yet to come: **In the *future*, I will become a doctor.**

G

group People, animals, or things that are together: **A *group* of six children played a game.**

group

hungry

H

heard Took in sounds through the ears: **Mike *heard* the truck before he saw it.**

her•self Done alone by a girl: **Carmen read a book by *herself* after her friends went home.**

hun•gry Wanting something to eat: **The lions are *hungry* because they have not eaten today.**

I

i•de•a A thought: **What a great *idea* to get everyone to help clean the classroom!**

im•por•tant Needing to be done: **She knew it was *important* to finish all her work.**

jungle

J

jun•gle A warm, wet forest with many trees and animals: **The tiger chased the monkey through the thick trees of the *jungle.***

K

kind Belongs in a certain group: **What *kind* of ice cream do you like?**

knew Was sure: **Suzanne *knew* the movie was good, so she went to see it.**

lies

L

laugh To make a sound showing that something is funny: **That joke made me *laugh.*** *syns.* giggle, chuckle

la•zy Not wanting to work: **Brenda felt *lazy* yesterday, so she didn't clean her room.**

lies To rest your body down flat: **John *lies* on his back to sleep.**

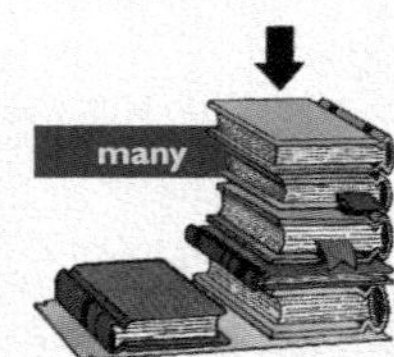

many

lone•ly Wanting others to be around: **Heidi felt *lonely* in her room by herself.**

loud Making a lot of sound; not quiet: **The music was so *loud* that I covered my ears.** *syn.* noisy

M

mountain

man•y A lot of: **Carlos got a prize for reading so *many* books.**

mind To think about: **We're so tired that we can hardly walk, never *mind* run!**

moun•tain A big hill: **That *mountain* is four times higher than this hill!**

neighbors

N

neigh•bors People who live near you: **I play with my *neighbors* who live next door.**

noise A loud sound: **Did you hear the *noise* that the car horn made?**

P

peo•ple Men, women, boys, and girls: **Many *people* were shopping at the store.**

per•fect Best; just right: **Right before bedtime is the *perfect* time for a good story.**

piece

piece A part of a whole: **John ate a *piece* of pie.** *syn.* part

prac•tice Doing something over and over in order to get better at it: **It takes a lot of *practice* to be a good baseball player.**

proud Feeling good about: **Romulo is *proud* because his picture won a prize.**

purple

pur•ple A color made from mixing red and blue: **Do you like to eat *purple* grapes?**

R

re•mem•ber To think of again; to not forget: **I *remember* the fun we had at the beach last week.**

S

says Speaks: **My mom *says* that I should be nice to others.**

scares Makes someone afraid: **Sometimes the dark *scares* me.** *syn.* frightens

shoes

scratched Scraped lightly with fingernails: **Sam *scratched* his bug bite.**

shoes Something worn on the feet: **Yoko will buy new *shoes* because her feet grew.**

sighed Let out a deep, loud breath: **Laura *sighed* when she could not untie the knot.**

some•times Not all the time: ***Sometimes* I like to wear a hat, but not every day.**

sor•ry Feeling a little bad about something: ***Sorry,* I cannot let you ride my bike.**

sound Something that is heard: **I heard the *sound* of the alarm.**

spare Extra: **I have a *spare* pencil in case I lose my other one.**

spe•cial Extra nice; different from the rest: **Alexandra's puppy is *special* because it is the only one with white paws.**

spread To open or unfold; to stretch out: **Alex *spread* his arms as if he were going to fly.**

squeezed

squeezed Pushed through a small place: **The mouse *squeezed* into the little hole.**

start To begin: **Everyone is here, so let's *start* the movie!**

strong Full of power; not weak: **A *strong* wind blew the man's hat off.**

sure Knowing something will happen: **Anya is *sure* she will get a bike someday.** *syn.* certain

T

ter•ri•ble Bad: **Billy had a *terrible* cold and had to stay in bed.** *syn.* horrible

thanks Something you say to let people know you like what they have done for you: ***Thanks* for your help.**

thorn

thorn A hard point on a plant: **Be careful of the *thorn* on that rose!**

touch To reach out and feel something: **Lynn likes to *touch* the rabbit because it is soft.**

touch

U

used Did something with: **I *used* a stick to stir the paint.**

W

whole All of something: **He ate the *whole* thing and didn't leave a piece for me.**

with•out Not having: **If you went out in the snow *without* a coat, you would be cold.**

wondered

won•dered Wanted to know about: **Mrs. Patel *wondered* who was knocking at the door.**

won•der•ful Great: **Candace had a *wonderful* time at the party.** *syns.* terrific, excellent

would Planned to do something: **When she was little, she *would* go to bed very early.**

wrong Not right; not correct: **The lock wouldn't open because I used the *wrong* key.**

Y

your•self You: **Please help *yourself* to some cake.**

Printed in the United States of America

Acknowledgments

For permission to reprint copyrighted material, grateful acknowledgment is made to the following sources:

Atheneum Books for Young Readers, an imprint of Simon & Schuster: Cover illustration by David S. Rose from *There's a Dragon in My Sleeping Bag* by James Howe. Illustration copyright © 1994 by David S. Rose.

Children's Book Press, San Francisco, CA: *Nine-In-One, Grr! Grr!*, told by Blia Xiong, adapted by Cathy Spagnoli, illustrated by Nancy Hom. Text copyright © 1989 by Cathy Spagnoli; illustrations copyright © 1989 by Nancy Hom.

Children's Television Workshop, New York: "What's for Lunch? Kids Chow Down Around the World" by Samantha Bonar, illustrations by David Goldin from *3-2-1 Contact* Magazine, March 1995. Copyright 1995 by Children's Television Workshop. "Rosie, the Visiting Dog" from *Sesame Street* Magazine, March 1995. Text copyright 1995 by Children's Television Workshop.

Clarion Books, a Houghton Mifflin Company imprint: Photographs by Justin Sutcliffe from *Rosie: A Visiting Dog's Story* by Stephanie Calmenson. Photographs © 1994 by Justin Sutcliffe.

Dial Books for Young Readers, a division of Penguin Books USA Inc.: Cover illustration by Susanna Natti from *Lionel at Large* by Stephen Krensky. Illustration copyright © 1986 by Susanna Natti.

Dutton Children's Books, a division of Penguin Books USA Inc.: *Abuela* by Arthur Dorros, illustrated by Elisa Kleven. Text copyright © 1991 by Arthur Dorros; illustrations copyright © 1991 by Elisa Kleven. Cover illustration from *Mary Ann* by Betsy James. Copyright © 1994 by Betsy James. *Matthew and Tilly* by Rebecca C. Jones, illustrated by Beth Peck. Text copyright © 1991 by Rebecca C. Jones; illustrations copyright © 1991 by Beth Peck.

Farrar, Straus & Giroux: "two friends" from *Spin a Soft Black Song* by Nikki Giovanni. Text copyright © 1971, 1985 by Nikki Giovanni.

Greenwillow Books, a division of William Morrow & Company, Inc.: "We Have a New Girl in Class" and "How Do You Feel?" from *Feelings* by Aliki. Copyright © 1984 by Aliki Brandenberg. Cover illustration from *Chester's Way* by Kevin Henkes. Copyright © 1988 by Kevin Henkes.

Harcourt Brace & Company: "The Trade" from *Emily and Alice Again* by Joyce Champion, illustrated by Suçie Stevenson. Text copyright © 1995 by Joyce Champion; illustrations copyright © 1995 by Suçie Stevenson. Cover illustration by Suçie Stevenson from *Emily and Alice* by Joyce Champion. Illustration copyright © 1993 by Suçie Stevenson. *Coyote: A Trickster Tale from the American Southwest* by Gerald McDermott. Copyright © 1994 by Gerald McDermott. *Mr. Putter and Tabby Pour the Tea* by Cynthia Rylant, illustrated by Arthur Howard. Text copyright © 1994 Cynthia Rylant; illustrations copyright © 1994 by Arthur Howard. From "Harcourt Brace Profiles" (Retitled: "Meet Cynthia Rylant") by Cynthia Rylant. Cover illustration from *Tops & Bottoms* by Janet Stevens. Copyright © 1995 by Janet Stevens.

HarperCollins Publishers: "Balloon Tom-Tom" from *Making Music: 6 Instruments You Can Create* by Eddie Herschel Oates, illustrated by Michael Koelsch. Text copyright © 1995 by Eddie Oates; illustration copyright © 1995 by Michael Koelsch.

HarperCollins Publishers (Australia) Pty. Ltd.: Cover illustration by Rod Clement from *Edward the Emu* by Sheena Knowles. Illustration copyright © by Rod Clement.

Henry Holt and Company, Inc.: Cover illustration from *Anansi the Spider* by Gerald McDermott. Copyright © 1972 by Landmark Production Inc.

Holiday House, Inc.: *Anansi and the Talking Melon*, retold by Eric A. Kimmel, illustrated by Janet Stevens. Text copyright © 1994 by Eric A. Kimmel; illustrations copyright © 1994 by Janet Stevens.

Homeland Publishing, a division of Troubadour Records Ltd.: From "Anansi" by Bert Simpson. Text copyright © 1979 by Homeland Publishing, a division of Troubadour Records Ltd.

Alfred A. Knopf, Inc.: Cover illustration from *Polka and Dot* by Dena Schutzer. Copyright © 1994 by Dena Schutzer.

Little, Brown and Company: From *Dinosaurs Alive and Well!* by Laurie Krasny Brown and Marc Brown. Copyright © 1990 by Laurie Krasny Brown and Marc Brown.

Lothrop, Lee & Shepard Books, a division of William Morrow & Company, Inc.: Cover illustration from *Jimmy Lee Did It* by Pat Cummings. Copyright © 1985 by Pat Cummings. Cover photograph by Ken Heyman from *Puddle Jumper: How a Toy Is Made* by Ann Morris. Photograph copyright © 1993 by Ken Heyman.

Vo-Dinh Mai: Cover illustration by Vo-Dinh Mai from *Angel Child, Dragon Child* by Michele Maria Surat. Illustration copyright © 1983 by Vo-Dinh Mai.

Morrow Junior Books, a division of William Morrow & Company, Inc.: From *Hopscotch Around the World* by Mary D. Lankford, illustrated by Karen Milone. Text copyright © 1992 by Mary Lankford; illustrations copyright © 1992 by Karen Milone.

National Geographic Society: From *Tricks Animals Play* by Jan Nagel Clarkson. Text copyright © 1975 by National Geographic Society.

Plays, Inc.: *Rabbit and Tiger* by F. C. Nicholson from *PLAYS: The Drama Magazine for Young People*, April 1993. Text copyright © 1993 by Plays, Inc. This play is for reading purposes only; for permission to produce, write to Plays, Inc., 120 Boylston Street, Boston, MA 02116.

G. P. Putnam's Sons, a division of The Putnam & Grosset Group: Cover illustration by Kathleen Kuchera from *The Rooster Who Went to His Uncle's Wedding*, retold by Alma Flor Ada. Illustration copyright © 1993 by Kathleen Kuchera.

Scholastic Inc.: *This Is the Way We Go to School* by Edith Baer, illustrated by Steve Björkman. Text copyright © 1990 by Edith Baer; illustrations copyright © 1990 by Steven Björkman.

Simon & Schuster Books for Young Readers, a division of Simon & Schuster: Cover illustration by Sheila Hamanaka from *The Terrible EEK* by Patricia A. Compton. Illustration copyright © 1991 by Sheila Hamanaka. *Six-Dinner Sid* by Inga Moore. Copyright © 1991 by Inga Moore. Originally published in Great Britain by Simon & Schuster Young Books. "Secret Messages" from *Dr. Zed's Science Surprises* by Gordon Penrose. Copyright © 1989 by Greey de Pencier Books. *Max Found Two Sticks* by Brian Pinkney. Copyright © 1994 by Brian Pinkney.

Albert Whitman & Company: Cover illustration from *Two of Everything* by Lily Toy Hong. Copyright © 1993 by Lily Toy Hong.

Photo Credits

Key: (t) top, (b) bottom, (c) center, (l) left, (r) right.

Alan Blank/ Bruce Coleman, Inc., 267 (tl,tr); John R. Brownlie/ Bruce Coleman, Inc., 265; Jane Burton/Bruce Coleman, Inc, 264; Stephen Collins/National Audubon Soc., 262; Stephen Cridland/Black Star/Harcourt Brace & Company, 257; Tim Davis/ Photo Res., 265(b); Sal DiMarco/Black Star/Harcourt Brace & Company, 60; Warren Faubel/Black Star/Harcourt Brace & Company, 37(b), 319; Rick Friedman/Black Star/Harcourt Brace & Company, 61, 116, 117; Dale Higgins/Harcourt Brace & Company, 179, 225(r); Ken Karp,118-119, 178-179, 260-261, 320-321; Z. Leszcyndki, 263(b); Tom Myers, 267 (br, bl); Carlo Ontal, 178(c); Edward S. Ross, 266; 267 (cr, cl); Joyce Sangirardi, 146-147; Tom Sobolik/Black Star/Harcourt Brace & Company, 37(t), 91; Justin Sutcliffe, 202-203; Frank Varney/Black Star/Harcourt Brace & Company, 256; Doug Wilson/Black Star/Harcourt Brace & Company, 225(l); Photos from Cynthia Rylant's autobiography "Best Wishes" copyright © 1992 published by Richard C. Owens Publishers, Inc.; Pablo Picasso *Ronde des Enfants* (1901), courtesy of Marc Arthur Kohn, Paris, 64-65; Pierre Auguste Renoir *Two Young Girls at the Piano*, The Metropolitan Museum of Art, Robert Lehman, 156-157; Michelle Paisano *Storyteller Doll*, Museum of the American Indian, 296-297

Illustration Credits

Gerald McDermott, Cover Art; Julia Gorton, 6-7, 13-17, 64, 120; Jennifer Beck Harris, 8-9, 121-125, 156-157, 228; Seymour Chwast, 10-11, 229-233, 296-297, 348; Aliki, 38-39; Richard Bernal, 324-345; Steve Björkman, 18-37; Marc Brown, 96- 117; Samantha Bonar, 42-43; David Goldin 42-43; Nancy Hom, 268-293; Arthur Howard, 158-177, 180-181; Elisa Kleven, 204-225; Michael Koelsch, 94-95; Mary Lankford, 150-155; Gerald McDermott, 298-319; Mercedes McDonald, 258-259; Inga Moore, 182-199; Beth Peck, 126-145; Brian Pinkney, 66-91; Janet Stevens, 234-257, 260-261; Suçie Stevenson, 44-61; Margaret Cusack, 226-227; Sharon Dodge, 294-295; Sudi McCollum 294-295; Scott Scheidly, 118-119 (t), 200-201, 346-347(t); Linda Solovic, 92-93; Peggy Tagel, 62-63; Matt Wawiorka, 40-41.

Handwriting

Uppercase Manuscript Alphabet

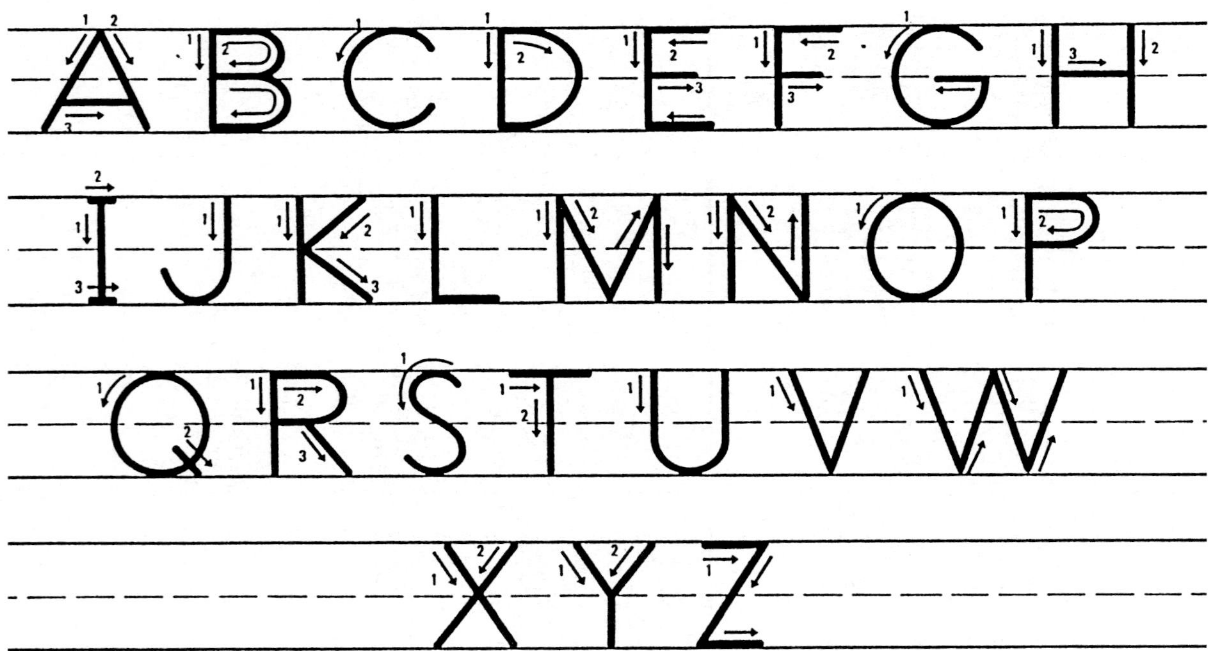

Handwriting

Lowercase Manuscript Alphabet

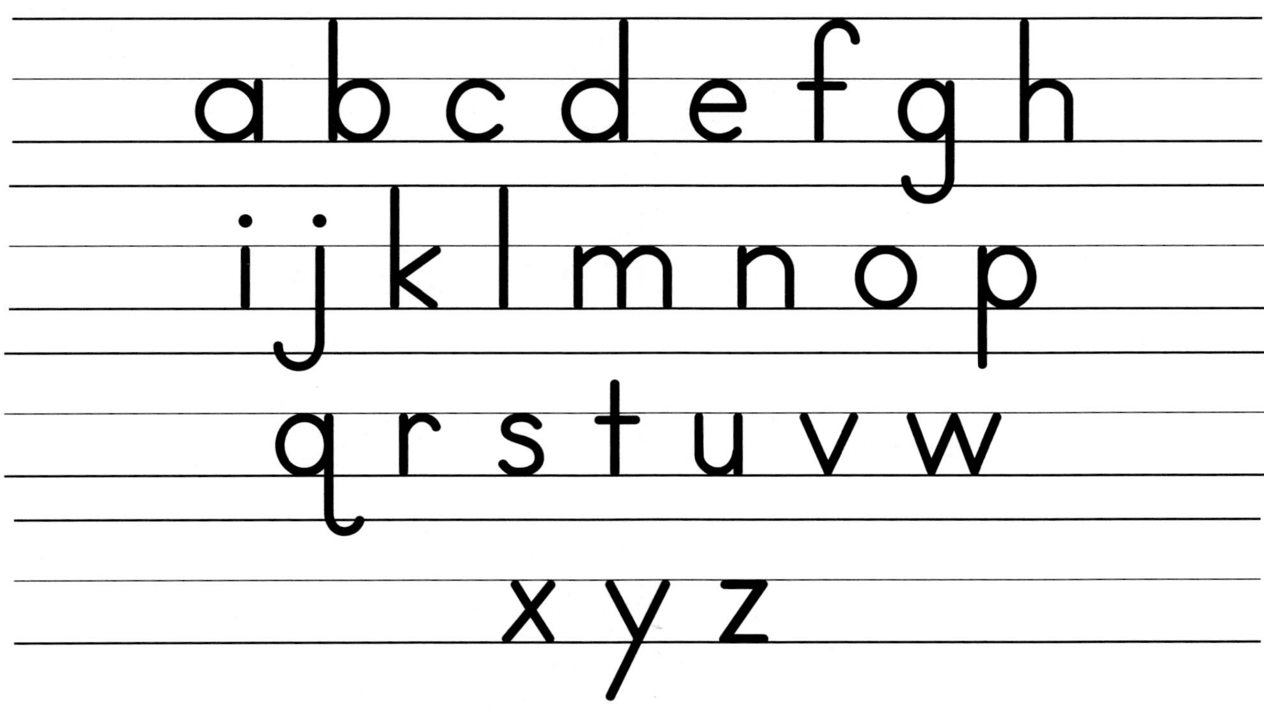

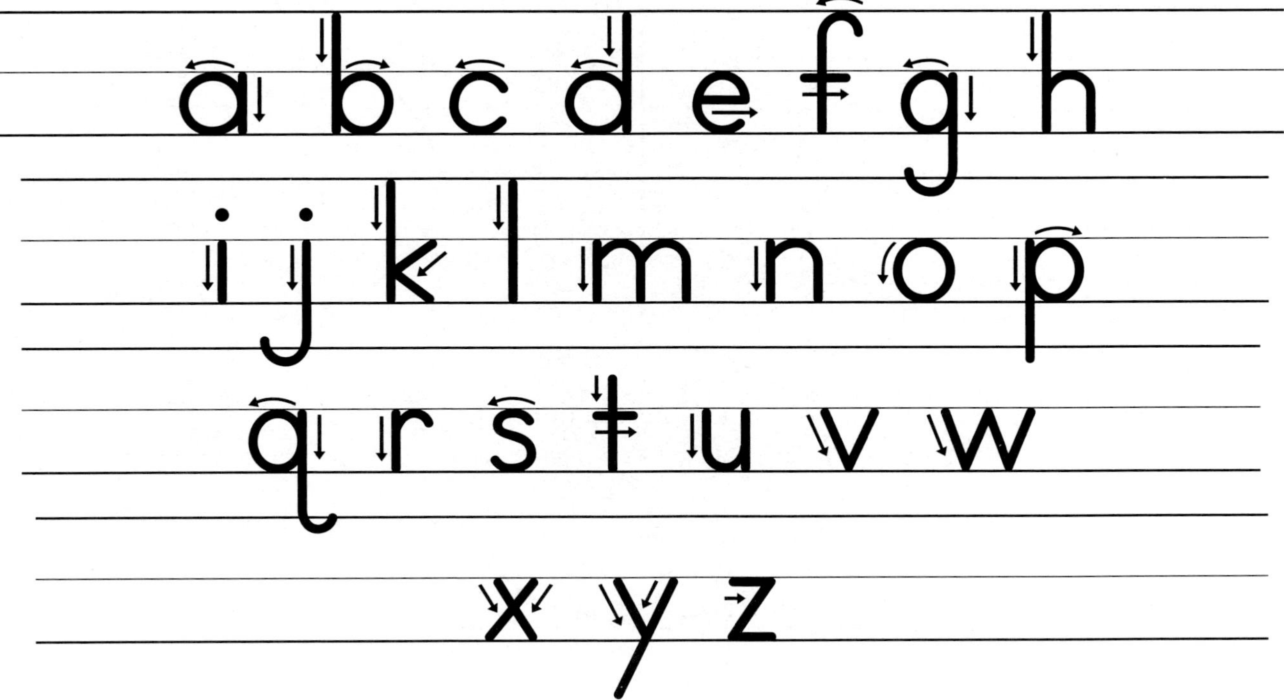

Harcourt Brace School Publishers

Idea Web

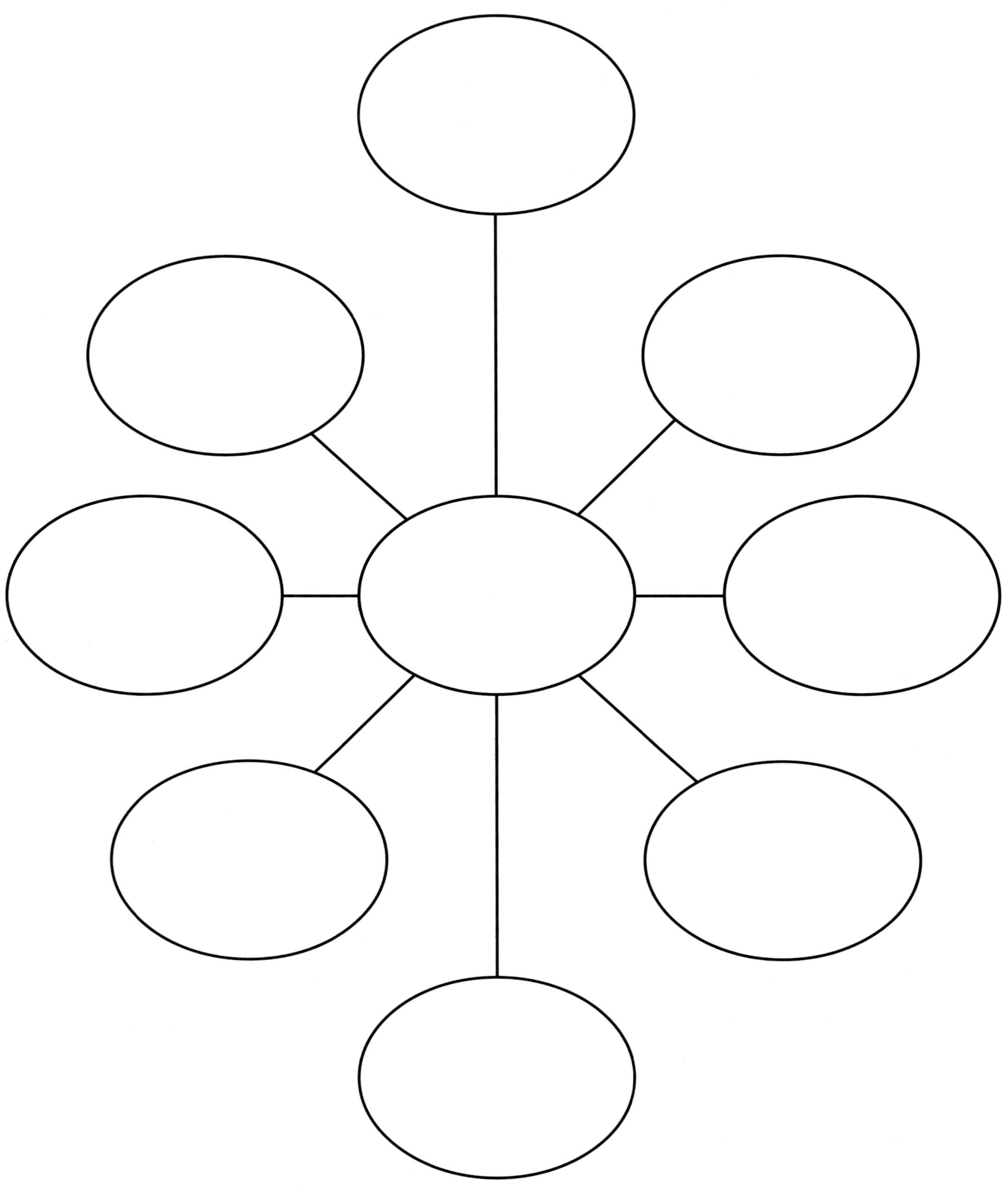

Story Map

Beginning

Who is in the story?

When and where does the story take place?

What is the problem?

Middle

What important things happen?

Ending

How is the problem solved?

Chart

K–W–L Chart

K	W	L
What I Know	What I Want to Know	What I Learned

Flowchart

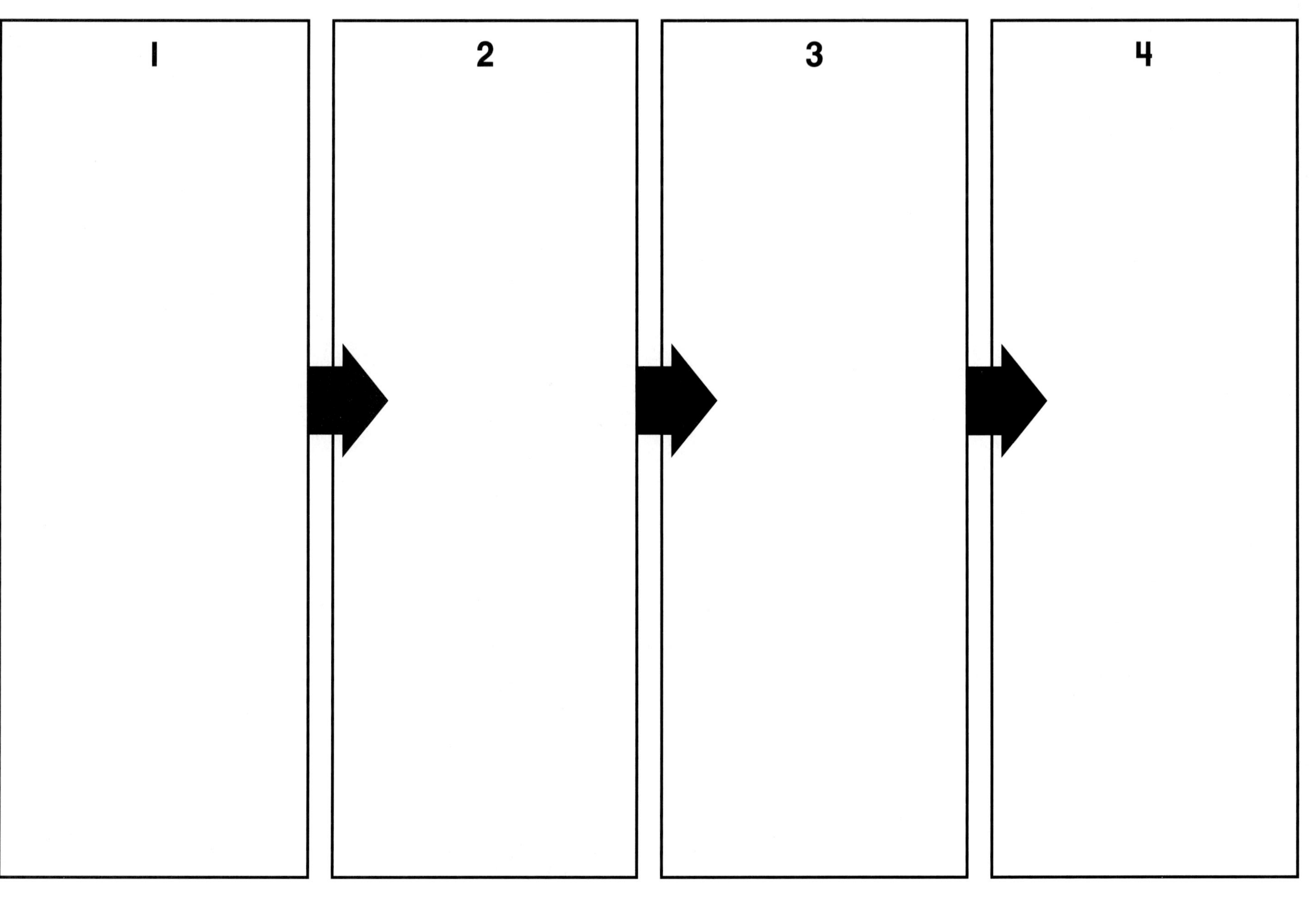

Venn Diagram

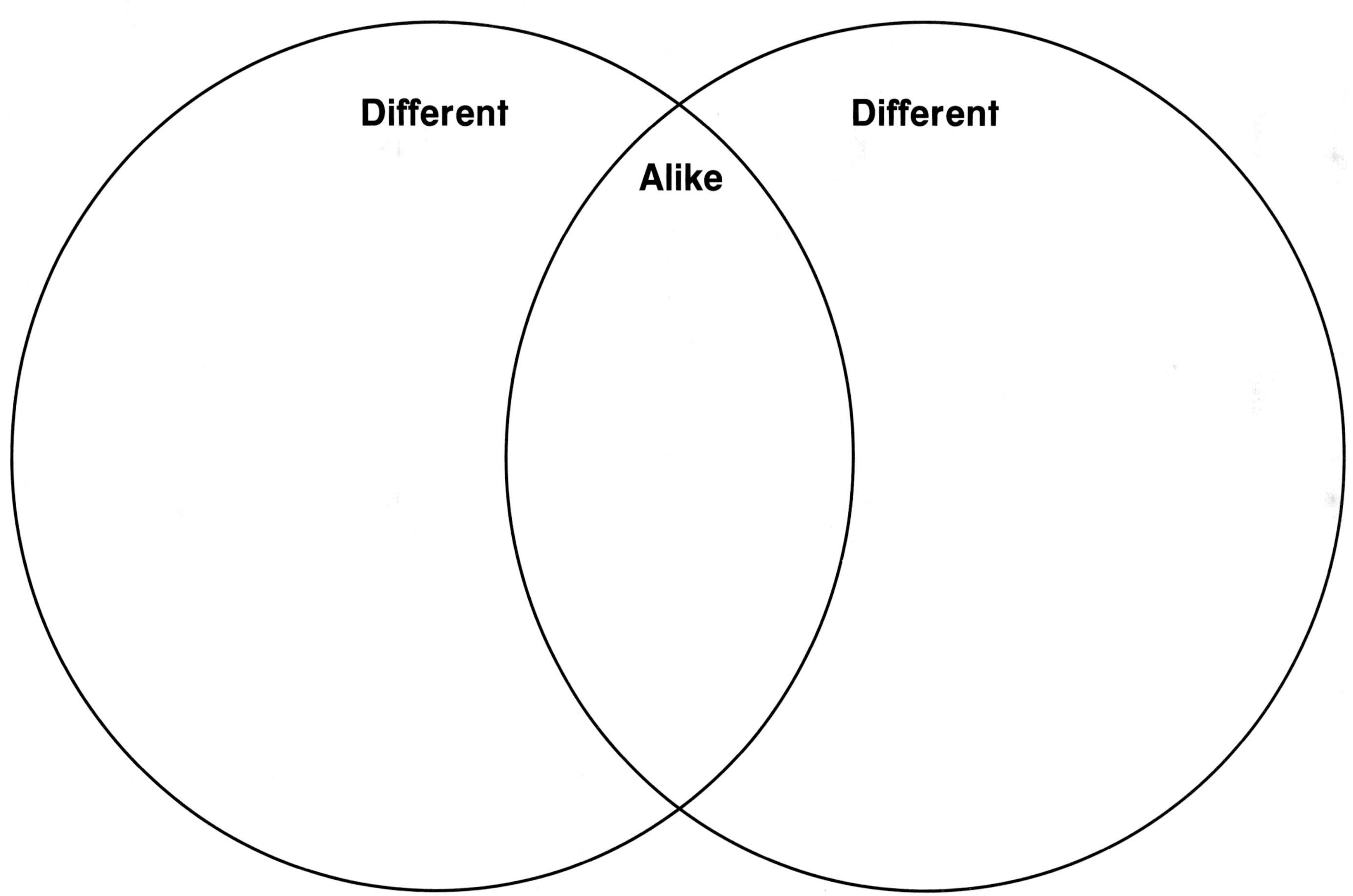

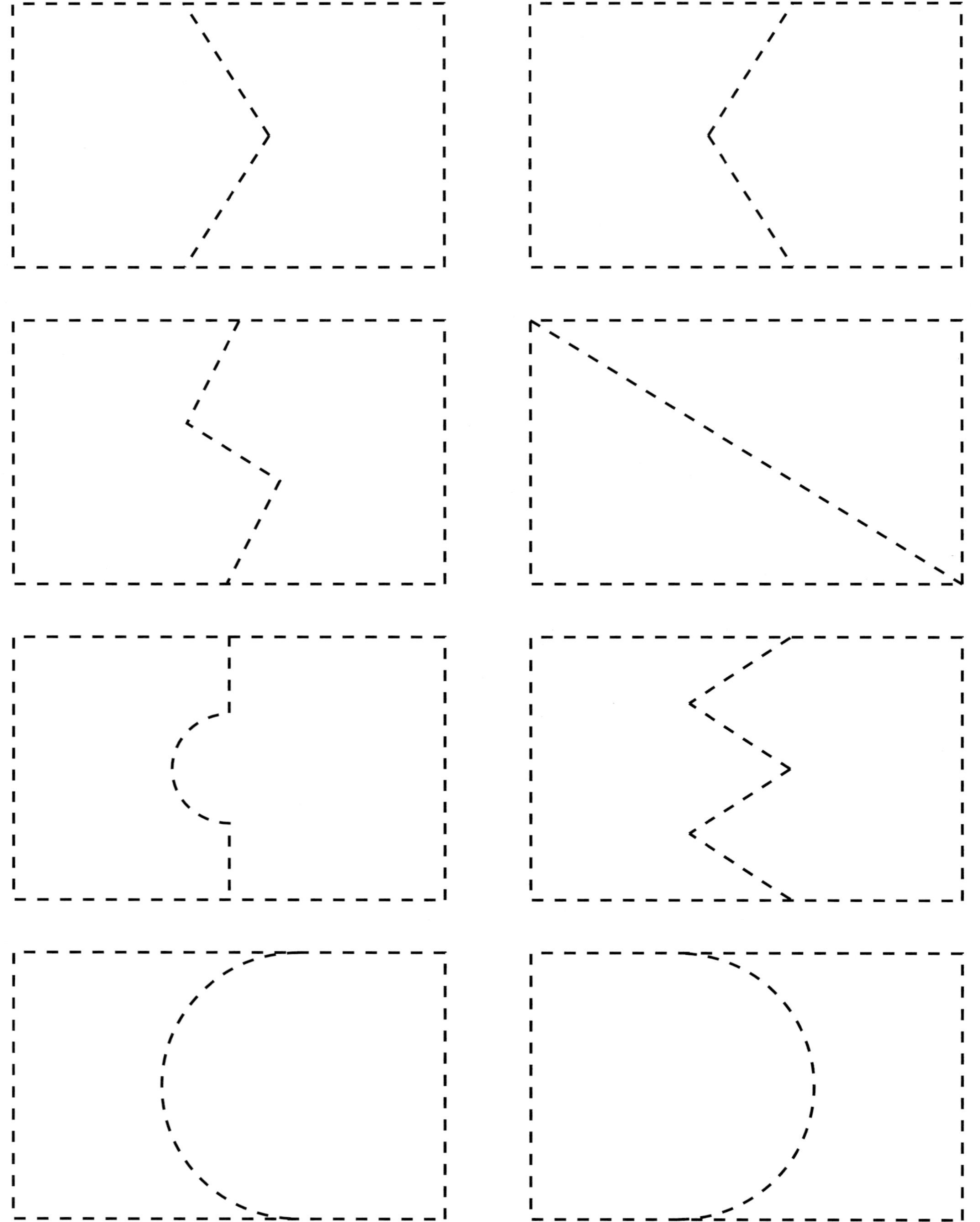

Form/Application

Felixville Animal Shelter

Application to Adopt a Pet

Name: ____________________

Address: ____________________

____

Telephone: ____________________

What kind of pet do you want?

Mark an **X** in the correct space.

____ cat ____ dog ____ other

Do you have any other pets? ____________________

How will you take care of your pet?

____

____

____

____

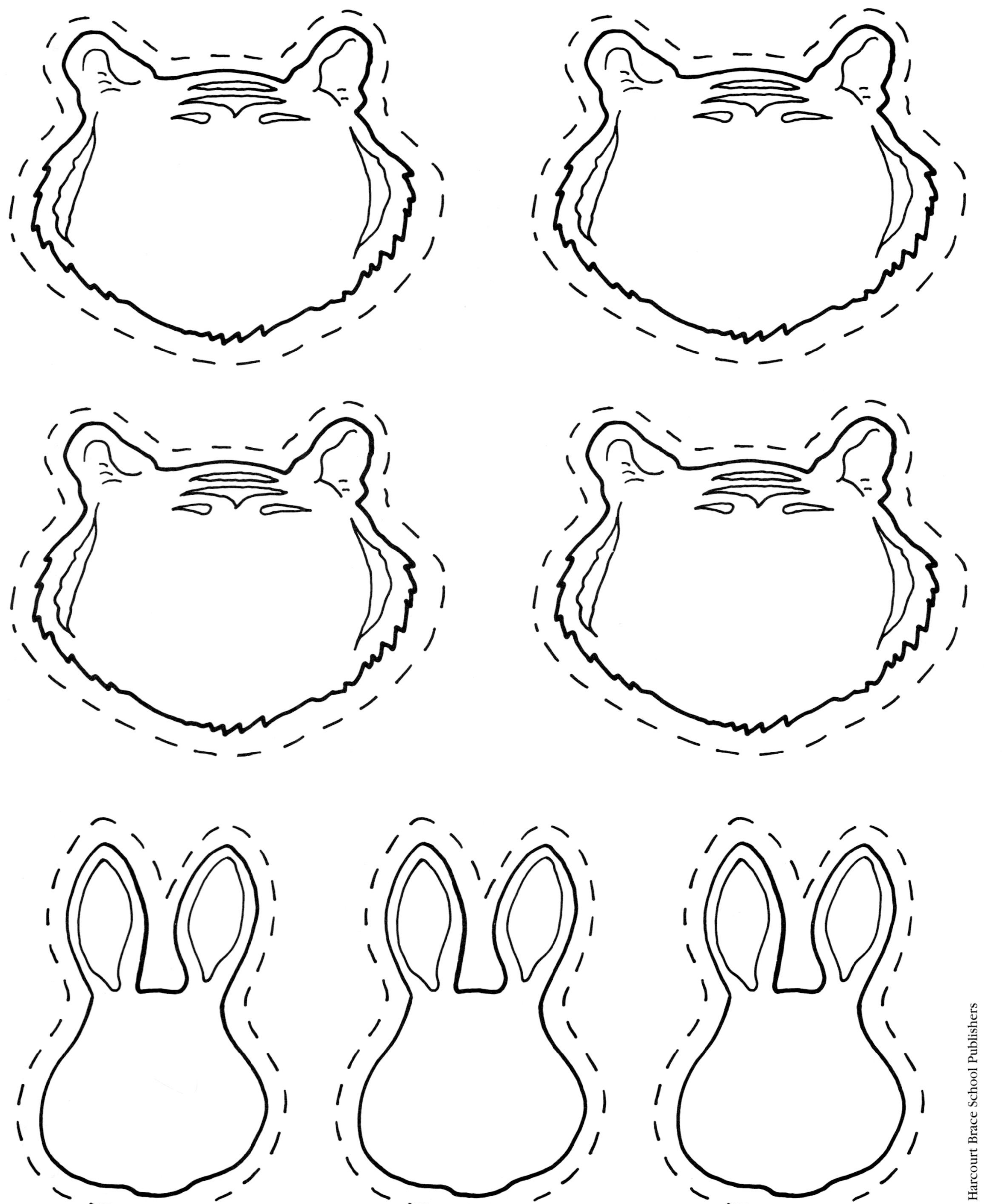

Setting

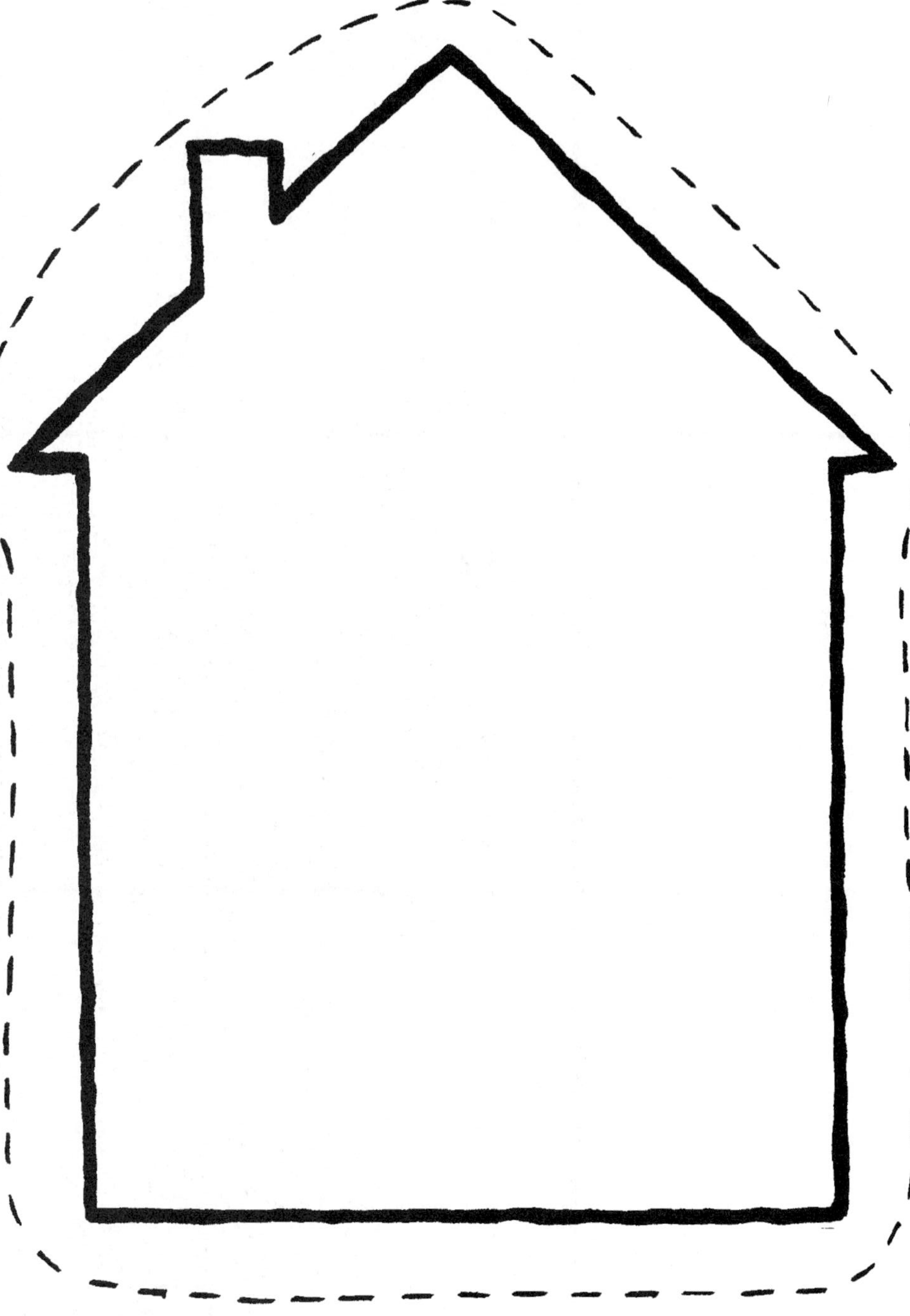

Character

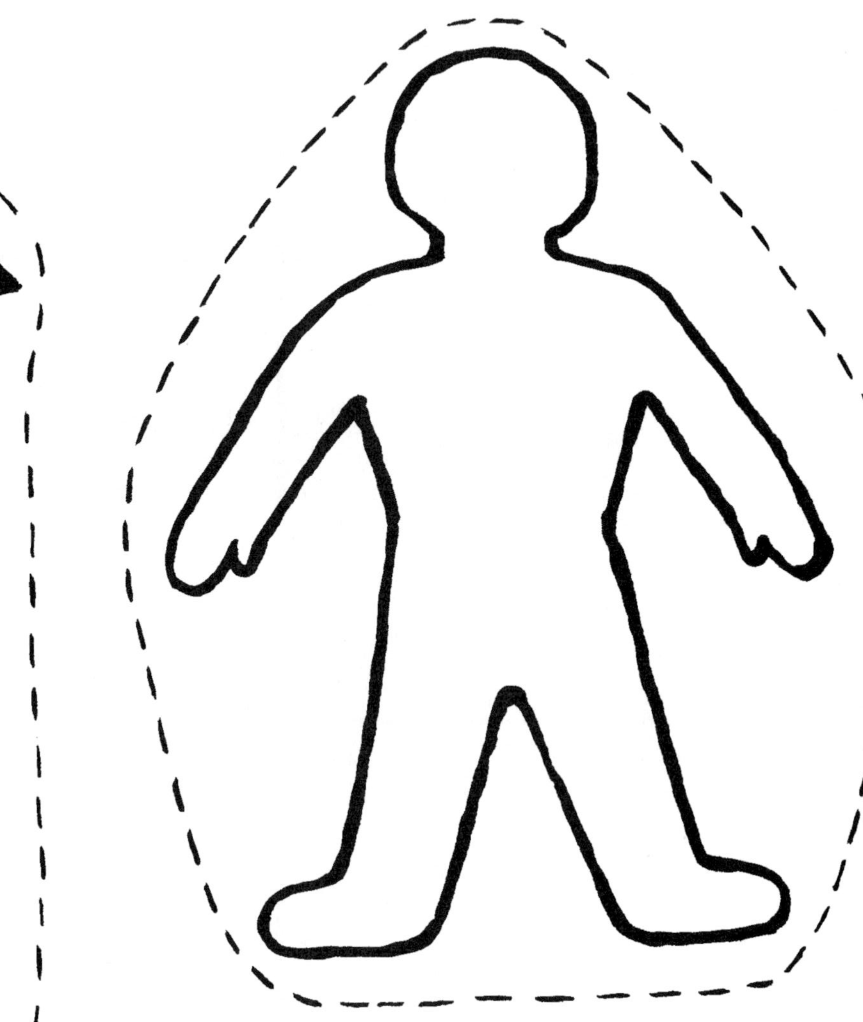

VIDEOCASSETTES
FOR USE WITH
SIGNATURES, Grade 2

The pages that follow are intended to help classroom teachers effectively integrate videocassettes into their instruction for SIGNATURES. Some of the videocassettes listed within this correlation are dramatizations or animations of the literature in the Student Anthologies of SIGNATURES. Others are videos of additional thematically related literature, while still others build background for understanding and appreciating the literature and themes in SIGNATURES.

These resources are listed and correlated in three columns. The first identifies a grade 2 theme within SIGNATURES. The second lists a related videocassette or videocassettes. And the third identifies the publisher or distributor of each videocassette.

This correlation was produced by Harcourt Brace School Publishers as a service to teachers using SIGNATURES. The videocassettes listed within this correlation are neither published nor distributed by Harcourt Brace School Publishers. The final page of the correlation lists the publishers and distributors, their addresses and telephone numbers, and the videocassettes each has available.

Grade 2

BOOK/THEME	TITLE	PUBLISHER/DISTRIBUTOR
2–1/		
Celebrate Me!	*Clean Your Room, Harvey Moon!*	Spoken Arts
	Pet Show!	Weston Woods
	The Day Jimmy's Boa Ate the Wash	Weston Woods
	The Bicycle Man	Perma-Bound
2–1/		
We Belong Together	*The Island of the Skog*	Weston Woods
	Bremen-Town Musicians	Perma-Bound
	The Adventures of Taxi Dog	Reading Rainbow; Perma-Bound
	Make Way for Ducklings!	Weston Woods
2–1/		
Tell a Tricky Tale	*Doctor De Soto*	Weston Woods
	Dr. Seuss on the Loose: Sneetches, Zax, Green Eggs and Ham	Perma-Bound
	Bartholomew and the Oobleck	Perma-Bound
	Stone Soup	Weston Woods
2–2/		
Families That Care and Share	*Thunder Cake*	Spoken Arts
	The Empty Pot	Spoken Arts
	Clean Your Room, Harvey Moon!	Spoken Arts
2–2/		
In the Night Sky	*Alistair in Outer Space*	GPN (Reading Rainbow Series)
2–2/		
Dare to Dream	*Digging Up Dinosaurs*	GPN (Reading Rainbow Series)
	The Empty Pot	Spoken Arts
	Dr. Seuss: The Lorax	Perma-Bound

VIDEOCASSETTE DISTRIBUTORS

Addresses and Phone Numbers

GPN
P.O. Box 80669
Lincoln, NE 68501-0669
1-800-228-4630
FAX (402) 472-4076

- *Alistair in Outer Space*
- *Digging Up Dinosaurs*
- *The Adventures of Taxi Dog*

Perma-Bound Books
617 E. Vandalia Rd.
Jacksonville, IL 62650
1-800-637-6581
FAX 1-800-551-1169

- *The Adventures of Taxi Dog*
- *Bartholomew and the Oobleck*
- *The Bicycle Man*
- *Bremen-Town Musicians*
- *Dr. Seuss on the Loose: Sneetches, Zax, Green Eggs and Ham*
- *Dr. Seuss: The Lorax*

Spoken Arts
8 Lawn Ave.
New Rochelle, NY 10801
1-800-326-4090
FAX (914) 633-4620

- *Clean Your Room, Harvey Moon!*
- *The Empty Pot*
- *Thunder Cake*

Weston Woods
Weston, CT 06883-1199
1-800-243-5020
FAX (203) 226-3818

- *The Day Jimmy's Boa Ate the Wash*
- *Doctor De Soto*
- *The Island of the Skog*
- *Make Way for Ducklings!*
- *Pet Show!*
- *Stone Soup*

INTEGRATED TECHNOLOGY COMPONENTS

FOR USE WITH SIGNATURES, Grade 2

This page focuses on technology resources that are integrated components of SIGNATURES. These components, all available from Harcourt Brace School Publishers, are referenced within SIGNATURES teaching plans at appropriate points of use to enhance, extend, and enliven instruction.

The Amazing Writing Machine, Harcourt Brace School Edition, is a rich, creative desktop publishing program that encourages children to write and illustrate their own SIGNATURES-related stories, letters, journals, essays, and poems.

Imagination Express, School Version, is a series of six CD-ROM programs that go a marvelous step beyond electronic books, enabling children to be not consumers, but creators of their own multimedia books and reports directly related to themes in SIGNATURES. The following destinations are cited in various themes: ***Castle, Neighborhood, Rain Forest,*** and ***Ocean.***

Bailey's Book House, School Version, is award-winning interactive software that delights children in the primary grades as they learn about sounds and letters, words, stories, and rhyme.

Kid Pix, School Edition, is an easy-to-use creative publishing tools program that enables children to create multimedia reports, animations, and slide shows.

Living Books, School Edition, is a series of electronic books that improves children's reading fluency, comprehension, and observation skills. Using the *Read to Me* option, children can listen to and view the animated version of a book. Using the *Let Me Play* option, they can explore the screen independently.

Trudy's Time & Place House, School Version, is interactive software that invites children to explore time and geography in five adventurous activities.

Thinkin' Things, School Versions, consists of three leveled collections of delightful activities that help children develop the logical reasoning and critical thinking skills necessary for successful problem solving in their daily lives. ***Thinkin' Things, Collections 1*** and ***2*** are cited in various themes.

Assessment Workshop: Scoring Student Writing is a software resource that instructs teachers in holistic scoring of children's writing. It is available in ***Primary, Intermediate,*** and ***Middle School*** levels.

Computer Management System provides a technology aid for scoring and recording children's reading skills.

Benchmarks

These benchmark statements represent a continuum of learning. The highlighted column describes observable behaviors most of your children should exhibit by the end of the school year.

LISTENING

Listens to a variety of texts	Listens to a variety of texts	Listens to a variety of texts
Listens to and follows directions	Listens to and follows directions	Listens to and follows directions
Responds to rhythm and rhyme	Responds to rhythm and rhyme	
Listens for a purpose	Listens for a purpose	Listens for a purpose
Listens for enjoyment	Listens for enjoyment	Listens for enjoyment
Listens and responds to peers in small groups	Listens and responds to peers in small groups	Listens and responds to peers in small groups
Participates in cooperative groups	Participates in cooperative groups	Participates in cooperative groups
Asks for repetition, restatement, or explanation to clarify meaning	Asks for repetition, restatement, or explanation to clarify meaning	Asks for repetition, restatement, or explanation to clarify meaning
		Recalls main idea, details, and facts after listening
		Listens to others' opinions and points of view

SPEAKING

Discusses a variety of texts	Discusses a variety of texts	Discusses a variety of texts
Participates in storytelling, retelling, rhyme, and song	Participates in storytelling, retelling, rhyme, and song	Participates in storytelling, retelling, rhyme, and song
Participates in group activities	Participates in group activities	Participates in group activities
Uses talk to clarify or explain ideas or experiences	Uses talk to clarify or explain ideas or experiences	Uses talk to clarify or explain ideas or experiences
Offers personal opinions	Offers personal opinions	Offers personal opinions
Describes personal ideas and experiences	Describes personal ideas and experiences	Describes personal ideas and experiences
Retells or reads orally	Retells or reads orally	Retells or reads orally
Speaks confidently in a variety of situations	Speaks confidently in a variety of situations	Speaks confidently in a variety of situations
	Gives oral reports	Gives oral reports

VIEWING

Enjoys a variety of illustrations and discusses them	Enjoys a variety of illustrations and discusses them	Discusses illustration styles and works of various illustrators
Uses rebuses	Uses rebuses	Uses pictures to get meaning from or support text
Predicts from visuals	Predicts from visuals	Predicts from visuals
"Reads" illustrations for details	"Reads" illustrations for details	Uses illustrations for details
Uses visuals to follow directions	Uses visuals to follow directions	Uses visuals to follow directions
Views critically	Views critically	Views critically
Tells own story from illustrations	Tells own story from illustrations	

Child ______________________ Teacher ______________________ Grade ____________

Listening, Speaking, and Viewing Checklist

	Date	Date	Date	Date	Date	Date
LISTENING						
Listens to a variety of texts						
Listens to and follows directions						
Listens for a purpose						
Listens for enjoyment						
Listens and responds to peers in small groups						
Participates in cooperative groups						
Asks for repetition, restatement, or explanation to clarify meaning						
SPEAKING						
Discusses a variety of texts						
Participates in storytelling, retelling, rhyme, and song						
Participates in group activities						
Uses talk to clarify or explain ideas or experiences						
Offers personal opinions						
Describes personal ideas and experiences						
Retells or reads orally						
Speaks confidently in a variety of situations						
Gives oral reports						
VIEWING						
Enjoys a variety of illustrations and discusses them						
Uses rebuses						
Predicts from visuals						
"Reads" illustrations for details						
Uses visuals to follow directions						
Views critically						
Tells own story from illustrations						

Comments:

Key:
N – Not Observed
O – Observed Occasionally
R – Observed Regularly

Benchmarks

These benchmark statements represent a continuum of learning. The highlighted column describes observable behaviors most of your children should exhibit by the end of the school year.

READING: COMPREHENSION

Discusses and retells stories
Uses clues from titles and illustrations to make predictions; reads to confirm
Writes or dictates a new ending for a story
Produces artwork and writing to reflect understanding of text
Identifies and recalls details, events, and ideas of familiar stories
Relates reading to personal experiences
Discusses characters' actions
Rereads to check predictions and clarify meaning
Uses commas, end punctuation, and quotation marks as clues to meaning
Follows written directions
Discriminates between reality and fantasy

Discusses and retells stories and articles
Uses clues from titles and illustrations to make predictions; reads to confirm
Writes a new ending for a story
Produces writing and artwork to reflect understanding of text
Identifies and recalls main idea, characters, events, setting, problem, and solution from text
Relates reading to own experiences before, during, and after reading
Identifies relationships between characters
Begins to reread and/or read on for meaning
Uses commas, end punctuation, and quotation marks as clues to meaning
Follows written directions
Discriminates between reality and fantasy, fact and fiction
Identifies and compares information

Discusses and retells stories and articles
Hypothesizes and predicts to infer story events or outcome; reads to confirm
Creates sequels and new endings for a story
Produces writing and artwork to reflect understanding of and response to text
Identifies and recalls main idea, characters, events, setting, problem, and solution from text
Relates reading to own knowledge and experiences before, during, and after reading
Discusses motives of characters and compares traits of characters
Rereads, reads on, and/or skips word when meaning breaks down
Uses punctuation as clues to meaning
Follows written directions
Discriminates between reality and fantasy, fact and fiction
Identifies and compares information
Relates one work to another
Supports ideas by reference to evidence in text
Uses strategies of purpose-setting, predicting, confirming, and self-correcting
Adjusts reading pace to accommodate purpose, style, and difficulty of material
Recognizes point of view
Recognizes use of literary devices

READING: VOCABULARY AND DECODING

Knows letter names
Recognizes environmental print
Recognizes and uses rhyming words
Segments and blends phonemes
Recognizes some high-frequency words both in and out of context
Applies basic letter/sound correspondences
Recognizes compound words and inflectional endings
Identifies words using graphophonic, semantic, and syntactic cues

Recognizes environmental print
Recognizes and uses rhyming words
Segments and blends phonemes
Recognizes some high-frequency words both in and out of context
Applies basic and complex letter/sound correspondences
Recognizes compound words and inflectional endings
Identifies words and constructs meaning based on graphophonic, semantic, and syntactic cues
Consults dictionary for pronunciation or meaning

Recognizes most high-frequency words
Applies basic and complex letter/sound correspondences
Recognizes word parts: base words, suffixes, prefixes; compound words; and inflectional endings
Identifies words and constructs meaning based on graphophonic, semantic, and syntactic cues
Consults dictionary or other reference materials for pronunciation or meaning
Uses familiar word parts to identify unknown words
Identifies synonyms, antonyms, and multiple-meaning words

Child ______________________ Teacher ______________________ Grade ____________

Reading Checklist

	Date	Date	Date	Date	Date	Date
COMPREHENSION						
Discusses and retells stories and articles						
Uses clues from titles and illustrations to make predictions; reads to confirm						
Writes a new ending for a story						
Produces writing and artwork to reflect understanding of text						
Identifies and recalls main idea, characters, events, setting, problem, and solution from text						
Relates reading to own experiences before, during, and after reading						
Identifies relationships between characters						
Begins to reread and/or read on for meaning						
Uses commas, end punctuation, and quotation marks as clues to meaning						
Follows written directions						
Discriminates between reality and fantasy, fact and fiction						
Identifies and compares information						
VOCABULARY AND DECODING						
Recognizes and uses rhyming words						
Segments and blends phonemes						
Recognizes some high-frequency words both in and out of context						
Applies basic and complex letter/sound correspondences						
Recognizes compound words and inflectional endings						
Identifies words and constructs meaning based on graphophonic, semantic, and syntactic cues						
Consults dictionary for pronunciation, meaning						

Comments:

Key:

N – Not Observed
O – Observed Occasionally
R – Observed Regularly

Benchmarks

These benchmark statements represent a continuum of learning. The highlighted column describes observable behaviors most of your children should exhibit by the end of the school year.

WRITING: CONTENT AND ORGANIZATION

Aims for a purpose and an audience through pictures and/or writing	Aims for a purpose and an audience through writing and/or pictures	Writes for a purpose and an audience
Writes some high-frequency words independently	Writes most high-frequency words independently	Writes most high-frequency words independently
Dictates/writes about pictures and draws pictures and tells stories about them	Writes a phrase or sentence that elaborates on another sentence	Writes a sentence that elaborates another sentence
Writes complete thoughts, and joins related sentences into a paragraph	Joins related sentences into paragraphs	Joins related sentences into paragraphs and uses paragraphs to organize information and ideas
Sequences ideas through dictation or writing	Stays on topic and sequences ideas	Stays on topic and sequences ideas
Dictates or writes stories with a sense of beginning, middle, end	Shows beginning, middle, and end in narrative writing	Includes introduction, development, and closing in writing
Expresses ideas, details, and topics through dictation, pictures, and writing	Uses detail in narrative and informational writing	Uses supporting ideas to develop topic and specific details to support ideas
Uses personal experiences as source of ideas for writing or dictation	Writes stories that draw on personal experience	Writes stories that draw on personal experience
	Uses appropriate word choice	Uses appropriate word choice
	Constructs several sentences on one topic in a logical order	Constructs several sentences on one topic in a logical order
		Uses concepts of order and time in writing
		Uses descriptive language
		Uses transitional words and phrases

WRITING: CONVENTIONS AND MECHANICS

Writes with left-to-right and top-to-bottom directionality	Writes with left-to-right and top-to-bottom directionality	Writes with left-to-right and top-to-bottom directionality
Uses appropriate spacing between words and/or sentences	Uses appropriate spacing between words and/or sentences	Uses appropriate spacing between words and/or sentences
Writes some sentences (simple in structure), some fragments	Writes mostly complete sentences in the S-V-O pattern	Recognizes and produces basic sentence patterns, compound sentences
Uses punctuation at the ends of sentences	Uses terminal and internal punctuation correctly most of the time	Uses punctuation correctly
Uses capitalization, especially at the beginning of sentences	Uses beginning capitalization correctly most of the time	Uses capitalization correctly
		Uses quotation marks
		Makes few errors in usage

WRITING: SPELLING

Spells some high-frequency words correctly	Spells high-frequency words correctly	Spells high-frequency words correctly
Spells using initial and final consonants and vowels—phonetically related approximations	Spells using phonetically related approximations that can generally be read by others	Applies spelling generalizations
	Uses conventional spelling most of the time	Uses conventional spelling most of the time

Child ____________ Teacher ____________ Grade ____________

Writing Checklist

	Date	Date	Date	Date	Date	Date
CONTENT AND ORGANIZATION						
Aims for a purpose and an audience through writing and/or pictures						
Writes a phrase or sentence that elaborates on another sentence						
Joins related sentences into paragraphs						
Stays on topic and sequences ideas						
Shows beginning, middle, and end in narrative writing						
Uses detail in narrative and informational writing						
Uses appropriate word choice						
Constructs several sentences on one topic in a logical order						
CONVENTIONS AND MECHANICS						
Writes with left-to-right and top-to-bottom directionality						
Uses appropriate spacing between words and/or sentences						
Writes mostly complete sentences in the S-V-O pattern						
Uses terminal and internal punctuation correctly most of the time						
Uses beginning capitalization correctly most of the time						
SPELLING						
Spells high-frequency words correctly						
Spells using phonetically related approximations that can generally be read by others						
Uses conventional spelling most of the time						

Comments:

Key:

N – Not Observed
O – Observed Occasionally
R – Observed Regularly

Scope and Sequence

GRADE/LEVEL	K/1	1-1	1-2	1-3	1-4	1-5	2	3	4	5	6
THINKING											
Observing											
Brainstorming											
Classifying and Categorizing											
Comparing and Contrasting											
Visualizing											
Evaluating											
Synthesizing											
Analyzing											
EMERGENT LITERACY											
Phonemic Awareness											
Print Awareness											
Concept of Letter, Word, Sentence											
STRATEGIC READING											
Active Reading Strategies											
Read Fiction (Narrative Text)											
Read Nonfiction (Expository Text; Text Structure)											
Analyze Details											
Synthesize Ideas/Information											
Make Inferences											
Decoding Strategy: Use phonemic/structural analysis plus context to unlock pronunciation											
Vocabulary Strategy: Use phonetic/structural/contextual clues to determine meanings											
Use Self-Assessment Strategies											
COMPREHENSION											
Cause-Effect							●	●	●	●	●
Classify/Categorize											
Compare and Contrast								●	●	●	●
Draw Conclusions							●	●	●	●	●
Fact-Fantasy/Nonfact											
Author's Purpose										●	●
Author's Viewpoint										●	●
Fact-Opinion								●	●	●	●
Main Idea (Global Meaning)/Details						●	●	●	●	●	●
Make Generalizations											
Make Judgments											
Make Predictions					●		●	●	●	●	●
Paraphrase								●	●	●	●
Referents											
Sequence				●			●	●	●	●	●
Summarize								●	●	●	●
VOCABULARY											
High-frequency Words											
Key Words/Selection Vocabulary	●	●	●	●	●	●	●	●	●	●	●
Vocabulary Strategy: Use phonetic/structural/contextual clues to determine meanings											
Synonyms/Antonyms											
Multiple-Meaning Words										●	
Homophones/Homographs											
Context Clues								●	●	●	●
Analogies											
Connotation/Denotation											
Glossary											
Dictionary (for Word Meaning)											
DECODING											
Phonics											
Initial/Medial/Final Consonants	●	●	●	●							
Phonograms and Word Patterns											
Short Vowels/Long Vowels		●	●	●	●	●	●				
Consonant Clusters/Digraphs (Initial/Final)					●	●					
R-Controlled Vowels							●				
Vowel Diphthongs/Vowel Digraphs/Variant Vowels							●				
Schwa											
Decoding Strategy: Use phonetic/structural analysis plus context to unlock pronunciation											
Decoding Strategy: Use graphophonic, semantic, and syntactic cues to decode or identify words											
Decoding Strategy: Use visual and graphophonic cues to decode long (multisyllabic) words											

Shaded Area **Modeling / Instruction / Application** ● **Tested**

Testing options include Skills Assessment, Holistic Reading Assessment, and Integrated Performance Assessment.

For a complete scope and sequence of the kindergarten program, see the Teacher's Edition for that level.

GRADE/LEVEL	K/1	1–1	1–2	1–3	1–4	1–5	2	3	4	5	6
Structural Analysis											
Inflected Forms (Nouns; Verbs With and Without Spelling Changes)		●			●	●	●				
Possessives, Comparatives, Superlatives											
Contractions			●	●							
Compound Words											
Syllables and Syllabication											
Suffixes/Prefixes								●	●	●	●
Greek and Latin Roots									●	●	●
Spelling Patterns											
STUDY SKILLS											
Locate Sources of Information											
Use the Library (Parts of, Card Catalog, Computerized Card Catalog, Call Numbers, Database Searching Strategies, *Books in Print, Readers' Guide to Periodical Literature*)											
Alphabet/Alphabetical Order					●		●				
Skimming/Scanning											
Select Appropriate Resources											
Use Sources of Information											
Book Parts											
Graphic Aids (Maps, Charts, Graphs, Tables/Schedules, Diagrams, Time Lines, Calendars)											
Compare Information from More Than One Source											
Use Reference Sources (Glossary/Dictionary, Thesaurus, Specialized Dictionary, Atlas/Globe, Encyclopedia, Almanac, Telephone Directory, Newspaper, Electronic and Audiovisual Media, *Books in Print, Readers' Guide to Periodical Literature*)								●	●	●	●
Organizing Information: Outlining, Note-Taking, Mapping, Webbing, Clustering, Classifying, Highlighting											
Study Strategies (K-W-L, SQ3R, How to Study)											
Content-Area Reading											
Adjust Method/Rate of Reading											
Test-Taking Strategies											
Follow Directions											
Forms/Applications											
LITERARY APPRECIATION											
Select Books for Individual Needs and Interests											
Read Full-length Books											
Literary Elements											
Plot Development											
Plot									●	●	●
Conflict (Internal/External)											
Climax											
Theme										●	●
Character (Emotions, Development, Traits)									●	●	●
Setting									●	●	●
Mood/Tone											
Point of View											
Narration											
Dialogue											
Author's Craft/Technique											
Figurative Language											
Characterization											
Imagery											
Humor											
Sound Devices (Rhythm/Rhyme/Alliteration/Onomatopoeia)											
Idiom, Slang, Dialect, Colloquialism											
Formal/Informal Language											
Literary Forms/Genre											
Fiction											
Realistic Fiction											
Historical Fiction											
Mystery											
Fantasy											
Science Fiction											
Full-length Book											
Riddle, Word Play, Pun											
Drama/Play											
Novel											
Short Story											
Pourquoi Tales											
Poetry/Song											

Shaded Area **Modeling / Instruction / Application** ● **Tested**

Testing options include Skills Assessment, Holistic Reading Assessment, and Integrated Performance Assessment. For a complete scope and sequence of the kindergarten program, see the Teacher's Edition for that level.

GRADE/LEVEL	K/1	1–1	1–2	1–3	1–4	1–5	2	3	4	5	6
Folklore (Folktale, Fairy Tale, Fable, Myth, Tall Tale, Legend, Nursery Rhyme)											
Nonfiction											
Biography/Autobiography											
Journal/Diary/Letters											
Essay											
Informational Article											
How-to Article											
Encyclopedia Article											
Magazine Article											
Newspaper Article/Feature											
Interview											
Speech											
Photo Essay											
Predictable and Patterned Text											
Personal Narrative											
MULTICULTURALISM											
Respond to Literature Representing Our Pluralistic Culture											
View Concepts/Issues from Diverse Perspectives											
Understand the Concept That All Groups Have Contributed to Society											
Acquire Attitudes/Skills/Knowledge to Interact Successfully with Members of Diverse Groups											
Recognize the Universality of Literary Themes Across Cultures and Languages											
LANGUAGE											
Composition											
Writing Process (Prewriting, Drafting, Revising, Proofreading, Publishing)											
Writer's Craft											
Capturing Reader's Interest											
Identifying Audience and Purpose							●	●	●	●	●
Using Appropriate Language							●	●	●	●	●
Writing Approaches											
Collaborative Writing											
Shared Writing											
Timed Writing											
Writing to Prompts							●	●	●	●	●
Responding to Essay Questions											
Forms of Writing											
Expository Writing (Compare/Contrast, Explanation, Directions, Speech, How-to, Friendly/Business Letters, News Story, Essay, Report)							●	●	●	●	●
Narrative Writing (Stories, Paragraphs, Personal Narrative, Personal Journal, Play, Poetry)							●	●	●	●	●
Descriptive Writing (Titles, Captions, Ad, Poster, Paragraphs, Stories, Poetry)							●	●	●	●	●
Persuasive Writing (Paragraph/s, Essay, Letter)								●	●	●	●
Cross-Curricular Writing											
Everyday Writing (Journals, Messages, Forms, Note-Taking, Summaries)											
Skills of Revision											
Correcting Sentence Fragments/Run-ons								●	●	●	●
Sentence Combining									●	●	●
Adding/Deleting/Rearranging Information											
Choosing Words Effectively (Exact/Precise Words, Vivid Words, Trite/Overused Words, Clichés)								●	●	●	●
Elaborating (Details, Examples, Dialogue, Quotations)								●	●	●	●
Unity and Coherence							●	●	●	●	●
Varying Sentence Structure, Word Order, and Sentence Length								●	●	●	●
Grammar											
Sentences											
Types (Declarative, Interrogative, Exclamatory, Imperative)							●	●	●	●	●
Structure (Simple, Compound, Complex)									●	●	●
Parts (Subjects/Predicates: Complete, Simple, Compound; Clauses: Independent, Subordinate; Phrases)								●	●	●	●
Complements (Direct/Indirect Objects; Predicate Nominatives/Adjectives)											●
Word Order							●				
Nouns (Singular, Plural, Common, Proper, Possessive, Collective, Abstract, Concrete; Abbreviations)							●	●	●	●	●
Verbs (Action, Helping, Linking, Transitive, Intransitive, Regular, Irregular)							●	●	●	●	●
Verb Tenses (Present, Past, Future; Present, Past, and Future Perfect)							●	●	●	●	●
Participles; Infinitives											
Adjectives (Common, Proper; Articles; Comparison)								●	●	●	●
Adverbs (Place, Time, Manner, Degree)								●	●	●	●
Pronouns (Subject, Object, Possessive, Reflexive, Demonstrative)							●	●	●	●	●
Prepositions; Prepositional Phrases										●	●
Conjunctions										●	●

Shaded Area **Modeling / Instruction / Application** ● **Tested**

Testing options include Skills Assessment, Holistic Reading Assessment, and Integrated Performance Assessment.
For a complete scope and sequence of the kindergarten program, see the Teacher's Edition for that level.

GRADE/LEVEL	K/1	1-1	1-2	1-3	1-4	1-5	2	3	4	5	6
Usage											
Nouns (Abbreviations, Plural Forms, Appositives)							●	●	●	●	●
Verbs (Subject-Verb Agreement)							●	●	●	●	●
Adjectives (Articles; Positive, Comparative, Superlative)								●	●	●	●
Adverbs (Positive, Comparative, Superlative)									●	●	●
Pronouns (Antecedents; Subject, Object, Possessive, and Reflexive Forms)							●	●	●	●	●
Troublesome words											
Mechanics											
Capitalization											
Punctuation											
Listening											
Participate in Cooperative Groups											
Participate in Reader Response Groups											
Receive Directions/Gain Information/Enhance Appreciation of Language											
Respond to a Speaker by Retelling What Was Heard, Asking Questions, and/or Contributing Information											
Analyze/Evaluate Intent and Content of Speaker's Message											
Note Details											
Visualize											
Determine Problem/Solution											
Make Justifiable Inferences											
Identify Supporting Details											
Recognize Persuasion											
Identify Mood/Tone											
Recognize Bias/Prejudice/Propaganda/Emotional Appeals											
Speaking											
Participate in Cooperative Groups											
Identify Audience/Purpose											
Use a Variety of Words to Convey Meaning											
Describe Personal Ideas, Feelings, Expressions, and Events											
Retell Orally/Summarize Stories											
Entertain Others with Stories, Poems, Dramatic Activities											
Give Directions											
Share Information											
Compare/Contrast											
Persuade Others											
Develop Skill in Using the Conventions of English											
Recite Rhyme, Chants, Poems											
Participate in Choral and Echo Reading											
Read Orally											
Present Oral Reports											
Read Fluently with Expression, Phrasing, and Intonation											
Conduct Interviews or Surveys											
Viewing											
Appreciate/Interpret Artists' Techniques											
View Information											
View Critically											
Compare Visual Materials											
Compare Visual and Written Versions of the Same Materials											
Handwriting											
Letter Forms (Manuscript, Cursive)											
Elements											
Common Errors											
Integrated Spelling											
Sound-Letter Relationship (Consonants, Vowels, Schwa, Double Letters, Stress and Accents)											
Word Structure (Plural Nouns/Inflected Verbs and Adjectives With and Without Spelling Changes, Prefixes, Suffixes, Greek and Latin Roots, Abbreviations, Contractions, Possessives, Compound Words)											
Word Analysis (Syllable/Letter Patterns, Pronunciation and Stress, Phonograms, Rhyming Words, Related Words, Word Origins)											
Study Methods and Strategies (Rhyming Words, Pronunciation, Word Shapes, Placeholders, Dictionary, Related Words, Mnemonic Devices, Proofreading)											
Apply Spelling Generalizations					●	●	●	●	●	●	●
Apply Spelling Strategies											
Master Frequently Misspelled Words											
Personal Spelling Lists											

Shaded Area **Modeling / Instruction / Application** ● **Tested**

Testing options include Skills Assessment, Holistic Reading Assessment, and Integrated Performance Assessment. For a complete scope and sequence of the kindergarten program, see the Teacher's Edition for that level.

Reviewers

TEACHERS, ADMINISTRATORS, AND READING SPECIALISTS

Pamela Atkins
Teacher
Artesia Intermediate School
Artesia, New Mexico

Darlene A. Beamon
Teacher
Liberty School
Springfield, Massachusetts

Kay L. Bollinger
Teacher
Coolbaugh Elementary
Tobyhanna, Pennsylvania

Joanne Boston
Supervisor of Reading
School District of the City of York
York, Pennsylvania

Margaret Burley
Teacher
Miller School
Pittsburgh, Pennsylvania

Linda Chick
Teacher
Paloma Elementary
San Marcos, California

Patricia L. DeJagger
Coordinator for Curriculum Differentiation
Rochester Community Schools
Rochester, Michigan

Carla B. Ford, Ph.D.
Coordinator, Office of Early Learning Years
City of Baltimore Department of Education
Baltimore, Maryland

James R. Gambardella
Administrator
Providence School Department
Providence, Rhode Island

Susan L. Guy
Teacher
Joslyn Elementary
Omaha, Nebraska

Catherine Hill
Elementary Education Consultant
New Mexico Department of Education
Santa Fe, New Mexico

Jacque Huffman
Teacher
Eastside Elementary
Clinton, Mississippi

Jody Irola-Pishione
Teacher
Susan B. Anthony Elementary
Fresno, California

Cynthia Ko
Teacher
Glenview Elementary
Oakland, California

Beverly Lynch
Director of Communication Arts
N.Y.C. Board of Education, District 20
Brooklyn, New York

Karen A. McGee
Reading Coordinator
Bullis Curriculum & Instruction Center
Reno, Nevada

Susan M. Middleton
Librarian
La Jolla Country Day School
La Jolla, California

Cynthia R. Muse
Teacher
Patterson School
Philadelphia, Pennsylvania

Lisbé P. Page
Teacher
Wacona Elementary
Waycross, Georgia

Ruby B. Pannoni
Supervisor of Language Arts
Boyertown Area School District
Boyertown, Pennsylvania

Dr. Anne M. Primavera
Coordinator of Language Arts
Brentwood Union Free School District
Brentwood, New York

Barbara Schweiger
Supervisor, Reading Services
Omaha Public School
Omaha, Nebraska

Barbara Singleton
Curriculum Coordinator
Harrison County School District
Gulfport, Mississippi

Denise Sontag
Reading Coordinator
Community School District #27
Ozone Park, New York

Kathy Stehr
Director of Curriculum
Chandler Unified School District
Chandler, Arizona

Karen Whitworth–Thompson
Teacher
Forest Street School
Orange, New Jersey

JoAnn Yerkes
Principal
St. Columba Elementary
Chicago, Illinois

Lillian Yoshimura
Teacher
Prisk Elementary
Long Beach, California

Linda Zankowsky
Principal
Townsend Elementary
Townsend, Delaware

PARENTS

Tracy Clark
Benicia, California

Sharon Dominguez
Hazel Crest, Illinois

James Dorsett
Los Angeles, California

Karen Fultz
Chicago, Illinois

Kari Kruger
Santa Barbara, California

Diana Lukenbill
Boise, Idaho

Susan Monken
Solana Beach, California

Amy Sather
Santa Rosa, California

Kaylene T. White
Spanish Fort, Alabama

KINDERGARTEN REVIEWERS

Dara Lothi-Phaisith
Des Moines, Iowa

Shannon Applegate
Solana Vista Elementary
Solana Vista, CA

Eleanor Skolnick
P.S. 131Q
Jamaica, NY

SPANISH REVIEWERS

Eduardo Nunez
Citrus Grove Elementary School
Miami, FL

Martha Estrella
Cesar Chavez Elementary School
San Francisco, CA

Sylvia Hernandez
Bilingual Coordinator
Sheridan Street Elementary School
Los Angeles, CA

Index

This index includes references to both Teacher's Editions *for grade 2 of* Signatures. *Page numbers for this level are in blue. The index is divided into seven color-coded sections, as shown below.*

KEY

2/1 *Out of the Blue*

2/2 *Living Colors*

✓= Tested

Emergent Literacy

Skills and Strategies

Reading

Comprehension

Literary Appreciation

KEY
✓ = Tested   Blue = Pages in this book

Index

Skills and Strategies

KEY
✓ = Tested   Blue = Pages in this book

Skills and Strategies

Index

Reading Activities

Reading Strategies

Real-Life Reading

Study Skills

KEY
✓ = Tested   Blue = Pages in this book

Index

Vocabulary

Thinking

KEY
✓ = Tested   Blue = Pages in this book

Skills and Strategies

Index

Skills and Strategies

Writing and Language

Composition

KEY
✓ = Tested   Blue = Pages in this book

Grammar

Listening

Mechanics

Oral Language Development

Skills and Strategies

KEY
✓ = Tested   Blue = Pages in this book

Speaking

Spelling

Usage

Viewing

KEY
✓ = Tested   Blue = Pages in this book

Assessment

Formal Assessment

Informal Assessment

Classroom Management

Connections

Flexible Grouping

Classroom Management

Intervention Strategies

KEY
✓ = Tested   Blue = Pages in this book

Meeting Individual Needs

KEY

✓ = Tested Blue = Pages in this book

Classroom Management

KEY
✓ = Tested   Blue = Pages in this book

Integrated Curriculum

Content-Area Reading

Integrated Curriculum Focus Topics

KEY
✓ = Tested   Blue = Pages in this book

Multiculturalism

Technology

CD-ROM

Floppy Disk

Internet

Video/Audio

Literature

Literary Forms/Genre

KEY
✓ = Tested   Blue = Pages in this book

Index

Responding to Literature

Selection Information

Artists

Authors

Author/Illustrators

Awards

Illustrators

Photographers

Themes

Trade Books

KEY
✓ = Tested   Blue = Pages in this book

Index

For permission to reprint copyrighted material, grateful acknowledgment is made to ·e following sources:

ıeum Books for Young Readers, an imprint of Simon & Schuster: Cover ıtion by Ron Barrett from *Cloudy With a Chance of Meatballs* by Judi Barrett. ıtion copyright © 1978 by Ron Barrett. Cover illustration from *Beat the Story-, Pum-Pum* by Ashley Bryan. Copyright © 1980 by Ashley Bryan. Cover ıtion from *Turtle Knows Your Name* by Ashley Bryan. Copyright © 1989 by · Bryan. Cover illustration from *A Story, A Story* retold by Gail E. Haley. Copyright 0 by Gail E. Haley. Cover illustration by Melissa Sweet from *Pinky and Rex and ·w Baby* by James Howe. Illustration copyright © 1993 by Melissa Sweet. Cover ıtion from *Three Stalks of Corn* by Leo Politi. Copyright © 1976 by Leo Politi. illustration by Lorna Tomei from *Rosie and Michael* by Judith Viorst. Illustration ght © 1974 by Lorna Tomei. Cover illustration from *Donkey Trouble* by Ed . Copyright © 1995 by Ed Young.

·Water Books, an imprint of Troll Communications, L. L. C.: Cover illustration ›in Spowart from *Lunch with Milly* by Jeanne Modesitt. Illustration copyright 5 by Robin Spowart.

ne House, Boyds Mills Press, Inc.: Cover photograph by Alvis Upitis from *Extra ·, Please! Mozzarella's Journey from Cow to Pizza* by Cris Peterson. Photograph ght © 1994 by Alvis Upitis.

hoda Books, Inc., Minneapolis, MN: Cover illustration by Peter J. Thornton from *›ody Cooks Rice* by Norah Dooley. Copyright © 1991 by Carolrhoda Books, Inc. illustration from *Miss Hindy's Cats* by Helena Clare Pittman. Copyright © 1990 ena Clare Pittman.

·n's Book Press, San Francisco, CA: Cover illustration by Mira Reisberg from *?attlesnake,* told by Te Ata, adapted by Lynn Moroney. Illustration copyright) by Mira Reisberg. Cover illustration by Nancy Hom from *The Little Weaver ·i-Yên Village/Cô Bé Tho-Dêt Làng Thái-Yên,* written in Vietnamese by Trân-·Tuyêt, translated into English by Christopher N. H. Jenkins and Trân-Khánh-Original edition © 1977 by Children's Book Press/Imprenta de Libros Infantiles; l edition © 1987. Cover illustration by Nancy Hom from *Judge Rabbit and the ›irit: A folktale from Cambodia,* told by Lina Mao Wall, adapted by Cathy ›li. Illustration copyright © 1991 by Nancy Hom.

ı Books, a Houghton Mifflin Company imprint: Cover illustration by Donald : from *The Wednesday Surprise* by Eve Bunting. Illustration copyright © 1989 ıald Carrick.

Publishers, Inc.: Cover illustration from *Stop That Noise!* by Paul Geraghty. ght © 1992 by Paul Geraghty. Cover illustration from *Tar Beach* by Faith ld. Illustration copyright © 1988 by Faith Ringgold. Illustration courtesy of omon R. Guggenheim Museum, New York City.

›oks, a division of Bantam Doubleday Dell Publishing Group, Inc.: Cover :ion from *The 13th Clue* by Ann Jonas. Copyright © 1992 by Ann Jonas.

›oks for Young Readers, a division of Penguin Books USA Inc.: Cover :ion by Leo and Diane Dillon from *Who's In Rabbit's House?,* retold by Verna ıa. Illustration copyright © 1977 by Leo and Diane Dillon. Cover illustration by l Diane Dillon from *Why Mosquitoes Buzz in People's Ears* by Verna Aardema. :ion copyright © 1975 by Leo and Diane Dillon. Cover illustration by Mark ·r from *The Adventures of Taxi Dog* by Debra and Sal Barracca. Illustration ·ht © 1990 by Mark Buehner. Cover illustration by Virginia A. Stroud from *The f The Milky Way* by Joseph Bruchac and Gayle Ross. Illustration copyright · by Virginia A. Stroud. Cover illustration by Susanna Natti from *Lionel in the* by Stephen Krensky. Illustration copyright © 1990 by Susanna Natti. Cover :ion from *A Boy, A Dog, A Frog and A Friend* by Mercer and Marianna Mayer. ·ht © 1971 by Mercer and Marianna Mayer.

Children's Books, a division of Penguin Books USA Inc.: Cover illustration *·e Lion and the Little Red Bird* by Elisa Kleven. Copyright © 1992 by Elisa Cover illustration from *The Garden in the City* by Gerda Muller. Copyright · by Ravensburger Buchverlag, Otto Maier GmbH; American edition copyright by Dutton Children's Books.

·rlag, Hamburg, Germany: Map of Puerto Rico.

·illow Books, a division of William Morrow & Company, Inc.: Cover ion from *Feelings* by Aliki. Copyright © 1984 by Aliki Brandenberg. Cover ion from *Window* by Jeannie Baker. Copyright © 1991 by Jeannie Baker. Cover ion from *City Sounds* by Craig Brown. Copyright © 1992 by Craig McFarland Cover illustration from *A Carpenter* by Douglas Florian. Copyright © 1991 by ; Florian. Cover illustration by Jim Fowler from *Dolphin Adventure* by Wayne Illustration copyright © 1990 by Jim Fowler. Cover illustration from *Chester's* Kevin Henkes. Copyright © 1988 by Kevin Henkes. Cover illustration by . Chess from *Once Around the Block* by Kevin Henkes. Illustration copyright by Victoria Chess. Cover illustration from *A Weekend with Wendell* by Kevin . Copyright © 1986 by Kevin Henkes.

·rt Brace & Company: Cover illustration from *The Trouble with Tyrannosaurus* Lorinda Bryan Cauley. Copyright © 1988 by Lorinda Bryan Cauley. Cover ion by Suçie Stevenson from *Emily and Alice* by Joyce Champion. Illustration ht © 1993 by Suçie Stevenson. Cover illustration from *The Armadillo from ·o* by Lynne Cherry. Copyright © 1994 by Lynne Cherry. Cover illustration from *·at Kapok Tree* by Lynne Cherry. Copyright © 1990 by Lynne Cherry. Cover ion by Louis Slobodkin from *Rufus M.* by Eleanor Estes. Copyright 1943 by Estes; copyright renewed 1970 by Eleanor Estes. Cover illustration by Terry from *Night Noises* by Mem Fox. Illustration copyright © 1989 by Terry . Cover illustration from *Check It Out! The Book About Libraries* by Gail ;. Copyright © 1985 by Gail Gibbons. Cover illustration by Margot Zemach from *The Chinese Mirror* by Mirra Ginsburg. Illustration copyright © 1988 by Margot Zemach. Cover illustration from *Papagayo: The Mischief Maker* by Gerald McDermott. Illustration copyright © 1992 by Gerald McDermott. Cover illustration from *Raven* by Gerald McDermott. Copyright © 1993 by Gerald McDermott. Cover illustration from *Zomo the Rabbit* by Gerald McDermott. Copyright © 1992 by Gerald McDermott. Cover illustration by Arthur Howard from *Mr. Putter and Tabby Pick the Pears* by Cynthia Rylant. Illustration copyright © 1995 by Arthur Howard. Cover illustration by Arthur Howard from *Mr. Putter and Tabby Bake the Cake* by Cynthia Rylant. Illustration copyright © 1994 by Arthur Howard. Cover illustration by Arthur Howard from *Mr. Putter and Tabby Walk the Dog* by Cynthia Rylant. Illustration copyright © 1994 by Arthur Howard. Cover illustration from *Tops & Bottoms*, adapted by Janet Stevens. Copyright © 1995 by Janet Stevens. Cover illustration from *How the Manx Cat Lost Its Tail,* retold and illustrated by Janet Stevens. Copyright © 1990 by Janet Stevens.

HarperCollins Publishers: Cover illustration from *The Day I Had to Play with My Sister* by Crosby Bonsall. Copyright © 1972 by Crosby Bonsall. Cover illustration from *Ant Cities* by Arthur Dorros. Copyright © 1987 by Arthur Dorros. Cover illustration from *Radio Man* by Arthur Dorros. Copyright © 1993 by Arthur Dorros. Cover illustration by Loretta Krupinski from *The Old Ladies Who Liked Cats* by Carol Greene. Illustration copyright © 1991 by Loretta Krupinski. Cover illustration from *Arthur's Camp-Out* by Lillian Hoban. Copyright © 1993 by Lillian Hoban. Cover illustration by Lillian Hoban from *A Bargain for Frances* by Russell Hoban. Illustration copyright © 1992 by Lillian Hoban. Cover illustration by Bob Marstall from *The Lady and the Spider* by Faith McNulty. Illustration copyright © 1986 by Bob Marstall. Cover illustration by Fritz Siebel from *Who Took the Farmer's Hat?* by Joan L. Nodset. Illustration copyright © 1963 by Fritz Siebel. Cover illustration from *Where the Wild Things Are* by Maurice Sendak. Copyright © 1963 by Maurice Sendak. Cover illustration by Pat Cummings from *Storm in the Night* by Mary Stolz. Illustration copyright © 1988 by Pat Cummings. Cover illustration from *Crictor* by Tomi Ungerer. Copyright © 1958 by Jean Thomas Ungerer; copyright renewed 1986 by Tomi Ungerer. Cover illustration by Margaret Bloy Graham from *Harry the Dirty Dog* by Gene Zion. Illustration copyright © 1956 by Margaret Bloy Graham; illustration copyright renewed 1984 by Margaret Bloy Graham. Cover illustration by William Pène du Bois from *William's Doll* by Charlotte Zolotow. Illustration copyright © 1972 by William Pène du Bois.

Holiday House, Inc.: Cover illustration by Janet Stevens from *Anansi Goes Fishing,* retold by Eric A. Kimmel. Illustration copyright © 1992 by Janet Stevens. Cover illustration by Janet Stevens from *Anansi and the Moss-Covered Rock*, retold by Eric A. Kimmel. Illustration copyright © 1988 by Janet Stevens. Cover illustration by Janet Stevens from *Nanny Goat and the Seven Little Kids,* retold from The Brothers Grimm by Eric A. Kimmel. Illustration copyright © 1990 by Janet Stevens. Cover illustration by Robert Rayevsky from *Three Sacks of Truth: A Story from France,* adapted by Eric A. Kimmel. Illustration copyright © 1993 by Robert Rayevsky. Cover illustration by Leonard Everett Fisher from *The Three Princes: A Tale from the Middle East,* retold by Eric A. Kimmel. Illustration copyright © 1994 by Leonard Everett Fisher. Cover illustration from *The Kids' Cat Book* by Tomie de Paola. Copyright © 1979 by Tomie de Paola. Cover illustration from *Coyote Steals the Blanket: A Ute Tale,* retold and illustrated by Janet Stevens. Copyright © 1993 by Janet Stevens.

Henry Holt and Company, Inc.: Cover illustration by Ann Grifalconi from *Everett Anderson's Friend* by Lucille Clifton. Illustration copyright © 1976 by Ann Grifalconi. Cover illustration by Tatyana Yuditskaya from *The Four Gallant Sisters* by Eric A. Kimmel. Illustration copyright © 1992 by Tatyana Yuditskaya. Cover illustration from *Anansi the Spider* by Gerald McDermott. Copyright © 1972 by Landmark Production, Inc.

Houghton Mifflin Company: Cover illustration by Deborah Kogan Ray from *I Know a Place* by Karen Ackerman. Illustration copyright © 1992 by Deborah Kogan Ray. Cover illustration from *Annie and the Wild Animals* by Jan Brett. Copyright © 1985 by Jan Brett. Cover illustration from *Imagine* by Alison Lester. Copyright © 1989 by Alison Lester. Cover illustration by Lynn Munsinger from *Tacky the Penguin* by Helen Lester. Illustration copyright © 1988 by Lynn Munsinger. Cover illustration by Simms Taback from *Too Much Noise* by Ann McGovern. Illustration copyright © 1967 by Simms Taback.

Ideals Children's Books, an imprint of Hambleton-Hill Publishing, Inc.: Cover illustration by Robert Quackenbush from *The Whole World in Your Hands* by Melvin and Gilda Berger. Illustration copyright © 1993 by Robert Quackenbush. Cover illustration from *Don't Forget to Write* by Martina Selway. Copyright © 1992 by Martina Selway.

Dorling Kindersley Limited, London: Cover photograph by Jerry Young from *Amazing Cats* by Alexandra Parsons. Photograph copyright © 1990 by Jerry Young. Published by Alfred A. Knopf, Inc.

Alfred A. Knopf, Inc.: Cover illustration by Petra Mathers from *Borreguita and the Coyote: A Tale from Ayutla, Mexico,* retold by Verna Aardema. Illustration copyright © 1991 by Petra Mathers. Cover illustration by Will Hillenbrand from *Traveling to Tondo: A Tale of the Nkundo of Zaire,* retold by Verna Aardema. Illustration copyright © 1991 by Will Hillenbrand. Cover illustration by Bryce Lee from *Germy Blew the Bugle* by Rebecca C. Jones. Illustration copyright © 1992 by Bryce Lee. Cover illustration from *How to Make an Apple Pie and See the World* by Marjorie Priceman. Copyright © 1994 by Marjorie Priceman. Cover illustration by Beatriz Vidal from *Rainbow Crow,* retold by Nancy Van Laan. Illustration copyright © 1989 by Beatriz Vidal.

Little, Brown and Company: Cover illustration from *Dinosaurs Divorce:A Guide for Changing Families* by Laurene Krasny Brown and Marc Brown. Illustration copyright © 1986 by Marc Brown and Laurene Krasny Brown. Cover illustration from *Dinosaurs to the Rescue!:A Guide to Protecting Our Planet* by Laurie Krasny Brown and Marc Brown. Copyright © 1992 by Laurene Krasny Brown and Marc Brown. Cover illustration from *Dinosaurs Travel:A Guide for Families On the Go* by Laurie Krasny Brown and Marc Brown. Copyright © 1988 by Laurie Krasny Brown and Marc Brown. Cover illustration from *Arthur's Pet Business* by Marc Brown. Copyright © 1990 by Marc Brown. Cover illustration from *Arthur's Teacher Trouble* by Marc Brown. Copyright © 1986 by Marc Brown. Cover illustration from *Arthur Meets the President* by Marc Brown. Copyright © 1991 by Marc Brown. Cover illustration from *The Bionic Bunny Show* by Marc Brown and Laurene Krasny Brown. Illustration copyright © 1984 by Marc Brown. Cover illustration by Victoria Chess from *The Bigness Contest* by Florence Parry Heide. Illustration copyright © 1994 by Victoria Chess. Cover illustration from *I Know an Old Lady Who Swallowed a Fly,* retold and illustrated by Nadine Bernard Westcott. Copyright © 1980 by Nadine Bernard Westcott.

Lothrop, Lee & Shepard Books, a division of William Morrow & Company, Inc.: Cover illustration by Jan Ormerod from *Grandmother and I* by Helen Buckley. Illustration copyright © 1994 by Jan Ormerod. Cover illustration from *Elmer* by David McKee. Illustration copyright © 1968 by David McKee. Cover photograph by Ken Heyman from *On the Go* by Ann Morris. Photograph copyright © 1990 by Ken Heyman. Cover illustration by Catherine Stock from *Galimoto* by Karen Lynn Williams. Illustration copyright © 1990 by Catherine Stock.

Margaret K. McElderry Books, an imprint of Simon & Schuster: Cover illustration by Mark Graham from *Charlie Anderson* by Barbara Abercrombie. Illustration copyright © 1990 by Mark Graham.

Joshua Morris, a subsidiary of Reader's Digest Young Families, Inc.: From *A Look Inside Spiders and Scorpions* by Dr. Paul Hillyard, illustrated by Steve Johnson, Gary Slater, Alex Pang and Andrew Barrowman. Copyright © 1995 by Stewart Cowley & Associates.

Morrow Junior Books, a division of William Morrow & Company, Inc.: Cover illustration by Beth Peck from *The House on Maple Street* by Bonnie Pryor. Illustration copyright © 1987 by Beth Peck.

Roxie Munro: Cover illustration from *The Inside-Outside Book of New York City* by Roxie Munro. Copyright © 1985 by Roxie Munro. Published by G.P. Putnam's Sons.

Open Hand Publishing Inc.: Cover illustration from *"T" is for "terrific"/"T" es por "terrífico"* by Mahji Hall. Copyright © 1989 by Open Hand Publishing Inc.

Orchard Books, New York: Cover illustration by Denys Cazet from *Annie, Bea, and Chi Chi Dolores* by Donna Maurer. Illustration copyright © 1993 by Denys Cazet.

Philomel Books: Cover illustration from *Anno's Math Games* by Mitsumasa Anno. Copyright © 1982 by Kuso-kobo.

Picture Book Studio, Ltd.: Cover illustration from *A House for Hermit Crab* by Eric Carle. Copyright © 1987 by Eric Carle Corp.

Puffin Books, a division of Penguin Books USA Inc.: Cover illustration from *I Like Me!* by Nancy Carlson. Copyright © 1988 by Nancy Carlson.

G. P. Putnam's Sons: Cover illustration by Petra Mathers from *Mrs. Merriwether's Musical Cat* by Carol Purdy. Illustration copyright © 1994 by Petra Mathers.

R & S Books, an imprint of Rabén & Sjögren, Stockholm: Cover illustration by Lena Anderson from *Linnea's Windowsill Garden* by Christina Björk. Illustration copyright © 1978 by Lena Anderson.

Random House, Inc.: Cover illustration by Ann Strugnell from *Julian, Dream Doctor* by Ann Cameron. Illustration copyright © 1990 by Ann Strugnell. Cover illustration from *Green Eggs and Ham* by Dr. Seuss.TM & © 1960, renewed 1988 by Dr. Seuss Enterprises, L.P. Cover illustration from *Oh, the Places You'll Go!* by Dr. Seuss. Copyright © 1990 by Theodor S. Geisel and Audrey S. Geisel. Cover illustration from *And to Think That I Saw It on Mulberry Street* by Dr. Seuss. Copyright 1937 by Dr. Seuss; copyright renewed 1964 by Theodor S. Geisel and Audrey S. Geisel.

Scholastic Inc.: Cover illustration by Marcia Brown from *How the Ostrich Got Its Long Neck,* retold by Verna Aardema. Illustration copyright © 1995 by Marcia Brown. Cover illustration by Steve Björkman from *This Is the Way We Eat Our Lunch* by Edith Baer. Illustration copyright © 1995 by Steve Björkman. Cover illustration by Bruce Degen from *The Magic School Bus: Lost in the Solar System* by Joanna Cole. Illustration copyright © 1990 by Bruce Degen. Cover illustration by Bruce Degen from *The Magic School Bus: In the Time of the Dinosaurs* by Joanna Cole. Illustration copyright © 1994 by Bruce Degen. THE MAGIC SCHOOL BUS is a registered trademark of Scholastic Inc. Cover illustration from *Animal Tracks* by Arthur Dorros. Copyright © 1991 by Arthur Dorros. Cover illustration by Mark Teague from *The Iguana Brothers* by Tony Johnston. Illustration copyright © 1995 by Mark Teague. Cover illustration by Steve Björkman from *I Hate English!* by Ellen Levine. Illustration copyright © 1989 by Steven Björkman. Cover illustration from *Ruby the Copycat* by Peggy Rathmann. Copyright © 1991 by Margaret Rathmann. Cover photographs from *Make Me a Peanut Butter Sandwich and a Glass of Milk* by Ken Robbins. Copyright © 1991 by Ken Robbins.

School Zone® Publishing Company: Cover illustration by John Sandford from *The Gum on the Drum* by Barbara Gregorich. © 1992 by School Zone® Publishing Company.

Silver Moon Press: Cover illustration from *Anna in the Garden* by Diane Dawson Hearn. Copyright © 1994 by Diane Dawson Hearn.

Simon & Schuster Books for Young Readers, a division of Simon & Schuster: Cover illustration from *Have You Seen My Cat?* by Eric Carle. Copyright © 1987 by Eric C Corp. Cover illustration from *Fortunately* by Remy Charlip. Copyright © 1964 by Charlip. Cover illustration from *One Fine Day* by Nonny Hogrogian. Copyright © by Nonny Hogrogian. Cover illustration from *Max* by Rachel Isadora. Copyright © by Rachel Isadora. Cover illustration by Virginia Wright-Frierson from *Down At the Bottom of the Deep Dark Sea* by Rebecca C. Jones. Illustration copyright © 1991 Virginia Wright-Frierson. Cover illustration by Jose Aruego and Ariane Dewey from *Musical Max* by Robert Kraus. Illustration copyright © 1990 by Jose Aruego and A Dewey. Cover photograph from *Farm Noises* by Jane Miller. Copyright © 1988 by Jane Miller. Cover illustration by Nancy Carpenter from *Sitti's Secrets* by Naomi Shibab Nye. Illustration copyright © 1994 by Nancy Carpenter. Cover illustration l Suçie Stevenson from *Henry and Mudge and the Best Day of All* by Cynthia Ryla Illustration copyright © 1995 by Suçie Stevenson. Cover illustration by Suçie Stevenson from *Henry and Mudge and the Wild Wind* by Cynthia Rylant. Illustrat copyright © 1993 by Suçie Stevenson. Cover illustration by Suçie Stevenson from *Henry and Mudge Take the Big Test* by Cynthia Rylant. Illustration copyright © 1 by Suçie Stevenson.

Ticknor & Fields Books for Young Readers, a Houghton Mifflin Company impri Cover illustration by Andrew McLean from *Switch Cat* by Garry Disher. Illustratio copyright © 1994 by Andrew McLean.

Viking Penguin, a division of Penguin Books USA Inc.: Cover illustration by Sus Davis from *The Dinosaur Who Lived In My Backyard* by B.G. Hennessy. Illustrati copyright © 1988 by Susan Davis. Cover illustration by Blanche Sims from *I Took Frog to the Library* by Eric A. Kimmel. Illustration copyright © 1990 by Blanche Cover illustration by Mavis Smith from *Let's Get a Pet* by Harriet Ziefert. Illustrati copyright © 1993 by Mavis Smith.

BIG BOOK OF RHYMES

Mae Galarza: "A Pear Is One" from *Very Very Short Nature Poems* by Ernesto Ga

HarperCollins Publishers: "Rope Rhyme" from *Honey, I Love and Other Poems* l Eloise Greenfield. Text copyright © 1978 by Eloise Greenfield.

Oxford University Press: "Misery" from *Black Misery* by Langston Hughes. Text copyright 1969 by Arna Bontemps and George Houston Bass, as Executors of the of Langston Hughes. Published by Oxford University Press, Inc., 1994.

Nina Payne: "Bubble Gum" from *All the Day Long* by Nina Payne. Text copyright © 1973 by Nina Payne.

Louise H. Sclove: Untitled poem (Retitled: "Chums") by Arthur Guiterman.